# Cisco IOS Dial Solutions

**Cisco Systems, Inc.**

Macmillan Technical Publishing
201 West 103rd Street
Indianapolis, IN 46290 USA

Cisco IOS Dial Solutions

Cisco Systems, Inc.



Published by:
Macmillan Technical Publishing
201 West 103rd Street
Indianapolis, IN 46290 USA



Printed in the United States of America 1 2 3 4 5 6 7 8 9 0

**Library of Congress Cataloging-in-Publication:** 97-80684

**ISBN:** 1-57870-055-8

**Warning and Disclaimer**

This book is designed to provide information about **Cisco IOS Dial Solutions**. Every effort has been made to make this book as complete and as accurate as possible, but no warranty or fitness is implied.

The information is provided on an "as is" basis. The author, Macmillan Technical Publishing, and Cisco Systems, Inc. shall have neither liability nor responsibility to any person or entity with respect to any loss or damages arising from the information contained in this book or from the use of the discs or programs that may accompany it.

The opinions expressed in this book belong to the author and are not necessarily those of Cisco Systems, Inc.

| | |
|---|---|
| **Associate Publisher** | Jim LeValley |
| **Executive Editor** | Julie Fairweather |
| **Cisco Systems Program Manager** | H. Kim Lew |
| **Managing Editor** | Caroline Roop |
| **Acquisitions Editor** | Tracy Hughes |
| **Development Editor** | Stacia Mellinger |
| **Project Editor** | Brian Sweany |
| **Team Coordinator** | Amy Lewis |
| **Book Designer** | Louisa Klucznik |
| **Cover Designer** | Jean Bisesi |
| **Production Manager** | Laurie Casey |
| **Production Team Supervisor** | Vic Peterson |
| **Production Team** | Aleata Howard<br>Nicole M R Ritch<br>Lisa Stumpf<br>Trina Wurst |
| **Indexer** | Tim Wright |
| **Director of Alliance Co-Marketing** | Kourtnaye Sturgeon |
| **Vice President of Brand Management** | Jim Price |
| **Brand Associate** | Kim Spilker |
| **Brand Coordinator** | Linda Beckwith |

# Trademark Acknowledgments

# Acknowledgments

The Cisco IOS Reference Library is the result of collaborative efforts of many Cisco technical writers and editors over the years. This bookset represents the continuing development and integration of user documentation for the ever-increasing set of Cisco IOS networking features and functionality.

The current team of Cisco IOS technical writers and editors includes Katherine Anderson, Jennifer Bridges, Joelle Chapman, Christy Choate, Meredith Fisher, Tina Fox, Marie Godfrey, Dianna Johansen, Sheryl Kelly, Yvonne Kucher, Doug MacBeth, Lavanya Mandavilli, Mary Mangone, Spank McCoy, Greg McMillan, Madhu Mitra, Oralee Murillo, Vicki Payne, Jane Phillips, George Powers, Teresa Oliver Schick, Wink Schuetz, Karen Shell, Grace Tai, and Bethann Watson.

The writing team wants to acknowledge the many engineering, customer support, and marketing subject-matter experts for their participation in reviewing draft documents and, in many cases, providing source material from which this bookset is developed.

# Contents at a Glance

# Table of Contents

# About the Cisco IOS Reference Library

The Cisco IOS Reference Library books are Cisco documentation that describe the tasks and commands necessary to configure and maintain your Cisco IOS network.

The Cisco IOS software bookset is intended primarily for users who configure and maintain access servers and routers, but are not necessarily familiar with the tasks, the relationship between tasks, or the commands necessary to perform particular tasks.

## Cisco IOS Reference Library Organization

The Cisco IOS Reference library consists of eight books. Each book contains technology-specific configuration chapters with corresponding command reference chapters. Each configuration chapter describes Cisco's implementation of protocols and technologies, related configuration tasks, and contains comprehensive configuration examples. Each command reference chapter complements the organization of its corresponding configuration chapter and provides complete command syntax information.

## Other Books Available in the Cisco IOS Reference Library

- Cisco IOS Configuration Fundamentals. 1-57870-044-2; Available December 1997

  This comprehensive guide details Cisco IOS software configuration basics. Cisco IOS Configuration Fundamentals offers thorough coverage of router and access server configuration and maintenance techniques. In addition to hands-on implementation and task instruction, this book also presents the complete syntax for router and access server commands, and individual examples for each command. Learn to configure interfaces in addition to system management, file loading, AutoInstall, and set up functions.

- Cisco IOS WAN Solutions. 1-57870-054-x; Available March 1998

  This book offers thorough, comprehensive coverage of internetworking technologies, particularly ATM, Frame Relay, SMDS, LAPB, and X.25, teaching the reader how to configure the technologies in a LAN/WAN environment.

- Cisco IOS Switching Services. 1-57870-053-1; Available March 1998

  This book is a comprehensive guide detailing available Cisco IOS switching alternatives. Cisco's switching services range from fast switching and Netflow switching to LAN Emulation.

- Cisco IOS IP Network Protocols, Vol. I. 1-57870-049-3; Available April 1998

  This book is a comprehensive guide detailing available IP and IP routing alternatives. It describes how to implement IP addressing and IP services and how to configure support for a wide range of IP routing protocols including BGP for ISP networks and basic and advanced IP Multicast functionality.

- Cisco IOS Networking Protocols, Vol. II. 1-57870-050-7, Available April 1998

  This book is a comprehensive guide detailing available network protocol alternatives. It describes how to implement various protocols in your network. This book includes documentation of the latest functionality for the IPX and AppleTalk desktop protocols as well as the following network protocols: Apollo Domain, Banyan VINES, DECNet, ISO CLNS, and XNS.

- Cisco IOS Bridging and IBM Networking Solutions. 1-57870-051-5, Available April 1998

  This book describes Cisco's support for networks in IBM and bridging environments. Support includes: transparent and source-route transparent bridging, source-route bridging (SRB), remote source-route bridging (RSRB), data link switching plus (DLS+), serial tunnel and block serial tunnel, SDLC and LLC2 parameter, IBM network media translation, downstream physical unit and SNA service point, SNA Frame Relay access support, Advanced Peer-to-Peer Networking, and native client interface architecture (NCIA).

- Cisco IOS Router Security. 1-57870-057-4, Available May 1998

  This book documents security configuration from a remote site and for a central enterprise or service provider network. It describes AAA, Radius, TACACS+, and Kerberos network security features. It also explains how to encrypt data across enterprise networks. The book includes many illustrations that show configurations and functionality, along with a discussion of network security policy choices and some decision-making guidelines.

## Book Conventions

Software and hardware documentation uses the following conventions:

- The caret character (^) represents the Control key.

For example, the key combinations ^D and Ctrl-D are equivalent: Both mean hold down the Control key while you press the D key. Keys are indicated in capitals, but are not case-sensitive.

- A string is defined as a nonquoted set of characters.

  For example, when setting an SNMP community string to *public*, do not use quotation marks around the string; otherwise, the string will include the quotation marks.

Command descriptions use these conventions:

- Vertical bars ( | ) separate alternative, mutually exclusive, elements.
- Square brackets ([ ]) indicate optional elements.
- Braces ({ }) indicate a required choice.
- Braces within square brackets ([{ }]) indicate a required choice within an optional element.
- **Boldface** indicates commands and keywords that are entered literally as shown.
- *Italics* indicate arguments for which you supply values; in contexts that do not allow italics, arguments are enclosed in angle brackets (< >).

Examples use these conventions:

- Examples that contain system prompts denote interactive sessions, indicating that the user enters commands at the prompt. The system prompt indicates the current command mode. For example, the prompt `Router(config)#` indicates global configuration mode.
- Terminal sessions and information the system displays are in `screen` font.
- Information you enter is in **`boldface screen`** font.
- Nonprinting characters, such as passwords, are in angle brackets (< >).
- Default responses to system prompts are in square brackets ([ ]).
- Exclamation points (!) at the beginning of a line indicate a comment line. They are also displayed by the Cisco IOS software for certain processes.

---

**CAUTION**

Means *reader be careful.* In this situation, you might do something that could result in equipment damage or loss of data.

---

**NOTES**

Means *reader take note.* Notes contain helpful suggestions or references to materials not contained in this manual.

---

**TIMESAVER**

Means *the described action saves time.* You can save time by performing the action described in the paragraph.

Within the Cisco IOS Reference Library, the term *router* is used to refer to both access servers and routers. When a feature is supported on the access server only, the term *access server* is used. When a feature is supported on one or more specific router platforms (such as the Cisco 4500), but not on other platforms (such as the Cisco 2500), the text specifies the supported platforms.

Within examples, routers and access servers are alternately shown. These products are used only for example purposes—an example that shows one product does not indicate that the other product is not supported.

# PART 1

# Business Applications and Scenarios

# CHAPTER 1

# Dial Networking Business Applications

This chapter provides an introduction to common dial networking scenarios used by service providers and enterprises.

Providing dial access refers to setting up one or more access servers or routers to allow on-demand connectivity for individual remote nodes or remote offices. The dial network solutions described in this chapter are based on business case scenarios. Depending on your business application, dial access has different meanings and implementations.

This chapter provides the following sections:

- Dial Networking for Service Providers and Enterprises
- Common Business Cases Applied to Dial Scenarios
- IP Addressing Strategies to Consider

## DIAL NETWORKING FOR SERVICE PROVIDERS AND ENTERPRISES

Service providers tend to supply public and private dial-in services for businesses or individual home users. Enterprises tend to provide private dial-in access for employees dialing in from remote LANs (such as a remote office) or individual remote nodes (such as a telecommuter). Additionally, there are hybrid forms of dial access—virtual private dial networks (VPDNs)—that are jointly owned, operated, and set up by both service providers and enterprises.

Figure 1–1 displays a common dial topology used by Internet service providers (ISPs). The central dial-in site is owned and controlled by the service provider, who only accepts dial-in calls. Enterprises and individual remote clients have no administrative control over the ISP's dial-in site.

**NOTES**

Many additional dial network strategies exist for different business applications. This overview is intended to provide only a sample of the most common dial business needs as experienced by Cisco Systems' dial escalation team.

*Figure 1–1*

*Sample Dial Network for an Internet Service Provider.*

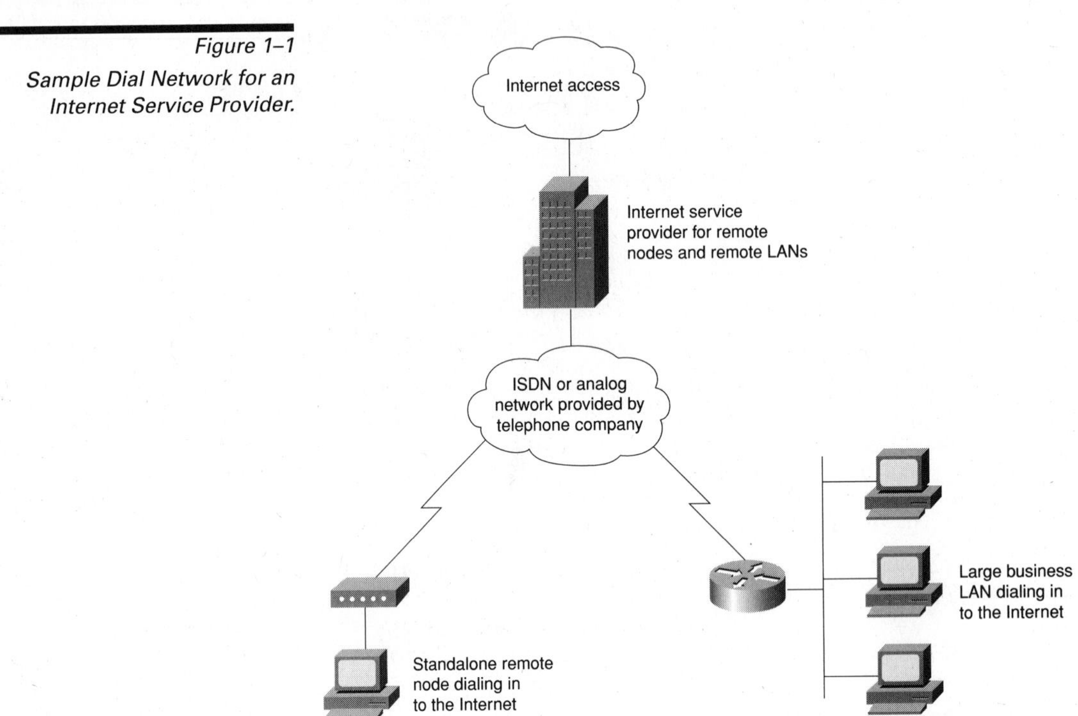


Enterprises can provide bidirectional access services with remote LANs and one-way dial-in access for stand-alone remote nodes. With bidirectional access, remote LANs can dial in to the enterprise, and the enterprise can dial out to the remote LANs. A remote LAN can be a large remote office or a small home office. A stand-alone remote node can be an individual PC that is dynamically assigned an IP address from the enterprise's modem pool. In most cases, an enterprise has complete administrative control over its local and remote devices. (See Figure 1–2.)

*Figure 1–2*
*Sample Dial Network for an Enterprise.*

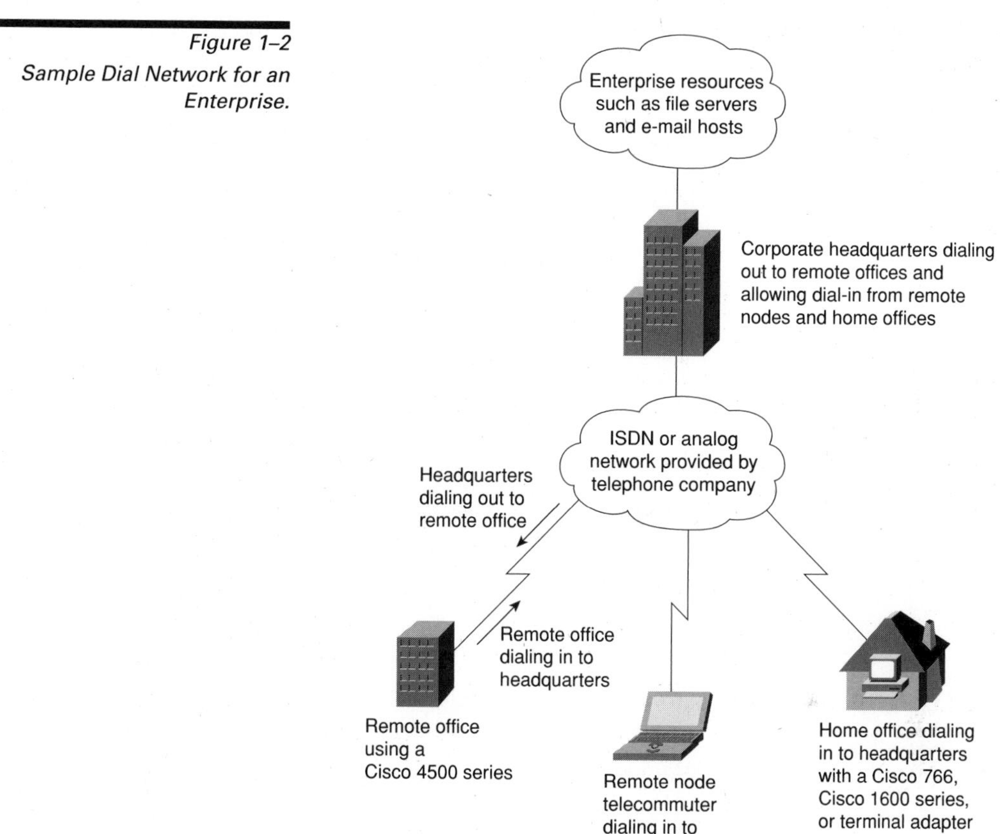


Service providers and enterprises both benefit from a hybrid dial solution called VPDN. Service providers offer virtually private access to enterprises by providing the dial-in access devices for the enterprise's use (for example, access servers and modem pools). In this solution, service providers construct the networking fabric for city-to-city dial connectivity for the enterprise. Enterprises provide only a home gateway router (with no attached modems) and a WAN connection to their service provider. VPDN dial solutions enable the enterprise to continue to maintain complete administrative control over its remote locations and network resource privileges. (See Figure 1–3.)

*Figure 1–3*
*Sample VPDN for Service Providers and Enterprises.*

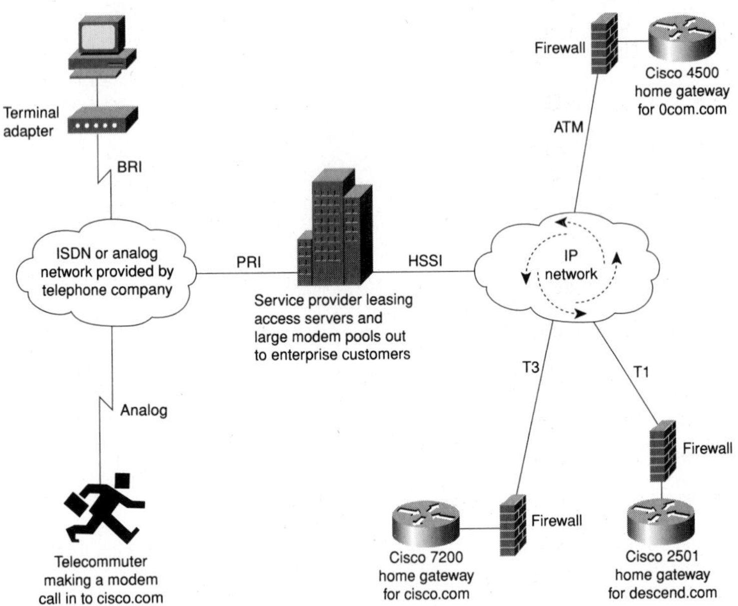


## Common Business Cases Applied to Dial Scenarios

The hardware and software configuration designs for dial networks are derived from business operations needs. This section describes several of the most common business dial scenarios that Cisco Systems is supporting for basic IP and security services.

Refer to the scenario that best describes your business or networking needs:

- The following dial scenarios are commonly used by service providers. For detailed description and configuration information, see Chapter 2, "Service Provider Dial Scenarios and Configurations."
  - Scenario 1, Remote PCs Dialing In to a Small- to Medium-Scale Dial-In Solution (one or two access servers at the central dial-in site)
  - Scenario 2, Remote PCs Dialing In to a Large-Scale Dial-In Solution (more than two access servers at the central dial-in site, multichassis, multilink PPP)
  - Scenario 3, Remote PCs Placing PPP Calls over X.25 Networks
  - Scenario 4, Remote PCs Dialing In to a Virtual Private Dial Network
- The following dial scenarios are commonly used by enterprises. For detailed description and configuration information, see Chapter 3, "Enterprise Dial Scenarios and Configurations."

- Scenario 1, Remote Offices and Telecommuters Dialing In to a Central Site
- Scenario 2, Bidirectional Dial Networking between a Central Site and Remote Offices or Telecommuters
- Scenario 3, Telecommuters Dialing In to a Mixed Protocol Environment

## IP Addressing Strategies to Consider

Exponential growth in the remote access router market has created new challenges for Internet service providers (ISPs) and enterprise customers in remote locations and small office/home office (SOHO) environments. Such customers seek internetworking solutions that will accomplish the following:

- Minimize Internet access costs for remote offices
- Minimize configuration requirements on remote access routers
- Enable transparent and dynamic IP address allocation for hosts in remote environments
- Improve network security capabilities at each remote SOHO site
- Conserve registered IP addresses
- Maximize IP address manageability

Remote networks have variable numbers of end systems that need access to the Internet; therefore, some ISPs are interested in allocating just one IP address to each remote LAN.

In enterprise networks where telecommuter populations are increasing in number, network administrators need solutions that ease configuration and management of remote routers and provide conservation and dynamic allocation of IP addresses within their networks. These solutions are especially important when network administrators implement large dial-up user pools in which ISDN plays a major role.

### Choose an Appropriate IP Addressing Scheme

You should use an IP addressing scheme that is appropriate for your business scenario as described in the following sections (found later in this chapter):

- Use a Classic Address Strategy for Remote LAN and Remote Client Dial-In
- Set Up Easy IP on a Router or Access Server

Additionally, here are some addressing issues to keep in mind while you evaluate different IP address strategies:

1. How many IP addresses do you need?
2. Do you want remote clients to dial in to your network and connect to server-based services, which require statically assigned IP addresses?
3. Is your primary goal to provide Internet services to a network (for example, surfing the Web, downloading e-mail, using TCP/IP applications)?

4. Can you conduct business with only a few registered IP addresses?
5. Do you need a single contiguous address space or can you function with two non-contiguous address spaces?

## *Use a Classic Address Strategy for Remote LAN and Remote Client Dial-In*

This section describes two classic IP addressing strategies you can use to set up dial-in access. Classic IP addresses are statically or dynamically assigned from your network to each site router or dial-in client. The IP address strategy you use depends on whether you are allowing remote LANs or individual remote clients to dial in.

A remote LAN usually consists of a single router at the gateway followed by multiple nodes, such as 50 PCs. The IP address on the gateway router is fixed or statically assigned (for example, 3.3.3.3). This device always uses the address 3.3.3.3 to dial in to the enterprise or service provider network. There is also a segment or subnet associated with the gateway router (for example, 2.1.1.0 255.255.255.0), which is defined by the dial-in security server.

For individual remote clients dialing in, a specific range or pool of IP addresses is defined by the gateway access server and dynamically assigned to each node. When a remote node dials in, it receives an address from the specified address pool. This pool of addresses usually resides locally on the network access server, whereas the remote LANs have predefined or statically assigned addresses. The accompanying subnet is usually statically assigned, as well. (See Figure 1–4.)

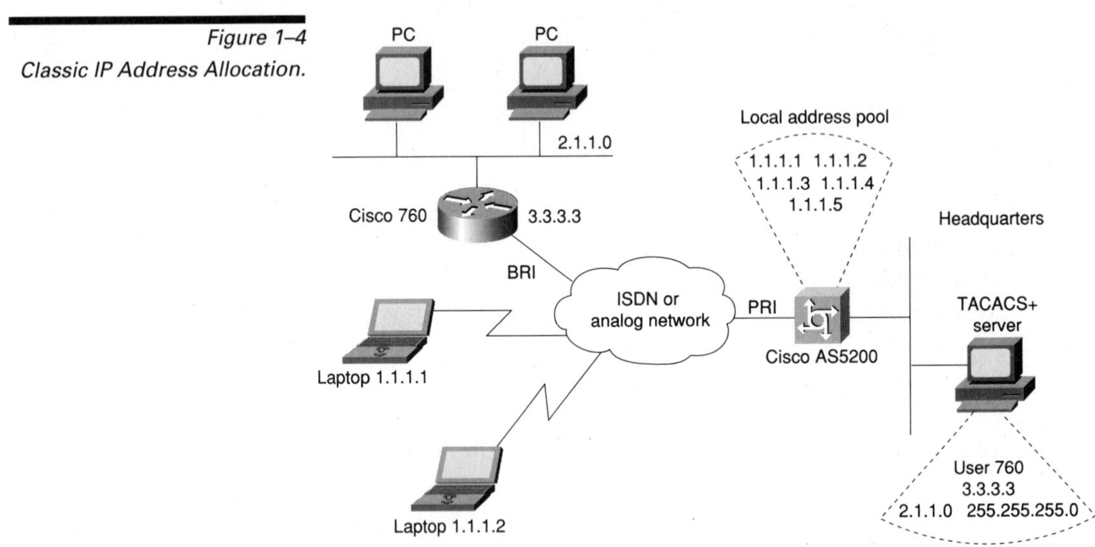


*Figure 1–4*
*Classic IP Address Allocation.*

Following are some advantages and disadvantages of manually assigning IP addresses:

- Advantages
  - Web servers or Xservers can be stationed at remote locations.
  - Because addresses are members of your network, they are perfectly transparent.
- Disadvantages
  - IP address assignments are difficult to both administer and manage. You may also need to use some complicated subnetting configurations.
  - Statically assigned IP addresses use up precious address space.
  - Strong routing configuration skills are usually required.

### Set Up Easy IP on a Router or Access Server

Two of the key problems facing the Internet are depletion of IP address space and scaling in routing. The Easy IP (Phase 1) feature combines Network Address Translation (NAT) and PPP/Internet Protocol Control Protocol (IPCP). This feature enables a Cisco router to automatically negotiate its own registered WAN interface IP address from a central server and allows all remote hosts to access the global Internet using this single registered IP address. Because Easy IP uses existing port-level multiplexed NAT functionality within the Cisco IOS software, IP addresses on the remote LAN are invisible to the Internet.

#### *Cisco IOS Easy IP (Phase 1) Component Technologies*

Cisco IOS Easy IP solution is a scalable, standards-based, "plug-and-play" solution that is comprised of a combination of the following technologies:

- NAT—Described in RFC 1631. NAT operates on a router that usually connects two or more networks together. Using Easy IP, at least one of these networks (designated as "inside" or "LAN") is addressed with private (RFC 1918) addresses that must be converted into a registered address before packets are forwarded onto the other registered network (designated as "outside" or "WAN"). Cisco IOS software provides the capability to define one-to-one translations (NAT), as well as many-to-one translations (Port Address Translation [PAT]). Within the context of Cisco IOS Easy IP, PAT is used to translate all internal private addresses to a single outside registered IP address.
- Point-to-Point Protocol/Internet Protocol Control Protocol (PPP/IPCP)—Defined in RFC 1332. This protocol enables users to dynamically configure IP addresses over PPP. A Cisco IOS Easy IP router uses PPP/IPCP to dynamically negotiate its own WAN interface address from a central access server or DHCP server.

Figure 1–5 shows an example of how Easy IP works. A range of registered or unregistered IP addresses are used inside a company's network. When a dial-up connection is initiated by an internal node, the router uses the Easy IP feature to rewrite the IP header belonging to each packet and translate the private address into the dynamically assigned and registered IP address, which can be borrowed from a service provider.

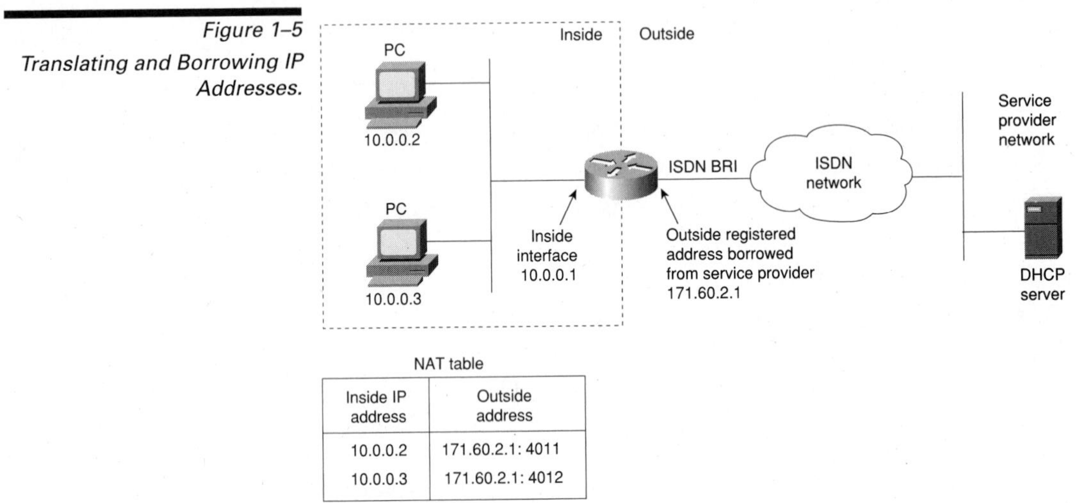


| Inside IP address | Outside address |
|---|---|
| 10.0.0.2 | 171.60.2.1: 4011 |
| 10.0.0.3 | 171.60.2.1: 4012 |

*Figure 1–5 Translating and Borrowing IP Addresses.*

For a more detailed description of how Easy IP (phase 1) works, see Chapter 78, "Configuring Easy IP."

### *Key Benefits of Using Easy IP*

The Easy IP feature provides the following benefits:

- Reduces Internet access costs by using dynamically allocated IP addresses. Using dynamic IP address negotiation (PPP/IPCP) at each remote site substantially reduces Internet access costs. Static IP addresses cost more to *purchase* compared to dynamically allocated or *rented* IP addresses. Easy IP enables you to rent IP addresses. In addition, dynamically assigned IP addresses save you time and money associated with subnet mask configuration tasks on hosts. It also eliminates the need to configure host IP addresses when moving from network to network.
- Simplifies IP address management. Easy IP enables ISPs to allocate a single registered IP address to each remote LAN. Because only a single registered IP address is required to provide global Internet access to all users on an entire remote LAN, customers and ISPs can use their registered IP addresses more efficiently.
- Conserves registered IP addresses. Suppose you want to connect to the Internet, but not all your hosts have globally unique IP addresses. NAT enables private IP internetworks that use nonregistered or overlapping IP addresses to connect to the Internet. NAT is configured on the router at the border of a stub domain (red to as the *inside network*) and a public network such as the Internet (referred to as the *outside network*). The private addresses

you set up on the inside of your network translate in to a *single* registered IP address on the outside of your network.

- Provides remote LAN IP address privacy. Because Easy IP uses existing port-level multiplexed NAT functionality within Cisco IOS software, IP addresses on the remote LAN are invisible to the Internet, making the LAN inherently more secure. As seen by the external network, the source IP address of all traffic from the remote LAN is the single registered IP address of the Easy IP router's WAN interface.

For step-by-step configuration information on how to set up the Easy IP feature on a router or access server, see Chapter 78.

CHAPTER 2

# Service Provider Dial Scenarios and Configurations

This chapter provides sample hardware and software configurations for specific dial scenarios used by service providers. Each configuration is designed to enable IP network traffic with basic security authentication.

The following scenarios are described:

- Scenario 1—Remote PCs Dialing In to a Small- to Medium-Scale Dial-In Solution
- Scenario 2—Remote PCs Dialing In to a Large-Scale Dial-In Solution
- Scenario 3—Remote PCs Placing PPP Calls over X.25 Networks
- Scenario 4—Remote PCs Dialing In to a Virtual Private Dial Network

**NOTES**

In many of these example scenarios, you can replace the Cisco AS5200 access server with a Cisco AS5300 access server. This hardware exchange provides higher call density performance and increases the number of PRI interfaces and modem ports on each chassis.

## REMOTE PCs DIALING IN TO A SMALL- TO MEDIUM-SCALE DIAL-IN SOLUTION

Many small- to medium-sized Internet service providers (ISPs) configure one or two access servers to provide dial-in access for their customers. Many of these dial-in customers use individual remote PCs that are not connected to local-area networks (LANs). Using an Internet access application such as Windows 95, remote clients initiate analog or digital connections using modems or home office terminal adapters.

This section provides three types of single user dial-in scenarios for ISPs plus a recommended client setup for Windows 95:

- Configuring Dial for Individual Remote PCs Using Modems
- Configuring Dial for Individual PCs Using Terminal Adapters
- Configuring Dial for a Mixture of Digital and Analog Incoming Calls
- Setting Up Windows 95 on the Remote PC Side of the Connection

**NOTES**

Be sure to include your own IP addresses, host names, and security passwords where appropriate. The following sample configurations assume that the dial-in clients are individual PCs running PPP, connecting to an IP network, and requiring only basic security authentication.

## Configuring Dial for Individual Remote PCs Using Modems

ISPs can configure a single Cisco AS5200 to receive analog calls from remote PCs connected to modems, as shown in Figure 2–1. The point of presence (POP) at the ISP central site can also be a Cisco 2511 access server connected to external modems.

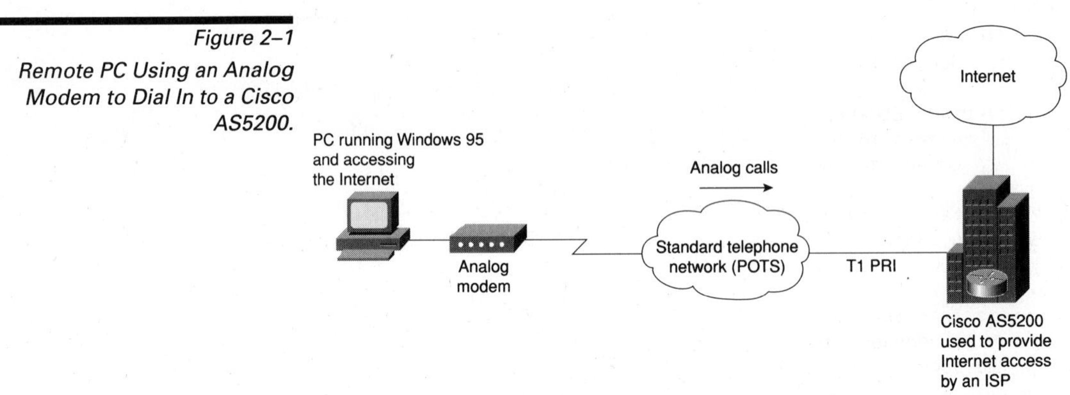


*Figure 2–1 Remote PC Using an Analog Modem to Dial In to a Cisco AS5200.*

### *Modem Calls over ISDN PRI Configuration for the Cisco AS5200 Access Server*

The following sample configuration runs on the Cisco AS5200, as shown in Figure 2–1, which enables remote analog users to dial in and surf the Internet:

```
!
version 11.2
service timestamps debug datetime msec
service timestamps log datetime msec
service password-encryption
no service udp-small-servers
no service tcp-small-servers
!
hostname NAS
!
```

```
aaa new-model
aaa authentication login console enable
aaa authentication login vty tacacs+
aaa authentication login dialin tacacs+
aaa authentication ppp default tacacs+
aaa authentication ppp dialin if-needed tacacs+
enable secret cisco
!
async-bootp dns-server 10.1.3.1 10.1.3.2
isdn switch-type primary-5ess
!
controller T1 0
 framing esf
 clock source line primary
 linecode b8zs
 pri-group timeslots 1-24
!
controller T1 1
 framing esf
 clock source line secondary
 linecode b8zs
 pri-group timeslots 1-24
!
interface Loopback0
 ip address 10.1.2.254 255.255.255.0
!
interface Ethernet0
 ip address 10.1.1.10 255.255.255.0
 ip summary address eigrp 10 10.1.2.0 255.255.255.0
!
interface Serial0
 no ip address
 shutdown
!
interface Serial1
 no ip address
 shutdown
!
interface Serial0:23
 no ip address
 encapsulation ppp
 isdn incoming-voice modem
!
interface Serial1:23
 no ip address
 isdn incoming-voice modem
!
interface Group-Async1
 ip unnumbered Loopback0
 encapsulation ppp
 async mode interactive
 peer default ip address pool dialin_pool
 no cdp enable
 ppp authentication chap pap dialin
```

```
 group-range 1 48
!
router eigrp 10
 network 10.0.0.0
 passive-interface Dialer0
 no auto-summary
!
ip local pool dialin_pool 10.1.2.1 10.1.2.50
ip default-gateway 10.1.1.1
ip classless
!
dialer-list 1 protocol ip permit
!
line con 0
 login authentication console
line 1 48
 autoselect ppp
 autoselect during-login
 login authentication dialin
 modem DialIn
line aux 0
 login authentication console
line vty 0 4
 login authentication vty
 transport input telnet rlogin
!
end
```

Some service providers use a remote TACACS+ or RADIUS security server in this dial-in scenario. The following example shows a TACACS+ entry that appears in a remote security server's configuration file:

```
user = PCuser1 {
            login = cleartext "dialpass1"
            chap = cleartext "dialpass1"
            service = ppp protocol = ip {
                         addr-pool = dialin_pool
            }
            service = exec {
                         autocmd = "ppp negotiate"
            }
}


user = PCuser2 {
            login = cleartext "dialpass2"
            chap = cleartext "dialpass2"
            service = ppp protocol = ip {
                         addr-pool = dialin_pool
            }
            service = exec {
                         autocmd = "ppp negotiate"
            }
}
```

```
user = PCuser3 {
            login = cleartext "dialpass3"
            chap = cleartext "dialpass3"
            service = ppp protocol = ip {
                        addr-pool = dialin_pool
            }
            service = exec {
                        autocmd = "ppp negotiate"
            }
}
```

### *Modem Dial-In Configuration for Robbed Bit Signaling*

The following configuration is for a single Cisco AS5200 to support remote client PCs dialing in with analog modems over T1 lines. Digital ISDN calls do not transmit across these older types of channelized lines. The configuration assumes that the client can dial in and connect to the router in either terminal emulation mode (text only) or PPP packet mode.

**NOTES**

The following configuration works only for analog modem calls. It includes no serial D channel configuration (Serial 0:23 and Serial 1:23). The next ISDN PRI example is for digital calls.

```
!
version 11.2
service timestamps debug datetime msec
service timestamps log datetime msec
service password-encryption
no service udp-small-servers
no service tcp-small-servers
!
hostname NAS
!
aaa new-model
aaa authentication login console enable
aaa authentication login vty tacacs+
aaa authentication login dialin tacacs+
aaa authentication ppp default tacacs+
aaa authentication ppp dialin if-needed tacacs+
enable secret cisco
!
async-bootp dns-server 10.1.3.1 10.1.3.2
isdn switch-type primary-5ess
!
controller T1 0
 framing esf
 clock source line primary
 linecode b8zs
 cas-group 0 timeslots 1-24 type e&m-fgb
!
controller T1 1
```

```
 framing esf
 clock source line secondary
 linecode b8zs
 cas-group 0 timeslots 1-24 type e&m-fgb
!
interface Loopback0
 ip address 10.1.2.254 255.255.255.0
!
interface Ethernet0
 ip address 10.1.1.10 255.255.255.0
 ip summary address eigrp 10 10.1.2.0 255.255.255.0
!
interface Serial0
 no ip address
 shutdown
!
interface Serial1
 no ip address
 shutdown
!
!
interface Group-Async1
 ip unnumbered Loopback0
 encapsulation ppp
 async mode interactive
 peer default ip address pool dialin_pool
 no cdp enable
 ppp authentication chap pap dialin
 group-range 1 48
!
router eigrp 10
 network 10.0.0.0
 passive-interface Dialer0
 no auto-summary
!
ip local pool dialin_pool 10.1.2.1 10.1.2.50
ip default-gateway 10.1.1.1
ip classless
!
dialer-list 1 protocol ip permit
!
line con 0
 login authentication console
line 1 48
 autoselect ppp
 autoselect during-login
 login authentication dialin
 modem DialIn
line aux 0
 login authentication console
line vty 0 4
 login authentication vty
 transport input telnet rlogin
!
end
```

## Configuring Dial for Individual PCs Using Terminal Adapters

ISPs can configure a single Cisco AS5200 to receive digital multilink calls from remote PCs connected to terminal adapters, as shown in Figure 2–2. The point of presence at the ISP's central site can be any Cisco router that supports ISDN PRI, such as the Cisco 4700-M loaded with a channelized T1 PRI network module.

*Figure 2–2 Remote PC Using a Terminal Adapter To Dial In to a Cisco AS5200.*

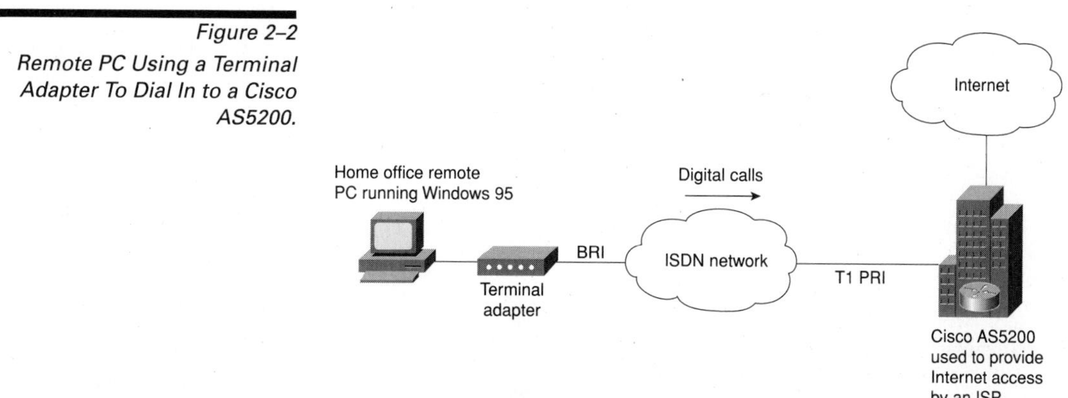


To configure one Cisco AS5200 to accept both incoming ISDN and analog calls from individual terminal adapters and modems, see the section in this chapter, "Configuring Dial for a Mixture of Digital and Analog Incoming Calls."

### *ISDN PRI Dial-In Configuration for the Cisco AS5200 Access Server*

The following example configures a Cisco AS5200 to enable PCs fitted with internal or external terminal adapters to dial in to an IP network. The terminal adapter configuration is set up for asynchronous to synchronous PPP conversion. In some cases, PPP authentication must be set up for the Password Authentication Protocol (PAP) because some terminal adapters only support PAP authentication.

```
!
version 11.2
service timestamps debug datetime msec
service timestamps log datetime msec
service password-encryption
no service udp-small-servers
no service tcp-small-servers
!
hostname NAS
!
aaa new-model
aaa authentication login console enable
aaa authentication login vty tacacs+
aaa authentication login dialin tacacs+
aaa authentication ppp default tacacs+
```

```
aaa authentication ppp dialin if-needed tacacs+
enable secret cisco
!
async-bootp dns-server 10.1.3.1 10.1.3.2
isdn switch-type primary-5ess
!
controller T1 0
 framing esf
 clock source line primary
 linecode b8zs
 pri-group timeslots 1-24
!
controller T1 1
 framing esf
 clock source line secondary
 linecode b8zs
 pri-group timeslots 1-24
!
interface Loopback0
 ip address 10.1.2.254 255.255.255.0
!
interface Ethernet0
 ip address 10.1.1.10 255.255.255.0
 ip summary address eigrp 10 10.1.2.0 255.255.255.0
!
interface Serial0
 no ip address
 shutdown
!
interface Serial1
 no ip address
 shutdown
!
interface Serial0:23
 no ip address
 encapsulation ppp
 dialer rotary-group 0
 dialer-group 1
 no fair-queue
 no cdp enable
!
interface Serial1:23
 no ip address
 encapsulation ppp
 dialer rotary-group 0
 dialer-group 1
 no fair-queue
 no cdp enable
!
interface Dialer0
 ip unnumbered Loopback0
 no ip mroute-cache
 encapsulation ppp
 peer default ip address pool dialin_pool
```

```
 dialer in-band
 dialer-group 1
 no fair-queue
 no cdp enable
 ppp authentication chap pap dialin
 ppp multilink
!
router eigrp 10
 network 10.0.0.0
 passive-interface Dialer0
 no auto-summary
!
ip local pool dialin_pool 10.1.2.1 10.1.2.50
ip default-gateway 10.1.1.1
ip classless
!
!
!
dialer-list 1 protocol ip permit
!
line con 0
 login authentication console
line 1 48
 autoselect ppp
 autoselect during-login
 login authentication dialin
 modem DialIn
line aux 0
 login authentication console
line vty 0 4
 login authentication vty
 transport input telnet rlogin
!
end
```

## Configuring Dial for a Mixture of Digital and Analog Incoming Calls

ISPs can configure a single Cisco AS5200 to receive calls from a mixture of remote PCs connected to terminal adapters and modems, as shown in Figure 2–3. In this scenario, the Cisco AS5200 is used as a hybrid access server, which is its primary network application.

### *Modem and ISDN Dial-In Configuration for the Cisco AS5200 Access Server*

The following configuration is a combination of the modem and ISDN dial-in configurations. The incoming ISDN calls carry information about whether they are data or voice, using the bearer capability information element in the call setup packet. After the call enters the access server, it is routed either to the serial configuration or to the modems and group asynchronous configuration.

*Figure 2–3*
*Remote PCs Making Digital Calls and Analog Calls to a Cisco AS5200.*

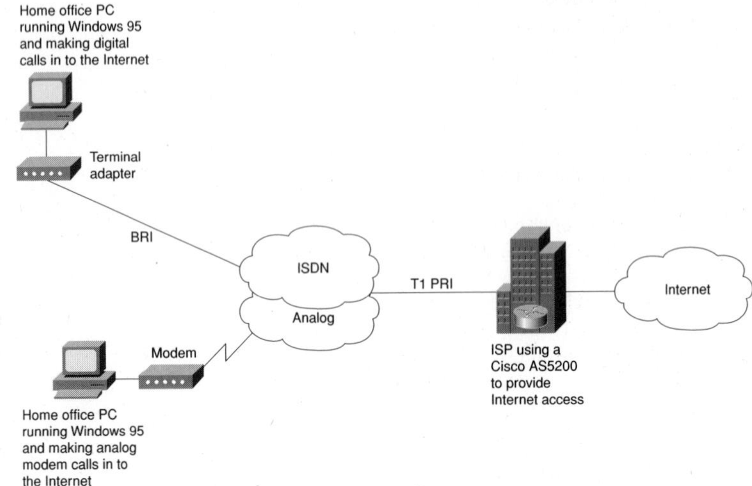


**NOTES**

This configuration assumes that only individual remote PCs are dialing in; no remote routers are dialing in. For a remote router dial-in configuration, see Chapter 3, "Enterprise Dial Scenarios and Configurations."

```
!
version 11.2
service timestamps debug datetime msec
service timestamps log datetime msec
service password-encryption
no service udp-small-servers
no service tcp-small-servers
!
hostname NAS
!
aaa new-model
aaa authentication login console enable
aaa authentication login vty tacacs+
aaa authentication login dialin tacacs+
aaa authentication ppp default tacacs+
aaa authentication ppp dialin if-needed tacacs+
enable secret cisco
!
async-bootp dns-server 10.1.3.1 10.1.3.2
isdn switch-type primary-5ess
!
controller T1 0
 framing esf
 clock source line primary
```

```
 linecode b8zs
 pri-group timeslots 1-24
!
controller T1 1
 framing esf
 clock source line secondary
 linecode b8zs
 pri-group timeslots 1-24
!
interface Loopback0
 ip address 10.1.2.254 255.255.255.0
!
interface Ethernet0
 ip address 10.1.1.10 255.255.255.0
 ip summary address eigrp 10 10.1.2.0 255.255.255.0
!
interface Serial0
 no ip address
 shutdown
!
interface Serial1
 no ip address
 shutdown
!
interface Serial0:23
 no ip address
 encapsulation ppp
 isdn incoming-voice modem
 dialer rotary-group 0
 dialer-group 1
 no fair-queue
 no cdp enable
!
interface Serial1:23
 no ip address
 encapsulation ppp
 isdn incoming-voice modem
 dialer rotary-group 0
 dialer-group 1
 no fair-queue
 no cdp enable
!
interface Group-Async1
 ip unnumbered Loopback0
 encapsulation ppp
 async mode interactive
 peer default ip address pool dialin_pool
 no cdp enable
 ppp authentication chap pap dialin
 group-range 1 48
!
interface Dialer0
 ip unnumbered Loopback0
 no ip mroute-cache
```

```
 encapsulation ppp
 peer default ip address pool dialin_pool
 dialer in-band
 dialer-group 1
 no fair-queue
 no cdp enable
 ppp authentication chap pap dialin
 ppp multilink
!
router eigrp 10
 network 10.0.0.0
 passive-interface Dialer0
 no auto-summary
!
ip local pool dialin_pool 10.1.2.1 10.1.2.50
ip default-gateway 10.1.1.1
ip classless
!
dialer-list 1 protocol ip permit
!
line con 0
 login authentication console
line 1 48
 autoselect ppp
 autoselect during-login
 login authentication dialin
 modem DialIn
line aux 0
 login authentication console
line vty 0 4
 login authentication vty
 transport input telnet rlogin
end
```

## Setting Up Windows 95 on the Remote PC Side of the Connection

This section describes how to install and configure Windows 95 client software to dial in to and access network resources through a Cisco access server.

This configuration procedure is intended only as a starting point. Because Cisco does not control the design and development efforts of other companies, the configuration requirements can change without notice. This configuration information is only one of many ways of configuring a Windows 95 client application for dial-in using PPP. To set up the built-in PPP application in Windows 95 to access the ISP's IP or NetBEUI network resources, perform the following steps:

**Step 1** Double-click on the My Computer icon located either in the Applications window or on the desktop.

The My Computer window appears.

**Step 2** If you are making a connection for the first time, double-click on the Make a New Connection icon. If you have already configured your connection profiles, additional icons appear in this window, and you can double-click on them for use in the future.

**Step 3** Give the connection session a name, such as MyConnection.

**Step 4** From the list of modems, select the type of modem connected to your PC (or built in to the PC).

**Step 5** When the dialog box appears, click on the **Configure** button.

The General, Connection, and Options folders appear stacked on top of one another. You can select each tab to configure the appropriate parameters.

**Step 6** Select the Connection tab. In the Connection folder, set data bits to 8, parity to No, and stop bits to 1. Click **Apply.**

The Advanced Connection Settings window appears.

**Step 7** Modems usually perform all necessary data compression; however, if you have a very old modem, select Data Compression and Hardware flow control and click **OK.**

**Step 8** Select the Options tab. In the Options folder, select "Bring up terminal window after dialing" and click on the **Next** button.

Selecting the option "Bring up terminal window after dialing" causes the access server to prompt you for your username and password (when you dial in), then to log you in to the EXEC facility.

A new dialog box appears that indicates you have finished configuring a dialup profile, and the "Myconnection" connectoid appears.

**Step 9** Click on the **Next** button.

**Step 10** In the Phone Number field, enter the phone number, area code, and country of the access server you intend to dial, and press Return.

You have just configured preliminary parameters to enable the Windows 95 client to dial in to an access server. You must now define additional properties:

**Step 1** Select the dialup profile connectoid. Click with the right mouse button, and pull down the menu. Select Properties.

**Step 2** In the Properties dialog box, select Server_Type.

The Server Types dialog box appears as shown in Figure 2–4.

**Step 3** Select PPP Windows 95 Windows NT 3.5 Internet.

**Step 4** In the Advanced Options area, be sure "Log on to network" and "Enable software compression" are both disabled.

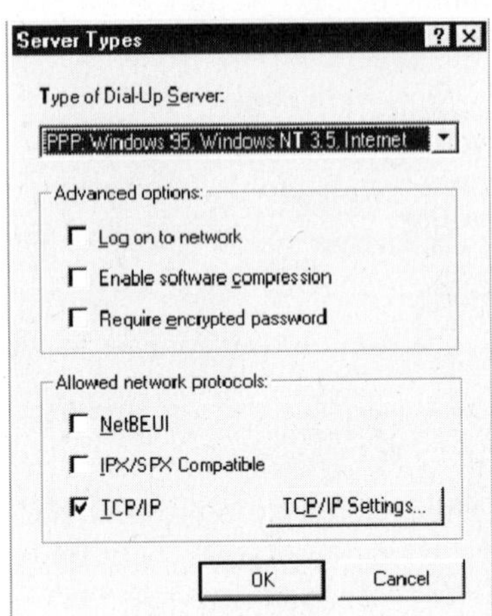


*Figure 2–4 Windows 95 Server Types Dialog Box.*

**Step 5** In the Allowed Network Protocols area, select "TCP/IP" if you want the PC to function as an IP client to access IP network resources.

**Step 6** Open the TCP/IP Settings pull-down menu at the bottom-right corner of the dialog box by clicking on the **TCP/IP Settings** button.

**Step 7** If you are getting your addresses from a server, select Server assigned IP and Name server addresses. Otherwise, enter an IP address.

**Step 8** Select "Use default gateway on remote network." Click **Apply**. Select IP compression if you intend to enable header compression of IP packets on the access server, which is enabled with the **ip tcp header-compression passive** interface configuration command.

**Step 9** Access the Control Panel, and select Internet.

**Step 10** If your PPP connection is the only modem or ISDN connection to the Internet, check the AutoDial checkbox. Uncheck this box if you have more than one outgoing connection.

**Step 11** Select MyConnection and click on the **Apply** button.

When you start an application that requires network access, you are prompted for a username and password. This username and password must match the username and password on the access server. When you select Connect, the client dials the number you entered. In a status box, you can see the information *dialing*, *verifying username/password*, and the dial-in application should run without problems. Figure 2–5 shows a successful connection.

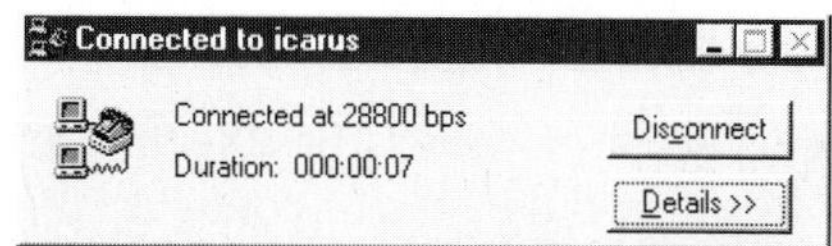


*Figure 2–5*
*Windows 95 Connection Status Box.*

## Remote PCs Dialing In to a Large-Scale Dial-In Solution

Because of the significant increase in demand for Internet access, large-scale dial-in solutions are required by many Internet service providers. Internet access configurations can be set up to enable users dialing in with individual computers to make mixed ISDN multilink or modem connections using a stack of Cisco AS5200 universal access servers running Multichassis Multilink PPP (MMP).

You must consider scalability and call density issues when designing a large-scale dial-in scenario. Because access servers have physical limitations, such as how many dial-in users can be supported on one device, you should consider the conditions and recommendations described in Table 2–1.

**Table 2–1** *Recommended Configurations for Different Remote Access Needs*

| Dial-in Demand You Need to Support | Recommended Configuration |
|---|---|
| PCs dialing in, 75 to 90% modem calls, 10 to 25% ISDN calls (terminal adapters or routers), and support for less than 96 (T1) to 116 (E1) simultaneous dial-in connections. | Two Cisco AS5200s configured for IP, basic security, MMP, L2F, and no offload server. |
| PCs dialing in, less than 50% modem calls, more than 50% ISDN calls (terminal adapters or routers), dial-in only, and 250 or more simultaneous links into the offload server. | Three or more Cisco AS5200s configured for IP, remote security, MMP, and L2F. Each Cisco AS5200 is configured to offload its segmentation and reassembly of the multilink sessions onto an offload server, such as a Cisco 7202 or Cisco 4700. |

**Notes**

In many of these example scenarios, you can replace the Cisco AS5200 access server with a Cisco AS5300 access server. This hardware exchange provides higher call density performance and increases the number of PRI interfaces and modem ports on each chassis.

The Cisco AccessPath Integrated Access System is an excellent solution designed to meet the demands of rapidly growing ISPs, telecommunication carriers, and other network service providers

*continues*

who offer managed Internet services. This universal connection server family also provides a ready solution for large enterprises as they expand their intranet requirements to include significant components of dial access.

## How a Large-Scale Dial-in Solution Works

Before you configure a stack of Cisco AS5200s for large-scale dial-in access, it is useful to understand the reasons why you would need to configure this setup. This section describes the following basic concepts and how they work together in a large-scale dial-in scenario:

- A Typical Multilink PPP Session
- Using Multichassis Multilink PPP
- Setting Up an Offload Server
- Using the Stack Group Bidding Protocol
- Using Layer 2 Forwarding

### A Typical Multilink PPP Session

A basic multilink session is an ISDN connection between two routing devices, such as a Cisco 766 and a Cisco AS5200. Figure 2–6 shows a remote PC connecting to a Cisco 766 ISDN router, which in turn opens two B-channel connections at 128 kbps across an ISDN network. The multilink PPP session is brought up. The Cisco 766 sends four packets across the network to the Cisco AS5200, which in turn reassembles the packets into the correct order and sends them out the LAN port to the Internet.

*Figure 2–6 A Typical Multilink PPP Session.*

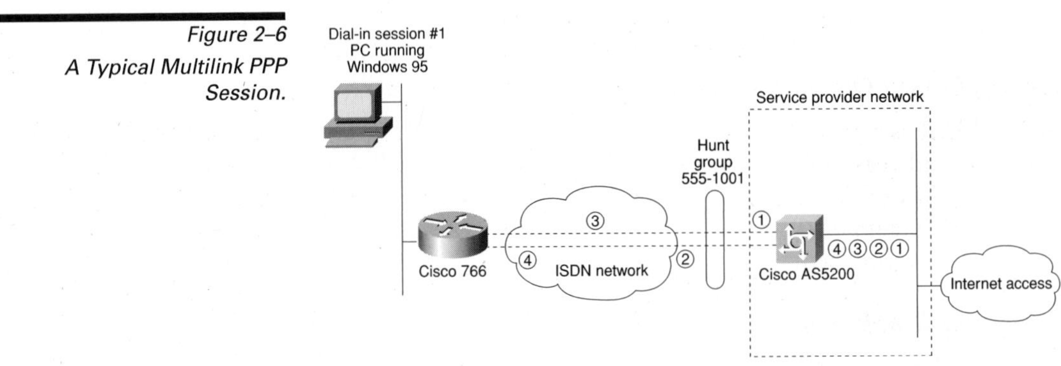


### Using Multichassis Multilink PPP

The dial solution becomes more complex when the scenario is scaled to include multiple multilink calls connecting across multiple chassis. Figure 2–7 shows a terminal adapter making a call in to the Cisco AS5200, labeled #1. However, only one of the access server's 46-B channels is available to accept the call. The other channels are busy with calls. The result is that one of the terminal adapter's two B-channels is redirected to device #2. At this point, a multilink multichassis session is shared between two Cisco AS5200s that belong to the same stack group. Packet fragments A and C go to device #1. Packet fragments B and D go to device #2.

Because device #1 is the first access server to receive a packet and establish a link, this access server creates a virtual interface and becomes the bundlemaster. The bundlemaster takes ownership of the multilink PPP session with the remote device. The Multichassis Multilink PPP protocol forwards the second link from device #2 to the bundlemaster, which in turn bundles the two B channels together and provides 128 kbps to the end user. Layer 2 forwarding (L2F) is the mechanism that device #2 uses to forward all packet fragments received from the terminal adapter to device #1. In this way, all packets and calls virtually appear to terminate at device #1.

*Figure 2–7 A Stackgroup of Access Servers Using MMP without an Offload Processor.*

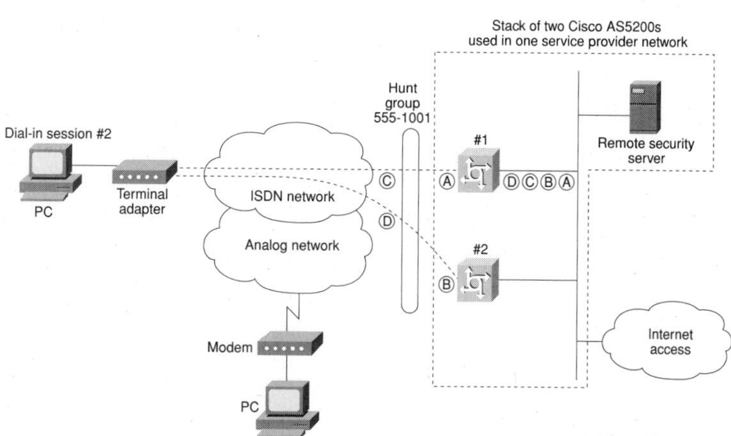


### Setting Up an Offload Server

Because MMP is a processor-intensive application, you might need to offload the processing or segmentation and reassemble from the Cisco AS5200s to a router with a higher CPU, such as the Cisco 4700-M or Cisco 7206. It is recommended here that you include an offload server for dial-in solutions that support more than 50% ISDN calls or more than 10 multilink sessions per Cisco AS5200. (See Figure 2–8.)

### Using the Stack Group Bidding Protocol

The Stack Group Bidding Protocol (SGBP) is a critical component used in multichassis multilink sessions. The SGBP unites each Cisco AS5200 in a virtual stack, which enables the access servers to become virtually tied together. Each independent stack member communicates with the other members and determines which device's CPU should be in charge of running the multilink session and packet reassembly—the bundlemaster's duty. The goal of SGBP is to find a common place to forward the links and ensure that this destination has enough CPU to perform the segmentation and packet reassembly. (See Figure 2–8.)

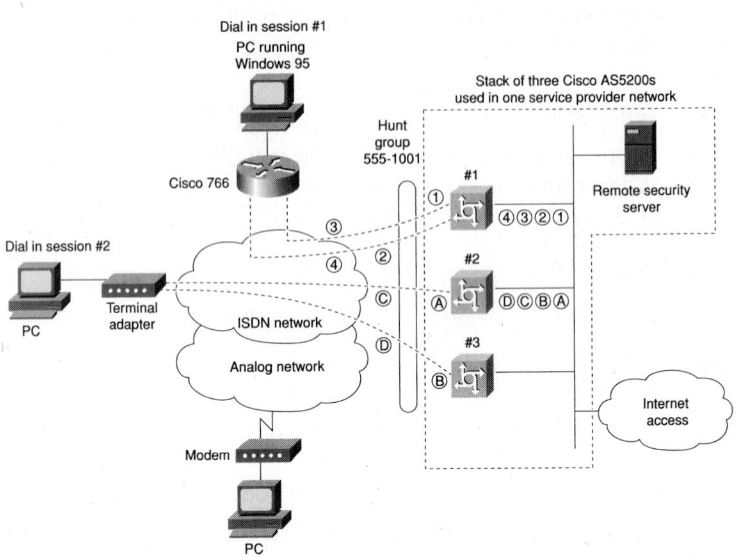


*Figure 2–8*
*A Stack Group of Access Servers Using MMP with an Offload Processor.*

When SGBP is configured on each Cisco AS5200, each access server sends out a query to each stack group member stating, for example, "I have a call coming in from walt@options.com. What is your bid for this user?" Each access server then consults the following default bidding criteria and answers the query accordingly:

1. Do I have an existing call or link for the user walt@options.com? If I do, then bid very high to get this second link in to me.
2. If I do not have an existing call for walt@options.com, then bid a value that is proportional to how much CPU I have.
3. How busy am I supporting other users?

**NOTES**

An offload server will always serve as the bundlemaster by bidding a higher value than the other devices.

### *Using Layer 2 Forwarding*

Layer 2 forwarding (L2F) is a critical component used in multichassis multilink sessions. If an access server is not in charge of a multilink session, the access server encapsulates the fragmented PPP frames and forwards them to the bundlemaster using L2F. The master device receives the calls, not through the dial port (such as a dual T1/PRI card), but through the LAN or Ethernet port. L2F simply tunnels packet fragments to the device that owns the multilink session for the call. If you include an offload server in your dial-in scenario, it creates all the virtual interfaces, owns all the multilink sessions, and reassembles all the fragmented packets received by L2F via the other stack-group members. (Refer to Figure 2–8.)

### Large-Scale Dial-In Configuration Examples

This section provides sample Cisco IOS configurations for the devices shown in Figure 2–8. The sample configurations are as follows:

- Cisco AS5200 #1 Configuration
- Cisco AS5200 #2 Configuration
- Cisco AS5200 #3 Configuration
- Cisco 7206 Configuration
- RADIUS Remote Security Examples

**NOTES**

Be sure to include your own IP addresses, host names, and security passwords where appropriate.

#### *Cisco AS5200 #1 Configuration*

The following configuration runs on the Cisco AS5200 labeled #1 in Figure 2–8:

```
!
version 11.2
service timestamps debug datetime msec
service timestamps log datetime msec
service password-encryption
no service udp-small-servers
no service tcp-small-servers
!
hostname AS5200-1
!
aaa new-model
aaa authentication login default local
aaa authentication login console enable
aaa authentication login vty local
aaa authentication login dialin radius
aaa authentication ppp default local
aaa authentication ppp dialin if-needed radius
aaa authorization exec local radius
aaa authorization network radius
aaa accounting network start-stop radius
aaa accounting exec start-stop radius
enable secret cisco
!
username admin password cisco
username MYSTACK password STACK-SECRET
sgbp group MYSTACK
sgbp member AS5200-2 10.1.1.12
sgbp member AS5200-3 10.1.1.13
```

```
sgbp member 7200 10.1.1.14
async-bootp dns-server 10.1.3.1 10.1.3.2
isdn switch-type primary-5ess
!
controller T1 0
 framing esf
 clock source line primary
 linecode b8zs
 pri-group timeslots 1-24
!
controller T1 1
 framing esf
 clock source line secondary
 linecode b8zs
 pri-group timeslots 1-24
!
interface Loopback0
 ip address 10.1.2.62 255.255.255.192
!
interface Ethernet0
 ip address 10.1.1.11 255.255.255.0
 ip summary address eigrp 10 10.1.2.0 255.255.255.192
!
interface Serial0
 no ip address
 shutdown
!
interface Serial1
 no ip address
 shutdown
!
interface Serial0:23
 no ip address
 encapsulation ppp
 isdn incoming-voice modem
 dialer rotary-group 0
 dialer-group 1
 no fair-queue
 no cdp enable
!
interface Serial1:23
 no ip address
 encapsulation ppp
 isdn incoming-voice modem
 dialer rotary-group 0
 dialer-group 1
 no fair-queue
 no cdp enable
!
interface Group-Async1
 ip unnumbered Loopback0
 encapsulation ppp
 async mode interactive
 peer default ip address pool dialin_pool
```

```
 no cdp enable
 ppp authentication chap pap dialin
 group-range 1 48
!
interface Dialer0
 ip unnumbered Loopback0
 no ip mroute-cache
 encapsulation ppp
 peer default ip address pool dialin_pool
 dialer in-band
 dialer-group 1
 no fair-queue
 no cdp enable
 ppp authentication chap pap dialin
 ppp multilink
!
router eigrp 10
 network 10.0.0.0
 passive-interface Dialer0
 no auto-summary
!
ip local pool dialin_pool 10.1.2.1 10.1.2.50
ip default-gateway 10.1.1.1
ip classless
!
!
!
dialer-list 1 protocol ip permit
radius-server host 10.1.1.23 auth-port 1645 acct-port 1646
radius-server host 10.1.1.24 auth-port 1645 acct-port 1646
radius-server key cisco
!
line con 0
 login authentication console
line 1 48
 autoselect ppp
 autoselect during-login
 login authentication dialin
 modem DialIn
line aux 0
 login authentication console
line vty 0 4
 login authentication vty
 transport input telnet rlogin
!
end
```

### Cisco AS5200 #2 Configuration

The following configuration runs on the Cisco AS5200 labeled #2 in Figure 2–8:

```
!
version 11.2
service timestamps debug datetime msec
service timestamps log datetime msec
```

```
service password-encryption
no service udp-small-servers
no service tcp-small-servers
!
hostname AS5200-2
!
aaa new-model
aaa authentication login default local
aaa authentication login console enable
aaa authentication login vty local
aaa authentication login dialin radius
aaa authentication ppp default local
aaa authentication ppp dialin if-needed radius
aaa authorization exec local radius
aaa authorization network radius
aaa accounting network start-stop radius
aaa accounting exec start-stop radius
enable secret cisco
!
username admin password cisco
username MYSTACK password STACK-SECRET
sgbp group MYSTACK
sgbp member AS5200-1 10.1.1.11
sgbp member AS5200-3 10.1.1.13
sgbp member 7200 10.1.1.14
async-bootp dns-server 10.1.3.1 10.1.3.2
isdn switch-type primary-5ess
!
controller T1 0
 framing esf
 clock source line primary
 linecode b8zs
 pri-group timeslots 1-24
!
controller T1 1
 framing esf
 clock source line secondary
 linecode b8zs
 pri-group timeslots 1-24
!
interface Loopback0
 ip address 10.1.2.126 255.255.255.192
!
interface Ethernet0
 ip address 10.1.1.12 255.255.255.0
 ip summary address eigrp 10 10.1.2.64 255.255.255.192
!
interface Serial0
 no ip address
 shutdown
!
interface Serial1
 no ip address
 shutdown
```

```
!
interface Serial0:23
 no ip address
 encapsulation ppp
 isdn incoming-voice modem
 dialer rotary-group 0
 dialer-group 1
 no fair-queue
 no cdp enable
!
interface Serial1:23
 no ip address
 encapsulation ppp
 isdn incoming-voice modem
 dialer rotary-group 0
 dialer-group 1
 no fair-queue
 no cdp enable
!
interface Group-Async1
 ip unnumbered Loopback0
 encapsulation ppp
 async mode interactive
 peer default ip address pool dialin_pool
 no cdp enable
 ppp authentication chap pap dialin
 group-range 1 48
!
interface Dialer0
 ip unnumbered Loopback0
 no ip mroute-cache
 encapsulation ppp
 peer default ip address pool dialin_pool
 dialer in-band
 dialer-group 1
 no fair-queue
 no cdp enable
 ppp authentication chap pap dialin
 ppp multilink
!
router eigrp 10
 network 10.0..0.0
 passive-interface Dialer0
 no auto-summary
!
ip local pool dialin_pool 10.1.2.65 10.1.2.114
ip default-gateway 10.1.1.1
ip classless
!
dialer-list 1 protocol ip permit
radius-server host 10.1.1.23 auth-port 1645 acct-port 1646
radius-server host 10.1.1.24 auth-port 1645 acct-port 1646
radius-server key cisco
!
```

```
line con 0
 login authentication console
line 1 48
 autoselect ppp
 autoselect during-login
 login authentication dialin
 modem DialIn
line aux 0
 login authentication console
line vty 0 4
 login authentication vty
 transport input telnet rlogin
!
end
```

### *Cisco AS5200 #3 Configuration*

The following configuration runs on the Cisco AS5200 labeled #3 in Figure 2–8:

```
!
version 11.2
service timestamps debug datetime msec
service timestamps log datetime msec
service password-encryption
no service udp-small-servers
no service tcp-small-servers
!
hostname AS5200-3
!
aaa new-model
aaa authentication login default local
aaa authentication login console enable
aaa authentication login vty local
aaa authentication login dialin radius
aaa authentication ppp default local
aaa authentication ppp dialin if-needed radius
aaa authorization exec local radius
aaa authorization network radius
aaa accounting network start-stop radius
aaa accounting exec start-stop radius
enable secret cisco
!
username admin password cisco
username MYSTACK password STACK-SECRET
sgbp group MYSTACK
sgbp member AS5200-1 10.1.1.11
sgbp member AS5200-2 10.1.1.12
sgbp member 7200 10.1.1.14
async-bootp dns-server 10.1.3.1 10.1.3.2
isdn switch-type primary-5ess
!
controller T1 0
 framing esf
 clock source line primary
 linecode b8zs
```

```
 pri-group timeslots 1-24
!
controller T1 1
 framing esf
 clock source line secondary
 linecode b8zs
 pri-group timeslots 1-24
!
interface Loopback0
 ip address 10.1.2.190 255.255.255.192
!
interface Ethernet0
 ip address 10.1.1.13 255.255.255.0
 ip summary address eigrp 10 10.1.2.128 255.255.255.192
!
interface Serial0
 no ip address
 shutdown
!
interface Serial1
 no ip address
 shutdown
!
interface Serial0:23
 no ip address
 encapsulation ppp
 isdn incoming-voice modem
 dialer rotary-group 0
 dialer-group 1
 no fair-queue
 no cdp enable
!
interface Serial1:23
 no ip address
 encapsulation ppp
 isdn incoming-voice modem
 dialer rotary-group 0
 dialer-group 1
 no fair-queue
 no cdp enable
!
interface Group-Async1
 ip unnumbered Loopback0
 encapsulation ppp
 async mode interactive
 peer default ip address pool dialin_pool
 no cdp enable
 ppp authentication chap pap dialin
 group-range 1 48
!
interface Dialer0
 ip unnumbered Loopback0
 no ip mroute-cache
 encapsulation ppp
```

```
 peer default ip address pool dialin_pool
 dialer in-band
 dialer-group 1
 no fair-queue
 no cdp enable
 ppp authentication chap pap dialin
 ppp multilink
!
router eigrp 10
 network 10.0.0.0
 passive-interface Dialer0
 no auto-summary
!
ip local pool dialin_pool 10.1.2.129 10.1.2.178
ip default-gateway 10.1.1.1
ip classless
!
dialer-list 1 protocol ip permit
radius-server host 10.1.1.23 auth-port 1645 acct-port 1646
radius-server host 10.1.1.24 auth-port 1645 acct-port 1646
radius-server key cisco
!
line con 0
 login authentication console
line 1 48
 autoselect ppp
 autoselect during-login
 login authentication dialin
 modem DialIn
line aux 0
 login authentication console
line vty 0 4
 login authentication vty
 transport input telnet rlogin
!
end
```

### *Cisco 7206 Configuration*

The following configuration runs on the Cisco 7206 router shown in Figure 2–8.

**NOTES**

Any Cisco router that has a strong CPU can be used as an offload server, such as a Cisco 4500-M, 4700-M, or 3640. However, the router must be configured to handle the necessary processing overhead demanded by each stack member.

```
!
version 11.2
service timestamps debug datetime msec
service timestamps log datetime msec
service password-encryption
```

```
no service udp-small-servers
no service tcp-small-servers
!
hostname 7200
!
aaa new-model
aaa authentication login default local
aaa authentication login console enable
aaa authentication login vty local
aaa authentication login dialin radius
aaa authentication ppp default local
aaa authentication ppp dialin if-needed radius
aaa authorization exec local radius
aaa authorization network radius
aaa accounting network start-stop radius
aaa accounting exec start-stop radius
enable secret cisco
!
username MYSTACK password STACK-SECRET
username admin password cisco
multilink virtual-template 1
sgbp group MYSTACK
sgbp member AS5200-1 10.1.1.11
sgbp member AS5200-2 10.1.1.12
sgbp member AS5200-3 10.1.1.13
sgbp seed-bid offload
async-bootp dns-server 10.1.3.1 10.1.3.2
!
interface Loopback0
 ip address 10.1.2.254 255.255.255.192
!
interface Ethernet2/0
 ip address 10.1.1.14 255.255.255.0
 ip summary address eigrp 10 10.1.2.192 255.255.255.192
!
interface Ethernet2/1
 no ip address
 shutdown
!
interface Ethernet2/2
 no ip address
 shutdown
!
interface Ethernet2/3
 no ip address
 shutdown
!
interface Virtual-Template1
 ip unnumbered Loopback0
 no ip mroute-cache
 peer default ip address pool dialin_pool
 ppp authentication chap pap dialin
 ppp multilink
!
```

```
router eigrp 10
 network 10.0.0.0
 passive-interface Virtual-Template1
 no auto-summary
!
ip local pool dialin_pool 10.1.2.193 10.1.2.242
ip default-gateway 10.1.1.1
ip classless
!
radius-server host 10.1.1.23 auth-port 1645 acct-port 1646
radius-server host 10.1.1.24 auth-port 1645 acct-port 1646
radius-server key cisco
!
line con 0
 login authentication console
line aux 0
 login authentication console
line vty 0 4
 login authentication vty
!
end
```

### *RADIUS Remote Security Examples*

The following RADIUS examples use the IETF syntax for the attributes. Depending on how the dictionary is set up, the syntax for these configurations might differ between versions of RADIUS daemons.

**NOTES**

You must have the **async dynamic address** command enabled on the network access server if you use Framed-IP-Address to statically assign IP addresses.

#### *Example 1*

The following example shows a user setup for PPP. The user's IP address comes from the configured default IP address that is set up on the interface (which can be a specific default IP address, a pointer to a local pool of addresses, or a pointer to a DHCP server). The special address that signals the default address is 255.255.255.254.

```
pppme Password = "cisco"
        CHAP-Password = "cisco"
        Service-Type = Framed,
        Framed-Protocol = PPP,
        Framed-IP-Address = 255.255.255.254
```

#### *Example 2*

The following example shows a user setup for PPP and a static IP address that stays with the user across all connections. Make sure your router is set up to support this configuration, especially for large or multiple POPs.

```
staticallypppme Password = "cisco"
        CHAP-Password = "cisco"
        Service-Type = Framed,
        Framed-Protocol = PPP,
        Framed-IP-Address = 1.1.1.1
```

### *Example 3*

The next example supports a router dialing in, which requires that a static IP address and a remote Ethernet interface be added to the network access server's routing table. The router's WAN port is assigned the address 1.1.1.2. The remote Ethernet interface is 2.1.1.0 with a class C mask. Be sure your routing table can support this requirement. You might need to redistribute the static route with a dynamic routing protocol.

```
routeme Password = "cisco"
        CHAP-Password = "cisco"
        Service-Type = Framed,
        Framed-Protocol = PPP,
        Framed-IP-Address = 1.1.1.1
        Framed-Route = "2.1.1.0/24 1.1.1.2"
```

### *Example 4*

The following example shows a user setup for the SLIP protocol. Remote users are assigned to the default address on the interface.

```
slipme Password = "cisco"
        Service-Type = Framed,
        Framed-Protocol = SLIP,
        Framed-IP-Address = 255.255.255.254
```

### *Example 5*

The following example shows a user setup for SLIP and a static IP address that stays with the user across all connections. Make sure your routing is set up to support this configuration, especially for large or multiple POPs.

```
staticallyslipme Password = "cisco"
        Service-Type = Framed,
        Framed-Protocol = SLIP,
        Framed-IP-Address = 1.1.1.13
```

### *Example 6*

This example automatically Telnets the user to a UNIX host. This configuration is useful for registering new users, providing basic UNIX shell services, or providing a guest account.

```
telnetme Password = "cisco"
        Service-Type = Login,
        Login-Service = Telnet,
        Login-IP-Host = 4.1.1.1
```

*Example 7*

This example automatically rlogins the user to a UNIX host:

```
rloginme Password = "cisco"
        Service-Type = Login,
        Login-Service = Rlogin,
        Login-IP-Host =4.1.1.2
```

If you want to prevent a second password prompt from being brought up, you must have the following two commands enabled on the router or access server:

- **rlogin trusted-remoteuser-source local**
- **rlogin trusted-localuser-source radius**

## Remote PCs Placing PPP Calls over X.25 Networks

Remote PCs stationed in X.25 PAD networks can access the Internet by dialing in to Cisco routers, which support PPP. By positioning a Cisco router at the corner of an X.25 network, ISPs and telcos can provide Internet and PPP access to PAD users. All remote PAD users, who dial in to X.25 networks, dial in to one Cisco router that allows PPP connections. Although connection performance is not optimal, these X.25-to-PPP calls utilize installed bases of X.25 equipment and cost less to operate than connecting over the standard telephone network.

**Notes**

This dial-in scenario can also be used as an enterprise solution. In this case, an enterprise consults with a third-party service provider that allows enterprises to leverage exiting X.25 enterprise equipment to provide connections back into enterprise environments.

Many cities throughout the world have large installed bases of PCs interfacing with older modems, PADs, and X.25 networks. These remote PCs or terminals dial in to PADs and make X.25 PAD calls or terminal connections to mainframe computers or other devices, which run the X.25 protocol. Unfortunately, the user interface is only a regular text-based screen in character mode (as opposed to packet mode). Therefore, many ISPs and telcos who have large investments in X.25 networks are upgrading their outdated equipment and creating separate networks for PPP connections. Because this upgrade process takes significant time and money to complete, using a Cisco router to allow PPP connections over an X.25 network is a good interim solution for a dead-end dial case.

Figure 2–9 shows a remote PC browsing the Internet through an X.25 PAD call and a Cisco 4500 router. This X.25 network is owned by an ISP or telco that is heavily invested in X.25 equipment, currently upgrading its outdated equipment, and creating separate networks for PPP connections. In this topology, the Cisco 4500 performs protocol translation between the protocols X.25 and PPP. The router is configured to accept an incoming X.25 PAD call, run and unpack PPP packets over the call, and enable the remote PC to function as if it were on the IP network.

For more information about configuring protocol translation, see Chapter 21, "Configuring Protocol Translation and Virtual Asynchronous Devices."

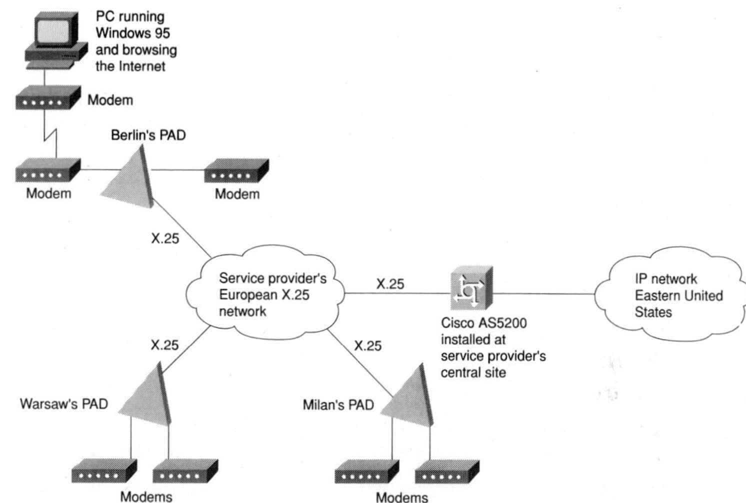


*Figure 2–9*
*Remote PC Browsing the Internet through an X.25 PAD Call and a Cisco 4500.*

## Cisco AS5200 Configuration

In the following example, PAD callers, who dial 4085551234, receive a router prompt. PAD callers who dial 4085555123401 start PPP and pick up an address from the IP pool called dialin_pool. These addresses are "borrowed" from the Ethernet interface on the Cisco AS5200. Additionally, you can create a loopback interface network and set the X.25 addresses. Be sure, however, to run a routing protocol to advertise the loopback interface network if you use this method.

**NOTES**

Be sure to include your own IP addresses, host names, and security passwords where appropriate

```
!
version 11.2
service timestamps debug datetime msec
service timestamps log datetime msec
service password-encryption
no service udp-small-servers
no service tcp-small-servers
!
hostname NAS
!
aaa new-model
aaa authentication login console enable
aaa authentication login vty tacacs+
```

```
aaa authentication login dialin tacacs+
aaa authentication ppp default tacacs+
aaa authentication ppp dialin if-needed tacacs+
enable secret cisco
!
async-bootp dns-server 10.1.3.1 10.1.3.2

vty-async
vty-async ppp authentication chap pap
!
interface Loopback0
 ip address 10.1.2.254 255.255.255.0
!
interface Ethernet0
 ip address 10.1.1.10 255.255.255.0
 ip summary address eigrp 10 10.1.2.0 255.255.255.0
!
interface Serial0
 no ip address
 encapsulation x25
 x25 address 4085551234
 x25 accept-reverse
 x25 default pad
!
router eigrp 10
 network 10.0.0.0
 passive-interface Dialer0
 no auto-summary
!
ip local pool dialin_pool 10.1.2.1 10.1.2.50
ip default-gateway 10.1.1.1

ip classless

translate x25 4085555123401 ppp ip-pool scope-name dialin_pool
!
!
dialer-list 1 protocol ip permit
!
line con 0
 login authentication console
line aux 0
 login authentication console
line vty 0 150
 login authentication vty
 transport input telnet rlogin
!
end
```

## REMOTE PCs DIALING IN TO A VIRTUAL PRIVATE DIAL NETWORK

A growing number of ISPs are providing virtual private dial networks (VPDNs) to enterprise customers, which are dial-in only solutions.

VPDN is described in the following sections:

- Exploring the Benefits of VPDNs and Who Uses Them
- Choosing the Right VPDN Scenario for Your Business Application
- Understanding How a VPDN Works
- Exploring VPDN Configuration Examples with Local Security
- Exploring a Large-Scale VPDN Example Using a Remote RADIUS Server

### Benefits of VPDNs and Who Uses Them

VPDNs are dial-in access services provided by ISPs to enterprise customers who choose not to purchase, configure, or maintain access servers or modem pools. Using this scenario, the enterprise customer avoids costly front-end access resources (such as hundreds of modems, access servers, and additional telephone lines) as well as support and maintenance costs. The VPDN scenario is also a solution for ISPs that have excess modem capacity and want to develop and offer a value-added dial-in service to their organization. Enterprises can save on capital investment by researching whether or not their ISP provides this kind of dial service.

### Choosing the Right VPDN Scenario for Your Business Application

There are two scenario-based approaches used to define or set up a VPDN solution. For ISPs that provide access for five or fewer enterprises or domains, Cisco Systems recommends a small-sized VPDN with a local security solution. For ISPs that provide access for six or more enterprises or domains, Cisco Systems recommends a large-sized VPDN with a remote access control security solution. Cisco also recommends a large-scale VPDN for ISPs that have a large pool of network access servers to maintain. The appropriate solution depends primarily on serviceability and scalability issues.

The difference between a small and large VPDN is the number of high-density access servers installed at the ISP's POP in addition to local versus remote security. Small-scale VPDNs require system administrators to maintain the security database on each dial-in access server. For large-scale VPDNs, the ISP's authentication process is easily maintained by a single access control security server using a UNIX-based application such as CiscoSecure. Each time a customer is added to a large-scale solution, a new domain name map entry does not need to be added locally to each access server's configuration file. Instead, the entry is recorded once in the security server's database. Remote security server solutions also take on the responsibility of defining L2F tunnel definitions and user names.

## How a VPDN Works

A sample network topology for a VPDN scenario is shown in Figure 2–10. An ISP has a stack of Cisco AS5200s connected to its 10.0.0.0 network, which provides a pool of integrated modems (for analog calls) and ISDN bearer channels (for digital calls) for three enterprise customers (cisco.com, 0com.com, and decend.com). The ISP provides each enterprise with its own home gateway router, firewall setup configured for authentication, and a common dial-in telephone number for each company's group of telecommuters or remote office users. Although the ISP provides the dial-in vehicle for the remote nodes, each enterprise customer assigns its own IP addresses and processes all the PPP packets sent by the remote PCs. All network resource security is owned and maintained by the enterprise customer. From the enterprise's point of view, the connections initiated by the remote clients are virtually private and maintained by the enterprise.

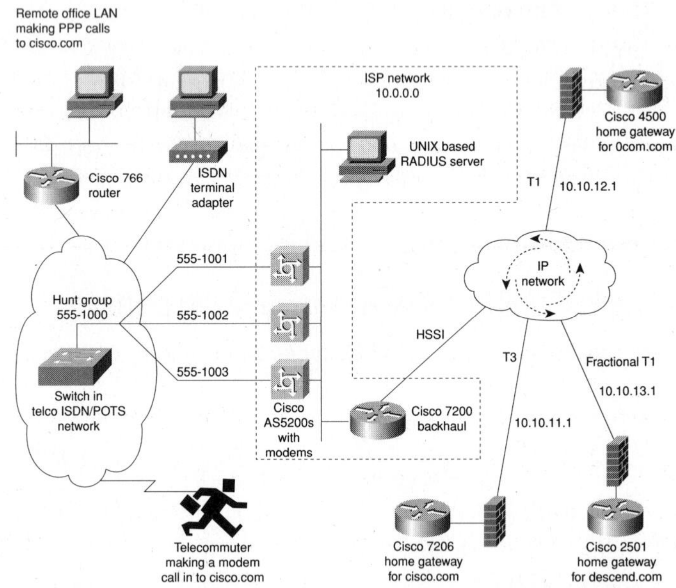


*Figure 2–10 Network Topology for a Virtual Private Dial-Up Network.*

All enterprise home gateways only allow incoming L2F UDP packets on the WAN connection to their service provider. This configuration effectively firewalls off any IP connectivity other than that which is needed for the forwarding of user traffic. These enterprise network connections are virtually private and owned by the enterprise.

On the ISP's side of the configuration, each T1 line is assigned its own dial-in telephone number. The telco groups all T1 lines that connect to each Cisco AS5200 into a single hunt group. Because T1 lines are limited to 24 channels, the telco creates a hunt group telephone number so that the dial-in access is not limited to only 24 simultaneous users. A hunt group telephone number (shown in Figure 2–10 as 555-1000) provides the dial-in access for the dial-in clients. The hunt group number is the only number that clients dial in to, regardless of whether they are using modems, terminal adapters, or routers. As soon as a call comes into the telco's network, the telco's switch searches or hunts for the first available channel on each of the Cisco AS5200's T1 lines. One hunt group telephone number on the telco side provides multiple dial-in services for the ISP.

Depending on the size of the VPDN solution needed, local or remote security is configured on the ISP's access network. For small-size VPDN solutions, the security database is configured and replicated locally on each Cisco AS5200. For larger-size VPDN solutions, the security database is configured on an access control server (for example, a TACACS+ or RADIUS server running CiscoSecure). Each Cisco AS5200 that receives a call queries the local or remote security database for information about where to tunnel or send the call (for example, user name, domain mapping, home gateway address, and user profile).

Here is an example of how the VPDN dial-in process works for a telecommuter dialing in to the Cisco System's network. The telecommuter dials in to the ISP's modem pool using the hunt group dial-in number provisioned for Cisco Systems. Based on the dial-in client's login information, a Cisco AS5200 creates an L2F tunnel and relays the client's PPP frames over an IP network to the cisco.com gateway router for authentication. After a tunnel is built to the cisco.com gateway router, a backhaul router (shown in Figure 2–10 as the Cisco 7200) forwards encapsulated PPP frames on top of UDP packets through an IP substrate—a networking base through which packets travel.

**NOTES**

Rather than basing the routing on the domain and username, an ISP can build an L2F tunnel based on the phone number that the remote clients dial. This dialed number identification service (DNIS) information is collected, however, only if you are using ISDN PRI lines, or if you have CT1 lines, and you must use MICA modem technology.

### VPDN Configuration Examples with Local Security

The following sample configurations run on the routers and access servers featured in Figure 2–10. The configurations include only basic IP and local security support.

- Cisco AS5200 Configuration for the Service Provider's Network Access Servers
- Cisco 2501 Home Gateway Configuration for descend.com
- Cisco 4500 Series Home Gateway Configuration for 0com.com
- Cisco 7206 Series Home Gateway Configuration for cisco.com

**NOTES**

Be sure to include your own IP addresses, host names, and security passwords where appropriate.

### *Cisco AS5200 Configuration for the Service Provider's Network Access Servers*

The following configuration is deployed on each of the Cisco AS5200s included in the service provider's stack group (refer to Figure 2–10. The only parts of the configuration that are configured differently on each access server are the Ethernet IP addresses and the IP addresses for the local pools.

```
!
version 11.2
service timestamps debug datetime msec
service timestamps log datetime msec
service password-encryption
no service udp-small-servers
no service tcp-small-servers
!
hostname NAS
!
aaa new-model
aaa authentication login default local
aaa authentication login console enable
aaa authentication login vty local
aaa authentication login dialin local
aaa authentication ppp default local
aaa authentication ppp dialin if-needed local
enable secret cisco
!
username admin password cisco
username ISP password ISP
username cisco.com password CISCO_SECRET
username 0com.com password 0COM_SECRET
username descend.com password DESCEND_SECRET
vpdn enable
vpdn outgoing cisco.com ISP ip 10.10.11.1
vpdn outgoing 0com.com ISP ip 10.10.12.1
vpdn outgoing descend.com ISP ip 10.10.13.1
async-bootp dns-server 10.1.3.1 10.1.3.2
isdn switch-type primary-5ess
!
controller T1 0
 framing esf
 clock source line primary
 linecode b8zs
 pri-group timeslots 1-24
!
controller T1 1
 framing esf
 clock source line secondary
 linecode b8zs
 pri-group timeslots 1-24
!
interface Loopback0
 ip address 10.1.2.254 255.255.255.0
!
interface Ethernet0
```

```
 ip address 10.1.1.10 255.255.255.0
 ip summary address eigrp 10 10.1.2.0 255.255.255.0
!
interface Serial0
 no ip address
 shutdown
!
interface Serial1
 no ip address
 shutdown
!
interface Serial0:23
 no ip address
 encapsulation ppp
 isdn incoming-voice modem
 dialer rotary-group 0
 dialer-group 1
 no fair-queue
 no cdp enable
!
interface Serial1:23
 no ip address
 encapsulation ppp
 isdn incoming-voice modem
 dialer rotary-group 0
 dialer-group 1
 no fair-queue
 no cdp enable
!
interface Group-Async1
 ip unnumbered Loopback0
 encapsulation ppp
 async mode interactive
 peer default ip address pool dialin_pool
 no cdp enable
 ppp authentication chap pap dialin
 group-range 1 48
!
interface Dialer0
 ip unnumbered Loopback0
 no ip mroute-cache
 encapsulation ppp
 peer default ip address pool dialin_pool
 dialer in-band
 dialer-group 1
 no fair-queue
 no cdp enable
 ppp authentication chap pap dialin
 ppp multilink
!
router eigrp 10
 network 10.0.0.0
 passive-interface Dialer0
 no auto-summary
```

```
!
ip local pool dialin_ppol 10.1.2.1 10.1.2.50
ip default-gateway 10.1.1.1
ip classless
!
!
!
dialer-list 1 protocol ip permit
!
line con 0
 login authentication console
line 1 48
 autoselect ppp
 autoselect during-login
 login authentication dialin
 modem DialIn
line aux 0
 login authentication console
line vty 0 4
 login authentication vty
 transport input telnet rlogin
!
end
```

### Cisco 2501 Home Gateway Configuration for descend.com

The following configuration runs on the Cisco 2501, which is used by descend.com in Figure 2–10.

```
!
version 11.2
no service udp-small-servers
no service tcp-small-servers
!
hostname DESCEND_HGW
!
aaa new-model
aaa authentication login default local
aaa authentication ppp default local
!
username descend.com password DESCEND_SECRET
username ISP password ISP
username pcuser@descend.com password cisco
vpdn enable
vpdn incoming ISP descend.com virtual-template 1
!
interface Ethernet0
 ip address 3.1.1.1 255.255.255.0
!
interface Serial0
 ip address 10.10.13.1 255.255.255.252
 ip access-group 101 in
 encapsulation ppp
!
interface Serial1
 no ip address
```

```
 shutdown
!
interface Virtual-Template1
 ip unnumbered Ethernet0
 peer default ip address pool descend-pool
 ppp authentication chap pap
!
router eigrp 3
 network 3.0.0.0
 no auto-summary
!
ip local pool descend-pool 3.1.1.3 3.1.1.22
ip classless
!
!
line con 0
line aux 0
line vty 0 4
!
end
```

You can also use the following access lists to firewall off this home gateway from the VPDN provider. These access lists, however, cut off all IP traffic on the router except for L2F information:

- **access-list 101 permit udp any host** *ip-address-of-serial-interface* **eq 1701**
- **access-list 101 deny ip any any**

### Cisco 4500 Series Home Gateway Configuration for 0com.com

The following configuration runs on the Cisco 4500, which is used by 0com.com in Figure 2–10.

```
!
version 11.2
no service udp-small-servers
no service tcp-small-servers
!
hostname 0COM_HGW
!
aaa new-model
aaa authentication login default local
aaa authentication ppp default local
!
username 0com.com password 0COM_SECRET
username ISP password ISP
username pcuser@0com.com password cisco
vpdn enable
vpdn incoming ISP 0com.com virtual-template 1
!
interface Ethernet0
 ip address 2.1.1.1 255.255.255.0
!
interface Ethernet1
 no ip address
```

```
 shutdown
!
interface Serial0
 ip address 10.10.12.1 255.255.255.252
 ip access-group 101 in
 encapsulation ppp
!
interface Serial1
 no ip address
 shutdown
!
interface Serial2
 no ip address
 shutdown
!
interface Serial3
 no ip address
 shutdown
!
interface Virtual-Template1
 ip unnumbered Ethernet0
 peer default ip address pool 0com-pool
 ppp authentication chap pap
!
router eigrp 2
 network 2.0.0.0
 no auto-summary
!
ip local pool 0com-pool 2.1.1.3 2.1.1.52
ip classless
!
!
line con 0
line aux 0
line vty 0 4
```

You can also use the following access lists to firewall off this home gateway from the VPDN provider. However, these access lists cut off all IP traffic on the router except for L2F information.

- **access-list 101 permit udp any host** *ip-address-of-serial-interface* **eq 1701**
- **access-list 101 deny ip any any**

### *Cisco 7206 Series Home Gateway Configuration for cisco.com*

The following configuration runs on the Cisco 7206, which is used by cisco.com in Figure 2–10.

```
!
version 11.2
no service udp-small-servers
no service tcp-small-servers
!
hostname CISCO_HGW
!
```

```
aaa new-model
aaa authentication login default local
aaa authentication ppp default local
!
username cisco.com password CISCO_SECRET
username ISP password ISP
username pcuser@cisco.com password cisco
vpdn enable
vpdn incoming ISP cisco.com virtual-template 1
!
interface Ethernet2/0
 ip address 1.1.1.1 255.255.255.0
!
interface Ethernet2/1
 no ip address
 shutdown
!
interface Ethernet2/2
 no ip address
 shutdown
!
interface Ethernet2/3
 no ip address
 shutdown
!
interface Serial3/0
 ip address 10.10.11.1 255.255.255.252
 ip access-group 101 in
 encapsulation ppp
!
interface Serial3/1
 no ip address
 shutdown
!
interface Serial3/2
 no ip address
 shutdown
!
interface Serial3/3
 no ip address
 shutdown
!
interface Virtual-Template1
 ip unnumbered Ethernet2/1
 peer default ip address pool cisco-pool
 ppp authentication chap pap
!
router eigrp 1
 network 1.0.0.0
 no auto-summary
!
ip local pool cisco-pool 1.1.1.3 1.1.1.102
ip classless
!
```

```
line con 0
line aux 0
line vty 0 4
!
end
```

You can also use the following access lists to firewall off this home gateway from the VPDN provider. However, these access lists cut off all IP traffic on the router except for L2F information.

- **access-list 101 permit udp any host** *ip-address-of-serial-interface* **eq 1701**
- **access-list 101 deny ip any any**

## Large-Scale VPDN Example Using a Remote RADIUS Server

Large-scale VPDNs can provide dial-in access for dozens of different home gateways owned and maintained by different customers. For these large-scale scenarios, it is impractical to configure the tunneling information for each home gateway on each network access server. Rather, the call tunneling information is set up on an access control server, such as a UNIX-based RADIUS server, which is owned and maintained by the service provider. All network resource security, however, is still maintained by the enterprise customers at their home gateways.

This section includes a Cisco AS5200 configuration using RADIUS security, which is deployed on each stack group member in the large-scale VPDN solution. This section also includes a user's file for a UNIX-based RADIUS server, which keeps track of all the incoming call tunneling information for multiple home gateways.

To compliment a remote RADIUS security solution, run the following configuration on each Cisco AS5200 in the VPDN stack group. See Figure 2–10.

**NOTES**

Be sure to include your own IP addresses, host names, and security passwords where appropriate.

```
!
version 11.2
service timestamps debug datetime msec
service timestamps log datetime msec
service password-encryption
no service udp-small-servers
no service tcp-small-servers
!
hostname ISP
!
aaa new-model
aaa authentication login default local
aaa authentication login console enable
aaa authentication login vty local
aaa authentication login dialin radius
aaa authentication ppp default local
aaa authentication ppp dialin if-needed radius
```

```
aaa authorization network radius
aaa accounting exec start-stop radius
aaa accounting network start-stop radius
enable secret cisco
!
username admin password cisco
vpdn enable
async-bootp dns-server 10.1.3.1 10.1.3.2
isdn switch-type primary-5ess
!
controller T1 0
 framing esf
 clock source line primary
 linecode b8zs
 pri-group timeslots 1-24
!
controller T1 1
 framing esf
 clock source line secondary
 linecode b8zs
 pri-group timeslots 1-24
!
interface Loopback0
 ip address 10.1.2.254 255.255.255.0
!
interface Ethernet0
 ip address 10.1.1.10 255.255.255.0
 ip summary address eigrp 10 10.1.2.0 255.255.255.0
!
interface Serial0
 no ip address
 shutdown
!
interface Serial1
 no ip address
 shutdown
!
interface Serial0:23
 no ip address
 encapsulation ppp
 isdn incoming-voice modem
 dialer rotary-group 0
 dialer-group 1
 no fair-queue
 no cdp enable
!
interface Serial1:23
 no ip address
 encapsulation ppp
 isdn incoming-voice modem
 dialer rotary-group 0
 dialer-group 1
 no fair-queue
 no cdp enable
```

```
!
interface Group-Async1
 ip unnumbered Loopback0
 encapsulation ppp
 async mode interactive
 peer default ip address pool dialin_pool
 no cdp enable
 ppp authentication chap pap dialin
 group-range 1 48
!
interface Dialer0
 ip unnumbered Loopback0
 no ip mroute-cache
 encapsulation ppp
 peer default ip address pool dialin_pool
 dialer in-band
 dialer-group 1
 no fair-queue
 no cdp enable
 ppp authentication chap pap dialin
 ppp multilink
!
router eigrp 10
 network 10.0.0.0
 passive-interface Dialer0
 no auto-summary
!
ip local pool dialin_pool 10.1.2.1 10.1.2.50
ip default-gateway 10.1.1.1
ip classless
!
dialer-list 1 protocol ip permit
radius-server host 10.1.1.23 auth-port 1645 acct-port 1646
radius-server host 10.1.1.24 auth-port 1645 acct-port 1646
radius-server key cisco
!
line con 0
 login authentication console
line 1 48
 autoselect ppp
 autoselect during-login
 login authentication dialin
 modem DialIn
line aux 0
 login authentication console
line vty 0 4
 login authentication vty
 transport input telnet rlogin
!
end
```

The following user's file runs on the UNIX-based RADIUS server shown in Figure 2–10. This user's file provides the L2F tunnel definitions and user names for ten different home gateway routers at ten different company sites. This configuration uses the cisco-avpair attribute, which is a vendor-specific attribute (attribute 26). The RADIUS server must support the vendor-specific option, as defined in RFC 2138. Otherwise, the configuration will not work.

```
corp1.com Password = "cisco", Service-Type = Outbound-User
        cisco-avpair = "vpdn:tunnel-id=NAS",
        cisco-avpair = "vpdn:nas-password=corp1secret",
        cisco-avpair = "vpdn:gw-password=corp1secret",
        cisco-avpair = "vpdn:ip-addresses=10.10.1.1"

corp2.com Password = "cisco", Service-Type = Outbound-User
        cisco-avpair = "vpdn:tunnel-id=NAS",
        cisco-avpair = "vpdn:nas-password=corp2secret",
        cisco-avpair = "vpdn:gw-password=corp2secret",
        cisco-avpair = "vpdn:ip-addresses=10.10.2.1"

corp3.com Password = "cisco", Service-Type = Outbound-User
        cisco-avpair = "vpdn:tunnel-id=NAS",
        cisco-avpair = "vpdn:nas-password=corp3secret",
        cisco-avpair = "vpdn:gw-password=corp3secret",
        cisco-avpair = "vpdn:ip-addresses=10.10.3.1"

corp4.com Password = "cisco", Service-Type = Outbound-User
        cisco-avpair = "vpdn:tunnel-id=NAS",
        cisco-avpair = "vpdn:nas-password=corp4secret",
        cisco-avpair = "vpdn:gw-password=corp4secret",
        cisco-avpair = "vpdn:ip-addresses=10.10.4.1"

corp5.com Password = "cisco", Service-Type = Outbound-User
        cisco-avpair = "vpdn:tunnel-id=NAS",
        cisco-avpair = "vpdn:nas-password=corp5secret",
        cisco-avpair = "vpdn:gw-password=corp5secret",
        cisco-avpair = "vpdn:ip-addresses=10.10.5.1"

corp6.com Password = "cisco", Service-Type = Outbound-User
        cisco-avpair = "vpdn:tunnel-id=NAS",
        cisco-avpair = "vpdn:nas-password=corp6secret",
        cisco-avpair = "vpdn:gw-password=corp6secret",
        cisco-avpair = "vpdn:ip-addresses=10.10.6.1"

corp7.com Password = "cisco", Service-Type = Outbound-User
        cisco-avpair = "vpdn:tunnel-id=NAS",
        cisco-avpair = "vpdn:nas-password=corp7secret",
        cisco-avpair = "vpdn:gw-password=corp7secret",
        cisco-avpair = "vpdn:ip-addresses=10.10.7.1"

corp8.com Password = "cisco", Service-Type = Outbound-User
        cisco-avpair = "vpdn:tunnel-id=NAS",
        cisco-avpair = "vpdn:nas-password=corp8secret",
        cisco-avpair = "vpdn:gw-password=corp8secret",
        cisco-avpair = "vpdn:ip-addresses=10.10.8.1"

corp9.com Password = "cisco", Service-Type = Outbound-User
        cisco-avpair = "vpdn:tunnel-id=NAS",
```

```
        cisco-avpair = "vpdn:nas-password=corp9secret",
        cisco-avpair = "vpdn:gw-password=corp9secret",
        cisco-avpair = "vpdn:ip-addresses=10.10.9.1"

corp10.com Password = "cisco", Service-Type = Outbound-User
        cisco-avpair = "vpdn:tunnel-id=NAS",
        cisco-avpair = "vpdn:nas-password=corp10secret",
        cisco-avpair = "vpdn:gw-password=corp10secret",
        cisco-avpair = "vpdn:ip-addresses=10.10.10.1"
```

The following configuration can run on a Cisco 4500 series home gateway router that is used in a large-scale VPDN solution:

```
!
version 11.2
no service udp-small-servers
no service tcp-small-servers
!
hostname CORP1_HomeGateway
!
aaa new-model
aaa authentication login default local
aaa authentication ppp default local
!
username NAS password corp1secret
username NAS password corp1secret
username pcuser@corp1.com password cisco
vpdn enable
vpdn incoming ISP corp1.com virtual-template 1
!
interface Ethernet0
 ip address 4.1.1.1 255.255.255.0
!
interface Ethernet1
 no ip address
 shutdown
!
interface Serial0
 ip address 10.10.1.1 255.255.255.252
 encapsulation ppp
!
interface Serial1
 no ip address
 shutdown
!
interface Serial2
 no ip address
 shutdown
!
interface Serial3
 no ip address
 shutdown
!
interface Virtual-Template1
 ip unnumbered Ethernet0
```

```
 peer default ip address pool corp1_pool
 ppp authentication chap pap
!
router eigrp 2
 network 2.0.0.0
 no auto-summary
!
ip local pool corp1_pool 4.1.1.3 4.1.1.52
ip classless
!
!
line con 0
line aux 0
line vty 0 4
```

CHAPTER 3

# Enterprise Dial Scenarios and Configurations

This chapter provides sample hardware and software configurations for specific dial scenarios used by enterprises. Each configuration is designed to support IP network traffic with basic security for the specified scenario.

The following scenarios are described:

- Scenario 1—Remote Offices and Telecommuters Dialing In to a Central Site
- Scenario 2—Bidirectional Dial Networking between a Central Site and Remote Offices or Telecommuters
- Scenario 3—Telecommuters Dialing In to a Mixed Protocol Environment

**NOTES**

If you use token card-based security in your dial network, Cisco recommends that you enable PAP authentication and disable multilink to maximize dial-in performance.

## SCALABILITY AND DESIGN ISSUES

You need to consider scalablility and design issues when building dial enterprise networks. As the number of company employees increases, the number of remote users needing to dial in increases. A scalable dial solution is needed as the demand for dial-in ports grows. It is not uncommon, for example, for a fast-growing enterprise to grow from a demand of 100 modems to 250 modems in less than one year.

You should always maintain a surplus of dial-in ports to accommodate company growth and occasional increases in access demand. In the early stages of a fast-growing company that has 100 modems installed for 6,000 registered remote users, only 50 to 60 modems might be active at the same time. One year later, however, 250 modems might be installed to support 10,000 registered token card holders.

During special company occasions, such as a worldwide convention, demand for remote access can also increase significantly. During such an activity, dial-in lines are heavily stressed throughout the day and evening by remote sales people using laptops to access e-mail and share files. This behavior is indicative of salespeople working from their home territories or sales offices. Network administrators need to prepare for these remote access bursts, which cause significant increases for remote access demand.

### REMOTE OFFICES AND TELECOMMUTERS DIALING IN TO A CENTRAL SITE

Employees stationed in remote offices or disparate locations often dial in to central sites or headquarter offices to download or upload files and check e-mail. These employees often dial in to the corporate network from a remote office LAN using ISDN or from another location such as a hotel room using a modem.

The following types of remote enterprise users dial in to enterprise networks:

- Full-time telecommuters—Employees using stationary workstations to dial in from a small office or home office (SOHO), making ISDN connections with terminal adapters or PC cards through the public telephone network, and operating at higher speeds over the network, which rules out the need for a modem.
- Travelers—Employees such as salespeople who are not in a steady location for more than 30% of the time, usually dial in to the network with a laptop and modem through the public telephone network, and primarily access the network to check e-mail or transfer a few files.
- Workday extenders—Employees who primarily work in the company office, occasionally dial in to the enterprise with a mobile or stationary workstation plus modem, and primarily access the network to check e-mail or transfer a few files.

Remote office LANs typically dial in to other networks using ISDN, which provides a larger bandwidth that cannot be attained over analog telephone connections. Remote offices that use Frame Relay to access other networks require a more costly dedicated link.

Connections initiated by remote offices or telecommuters are brought up on an as-needed basis, which results in substantial cost savings for the company. In dial-on-demand scenarios, users are not connected for long periods of time. The number of remote nodes requiring access is relatively low, and the completion time for the dial-in task is short.

Central or headquarter sites typically do not dial out to the remote LANs or devices. Instead, central sites respond to calls. Remote sites initiate calls. A field sales office, for example, might use ISDN to dial in to and browse a central site's intranet. Additionally, a warehouse comprised of five employees can use ISDN to log in to a remote network server to download or upload product order information. For an example of bidirectional dialing, see the section "Bidirectional Dial Networking between a Central Site and Remote Offices or Telecommuters," later in this chapter.

**NOTES**

When using dial-on-demand routing, you must make a fundamental decision about how your routing will be set up: to use static routes or snapshot routing. For IP-only configurations, static routes are commonly used for remote dial-in. For IPX networking, snapshot routing is often used to minimize configuration complexity.

---

Figure 3–1 shows an example of a remote office placing digital calls in to a central site network. The remote office router can be any Cisco router with a BRI physical interface, such as a Cisco 766 or Cisco 1604. The central office gateway router can be any Cisco router that supports PRI connections, such as a Cisco 3600 series, 4000 series, or 7000 series router.

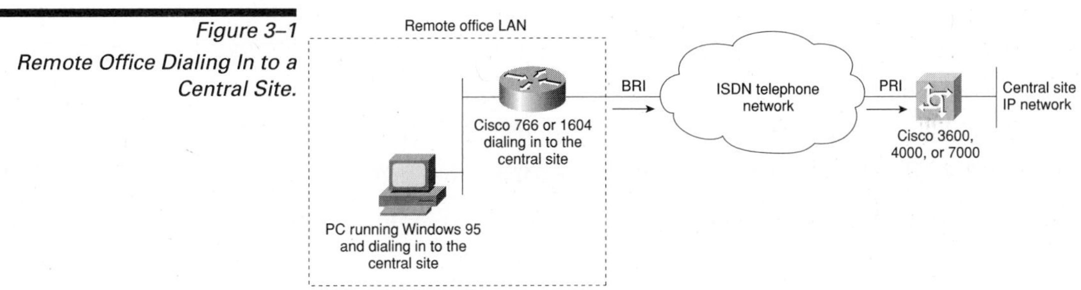


*Figure 3–1 Remote Office Dialing In to a Central Site.*

Figure 3–2 shows an example of a remote office and telecommuter dialing in to a central site. The remote office places digital calls. The telecommuter places analog calls. The remote office router can be any Cisco router with a BRI interface, such as a Cisco 766, 1604, or 2503. The central office gateway router is a Cisco AS5200 or Cisco 3640, which supports both PRI and analog connections.

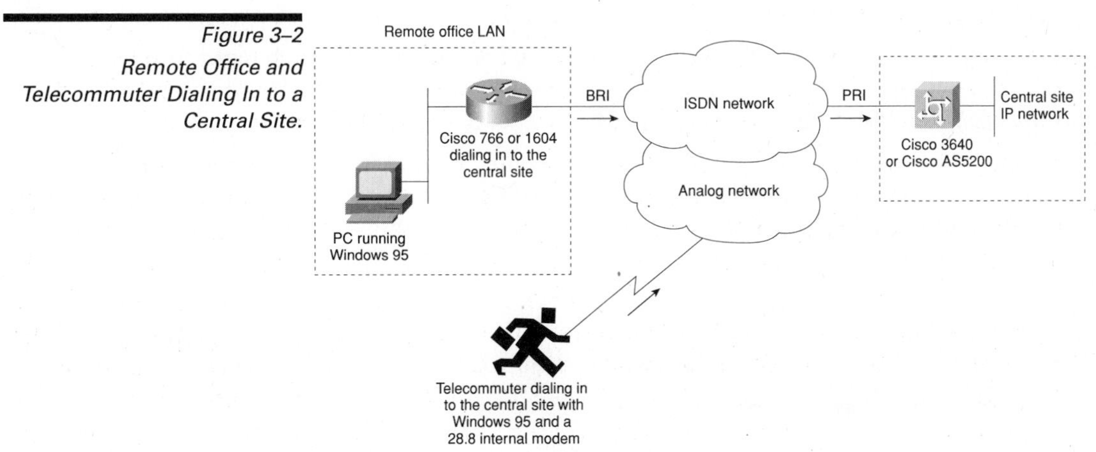


*Figure 3–2 Remote Office and Telecommuter Dialing In to a Central Site.*

## Sample Configurations for Remote Offices and Telecommuters

The following sample configurations are provided for different combinations of dial-in scenarios, which can be derived from Figure 3–1 and Figure 3–2:

- Cisco 1604 Dialing In to a Cisco 3620 Central Site Router
- Cisco 700 Series Router Dialing In to a Cisco 3620 Central Site Access Router
- Cisco 700 Series Router Using PAT to Dial In to a Cisco AS5200 Central Site Access Server
- Cisco 1600 Using Easy IP to Dial In to a Central Site
- Cisco 3640 Central Site Configuration to Support ISDN and Modem Calls
- Cisco AS5200 Central Site Configuration Using Remote Security

**NOTES**

Be sure to include your own IP addresses, host names, and security passwords where appropriate.

### *Cisco 1604 Dialing In to a Cisco 3620 Central Site Router*

This section provides a common configuration for a Cisco 1604 remote office router dialing in to a Cisco 3620 access router positioned at a central enterprise site. Only ISDN digital calls are supported in this scenario. No analog modem calls are supported. All calls are initiated by the remote router on an as-needed basis. The Cisco 3620 is not set up to dial out to the Cisco 1604 (refer to Figure 3–1).

The following configurations for the Cisco 1604 and Cisco 3620 use the IP unnumbered address configuration, Multilink PPP, and the dial-load threshold feature, which brings up the second B channel when the first B channel exceeds a certain limit. Because static routes are used, a routing protocol is not configured. A default static route is configured on the Cisco 1604, which points back to the central site. The central site also has a static route that points back to the remote LAN. Static route configurations assume that you have only one LAN segment at each remote office.

#### *Configuration for the Remote Cisco 1604*

The following example runs on the Cisco 1604 router, shown in Figure 3–1. This SOHO router places digital calls in to the Cisco 3620 central site access router. See the next example for the Cisco 3620 router's running configuration.

```
!
version 11.2
service timestamps debug datetime msec
service timestamps log datetime msec
service password-encryption
no service udp-small-servers
no service tcp-small-servers
!
hostname remotelan1
!
```

```
enable secret cisco
!
username NAS password dialpass
username admin password cisco

isdn switch-type basic-5ess
!
interface Ethernet0
 ip address 10.2.1.1 255.255.255.0
!
interface BRI0
 ip unnumbered Ethernet0
 encapsulation ppp
 dialer map ip 10.1.1.10 name NAS 5551234
 dialer load-threshold 100 either
 dialer-group 1
 no fair-queue
 ppp authentication chap pap callin
 ppp multilink
!
ip classless
ip route 0.0.0.0 0.0.0.0 10.1.1.10
ip route 10.1.1.10 255.255.255.255 BRI0
dialer-list 1 protocol ip permit
!
line con 0
line vty 0 4
 login local
!
end
```

### *Configuration for the Cisco 3620 Central Site Access Router*

The following sample configuration runs on the Cisco 3620 shown in Figure 3–1. This modular access router has one 2-port PRI network module installed in slot 1 and one 1-port Ethernet network module installed in slot 0. The router receives only digital ISDN calls from the Cisco 1604. The configuration for the Cisco 1604 is provided in the previous example.

```
!
version 11.2
service timestamps debug datetime msec
service timestamps log datetime msec
service password-encryption
no service udp-small-servers
no service tcp-small-servers
!
hostname NAS
!
aaa new-model
aaa authentication login default local
aaa authentication login console enable
aaa authentication login vty local
aaa authentication login dialin local
aaa authentication ppp default local
```

```
aaa authentication ppp dialin if-needed local
enable secret cisco
!
username admin password cisco
username remotelan1 password dialpass

async-bootp dns-server 10.1.3.1 10.1.3.2
isdn switch-type primary-5ess
!
controller T1 1/0
 framing esf
 clock source line
 linecode b8zs
 pri-group timeslots 1-24
!
controller T1 1/1
 framing esf
 clock source line
 linecode b8zs
 pri-group timeslots 1-24
!
interface Loopback0
 ip address 10.1.2.254 255.255.255.0
!
interface Ethernet 0/0
 ip address 10.1.1.10 255.255.255.0
 ip summary address eigrp 10 10.1.2.0 255.255.255.0
!
interface Serial 1/0:23
 no ip address
 encapsulation ppp
 isdn incoming-voice modem
 dialer rotary-group 0
 dialer-group 1
 no fair-queue
 no cdp enable
!
interface Serial 1/1:23
 no ip address
 encapsulation ppp
 isdn incoming-voice modem
 dialer rotary-group 0
 dialer-group 1
 no fair-queue
 no cdp enable
!
interface Dialer0
 ip unnumbered Loopback0
 no ip mroute-cache
 encapsulation ppp
 peer default ip address pool dialin_pool
 dialer in-band
 dialer-group 1
 no fair-queue
 no cdp enable
```

```
 ppp authentication chap pap dialin
 ppp multilink
!
router eigrp 10
 network 10.0.0.0
 passive-interface Dialer0
 default-metric 64 100 250 100 1500
 redistribute static
 no auto-summary
!
ip local pool dialin_pool 10.1.2.1 10.1.2.50
ip default-gateway 10.1.1.1

ip route 10.2.1.1 255.255.255.255 Dialer0
ip route 10.2.1.0 255.255.255.0 10.2.1.1

ip classless
!
dialer-list 1 protocol ip permit
!
line con 0
 login authentication console
line aux 0
 login authentication console
line vty 0 4
 login authentication vty
 transport input telnet rlogin
!
end
```

### Cisco 700 Series Router Dialing In to a Cisco 3620 Central Site Access Router

This section provides a common configuration for a Cisco 760 or Cisco 770 series remote office router placing digital calls in to a Cisco 3620 router positioned at a central enterprise site. All calls are initiated by the remote router on an as-needed basis. The Cisco 3620 is not set up to dial out to the remote office router (refer to Figure 3–1).

#### Configuration for the Remote Cisco 700 Series Router

The following example is for a Cisco 760 or Cisco 770 series ISDN router placing digital calls in to a central site router that supports ISDN PRI, such as the Cisco 3620. In this scenario, ISDN unnumbered interfaces with static routes are pointing back to the Cisco 3620.

To configure the router, perform the following tasks. This configuration assumes that you are starting from the router's default configuration. To return the router to its default configuration, issue the **set default** command.

| Step | Command | Purpose |
|---|---|---|
| 1 | ><br>> **set systemname remotelan1**<br>remotelan1> | At the system prompt level, specify the router's host name, which is also used when responding to CHAP authentication with the Cisco 3620. For CHAP authentication, the system's name must match the username configured on the Cisco 3620. |

| Step | Command | Purpose |
|---|---|---|
| 2 | remotelan1> **set ppp secret client**<br>remotelan1> Enter new password: **dialpass**<br>remotelan1> Enter new password: **dialpass** | Set the transmit and receive password for the client. This is the password that is used in response to CHAP authentication requests, and it must match the username password configured on the Cisco 3620. |
| 3 | remotelan1> **set encapsulation ppp** | Set PPP encapsulation for incoming and outgoing authentication instead of CPP. |
| 4 | remotelan1> **set ppp multilink on** | Enable PPP multilink. |
| 5 | remotelan1> **set user nas**<br>remotelan1> New user nas being created | Create the profile *nas*, which is reserved for the Cisco 3620. |
| 6 | remotelan1:nas> **set ip 0.0.0.0** | Specify the LAN IP address 0.0.0.0. |
| 7 | remotelan1:nas> **set ip framing none** | Configure the profiles to not use Ethernet framing. |
| 8 | remotelan1:nas> **set ip route destination 0.0.0.0 gateway 10.1.1.10** | Set the default route to point to the Cisco 3620 router's Ethernet IP address. |
| 9 | remotelan1:nas> **set timeout 300** | Set the idle time at which the B channel will be dropped. In this case, the line is dropped after 300 seconds of idle time. |
| 10 | remotelan1:nas> **set 1/2 number 5551234** | Set the number to call when dialing out of the first and second B channel. |
| 11 | remotelan1:nas> **cd lan** | Enter LAN profile mode. |
| 12 | remotelan1:LAN> **set bridging off** | Turn bridging off. |
| 13 | remotelan1:LAN> **set ip routing on** | Turn on IP routing. |
| 14 | remotelan1:LAN> **set ip 10.2.1.1** | Set the LAN IP address for the interface. |

After you configure the Cisco 760 or Cisco 770 series router, the final configuration should look like this:

```
set systemname remotelan1
set ppp secret client
set encapsulation ppp
set ppp multilink on
cd lan
set bridging off
set ip routing on
set ip 10.2.1.1
set subnet 255.255.255.0
```

```
set user nas
set bridging off
set ip 0.0.0.0
set ip netmask 0.0.0.0
set ip framing none
set ip route destination 0.0.0.0 gateway 10.1.1.10
set timeout 300
set 1 number 5551234
set 2 number 5551234
```

The previous software configuration does not provide for any access security. The following optional commands provide access security.

| Command | Purpose |
|---|---|
| **set ppp authentication incoming chap** | Provides CHAP authentication to incoming calls. |
| **set callerid** | Requires the calling party's number to be matched against the configured receive numbers (such as set by the **set callidreceive #** command). This command also denies all incoming calls if no callidreceive number is configured. |
| **set remoteaccess protected** | Specifies a remote system password, which enables you to make changes on the Cisco 700 series router from a remote location. |
| **set localaccess protected** | Specifies a local system password, which enables you to make changes on the Cisco 700 series router from a local console connection. |
| **set password system** | Sets the system password for the above access configurations. |

### *Configuration for the Cisco 3620 Central Site Access Router*

The following example provides a sample configuration for the Cisco 3620 router. This modular access router has one 2-port PRI network module installed in slot 1 and one 1-port Ethernet network module installed in slot 0. The router receives only digital ISDN calls over T1 lines from the Cisco 700 series remote office router, which is described in the previous example.

```
!
version 11.2
service timestamps debug datetime msec
service timestamps log datetime msec
service password-encryption
no service udp-small-servers
no service tcp-small-servers
!
hostname NAS
!
```

```
aaa new-model
aaa authentication login default local
aaa authentication login console enable
aaa authentication login vty local
aaa authentication login dialin local
aaa authentication ppp default local
aaa authentication ppp dialin if-needed local
enable secret cisco
!
username admin password cisco
username remotelan1 password dialpass
!
async-bootp dns-server 10.1.3.1 10.1.3.2
isdn switch-type primary-5ess
!
controller T1 1/0
 framing esf
 clock source line
 linecode b8zs
 pri-group timeslots 1-24
!
controller T1 1/1
 framing esf
 clock source line
 linecode b8zs
 pri-group timeslots 1-24
!
interface Loopback0
 ip address 10.1.2.254 255.255.255.0
!
interface Ethernet 0/0
 ip address 10.1.1.10 255.255.255.0
 ip summary address eigrp 10 10.1.2.0 255.255.255.0
!
interface Serial 1/0:23
 no ip address
 encapsulation ppp
 isdn incoming-voice modem
 dialer rotary-group 0
 dialer-group 1
 no fair-queue
 no cdp enable
!
interface Serial 1/1:23
 no ip address
 encapsulation ppp
 isdn incoming-voice modem
 dialer rotary-group 0
 dialer-group 1
 no fair-queue
 no cdp enable
!
interface Dialer0
 ip unnumbered Loopback0
```

```
 no ip mroute-cache
 encapsulation ppp
 peer default ip address pool dialin_pool
 dialer in-band
 dialer-group 1
 no fair-queue
 no cdp enable
 ppp authentication chap pap dialin
 ppp multilink
!
router eigrp 10
 network 10.0.0.0
 passive-interface Dialer0
 default-metric 64 100 250 100 1500
 redistribute static
 no auto-summary
!
ip local pool dialin_pool 10.1.2.1 10.1.2.50
ip default-gateway 10.1.1.1

ip route 10.2.1.1 255.255.255.255 Dialer0
ip route 10.2.1.0 255.255.255.0 10.2.1.1

ip classless
!
dialer-list 1 protocol ip permit
!
line con 0
 login authentication console
line aux 0
 login authentication console
line vty 0 4
 login authentication vty
 transport input telnet rlogin
!
end
```

## Cisco 700 Series Router Using PAT to Dial In to a Cisco AS5200 Central Site Access Server

This section shows a Cisco 700 series router using the port address translation (PAT) feature to dial in to a Cisco AS5200 central site access server. IP addresses are assigned from the central site, which leverages the PAT feature to streamline multiple devices at the remote site through a single assigned address. In this example, the Cisco 700 series router has a private range of IP addresses used on the Ethernet side. The router, however, is able to translate between the local private addresses and the dynamically registered address on the WAN interface (refer to Figure 3–1).

### Configuration for the Cisco 700 Remote Router

The sample configuration in this section allows PCs on a LAN to boot up and acquire their IP address dynamically from a Cisco 700 series router, which in turn translates the private addresses into a single IP address assigned from a Cisco AS5200 central site router. The Cisco 700 series router also passes information via DHCP regarding the DNS server (in this example, 10.2.10.1) and the WINS server (in this example, 10.2.11.1) along with the domain name.

A possible sequence of events would be a remote PC running Windows 95 boots up on the Ethernet segment and gets its IP address and network information from the Cisco 700 series router. The PC then opens up Netscape and attempts to view a Web page at the central site, which causes the Cisco 700 series router to dial in to the central site. The Cisco 700 series router dynamically obtains its address from the central site pool of addresses and uses it to translate between the private address on the local Ethernet segment and the registered IP address borrowed from the central site router.

To configure the Cisco 700 series remote router, perform the following tasks beginning in system configuration mode:

| Step | Command | Purpose |
|---|---|---|
| 1 | ><br>> **set systemname remotelan1**<br>remotelan1> | At the system prompt level, specify the router's host name, which is also used when responding to CHAP authentication with the Cisco 3620. For CHAP authentication, the system's name must match the username configured on the Cisco 3620. |
| 2 | remotelan1> **set ppp secret client**<br>remotelan1> Enter new password:**dialpass**<br>remotelan1> Enter new password: **dialpass** | Set the transmit and receive password for the client. This is the password that is used in response to CHAP authentication requests, and it must match the username password configured on the Cisco 3620. |
| 3 | remotelan1> **set encapsulation ppp** | Set PPP encapsulation for incoming and outgoing authentication instead of CPP. |
| 4 | remotelan1> **set ppp multilink on** | Enable PPP multilink. |
| 5 | remotelan1> **set dhcp server** | Enable the router to act as a DHCP server and assign addresses from the private network. By default, all DHCP client addresses are assigned from the 10.0.0.0 network. |
| 6 | remotelan1> **set dhcp dns primary 10.2.10.1** | Pass the DNS server IP address to the DHCP client. |
| 7 | remotelan1> **set dhcp wins 10.2.11.1** | Pass the IP address of the WINs server to the DHCP client. |

| Step | Command | Purpose |
|---|---|---|
| 8 | `remotelan1>` **`set dhcp domain nas.com`** | Set the DHCP domain name for the Cisco 3620 central site router. |
| 9 | `remotelan1>` **`set user nas`**<br>`remotelan1> New user nas being created` | Create the profile *nas*, which is set up for the Cisco 3620. |
| 10 | `remotelan1:nas>` **`set ip pat on`** | Enable Port Address Translation (PAT) on the router. |
| 11 | `remotelan1:nas>` **`set ip framing none`** | Configure the profiles to not use Ethernet framing. |
| 12 | `remotelan1:nas>` **`set ip route destination 0.0.0.0 gateway 10.1.1.0`** | Set the default route to point to the Cisco 3620 router's Ethernet IP address. |
| 13 | `remotelan1:nas>` **`set 1 number 5551234`** | Set the number to call when dialing out of the first B channel. |
| 14 | `remotelan1:nas>` **`set 2 number 5551234`** | Set the number to call when dialing out of the second B channel. |
| 15 | `remotelan1:nas>` **`cd lan`** | Enter LAN profile mode. |
| 16 | `remotelan1:LAN>` **`set bridging off`** | Turn bridging off. |
| 17 | `remotelan1:LAN>` **`set ip routing on`** | Turn IP routing on. |

After you configure the router, the configuration should look like this:

```
set systemname remotelan1
set encapsulation ppp
set ppp secret client
set ppp multilink on
set dhcp server
set dhcp dns primary 10.2.10.1
set dhcp wins 10.2.11.1
set dhcp domain nas.com
set user nas
set bridging off
set ip routing on
set ip framing none
set ip pat on
set ip route destination 0.0.0.0 gateway 10.1.1.0
set 1 number 5551234
set 2 number 5551234
```

### *Configuration for a Cisco AS5200 Central Site Access Server*

This example provides a sample configuration for a Cisco AS5200 receiving calls from the Cisco 700 series router in the previous example.

**NOTES**

This configuration can also run on a Cisco 4000, 3600, or 7000 series router. The interface numbering scheme, however, for these routers will be in the form of slot/port. Additionally, the clocking will be set differently. See your product's hardware and software configuration guides and configuration notes for more details.

```
!
version 11.2
service timestamps debug datetime msec
service timestamps log datetime msec
service password-encryption
no service udp-small-servers
no service tcp-small-servers
!
hostname NAS
!
aaa new-model
aaa authentication login default local
aaa authentication login console enable
aaa authentication login vty local
aaa authentication login dialin local
aaa authentication ppp default local
aaa authentication ppp dialin if-needed local
enable secret cisco
!
username admin password cisco
username remotelan1 password dialpass

async-bootp dns-server 10.1.3.1 10.1.3.2
isdn switch-type primary-5ess
!
controller T1 0
 framing esf
 clock source line primary
 linecode b8zs
 pri-group timeslots 1-24
!
controller T1 1
 framing esf
 clock source line secondary
 linecode b8zs
 pri-group timeslots 1-24
!
interface Loopback0
 ip address 10.1.2.254 255.255.255.0
!
interface Ethernet0
 ip address 10.1.1.10 255.255.255.0
 ip summary address eigrp 10 10.1.2.0 255.255.255.0
!
interface Serial0
```

```
 no ip address
 shutdown
!
interface Serial1
 no ip address
 shutdown
!
interface Serial0:23
 no ip address
 encapsulation ppp
 isdn incoming-voice modem
 dialer rotary-group 0
 dialer-group 1
 no fair-queue
 no cdp enable
!
interface Serial1:23
 no ip address
 encapsulation ppp
 isdn incoming-voice modem
 dialer rotary-group 0
 dialer-group 1
 no fair-queue
 no cdp enable
!
interface Dialer0
 ip unnumbered Loopback0
 no ip mroute-cache
 encapsulation ppp
 peer default ip address pool dialin_pool
 dialer in-band
 dialer-group 1
 no fair-queue
 no cdp enable
 ppp authentication chap pap dialin
 ppp multilink
!
router eigrp 10
 network 10.0.0.0
 passive-interface Dialer0
 default-metric 64 100 250 100 1500
 redistribute static
 no auto-summary
!
ip local pool dialin_pool 10.1.2.1 10.1.2.50
ip default-gateway 10.1.1.1

ip route 10.2.1.1 255.255.255.255 Dialer0
ip route 10.2.1.0 255.255.255.0 10.2.1.1

ip classless
!
dialer-list 1 protocol ip permit
!
```

```
line con 0
 login authentication console
line aux 0
 login authentication console
line vty 0 4
 login authentication vty
 transport input telnet rlogin
!
end
```

In this configuration, the local pool is using a range of unused addresses on the same subnet that the Ethernet interface is configured on. The addresses will be used for the remote devices dialing in to the Cisco AS5200.

### *Cisco 1600 Using Easy IP To Dial In to a Central Site*

The following example shows the running configuration on a Cisco 1600 series router using the Easy IP (Phase 1) feature. Unlike the PAT feature for the Cisco 700 series routers, Easy IP (Phase 1) does not support DHCP server functionality. However, Easy IP (Phase 2) will support this feature. For Easy IP (Phase 1) configuration, you must statically configure the IP addresses for the hosts (PCs) on the Cisco 1600 series side of the connection. For additional information about using Easy IP, see Chapter 78, "Configuring Easy IP."

```
!
version 11.3
service timestamps debug datetime msec
service timestamps log datetime msec
service password-encryption
no service udp-small-servers
no service tcp-small-servers
!
hostname remotelan1
!
enable secret cisco
!
username NAS password dialpass
username admin password cisco
ip nat inside source list 1 interface BRI0 overload
!
isdn switch-type basic-5ess
!
interface Ethernet0
 ip address 13.1.1.1 255.255.255.0
 ip nat inside
!
interface BRI0
 ip address negotiated
 ip nat outside
 encapsulation ppp
 dialer map ip 10.1.1.10 name NAS 5551234
 dialer load-threshold 100 either
 dialer-group 1
```

```
 no fair-queue
 ppp authentication chap pap callin
 ppp multilink
!
ip classless
ip route 0.0.0.0 0.0.0.0 10.1.1.10
ip route 10.1.1.10 255.255.255.255 BRI0
access-list 1 permit 13.1.1.0 0.0.0.255
dialer-list 1 protocol ip permit
!
line con 0
line vty 0 4
 login local
!
end
```

### Cisco 3640 Central Site Configuration To Support ISDN and Modem Calls

The following configuration allows remote LANs and stand-alone remote users with modems to dial in to a central site. Figure 3–2 shows the network topology.

The Cisco 3640 has the following hardware configuration for this scenario:

- One 2-port ISDN-PRI network module installed in slot 1.
- One digital modem network module installed in slot 2 and slot 3.
- One 1-port Ethernet network module installed in slot 0.

**NOTES**

Each MICA digital modem card has its own group async configuration. Additionally, a single range of async lines is used for each modem card.

```
!
version 11.2
service timestamps debug datetime msec
service timestamps log datetime msec
service password-encryption
no service udp-small-servers
no service tcp-small-servers
!
hostname NAS
!
aaa new-model
aaa authentication login default local
aaa authentication login console enable
aaa authentication login vty local
aaa authentication login dialin local
aaa authentication ppp default local
aaa authentication ppp dialin if-needed local
enable secret cisco
!
```

```
username admin password cisco
username remotelan1 password dialpass1
username remotelan2 password dialpass2
username PCuser1 password dialpass3
username PCuser2 password dialpass4

async-bootp dns-server 10.1.3.1 10.1.3.2
isdn switch-type primary-5ess
!
controller T1 1/0
 framing esf
 clock source line
 linecode b8zs
 pri-group timeslots 1-24
!
controller T1 1/1
 framing esf
 clock source line
 linecode b8zs
 pri-group timeslots 1-24
!
interface Loopback0
 ip address 10.1.2.254 255.255.255.0
!
interface Ethernet0/0
 ip address 10.1.1.10 255.255.255.0
 ip summary address eigrp 10 10.1.2.0 255.255.255.0
!
interface Serial 1/0:23
 no ip address
 encapsulation ppp
 isdn incoming-voice modem
 dialer rotary-group 0
 dialer-group 1
 no fair-queue
 no cdp enable
!
interface Serial 1/1:23
 no ip address
 encapsulation ppp
 isdn incoming-voice modem
 dialer rotary-group 0
 dialer-group 1
 no fair-queue
 no cdp enable
!
interface Group-Async1
 ip unnumbered Loopback0
 encapsulation ppp
 async mode interactive
 peer default ip address pool dialin_pool
 no cdp enable
 ppp authentication chap pap dialin
 group-range 65 88
!
```

```
interface Group-Async2
 ip unnumbered Loopback0
 encapsulation ppp
 async mode interactive
 peer default ip address pool dialin_pool
 no cdp enable
 ppp authentication chap pap dialin
 group-range 97 120
!
interface Dialer0
 ip unnumbered Loopback0
 no ip mroute-cache
 encapsulation ppp
 peer default ip address pool dialin_pool
 dialer in-band
 dialer-group 1
 no fair-queue
 no cdp enable
 ppp authentication chap pap dialin
 ppp multilink
!
router eigrp 10
 network 10.0.0.0
 passive-interface Dialer0
 no auto-summary
!
ip local pool dialin_pool 10.1.2.1 10.1.2.50
ip default-gateway 10.1.1.1
ip classless
!
dialer-list 1 protocol ip permit
!
line con 0
 login authentication console
line 65 88
 autoselect ppp
 autoselect during-login
 login authentication dialin
 modem DialIn
line 97 120
 autoselect ppp
 autoselect during-login
 login authentication dialin
 modem DialIn
line aux 0
 login authentication console
line vty 0 4
 login authentication vty
 transport input telnet rlogin
!
end
```

### *Cisco AS5200 Central Site Configuration Using Remote Security*

The previous examples in this section configure static CHAP authentication on the central router using the **username** command. A more common configuration to support modem and ISDN calls on a single chassis is to use the AAA security model and an external security server at the central site. Cisco recommends that you have a solid understanding of basic security principles and the AAA model before you set up this configuration.

### *Central Site Cisco AS5200 Configuration Using TACACS+ Authentication*

The following example assumes you are running TACACS+ on the remote security server:

```
!
version 11.2
service timestamps debug datetime msec
service timestamps log datetime msec
service password-encryption
no service udp-small-servers
no service tcp-small-servers
!
hostname NAS
!
aaa new-model
aaa authentication login console enable
aaa authentication login vty tacacs+
aaa authentication login dialin tacacs+
aaa authentication ppp default tacacs+
aaa authentication ppp dialin if-needed tacacs+
enable secret cisco
!
async-bootp dns-server 10.1.3.1 10.1.3.2
isdn switch-type primary-5ess
!
controller T1 0
 framing esf
 clock source line primary
 linecode b8zs
 pri-group timeslots 1-24
!
controller T1 1
 framing esf
 clock source line secondary
 linecode b8zs
 pri-group timeslots 1-24
!
interface Loopback0
 ip address 10.1.2.254 255.255.255.0
!
interface Ethernet0
 ip address 10.1.1.10 255.255.255.0
 ip summary address eigrp 10 10.1.2.0 255.255.255.0
!
interface Serial0
 no ip address
 shutdown
!
interface Serial1
 no ip address
```

```
 shutdown
!
interface Serial0:23
 no ip address
 encapsulation ppp
 isdn incoming-voice modem
 dialer rotary-group 0
 dialer-group 1
 no fair-queue
 no cdp enable
!
interface Serial1:23
 no ip address
 encapsulation ppp
 isdn incoming-voice modem
 dialer rotary-group 0
 dialer-group 1
 no fair-queue
 no cdp enable
!
interface Group-Async1
 ip unnumbered Loopback0
 encapsulation ppp
 async mode interactive
 peer default ip address pool dialin_pool
 no cdp enable
 ppp authentication chap pap dialin
 group-range 1 48
!
interface Dialer0
 ip unnumbered Loopback0
 no ip mroute-cache
 encapsulation ppp
 peer default ip address pool dialin_pool
 dialer in-band
 dialer-group 1
 no fair-queue
 no cdp enable
 ppp authentication chap pap dialin
 ppp multilink
!
router eigrp 10
 network 10.0.0.0
 passive-interface Dialer0
 redistribute static
 default-metric 64 100 250 100 1500
 no auto-summary
!
ip local pool dialin_pool 10.1.2.1 10.1.2.50
ip default-gateway 10.1.1.1
ip classless
!
dialer-list 1 protocol ip permit
!
```

```
line con 0
 login authentication console
line 1 48
 autoselect ppp
 autoselect during-login
 login authentication dialin
 modem DialIn
line aux 0
 login authentication console
line vty 0 4
 login authentication vty
 transport input telnet rlogin
!
end
```

### *TACACS+ Security Server Entry*

The following configuration file entry runs on the remote TACACS+ security server, which compliments the Cisco AS5200 configuration in the previous example:

```
user = remotelan1 {
           chap = cleartext "dialpass1"
           service = ppp protocol = ip {
                       addr = 10.2.1.1
                       route = "10.2.1.0 255.255.255.0"
           }
}


user = PCuser1 {
           login = cleartext "dialpass2"
           chap = cleartext "dialpass2"
           service = ppp protocol = ip {
                       addr-pool = dialin_pool
           }
           service = exec {
                       autocmd = "ppp negotiate"
           }
}

user = PCuser2 {
           login = cleartext "dialpass3"
           chap = cleartext "dialpass3"
           service = ppp protocol = ip {
                       addr-pool = dialin_pool
           }
           service = exec {
                       autocmd = "ppp negotiate"
           }
```

## BIDIRECTIONAL DIAL NETWORKING BETWEEN A CENTRAL SITE AND REMOTE OFFICES OR TELECOMMUTERS

Sometimes a headquarter's gateway access server is required to dial out to a remote site while receiving incoming calls. This type of networking need is designed around a specific business support model, such as that shown in Figure 3–3.

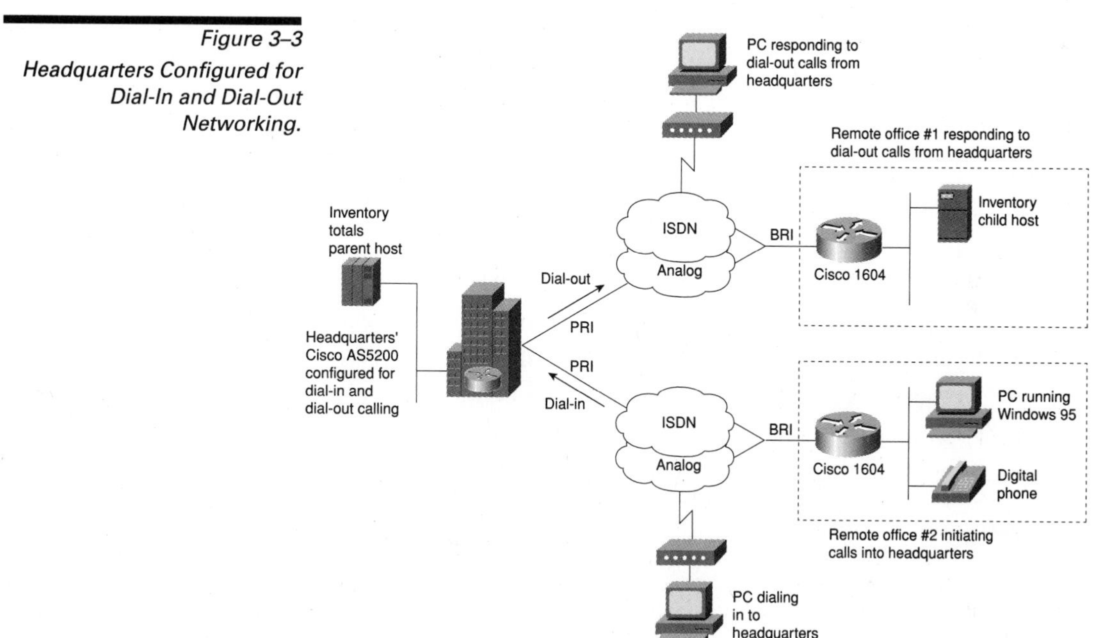


*Figure 3–3 Headquarters Configured for Dial-In and Dial-Out Networking.*

Figure 3–3 shows a typical dial-in and dial-out network scenario, which amounts to only 25% of all dial topologies. The headquarters' Cisco AS5200 initiates a connection with a Cisco 1604 at remote office 1. After a connection is established, the remote site's file server (shown as *Inventory child host*) runs a batch-processing application with the headquarters' mainframe (shown as *Inventory totals parent host*). While files are being transferred between remote office 1 and headquarters, remote office 2 is successfully dialing in to headquarters.

There are some restrictions for dial-out calling. Dial-out analog and digital calls are commonly made to remote ISDN routers, such as the Cisco 1604. On the whole, dial-out calls are not made from a central site router to a remote PC but rather from a remote PC in to the central site. Central site post offices, however, often call remote office routers on demand to deliver e-mail. Callback is enabled on dial-in scenarios only. The majority of a dial-out software configuration is set up on the headquarters' router, not the remote office router. Dialing out to a stack group of multiple chassis is not supported by Cisco IOS software. Note that Multichassis Multilink PPP and virtual private dial networks (VPDNs) are dial-in only solutions.

## Dialer Profiles and Virtual Profiles

You can set up profiles in your dial solution to discriminate access on a user-specific basis. For example, if the chief network administrator is dialing in to the enterprise, a unique user profile can be created with an idle timeout of one year, and universal access privileges set up to all networks in the company. For less fortunate users, access can be restricted to an idle timeout of 10 seconds and network connections set up for only a few addresses.

Depending on the size and scope of your dial solution, you can set up two different types of profiles: dialer profiles or virtual profiles. Dialer profiles are individual user profiles set up on routers or access servers in a small scale-dial solution. This type of profile is configured locally on the router and is limited by the number of interfaces that exist on the router. When an incoming call comes into the dial pool, the dialer interface binds the caller to a dialer profile via the caller ID or the caller name.

Figure 3–4 shows an example of how dialer profiles can be used:

- You need to bridge over multiple ISDN channels.
- You want to use ISDN to back up a WAN link, but still have the ISDN interface available during those times that the WAN link is up.
- A security server, such as a AAA TACACS or RADIUS server, is not available for use.

For more information about dialer profiles, see Chapter 44, "Configuring Peer-to-Peer DDR with Dialer Profiles" and Chapter 48, "Configuring Dial Backup with Dialer Profiles."

*Figure 3–4*
*Dial-In Scenario for Dialer Profiles.*

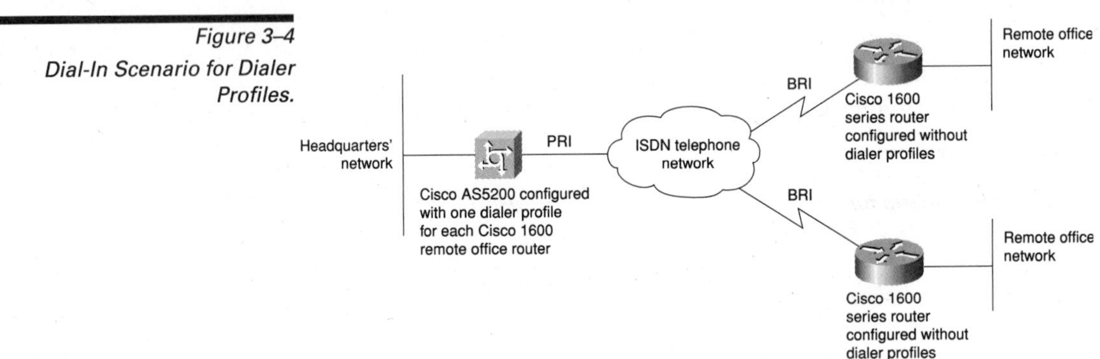


Virtual profiles are user-specific profiles for large-scale dial solutions; however, these profiles are not manually configured on each router or access server. A virtual profile is a unique Point-to-Point Protocol (PPP) application that can create and configure a virtual access interface dynamically when a dial-in call is received, and tear down the interface dynamically when the call ends.

The configuration information for a virtual profile's virtual access interface can come from a virtual template interface, or from user-specific configuration stored on an AAA server, or both. The virtual profile user-specific configuration stored on the AAA server is identified by the authentication name for the call-in user. (That is, if the AAA server authenticates the user as samson, the user-specific configuration is listed under samson in the AAA users file.) The virtual profile user-specific configuration should include only the configuration that is not shared by multiple users. Shared configuration should be placed in the virtual template interface where it can be cloned on many virtual access interfaces as needed.

AAA configurations are much easier to manage for large numbers of dial-in users. Virtual profiles can span across a group of access servers, but a AAA server is required. Virtual profiles are set up independently of which access server, interface, or port number users connect to. For users that share duplicate configuration information, it is best to enclose the configuration in a virtual template. This eliminates the duplication of commands in each of the user records on the AAA server.

The user-specific AAA configuration used by virtual profiles is interface configuration information and downloaded during LCP negotiations. Another feature, called Per-User Configuration, also uses configuration information gained from a AAA server. However, Per-User Configuration uses *network* configuration (such as access lists and route filters) downloaded during NCP negotiations.

Figure 3–5 shows an example of how virtual profiles are used:

- A large dial-in solution is available, which includes many access servers or routers (for example, three or more devices stacked together in a multichassis multilink PPP scenario).
- Discrimination between large numbers of users is needed.
- Setup and maintenance of a user profile for each dial-in user on each access server or router is much too time consuming.
- A security server, such as a AAA TACACS or RADIUS server, is available for use.

For a virtual profile configuration example, see the section "Large Scale Dial-In Configuration Using Virtual Profiles" found later in this chapter. For more information about virtual profiles, see Chapter 58, "Configuring Virtual Profiles," and Chapter 60, "Per-User Configuration."

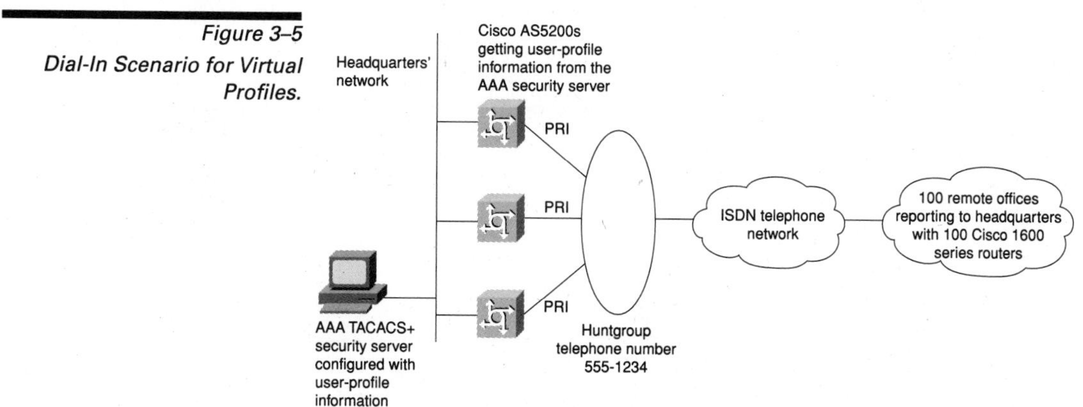


*Figure 3–5 Dial-In Scenario for Virtual Profiles.*

## Configuration Examples

In most cases, dialer profiles are configured on access servers or routers that receive calls and must discriminate between users, such as many different remote routers dialing in. See Figure 3–6.

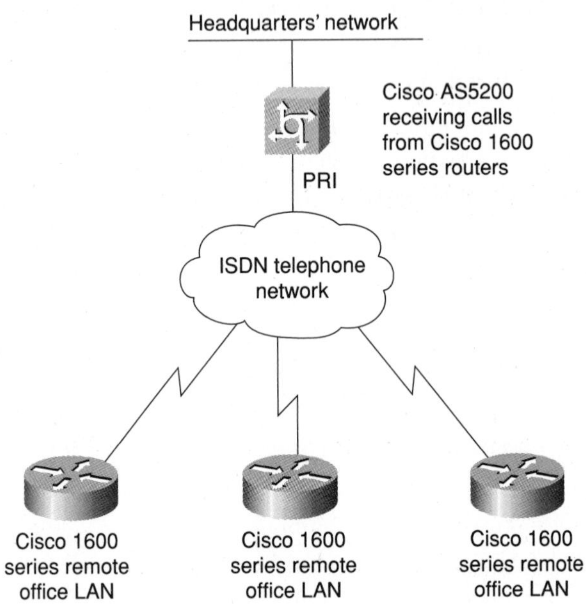


*Figure 3–6*
*Remote Cisco 1600s Dialing In to a Cisco AS5200 at the Central Site.*

Access servers or routers that only place calls (not receive calls) do not need any awareness of dialer profiles configured. Remote routers do not need to discriminate based on which device they are calling in to. If multiple Cisco 1600 series routers are dialing in to one Cisco AS5200, for example, the Cisco 1600s should not be configured with dialer profiles. The Cisco AS5200 should be configured with dialer profiles. Do not configure dialer profiles on devices that *only* make calls.

The following sample configurations are provided for different types of dial scenarios, which can be derived from Figure 3–3 through Figure 3–6:

- Examples with dialer profiles
  - Cisco AS5200 Configuration with Dialer Profiles
  - Cisco 1604 ISDN Configuration with Dialer Profiles
  - Cisco 1604 Async Configuration with Dialer Profiles
- Examples without dialer profiles
  - Cisco AS5200 Configuration without Dialer Profiles
  - Cisco 1604 ISDN Configuration without Dialer Profiles
  - Cisco 1604 Async Configuration without Dialer Profiles
- Large-Scale Dial-In Configuration Using Virtual Profiles

**NOTES**

Be sure to include your own IP addresses, host names, and security passwords where appropriate.

### *Cisco AS5200 Configuration with Dialer Profiles*

The following bidirectional dial configuration runs on the headquarters' Cisco AS5200 in Figure 3–3. This configuration enables calls to be sent to the SOHO router and received from remote hosts and clients. The calling is bidirectional.

```
!
version 11.2
service udp-small-servers
service tcp-small-servers
!
hostname 5200
!
aaa new-model
aaa authentication login default local
aaa authentication login console enable
aaa authentication login vty local
aaa authentication login dialin local
aaa authentication ppp default local
aaa authentication ppp dialin if-needed local
enable secret cisco
!
username async1 password cisco
username async2 password cisco
username async3 password cisco
username async4 password cisco
username async5 password cisco
username async6 password cisco
username async7 password cisco
username async8 password cisco
username isdn1 password cisco
username isdn2 password cisco
username isdn3 password cisco
username isdn4 password cisco
username isdn5 password cisco
username isdn6 password cisco
username isdn7 password cisco
username isdn8 password cisco
username DialupAdmin password cisco
!
isdn switch-type primary-dms100
chat-script cisco-default ABORT ERROR "" "AT" OK "ATDT\T" TIMEOUT 60 CONNECT
!
controller T1 0
 framing esf
 clock source line primary
 linecode b8zs
 pri-group timeslots 1-24
!
controller T1 1
 framing esf
```

```
 clock source line secondary
 linecode b8zs
 pri-group timeslots 1-24
!
interface loopback 1
 ip address 131.108.38.40 255.255.255.128
!
interface loopback 2
 ip address 131.108.38.130 255.255.255.128
!
interface Ethernet0
 ip address 131.108.39.40 255.255.255.0
 no ip mroute-cache
 ip ospf priority 0
!
interface Serial0:23
 no ip address
 no ip mroute-cache
 encapsulation ppp
 isdn incoming-voice modem
 dialer pool-member 2
!
interface Serial1:23
 no ip address
 no ip mroute-cache
 encapsulation ppp
 isdn incoming-voice modem
 dialer pool-member 2
!
interface Group-Async1
 no ip address
 no ip mroute-cache
 encapsulation ppp
 async mode interactive
 dialer in-band
 dialer pool-member 1
 ppp authentication chap pap
 group-range 1 48
!
interface Dialer10
 ip unnumbered loopback 1
 encapsulation ppp
 peer default ip address dialin_pool
 dialer remote-name async1
 dialer string 14085268983
 dialer hold-queue 10
 dialer pool 1
 dialer-group 1
 ppp authentication pap chap callin
 ppp pap sent-username DialupAdmin password 7 07063D11542
!
interface Dialer11
 ip unnumbered loopback 1
 encapsulation ppp
```

```
 no peer default ip address pool
 dialer remote-name async2
 dialer string 14085262012
 dialer hold-queue 10
 dialer pool 1
 dialer-group 1
 ppp authentication pap chap callin
 ppp pap sent-username DialupAdmin password 7 07063D11542
!
interface Dialer12
 ip unnumbered loopback 1
 encapsulation ppp
 no peer default ip address pool
 dialer remote-name async3
 dialer string 14085260706
 dialer hold-queue 10
 dialer pool 1
 dialer-group 1
 ppp authentication pap chap callin
 ppp pap sent-username DialupAdmin password 7 07063D11542
!
interface Dialer13
 ip unnumbered loopback 1
 encapsulation ppp
 no peer default ip address pool
 dialer remote-name async4
 dialer string 14085262731
 dialer hold-queue 10
 dialer pool 1
 dialer-group 1
 ppp authentication pap chap callin
 ppp pap sent-username DialupAdmin password 7 07063D11542
!
interface Dialer14
 ip unnumbered loopback 1
 encapsulation ppp
 no peer default ip address pool
 dialer remote-name async5
 dialer string 14085264431
 dialer hold-queue 10
 dialer pool 1
 dialer-group 1
 ppp authentication pap chap callin
 ppp pap sent-username DialupAdmin password 7 07063D11542
!
interface Dialer15
 ip unnumbered loopback 1
 encapsulation ppp
 no peer default ip address pool
 dialer remote-name async6
 dialer string 14085261933
 dialer hold-queue 10
 dialer pool 1
 dialer-group 1
```

```
 ppp authentication pap chap callin
 ppp pap sent-username DialupAdmin password 7 07063D11542
!
interface Dialer16
 ip unnumbered loopback 1
 encapsulation ppp
 no peer default ip address pool
 dialer remote-name async7
 dialer string 14085267631
 dialer hold-queue 10
 dialer pool 1
 dialer-group 1
 ppp authentication pap chap callin
 ppp pap sent-username DialupAdmin password 7 07063D11542
!
interface Dialer17
 ip unnumbered loopback 2
 encapsulation ppp
 no peer default ip address pool
 dialer remote-name async8
 dialer string 14085265153
 dialer hold-queue 10
 dialer pool 2
 dialer-group 1
 ppp authentication chap pap
!
interface Dialer18
 ip unnumbered loopback 2
 encapsulation ppp
 no peer default ip address pool
 dialer remote-name isdn1
 dialer string 14085267887
 dialer hold-queue 10
 dialer pool 2
 dialer-group 1
 ppp authentication chap pap
!
interface Dialer19
 ip unnumbered loopback 2
 encapsulation ppp
 no peer default ip address pool
 dialer remote-name isdn2
 dialer string 14085261591
 dialer hold-queue 10
 dialer pool 2
 dialer-group 1
 ppp authentication chap pap
!
interface Dialer20
 ip unnumbered loopback 2
 encapsulation ppp
 no peer default ip address pool
 dialer remote-name isdn3
 dialer string 14085262118
```

```
 dialer hold-queue 10
 dialer pool 2
 dialer-group 1
 ppp authentication chap pap
!
interface Dialer21
 ip unnumbered loopback 2
 encapsulation ppp
 no peer default ip address pool
 dialer remote-name isdn4
 dialer string 14085263757
 dialer hold-queue 10
 dialer pool 2
 dialer-group 1
 ppp authentication chap pap
!
interface Dialer22
 ip unnumbered loopback 2
 encapsulation ppp
 no peer default ip address pool
 dialer remote-name isdn5
 dialer string 14085263769
 dialer hold-queue 10
 dialer pool 2
 dialer-group 1
 ppp authentication chap pap
!
interface Dialer23
 ip unnumbered loopback 2
 encapsulation ppp
 no peer default ip address pool
 dialer remote-name isdn6
 dialer string 14085267884
 dialer hold-queue 10
 dialer pool 2
 dialer-group 1
 ppp authentication chap pap
!
interface Dialer24
 ip unnumbered loopback 2
 encapsulation ppp
 no peer default ip address pool
 dialer remote-name isdn7
 dialer string 14085267360
 dialer hold-queue 10
 dialer pool 2
 dialer-group 1
 ppp authentication chap pap
!
interface Dialer25
 ip unnumbered loopback 2
 encapsulation ppp
 no peer default ip address pool
 dialer remote-name isdn8
```

```
 dialer string 14085260361
 dialer hold-queue 10
 dialer pool 2
 dialer-group 1
 ppp authentication chap pap
!
router ospf 1
redistribute static subnets
passive-interface Dialer1
passive-interface Dialer2
network 131.108.0.0 0.0.255.255 area 0
!
ip local pool dialin_pool 10.1.2.1 10.1.2.50
ip domain-name cisco.com
ip classless
!
dialer-list 1 protocol ip permit
!
line con 0
 exec-timeout 0 0
line 1 24
 no exec
 exec-timeout 0 0
 autoselect during-login
 autoselect ppp
 script dialer cisco-default
 login local
 modem InOut
 modem autoconfigure type microcom_hdms
 transport input telnet
line aux 0
line vty 0 1
 exec-timeout 60 0
 password cisco
 login
line vty 2 5
 exec-timeout 5 0
 password cisco
 login
!
end
```

### *Cisco 1604 ISDN Configuration with Dialer Profiles*

The following configuration runs on the remote office Cisco 1604 router, which receives calls from the Cisco AS5200 central site access server. Refer to Figure 3–3.

```
!
version 11.2
service udp-small-servers
service tcp-small-servers
!
hostname isdn1
!
enable password cisco
!
```

```
username 5200 password cisco
username isdn1 password cisco
isdn switch-type basic-5ess
!
interface Ethernet0
 ip address 131.108.40.1 255.255.255.0
!
interface BRI0
 no ip address
 encapsulation ppp
 dialer pool-member 1
 ppp authentication chap pap
!
interface Dialer1
 ip address 131.108.38.131 255.255.255.128
 encapsulation ppp
 no peer default ip address pool
 dialer remote-name 5200
 dialer string 14085269328
 dialer hold-queue 10
 dialer pool 2
 dialer-group 1
 ppp authentication chap pap
!
ip classless
ip route 0.0.0.0 0.0.0.0 131.108.38.130
dialer-list 1 protocol ip permit
!
line con 0
line vty 0 4
 password cisco
 login
 password cisco
 login
!
end
```

### *Cisco 1604 Async Configuration with Dialer Profiles*

The following asynchronous configuration runs on the remote office Cisco 1604 router, which receives calls from the Cisco AS5200 central site access server (refer to Figure 3–3).

```
!
version 11.2
service udp-small-servers
service tcp-small-servers
!
hostname async1
!
enable password cisco
!
username 5200 password cisco
username async1 password cisco
chat script dial_out "" "ATDT\T" timeout 60 connect \c
!
interface Ethernet0
 ip address 131.108.41.1 255.255.255.0
```

```
!
interface serial 0
 physical-layer async
 no ip address
 encapsulation ppp
 dialer pool-member 1
 ppp authentication chap pap
!
interface Dialer10
 ip address 131.108.38.41 255.255.255.128
 encapsulation ppp
 no peer default ip address pool
 dialer remote-name 5200
 dialer string 14085269328
 dialer hold-queue 10
 dialer pool 1
 dialer-group 1
 ppp authentication chap pap
!
ip classless
ip route 0.0.0.0 0.0.0.0 131.108.38.40
dialer-list 1 protocol ip permit
!
line con 0
line 1
password cisco
login
script modem dial_out
!
end
```

### Cisco AS5200 Configuration without Dialer Profiles

The following bidirectional dial configuration runs on the headquarters' Cisco AS5200 in Figure 3–3. This configuration enables calls to be sent to the SOHO router and received from remote hosts and clients. The calling is bidirectional.

```
!
version 11.2
service udp-small-servers
service tcp-small-servers
!
hostname 5200
!
aaa new-model
aaa authentication login default local
aaa authentication login console enable
aaa authentication login vty local
aaa authentication login dialin local
aaa authentication ppp default local
aaa authentication ppp dialin if-needed local
enable secret cisco
!
username async1 password cisco
username async2 password cisco
username async3 password cisco
```

```
username async4 password cisco
username async5 password cisco
username async6 password cisco
username async7 password cisco
username async8 password cisco
username isdn1 password cisco
username isdn2 password cisco
username isdn3 password cisco
username isdn4 password cisco
username isdn5 password cisco
username isdn6 password cisco
username isdn7 password cisco
username isdn8 password cisco
username DialupAdmin password cisco
!
isdn switch-type primary-dms100
chat-script cisco-default ABORT ERROR "" "AT" OK "ATDT\T" TIMEOUT 60 CONNECT
!
controller T1 0
 framing esf
 clock source line primary
 linecode b8zs
 pri-group timeslots 1-24
 description ISDN Controller 0
!
controller T1 1
 framing esf
 clock source line secondary
 linecode b8zs
 pri-group timeslots 1-24
 description ISDN Controller 1
!
interface Ethernet0
 ip address 131.108.39.40 255.255.255.0
 no ip mroute-cache
 ip ospf priority 0
!
interface Serial0:23
 no ip address
 no ip mroute-cache
 encapsulation ppp
 isdn incoming-voice modem
 dialer rotary-group 2
!
interface Serial1:23
 no ip address
 no ip mroute-cache
 encapsulation ppp
 isdn incoming-voice modem
 dialer rotary-group 2
!
interface Group-Async1
 no ip address
 no ip mroute-cache
 encapsulation ppp
```

```
 async dynamic address
 async mode interactive
 dialer in-band
 dialer rotary-group 1
 ppp authentication pap callin
 ppp pap sent-username HQ5200 password 7 09434678520A
 group-range 1 24
!
interface Dialer1
 ip address 131.108.38.40 255.255.255.128
 encapsulation ppp
 no peer default ip address pool
 dialer in-band
 dialer map ip 131.108.38.41 name async1 14085268983
 dialer map ip 131.108.38.42 name async2 14085262012
 dialer map ip 131.108.38.43 name async3 14085260706
 dialer map ip 131.108.38.44 name async4 14085262731
 dialer map ip 131.108.38.45 name async5 14085264431
 dialer map ip 131.108.38.46 name async6 14085261933
 dialer map ip 131.108.38.47 name async7 14085267631
 dialer map ip 131.108.38.48 name async8 14085265153
 dialer hold-queue 10
 dialer-group 1
 ppp authentication pap chap callin
 ppp pap sent-username DialupAdmin password 7 07063D11542
!
interface Dialer2
 ip address 131.108.38.130 255.255.255.128
 encapsulation ppp
 no peer default ip address pool
 dialer in-band
 dialer map ip 131.108.38.131 name isdn1 14085267887
 dialer map ip 131.108.38.132 name isdn2 14085261591
 dialer map ip 131.108.38.133 name isdn3 14085262118
 dialer map ip 131.108.38.134 name isdn4 14085263757
 dialer map ip 131.108.38.135 name isdn5 14085263769
 dialer map ip 131.108.38.136 name isdn6 14085267884
 dialer map ip 131.108.38.137 name isdn7 14085267360
 dialer map ip 131.108.38.138 name isdn8 14085260361
 dialer hold-queue 10
 dialer-group 1
 ppp authentication chap pap
 ppp multilink
!
router ospf 1
 redistribute static subnets
 passive-interface Dialer1
 passive-interface Dialer2
 network 131.108.0.0 0.0.255.255 area 0
!
ip domain-name cisco.com
ip classless
!
dialer-list 1 protocol ip permit
!
```

```
line con 0
 exec-timeout 0 0
line 1 24
 no exec
 exec-timeout 0 0
 autoselect during-login
 autoselect ppp
 script dialer cisco-default
 login local
 modem InOut
 modem autoconfigure type microcom_hdms
 transport input telnet
line aux 0
line vty 0 1
 exec-timeout 60 0
 password cisco
 login
line vty 2 5
 exec-timeout 5 0
 password cisco
 login
!
end
```

### *Cisco 1604 ISDN Configuration without Dialer Profiles*

The following configuration runs on the remote office Cisco 1604 router, which dials into the headquarters' Cisco AS5200. This configuration does not receive calls from the Cisco AS5200 (refer to Figure 3–3).

```
!
version 11.1
service udp-small-servers
service tcp-small-servers
!
hostname isdn1
!
enable password cisco
!
username 5200 password cisco
username isdn1 password cisco
isdn switch-type basic-5ess
!
interface Ethernet0
 ip address 131.108.40.1 255.255.255.0
!
interface BRI0
 ip address 131.108.38.131 255.255.255.128
 encapsulation ppp
 dialer map ip 131.108.38.130 name 5200 14085269328
 dialer-group 1
 ppp authentication chap pap
!
ip classless
ip route 0.0.0.0 0.0.0.0 131.108.38.130
dialer-list 1 protocol ip permit
```

```
!
line con 0
line vty 0 4
 password cisco
 login
 password cisco
 login
!
end
```

### *Cisco 1604 Async Configuration without Dialer Profiles*

The following asynchronous configuration runs on the remote office Cisco 1604 router, which dials into the headquarters' Cisco AS5200. This configuration does not receive calls from the Cisco AS5200 (refer to Figure 3–3).

```
!
version 11.2
service udp-small-servers
service tcp-small-servers
!
hostname async1
!
enable password cisco
!
username 5200 password cisco
username async1 password cisco
chat script dial_out "" "ATDT\T" timeout 60 connect \c
!
interface Ethernet0
 ip address 131.108.41.1 255.255.255.0
!
interface serial 0
 physical-layer async
 ip address 131.108.38.41 255.255.255.128
 encapsulation ppp
 dialer in-band
 dialer map ip 131.108.38.40 name 5200 modem-script dial_out 14085269328
 dialer-group 1
 ppp authentication chap pap
!
ip classless
ip route 0.0.0.0 0.0.0.0 131.108.38.40
dialer-list 1 protocol ip permit
!
line con 0
line 1
 password cisco
 login
 password cisco
 login
!
end
```

### *Large-Scale Dial-In Configuration Using Virtual Profiles*

The following example configuration is used on each central site stack member shown in Figure 3–5. This configuration is for a large scale dial-in scenario.

```
!
aaa new-model
aaa authentication login default none
aaa authentication ppp default radius
aaa authentication ppp admin local
aaa authorization network radius
isdn switch-type primary-5ess
!
interface Serial0:23
 no ip address
 no ip mroute-cache
 no cdp enable
 ppp authentication chap
!
tacacs-server host 171.68.203.45
virtual-profile aaa
```

The following is a sample configuration entry running on a RADIUS security server, which is queried by each central site stack member when a call comes in. This entry includes the virtual profile configuration information for remote users dialing in to the central site stack solution.

In this example, virtual profiles are configured by both virtual templates and AAA configuration. John and Rick can dial in from anywhere and have their same keepalive settings and their own IP addresses.

The remaining AV-pair settings are not used by virtual profiles. They are the network-protocol access lists and route filters used by AAA-based Per-User Configuration.

In the AAA configuration cisco-avpair lines, "\n" is used to indicate the start of a new Cisco IOS command line.

```
john Password = "welcome"
     User-Service-Type = Framed-User,
     Framed-Protocol = PPP,
        cisco-avpair = "lcp:interface-config=keepalive 75\nip address 100.100.100.100
255.255.255.0",
        cisco-avpair = "ip:rte-fltr-out#0=router igrp 60",
        cisco-avpair = "ip:rte-fltr-out#3=deny 171.0.0.0 0.255.255.255",
        cisco-avpair = "ip:rte-fltr-out#4=deny 172.0.0.0 0.255.255.255",
        cisco-avpair = "ip:rte-fltr-out#5=permit any"
rick Password = "emoclew"
     User-Service-Type = Framed-User,
     Framed-Protocol = PPP,
        cisco-avpair = "lcp:interface-config=keepalive 100\nip address 200.200.200.200
255.255.255.0",
        cisco-avpair = "ip:inacl#3=permit ip any any precedence immediate",
        cisco-avpair = "ip:inacl#4=deny igrp 0.0.1.2 255.255.0.0 any",
        cisco-avpair = "ip:outacl#2=permit ip any any precedence immediate",
        cisco-avpair = "ip:outacl#3=deny igrp 0.0.9.10 255.255.0.0 any"
```

## TELECOMMUTERS DIALING IN TO A MIXED PROTOCOL ENVIRONMENT

This scenario describes how to provide remote access to employees dialing in to a mixed protocol enterprise network. The sample configurations provided in this section assume that enterprise telecommuters are dialing in with modems or terminal adapters from outside the headquarters' LAN.

The following sections are provided:

- Describing a Mixed Protocol Enterprise Environment
- Exploring a Sample Enterprise Network for Dial-In Access
- Exploring Mixed Protocol Configuration Examples

### Description of a Mixed Protocol Enterprise Environment

Sometimes an enterprise conducts its daily business operations across internal mixed protocol environments (see Figure 3–7 and Table 3–1). An enterprise might deploy an IP base across the entire intranet, for example, while still allowing file-sharing with other protocols, such as AppleTalk and AppleTalk Remote Access (ARA).

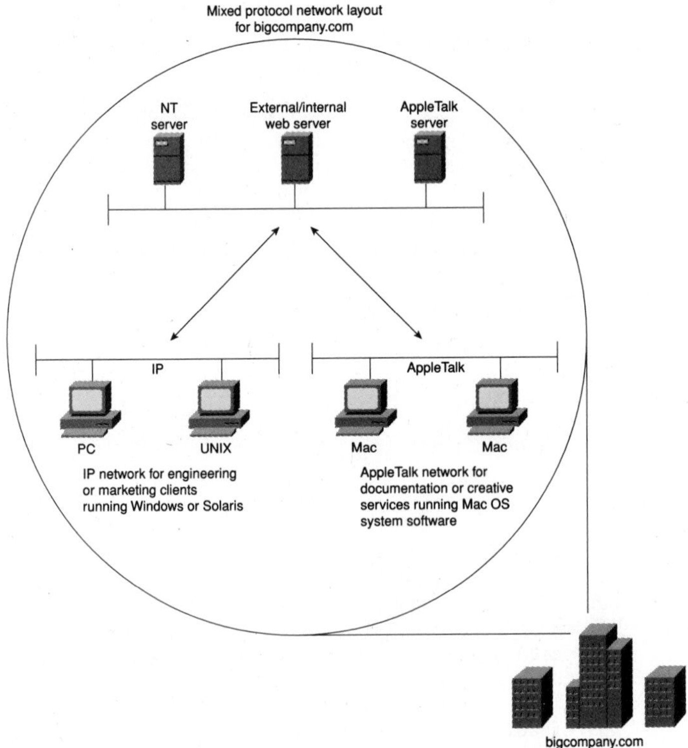


*Figure 3–7 Large Enterprise with a Multiprotocol Network.*

**Table 3–1** *Typical Mixed Protocol Environment*

| Applications Running on the Network Server | Remote or Local Client Applications | Protocol Used to Support the Network | Internal Supporting Department |
|---|---|---|---|
| Windows NT | Windows 95 or Windows 3.1 running on PCs | IP | Marketing, human resources, engineering, customer support |
| UNIX | SunOS or Solaris running on a UNIX-based workstation or NCD | IP | Engineering and customer support |
| AppleTalk | Mac OS System Software 7.5 running on Macintosh computers | AppleTalk | Documentation and creative services |
| NetWare | Novell NetWare client software | IPX | Marketing, human resources, engineering, customer support |

## Sample Enterprise Network for Dial-In Access

Figure 3–8 shows a sample enterprise network, which supports 10,000 registered token card holders. Some registered users might use their access privileges each day; others might use their access privileges very infrequently, such as only on business trips. The dial-in access provisioned for outsiders, such as partners or vendors, is supported separately in a firewalled setup.

Five Cisco AS5200s are positioned to provide 250 dial-in ports for incoming modem calls. A Catalyst 1900 is used as a stand-alone switch to provide Ethernet switching between the Cisco AS5200s and the 100BaseT interfaces on the backbone routers. Two Cisco 7200 series routers are used to reduce the processing workload on the access servers and provide access to the company's backbone. If the Cisco 7200 series devices were not used in the network solution, the Cisco AS5200s could not update routing tables, especially if 20 to 30 additional routers existed on the company's backbone. Two additional backbone switches are used to provide access to the company network.

**NOTES**

Depending on your networking needs, the Cisco 7200 series can be substituted by one or more Cisco 4500s, 4700s, or 3640s. Additionally, the Cisco AS5200s can be replaced by Cisco 3640s loaded with MICA digital modem cards.

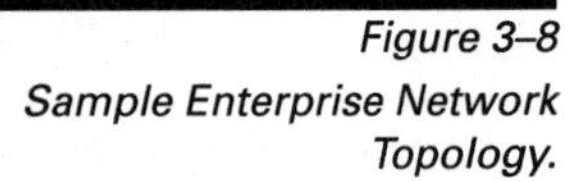

*Figure 3–8*
*Sample Enterprise Network Topology.*

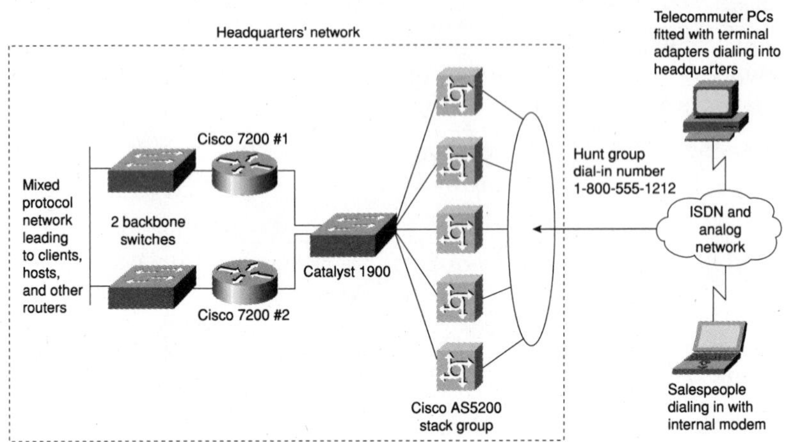


If you are setting up dial-in access for remote terminal adapters, the settings configured on the terminal adapters must match the setting on the access server or router. Depending on your business application, terminal adapters can operate in many different modes (refer toTable 3–2).

**Table 3–2** *Options for Terminal Adapter Settings*

| **Terminal Adapter Mode** | **Comments** |
|---|---|
| Synchronous PPP | Cisco recommends you use this mode for most terminal adapter scenarios. By default, Cisco access servers and routers have synchronous PPP enabled. Therefore, additional configuration is required on the router or access server. |
| V.120 | Use this mode for asynchronous-to-synchronous communication, which can be used to tunnel character mode sessions over synchronous ISDN. Cisco recommends you use this mode with mid-range routers, such as the Cisco 4500. |
| V.110 | Use this modem for setting up cellular modem access. |

## Mixed Protocol Configuration Examples

These sample configurations are intended to run on each network device featured in Figure 3–8, which allows remote users to dial in to a mixed protocol environment:

- Cisco 7200 #1 Backbone Router
- Cisco 7200 #2 Backbone Router
- Cisco AS5200 Universal Access Server

**NOTES**

Be sure to include your own IP addresses, host names, and security passwords where appropriate.

### *Cisco 7200 #1 Backbone Router*

The following configuration runs on the router labeled Cisco 7200 #1 in Figure 3–8. The Fast Ethernet interface 0/0 connects to the corporate backbone switch. The Fast Ethernet interface 1/0 connects to the Catalyst 1900 switch, which in turn connects to the Cisco AS5200 access servers.

```
!
version 11.2
no service udp-small-servers
no service tcp-small-servers
!
hostname bbone-dial1
!
aaa new-model
aaa authentication login default local
aaa authentication login console enable
!
username admin password cisco
!
boot system flash slot0:
enable secret <password>
appletalk routing
ipx routing
!
interface FastEthernet0/0
 ip address 10.0.1.52 255.255.255.192
 appletalk cable-range 1000-1000
 appletalk zone Networking Infrastructure
 ipx network 1000
!
interface FastEthernet1/0
 ip address 10.1.1.2 255.255.255.224
 no ip redirects
 appletalk cable-range 7650-7650 7650.1
 appletalk zone Dial-Up Net
 ipx network 7650
!
 standby ip 10.1.1.1
 standby priority 101
 standby preempt
!
router eigrp 109
 redistribute static
 network 10.0.0.0
 no auto-summary
!
ip classless
ip http server
no logging console
```

```
!
ip route 10.1.2.0 255.255.255.192 10.1.1.10
!
line con 0
login authentication console
!
line vty 0 4
 login authentication default
!
end
```

### *Cisco 7200 #2 Backbone Router*

The following configuration runs on the router labeled Cisco 7200 #2 in Figure 3–8. The Fast Ethernet interface 0/0 connects to the corporate backbone switch. The Fast Ethernet interface 1/0 connects to the Catalyst 1900 switch, which in turn connects to the Cisco AS5200 access servers.

```
!
version 11.2
no service udp-small-servers
no service tcp-small-servers
!
hostname bbone-dial2
!
aaa new-model
aaa authentication login default local
aaa authentication login console enable
!
username admin password cisco
!
boot system flash slot0:
enable secret <password>
appletalk routing
ipx routing
!
interface FastEthernet0/0
 ip address 10.0.1.116 255.255.255.192
 appletalk cable-range 1001-1001
 appletalk zone Networking Infrastructure
 ipx network 1001
!
interface FastEthernet1/0
 ip address 10.1.1.3 255.255.255.224
 no ip redirects
 appletalk cable-range 7650-7650 7650.2
 appletalk zone Dial-Up Net
 ipx network 7650
!
 standby ip 10.1.1.1
!
router eigrp 109
 redistribute static
 network 10.0.0.0
 no auto-summary
```

```
!
ip classless
ip http server
no logging console
!
ip route 10.1.2.0 255.255.255.192 10.1.1.10
!
line con 0
login authentication console
!
line vty 0 4
 login authentication console
!
end
```

### *Cisco AS5200 Universal Access Server*

The following sample configuration runs on each Cisco AS5200 in the stackgroup shown in Figure 3–8:

```
!
version 11.2
service timestamps debug datetime msec
service timestamps log datetime msec
service password-encryption
no service udp-small-servers
no service tcp-small-servers
!
appletalk routing
ipx routing
appletalk virtual net 7651 Dial-Up Net
arap network 7652 Dial-Up Net
!
hostname NAS
!
aaa new-model
aaa authentication login default local
aaa authentication login console enable
aaa authentication login vty local
aaa authentication login dialin local
aaa authentication ppp default local
aaa authentication ppp dialin if-needed local
aaa authentication arap default auth-guest local
enable secret cisco
!
username admin password cisco
username pcuser1 password mypass
isdn switch-type primary-5ess
!
controller T1 0
 framing esf
 clock source line primary
 linecode b8zs
 pri-group timeslots 1-24
!
```

```
controller T1 1
 framing esf
 clock source line secondary
 linecode b8zs
 pri-group timeslots 1-24
!
interface loopback 0
 ip address 10.1.2.0 255.255.255.192
 ipx network 7651
!
interface Ethernet0
 ip address 10.1.1.10 255.255.255.0
 appletalk cable-range 7650
 appletalk zone Dial-Up-Net
 ipx network 7650
!
interface Serial0
 no ip address
 shutdown
!
interface Serial1
 no ip address
 shutdown
!
interface Serial0:23
 no ip address
 encapsulation ppp
 isdn incoming-voice modem
 dialer rotary-group 0
 dialer-group 1
 no fair-queue
 no cdp enable
!
interface Serial1:23
 no ip address
 encapsulation ppp
 isdn incoming-voice modem
 dialer rotary-group 0
 dialer-group 1
 no fair-queue
 no cdp enable
!
interface Group-Async1
 ip unnumbered Ethernet0
 encapsulation ppp
 async mode interactive
 peer default ip address pool dialin_pool
 appletalk client-mode
 ipx ppp-client
 no cdp enable
 ppp authentication chap pap dialin
 group-range 1 48
!
interface Dialer0
 ip unnumbered Ethernet0
```

```
 no ip mroute-cache
 encapsulation ppp
 peer default ip address pool dialin_pool
 ipx ppp-client
 appletalk client-mode
 dialer in-band
 dialer-group 1
 no fair-queue
 no cdp enable
 ppp authentication chap pap dialin
 ppp multilink
!
ip local pool dialin_pool 10.1.2.1 10.1.2.62
ip default-gateway 10.1.1.1
ip classless
ip route 0.0.0.0 0.0.0.0 10.1.1.1
!
dialer-list 1 protocol ip permit
!
async-bootp dns-server 10.1.0.40 10.1.0.170
async-bootp nbns-server 10.0.235.228 10.0.235.229
!
xremote buffersize 72000
xremote tftp host 10.0.2.74
!
line con 0
 login authentication console
line 1 48
 autoselect ppp
 autoselect during-login
 autoselect arap
 arap enable
 arap authentication default
 arap timelimit 240
 arap warningtime 15
 login authentication dialin
 modem DialIn
 terminal-type dialup
line aux 0
 login authentication console
line vty 0 4
 login authentication vty
 transport input telnet rlogin
!
end
```

PART 2

# Dial-In Port Set-Up

# CHAPTER 4

# Overview of Lines, Interfaces, and Controllers on Cisco Routers

This chapter provides information about the different types of calls, interfaces, internal software constructs, and lines used for remote access.

The following sections are provided in this chapter:

- Types of Calls Sent and Received in Dial Networking
- Logical Constructs for Remote Access
- Logical Interfaces for Remote Access
- Lines Used for Remote Access

## TYPES OF CALLS SENT AND RECEIVED IN DIAL NETWORKING

There are three basic types of calls sent and received in dial networking:

- Digital Calls
- Analog Modem Calls
- Asynchronous Character Stream Calls

### Digital Calls

Digital calls are generally ISDN 56Kbps or 64Kbps data or voice calls that use the point-to-point protocol (PPP). These calls usually originate from a PC, Macintosh, or digital telephone connected to an ISDN router or terminal adapter and terminate at another access server's or router's ISDN interface. Digital calls are also assigned to use B channels when traveling across ISDN networks. (See Figure 4–1.)

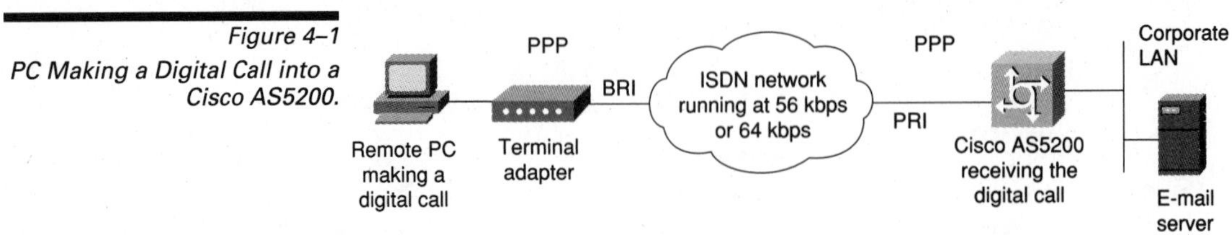


*Figure 4–1*
*PC Making a Digital Call into a Cisco AS5200.*

### Analog Modem Calls

Analog modem calls travel through standard telephone lines (POTS) or ISDN lines. Regardless of whether analog calls travel through an asynchronous POTS line or ISDN line, these calls are eventually routed to an internal modem (such as with the Cisco AS5200) or an external modem (such as with the Cisco 2500 series). (See Figure 4–2.)

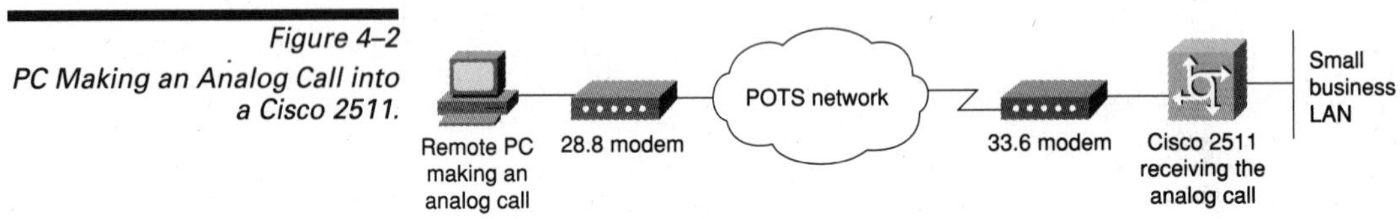


*Figure 4–2*
*PC Making an Analog Call into a Cisco 2511.*

### Asynchronous Character Stream Calls

These calls get routed to virtual terminal (VTY) lines and virtual asynchronous interfaces (VTY-async), which are used to terminate incoming character streams that do not have a physical connection (such as a physical interface) to the access server or router. A virtual asynchronous interface is the place where inbound Telnet, LAT, V.120, TN3270, and PAD calls or sessions terminate on the router. Virtual terminal lines are used for attaching to the router in a non-physical way. If you begin a PPP session over an asynchronous character stream, for example, a VTY-async interface is created to support the call. (See Figure 4–3.)

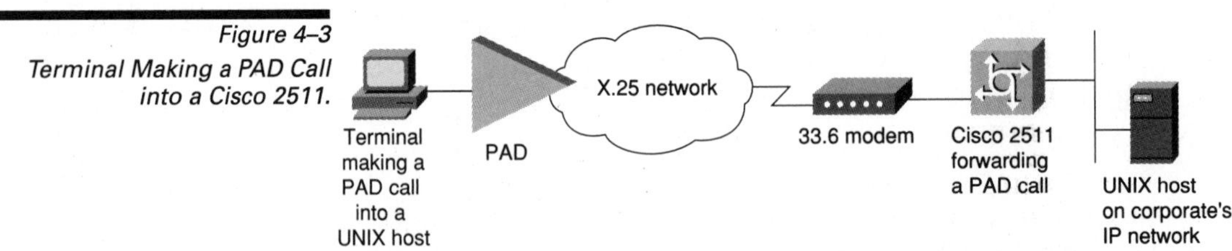


*Figure 4–3*
*Terminal Making a PAD Call into a Cisco 2511.*

## Logical Constructs for Remote Access

A logical construct is an intangible device in an access server or router that stores data or configuration information for physical interfaces. No data packets are forwarded to a logical construct. Cisco uses two types of logical constructs in its access servers and routers:

- Group Asynchronous Interfaces
- Virtual Interface Templates

## Group Asynchronous Interfaces

A group asynchronous interface is a parent interface that applies specified protocol characteristics to a specified range of asynchronous ports. This convenient interface stores and projects configuration information to asynchronous ports, which usually connect to modems. This feature, for example, facilitates applying asynchronous configurations, such as autoselect PPP, to several interfaces at once. No data packets arrive in a group asynchronous interface (see Figure 4–4).

*Figure 4–4*
*Logical Construct for Group Asynchronous Interface.*

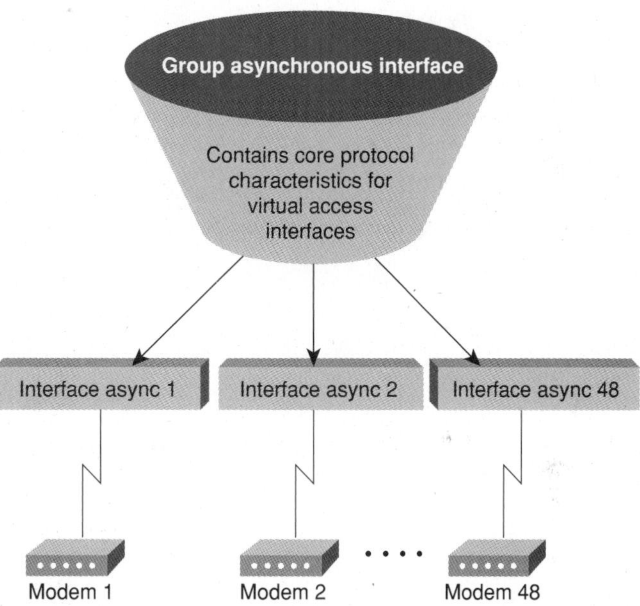


Configuring a group asynchronous interface eliminates the need to repeatedly configure identical configuration information across several asynchronous interfaces. To configure a group interface, use the **interface group-async** global configuration command.

You must specify the group async number (an arbitrary number) and the group range (beginning and ending asynchronous interface number). The following example shows the process of creating a group asynchronous interface for asynchronous interfaces 1 through 16 on a Cisco 2511 access server:

```
router(config)# interface group-async 1
router(config-if)# group-range 1 16

Building configuration...

router(config-if)#
```

For additional information about configuring group asynchronous interfaces, see Chapter 5, "Configuring Modem Support and Asynchronous Devices."

### Virtual Interface Templates

A virtual interface template exists inside the router and stores protocol configuration information that is projected or applied to protocol translation sessions or virtual access interfaces. The template is not a physical interface; it is a logical interface. No data packets ever arrive in a virtual interface template (see Figure 4–5).

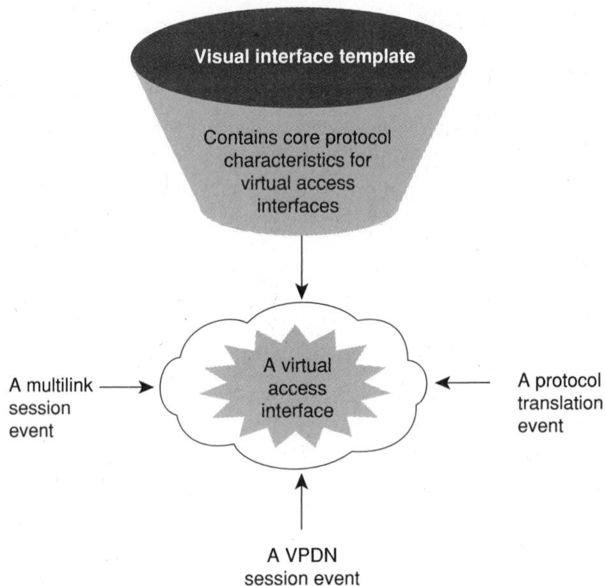


*Figure 4–5 Logical Construct for a Virtual Interface Template.*

Additionally, a virtual interface template enables you to simplify the process of configuring protocol translation to tunnel PPP or SLIP across X.25, TCP, and LAT networks. A virtual interface template is configured independently and is applied to any protocol translation session. You can create a virtual interface template with the **interface virtual-template** command and use it for one-step and two-step protocol translation. When a user dials in through a virtual terminal (VTY) line and a tunnel connection is established, the router clones the attributes of the virtual interface template onto a *virtual access interface*. This virtual access interface is a temporary interface that supports the asynchronous protocol configuration specified in the virtual interface template. This virtual access interface is created dynamically and lasts only as long as the tunnel session is active.

A virtual interface template is also used to project configuration information to virtual access interfaces that spawn due to multilink or virtual private dial-up network sessions. When a virtual access interface is created, the configuration information in the virtual template is leveraged and the negotiated parameters are implemented thereon to the connection.

For information about applying virtual templates to protocol translation, see Chapter 21, "Configuring Protocol Translation and Virtual Asynchronous Devices."

## LOGICAL INTERFACES FOR REMOTE ACCESS

A logical interface is a device in an access server or router that receives and transmits data packets and controls physical interfaces. The Cisco IOS software provides three logical interfaces:

- Dialer Interfaces
- Virtual Access Interfaces
- Virtual Asynchronous Interfaces

### Dialer Interfaces

A dialer interface is a parent interface that holds central protocol characteristics for ISDN D channels, which are part of specified dialer rotary groups. Data packets are delivered to dialer interfaces, which in turn initiate dialing for inbound calls. In most cases, D channels get their core protocol intelligence from dialer interfaces (see Figure 4–6).

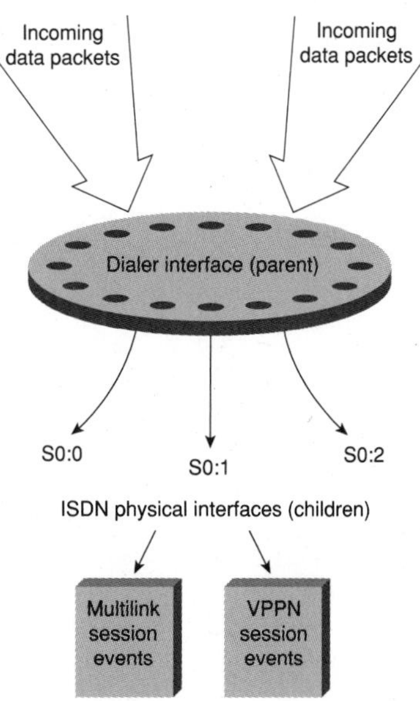


*Figure 4–6 Dialer Interface and Its Neighboring Components.*

A dialer interface is user configurable and linked to individual B channels (such as S0:0, S0:1, S0:2), where it delivers data packets to their physical destinations. Dialer interfaces seize physical interfaces to cause packet delivery. If a dialer interface spawns a multilink session, a dialer interface can be in control of a virtual access interface, which in turn controls S0:3 or chassis 2 S0:3 for example. A dialer interface is created with the **interface dialer** global configuration command.

### Virtual Access Interfaces

A virtual access interface is a mechanism that is used to terminate incoming PPP steams that do not have a physical connection. PPP streams and L2F frames coming in on multiple channels (also known as multilink sessions) get reassembled by a virtual access interface, which is an interface construct to terminate packets into. (All packets must have some kind of interface to arrive on or land on.) A virtual access interface is also used to clone attributes from a virtual interface template, which is used in protocol translation to tunnel PPP or SLIP across X.25, TCP, and LAT networks.

A virtual access interface is not directly user-configurable. All negotiated protocol parameters are configured at the virtual interface template. Use a virtual template to project how a virtual access interface will be configured or spawned. A virtual access interface is created dynamically and lasts only as long as a tunnel or multilink session is active.

Figure 4–7 shows how a virtual access interface functions to accommodate a multilink session event. Two physical interfaces on two different access servers are involved in a multilink call that originates from one PC. Only one B channel, however, on each Cisco AS5200 is available to receive the call. All four packets, therefore, are equally distributed between the two separate devices. Each Cisco AS5200 receives only half the total packets. A virtual access interface is dynamically created upstream to receive the multilink protocol, track the multilink frames, and reassemble the packets.

*Figure 4–7*
*A Virtual Access Interface Used for a Multilink Session Event.*

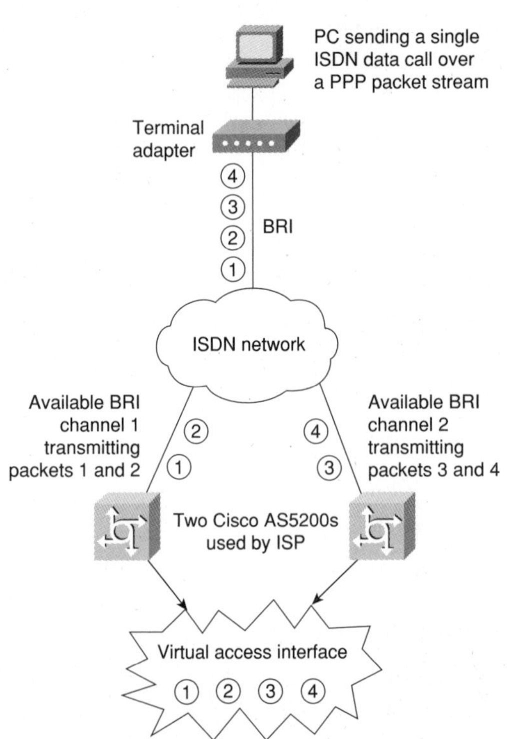

### Virtual Asynchronous Interfaces

A virtual asynchronous interface (also known as VTY-async) is created on demand to support calls that enter the router through a non-physical interface. Asynchronous character stream calls, for example, arrive on non-physical interfaces. These types of calls include inbound Telnet, LAT, PPP over character-oriented protocols (such as V.120 or X.25), and PAD calls. A virtual asynchronous interface is also used to terminate L2F tunnels, which are often traveling companions with multilink sessions. Virtual asynchronous interfaces are not user-configurable; rather, they are dynamically created and torn down on demand. A virtual asynchronous line is used to access a virtual asynchronous interface (see Figure 4–8).

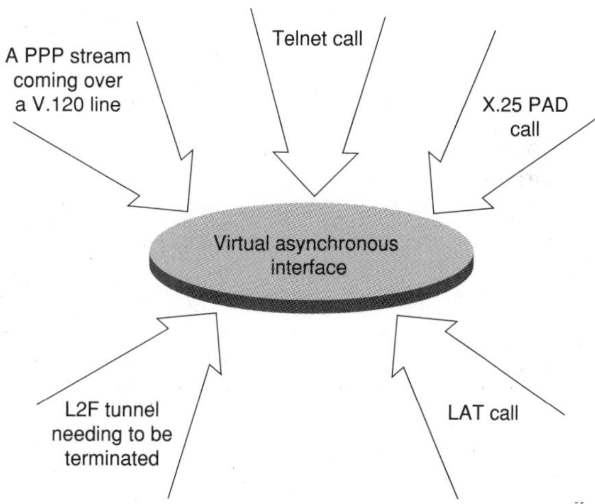


*Figure 4–8*
*Types of Calls that Terminate on a Virtual Asynchronous Interface.*

### Physical Interfaces, Lines, and Controllers for Remote Access

Data packets travel through physical interfaces and controllers in dial access servers and routers. This section describes different types of physical interfaces and controllers, as follows:

- Asynchronous Interfaces
- Asynchronous Modem Lines
- ISDN Interfaces
- Channelized T1 and Channelized E1
- Controllers for T1 or E1 Networks

### Asynchronous Interfaces

Remote clients dial in to the network through asynchronous ports, which can be on the back of an access server (for example, the Cisco 2511) or inside an access server (for example, the Cisco AS5300).

To enable clients to dial in, you configure two components of each asynchronous port: lines and interfaces. Asynchronous interfaces correspond to physical terminal (TTY) lines. Asynchronous interface 1, for example, corresponds to TTY line 1.

Generally, commands entered in asynchronous interface mode enable you to configure protocol-specific parameters for asynchronous interfaces, whereas commands entered in line configuration mode let you configure the physical aspects for the same port.

Specifically, you configure asynchronous interfaces to support PPP connections. An asynchronous interface on an access server or router can be configured to support the following functions:

- Network protocol support (such as IP, IPX, or AppleTalk)
- Encapsulation support (such as PPP)
- IP client addressing options (default and/or dynamic)
- IPX network addressing options
- PPP authentication
- ISDN BRI and PRI configuration

For additional information about configuring asynchronous interfaces, see Chapter 5.

### Asynchronous Modem Lines

Asynchronous line configuration commands configure ports for the following options:

- Physical layer options (such as modem configuration)
- Security for EXEC mode
- ARA protocol configuration (PPP is configured in interface configuration mode)
- Autoselect to detect incoming protocols (ARA and PPP)

To enter line configuration mode, first connect to the console port of the access server and enter privileged EXEC mode. Then enter global configuration mode, and finally, enter line configuration mode for the asynchronous lines that you want to configure. The following example shows the process of entering line configuration mode for lines 1 through 16:

```
router> enable
router# configure terminal
router(config)# line 1 16
router(config-line)#
```

For additional information about configuring asynchronous modem lines, see Chapter 5.

### ISDN Interfaces

There are two types of ISDN interfaces or services that Cisco routers and access servers provide—Basic Rate Interface (BRI) and Primary Rate Interface (PRI).

#### *ISDN BRI*

ISDN BRI operates over most of the copper twisted-pair telephone wiring in place today. ISDN BRI delivers a total bandwidth of 144Kbps via three separate channels. Two of the channels, called B

(Bearer) channels, operate at 64Kbps and are used to carry voice, video, or data traffic. The third channel, the D (Data) channel, is a 16-Kbps signaling channel used to carry instructions that tell the telephone network how to handle each of the B channels. ISDN BRI is often referred to as "2 B+D."

The flexibility of ISDN comes from its ability to use each of the B channels for separate voice or data applications. A long document, for example, can be downloaded from the corporate network over one ISDN 64-kbps B channel connection. While that document is downloading, another B channel can be connected to the Internet to browse a Web page.

A D channel notifies the central office switch to send the incoming call to particular timeslots on the router. Each one of the bearer or B channels carries data or voice. The D channel carries signaling for the B channels. The D channel also identifies whether the call is a digital call or an analog call. Analog calls are decoded and then sent off to the modems. Digital calls are directly relayed off to the ISDN processor in the router.

Enter the **interface bri** command to bring up and configure a single BRI interface, which is the overseer of the 2 B+D channels. As soon as this command is issued, the BRI interface is set up to support traffic on both B and D channels. Other than protocol and dialer map information, you do not need to enter any additional configuration commands to prepare the B channels to transmit network traffic. The D channel is not user-configurable.

### ISDN PRI

ISDN PRI is often referred to as "23 B+D" (U.S.) or "30 B+D" (non-U.S.). PRI is designed to carry large numbers of incoming ISDN calls at corporate offices or other central site locations. All the reliability and performance features of ISDN BRI apply to ISDN PRI, but ISDN PRI also has 23 B channels of 64Kbps each that carry user traffic and a shared 64-kbps D channel that carries signaling traffic. The logical contents of a PRI interface include 24 virtual serial interfaces, 24 timeslots, 23 B channels, and one D channel. (See Figure 4–9.)

ISDN PRI is configured on a T1 or E1 controller, which is also set up to support an ISDN switch type, framing, linecode, and a PRI timeslot range. In T1 networks, the D channel is brought up by specifying the **interface serial 0:23** and **interface serial 1:23** commands in the Cisco IOS software. In E1 networks, the D channel is brought up by specifying the **interface serial 0:15** and **interface serial 1:15** commands. D channels are user-configurable and behave precisely like dialer interfaces, which are areas where packets go to initiate dialing. In Figure 4–9, the D channel Serial 0:23 in turn controls virtual interfaces Serial 0:0 through Serial 0:22. If Figure 4–9 were for an E1 configuration, the D channel Serial 0:15 would control virtual interfaces Serial 0:0 through Serial 0:14.

*Figure 4–9*
*Logical Flow of Traffic Between ISDN PRI and an Access Server or Router.*

| Channel type | | Timeslot number | Virtual serial interface number |
|---|---|---|---|
| B | (data channel) | 1 | S0:0 |
| B | (data channel) | 2 | S0:1 |
| B | (data channel) | 3 | S0:2 |
| B | (data channel) | 4 | S0:3 |
| • | | • | • |
| • | | • | • |
| • | | • | • |
| • | | • | • |
| • | | • | • |
| B | (data channel) | 21 | S0:20 |
| B | (data channel) | 22 | S0:21 |
| B | (data channel) | 23 | S0:22 |
| Ⓓ | (voice signaling channel) | 24 | S0:23 |

Logical contents of a PRI interface

## Channelized T1 and Channelized E1

A channelized T1 (CT1) or E1(CE1) is an analog line that was originally intended to support analog voice calls but has evolved to support analog data calls. ISDN or digital calls do not transmit across CT1 or CE1 lines. Cisco routers and access servers can directly connect to channelized lines.

The key difference between traditional channelized lines (analog) and non-channelized lines (digital or ISDN) is that channelized lines do not have built-in D-channel signaling. All 24 channels on a T1 line, for example, only carry data. The signaling is in-band or associated to the data channels (also known as robbed-bit signaling for T1 lines or channel-associated signaling for E1 lines). A traditional channelized line cannot support a digitized data call (for example, BRI with 2B+D). The only supported signals on a traditional channelized line are onhook, offhook, relay open, and relay closed. The Cisco AS5200, Cisco AS5300, and Cisco 3600 series support different types of channel-associated signalling for receiving and transmitting analog calls, such as ground start, loop start, wink start, immediate start, and E&M. Signaling for CT1 or CE1 is turned on or enabled with the **cas-group** command, which is configured on a T1 or E1 controller.

## Controllers for T1 or E1 Networks

A T1 or E1 controller is a device that exists inside a router or access server. You configure the controller to inform the router how to distribute or provision individual timeslots for a connected T1 or E1 line. A controller communicates with the telephone company in a way similar to line coding and framing. Typically, timeslots are distributed to meet the needs of a particular business scenario. To support traffic flow for a ISDN PRI interface, for example, the **pri-group 1-24** command is configured. To support traffic flow for analog calls over a channelized T1 line provisioned for E&M signaling (such as feature group b ear and mouth), the **cas-group e&m-fgb 1-24** command is configured. Although supported on Cisco routers, most telephone companies will not provision their switches to support a single T1 or E1 line with a combination of PRI, channel-associated signaling, and leased-line grouping, such as communicated by the following router configuration statement on a controller T1:

```
pri-group timeslots 1-10
channel-group 11 timeslots 11-16
cas-group 17 timeslots 17-23 type e&m-fgb.
```

## Lines Used for Remote Access

This section describes the different line types used for dial access on Cisco access servers and routers. It also describes the relationship between lines and interfaces. The following sections are included:

- Line Types
- Relationship Between Lines and Interfaces on Cisco Routers
- Absolute Versus Relative Line Numbers
- Interface and Line Numbering Schemes for Specific Access Servers and Routers

**Notes**

Cisco devices have four types of lines: console, auxiliary, asynchronous, and virtual terminal lines. Different routers have different numbers of these line types. Refer to the hardware and software configuration guides that shipped with your device for exact configurations.

### Line Types

Table 4–1 shows the types of lines that can be configured on Cisco routers.

**Table 4–1** *Line Types Available on Cisco Routers*

| Line Type | Port | Description | Numbering Rules |
|---|---|---|---|
| CON or CTY | Console | Typically used to log in to the router for configuration purposes. | Line 0. |
| AUX | Auxiliary | RS-232 DTE port used as a backup asynchronous port (TTY). Cannot be used as a second console port. | Last TTY line number plus 1. |
| TTY | Asynchronous | Same as asynchronous interface. Used typically for remote-node dial-in sessions that use such protocols as SLIP, PPP, and XRemote. | The numbering widely varies between platforms. |
| VTY | Virtual terminal | Used for incoming Telnet, LAT, X.25 PAD, and protocol translation connections into synchronous ports (such as Ethernet and serial interfaces) on the router. | Last TTY line number plus 2 through the maximum number of VTY lines specified.* |

* Increase the number of VTY lines on a router using the **line vty** command. Delete VTY lines with the **no line vty** *line-number* global configuration command. The **line vty** command accepts any line number larger than 5 up to the maximum number of lines supported by your router with its current configuration.

## Relationship Between Lines and Interfaces on Cisco Routers

This section describes the relationship between lines and interfaces on Cisco routers:

- Asynchronous Interfaces and TTY Lines
- Synchronous Interfaces and VTY Lines

### *Asynchronous Interfaces and TTY Lines*

Asynchronous interfaces correspond to physical terminal (TTY) lines. Commands entered in asynchronous interface mode enable you to configure protocol-specific parameters for asynchronous interfaces; commands entered in line configuration mode let you configure the physical aspects of the line's port.

To enable IP resources to dial in to a network, for example, configure the lines and asynchronous interfaces as follows:

**Step 1** Configure the physical aspect of a line that leads to a port. You might enter the following commands to configure lines 1 through 16 (asynchronous TTY lines on a Cisco 2511 access server):

```
line 1 16
 login local
 modem inout
 speed 115200
 flowcontrol hardware
 ! configures the line to autosense PPP; physical line attribute
 autoselect ppp
```

**Step 2** On asynchronous interface 1, configure your protocol-specific commands. You might enter the following commands:

```
interface async 1
 encapsulation ppp
 async mode interactive
 async dynamic address
 async dynamic routing
 async default ip address 198.192.16.132
 ppp authentication chap
```

The remote node services SLIP, PPP, and XRemote are configured in asynchronous interface mode. AppleTalk Remote Access (ARA) is configured in line configuration mode on virtual terminal (VTY) lines or TTY lines.

### *Synchronous Interfaces and VTY Lines*

Virtual terminal (VTY) lines provide access to the router through a synchronous interface. VTY lines do not correspond to synchronous interfaces in the same way that TTY lines correspond to asynchronous interfaces. This difference is due to the face that VTY lines are created dynamically on the router, whereas TTY lines are static physical ports. When a user connects to the router on a VTY line, that user is connecting into a *virtual* port on an interface. You can have multiple virtual ports for each synchronous interface.

Several Telnet connections, for example, can be made to an interface (such as an Ethernet or serial interface).

The number of VTY lines available on a router are defined using the **line vty** *number-of-lines* global configuration command.

Use the **show line** command to see the status of each of the lines available on a router (see Figure 4–10).

*Figure 4–10*
*Sample Show Line Output Showing CTY, TTY, AUX, and VTY Line Statistics.*

Rotary group #
Access class In/out
Autoselect state
Absolute line number
Line speed
Modem setting
Number of TCP connections made
This is VTY2 (3rd VTY) line 20

```
sankara> show line
  Tty Typ      Tx/Rx         A Modem  Roty ACCO ACCI  Uses    Noise   Overruns
*   0 CTY                    -   -      -     -    -     0        0        0/0
*   1 TTY 115200/115200      - inout    -     4    -    31       26        0/0
*   2 TTY 115200/115200      - inout    - 21630    -    37       23        0/0
A   3 TTY 115200/115200      - inout    -    25    -    10       24        1/0
*   4 TTY 115200/115200      - inout    -     4    -    20       63        1/0
*   5 TTY 115200/115200      - inout    - 32445    -    18      325       22/0
A   6 TTY 115200/115200      - inout    -    25    -     7        0        0/0
I   7 TTY 115200/115200      - inout    -     6    -     6       36        1/0
I   8 TTY 115200/115200      - inout    -     -    -     3       25        3/0
*   9 TTY 115200/115200      - inout    -     4    -     2        0        0/0
A  10 TTY 115200/115200      - inout    -    56    -     2      470      216/0
I  11 TTY 115200/115200      - inout    -     4    -    31       26        0/0
I  12 TTY 115200/115200      - inout    -     4    -    31       26        0/0
I  13 TTY 115200/115200      - inout    -     4    -    31       26        0/0
I  14 TTY 115200/115200      - inout    -     4    -    31       26        0/0
I  15 TTY 115200/115200      - inout    -     4    -    31       26        0/0
I  16 TTY 115200/115200      - inout    -     4    -    31       26        0/0
   17 AUX   9600/9600        -   -      -     -    -     2        1        2/104800
*  18 VTY   9600/9600        -   -      -     -    -   103        0        0/0
   19 VTY   9600/9600        -   -      -     -    -     6        0        0/0
   20 VTY   9600/9600        -   -      -     -    -     1        0        0/0
   21 VTY   9600/9600        -   -      -     -    -     0        0        0/0
   22 VTY   9600/9600        -   -      -     -    -     0        0        0/0
   23 VTY   9600/9600        -   -      -     -    -     0        0        0/0
   24 VTY   9600/9600        -   -      -     -    -     0        0        0/0
   25 VTY   9600/9600        -   -      -     -    -     0        0        0/0
   26 VTY   9600/9600        -   -      -     -    -     0        0        0/0
   27 VTY   9600/9600        -   -      -     -    -     0        0        0/0
   28 VTY   9600/9600        -   -      -     -    -     0        0        0/0
   29 VTY   9600/9600        -   -      -     -    -     0        0        0/0
   30 VTY   9600/9600        -   -      -     -    -     0        0        0/0
   31 VTY   9600/9600        -   -      -     -    -     0        0        0/0
   32 VTY   9600/9600        -   -      -     -    -     0        0        0/0
   33 VTY   9600/9600        -   -      -     -    -     0        0        0/0
```

## Absolute Versus Relative Line Numbers

When you enter line configuration mode, you can specify an *absolute line number* or a *relative line number.* In Figure 4–10, for example, absolute line number 20 is VTY2 (line 18 is VTY0). Referring to lines in a relative format is often easier than attempting to recall the absolute number of a line on a large system. Internally, the router uses absolute line numbers.

You can view all of the absolute and relative line numbers with the **show users all** EXEC command. In the following sample display, absolute line numbers are listed at the far left under the heading "Line." Relative line numbers are in the third column, after the line type. In this example, the second virtual terminal line, VTY 1, is absolute line number 3.

```
Line       User      Host(s)                Idle Location
0 con 0
1 aux 0
2 vty 0              incoming               0 SERVER.COMPANY.COM
3 vty 1
```

```
4 vty 2
5 vty 3
6 vty 4
```

Compare the line numbers in this sample display to the output from the **show line** command, as shown in Figure 4–10.

## Interface and Line Numbering Schemes for Specific Access Servers and Routers

Interface and line numbering schemes vary between access servers and routers and the type of assembled hardware configuration. Refer to the hardware and software configuration guides that shipped with your device for specific interface and line numbering information.

CHAPTER 5

# Configuring Modem Support and Asynchronous Devices

This chapter describes how to configure the Cisco IOS software for line, terminal, and modem connections. Cisco devices have four types of lines: console, auxiliary, asynchronous, and virtual terminal lines. Different routers have different numbers of these line types. Refer to the hardware or software configuration guide that shipped with your device for exact line numbering schemes.

The following sections are provided in this chapter:

- General Concepts
- Modem Support Configuration Task List
- Asynchronous Configuration Task List
- Configuring Support for Extended BOOTP Requests
- Monitoring and Maintaining Asynchronous Devices
- Configuring Chat Scripts for Asynchronous Lines
- Configuring Additional Asynchronous Features
- Asynchronous Configuration Examples

For a complete description of the commands in this chapter, see Chapter 6, "Modem Support and Asynchronous Device Commands."

## GENERAL CONCEPTS

Asynchronous ports can be on the outside of your access server (for example, the Cisco AS2511-RJ) or on the inside of your device (for example, the Cisco AS5200). In both cases, external or internal modems connect to these interfaces. The remote clients referenced in this chapter are making analog calls in to the network via asynchronous ports.

To enable clients to dial in, you configure two components of each asynchronous port: lines and interfaces. Asynchronous interfaces correspond to physical terminal (TTY) lines. Asynchronous interface 1, for example, corresponds to TTY line 1.

Generally, commands entered in asynchronous interface mode enable you to configure protocol-specific parameters for asynchronous interfaces, whereas commands entered in line configuration mode permit you to configure the physical aspects for the same port. In Figure 5–1, which shows the **show line** output on a Cisco 2511, TTY line 1 corresponds with asynchronous interface 1, TTY line 16 corresponds with asynchronous interface 16, and so on.

*Figure 5–1*
*Show Line Output—Comparing TTY Lines to Asynchronous Interfaces.*

Rotary group #
Access class In/out
Autoselect state
Absolute line number
Line speed
Modem setting
Number of TCP connections made
This is VTY2 (3rd VTY) line 20

```
sankara> show line
 Tty Typ     Tx/Rx        A Modem  Roty ACCO ACCI  Uses   Noise  Overruns
*  0 CTY                  -    -      -    -    -     0       0       0/0
*  1 TTY 115200/115200 - inout      -     4    -    31      26       0/0
*  2 TTY 115200/115200 - inout      - 21630    -    37      23       0/0
A  3 TTY 115200/115200 - inout      -    25    -    10      24       1/0
*  4 TTY 115200/115200 - inout      -     4    -    20      63       1/0
*  5 TTY 115200/115200 - inout      - 32445    -    18     325      22/0
A  6 TTY 115200/115200 - inout      -    25    -     7       0       0/0
I  7 TTY 115200/115200 - inout      -     6    -     6      36       1/0
I  8 TTY 115200/115200 - inout      -     -    -     3      25       3/0
*  9 TTY 115200/115200 - inout      -     4    -     2       0       0/0
A 10 TTY 115200/115200 - inout      -    56    -     2     470     216/0
I 11 TTY 115200/115200 - inout      -     4    -    31      26       0/0
I 12 TTY 115200/115200 - inout      -     4    -    31      26       0/0
I 13 TTY 115200/115200 - inout      -     4    -    31      26       0/0
I 14 TTY 115200/115200 - inout      -     4    -    31      26       0/0
I 15 TTY 115200/115200 - inout      -     4    -    31      26       0/0
I 16 TTY 115200/115200 - inout      -     4    -    31      26       0/0
  17 AUX    9600/9600  -    -       -     -    -     2       1       2/104800
* 18 VTY    9600/9600  -    -       -     -    -   103       0       0/0
  19 VTY    9600/9600  -    -       -     -    -     6       0       0/0
  20 VTY    9600/9600  -    -       -     -    -     1       0       0/0
  21 VTY    9600/9600  -    -       -     -    -     0       0       0/0
  22 VTY    9600/9600  -    -       -     -    -     0       0       0/0
  23 VTY    9600/9600  -    -       -     -    -     0       0       0/0
  24 VTY    9600/9600  -    -       -     -    -     0       0       0/0
  25 VTY    9600/9600  -    -       -     -    -     0       0       0/0
  26 VTY    9600/9600  -    -       -     -    -     0       0       0/0
  27 VTY    9600/9600  -    -       -     -    -     0       0       0/0
  28 VTY    9600/9600  -    -       -     -    -     0       0       0/0
  29 VTY    9600/9600  -    -       -     -    -     0       0       0/0
  30 VTY    9600/9600  -    -       -     -    -     0       0       0/0
  31 VTY    9600/9600  -    -       -     -    -     0       0       0/0
  32 VTY    9600/9600  -    -       -     -    -     0       0       0/0
  33 VTY    9600/9600  -    -       -     -    -     0       0       0/0
```

## Asynchronous Modem Lines

Asynchronous line configuration commands configure ports for the following options:

- Physical layer options (such as modem configuration)
- Security for EXEC mode
- ARA protocol configuration (PPP is configured in interface configuration mode)
- Autoselect to detect incoming protocols (ARA and PPP)

To enter line configuration mode, first connect to the console port of the access server and enter privileged EXEC mode. Then enter global configuration mode and finally enter line configuration mode for the asynchronous lines that you want to configure. The following example shows the process of entering line configuration mode for lines 1 through 16:

```
router> enable
router# configure terminal
router(config)# line 1 16
router(config-line)#
```

### Asynchronous Interfaces

Generally, interfaces enable the Cisco IOS software to use routing functions. Specifically, you configure asynchronous interfaces to support PPP connections. You configure interfaces on an access server for the following functions:

- Network protocol support (such as IP, IPX, or AppleTalk)
- Encapsulation support (such as PPP)
- IP client addressing options (default and/or dynamic)
- IPX network addressing options
- PPP authentication
- ISDN BRI and PRI configuration

### Line Numbering Issues

The TTY line numbering scheme used by your access server or router is specific to your product and its hardware configuration. (Refer to the product-specific documentation that came with your product for line numbering scheme information.)

The Cisco AS5200 access server, for example, has TTY lines that map directly to integrated modems as shown in Table 5–1. The TTY lines 1 through 24 directly connect to modems 1/0 through 1/23, which are installed in the first chassis slot in this example. The TTY lines 25 through 48 directly connect to modems 2/0 through 2/23, which are installed in the second chassis slot.

**Table 5–1** *TTY Lines Associated to Integrated AS5200 Modems*

| TTY Line | Slot/Modem Number | TTY Line | Slot/Modem Number |
|---|---|---|---|
| 1 | 1/0 | 25 | 2/0 |
| 2 | 1/1 | 26 | 2/1 |
| 3 | 1/2 | 27 | 2/2 |
| 4 | 1/3 | 28 | 2/3 |
| 5 | 1/4 | 29 | 2/4 |
| 6 | 1/5 | 30 | 2/5 |
| 7 | 1/6 | 31 | 2/6 |

**Table 5–1** *TTY Lines Associated to Integrated AS5200 Modems, Continued*

| TTY Line | Slot/Modem Number | TTY Line | Slot/Modem Number |
|---|---|---|---|
| 8 | 1/7 | 32 | 2/7 |
| 9 | 1/8 | 33 | 2/8 |
| 10 | 1/9 | 34 | 2/9 |
| 11 | 1/10 | 35 | 2/10 |
| 12 | 1/11 | 36 | 2/11 |
| 13 | 1/12 | 37 | 2/12 |
| 14 | 1/13 | 38 | 2/13 |
| 15 | 1/14 | 39 | 2/14 |
| 16 | 1/15 | 40 | 2/15 |
| 17 | 1/16 | 41 | 2/16 |
| 18 | 1/17 | 42 | 2/17 |
| 19 | 1/18 | 43 | 2/18 |
| 20 | 1/19 | 44 | 2/19 |
| 21 | 1/20 | 45 | 2/20 |
| 22 | 1/21 | 46 | 2/21 |
| 23 | 1/22 | 47 | 2/22 |
| 24 | 1/23 | 48 | 2/23 |

## Group Asynchronous Interfaces

To configure multiple asynchronous interfaces at the same time (with the same parameters), you can assign each asynchronous interface to a group and then configure the group. Configurations throughout this book configure group asynchronous interfaces, rather than configuring each interface separately.

**NOTES**

After assigning asynchronous interfaces to a group, you cannot configure these interfaces separately. If you want to configure different attributes on different asynchronous interfaces, do not assign them to the group or assign different interfaces to different groups. On a Cisco 2511 access server, for example, you can assign asynchronous interfaces 1 to 8 as part of one group (such as group-async1) and asynchronous interfaces 9 to 16 as part of another group (group-async2).

To configure a group asynchronous interface, specify the group async number (an arbitrary number) and the group range (beginning and ending asynchronous interface number). The following example shows the process of creating and configuring a group asynchronous interface for asynchronous interfaces 1 through 48 on a Cisco AS5200 access server, which is loaded with 48 V.34 Microcom modems:

```
router(config)# interface group-async 1
router(config-if)# ip unnumbered ethernet 0
router(config-if)# encapsulation ppp
router(config-if)# async mode interactive
router(config-if)# ppp authentication chap pap
router(config-if)# peer default ip address pool default
router(config-if)# group-range 1 48
Building configuration...
router(config-if)#
```

## Modem Support Configuration Task List

The tasks in the following sections are to be performed to set up externally or internally connected modems. The first three tasks are required. The last task is optional.

- Attach the Modems
- Configure the Modem Lines
- Configure the Modems
- Configure Additional Modem Control Parameters

### Attach the Modems

Before configuring lines on a Cisco access server, you must attach your modems to the asynchronous ports. To attach a modem, refer to the user guide or installation guide that accompanied your access server.

Some Cisco access servers (such as the Cisco AS5200 universal access server), have integrated modems and do not require that you attach an external modem. If you have an access server with integrated modems, proceed directly to the next section, "Configure the Modem Lines."

### Configure the Modem Lines

You must configure the lines to which you attach modems and allow dial-in access. To configure lines, enter line configuration mode for the specific lines you need to configure. The following example shows lines 1 through 16 being configured on a Cisco 2511 access server (remember, **bold screen font** indicates what you type):

```
router> enable
Password: <password>
router# configure terminal
Enter configuration commands, one per line. End with CNTL/Z.
router(config)# line 1 X (X = the highest number of lines the router has; 8 or 16)
router(config-line)#
```

After you enter line configuration mode for the lines to which your modems are attached, configure the lines using the required commands listed in the following task table. These are the most common commands necessary for basic modem communications.

| Task | | Command |
|---|---|---|
| **Step 1** | Sets line speed to the highest common speed for the modem and the access server port. See Table 5–2 for a list of modem transmission rates and line speeds to be set on the access server.* | **speed 115200** or **speed 57600** or **speed 38400** |
| **Step 2** | Sets RTS/CTS flow control on the line. | **flowcontrol hardware** |
| **Step 3** | Configures the line to drop the connection when the Carrier Detect (CD) signal is lost (cycle DTR to close the connection). The **modem dialin** command can be used rather than the **modem inout** command to enhance security because the **modem dialin** command restricts outgoing connections from the access server to the modem. Use the **modem inout** command during setup so that you can configure the modem from the access server, and change to the **modem dialin** command when testing is completed. Use the **modem host** command to attach or connect to a printer or host device. | **modem inout** |

* Cisco Systems assumes that your modem supports flow control. Refer to your modem documentation to determine whether your modem supports flow control, and to learn the maximum transmission speed of your modem.

**Table 5–2** *Matching the Access Server Line Speed to Your Modem Speed*

| Modem Transmission Rate | Line Speed on the Access Server |
|---|---|
| 9600 | 38400 |
| 14400 | 57600 |
| 28800 | 115200 |

## Configure the Modems

This section describes the tasks required to configure modems that are externally attached to the access server:

- Communicating with the Modem
- Automatically Configuring Your External Modem

- Manually Configuring Your External Modem
- Testing the Dial-In Connection

When you configure modems to function with your access server, you must provide initialization strings and other settings on the modem to tell it how to function with the access server.

For modem configuration information about specific access servers that have integrated modems, see the section "Checking Other Modem Settings," later in this chapter.

## *Communicating with the Modem*

This section assumes you have already physically attached the modem to the access server. If not, refer to the user guide or installation and configuration guide for your access server for information about attaching modems.

Before you can configure the modem, you must establish communication with it, which requires terminal access to the modem's command environment. The process of manually configuring a modem consists of the following tasks:

1. Establishing a Direct Telnet Session to the Modem
2. Testing the Modem Connection
3. Suspending and Terminating Telnet Sessions

### *Establishing a Direct Telnet Session to the Modem*

You communicate with the modem by establishing a direct Telnet session from the access server's asynchronous line, which is connected to the modem.

**NOTES**

This process is also referred to as *reverse Telnet*. Performing a reverse Telnet means that you are initiating a Telnet session out the asynchronous line, instead of accepting a connection into the line (called a *forward* connection).

This section explains how to establish a direct Telnet session with an external modem (existing outside the router) that is connected through an asynchronous port. Internal or integrated modems, such as used with the Cisco AS5200, are connected to through a direct connect session issued from the Cisco IOS software, which is described later.

To establish a direct Telnet session to an external modem, determine the IP address of your LAN (Ethernet) interface, then enter a Telnet command to port 2000 + *n* on the access server, where *n* is the line number to which the modem is connected. To connect to the modem attached to line 1, for example, enter the following command from an EXEC session on the access server:

```
router# telnet 172.16.1.10 2001
Trying 172.16.1.10, 2001 ... Open
```

This example enables you to communicate with the modem on line 1 using the AT (attention) command set defined by the modem vendor.

**TIMESAVER**

Use the **ip host** configuration command to simplify direct Telnet sessions with modems. The **ip host** command maps an IP address of a port to a device name. The **modem1 2001 172.16.1.10** command, for example, enables you to enter **modem1** to initiate a connection with the modem, instead of repeatedly entering **telnet 172.16.1.10 2001** each time you want to communicate with the modem.

If you are unable to connect to the modem, check the following:

1. Issue the **show users** EXEC command. It should not indicate the line is in use.
2. Verify that the line is configured for **modem inout**.
3. Issue the **show line** EXEC command. The output should contain the following two lines:

```
Modem state: Idle
Modem hardware state: CTS noDSR  DTR RTS
```

4. Check to see if the virtual terminal connections to lines in the access server require passwords.
5. Check to see if the speed between the modem and the access server are the same. They are likely to be different. If they are different, switch off the modem, then switch it back on. This should match the speed of the modem with the speed of the access server.

### *Testing the Modem Connection*

After you make a direct Telnet connection to the modem, you need to test the connection. Send the modem the **AT** command to request its attention. It should respond with OK. For example:

```
at
OK
```

If the modem does not reply to the **AT** command, check the following:

1. Look at the output of the **show line 1** command. If it displays "no CTS" for the modem hardware state, the modem is not connected, powered on, and waiting for data, or the modem might not be configured for hardware flow control.
2. Check your cabling (for modems connected externally only) and the modem configuration (echo or result codes might be off). Enter the appropriate **AT modem** command to view the modem configuration, or enter the command **at&f** to return to factory defaults. Refer to your modem documentation to learn the appropriate **AT** command to view your modem configuration.

### *Suspending and Terminating Telnet Sessions*

If you are connected to an external modem, the direct Telnet session must be terminated before the line can accept incoming calls. If you do not terminate the session, it will be indicated in the output of the **show users** command when it returns a modem state of ready if the line is still in use. If the line is no longer in use, the output of the **show line** *value* command will return a state of idle. For routers that support integrated modems (for example, the Cisco AS5200), calls will not be interrupted unless you enter an AT command that requires extra processing power from the modem's CPU, such as the **ATH** command.

Terminating the Telnet session requires first suspending it, then disconnecting it. To suspend a Telnet session, enter the escape sequence **Ctrl-Shift-6 x** (press **Control-Shift-6**, let go, then press **x**). Enter the **disconnect** EXEC command to terminate the Telnet session.

**NOTES**

Ensure that you can reliably issue the escape sequence to suspend a Telnet session. Some terminal emulation packages have difficulty sending the **Ctrl-Shift-6 x** sequence. Refer to your terminal emulation documentation for more information about escape sequences.

To suspend and then disconnect a Telnet session, perform the following steps:

**Step 1** Enter **Ctrl-Shift-6 x** to suspend the Telnet session:

```
- suspend keystroke -
router#
```

**Step 2** Enter the **where** EXEC command to check for open sessions:

```
router# where
Conn Host                  Address                 Byte  Idle Conn Name
*  1 172.16.1.10           172.16.1.10                0     0  172.16.1.10
   2 172.16.1.11           172.16.1.11                0    12  modem2
```

**Step 3** After suspending a session with one modem, you can connect to another modem (then suspend it):

```
router# telnet modem2
Trying modem2 (172.16.1.11, 2002) ... Open

- suspend keystroke -
router#
```

**Step 4** To disconnect (completely close) a session, issue the **disconnect** EXEC command:

```
router# disconnect line 1
Closing connection to 172.16.1.10 [confirm] y
router# disconnect line 2
Closing connection to 172.16.1.11 [confirm] y
router#
```

**NOTES**

Before attempting to allow inbound connections, make sure you close all open connections to the modems attached to the access server. If you have a modem port in use, the modem will not accept a call properly.

---

After you have established and tested the connection to the modem, you can proceed with the next section, "Automatically Configuring Your External Modem."

### *Automatically Configuring Your External Modem*

The Cisco IOS software can issue initialization strings automatically for most types of modems externally attached to the access server. A modem initialization string is a series of parameter settings that are sent to your modem to configure it to interact with the access server in a specified way. The Cisco IOS software defines seven initialization strings that have been found to properly initialize most modems so that the modems function properly with Cisco access servers. These initialization strings have the following names:

- Codex_3260
- Usr_courier
- Usr_sportster
- Hayes_optima
- Global_village
- Viva
- Telebit_t3000

**NOTES**

Internal or integrated modems, such as those used by the Cisco AS5200, are preconfigured by Cisco Systems and do not need to be initialized.

---

If you do not know which of these modem strings is appropriate for your modems, issue the **modem autoconfigure discovery** line configuration command, as shown in the following example:

```
router# configure terminal
router(config)# line 1 16
router(config-line)# modem autoconfigure discovery
router(config-line)# Ctrl-Z
router# copy running-config startup-config
```

The Cisco IOS software first tries the first of these strings to see if the modem initializes properly. If not, the Cisco IOS software cycles to the next string and repeats the process until the appropriate string is found. If none of the strings properly initializes the modem, you must manually configure the modem (see the following section, "Manually Configuring Your External Modem").

If you know that your modem can be configured using an initialization string from one of these scripts, you can issue the **modem autoconfigure type** *type* command, where *type* is one of the strings in the preceding list. If you list a specific modem type, initialization proceeds more quickly.

To display the list of modems for which the router has modem string entries, issue the **show modemcap** command. You can change a modem value that was returned from the **show modemcap** EXEC command. You might, for example, want to add the factory default, &F, entry to the configuration file. To do this, enter the **modemcap edit** *modem-name attribute value* line configuration command. Configure one attribute of one modem at a time.

The following example shows how to enter line configuration mode and issue the **modem autoconfigure type** *type* command for a U.S. Robotics Sportster modem:

```
router(config-line)# modem autoconfigure type usr_sportster
```

For more information about the recommended strings for any type of modem, see the section "Sample Modem Strings," in Appendix A, "Configuring Modem Support and Chat Scripts." If you have access to Cisco Connection Online (CCO), you can also access the following URL for more information:

```
http://www.cisco.com/warp/customer/76/4.html
```

**NOTES**

Note that this URL is subject to change without notice.

### *Manually Configuring Your External Modem*

If you cannot configure your modem automatically, you must configure it manually. The following sections describe how to configure your externally attached modem manually:

- Configuring Modem Initialization Strings
- Checking Other Modem Settings
- Initializing the Modem

#### *Configuring Modem Initialization Strings*

This section describes the process of determining and issuing the correct initialization string for your modem and configuring your modem with it.

Modem command sets vary widely. Although most modems use the **Hayes** command set (prefixing commands with **AT**), Hayes-compatible modems do not use identical **AT** command sets.

Refer to your modem manufacturer's documentation to learn how to examine the current and stored configuration of the modem you are using. Generally, you enter **AT** commands such as **&v**, **i4**, or ***o** to view, inspect, or observe the settings.

**NOTES**

You must first create a direct Telnet or connection session to the modem before you can send an initialization string. You can use **AT&F** as a basic modem initialization string in most cases.

A sample modem initialization string for a U.S. Robotics Courier modem is as follows:

```
&b1&h1&r2&c1&d3&m4&k1s0=1
```

Modem initialization strings enable the following functions:

- Locks the speed of the modem to the speed of the serial port on the access server
- Sets Hardware Flow Control (RTS/CTS)
- Ensures Correct DCD Operation
- Ensures Proper DTR Interpretation
- Answers Calls on the First Ring

**TIMESAVER**

Initialization strings for other modems are listed in Appendix A and on Cisco Connection Online (CCO), in Tech Tips (http://www.cisco.com). Note that these URLs are subject to change without notice.

**NOTES**

Make sure to turn off automatic baud rate detection because the modem speeds must be set to a fixed value.

The port speed must not change when a session is negotiated with a remote modem. If the speed of the port on the access server is changed, you must establish a direct Telnet session to the modem and send an **AT** command so that the modem can learn the new speed.

Modems differ in the method they use to lock the EIA/TIA-232 (serial) port speed. In the modem documentation, vendors use terms such as, port-rate adjust, speed conversion, or buffered mode. Enabling error correction often puts the modem in the buffered mode. Refer to your modem documentation to see how your modem locks speed (check the settings **&b**, **\j**, **&q**, **\n**, or s-register settings).

Ready-To-Send (RTS) and Clear-To-Send (CTS) signals must be used between the modem and the access server to control the flow of data. Misconfiguring flow control for software or setting no flow control can result in hung sessions and loss of data. Modems differ in the method they use to enable hardware flow control. Refer to your modem documentation to see how to enable hardware flow control (check the settings **&e**, **&k**, **&h**, **&r**, or s-register).

The modem must use the data carrier detect (DCD) wire to indicate to the access server when a session has been negotiated and is established with a remote modem. Most modems use the setting **&c1**. Refer to your modem documentation for the DCD settings used with your modem.

The modem must interpret a toggle of the Data Terminal Ready (DTR) signal as a command to drop any active call and return to the stored settings. Most modems use the settings **&d2** or **&d3**. Refer to your modem documentation for the DTR settings used with your modem.

If a modem is used to service incoming calls, it must be configured to answer a call after a specific number of rings. Most modems use the setting **s0=1** to answer the call after one ring. Refer to your modem documentation for the settings used with your modem.

### *Checking Other Modem Settings*

This section defines other settings that might be needed or desirable depending on your modem.

Error correction can be negotiated between two modems to ensure a reliable data link. Error correction standards include LAPM and MNP4. V.42 error correction allows either LAPM or MNP4 error correction to be negotiated. Modems differ in the way they enable error correction. Refer to your modem documentation for the error correction methods used with your modem.

Data compression can be negotiated between two modems for greater data throughput. Data compression standards include V.42 bis and MNP5. Modems differ in the way they enable data compression. Refer to your modem documentation for the data compression settings used with your modem.

To establish a direct connect session to an internal or integrated modem (existing inside the router), such as required for Microcom modems in the Cisco AS5200, first open a directly connected session with the **modem at-mode** command, then send an AT command to the specified modem. The following, for example, sends the AT command **at\s** to modem 1/1:

```
AS5200# modem at-mode 1/1
You are now entering AT command mode on modem (slot 1 / port 1).
Please type CTRL-C to exit AT command mode.
at%v

MNP Class 10 V.34/V.FC Modem Rev 1.0/85

OK
at\s

IDLE            000:00:00
LAST DIAL

NET ADDR:       FFFFFFFFFFFF
MODEM HW: SA 2W United States
4 RTS 5 CTS 6 DSR - CD 20 DTR - RI
MODULATION      IDLE
MODEM BPS       28800  AT%G0
MODEM FLOW      OFF    AT\G0
MODEM MODE      AUT    AT\N3
V.23 OPR.       OFF    AT%F0
AUTO ANS.       ON     ATS0=1
```

```
SERIAL BPS       115200 AT%U0
BPS ADJUST       OFF     AT\J0
SPT BPS ADJ.     0       AT\W0
ANSWER MESSGS    ON      ATQ0
SERIAL FLOW      BHW     AT\Q3
PASS XON/XOFF    OFF     AT\X0
PARITY           8N      AT
```

### *Initializing the Modem*

This section is important if you cannot or choose not to initialize your modems automatically, as described in the section "Automatically Configuring Your External Modem," earlier in this chapter.

After the modem initialization string has been determined, perform the following steps to configure the modem. This example configures a U.S. Robotics Courier modem on line 1 (decimal number 2000 + line number 1 = 2001):

**Step 1** Map a host name to a decimal port. The port number is 200x, plus the number of the TTY line. The following example maps port 2001 to the IP address of the Ethernet0 interface on the access server (172.16.1.10):

```
router(config)# ip host modem1 2001 172.16.1.10
router(config)# exit
router#
```

**Step 2** Establish a direct Telnet session to the modem:

```
router# telnet modem1
Trying modem1 (172.16.1.10, 2001)... Open
```

**Step 3** Return the modem to its factory defaults (this step is optional):

```
at&f
OK
```

**Step 4** Configure the modem with an initialization string. The following example string is for a U.S. Robotics Courier modem:

```
at&b1&h1&r2&c1&d3&m4&k1s0=1
OK
```

**Step 5** Store the modem settings in NVRAM on the modem:

```
at&w
OK
```

**NOTES**

Some modems need to be "strapped" so that they start up with saved settings when powered on, rather than using defaults. You should make sure your modem is strapped accordingly.

**Step 6** Suspend and disconnect your Telnet session:

```
- suspend keystroke -
router# disconnect
Closing connection to modem1 [confirm] y
router#
```

**TIMESAVER**

The **script-reset** line configuration command can automate the configuration of your modems. See the "Technical Tips" section on CCO for more information.

### *Testing the Dial-In Connection*

The access server and modem are now correctly configured for dial-in access. Before configuring any additional protocols for the line (such as SLIP, PPP, or ARA), test the dial-in connection.

**NOTES**

The same configuration issues exist between the client data terminal equipment (DTE) and client modem. Make sure you have the correct EIA/TIA-232 cabling and modem initialization string for your client modem.

The following is an example of a successful connection from a PC using a U.S. Robotics Courier modem to dial in to a Cisco 2500 series access server:

```
at&f&c1&d3&h1&r2&b1&m4&k1&w
OK
atdt9,5551234
CONNECT 14400/ARQ/V32/LAPM/V42BIS
User Access Verification
Username: janedoe
Password:
router>
```

## Configure Additional Modem Control Parameters

Cisco routers use six EIA/TIA-232 signals for each port, so one 50-pin telco, RJ-11, or RJ-45 connector can support eight sessions. The router can support the most popular forms of modem control and hardware flow control, as well as high-speed dial-up modems.

The EIA/TIA-232 output signals are Transmit Data (TXDATA), Data Terminal Ready (DTR), and Ready To Send (RTS, 2500 only). The input signals are Receive Data (RXDATA), Clear to Send (CTS), and RING. The sixth signal is ground. Depending on the type of modem control your modem uses, these names may or may not correspond to the standard EIA/TIA-232 signals.

Dial-up modems that operate over normal telephone lines at speeds of 28,800 bits per second (bps) use hardware flow control to stop the data from reaching the host by toggling an EIA/TIA-232 signal when their limit is reached.

In addition to hardware flow control, modems require special software configuring. They must be configured to create an EXEC session when a user dials in, for example, and to hang up when the user exits the EXEC. These modems also must be configured to close any existing network connections if the telephone line hangs up in the middle of a session.

The Cisco IOS software supports hardware flow control on its CTS input signal, which is also used by the normal modem handshake.

The following modem line characteristics and modem features are discussed in the following sections:

- Configure Automatic Dialing
- Automatically Answer a Modem
- Support Dial-In and Dial-Out Modems
- Configure a Line Timeout Interval
- Close Modem Connections
- Configure a Line To Automatically Disconnect
- Support Old-Style Dial-In Modems
- Support Reverse Modem Connections and Prevent Incoming Calls

Signal and line state diagrams accompany some of the tasks in the following sections to illustrate how the modem control works. The diagrams show two processes:

- The "create daemon" process creates a TTY daemon that handles the incoming network connection.
- The "create EXEC" process creates the process that interprets user commands. (Refer to Figures 5–2 through 5–7.)

In the diagrams, the current signal state and the signal the line is watching are listed inside each box. The state of the line (as displayed by the **show line** EXEC command) is listed next to the box. Events that change that state appear in italics along the event path, and actions that the software performs are described within the ovals.

Figure 5–2 illustrates line states when no modem control is set. The DTR output is always high, and CTS and RING are completely ignored. The Cisco IOS software starts an EXEC session when the user types the activation character. Incoming TCP connections occur instantly if the line is not in use and can be closed only by the remote host.

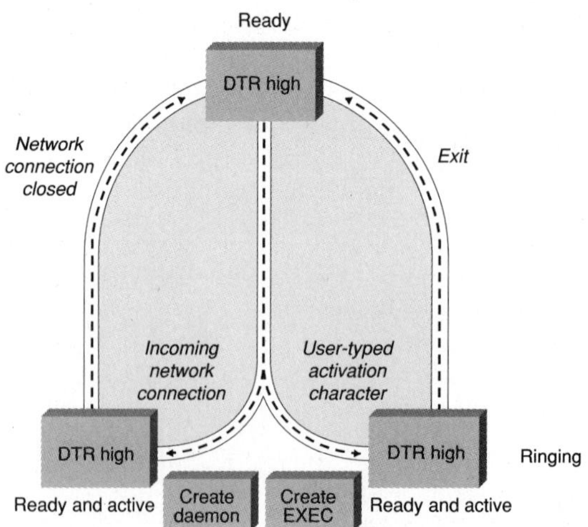


*Figure 5–2*
*EXEC and Daemon Creation on a Line with No Modem Control.*

### Configure Automatic Dialing

With the dial-up capability, you can set a modem to dial the phone number of a remote router automatically. This feature offers cost savings because phone line connections are made only when they are needed—you only pay for using the phone line when there is data to be received or sent. To configure a line for automatic dialing, perform the following task in line configuration mode:

| Task | Command |
|---|---|
| Configure a line to initiate automatic dialing. | **modem dtr-active** |

Using the **modem dtr-active** command causes a line to raise DTR signal only when there is an outgoing connection (such as reverse Telnet, NASI, or DDR), rather than leave DTR raised all the time. When raised, DTR potentially tells the modem that the router is ready to accept a call.

### Automatically Answer a Modem

You can configure a line to answer a modem automatically. You also can configure the modem to answer the telephone on its own (as long as DTR is high), drop connections when DTR is low, and use its Carrier Detect (CD) signal to accurately reflect the presence of the carrier. (Configuring the modem is a modem-dependent process.) Wire the modem's CD signal (generally pin-8) to the router's RING input (pin-22), and perform the following task in line configuration mode:

| Task | Command |
|---|---|
| Configure a line to automatically answer a modem. | **modem dialin** |

You can turn on the modem's hardware flow control independently to respond to the status of the router's CTS input. Wire CTS to whatever signal the modem uses for hardware flow control. If the modem expects to control hardware flow in both directions, you might also need to wire the modem's flow control input to some other signal that the router always has high (such as the DTR signal).

Figure 5–3 illustrates the **modem dialin** process with a high-speed dial-up modem. When the Cisco IOS software detects a signal on the RING input of an idle line, it starts an EXEC or autobaud process on that line. If the RING signal disappears on an active line, the Cisco IOS software closes any open network connections and terminates the EXEC facility. If the user exits the EXEC or the software terminates because of no user input, the line makes the modem hang up by lowering the DTR signal for five seconds. After five seconds, the modem is ready to accept another call.

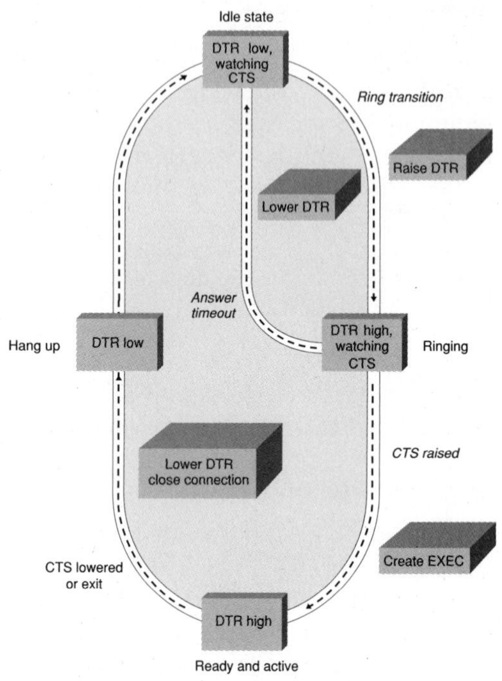


*Figure 5–3 EXEC Creation on a Line Configured for a High-Speed Modem.*

## *Support Dial-In and Dial-Out Modems*

You can configure a line for both incoming and outgoing calls by performing the following task in line configuration mode:

| Task | Command |
|---|---|
| Configure a line for both incoming and outgoing calls. | **modem inout** |

Figure 5–4 illustrates the **modem inout** command. If the line is activated by raising the data set ready (DSR) signal, it functions exactly as a line configured with the **modem dialin** line configuration command described in the section "Automatically Answer a Modem," earlier in this chapter. If the line is activated by an incoming TCP connection, the line functions similarly to lines not used with modems.

*Figure 5–4*
*EXEC and Daemon Creation for Incoming and Outgoing Calls.*

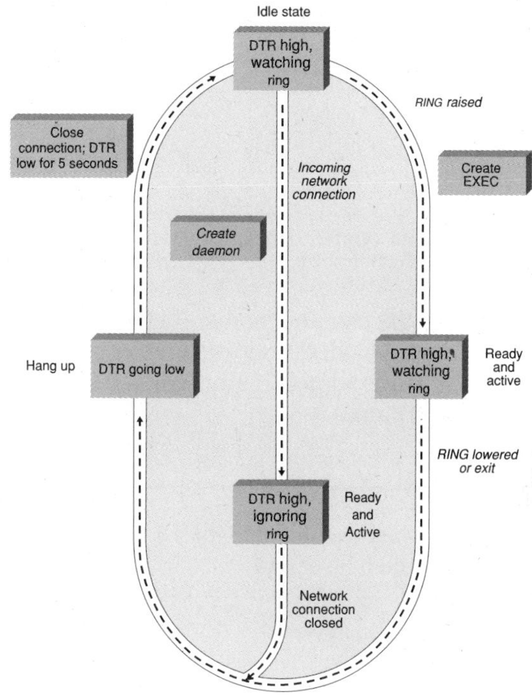


**NOTES**

If your system incorporates dial-out modems, consider using access lists to prevent unauthorized use.

### Configure a Line Timeout Interval

You can change the interval that the Cisco IOS software waits for the CTS signal after raising the DTR signal in response to the DSR (the default is 15 seconds). To do so, perform the following task in line configuration mode. The timeout applies to the **modem callin** command only.

| Task | Command |
|---|---|
| Configure modem line timing. | **modem answer-timeout** *seconds* |

**NOTES**

The DSR signal is called RING on older ASM-style chassis.

### Close Modem Connections

You can configure a line to close connections from a user's terminal when the terminal is turned off and prevent inbound connections to devices that are out of service. To do so, perform the following task in line configuration mode:

| Task | Command |
|---|---|
| Configure a line to close connections. | **modem cts-required** |

Figure 5–5 illustrates the **modem cts-required** command operating in the context of a continuous CTS signal. This form of modem control requires that the CTS signal be high for the entire session. If CTS is not high, the user's input is ignored, and incoming connections are refused (or sent to the next line in a rotary group).

**NOTES**

For the Cisco IOS software to reliably detect a CTS signal change, the CTS signal must remain in the new state for at least one full second.

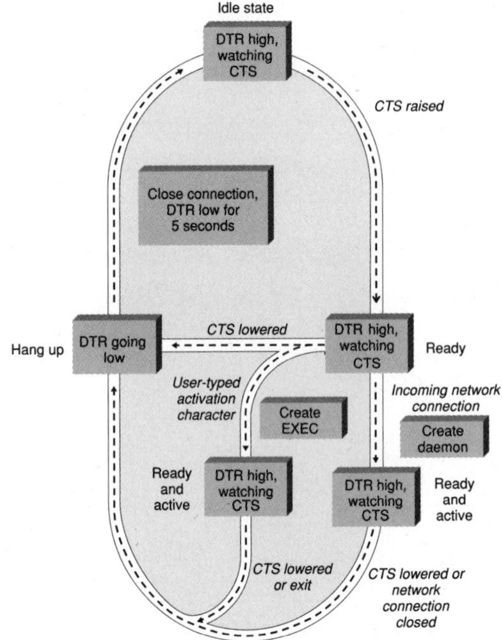


*Figure 5–5 EXEC and Daemon Creation on a Line Configured for Continuous CTS.*

### *Configure a Line to Automatically Disconnect*

You can configure automatic line disconnect by performing the following task in line configuration mode:

| Task | Command |
|---|---|
| Configure automatic line disconnect. | **autohangup** |

The **autohangup** command causes the EXEC facility to issue the **exit** command when the last connection closes. This feature is useful for UNIX-to-UNIX copy program (UUCP) applications because UUCP scripts cannot issue a command to hang up the telephone. This feature is not often used.

### *Support Old-Style Dial-In Modems*

The Cisco IOS software supports dial-in modems that use DTR to control the off-hook status of the telephone line. This feature is supported primarily on old-style modems, especially those in Europe. To configure the line to support this feature, perform the following task in line configuration mode:

| Task | Command |
|---|---|
| Configure a line for a dial-in modem. | **modem callin** |

Figure 5–6 illustrates the **modem callin** command. When a modem dialing line is idle, it has its DTR signal at a low state and waits for a transition to occur on the DSR (RING) input. This transition causes the line to raise the DTR signal and start watching the CTS signal from the modem. After the modem raises CTS, the Cisco IOS software creates an EXEC session on the line. If the timeout interval (set with the **modem answer-timeout** command) passes before the modem raises the CTS signal, the line lowers the DTR signal and returns to the idle state.

**NOTES**

The **modem callin** and **modem cts-required** line configuration commands are useful for SLIP operation. These commands ensure that when the line is hung up or the CTS signal drops, the line reverts from SLIP mode to normal interactive mode. These commands do not work if you put the line in network mode permanently.

Although you can use the **modem callin** line configuration command with newer modems, the **modem dialin** line configuration command described in this section is more appropriate. The **modem dialin** command frees up CTS input for hardware flow control. Modern modems do not require the assertion of DTR to answer a phone line (that is, to take the line off-hook).

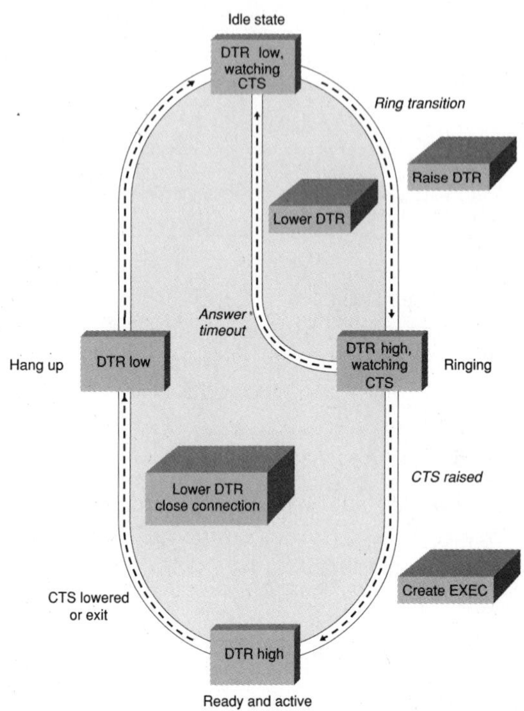


*Figure 5–6 EXEC Creation on a Line Configured for Modem Call-In.*

### Support Reverse Modem Connections and Prevent Incoming Calls

In addition to initiating connections, the Cisco IOS software can receive incoming connections. This capability allows you to attach serial and parallel printers, modems, and other shared peripherals to the router or access server and drive them remotely from other modem-connected systems. The Cisco IOS software supports reverse TCP, XRemote, and LAT connections.

The specific TCP port or socket, to which you attach the device, determines the type of service that the Cisco IOS software provides on a line. When you attach the serial lines of a computer system or a data terminal switch to the serial lines of the access server, the access server can act as a network front-end device for a host that does not support the TCP/IP protocols. This arrangement is sometimes called *front-ending*, or *reverse connection mode.*

The Cisco IOS software supports ports connected to computers that are connected to modems. You can configure the Cisco IOS software to function somewhat like a modem by performing the following task in line configuration mode. This command also prevents incoming calls.

| Task | Command |
|---|---|
| Configure a line for reverse connections and prevent incoming calls. | **modem callout** |

Figure 5–7 illustrates the **modem callout** process. When the Cisco IOS software receives an incoming connection, it raises the DTR signal and waits to see if the CTS signal is raised to indicate that the host has noticed the router's DTR signal. If the host does not respond within the interval set by the **modem answer-timeout** line configuration command, the software lowers the DTR signal and drops the connection.

*Figure 5–7 Daemon Creation on a Line Configured for Modem Call-Out.*

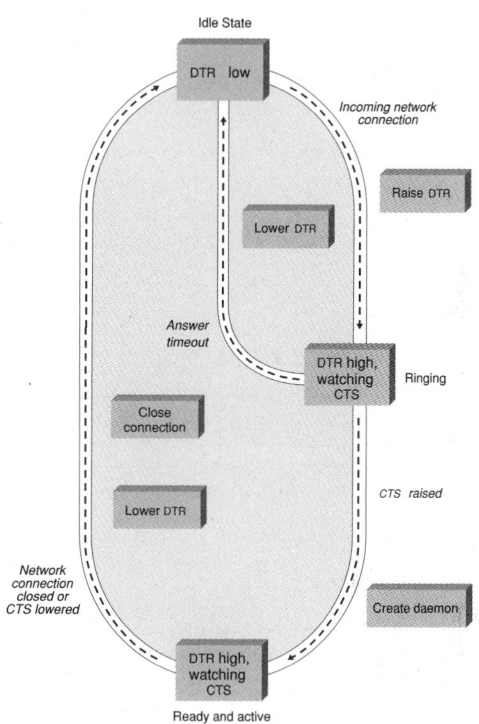


## Asynchronous Configuration Task List

This section describes the processing of configuring basic functionality on asynchronous interfaces, and then customizing the interfaces for your environment. Basic configuration tasks include the following:

- Specify an Asynchronous Interface
- Configure Group and Member Asynchronous Interfaces
- Configure Dual-Purpose Ports
- Assign IP Addresses for Local Devices
- Configure the Interface Addressing Method for Remote Devices
- Configure Asynchronous Serial Encapsulation

- Configure Dedicated or Interactive PPP and SLIP Sessions
- Enable Routing on Asynchronous Interfaces

If you want to call back a PPP client requesting asynchronous callback, see Chapter 65, "Configuring Asynchronous Callback."

See the section, "Asynchronous Configuration Examples," later in this chapter for examples of asynchronous configuration files. Tasks are performed in global configuration mode unless otherwise specified.

## Specify an Asynchronous Interface

On an access server, you can configure asynchronous interfaces. The auxiliary port (labeled AUX on the back of the product) can also be configured as an asynchronous serial interface, although performance on the AUX port is much slower than on standard asynchronous interfaces and does not support some features. Table 5–3 illustrates why asynchronous interfaces permit substantially better performance than AUX ports configured as asynchronous interfaces.

**Table 5–3** *Differences between Auxiliary (AUX) Port and Asynchronous Port*

| Feature | Asynchronous Interface | Auxiliary Port |
|---|---|---|
| Maximum speed | 115200 Kbps | 38400 Kbps |
| Supports DMA buffering* | Yes | No |
| PPP framing on chip† | Yes | No |
| IP fast switching‡ | Yes | No |

* Direct Memory Access (DMA) buffering moves data packets directly to and from system memory without interrupting the main CPU. This process removes overhead from the CPU and increases overall system performance.
† PPP framing on a hardware chip removes overhead from the router's CPU, which enables the router to sustain 115.2-Kbps throughput on all asynchronous ports simultaneously.
‡ After the destination of the first IP packet is added to the fast switching cache, it is fast switched to and from other interfaces with Ainimal involvement from the main processor.

On routers without built-in asynchronous interfaces, only the AUX port can be configured as an asynchronous serial interface. To configure the AUX port as an asynchronous interface, you must also configure it as an auxiliary line with the **line aux 1** command.

Use the **line** command with the appropriate line configuration commands for modem control, such as speed. Perform the following task in global configuration mode to specify a port as an asynchronous interface:

| Task | Command |
|---|---|
| Specify an asynchronous serial interface. | **interface async** *port-number* |

## Configure Group and Member Asynchronous Interfaces

You can create an asynchronous interface to be used as a group interface, which can be associated with other, *member* asynchronous interfaces.

This association allows you to configure the group interface and all of its member interfaces with a single command entered at the asynchronous group interface command line. You can have more than one group interface on a device; however, a member interface can be associated with only one group.

See the section "Group and Member Asynchronous Interfaces Examples," later in this chapter for an example of group and member interfaces.

Figure 5–8 illustrates the group-member interface concept.

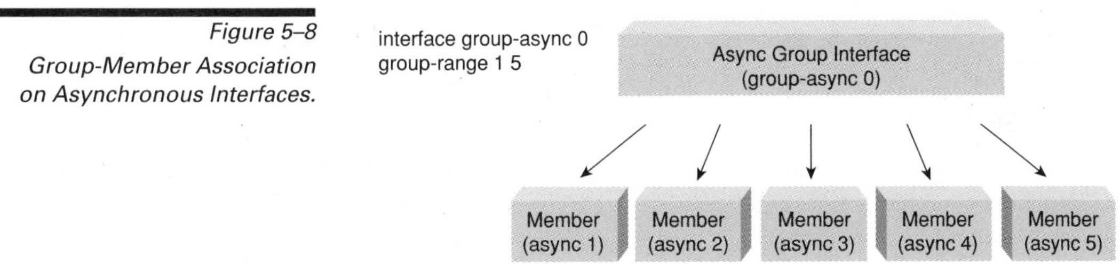


*Figure 5–8 Group-Member Association on Asynchronous Interfaces.*

### *Create the Group Interface and the Member Interfaces*

To create an asynchronous group interface and associate member interfaces to this group interface, perform the following commands starting in global configuration mode:

| Task | Command |
|---|---|
| Create an asynchronous group interface. | **interface group-async** *unit-number* |
| Associate one or more asynchronous interfaces (members) to the group interface so that all associated interfaces can be configured through the group interface. | **group-range** *low-end-of-range high-end-of-range* |

See the section "Group and Member Asynchronous Interfaces Examples," later in this chapter for an example configuration.

### *Define Member Asynchronous Interface Characteristics*

Member interfaces can have certain interface configurations that differ from their group. The following are valid interface configuration commands:

- **async default ip address**
- **description**

To configure a member with two or more interface configurations that are different from its group, enter the following command in interface configuration mode, where *interface-command* is one of the commands listed in the preceding list:

| Task | Command |
|---|---|
| Configure a member to have specific differences from its group. | **member** *interface-number interface-command* |

## Configure Dual-Purpose Ports

To specify the mode of a low-speed serial interface as either synchronous or asynchronous, perform the following task in interface configuration mode:

| Task | Command |
|---|---|
| Specify the mode of a low-speed interface as either synchronous or asynchronous. | **physical-layer** {**sync** \| **async**} |

This command applies only to low-speed serial interfaces available on Cisco 2520 through Cisco 2523 routers.

In synchronous mode, low-speed serial interfaces support all interface configuration commands available for high-speed serial interfaces, except the following two commands:

- **sdlc cts-delay**
- **sdlc rts-timeout**

When placed in asynchronous mode, low-speed serial interfaces support all commands available for standard asynchronous interfaces. The default is synchronous mode.

Note that when you enter this command, it does not appear in the output of **show running config** and **show startup config** commands, because the command is a physical-layer command.

## Assign IP Addresses for Local Devices

The local address is set using the **ip address** or **ip unnumbered** command. IP addresses identify locations to which IP datagrams can be sent. You must assign each router interface an IP address.

To assign an IP address to a network interface, perform the following task in interface configuration mode:

| Task | Command |
|---|---|
| Set an IP address for an interface. | **ip address** *address mask* [**secondary**] |

A subnet mask identifies the subnet field of a network address.

### *Conserve Network Addresses*

When asynchronous routing is enabled, you might find it necessary to conserve network addresses by configuring the asynchronous interfaces as *unnumbered*. An unnumbered interface does not have an address. Network resources are therefore conserved because fewer network numbers are used and routing tables are smaller.

To configure an unnumbered interface, perform the following task in interface configuration mode:

| Task | Command |
|---|---|
| Configure the asynchronous interface to be unnumbered. | **ip unnumbered** *type number* |

Whenever the unnumbered interface generates a packet (for example, a routing update), it uses the address of the specified interface as the source address of the IP packet. It also uses the address of the specified interface to determine which routing processes are sending updates over the unnumbered interface.

You can use the IP unnumbered feature even if the system on the other end of the asynchronous link does not support it. The IP unnumbered feature is transparent to the other end of the link because each system bases its routing activities on information in the routing updates it receives and on its own interface address.

## Configure the Interface Addressing Method for Remote Devices

You can control whether addressing is dynamic (the user specifies the address at the EXEC level when making the connection), or whether default addressing is used (the address is forced by the system). If you specify dynamic addressing, the router must be in interactive mode and the user will enter the address at the EXEC level.

It is common to configure an asynchronous interface to have a default address and to allow dynamic addressing. With this configuration, the choice between the default address or a dynamic addressing is made by the users when they enter the **slip** or **ppp** EXEC command. If the user enters an address, that address is used, and if the user enters the **default** keyword, the default address is used.

This section describes the following tasks:

- Assign a default asynchronous address
- Allow an asynchronous address to be assigned dynamically

### *Assign a Default Asynchronous Address*

Perform the following task in interface configuration mode to assign a permanent default asynchronous address:

| Task | Command |
|---|---|
| Assign a default IP address to an asynchronous interface. | **peer default ip address** *address* |

Use the **no** form of this command to disable the default address. If the server has been configured to authenticate asynchronous connections, you are prompted for a password after entering the **slip default** or **ppp default** EXEC command before the line is placed into asynchronous mode.

The assigned default address is implemented when the user enters the **slip default** or **ppp default** EXEC command. The transaction is validated by the Terminal Access Controller Access System (TACACS) server, when enabled, and the line is put into network mode using the address that is in the configuration file.

Configuring a default address is useful when the user is not required to know the IP address to gain access to a system (for example, users of a server that is available to many students on a campus). Instead of requiring each user to know an IP address, they only need to enter the **slip default** or **ppp default** EXEC command and let the server select the address to use.

### *Allow an Asynchronous Address To Be Assigned Dynamically*

When a line is configured for dynamic assignment of asynchronous addresses, the user enters the **slip** or **ppp** EXEC command and is prompted for an address or logical host name. The address is validated by TACACS, when enabled, and the line is assigned the given address and put into asynchronous mode. Assigning asynchronous addresses dynamically is also useful when you want to assign set addresses to users. An application on a personal computer that automatically dials in using SLIP, for example, and polls for electronic mail messages can be set up to dial in periodically and enter the required IP address and password.

To assign asynchronous addresses dynamically, perform the following task in interface configuration mode:

| Task | Command |
|---|---|
| Allow the IP address to be assigned when the protocol is initiated. | **async dynamic address** |

The dynamic addressing features of the internetwork allow packets to get to their destination and back regardless of the access server, router, or network they are sent from. If a host such as a laptop computer, for example, moves from place to place, it can keep the same address no matter where it is dialing in from.

Logical host names are first converted to uppercase and then sent to the TACACS server for authentication.

## Configure Asynchronous Serial Encapsulation

To configure an asynchronous serial interface on a routing device, you must set up the interface to send SLIP or PPP packets. PPP and SLIP define methods of sending Internet packets over a standard EIA-232 asynchronous serial line. PPP also defines methods for sending IPX and ARA packets during PPP sessions.

There are two asynchronous serial encapsulation methods:

- Serial Line Internet Protocol (SLIP)
- Point-to-Point Protocol (PPP)

Only IP packets can be sent across lines configured for SLIP. PPP supports transmission of IP, IPX, and ARA packets on an asynchronous serial interface.

For information about configuring PPP and SLIP, see Chapter 27, "Configuring Asynchronous PPP and SLIP."

## Configure Dedicated or Interactive PPP and SLIP Sessions

You can configure one or more asynchronous interfaces on your access server (and one on a router) to be in dedicated network interface mode. In dedicated mode, an interface is automatically configured for SLIP or PPP connections. There is no user prompt or EXEC level, and no end-user commands are required to initiate remote-node connections. If you want a line to be used only for SLIP or PPP connections, configure the line for dedicated mode.

In interactive mode, a line can be used to make any type of connection, depending on the EXEC command entered by the user. For example, depending on its configuration, the line can be used for Telnet or XRemote connections, or SLIP or PPP encapsulation. The user is prompted for an EXEC command before a connection is initiated.

### *Configure Dedicated Network Mode or Interactive Mode*

You can configure an asynchronous interface to be in dedicated network mode. When the interface is configured for dedicated mode, the end user cannot change the encapsulation method, address, or other parameters.

To configure an interface for dedicated network mode or return it back to interactive mode, perform one of the following tasks in interface configuration mode.

| Task | Command |
|---|---|
| Place the line into dedicated asynchronous network mode. | **async mode dedicated** |
| Return the line to interactive mode. | **async mode interactive** |

By default, no asynchronous mode is configured. In this state, the line is not available for inbound networking because the SLIP and PPP connections are disabled.

### Enable Routing on Asynchronous Interfaces

To route IP packets on an asynchronous interface, perform one of the following tasks in interface configuration mode:

| Task | Command |
|---|---|
| Configure an asynchronous interface for dynamic routing. | **async dynamic routing** |
| Automatically configure an asynchronous interface for routing. | **async default routing** |

This **async dynamic routing** command routes IP packets on an asynchronous interface, which permits you to enable the IGRP, RIP, and OSPF routing protocols for use when the user makes a connection using the **ppp** or **slip** EXEC commands. The user must, however, specify the **/routing** keyword at the SLIP or PPP command line.

For asynchronous interfaces in interactive mode, the **async default routing** command causes the **ppp** and **slip** EXEC commands to be interpreted as though the **/route** switch had been included in the command. For asynchronous interfaces in dedicated mode, the **async dynamic routing** command enables routing protocols to be used on the line. Without the **async default routing** command, there is no way to enable the use of routing protocols automatically on a dedicated asynchronous interface.

## Configuring Support for Extended BOOTP Requests

To configure Cisco IOS software to respond to BOOTP requests from client machines, perform the following task in global configuration mode:

| Task | Command |
|---|---|
| Specify the router network information that is sent in response to BOOTP requests. | **async-bootp** *tag* [:*hostname*] *data* |

## Monitoring and Maintaining Asynchronous Devices

This section describes the following monitoring and maintenance tasks that you can perform on asynchronous interfaces:

- Monitor and maintain asynchronous activity
- Debug asynchronous interfaces
- Debug PPP

To monitor and maintain asynchronous activity, perform one or more of the following tasks in privileged EXEC mode:

| Task | Command |
|---|---|
| Return a line to its idle state. | **clear line** *line-number* |
| Display parameters that have been set for extended BOOTP requests. | **show async bootp** |
| Display statistics for asynchronous interface activity. | **show async status** |
| Display the status of asynchronous line connections. | **show line** [*line-number*] |

To debug asynchronous interfaces, perform the following task in privileged EXEC mode:

| Task | Command |
|---|---|
| Displays errors, changes in interface state, and log input and output. | **debug async {framing \| state \| packets}** |

To debug PPP links, perform the following tasks in privileged EXEC mode:

| Task | Command |
|---|---|
| Enable debugging of PPP protocol negotiation process. | **debug ppp negotiation** |
| Display PPP protocol errors. | **debug ppp error** |
| Display PPP packets sent and received. | **debug ppp packet** |
| Display errors encountered during remote or local system authentication. | **debug ppp chap** |

### CONFIGURING CHAT SCRIPTS FOR ASYNCHRONOUS LINES

*Chat scripts* are strings of text used to send commands for modem dialing, logging on to remote systems, and initializing asynchronous devices connected to an asynchronous line. On a router, chat scripts can be configured on the auxiliary port only. A chat script must be configured to dial out on asynchronous lines. You also can configure chat scripts so that they are executed automatically for other specific events on a line, or so that they are executed manually. Each chat script is defined for a different event. These events can include the following:

- Line activation
- Incoming connection initiation
- Asynchronous dial-on-demand routing
- Line resets
- Startup

To use a chat script, perform the following steps:

**Step 1** Define the chat script in global configuration mode using the **chat-script** command.

**Step 2** Configure the line so that a chat script is activated when a specific event occurs (using the **script** line configuration command), or start a chat script manually (using the **start-chat** privileged EXEC command).

### Create a Chat Script

To define a chat script, perform the following task in global configuration mode:

| Task | Command |
|---|---|
| Create a script that will place a call on a modem, log on to a remote system, or initialize an asynchronous device on a line. | **chat-script** *script-name expect send...* |

A limited list of keywords are supported, along with expect/send pairs. Send strings can have special escape modifiers.

Cisco recommends that one chat script (a "modem" chat script) be written for placing a call and another chat script (a "system" or "login" chat script) be written to log on to remote systems, where required.

Chat scripts are not supported on lines where modem control is set for inbound activity that only uses the **modem dialin** command.

### Suggested Chat Script Naming Conventions (for Dial Scripts only)

When you create a script name, include the modem vendor, type, and modulation, separated by hyphens. For example, if you have a Telebit t3000 modem that uses V.32bis modulation, your script name would be *telebit-t3000-v32bis.*

A suggested naming convention for chat scripts used to dial is as follows:

*vendor-type-modulation*

In other words, the syntax of the **chat-script** command becomes the following:

**chat-script** *vendor-type-modulation expect send...*

For example, if you have a Telebit t3000 modem that uses V.32bis modulation, you would name your chat script as follows:

```
telebit-t3000-v32bis
```

The **chat-script** command could become the following:

```
router(config)# chat-script telebit-t3000-v32bis ABORT ERROR ABORT BUSY ABORT
"NO ANSWER" "" "ATH" OK "ATDT\T" TIMEOUT 30 CONNECT
```

Adhering to this naming convention allows you to specify a range of chat scripts using partial chat script names with regular expressions. This is particularly useful for dialer rotary groups.

### Configure the Line to Activate Chat Scripts

Chat scripts can be activated by any of five events, each corresponding to a different version of the **script** line configuration command. To start a chat script manually at any point, refer to the following section, "Start a Chat Script Manually on an Asynchronous Line."

To define a chat script to start automatically when a specific event occurs, perform the following tasks in line configuration mode:

| Task | Command |
|---|---|
| Start a chat script on a line when the line is activated (every time a command EXEC is started on the line). | **script activation** *regexp*[*] |
| Start a chat script on a line when a network connection is made to the line. | **script connection** *regexp* |
| Specify a modem script for DDR on a line. | **script dialer** *regexp* |
| Start a chat script on a line whenever the line is reset. | **script reset** *regexp* |
| Start a chat script on a line whenever the system is started up. | **script startup** *regexp* |

[*] The argument *regexp* is a regular expression that is matched to a script name that has already been defined using the **chat-script** command.

**NOTES**

Outbound chat scripts are not supported on lines where modem control is set for inbound activity only (using the **modem dialin** command).

### Start a Chat Script Manually on an Asynchronous Line

You can start a chat script manually on any line that is currently not active by performing the following task in privileged EXEC mode:

| Task | Command |
|---|---|
| Start a chat script manually on any asynchronous line. | **start-chat** *regexp* [*line-number* [*dialer-string*]] |

If you do not specify the line number, the script runs on the current line. If the line specified is already in use, you cannot start the chat script. A message appears indicating that the line is already in use.

## Configuring Additional Asynchronous Features

You can configure the following asynchronous features:

- Establish and Control the EXEC Process
- Configure the Auxiliary (AUX) Port
- Configure the Line to Automatically Detect the Incoming Protocol and Start a Session
- Define a Command String for Automatic Execution
- Configure Rotary Groups
- Specify Decimal TCP Port Numbers when Connecting to Lines
- Optimize Available Bandwidth

### Establish and Control the EXEC Process

By default, the Cisco IOS software starts an EXEC process on all lines. However, you can control EXEC processes, as follows:

- Turn the EXEC process on or off.

  A serial printer, for example, should not have an EXEC session started.
- Set the idle terminal timeout interval.

The EXEC command interpreter waits for a specified amount of time to receive user input. If no input is detected, the EXEC facility resumes the current connection. If no connections exist, it returns the terminal to the idle state and disconnects the incoming connection. To control the EXEC process, perform the following tasks in line configuration mode:

| Task | Command |
|---|---|
| Turn on EXEC processes. | **exec** |
| Set the idle terminal timeout interval. | **exec-timeout** *minutes* [*seconds*] |

### Configure the Auxiliary (AUX) Port

The AUX port is typically configured as an asynchronous serial interface on routers without built-in asynchronous interfaces. To configure the AUX port as an asynchronous interface, configure it first as an auxiliary line with the **line aux 1** global configuration command.

The AUX port sends a DTR signal only when a Telnet connection is established. The auxiliary port does not use Ready to Send/Clear to Send (RTS/CTS) handshaking for flow control. To understand the differences between standard asynchronous interfaces and AUX ports configured as an asynchronous interface, see Table 5–4. To enable the auxiliary port, perform the following task:

You cannot use the auxiliary (AUX) port as a second console port. To use the AUX port as a console port, you must order a special cable from your technical support personnel.

| Task | Command |
|---|---|
| Enable the auxiliary serial DTE port. | **line aux** *line-number* |

On an access server, you can configure any of the available asynchronous interfaces (1 through 8, 16, or 48). The auxiliary port (labeled AUX on the back of the product) can also be configured as an asynchronous serial interface, although performance on the AUX port is much slower than on standard asynchronous interfaces and does not support some features. Table 5–4 illustrates why asynchronous interfaces permit substantially better performance than AUX ports configured as asynchronous interfaces.

**Table 5–4** *Differences between the Auxillary (AUX) Port and the Asynchronous Port*

| Feature | Asynchronous Interface | Auxiliary Port |
|---|---|---|
| Maximum speed | 115,200 Kbps | 38,400 Kbps |
| Supports DMA buffering* | Yes | No |
| PPP framing on chip† | Yes | No |
| IP fast switching‡ | Yes | No |

* Direct Memory Access (DMA) buffering moves data packets directly to and from system memory without interrupting the main central processing unit (CPU). This process removes overhead from the CPU and increases overall system performance.

† PPP framing on a hardware chip removes overhead from the router's CPU, which enables the router to sustain 115.2-Kbps throughput on all asynchronous ports simultaneously.

‡ After the destination of the first IP packet is added to the fast switching cache, it is fast switched to and from other interfaces with minimal involvement from the main processor.

On routers without built-in asynchronous interfaces, only the AUX port can be configured as an asynchronous serial interface. To configure the AUX port as an asynchronous interface, you must also configure it as an auxiliary line with the **line aux 1** command. Access servers do not have this restriction. Use the line command with the appropriate line configuration commands for modem control, such as speed.

Only IP packets can be sent across lines configured for SLIP. PPP supports transmission of IP, IPX, and AppleTalk packets on an asynchronous serial interface.

## Configure the Line to Automatically Detect the Incoming Protocol and Start a Session

To configure the Cisco IOS software to allow an AppleTalk Remote Access (ARA), Point-to-Point Protocol (PPP), or Serial Line Internet Protocol (SLIP) session to start automatically, perform the following task in line configuration mode:

| Task | Command |
|---|---|
| Configure a line to automatically start an ARA, PPP, or SLIP session. | **autoselect** {**arap** \| **ppp** \| **slip** \| **during login**} |

The **autoselect** command enables the Cisco IOS software to start a process automatically when a start character is received. The Cisco IOS software detects either a Return character (which is the start character for an EXEC session, or the start character for the ARA protocol).

The **autoselect** command bypasses the login prompt and enables the specified session to begin automatically. However, by entering the **autoselect** command with the **during login** keyword, the username or password prompt appears without pressing the Return key. While the username or password prompt is displayed, you can choose either to answer these prompts or to send packets from an autoselected protocol.

**NOTES**

When you use the **autoselect** command, the activation character should be set to the default Return, and exec-character-bits to 7. If you change these defaults, the application cannot recognize the activation request.

### Define a Command String for Automatic Execution

You can set up a command to execute automatically when the router connects to another host. The Cisco IOS can execute any appropriate EXEC command and any switch or host name that occurs with the EXEC command. To define a command, perform the following task in line configuration mode:

| Task | Command |
|---|---|
| Define a command to be automatically executed. | **autocommand** *command* |

### Configure Rotary Groups

Connections can be made to the next free line in a group of lines, also called a *rotary group* or *hunt group*. A line can be in only one rotary group; a rotary group can consist of a single line or several contiguous lines. The console line (line 0) cannot be in a rotary group.

To configure a rotary group, perform the following task in line configuration mode:

| Task | Command |
|---|---|
| Add a line to the specified rotary group. | **rotary** *group* |

### Specify Decimal TCP Port Numbers when Connecting to Lines

Connections to an individual line are most useful when a dial-out modem, parallel printer, or serial printer is attached to that line. To connect to an individual line, the remote host or terminal must specify a particular TCP port on the router.

If reverse XRemote is required, that port is 9000 (decimal) plus the decimal value of the line number.

If a raw TCP stream is required, the port is 4000 (decimal) plus the decimal line number. The raw TCP stream is usually the required mode for sending data to a printer.

If Telnet protocols are required, that port is 2000 (decimal) plus the decimal value of the line number. The Telnet protocol might require that Return characters be translated into Return and line-feed character pairs. You can turn off this translation by specifying the Telnet binary mode option. To specify this option, connect to port 6000 (decimal) plus the decimal line number.

For example, a laser printer is attached to line 10 of a Cisco 2511 router. Such a printer usually uses XON/XOFF software flow control. Because the Cisco IOS software cannot receive an incoming connection if the line already has a process, you must ensure that an EXEC session is not accidentally started. You must, therefore, configure it as follows:

```
line 10
 flowcontrol software
 no exec
```

A host that wants to send data to the printer would connect to the router on TCP port 4008, send the data, and then close the connection. (Remember that line number 10 octal equals 8 decimal.)

### Optimize Available Bandwidth

Asynchronous lines have relatively low bandwidth and can easily be overloaded, resulting in slow traffic across these lines.

To optimize available bandwidth, perform either of the following tasks:

- Configure Header Compression
- Force Header Compression at the EXEC Level

#### *Configure Header Compression*

One way to optimize available bandwidth is by using TCP header compression. Van Jacobson TCP header compression (defined by RFC 1144) can increase bandwidth availability between two and five times when compared to lines not using header compression. Theoretically, it can improve bandwidth availability by a ratio of seven to one.

To configure header compression, perform the following task in interface configuration mode:

| Task | Command |
|---|---|
| Configure Van Jacobson TCP header compression on the asynchronous link. | **ip tcp header-compression** [**on** \| **off** \| **passive**] |

### *Force Header Compression at the EXEC Level*

On SLIP interfaces, you can force header compression at the EXEC prompt on a line on which header compression has been set to passive. This action allows more efficient use of the available bandwidth and does not require entering privileged configuration mode.

To implement header compression, perform the following task in interface configuration mode:

| Task | Command |
|---|---|
| Allow status of header compression to be assigned at the user level. | **ip tcp header compression passive** |

For PPP interfaces, the **passive** option functions the same as the **on** option.

## ASYNCHRONOUS CONFIGURATION EXAMPLES

This section illustrates different communication requirements for the following asynchronous scenarios:

- Restricting Access on the Asynchronous Interface Example
- Address Pooling on Asynchronous Interfaces Examples
- Group and Member Asynchronous Interfaces Examples
- Dedicated Asynchronous Interface Configuration Example
- IP–SLIP—Asynchronous Interface Example
- AppleTalk–PPP Example
- IP–PPP Example
- IPX–PPP—Loopback Interface Example
- IPX–PPP—Using Dedicated IPX Network Numbers for Each Interface Example
- IPX–PPP over X.25 to an IPX Network on VTY Lines Example
- Remote Node NetBEUI Example
- Asynchronous Routing and Dynamic Addressing Configuration Example
- TCP Header Compression Configuration Example
- Conserving Network Addresses Using the IP Unnumbered Feature Example

- Configuring Routing on a Dedicated Dial-In Router Example
- Configuring an Asynchronous Interface as the Only Network Interface Example
- Configuring IGRP Example
- Configuring an Interface Example
- Remote Network Access Using PPP—A Basic Configuration Example
- Remote Network Access Using PPP—Routing IP Example
- Remote Network Access—Leased Line with Dial-Backup Using PPP Example

### Restricting Access on the Asynchronous Interface Example

The following example assumes that users are restricted to certain servers designated as asynchronous servers, but that normal terminal users can access anything on the local network.

```
! access list for normal connections
access-list 1 permit 131.108.0.0 0.0.255.255
!
access-list 2 permit 131.108.42.55
access-list 2 permit 131.108.111.1
access-list 2 permit 131.108.55.99
!
line 1
 speed 19200
 flow hardware
 modem inout
interface async 1
 async mode interactive
 async dynamic address
 ip access-group 1 out
 ip access-group 2 in
```

### Address Pooling on Asynchronous Interfaces Examples

The following sections provide examples of the use of DHCP and local pooling mechanisms.

#### *DHCP Pooling Examples*

The following global configuration example enables DHCP proxy-client status on all asynchronous interfaces on the access server:

```
ip address-pool dhcp-proxy-client
```

The following global configuration example illustrates how to specify which DHCP servers are used on your network. You can specify up to four servers using IP addresses or names. If you do not specify servers, the default is to use the IP limited broadcast address of 255.255.255.255 for transactions with any and all discovered DHCP servers.

```
ip dhcp-server jones smith wesson
```

The following interface configuration example illustrates how to disable DHCP proxy-client functionality on asynchronous interface 1:

```
async interface
interface 1
 no peer default ip address
```

### *Local Pooling Example*

The following example shows how to select the IP pooling mechanism and how to create a pool of local IP addresses that are used when a client dials in on an asynchronous line. The default address pool comprises IP addresses 172.30.0.1 through 172.30.0.28.

```
! this command tells the access server to use a local pool
ip address-pool local
! this command defines the ip address pool.
! The address pool is named group1 and comprised of addresses
! 10.1.2.1through 10.1.2.5 inclusive
ip local-pool group1 10.1.2.1 10.1.2.5
```

### *Configure Specific IP Addresses for an Interface Example*

This example shows how to configure the access server so that it will use the default address pool on all interfaces except interface 7, on which it will use an address pool called lass:

```
ip address-pool local
ip local-pool lass 172.30.0.1
 async interface
 interface 7
 peer default ip address lass
```

## Group and Member Asynchronous Interfaces Examples

The following example shows how to create an asynchronous group interface 0 with group interface members 2 through 7, starting in global configuration mode:

```
interface group-async 0
 group-range 2 7
```

The following example shows how you need to configure asynchronous interfaces 1, 2, and 3 separately if you do not have a group interface configured:

```
interface Async1
 ip unnumbered Ethernet0
 encapsulation ppp
 async default ip address 172.30.1.1
 async mode interactive
 async dynamic routing
!
interface Async2
 ip unnumbered Ethernet0
 encapsulation ppp
 async default ip address 172.30.1.2
 async mode interactive
 async dynamic routing
!
interface Async3
```

```
 ip unnumbered Ethernet0
!
 encapsulation ppp
 async default ip address 172.30.1.3
 async mode interactive
 async dynamic routing
```

The following example configures the same interfaces, but from a single group asynchronous interface:

```
!
interface Group-Async 0
 ip unnumbered Ethernet0
 encapsulation ppp
 async mode interactive
 async dynamic routing
 group-range 1 3
 member 1 async default ip address 172.30.1.1
 member 2 async default ip address 172.30.1.2
 member 3 async default ip address 172.30.1.3
```

### Dedicated Asynchronous Interface Configuration Example

The following example assigns an IP address to an asynchronous interface and places the line in dedicated network mode. Setting the stop bit to 1 is a performance enhancement.

```
line 20
 location Department PC Lab
 stopbits 1
 speed 19200
!
interface async 20
 async default ip address 182.32.7.51
 async mode dedicated
```

### IP–SLIP—Asynchronous Interface Example

The following example configures IP–SLIP on asynchronous interface 6. The IP address for the interface is assigned to Ethernet 0, interactive mode has been enabled, and the IP address of the client PC running SLIP has been specified.

IP and the appropriate IP routing protocols have already been enabled on the access server or router.

```
interface async 6
 ip unnumbered ethernet 0
 encapsulation slip
 async mode interactive
 async default ip address 172.18.1.128
```

### AppleTalk–PPP Example

The following example configures asynchronous interface 4 on the router so that users can access AppleTalk zones by dialing in to the router via PPP to this interface. Users accessing the network can run AppleTalk and IP natively on a remote Macintosh, access any available AppleTalk zones from Chooser, use networked peripherals, and share files with other Macintosh users. Routing is not supported on the asynchronous interface 6.

```
interface async 6
 encapsulation ppp
 appletalk virtual-net 12345 saivite
 appletalk client-mode
```

### IP–PPP Example

The following example configures IP–PPP on asynchronous interface 6. The IP address for the interface is assigned to Ethernet 0, interactive mode has been enabled, and the IP address of the client PC running PPP has been specified.

IP and the appropriate IP routing protocols have already been enabled on the access server or router.

```
interface async 6
 ip unnumbered ethernet 0
 encapsulation ppp
 async mode interactive
 peer default ip address 172.18.1.128
```

### IPX–PPP—Loopback Interface Example

The following example shows how to configure IPX to run over PPP on an asynchronous interface. The asynchronous interface is associated with a loopback interface configured to run IPX. This example enables a non-routing IPX client to connect to the router.

```
ipx routing 0000.0c07.b509
interface loopback0
 no ip address
 ipx network 544
 ipx sap-interval 2000
interface ethernet0
 ip address 172.21.14.64
 ipx network AC150E00
 ipx encapsulation SAP
interface async 3
 ip unnumbered ethernet0
 encapsulation ppp
 async mode interactive
 async default ip address 172.18.1.128
 ipx ppp-client loopback0
 ipx sap-interval 0
```

In this example, IPX client connections are permitted to asynchronous interface 3, which is associated with loopback interface 0. Loopback interface 0 is configured to run IPX. Routing updates have been filtered on asynchronous interface 3. Routing updates take up a great deal of bandwidth, and asynchronous interfaces have low bandwidth.

### IPX–PPP—Using Dedicated IPX Network Numbers for Each Interface Example

The following example shows how to configure IPX to run over PPP on an asynchronous interface. A dedicated IPX network number has been specified for each interface, which can require a substantial number of network numbers for a large number of interfaces. This example permits an IPX client with routing enabled to connect with the router.

```
ipx routing 0000.0c07.b509
interface async 6
 ip unnumbered ethernet0
 encapsulation ppp
 async mode interactive
 ipx network AC150E00
 ipx sap-interval 0
```

In this example, IPX client connections are permitted to asynchronous interface 6, which has a unique IPX network number. Routing updates have been filtered on asynchronous interface 6. Routing updates take up a great deal of bandwidth, and asynchronous interfaces have low bandwidth.

### IPX–PPP over X.25 to an IPX Network on VTY Lines Example

The following example shows how to enable IPX–PPP on VTY lines. First, enable PPP to run on VTY lines, then associate the VTY line with a loopback interface configured to run IPX. This example enables a non-routing IPX client to connect to the router.

```
ipx routing 0000.0c07.b509
interface loopback0
 no ip address
 ipx network 544
vty-async ipx ppp-client loopback0
```

In this example, IPX client connections are permitted to VTY lines, which have been associated with loopback interface 0. Loopback interface 0 is configured with an IPX network number that is used by the VTY lines.

### Remote Node NetBEUI Example

In the following example, asynchronous interface 7 and ethernet interface 0 are configured to enable NetBEUI connectivity between the corporate telecommuter's client and the remote access (NetBEUI) server. The PC client is running a legacy application—Chat—in Windows NT, to connect with the remote server. Refer to Figure 5–9.

The configuration for the router is as follows:

```
interface async 7
 netbios nbf
 encapsulation ppp
```

You would also need to configure security, such as TACACS+, RADIUS, or another form of login authentication on the router.

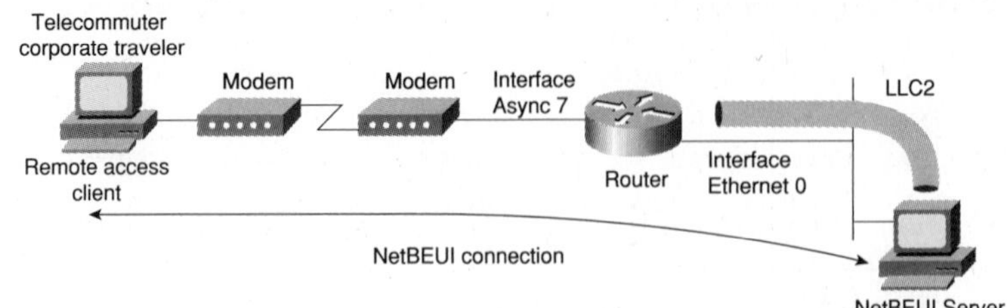


*Figure 5–9 Connecting a Remote NetBEUI Client to a Server through a Router.*

## Asynchronous Routing and Dynamic Addressing Configuration Example

The following example shows a simple configuration that allows routing and dynamic addressing. With this configuration, if the user specifies **/routing** in the EXEC **slip** or **ppp** command, routing protocols will be sent and received.

```
interface async 6
 async dynamic routing
 async dynamic address
```

## TCP Header Compression Configuration Example

The following example configures async interface 7 with a default IP address, allowing header compression if it is specified in the **slip** or **ppp** connection command entered by the user or if the connecting system sends compressed packets.

```
interface async 7
 ip address 172.31.79.1
 async default ip address 172.31.79.2
 ip tcp header-compression passive
```

## Conserving Network Addresses Using the IP Unnumbered Feature Example

The following example shows how to configure your router for routing using unnumbered interfaces. The source (local) address is shared between Ethernet 0 and async 6 (172.18.1.1). The default remote address is 172.18.1.2.

```
interface ethernet 0
 ip address 172.18.1.1 255.255.255.0
!
interface async 6
 ip unnumbered ethernet 0
 async dynamic routing
! default address is on the local subnet
 async dynamic address
 async default ip address 172.18.1.2
 ip tcp header-compression passive
```

The following example shows how the IP unnumbered configuration works. Although the user assigned an address, the system response shows the interface as unnumbered, and the address entered by the user will be used only in response to BOOTP requests.

```
router> slip /compressed 10.11.11.254
Password:
```

```
Entering async mode.
Interface IP address is unnumbered, MTU is 1500 bytes.
Header compression is On.
```

## Configuring Routing on a Dedicated Dial-In Router Example

In the following example, the router is set up as a dedicated dial-in router. Interfaces are configured as IP unnumbered to conserve network resources, primarily IP addresses.

```
ip routing
interface ether 0
 ip address 10.129.128.2 255.255.255.0
!
interface async 1
 ip unnumbered ethernet 0
 async dynamic routing
! The addresses assigned with SLIP or PPP EXEC commands are not used except
! to reply to BOOTP requests.
! Normally, the routers dialing in will have their own address
! and not use BOOTP at all.
 async default ip address 10.11.11.254
!
interface async 2
 ip unnumbered ethernet 0
 async default ip address 10.11.12.16
 ip tcp header-compression passive
 async mode dedicated
!
! run RIP on the asynchronous lines, because few implementations of SLIP
! understand IGRP. Run IGRP on the ethernet (and in the local network).
!
router igrp 110
 network 10.11.12.0
! send routes from the asynchronous lines on the production network.
 redistribute RIP
! don't send IGRP updates on the async interfaces
 passive-interface async 1
!
 router RIP
 network 10.11.12.0
 redistribute igrp
 passive-interface ethernet 0
! consider filtering everything except a default route from the routing
! updates sent on the (slow) asynchronous lines
 distribute-list 1 out
 ip unnumbered async 2
 async dynamic routing
```

## Configuring an Asynchronous Interface as the Only Network Interface Example

In the following example, one of the asynchronous lines is used as the only network interface. The router is used primarily as a terminal server, but is at a remote location and dials in to the central site for its only network connection.

```
ip default-gateway 10.11.12.2
interface ethernet 0
 shutdown
interface async 1
 async dynamic routing
 ip tcp header-compression on
 async default ip address 10.11.16.12
 async mode dedicated
 ip address 10.11.12.32 255.255.255.0
```

## Configuring IGRP Example

In the following example, only the IGRP TCP/IP routing protocol is running; it is assumed that the systems that are dialing in to use routing will either support IGRP or have some other method (for example, a static default route) of determining that the router is the best place to send most of its packets.

```
router igrp 111
 network 10.11.12.0
interface ethernet 0
 ip address 10.11.12.92 255.255.255.0
!
interface async 1
 async default ip address 10.11.12.96
 async dynamic routing
 ip tcp header-compression passive
 ip unnumbered ethernet 0

line 1
 modem ri-is-cd
```

## Configuring an Interface Example

The following configuration shows interface and line configuration. The interface is configured with access lists, passive header compression and a default address. The line is configured for TACACS authentication.

```
interface async 1
 ip access-group 1 in
 ip access-group 1 out
 ip tcp header-compression passive
 async default ip address 172.31.176.201

line 1
 login tacacs
 location 457-5xxx
 exec-timeout 20 0
 password XXXXXXXX
 session-timeout 20
 stopbits 1
```

### Remote Network Access Using PPP—A Basic Configuration Example

Figure 5–10 illustrates a simple network configuration comprised of remote PCs with modems connected via modem to a router. The cloud is a public switched telephone network (PSTN). The modems are connected via asynchronous lines, and the access server is connected to a local network.

In this configuration you need to configure the following:

- An asynchronous line on the access server configured to use PPP encapsulation
- An interface on the access server for the modem connection; this interface also needs to be configured to accept incoming modem calls
- A default IP address for each incoming line

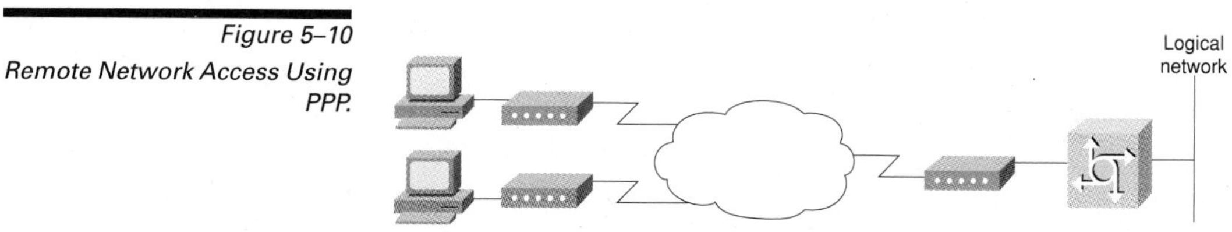


*Figure 5–10*
*Remote Network Access Using PPP.*

This default address indicates the address of the remote PC to the server, unless the user explicitly specifies another when starting the PPP session.

The server is configured for interactive mode with autoselect enabled, which allows the user to automatically begin a PPP session upon detection of a PPP packet from the remote PC; or, the remote PC can explicitly begin a PPP session by typing PPP at the prompt.

The configuration is as follows:

```
ip routing
!
interface ethernet 0
 ip address 192.168.32.12 255.255.255.0
!
interface async 1
 encapsulation ppp
 async mode interactive
 async default ip address 192.168.32.51
 async dynamic address
 ip unnumbered ethernet 0

line 1
 autoselect ppp
 modem callin
 speed 19200
```

### Remote Network Access Using PPP—Routing IP Example

Figure 5–11 illustrates a network configuration that provides routing functionality, allowing routing updates to be passed across the asynchronous lines.

This network is comprised of remote and local PCs connected via modem and network connections to an access server. This access server is connected to a second access server via an asynchronous line running TCP/IP. The second access server is connected to a local network via modem.

For this scenario, you will need to configure the following:

- An asynchronous line on both access servers configured to use PPP encapsulation
- An interface on both access servers for the modem connection and for this interface to be configured to accept incoming modem calls
- A default IP address for each incoming line
- IP routing on all configured interfaces

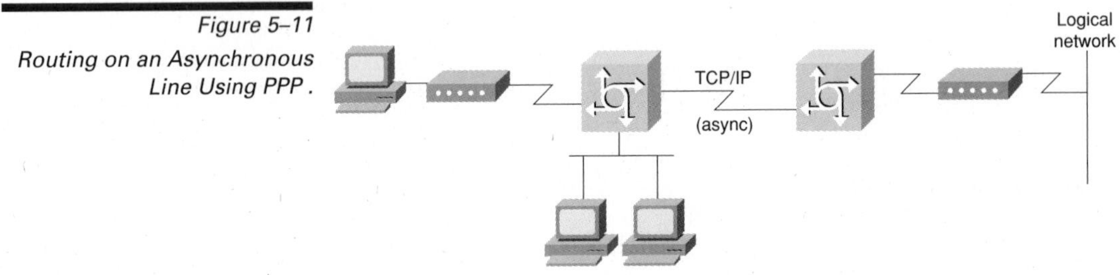


*Figure 5–11*
*Routing on an Asynchronous Line Using PPP.*

The configuration is as follows:

```
interface async 1
 encapsulation ppp
 async mode interactive
 async default ip address 192.168.32.10
 async dynamic address
 ip unnumbered ethernet 0
 async dynamic routing
```

If you want to pass IP routing updates across the asynchronous link, issue the following commands:

```
line 1
 autoselect ppp
 modem callin
 speed 19200
```

Next, enter these commands to configure the asynchronous lines between the access servers, starting in global configuration mode:

```
interface async 2
 async default ip address 192.168.32.55
 ip tcp header compression passive
```

Finally, configure routing using one of the following methods:

1. Use ARP, which is the default behavior.
2. Use a default-gateway by issuing the command **ip default-gateway** *x.x.x.x*, where *x.x.x.x* is the IP address of a locally attached router.
3. Run an IP routing protocol (RIP, IGRP, EIGRP, or OSPF).

### Remote Network Access—Leased Line with Dial-Backup Using PPP Example

Figure 5–12 illustrates a scenario where two networks are connected via access servers on a leased line. Redundancy is provided by a dial-backup line over the public switched telephone network so that if the primary leased line goes down, the dial-backup line will be automatically brought up to restore the connection. This configuration would be useful for using an auxiliary port as the backup port for a synchronous port.

In this scenario, you will need to configure the following:

- Two asynchronous interfaces on each access server
- Two modem interfaces
- A default IP address for each interface
- Dial-backup on one modem interface per access server
- An interface connecting to the access server's related network

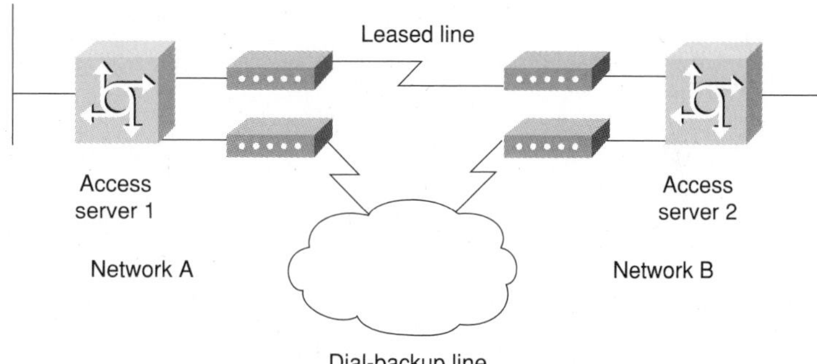


*Figure 5–12 Asynchronous Leased Line with Backup.*

The configuration is as follows:

```
hostname routerA
!
username routerB password cisco
chat-script backup "" "AT" TIMEOUT 30 OK atdt\T TIMEOUT 30 CONNECT \c !
!
interface Serial0
 backup interface Async1
 ip address 192.168.222.12 255.255.255.0
!
interface Async1
```

```
 ip address 172.16.199.1 255.255.255.0
 encapsulation ppp
 async default ip address 172.16.199.2
 async dynamic address
 async dynamic routing
 async mode dedicated
 dialer in-band
 dialer map IP 172.16.199.2 name routerB modem-script backup broadcast 3241129
 dialer-group 1
 ppp authentication chap
!
 dialer-list 1 protocol ip permit
!
line aux 0
 modem InOut
 rxspeed 38400
 txspeed 38400
```

# CHAPTER 6

# Modem Support and Asynchronous Device Commands

The configuration commands described in this chapter are used to configure modems and modem lines on access servers and routers.

**NOTES**

Some commands previously documented in this chapter have been replaced by new commands. Although the commands found in this chapter continue to perform their normal functions in the current release, support for these commands will cease in future releases.

For line configuration information and examples, see Chapter 5, "Configuring Modem Support and Asynchronous Devices."

## ASYNC-BOOTP

To support the extended BOOTP request specified in RFC 1084, and to specify information that is to be sent in response to BOOTP requests, use the **async-bootp** global configuration command. To clear the list, use the **no** form of this command.

**async-bootp** *tag* [:*hostname*] *data*
**no async-bootp** *tag* [:*hostname*] *data*

| *Syntax* | *Description* |
|---|---|
| *tag* | Item being requested; expressed as filename, integer, or IP dotted decimal address. See Table 6–1 for possible values. |
| :*hostname* | (Optional) This entry applies only to the specified host. The argument can be either an IP address or a logical host name. |
| *data* | List of IP addresses entered in dotted decimal notation or as logical host names, a number, or a quoted string. |

**Table 6–1** *Supported External BOOTP Requests*

| Keyword and Argument Pair | Use |
|---|---|
| *bootfile* | Server boot file from which to download the boot program. Use the optional *:hostname* and *data* arguments to specify the host or hosts. |
| **subnet-mask** *mask* | Dotted decimal address specifying the network and local subnetwork mask (as defined by RFC 950). |
| **time-offset** *offset* | A signed 32-bit integer specifying the time offset of the local subnetwork in seconds from Coordinated Universal Time. |
| **gateway** *address* | Dotted decimal address specifying the IP addresses of gateways for this subnetwork. A preferred gateway should be listed first. |
| **time-server** *address* | Dotted decimal address specifying the IP address of time servers (as defined by RFC 868). |
| **ien116-server** *address* | Dotted decimal address specifying the IP address of name servers (as defined by IEN.116). |
| **dns-server** *address* | Dotted decimal address specifying the IP address of Domain Name Servers (as defined by RFC 1034). |
| **log-server** *address* | Dotted decimal address specifying the IP address of an MIT-LCS UDP log server. |
| **quote-server** *address* | Dotted decimal address specifying the IP address of Quote of the Day servers (as defined in RFC 865). |
| **lpr-server** *address* | Dotted decimal address specifying the IP address of Berkeley UNIX Version 4 BSD servers. |
| **impress-server** *address* | Dotted decimal address specifying the IP address of Impress network image servers. |
| **rlp-server** *address* | Dotted decimal address specifying the IP address of Resource Location Protocol (RLP) servers (as defined in RFC 887). |
| **hostname** *name* | Name of the client (which might or might not be domain qualified, depending upon the site). |
| **bootfile-size** *value* | Two-octet value specifying the number of 512 octet (byte) blocks in the default boot file. |

### Default

If no extended BOOTP commands are entered, the software generates a gateway and subnet mask appropriate for the local network.

### Command Mode

Global configuration

### Usage Guidelines

This command first appeared in Cisco IOS Release 10.3.

Each of the *tag* keyword-argument pairs is a field that can be filled in and sent in response to BOOTP requests from clients.

BOOTP supports the extended BOOTP requests specified in RFC 1084 and works for both SLIP and PPP encapsulation.

Use the **show async bootp** EXEC command to list the configured parameters. BOOTP works for both SLIP and PPP.

### Examples

The following example specifies different boot files: one for a PC and one for a Macintosh. With this configuration, a BOOTP request from the host on 192.168.31.1 results in a reply listing the boot filename as pcboot. A BOOTP request from the host named mac results in a reply listing the boot filename as macboot.

```
async-bootp bootfile :192.168.31.1 "pcboot"
async-bootp bootfile :mac "macboot"
```

The following example specifies a subnet mask of 255.255.0.0:

```
async-bootp subnet-mask 255.255.0.0
```

The following example specifies a negative time offset of the local subnetwork of -3600 seconds:

```
async-bootp time-offset -3600
```

The following example specifies the IP address of a time server:

```
async-bootp time-server 192.168.31.1
```

### Related Commands

Search online to find documentation for related commands.

**service old-slip-prompts**

## ASYNC DEFAULT IP ADDRESS

The **peer default ip address** command replaces the **async default ip address** command.

Refer to the description of the **peer default ip address** command for more information.

## ASYNC DEFAULT ROUTING

To enable RIP, OSPF, and IGRP routing protocols on an asynchronous interfaces when using the **/routing** keyword with the **ppp** and **slip** EXEC commands, use the **async default routing** interface command. To disable this function, use the **no** form of this command.

**async default routing**
**no async default routing**

### *Syntax Description*

This command has no arguments or keywords.

### *Default*

Disabled

### *Command Mode*

Interface configuration

### *Usage Guidelines*

This command first appeared in Cisco IOS Release 11.1.

For asynchronous interfaces in interactive mode, the **async default routing** command causes the **ppp** and **slip** EXEC commands to be interpreted as though the **/route** keyword had been included in the command. For asynchronous interfaces in dedicated mode, the **async default routing** command turns on the use of routing protocols on the line. Without the **async default routing** command, there is no way to enable the use of routing protocols automatically on a dedicated asynchronous interface.

### *Example*

The following example enables the use of routing protocols on asynchronous interface 4. In this example, asynchronous interface 4 is dedicated for asynchronous use.

```
interface async 4
 ip address 191.191.191.191 255.255.255.0
 async default routing
 async mode dedicated
```

### *Related Commands*

Search online to find documentation for related commands.

**async dynamic routing**
**async mode dedicated**
**async mode interactive**
**ppp**
**slip**

## ASYNC DYNAMIC ADDRESS

To specify dynamic asynchronous addressing, use the **async dynamic address** interface configuration command. To disable dynamic addressing, use the **no** form of this command.

**async dynamic address**
**no async dynamic address**

### *Syntax Description*

This command has no arguments or keywords.

### *Default*

Dynamic addressing is disabled.

### *Command Mode*

Interface configuration

### *Usage Guidelines*

This command first appeared in Cisco IOS Release 10.0.

You can control whether addressing is dynamic (the user specifies the address at the EXEC level when making the connection), or whether default addressing is used (the address is forced by the system). If you specify dynamic addressing, the router must be in interactive mode and the user will enter the address at the EXEC level.

It is common to configure an asynchronous interface to have a default address and to allow dynamic addressing. With this configuration, the choice between the default address or a dynamic addressing is made by the user when he or she enters the **slip** or **ppp** EXEC command. If the user enters an address, it is used, and if the user enters the **default** keyword, the default address is used.

### *Example*

The following example shows dynamic addressing assigned to async interface 6.

```
interface ethernet 0
 ip address 10.0.0.1 255.0.0.0
interface async 6
 async dynamic address
```

### *Related Commands*

Search online to find documentation for related commands.

**peer default ip address**

## ASYNC DYNAMIC ROUTING

To allow the use of routing protocols on an interface, use the **async dynamic routing** interface configuration command. To disable the use of routing protocols, use the **no** form of this command.

**async dynamic routing**
**no async dynamic routing**

### *Syntax Description*

This command has no arguments or keywords.

### *Default*

Dynamic routing is disabled.

### *Command Mode*

Interface configuration

### *Usage Guidelines*

This command first appeared in Cisco IOS Release 10.0.

The use of routing protocols is further controlled by the use of the **/routing** keyword in the **slip** and **ppp** EXEC command.

### *Example*

The following example shows how to enable asynchronous routing on async interface 6. The **ip tcp header-compression passive** command enables Van Jacobson TCP header compression and prevents transmission of compressed packets until a compressed packet arrives from the asynchronous link.

```
interface async 6
 async dynamic routing
 async dynamic address
 async default ip address 10.11.14.2
 ip tcp header-compression passive
 ip unnumbered ethernet 0
```

### *Related Commands*

Search online to find documentation for related commands.
**async dynamic address**
**ip tcp header-compression**

## AUTOCOMMAND

To configure the Cisco IOS software to automatically execute a command when a user connects to a particular line, use the **autocommand** line configuration command.

**autocommand** *command*

| *Syntax* | *Description* |
|---|---|
| *command* | Any appropriate EXEC command, including the host name and any switches that occur with the EXEC command. |

#### *Default*

No commands are configured to automatically execute.

#### *Command Mode*

Line configuration

#### *Usage Guidelines*

This command first appeared in Cisco IOS Release 10.0.

This command enables you to automatically execute an EXEC command when a user connects to a line.

#### *Example*

The following example forces an automatic connection to a host named *host21* (which could be an IP address):

```
line vty 4
 autocommand connect host21
```

### AUTOHANGUP

To configure automatic line disconnect, use the **autohangup** line configuration command. This command causes the EXEC to issue the **exit** command when the last connection closes.

**autohangup**

#### *Syntax Description*

This command has no arguments or keywords.

#### *Default*

Disabled

#### *Command Mode*

Line configuration

#### *Usage Guidelines*

This command first appeared in Cisco IOS Release 10.0.

This command is useful for UNIX UUCP applications that automatically disconnect lines because UUCP scripts cannot issue the **exit** command to hang up the telephone.

### *Example*

The following example enables automatic line disconnect on lines 5 through 10:

```
line 5 10
 autohangup
```

## CLEAR LINE

To return a terminal line to idle state, use the **clear line** EXEC command.

**clear line** *line-number*

| *Syntax* | *Description* |
|---|---|
| *line-number* | Absolute line number. |

### *Command Mode*

EXEC

### *Usage Guidelines*

This command first appeared in Cisco IOS Release 10.0.

Use this command to log out of a specific session running on another line. If the line uses a modem, the modem is disconnected.

### *Example*

In the following example, line 3 is reset to idle state:

```
clear line 3
```

## EXEC

To allow an EXEC process on a line, use the **exec** line configuration command. Use the **no** form of this command to turn off the EXEC process for the specified line.

**exec**
**no exec**

### *Syntax Description*

This command has no arguments or keywords.

### *Default*

The EXEC process is activated automatically on all lines.

*Command Mode*

Line configuration

*Usage Guidelines*

This command first appeared in Cisco IOS Release 10.0.

When you want to allow an outgoing connection *only* for a line, use the **no exec** command. When a user tries to Telnet to a line with the **no exec** command configured, the user will get no response when pressing the Return key at the login screen.

*Example*

The following example turns off the EXEC on line 7. You might want to do this on the auxiliary port if the attached device (for example, the control port of a rack of modems) sends unsolicited data. If this happens, an EXEC process starts, which makes the line unavailable.

```
line 7
 no exec
```

### EXEC-TIMEOUT

To set the interval that the EXEC command interpreter waits until user input is detected, use the **exec-timeout** line configuration command. Use the **no** form of this command to remove the timeout definition.

**exec-timeout** *minutes* [*seconds*]
**no exec-timeout**

| *Syntax* | *Description* |
|---|---|
| *minutes* | Integer that specifies the number of minutes. |
| *seconds* | (Optional) Additional time intervals in seconds. An interval of zero specifies no timeouts. |

*Default*

10 minutes

*Command Mode*

Line configuration

*Usage Guidelines*

This command first appeared in Cisco IOS Release 10.0.

If no input is detected, the EXEC facility resumes the current connection, or if no connections exist, it returns the terminal to the idle state and disconnects the incoming session. It is the same as entering **exec-timeout** 0.

### *Examples*

The following example sets a time interval of 2 minutes, 30 seconds:

```
line console
 exec-timeout 2 30
```

The following example sets a time interval of 10 seconds:

```
line console
 exec-timeout 0 10
```

## FLOWCONTROL

To set the method of data flow control between the terminal or other serial device and the router, use the **flowcontrol** line configuration command. Use the **no** form of this command to disable flow control.

**flowcontrol** {**none** | **software** [**lock**] [**in** | **out**] | **hardware** [**in** | **out**]}
**no flowcontrol** {**none** | **software** [**in** | **out**] | **hardware** [**in** | **out**]}

| *Syntax* | *Description* |
|---|---|
| **none** | Turns off flow control. |
| **software** | Sets software flow control. An optional keyword specifies the direction: **in** causes the Cisco IOS software to listen to flow control from the attached device, and **out** causes the software to send flow control information to the attached device. If you do not specify a direction, both are assumed. |
| **lock** | Used to make it impossible to turn off flow control from the remote host when the connected device *needs* software flow control. This option applies to connections using the Telnet or rlogin protocols. |
| **hardware** | Sets hardware flow control. An optional keyword specifies the direction: **in** causes the software to listen to flow control from the attached device, and **out** causes the software to send flow control information to the attached device. If you do not specify a direction, both are assumed. For more information about hardware flow control, see the hardware manual that was shipped with your router. |

### *Default*

No flow control

### Command Mode

Line configuration

### Usage Guidelines

This command first appeared in Cisco IOS Release 10.0.

When software flow control is set, the default stop and start characters are Ctrl-S and Ctrl-Q (XOFF and XON). You can change them with the **stop-character** and **start-character** commands.

If a remote Telnet device requires software flow control, the remote system should not be able to turn it off. Using the **lock** option makes it possible to refuse "dangerous" Telnet negotiations if they are inappropriate.

### Example

The following example sets hardware flow control on line 7:

```
line 7
 flowcontrol hardware
```

### Related Commands

Search online to find documentation for related commands.

**start-character**
**stop-character**
**terminal flowcontrol**

## GROUP-RANGE

To create a list of member asynchronous interfaces (associated with a group interface), use the **group-range** interface configuration command. Use the **no** form of the command to remove an interface from the member list.

**group-range** *low-end-of-range high-end-of-range*
**no group**-range interface

| *Sytax* | *Description* |
|---|---|
| *low-end-of-range* | Beginning interface number to be made a member of the group interface. |
| *high-end-of-range* | Ending interface number to be made a member of the group interface. |

### Default

No interfaces are designated as members of a group.

### *Command Mode*

Interface configuration

### *Usage Guidelines*

Using the **group-range** command, you create a group of asynchronous interfaces that are associated with a group asynchronous interface on the same device. This group interface is configured by using the **interface group-async** command. This one-to-many structure allows you to configure all associated member interfaces by entering one command on the group interface, rather than entering this command on each interface. You can customize the configuration on a specific interface by using the **member** command.

### *Examples*

The following example defines interfaces 2, 3, 4, 5, 6, and 7 as members of asynchronous group interface 0:

```
interface group-async 0
 group range 2 7
```

### *Related Commands*

Search online to find documentation for related commands.

**interface group-async**
**member**

## HOLD-QUEUE

To limit the size of the IP output queue, use the **hold-queue** interface configuration command. To return the output queue to the default size, use the **no** form of this command.

**hold-queue** *packets*
**no hold-queue**

| *Syntax* | *Description* |
|---|---|
| *packets* | Maximum number of packets. The range of values is 0 to 65535. |

### *Default*

10 packets (default for asynchronous interfaces only)

### *Command Mode*

Interface configuration

### *Usage Guidelines*

This command first appeared in Cisco IOS Release 10.0. The **no hold-queue** command first appeared in Cisco IOS Release 11.1.

The default of 10 packets allows the Cisco IOS software to queue a number of back-to-back routing updates. This is the default for asynchronous interfaces only; other media types have different defaults.

The hold queue stores packets received from the network that are waiting to be sent to the client. It is recommended that the queue size not exceed ten packets on asynchronous interfaces. For most other interfaces, queue length should not exceed 100.

### *Example*

The following example changes the packet queue length of a line to five packets:

```
interface async 2
 async default ip address 172.31.7.5
 hold-queue 5
```

## IP ACCESS-GROUP

To configure an access list to be used for packets transmitted to and from the asynchronous host, use the **ip access-group** interface configuration command. To disable control over packets transmitted to or from an asynchronous host, use the **no** form of this command.

**ip access-group** *access-list-number* {**in** | **out**}
**no ip access-group** *access-list-number*

| *Syntax* | *Description* |
|---|---|
| *access-list-number* | Assigned IP access list number. |
| **in** | Defines access control on packets transmitted *from* the asynchronous host. |
| **out** | Defines access control on packets being sent *to* the asynchronous host. |

### *Default*

Disabled

### *Command Mode*

Interface configuration

### *Usage Guidelines*

This command first appeared in Cisco IOS Release 10.0.

With this command in effect, the IP destination address of each packet is run through the access list for acceptability and dropped or passed.

### *Example*

The following example assumes that users are restricted to certain servers designated as SLIP or PPP servers, but that normal terminal users can access anything on the local network:

```
! access list for normal connections
access-list 1 permit 172.16.0.0 0.0.255.255
!
! access list for SLIP packets.
access-list 2 permit 172.16.42.55
access-list 2 permit 172.16.111.1
access-list 2 permit 172.16.55.99
!
! Specify the access list
interface async 6
 async dynamic address
 ip access-group 1 out
 ip access-group 2 in
```

## IP MTU

To specify the size of the largest Internet packet, use the **ip mtu** interface configuration command. To return to the default MTU size of 1,500 bytes, use the **no** form of this command.

**ip mtu** *bytes*
**no ip mtu**

| *Syntax* | *Description* |
|---|---|
| *bytes* | Maximum number of bytes. The range of values is 64 to 1,000,000. |

### *Default*

1,500 bytes

### *Command Mode*

Interface configuration

### *Usage Guidelines*

This command first appeared in Cisco IOS Release 10.0.

### *Example*

The following example sets the packet MTU size to 200 bytes:

```
interface async 5
 async default ip address 172.31.7.5
 ip mtu 200
```

## LINE

To identify a specific line for configuration and start the line configuration command collection mode, use the **line** global configuration command.

**line** [**aux** | **console** | **tty** | **vty**] *line-number* [*ending-line-number*]

| *Syntax* | *Description* |
|---|---|
| **aux** | (Optional) Auxiliary EIA/TIA-232 DTE port. Must be addressed as relative line 0. The auxiliary port can be used for modem support and asynchronous connections. |
| **console** | (Optional) Console terminal line. The console port is DCE. |
| **tty** | (Optional) Standard asynchronous line. |
| **vty** | (Optional) Virtual terminal for remote console access. |
| *line-number* | The relative number of the terminal line (or the first line in a contiguous group) that you want to configure when the line type is specified. Numbering begins with zero. |
| *ending-line-number* | (Optional) The relative number of the last line in a contiguous group that you want to configure. If you omit the keyword, then *line-number* and *ending-line-number* are absolute rather than relative line numbers. |

### *Default*

There is no default line.

### *Command Mode*

Global configuration

### *Usage Guidelines*

This command first appeared in Cisco IOS Release 10.0.

You can address a single line or a consecutive range of lines with the **line** command. A line number is necessary, though, and you will receive an error message if you forget to include it.

Entering the **line** command with the optional line type (**AUX**, **CON**, **TTY**, or **VTY**) designates the line number as relative. For example, to configure line parameters for line 7 (a TTY line), you can enter the following:

```
Router(config)# line tty 7
```

You also can enter the **line** command without specifying a line type. In this case, the line number is treated as an absolute line number. For example, to configure line parameters for line 5, which can be of any type, you can enter the following:

```
Router(config)# line 5
```

Absolute line numbers increment consecutively and can be difficult to manage on large systems. Relative line numbers are a shorthand notation used in configuration. Internally, the Cisco IOS software uses absolute line numbers. You cannot use relative line numbers everywhere, but you can use absolute line numbers everywhere.

The absolute line number of the auxiliary port is 1. The relative line number of the auxiliary port is 0. See the **modem** line configuration command to set up modem support on the auxiliary port.

The software keeps a table of absolute and relative line numbers that you can display with the EXEC command **show users all**. A sample display follows:

```
Router> show users all
  Line       User      Host(s)                 Idle   Location
   0 con 0                                            chaff console
   1 tty 1                                            Engineering printer
   2 tty 2
   3 tty 3             DREGGS                  1:07   Katy x1111
   4 tty 4                                            Console E3-D
   5 tty 5                                            Mkt. demo area
   6 tty 6
   7 tty 7             DREGGS                    14   Marie x1112
  10 tty 10
 .  .  .
 135 tty 135
 136 tty 136
 137 tty 137                                          rp4-printer
 140 tty 140                                          Braille printer
 141 aux 0
 142 vty 0   Denise      idle                         DENISE-MAC.CISCO.COM
 143 vty 1   Michael     idle                       0 DREGGS.CISCO.COM
 144 vty 2
 145 vty 3
 146 vty 4
 147 vty 5
```

The absolute line numbers are listed at the far left, followed by the line type, and then the relative line number. Relative line numbers always begin numbering at zero and define the type of line. Addressing the second virtual terminal line as line VTY 1, for example, is easier than remembering it as line 143—its absolute line number.

The line types are ranked as follows in the line table:

1. Console 0 (con 0)
2. Standard asynchronous line (TTY)
3. Auxiliary port (aux)
4. Virtual terminal line (VTY)
5. Printer

The terminal from which you locally configure the router is attached to the console port. To configure line parameters for the console port, enter the following:

```
Router(config)# line con 0
```

The console relative line number must be 0.

Virtual terminal lines are used to allow remote access to the router. A virtual terminal line is not associated with either the auxiliary or console port. The router has five virtual terminal lines by default. However, you can create additional virtual terminal lines as described in the section "Create Additional Virtual Terminal Lines," found in Chapter 21, "Configuring Protocol Translation and Virtual Asynchronous Devices."

Configuring the console port or virtual terminal lines allows you to perform such tasks as setting communication parameters, specifying autobaud connections, and configuring terminal operating parameters for the terminal you are using.

### *Examples*

The following example starts configuration for virtual terminal lines 0 to 4:

```
line vty 0 4
```

In the following example, the user creates and configures the maximum 100 virtual terminal lines with the **no login** command:

```
line vty 0 99
 no login
```

In the following example, the user eliminates virtual terminal line number 5 and all higher-numbered virtual terminal lines. Only virtual terminal lines 0 to 4 will remain.

```
no line vty 5
```

In the following example, the user configures console line 0, auxiliary line 0, and virtual terminal lines 0 to 4:

```
line vty 0 4
 login
line con 0
 password baskerville
line aux 0
 password Mypassword
 no exec
 access-class 1 in
 speed 19200
line vty 0
 exec-timeout 0 0
 password Mypassword
line vty 1
 exec-timeout 0 0
 password Mypassword
line vty 2
 exec-timeout 0 0
 password Mypassword
line vty 3
 password Mypassword
line vty 4
 password Mypassword
```

### *Related Commands*

Search online to find documentation for related commands.

**show line**
**show users all**

## MEMBER

To alter the configuration of an asynchronous interface that is a member of a group, use the **member** interface configuration command. Use the **no** form of the command to restore defaults set at the group master interface.

**member** *number interface-command*
**no member** *number interface-command*

| *Syntax* | *Description* |
|---|---|
| *number* | Number of the asynchronous interface to be altered. |
| *interface-command* | One or more of the following commands entered for this specific interface:<br>• **peer default ip address**<br>• **description** |

### *Default*

No individual configurations are set for member interfaces.

### *Command Mode*

Interface configuration

### *Usage Guidelines*

You can customize a member interface by using the **member** command. (Interfaces are designated as members of a group by using the **interface group-async** and **group-range** commands.) To restore the defaults set at the group master interface, use the **no** form of this command.

### *Examples*

The following example defines interface 3 with a description of line 3, which is attached to a Hayes Optima modem:

```
interface group-async 0
 member 3 description line #3 Hayes Optima
```

### *Related Commands*

Search online to find documentation for related commands.

**group-range**
**interface group-async**

## MODEM CALLIN

To support dial-in modems that use the data terminal ready (DTR) signal to control the off-hook status of the modem, use the **modem callin** line configuration command. Use the **no** form of this command to disable this feature.

**modem callin**
**no modem callin**

### *Syntax Description*

This command has no arguments or keywords.

### *Default*

No modem control

### *Command Mode*

Line configuration

### *Usage Guidelines*

This command first appeared in Cisco IOS Release 10.0.

In response to RING, the router raises the DTR signal, which indicates to the modem that it should answer the call. At the end of the session, the Cisco IOS software lowers DTR, which disconnects the modem. This command is useful for older modems that do not support auto answer.

This command uses CTS, whereas newer modem commands in the Cisco IOS software use DSR.

Only use the **modem callin** command on the ASM terminal server, where hardware flow control is not possible. If you have a more recent device (such as a Cisco 2509 through 2512, Cisco 2520 through 2523, a Cisco AS5100, Cisco 3600 series, or Cisco AS5200), use the **modem dialin** command instead.

### *Example*

The following example configures lines 10 through 16 for dial-in modems that can run at speeds from 300 to 19,200 bps:

```
line 10 16
 modem callin
 autobaud
```

### *Related Commands*

Search online to find documentation for related commands.

**modem answer-timeout**
**modem inout**

## MODEM CALLOUT

To configure a line for reverse connections, use the **modem callout** line configuration command. Use the **no** form of this command to disable this feature.

**modem callout**
**no modem callout**

### *Syntax Description*

This command has no arguments or keywords.

### *Default*

No modem control

### *Command Mode*

Line configuration

### *Usage Guidelines*

This command first appeared in Cisco IOS Release 10.0.

This command supports ports connected to computers that would normally be connected to modems. It causes the access server to act somewhat like a modem.

This command uses CTS and should be used only on access servers that do not support hardware flow control. If you have an access server that is newer than the ASM terminal server (such as a Cisco 2509 through 2512, Cisco 2520 through 2523, a Cisco AS5100, Cisco 3600 series, or a Cisco AS5200), use the **modem host** command instead. The **modem callout** command uses CTS, whereas the **modem host** command uses DSR/DCD. If CTS is used for modem control instead of DSR/DCD, it prevents CTS from being used by hardware flow control.

### *Example*

The following example configures lines 17 through 32 in reverse connection mode to a large terminal switch. By using Telnet to connect to a TCP port on this host, the user gets the next free line in the rotary group.

```
line 17 32
 rotary 1
 modem callout
```

### *Related Commands*

Search online to find documentation for related commands.

**modem inout**
**rotary**

## MODEM CTS-REQUIRED

The **modem printer** command replaces the **modem cts-required** command. Refer to the description of the **modem printer** command for more information.

## MODEM DIALIN

To configure a line to enable a modem attached to the router to accept incoming calls only, use the **modem dialin** line configuration command. Use the **no** form of this command to disable this feature.

**modem dialin**
**no modem dialin**

### *Syntax Description*

This command has no arguments or keywords.

### *Default*

Do not permit incoming calls to the modem.

### *Command Mode*

Line configuration

### *Usage Guidelines*

This command first appeared in Cisco IOS Release 11.1.

This command supports modems that can automatically handle telephone line activity, such as answering the telephone after a certain number of rings.

### *Example*

The following example configures a line for a high-speed modem:

```
line 5
 modem dialin
```

### *Related Commands*

Search online to find documentation for related commands.

**dialer**
**modem inout**
**parity**

### MODEM DTR-ACTIVE

To configure a line to leave data terminal ready (DTR) signals low, unless the line has an active incoming connection or an EXEC process, use the **modem dtr-active** line configuration command. Use the **no** form of this command to disable this feature.

**modem dtr-active**
**no modem dtr-active**

#### *Syntax Description*

This command has no arguments or keywords.

#### *Default*

No modem control

#### *Command Mode*

Line configuration

#### *Usage Guidelines*

This command first appeared in Cisco IOS Release 10.0.

This command does not use the Carrier Detect (CD) signal.

This command can be useful if the line is connected to an external device (for example, a time-sharing system) that must know whether a line is in active use. The **modem dtr-active** command is similar to the **no modem** line configuration command.

#### *Example*

The following example configures a line for low DTR:

```
line 5
 modem dtr-active
```

#### *Related Commands*

Search online to find documentation for related commands.

**modem cts-required**

### MODEM HOST

To configure a line for reverse connections where hardware flow control is also required, use the **modem host** line configuration command. Use the **no** form of this command to disable the line modem control for reverse connections.

**modem host**
**no modem host**

### *Syntax Description*

This command has no arguments or keywords.

### *Default*

No modem control

### *Command Mode*

Line configuration

### *Usage Guidelines*

This command first appeared in Cisco IOS Release 11.1.

This command supports ports connected to computers that would normally be connected to modems. This command causes the access server to act like a modem.

The **modem host** command is identical in operation to the **modem callout** command except that DSR/DCD is used for modem control instead of CTS. This frees CTS for use by hardware flow control.

### *Example*

The following example configures a line to send a DSR/CD active signal to the modem for data switches and hosts:

```
line 5
 modem host
```

### *Related Commands*

Search online to find documentation for related commands.

**modem callout**
**modem printer**

## MODEM INOUT

To configure a line for both incoming and outgoing calls, use the **modem inout** line configuration command. Use the **no** form of this command to disable this feature.

**modem inout**
**no modem inout**

### *Syntax Description*

This command has no arguments or keywords.

### *Default*

No modem control

### *Command Mode*

Line configuration

### *Usage Guidelines*

This command first appeared in Cisco IOS Release 10.0.

This command uses DSR and RING signals for carrier detection.

The Cisco IOS software does not support any dialing protocols; therefore, the host system software or the user must provide any special dialing commands when using the modem for outgoing calls.

### *Example*

The following example configures a line for both incoming and outgoing calls:

```
line 5
 modem inout
```

### *Related Commands*

Search online to find documentation for related commands.

**dialer**
**parity**

## MODEM PRINTER

To configure a line to require a data set ready (DSR) signal, use the **modem printer** line configuration command. Use the **no** form of this command to use CTS instead of DSR.

**modem printer**
**no modem printer**

### *Syntax Description*

This command has no arguments or keywords.

### *Default*

No modem control

### *Command Mode*

Line configuration

### *Usage Guidelines*

This command first appeared in Cisco IOS Release 11.1.

This command uses RING/DCD (Data Carrier Detect) /DSR as the modem control signal instead of CTS. This leaves CTS free for use in hardware flow control. You can configure hardware flow control concurrently with the **modem printer** command.

The **modem dialin** command supports modems concurrently with hardware flow control, yet the other auxiliary modem control options for printers, such as **modem cts-required**, use CTS instead of DSR/CD, as the CD signal.

### *Example*

The following example configures a line to send a DSR signal to the modem:

```
line 5
 modem printer
```

## MODEM RI-IS-CD

The **modem dialin** command replaces the **modem ri-is-cd** command. Refer to the description of the **modem dialin** command for more information.

## NETBIOS NBF

To enable the NetBIOS Frames Protocol (NBF) on an interface, use the **netbios nbf** interface configuration command. To disable NetBIOS Frames Protocol support on an interface, use the **no** form of this command.

**netbios nbf**
**no netbios nbf**

### *Syntax Description*

This command has no arguments or keywords.

### *Default*

Disabled

### *Command Mode*

Interface configuration

### *Usage Guidelines*

This command first appeared in Cisco IOS Release 11.1.

### *Example*

The following example enables NetBIOS Frames Protocol on asynchronous interface 1 (connected to remote access client using a NetBEUI application) and Ethernet interface 0 (connected to the remote router):

```
interface async 1
 netbios nbf
interface ethernet 0
 netbios nbf
```

#### *Related Commands*

Search online to find documentation for related commands.

**netbios name-cache**
**show netbios cache**
**show nbf sessions**

### PHYSICAL-LAYER

To specify the mode of a slow-speed serial interface on a router as either synchronous or asynchronous, use the **physical-layer** interface configuration command. Use the **no** form of this command to return the interface to its default mode, which is synchronous.

**physical-layer {sync | async}**
**no physical-layer**

| *Syntax* | *Description* |
|---|---|
| **sync** | Place the interface in synchronous mode. |
| **async** | Place the interface in asynchronous mode. |

#### *Default*

Synchronous mode

#### *Command Mode*

Interface configuration

#### *Usage Guidelines*

This command first appeared in Cisco IOS Release 11.2.

This command applies only to low-speed serial interfaces available on Cisco 2520 through Cisco 2523 routers.

If you specify the **no physical-layer** command, you return the interface to its default mode (synchronous).

In synchronous mode, low-speed serial interfaces support all interface configuration commands available for high-speed serial interfaces, except the following two commands:

- **sdlc cts-delay**
- **sdlc rts-timeout**

When placed in asynchronous mode, low-speed serial interfaces support all commands available for standard asynchronous interfaces.

When you enter this command, it does not appear in the output of **show running config** and **show startup config** commands, because the command is a physical layer command.

#### *Example*

The following example changes a low-speed serial interface from synchronous to asynchronous mode:

```
interface serial 2
 physical-layer async
```

### ROTARY

To define a group of lines consisting of one or more lines, use the **rotary** line configuration command. Use the **no** form of this command to remove a line or group of lines from a rotary group.

**rotary** *group*
**no rotary**

| *Syntax* | *Description* |
|---|---|
| *group* | Integer between 1 and 100 that you choose to identify the rotary group. |

#### *Default*

No group of lines is defined.

#### *Command Mode*

Line configuration

#### *Usage Guidelines*

This command first appeared in Cisco IOS Release 10.0.

Typically, rotary groups are used on devices with multiple modem connections to allow connections to the next free line in a hunt group.

Connections to a rotary group can take advantage of the following features:

- Clear To Send (CTS)—If a line in a rotary group is configured to require CTS, the Cisco IOS software skips that line if CTS from the attached device is low. This feature enables the software to avoid inactive host ports automatically. To enable this feature, use the **modem bad** line configuration command.
- EIA/TIA-232 handshaking—Rotary groups are often associated with large terminal switches that require an EIA/TIA-232 handshake before forming a connection. In this case, use the **modem callout** line configuration command to configure the lines in the group. If

the EIA/TIA-232 handshake fails on a line, the Cisco IOS software steps to the next free line in the rotary group and restarts the negotiation.

- Access control—You can use access lists for groups of virtual terminal lines.
- Session timeout—Use the **session-timeout** line configuration command to set an interval for a line so that if no activity occurs on a remotely initiated connection for that interval the Cisco IOS software closes the connection. The software assumes that the host has crashed or is otherwise inaccessible.

The remote host must specify a particular TCP port on the router to connect to a rotary group with connections to an individual line. The available services are the same, but the TCP port numbers are different. Table 6–2 lists the services and port numbers for both rotary groups and individual lines.

**Table 6–2** *Services and Port Numbers for Rotary Groups and Lines*

| Services Provided | Base TCP Port for Rotaries | Base TCP Port for Individual Lines |
|---|---|---|
| Telnet protocol | 3000 | 2000 |
| Raw TCP protocol (no Telnet protocol) | 5000 | 4000 |
| Telnet protocol, binary mode | 7000 | 6000 |
| XRemote protocol | 10000 | 9000 |

For example, if Telnet protocols are required, the remote host connects to the TCP port numbered 3000 (decimal) plus the rotary group number. If the rotary group identifier is 13, the corresponding TCP port is 3013.

If a raw TCP stream is required, the port is 5000 (decimal) plus the rotary group number. If rotary group 5 includes a raw TCP (printer) line, the user connects to port 5005 and is connected to one of the raw printers in the group.

If Telnet binary mode is required, the port is 7000 (decimal) plus the rotary group number.

### *Example*

The following example establishes a rotary group consisting of virtual terminal lines 2 through 4 and defines a password on those lines. By using Telnet to connect to TCP port 3001, the user gets the next free line in the rotary group. The user does not have to remember the range of line numbers associated with the password.

```
line vty 2 4
 rotary 1
 password letmein
login
```

### *Related Commands*

Search online to find documentation for related commands.

**dialer**
**modem bad**
**modem callout**
**session-timeout**

## SCRIPT ACTIVATION

To specify that a chat script start on a physical terminal line any time the line is activated, use the **script activation** line configuration command. Use the **no** form of this command to disable this feature.

**script activation** *regexp*
no **script activation**

| *Syntax* | *Description* |
|---|---|
| *regexp* | Regular expression that specifies the set of modem scripts that might be executed. The first script name that matches the argument *regexp* is used. |

### *Default*

Not assigned to terminal lines

### *Command Mode*

Line configuration

### *Usage Guidelines*

This command first appeared in Cisco IOS Release 10.0.

This command provides an asynchronous handshake to a user or device that activates the line. It can be activated by several events, such as a user issuing a carriage return on a vacant line, by a modem on the line sensing an incoming carrier, or an asynchronous device (such as another router) sending data. Each time an EXEC session is started on a line, the system checks to see if a **script activation** command is configured on the line. If so, and the argument *regexp* (a regular expression) matches an existing chat script name, the matched script is run on the line. For more information about regular expressions, see Appendix C, "Regular Expressions."

The **script activation** command can mimic a login handshake of another system. For example, a system that dials in to a line on a router and expects an IBM mainframe login handshake can be satisfied with an appropriate activation script.

This command also can send strings to asynchronous devices that are connecting or dialing in to a router.

The **script activation** command functions only on physical terminal (TTY) lines. It does not function on virtual terminal (VTY) lines.

### *Example*

The following example specifies that the chat script with a name that includes *telebit* is to be activated whenever line 4 is activated:

```
line 4
 script activation telebit
```

### *Related Commands*

Search online to find documentation for related commands.

**chat-script**
**dialer map modem-script system-script**
**dialer map modem-script system-script name**
**script activation**
**script connection**
**script dialer**
**script reset**
**script startup**
**start-chat**

## SCRIPT CONNECTION

To specify that a chat script start on a physical terminal line any time a remote network connection is made to a line, use the **script connection** line configuration command. Use the **no** form of this command to disable this feature.

**script connection** *regexp*
**no script connection**

| *Syntax* | *Description* |
|---|---|
| *regexp* | Specifies the set of modem scripts that might be executed. The first script name that matches the argument regexp is used. |

### *Default*

Not assigned to terminal lines

### *Command Mode*

Line configuration

### *Usage Guidelines*

This command first appeared in Cisco IOS Release 10.0.

This command provides modem dialing commands and commands for logging on to remote systems. The **script connection** command functions only on physical terminal (TTY) lines. It does not function on virtual terminal (VTY) lines.

This command can be used to initialize an asynchronous device sitting on a line to which a reverse network connection is made.

For information about regular expressions, see Appendix C.

### *Example*

The following example specifies that the chat script with a name that includes *inband* will be activated whenever a remote connection to line 4 is established. The router can send a login string and password to the UNIX server when a network tunneling connection comes in to line 4:

```
line 4
 script connection inband
```

Using this example and the topology in Figure 6–1, the access server or router can send a login string and password to the UNIX server when a network tunneling connection comes in to line 4.

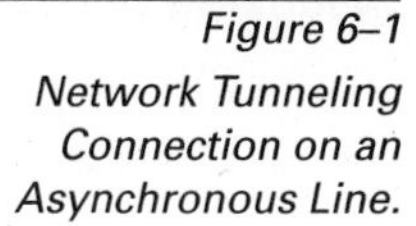

*Figure 6–1*
*Network Tunneling Connection on an Asynchronous Line.*

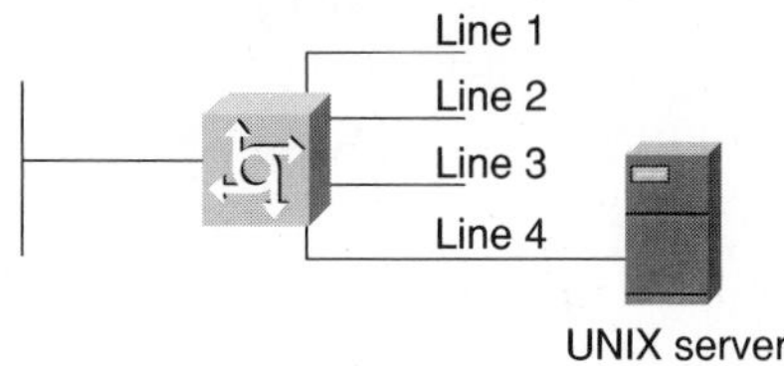


### *Related Commands*

Search online to find documentation for related commands.

**chat-script**
**dialer map modem-script system-script**
**dialer map modem-script system-script name**
**script activation**
**script dialer**
**script reset**
**script startup**
**start-chat**

## SCRIPT RESET

To specify that a chat script start on a physical terminal line any time the specified line is reset, use the **script reset** line configuration command. Use the **no** form of this command to disable this feature.

**script reset** *regexp*
**no script reset**

| *Syntax* | *Description* |
|---|---|
| *regexp* | Specifies the set of modem scripts that might be executed. The first script name that matches the argument *regexp* is used. |

### *Default*

Not assigned to terminal lines

### *Command Mode*

Line configuration

### *Usage Guidelines*

This command first appeared in Cisco IOS Release 10.0.

Chat scripts provide modem dialing commands and commands for logging on to remote systems. Use this command to reset a modem attached to a line every time a call is dropped.

The **script reset** command functions only on physical terminal (TTY) lines. It does not function on virtual terminal (VTY) lines.

For information about regular expressions, see Appendix C.

### *Examples*

The following example specifies that any chat script name with the word *linebackup* in it will be activated any time line 7 is reset:

```
line 7
 script reset linebackup
```

The following example resets a modem sitting on a line each time a call is dropped:

```
chat-script drop-line ""+++"" " " ATH OK "ATS0=1" OK "ATS9=21"
line 4
 script reset drop-line
```

### *Related Commands*

Search online to find documentation for related commands.

**chat-script**
**dialer map modem-script system-script**
**dialer map modem-script system-script name**
**script activation**
**script connection**
**script dialer**

**script startup**
**start-chat**

## SCRIPT STARTUP

To specify that a chat script start on a physical terminal line any time the router is powered up, use the **script startup** line configuration command. Use the **no** form of this command to disable this feature.

**script startup** *regexp*
**no script startup**

| *Syntax* | *Description* |
|---|---|
| *regexp* | Specifies the set of modem scripts that might be executed. The first script that matches the argument *regexp* is used. |

### *Default*

Not assigned to terminal lines

### *Command Mode*

Line configuration

### *Usage Guidelines*

This command first appeared in Cisco IOS Release 10.0.

Use this command to initialize asynchronous devices connected to a line when the router is started up or reloaded. You can also use it to start up a banner other than the default banner on lines. The **script startup** command functions only on physical terminal (TTY) lines. It does not function on virtual terminal (VTY) lines.

For information about regular expressions, see Appendix C.

### *Example*

The following example specifies that a chat script with the word *linestart* in its name will be activated whenever line 5 is started up:

```
line 5
 script startup linestart
```

### *Related Commands*

Search online to find documentation for related commands.

**chat-script**
**dialer map modem-script system-script**
**dialer map modem-script system-script name**

**script activation**
**script connection**
**script dialer**
**script reset**
**start-chat**

## SHOW ASYNC BOOTP

To display the parameters that have been configured for extended BOOTP requests, use the **show async bootp** privileged EXEC command.

**show async bootp**

### *Syntax Description*

This command has no arguments or keywords.

### *Command Mode*

Privileged EXEC

### *Usage Guidelines*

This command first appeared in Cisco IOS Release 10.0.

### *Sample Display*

The following is sample output from the **show async bootp** command.

```
sloth# show async bootp

The following extended data will be sent in BOOTP responses:

bootfile (for address 192.168.31.1) "pcboot"
bootfile (for address 172.16.1.110) "dirtboot"
subnet-mask 255.255.0.0
time-offset -3600
time-server 192.168.31.1
```

Table 6–3 describes significant fields shown in the display.

**Table 6–3** *Show Async BOOTP Field Descriptions*

| Field | Description |
|---|---|
| bootfile... “pcboot” | Indicates that the boot file for address 192.168.31.1 is named pcboot. |
| subnet-mask 255.255.0.0 | Specifies the subnet mask. |

**Table 6–3** *Show Async BOOTP Field Descriptions, Continued*

| Field | Description |
|---|---|
| time-offset -3600 | Indicates that the local time is one hour (3,600 seconds) earlier than Coordinated Universal Time (UTC). |
| time-server 192.168.31.1 | Indicates the address of the time server for the network. |

## SHOW ASYNC STATUS

To display the status of activity on all lines configured for asynchronous support, use the **show async status** privileged EXEC command.

**show async status**

### *Syntax Description*

This command has no arguments or keywords.

### *Command Mode*

Privileged EXEC

### *Usage Guidelines*

This command first appeared in Cisco IOS Release 10.0.

The display resulting from this command shows all asynchronous sessions, whether they are using SLIP or PPP encapsulation.

### *Sample Display*

The following is sample output from the **show async status** command:

```
router# show async status

Async protocol statistics:
  Rcvd: 5448 packets, 7682760 bytes
        1 format errors, 0 checksum errors, 0 overrun, 0 no buffer
  Sent: 5455 packets, 7682676 bytes, 0 dropped


 Tty           Local            Remote Qd InPack OutPac Inerr  Drops  MTU Qsz
   1      192.168.7.84         Dynamic  0      0      0     0      0 1500  10
*  3      192.168.7.98            None  0   5448   5455     1      0 1500  10
```

Table 6–4 describes significant fields shown in the display.

**Table 6–4** *Show Async Status Field Descriptions*

| Field | Description |
|---|---|
| Rcvd | Statistics on packets received. |
| 5448 packets | Packets received. |
| 7,682,760 bytes | Total number of bytes. |
| 1 format errors | Spurious characters received when a packet start delimiter is expected. |
| 0 checksum errors | Count of checksum errors. |
| 0 overrun | Number of giants received. |
| 0 no buffer | Number of packets received when no buffer was available. |
| Sent | Statistics on packets sent. |
| 5455 packets | Packets sent. |
| 7682676 bytes | Total number of bytes. |
| 0 dropped | Number of packets dropped. |
| Tty | Line number. |
| * | Line currently in use. |
| Local | Local IP address on the link. |
| Remote | Remote IP address on the link; "Dynamic" indicates that a remote address is allowed but has not been specified; "None" indicates that no remote address is assigned or being used. |
| Qd | Number of packets on hold queue (Qsz is the maximum). |
| InPack | Number of packets received. |
| OutPac | Number of packets sent. |
| Inerr | Number of total input errors; sum of format errors, checksum errors, overruns and no buffers. |
| Drops | Number of packets received that would not fit on the hold queue. |
| MTU | Current maximum transmission unit size. |
| Qsz | Current output hold queue size. |

### SHOW LINE

To display a terminal line's parameters, use the **show line** EXEC command.

**show line** [*line-number*]

| *Syntax* | *Description* |
|---|---|
| *line-number* | (Optional) Absolute line number of the line for which you want to list parameters. |

#### Command Mode

EXEC

#### Usage Guidelines

This command first appeared in Cisco IOS Release 10.0.

#### Sample Display

The following sample output from the **show line** command indicates that line 17 is a virtual terminal line with a transmit and receive rate of 9600 bps. Also shown is the modem state, terminal screen width and length, and so on.

```
router# show line 17

Tty Typ     Tx/Rx      A Modem  Roty AccO AccI  Uses    Noise   Overruns
A 17 VTY   9600/9600   -    -       -    -    -     1        0        0/0

Line 17, Location: "", Type: ""
Length: 24 lines, Width: 80 columns
Baud rate (TX/RX) is 9600/9600
Status: Ready, Connected, Active, No Exit Banner, Async interface active
Capabilities: Line usable as async interface
Modem state: Ready
Special Chars: Escape  Hold  Stop  Start  Disconnect  Activation
                ^^x    none   -     -       none
Timeouts:      Idle EXEC    Idle Session   Modem Answer  Session   Dispatch
                never         never                       none     not set
Session limit is not set.
Time since activation: never
Editing is enabled.
History is enabled, history size is 10.
Full user help is disabled
Allowed transports are lat telnet rlogin mop.  Preferred is lat.
No output characters are padded
No special data dispatching characters

Line is running SLIP routing for address 1.0.0.2.
0 output packets queued, 0 input packets.
Group codes:    0
```

Table 6–5 describes the fields in the **show line** output.

**Table 6–5** *Show Line Field Descriptions*

| Field | Description |
|---|---|
| Tty | Line number. In this case, 17. |
| Typ | Type of line. In this case, a virtual terminal line (VTY), which is active, in asynchronous mode denoted by the preceding 'A.' Other possible values are:<br>• CTY—console<br>• AUX—auxiliary port<br>• TTY—asynchronous terminal port<br>• lpt—parallel printer |
| Tx/Rx | Transmit rate/receive rate of the line. |
| A | Indicates whether autobaud has been configured for the line. A value of F indicates that autobaud has been configured; a hyphen indicates that it has not been configured. |
| Modem | Types of modem signals that have been configured for the line. Possible values include:<br>• callin<br>• callout<br>• cts-req<br>• DTR-Act<br>• inout<br>• RIisCD |
| Roty | Rotary group configured for the line. |
| AccO, AccI | Output or Input access list number configured for the line. |
| Uses | Number of connections established to or from the line since the system was restarted. |
| Noise | Number of times noise has been detected on the line since the system restarted. |

**Table 6–5** *Show Line Field Descriptions, Continued*

| Field | Description |
|---|---|
| Overruns | Hardware (UART) overruns and/or software buffer overflows, both defined as the number of overruns or overflows that have occurred on the specified line since the system was restarted. Hardware overruns are buffer overruns; the UART chip has received bits from the software faster than it can process them. A software overflow occurs when the software has received bits from the hardware faster than it can process them. |
| Line | Current line. |
| Location | Location of the current line. |
| Type | Type of line, as specified by the **line** global configuration command. |
| Length | Length of the terminal or screen display. |
| Width | Width of the terminal or screen display. |
| Baud rate (TX/RX) | Transmit rate/receive rate of the line. |
| Status | State of the line: Ready or not, connected or disconnected, active or inactive, exit banner or no exit banner, async interface active or inactive. |
| Capabilities | Current terminal capabilities. In this case, the line is usable as an asynchronous interface. |
| Modem state | Modem control state. This field should always read READY. |
| Special Chars | Current settings of special characters that were input by the user (or taken by default) from the following global configuration commands:<br>• **escape-character**<br>• **hold-character**<br>• **stop-character**<br>• **start-character**<br>• **disconnect-character**<br>• **activation-character** |
| Timeouts | Current settings that were input by the user (or taken by default) from the following global configuration commands:<br>• **exec-timeout**<br>• **session-timeout**<br>• **dispatch-timeout**<br>• **modem answer-timeout** |

**Table 6–5** *Show Line Field Descriptions, Continued*

| Field | Description |
|---|---|
| Session limit | Maximum number of sessions. |
| Time since activation | Last time start_process was run. |
| Editing | Whether or not command line editing is enabled. |
| History | Current history length, set by the user (or taken by default) from the **history** configuration command. |
| Full user help | Whether or not full user help has been set by the user with the **terminal full-help** command or by the administrator with the **full-help** line configuration command. |
| Allowed transports are... | Current set transport method, set by the user (or taken by default) from the **transport preferred** line configuration command. |
| Characters are padded | Current set padding, set by the user (or taken by default) from the **padding** line configuration command. |
| Data dispatching characters | Current dispatch character set by the user (or taken by default) from the **dispatch-character** line configuration command. |
| Line | Definition of the specified line's protocol and address. |
| Output, input packets | Number of output and input packets queued on this line. |
| Group codes | AT group codes. |

## SHOW MODEMCAP

To display the values set for the current modem, use the **show modemcap** command. This display lists the modems for which the router has entries. To display the attributes associated with a specific modem, use the **show modemcap** *modem-name* command.

**show modemcap** *modem-name*

| *Syntax* | *Description* |
|---|---|
| *modem-name* | The name of the modem (such as Codex_3260). |

### *Default*

The list of modems for which the router has entries.

### *Command Mode*

EXEC

### *Usage Guidelines*

This command first appeared in Cisco IOS Release 11.1.

When a modem name is supplied, this command displays the available modem values. Table 6–6 identifies the list of attributes and their description:

**Table 6–6** *Modem Attributes*

| Modem Attribute | Description |
|---|---|
| Factory defaults (FD) | Returns the modem to factory default configuration. This is commonly "&F." |
| Autoanswer (AA) | Sets the modem to answer the phone if DTR is high, preferably on the first ring. This is commonly "S0=1." |
| Carrier detect (CD) | Instructs the modem to raise a CD signal when a carrier is detected. Cisco configures modems into auto-answer mode by default. Oddly, this is not the default for most modems, which just raise CD and leave it high. This is commonly "&C1."<br>In auto-answer mode, the modem waits until it detects a ring, then responds to the incoming call and negotiates an end-to-end connection with the other modem. At this point, the modem receiving the call informs the router that it has a call ready to be processed; this notification is performed by raising the signal on RS-232 pin 8 (the Data Carrier Detect signal) to high. |
| Drop with DTR (DTR) | Drops the connection if DTR signal drops. There is frequently an option to reset the configuration while doing this. However, this option should *not* be used. The connection should only drop. The correct value for this is commonly "&D2." |
| Set hardware flow control (HFL) | Uses RTS/CTS (out-of-band) flow control. |
| Set software flow control (SFL) | Uses XON/XOFF (in-band) flow control. |

**Table 6–6** *Modem Attributes, Continued*

| Modem Attribute | Description |
|---|---|
| Lock to maximum DTE speed (SPD) | Instructs the modem to lock the speed at which it communicates to the router to a single rate, preferably the highest. This attribute is important and is often hard to find in manuals.<br>SPD is often linked to the hardware flow control variable. Look for phrases like "bps rate adjust" and "bit rate adjust."<br>Some modems set the speed to a value that depends on an S-register; other modems simply lock to the speed that was used when the last AT command was issued. Locking to the speed that was last used is handled automatically. To enable the S-register to set the speed, you must include the proper S-register value for the fastest possible DTE speed. |
| Best error control (BER) | Instructs the modem to negotiate its best error control with remote modems. For ARAP users, this is MNP5/LAPB, but not MNP4. |
| Best compression (BCP) | Instructs the modem to negotiate its best compression with remote modems. |
| No error control (NER) | Instructs the modem to negotiate no error control with remote modems. This will be used when placing outgoing (callback) ARAP calls. |
| No compression (NCP) | Instructs the modem to negotiate no compression with remote modems. This is used when placing outgoing (callback) ARAP calls. |
| No echo (NEC) | Requests the modem *not* to echo characters. This is commonly "E0." |
| No response codes (NRS) | Requests the modem *not* to send a response when you issue a command. This is commonly "Q1." |
| Set Caller ID (CID) | Requests that Caller ID information be returned when dialin occurs. Currently not used. |
| Miscellaneous strings (MSC) | Sends any extra commands that are needed for the modem to work (possibly with specific platforms). |
| Template entry (TPL) | This is the name of another modem type. It is referenced as the value of any of the previously listed attributes if they are not set on the current modem type. |

As an alternative to repeatedly entering the same data, use templates as a way to join modemcap entries. For example, consider the following modemcap entries:

```
modemcap entry gv_basics:FD=&F:AA=S0=1:CD=&C1:DTR=&D2:NEC=E0:NRS=Q1
modemcap entry global_village:HFL=&K3\\X1:BCP=%C1:NCP=%C0:TPL=gv_basics
modemcap entry gv_teleport:NCP=%C0:TPL=gv_basics
```

To look up the factory default for a global_village modem, perform the following steps:

**Step 1** Look at the global_village modemcap entry for the factory default (FD).

**Step 2** If you fail to find FD in global_village, look at the global_village modemcap entry for a template (TPL).

**Step 3** Find a TPL called "gv_basics."

**Step 4** Look in the gv_basics modemcap entry for the FD.

**Step 5** Find FD=&F in the gv_basics modemcap entry.

**Step 6** Use &F as the FD for the global_village.

### *Sample Display*

The following example shows the modem values in a Codex_3260:

```
show modemcap Codex_3260
```

### *Related Commands*

Search online to find documentation for related commands.

**modemcap edit**
**modemcap entry**

## SHOW NBF CACHE

Use the **show nbf cache** user level EXEC command to display NetBIOS name cache contents.

**show nbf cache**

### *Syntax Description*

This command has no arguments or keywords.

### *Command Mode*

EXEC

### *Usage Guidelines*

This command first appeared in Cisco IOS Release 11.1.

### *Sample Display*

The following is sample output from the **show nbf cache** command:

```
router> show nbf cache
 HW Addr            Name          How      Idle   NetBIOS Packet Savings
1000.5a89.449a    IKBA          E0       6      0
0000.0000.0000    NANOO         async1   21     0
```

Table 6–7 describes significant fields shown in the display.

**Table 6–7** *Show NBF Cache Field Descriptions*

| Field | Description |
|---|---|
| HW Addr | MAC address mapped to the NetBIOS name in this entry. |
| Name | NetBIOS name mapped to the MAC address in this entry. |
| How | Interface through which this information was learned. |
| Idle | Period of time (in seconds) since this entry was last accessed. A hyphen in this column indicates a static entry in the NetBIOS name cache. |
| NetBIOS Packet Savings | Number of packets to which local replies were made (thus preventing transmission of these packets over the network). |

### *Related Commands*

Search online to find documentation for related commands.

**netbios access-list**
**netbios input-access-filter**
**netbios name-cache**
**netbios nbf**
**netbios output-access-filter**
**show nbf sessions**

## SHOW NBF SESSIONS

Use the **show nbf sessions** user level EXEC command to view NetBEUI connection information.

**show nbf sessions**

### *Syntax Description*

This command has no arguments or keywords.

### *Command Mode*

EXEC

### Usage Guidelines

This command first appeared in Cisco IOS Release 11.1.

### Sample Display

The following is sample output from the **show nbf sessions** command:

```
router> show nbf sessions

Async6 NetBIOS Session Table:
Srcnum   Destnum  Dest-Interface DestMAC
8        6          Ethernet0 00aa.005b.c17b

NetBIOS Global Session Table:
Srcnum   Destnum    Dest-Interface DestMAC  Src-Interface SrcMac(I)


6        8          Async7 0000.0000.0000  Ethernet0 00aa.005b.c17b(95)
ADD_[GROUP]NAME_QUERY queuesize=0
STATUS_QUERY queuesize=0
STATUS_RESPONSE queuesize=0
NAME_QUERY queuesize=0
NAME_RECOGNIZED queuesize=0
SESSION_INITIALIZE queuesize=0
SESSION_INITIALIZE (pending) queuesize=0
```

Table 6–8 describes significant fields shown in the display.

**Table 6–8** *Show NBF Sessions Field Descriptions*

| Field | Description |
|---|---|
| **Interface NetBIOS Session Table:** | Summarizes Async/ISDN interface NetBIOS connection information. |
| Srcnum, Destnum | Source and destination connection numbers. |
| Dest-Interface, DestMAC | Destination interface and MAC address. |
| **Global NetBIOS Session Table:** | Summarizes LAN NetBIOS connection information. |
| Dest-Interface DestMAC | Destination interface (`Async7` in this case) and MAC address (`0000.0000.0000` in this case). |
| Src-Interface SrcMac | Source interface (`Ethernet0` in this case) and MAC address (`00aa.005b.c17b(95)` in this case). |
| **NetBIOS Datagram Queue Summary** | Summarizes NetBIOS pending datagram queues. |
| ADD_[GROUP]NAME_ QUERY | Add Group Name Query packets. |
| STATUS_QUERY | Status Query packets. |

**Table 6–8** *Show NBF Sessions Field Descriptions, Continued*

| Field | Description |
|---|---|
| STATUS_RESPONSE | Status Response packets. |
| NAME_QUERY | Name Query packets. |
| NAME_RECOGNIZED | Name Recognized packets. |
| SESSION_INITIALIZE (pending) | NetBIOS session Initialize packets. |

### *Related Commands*

Search online to find documentation for related commands.

**netbios access-list**
**netbios input-access-filter**
**netbios output-access-filter**
**netbios name-cache**
**netbios nbf**
**show nbf cache**

## SHOW USERS

To display information about the active lines on the router, use the **show users** user EXEC command.

**show users** [**all**]

| *Syntax* | *Description* |
|---|---|
| **all** | (Optional) Specifies that all lines be displayed, regardless of whether anyone is using them or not. |

### *Command Mode*

User EXEC

### *Usage Guidelines*

This command first appeared in a release prior to Cisco IOS Release 10.0.

This command displays the line number, connection name, idle time, and terminal location.

### *Sample Displays*

The following is sample output from the **show users** command:

```
router# show users
      Line            User            Host(s)         Idle Location
```

```
      0 con 0                         idle
*     2 vty 0        rose             idle           0    BASHFUL.CISCO.COM
```

The following is sample output from the **show users all** command:

```
router# show users all
   Line       User           Host(s)      Idle  Location
*  0 vty 0    rose           idle           0   BASHFUL.CISCO.COM
   1 vty 1
   2 con 0
   3 aux 0
   4 vty 2
```

The asterisk (*) indicates the current terminal session.

Table 6–9 describes significant fields shown in the displays.

**Table 6–9** *Show Users Field Descriptions*

| Field | Description |
|---|---|
| Line | Contains three subfields.<br>• The first subfield (0 in the sample output) is the absolute line number.<br>• The second subfield (VTY) indicates the type of line. Possible values follow:<br>con—Console<br>aux—Auxiliary port<br>tty—Asynchronous terminal port<br>vty—Virtual terminal<br>• The third subfield (0 in the * sample output) indicates the relative line number within the type. |
| User | User using the line. If no user is listed in this field, no one is using the line. |
| Host(s) | Host to which the user is connected (outgoing connection). A value of idle means that there is no outgoing connection to a host. |
| Idle | Interval (in minutes) since the user has entered something. |
| Location | Either the hard-wired location for the line or, if there is an incoming connection, the host from which incoming connection came. |

### *Related Commands*

Search online to find documentation for related commands.

**show users**

## START-CHARACTER

To set the flow control start character, use the **start-character** line configuration command. Use the **no** form of this command to remove the character.

**start-character** *ascii-number*
**no start-character**

| *Syntax* | *Description* |
| --- | --- |
| *ascii-number* | Decimal representation of the start character. |

### *Default*

Decimal 17

### *Command Mode*

Line configuration

### *Usage Guidelines*

This command first appeared in Cisco IOS Release 10.0.

This command defines the character that signals the start of data transmission when software flow control is in effect.

### *Example*

The following example changes the start character to Ctrl-B, which is decimal 2:

```
line 2
 start-character 2
```

### *Related Commands*

Search online to find documentation for related commands.

**flowcontrol**
**stop-character**
**terminal start-character**

## START-CHAT

To specify that a chat script start on a specified line at any point, use the **start-chat** privileged EXEC command. Use the **no** form of this command to stop the chat script.

**start-chat** *regexp* [*line-number* [*dialer-string*]]
**no start-chat**

| *Syntax* | *Description* |
|---|---|
| *regexp* | Specifies the name of a regular expression or modem script to be executed. If there is more than one script with a name that matches the argument *regexp*, the first script found is used. |
| *line-number* | (Optional) Indicates the line number on which to execute the chat script. If you do not specify a line number, the current line number is selected. If the specified line is busy, the script is not executed and an error message appears. If the dialer-string argument is specified, line-number must be entered; it is not optional if you specify a dialer string. This command functions only on physical terminal (TTY) lines. It does not function on virtual terminal (VTY) lines. |
| *dialer-string* | (Optional) String of characters (often a telephone number) to be sent to a DCE. If you enter a dialer string, you must also specify line-number, or the chat script *regexp* will not start. |

### *Command Mode*

Privileged EXEC

### *Usage Guidelines*

This command first appeared in Cisco IOS Release 10.0.

This command provides modem dialing commands for a chat script that you want to apply immediately to a line. If you do not specify a line, the script runs on the current line. If the specified line is already in use, the script is not activated and an error message appears.

The argument *regexp* is used to specify the name of the modem script that is to be executed. The first script that matches the argument in this command and the **dialer map** command is used. For more information about regular expressions, see Appendix C.

This command functions only on physical terminal (TTY) lines. It does not function on virtual terminal (VTY) lines.

### *Example*

The following example forces a dialout on line 8 using the script *telebit*:

```
start-chat telebit line 8
```

### *Related Commands*

Search online to find documentation for related commands.

**chat-script**
**dialer map modem-script system-script**
**dialer map modem-script system-script name**
**script activation**
**script connection**
**script dialer**
**script reset**
**script startup**

## STOP-CHARACTER

To set the flow control stop character, use the **stop-character** line configuration command. Use the **no** form of this command to remove the character.

**stop-character** *ascii-number*
**no stop-character**

| *Syntax* | *Description* |
|---|---|
| *ascii-number* | Decimal representation of the stop character. |

### *Default*

Decimal 19

### *Command Mode*

Line configuration

### *Usage Guidelines*

This command first appeared in Cisco IOS Release 10.0.

This command defines the character that signals the end of data transmission when software flow control is in effect.

### *Example*

The following example changes the stop character to Ctrl-E, which is decimal 5:

```
line 3
 stop-character 5
```

### *Related Commands*

Search online to find documentation for related commands.

**flowcontrol**
**start-character**
**terminal stop-character**

# CHAPTER 7

# Managing Modems

The Cisco IOS software provides commands that manage modems that reside inside access servers or routers in the form of modem cards. Cisco Systems does not consider external modems, which physically connect to an access server or router with an asynchronous cable or modem line, to be part of its modem management paradigm. For a complete description of the commands in this chapter, see Chapter 8, "Modem Management Commands."

This chapter consists of the following sections:

- Business Scenarios that Benefit from Managing Modems
- Cisco's Modem and Terminal Adapter Technology
- Manageable Versus Nonmanageable Modems
- Verifying Connection Speed Performance
- Automatically Running a Modem Diagnostics Test
- Displaying Local Disconnect Reasons
- Upgrading Modem Firmware for 56K, V.34, and V.110 Cards
- Controlling Modems
- Collecting Modem Statistics
- Changing Modem Configuration

## Business Scenarios that Benefit from Managing Modems

Figure 7–1 shows a typical large-scale dial scenario for an Internet service provider. Modem management commands are useful for gathering call statistics and upgrading modem firmware for large modem pools.

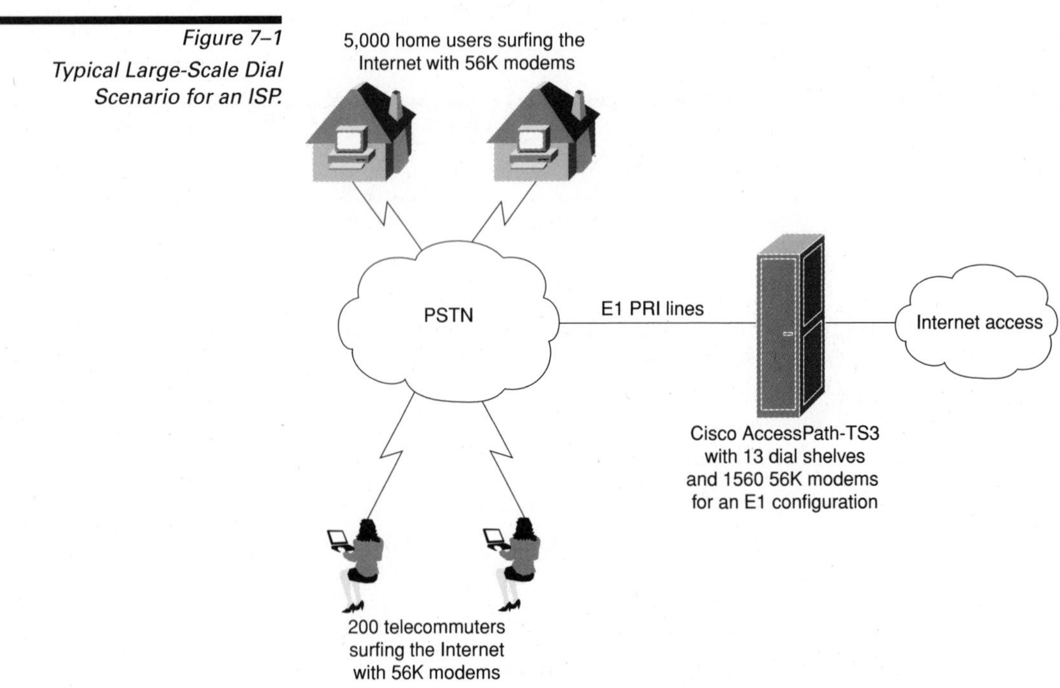


*Figure 7–1 Typical Large-Scale Dial Scenario for an ISP.*

Figure 7–2 shows a typical dial scenario for an enterprise network.

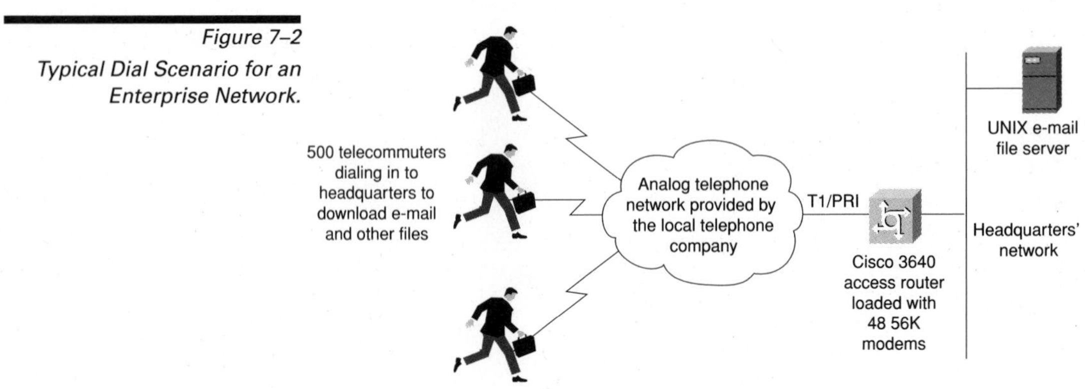


*Figure 7–2 Typical Dial Scenario for an Enterprise Network.*

## CISCO'S MODEM AND TERMINAL ADAPTER TECHNOLOGY

Cisco Systems installs the following different types of modems and terminal adapter cards in some of its access devices:

- 56K Modems
- V.110 Terminal Adapters
- V.34 Modems

Table 7-1 shows which Cisco access devices provide hardware support for these dial technologies.

**Table 7–1** *Available Modems and Terminal Adapters*

| Type of Modem or Terminal Adapter | Cisco AS5200 | Cisco AS5300 | Cisco 3600 Series | Cisco AccessPath Integrated Access System |
|---|---|---|---|---|
| 56K modem card | Yes | Yes | Yes | Yes |
| V.110 terminal adapter module | Yes | No | No | No |
| V.34 modem card | Yes | Yes | Yes | Yes |

### 56K Modems

The 56K modems are used for making high-speed connections across digital networks. Ultimately, this means that files transmitted at up to 56 Kbps arrive at the desktop nearly twice as fast as standard V.34 (28.8-Kbps) connections. The wait for information is reduced by nearly 50 percent.

The 56K modems are ideal for serious Internet users who want to quickly dial in to corporate LANs or download Web pages containing sound, video, graphics, and other large files over digital networks using standard telephone lines.

Traditional modems assume that both ends of a modem conversation use an analog connection over the public switched telephone network. Data signals are converted from digital to analog and back again to digital, limiting transmission speeds to 33.6 Kbps. The 56K modems, however, assume that one end of the modem conversation has a pure digital connection to the phone network and takes advantage of the high-speed digital connection. This is a new technique where the network is viewed as a digital transmission medium and the data is encoded for transmission over an end user's telephone line, which is also known as the local loop. The downstream data is digitally encoded instead of being modulated. Upstream analog-to-digital communication at the local loop can transmit up to 33.6 Kbps. Downstream digital-to-analog communication at the local loop can transmit up to 56 Kbps. To maximize channel bandwidth for 56 Kbps connections, the Integrated Services Digital Network Primary Rate Interface (ISDN PRI) must be used. (See Figure 7–3.)

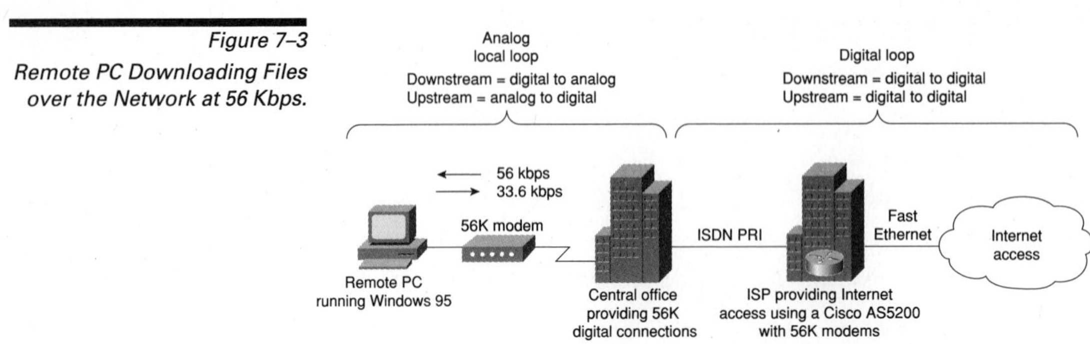


*Figure 7–3 Remote PC Downloading Files over the Network at 56 Kbps.*

Special digital signal processor (DSP) software is used in conjunction with 56K modem firmware to enable speeds up to 56 Kbps. Both DSP and modem firmware are posted on the Cisco Connection Online (CCO) FTP server for upgrading purposes. Upgrade instructions are provided in section "Upgrading Modem Firmware for 56K, V.34, and V.110 Cards," found later in this chapter.

The following prerequisites apply to 56K modems:

- K56flex-compatible modems must be present at both ends of a digital connection in a digital network. K56 requires a client-side modem and a server-side modem. If not, this speed cannot be achieved. All modem connections fall back to V.34 speeds.
- Only one analog loop can be in the end-to-end communications path.
- You cannot have any A-law to U-law conversions, which exist at some international gateways.

### V.110 Terminal Adapters

V.110 is a bit rate adaptation protocol defined by International Telecommunication Union (ITU). V.110 provides a standard method of encapsulating data over Global System for Mobile Telecommunications (GSM) and ISDN networks. A Cisco AS5200 loaded with V.110 terminal adapter modules provides corporate or Internet access to GSM mobile users.

The 12 port V.110 terminal adapter connects to the AS5200 TDM bus via the universal carrier card. There can be up to five V.110 modules in one Cisco AS5200, which is capable of terminating 60 V.110 sessions. Modem and V.110 terminal adapter port modules can coexist in the same Cisco AS5200. Based on ISDN Q.931 call bearer information, the Cisco IOS software calls to the appropriate port module for termination. For example, analog calls are terminated by the modem modules, GSM calls are serviced by the V.110 terminal adapter modules, and ISDN calls are sent to the PPP termination engine. This flexibility allows for the providing of one telephone number to users for analog, GSM, and ISDN data calls.

Figure 7–4 shows a dial-in scenario demonstrating how V.110 technology can be used with Cisco AS5200 access servers.

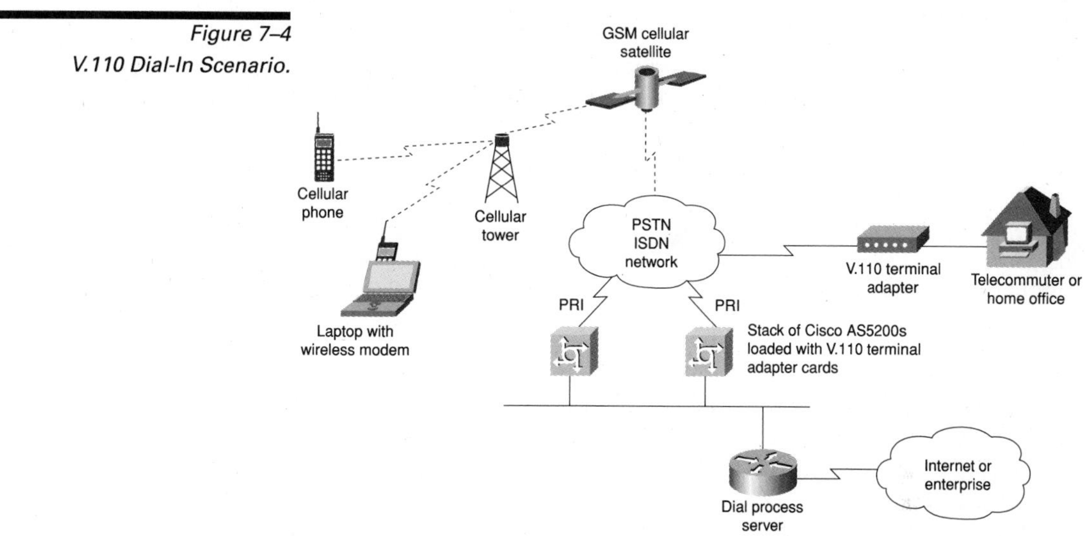


*Figure 7–4*
*V.110 Dial-In Scenario.*

### V.34 Modems

Recommendation V.34 is the name of the standard that defines how modems should operate at 28.8 Kbps. The previous standard for high-speed modem communication was V.32bis, which defined how modems should operate at 14.4 Kbps.

## Manageable Versus Nonmanageable Modems

Depending on which modem license you purchase with your access server or router, Cisco modems are either manageable or not manageable by the Cisco IOS software.

Manageable modems support the one out-of-band feature, which is used for gathering modem performance statistics and transmitting attention (AT) commands. Nonmanageable modems do not support the out-of-band feature nor the functionality associated with manageable modems. As you read through this chapter, note which commands apply to manageable versus nonmanageable modems.

Table 7–2 provides a summary of the Cisco IOS commands supported by manageable modems versus nonmanageable modems.

**Table 7–2** *Commands for Manageable versus Nonmanageable Modems*

| Modem Commands | Supported by Manageable Modems | Supported by Nonmanageable Modems |
|---|---|---|
| clear modem | Yes | Yes |
| clear modem at-mode | Yes | No |

**Table 7–2** *Commands for Manageable versus Nonmanageable Modems, Continued*

| Modem Commands | Supported by Manageable Modems | Supported by Nonmanageable Modems |
|---|---|---|
| clear modem counters | Yes | No |
| copy modem | Yes | Yes |
| modem at-mode | Yes | No |
| modem at-mode-permit | Yes | No |
| modem autotest | Yes | Yes |
| modem bad | Yes | Yes |
| modem buffer-size | Yes | No |
| modem busyout | Yes | Yes |
| modem hold-reset | Yes | Yes |
| modem poll time | Yes | No |
| modem recovery-time | Yes | No |
| modem shutdown | Yes | Yes |
| modem startup-test | Yes | Yes |
| modem status-poll | Yes | No |
| show modem | Yes | Yes |
| show modem at-mode | Yes | No |
| show modem call-stats | Yes | No |
| show modem connect-speeds | Yes | No |
| show modem cookie | Yes | Yes |
| show modem csm | Yes | Yes |
| show modem log | Yes | Yes |
| show modem summary | Yes | No |
| show modem test | Yes | Yes |
| show modem version | Yes | Yes |
| test modem back-to-back | Yes | Yes |

### VERIFYING CONNECTION SPEED PERFORMANCE

Making sure that your modems are connecting at the correct connection speeds is an important aspect of managing modems. To display modem connection speed statistics for a specific modem or range of modems, use the following EXEC commands:

| Command | Purpose |
|---|---|
| **show modem connect-speeds** [*max-speed* [slot]] | Displays connection speed statistics for all the modems. |
| **show modem** [*slot/port* \| **group** *number*] | Displays a high-level performance report for all the modems or a single modem. |

These commands also provide performance information to investigate possible bad or corrupt modems or T1/E1 lines. For example, suppose you have an access server that is fully populated with V.34 modems. If you notice that modem 1/0 is only getting V.34 connections 50% of the time, whereas all the other modems are getting V.34 connections 80% of the time, then modem 1/0 is probably malfunctioning or bad. If you are reading low connection speeds across all the modems, you may have a faulty channelized T1 or ISDN PRI line connection.

To display connection speed information for all modems running in your system, use the **show modem connect-speeds** *max-speed* EXEC command. Because most terminal screens are not wide enough to display the entire range of connection speeds at one time (for example, 75 to 56,000 bps), the *max-speed* variable is used. This variable specifies the contents of a shifting baud-rate window, which provides you with a snapshot of the modem connection speeds for your system. Replace the *max-speed* argument with the maximum connect speed that you want to view. You can specify from 12,000 to 56,000 bps. If you are interested in viewing a snapshot of lower baud rates, specify a lower connection speed. If you are interested in viewing a snapshot of higher baud rates, specify a higher connection speed.

See Chapter 8 for a complete description of each of the fields displayed in the following Microcom modem example:

```
router# show modem connect-speeds 33600

  transmit connect speeds

  Mdm    14400  16800  19200  21600  24000  26400  28800  31200  33600 TotCnt
* 0/0        0      0      0      0      0      0      4      4      1      9
* 0/1        2      0      0      0      0      0      3      3      1      9
  0/2        2      0      0      0      0      1      2      4      1     10
* 0/3        0      0      0      1      0      0      3      4      1      9
* 0/4        1      0      0      0      0      2      2      1      1      7
* 0/5        0      0      0      0      0      0      4      4      1      9
* 0/6        0      0      0      0      0      1      3      3      1      8
* 0/7        0      0      0      2      0      0      4      3      1     10
* 0/8        2      0      0      0      0      0      3      4      1     10
```

```
* 0/9       0     0     0     0     0     0     4     3     0     7
* 0/10      1     0     0     0     0     1     3     2     1     8
* 0/11      0     0     0     0     0     0     4     3     1     8
  0/12      1     0     0     0     0     0     4     2     1     8
* 0/13      0     0     0     0     0     0     4     2     1     7
* 0/14      1     0     0     0     0     1     2     2     1     7
* 0/15      0     0     0     0     0     0     4     2     1     7
* 0/16      0     0     0     1     0     0     3     2     1     7
* 0/17      1     0     0     0     0     0     4     2     1     8
* 0/18      1     0     0     0     0     0     3     3     1     8
* 0/19      0     0     0     0     0     0     5     3     1     9
* 0/20      0     0     0     0     0     0     4     2     1     7
* 0/21      1     0     0     0     0     0     4     2     0     7
* 0/22      0     0     0     0     0     0     7     9     1    17
* 0/23      0     0     0     0     0     2     2     3     1     8
* 2/0       0     0     0     1     0     0     3     3     1     8
* 2/1       0     0     0     0     0     0     5     2     1     8
* 2/2       0     0     0     1     0     0     4     1     1     7
* 2/3       1     0     0     0     0     0     4     2     1     8
* 2/4       0     0     0     0     0     0     5     2     1     8
* 2/5       0     0     0     0     0     0     4     3     1     8
* 2/6       0     0     0     0     0     0     3     2     1     6
* 2/7       1     0     0     0     0     1     3     2     0     7
* 2/8       1     0     0     0     0     0     3     2     1     7
* 2/9       0     0     0     0     0     1     3     2     1     7
* 2/10      2     0     0     0     0     2     1     0     1     6
* 2/11      0     0     0     1     0     1     3     5     1    11
* 2/12      0     0     0     0     0     0     5     2     1     8
* 2/13      1     0     0     0     0     0     5     0     1     7
* 2/14      1     0     0     0     0     0     3     3     1     8
* 2/15      1     0     0     0     0     1     2     3     1     8
* 2/16      0     0     0     0     0     0     4     3     1     8
* 2/17      0     0     0     0     0     0     5    11     0    16
* 2/18      0     0     0     1     0     1     1     2     1     6
* 2/19      0     0     0     0     0     0     2     3     1     6
* 2/20      1     0     0     0     0     2     3     9     1    16
* 2/21      1     0     0     0     0     0     4     1     1     7
* 2/22      0     0     0     1     0     0     2     3     1     7
* 2/23      0     0     0     0     0     1     3     3     1     8
  Tot      23     0     0     9     0    18   165   141    44   400
  Tot %     5     0     0     2     0     4    41    35    11

  receive connect speeds

  Mdm   14400 16800 19200 21600 24000 26400 28800 31200 33600 TotCnt
* 0/0       0     0     0     0     0     4     1     3     1     9
* 0/1       2     0     0     0     0     3     1     2     1     9
  0/2       2     0     0     0     0     3     1     3     1    10
* 0/3       0     0     0     1     0     3     4     0     1     9
* 0/4       1     0     0     0     0     4     0     1     1     7
* 0/5       0     0     0     0     0     4     3     1     1     9
* 0/6       0     0     0     0     0     4     0     3     1     8
* 0/7       0     0     0     2     0     4     1     2     1    10
* 0/8       2     0     0     0     0     3     0     5     0    10
```

```
  * 0/9      0     0     0     0     0     4     2     0     1     7
  * 0/10     1     0     0     0     0     4     0     2     1     8
  * 0/11     0     0     0     0     0     4     0     3     1     8
    0/12     1     0     0     0     0     2     2     2     1     8
  * 0/13     0     0     0     0     0     4     1     1     1     7
  * 0/14     1     0     0     0     0     2     3     0     1     7
  * 0/15     0     0     0     0     0     4     1     1     1     7
  * 0/16     0     0     0     1     0     3     2     0     1     7
  * 0/17     1     0     0     0     0     4     1     1     1     8
  * 0/18     1     0     0     0     0     3     2     1     1     8
  * 0/19     0     0     0     0     0     5     1     2     1     9
  * 0/20     0     0     0     0     0     4     0     3     0     7
  * 0/21     1     0     0     0     0     4     0     1     1     7
  * 0/22     0     0     0     0     0     6     6     4     1    17
  * 0/23     0     0     0     0     0     4     2     1     1     8
  * 2/0      0     0     0     1     0     3     1     2     1     8
  * 2/1      0     0     0     0     0     3     3     1     1     8
  * 2/2      0     0     0     1     0     4     0     1     1     7
  * 2/3      1     0     0     0     0     3     2     1     1     8
  * 2/4      0     0     0     0     0     4     2     1     1     8
  * 2/5      0     0     0     0     0     4     1     2     1     8
  * 2/6      0     0     0     0     0     3     0     3     0     6
  * 2/7      1     0     0     0     1     2     2     0     1     7
  * 2/8      1     0     0     0     0     3     0     2     1     7
  * 2/9      0     0     0     0     0     4     1     1     1     7
  * 2/10     2     0     0     0     0     3     0     0     1     6
  * 2/11     0     0     0     1     0     3     1     5     1    11
  * 2/12     0     0     0     0     0     4     3     0     1     8
  * 2/13     1     0     0     0     0     2     3     0     1     7
  * 2/14     1     0     0     0     0     3     2     1     1     8
  * 2/15     1     0     0     0     0     3     0     3     1     8
  * 2/16     0     0     0     0     0     4     0     4     0     8
  * 2/17     0     0     0     0     0     5     2     8     1    16
  * 2/18     0     0     1     0     0     2     1     1     1     6
  * 2/19     0     0     0     0     0     2     2     1     1     6
  * 2/20     1     0     0     0     0     4     2     8     1    16
  * 2/21     1     0     0     0     0     4     0     1     1     7
  * 2/22     0     0     1     0     0     2     0     3     1     7
  * 2/23     0     0     0     0     0     4     2     1     1     8
   Tot      23     0     2     7     1   167    64    92    44   400
   Tot %     5     0     0     1     0    41    16    23    11
```

The following example shows the connection statistics for modem 1/2, which is a V.34 Microcom modem. See Chapter 8 for a complete description of each of the displayed fields:

```
router# show modem 1/2
Mdm  Typ    Status     Tx/Rx        G  Duration  TX  RX  RTS  CTS  DSR  DCD  DTR
1/2  V34    Idle     26400/28800    1  00:18:42           x    x    x         x

Modem 1/2, Microcom (Select), Async3, TTY3
Firmware (Boot) Rev: 3.1(30) (3.0(4))
DSP Controller (SPX) Rev: 1.1(0) (1.1(0))
Modem config: Incoming and Outgoing
Protocol: reliable/LAPM, Compression: V42bis
Management port config: Status polling and AT session
```

```
Management port status: Status polling and AT session
TX signals: -13 dBm, RX signals: -19 dBm

  Last clearing of "show modem" counters never
    122 incoming completes, 6 incoming failures
    0 outgoing completes, 0 outgoing failures
    0 failed dial attempts, 0 ring no answers, 0 busied outs
    0 no dial tones, 0 dial timeouts, 0 watchdog timeouts
    6 no carriers, 0 link failures, 2 resets, 0 recover oob
    0 protocol timeouts, 0 protocol errors, 0 lost events

Transmit Speed Counters:

Connection Speeds         75      300      600     1200     2400     4800
# of connections           0        0        0        0        0        0
Connection Speeds       7200     9600    12000    14400    16800    19200
# of connections           0        0        1        1        2        3
Connection Speeds      21600    24000    26400    28800    31200    32000
# of connections          18       13       51       32        1        0
Connection Speeds      33600    34000    36000    38000    40000    42000
# of connections           0        0        0        0        0        0
Connection Speeds      44000    46000    48000    50000    52000    54000
# of connections           0        0        0        0        0        0
Connection Speeds      56000
# of connections           0

Receive Speed Counters:

Connection Speeds         75      300      600     1200     2400     4800
# of connections           0        0        0        0        0        0
Connection Speeds       7200     9600    12000    14400    16800    19200
# of connections           0        0        1        1        0        3
Connection Speeds      21600    24000    26400    28800    31200    32000
# of connections           2       16       60       39        0        0
Connection Speeds      33600    34000    36000    38000    40000    42000
# of connections           0        0        0        0        0        0
Connection Speeds      44000    46000    48000    50000    52000    54000
# of connections           0        0        0        0        0        0
Connection Speeds      56000
# of connections           0
```

The next example shows example output for the **show modem** command. See Chapter 8 for a complete description of each of the displayed fields:

```
router# show modem
                Inc calls      Out calls     Busied   Failed  No      Succ
  Mdm  Usage    Succ   Fail    Succ   Fail   Out      Dial    Answer  Pct.
* 1/0    37%      98      4      0      0        0       0       0     96%
  1/1    38%      98      2      0      0        0       0       0     98%
  1/2    35%     122      6      0      0        0       0       0     95%
  1/3    37%     104      4      0      0        0       0       0     96%
* 1/4    39%     104      5      0      0        0       1       1     95%
* 1/5    37%      96      4      0      0        0       0       0     96%
* 1/6    37%     120      6      0      0        0       0       0     95%
  1/7    34%     130      5      0      0        0       0       0     96%
```

```
  1/8     39%    111     6     0     0     0     1     1    94%
  1/9     37%    108     4     0     0     0     0     0    96%
* 1/10    39%    115     8     0     0     0     0     0    93%
* 1/11    37%     86     3     0     0     0     0     0    96%
* 1/12    38%    121     3     0     0     0     1     1    97%
  1/13    35%    107     6     0     0     0     0     0    94%
* 1/14    37%     92     5     0     0     0     0     0    94%
  1/15    41%    106     9     0     0     0     0     0    92%
  1/16    35%    112     6     0     0     0     0     0    94%
  1/17    39%    101     3     0     0     0     0     0    97%
  1/18    40%    102     7     0     0     0     0     0    93%
  1/19    37%     93     3     0     0     0     0     0    96%
  1/20    42%     97     4     0     0     0     0     0    96%
  1/21    38%     86     5     0     0     0     0     0    94%
* 1/22    40%    104    10     0     0     0     0     0    91%
  1/23    41%     76     5     0     0     0     0     0    93%
```

## AUTOMATICALLY RUNNING A MODEM DIAGNOSTICS TEST

You can automatically run a diagnostics test on modems inside access servers, such as a Cisco AS5200 loaded with Microcom modems. Modems that fail the test are automatically busied out of service. To run the test, issue the **modem autotest** global configuration command, which is described in the following sections:

- How the Modem Autotest Works
- Preliminary Usage Guidelines
- Setting Up the Modem Autotest
- Modem Autotest Example
- Manually Isolating a Back-to-Back Modem Test Example

**NOTES**

The modem autotest feature is not supported on the Cisco 3600 series routers populated with MICA digital modem cards. However, the Cisco 3600 series does support a limited power on startup test, which automatically removes inoperable modems from dial-up services.

### How the Modem Autotest Works

The access server or router performs the test by automatically conducting a series of back-to-back connections and data transfers between two internal modems. The data transfer consists of sending one packet that is 10-bytes large between two modems. All modem test connections occur inside the system. A modem involved in a back-to-back modem test is temporarily marked as busy, which means the modem will not accept a call while the test is running.

If all modems are currently active and the modem autotest is activated, the test will wait until at least two modems drop their calls and become available. The modem autotest moves on to test a second pair of modems as soon as two additional modems become available, and so on. To disable the modem autotest at any time, issue the **no modem autotest** command.

### Preliminary Usage Guidelines

It is recommended that you set the modem autotest to run during off-peak hours. This timing provides maximum access to your remote users. For example, if you are an Internet service provider and your peak dial-in hours are between 5:00 p.m. and 12:00 p.m. on weekdays, configure the test to run automatically at 3:00 a.m. on Saturday mornings. Bad or inoperable modems detected by the test will automatically be busied out. See Figure 7–5.

*Figure 7–5*
*Sample Demand Curve for Dial Access.*

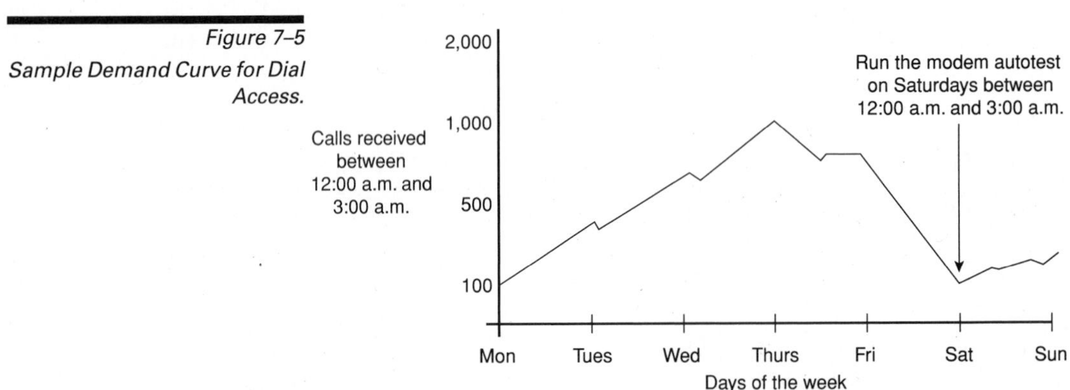


There are specific syntax functions used for the **modem autotest time** ***hh:mm*** [*interval#*] command. The required **time** ***hh:mm*** parameter specifies the start time to initiate the test in hours and minutes (hh:mm; for example 1:00 a.m. is specified as 01:00). By default, the test runs once every 24 hours when enabled. The modem autotest feature synchronizes its timing with the access server's internal clock. The *interval#* parameter gives you the opportunity to specify which day and hour of the week you want the test to run. In place of the interval parameter specify the hour that you want to start the test, which can be between 1 and 168 hours ahead of the current time. For example, suppose that today is Friday and the current time on the access server is 3:00 p.m. If you want the test to run once every Saturday at 3:00 a.m., enter the **modem autotest time 03:00 168** command (03:00 = 3:00 a.m. in military time; 168 = 7 days).

Use the **show clock** EXEC command to determine the current time set on the access server.

Use the **show modem test** EXEC command to see the results of the modem autotest. This command displays which modems were tested and the results of the test. You can also use the **show modem** EXEC command to see which modems are marked bad by the **modem autotest** command. To disable the test at any time, issue the **no modem autotest** command.

### Setting Up the Modem Autotest

To set up the modem autotest, perform the following tasks beginning in EXEC mode:

| Task | | Command |
|---|---|---|
| **Step 1** | Take note of the current time set on the access server or router. The modem autotest synchronizes with this time. Be sure this clock matches the current actual time in your time zone. | **show clock** |
| **Step 2** | Enter global configuration mode. | **configure terminal** |
| **Step 3** | Specify the time you want the modem test to automatically begin. Express it in hours and minutes in military time.* | **modem autotest time** *hh*:*mm* [*interval*] |
| **Step 4** | Set the minimum number of modems that will remain untested and available to accept calls during each test cycle. The default is six modems. | **modem autotest minimum** *number* |
| **Step 5** | Specify a maximum consecutive modem error count that will trigger the modem autotest. You can configure the system to watch for between 3 and 50 errors before the modem autotest begins. To view the list of monitored errors, issue the **show modem call-stats** command. | **modem autotest error** *threshold* |
| **Step 6** | Return to EXEC mode. | **exit** |
| **Step 7** | Display the results of the modem autotest after it has run. | **show modem test** |
| **Step 8** | Display the complete list of which modems are marked bad versus good.† | **show modem** |
| **Step 9** | Clear the log or test report that is displayed by the **show modem test** command. If you do not clear the test regularly, eventually the oldest test report will replace by the current test report. | **clear modem test** |

*Do not forget to include the required colon (:) between the hours parameter (hh) and the minutes parameter (mm).
†Inoperable or bad modems are marked with a "B" appearing before the slot/port.

### Modem Autotest Example

The following example shows how to set the modem autotest to run once per week on Tuesdays at 3:00 a.m. Additionally, the autotest will activate if the system detects a modem error count higher than 40 errors.

**Step 1** Use the **set clock** EXEC command to determine the current time set on the router or access server. In this example, the time and date set on the following router is 3:00 p.m, Monday, August 25, 1997.

```
router# show clock
*15:00:01.031 EST Aug 25 1997
```

**Step 2** Enter global configuration mode and set the modem autotest using the **modem autotest time** command. In this example, the access server is configured to run the modem autotest every Tuesday at 3:00 a.m.

```
router# configure terminal
Enter configuration commands, one per line.  End with CNTL/Z.
router(config)# modem autotest time 03:00 168
```

**Step 3** Configure the autotest to activate if the system detects a high modem error count. In this example, the autotest activates if the system detects a modem error count higher than 40 errors. To view the list of monitored errors, issue the **show modem call-stats** EXEC command.

```
router(config)# modem autotest error 40
router(config)# exit
router#
%SYS-5-CONFIG_I: Configured from console by console
router#
```

**Step 4** Display the results of the modem autotest after the test has run through a test cycle by issuing the **show modem test** EXEC command:

```
router# show modem test
 Date  Time     Modem        Test              Reason         State    Result
 5/15 07:25:17 AM  1/0     Back-To-Back        TIME INTERVAL   Idle       FAIL
 5/15 07:25:17 AM  1/1     Back-To-Back        TIME INTERVAL   Idle       PASS
 5/15 07:25:17 AM  1/2     Back-To-Back        TIME INTERVAL   Idle       PASS
 5/15 07:25:17 AM  1/3     Back-To-Back        TIME INTERVAL   Idle       FAIL
 5/15 07:25:17 AM  1/4     Back-To-Back        TIME INTERVAL   Idle       PASS
 5/15 07:25:17 AM  1/5     Back-To-Back        TIME INTERVAL   Idle       PASS
 5/15 07:25:17 AM  1/6     Back-To-Back        TIME INTERVAL   Idle       PASS
 5/15 07:25:17 AM  1/7     Back-To-Back        TIME INTERVAL   Idle       PASS
 5/15 07:25:17 AM  1/8     Back-To-Back        TIME INTERVAL   Idle       PASS
 5/15 07:25:17 AM  1/9     Back-To-Back        TIME INTERVAL   Idle       PASS
...
```

Alternatively, you can view which modems were marked bad by the modem autotest by issuing the **show modem** EXEC command. Bad modems are marked by the letter B. In this example, modem 1/0 and 1/3 are marked bad, which takes them out of commission and makes them unable to participate in dial services.

```
router# show modem
%SYS-5-CONFIG_I: Configured from console by consolem
                 Inc calls       Out calls      Busied   Failed  No        Succ
  Mdm   Usage   Succ     Fail   Succ     Fail   Out      Dial    Answer    Pct.
B 1/0     0%       0        0      0        0        1       0        0      0%
  1/1     0%       0        0      0        0        3       0        0      0%
  1/2     0%       0        0      0        0        1       0        0      0%
B 1/3     0%       0        0      0        0        1       0        0      0%
  1/4     0%       0        0      0        0        1       0        0      0%
  1/5     0%       0        0      0        0        1       0        0      0%
  1/6     0%       0        0      0        0        1       0        0      0%
  1/7     0%       0        0      0        0        1       0        0      0%
  1/8     0%       0        0      0        0        1       0        0      0%
  1/9     0%       0        0      0        0        1       0        0      0%
  1/10    0%       0        0      0        0        1       0        0      0%
  1/11    0%       0        0      0        0        1       0        0      0%
  1/12    0%       0        0      0        0        1       0        0      0%
  1/13    0%       0        0      0        0        1       0        0      0%
  1/14    0%       0        0      0        0        1       0        0      0%
  1/15    0%       0        0      0        0        1       0        0      0%
  1/16    0%       0        0      0        0        1       0        0      0%
  1/17    0%       0        0      0        0        1       0        0      0%
  1/18    0%       0        0      0        0        0       0        0      0%
  1/19    0%       0        0      0        0        0       0        0      0%
  1/20    0%       0        0      0        0        0       0        0      0%
  1/21    0%       0        0      0        0        0       0        0      0%
  1/22    0%       0        0      0        0        0       0        0      0%
  1/23    0%       0        0      0        0        0       0        0      0%
```

## Manually Isolating a Back-to-Back Modem Test Example

You can also manually isolate an internal back-to-back connection and data transfer between two modems for focused troubleshooting purposes. For example, if mobile users cannot dial in to modem 2/5 (which is the sixth modem port on the modem board in the second chassis slot), attempt a back-to-back test with modem 2/5 and a modem known to be functioning, such as modem 2/6. To do this, issue the **test modem back-to-back** *slot/port slot/port*.

You might need to enable this command on several different combinations of modems to determine which one is not functioning properly. A pair of operable modems successfully connect and complete transmitting data in both directions. An operable modem and an inoperable modem do not successfully connect with each other. Perform the following steps:

**Step 1** Perform a back-to-back modem test between two normal functioning modems. This example shows a successful connection between modem 1/1 and modem 1/0, which verifies normal operating conditions between these two modems.

```
AS5200# test modem back-to-back 1/1 1/0
Repetitions (of 10-byte packets) [1]: 10
AS5200#
%MODEM-5-B2BCONNECT: Modems (1/1) and (1/0) connected in back-to-back test:
CONN
ECT9600/REL-MNP
```

```
%MODEM-5-B2BMODEMS: Modems (1/0) and (1/1) completed back-to-back test:
success/
packets = 20/20
```

After you enter the **test modem back-to-back** command, you must define the number of packets transmitted between modems at the *Repetitions* prompt. The ideal range of packets to transmit and receive is from 1 to 100. The default is 1 packet that is 10-bytes large. The response message (for example, "success/packets = 2/2") tells you how many packets were successfully sent in *both* directions compared to the total number of packets attempted to be sent in both directions. Because the software reports the packet total in both directions, the reported numbers are *two times* the number you originally specify.

**Step 2** When modem 1/1 is tested against modem 1/3, the back-to-back modem test fails. Therefore, modem 1/3 is suspected or proven to be inoperable or bad.

```
router# test modem back-to-back 1/1 1/3
Repetitions (of 10-byte packets) [1]: 10
router#
%MODEM-5-BADMODEMS: Modems (1/3) and (1/1) failed back-to-back test:
NOCARRIER
```

**Step 3** Manually mark modem 1/3 as an inoperable or bad modem. To do this, you must first find out which line number corresponds with modem 1/3. By issuing the **show modem 1/3** EXEC command, you can see that TTY line number 4 (shown as TTY4) is used for modem 1/3.

```
router# show modem 1/3
Mdm  Typ    Status     Tx/Rx       G  Duration  TX  RX  RTS  CTS  DSR  DCD  DTR
1/3  V34    Idle    28800/28800    0  00:00:00           x    x    x    x    x

Modem 1/3, Microcom MNP10 V34 Modem (Managed), TTY4
Firmware (Boot) Rev: 1.0(23) (1.0(5))
Modem config: Incoming and Outgoing
Protocol: reliable/MNP, Compression: V42bis
Management port config: Status polling and AT session
Management port status: Status polling and AT session
TX signals: -15 dBm, RX signals: -17 dBm

  Last clearing of "show modem" counters never
    0 incoming completes, 0 incoming failures
    0 outgoing completes, 0 outgoing failures
    0 failed dial attempts, 0 ring no answers, 1 busied outs
    0 no dial tones, 0 dial timeouts, 0 watchdog timeouts
    0 no carriers, 0 link failures, 0 resets, 0 recover oob
    0 protocol timeouts, 0 protocol errors, 0 lost events

Transmit Speed Counters:

Connection Speeds           75      300      600     1200     2400     4800
# of connections             0        0        0        0        0        0
Connection Speeds         7200     9600    12000    14400    16800    19200
# of connections             0        0        0        0        0        0
Connection Speeds        21600    24000    26400    28800    31200    32000
```

```
# of connections             0        0        0        1        0        0
Connection Speeds        33600    34000    36000    38000    40000    42000
# of connections             0        0        0        0        0        0
Connection Speeds        44000    46000    48000    50000    52000    54000
# of connections             0        0        0        0        0        0
Connection Speeds        56000
# of connections             0
```

**Step 4** Enter line configuration mode and manually remove modem 1/3 from dial services by issuing the **modem bad** command on line 4:

```
router# configure terminal
router(config)# line 4
router(config-line)# modem bad
router(config-line)# exit
router(config)# exit
router#
```

**Step 5** Issue the **show modem** EXEC command or the **show modem** *slot/port* command to display the bad modem status.

Bad modems are marked with the letter B in the **show modem** command display output:

```
router# show modem
%SYS-5-CONFIG_I: Configured from console by consolem
                   Inc calls       Out calls     Busied    Failed  No        Succ
  Mdm    Usage    Succ    Fail    Succ    Fail    Out       Dial    Answer    Pct.
  1/0      0%       0       0       0       0       1        0        0        0%
  1/1      0%       0       0       0       0       3        0        0        0%
  1/2      0%       0       0       0       0       1        0        0        0%
B 1/3      0%       0       0       0       0       1        0        0        0%
  1/4      0%       0       0       0       0       1        0        0        0%
  1/5      0%       0       0       0       0       1        0        0        0%
  1/6      0%       0       0       0       0       1        0        0        0%
  1/7      0%       0       0       0       0       1        0        0        0%
  1/8      0%       0       0       0       0       1        0        0        0%
  1/9      0%       0       0       0       0       1        0        0        0%
  1/10     0%       0       0       0       0       1        0        0        0%
  1/11     0%       0       0       0       0       1        0        0        0%
  1/12     0%       0       0       0       0       1        0        0        0%
  1/13     0%       0       0       0       0       1        0        0        0%
  1/14     0%       0       0       0       0       1        0        0        0%
  1/15     0%       0       0       0       0       1        0        0        0%
  1/16     0%       0       0       0       0       1        0        0        0%
  1/17     0%       0       0       0       0       1        0        0        0%
  1/18     0%       0       0       0       0       0        0        0        0%
  1/19     0%       0       0       0       0       0        0        0        0%
  1/20     0%       0       0       0       0       0        0        0        0%
  1/21     0%       0       0       0       0       0        0        0        0%
  1/22     0%       0       0       0       0       0        0        0        0%
  1/23     0%       0       0       0       0       0        0        0        0%
```

Bad modems are also marked as *Bad* in the Status column of the **show modem** *slot/port* command's display output:

```
router# show modem 1/3
Mdm  Typ    Status     Tx/Rx        G  Duration  TX  RX  RTS  CTS  DSR  DCD  DTR
1/3  V34     Bad     28800/28800   0  00:00:00              x    x    x    x    x

Modem 1/3, Microcom MNP10 V34 Modem (Managed), TTY4
Firmware (Boot) Rev: 1.0(23) (1.0(5))
Modem config: Incoming and Outgoing
Protocol: reliable/MNP, Compression: V42bis
Management port config: Status polling and AT session
Management port status: Status polling and AT session
TX signals: -15 dBm, RX signals: -17 dBm

  Last clearing of "show modem" counters never
    0 incoming completes, 0 incoming failures
    0 outgoing completes, 0 outgoing failures
    0 failed dial attempts, 0 ring no answers, 1 busied outs
    0 no dial tones, 0 dial timeouts, 0 watchdog timeouts
    0 no carriers, 0 link failures, 0 resets, 0 recover oob
    0 protocol timeouts, 0 protocol errors, 0 lost events

Transmit Speed Counters:

Connection Speeds        75      300      600     1200     2400     4800
# of connections          0        0        0        0        0        0
Connection Speeds      7200     9600    12000    14400    16800    19200
# of connections          0        0        0        0        0        0
Connection Speeds     21600    24000    26400    28800    31200    32000
# of connections          0        0        0        1        0        0
Connection Speeds     33600    34000    36000    38000    40000    42000
# of connections          0        0        0        0        0        0
Connection Speeds     44000    46000    48000    50000    52000    54000
# of connections          0        0        0        0        0        0
Connection Speeds     56000
# of connections          0
```

## DISPLAYING LOCAL DISCONNECT REASONS

Use the **show modem call-stats** [*slot*] EXEC command to find out why a modem ended its connection or why a modem is not operating at peek performance.

Local disconnect reasons are listed across the top of the screen display (for example, wdogTimr, compress, retrain, inacTout, linkFail, moduFail, mnpProto, and lapmProt). In the body of the screen display, the number of times each modem disconnected is displayed (see the # column). For a particular disconnect reason, the % column indicates the percent that a modem was logged for the specified disconnect reason with respect to the entire modem pool for that given reason. For example, out of all the times the rmtLink error occurred on all the modems in the system, the rmtLink error occurred 10% of the time on modem 0/22.

Bad or malfunctioning modems are detected by an unusually high number of disconnect counters for a particular disconnect reason. For example, if modem 1/0 had an astronomically high number of compression errors compared to the remaining modems in the system, modem 1/0 would probably be bad or inoperable.

To reset the counters displayed by the **show modem call-stats** command, issue the **clear modem counters** command.

**NOTES**

For a complete description of each of the error display fields, see Chapter 8. Remote disconnect reasons are not described by this command.

The following example displays output for the **show modem call-stats** command. Due to the screen size limitation of most terminal screen displays, not all the possible disconnect reasons are displayed at one time. Only the eight most frequently experienced disconnect reasons are displayed at one time.

```
router# show modem call-stats

  dial-in/dial-out call statistics

        lostCarr  dtrDrop   rmtLink wdogTimr compress  retrain inacTout linkFail
   Mdm    #   %    #   %     #   %    #   %    #   %    #   %    #   %    #   %
 * 0/0    6   2    2   3     1   0    0   0    0   0    0   0    0   0    0   0
 * 0/1    5   2    2   3     2   1    0   0    0   0    0   0    0   0    0   0
   0/2    5   2    2   3     4   3    0   0    0   0    0   0    0   0    0   0
 * 0/3    5   2    2   3     2   1    0   0    0   0    0   0    0   0    0   0
 * 0/4    5   2    1   1     1   0    0   0    0   0    0   0    0   0    0   0
 * 0/5    5   2    2   3     2   1    0   0    0   0    0   0    0   0    0   0
 * 0/6    4   1    2   3     2   1    0   0    0   0    0   0    0   0    0   0
 * 0/7    4   1    2   3     4   3    0   0    0   0    0   0    0   0    0   0
 * 0/8    6   2    1   1     3   2    0   0    0   0    0   0    0   0    0   0
 * 0/9    5   2    1   1     1   0    0   0    0   0    0   0    0   0    0   0
 * 0/10   5   2    1   1     2   1    0   0    0   0    0   0    0   0    0   0
 * 0/11   5   2    1   1     2   1    0   0    0   0    0   0    0   0    0   0
   0/12   5   2    2   3     2   1    0   0    0   0    0   0    0   0    0   0
 * 0/13   5   2    1   1     1   0    0   0    0   0    0   0    0   0    0   0
 * 0/14   5   2    1   1     1   0    0   0    0   0    0   0    0   0    0   0
 * 0/15   5   2    1   1     1   0    0   0    0   0    0   0    0   0    0   0
 * 0/16   5   2    1   1     1   0    0   0    0   0    0   0    0   0    0   0
 * 0/17   5   2    1   1     2   1    0   0    0   0    0   0    0   0    0   0
 * 0/18   5   2    1   1     2   1    0   0    0   0    0   0    0   0    0   0
 * 0/19   5   2    1   1     3   2    0   0    0   0    0   0    0   0    0   0
 * 0/20   5   2    1   1     1   0    0   0    0   0    0   0    0   0    0   0
 * 0/21   5   2    1   1     1   0    0   0    0   0    0   0    0   0    0   0
 * 0/22   5   2    1   1    11  10    0   0    0   0    0   0    0   0    0   0
 * 0/23   5   2    1   1     2   1    0   0    0   0    0   0    0   0    0   0
 * 2/0    4   1    2   3     2   1    0   0    0   0    0   0    0   0    0   0
 * 2/1    5   2    1   1     2   1    0   0    0   0    0   0    0   0    0   0
 * 2/2    5   2    2   3     0   0    0   0    0   0    0   0    0   0    0   0
```

```
* 2/3     5   2    1   1    2   1    0   0    0   0    0   0    0   0    0   0
* 2/4     5   2    1   1    2   1    0   0    0   0    0   0    0   0    0   0
* 2/5     5   2    1   1    2   1    0   0    0   0    0   0    0   0    0   0
* 2/6     4   1    1   1    1   0    0   0    0   0    0   0    0   0    0   0
* 2/7     5   2    1   1    1   0    0   0    0   0    0   0    0   0    0   0
* 2/8     5   2    1   1    1   0    0   0    0   0    0   0    0   0    0   0
* 2/9     4   1    1   1    2   1    0   0    0   0    0   0    0   0    0   0
* 2/10    5   2    1   1    0   0    0   0    0   0    0   0    0   0    0   0
* 2/11    5   2    1   1    5   4    0   0    0   0    0   0    0   0    0   0
* 2/12    5   2    1   1    2   1    0   0    0   0    0   0    0   0    0   0
* 2/13    5   2    1   1    1   0    0   0    0   0    0   0    0   0    0   0
* 2/14    5   2    1   1    2   1    0   0    0   0    0   0    0   0    0   0
* 2/15    4   1    1   1    3   2    0   0    0   0    0   0    0   0    0   0
* 2/16    4   1    1   1    3   2    0   0    0   0    0   0    0   0    0   0
* 2/17    5   2    2   3    9   8    0   0    0   0    0   0    0   0    0   0
* 2/18    4   1    1   1    1   0    0   0    0   0    0   0    0   0    0   0
* 2/19    3   1    1   1    2   1    0   0    0   0    0   0    0   0    0   0
* 2/20    7   3    1   1    8   7    0   0    0   0    0   0    0   0    0   0
* 2/21    5   2    1   1    1   0    0   0    0   0    0   0    0   0    0   0
* 2/22    4   1    1   1    2   1    0   0    0   0    0   0    0   0    0   0
* 2/23    5   2    1   1    2   1    0   0    0   0    0   0    0   0    0   0
  Total 233       59      110        0        0        0        0        0

  dial-out call statistics

        noCarr noDitone     busy     abort dialStrg autoLgon dialTout  rmtHgup
  Mdm     #   %    #   %    #   %    #   %    #   %    #   %    #   %    #   %
* 0/0     1   1    0   0    0   0    0   0    0   0    0   0    0   0    0   0
* 0/1     0   0    0   0    0   0    0   0    0   0    0   0    0   0    0   0
  0/2     0   0    0   0    0   0    0   0    0   0    0   0    0   0    0   0
* 0/3     1   1    0   0    0   0    0   0    0   0    0   0    0   0    0   0
* 0/4     1   1    0   0    0   0    0   0    0   0    0   0    0   0    0   0
* 0/5     0   0    0   0    0   0    0   0    0   0    0   0    0   0    0   0
* 0/6     1   1    0   0    0   0    0   0    0   0    0   0    0   0    0   0
* 0/7     5   5    0   0    0   0    0   0    0   0    0   0    0   0    0   0
* 0/8     0   0    0   0    0   0    0   0    0   0    0   0    0   0    0   0
* 0/9     1   1    0   0    0   0    0   0    0   0    0   0    0   0    0   0
* 0/10    0   0    0   0    0   0    0   0    0   0    0   0    0   0    0   0
* 0/11    5   5    0   0    0   0    0   0    0   0    0   0    0   0    0   0
  0/12    0   0    0   0    0   0    0   0    0   0    0   0    0   0    0   0
* 0/13    0   0    0   0    0   0    0   0    0   0    0   0    0   0    0   0
* 0/14    1   1    0   0    0   0    0   0    0   0    0   0    0   0    0   0
* 0/15    1   1    0   0    0   0    0   0    0   0    0   0    0   0    0   0
* 0/16    2   2    0   0    0   0    0   0    0   0    0   0    0   0    0   0
* 0/17    4   4    0   0    0   0    0   0    0   0    0   0    0   0    0   0
* 0/18    5   5    0   0    0   0    0   0    0   0    0   0    0   0    0   0
* 0/19    1   1    0   0    0   0    0   0    0   0    0   0    0   0    0   0
* 0/20    0   0    0   0    0   0    0   0    0   0    0   0    0   0    0   0
* 0/21    0   0    0   0    0   0    0   0    0   0    0   0    0   0    0   0
* 0/22    5   5    0   0    0   0    0   0    0   0    0   0    0   0    0   0
* 0/23    1   1    0   0    0   0    0   0    0   0    0   0    0   0    0   0
* 2/0     2   2    0   0    0   0    0   0    0   0    0   0    0   0    0   0
* 2/1     3   3    0   0    0   0    0   0    0   0    0   0    0   0    0   0
* 2/2     0   0    0   0    0   0    0   0    0   0    0   0    0   0    0   0
```

```
* 2/3     0   0    0   0    0   0    0   0    0   0    0   0    0   0    0   0
* 2/4     0   0    0   0    0   0    0   0    0   0    0   0    0   0    0   0
* 2/5     1   1    0   0    0   0    0   0    0   0    0   0    0   0    0   0
* 2/6     1   1    0   0    0   0    0   0    0   0    0   0    0   0    0   0
* 2/7     4   4    0   0    0   0    0   0    0   0    0   0    0   0    0   0
* 2/8     7   8    0   0    0   0    0   0    0   0    0   0    0   0    0   0
* 2/9     4   1    1   1    2   1    0   0    0   0    0   0    0   0    0   0
* 2/10    1   1    0   0    0   0    0   0    0   0    0   0    0   0    0   0
* 2/11    1   1    0   0    0   0    0   0    0   0    0   0    0   0    0   0
* 2/12    1   1    0   0    0   0    0   0    0   0    0   0    0   0    0   0
* 2/13    1   1    0   0    0   0    0   0    0   0    0   0    0   0    0   0
* 2/14    4   4    0   0    0   0    0   0    0   0    0   0    0   0    0   0
* 2/15    1   1    0   0    0   0    0   0    0   0    0   0    0   0    0   0
* 2/16    1   1    0   0    0   0    0   0    0   0    0   0    0   0    0   0
* 2/17    5   5    0   0    0   0    0   0    0   0    0   0    0   0    0   0
* 2/18    5   5    0   0    0   0    0   0    0   0    0   0    0   0    0   0
* 2/19    3   3    0   0    0   0    0   0    0   0    0   0    0   0    0   0
* 2/20    0   0    0   0    0   0    0   0    0   0    0   0    0   0    0   0
* 2/21    4   4    0   0    0   0    0   0    0   0    0   0    0   0    0   0
* 2/22    2   2    0   0    0   0    0   0    0   0    0   0    0   0    0   0
* 2/23    0   0    0   0    0   0    0   0    0   0    0   0    0   0    0   0
  Total  84        0        0        0        0        0        0        0
```

## Upgrading Modem Firmware for 56K, V.34, and V.110 Cards

New versions of modem firmware are regularly posted to the Cisco Connection Online (CCO) server for you to download to your system. However, you must be a CCO registered user to access these files. These new versions of firmware contain bug fixes or new modem features, which can improve your system's overall modem performance.

**Notes**

The modem download procedures described in this section do not apply to MICA digital modems. Only Microcom modem support is described.

---

The typical way to download firmware is shown in Figure 7–6. Use a PC or UNIX workstation to access CCO and download the new firmware to your desktop computer. After the firmware is downloaded, transfer it to a TFTP server somewhere on your LAN. You might be able to set up your workstation as a TFTP server. Next, log on to the access server or router to which you want to upgrade modem firmware and issue the Cisco IOS **copy** command to copy the file to the integrated modems.

Perform the following two steps to download modem firmware from CCO to your integrated modems:

Step 1—Download the Modem Firmware from CCO to Your Workstation

Step 2—Copy the Firmware from a Local TFTP Server to the Access Server or Router

These steps are explained in detail in the following sections.

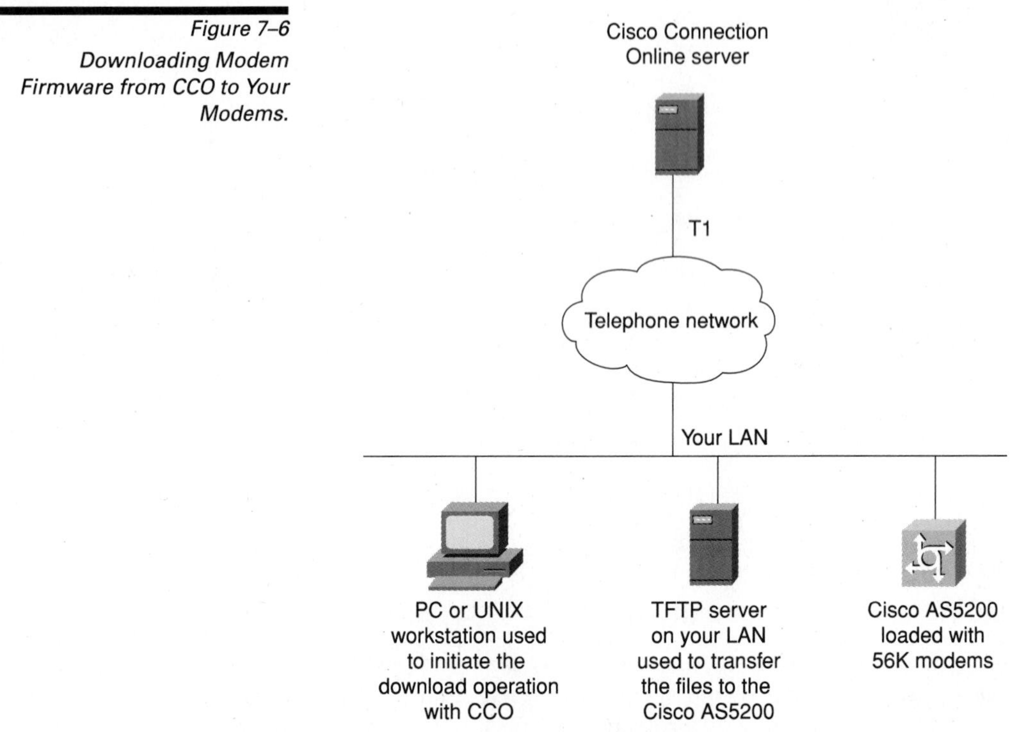


*Figure 7-6 Downloading Modem Firmware from CCO to Your Modems.*

## Step 1—Download the Modem Firmware from CCO to Your Workstation

Choose a method to download these files from Cisco Systems:

- Download Method 1—Use an Internet Browser
- Download Method 2—Use a Traditional FTP Application

### *Download Method 1—Use an Internet Browser*

This section describes the procedure for logging on to Cisco System's Software Center and downloading new modem firmware to a workstation. You must log in as a Cisco registered user.

**NOTES**

After the files are downloaded to your desktop computer, you must transfer them to a TFTP server on your network using an FTP application. The Cisco IOS software uses the **copy tftp** command to copy files from remote servers to access servers or routers. However, check to see if your workstation can be set up as TFTP server. If so, you do not need to transfer the files. Use your workstation as a server instead.

Perform the following steps:

**Step 1** Launch an Internet browser.

**Step 2** Bring up Cisco Systems' Software Center home page at the following URL, which is subject to change without notice, and enter your CCO registered username and password at the prompt:

http://www.cisco.com/kobayashi/sw-center

**Step 3** Find the firmware you want. Download it to your local workstation. For example, suppose you are looking for the latest Microcom firmware for the Cisco AS5200. Click the **Access Products** hot link. The Access Products window is displayed.

**Step 4** Click **Cisco AS5200 Series Software.**

**Step 5** Click **Download Microcom Modem Firmware** (for the type of modems installed in your access server or router).

**Step 6** Select the version of firmware you want to download.

**Step 7** Follow the remaining download instructions.

**Step 8** After the firmware is downloaded to your workstation, you must transfer the file to a TFTP server somewhere in your LAN using a terminal emulation software application.

### *Download Method 2—Use a Traditional FTP Application*

Take the following steps to download firmware files from Cisco's CCO FTP server using an FTP client application.

**NOTES**

The directory path leading to the firmware files on cco.cisco.com is subject to change without notice. If you cannot access the files using an FTP application, try taking the URL route at http://www.cisco.com/kobayashi/sw-center.

---

**Step 1** Log in to Cisco Systems' CCO FTP server, which is called cco.cisco.com:

```
terminal> ftp cco.cisco.com
Connected to cio-sys.cisco.com.

   Cisco Connection Online       |         |       Cisco Systems, Inc.
   Email: cco-team@cisco.com    |||       |||      170 West Tasman Drive
   Phone: +1.800.553.2447     .:|||||:..:|||||:.   San Jose, CA 95134

   NOTE: As of February 1, 1997 ftp.cisco.com will now point to this
   service.  Please be advised.  To use the former ftp.cisco.com after
   February 1, connect to ftpeng.cisco.com

   You may login with:
          + Your CCO username and password, or
          + A special access code followed by your e-mail address, or
          + "anonymous" followed by your e-mail address for guest access.
```

```
cio-sys FTP server (CIOESD #103 Sun Dec 15 14:43:43 PST 1996) ready.
```

**Step 2** Enter your CCO registered username and password (for example, **harry** and **letmein**):

```
Name (cco.cisco.com:harry): harry
Password required for harry.
Password: letmein
###########################################################################
#  Welcome to the Cisco Systems CCO FTP server.
#  This server has a number of restrictions.  If you are not familiar
#  with these, please first get and read the /README or /README.TXT
#  file.http://www.cisco.com/acs/info/cioesd.html for more info.
###########################################################################

*****  NOTE: As of February 1, 1997, "cco.cisco.com",     *****
*****  "www.cisco.com" and "ftp.cisco.com" are now all    *****
*****  logical names for the same machine.                *****
*****                                                     *****
*****  The old "ftp.cisco.com" is an entirely             *****
*****  different machine, which is now known as           *****
*****  "ftpeng.cisco.com" or "ftp-eng.cisco.com".         *****
*****                                                     *****
*****  In general, "ftpeng.cisco.com" is used only for    *****
*****  distribution of Cisco Engineering-controlled       *****
*****  projects, such as beta programs, early field       *****
*****  trials, developing standards documents, etc.       *****
*****                                                     *****
*****  Be sure to confirm you have connected to           *****
*****  the machine you need to interact with.             *****

If you have any odd problems, try logging in with a minus sign (-)
as the first character of your password.  This will turn off a feature
that may be confusing your ftp client program.
Please send any questions, comments, or problem reports about this
server to cco-team@cisco.com.

NOTE:
To download files from CCO, you must be running a *passive-mode*
capable FTP client.
To drop files on this system, you must cd to the /drop directory.
Mirrors of this server can be found at

+ ftp://www-europe.cisco.com European (Amsterdam)
+ ftp://www-fr.cisco.com     France     (Paris)
+ ftp://www-au.cisco.com     Australia  (Sydney)
+ ftp://www-jp.cisco.com     Japan      (Tokyo)
+ ftp://www-kr.cisco.com     Korea      (Seoul)


Please read the file README
it was last modified on Sat Feb  1 12:49:31 1997 - 163 days ago
ser harry logged in.  Access restrictions apply.
```

```
Remote system type is UNIX.
Using binary mode to transfer files.
```

**Step 3** Specify the directory path that holds the modem firmware you want to download. Suppose you want 56K modem firmware for the Cisco AS5200, the directory path would be /cisco/access/5200/56k:

```
ftp> cd /cisco/access/5200/56k
Please read the file README
it was last modified on Tue May 27 10:07:38 1997 - 48 days ago
Please read the file README.txt
it was last modified on Tue May 27 10:07:38 1997 - 48 days ago
WD command successful.
```

**Step 4** View the contents of the directory with the **ls** command:

```
ftp> ls
Entering Passive Mode (192,31,7,130,218,128)
Opening ASCII mode data connection for /bin/ls.
total 2688
drwxr-s--T   2 ftpadmin ftpcio       512 Jun 30 18:11 .
drwxr-sr-t  19 ftpadmin ftpcio       512 Jun 23 10:26 ..
lrwxrwxrwx   1 root     3             10 Aug  6  1996 README -> README.txt
-rw-rw-r--   1 root     ftpcio      2304 May 27 10:07 README.txt
-r--r--r-- 1 ftpadmin ftpint 96708 Jul 10 18:08
mcom-modem-dsp-3.1.30-1.1.0.bin
-r--r--r-- 1 ftpadmin ftpint 280208 Jul 10 18:08
mcom-modem-fw-3.1.30-1.1.0.bin
Transfer complete.
```

**Step 5** Specify a binary image transfer:

```
ftp> binary
Type set to I.
```

**Step 6** Copy the modem firmware files from the server to your local environment with the **get** command.

The following example downloads the modem firmware file mcom-modem-fw-3.1.30-1.1.0.bin:

```
ftp> get mcom-modem-fw-3.1.30-1.1.0.bin
PORT command successful.
Opening BINARY mode data connection for mcom-modem-fw-3.1.30-1.1.0.bin
(280208 bytes).
Transfer complete.
local: mcom-modem-fw-3.1.30-1.1.0.bin remote:
mcom-modem-fw-3.1.30-1.1.0.bin
280208 bytes received in 0.63 seconds (4.4e+02 Kbytes/s)
```

**Step 7** Quit your terminal session:

```
ftp> quit
Goodbye.
```

**Step 8** Verify that you successfully transferred the files to your local directory:

```
server% ls -al
total 596
-r--r--r-- 1 96708 Jul 10 18:08 mcom-modem-dsp-3.1.30-1.1.0.bin
-r--r--r-- 1 280208 Jul 10 18:08 mcom-modem-fw-3.1.30-1.1.0.bin
```

```
server% pwd
/auto/tftpboot
```

If you haven't already done so, you must now transfer these files to a local TFTP or rcp server that your access server or router can access.

### Step 2—Copy the Firmware from a Local TFTP Server to the Access Server or Router

Depending on the type of modems installed in your system, the download instructions vary. Refer to the instructions that best describe your scenario:

- 56K Firmware and DSP Upgrades
- V.34 Firmware Upgrades
- V.110 Firmware Upgrades

#### *56K Firmware and DSP Upgrades*

Perform the following steps to upgrade Microcom 56K modem firmware and DSP software. This section provides an example to upgrade the firmware on 56K modems loaded in a Cisco AS5200 access server.

**NOTES**

This section describes the two file download methods for Microcom modem cards. It does not describe how to download firmware for MICA modems nor the single file download method for Microcom modems (a single file downloaded from Cisco's CCO FTP server, which contains both modem firmware and DSP software). Refer to your product-specific documentation for information about single file 56K downloads and MICA downloads.

- Step 1—Create an Empty Boot Flash Memory Image File on Your TFTP Server
- Step 2—Back Up the Boot Flash Image and Disable Modem Autoconfigure
- Step 3—Upgrade to the Latest 56K Modem Firmware
- Step 4—Download the RAM-Based DSP Software to Boot Flash Memory
- Step 5—Copy the RAM-Based DSP Software from Boot Flash Memory to the 56K Modems

Before 56K modems were introduced, modem firmware was upgraded with a single firmware file stored in the modem's Flash memory. The file remained in the modem's Flash memory. However, with 56K modems, the modem's Flash memory is not large enough to retain the necessary software to transmit at 56 Kbps. Therefore, the software is divided into two parts—56K modem firmware and DSP software. The firmware resides in the modem's Flash memory. The DSP software, which is the core intelligence of K56flex technology, runs from the access server's RAM. Because the DSP software is not retained across reloads or power cycles, the image is stored in the access server's boot Flash memory. (See Figure 7–7.)

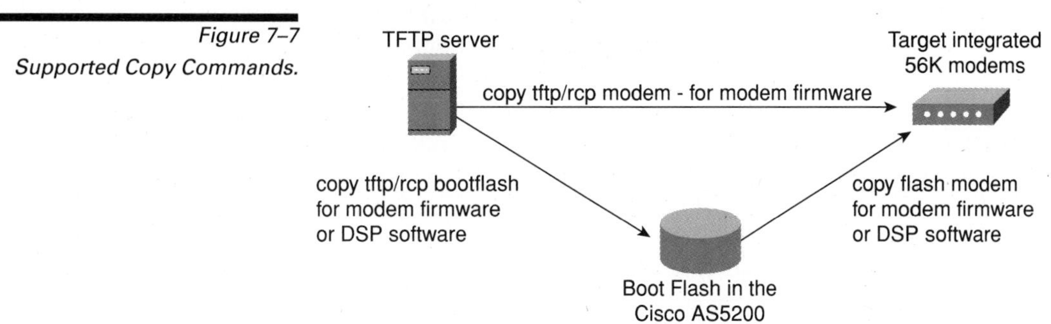


*Figure 7–7*
*Supported Copy Commands.*

### *Step 1—Create an Empty Boot Flash Memory Image File on Your TFTP Server*

Before you back up your boot Flash image with the **copy bootflash tftp** command, you must create an empty destination file on your local TFTP server:

**Step 1** Log on to the Cisco AS5200 and find out the name of the boot image file in boot Flash memory with the **show bootflash** command:

```
router> enable
Password: letmein
router# show bootflash

Boot flash directory:
File  Length   Name/status
  1   6465584  c5200-is-l.112-6.4
[6465648 bytes used, 1922960 available, 8388608 total]
8192K bytes of processor board Boot flash (Read/Write)

router#
```

**Step 2** Go to your TFTP server and create an empty file using your boot image's filename, then change its permissions to be world writable:

```
henry-sun:/tftpboot> touch c5200-is-l.112-6.4
henry-sun:/tftpboot> chmod 666 c5200-is-l.112-6.4
henry-sun:/tftpboot> ls -l c5200-is-l.112-6.4
-rw-rw-rw-   1 henry cisco     6465584 Jul 14 15:25 c5200-is-l.112-6.4
```

The placeholder or destination file is now created and prepared for the backup copy operation.

### *Step 2—Back Up the Boot Flash Image and Disable Modem Autoconfigure*

For example, complete the following steps for a Cisco AS5200:

**Step 1** Back up your boot Flash image to a local TFTP server on your network with the **copy bootflash tftp** command. This provides a recovery mechanism for you in case you accidentally erase or damage your boot Flash image in one of the later steps.

```
router# copy bootflash tftp
```

**Step 2** Enter global configuration mode and disable the **modem autoconfigure** command on the TTY lines that correspond with the 56K modems. Ignore this step if this command is not enabled in your system configuration. In the following example, one 12-port 56K modem card is installed in slot 2:

```
router# configure terminal
Enter configuration commands, one per line.  End with CNTL/Z.
router(config)# line 13 24
router(config-line)# no modem autoconfigure
router(config-line)# exit
router(config)# exit
router#
%SYS-5-CONFIG_I: Configured from console by console
```

The boot image is now backed up, and modem autoconfigure is disabled.

### *Step 3—Upgrade to the Latest 56K Modem Firmware*

For example, complete the following steps for a Cisco AS5200:

**Step 1** Log in to the Cisco AS5200 and copy the new modem firmware file from your TFTP server directly to the installed 56K modems using the **copy tftp modem** Privileged EXEC command:

```
router# copy tftp modem
```

**Step 2** Specify the range of 56K modems that you want to upgrade. This example shows the range of modems to be 2/12 through 2/23:

```
Modem Numbers (<slot>/<port>[-<slot>/<port>] ¦ group <number> ¦ all)?
2/12-2/23
```

**Step 3** Specify the name or address of the TFTP server holding the new modem firmware. Press the **Return** key to accept the default name or IP address enclosed in the brackets [ ]. Also specify the source path/filename of the firmware.

```
Address or name of remote host [255.255.255.255]? tftp-server
Source file name? mcom-modem-fw-3.1.30-1.1.0.bin
Accessing file 'mcom-modem-fw-3.1.30-1.1.0.bin' on tftp-server...
Loading mcom-modem-fw-3.1.30-1.1.0.bin from 172.16.1.129 (via Ethernet0):
!!!!!!!!!!!!!!!!!!!!!!!!!!!!!!!!!!!!!!!!!!!!!!!!!!!!!!!!!!!
[OK - 280208/557056 bytes]

router#
*Mar  2 08:18:49.143: %MODEM-5-DL_START: Modem (2/12) started firmware
download
*Mar  2 08:18:51.147: %MODEM-5-DL_START: Modem (2/13) started firmware
download
```

```
*Mar  2 08:18:53.151: %MODEM-5-DL_START: Modem (2/14) started firmware
download
*Mar  2 08:18:55.155: %MODEM-5-DL_START: Modem (2/15) started firmware
download
*Mar  2 08:18:57.159: %MODEM-5-DL_START: Modem (2/16) started firmware
download
*Mar  2 08:18:59.163: %MODEM-5-DL_START: Modem (2/17) started firmware
download
*Mar  2 08:19:01.167: %MODEM-5-DL_START: Modem (2/18) started firmware
download
*Mar  2 08:19:03.171: %MODEM-5-DL_START: Modem (2/19) started firmware
download
*Mar  2 08:19:05.175: %MODEM-5-DL_START: Modem (2/20) started firmware
download
*Mar  2 08:19:07.179: %MODEM-5-DL_START: Modem (2/21) started firmware
download
*Mar  2 08:19:09.179: %MODEM-5-DL_START: Modem (2/22) started firmware
download
*Mar  2 08:19:11.183: %MODEM-5-DL_START: Modem (2/23) started firmware
download
*Mar  2 08:20:01.959: %MODEM-5-DL_GOOD: Modem (2/17) completed firmware
download: MNPClass10K56flexModemRev3.1.30/85
*Mar  2 08:20:02.251: %MODEM-5-DL_GOOD: Modem (2/18) completed firmware
download: MNPClass10K56flexModemRev3.1.30/85
*Mar  2 08:20:03.019: %MODEM-5-DL_GOOD: Modem (2/15) completed firmware
download: MNPClass10K56flexModemRev3.1.30/85
*Mar  2 08:20:03.023: %MODEM-5-DL_GOOD: Modem (2/16) completed firmware
download: MNPClass10K56flexModemRev3.1.30/85
*Mar  2 08:20:03.347: %MODEM-5-DL_GOOD: Modem (2/14) completed firmware
download: MNPClass10K56flexModemRev3.1.30/85
*Mar  2 08:20:03.355: %MODEM-5-DL_GOOD: Modem (2/19) completed firmware
download: MNPClass10K56flexModemRev3.1.30/85
*Mar  2 08:20:04.711: %MODEM-5-DL_GOOD: Modem (2/13) completed firmware
download: MNPClass10K56flexModemRev3.1.30/85
*Mar  2 08:20:05.739: %MODEM-5-DL_GOOD: Modem (2/12) completed firmware
download: MNPClass10K56flexModemRev3.1.30/85
*Mar  2 08:20:05.747: %MODEM-5-DL_GOOD: Modem (2/20) completed firmware
download: MNPClass10K56flexModemRev3.1.30/85
*Mar  2 08:20:05.751: %MODEM-5-DL_GOOD: Modem (2/21) completed firmware
download: MNPClass10K56flexModemRev3.1.30/85
*Mar  2 08:20:06.007: %MODEM-5-DL_GOOD: Modem (2/22) completed firmware
download: MNPClass10K56flexModemRev3.1.30/85
*Mar  2 08:20:09.375: %MODEM-5-DL_GOOD: Modem (2/23) completed firmware
download: MNPClass10K56flexModemRev3.1.30/85
```

The 56K modems are now upgraded to the latest version of modem firmware. The procedure for copying the DSP software from a local file server to the access server's boot Flash memory is described next.

- Step 4—Download the RAM-Based DSP Software to Boot Flash Memory
- Step 5—Copy the RAM-Based DSP Software from Boot Flash Memory to the 56K Modems

These two steps are performed only once. Although the DSP software runs from RAM, the Cisco IOS software automatically copies the DSP code from boot Flash memory to the 56K modems each time the access server power cycles in the future. After you copy the DSP software to boot Flash memory for the first time, you should not have to perform these steps again.

### *Step 4—Download the RAM-Based DSP Software to Boot Flash Memory*

**Step 1** Copy the DSP software file from your TFTP server to the access server's boot Flash memory using the **copy tftp bootflash** command. The Cisco IOS software prompts you with a sequence of questions such as name/address of the TFTP server and the DSP filename to be copied. Answer all of the questions accordingly.

```
router# copy tftp bootflash

Boot flash directory:
File  Length   Name/status
1    2348148   as5200-boot-l.111-7.AA
[2348212 bytes used, 6040396 available, 8388608 total]
```

**Step 2** Specify the address or name of the server that currently holds the DSP software. You must also specify the source path/filename of the DSP software and the destination filename. The system software proposes a destination filename for you, which is enclosed in square brackets [ ]. Press the **Return** key to accept the default destination name.

```
Address or name of remote host [255.255.255.255]? tftp-server
Source file name? mcom-modem-dsp-3.1.30-1.1.0.bin
Destination file name [mcom-modem-dsp-3.1.30-1.1.0.bin]?
Accessing file 'mcom-modem-dsp-3.1.30-1.1.0.bin' on tftp-server...
Loading mcom-modem-dsp-3.1.30-1.1.0.bin from 172.16.1.129 (via Ethernet0):
! [OK]
```

**Step 3** When the system asks to confirm erasing the Flash memory device before copying the DSP file, enter **no**. You will now see a warning message appear that says the DSP file cannot be executed on the system (unlike a feature set or system image). Ignore this message, because you do not want to erase the system's Flash memory.

```
Erase flash device before writing? [confirm] no
%Warning: File not a valid executable for this system
```

**Step 4** Initiate the copy operation by entering **y** then pressing the **Return** key at the [confirm] prompt:

```
Copy file? [confirm] y
```

**Step 5** Continue with the copy operation by entering **yes** and pressing the **Return** key:

```
Copy 'mcom-modem-dsp-3.1.30-1.1.0.bin' from server as
'mcom-modem-dsp-3.1.30-1.1.0.bin' into Flash WITHOUT erase? [yes/no] yes
Loading mcom-modem-dsp-3.1.30-1.1.0.bin from 172.16.1.129 (via Ethernet0):
!!!!!!!!!!!!!!!!!!![OK - 96708/6040396 bytes]

Verifying checksum...  OK (0x9B87) Flash device copy took 00:00:02 [hh:mm:ss]
```

Now the DSP software is in the access server's boot Flash memory. Proceed to the next section, "Step 5—Copy the RAM-Based DSP Software from Boot Flash Memory to the 56K Modems," for step-by-step instructions on how to transfer the DSP image to the 56K modems.

### *Step 5—Copy the RAM-Based DSP Software from Boot Flash Memory to the 56K Modems*

**Step 1** Copy the DSP software to the 56K modems by entering the **copy flash modem** Privileged EXEC command. After you enter this command, specify the range of 56K modems that you want to target with the DSP software. In this example, only one 12-port 56K modem board is installed in the Cisco AS5200.

```
router# copy flash modem
Modem Numbers (<slot>/<port>[-<slot>/<port>] ¦ group <number> ¦ all)?
2/12-2/23
```

**Step 2** Specify the filename of the DSP software and press the **Return** key. Note that the filename must be preceded by **bootflash:**, which is necessary to address the file that is stored in boot Flash memory.

```
Name of file to copy? bootflash:mcom-modem-dsp-3.1.30-1.1.0.bin
[OK - 96708/278528 bytes]

Downloading modem DSP file: bootflash:mcom-modem-dsp-3.1.30-1.1.0.bin
DSP Rev: 1.1(0)
```

**Step 3** Proceed with the DSP download by entering **y** and pressing the **Return** key:

```
Proceed with DSP download? [n]: y
Downloading modem DSP file. Check current modem firmware version.
If firmware version is not the correct version to run with DSP image,
the correct firmware version must also be downloaded.
router#
*Mar  2 08:22:10.535: %MODEM-5-DL_DSP_START: Modem (2/12) started DSP
download
*Mar  2 08:22:12.539: %MODEM-5-DL_DSP_START: Modem (2/13) started DSP
download
*Mar  2 08:22:14.543: %MODEM-5-DL_DSP_START: Modem (2/14) started DSP
download
*Mar  2 08:22:16.543: %MODEM-5-DL_DSP_START: Modem (2/15) started DSP
download
*Mar  2 08:22:18.563: %MODEM-5-DL_DSP_START: Modem (2/16) started DSP
download
*Mar  2 08:22:20.567: %MODEM-5-DL_DSP_START: Modem (2/17) started DSP
download
*Mar  2 08:22:22.567: %MODEM-5-DL_DSP_START: Modem (2/18) started DSP
download
*Mar  2 08:22:24.567: %MODEM-5-DL_DSP_START: Modem (2/19) started DSP
download
*Mar  2 08:22:26.567: %MODEM-5-DL_DSP_START: Modem (2/20) started DSP
download
*Mar  2 08:22:28.571: %MODEM-5-DL_DSP_START: Modem (2/21) started DSP
download
```

```
*Mar  2 08:22:30.575: %MODEM-5-DL_DSP_START: Modem (2/22) started DSP
download
*Mar  2 08:22:32.579: %MODEM-5-DL_DSP_START: Modem (2/23) started DSP
download
*Mar  2 08:22:56.795: %MODEM-5-DL_DSP_GOOD: Modem (2/13) completed DSP
download: MNPClass10K56flexModemRev3.1.30/85
*Mar  2 08:22:57.055: %MODEM-5-DL_DSP_GOOD: Modem (2/12) completed DSP
download: MNPClass10K56flexModemRev3.1.30/85
*Mar  2 08:22:57.311: %MODEM-5-DL_DSP_GOOD: Modem (2/14) completed DSP
download: MNPClass10K56flexModemRev3.1.30/85
*Mar  2 08:22:57.315: %MODEM-5-DL_DSP_GOOD: Modem (2/15) completed DSP
download: MNPClass10K56flexModemRev3.1.30/85
*Mar  2 08:22:57.575: %MODEM-5-DL_DSP_GOOD: Modem (2/17) completed DSP
download: MNPClass10K56flexModemRev3.1.30/85
*Mar  2 08:22:57.835: %MODEM-5-DL_DSP_GOOD: Modem (2/18) completed DSP
download: MNPClass10K56flexModemRev3.1.30/85
*Mar  2 08:22:58.091: %MODEM-5-DL_DSP_GOOD: Modem (2/16) completed DSP
download: MNPClass10K56flexModemRev3.1.30/85
*Mar  2 08:22:58.351: %MODEM-5-DL_DSP_GOOD: Modem (2/19) completed DSP
download: MNPClass10K56flexModemRev3.1.30/85
*Mar  2 08:22:58.355: %MODEM-5-DL_DSP_GOOD: Modem (2/20) completed DSP
download: MNPClass10K56flexModemRev3.1.30/85
*Mar  2 08:23:00.059: %MODEM-5-DL_DSP_GOOD: Modem (2/21) completed DSP
download: MNPClass10K56flexModemRev3.1.30/85
*Mar  2 08:23:04.119: %MODEM-5-DL_DSP_GOOD: Modem (2/22) completed DSP
download: MNPClass10K56flexModemRev3.1.30/85
*Mar  2 08:23:05.387: %MODEM-5-DL_DSP_GOOD: Modem (2/23) completed DSP
download: MNPClass10K56flexModemRev3.1.30/85
```

**NOTES**

Now the 56K modems are equipped with the DSP software. The modems are configured to transmit at speeds up to 56 Kbps. Each time the access server is power cycled, the system software automatically loads the 56K modems with the DSP software in boot Flash memory. If you erase the DSP software file from boot Flash memory, the 56K modems will revert to V.34 operation on the next power cycle.

**Step 4** Verify that the DSP software copied to the 56K modems with the **show modem version** command. In this example, modems 2/12 through 2/23 are loaded with the new DSP software:

```
router# show modem version

          Modem module      Firmware   Boot         DSP
Mdm       Number            Rev        Rev          Rev
2/0        0                2.2(8)     1.0(5)
2/1        0                2.2(8)     1.0(5)
2/2        0                2.2(7)     1.0(5)
2/3        0                2.2(7)     1.0(5)
2/4        0                2.2(7)     1.0(5)
2/5        0                2.2(7)     1.0(5)
2/6        0                2.2(7)     1.0(5)
```

```
2/7     0          2.2(7)     1.0(5)
2/8     0          2.2(7)     1.0(5)
2/9     0          2.2(7)     1.0(5)
2/10    0          2.2(7)     1.0(5)
2/11    0          2.2(7)     1.0(5)
2/12    1          3.1(30)    3.0(4)        1.1(0)/1.1(0)
2/13    1          3.1(30)    3.0(4)        1.1(0)/1.1(0)
2/14    1          3.1(30)    3.0(4)        1.1(0)/1.1(0)
2/15    1          3.1(30)    3.0(4)        1.1(0)/1.1(0)
2/16    1          3.1(30)    3.0(4)        1.1(0)/1.1(0)
2/17    1          3.1(30)    3.0(4)        1.1(0)/1.1(0)
2/18    1          3.1(30)    3.0(4)        1.1(0)/1.1(0)
2/19    1          3.1(30)    3.0(4)        1.1(0)/1.1(0)
2/20    1          3.1(30)    3.0(4)        1.1(0)/1.1(0)
2/21    1          3.1(30)    3.0(4)        1.1(0)/1.1(0)
2/22    1          3.1(30)    3.0(4)        1.1(0)/1.1(0)
2/23    1          3.1(30)    3.0(4)        1.1(0)/1.1(0)

Modem board HW version info:

Slot 2:
  Carrier card:
    hw version= 8, number_of_ports= 24, max_modules= 2, max_oob_ports= 2
  Modem Module 0:
    number_of_modems= 12, option_bits= 1,
    rev_num= 03.00, vendor_model_number= 01,
    vendor_banner= Microcom MNP10 V34 Modem
  Modem Module 1:
    number_of_modems= 12, option_bits= 1,
    rev_num= 03.00, vendor_model_number= 02,
    vendor_banner= Microcom MNP10 K56 Modem
```

### *V.34 Firmware Upgrades*

The following example copies the Microcom modem firmware file called mcom-modem-firmware.2.2.8.bin from the TFTP server Modem_Server to all the V.34 Microcom modems installed in a Cisco AS5200 access server:

```
router# copy tftp modem
Modem Numbers (<slot>/<port>[-<slot>/<port>] ¦ group <number> ¦ all)? all

Address or name of remote host [UNKNOWN]? Modem_Server
Source file name? images/mcom-modem-firmware.2.2.8.bin
Accessing file 'images/mcom-modem-firmware.2.2.8.bin on Modem_Server...
Loading images/mcom-modem-firmware.2.2.8.bin .from 172.16.254.254 (via Ethernet0): ! [OK]

Loading images/mcom-modem-firmware.2.2.8.bin from 172.16.254.254 (via Ethernet0):
!!!!!!!!!!!!!!!!!!!!!!!!!!!!!!!!!!!!!!!!!!!!!!!!!!
[OK - 237503/278528 bytes]

router#
%MODEM-5-DL_START: Modem (2/0) started firmware download
%MODEM-5-DL_START: Modem (2/1) started firmware download
%MODEM-5-DL_START: Modem (2/2) started firmware download
```

```
%MODEM-5-DL_START: Modem (2/3) started firmware download
%MODEM-5-DL_START: Modem (2/4) started firmware download
%MODEM-5-DL_START: Modem (2/5) started firmware download
%MODEM-5-DL_START: Modem (2/6) started firmware download
%MODEM-5-DL_START: Modem (2/7) started firmware download
%MODEM-5-DL_START: Modem (2/8) started firmware download
%MODEM-5-DL_START: Modem (2/9) started firmware download
%MODEM-5-DL_START: Modem (2/10) started firmware download
%MODEM-5-DL_START: Modem (2/11) started firmware download
%MODEM-5-DL_START: Modem (2/12) started firmware download
%MODEM-5-DL_START: Modem (2/13) started firmware download
%MODEM-5-DL_START: Modem (2/14) started firmware download
%MODEM-5-DL_START: Modem (2/15) started firmware download
%MODEM-5-DL_START: Modem (2/16) started firmware download
%MODEM-5-DL_START: Modem (2/17) started firmware download
%MODEM-5-DL_START: Modem (2/18) started firmware download
%MODEM-5-DL_START: Modem (2/19) started firmware download
%MODEM-5-DL_START: Modem (2/20) started firmware download
%MODEM-5-DL_START: Modem (2/21) started firmware download
%MODEM-5-DL_START: Modem (2/22) started firmware download
%MODEM-5-DL_START: Modem (2/23) started firmware download
%MODEM-5-DL_GOOD: Modem (2/2) completed firmware download:
MNPClass10V.34/V.FCModemRev1.0.23/85.23/85
%MODEM-5-DL_GOOD: Modem (2/10) completed firmware download:
MNPClass10V.34/V.FCModemRev1.0.23/85.23/85
%MODEM-5-DL_GOOD: Modem (2/4) completed firmware download:
MNPClass10V.34/V.FCModemRev1.0.23/85.23/85
%MODEM-5-DL_GOOD: Modem (2/6) completed firmware download:
MNPClass10V.34/V.FCModemRev1.0.23/85.23/85
%MODEM-5-DL_GOOD: Modem (2/7) completed firmware download:
MNPClass10V.34/V.FCModemRev1.0.23/85.23/85
%MODEM-5-DL_GOOD: Modem (2/12) completed firmware download:
MNPClass10V.34/V.FCModemRev1.0.23/85.23/85
%MODEM-5-DL_GOOD: Modem (2/11) completed firmware download:
MNPClass10V.34/V.FCModemRev1.0.23/85.23/85
%MODEM-5-DL_GOOD: Modem (2/13) completed firmware download:
MNPClass10V.34/V.FCModemRev1.0.23/85.23/85
%MODEM-5-DL_GOOD: Modem (2/1) completed firmware download:
MNPClass10V.34/V.FCModemRev1.0.23/85.23/85
%MODEM-5-DL_GOOD: Modem (2/14) completed firmware download:
MNPClass10V.34/V.FCModemRev1.0.23/85.23/85
%MODEM-5-DL_GOOD: Modem (2/19) completed firmware download:
MNPClass10V.34/V.FCModemRev1.0.23/85.23/85
%MODEM-5-DL_GOOD: Modem (2/22) completed firmware download:
MNPClass10V.34/V.FCModemRev1.0.23/85.23/85
%MODEM-5-DL_GOOD: Modem (2/5) completed firmware download:
MNPClass10V.34/V.FCModemRev1.0.23/85.23/85
%MODEM-5-DL_GOOD: Modem (2/8) completed firmware download:
MNPClass10V.34/V.FCModemRev1.0.23/85.23/85
%MODEM-5-DL_GOOD: Modem (2/9) completed firmware download:
MNPClass10V.34/V.FCModemRev1.0.23/85.23/85
%MODEM-5-DL_GOOD: Modem (2/17) completed firmware download:
MNPClass10V.34/V.FCModemRev1.0.23/85.23/85
```

```
%MODEM-5-DL_GOOD: Modem (2/0) completed firmware download:
MNPClass10V.34/V.FCModemRev1.0.23/85.23/85
%MODEM-5-DL_GOOD: Modem (2/3) completed firmware download:
MNPClass10V.34/V.FCModemRev1.0.23/85.23/85
%MODEM-5-DL_GOOD: Modem (2/21) completed firmware download:
MNPClass10V.34/V.FCModemRev1.0.23/85.23/85
%MODEM-5-DL_GOOD: Modem (2/16) completed firmware download:
MNPClass10V.34/V.FCModemRev1.0.23/85.23/85
%MODEM-5-DL_GOOD: Modem (2/15) completed firmware download:
MNPClass10V.34/V.FCModemRev1.0.23/85.23/85
%MODEM-5-DL_GOOD: Modem (2/18) completed firmware download:
MNPClass10V.34/V.FCModemRev1.0.23/85.23/85
%MODEM-5-DL_GOOD: Modem (2/20) completed firmware download:
MNPClass10V.34/V.FCModemRev1.0.23/85.23/85
%MODEM-5-DL_GOOD: Modem (2/23) completed firmware download:
MNPClass10V.34/V.FCModemRev1.0.23/85.23/85
```

### V.110 Firmware Upgrades

The following example copies the modem firmware file v110-ta-firmware.2.8.7.bin from the local TFTP server Modem_Server to all the V.34 terminal adapters installed in a Cisco AS5200 access server:

```
router# copy tftp modem
Modem Numbers (<slot>/<port>[-<slot>/<port>] ¦ group <number> ¦ all)? all
Address or name of remote host [UNKNOWN]? Modem_Server
Source file name? images/v110-ta-firmware.2.8.7.bin
Accessing file 'images/v110-ta-firmware.2.8.7.bin on Modem_Server...
Loading images/v110-ta-firmware.2.8.7.bin .from 172.16.254.254 (via Ethernet0): ! [OK]

Loading images/v110-ta-firmware.2.8.7.bin from 172.16.254.254 (via Ethernet0):
!!!!!!!!!!!!!!!!!!!!!!!!!!!!!!!!!!!!!!!!!!!!!!
[OK - 237503/278528 bytes]
router#
%MODEM-5-DL_START: Modem (2/0) started firmware download
%MODEM-5-DL_START: Modem (2/1) started firmware download
%MODEM-5-DL_START: Modem (2/2) started firmware download
%MODEM-5-DL_START: Modem (2/3) started firmware download
%MODEM-5-DL_START: Modem (2/4) started firmware download
%MODEM-5-DL_START: Modem (2/5) started firmware download
%MODEM-5-DL_START: Modem (2/6) started firmware download
%MODEM-5-DL_START: Modem (2/7) started firmware download
%MODEM-5-DL_START: Modem (2/8) started firmware download
%MODEM-5-DL_START: Modem (2/9) started firmware download
%MODEM-5-DL_START: Modem (2/10) started firmware download
%MODEM-5-DL_START: Modem (2/11) started firmware download
%MODEM-5-DL_START: Modem (2/12) started firmware download
%MODEM-5-DL_START: Modem (2/13) started firmware download
%MODEM-5-DL_START: Modem (2/14) started firmware download
%MODEM-5-DL_START: Modem (2/15) started firmware download
%MODEM-5-DL_START: Modem (2/16) started firmware download
%MODEM-5-DL_START: Modem (2/17) started firmware download
%MODEM-5-DL_START: Modem (2/18) started firmware download
%MODEM-5-DL_START: Modem (2/19) started firmware download
```

```
%MODEM-5-DL_START: Modem (2/20) started firmware download
%MODEM-5-DL_START: Modem (2/21) started firmware download
%MODEM-5-DL_START: Modem (2/22) started firmware download
%MODEM-5-DL_START: Modem (2/23) started firmware download
%MODEM-5-DL_GOOD: Modem (2/2) completed firmware download:
MNPClass10v110/V.FCModemRev1.0.23/85.23/85
%MODEM-5-DL_GOOD: Modem (2/10) completed firmware download:
MNPClass10v110/V.FCModemRev1.0.23/85.23/85
%MODEM-5-DL_GOOD: Modem (2/4) completed firmware download:
MNPClass10v110/V.FCModemRev1.0.23/85.23/85
%MODEM-5-DL_GOOD: Modem (2/6) completed firmware download:
MNPClass10v110/V.FCModemRev1.0.23/85.23/85
%MODEM-5-DL_GOOD: Modem (2/7) completed firmware download:
MNPClass10v110/V.FCModemRev1.0.23/85.23/85
%MODEM-5-DL_GOOD: Modem (2/12) completed firmware download:
MNPClass10v110/V.FCModemRev1.0.23/85.23/85
%MODEM-5-DL_GOOD: Modem (2/11) completed firmware download:
MNPClass10v110/V.FCModemRev1.0.23/85.23/85
%MODEM-5-DL_GOOD: Modem (2/13) completed firmware download:
MNPClass10v110/V.FCModemRev1.0.23/85.23/85
%MODEM-5-DL_GOOD: Modem (2/1) completed firmware download:
MNPClass10v110/V.FCModemRev1.0.23/85.23/85
%MODEM-5-DL_GOOD: Modem (2/14) completed firmware download:
MNPClass10v110/V.FCModemRev1.0.23/85.23/85
%MODEM-5-DL_GOOD: Modem (2/19) completed firmware download:
MNPClass10v110/V.FCModemRev1.0.23/85.23/85
%MODEM-5-DL_GOOD: Modem (2/22) completed firmware download:
MNPClass10v110/V.FCModemRev1.0.23/85.23/85
%MODEM-5-DL_GOOD: Modem (2/5) completed firmware download:
MNPClass10v110/V.FCModemRev1.0.23/85.23/85
%MODEM-5-DL_GOOD: Modem (2/8) completed firmware download:
MNPClass10v110/V.FCModemRev1.0.23/85.23/85
%MODEM-5-DL_GOOD: Modem (2/9) completed firmware download:
MNPClass10v110/V.FCModemRev1.0.23/85.23/85
%MODEM-5-DL_GOOD: Modem (2/17) completed firmware download:
MNPClass10v110/V.FCModemRev1.0.23/85.23/85
%MODEM-5-DL_GOOD: Modem (2/0) completed firmware download:
MNPClass10v110/V.FCModemRev1.0.23/85.23/85
%MODEM-5-DL_GOOD: Modem (2/3) completed firmware download:
MNPClass10v110/V.FCModemRev1.0.23/85.23/85
%MODEM-5-DL_GOOD: Modem (2/21) completed firmware download:
MNPClass10v110/V.FCModemRev1.0.23/85.23/85
%MODEM-5-DL_GOOD: Modem (2/16) completed firmware download:
MNPClass10v110/V.FCModemRev1.0.23/85.23/85
%MODEM-5-DL_GOOD: Modem (2/15) completed firmware download:
MNPClass10v110/V.FCModemRev1.0.23/85.23/85
%MODEM-5-DL_GOOD: Modem (2/18) completed firmware download:
MNPClass10v110/V.FCModemRev1.0.23/85.23/85
%MODEM-5-DL_GOOD: Modem (2/20) completed firmware download:
MNPClass10v110/V.FCModemRev1.0.23/85.23/85
%MODEM-5-DL_GOOD: Modem (2/23) completed firmware download:
MNPClass10v110/V.FCModemRev1.0.23/85.23/85
```

## CONTROLLING MODEMS

This section describes how to manually remove inoperable or bad modems from dial-up services. You can perform the following optional tasks in line configuration mode:

| Task | Command |
|---|---|
| Remove an idle modem from service and indicate it as suspected or proven to be inoperable. | **modem bad** |
| Reset and isolate the modem hardware for extensive troubleshooting. | **modem hold-reset** |
| Gracefully disable a modem from dial services. | **modem busyout** |
| Abruptly shut down a modem from dial service. | **modem shutdown** |
| Set the maximum amount of time the call-switching module waits for a local modem to respond to a request before it is considered locked in a suspended state. The default is five minutes. | **modem recovery-time** *minutes* |

If you use the **modem bad** command to remove an idle modem from dial services and mark it as inoperable, the letter B is used to identify the modem as bad. You can see the letter B for modems that are marked bad by looking at the *Status* column in the **show modem** *slot/port* command's output. Additionally, look at the far left column in the **show modem** command's output. Use the **no modem bad** command to unmark a modem as B and restore it for dial-up connection services. If the letter b appears next to a modem number, it means the modem was removed from service with the **modem shutdown** command or the **modem busyout** command.

**NOTES**

Only idle modems can be marked bad by the **modem bad** command. If you want to mark a modem bad that is actively supporting a call, first issue the **modem shutdown** command then issue the **modem bad** command.

Use the **modem hold-reset** command if you are experiencing extreme modem behavior (for example, if the modem is uncontrollably dialing in to the network). This command prevents the modem from establishing software relationships such as those created by the **test back-to-back modem** command and the **modem autotest** command. The modem is unusable while the **modem hold-reset** command is configured. The **modem hold-reset** command also resets a modem that is frozen in a suspended state. Disable the suspended modem with the **modem hold-reset** command, and then restart hardware initialization with the **no modem hold-reset** command.

The following example disables a suspended modem and resets its hardware initialization:

```
router# configure terminal
router(config)# line 4
```

```
router(config-line)# modem hold-reset
router(config-line)# no modem hold-reset
```

The following example gracefully disables the modem associated with line 1 from dialing and answering calls. The modem is disabled only after all active calls on the modem are dropped.

```
router# configure terminal
router(config)# line 1
router(config)# modem busyout
```

The following example abruptly shuts down the modem associated with line 2. All active calls on the modem are dropped immediately.

```
router# configure terminal
router(config)# line 2
router(config)# modem shutdown
```

In the following example, the modem using TTY line 3 is actively supporting a call. However, we want to mark the modem bad because it has poor connection performance. First abruptly shut down the modem and drop the call with the **modem shutdown** command, then issue the **modem bad** command to take the modem out of service.

```
router# show modem
                  Inc calls     Out calls     Busied   Failed  No       Succ
  Mdm  Usage      Succ    Fail  Succ    Fail  Out      Dial    Answer   Pct.
  1/0    37%       98       4    0        0       0        0        0    96%
  1/1    38%       98       2    0        0       0        0        0    98%
* 1/2     2%        3      99    0        0       0        0        0     1%

...

router# configure terminal
router(config)# line 3
router(config)# modem shutdown
router(config)# modem bad
router(config)# exit
router# show modem
                  Inc calls     Out calls     Busied   Failed  No       Succ
  Mdm  Usage      Succ    Fail  Succ    Fail  Out      Dial    Answer   Pct.
  1/0    37%       98       4    0        0       0        0        0    96%
  1/1    38%       98       2    0        0       0        0        0    98%
B 1/2     2%        3      99    0        0       0        0        0     1%
```

## Collecting Modem Statistics

There are many commands that enable you to display or poll various modem statistics.To show modem performance statistics, perform the following tasks in EXEC mode:

| Task | Command |
|---|---|
| Show various performance statistics for a modem or group of modems. | **show modem** [*slot/port* \| **group** *number*] |
| Show the call-switching module status for a modem or group of modems. | **show modem csm** [*slot/port* \| **group** *number*] |
| Show the event log status for a modem or group of modems. | **show modem log** [*slot/port* \| **group** *number*]* |
| Display the cumulative system statistics for all modems installed in the access server. | **show modem summary*** |
| Display all the active direct connect AT sessions for Microcom modems. | **show modem at-mode*** |

*This command does not apply to nonmanageable modems.

Manageable Microcom modems have an out-of-band feature, which is used for polling modem statistics. To configure the system to poll for modem statistics, perform the tasks in the following task table. Unless otherwise specified, all tasks are performed in global configuration mode.

| Task | | Command |
|---|---|---|
| **Step 1** | Specify the number of seconds between statistical modem polling for Microcom modems. The default is 12 seconds.The configuration range is 2 to 120 seconds. | **modem poll time** *seconds* |
| **Step 2** | Set maximum number of polling attempts to Microcom modems. The default is three polling attempts. The configuration range is from 0 to 10 attempts.* | **modem poll retry** *number* |
| **Step 3** | In line configuration mode, poll for a Microcom modem's status and statistics. | **modem status-poll** |
| **Step 4** | Define the number of modem events that each modem is able to store. The default is 100 events for each modem. Use the **show modem log** command to view modem events. | **modem buffer-size** *number* |

*If the number of attempts to retrieve modem status or statistics exceeds the number you define, the out-of-band feature is removed from operation. In this case, you must reset the modem hardware using the **clear modem** command.

### Show Modem Example

The following example shows example output for the **show modem** command:

```
router# show modem
                     Inc calls         Out calls        Busied    Failed   No         Succ
  Mdm   Usage      Succ     Fail     Succ     Fail     Out       Dial     Answer     Pct.
* 1/0     17%        74        3        0        0        0         0         0       96%
* 1/1     15%        80        4        0        0        0         1         1       95%
* 1/2     15%        82        0        0        0        0         0         0      100%
  1/3     21%        62        1        0        0        0         0         0       98%
  1/4     21%        49        5        0        0        0         0         0       90%
* 1/5     18%        65        3        0        0        0         0         0       95%
* 1/6     19%        58        2        0        0        0         0         0       96%
* 1/7     17%        67        5        0        0        0         1         1       93%
* 1/8     20%        68        3        0        0        0         0         0       95%
  1/9     16%        67        2        0        0        0         0         0       97%
  1/10    18%        56        2        0        0        0         1         1       96%
* 1/11    15%        76        3        0        0        0         0         0       96%
* 1/12    16%        62        1        0        0        0         0         0       98%
  1/13    17%        51        4        0        0        0         0         0       92%
  1/14    16%        51        5        0        0        0         0         0       91%
  1/15    17%        65        0        0        0        0         0         0      100%
  1/16    15%        73        3        0        0        0         0         0       96%
  1/17    17%        67        2        0        0        0         0         0       97%
  1/18    17%        61        2        0        0        0         0         0       96%
* 1/19    17%        74        2        0        0        0         0         0       97%
  1/20    16%        65        1        0        0        0         0         0       98%
* 1/21    16%        58        3        0        0        0         0         0       95%
* 1/22    18%        56        4        0        0        0         0         0       93%
* 1/23    20%        60        4        0        0        0         0         0       93%
```

### Show Modem Summary Example

You can display a high level summary of the modems' performance with the **show modem summary** command:

```
router# show modem summary
          Incoming calls         Outgoing calls         Busied    Failed   No     Succ
Usage   Succ    Fail   Avail    Succ    Fail   Avail    Out       Dial     Ans    Pct.
  14%   2489     123      15       0       0      15          0        3      3     95%
```

### Show Modem Log Example

The following example shows the event log status for a manageable modem. It also identifies the time elapsed since each modem event was performed (for example, 01:02:41 means the modem event occurred 1 hour, 2 minutes, and 41 seconds ago):

```
router# show modem log 0/0
Modem 0/0 Events Log:
  01:03:03: Startup Response: Microcom MNP10 K56 Modem (Select)
            Modem (boot) firmware = 3.1(16) (3.0(4))
            DSP Controller (SPX) rev = 204.173(0) (143.191(0))
  01:03:03: Control Reply: 0xFF1F
  01:03:03: RS232 event: RTS  noDTR* CTS* DSR* noDCD* noRI  noTST
  01:03:03: RS232 event: RTS  noDTR  CTS  DSR  noDCD  noRI  noTST
```

```
01:03:03: Modem State event: Idle
01:03:03: End connection event: Retransmits for MNP block (TX/RX) = 0/0
          Duration = 0:00:00, Number of TX/RX char = 0/0
          Local Disc Reason = Lost Carrier
          Remote Disc Reason = Unknown
01:03:04: Phone number event:
01:02:51: DTR event: DTR On
01:02:51: RS232 event: RTS  DTR* CTS  DSR  noDCD  noRI  noTST
00:39:52: Startup Response: Microcom MNP10 K56 Modem (Select)
          Modem (boot) firmware = 3.1(16) (3.0(4))
          DSP Controller (SPX) rev = 1.1(0) (1.1(0))
```

### Show Modem AT-Mode Example

The following example shows that modem 1/1 has one open AT directly connected session:

```
router# show modem at-mode
Active AT-MODE management sessions:
Modem    User's Terminal
1/1 0 cty 0
```

### Time Interval Example

The following example sets the time interval between polls to 10 seconds using the **modem poll time** configuration command:

```
router# configure terminal
router(config)# modem poll time 10
```

### Modem Polling Example

The following example enables modem status polling through the out-of-band feature, which is associated to line 1:

```
router# configure terminal
router(config)# line 1
router(config-line)# modem status-poll
```

### Polling Attempts Example

The following example configures the server to attempt to retrieve statistics from a local modem up to five times before discontinuing the polling effort:

```
router# configure terminal
router(config)# modem poll retry 5
```

## CHANGING MODEM CONFIGURATION

You can automatically change the running configuration for external modems (not embedded in modem cards) by issuing a single command. Additionally, you can change an integrated modem's running configuration by sending individual AT commands:

- Change Automatically for External Modems
- Change Manually by Sending AT Commands to Integrated Modems

### Change Automatically for External Modems

The Cisco IOS software can issue initialization strings automatically for most types of modems externally attached to an access server. A modem initialization string is a series of parameter settings that are sent to your modem to configure it to interact with the access server in a specified way. The Cisco IOS software defines seven initialization strings that have been found to properly initialize most modems so that the modems function properly with Cisco access servers. These initialization strings have the following names:

- Codex_3260
- Usr_courier
- Usr_sportster
- Hayes_optima
- Global_village
- Viva
- Telebit_t3000

**NOTES**

Internal or integrated modems, such as those used by the Cisco AS5200 and Cisco AS5300, are preconfigured by Cisco Systems and do not need to be initialized.

If you do not know which of these modem strings is appropriate for your modems, issue the **modem autoconfigure discovery** line configuration command, as shown in the following example:

```
2511# configure terminal
2511(config)# line 1 16
2511(config-line)# modem autoconfigure discovery
2511(config-line)# Ctrl-Z
2511# copy running-config startup-config
```

The Cisco IOS software first tries the first of these strings to see if the modem initializes properly. If not, the Cisco IOS software cycles to the next string and repeats the process until the appropriate string is found. If none of the strings properly initializes the modem, you must manually configure the modem.

If you know that your modem can be configured using an initialization string from one of these scripts, you can issue the **modem autoconfigure type** *type* command, where *type* is one of the strings in the preceding list. If you list a specific modem type, initialization proceeds more quickly.

To display the list of modems for which the router has modem string entries, issue the **show modemcap** command. You can change a modem value that was returned from the **show modemcap** EXEC command. For example, you might want to add the factory default, **&F**, entry to the configuration file. To do this, enter the **modemcap edit** *modem-name attribute value* line configuration command. Configure one attribute of one modem at a time.

The following example shows how to enter line configuration mode and issue the **modem autoconfigure type** *type* command for a US Robotics Sportster modem.

```
2511(config-line)# modem autoconfigure type usr_sportster
```

For more information about the recommended strings for any type of modem, see section, "Sample Modem Strings," found in Appendix A, "Configuring Modem Support and Chat Scripts." If you have access to Cisco Connection Online (CCO), you can also access the following URL for more information (which is subject to change without notice):

http://www.cisco.com/warp/customer/76/4.html

### Change Manually by Sending AT Commands to Integrated Modems

Manageable Microcom modems have an out-of-band feature, which is used to poll modem statistics and transmit AT commands. The Cisco IOS software uses a direct connect session to transfer information through this out-of-band feature. To send AT commands to a Microcom modem, you must permit a direct connect session for a specified modem, open a direct connect session, send AT commands to a modem, and clear the directly connected session from the modem when you are finished.

**NOTES**

This section does not describe how to send AT commands to MICA digital modems.

---

Open a direct connect session by issuing the **modem at-mode** *slot/port* command in Privileged EXEC mode. From here, you can transmit AT commands directly from your terminal session window to the internal Microcom modems. Most incoming or outgoing calls on the modems are not interrupted when you open a direct connect session and transmit AT commands. However, some AT commands interrupt a call—for example, the **ATH** command, which hangs up a call. Open and close one direct connect session at a time. Beware that multiple open sessions slow down modem performance.

Refer to the AT command set that came with your router for a complete list of AT commands that you can transmit to the modems.

For Microcom modems, you can clear or terminate an active directly connected session in two ways:

- Press **Ctrl-C** after transmitting all AT commands as instructed by the system when you enter AT command mode.
- Enter a second Telnet session and enable the **clear modem at-mode** *slot/port* command in EXEC configuration mode. This method is used for closing a directly connected session that may have been mistakenly left open by the first Telnet session.

#### *Transmit AT Command Example*

The following example opens a directly connected session on modem 1/1, enters AT command mode on modem 1/1, and transmits the **at%v** and **at\s** commands via the out-of-band feature on modem 1/1:

```
router# modem at-mode 1/1
You are now entering AT command mode on modem (slot 1 / port 1).
Please type CTRL-C to exit AT command mode.
at%v

MNP Class 10 V.34/V.FC Modem Rev 1.0/85

OK
at\s

IDLE            000:00:00
LAST DIAL

NET ADDR:       FFFFFFFFFFFF
MODEM HW: SA 2W United States
4 RTS 5 CTS 6 DSR - CD 20 DTR - RI
MODULATION      IDLE
MODEM BPS       28800  AT%G0
MODEM FLOW      OFF    AT\G0
MODEM MODE      AUT    AT\N3
V.23 OPR.       OFF    AT%F0
AUTO ANS.       ON     ATS0=1
SERIAL BPS      115200 AT%U0
BPS ADJUST      OFF    AT\J0
SPT BPS ADJ.    0      AT\W0
ANSWER MESSGS   ON     ATQ0
SERIAL FLOW     BHW    AT\Q3
PASS XON/XOFF   OFF    AT\X0
PARITY          8N     AT
```

The manageable modem returns "OK" if the AT command you transmit is successfully enabled.

### *Clear a Direct Connect Session from a Second Telnet Session Example*

The following examples are for Microcom modems.

The following example shows how to execute the **modem at-mode** command from a Telnet session:

```
router# modem at-mode 1/1
```

The following example shows how to execute the **clear modem at-mode** command from a second Telnet session while the first Telnet session is connected to the modem:

```
router# clear modem at-mode 1/1
clear "modem at-mode" for modem 1/1 [confirm] <press Return>
router#
```

The following output is displayed in the first Telnet session after the modem is cleared by the second Telnet session:

```
Direct connect session cleared by vty0 (171.69.1.164)
```

# CHAPTER 8

# Modem Management Commands

This chapter describes the commands that manage modems existing inside access servers or routers. Cisco Systems does not consider external modems, which physically connect to an access server or router through an asynchronous cable, to be part of its modem management paradigm.

For configuration information and examples, see Chapter 7, "Managing Modems."

## CLEAR MODEM

To reset a manageable modem's hardware on an access server or router, use the **clear modem** EXEC command.

**clear modem** [*slot/port* | **group** *group-number*]

| *Syntax* | *Description* |
|---|---|
| *slot/port* | Slot and modem port number. Remember to include the forward slash (/) when entering this variable. |
| **group** *group-number* | Modem group. |

### *Default*

Disabled

### *Command Mode*

EXEC

### *Usage Guidelines*

This command first appeared in Cisco IOS Release 11.2.

This command resets the specified modem or group of modems, or all the modems in the system. The modem hardware is reset for modems that are idle or busied out for long periods of time.

You can construct a logical modem group using the **interface group-async** command.

### *Example*

The following example resets the hardware for manageable modem 1/1:

```
clear modem 1/1
```

## CLEAR MODEM AT-MODE

To clear an attention (AT) directly connected session to a manageable Microcom modem from a second Telnet session, use the **clear modem at-mode** EXEC command.

**clear modem at-mode** *slot/port*

| *Syntax* | *Description* |
|---|---|
| **at-mode** | An AT directly connected session. |
| *slot/port* | Slot and modem port number. Remember to include the forward slash (/) when entering this variable. |

### *Default*

Disabled

### *Command Mode*

EXEC

### *Usage Guidelines*

This command first appeared in Cisco IOS Release 11.2.

An AT directly connected session is usually initiated and closed from the same Telnet session by using the **modem at-mode** command and **Ctrl-C**. However, you can clear an AT directly connected session that was mistakenly left open by enabling the **clear modem at-mode** command from a second Telnet session in to the access server.

### *Examples*

The following example executes the **modem at-mode** command from a Telnet session:

```
modem at-mode 1/1
```

The following example executes the **clear modem at-mode** command from a second Telnet session while the first Telnet session is connected to the modem:

```
router# clear modem at-mode 1/1
clear "modem at-mode" for modem 1/1 [confirm]
router#
```

The following output is displayed in the first Telnet session after the modem is cleared by the second Telnet session:

```
Direct connect session cleared by vty0 (171.69.1.164)
```



### *Related Commands*

Search online to find documentation for related commands.

**modem at-mode**

## CLEAR MODEM COUNTERS

To clear the statistical counters on a manageable modem installed in an access server, use the **clear modem counters** EXEC command.

**clear modem counters** [*slot/port* | **group** *group-number*]

| *Syntax* | *Description* |
|---|---|
| *slot/port* | (Optional) Slot and modem port number. Remember to include the forward slash (/) when entering this variable. |
| **group** *group-number* | (Optional) Modem group. |

### *Default*

Disabled

### *Command Mode*

EXEC

### *Usage Guidelines*

This command first appeared in Cisco IOS Release 11.2.

Entering the **clear modem counters** command without specifying an optional keyword or argument resets the modem statistics on each modem and the summary statistics displayed in the **show modem summary** command.

You can create a logical modem group using the **interface group-async** command.

### *Example*

The following example clears the statistical counters on manageable modem 1/1:

```
clear modem counters 1/1
```

### COPY MODEM

To copy modem firmware to integrated modems in an access server, use the **copy modem** EXEC command.

**copy** {**flash** | **tftp** | **rcp**} **modem**

| *Syntax* | *Description* |
|---|---|
| **flash** | Copies firmware from Flash memory to the modems. |
| **tftp** | Copies firmware from a local TFTP server on your network to the modems. |
| **rcp** | Copies firmware from a local rcp server on your network to the modems. |

#### *Default*

Disabled

#### *Command Mode*

EXEC

#### *Usage Guidelines*

This command first appeared in Cisco IOS Release 11.2.

After you enable this command, you are asked to provide the download destination (a *slot/port* or **all**), the remote host name, and the path leading to the source modem firmware.

If a modem that you want to upgrade is busy with a call when the **copy modem** command is enabled, the upgrade for that modem yields until the active call is dropped. All other idle modems in the upgrade range proceed with the downloading operation.

#### *Examples*

The following example copies the modem firmware file called modem_upgrade from the TFTP server called Modem_Server to modem 2/0, which is installed in a Cisco AS5200 access server:

```
router# copy tftp modem
Modem Numbers (<slot>/<port>[-<slot>/<port>] ¦ group <number> ¦ all)? 2/0
Address or name of remote host [UNKNOWN]? Modem_Server
Source file name? dirt/elem/modem_upgrade
Accessing file 'dirt/elem/modem_upgrade on Modem_Server...
Loading dirt/elem/modem_upgrade .from 223.255.254.254 (via Ethernet0): ! [OK]

Loading dirt/elem/modem_upgrade from 223.255.254.254 (via Ethernet0):
!!!!!!!!!!!!!!!!!!!!!!!!!!!!!!!!!!!!!!!!!!!!!!!!!
[OK - 237503/278528 bytes]

router#
%MODEM-5-DL_START: Modem (2/0) started firmware download
%MODEM-5-DL_GOOD: Modem (2/0) completed firmware download:
MNPClass10V.34/V.FCModemRev1.0.23/85.23/85
```

As shown in this example, you might want to upgrade and test one modem's firmware before upgrading the firmware of all the modems on the access server, as shown in the next example.

This example downloads the same modem firmware file from the TFTP server to all the modems in the Cisco AS5200 access server:

```
router# copy tftp modem
Modem Numbers (<slot>/<port>[-<slot>/<port>] ¦ group <number> ¦ all)? all
Address or name of remote host [UNKNOWN]? Modem_Server
Source file name? dirt/elem/modem_upgrade
Accessing file 'dirt/elem/modem_upgrade on Modem_Server...
Loading dirt/elem/modem_upgrade .from 223.255.254.254 (via Ethernet0): ! [OK]

Loading dirt/elem/modem_upgrade from 223.255.254.254 (via Ethernet0):
!!!!!!!!!!!!!!!!!!!!!!!!!!!!!!!!!!!!!!!!!!!!!!!
[OK - 237503/278528 bytes]

router#
%MODEM-5-DL_START: Modem (2/0) started firmware download
%MODEM-5-DL_START: Modem (2/1) started firmware download
%MODEM-5-DL_START: Modem (2/2) started firmware download
%MODEM-5-DL_START: Modem (2/3) started firmware download
%MODEM-5-DL_START: Modem (2/4) started firmware download
%MODEM-5-DL_START: Modem (2/5) started firmware download
%MODEM-5-DL_START: Modem (2/6) started firmware download
%MODEM-5-DL_START: Modem (2/7) started firmware download
%MODEM-5-DL_START: Modem (2/8) started firmware download
%MODEM-5-DL_START: Modem (2/9) started firmware download
%MODEM-5-DL_START: Modem (2/10) started firmware download
%MODEM-5-DL_START: Modem (2/11) started firmware download
%MODEM-5-DL_START: Modem (2/12) started firmware download
%MODEM-5-DL_START: Modem (2/13) started firmware download
%MODEM-5-DL_START: Modem (2/14) started firmware download
%MODEM-5-DL_START: Modem (2/15) started firmware download
%MODEM-5-DL_START: Modem (2/16) started firmware download
%MODEM-5-DL_START: Modem (2/17) started firmware download
%MODEM-5-DL_START: Modem (2/18) started firmware download
%MODEM-5-DL_START: Modem (2/19) started firmware download
%MODEM-5-DL_START: Modem (2/20) started firmware download
%MODEM-5-DL_START: Modem (2/21) started firmware download
%MODEM-5-DL_START: Modem (2/22) started firmware download
%MODEM-5-DL_START: Modem (2/23) started firmware download
%MODEM-5-DL_GOOD: Modem (2/2) completed firmware download:
MNPClass10V.34/V.FCModemRev1.0.23/85.23/85
%MODEM-5-DL_GOOD: Modem (2/10) completed firmware download:
MNPClass10V.34/V.FCModemRev1.0.23/85.23/85
%MODEM-5-DL_GOOD: Modem (2/4) completed firmware download:
MNPClass10V.34/V.FCModemRev1.0.23/85.23/85
%MODEM-5-DL_GOOD: Modem (2/6) completed firmware download:
MNPClass10V.34/V.FCModemRev1.0.23/85.23/85
%MODEM-5-DL_GOOD: Modem (2/7) completed firmware download:
MNPClass10V.34/V.FCModemRev1.0.23/85.23/85
%MODEM-5-DL_GOOD: Modem (2/12) completed firmware download:
MNPClass10V.34/V.FCModemRev1.0.23/85.23/85
```

```
%MODEM-5-DL_GOOD: Modem (2/11) completed firmware download:
MNPClass10V.34/V.FCModemRev1.0.23/85.23/85
%MODEM-5-DL_GOOD: Modem (2/13) completed firmware download:
MNPClass10V.34/V.FCModemRev1.0.23/85.23/85
%MODEM-5-DL_GOOD: Modem (2/1) completed firmware download:
MNPClass10V.34/V.FCModemRev1.0.23/85.23/85
%MODEM-5-DL_GOOD: Modem (2/14) completed firmware download:
MNPClass10V.34/V.FCModemRev1.0.23/85.23/85
%MODEM-5-DL_GOOD: Modem (2/19) completed firmware download:
MNPClass10V.34/V.FCModemRev1.0.23/85.23/85
%MODEM-5-DL_GOOD: Modem (2/22) completed firmware download:
MNPClass10V.34/V.FCModemRev1.0.23/85.23/85
%MODEM-5-DL_GOOD: Modem (2/5) completed firmware download:
MNPClass10V.34/V.FCModemRev1.0.23/85.23/85
%MODEM-5-DL_GOOD: Modem (2/8) completed firmware download:
MNPClass10V.34/V.FCModemRev1.0.23/85.23/85
%MODEM-5-DL_GOOD: Modem (2/9) completed firmware download:
MNPClass10V.34/V.FCModemRev1.0.23/85.23/85
%MODEM-5-DL_GOOD: Modem (2/17) completed firmware download:
MNPClass10V.34/V.FCModemRev1.0.23/85.23/85
%MODEM-5-DL_GOOD: Modem (2/0) completed firmware download:
MNPClass10V.34/V.FCModemRev1.0.23/85.23/85
%MODEM-5-DL_GOOD: Modem (2/3) completed firmware download:
MNPClass10V.34/V.FCModemRev1.0.23/85.23/85
%MODEM-5-DL_GOOD: Modem (2/21) completed firmware download:
MNPClass10V.34/V.FCModemRev1.0.23/85.23/85
%MODEM-5-DL_GOOD: Modem (2/16) completed firmware download:
MNPClass10V.34/V.FCModemRev1.0.23/85.23/85
%MODEM-5-DL_GOOD: Modem (2/15) completed firmware download:
MNPClass10V.34/V.FCModemRev1.0.23/85.23/85
%MODEM-5-DL_GOOD: Modem (2/18) completed firmware download:
MNPClass10V.34/V.FCModemRev1.0.23/85.23/85
%MODEM-5-DL_GOOD: Modem (2/20) completed firmware download:
MNPClass10V.34/V.FCModemRev1.0.23/85.23/85
%MODEM-5-DL_GOOD: Modem (2/23) completed firmware download:
MNPClass10V.34/V.FCModemRev1.0.23/85.23/85
```

The following example copies the modem firmware file called STAR.M from Flash memory to the integrated modem 1/2:

```
router# copy flash modem
Modem Numbers (<slot>/<port> | group <number> | all)? 1/2

System flash directory:
File  Length   Name/status
  1   3539820  as5200-i-m.allcookies
  2   239203   STAR.M
  3   23072    BOOT.105 [3802288 bytes used, 4586320 available, 8388608 total]
Source file name? STAR.M
router#
%MODEM-5-DL_START: Modem (1/2) started firmware download
%MODEM-5-DL_GOOD: Modem (1/2) completed firmware download:
MNPClass10V.34/V.FCModemRev1.0.23/85.23/85
router#
```

## MODEM ANSWER-TIMEOUT

To set the amount of time that the Cisco IOS software waits for the Clear to Send (CTS) signal after raising the data terminal ready (DTR) signal in response to RING, use the **modem answer-timeout** line configuration command. Use the **no** form of this command to revert to the default value.

**modem answer-timeout** *seconds*
**no modem answer-timeout**

| *Syntax* | *Description* |
|---|---|
| *seconds* | Specifies the timeout interval in seconds. |

### *Default*

15 seconds

### *Command Mode*

Line configuration

### *Usage Guidelines*

This command first appeared in Cisco IOS Release 10.0.

This command is useful for modems that take a long time to synchronize to the appropriate line speed.

For more information, see Chapter 5, "Configuring Modem Support and Asynchronous Devices."

### *Example*

The following example sets the timeout interval to 20 seconds for the modem connected to lines 3 through 13:

```
line 3 13
 modem answer-timeout 20
```

### *Related Commands*

Search online to find documentation for related commands.

**modem callin**
**modem inout**

## MODEM AT-MODE

To open a directly connected session and enter AT command mode, which is used for sending AT commands to Microcom manageable modems, use the **modem at-mode** EXEC command.

**modem at-mode** *slot/port*

| *Syntax* | *Description* |
|---|---|
| *slot/port* | Slot and modem port number. Remember to include the forward slash (/) when entering this variable. |

### Default

Disabled

### Command Mode

EXEC

### Usage Guidelines

This command first appeared in Cisco IOS Release 11.2.

Manageable modems return "OK" if the AT command you transmit is successfully enabled. Press **Ctrl-C** after transmitting an AT command to close the directly connected session.

**NOTES**

This command does not apply to nonmanageable modems, which do not have out-of-band ports.

### Example

The following example opens a directly connected session on modem 1/1, enters AT command mode on modem 1/1, and transmits the AT command **ATH** through the out-of-band feature of modem 1/1:

```
router# modem at-mode 1/1
You are now entering AT command mode on modem (slot 1 / port 1).
Please type CTRL-C to exit AT command mode.
at%v

MNP Class 10 V.34/V.FC Modem Rev 1.0/85

OK
at\s

IDLE           000:00:00
LAST DIAL

NET ADDR:      FFFFFFFFFFFF
MODEM HW: SA 2W United States
4 RTS 5 CTS 6 DSR - CD 20 DTR - RI
MODULATION     IDLE
MODEM BPS      28800  AT%G0
MODEM FLOW     OFF    AT\G0
MODEM MODE     AUT    AT\N3
V.23 OPR.      OFF    AT%F0
```

```
AUTO ANS.       ON     ATS0=1
SERIAL BPS      115200 AT%U0
BPS ADJUST      OFF    AT\J0
SPT BPS ADJ.    0      AT\W0
ANSWER MESSGS   ON     ATQ0
SERIAL FLOW     BHW    AT\Q3
PASS XON/XOFF   OFF    AT\X0
PARITY          8N     AT
```

### *Related Commands*

Search online to find documentation for related commands.

**clear modem at-mode**

## MODEM AT-MODE-PERMIT

To permit a Microcom modem to accept a directly connected session, use the **modem at-mode-permit** line configuration command. The **no** form of this command disables permission for modems to accept a direct connection.

**modem at-mode-permit**
**no modem at-mode-permit**

### *Syntax Description*

This command has no keywords or arguments.

### *Default*

Enabled

### *Command Mode*

Line configuration

### *Usage Guidelines*

This command first appeared in Cisco IOS Release 11.2.

After you enter this command, enter the **modem at-mode** command to enable a directly connected session on the modem. From AT command mode, you can enter AT commands directly from your terminal session.

For a complete list of supported AT commands, refer to the AT command documentation that came with your access server or router.

The **no modem at-mode-permit** command disables a modem from accepting a direct connection, which is useful for ensuring modem security.

**NOTES**

This command does not apply to nonmanageable modems, which do not have out-of-band ports.

### *Example*

The following example permits the modem connected to TTY line 1 to accept a directly connected session:

```
line 1
 modem at-mode-permit
```

### *Related Commands*

Search online to find documentation for related commands.

**clear modem at-mode**
**modem at-mode**

## MODEM AUTOCONFIGURE DISCOVERY

To configure a line to discover what kind of modem is connected to the router and to configure that modem automatically, use the **modem autoconfigure discovery** line configuration command. Use the **no** form of this command to disable this feature.

**modem autoconfigure discovery**

### *Syntax Description*

This command has no arguments or keywords.

### *Default*

This command has no default.

### *Command Mode*

Line configuration

### *Usage Guidelines*

This command first appeared in Cisco IOS Release 11.1.

The modem is identified each time the line is reset. If a modem cannot be detected, the line continues retrying for 10 seconds. When the modem type is determined, this information remains stored until the modem is recycled or disconnected. Discovery mode is much slower than configuring a line directly.

Each time the modem is reset (every time a chat reset script is executed), a string of commands is sent to the modem, the first one being "return to factory-defaults."

### *Example*

The following example discovers whatever kind of modem is attached to the router or access server:

```
modem autoconfigure discovery
```

### *Related Commands*

Search online to find documentation for related commands.

**modem autoconfigure type**

## MODEM AUTOCONFIGURE TYPE

To direct a line to attempt to configure the attached modem using the entry for *modem-name*, use the **modem autoconfigure type** line configuration command. Use the **no** form of this command to disable this feature.

**modem autoconfigure type** *modem-name*
**no modem autoconfigure type**

| *Syntax* | *Description* |
|---|---|
| *modem-name* | The name of the modem (such as Codex_3260). |

### *Default*

This command has no default.

### *Command Mode*

Line configuration

### *Usage Guidelines*

This command first appeared in Cisco IOS Release 11.1.

The modem is reconfigured each time the line goes down.

### *Example*

The following example automatically configures the attached modem using the codex_3260 modemcap entry:

```
modem autoconfigure type Codex_3260
```

### *Related Commands*

Search online to find documentation for related commands.

**modem autoconfigure discovery**

### MODEM AUTOTEST

To automatically and periodically perform a modem diagnostics test for modems inside the access server or router, use the **modem autotest** global configuration command. Use the **no** form of this command to disable or turn off the modem autotest service.

**modem autotest** {**error** *threshold* | **minimum** *modem* | **time** *hh:mm* [*interval*]}
**no modem autotest**

| Syntax | Description |
|---|---|
| **error** *threshold* | Maximum modem error threshold. When the system detects this many errors with the modems, the modem diagnostics test is automatically triggered. Specify a *threshold* count between 3 and 50. |
| **minimum** *modem* | Minimum number of modems that will remain untested and available to accept calls during each test cycle. You can specify between 5 and 48 modems. The default is 6 modems. |
| **time** *hh:mm* | Time you want the modem autotest to begin. You must use the military time convention and a required colon (:) between the hours and minutes variables for this feature. For example, 1:30 a.m. is issued as 01:30. |
| *interval* | (Optional) Long-range time variable used to set the modem autotest more than one day in advance. The range of hours is between 1 hour and 168 hours. For example, if you want to run the test once per week, issue 168. There are 168 hours in one week. |

#### *Default*

Disabled

#### *Command Mode*

Global configuration

#### *Usage Guidelines*

This command first appeared in Cisco IOS Release 11.3.

#### *Example*

The following example shows how to set the modem autotest to run once per week at 3:00 a.m. Additionally, the autotest will activate if the system detects a modem error count higher than 40 errors.

**Step 1** Determine the current time set on the access server with the **show clock** EXEC command. In this example, the time and date set is 3:00 p.m, Monday, August 25, 1997:

```
router# show clock
*15:00:01.031 EST Aug 25 1997
```

**Step 2** Enter global configuration mode and set the time you want the modem autotest to activate. In this example, the access server is configured to run the modem autotest each ongoing Tuesday at 3:00 a.m:

```
router# configure terminal
Enter configuration commands, one per line.  End with CNTL/Z.
router(config)# modem autotest time 03:00 168
```

**Step 3** Configure the autotest to activate if the system detects a high modem error count. In this example, the autotest activates if the system detects a modem error count higher than 40 errors. For the list of modem errors that are monitored by the **modem autotest** command, see the **show modem call-stats** command.

```
router(config)# modem autotest error 40
router(config)# exit
router#
%SYS-5-CONFIG_I: Configured from console by console
router#
```

**Step 4** Display the results of the modem autotest once the test has run through a test cycle by issuing the **show modem test** EXEC command:

```
router# show modem test

Date Time          Modem   Test                  Reason               State Resul
t
 5/15 07:25:17 AM  1/0     Back-To-Back          TIME INTERVAL        Idle   FAIL
 5/15 07:25:17 AM  1/1     Back-To-Back          TIME INTERVAL        Idle   PASS
 5/15 07:25:17 AM  1/2     Back-To-Back          TIME INTERVAL        Idle   PASS
 5/15 07:25:17 AM  1/3     Back-To-Back          TIME INTERVAL        Idle   FAIL
 5/15 07:25:17 AM  1/4     Back-To-Back          TIME INTERVAL        Idle   PASS
 5/15 07:25:17 AM  1/5     Back-To-Back          TIME INTERVAL        Idle   PASS
 5/15 07:25:17 AM  1/6     Back-To-Back          TIME INTERVAL        Idle   PASS
 5/15 07:25:17 AM  1/7     Back-To-Back          TIME INTERVAL        Idle   PASS
 5/15 07:25:17 AM  1/8     Back-To-Back          TIME INTERVAL        Idle   PASS
 5/15 07:25:17 AM  1/9     Back-To-Back          TIME INTERVAL        Idle   PASS
...
```

Alternatively, you can view which modems were marked bad by the modem autotest by issuing the **show modem** EXEC command. Bad modems are marked by the letter B. In this example, modems 1/0 and 1/3 are marked bad (identified with a B), which takes them out of commission and unable to participate in dial services:

```
router# show modem

                         Inc calls     Out calls     Busied     Failed   No        Succ
```

```
       Mdm   Usage    Succ   Fail   Succ   Fail    Out     Dial   Answer  Pct.
     B 1/0    0%       0      0      0      0       1       0       0      0%
       1/1    0%       0      0      0      0       3       0       0      0%
       1/2    0%       0      0      0      0       1       0       0      0%
     B 1/3    0%       0      0      0      0       1       0       0      0%
       1/4    0%       0      0      0      0       1       0       0      0%
       1/5    0%       0      0      0      0       1       0       0      0%
       1/6    0%       0      0      0      0       1       0       0      0%
       1/7    0%       0      0      0      0       1       0       0      0%
       1/8    0%       0      0      0      0       1       0       0      0%
       1/9    0%       0      0      0      0       1       0       0      0%
       1/10   0%       0      0      0      0       1       0       0      0%
       1/11   0%       0      0      0      0       1       0       0      0%
       1/12   0%       0      0      0      0       1       0       0      0%
       1/13   0%       0      0      0      0       1       0       0      0%
       1/14   0%       0      0      0      0       1       0       0      0%
       1/15   0%       0      0      0      0       1       0       0      0%
       1/16   0%       0      0      0      0       1       0       0      0%
       1/17   0%       0      0      0      0       1       0       0      0%
       1/18   0%       0      0      0      0       0       0       0      0%
       1/19   0%       0      0      0      0       0       0       0      0%
       1/20   0%       0      0      0      0       0       0       0      0%
       1/21   0%       0      0      0      0       0       0       0      0%
       1/22   0%       0      0      0      0       0       0       0      0%
       1/23   0%       0      0      0      0       0       0       0      0%
```

## MODEM BAD

To remove an integrated modem from service and indicate it as suspected or proven to be inoperable, use the **modem bad** line configuration command. Use the **no** form of this command to restore a modem to service.

**modem bad**
**no modem bad**

### *Syntax Description*

This command has no keywords or arguments.

### *Default*

Disabled

### *Command Mode*

Line configuration

### *Usage Guidelines*

This command first appeared in Cisco IOS Release 11.2.

If you mark a modem as inoperable, it appears as *Bad*—without the asterisk (*)—in the *Status* column of the **show modem** command output. A modem marked inoperable by the **modem startup-test** command appears as *Bad** in the **show modem** command output. Use the **no modem bad** command to unmark a modem as *Bad** or *Bad* and restore it for dial-up connection services.

**NOTES**

Only idle modems can be marked bad by the **modem bad** command. If you want to mark a modem bad that is actively supporting a call, first issue the **modem shutdown** command, then issue the **modem bad** command.

### *Example*

The first part of the following example shows a successful connection between modem 2/1 and modem 2/0, which verifies normal operating conditions between these two modems. However, when modem 2/1 is tested against modem 2/3, the back-to-back modem test fails. Therefore, modem 2/3 is suspected or proven to be inoperable. Modem 2/3 is removed from dial-up services through the use of the **modem bad** command on line 28.

```
router# test modem back-to-back 2/1 2/0
Repetitions (of 10-byte packets) [1]: 10
router#
%MODEM-5-B2BCONNECT: Modems (2/1) and (2/0) connected in back-to-back test: CONN
ECT9600/REL-MNP
%MODEM-5-B2BMODEMS: Modems (2/0) and (2/1) completed back-to-back test: success/
packets = 20/20
router# test modem back-to-back 2/1 2/3
Repetitions (of 10-byte packets) [1]: 10
router#
%MODEM-5-BADMODEMS: Modems (2/3) and (2/1) failed back-to-back test: NOCARRIER
router# configure terminal
router(config)# line 28
router(config-line)# modem bad
router(config-line)# end
```

### *Related Commands*

Search online to find documentation for related commands.

**modem startup-test**
**show modem**
**test modem back-to-back**

### MODEM BUFFER-SIZE

To configure the size of the history event queue buffer for integrated modems installed in an access server or router, use the **modem buffer-size** command.

**modem buffer-size** *number*

| *Syntax* | *Description* |
|---|---|
| *number* | Defined number of modem events that each manageable modem is able to store. |

#### *Default*

100 modem events

#### *Command Mode*

Global configuration

#### *Usage Guidelines*

This command first appeared in Cisco IOS Release 11.2.

A large buffer size uses significant amounts of processing memory. If the processing memory is running low, reduce the modem buffer size.

To view modem events, use the **show modem log** command.

**NOTES**

This command does not apply to nonmanageable modems, which do not have out-of-band ports.

#### *Example*

The following example enables each modem in the access server to store 150 modem events:

```
modem buffer-size 150
```

#### *Related Commands*

Search online to find documentation for related commands.

**show modem log**

### MODEM BUSYOUT

To gracefully disable a modem from dialing or answering calls, use the **modem busyout** line configuration command. Use the **no** form of this command to re-enable a modem.

**modem busyout**
**no modem busyout**

### *Syntax Description*

This command has no keywords or arguments.

### *Default*

Disabled

### *Command Mode*

Line configuration

### *Usage Guidelines*

This command first appeared in Cisco IOS Release 11.2.

The disabling action is not executed until the active modem returns to an idle state. No active connections are interrupted when you use this command.

### *Example*

The following example disables the modem associated with line 1 from dialing and answering calls. You do not specify a *slot/port* number with this command:

```
line 1
 modem busyout
```

### *Related Commands*

Search online to find documentation for related commands.

**modem shutdown**

## MODEMCAP EDIT

To change a modem value that was returned from the **show modemcap** command, use the **modemcap edit** global configuration command.

**modemcap edit** *modem-name attribute value*

| *Syntax* | *Description* |
|---|---|
| *modem-name* | Name of the modem whose values are being edited. |
| *attribute* | Modem capability, or attribute, as defined by the **show modemcap** command. |
| *value* | The AT command equivalent (such as &F). |

### *Default*

This command has no default.

### *Command Mode*

Global configuration

### *Usage Guidelines*

This command first appeared in Cisco IOS Release 11.1.

Modemcaps are printed within the configuration file. You can edit them using this command.

Configure one attribute of one modem at a time. See the modem-capability values defined by **show modemcap** command.

### *Example*

The following example adds the factory default entry, &F, to the configuration file. This entry, and others like it, are stored in a database that is referenced by the configuration file.

```
modemcap edit Codex_3250 factory-default &F
```

### *Related Commands*

Search online to find documentation for related commands.

**modemcap entry**
**show modemcap**

## MODEMCAP ENTRY

To store and compress information about the capability of a specified modem, use the **modemcap entry** global configuration command. Use the **no** form of this command to disable this feature.

**modemcap entry** *modem-type*

| *Syntax* | *Description* |
| --- | --- |
| *modem-type* | Type of supported modem as specified in Table 8–1. |

### *Default*

The capability values that exist in the specified modem at the time that the command is issued

### *Command Mode*

Global configuration

### *Usage Guidelines*

This command first appeared in Cisco IOS Release 11.1.

This command displays the capability of the specified modem.

Modemcaps are printed within the configuration file and are intended to be edited using the **modemcap edit** command. The **modemcap entry** command does not display values that are not set in the modem.

Use **modemcap entry** with the **show modemcap** command to interpret the capability of the specified modem. Table 8–1 lists the modemcap entries for supported modems.

**Table 8–1** *Modemcap Entries for Supported Modems*

| Modem Type | Output |
|---|---|
| hayes_optima | FD=&F:AA=S0=1:DTR=&D2:CD=&C1:TPL=default. |
| codex_3260 | FD=&F:AA=S0=1:CD=&C1:DTR=&D2:HFL=*FL3:SPD=*SC1:BER=*SM3:BCP=*DC1:NER=*SM1:NCP=*DC0:NEC=E0:NRS=Q1:CID=&S1. |
| usr_courier | HFL=&H1&R2:SPD=&B1:BER=&M4:BCP=&K1:NER=&M0:NCP=&K0:TPL=default. |
| usr_sportster | TPL=usr_courier. |
| hayes_optima | HFL=&K3:BER=&Q5:BCP=&Q9:NER=&Q0:NCP=&Q0:TPL=default |
| viva | HFL=&K3:BER=&Q5:BCP=%C1:NER=&Q6:NCP=%C0:TPL=default |
| telebit_t3000 | HFL=S58=2:BER=S180=3:BCP=S190=1:NER=S180=0:NCP=S190=0:TPL=default. |

### *Related Commands*

Search online to find documentation for related commands.

**modemcap edit**
**show modemcap**

## MODEM HOLD-RESET

To reset and isolate integrated modems for extensive troubleshooting, use the **modem hold-reset** line configuration command. Use the **no** form of this command to restart a modem.

**modem hold-reset**
**no modem hold-reset**

### *Syntax Description*

This command has no keywords or arguments.

*Default*

Disabled

*Command Mode*

Line configuration

*Usage Guidelines*

This command first appeared in Cisco IOS Release 11.2.

This command is also used to reset a modem that is frozen in a suspended state. Disable the suspended modem with the **modem hold-reset** command, and then restart initialization with the **no modem hold-reset** command.

The **modem hold-reset** command for the V.110 port module resets the processor on board the module only if the command is executed on all 12 ports. If the **modem hold-reset** command is issued on only a portion of the V.110 ports, the processor will not reset.

*Example*

The following example disables the suspended modem using tty line 4 and resets the modem's initialization:

```
router# configure terminal
Enter configuration commands, one per line.  End with CNTL/Z.
router(config)# line 4
router(config-line)# modem hold-reset
router(config-line)# no modem hold-reset
```

The following example resets a 12-port V.110 port module. You must specify the entire tty line range for the entire bank of ports.

```
router# configure terminal
Enter configuration commands, one per line.  End with CNTL/Z.
router(config)# line 1 12
router(config-line)# modem hold-reset
router(config-line)# no modem hold-reset
router(config-line)# exit
router(config)#
```

*Related Commands*

Search online to find documentation for related commands.

**modem autotest**

## MODEM POLL RETRY

To set the maximum number of polling attempts used to retrieve performance statistics from a modem installed in an access server or router, use the **modem poll retry** global configuration command.

**modem poll retry** *number*

| *Syntax* | *Description* |
| --- | --- |
| *number* | Maximum number of polling attempts. The configuration range is from 0 to 10 attempts. |

### *Default*

Three polling attempts

### *Command Mode*

Global configuration

### *Usage Guidelines*

This command first appeared in Cisco IOS Release 11.2.

Higher settings cause the software to keep polling one modem for status and to avoid polling other modems, which decreases the amount of statistics that are gathered.

**NOTES**

This command does not apply to nonmanageable modems, which do not have out-of-band ports.

### *Example*

The following example configures the server to attempt to retrieve statistics from a local modem up to five times before discontinuing the polling effort:

```
modem poll retry 5
```

### *Related Commands*

Search online to find documentation for related commands.

**clear modem**
**modem poll time**
**modem status-poll**

## MODEM POLL TIME

To set the time interval between modem polls, which are used to periodically retrieve and report modem statistics, use the **modem poll time** global configuration command. To restore the 12-second default setting, use the **no** form of this command.

**modem poll time** *seconds*
**no modem poll time** *seconds*

| Syntax | Description |
|---|---|
| *seconds* | Number of seconds between polls. The configuration range is from 2 to 120 seconds. |

### Default

12 seconds

### Command Mode

Global configuration

### Usage Guidelines

This command first appeared in Cisco IOS Release 11.2.

This command does not apply to nonmanageable modems, which do not have out-of-band ports.

### Example

The following example sets the time interval between polls to 10 seconds:

```
modem poll time 10
```

### Related Commands

Search online to find documentation for related commands.

**modem poll retry**
**modem status-poll**

## MODEM RECOVERY-TIME

To set the maximum amount of time the call-switching module waits for a local modem to respond to a request before it is considered locked in a suspended state, use the **modem recovery-time** global configuration command. The **no** form of this command sets a 5-minute response time, which is the default setting.

**modem recovery-time** *minutes*
**no modem recovery-time**

| Syntax | Description |
|---|---|
| *minutes* | Maximum amount of time local modems wait for a response. |

### Default

5 minutes

### *Command Mode*

Global configuration

### *Usage Guidelines*

This command first appeared in Cisco IOS Release 11.2.

**NOTES**

This command does not apply to nonmanageable modems, which do not have out-of-band ports.

After the call-switching module resets a suspended modem, it recovers to a default call-switching module state.

### *Example*

The following example configures the call-switching module to wait for 8 minutes:

```
modem recovery-time 8
```

## MODEM SHUTDOWN

To abruptly shut down an active or idle modem installed in an access server or router, use the **modem shutdown** line configuration command. Use the **no** form of this command to take the modem out of a shutdown state and place it back in service.

**modem shutdown**
**no modem shutdown**

### *Syntax Description*

This command has no keywords or arguments.

### *Default*

Disabled

### *Command Mode*

Line configuration

### *Usage Guidelines*

This command first appeared in Cisco IOS Release 11.2.

Enable the **no modem shutdown** command to restore to service a modem that has been shut down.

### Example

The following example abruptly shuts down the modem associated with line 2. All active calls on the modem are dropped immediately.

```
configure terminal
 line 2
  modem shutdown
```

### Related Commands

Search online to find documentation for related commands.

**modem busyout**

## MODEM STARTUP-TEST

To perform diagnostic testing on each integrated modem during the rebooting process, use the **modem startup-test** global configuration command. Use the **no** form of this command to disable startup testing.

**modem startup-test**
**no modem startup-test**

### Syntax Description

This command has no keywords or arguments.

### Default

Enabled

### Command Mode

Global configuration

### Usage Guidelines

This command first appeared in Cisco IOS Release 11.2.

The results of the modem startup test are displayed in the *Status* column of the **show modem** command's output. Modems that pass the diagnostic test are marked as *Idle*, *Busy*, *Downloading*, and *Reset*. Modems that fail the diagnostic test are marked as *Bad**. These modems cannot be used for call connections. Depending on how many modems are installed, this diagnostic test may take from 5 to 15 minutes to complete.

Perform additional testing on an inoperative modem by executing the **test modem back-to-back** command. The **no modem startup-test** command disables startup testing.

### Example

The following example performs a startup test on the integrated Cisco AS5200 modems:

```
configure terminal
 modem startup-test
```

Display the results of the modem startup test after you restart the system by enabling the **show modem** command.

### *Related Commands*

Search online to find documentation for related commands.

**modem autotest**
**show modem**
**test modem back-to-back**

## MODEM STATUS-POLL

To poll for modem statistics through a modem's out-of-band feature, use the **modem status-poll** line configuration command. Use the **no** form of this command to disable status polling through the out-of-band feature for a specified modem.

**modem status-poll**
**no modem status-poll**

### *Syntax Description*

This command has no keywords or arguments.

### *Default*

Enabled

### *Command Mode*

Line configuration

### *Usage Guidelines*

This command first appeared in Cisco IOS Release 11.2.

This command applies only to manageable modems that have out-of-band ports.

**NOTES**

This command does not apply to nonmanageable modems, which do not have out-of-band ports.

### *Example*

The following example enables modem status polling through TTY line 1:

```
configure terminal
 line 1
  modem status-poll
```

### *Related Commands*

Search online to find documentation for related commands.

**modem poll retry**
**modem poll time**

## SHOW MODEM

To display a high-level performance report for all the modems or a single modem inside an access server or router, use the **show modem** EXEC command.

**show modem** [*slot/port* | **group** *number*]

| *Syntax* | *Description* |
|---|---|
| *slot/port* | (Optional) Specifies the location of a slot and modem port. If this number is not specified, statistics for all connected modems are displayed. Remember to include the forward slash (/) when entering this variable. |
| **group** *number* | (Optional) Specifies a modem group to which a specified modem belongs. The group number range is between 1 and 200. |

### *Command Mode*

User and Privileged EXEC

### *Usage Guidelines*

This command first appeared in Cisco IOS Release 11.2.

### *Sample Displays*

The following display shows output information for the **show modem** command for two V.34 modem cards inserted in a Cisco AS5200:

```
router# show modem
                    Inc calls      Out calls      Busied   Failed  No       Succ
  Mdm   Usage    Succ    Fail   Succ    Fail   Out      Dial    Answer   Pct.
* 1/0    17%      74       3      0       0       0        0       0      96%
* 1/1    15%      80       4      0       0       0        1       1      95%
* 1/2    15%      82       0      0       0       0        0       0     100%
  1/3    21%      62       1      0       0       0        0       0      98%
  1/4    21%      49       5      0       0       0        0       0      90%
* 1/5    18%      65       3      0       0       0        0       0      95%
* 1/6    19%      58       2      0       0       0        0       0      96%
* 1/7    17%      67       5      0       0       0        1       1      93%
* 1/8    20%      68       3      0       0       0        0       0      95%
  1/9    16%      67       2      0       0       0        0       0      97%
  1/10   18%      56       2      0       0       0        1       1      96%
* 1/11   15%      76       3      0       0       0        0       0      96%
* 1/12   16%      62       1      0       0       0        0       0      98%
```

```
   1/13    17%        51       4       0       0        0         0       0      92%
   1/14    16%        51       5       0       0        0         0       0      91%
   1/15    17%        65       0       0       0        0         0       0     100%
   1/16    15%        73       3       0       0        0         0       0      96%
   1/17    17%        67       2       0       0        0         0       0      97%
   1/18    17%        61       2       0       0        0         0       0      96%
 * 1/19    17%        74       2       0       0        0         0       0      97%
   1/20    16%        65       1       0       0        0         0       0      98%
 * 1/21    16%        58       3       0       0        0         0       0      95%
 * 1/22    18%        56       4       0       0        0         0       0      93%
 * 1/23    20%        60       4       0       0        0         0       0      93%
```

The following display shows output information for the **show modem** command for two V.110 modem cards inserted in a Cisco AS5200:

```
router# show modem
                    Inc calls      Out calls     Busied    Failed  No        Succ
   Mdm  Usage      Succ    Fail   Succ    Fail   Out       Dial    Answer    Pct.
   0/0      0%        -       -      -       -        0         0       0      -
   0/1      0%        -       -      -       -        0         0       0      -
   0/2      0%        -       -      -       -        0         0       0      -
   0/3      0%        -       -      -       -        0         0       0      -
   0/4      0%        -       -      -       -        0         0       0      -
   0/5      0%        -       -      -       -        0         0       0      -
   0/6      0%        -       -      -       -        0         0       0      -
   0/7      0%        -       -      -       -        0         0       0      -
   0/8      0%        -       -      -       -        0         0       0      -
   0/9      0%        -       -      -       -        0         0       0      -
   0/10     0%        -       -      -       -        0         0       0      -
   0/11     0%        -       -      -       -        0         0       0      -
   1/0      0%        -       -      -       -        0         0       0      -
   1/1      0%        -       -      -       -        0         0       0      -
   1/2      0%        -       -      -       -        0         0       0      -
   1/3      0%        -       -      -       -        0         0       0      -
   1/4      0%        -       -      -       -        0         0       0      -
   1/5      0%        -       -      -       -        0         0       0      -
   1/6      0%        -       -      -       -        0         0       0      -
   1/7      0%        -       -      -       -        0         0       0      -
   1/8      0%        -       -      -       -        0         0       0      -
   1/9      0%        -       -      -       -        0         0       0      -
   1/10     0%        -       -      -       -        0         0       0      -
   1/11     0%        -       -      -       -        0         0       0      -
```

Table 8–2 describes the fields in the previous display.

**Table 8–2** *Slow Modem Field Descriptions*

| Field | Description |
|---|---|
| Mdm | Slot and modem port number. Also, the following modem states can appear to the left of a slot/modem port number:<br>b—Modem was removed from service with the **modem shutdown** command or the **modem busyout** command.<br>B—Modem is suspected to be inoperable or bad. No calls can be made with this modem. The letter B can also mean that a modem firmware download failed for the specified modem. In this case, try unmarking the modem as bad with the **no modem bad** command and upgrading the modem firmware again.<br>d—The RAM-based DSP code, which supports K56flex, is not configured. The modem will revert to transmitting at 33.6 Kbps.<br>D—Modem is currently downloading firmware. |
| | R—Modem is held and isolated in a suspended state by the **modem hold-reset** command.<br>T—Modem is conducting a back-to-back test with another modem.<br>*—Modem is connected or dialing. |
| Usage | Percentage of the total system uptime that all modems are in use. |
| Inc calls | Number of incoming calls that successfully and unsuccessfully connected to a modem. |
| Out calls | Number of outgoing calls that successfully and unsuccessfully dialed out from an available modem. |
| Busied Out | Number of modems that have been manually removed from service. |
| Failed Dial | Number of modems that attempted to dial in to the network but failed to make a connection. |
| No Answer | Number of modems that detected an incoming ring but failed to answer the call. |
| Succ Pct. | Successful connection percentage of total available modems. |

The following example shows the statistics and current configurations for the manageable modem 2/10, which exists on a V.34 modem card in a Cisco AS5200. A dash (-) indicates a field that is not available on nonmanageable modems. An *x* indicates a field that is available and active on manageable modems. See Table 8–3 for a description of the fields displayed by the **show modem** command.

```
router> show modem 2/10
Mdm  Typ    Status      Tx/Rx       G  Duration  TX  RX  RTS  CTS  DSR  DCD  DTR
2/10 V34    Idle    33600/33600     1  00:00:00           x    x    x         x

Modem 2/10, Microcom MNP10 V34 Modem (Select), Async35, TTY35
Firmware (Boot) Rev: 2.1(9) (1.0(5))
Modem config: Incoming and Outgoing
Protocol: reliable/MNP, Compression: V42bis
Management port config: Status polling and AT session
Management port status: Status polling and AT session
TX signals: 0 dBm, RX signals: 0 dBm

  Last clearing of "show modem" counters never
    0 incoming completes, 0 incoming failures
    0 outgoing completes, 0 outgoing failures
    0 failed dial attempts, 0 ring no answers, 0 busied outs
    0 no dial tones, 0 dial timeouts, 0 watchdog timeouts
    0 no carriers, 0 link failures, 0 resets 0 recover oob
    0 protocol timeouts, 0 protocol errors, 0 lost events
Connection Speeds         75      300      600     1200     2400     4800
# of connections           0        0        0        0        0        0
Connection Speeds       7200     9600    12000    14400    16800    19200
# of connections           0        0        0        0        0        0
Connection Speeds      21600    24000    26400    28800    31200    33600
# of connections           0        0        0        0        0        1
```

The following example displays example output for a nonmanageable V.34 modem module. Notice that unavailable fields are marked with dashes (-):

```
router# show modem 1/1
Mdm  Typ  Status    Tx/Rx       G  Duration  TX  RX  RTS  CTS  DSR  DCD  DTR
1/1   -   Idle   19200/19200    0  00:01:05   -   -   -    -    -    -    -

Modem 1/1, AS5200 Non-Manageable Modem
Firmware (Boot) Rev: Unknown
Modem config: Unknown
Management config: Not Manageable Modem

Last clearing of "show modem" counters never
- incoming completes, - incoming failures
- outgoing completes, - outgoing failures,
0 failed dial attempts, 0 ring no answers, 0 busied outs
0 no dial tones, 0 dial timeouts, 0 watchdog timeouts
- no carriers, - link failures, 0 resets
- protocol timeouts, - protocol errors, - lost events

Connection Speeds         75      300      600     1200     2400     4800
# of connections           0        0        0        0        0        0
Connection Speeds       7200     9600    12000    14400    16800    19200
# of connections           0        0        0        0        0        0
Connection Speeds      21600    24000    26400    28800    31200    33600
# of connections           0        0        0        0        0        0
```

The following display shows output information for the **show modem** *slot/port* command for V.110 modem cards:

```
router# show modem 0/1
Mdm  Typ    Status     Tx/Rx     G  Duration  TX  RX  RTS  CTS  DSR  DCD  DTR
0/1         Idle        -/-      1  00:00:00  -   -   -    -    -    -    -

Modem 0/1, V.110 Terminal Adaptor (Unmanaged), Async2, TTY2
Firmware (Boot) Rev: Unmanaged (Unmanaged)
Modem config: Incoming and Outgoing
Management config: Unmanaged

  Last clearing of "show modem" counters never
    - incoming completes, - incoming failures
    - outgoing completes, - outgoing failures
    0 failed dial attempts, 0 ring no answers, 0 busied outs
    - no dial tones, - dial timeouts, 0 watchdog timeouts
    - no carriers, - link failures, 0 resets, - recover oob
    - protocol timeouts, - protocol errors, - lost events

Connection Speeds        75       300      600      1200     2400     4800
# of connections          -         -        -         -        -        -
Connection Speeds      7200      9600    12000     14400    16800    19200
# of connections          -         -        -         -        -        -
Connection Speeds     21600     24000    26400     28800    31200    32000
# of connections          -         -        -         -        -        -
Connection Speeds     33600     34000    36000     38000    40000    42000
# of connections          -         -        -         -        -        -
Connection Speeds     44000     46000    48000     50000    52000    54000
# of connections          -         -        -         -        -        -
Connection Speeds     56000
# of connections          -
```

The type of display output generated from the **show modem** *slot/port* command depends on the version of Cisco IOS software running on the router or access server. For example, the following shows example output for a 56K modem card, which carries digital modems that transmit at 56 Kbps. (In truth, 56K modems do not modulate or demodulate data. A pure digital-to-digital connection is made.) See Table 8–3 for a description of the fields displayed by this modem card.

```
router# show modem 0/0
Mdm  Typ    Status     Tx/Rx     G  Duration  TX  RX  RTS  CTS  DSR  DCD  DTR
0/0         Idle        0/0      0  00:00:00          x    x    x         x

Modem 0/0, Microcom MNP10 K56 Modem (Select), TTY1
Firmware (Boot) Rev: 3.1(16) (3.0(4))
DSP Controller (SPX) Rev: 1.1(0) (1.1(0))
Modem config: Incoming and Outgoing
Protocol: Normal, Compression: None
Management port config: Status polling and AT session
Management port status: Status polling and AT session
TX signals: 0 dBm, RX signals: 0 dBm

  Last clearing of "show modem" counters never
    0 incoming completes, 0 incoming failures
```

```
    0 outgoing completes, 0 outgoing failures
    0 failed dial attempts, 0 ring no answers, 0 busied outs
    0 no dial tones, 0 dial timeouts, 0 watchdog timeouts
    0 no carriers, 0 link failures, 1 resets 0 recover oob
    0 protocol timeouts, 0 protocol errors, 0 lost events

Transmit Speed Counters:

Connection Speeds        75     300     600    1200    2400    4800
# of connections          0       0       0       0       0       0
Connection Speeds      7200    9600   12000   14400   16800   19200
# of connections          0       0       0       0       0       0
Connection Speeds     21600   24000   26400   28800   31200   32000
# of connections          0       0       0       0       0       0
Connection Speeds     33600   34000   36000   38000   40000   42000
# of connections          0       0       0       0       0       0
Connection Speeds     44000   46000   48000   50000   52000   54000
# of connections          0       0       0       0       0       0
Connection Speeds     56000
# of connections          0

Receive Speed Counters:
Connection Speeds        75     300     600    1200    2400    4800
# of connections          0       0       0       0       0       0
Connection Speeds      7200    9600   12000   14400   16800   19200
# of connections          0       0       0       0       0       0
Connection Speeds     21600   24000   26400   28800   31200   32000
# of connections          0       0       0       0       0       0
Connection Speeds     33600   34000   36000   38000   40000   42000
# of connections          0       0       0       0       0       0
Connection Speeds     44000   46000   48000   50000   52000   54000
# of connections          0       0       0       0       0       0
Connection Speeds     56000
# of connections          0
```

Table 8–3 describes the fields in the previous four displays, which were created using the **show modem** *slot/port* command. This table applies to all modem module types.

The following example shows the sample display for modem group 1, which is composed of modem 1/0 through modem 1/23:

```
router# show modem group 1
              Incoming calls       Outgoing calls     Busied    Failed  No    Succ
Grp  Usage  Succ    Fail   Avail   Succ    Fail  Avail  Out       Dial    Ans   Pct.
1     0%    0       0      24      0       0     24       0          0  0     0%
```

```
Modem Group 1: 1/0, 1/1, 1/2, 1/3, 1/4, 1/5, 1/6, 1/7, 1/8, 1/9, 1/10, 1/11, 1/12, 1/13,
1/14, 1/15, 1/16, 1/17, 1/18, 1/19, 1/20, 1/21, 1/22, 1/23
```

**Table 8–3** *Show Modem Slot/Port Descriptions*

| Field | Description |
|---|---|
| Mdm | Slot and modem number. |
| Typ | Modulation type, which can be any of the following values: Bel103, Bel212, V21, V22, V22bis, V23, V32, V32bis, VFC, V34, V17, V27, V33 and K56Flx |
| Status | Current status of the modem. Possible values include:<br>• Conn—Modem is connected to a remote host.<br>• B—Inoperable state, which is configured by the **modem bad** command.<br>• B*—Inoperable state, which is configured by the **modem startup-test** command during initial power-up testing.<br>• b—Modem is busied out. This can be manually configured by the **modem busyout** line configuration command.<br>• Reset—Modem is in reset mode.<br>• D/L—Modem is downloading firmware.<br>• Bad FW—Downloaded modem firmware is not operational.<br>• Busy—Modem is out of service and not available for calls.<br>• Idle—Modem is ready for incoming and outgoing calls. |
| Tx/Rx | Transmission and receiving speed for the most recently connected call. |
| G | Modem group number assigned to the modem. The group number 0 means the modem is not part of any group. |
| Duration | Time duration of the current call or the last call. |

**Table 8–3** *Show Modem Slot/Port Descriptions, Continued*

| Field | Description |
|---|---|
| Modem functions | The following modem functions are displayed on manageable modems. A field that is available and turned on is marked with an *x*. An unavailable field is marked with a dash (-).<br>TX—Transmit Data. The DTE transmits data to the DCE.<br>RX—Receive Data. The DCE receives data from the DTE.<br>RTS—Request To Send. The DTE signals to the DCE that the DTE accepts data into its buffers.<br>CTS—Clear To Send. The DCE signals to the DTE that the DCE accepts data into its buffers.<br>DSR—Data Set Ready. The modem is ready to start communication.<br>DCD—Data Carrier Detect. The DCE indicates to the DTE that a call is present and established with a remote modem. Dropping the DCD function terminates the session.<br>DTR—Data Terminal Ready. The DTE indicates to the DCE that it accepts calls. |
| Firmware | Installed modem firmware. |
| Modem config | Current modem configuration, which includes the fields Incoming, Outgoing, Incoming and Outgoing, and Unknown. |
| Protocol | Protocol the modem is running such as Normal, Direct, reliable/MNP4, and reliable/LAPM (Link Access Procedure for Modems). |
| Compression | Compression algorithm running on the modem, such as None, V42bis, and MNP5. |
| Management config | Indicates if the modem is configured for out-of-band feature polling. |
| TX signals | Transmit signal levels. For modulations that do not support signal-to-noise calculations, the ratio is 0. |
| RX signals | Transmit signal levels. |

**Table 8–3** *Show Modem Slot/Port Descriptions, Continued*

| Field | Description |
|---|---|
| Last clearing of "show modem" counters | Last time the modem's counters were cleared using the **clear modem counters** command. A summary of modem events also appears.<br>• Incoming completes and failures—Total number of incoming connection requests that the modem answered and successfully or unsuccessfully connected with the remote DCE.<br>• Outgoing completes and failures—Total number of outgoing connection requests that the modem dialed and successfully or unsuccessfully connected with the remote DCE.<br>• Failed dial attempts—Number of times the modem attempted to dial out but the call failed to leave the modem.<br>• Ring no answers—Number of times the integrated modem detected ringing but did not answer the incoming call.<br>• Busied outs—Number of times the integrated modem was intentionally taken out of service (for example, the **modem busyout** command was enabled on the modem).<br>• No dial tones—Number of times the dial-out attempt failed because the modem failed to detect a dial tone.<br>• Dial timeouts—Number of times the modem has timed out while attempting to dial.<br>• Watchdog timeouts—Number of times the modem internal watchdog timer has expired.<br>• No carriers—Number of times the modem disconnected because no carrier was present.<br>• Link failures—Number of times the modem has detected a link failure.<br>• Resets—Number of times the modem has been reset.<br>• recover oob—Number of times the out-of-band feature has been cleared and re-initialized.<br>• Protocol timeouts and errors—Number of times the modem protocol failed to make a call connection.<br>• Lost events—Number of incomplete modem events performed by the modem. |
| Transmit Speed Counters: | List of connection speeds that were transmitted by the modem. |

**Table 8–3** *Show Modem Slot/Port Descriptions, Continued*

| Field | Description |
|---|---|
| Receive Speed Counters: | List of connection speeds that were received by the modem. |
| Connection Speeds # of connections | A complete summary of possible connection speeds and the actual number of connections that occurred at those speeds. Depending on which modem port module and version of software you are running, possible connection speeds range from 75 to 56,000 bps. The number of successful connections are displayed directly beneath the connection speed identifier. For example, the following output shows that three connections were made at 56 Kbps.<br>Connection Speeds 56000<br># of connections 3 |

The following example show the sample display for modem group 1, which is composed of modem 1/0 through modem 1/23:

```
router# show modem group 1
                  Incoming calls       Outgoing calls    Busied    Failed  No    Succ
Grp  Usage    Succ    Fail  Avail    Succ    Fail  Avail  Out       Dial    Ans   Pct.
1    0%       0       0     24       0       0     24       0         0     0     0%

Modem Group 1: 1/0, 1/1, 1/2, 1/3, 1/4, 1/5, 1/6, 1/7, 1/8, 1/9, 1/10, 1/11, 1/12, 1/13,
1/14, 1/15, 1/16, 1/17, 1/18, 1/19, 1/20, 1/21, 1/22, 1/23
```

## SHOW MODEM AT-MODE

To display a list of the manageable Microcom modems that have open AT sessions and a list of users logged in to those sessions, use the **show modem at-mode** EXEC command.

**show modem at-mode**

### *Syntax Description*

This command has no arguments or keywords.

### *Command Mode*

User and Privileged EXEC

### *Usage Guidelines*

This command first appeared in Cisco IOS Release 11.2.

### *Sample Displays*

The following output shows that modem 1/1 has one open AT directly connected session:

```
router# show modem at-mode
Active AT-MODE management sessions:
```

```
Modem    User's Terminal
1/1 0 cty 0
```

## SHOW MODEM CALL-STATS

To display the local disconnect reasons for all modems inside an access server or router, use the **show modem call-stats** EXEC command.

**show modem call-stats** [*slot*]

| Syntax | Description |
|---|---|
| *slot* | (Optional) Specifies the slot number, which limits the display output to a particular range of modems in the system. |

### *Command Mode*

User and Privileged EXEC

### *Usage Guidelines*

This command first appeared in Cisco IOS Release 11.3.

Use this command to find out why a modem ended its connection or why a modem is not operating at peak performance.

Local disconnect reasons for a particular modem are listed across the top of the screen display. For example, see lostCarr, dtrDrop, rmtLink, wdogTimr, compress, retrain, inacTout, and linkFail in the following output:

```
router# show modem call-stats

  dial-in/dial-out call statistics

       lostCarr  dtrDrop  rmtLink wdogTimr compress  retrain inacTout linkFail
  Mdm
* 0/0
* 0/1
```

In the body of the screen display, the number of times an error occured on a specific modem is displayed (see the # column). The % column shows the total running percent that a modem was logged for the specified disconnect reason with respect to the entire modem pool. For example, out of all the times the lostCarr error occurred on all the modems in the system, the lostCarr error occurred 2% of the time on modem 0/0.

```
router# show modem call-stats

  dial-in/dial-out call statistics

       lostCarr  dtrDrop  rmtLink wdogTimr compress  retrain inacTout linkFail
  Mdm    #   %    #   %    #   %    #   %    #   %    #   %    #   %    #   %
* 0/0    6   2    2   3    1   0    0   0    0   0    0   0    0   0    0   0
* 0/1    5   2    2   3    2   1    0   0    0   0    0   0    0   0    0   0
```

Bad or malfunctioning modems are detected by an unusually high number of disconnect counters for a particular disconnect reason. For example, if modem 1/0 had an astronomically high number of compression errors compared to the remaining modems in system, modem 1/0 would probably be bad or inoperable.

To reset the counters displayed by the **show modem call-stats** command, issue the **clear modem counters** command.

**NOTES**

Remote disconnect reasons are not described by this command.

### *Sample Displays*

The following example shows call statistics for the **show modem call-stats** command. Due to the screen-size limitation of most terminal screen displays, all the possible disconnect reasons cannot be displayed at the same time. Only the top eight most frequently experienced disconnect reasons are displayed.

See Table 8–4 for descriptions of the fields and end-connection events in the following sample display.

```
router# show modem call-stats

  dial-in/dial-out call statistics

        lostCarr  dtrDrop  rmtLink wdogTimr compress  retrain inacTout linkFail
  Mdm     #   %    #   %    #   %    #   %    #   %    #   %    #   %    #   %
* 0/0     6   2    2   3    1   0    0   0    0   0    0   0    0   0    0   0
* 0/1     5   2    2   3    2   1    0   0    0   0    0   0    0   0    0   0
  0/2     5   2    2   3    4   3    0   0    0   0    0   0    0   0    0   0
* 0/3     5   2    2   3    2   1    0   0    0   0    0   0    0   0    0   0
* 0/4     5   2    1   1    1   0    0   0    0   0    0   0    0   0    0   0
* 0/5     5   2    2   3    2   1    0   0    0   0    0   0    0   0    0   0
* 0/6     4   1    2   3    2   1    0   0    0   0    0   0    0   0    0   0
* 0/7     4   1    2   3    4   3    0   0    0   0    0   0    0   0    0   0
* 0/8     6   2    1   1    3   2    0   0    0   0    0   0    0   0    0   0
* 0/9     5   2    1   1    1   0    0   0    0   0    0   0    0   0    0   0
* 0/10    5   2    1   1    2   1    0   0    0   0    0   0    0   0    0   0
* 0/11    5   2    1   1    2   1    0   0    0   0    0   0    0   0    0   0
  0/12    5   2    2   3    2   1    0   0    0   0    0   0    0   0    0   0
* 0/13    5   2    1   1    1   0    0   0    0   0    0   0    0   0    0   0
* 0/14    5   2    1   1    1   0    0   0    0   0    0   0    0   0    0   0
* 0/15    5   2    1   1    1   0    0   0    0   0    0   0    0   0    0   0
* 0/16    5   2    1   1    1   0    0   0    0   0    0   0    0   0    0   0
* 0/17    5   2    1   1    2   1    0   0    0   0    0   0    0   0    0   0
* 0/18    5   2    1   1    2   1    0   0    0   0    0   0    0   0    0   0
* 0/19    5   2    1   1    3   2    0   0    0   0    0   0    0   0    0   0
* 0/20    5   2    1   1    1   0    0   0    0   0    0   0    0   0    0   0
* 0/21    5   2    1   1    1   0    0   0    0   0    0   0    0   0    0   0
* 0/22    5   2    1   1   11  10    0   0    0   0    0   0    0   0    0   0
```

```
  * 0/23    5    2     1    1     2    1     0    0     0    0     0    0     0    0     0    0
  * 2/0     4    1     2    3     2    1     0    0     0    0     0    0     0    0     0    0
  * 2/1     5    2     1    1     2    1     0    0     0    0     0    0     0    0     0    0
  * 2/2     5    2     2    3     0    0     0    0     0    0     0    0     0    0     0    0
  * 2/3     5    2     1    1     2    1     0    0     0    0     0    0     0    0     0    0
  * 2/4     5    2     1    1     2    1     0    0     0    0     0    0     0    0     0    0
  * 2/5     5    2     1    1     2    1     0    0     0    0     0    0     0    0     0    0
  * 2/6     4    1     1    1     1    0     0    0     0    0     0    0     0    0     0    0
  * 2/7     5    2     1    1     1    0     0    0     0    0     0    0     0    0     0    0
  * 2/8     5    2     1    1     1    0     0    0     0    0     0    0     0    0     0    0
  * 2/9     4    1     1    1     2    1     0    0     0    0     0    0     0    0     0    0
  * 2/10    5    2     1    1     0    0     0    0     0    0     0    0     0    0     0    0
  * 2/11    5    2     1    1     5    4     0    0     0    0     0    0     0    0     0    0
  * 2/12    5    2     1    1     2    1     0    0     0    0     0    0     0    0     0    0
  * 2/13    5    2     1    1     1    0     0    0     0    0     0    0     0    0     0    0
  * 2/14    5    2     1    1     2    1     0    0     0    0     0    0     0    0     0    0
  * 2/15    4    1     1    1     3    2     0    0     0    0     0    0     0    0     0    0
  * 2/16    4    1     1    1     3    2     0    0     0    0     0    0     0    0     0    0
  * 2/17    5    2     2    3     9    8     0    0     0    0     0    0     0    0     0    0
  * 2/18    4    1     1    1     1    0     0    0     0    0     0    0     0    0     0    0
  * 2/19    3    1     1    1     2    1     0    0     0    0     0    0     0    0     0    0
  * 2/20    7    3     1    1     8    7     0    0     0    0     0    0     0    0     0    0
  * 2/21    5    2     1    1     1    0     0    0     0    0     0    0     0    0     0    0
  * 2/22    4    1     1    1     2    1     0    0     0    0     0    0     0    0     0    0
  * 2/23    5    2     1    1     2    1     0    0     0    0     0    0     0    0     0    0
   Total  233         59        110          0          0          0          0          0

    dial-out call statistics

          noCarr  noDitone      busy      abort  dialStrg  autoLgon  dialTout   rmtHgup
    Mdm    #    %     #    %     #    %     #    %     #    %     #    %     #    %     #    %
  * 0/0    1    1     0    0     0    0     0    0     0    0     0    0     0    0     0    0
  * 0/1    0    0     0    0     0    0     0    0     0    0     0    0     0    0     0    0
    0/2    0    0     0    0     0    0     0    0     0    0     0    0     0    0     0    0
  * 0/3    1    1     0    0     0    0     0    0     0    0     0    0     0    0     0    0
  * 0/4    1    1     0    0     0    0     0    0     0    0     0    0     0    0     0    0
  * 0/5    0    0     0    0     0    0     0    0     0    0     0    0     0    0     0    0
  * 0/6    1    1     0    0     0    0     0    0     0    0     0    0     0    0     0    0
  * 0/7    5    5     0    0     0    0     0    0     0    0     0    0     0    0     0    0
  * 0/8    0    0     0    0     0    0     0    0     0    0     0    0     0    0     0    0
  * 0/9    1    1     0    0     0    0     0    0     0    0     0    0     0    0     0    0
  * 0/10   0    0     0    0     0    0     0    0     0    0     0    0     0    0     0    0
  * 0/11   5    5     0    0     0    0     0    0     0    0     0    0     0    0     0    0
    0/12   0    0     0    0     0    0     0    0     0    0     0    0     0    0     0    0
  * 0/13   0    0     0    0     0    0     0    0     0    0     0    0     0    0     0    0
  * 0/14   1    1     0    0     0    0     0    0     0    0     0    0     0    0     0    0
  * 0/15   1    1     0    0     0    0     0    0     0    0     0    0     0    0     0    0
  * 0/16   2    2     0    0     0    0     0    0     0    0     0    0     0    0     0    0
  * 0/17   4    4     0    0     0    0     0    0     0    0     0    0     0    0     0    0
  * 0/18   5    5     0    0     0    0     0    0     0    0     0    0     0    0     0    0
  * 0/19   1    1     0    0     0    0     0    0     0    0     0    0     0    0     0    0
  * 0/20   0    0     0    0     0    0     0    0     0    0     0    0     0    0     0    0
  * 0/21   0    0     0    0     0    0     0    0     0    0     0    0     0    0     0    0
  * 0/22   5    5     0    0     0    0     0    0     0    0     0    0     0    0     0    0
```

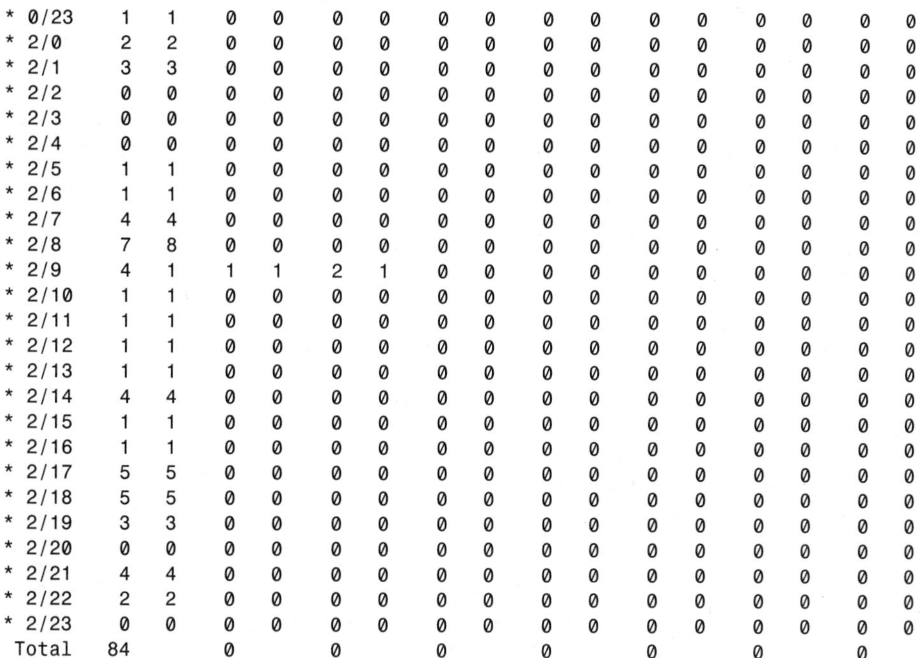

```
* 0/23    1  1   0  0   0  0   0  0   0  0   0  0   0  0   0  0
* 2/0     2  2   0  0   0  0   0  0   0  0   0  0   0  0   0  0
* 2/1     3  3   0  0   0  0   0  0   0  0   0  0   0  0   0  0
* 2/2     0  0   0  0   0  0   0  0   0  0   0  0   0  0   0  0
* 2/3     0  0   0  0   0  0   0  0   0  0   0  0   0  0   0  0
* 2/4     0  0   0  0   0  0   0  0   0  0   0  0   0  0   0  0
* 2/5     1  1   0  0   0  0   0  0   0  0   0  0   0  0   0  0
* 2/6     1  1   0  0   0  0   0  0   0  0   0  0   0  0   0  0
* 2/7     4  4   0  0   0  0   0  0   0  0   0  0   0  0   0  0
* 2/8     7  8   0  0   0  0   0  0   0  0   0  0   0  0   0  0
* 2/9     4  1   1  1   2  1   0  0   0  0   0  0   0  0   0  0
* 2/10    1  1   0  0   0  0   0  0   0  0   0  0   0  0   0  0
* 2/11    1  1   0  0   0  0   0  0   0  0   0  0   0  0   0  0
* 2/12    1  1   0  0   0  0   0  0   0  0   0  0   0  0   0  0
* 2/13    1  1   0  0   0  0   0  0   0  0   0  0   0  0   0  0
* 2/14    4  4   0  0   0  0   0  0   0  0   0  0   0  0   0  0
* 2/15    1  1   0  0   0  0   0  0   0  0   0  0   0  0   0  0
* 2/16    1  1   0  0   0  0   0  0   0  0   0  0   0  0   0  0
* 2/17    5  5   0  0   0  0   0  0   0  0   0  0   0  0   0  0
* 2/18    5  5   0  0   0  0   0  0   0  0   0  0   0  0   0  0
* 2/19    3  3   0  0   0  0   0  0   0  0   0  0   0  0   0  0
* 2/20    0  0   0  0   0  0   0  0   0  0   0  0   0  0   0  0
* 2/21    4  4   0  0   0  0   0  0   0  0   0  0   0  0   0  0
* 2/22    2  2   0  0   0  0   0  0   0  0   0  0   0  0   0  0
* 2/23    0  0   0  0   0  0   0  0   0  0   0  0   0  0   0  0
  Total  84      0      0      0      0      0      0      0
```

**Table 8–4** *Show Modem Call-Stats Field Descriptions*

| Field | Description |
|---|---|
| dial-in/dial-out call statistics | This category of disconnect reasons can happen only in dial-in or dial-out scenarios. |
| wdogTimr | Watchdog timeout. An obscure firmware problem occurred. This is a rare disconnect reason. |
| compress | Compression. An error was detected during decompression, which caused the internal decompression dictionary to overflow. This can be caused by a modem dialing in that is using a slightly different compression algorithm. |
| retrain | Retrain failure. A connection was lost and not re-established after three attempts. |
| inacTout | Inactivity timeout. The time specified in the AT/T command has expired. No modem data transfers were detected during that period. |
| linkFail | Link failure. The protocol level link failed while using MNP-10 or LAPM in reliable mode. |
| moduFail | Modulation error. An error was detected at the DSP chip level, which caused a disconnect. |

**Table 8–4** *Show Modem Call-Stats Field Descriptions, Continued*

| Field | Description |
|---|---|
| mnpProto | MNP10 protocol error. An uncorrectable error occurred during a MNP-10 connection. |
| lapmProt | LAPM protocol error. An uncorrectable error occurred during a LAPM connection. |
| lostCarr | Lost carrier. The modem firmware detected a carrier drop during a connection. The cause for the carrier drop could be the loss of signal from the remote modem or the result of a error detection. |
| dtrDrop | DTR drop. The modem disconnected because the DTR signal from the host became inactive. |
| userHgup | User hangup. The modem disconnected because a command such as ATH was detected. |
| rmtlink | Remote link disconnect. If an MNP-10 reliable link is established, the remote modem sends the disconnect reason across the link before disconnecting. The disconnect reason displayed is LOCAL (remote link disconnect) and REMOTE (the reason the remote modem disconnected). |
| trminate | Terminate. A password security error occurred in the Microcom HDMS. This error occurs only with Microcom modems. |
| callBkfa | Callback failed. This error applies to leased line connections only. A switched line connection failed and a connection still cannot be made on the leased line. |
| dial-out call statistics | This category of disconnect reasons can happen only in a dial-out scenario. |
| noCarr | No carrier. The called number answered, but no answer tone was detected after the appropriate wait. |
| noDitone | No dialtone. No dial tone was detected after the modem went off hook. |
| busy | Busy. A busy signal was detected while the local modem was attempting to dial. |
| abort | Abort. A character was received from the remote host after the dial command was issued and before a connection was established. |
| dialStrg | Dialstring error. An invalid character was detected in the dial string, which forced the dial attempt to terminate. |
| autoLgon | Autologon error. An autologon sequence did not successfully complete. |

**Table 8–4** *Show Modem Call-Stats Field Descriptions, Continued*

| Field | Description |
|---|---|
| dialTout | Dial timeout. When a semicolon is used as a dial modifier, the modem returns to the command state as indicated by an "OK." This allows a continuation of the dial string. If a period of time elapses as specified in the S7 register without the dial string completing, the attempt is aborted with dial timeout as the disconnect reason. |
| rmtHgup | Remote hangup. The modem disconnected because the remote modem disconnected the call and dropped DTR. |
| blacklst | Blacklist. In a country that supports blacklisting, an attempt was made to go off hook with a null dial string (ATD). |
| ccpNssn | CCP not seen. The credit card prompt (also known as Bong) was not detected. |
| faxClasz | FAX class 2 error. An abnormal termination to a fax transmission was detected. |
| Total | Total number of times the disconnect reason occurred among all the modems in the system. |

## SHOW MODEM CONNECT-SPEEDS

To display connection speed statistics for all the modems running in an access server or router, use the **show modem connect-speeds** EXEC command.

**show modem connect-speeds** [*max-speed* [*slot*]]

| *Syntax* | *Description* |
|---|---|
| *max-speed* | (Optional) Maximum speed you want displayed in the shifting speed window. You can specify from 12,000 to 56,000 bps. |
| *slot* | (Optional) Specifies the slot number, which limits the display output to a particular range of modems in the system. |

### *Default*

The maximum speed displayed is 12,000 bps.

### *Command Mode*

User and Privileged EXEC

### *Usage Guidelines*

This command first appeared in Cisco IOS Release 11.3.

Because most terminal screens are not wide enough to display the entire range of connection speeds at one time (for example, 75 to 56000 bps), the *max-speed* variable is used. This variable specifies the contents of a shifting baud-rate window, which provides you with a snapshot of modem connection speeds for your system. If you want to see a snapshot of lower baud rates, specify a lower connection speed. If you want to see a snapshot of higher baud rates, specify a higher connection speed.

The *max-speed* variable also rounds up to the nearest recognizable baud rate by the software, so you do not need to memorize or enter exact connection speeds. For example, if you enter a maximum baud rate of **22059**, the system software automatically rounds the value up to **24000**.

To display a complete picture of all the connection speeds and counters on the system, you must enter a series of commands. Each time you issue the **show modem connect-speeds** *max-speed* command, only nine baud-rate columns can be displayed at the same time. Table 8–5 shows a range of commands that you can issue, one at a time, to see a complete picture of the total possible connection speeds on your access server.

**Table 8–5** *Connect Speed Displays for the Show Modem Connect-Speeds Command*

| Command | Connect Speed Range Displayed |
|---|---|
| **show modem connect-speeds 56000** | 40,000 to 56,000 bps |
| **show modem connect-speeds 38000** | 24,000 to 38,000 bps |
| **show modem connect-speeds 21600** | 2,400 to 21,600 bps |
| **show modem connect-speeds 12000** | 75 to 1200 bps |

The **show modem connect-speeds** command displays a log of connection speed statistics starting from the last time the access servers or router was power cycled or the **clear modem counters** command was issued. If you want to create a monthly report of the connection speeds achieved by the modems, issue the **clear modem counters** command at the beginning of the month and issue the **show modem connect-speeds** command at the end of the month.

**NOTES**

The Cisco IOS software does not accept commas (,) in the connect speed field. For example, enter 28000 not 28,000.

### *Sample Displays*

See Table 8–6 for descriptions of the fields shown in the following displays.

The following display shows connection speed statistics up to 28000 bps:

```
router# show modem connect-speeds 28800

  transmit connect speeds

  Mdm     9600  12000  14400  16800  19200  21600  24000  26400  28800 TotCnt
* 1/0        0      0      0      0      3      4      6     37     23     74
* 1/1        0      0      3      1      0      4      9     41     20     80
* 1/2        0      0      2      0      1      3     10     37     26     82
  1/3        1      0      0      0      0      3     15     35      7     62
  1/4        0      0      0      0      4      2      8     20     13     49
* 1/5        0      0      4      0      1      0      4     38     17     65
* 1/6        0      0      2      1      0      1      9     32     11     57
* 1/7        1      0      2      0      0      5     10     31     18     67
* 1/8        0      0      0      1      1      1     10     42     11     68
  1/9        0      0      2      1      2      4      4     30     23     67
  1/10       0      0      0      0      0      2      5     26     22     56
* 1/11       0      0      0      0      3      1     16     38     17     76
* 1/12       0      0      0      0      0      3      7     40     12     62
  1/13       0      0      0      1      2      3     11     20     14     51
  1/14       0      0      2      0      0      2      7     26     12     51
  1/15       0      0      1      1      1      2      6     29     25     65
  1/16       2      0      2      0      1      5     10     37     15     73
  1/17       0      0      0      0      0      2     10     33     22     67
  1/18       0      0      2      2      0      2     12     17     25     61
* 1/19       2      0      3      0      1      2      9     35     20     74
  1/20       0      0      2      2      2      2      8     28     21     65
* 1/21       0      1      2      0      1      2      5     23     21     58
* 1/22       0      0      1      0      1      1      5     27     21     56
* 1/23       0      0      2      0      0      4      8     30     15     60
 Tot         6      1     32     10     24     60    204    752    431   1546
 Tot %       0      0      2      0      1      3     13     48     27

  receive connect speeds

  Mdm     9600  12000  14400  16800  19200  21600  24000  26400  28800 TotCnt
* 1/0        0      0      1      0      1      2      9     35     25     74
* 1/1        0      0      3      0      1      3     10     42     18     80
* 1/2        0      0      2      0      1      4      8     40     26     82
  1/3        1      0      0      0      0      1     10     36     14     62
  1/4        0      0      1      0      2      2      8     22      8     49
* 1/5        0      1      4      0      0      0      9     32     17     65
* 1/6        0      0      2      0      0      0      7     33     14     57
* 1/7        0      0      2      1      1      0      6     39     18     67
* 1/8        0      0      0      0      1      0     11     43     12     68
  1/9        1      0      3      0      0      0      8     33     22     67
  1/10       0      0      0      0      1      1      6     31     17     56
* 1/11       0      0      0      1      1      1     14     43     16     76
* 1/12       0      0      0      0      0      0      5     43     12     62
  1/13       0      0      0      0      0      2     10     26     13     51
  1/14       0      0      2      1      0      0      5     27     14     51
  1/15       0      0      1      0      1      2      3     36     22     65
  1/16       1      0      3      1      2      0      8     37     20     73
  1/17       0      0      0      0      0      0      8     36     22     67
  1/18       0      1      1      0      0      2      4     30     20     61
```

```
* 1/19     0     0     3     2     1     1     6    42    18    74
  1/20     0     1     2     1     2     1     2    37    18    65
* 1/21     0     0     3     3     1     2     2    28    18    58
* 1/22     0     0     1     0     1     0     5    32    16    56
* 1/23     0     0     2     0     0     1     8    35    13    60
 Tot       3     3    36    10    17    25   172   838   413  1546
 Tot %     0     0     2     0     1     1    11    54    26
```

The following display shows connection speed statisitics up to 56000 bps:

```
router# show modem connect-speeds 56000

  transmit connect speeds

  Mdm   40000  42000  44000  46000  48000  50000  52000  54000  56000 TotCnt
  1/0       0      0      0      0      0      0      0      0      0      0
  1/1       0      0      0      0      0      0      0      0      0      0
  1/2       0      0      0      0      0      0      0      0      0      0
  1/3       0      0      0      0      0      0      0      0      0      0
  1/4       0      0      0      0      0      0      0      0      0      0
  1/5       0      0      0      0      0      0      0      0      0      0
  1/6       0      0      0      0      0      0      0      0      0      0
  1/7       0      0      0      0      0      0      0      0      0      0
  1/8       0      0      0      0      0      0      0      0      0      0
  1/9       0      0      0      0      0      0      0      0      0      0
  1/10      0      0      0      0      0      0      0      0      0      0
  1/11      0      0      0      0      0      0      0      0      0      0
  1/12      0      0      0      0      0      0      0      0      0      0
  1/13      0      0      0      0      0      0      0      0      0      0
  1/14      0      0      0      0      0      0      0      0      0      0
  1/15      0      0      0      0      0      0      0      0      0      0
  1/16      0      0      0      0      0      0      0      0      0      0
  1/17      0      0      0      0      0      0      0      0      0      0
  1/18      0      0      0      0      0      0      0      0      0      0
  1/19      0      0      0      0      0      0      0      0      0      0
  1/20      0      0      0      0      0      0      0      0      0      0
  1/21      0      0      0      0      0      0      0      0      0      0
  1/22      0      0      0      0      0      0      0      0      0      0
  1/23      0      0      0      0      0      0      0      0      0      0
 Tot        0      0      0      0      0      0      0      0      0      0
 Tot %      0      0      0      0      0      0      0      0      0

  receive connect speeds

  Mdm   40000  42000  44000  46000  48000  50000  52000  54000  56000 TotCnt
  1/0       0      0      0      0      0      0      0      0      0      0
  1/1       0      0      0      0      0      0      0      0      0      0
  1/2       0      0      0      0      0      0      0      0      0      0
  1/3       0      0      0      0      0      0      0      0      0      0
  1/4       0      0      0      0      0      0      0      0      0      0
  1/5       0      0      0      0      0      0      0      0      0      0
  1/6       0      0      0      0      0      0      0      0      0      0
  1/7       0      0      0      0      0      0      0      0      0      0
  1/8       0      0      0      0      0      0      0      0      0      0
```

```
  1/9      0     0     0     0     0     0     0     0     0     0
  1/10     0     0     0     0     0     0     0     0     0     0
  1/11     0     0     0     0     0     0     0     0     0     0
  1/12     0     0     0     0     0     0     0     0     0     0
  1/13     0     0     0     0     0     0     0     0     0     0
  1/14     0     0     0     0     0     0     0     0     0     0
  1/15     0     0     0     0     0     0     0     0     0     0
  1/16     0     0     0     0     0     0     0     0     0     0
  1/17     0     0     0     0     0     0     0     0     0     0
  1/18     0     0     0     0     0     0     0     0     0     0
  1/19     0     0     0     0     0     0     0     0     0     0
  1/20     0     0     0     0     0     0     0     0     0     0
  1/21     0     0     0     0     0     0     0     0     0     0
  1/22     0     0     0     0     0     0     0     0     0     0
  1/23     0     0     0     0     0     0     0     0     0     0
 Tot       0     0     0     0     0     0     0     0     0     0
 Tot %     0     0     0     0     0     0     0     0     0
```

**Table 8–6** *Show Modem Connect-Speeds Field Descriptions*

| Field | Description |
|---|---|
| transmit connect speeds | Connection speeds for calls initiated by the system. |
| Mdm *slot/port* | Specified slot and port number assigned to the modem. |
| speed counters | The transmit and receive speed counters are 75, 300, 600, 1200, 2400, 4800, 7200, 9600, 12000, 14400, 16800, 19200, 21600, 24000, 26400, 28800, 31200, 33600, 32000, 34000, 36000, 38000, 40000, 42000, 44000, 46000, 48000, 50000, 52000, 54000, and 56000 bps. |
| TotCnt | For the specified modem, the sum of the number of times a connection was initiated or received at one of the specified connection rates (75 to 56,000 bps). |
| Tot | For all modems loaded in the system, the total number of times a call was initiated or received at the specified speed. |
| Tot % | Percentage of the total number of calls that were initiated or received at the specified speed. |
| receive connect speeds | Connection speeds for incoming calls. |

## SHOW MODEM COOKIE

To display information about the modem cookie, use the **show modem cookie** EXEC command.

**show modem cookie**

### Syntax Description

This command has no arguments or keywords.

### Command Mode

User and Privileged EXEC

### Usage Guidelines

This command first appeared in Cisco IOS Release 11.2.

### Sample Displays

The following display shows output information for the **show modem cookie** command for a V.34 carrier card and two modem cards:

```
router# show modem cookie

 Hex dump of modem board HW version info:

 Slot 1:
   Carrier card:
     0000:  1802 0200 0000 0000 0000 0000 0000 0000
     0010:  0000 0000 0000 0000 0000 0000 0000 0000
   Modem Module 0:
     0000:  0C01 3033 3030 3031 4D69 6372 6F63 6F6D
     0010:  204D 4E50 3130 2056 3334 204D 6F64 656D
   Modem Module 1:
     0000:  0C01 3033 3030 3031 4D69 6372 6F63 6F6D
     0010:  204D 4E50 3130 2056 3334 204D 6F64 656D
```

Table 8–7 describes significant fields in the previous display.

**Table 8–7** *Show Modem Cookie Field Descriptions*

| Field | Description |
|---|---|
| Slot 1: | The slot carrying the carrier and modem card. |
| Carrier card: | Carrier card and its cookie parameters. |
| Modem Module 0: | Modem card and its cookie parameters. |

## SHOW MODEM CSM

To display the internal status of the call-switching module for modems inside access servers or routers, use the **show modem csm** EXEC command.

**show modem csm** [*slot/port* | **group** *number*]

| *Syntax* | *Description* |
|---|---|
| *slot/port* | (Optional) Specifies the location of a slot and modem port. If this number is not specified, statistics for all connected modems are displayed. Remember to include the forward slash (/) when entering this variable. |
| **group** *number* | (Optional) Specifies the location of a specific group of modems. If this number is not specified, statistics for all modems in the access server are displayed. The group number range is between 1 and 200. |

### *Command Mode*

User and Privileged EXEC

### *Usage Guidelines*

This command first appeared in Cisco IOS Release 11.2.

### *Sample Displays*

The following example displays the call switching module information for modem 1/2 on a Cisco AS5200:

```
router# show modem csm 1/2

MODEM_INFO: slot 1, port 2, unit 130, modem_mask=0x0004, modem_port_offset=0
tty_hwidb=0x00000000, modem_tty=0x004370A8, mgmt_tty=0x004370A8, modem_pool=0x0041D99C
csm_status(0): CSM_STATUS_UNLOCKED
csm_state(0x00000000)=CSM_OC_STATE, csm_event_proc=0x0005B448
invalid_event_count=0, wdt_timeout_count=0
wdt_timestamp_started is not activated
wait_for_dialing:False, wait_for_bchan:False
pri_chnl=TDM_ISDN_STREAM(s0, c0), modem_chnl=TDM_ISDN_STREAM(s0, c0)
dchan_idb_start_index=0, dchan_idb_index=0, call_id=0x0000, bchan_num=0
csm_event=CSM_EVENT_NONE, cause=0x0000, phone_num=
ring_indicator=0, oh_state=0, oh_int_enable=0, modem_reset=0
ring_no_answer=0, ic_failure=0, ic_complete=0
dial_failure=0, oc_failure=0, oc_complete=0
oc_busy=0, oc_no_dial_tone=0, oc_dial_timeout=0
remote_link_disc=0, busyout=0, modem_reset=0
call_duration_started=00:00:00, call_duration_ended=00:00:00,
total_call_duration=00:00:00
The calling party phone number = 4082968388
The called party phone number = 4085267406
```

Table 8–8 describes significant fields in the previous display.

**Table 8–8** *Show Modem CSM Field Descriptions*

| Field | Description |
|---|---|
| MODEM_INFO | Displays internal data structure information. |
| csm_status | Displays the status of the call-switching module. Possible displays include unlocked, active call, busyout req, shutdown, bad modem, modem hold, back-to-back, file downloading, and reset. |
| csm_state | Displays the current state of the call-switching module. Possible states include idle and connected. Incoming calls are marked *IC* and outgoing calls are marked *OC*. |
| Modem counters | Counters for different modem events. |
| The calling party phone number<br>The called party phone number | Phone numbers for the dialing integrated modem and the remote modem. |

## SHOW MODEM LOG

To display the modem history event status performed on a manageable modem or group of modems, use the **show modem log** EXEC command.

**show modem log** [*slot/port* | **group** *number*]

### *Syntax Description*

*slot/port* (Optional) Specifies the location of a slot and modem port. If this number is not specified, statistics for all connected modems are displayed. Remember to include the forward slash (/) when entering this variable.

**group** *number* (Optional) Specifies the location of a specific group of modems. If this number is not specified, statistics for all modems in the access server are displayed. The group number range is between 1 and 200.

### *Command Mode*

User and Privileged EXEC

### *Usage Guidelines*

This command first appeared in Cisco IOS Release 11.2.

### *Sample Display*

The following example shows the event log status for a manageable modem. It also identifies the time elapsed since each modem event was performed (for example, 01:02:41 means the modem event occurred 1 hour, 2 minutes, and 41 seconds ago). To escape from the log display mode, press the keys **Ctrl-C**.

```
router# show modem log 0/0

Modem 0/0 Events Log:
  01:03:03: Startup Response: Microcom MNP10 K56 Modem (Select)
            Modem (boot) firmware = 3.1(16) (3.0(4))
            DSP Controller (SPX) rev = 204.173(0) (143.191(0))
  01:03:03: Control Reply: 0xFF1F
  01:03:03: RS232 event: RTS  noDTR* CTS* DSR* noDCD* noRI  noTST
  01:03:03: RS232 event: RTS  noDTR  CTS  DSR  noDCD  noRI  noTST
  01:03:03: Modem State event: Idle
  01:03:03: End connection event: Retransmits for MNP block (TX/RX) = 0/0
            Duration = 0:00:00, Number of TX/RX char = 0/0
            Local Disc Reason = Lost Carrier
            Remote Disc Reason = Unknown
  01:03:04: Phone number event:
  01:02:51: DTR event: DTR On
  01:02:51: RS232 event: RTS  DTR* CTS  DSR  noDCD  noRI  noTST
  00:39:52: Startup Response: Microcom MNP10 K56 Modem (Select)
            Modem (boot) firmware = 3.1(16) (3.0(4))
            DSP Controller (SPX) rev = 1.1(0) (1.1(0))
  00:39:52: Control Reply: 0xFF1F
  00:39:52: RS232 event: RTS  noDTR* CTS* DSR* noDCD* noRI  noTST
  00:39:52: RS232 event: RTS  noDTR  CTS  DSR  noDCD  noRI  noTST
  00:39:53: Modem State event: Idle
  00:39:53: End connection event: Retransmits for MNP block (TX/RX) = 0/0
            Duration = 0:00:00, Number of TX/RX char = 0/0
            Local Disc Reason = Lost Carrier
            Remote Disc Reason = Unknown
  00:39:53: Phone number event:
  00:39:32: DTR event: DTR On
  00:39:32: RS232 event: RTS  DTR* CTS  DSR  noDCD  noRI  noTST
```

Table 8–9 describes significant fields in the previous display.

**Table 8–9** *Show Modem Log Field Description*

| Field | Description |
|---|---|
| Modem <slot/port> Events Log: | The modem for which log events are currently displayed. |
| Startup Response: | List of information describing the modem type, modem firmware, and DSP controller version (for 56K modems only). |
| Control Reply | Indicates the events the modem will be monitoring. |
| RS232 event | Detected modem signaling. |

**Table 8–9** *Show Modem Log Field Description, Continued*

| **Field** | **Description** |
|---|---|
| Modem State event | Current state of the modem, which can be any of the following:<br>• Conn—Modem is connected to a remote host.<br>• Bad—Inoperable state, which is configured by the **modem bad** command.<br>• Bad*—Inoperable state, which is configured by the **modem startup-test** command during initial power-up testing.<br>• Reset—Modem is in reset mode.<br>• D/L—Modem is downloading firmware.<br>• Bad FW—Downloaded modem firmware is not operational.<br>• Busy—Modem is out of service and not available for calls.<br>• Idle—Modem is ready for incoming and outgoing calls. |
| End connection event | Descriptions or reasons why a connection was terminated:<br>• Duration—Time a connection was up between the local and remote devices.<br>• Number of TX/RX char—Transmit and receive characters exchanged during the connection time.<br>• Local or remote disc reason—Reason the local or remote modem disconnected:<br>— Lost Carrier—The modem firmware detects a drop in Carrier Detect during a connection.<br>— DSP Task Hung—The DSP chip malfunctioned and failed to reset. |
| Phone number event | Descriptive information about the last dialed or current phone number. |

## SHOW MODEM SUMMARY

To display a high-level report for all manageable modems dialing in to and out of the network, use the **show modem summary** EXEC command.

**show modem summary**

### *Syntax Description*

This command has no arguments or keywords.

### Command Mode

User and Privileged EXEC

### Usage Guidelines

This command first appeared in Cisco IOS Release 11.2.

### Sample Display

The following is sample display output for the **show modem summary** command:

```
router# show modem summary

          Incoming calls         Outgoing calls        Busied    Failed    No     Succ
Usage  Succ    Fail  Avail    Succ    Fail  Avail     Out       Dial      Ans    Pct.
  17%  1547      64     11       0       0     11         0         3       3     96%
```

Table 8–10 describes the fields in the previous display.

**Table 8–10** *Show Modem Summary Field Descriptions*

| Fields | Descriptions |
|---|---|
| Incoming and Outgoing calls | Calls dialing in to and out of the modem.<br>• Usage—Percentage of the total system uptime that all the modems are in use.<br>• Succ—Total calls successfully connected.<br>• Fail—Total calls that did not successfully connect.<br>• Avail—Total modems available for use in the system. |
| Busied Out | Total number of times the modems were taken out of service with the **modem busy** command or the **modem shutdown** command. |
| Failed Dial | Total number of attempts the modems did not hang up or there was no dial tone. |
| No Ans | Total number of times call ringing was detected, but the calls were not answered by a modem. |
| Succ Pct. | Successful connection percentage of total available modems. |

## SHOW MODEM TEST

To display the modem test log, use the **show modem test** EXEC command.

**show modem test**

### Syntax Description

This command has no arguments or keywords.

### *Command Mode*

User and Privileged EXEC

### *Usage Guidelines*

This command first appeared in Cisco IOS Release 11.2.

The modem test log displays the results of the modem diagnostics test, which is issued with the **modem autotest** global configuration command.

### *Sample Display*

The following display shows output information for the **show modem test** command for a V.34 modem card:

```
router# show modem test
 Date Time           Modem  Test              Reason           State Result
 5/15 07:25:17 AM    1/0    Back-To-Back      TIME INTERVAL    Idle  FAIL
 5/15 07:25:17 AM    1/1    Back-To-Back      TIME INTERVAL    Idle  PASS
 5/15 07:25:17 AM    1/2    Back-To-Back      TIME INTERVAL    Idle  PASS
 5/15 07:25:17 AM    1/3    Back-To-Back      TIME INTERVAL    Idle  FAIL
 5/15 07:25:17 AM    1/4    Back-To-Back      TIME INTERVAL    Idle  PASS
 5/15 07:25:17 AM    1/5    Back-To-Back      TIME INTERVAL    Idle  PASS
 5/15 07:25:17 AM    1/6    Back-To-Back      TIME INTERVAL    Idle  PASS
 5/15 07:25:17 AM    1/7    Back-To-Back      TIME INTERVAL    Idle  PASS
 5/15 07:25:17 AM    1/8    Back-To-Back      TIME INTERVAL    Idle  PASS
 5/15 07:25:17 AM    1/9    Back-To-Back      TIME INTERVAL    Idle  PASS
...
```

Table 8–11 describes the field in the previous display.

**Table 8–11** *Show Modem Test Field Descriptions*

| **Fields** | **Descriptions** |
|---|---|
| Date | Date the back-to-back test occured for the specified modem. |
| Time | Time the test occured. |
| Modem | Specified modem that performed a back-to-back test. |
| Test | Operation performed by the specified modem. |
| Reason | Reason the modem performed a back-to-back test. |
| State | Current operational state of the modem. |
| Result | Result of the back-to-back test for the specified modem. |

## SHOW MODEM VERSION

To display version information about the modem firmware, controller and DSP code (for 56K modems only), and boot code, use the **show modem version** EXEC command.

**show modem version**

### *Syntax Description*

This command has no arguments or keywords.

### *Command Mode*

User and Privileged EXEC

### *Usage Guidelines*

This command first appeared in Cisco IOS Release 11.2.

This command is very useful for verifying the version of modem firmware running on the system after a modem firmware upgrade.

### *Sample Displays*

The following example displays information for modem firmware, which includes modem firmware version, boot code version, controller and DSP code version (56K modem modules only), modem board hardware version, and carrier card information. This particular example displays information for 56K modem cards installed in a Cisco AS5200.

If the version number is displayed as 0.0.0, verify that out-of-band status polling is functioning.

```
router# show modem version

          Modem module    Firmware    Boot           DSP
Mdm       Number          Rev         Rev            Rev
0/0                  0      3.1(21)  3.0(4)     1.1(0)/1.1(0)
0/1                  0      3.1(21)  3.0(4)     1.1(0)/1.1(0)
0/2                  0      3.1(21)  3.0(4)     1.1(0)/1.1(0)
0/3                  0      3.1(21)  3.0(4)     1.1(0)/1.1(0)
0/4                  0      3.1(21)  3.0(4)     1.1(0)/1.1(0)
0/5                  0      3.1(21)  3.0(4)     1.1(0)/1.1(0)
0/6                  0      3.1(21)  3.0(4)     1.1(0)/1.1(0)
0/7                  0      3.1(21)  3.0(4)     1.1(0)/1.1(0)
0/8                  0      3.1(21)  3.0(4)     1.1(0)/1.1(0)
0/9                  0      3.1(21)  3.0(4)     1.1(0)/1.1(0)
0/10                 0      3.1(21)  3.0(4)     1.1(0)/1.1(0)
0/11                 0      3.1(21)  3.0(4)     1.1(0)/1.1(0)
0/12                 1      2.2(8)   1.0(5)
0/13                 1      2.2(8)   1.0(5)
0/14                 1      2.2(8)   1.0(5)
0/15                 1      2.2(8)   1.0(5)
0/16                 1      2.2(8)   1.0(5)
0/17                 1      2.2(8)   1.0(5)
0/18                 1      2.2(8)   1.0(5)
0/19                 1      2.2(8)   1.0(5)
0/20                 1      2.2(8)   1.0(5)
0/21                 1      2.2(8)   1.0(5)
0/22                 1      2.2(8)   1.0(5)
0/23                 1      2.2(8)   1.0(5)
2/0                  0      3.1(21)  3.0(4)     1.1(0)/1.1(0)
2/1                  0      3.1(21)  3.0(4)     1.1(0)/1.1(0)
```

```
2/2              0       3.1(21)  3.0(4)    1.1(0)/1.1(0)
2/3              0       3.1(21)  3.0(4)    1.1(0)/1.1(0)
2/4              0       3.1(21)  3.0(4)    1.1(0)/1.1(0)
2/5              0       3.1(21)  3.0(4)    1.1(0)/1.1(0)
2/6              0       3.1(21)  3.0(4)    1.1(0)/1.1(0)
2/7              0       3.1(21)  3.0(4)    1.1(0)/1.1(0)
2/8              0       3.1(21)  3.0(4)    1.1(0)/1.1(0)
2/9              0       3.1(21)  3.0(4)    1.1(0)/1.1(0)
2/10             0       3.1(21)  3.0(4)    1.1(0)/1.1(0)
2/11             0       3.1(21)  3.0(4)    1.1(0)/1.1(0)
2/12             1       3.1(21)  3.0(4)    1.1(0)/1.1(0)
2/13             1       3.1(21)  3.0(4)    1.1(0)/1.1(0)
2/14             1       3.1(21)  3.0(4)    1.1(0)/1.1(0)
2/15             1       3.1(21)  3.0(4)    1.1(0)/1.1(0)
2/16             1       3.1(21)  3.0(4)    1.1(0)/1.1(0)
2/17             1       3.1(21)  3.0(4)    1.1(0)/1.1(0)
2/18             1       3.1(21)  3.0(4)    1.1(0)/1.1(0)
2/19             1       3.1(21)  3.0(4)    1.1(0)/1.1(0)
2/20             1       3.1(21)  3.0(4)    1.1(0)/1.1(0)
2/21             1       3.1(21)  3.0(4)    1.1(0)/1.1(0)
2/22             1       3.1(21)  3.0(4)    1.1(0)/1.1(0)
2/23             1       3.1(21)  3.0(4)    1.1(0)/1.1(0)

Modem board HW version info:

Slot 0:
  Carrier card:
    hw version= 8, number_of_ports= 24, max_modules= 2, max_oob_ports= 2
  Modem Module 0:
    number_of_modems= 12, option_bits= 1,
    rev_num= 02.00, vendor_model_number= 02,
    vendor_banner= Microcom MNP10 K56 Modem
  Modem Module 1:
    number_of_modems= 12, option_bits= 1,
    rev_num= 03.00, vendor_model_number= 01,
    vendor_banner= Microcom MNP10 V34 Modem

Slot 2:
  Carrier card:
    hw version= 7, number_of_ports= 24, max_modules= 2, max_oob_ports= 2
  Modem Module 0:
    number_of_modems= 12, option_bits= 1,
    rev_num= 02.00, vendor_model_number= 02,
    vendor_banner= Microcom MNP10 K56 Modem
  Modem Module 1:
    number_of_modems= 12, option_bits= 1,
    rev_num= 02.00, vendor_model_number= 02,
    vendor_banner= Microcom MNP10 K56 Modem
```

The next example displays modem version information for V.110 modem cards for unmanaged modems:

```
router# show modem version

                   Modem module        Firmware     Boot
Mdm                   Number           Rev          Rev
0/0                     0              Unmanaged    Unmanaged
0/1                     0              Unmanaged    Unmanaged
0/2                     0              Unmanaged    Unmanaged
0/3                     0              Unmanaged    Unmanaged
0/4                     0              Unmanaged    Unmanaged
0/5                     0              Unmanaged    Unmanaged
0/6                     0              Unmanaged    Unmanaged
0/7                     0              Unmanaged    Unmanaged
0/8                     0              Unmanaged    Unmanaged
0/9                     0              Unmanaged    Unmanaged
0/10                    0              Unmanaged    Unmanaged
0/11                    0              Unmanaged    Unmanaged
1/0                     0              Unmanaged    Unmanaged
1/1                     0              Unmanaged    Unmanaged
1/2                     0              Unmanaged    Unmanaged
1/3                     0              Unmanaged    Unmanaged
1/4                     0              Unmanaged    Unmanaged
1/5                     0              Unmanaged    Unmanaged
1/6                     0              Unmanaged    Unmanaged
1/7                     0              Unmanaged    Unmanaged
1/8                     0              Unmanaged    Unmanaged
1/9                     0              Unmanaged    Unmanaged
1/10                    0              Unmanaged    Unmanaged
1/11                    0              Unmanaged    Unmanaged
1/12                    1              Unmanaged    Unmanaged
1/13                    1              Unmanaged    Unmanaged
1/14                    1              Unmanaged    Unmanaged
1/15                    1              Unmanaged    Unmanaged
1/16                    1              Unmanaged    Unmanaged
1/17                    1              Unmanaged    Unmanaged
1/18                    1              Unmanaged    Unmanaged
1/19                    1              Unmanaged    Unmanaged
1/20                    1              Unmanaged    Unmanaged
1/21                    1              Unmanaged    Unmanaged
1/22                    1              Unmanaged    Unmanaged
1/23                    1              Unmanaged    Unmanaged
2/0                     0              Unmanaged    Unmanaged
2/1                     0              Unmanaged    Unmanaged
2/2                     0              Unmanaged    Unmanaged
2/3                     0              Unmanaged    Unmanaged
2/4                     0              Unmanaged    Unmanaged
2/5                     0              Unmanaged    Unmanaged
2/6                     0              Unmanaged    Unmanaged
2/7                     0              Unmanaged    Unmanaged
2/8                     0              Unmanaged    Unmanaged
2/9                     0              Unmanaged    Unmanaged
2/10                    0              Unmanaged    Unmanaged
```

```
2/11            0          Unmanaged   Unmanaged
2/12            1          Unmanaged   Unmanaged
2/13            1          Unmanaged   Unmanaged
2/14            1          Unmanaged   Unmanaged
2/15            1          Unmanaged   Unmanaged
2/16            1          Unmanaged   Unmanaged
2/17            1          Unmanaged   Unmanaged
2/18            1          Unmanaged   Unmanaged
2/19            1          Unmanaged   Unmanaged
2/20            1          Unmanaged   Unmanaged
2/21            1          Unmanaged   Unmanaged
2/22            1          Unmanaged   Unmanaged
2/23            1          Unmanaged   Unmanaged


Modem board HW version info:

Slot 0:
  Carrier card:
    hw version= 3, number_of_ports= 12, max_modules= 1, max_oob_ports= 1
  Modem Module 0:
    number_of_modems= 12, option_bits= 1,
    rev_num= 03.01, vendor_model_number= 01,
    vendor_banner= V.110 Terminal Adaptor

Slot 1:
  Carrier card:
    hw version= 8, number_of_ports= 24, max_modules= 2, max_oob_ports= 2
  Modem Module 0:
    number_of_modems= 12, option_bits= 1,
    rev_num= 03.01, vendor_model_number= 01,
    vendor_banner= V.110 Terminal Adaptor
  Modem Module 1:
    number_of_modems= 12, option_bits= 1,
    rev_num= 03.01, vendor_model_number= 01,
    vendor_banner= V.110 Terminal Adaptor

Slot 2:
  Carrier card:
    hw version= 8, number_of_ports= 24, max_modules= 2, max_oob_ports= 2
  Modem Module 0:
    number_of_modems= 12, option_bits= 1,
    rev_num= 03.00, vendor_model_number= 01,
    vendor_banner= V.110 Terminal Adaptor
  Modem Module 1:
    number_of_modems= 12, option_bits= 1,
    rev_num= 03.00, vendor_model_number= 01,
    vendor_banner= V.110 Terminal Adaptor
```

Table 8–12 describes the fields shown in the previous displays of the **show modem version** command.

**Table 8–12** *Show Modem Field Descriptions*

| Fields | Descriptions |
|---|---|
| Mdm | Slot and port number for the specified modem. |
| Modem module Number | Card number associated with the carrier card. |
| Firmware Rev | Modem firmware version, or one of the following:<br>• Unknown—Indicates that the retrieved version is 0.0.0.<br>• Unknown (F)—Indicates that the modem's out-of-band feature has failed.<br>• Unknown (NP)—Indicates that the user has disabled the status polling for this modem using the no modem status-polling command. |
| Boot Rev | Modem boot version, or one of the following:<br>• Unknown—Indicates that the retrieved version is 0.0.0.<br>• Unknown (F)—Indicates that the modem's out-of-band feature has failed.<br>• Unknown (NP)—Indicates that the user has disabled the status polling for this modem using the no modem status-polling command. |
| DSP Rev | Controller and DSP version, which is displayed for the 56K modems only. The first column of numbers correspond to the controller version. The second column of numbers, which begin with a forward slash (/), correspond to the DSP version. |
| Modem board HW version info: | Modem hardware board information. |
| Slot | Slot number used for the carrier card. |
| Carrier card | Modem carrier card. |
| hw version | Modem carrier card hardware version. |
| number_of_ports | Maximum number of modem ports that can be installed in the carrier card. |
| max_modules | Maximum number of modem cards that can be installed in a carrier card. |

**Table 8–12** *Show Modem Field Descriptions, Continued*

| Fields | Descriptions |
|---|---|
| max_oob_ports | Maximum out-of-band ports used in the carrier card. |
| Modem Module | Modem card. |
| number_of_modems | Number of modems installed in the modem card. |
| option_bits | Signal level of the modem A-law and the U-law. |
| rev_num | Modem card version number. |
| vendor_model_number | Vendor modem model number. |
| vendor_banner | Type of banner displayed by the modem vendor. |

## TEST MODEM BACK-TO-BACK

To diagnose an integrated modem that may not be functioning properly, use the **test modem back-to-back** EXEC command.

**test modem back-to-back** *first-slot/port second-slot/port*

| *Syntax* | *Description* |
|---|---|
| *first-slot/port* | Slot and modem number of the first test modem. Remember to include the forward slash (/) when entering this variable. |
| *second-slot/port* | Slot and modem number of the second test modem. Remember to include the forward slash (/) when entering this variable. |

### *Default*

Disabled

### *Command Mode*

EXEC

### *Usage Guidelines*

This command first appeared in Cisco IOS Release 11.2.

Use this command to perform back-to-back testing of two modems. You might need to enable this command on several different combinations of modems to determine which one is not functioning properly.

### *Example*

The following example performs a back-to-back modem test between modem 2/0 and modem 2/1 and removes modem 2/1 (which is associated with TTY line 26) from all dial-in and dial-out services:

```
router# test modem back-to-back 2/0 2/1
back2back 2/0 2/1
Repetitions (of 10-byte packets) [1]:
router#
%MODEM-5-B2BCONNECT: Modems (2/0) and (2/1) connected in back-to-back test:
CONNECT9600/REL-MNPM
%MODEM-5-B2BMODEMS: Modems (2/0) and (2/1) completed back-to-back test: success/packets =
2/2
```

### *Related Commands*

Search online to find documentation for related commands.

**modem bad**

CHAPTER 9

# Configuring Terminal Operating Characteristics for Dial-In Sessions

This chapter describes the process for setting operating characteristics for remote terminal service connections. In line configuration mode, you can set terminal operating characteristics that will be in operation for that line until the next time you change the line parameters. Alternatively, you can change the line setting temporarily with the **terminal** EXEC commands as described later in this chapter.

First, select a preferred connection protocol, then configure the appropriate communication parameters. The main sections in this chapter reflect these two tasks accrodinglingly:

- Selecting a Preferred Connection Protocol
- Configuring Communication Parameters for Terminal Ports

For a complete description of the terminal characteristic commands in this chapter, see Chapter 10, "Terminal Characteristics Commands for Dial Sessions."

## SELECTING A PREFERRED CONNECTION PROTOCOL

The preferred transport type is your preferred connection protocol. This section describes how to configure the router to support specific protocols for connection sessions over a line, as follows:

- All Sessions on a Line
- Individual Sessions

### All Sessions on a Line

Use the **transport preferred** command to specify which transport protocol is used on connections. Use the **transport input** and **transport output** commands to explicitly specify the protocols allowed on individual lines for both incoming and outgoing connections.

**NOTES**

Cisco routers do not accept incoming network connections to asynchronous ports (TTY lines) by default. You have to specify an incoming transport protocol, or specify **transport input all** before the line will accept incoming connections. For example, if you are using your router as a terminal server to make console-port connections to routers or other devices, you will not be able to use Telnet to connect to these devices. You will receive the message "Connection Refused."

For routers that support LAT, the default protocol for outgoing connections is LAT. For those that do not support LAT, the default protocol for outgoing connections is Telnet. For incoming connections, all the supported network protocols are accepted (the default protocol is **all**).

Perform one or more of the following tasks in line configuration mode to specify transport protocols:

| Task | Command |
|---|---|
| Define which protocols can be used to connect to a specific line. | **transport input** {**all** \| **lat** \| **mop** \| **nasi** \| **none** \| **pad** \| **rlogin** \| **telnet** \| **v120**} |
| Determine the protocols that can be used for outgoing connections from a line. | **transport output** {**all** \| **lat** \| **mop** \| **nasi** \| **none** \| **pad** \| **rlogin** \| **telnet** \| **v120**} |
| Specify the protocol for the router to use if the user did not specify a protocol. | **transport preferred** {**all** \| **lat** \| **mop** \| **nasi** \| **pad** \| **rlogin** \| **telnet** \| **v120**} |
| Prevent errant connection attempts. | **transport preferred none** |

The router accepts a host name entry at the EXEC system prompt as a Telnet command. If you enter the host name incorrectly, the router interprets the entry as an incorrect Telnet command and provides an error message indicating that the host does not exist. The **transport preferred none** command disables this option so that if you enter a command incorrectly at the EXEC prompt, the router does not attempt to make a Telnet connection to a host that it cannot find.

The **preferred transport** setting specifies a search order when attempting to resolve names that might be valid for multiple protocols. If the address or service does not match the preferred protocol, all other valid output protocols are searched to find a valid match.

## Individual Sessions

You can configure the Cisco IOS software to save local parameters between sessions. These local parameters are set with the EXEC **terminal** commands.

To specify the preferred protocol to use for the current session when a command does not specify one, perform the following task in EXEC mode:

| Task | Command |
|---|---|
| Specify the protocol for the Cisco IOS software to use for the current session if the user did not specify a protocol. | **terminal transport preferred {all \| lat \| mop \| nasi \| none \| pad \| rlogin \| telnet \| v120}** |

The preferred transport type is your preferred connection protocol. This setting specifies a protocol search order that the Cisco IOS software uses when it attempts to resolve a device name that you enter, but you do not specify a connection protocol. For example, if you want to connect to a TCP/IP host named host1 and want to use Telnet, you type **telnet host1**. However, if your preferred connection protocol is set to Telnet, you can type **host1** and be connected to the device. A host name might be valid for multiple protocols. If the address or service does not match the preferred protocol, all other valid connection protocols are searched to find a valid match for the name.

For router software images that support LAT, the default protocol for outgoing connections is LAT. For router software images that do not support LAT, the default protocol for outgoing connections is Telnet. For incoming connections, all the supported network protocols are accepted (the default protocol is **all**).

The Cisco IOS software accepts a host name entry at the EXEC prompt as a Telnet command. If you enter the host name incorrectly, the Cisco IOS software interprets the entry as an incorrect Telnet command and provides an error message indicating that the host does not exist. The **transport preferred none** command disables this option so that if you enter a command incorrectly at the EXEC prompt, the Cisco IOS software does not attempt to make a Telnet connection.

## Configuring Communication Parameters for Terminal Ports

The following communication parameters can be configured:

- Configure All Sessions on a Line
- Configure Individual Sessions
- Change the Default Privilege Level for Lines
- Enable Password Checking at Login
- Display Line Connection Information after the Login Prompt
- Establish Terminal Session Limits

### Configure All Sessions on a Line

The Cisco IOS software supplies the following default serial communication parameters for terminal and other serial device operation:

- 9600 bits per second (bps) line speed
- 8 data bits
- 2 stop bits
- No parity bit

You can change these parameters as necessary to meet the requirements of the terminal or host to which you are connected. To do so, perform one or more of the following tasks in line configuration mode:

| Task | Command |
|---|---|
| Set the line speed. Choose from line speed, transmit speed, or receive speed. | **speed** *bps*<br>**txspeed** *bps*<br>**rxspeed** *bps* |
| Set the data bits. | **databits** {**5** \| **6** \| **7** \| **8**} |
| Set the stop bits. | **stopbits** {**1** \| **1.5** \| **2**} |
| Set the parity bit. | **parity** {**none** \| **even** \| **odd** \| **space** \| **mark**} |

### Configure Individual Sessions

You can change these parameters as necessary to meet the requirements of the terminal or host to which you are attached. To do so, perform one or more of the following tasks in EXEC mode:

| Task | Command |
|---|---|
| Set the line speed for the current session. Choose from line speed, transmit speed, or receive speed. | **terminal speed** *bps*<br>**terminal txspeed** *bps*<br>**terminal rxspeed** *bps* |
| Set the data bits for the current session. | **terminal databits** {**5** \| **6** \| **7** \| **8**} |
| Set the stop bits for the current session. | **terminal stopbits** {**1** \| **1.5** \| **2**} |
| Set the parity bit for the current session. | **terminal parity** {**none** \| **even** \| **odd** \| **space** \| **mark**} |

### Change the Default Privilege Level for Lines

To change the default privilege level for a given line or a group of lines, perform the following task in line configuration mode:

| Task | Command |
|---|---|
| Specify a default privilege level for a line. | **privilege level** *level* |

### Enable Password Checking at Login

You can enable password checking on a particular line so that the user is prompted to enter a password at the system login screen. You must then also specify a password. To do so, perform the following steps in line configuration mode:

| Task | | Command |
|---|---|---|
| **Step 1** | Enable password checking on a per-line basis using the password specified with the **password** command. | **login** |
| **Step 2** | Assign a password to a particular line. | **password** *password* |

You can enable password checking on a per-user basis, in which case authentication is based on the username specified with the **username** global configuration command. To enable password checking on a per-user basis, perform one of the following tasks in line configuration mode:

| Task | Command |
|---|---|
| Enable password checking on a per-user basis using the username and password specified with the **username** global configuration command. | **login local** |
| Select the TACACS-style user ID and password-checking mechanism. | **login tacacs**<br>or<br>**login authentication** {**default** \| *list-name*} |

Use the **login tacacs** command with Terminal Access Controller Access Control System (TACACS) and Extended TACACS. Use the **login authentication** command with AAA/TACACS+.

By default, virtual terminals require passwords. If you do not set a password for a virtual terminal, the router displays an error message and closes the attempted connection. Use the **no login** command to disable this function and allow connections without a password.

## Establish Terminal Session Limits

You might need to control terminal sessions in high-traffic areas to provide resources for all users. You can define the following limitations for terminal sessions:

- The maximum number of sessions
- The idle session timeout interval or the absolute timeout interval

To establish terminal session limits, perform one of the following tasks in line configuration mode:

| Task | Command |
|---|---|
| Set the maximum number of simultaneous sessions. | **session-limit** *session-number*[*] |

| Task | Command |
|---|---|
| Set the idle session timeout interval. | **session-timeout** *minutes* [**output**] |
| or | or |
| Set the absolute timeout interval. | **absolute-timeout** *minutes* |
| Warn users of impending timeouts set with the **absolute-timeout** command. | **logout-warning** [*seconds*] |

*There is no inherent upper limit to the number of sessions you can create.

**NOTES**

The **absolute-timeout** command overrides any timeouts set through the AppleTalk Remote Access (ARA) protocol.

### Display Line Connection Information after the Login Prompt

You can display the host name, line number, and location of the host each time an EXEC session is started or an incoming connection is made. The line number banner appears immediately after the EXEC banner or incoming banner. This feature is useful for tracking problems with modems because it lists the host and line for the modem connection. Modem type information is also included if applicable.

To provide line information, perform the following task in global configuration mode:

| Task | Command |
|---|---|
| Provide service line-number information after the EXEC banner or incoming banner. | **service linenumber** |

# CHAPTER 10

# Terminal Characteristics Commands for Dial Sessions

This chapter describes the commands for setting operating characteristics for remote terminal service connections. It also describes the commands used to monitor and manage these connections.

Configuring support for terminal service connections refers to enabling network devices running the same protocol—such as local-area transport (LAT) or Transmission Control Protocol (TCP)--to connect across a LAN or WAN through network and terminal-emulation software such as Telnet, rlogin, TN3270, LAT, and NetWare Access Server Interface (NASI).

The following terminal connections can be performed by configuring terminal operating characteristic using the Cisco IOS software:

- Terminal services permit asynchronous devices to be connected to a LAN or WAN through network and terminal-emulation software including Telnet, rlogin, NASI, Digital's LAT protocol, and IBM TN3270.
- Access services permit terminals to connect with remote hosts using virtual terminal protocols including Telnet, NASI, LAT, TN3270, rlogin, and X.25 packet assembler/disassembler (PAD). You can use a router that supports access services to function as a terminal server to provide terminal access to devices on the network.
- A host can also connect directly to an access server. In IBM environments, TN3270 allows a standard ASCII terminal to emulate a 3278 terminal and access an IBM host across an IP network.
- In Digital environments, LAT support provides a terminal with connections to VMS hosts. X.25 PAD allows terminals to connect directly to an X.25 host over an X.25 network through the router. X.25 PAD eliminates the need for a separate PAD device. This connection requires use of one of the synchronous serial interfaces on the router supporting access services.

For configuration tasks and examples, see Chapter 9, "Configuring Terminal Operating Characteristics for Dial-In Sessions."

### ABSOLUTE-TIMEOUT

To set the interval for closing the connection, use the **absolute-timeout** line configuration command. Use the **no** form of this command to restore the default.

**absolute-timeout** *minutes*
**no absolute-timeout**

| *Syntax* | *Description* |
|---|---|
| *minutes* | The number of minutes after which the user's session will be terminated. |

#### *Default*

No timeout interval is automatically set.

#### *Command Mode*

Line configuration

#### *Usage Guidelines*

This command first appeared in Cisco IOS Release 11.0.

This command terminates the connection after the specified time period has elapsed, regardless of whether the connection is being used at the time of termination. You can specify an absolute-timeout value for each port. The user is given 20-seconds notice before the session is terminated. You can use this command in conjunction with the **logout-warning** command, which notifies the user of an impending logout.

**NOTES**

You can set this command and an AppleTalk Remote Access Protocol (ARAP) timeout for the same line; however, this command supersedes any timeouts set in ARAP. Additionally, ARAP users will receive no notice of any impending termination if you use this command.

#### *Example*

The following example sets an interval of 60 minutes on line 5:

```
line 5
 absolute-timeout 60
```

### *Related Commands*

Search online to find documentation for related commands.

**logout-warning**
**session-timeout**

## EDITING

To enable enhanced editing mode for a particular line, use the **editing** line configuration command. Use the **no** form of this command to disable the enhanced editing mode.

**editing**
**no editing**

### *Syntax Description*

This command has no arguments or keywords.

### *Default*

Enabled

### *Command Mode*

Line configuration

### *Usage Guidelines*

This command first appeared in Cisco IOS Release 10.0.

Table 10–1 provides a description of the keys used to enter and edit commands. "Ctrl" indicates the Control key. It must be pressed simultaneously with its associated letter key. "Esc" indicates the Escape key. It must be pressed first, followed by its associated letter key. Keys are *not* case-sensitive.

**Table 10–1** *Editing Keys and Functions for Software Release 9.21 and Later*

| Keys | Function |
|---|---|
| Tab | Completes a partial command name entry. When you enter a unique set of characters and press the Tab key, the system completes the command name. If you enter a set of characters that can indicate more than one command, the system beeps to indicate an error. Enter a question mark (?) immediately following the partial command (no space). The system provides a list of commands that begin with that string. |
| Delete or Backspace | Erases the character to the left of the cursor. |
| Return | At the command line, pressing the Return key performs the function of processing a command. At the `---More---` prompt on a terminal screen, pressing the Return key scrolls down a line. |

**Table 10–1** *Editing Keys and Functions for Software Release 9.21 and Later, Continued*

| Keys | Function |
|---|---|
| Spacebar | Allows you to see more output on the terminal screen. Press the Spacebar when you see the line `---More---` on the screen to display the next screen. |
| Left arrow* | Moves the cursor one character to the left. When you enter a command that extends beyond a single line, you can press the Left Arrow key repeatedly to scroll back toward the system prompt and verify the beginning of the command entry. |
| Right arrow | Moves the cursor one character to the right. |
| Up arrow or Ctrl-P | Recalls commands in the history buffer, beginning with the most recent command. Repeat the key sequence to recall successively older commands. |
| Down arrow* or Ctrl-N | Return to more recent commands in the history buffer after recalling commands with the Up arrow or Ctrl-P. Repeat the key sequence to recall successively more recent commands. |
| Ctrl-A | Moves the cursor to the beginning of the line. |
| Ctrl-B | Moves the cursor back one character. |
| Ctrl-D | Deletes the character at the cursor. |
| Ctrl-E | Moves the cursor to the end of the command line. |
| Ctrl-F | Moves the cursor forward one character. |
| Ctrl-K | Deletes all characters from the cursor to the end of the command line. |
| Ctrl-L and Ctrl-R | Redisplays the system prompt and command line. |
| Ctrl-T | Transposes the character to the left of the cursor with the character located at the cursor. |
| Ctrl-U and Ctrl-X | Deletes all characters from the cursor back to the beginning of the command line. |
| Ctrl-V and Esc Q | Inserts a code to indicate to the system that the keystroke immediately following should be treated as a command entry, *not* as an editing key. |
| Ctrl-W | Deletes the word to the left of the cursor. |
| Ctrl-Y | Recalls the most recent entry in the delete buffer. The delete buffer contains the last ten items you have deleted or cut. Ctrl-Y can be used in conjunction with Esc Y. |

**Table 10–1** *Editing Keys and Functions for Software Release 9.21 and Later, Continued*

| Keys | Function |
|---|---|
| Ctrl-Z | Ends configuration mode and returns you to the EXEC prompt. |
| Esc B | Moves the cursor back one word. |
| Esc C | Capitalizes the word at the cursor. |
| Esc D | Deletes from the cursor to the end of the word. |
| Esc F | Moves the cursor forward one word. |
| Esc L | Changes the word at the cursor to lowercase. |
| Esc U | Capitalizes from the cursor to the end of the word. |
| Esc Y | Recalls the next buffer entry. The buffer contains the last 10 items you have deleted. Press **Ctrl-Y** first to recall the most recent entry. Then press **Esc Y** up to nine times to recall the remaining entries in the buffer. If you bypass an entry, continue to press **Esc Y** to cycle back to it. |

* The arrow keys function only with ANSI-compatible terminals.

### *Example*

In the following example, enhanced editing mode is disabled on virtual terminal line 3:

```
line vty 3
 no editing
```

### *Related Commands*

Search online to find documentation for related commands.

**terminal editing**

## LOGIN (LINE)

To enable password checking at login, use the **login** line configuration command. Use the **no** form of this command to disable password checking and allow connections without a password.

**login** [**local** | **tacacs**]
**no login**

| *Syntax* | *Description* |
|---|---|
| **local** | (Optional) Selects local password checking. Authentication is based on the username specified with the **username** global configuration command. |
| **tacacs** | (Optional) Selects the Terminal Access Controller Access Control System (TACACS)-style user ID and password-checking mechanism. |

### *Default*

Virtual terminals require a password. If you do not set a password for a virtual terminal, it responds to attempted connections by displaying an error message and closing the connection.

### *Command Mode*

Line configuration

### *Usage Guidelines*

This command first appeared in Cisco IOS Release 10.0.

If you specify the **login** command without the **local** or **tacacs** option, authentication is based on the password specified with the **password** line configuration command.

**NOTES**

This command cannot be used with authentication, authorization, and accounting (AAA)/TACACS+. Use the **login authentication** command instead.

### *Examples*

The following example sets the password letmein on virtual terminal line 4:

```
line vty 4
 password letmein
 login
```

The following example enables the TACACS-style user ID and password-checking mechanism:

```
line 0
 password mypassword
 login tacacs
```

### *Related Commands*

Search online to find documentation for related commands.

**enable password**
**password**
**username**

## LOGIN AUTHENTICATION

To enable AAA/TACACS+ authentication for logins, use the **login authentication** line configuration command. Use the **no** form of the command to return to the default.

**login authentication** [**default** | *list-name*]
**no login authentication** [**default** | *list-name*]

| *Syntax* | *Description* |
|---|---|
| **default** | Uses the default list created with the **aaa authentication login** command. |
| *list-name* | Use the list specified. |

### *Default*

Login authentication uses the default set with the **aaa authentication login** command. If no default is set, the local user database is checked. No authentication is performed on the console.

### *Command Mode*

Line configuration

### *Usage Guidelines*

This command first appeared in Cisco IOS Release 10.3.

This command is a per-line command used with AAA authentication and specifies a list of TACACS+ authentication processes that are tried at login. If no list is specified, the default list is used (whether or not it is specified in the command line). Defaults and lists are created with the **aaa authentication login** command. Note that entering the **no** version of **login authentication** has the same effect as entering the command with the **default** argument.

Before issuing this command, create a list of authentication processes with the **aaa authentication login** global configuration command.

**CAUTION**

If you use a *list-name* that has not been configured with the **aaa authentication login** command, you will disable logins on this line.

### *Examples*

The following example specifies that the default AAA authentication is to be used on line 4:

```
line 4
 login authentication default
```

The following example specifies that the AAA authentication list called MIS-access is to be used on line 7:

```
line 7
 login authentication MIS-access
```

### *Related Commands*

Search online to find documentation for related commands.

**aaa authentication login**

## PASSWORD

To specify a password on a line, use the **password** line configuration command. Use the **no** form of this command to remove the password.

**password** *password*
**no password**

| *Syntax* | *Description* |
|---|---|
| *password* | Character string that specifies the line password. The first character cannot be a number. The string can contain any alphanumeric characters, including spaces, up to 80 characters. You cannot specify the password in the format number-space-anything. The space after the number causes problems. For example, hello 21 is a legal password, but 21 hello is not. The password checking is case-sensitive. For example, the password Secret is different than the password secret. |

### *Default*

No password is specified.

### *Command Mode*

Line configuration

### *Usage Guidelines*

This command first appeared in Cisco IOS Release 10.0.

When an EXEC process is started on a line with password protection, the EXEC prompts for the password. If the user enters the correct password, the EXEC prints its normal privileged prompt. The user can try three times to enter a password before the EXEC exits and returns the terminal to the idle state.

### *Example*

The following example removes the password from virtual terminal lines 1 to 4:

```
line vty 1 4
 no password
```

### *Related Commands*

Search online to find documentation for related commands.

**enable password**
**login (line)**

## RXSPEED

To set the terminal receive speed (how fast the terminal receives information from the modem), use the **rxspeed** line configuration command.

**rxspeed** *bps*

| *Syntax* | *Description* |
|---|---|
| *bps* | Baud rate in bits per second (bps). |

### *Default*

9600 bps

### *Command Mode*

Line configuration

### *Usage Guidelines*

This command first appeared in Cisco IOS Release 10.0.

Set the speed to match the baud rate of whatever device you have connected to the port. Some baud rates available on devices connected to the port might not be supported on the system. The system will indicate if the speed you select is not supported.

### *Example*

The following example sets the line 5 receive rate to 2400 bps:

```
line 5
 rxspeed 2400
```

### *Related Commands*

Search online to find documentation for related commands.

**speed**
**terminal rxspeed**
**txspeed**

## SESSION-LIMIT

To set the maximum number of terminal sessions per line, use the **session-limit** line configuration command. Use the **no** form of this command to remove any specified session limit.

**session-limit** *session-number*
**no session-limit**

### *Default*

The default and set session limits are displayed with the **show terminal** EXEC command.

| *Syntax* | *Description* |
|---|---|
| *session-number* | Specifies the maximum number of sessions. |

*Command Mode*

Line configuration

*Usage Guidelines*

This command first appeared in Cisco IOS Release 10.0.

*Example*

The following example limits the number of sessions to 8 on a 10-line range:

```
line 2 12
 session-limit 8
```

*Related Commands*

Search online to find documentation for related commands.

**line vty**

### SESSION-TIMEOUT

To set the interval for closing the connection when there is no input or output traffic, use the **session-timeout** line configuration command. Use the **no** form of this command to remove the timeout definition.

**session-timeout** *minutes* [output]
**no session-timeout**

| *Syntax* | *Description* |
|---|---|
| *minutes* | Specifies the timeout interval in minutes. |
| **output** | (Optional) Specifies that when traffic is sent to an asynchronous line from the router (within the specified interval), the connection is retained. |

*Default*

The default interval is zero, indicating the router maintains the connection indefinitely.

*Command Mode*

Line configuration

*Usage Guidelines*

This command first appeared in Cisco IOS Release 10.0.

This command sets the interval that the Cisco IOS software waits for traffic before closing the connection to a remote computer and returning the terminal to an idle state. If only **session timeout** is the specified command, the session timeout interval is based solely on detected input from the user. If **session-timeout output** is the specified command, the interval is based on input and output traffic. You can specify a session timeout on each port.

### *Examples*

The following example sets an interval of 20 minutes and specifies that the timeout is subject to traffic detected from the user (input only):

```
line 5
 session-timeout 20
```

The following example sets an interval of 10 minutes, subject to traffic on the line in either direction:

```
line 5
 session-timeout 10 output
```

## SHOW TERMINAL

To obtain information about the terminal configuration parameter settings for the current terminal line, use the **show terminal** EXEC command.

**show terminal**

### *Syntax Description*

This command has no arguments or keywords.

### *Command Mode*

EXEC

### *Usage Guidelines*

This command first appeared in Cisco IOS Release 10.0.

### *Sample Display*

The following is sample output from the **show terminal** command:

```
 router# show terminal

Line 2, Location: "", Type: ""
Length: 24 lines, Width: 80 columns
Baud rate (TX/RX) is 9600/9600
Status: Ready, Active, No Exit Banner
Capabilities: Enabled
Modem state: Ready
Special Chars: Escape  Hold  Stop  Start  Disconnect  Activation
                ^^x    none   -      -       none
```

```
Timeouts:      Idle EXEC    Idle Session   Modem Answer  Session   Dispatch
                never         never          0:00:15      not imp   not set
Session limit is not set.
Allowed transports are telnet rlogin.  Preferred is telnet
No output characters are padded
```

Table 10–2 describes the fields in the first three lines of **show terminal** output.

**Table 10–2** *Show Terminal Field Descriptions—First Three Lines of Output*

| Field | Description |
|---|---|
| Line 2 | Current terminal line. |
| Location: " " | Location of the current terminal line, as specified using the **location** line configuration command. |
| Type: " " | Type of the current terminal line, as specified using the **line** global configuration command. |
| Length: 24 lines | Length of the terminal display. |
| Width: 80 columns | Width of the terminal display, in character columns. |
| Baud rate (TX/RX) is 9600/9600 | Transmit rate/receive rate of the line. |

The following line of output indicates the status of the line:

```
Status: Ready, Active, No Exit Banner
```

Table 10–3 describes possible values for the Status field.

**Table 10–3** *Show Terminal Field Description—Status Field*

| Field | Description |
|---|---|
| Active | A process is actively using the line. |
| Autobauding | The line is running the autobaud process. |
| Carrier Dropped | Some sense of "carrier" has been dropped, so the line process should be killed. |
| Connected | The line has at least one active connection. |
| Dialing Out | A DDR asynchronous interface is dialing a remote site on this line. |
| Echo Off | The line is not echoing what the user types in (for example because a password must be entered). |
| Escape Started | The first character of the escape sequence has been typed. |

**Table 10–3** *Show Terminal Field Description—Status Field, Continued*

| Field | Description |
|---|---|
| Escape Typed | Both characters of the escape sequence have been typed. |
| Hanging Up | The line state is "hanging up." |
| Hardware XON/XOFF | The line uses a UART that supports XON/XOFF flow control in hardware. (This does not mean that the line is currently using software flow control.) |
| Hold Typed | The user typed the "hold character" (and the line is paused). |
| Idle | The line modem state is "idle" (see modem state diagrams). |
| Idle Timeout | An idle timeout has occurred. |
| Input Stopped | The input has been turned off because of hardware flow control or overflow. |
| No Exit Banner | The normal exit banner will not be displayed on this line. |
| PSI Enabled | The line is paying attention to typed escape characters. |
| Rcvd BREAK | A BREAK sequence has been received on the line. |
| Rcvd Command | The line has received a special command sequence (for example, ^^B for send break). |
| Rcvd CR | The last character received was a carriage return. |
| Ready | The line state is "ready." |
| Ring Transition | A transition has occurred on the RING signal of the line. |
| Send Break Soon | You need to send a BREAK on the line soon. |
| Send XOFF Soon | Your buffers are full and you should send an XOFF soon. |
| Sending Break | You are in the process of sending a BREAK sequence on the line. |
| Sent XOFF | Your buffers were full, so we sent an XOFF. |
| SLIP Mode | The line is running SLIP or PPP. |

The following line of output indicates the status of the capabilities of the line. These capabilities correspond closely to configurable parameters that can be set using configuration commands.

```
Capabilities: Enabled
```

Table 10–4 describes possible values for the Capabilities field.

**Table 10–4** *Show Terminal Field Descriptions—Capabilities Field*

| Field | Description |
|---|---|
| Autobaud Full Range | Corresponds to the **autobaud** command. |
| Character Padding | At least one **pad** *c x* configuration command has been used. |
| Enabled | The user has "enabled" successfully. |
| EXEC Suppressed | Corresponds to the **no exec** command. |
| Hangup on Last Close | Corresponds to the **autohangup** command. |
| Hardware Flowcontrol In | Corresponds to the **flowcontrol hardware in** command. |
| Hardware Flowcontrol Out | Corresponds to the **flowcontrol hardware out** command. |
| Insecure | Corresponds to the **insecure** command. |
| Lockable | Corresponds to the **lockable** command. |
| Modem Callin | Corresponds to the **modem callin** command. |
| Modem Callout | Corresponds to the **modem callout** command. |
| Modem CTS-Required | Corresponds to the **modem cts-required** command. |
| Modem DTR-Active | Corresponds to the **modem dtr-active** command. |
| Modem RI is CD | Corresponds to the **modem ri-is-cd** command. |
| No Login Banner | Corresponds to the **no exec-banner** command. |
| Notification Set | Corresponds to the **notify** command. |
| Output Non-Idle | Corresponds to the **session-timeout** command. |
| Permanent SLIP | Corresponds to the **slip-dedicated** command |
| Private Line | Corresponds to the **private** command. |
| Refuse Suppress-GA | Corresponds to the **telnet refuse** command. |
| Receives Logging Output | Corresponds to the **monitor** command. |
| Refuse Telnet Echo | Corresponds to the **telnet refuse** command. |
| Send BREAK on IP | Corresponds to the **telnet break-on-ip** command. |
| SLIP allowed | Corresponds to the **slip address** command. |
| Software Flowcontrol In | Corresponds to the **flowcontrol software in** command. |

**Table 10–4** *Show Terminal Field Descriptions—Capabilities Field, Continued*

| Field | Description |
|---|---|
| Software Flowcontrol Out | Corresponds to the **flowcontrol software out** command. |
| Telnet Transparent Mode | Corresponds to the **telnet transparent** command. |

The following line of output indicates the modem state. Possible values include Autobauding, Carrier Dropped, Hanging Up, Idle, and Ready.

```
Modem state: Ready
```

The following lines of output indicate the special characters that can be entered to activate various terminal operations. The none or hyphen (-) values imply that no special characters are set.

```
Special Chars: Escape  Hold  Stop  Start  Disconnect  Activation
                ^^x    none  -     -        none
```

The following lines of output indicate the timeout values that have been configured for the line:

```
Timeouts:      Idle EXEC    Idle Session   Modem Answer  Session   Dispatch
                never          never         0:00:15     not imp   not set
```

Table 10–5 describes the fields in the preceding lines of output.

**Table 10–5** *Show Terminal Field Descriptions—Timeouts Field*

| Field | Description |
|---|---|
| Idle EXEC | Interval that the EXEC command interpreter waits for user input before resuming the current connection; or if no connections exist, returning the terminal to the idle state and disconnecting the incoming session. This interval is set using the **exec-timeout** command. |
| Idle Session | Interval that the Cisco IOS software waits for traffic before closing the connection to a remote computer and returning the terminal to an idle state. This interval is set using the **session-timeout** command. |
| Modem Answer | Interval during which the software raises DTR in response to RING and the modem response to CTS. This interval is set using the **modem answer-timeout** command. |
| Session | Not implemented in this release. |
| Dispatch | Number of milliseconds the software waits after putting the first character into a packet buffer before sending the packet. This interval is set using the **dispatch-timeout** command. |

The following lines of output indicate how various options have been configured:

```
Session limit is not set.
Allowed transports are telnet rlogin. Preferred is telnet
No output characters are padded
```

## SPEED

To set the terminal baud rate, use the **speed** line configuration command. This command sets both the transmit (to terminal) and receive (from terminal) speeds.

**speed** *bps*

| *Syntax* | *Description* |
|---|---|
| *bps* | Baud rate in bits per second (bps). The default is 9600 bps. |

### *Default*

9600 bps

### *Command Mode*

Line configuration

### *Usage Guidelines*

This command first appeared in Cisco IOS Release 10.0.

Set the speed to match the transmission rate of whatever device you have connected to the port. Some baud rates available on devices connected to the port might not be supported on the router. The router indicates whether the speed you selected is not supported.

### *Example*

The following example sets lines 1 and 2 on a Cisco 2509 access server to 115200 bps:

```
line 1 2
 speed 115200
```

### *Related Commands*

Search online to find documentation for related commands.

**rxspeed**
**terminal speed**
**txspeed**

## START-CHARACTER

To set the flow control start character, use the **start-character** line configuration command. Use the **no** form of this command to remove the character.

**start-character** *ascii-number*
**no start-character**

| *Syntax* | *Description* |
|---|---|
| *ascii-number* | Decimal representation of the start character. |

### *Default*

Decimal 17

### *Command Mode*

Line configuration

### *Usage Guidelines*

This command first appeared in Cisco IOS Release 10.0.

This command defines the character that signals the start of data transmission when software flow control is in effect.

### *Example*

The following example changes the start character to Ctrl-B, which is decimal 2:

```
line 2
 start-character 2
```

### *Related Commands*

Search online to find documentation for related commands.

**flowcontrol**
**stop-character**
**terminal start-character**

## TRANSPORT INPUT

To define which protocols to use to connect to a specific line of the router, use the **transport input** line configuration command.

**transport input** {**all** | **lat** | **mop** | **nasi** | **none** | **pad** | **rlogin** | **telnet** | **v120**}

| Syntax | Description |
|---|---|
| **all** | Selects all protocols. Restores the default configuration. |
| **lat** | Selects the Digital LAT protocol and specifies both incoming reverse LAT and host-initiated connections. |

| | |
|---|---|
| **mop** | Selects Maintenance Operation Protocol (MOP). |
| **nasi** | Select NetWare Access Servers Interface (NASI) as the input transport protocol. |
| **none** | Prevents any protocol selection on the line. This makes the port unusable by incoming connections. |
| **pad** | Selects X.3 PAD incoming connections. |
| **rlogin** | Selects the UNIX rlogin protocol. |
| **telnet** | Specifies all types of incoming TCP/IP connections. |
| **v120** | Select the V.120 protocol for incoming async over ISDN connections. |

### *Default*

No protocols allowed on the line (**none**)

### *Command Mode*

Line configuration

### *Usage Guidelines*

This command first appeared in Cisco IOS Release 10.0. The **lat**, **pad**, **all**, and **v120** keywords first appeared in Cisco IOS Release 11.1. The **none** option became the default in Cisco IOS Release 11.1. Before Release 11.1, the default was **all**.

**CAUTION**

Cisco routers do not accept incoming network connections to asynchronous ports (TTY lines) by default. You have to specify an incoming transport protocol, or specify **transport input all** before the line will accept incoming connections. For example, if you are using your router as a terminal server to make console-port connections to routers or other devices, you will not be able to use Telnet to connect to these devices. You will receive the message "Connection Refused." This behavior is new as of Cisco IOS Software Release 11.1. Previous to release 11.1, the default was **transport input all**. If you are upgrading to Cisco IOS software version 11.1(1) or later from Cisco IOS software Release 11.0 or earlier, you must add the **transport input** {*protocol* | **all**} command, or you will be locked out of your router.

You can specify one protocol, multiple protocols, all protocols, or no protocols. To specify multiple protocols, enter the keyword for each protocol, separated by a space.

This command can be useful in distributing resources among different types of users, or making certain that only specific hosts can access a particular port. When using two-step protocol translation, the **transport input** command is useful in controlling exactly which protocols can be translated to other protocols.

Access lists for each individual protocol can be defined in addition to the allowances created by the **transport input** command. Any settings made with the **transport input** command override settings made with the **transport preferred** command.

### *Example*

The following example sets the incoming protocol to Telnet for vtys 0 to 32:

```
line vty 0 32
 transport input telnet
```

### *Related Commands*

Search online to find documentation for related commands.

**terminal transport input**
**transport output**
**transport preferred**

## TRANSPORT OUTPUT

To determine the protocols that can be used for outgoing connections from a line, use the **transport output** line configuration command.

**transport output** {**all** | **lat** | **mop** | **nasi** | **none** | **pad** | **rlogin** | **telnet** | **v120**}

| *Syntax* | *Description* |
|---|---|
| **all** | Selects all protocols. |
| **lat** | Selects the Digital LAT protocol, which is the protocol used most often to connect routers to Digital hosts. |
| **mop** | Selects Maintenance Operation Protocol (MOP). |
| **nasi** | Selects NetWare Access Server Interface (NASI) as the output transport protocol. |
| **none** | Prevents any protocol selection on the line. The system normally assumes that any unrecognized command is a host name. If the protocol is set to none, the system no longer makes that assumption. No connection will be attempted if the command is not recognized. |
| **pad** | Selects X.3 PAD, used most often to connect routers to X.25 hosts. |

| | |
|---|---|
| **rlogin** | Selects the UNIX rlogin protocol for TCP connections. The rlogin setting is a special case of Telnet. If an rlogin attempt to a particular host has failed, the failure will be tracked, and subsequent connection attempts will use Telnet instead. |
| **telnet** | Selects the TCP/IP Telnet protocol. It allows a user at one site to establish a TCP connection to a login server at another site. |
| **v120** | Select the V.120 protocol for outgoing asynchronous over ISDN connections. |

### *Default*

Telnet

### *Command Mode*

Line configuration

### *Usage Guidelines*

This command first appeared in Cisco IOS Release 10.0. The **all, lat, pad, rlogin**, and **v120** commands first appeared in IOS Release 11.1.

You can specify one protocol, multiple protocols, all protocols, or no protocols. To specify multiple protocols, enter the keyword for each protocol, separated by a space.

Any settings made with the **transport output** command override settings made with the **transport preferred** command.

### *Example*

The following example prevents any protocol selection:

```
transport output none
```

### *Related Commands*

Search online to find documentation for related commands.

**terminal transport output**
**transport input**
**transport preferred**

## TRANSPORT PREFERRED

To specify the transport protocol that the Cisco IOS software uses if the user does not specify one when initiating a connection, use the **transport preferred** line configuration command.

**transport preferred** {**all** | **lat** | **mop** | **nasi** | **none** | **pad** | **rlogin** | **telnet** | **v120**}

| *Syntax* | *Description* |
|---|---|
| **all** | Specifies all recognized protocols. |
| **lat** | Selects the Digital LAT protocol, which is the protocol used most often to connect routers to Digital hosts. |
| **mop** | Specifies the Maintenance Operation Protocol (MOP). |
| **nasi** | Specifies the NetWare Access Server Interface (NASI) protocol. |
| **none** | Prevents any protocol selection on the line. The system normally assumes that any unrecognized command is a host name. If the protocol is set to **none**, the system no longer makes that assumption. No connection is attempted if the command is not recognized. |
| **pad** | Selects X.3 PAD, used most often to connect routers to X.25 hosts. |
| **rlogin** | Selects the UNIX rlogin protocol for TCP connections. The rlogin setting is part of the Telnet protocol. If an rlogin attempt to a particular host fails, the failure is tracked, and subsequent connection attempts will use Telnet instead. |
| **telnet** | Selects the TCP/IP Telnet protocol. It allows a user at one site to establish a TCP connection to a login server at another site. |
| **v120** | Specifies asynchronous protocols over ISDN. |

### *Default*

Telnet

### *Command Mode*

Line configuration

### *Usage Guidelines*

This command first appeared in Cisco IOS Release 10.0. The **lat, pad**, and **rlogin** commands first appeared in Cisco IOS Release 11.1.

Specify **transport preferred none** to prevent errant connection attempts.

Any settings made with the **transport input** or **transport output** commands override settings made with the **transport preferred** command.

### *Example*

The following example sets the preferred protocol to Telnet on physical terminal line 1:

```
line tty 1
 transport preferred telnet
```

### *Related Commands*

Search online to find documentation for related commands.

**terminal transport preferred**
**transport input**
**transport output**

## TXSPEED

To set the terminal transmit speed (how fast the terminal sends information to the modem), use the **txspeed** line configuration command.

**txspeed** *bps*

| *Syntax* | *Description* |
|---|---|
| *bps* | Baud rate in bits per second (bps). |

### *Default*

9600 bps

### *Command Mode*

Line configuration

### *Usage Guidelines*

This command first appeared in Cisco IOS Release 10.0.

Set the speed to match the baud rate of whatever device you have connected to the port. Some baud rates available on devices connected to the port might not be supported on the router. The Cisco IOS software will indicate if the speed you select is not supported.

### *Example*

The following example sets the transmit speed for line 5 to 2400 bps:

```
line 5
 txspeed 2400
```

### *Related Commands*

Search online to find documentation for related commands.

**rxspeed**
**speed**
**terminal txspeed**

# CHAPTER 11

# Setting Up ISDN Basic Rate Service

This chapter describes tasks that are required to make an ISDN BRI line and interface operational, and it describes features involved in configuring ISDN in a circuit-switched internetworking environment.

This chapter does not address routing issues, dialer configuration, and dial backup. For information about those topics, see the chapters in Part V, "Dial-on-Demand Routing."

For hardware technical descriptions, and for information about installing the router interfaces, refer to the hardware installation and maintenance publication for your particular product.

For a complete description of the BRI commands in this chapter, see Chapter 12, "ISDN Basic Rate Service Setup Commands."

## ISDN BRI TASK LIST

Perform the tasks in the following sections to configure ISDN lines and interfaces:

- Requesting BRI Line and Switch Configuration from a Telco Service Provider
- Checking and Setting the Buffers
- Configuring Global Characteristics for ISDN BRI
- Specifying Interface Characteristics for an ISDN BRI

You can also perform the following ISDN troubleshooting and maintenance tasks:

- Performing Configuration Self-Tests
- Monitoring and Maintaining ISDN Interfaces

You can also optionally configure *snapshot routing* for ISDN interfaces. Snapshot routing is a method of learning remote routes dynamically and keeping the routes available for a specified period of time, even though routing updates are not exchanged during that period. See Chapter 69, "Configuring Snapshot Routing," for detailed information on the topic.

To place calls on an ISDN interface, you must configure it with dial-on-demand routing (DDR). For configuration information about ISDN using DDR, see the chapters in Part V. For command information, see Chapter 12.

To configure bandwidth on demand, see Chapter, 40, "Configuring Legacy DDR Spokes" or Chapter 42, "Configuring Legacy DDR Hubs."

ISDN BRI configuration examples can be found at the end of this chapter.

## Requesting BRI Line and Switch Configuration from a Telco Service Provider

Before configuring the ISDN interfaces on your Cisco router, it is necessary to order a correctly configured ISDN line from your telecommunications service provider.

This process varies dramatically from provider to provider on a national and international basis. However, some general guidelines follow:

- On a BRI, ask for two channels to be called by one number.
- Ask for delivery of calling line identification. Providers sometimes call this *CLI* or *Automatic Number Identification* (ANI).
- If the router is going to be the only device attached to the BRI, ask for point-to-point service and a data-only line.
- If the router is going to be attached to an ISDN bus (to which other ISDN devices might be attached), ask for point-to-multipoint service (subaddressing is required) and a voice-and-data line.

When you order ISDN service, request the BRI switch configuration attributes specified in Table 11–1.

**Table 11–1** *ISDN BRI Switch Type Configuration Information*

| Switch Type | Configuration |
|---|---|
| **DMS-100 BRI** | 2 B channels for voice and data.<br>2 directory numbers assigned by service provider.<br>2 SPIDs required; assigned by service provider.<br>Functional signaling.<br>Dynamic terminal endpoint identifier (TEI) assignment.<br>Maximum number of keys = 64.<br>Release key = no, or key number = no.<br>Ringing indicator = no.<br>EKTS = no.<br>PVC = 2.<br>Request delivery of calling line ID on Centrex lines.<br>Set speed for ISDN calls to 56 Kbps outside local exchange.<br>Directory number 1 can hunt to directory number 2. |

**Table 11–1** *ISDN BRI Switch Type Configuration Information, Continued*

| Switch Type | Configuration |
|---|---|
| **5ESS Custom BRI** | **For Data Only**<br>2 B channels for data.<br>Point to point.<br>Terminal type = E.<br>1 directory number (DN) assigned by service provider.<br>MTERM = 1.<br>Request delivery of calling line ID on Centrex lines.<br>Set speed for ISDN calls to 56 Kbps outside local exchange.<br><br>**For Voice and Data**<br>(Use these values only if you have an ISDN telephone connected.)<br>2 B channels for voice or data.<br>Multipoint.<br>Terminal type = D.<br>2 directory numbers assigned by service provider.<br>2 service profile identifiers (SPIDs) required, assigned by service provider.<br>MTERM = 2.<br>Number of call appearances = 1.<br>Display = No.<br>Ringing/idle call appearances = idle.<br>Autohold= no.<br>Onetouch = no.<br>Request delivery of calling line ID on Centrex lines.<br>Set speed for ISDN calls to 56 Kbps outside local exchange.<br>Directory number 1 can hunt to directory number 2. |
| **5ESS National ISDN (NI-1) BRI** | Terminal type = A.<br>2 B channels for voice and data.<br>2 directory numbers assigned by service provider.<br>2 SPIDs required; assigned by service provider.<br>Set speed for ISDN calls to 56 Kbps outside local exchange.<br>Directory number 1 can hunt to directory number 2. |

## Checking and Setting the Buffers

When configuring a BRI, after the system comes up, make sure enough buffers are in the free list of the buffer pool that matches the maximum transmission unit (MTU) of your BRI interface. If not, you must reconfigure buffers in order for the BRI interfaces to function properly.

To check the MTU size and the buffers and, if necessary, to configure the buffers and the MTU size, complete the following tasks beginning in EXEC mode:

| Task | Command |
|---|---|
| Check the MTU size. | **show interfaces bri** *number* |
| Check the free buffers. | **show buffers** |
| Configure the buffers. | **configure terminal**<br><br>**buffers big permanent** *number*<br>**buffers big max-free** *number*<br>**buffers big min-free** *number*<br>**buffers big initial** *number* |

## Configuring Global Characteristics for ISDN BRI

To configure the ISDN global characteristics, complete the tasks in the following sections:

- Configure the Switch Type
- Configure TEI Negotiation Timing

### Configure the Switch Type

To configure the switch type, complete the following task in global configuration mode:

| Task | Command |
|---|---|
| Select the service provider switch type.* | **isdn switch-type** *switch-type* |

* Any router with an MBRI must be connected to the same switch type on all its ISDN interfaces.

Table 11–2 lists the ISDN BRI switch types by geographic areas.

**Table 11–2** *ISDN Service Provider Switch Types*

| Keywords by Area | Switch Type |
|---|---|
| none | No switch defined |
| **Australia** | |
| basic-ts013 | Australian TS013 switches |
| **Europe** | |
| basic-1tr6 | German 1TR6 ISDN switches |
| basic-nwnet3 | Norway NET3 switches (phase 1) |

**Table 11–2** *ISDN Service Provider Switch Types, Continued*

| Keywords by Area | Switch Type |
|---|---|
| basic-net3 | NET3 ISDN switches; covers the Euro-ISDN E-DSS1 signaling system and is ETSI-compliant. |
| vn2 | French VN2 ISDN BRI switches |
| vn3 | French VN3 ISDN BRI switches |
| vn4 | French VN4 ISDN BRI switches |
| **Japan** | |
| ntt | Japanese NTT ISDN switches |
| **North America** | |
| basic-5ess | AT&T basic rate switches |
| basic-dms100 | NT DMS-100 basic rate switches |
| basic-ni1 | National ISDN-1 switches |
| **New Zealand** | |
| basic-nznet3 | New Zealand Net3 switches |

### Configure TEI Negotiation Timing

You can specify when Layer 2 ISDN terminal endpoint identifier (TEI) negotiation occurs. TEI negotiation is useful in Europe and also useful for switches that might deactivate Layer 2 when no calls are active.

By default, TEI negotiation occurs when the router is powered on. To define when TEI negotiation will occur, perform the following task in global configuration mode:

| Task | Command |
|---|---|
| Determine when ISDN TEI negotiation occurs. | **isdn tei [first-call \| powerup]** |

## SPECIFYING INTERFACE CHARACTERISTICS FOR AN ISDN BRI

Perform the tasks in the following sections to set interface characteristics for an ISDN BRI. Whether it is the only BRI in a router or is one of many, each of the BRIs can be configured separately. You must perform the tasks in the following sections:

- Specify the Interface and Its IP Address
- Configure Encapsulation
- Configure Network Addressing

In addition, you can configure the following optional interface characteristics on the BRI:

- Specify ISDN Service Profile Identifiers (SPIDs)
- Configure Calling Line Identification Screening
- Configure Called-Party Number Verification
- Configure ISDN Calling Number Identification
- Configure the Line Speed for Calls Not ISDN End-To-End
- Configure a Fast Rollover Delay
- Configure Inclusion of the Sending Complete Information Element

### Specify the Interface and Its IP Address

To specify an ISDN Basic Rate Interface (BRI) and enter interface configuration mode, perform the following task in global configuration mode:

| Task | Command |
|---|---|
| Specify the interface and enter interface configuration mode. | **interface bri** *number*<br>**interface bri** *slot/port* (Cisco 7200 series) |
| Specify an IP protocol address for the interface. | **ip address** *ip-address mask* |

### Configure Encapsulation

PPP encapsulation is configured for most ISDN communication.

Each ISDN B channel is treated as a synchronous serial line and supports HDLC and PPP encapsulation. The default serial encapsulation is HDLC. To configure PPP encapsulation, perform the following task in interface configuration mode:

| Task | Command |
|---|---|
| Configure PPP Encapsulation | **encapsulation ppp** |

The router might need to communicate with devices that require a different encapsulation protocol or the router might send traffic over a Frame Relay or X.25 network. For more information, see Chapter 74, "Configuring X.25 on ISDN."

To configure the router for automatic detection of encapsulation type on incoming calls, or to configure encapsulation for Combinet compatibility, see Chapter 17, "Configuring ISDN Special Signaling."

### Configure Network Addressing

The steps in this section support the primary goals of network addressing:

- Define which packets are *interesting*—and will thus cause the router to make an outgoing call.
- Define the remote host where the calls are going.
- Specify whether broadcast messages will be sent.
- Specify the dialing string to use in the call.

Intermediate steps that use shared argument values tie the host identification and dial string to the interesting packets to be transmitted to that host.

To configure network addressing, complete the following tasks beginning in interface configuration mode:

| Task | | Command |
|---|---|---|
| **Step 1** | (Most locations) Define the remote recipient's protocol address, host name, and dialing string; optionally, provide the ISDN subaddress; set the dialer speed to 56 or 64 Kbps, as needed.<br>or<br>(Germany) Use the command keyword that enables ISDN semipermanent connections. | **dialer map** *protocol next-hop-address* **name** *hostname* **speed 56\|64** *dial-string*[*:isdn-subaddress*]<br><br><br><br><br>**dialer map** *protocol next-hop-address* **name** *hostname* **spc** [**speed 56** \| **64**] [**broadcast**] *dial-string*[*:isdn-subaddress*] |
| **Step 2** | Assign the interface to a dialer group to control access to the interface. | **dialer-group** *group-number* |
| **Step 3** | Associate the dialer group number with an access list number. | **dialer-list** *dialer-group* **list** *access-list-number* |
| **Step 4** | Define an access list permitting or denying access to specified protocols, sources, or destinations. Permitted packets cause the router to place a call to the destination protocol address. | **access-list** *access-list-number* {**deny** \| **permit**} *protocol source address source-mask destination destination-mask* |

German networks allow semipermanent connections between customer routers with BRIs, and the 1TR6 basic rate switches in the exchange. Semipermanent connections are offered at better pricing than leased lines.

**NOTES**

The access list reference in Step 4 of this task list is an example of the access list commands allowed by different protocols. Some protocols might require a different command form or might require multiple commands.

For more information about defining outgoing call numbers, see Part V.

### Specify ISDN Service Profile Identifiers (SPIDs)

Some service providers use service profile identifiers (SPIDs) to define the services subscribed to by the ISDN device that is accessing the ISDN service provider. The service provider assigns the ISDN device one or more SPIDs when you first subscribe to the service. If you are using a service provider that requires SPIDs, your ISDN device cannot place or receive calls until it sends a valid, assigned SPID to the service provider when accessing the switch to initialize the connection.

Currently, only the DMS-100 and NI-1 switch types require SPIDs. The AT&T 5ESS switch type may support a SPID, but it is recommended that you set up that ISDN service without SPIDs. In addition, SPIDs have significance at the local access ISDN interface only. Remote routers are never sent the SPID.

A SPID is usually a seven-digit telephone number with some optional numbers. However, service providers may use different numbering schemes. For the DMS-100 switch type, two SPIDs are assigned, one for each B channel.

To define the SPIDs and the local directory number (LDN) on the router, perform the following tasks in interface configuration mode:

| Task | Command |
|---|---|
| Specify a SPID and local directory number for the B1 channel. | **isdn spid1** *spid-number* [*ldn*] |
| Specify a SPID and local directory number for the B2 channel. | **isdn spid2** *spid-number* [*ldn*] |

The LDN is optional but might be necessary if the router is to answer calls made to the second directory number.

### Configure Calling Line Identification Screening

This task applies only to Cisco 2500 series, Cisco 3000 series, and Cisco 4000 series routers that have a BRI.

Calling line identification (CLI, also called *caller ID*) screening adds a level of security by allowing you to screen incoming calls. You can verify that the calling line ID is from an expected origin. CLI screening requires a local switch that is capable of delivering the CLI to the router.

To configure caller ID screening, perform the following task in interface configuration mode:

| Task | Command |
|---|---|
| Configure caller ID screening. | **isdn caller** *number* |

**NOTES**

If caller ID screening is configured and the local switch does not deliver caller IDs, the router rejects all calls.

### Configure Called-Party Number Verification

When multiple devices are attached to an ISDN BRI, you can ensure that only a single device answers an incoming call by verifying the number or subaddress in the incoming call against the device's configured number or subaddress or both.

You can specify that the router verify a called-party number or subaddress number in the incoming setup message for ISDN BRI calls, if the number is delivered by the switch. You can do so by configuring the number that is allowed. To configure verification, perform the following task in interface configuration mode:

| Task | Command |
|---|---|
| Specify that the router verify a called-party number or subaddress number in the incoming setup message. | **isdn answer1** [*called-party-number*][:*subaddress*] |

Verifying the called-party number ensures that only the desired router responds to an incoming call. If you want to allow an additional number for the router, you can configure it, too. To configure a second number to be allowed, perform the following task in interface configuration mode:

| Task | Command |
|---|---|
| Specify that the router verify a second called-party number or subaddress number in the incoming setup message. | **isdn answer2** [*called-party-number*][:*subaddress*] |

### Configure ISDN Calling Number Identification

A router with an ISDN BRI interface might need to supply the ISDN network with a billing number for outgoing calls. Some networks offer better pricing on calls in which the number is presented. When configured, this information is included in the outgoing call Setup message.

To configure the interface to identify the billing number, perform the following task in interface configuration mode:

| Task | Command |
|---|---|
| Specify the calling-party number. | **isdn calling-number** *calling-number* |

This command can be used with all switch types except German 1TR6 ISDN BRI switches.

### Configure the Line Speed for Calls Not ISDN End-To-End

When calls are made at 56 Kbps but delivered by the ISDN network at 64 Kbps, the incoming data can be corrupted.

On ISDN calls, however, if the receiving side is informed that the call is not an ISDN call from end to end, it can set the line speed for the incoming call.

To set the speed for incoming calls recognized as not ISDN end-to-end, complete the following task in interface configuration mode:

| Task | Command |
|---|---|
| Set the speed to be used for incoming calls recognized as not ISDN end-to-end. | **isdn not-end-to-end** {**56** \| **64**} |

### Configure a Fast Rollover Delay

Sometimes a router attempts to dial a call on an ISDN B channel before a previous, failed call is completely torn down. The fast rollover fails because the second call is made to a different number before the B channel is released from the unsuccessful call. This might occur in ISDN configurations where:

- The two B channels of the BRI are not configured as a hunt group, but have separate numbers defined, and
- The B channel is not released by the ISDN switch until after Release Complete signal is processed.

You need to configure this delay if a BRI on a remote peer has two phone numbers configured (one for each B channel), if you are dialing in to this BRI, if you have a dialer map for each phone number, and if the first call succeeds but a second call fails with no channel available.

To configure a fast rollover delay, complete the following task in interface configuration mode:

| Task | Command |
|---|---|
| Define a fast rollover delay. | **isdn fast-rollover-delay** *seconds* |

A delay of 5 seconds should cover most cases. Configure sufficient delay to make sure the ISDN RELEASE_COMPLETE message has been sent or received before making the fast rollover call. Use the **debug isdn q931** command to display this information.

This pattern of failed second calls is a rare occurrence.

### Configure Inclusion of the Sending Complete Information Element

In some geographic locations, such as Hong Kong and Taiwan, ISDN switches require that the Sending Complete information element be included in the outgoing Setup message to indicate that the entire number is included. This information element is not required in other locations.

To configure the interface to include the Sending Complete information element in the outgoing call Setup message, complete the following task in interface configuration mode:

| Task | Command |
|---|---|
| Include the Sending Complete information element in the outgoing call Setup message. | **isdn sending-complete** |

### PERFORMING CONFIGURATION SELF-TESTS

To test the router's ISDN configuration, it is suggested that you perform the following tasks:

| Task | Command |
|---|---|
| Check Layer 1 (physical layer) of the BRI. | **show controllers bri** *number* |
| Check Layer 2 (data link layer). | **debug q921** |
| Check Layer 3 (network layer). | **debug isdn events**<br>debug q931<br>**debug dialer**<br>show dialer |

### MONITORING AND MAINTAINING ISDN INTERFACES

Use the following commands to monitor and maintain ISDN interfaces:

| Task | Command |
|---|---|
| Display information about the physical attributes of the ISDN BRI B and D channels. | **show interfaces bri** *number*<br>**show interfaces bri** *slot/port* (Cisco 7200 series) |
| Display protocol information about the ISDN B and D channels. | **show controllers bri** *number*<br>**how controllers bri** *slot/port* (Cisco 7200 series) |
| Display information about calls, history, memory, status, and Layer 2 and Layer 3 timers. | **show isdn** {**active** \| **history** \| **memory** \| **status** \| **timers**} |
| Obtain general diagnostic information about the specified interface. | **show dialer interface bri** *number* |

### ISDN BRI CONFIGURATION EXAMPLES

This section provides the following ISDN BRI configuration examples:

- BRI Connected to a PBX Example
- Multilink PPP on a BRI Interface Example
- Dialer Rotary Groups Example
- Compression Examples
- Voice over ISDN Examples

### BRI Connected to a PBX Example

The following example provides a simple partial configuration of a BRI interface that is connected to a PBX. This interface is connected to a switch that uses SPID numbers.

```
interface BRI0
 description connected to pbx line 61885
 ip address 7.1.1.3 255.255.255.0
 encapsulation ppp
 isdn spid1 123
 dialer map ip 7.1.1.1 name oldie 61886
 dialer map ip 7.1.1.2 name rudder 61884
 dialer map ip 7.1.1.4 name seinfeld 61888
 dialer-group 1
 no fair-queue
 ppp authentication chap
```

### Multilink PPP on a BRI Interface Example

The following example enables Multilink PPP on BRI 0:

```
interface BRI0
 description Enables PPP Multilink on BRI 0
 ip address 7.1.1.1 255.255.255.0
 encapsulation ppp
 dialer map ip 7.1.1.2 name starbuck 14195291357
 dialer map ip 7.1.1.3 name roaster speed 56 14098759854
 ppp authentication chap
 ppp multilink
 dialer-group 1
```

### Dialer Rotary Groups Example

The following example configures BRI interfaces to connect into a rotary group (dialer group) and then configures a dialer interface for that dialer group. This configuration permits IP packets to trigger calls.

```
interface BRI 0
 description connected into a rotary group
 encapsulation ppp
 dialer rotary-group 1

interface BRI 1
 no ip address
 encapsulation ppp
 dialer rotary-group 1
```

```
interface BRI 2
 encapsulation ppp
 dialer rotary-group 1

interface BRI 3
 no ip address
 encapsulation ppp
 dialer rotary-group 1

interface BRI 4
 encapsulation ppp
 dialer rotary-group 1

interface Dialer 0
 description Dialer group controlling the BRIs
 ip address 8.1.1.1 255.255.255.0
 encapsulation ppp
 dialer map ip 8.1.1.2 name angus 14802616900
 dialer-group 1
 ppp authentication chap

dialer-list 1 protocol ip permit
```

## Compression Examples

The following example enables predictor compression on BRI 0:

```
interface BRI0
 description Enables predictor compression on BRI 0
 ip address 7.1.1.1 255.255.255.0
 encapsulation ppp
 dialer map ip 7.1.1.2 name starbuck 14195291357
 compress predictor
 ppp authentication chap
 dialer-group 1
```

The following example enables Stacker compression on BRI 0:

```
interface BRI0
 description Enables stac compression on BRI 0
 ip address 7.1.1.1 255.255.255.0
 encapsulation ppp
 dialer map ip 7.1.1.2 name starbuck 14195291357
 compress stac
 ppp authentication chap
 dialer-group 1
```

## Multilink PPP and Compression Example

The following example enables PPP Multilink and Stacker compression on BRI 0:

```
interface BRI0
 description Enables PPP Multilink and stac compression on BRI 0
 ip address 7.1.1.1 255.255.255.0
 encapsulation ppp
 dialer map ip 7.1.1.2 name starbuck 14195291357
 ppp authentication chap
```

```
 compress stac
 ppp multilink
 dialer-group 1
```

## Voice over ISDN Examples

The following example allows incoming voice calls to be answered on BRI 0:

```
interface bri0
 description Allows incoming voice calls to be answered on BRI 0
 ip address 7.1.1.1 255.255.255.0
 encapsulation ppp
 isdn incoming-voice data
 dialer map ip 7.1.1.2 name starstruck 14038182344
 ppp authentication chap
 dialer-group 1
```

The following example places an outgoing call as a voice call on BRI 1:

```
interface bri1
 description Places an outgoing call as a voice call on BRI 1
 ip address 9.1.1.1 255.255.255.0
 encapsulation ppp
 dialer map ip 9.1.1.2 name angus class calltype 19091238877
 ppp authentication chap
 dialer-group 1

map-class dialer calltype
 dialer voice-call
```

CHAPTER 12

# ISDN Basic Rate Service Setup Commands

This chapter describes the commands available to configure ISDN basic rate interfaces for dial-up solutions on your router.

**NOTES**

For configuration tasks and examples to get the ISDN line up and running, see Chapter 11, "Setting Up ISDN Basic Rate Service." To complete the configuration for dial-in or dial-out routing or bridging, see the relevant chapters in Part V, "Dial-on-Demand Routing."

## INTERFACE BRI

To configure a Basic Rate Interface (BRI) interface and enter interface configuration mode, use the **interface bri** global configuration command.

**interface bri** *number*
**interface bri** *slot/port* (Cisco 7200 series)

To configure a BRI subinterface only, use the following form of the **interface bri** global configuration command:

**interface bri** *number.subinterface-number* [**multipoint** | **point-to-point**]
**interface bri** *slot/port.subinterface-number* [**multipoint** | **point-to-point**] (Cisco 7200 series)

| *Syntax* | *Description* |
|---|---|
| *number* | Port, connector, or interface card number. The numbers are assigned at the factory at the time of installation or when added to a system, and can be displayed with the **show interfaces** command. |
| *slot/port* | Backplane slot number and port number on the interface. See your hardware installation manual for the specific slot and port numbers. |

| | |
|---|---|
| *.subinterface-number* | Subinterface number in the range 1 to 4294967293. The *number* or *slot/port* that precedes the period (.) must match that of the interface this subinterface belongs to. |
| **multipoint \| point-to-point** | (Optional) Specifies a multipoint or point-to-point subinterface. The default is **multipoint.** |

### Default

The default mode for subinterfaces is multipoint.

### Command Mode

Global configuration

### Usage Guidelines

This command first appeared in Cisco IOS Release 10.3.

This command was modified in Cisco IOS Release 11.2 P to include slot/port syntax for the PA-8B-ST and PA-4B-U port adapters on Cisco 7200 series routers.

Subinterfaces can be configured to support partially meshed Frame Relay networks.

### Example

The following example configures BRI 0 to call and receive calls from two sites, use Point-to-Point Protocol (PPP) encapsulation on outgoing calls, and use Challenge Handshake Authentication Protocol (CHAP) authentication on incoming calls:

```
interface bri 0
 encapsulation ppp
 no keepalive
 dialer map ip 131.108.36.10 name EB1 234
 dialer map ip 131.108 36.9 name EB2 456
 dialer-group 1
 isdn spid1 0146334600
 isdn spid2 0146334610
 isdn T200 1000
 ppp authentication chap
```

### Related Commands

Search online to find documentation for related commands.

**dialer map**
**dialer-group**
**encapsulation ppp**
**isdn spid1**
**isdn spid2**
**ppp authentication chap**

**ppp authentication pap**
**show interfaces bri**

## ISDN ANSWER1, ISDN ANSWER2

To have the router verify a called-party number or subaddress number in the incoming setup message for ISDN BRI calls, if the number is delivered by the switch, use the **isdn answer1** interface configuration command. To remove the verification request, use the **no** form of this command.

**isdn answer1** [*called-party-number*] [*:subaddress*]
**no isdn answer1** [*called-party-number*][*:subaddress*]

To have the router verify an *additional* called-party number or subaddress number in the incoming setup message for ISDN BRI calls, if the number is delivered by the switch, use the **isdn answer2** interface configuration command. To remove this second verification request, use the **no** form of this command.

**isdn answer2** [*called-party-number*][*:subaddress*]
**no isdn answer2** [*called-party-number*][*:subaddress*]

| *Syntax* | *Description* |
|---|---|
| *called-party-number* | (Optional) Telephone number of the called party. At least one value—*called-party-number* or *subaddress*—must be specified. |
| : | Identifies the number that follows as a subaddress. Use the colon (:) when you configure both the called-party number and the subaddress, or when you configure only the subaddress. |
| *subaddress* | (Optional) Subaddress number, 20 or fewer characters long, used for ISDN multipoint connections. At least one value—*called-party-number* or *subaddress*—must be specified. |

### *Default*

The router does not verify the called-party or subaddress number.

### *Command Mode*

Interface configuration

### *Usage Guidelines*

This command first appeared in Cisco IOS Release 10.3.

If you do not specify the **isdn answer1** or **isdn answer2** command, all calls are processed and/or accepted. If you specify the **isdn answer1** or **isdn answer2** command, the router must verify the incoming called-party number and the subaddress before processing and/or accepting the call. The verification proceeds from right to left for the called-party number; it also proceeds from right to left for the subaddress number.

You can configure just the called-party number or just the subaddress. In such a case, only that part is verified. To configure a subaddress only, include the colon (:) before the subaddress number.

You can declare a digit a "don't care" digit by configuring it as an *x* or *X*. In such a case, any incoming digit is allowed.

### Examples

In the following example, 5552222 is the called-party number and 1234 is the subaddress:

```
interface bri 0
 isdn answer1 5552222:1234
```

In the following example, only the subaddress is configured:

```
interface bri 0
 isdn answer1 :1234
```

## ISDN CALLER

To configure ISDN caller ID screening, use the **isdn caller** interface configuration command. To disable this feature, use the **no** form of this command.

**isdn caller** *number*
**no isdn caller** *number*

| Syntax | Description |
|---|---|
| *number* | Telephone number for which to screen. Specify an *x* to represent a single "don't-care" character. The maximum length of each number is 25 characters. |

### Default

Disabled

### Command Mode

Interface configuration

### Usage Guidelines

This command first appeared in Cisco IOS Release 10.3.

This command configures the router to accept calls from the specified number.

Caller ID screening is available on Cisco 7000 series with RSP7000, Cisco 4000 series, Cisco 3000 series, and Cisco 2500 series routers that have one or more BRIs.

The maximum length of each number is 25 characters. You can specify up to 64 numbers per interface.

**NOTES**

Caller ID screening requires a local switch that is capable of delivering the caller ID to the router. If you enable caller ID screening but do not have such a switch, no calls are allowed in.

### *Examples*

The following example configures the router to accept a call with a delivered caller ID equal to 4155551234:

```
isdn caller 4155551234
```

The following example configures the router to accept a call with a delivered caller ID having 41555512 and any numbers in the last two positions:

```
isdn caller 41555512xx
```

### *Related Commands*

Search online to find documentation for related commands.

**show dialer**

## ISDN CALLING-NUMBER

To configure an ISDN BRI interface to present a billing number of the device making the outgoing call, use the **isdn calling-number** interface configuration command. To remove a previously configured calling number, use the **no** form of this command.

**isdn calling-number** *calling-number*
**no isdn calling number**

| *Syntax* | *Description* |
| --- | --- |
| *calling-number* | Number of the device making the outgoing call; only one entry is allowed, and it is limited to 16 digits. |

### *Default*

No calling number is presented.

### *Command Mode*

Interface configuration

### *Usage Guidelines*

This command first appeared in Cisco IOS Release 10.3.

An interface can have only one ISDN calling-number entry.

This command is intended for use when the ISDN network offers better pricing on calls in which devices present the calling number (that is, the billing number).

**NOTES**

This command cannot be used with German 1TR6 ISDN BRI switches. It can be used with all other switches.

### *Example*

In the following example, the ISDN BRI interface is configured to present the number 5551212 when it makes outgoing calls:

```
interface bri 0
 isdn calling-number 5551212
```

### *Related Commands*

Search online to find documentation for related commands.

**interface bri**

## ISDN FAST-ROLLOVER-DELAY

To specify the time delay between successive attempts to dial out to a number, use the **isdn fast-rollover-delay** interface configuration command.

**isdn fast-rollover-delay** *seconds*

| Syntax | Description |
|---|---|
| *seconds* | Number of seconds to delay before dialing the next dialer map after receiving an ISDN message indicating the current call will not succeed. |

### *Default*

This command is disabled by default. If enabled, the default value of the timer is 0 seconds.

### *Command Mode*

Interface configuration

### *Usage Guidelines*

This command first appeared in Cisco IOS Release 11.1.

This command provides a timer separate from the dialer wait-for-carrier timer to control the amount of time that elapses before calls are redialed. This delay is provided to allow the old call to be torn down completely before the new call is attempted.

When using PPP callback, this command specifies the time delay before the callback is done. This command is necessary on some ISDN switches because the new call may be attempted before the old call is completely torn down. This causes the second call or the callback to fail.

Use this command when *all* the following conditions are true:

- A BRI has two phone numbers configured, one for each B channel.
- You are dialing in to this BRI.
- You have a dialer map for each phone number.
- The first call succeeds, but the second call fails with no channel available.

If this has occurred, set **isdn fast-rollover-delay** to 5 seconds and try again.

A delay of 5 seconds should cover most cases. Configure sufficient delay to make sure the ISDN RELEASE_COMPLETE message has been sent or received before making the fast-rollover call. Use the **debug isdn q931** command to display this information.

### *Example*

The following partial example sets the fast-rollover delay that is suggested when all the conditions specified above are true.

```
isdn fast-rollover-delay 5
```

### *Related Commands*

Search online to find documentation for related commands.

**dialer map**
**dialer wait-for-carrier**
**ppp callback**

## ISDN INCOMING-VOICE DATA

To answer incoming voice calls at a configured rate (overriding the incoming data rate in the call), use the **isdn incoming-voice** interface configuration command.

**isdn incoming-voice data** [56 | 64]

| *Syntax* | *Description* |
|---|---|
| 56 | Answers all voice calls at 56 Kbps. |
| 64 | Answers all voice calls at 64 Kbps. |

### *Default*

None

### *Command Mode*

Interface configuration

### *Usage Guidelines*

When used without a keyword, this command checks the bearer capacity.

If this command is used, the dialing side must dial at 56 Kbps.

Ordinarily, a data device ignores incoming voice calls, but the tariff structure for data and voice calls might make it less expensive to do "data over voice" calls.

### *Example*

The following partial example BRI 0 to answer all incoming voice calls at 56 Kbps:

```
interface bri 0
 isdn incoming-voice data 56
```

## ISDN NOT-END-TO-END

For incoming calls, to override the speed that the network reports it will use to deliver the call data, use the **isdn not-end-to-end** interface configuration command.

**isdn not-end-to-end** {**56** | **64**}

| *Syntax* | *Description* |
|---|---|
| 56 | Answers all voice calls at 56 Kbps. |
| 64 | Answers all voice calls at 64 Kbps. |

### *Default*

The default line speed is 64 Kbps.

### *Command Mode*

Interface configuration

### *Usage Guidelines*

This command might be needed to handle incoming calls properly. Although a call might originate at a speed of 56 Kbps, the network or internetworking networks might improperly deliver the call to the user at a speed of 64 Kbps. This creates a speed mismatch and causes the data to be garbled. Enabling this command makes the router look more closely at the information elements of the incoming call to determine a speed.

A speed mismatch can occur when the source and destination ISDN ports do not belong to the same network.

### *Example*

In the following example, the line speed for incoming calls is set to 56 Kbps:

```
isdn not-end-to-end 56
```

### ISDN SENDING-COMPLETE

To specify that the Sending Complete information element (IE) is included in the outgoing Setup message, use the **isdn sending-complete** interface configuration command.

**isdn sending-complete**

#### *Syntax Description*

This command has no arguments or keywords.

#### *Default*

This command is disabled by default.

#### *Command Mode*

Interface configuration

#### *Usage Guidelines*

Some switches in some countries want a Sending Complete information element to be included in the outgoing Setup message to indicate that the entire number is included. The Sending Complete IE is required in Hong Kong and Taiwan, and the **isdn sending-complete** command forces it to be sent.

#### *Example*

In the following example, the **isdn sending-complete** command applies to an ISDN BRI interface:

```
interface BRI0
 description connected to PBX 61886
 ip address 172.1.1.1 255.255.255.0
 encapsulation ppp
 isdn sending-complete
 dialer idle-timeout 20
 dialer map ip 172.1.1.2 name rudder 61884
 dialer map ip 172.1.1.3 name bosun 61885
 dialer-group 1
 ppp authentication chap
!
```

### ISDN SPID1

Use the **isdn spid1** interface configuration command to define at the router the service profile identifier (SPID) number that has been assigned by the ISDN service provider for the B1 channel. Use the **no** form of this command to disable the specified SPID, thereby preventing access to the switch.

**isdn spid1** *spid-number* [*ldn*]
**no isdn spid1** *spid-number* [*ldn*]

| *Syntax* | *Description* |
|---|---|
| *spid-number* | Number identifying the service to which you have subscribed. This value is assigned by the ISDN service provider and is usually a 10-digit telephone number with some extra digits. |
| *ldn* | (Optional) Local directory number (LDN), as delivered by the service provider in the incoming setup message. This is a 7-digit number assigned by the service provider.<br>If you include the local directory number in the **no** form of this command, access to the switch is permitted, but the other B channel may not be able to receive incoming calls. |

#### *Default*

No SPID number is defined.

#### *Command Mode*

Interface configuration

#### *Usage Guidelines*

This command is required for DMS-100 and National ISDN-1 (NI-1) switches only.

On these switches, you must define the LDN if you want to receive any incoming calls on the B2 channel. The ISDN switch checks for the LDN to determine whether both channels can be used to transmit and receive data. If the LDN is not present, then only the B1 channel can be used for full-duplex communication. However, the other channel can still be used for making outgoing calls.

#### *Example*

The following example defines, on the router, a SPID and LDN for the B1 channel:

```
isdn spid1 415555121301 5551215
```

### ISDN SPID2

Use the **isdn spid2** interface configuration command to define at the router the SPID number that has been assigned by the ISDN service provider for the B2 channel. Use the **no** form of this command to disable the specified SPID, thereby preventing access to the switch.

**isdn spid2** *spid-number* [*ldn*]
**no isdn spid2** *spid-number* [*ldn*]

#### *Default*

No SPID number is defined.

#### *Command Mode*

Interface configuration

| *Syntax* | *Description* |
|---|---|
| *spid-number* | Number identifying the service to which you have subscribed. This value is assigned by the ISDN service provider and is usually a 10-digit telephone number with some extra digits. |
| *ldn* | (Optional) Local directory number, as delivered by the service provider in the incoming setup message. This is a 7-digit number also assigned by the service provider.<br>If you include the LDN in the **no** form of this command, the access to the switch is permitted, but the other B channel might not be able to receive incoming calls. |

### *Usage Guidelines*

This command is required for DMS-100 and National ISDN-1 (NI-1) switches only.

You must define the LDN if you want to receive any incoming calls on the B1 channel. The ISDN switch checks for the LDN to determine whether both channels can be used to transmit and receive data. If the LDN is not present, then only the B2 channel can be used for full-duplex communication. However, the other channel can still be used for making outgoing calls.

### *Example*

The following example defines, on the router, a SPID and LDN for the B2 channel:

```
isdn spid2 415555121202 5551214
```

## ISDN SWITCH-TYPE

To specify the central office switch type on the ISDN interface, use the **isdn switch-type** global configuration command.

**isdn switch-type** *switch-type*

| *Syntax* | *Description* |
|---|---|
| *switch-type* | Service provider switch type; see Table 12–1 for a list of supported switches. |

### *Default*

The switch type defaults to **none**, which disables the switch on the ISDN interface.

### *Command Mode*

Global configuration

### *Usage Guidelines*

To disable the switch on the ISDN interface, specify **isdn switch-type none**.

Table 12–1 lists supported switch types by geographic area.

**Table 12–1** *ISDN Service Provider BRI Switch Types*

| Keywords by Area | Switch Type |
|---|---|
| none | No switch defined |
| **Australia** | |
| basic-ts013 | Australian TS013 switches |
| **Europe** | |
| basic-1tr6 | German 1TR6 ISDN switches |
| basic-nwnet3 | NET3 switch type for Norway (phase 1) |
| basic-net3 | NET3 ISDN switch type for Europe; covers the Euro-ISDN E-DSS1 signaling system |
| vn2 | French VN2 ISDN switches |
| vn3 | French VN3 ISDN switches |
| **Japan** | |
| ntt | Japanese NTT ISDN switches |
| **North America** | |
| basic-5ess | AT&T basic rate switches |
| basic-dms100 | Northern Telecom DMS-100 basic rate switches |
| basic-ni1 | National ISDN-1 switches |
| **New Zealand** | |
| basic-nznet3 | New Zealand Net3 switches |

*Example*

The following example configures the French VN3 ISDN switch type:

```
isdn switch-type vn3
```

### ISDN TEI

To configure when ISDN Layer 2 terminal endpoint identifier (TEI) negotiation should occur, use the **isdn tei** global configuration command. Use the **no** form of this command to restore the default.

**isdn tei [first-call | powerup]**
**no isdn tei**

| *Syntax* | *Description* |
|---|---|
| **first-call** | (Optional) ISDN TEI negotiation occurs when the first ISDN call is placed or received. |
| **powerup** | (Optional) ISDN TEI negotiation occurs when the router is powered on. |

### *Default*

**powerup**

### *Command Mode*

Global configuration

### *Usage Guidelines*

Use this command with care. This command is for BRI configuration only.

### *Example*

The following example configures the router to negotiate TEI when the first ISDN call is placed or received:

```
isdn tei first-call
```

## ISDN TWAIT-DISABLE

To delay a National ISDN (NI-1) BRI switch a random time before activating the Layer 2 interface when the switch starts up, use the **isdn twait-disable** interface configuration command.

**isdn twait-disable**

### *Syntax Description*

This command has no arguments or keywords.

### *Default*

This command is enabled by default.

### *Command Mode*

Interface configuration

### *Usage Guidelines*

This random-length delay prevents mass power failures from causing the network ISDN switches to be overwhelmed when power returns and all the devices start up at the same time.

The random delay is in the range 1 to 300 seconds.

### *Example*

The following example configures a random wait period after a power failure:

```
isdn twait-disable
```

## SHOW CONTROLLERS BRI

To display information about the ISDN Basic Rate Interface (BRI), use the **show controllers bri** privileged EXEC command.

**show controllers bri** *number*
**show controllers bri** *slot/port* (Cisco 7200 series)

| *Syntax* | *Description* |
|---|---|
| *number* | Interface number. The value is 0 through 7 if the router has one 8-port BRI network interface module (NIM), or 0 through 15 if the router has two 8-port BRI NIMs. |
| *slot/port* | Backplane slot number and port number on the interface. See your hardware installation manual for the specific slot and port numbers. |

### *Command Mode*

Privileged EXEC

### *Usage Guidelines*

This command first appeared in Cisco IOS Release 10.3.

This command was modified in Cisco IOS Release 11.2 P to include slot/port syntax for the PA-8B-ST and PA-4B-U port adapters on Cisco 7200 series routers.

### *Sample Display*

The following is sample output from the **show controllers bri** command:

```
Router# show controllers bri 0

BRI unit 0
D Chan Info:
Layer 1 is ACTIVATED
idb 0x32089C, ds 0x3267D8, reset_mask 0x2
buffer size 1524
RX ring with 2 entries at 0x2101600 : Rxhead 0
00 pak=0x4122E8 ds=0x412444 status=D000 pak_size=0
01 pak=0x410C20 ds=0x410D7C status=F000 pak_size=0
TX ring with 1 entries at 0x2101640: tx_count = 0, tx_head = 0, tx_tail = 0
00 pak=0x000000 ds=0x000000 status=7C00 pak_size=0
0 missed datagrams, 0 overruns, 0 bad frame addresses
0 bad datagram encapsulations, 0 memory errors
0 transmitter underruns
B1 Chan Info:
```

```
Layer 1 is ACTIVATED
idb 0x3224E8, ds 0x3268C8, reset_mask 0x0
buffer size 1524
RX ring with 8 entries at 0x2101400 : Rxhead 0
00 pak=0x421FC0 ds=0x42211C status=D000 pak_size=0
01 pak=0x4085E8 ds=0x408744 status=D000 pak_size=0
02 pak=0x422EF0 ds=0x42304C status=D000 pak_size=0
03 pak=0x4148E0 ds=0x414A3C status=D000 pak_size=0
04 pak=0x424D50 ds=0x424EAC status=D000 pak_size=0
05 pak=0x423688 ds=0x4237E4 status=D000 pak_size=0
06 pak=0x41AB98 ds=0x41ACF4 status=D000 pak_size=0
07 pak=0x41A400 ds=0x41A55C status=F000 pak_size=0
TX ring with 4 entries at 0x2101440: tx_count = 0, tx_head = 0, tx_tail = 0
00 pak=0x000000 ds=0x000000 status=5C00 pak_size=0
01 pak=0x000000 ds=0x000000 status=5C00 pak_size=0
02 pak=0x000000 ds=0x000000 status=5C00 pak_size=0
03 pak=0x000000 ds=0x000000 status=7C00 pak_size=0
0 missed datagrams, 0 overruns, 0 bad frame addresses
0 bad datagram encapsulations, 0 memory errors
0 transmitter underruns
B2 Chan Info:
Layer 1 is ACTIVATED
idb 0x324520, ds 0x3269B8, reset_mask 0x2
buffer size 1524
RX ring with 8 entries at 0x2101500 : Rxhead 0
00 pak=0x40FCF0 ds=0x40FE4C status=D000 pak_size=0
01 pak=0x40E628 ds=0x40E784 status=D000 pak_size=0
02 pak=0x40F558 ds=0x40F6B4 status=D000 pak_size=0
03 pak=0x413218 ds=0x413374 status=D000 pak_size=0
04 pak=0x40EDC0 ds=0x40EF1C status=D000 pak_size=0
05 pak=0x4113B8 ds=0x411514 status=D000 pak_size=0
06 pak=0x416ED8 ds=0x417034 status=D000 pak_size=0
07 pak=0x416740 ds=0x41689C status=F000 pak_size=0
TX ring with 4 entries at 0x2101540: tx_count = 0, tx_head = 0, tx_tail = 0
00 pak=0x000000 ds=0x000000 status=5C00 pak_size=0
01 pak=0x000000 ds=0x000000 status=5C00 pak_size=0
02 pak=0x000000 ds=0x000000 status=5C00 pak_size=0
03 pak=0x000000 ds=0x000000 status=7C00 pak_size=0
0 missed datagrams, 0 overruns, 0 bad frame addresses
0 bad datagram encapsulations, 0 memory errors
0 transmitter underruns
```

Table 12–2 describes the significant fields in the display.

**Table 12–2** *Show Controllers BRI Field Descrptions*

| Field | Description |
|---|---|
| BRI unit 0 | Interface type and unit number. |
| Chan Info | D and B channel numbers. |
| Layer 1 is ACTIVATED | Status can be DEACTIVATED, PENDING ACTIVATION, or ACTIVATED. |

**Table 12–2** *Show Controllers BRI Field Descrptions, Continued*

| Field | Description |
|---|---|
| idb<br>ds<br>reset_mask | Information about internal data structures and parameters. |
| buffer size | Number of bytes allocated for buffers. |
| RX ring with - entries at - | Information about the Receiver Queue. |
| Rxhead | Start of the Receiver Queue. |
| pak<br>ds<br>status<br>pak_size | Information about internal data structures and parameters. |
| TX ring with - entries at - | Information about the Transmitter Queue. |
| tx_count | Number of packets to transmit. |
| tx_head | Start of the transmit list. |
| tx_tail | End of the transmit list. |
| missed datagrams | Incoming packets missed due to internal errors. |
| overruns | Number of times the receiver hardware was unable to hand received data to a hardware buffer because the input rate exceeded the receiver's ability to handle the data. |
| bad frame addresses | Frames received with a cyclic redundancy check (CRC) error and noninteger number of octets. |
| bad datagram encapsulations | Packets received with bad encapsulation. |
| memory errors | Internal direct memory access (DMA) memory errors. |
| transmitter underruns | Number of times that the transmitter has been running faster than the router can handle. |

The following is a partial sample output from the **show controllers bri** command on a Cisco 7200 series router:

```
BRI slot 2 interface 0 with integrated NT1
Layer 1 is ACTIVATED. (ISDN L1 State F7)
Master clock for slot 2 is bri interface 0.
Total chip configuration successes: 193, failures: 0, timeouts: 0
D Channel Information:
  Channel state: UP  Channel IDB: 6092AC64
  RX ring entries: 5, buffer size 512
```

```
RX descriptor ring: head = 165F4D8, tail = 165F508
RX buffer ring: head = 6093A260, tail = 6093A290
00 params=0x2000000 status=0x0 data ptr=0x1650F84 next ptr=0x165F4D8
01 params=0x2000000 status=0xC0080000 data ptr=0x1651884 next ptr=0x165F4E8
02 params=0x2000000 status=0xC0080000 data ptr=0x1651644 next ptr=0x165F4F8
03 params=0x2000000 status=0x0 data ptr=0x1651404 next ptr=0x165F508
04 params=0x42000000 status=0x0 data ptr=0x16511C4 next ptr=0x165F4C8
TX ring entries: 5, in use: 0, buffer size 512
TX descriptor ring: head = 3C2049C0, tail = 3C2049C0
TX buffer ring: head = 608EC0C4, tail = 608EC0C4
00 params=0x80000000 data ptr=0x0000000 next ptr=0x4D0049A8
01 params=0x80000000 data ptr=0x0000000 next ptr=0x4D0049B4
02 params=0x80000000 data ptr=0x0000000 next ptr=0x4D0049C0
03 params=0xC0000000 data ptr=0x0000000 next ptr=0x4D0049CC
04 params=0x0 data ptr=0x0000000 next ptr=0x4D00499C
List of timeslots (sw): 2
```

Table 12–3 describes the significant fields in the display.

**Table 12–3** *Show Controllers BRI Field Descriptions*

| Field | Description |
|---|---|
| BRI slot 2 interface 0 with integrated NTI | Interface type and slot and port number. |
| Layer 1 is ACTIVATED | Status can be DEACTIVATED, PENDING ACTIVATION, or ACTIVATED. |
| Master clock | The first interface that comes up on an MBRI port adapter holds the master clock. This clock is used for all interfaces on that port adapter. If the master clock interface goes down, the second interface that came up becomes the master clock interface. |
| Total chip configuration successes | Counters of successful chip configuration. |
| failures | Counters of bad chip configuration. |
| timeouts | Counters of failing to initialize chip. |
| D Channel Information | Information related to D channel status. |
| Channel state | Channel state can be UNUSED, IDLE, DOWN, STANDBY, UP, THROTTLED, ILLEGAL. |
| Channel IDB | Internal interface channel description. |
| RX (or TX) ring entries | Internal receive queue. |
| RX (or TX) descriptor ring | Internal receive queue to manage hardware chip. |
| RX (or TX) buffer ring | Internal receive queue to hold inbound packets. |

**Table 12–3** *Show Controllers BRI Field Descriptions, Continued*

| Field | Description |
|---|---|
| Rxhead | Start of the receiver queue. |
| params, status, data ptr, next ptr | Information about internal data structures and params. |
| List of timeslots (sw) | Timeslots assigned to this channel. |

### SHOW DIALER INTERFACE BRI

To display general diagnostic information for ISDN BRI interfaces configured for DDR, use the **show dialer interface bri** EXEC command.

**show dialer interface bri** *number*

| *Syntax* | *Description* |
|---|---|
| *number* | (Optional) BRI interface number. |

#### *Command Mode*

EXEC

#### *Sample Displays*

If you enter the **show dialer interface bri** command for the D channel of an ISDN BRI, the command output also displays the B channels. That is, the command **show dialer interface bri 0** displays information of interfaces bri 0, bri 0:1, and bri 0:2. Similarly, use of the related command **show dialer interface serial 0:23** (for a channelized T1 line configured for ISDN PRI) displays information for serial interfaces 0:23, 0:0, 0:1, and so forth to 0:22.

If you have defined a dialer group that consists of the interfaces serial 0, serial 1, and bri 2, the command **show dialer interface dialer 1** displays information for interfaces bri 0, bri 0:1, bri 0:2, serial 1, and serial 0.

The following is sample output from the **show dialer interface bri** command for a BRI interface when dialer profiles are configured:

```
impulse# show dialer interface bri 0

BRI0 - dialer type = ISDN

Dial String      Successes   Failures    Last called   Last status

0 incoming call(s) have been screened.

BRI0: B-Channel 1
Idle timer (120 secs), Fast idle timer (20 secs)
Wait for carrier (30 secs), Re-enable (15 secs)

Dialer state is data link layer up
```

```
Dial reason: ip (s=6.1.1.8, d=6.1.1.1)

Interface bound to profile Dialer0

Time until disconnect 102 secs
Current call connected 00:00:19
Connected to 5773872 (wolfman)

BRI0: B-Channel 2
Idle timer (120 secs), Fast idle timer (20 secs)
Wait for carrier (30 secs), Re-enable (15 secs)
Dialer state is idle
```

Table 12–4 describes significant fields shown in the display.

**Table 12–4** *Show Dialer Interface BRI Field Descriptions*

| Field | Description |
|---|---|
| BRI0 - dialer type = ISDN | ISDN dialer. |
| Dial string | Dial strings of logged calls (telephone numbers). On ISDN BRI interfaces, if you have specified a subaddress number in the **dialer string**, this number is included in the dial string after a colon. |
| Successes | Successful connections (even if no data is passed). |
| Failures | Failed connections; call not successfully completed. |
| Last called | Time that last call occurred to specific dial string. |
| Last status | Status of last call to specific dial string (successful or failed). |
| 0 incoming call(s) have been screened. | Number of calls subjected to Dialer Profiles screening to determine how the call is to be treated. |
| BRI0: B-Channel 1 | Header indicating the following data is for B channel 1. |
| Idle timer (120 secs), Fast idle timer (20 secs) | Settings (in seconds) for the idle timer and the fast idle timer. |
| Wait for carrier (30 secs), Re-enable (15 secs) | Settings (in seconds) for the wait for carrier timer and the re-enable timer. |

**Table 12–4** *Show Dialer Interface BRI Field Descriptions, Continued*

| Field | Description |
|---|---|
| Dialer state is data link layer up | The message "data link layer up" suggests that the dialer came up properly; if it says anything else, then dialer did not come up properly. The message "physical layer up" means the line protocol (LCP) came up, but the NCP did not come up. The **show interfaces** command also provides the similar information. |
| Dial reason: ip (s=6.1.1.8, d=6.1.1.1) | What initiated the dial, namely an IP packet, plus source and destination address in the packet. |
| Interface bound to profile Dialer0 | Dialer profile that is bound to this interface or B channel. |
| Time until disconnect | Time until line is configured to disconnect. This field is displayed if the interface is currently connected to a destination. |
| Current call connected | Time at which the current call was connected. |
| Connected to | Dial string to which line is currently connected. |

If an interface is connected to a destination, a display is provided that indicates the idle time before the line is disconnected. (The value decreases incrementally each second.) Then the duration of the current connection is shown. The following shows an example of this display; it appears after the third line in the **show dialer** display:

```
Time until disconnect 596 secs
Current call connected 0:00:25
```

After a call disconnects, the system displays the time remaining before it can dial again. The following is an example of this display; it appears after the third line in the **show dialer** display:

```
Time until interface enabled 8 secs
```

If caller ID screening is configured on an ISDN BRI, the **show dialer** command display includes a line similar to the following:

```
1 incoming call(s) have been screened.
```

This line reports the number of calls that have been screened.

### SHOW INTERFACES BRI

Use the **show interfaces bri** privileged EXEC command to display information about the BRI D channel or about one or more B channels.

**show interfaces bri** *number*[[*:bchannel*] | [*first*] [*last*]] [**accounting**]
**show interfaces bri** *slot/port* (Cisco 7200 series)

| *Syntax* | *Description* |
|---|---|
| *number* | Interface number. The value is 0 through 7 if the router has one 8-port BRI NIM, or 0 through 15 if the router has two 8-port BRI NIMs. Specifying just the number will display the D channel for that BRI interface. |
| *slot/port* | On the Cisco 7200 series, slot location and port number of the interface. |
| *:bchannel* | (Optional) Colon (:) followed by a specific B channel number. |
| *first* | (Optional) Specifies the first of the B channels; the value can be either 1 or 2. |
| *last* | (Optional) Specifies the last of the B channels; the value can only be 2, indicating B channels 1 and 2. |
| **accounting** | (Optional) Displays the number of packets of each protocol type that have been sent through the interface. |

### *Command Mode*

Privileged EXEC

### *Usage Guidelines*

This command first appeared in Cisco IOS Release 10.3.

This command was modified in Cisco IOS Release 11.2 P to include slot/port syntax for the PA-8B-ST and PA-4B-U port adapters on Cisco 7200 series routers.

Use either the *:bchannel-number* argument or the *first* or *last* arguments to display information about specified B channels.

Use the **show interfaces bri** *number* form of the command (without the optional *:bchannel,* or *first* and *last* arguments) to obtain D channel information.

Use the command syntax sample combinations in Table 12–5 to display the associated output.

**Table 12–5** *Sample Show Interface*

| **Command Syntax** | **Displays** |
|---|---|
| **show interfaces** | All interfaces in the router |
| **show interfaces bri 2** | Channel D for BRI interface 2 |
| **show interfaces bri 2:1** | Channel B1 on BRI interface 2 |
| **show interfaces bri 2:2** | Channel B2 on BRI interface 2 |
| **show interfaces bri 4 1** | Channel B1 on BRI interface 4 |

**Table 12–5** *Sample Show Interface, Continued*

| Command Syntax | Displays |
|---|---|
| show interfaces bri 4 2 | Channel B2 on BRI interface 4 |
| show interfaces bri 4 1 2 | Channels B1 and B2 on BRI interface 4 |
| show interfaces bri | Error message: "% Incomplete command." |

### *Sample Displays*

The following is sample output from the **show interfaces bri** command:

```
Router# show interfaces bri 0:1

BRI0:1 is down, line protocol is down
  Hardware is BRI
  MTU 1500 bytes, BW 64 Kbit, DLY 20000 usec, rely 255/255, load 1/255
  Encapsulation PPP, loopback not set, keepalive not set
  LCP Closed
  Closed: IPCP
  Last input never, output never, output hang never
  Last clearing of "show interface" counters never
  Queueing strategy: fifo
  Output queue 0/40, 0 drops; input queue 0/75, 0 drops
  5 minute input rate 0 bits/sec, 0 packets/sec
  5 minute output rate 0 bits/sec, 0 packets/sec
     0 packets input, 0 bytes, 0 no buffer
     Received 0 broadcasts, 0 runts, 0 giants
     0 input errors, 0 CRC, 0 frame, 0 overrun, 0 ignored, 0 abort
     0 packets output, 0 bytes, 0 underruns
     0 output errors, 0 collisions, 7 interface resets
     0 output buffer failures, 0 output buffers swapped out
     0 carrier transitions
```

The following is sample output from the **show interfaces bri** command on a Cisco 7200 series router:

```
Router# show interfaces bri 2/0

BRI2/0 is up, line protocol is up (spoofing)
  Hardware is BRI
  Internet address is 11.1.1.3/27
  MTU 1500 bytes, BW 64 Kbit, DLY 20000 usec, rely 255/255, load 1/255
  Encapsulation PPP, loopback not set
  Last input 00:00:01, output 00:00:01, output hang never
  Last clearing of "show interface" counters never
  Input queue: 0/75/0 (size/max/drops); Total output drops: 0
  Queueing strategy: weighted fair
  Output queue: 0/64/0 (size/threshold/drops)
     Conversations  0/1 (active/max active)
     Reserved Conversations 0/0 (allocated/max allocated)
  5 minute input rate 0 bits/sec, 0 packets/sec
  5 minute output rate 0 bits/sec, 0 packets/sec
     609 packets input, 2526 bytes, 0 no buffer
```

```
Received 0 broadcasts, 0 runts, 0 giants
0 input errors, 0 CRC, 0 frame, 0 overrun, 0 ignored, 0 abort
615 packets output, 2596 bytes, 0 underruns
0 output errors, 0 collisions, 5 interface resets
0 output buffer failures, 0 output buffers swapped out
3 carrier transitions
```

Table 12–6 describes the fields shown in the display.

**Table 12–6** *Show Interfaces BRI Field Descriptions*

| Field | Description |
|---|---|
| BRI... is {up \| down \| administratively down} | Indicates whether the interface hardware is currently active (whether line signal is present) and if it has been taken down by an administrator. |
| line protocol is {up \| down \| administratively down} | Indicates whether the software processes that handle the line protocol consider the line usable (that is, whether keepalives are successful). |
| Hardware is | Hardware type. |
| Internet address is | IP address and subnet mask, followed by packet size. |
| MTU | Maximum transmission unit of the interface. |
| BW | Bandwidth of the interface in kilobits per second. |
| DLY | Delay of the interface in microseconds. |
| rely | Reliability of the interface as a fraction of 255 (255/255 is 100 percent reliability), calculated as an exponential average over 5 minutes. |
| load | Load on the interface as a fraction of 255 (255/255 is completely saturated), calculated as an exponential average over 5 minutes. |
| Encapsulation | Encapsulation method assigned to interface. |
| loopback | Indicates whether loopback is set or not. |
| keepalive | Indicates whether keepalives are set or not. |
| Last input | Number of hours, minutes, and seconds since the last packet was successfully received by an interface. Useful for knowing when a nonfunctioning interface failed. |
| output | Number of hours, minutes, and seconds since the last packet was successfully transmitted by an interface. |

**Table 12–6** *Show Interfaces BRI Field Descriptions, Continued*

| Field | Description |
|---|---|
| output hang | Number of hours, minutes, and seconds (or never) since the interface was last reset because of a transmission that took too long. When the number of hours in any of the "last" fields exceeds 24 hours, the number of days and hours is printed. If that field overflows, asterisks (**) are printed. |
| Output queue, drops<br>Input queue, drops | Number of packets in output and input queues. Each number is followed by a slash (/), the maximum size of the queue, and the number of packets dropped due to a full queue. |
| Five minute input rate<br>Five minute output rate | Average number of bits and packets transmitted per second in the last 5 minutes. |
| packets input | Total number of error-free packets received by the system. |
| bytes | Total number of bytes, including data and media access control (MAC) encapsulation, in the error-free packets received by the system. |
| no buffer | Number of received packets discarded because there was no buffer space in the main system. Compare with ignored count. Broadcast storms on Ethernets and bursts of noise on serial lines are often responsible for no input buffer events. |
| broadcasts | Total number of broadcast or multicast packets received by the interface. |
| runts | Number of packets that are discarded because they are smaller than the medium's minimum packet size. |
| giants | Number of packets that are discarded because they exceed the medium's maximum packet size. |
| input errors | Total number of no buffer, runts, giants, CRCs, frame, overrun, ignored, and abort counts. Other input-related errors can also increment the count, so this sum may not balance with the other counts. |
| CRC | Cyclic redundancy checksum generated by the originating station or far-end device does not match the checksum calculated from the data received. On a serial link, CRCs usually indicate noise, gain hits, or other transmission problems on the data link. |

**Table 12–6** *Show Interfaces BRI Field Descriptions, Continued*

| Field | Description |
|---|---|
| frame | Number of packets received incorrectly having a CRC error and a noninteger number of octets. On a serial line, this is usually the result of noise or other transmission problems. |
| overrun | Number of times the serial receiver hardware was unable to hand received data to a hardware buffer because the input rate exceeded the receiver's ability to handle the data. |
| ignored | Number of received packets ignored by the interface because the interface hardware ran low on internal buffers. Broadcast storms and bursts of noise can increase the ignored count. |
| abort | Illegal sequence of one bits on a serial interface. This usually indicates a clocking problem between the serial interface and the data link equipment. |
| packets output | Total number of messages transmitted by the system. |
| bytes | Total number of bytes, including data and MAC encapsulation, transmitted by the system. |
| underruns | Number of times that the transmitter has been running faster than the router can handle. This may never be reported on some interfaces. |
| output errors | Sum of all errors that prevented the final transmission of datagrams out of the interface being examined. Note that this may not balance with the sum of the enumerated output errors, because some datagrams may have more than one error, and others may have errors that do not fall into any of the specifically tabulated categories. |
| collisions | Number of collisions. These can occur when you have several devices connected on a multiport line. |
| interface resets | Number of times an interface has been completely reset. This can happen if packets queued for transmission were not sent within several seconds. On a serial line, this can be caused by a malfunctioning modem that is not supplying the transmit clock signal or by a cable problem. If the system recognizes that the carrier detect line of a serial interface is up, but the line protocol is down, it periodically resets the interface in an effort to restart it. Interface resets can also occur when an interface is looped back or shut down. |

**Table 12–6** *Show Interfaces BRI Field Descriptions, Continued*

| Field | Description |
|---|---|
| restarts | Number of times the controller was restarted because of errors. |
| carrier transitions | Number of times the carrier detect signal of a serial interface has changed state. Check for modem or line problems if the carrier detect line is changing state often. |

### SHOW ISDN

To display the information about calls, history, memory, status, and Layer 2 and Layer 3 timers, use the **show isdn** EXEC command.

**show isdn** {**active** | **history** | **memory** | **status** [*dsl* | *interface-type number*] | **timers**}

| *Syntax* | *Description* |
|---|---|
| **active** | Displays current call information, including called number, the time until the call is disconnected, AOC charging units used during the call, and whether the AOC information is provided during calls or at the end of calls. |
| **history** | Displays historic and current call information, including the called number, the time until the call is disconnected, AOC charging time units used during the call, and whether the AOC information is provided during calls or at the end of calls. |
| **memory** | Displays memory pool statistics. This keyword is for use by technical development staff only. |
| **status** [*dsl* \| *interface-type number*] | Displays the status of all ISDN interfaces or, optionally, a specific digital signal link (DSL) or a specific ISDN interface. Values of *dsl* range from 0 to 15. *Interface-type* can be **bri** or **serial**. |
| **timers** | Displays the values of Layer 2 and Layer 3 timers. |

#### *Command Mode*

EXEC

#### *Sample Displays*

The following is sample output from the **show isdn active** command:

```
Router# show isdn active

--------------------------------------------------------------------------------
                              ISDN ACTIVE CALLS
--------------------------------------------------------------------------------
History Table MaxLength = 320 entries
```

```
History Retain Timer = 15 Minutes
------------------------------------------------------------------------------
Call Calling      Called          Duration  Remote    Time until   Recorded Charges
Type Number       Number          Seconds   Name      Disconnect   Units/Currency
------------------------------------------------------------------------------
Out              9876543222        Active(10)  idacom                11       u(E)
Out              9876543210        Active(34)  idacom 115            5        u(D)
------------------------------------------------------------------------------
```

The following is sample output from the **show isdn history** command:

```
Router# show isdn history

------------------------------------------------------------------------------
                              ISDN CALL HISTORY
------------------------------------------------------------------------------
History Table MaxLength = 320 entries
History Retain Timer = 15 Minutes
------------------------------------------------------------------------------
Call Calling      Called          Duration  Remote    Time until   Recorded Charges
Type Number       Number          Seconds   Name      Disconnect   Units/Currency
------------------------------------------------------------------------------
Out              47887654         240       blackcanary              5       u(D)
In    67893                       90        delorean
Out              56745678         Active(90)  blackcanary  240       13      u(D)
------------------------------------------------------------------------------
```

Table 12–7 describes the fields in the **show isdn active** and **show isdn history** output displays.

**Table 12–7** *Show ISDN Active and Show ISDN History Field Descriptions*

| Field | Description |
|---|---|
| History Table MaxLength | Maximum number of entries that can be retained in the Call History table. |
| History Retain Timer | Maximum number of seconds any entry can be retained in Call History table. |
| Call Type | Type of call: incoming or outgoing. |
| Calling Number | For incoming calls, the number from which the call was received. |
| Called Number | For outgoing calls, the number to which the call was placed. |
| Duration Seconds | Number of seconds the call lasted. Indicates whether the call is still active, and how many seconds it has lasted so far. |
| Remote Name | Name of the host placing the call or the host called. |
| Time until Disconnect | Number of seconds before the call is configured to disconnect because of the static idle timer for the map class or the interface. |
| Recorded Charges Units/Currency | For outgoing calls, number of ISDN AOC charging units used or the currency cost of the call. |

The following is sample output from the **show isdn timers** command:

```
Router# show isdn timers

ISDN Layer 2 values:
                  K    = 0   outstanding I-frames
                  N200 = 0   max number of retransmits
                  T200 = 0   seconds
                  T202 = 2   seconds
                  T203 = 0   seconds
ISDN Layer 3 values:
                  T303 = 0   seconds
                  T305 = 0   seconds
                  T308 = 0   seconds
                  T310 = 0   seconds
                  T313 = 0   seconds
                  T316 = 0   seconds
                  T318 = 0   seconds
                  T319 = 0   seconds
```

Table 12–8 displays some typical values of the timers shown in the **show isdn timers** display. The values of the timers depend on the switch type and typically are used only for homologation purposes. See the Q.921 specifications for detailed technical definitions of the Layer 2 timers; see the Q.931 specifications for detailed technical definitions of the Layer 3 timers.

**Table 12–8** *Show ISDN Timers Command Output*

| Field | Typical Value |
|---|---|
| **ISDN Layer 2 values:** | |
| K = 0 outstanding I-frames | 1 |
| N200 = 0 max number of retransmits | 3 |
| T200 = 0 seconds | 1 |
| T202 = 2 seconds | 2 |
| T203 = 0 seconds | 10 |
| **ISDN Layer 3 values:** | |
| T303 = 0 seconds | 4 |
| T305 = 0 seconds | 30 |
| T308 = 0 seconds | 4 |
| T310 = 0 seconds | 40 |
| T313 = 0 seconds | 0 |
| T316 = 0 seconds | 4 |

**Table 12–8** *Show ISDN Timers Command Output, Continued*

| Field<br>**ISDN Layer 2 values:** | Typical Value |
|---|---|
| T318 = 0 seconds | 4 |
| T319 = 0 seconds | 4 |

The following is sample output from the **show isdn status** command when no calls are active:

```
Router# show isdn status

The current ISDN Switchtype = basic-5ess
ISDN BRI0 interface
    Layer 1 Status:
        ACTIVE
    Layer 2 Status:
        TEI = 65, State = MULTIPLE_FRAME_ESTABLISHED
    Spid Status:
        TEI 65, ces = 1, state = 5(init)
            spid1 configured, no LDN, spid1 sent, spid1 valid
            Endpoint ID Info: epsf = 0, usid = 3, tid = 7F
    Layer 3 Status:
        0 Active Layer 3 Call(s)
    Activated dsl 0 CCBs = 0
    Number of active calls = 0
    Number of available B-channels = 2
    Total Allocated ISDN CCBs = 0
```

The following is sample output from the **show isdn status** command with one active call:

```
Router# show isdn status
    The current ISDN Switchtype = ntt
    ISDN BRI0 interface
        Layer 1 Status:
            ACTIVE
        Layer 2 Status:
            TEI = 64, State = MULTIPLE_FRAME_ESTABLISHED
        Layer 3 Status:
            1 Active Layer 3 Call(s)
        Activated dsl 0 CCBs = 1
            CCB:callid=8003, callref=0, sapi=0, ces=1, B-chan=1
        Number of active calls = 1
        Number of available B-channels = 1
        Total Allocated ISDN CCBs = 1
```

Table 12–9 describes the fields in the **show isdn status** command output.

**Table 12–9** *Show ISDN Status Field Descriptions*

| Field | Description |
|---|---|
| **Layer 1 Status** | |
| ACTIVE | Status of ISDN Layer 1. |
| **Layer 2 Status** | |
| TEI = 65,<br>State = MULTIPLE_FRAME_ESTABLISHED | Status of ISDN Layer 2. Terminal endpoint identifier number and multiframe structure state. |
| **Spid Status** | |
| TEI 65, ces = 1, state = 5(init) | Terminal endpoint identifier number and state. |
| spid1 configured, no LDN, spid1 sent, spid1 valid | SPID configuration information. For example, local directory number is defined. |
| Endpoint ID Info: epsf = 0, usid = 3, tid = 7F | Endpoint identifier information. |
| **Layer 3 Status:** | |
| 1 Active Layer 3 Call(s) | Number of active calls. |
| Activated dsl 0 CCBs = | Number of the Digital Signal Link activated. Number of call control blocks in use. |
| CCB:callid=8003, callref=0, sapi=0, ces=1, B-chan=1 | Information about the active call. |
| Number of active calls = | Number of active calls. |
| Number of available B-channels = | Number of B channels that are not being used. |
| Total Allocated ISDN CCBs = | Number of ISDN call control blocks that are allocated. |

CHAPTER 13

# Configuring Synchronous Serial Ports

Synchronous serial ports can be used for leased-line or dial-up communications. In addition, high-speed lines (E1 or T1) can be configured to support multiple serial interfaces that can themselves be configured as if they were attached to dial-up lines. Finally, dialers can be configured on synchronous serial lines to support dial-on-demand routing.

This chapter presents configuration tasks required to make a serial interface operational. To configure routing and dial capabilities, additional configuration is required. For information about dial-up uses of the serial interfaces, see Chapter 15, "Configuring Channelized E1 and Channelized T1," as well as the chapters in Part V, "Dial-on-Demand Routing."

For a complete description of the synchronous interface commands in this chapter, see Chapter 14, "Synchronous Serial Port Setup Commands."

**NOTES**

In Cisco IOS Release 11.3, all commands supported on the Cisco 7500 series are also supported on the Cisco 7000 series.

## SYNCHRONOUS SERIAL INTERFACE TASK LIST

Perform the tasks in the following sections to configure a synchronous serial interface. The first task is required; the remaining tasks are optional.

- Specifying a Synchronous Serial Interface
- Specifying Synchronous Serial Encapsulation
- Configuring PPP
- Configuring Compression of HDLC Data
- Configuring the CRC

- Using the Line-Coding Format
- Enabling the Internal Clock
- Inverting the Transmit Clock Signal
- Setting Transmit Delay
- Configuring DTR Signal Pulsing
- Ignoring DCD and Monitoring DSR as Line Up/Down Indicator
- Configuring the Clock Rate for an DCE Mode Interface
- Specifying the Timing Signal Configuration
- Specifying G.703 Interface Options

Synchronous serial interface configuration examples can be found at the end of this chapter.

## Specifying a Synchronous Serial Interface

To specify a synchronous serial interface and enter interface configuration mode, perform the following task in global configuration mode:

| Task | Command |
|---|---|
| Specify an interface and enter interface configuration mode. | **interface serial** *number*<br>**interface serial** *slot/port*<br>(Cisco 7500 series or Cisco 7200 series)<br>**interface serial** *slot/port-adapter/port* (Cisco 7200 series)<br>**interface serial** *slot/port:channel-group*<br>(channelized T1 or E1 interface on the Cisco 7500 series)<br>**interface serial** *number:channel-group*<br>(channelized T1 or E1 interface on the Cisco 4000 series) |

## Specifying Synchronous Serial Encapsulation

Encapsulation methods are set according to the type of protocol or application you configure in the Cisco IOS software.

By default, synchronous serial lines use the High-Level Data Link Control (HDLC) serial encapsulation method, which provides the synchronous framing and error-detection functions of HDLC without windowing or retransmission. Synchronous serial interfaces support the following serial encapsulation methods for dial solutions:

- High-Level Data Link Control (HDLC)
- Point-to-Point Protocol (PPP)

In addition, synchronous serial interfaces support the following encapsulation methods:

- Asynchronous Transfer Mode-Data Exchange Interface (ATM-DXI)
- Frame Relay
- Synchronous Data Link Control (SDLC)
- Switched Multimegabit Data Services (SMDS)
- Cisco Serial Tunnel (STUN)
- X.25-based encapsulations

You can define the encapsulation method for dial solutions by performing the following task in interface configuration mode:

| Task | Command |
|---|---|
| Configure synchronous serial encapsulation for dial solutions. | **encapsulation** {**hdlc** \| **ppp**} |

The default is HDLC encapsulation.

## Configuring PPP

To configure PPP (including PPP compression), see Chapter 25, "Configuring Media-Independent PPP and Multilink PPP."

## Configuring Compression of HDLC Data

You can configure point-to-point software compression on serial interfaces that use HDLC encapsulation. Compression reduces the size of a HDLC frame via lossless data compression. The compression algorithm used is a Stacker (LZS) algorithm.

Compression is performed in software and might significantly affect system performance. It is recommended that you disable compression if CPU load exceeds 65 percent. To display the CPU load, use the **show process cpu** EXEC command.

If the majority of your traffic is already compressed files, you should not use compression.

To configure compression over HDLC, perform the following tasks in interface configuration mode:

| Task | | Command |
|---|---|---|
| **Step 1** | Enable encapsulation of a single protocol on the serial line. | **encapsulation hdlc** |
| **Step 2** | Enable compression. | **compress stac** |

### Configuring the CRC

The cyclic redundancy check (CRC) on a serial interface defaults to a length of 16 bits. To change the length of the CRC to 32 bits on an FSIP or HIP of the Cisco 7000 series with RSP7000 only, complete the following task in interface configuration mode:

| Task | Command |
|---|---|
| Set the length of the CRC. | **crc** *size* |

### Using the Line-Coding Format

All FSIP interface types on the Cisco 7000 series with RSP7000 support nonreturn-to-zero (NRZ) and nonreturn-to-zero inverted (NRZI) format. This is a line-coding format that is required for serial connections in some environments. NRZ encoding is most common. NRZI encoding is used primarily with EIA/TIA-232 connections in IBM environments.

The default configuration for all serial interfaces is NRZ format. The default is **no nrzi-encoding**. To enable NRZI format, complete the following task in interface configuration mode:

| Task | Command |
|---|---|
| Enable NRZI encoding format. | **nrzi-encoding** |

### Enabling the Internal Clock

When a DTE does not return a transmit clock, use the following interface configuration command on the Cisco 7000 series with RSP7000 to enable the internally generated clock on a serial interface:

| Task | Command |
|---|---|
| Enable the internally generated clock on a serial interface. | **transmit-clock-internal** |

### Inverting the Transmit Clock Signal

Delays between the SCTE clock and data transmission indicate that the transmit clock signal might not be appropriate for the interface rate and length of cable being used. Different ends of the wire may have variances that differ slightly. Invert the clock signal to compensate for these factors by completing the following task in interface configuration mode on a Cisco 7000 series with RSP7000, Cisco 7200 series, and Cisco 7500 series router:

| Task | Command |
|---|---|
| Invert the clock signal on an interface. | **invert-transmit-clock** |

### Setting Transmit Delay

It is possible to send back-to-back data packets over serial interfaces faster than some hosts can receive them. You can specify a minimum dead time after transmitting a packet to alleviate this condition. This setting is available for serial interfaces on the MCI and SCI interface cards and for the HSSI or MIP. Perform one of the following tasks, as appropriate for your system, in interface configuration mode:

| Task | Command |
|---|---|
| Set the transmit delay on the MCI and SCI synchronous serial interfaces. | **transmitter-delay** *microseconds* |
| Set the transmit delay on the HSSI or MIP. | **transmitter-delay** *hdlc-flags* |

### Configuring DTR Signal Pulsing

You can configure pulsing DTR signals on all serial interfaces. When the serial line protocol goes down (for example, because of loss of synchronization), the interface hardware is reset and the DTR signal is held inactive for at least the specified interval. This function is useful for handling encrypting or other similar devices that use the toggling of the DTR signal to resynchronize. To configure DTR signal pulsing, perform the following task in interface configuration mode:

| Task | Command |
|---|---|
| Configure DTR signal pulsing. | **pulse-time** *seconds* |

### Ignoring DCD and Monitoring DSR as Line Up/Down Indicator

This task applies to Quad Serial NIM interfaces on the Cisco 4000 series and Hitachi-based serial interfaces on the Cisco 2500 series and Cisco 3000 series.

By default, when the serial interface is operating in DTE mode, it monitors the Data Carrier Detect (DCD) signal as the line up/down indicator. By default, the attached DCE device sends the DCD signal. When the DTE interface detects the DCD signal, it changes the state of the interface to up.

In some configurations, such as an SDLC multidrop environment, the DCE device sends the Data Set Ready (DSR) signal rather than the DCD signal, which prevents the interface from coming up. To tell the interface to monitor the DSR signal rather than the DCD signal as the line up/down indicator, perform the following task in interface configuration mode:

| Task | Command |
|---|---|
| Configure the serial interface to monitor the DSR signal as the line up/down indicator. | **ignore-dcd** |

### CONFIGURING THE CLOCK RATE FOR A DCE MODE INTERFACE

You can configure the clock rate for the connector hardware of the serial interface to an acceptable bit rate. To do so, perform the following task in interface configuration mode:

| Task | Command |
|---|---|
| Configure the clock rate on serial interfaces. | **clock rate** *bps* |

### SPECIFYING THE TIMING SIGNAL CONFIGURATION

On Cisco 4000 series routers, you can specify the serial NPM timing signal configuration. When the board is operating as a DCE and the DTE provides terminal timing (SCTE or TT), you can configure the DCE to use SCTE from the DTE. When running the line at high speeds and long distances, this strategy prevents phase shifting of the data with respect to the clock.

To configure the DCE to use SCTE from the DTE, perform the following task in interface configuration mode:

| Task | Command |
|---|---|
| Configure the DCE to use SCTE from the DTE. | **dce-terminal-timing enable** |

When the board is operating as a DTE, you can invert the TXC clock signal it gets from the DCE that the DTE uses to transmit data. Invert the clock signal if the DCE cannot receive SCTE from the DTE, the data is running at high speeds, and the transmission line is long. Again, this prevents phase shifting of the data with respect to the clock.

To configure the interface so that the router inverts the TXC clock signal, perform the following task in interface configuration mode:

| Task | Command |
|---|---|
| Specify timing configuration to invert TXC clock signal. | **dte-invert-txc** |

### SPECIFYING G.703 INTERFACE OPTIONS

This section describes the optional tasks for configuring a G.703 serial interface:

- Enable Framed Mode
- Enable CRC4 Generation
- Use Timeslot 16 for Data
- Specify a Clock

Interfaces that meet the G.703 electrical and mechanical specifications operate at E1 data rates (2.048 Mbps).

## Enable Framed Mode

G.703 interfaces have two modes of operation: framed and unframed. By default, serial interfaces on a G.703 port adapter are configured for unframed mode. To enable framed mode, perform the following task in interface configuration mode:

| Task | Command |
|---|---|
| Enable framed mode. | **timeslot** *start-slot* - *stop-slot* |

To restore the default, use the **no** form of this command or set the starting time slot to 0.

## Enable CRC4 Generation

By default, the G.703 CRC4 is not generated. To enable generation of the G.703 CRC4, which is useful for checking data integrity while operating in framed mode, perform the following task in interface configuration mode:

| Task | Command |
|---|---|
| Enable CRC4 generation. | **crc4** |

## Use Timeslot 16 for Data

By default, timeslot 16 is used for signaling. It can also be used for data. To control the use of timeslot 16 for data, perform the following task in interface configuration mode:

| Task | Command |
|---|---|
| Specify that timeslot 16 is used for data. | **ts16** |

## Specify a Clock

A G.703 interface can clock its transmitted data from either its internal clock or from a clock recovered from the line's receive data stream. By default, the clock source is the line's receive data stream. To control which clock is used, perform the following task in interface configuration mode:

| Task | Command |
|---|---|
| Specify the clock used for transmitted data. | **clock source** {**line** \| **internal**} |

## Synchronous Serial Interface Configuration Examples

This section contains the following examples:

- Beginning the Interface Configuration Examples
- Configuring a Serial Interface for DCE Mode Examples
- G.703 Serial Interface Configuration Example
- JT2 6.3-MHz Serial Interface Configuration Example
- Signal Inversion Examples
- Channelized T1 Controller and Interface Examples
- Channelized E1 Controller Example
- Interface Shutdown Examples

For more information about synchronous serial interfaces configured on channelized E1/T1 and used for dialing, see Chapter 15.

### Beginning the Interface Configuration Examples

The following example illustrates how to begin interface configuration on a serial interface. It assigns Point-to-Point (PPP) encapsulation to serial interface 0.

```
interface serial 0
 encapsulation ppp
```

The same example on a Cisco 7500 requires the following commands:

```
interface serial 1/0
 encapsulation ppp
```

### Configuring a Serial Interface for DCE Mode Examples

The following example configures a serial interface for DCE mode on a Cisco 7500 series. Because the DTE does not return the Synchronous Clock Transmit Enable (SCTE) signal, the **transmit-clock-internal** is needed.

```
interface serial 0/0
 ip address 170.1.8.2 255.255.255.0
 clockrate 72000
 transmit-clock-internal
```

The following example configures a serial interface for DCE mode on a Cisco 4000 series router. Because the DTE does not return the Synchronous Clock Transmit Enable (SCTE) signal, the **dce-terminal-timing-enable** is needed. In this example, the default NRZ encoding and 16-bit CRC are accepted.

```
interface serial 1
 clockrate 72000
 dce-terminal-timing-enable
 nrz-encoding
```

### G.703 Serial Interface Configuration Example

The following example shows a basic configuration for serial interface 9/1/3 on a E1-G.703/G.704 serial port adapter in a Cisco 7500 series router. In this example, the interface is configured for framed (G.704) operation, and timeslot 16 is used for data.

```
interface serial 9/1/3
 ip address 1.1.1.10 255.255.255.0
 no keepalive
 no fair-queue
 timeslot 1-31
 crc4
 ts16
```

### JT2 6.3-MHz Serial Interface Configuration Example

The following example shows a configuration for serial interface 1/0/0 on a PA-2JT2 serial port adapter in a Cisco 7500 series router. In this example, the interface is configured to clock data using an internal clock source rather than the default line-derived clock source and to allow the frame alignment search criteria to use CRC5.

```
interface serial 1/0/0
 ip address 1.1.1.10 255.255.255.0
 clock source internal
 crc bits 5
 no shutdown
```

### Signal Inversion Examples

The following example inverts data on serial interface 3/1/0:

```
interface serial 3/1/0
 invert data
```

The following example inverts the clock signal on serial interface 3/0:

```
interface serial 3/0
 invert txclock
```

The following example, specifies NRZI mark encoding for serial interface 4/0/2:

```
interface serial 4/0/2
 nrzi-encoding mark
```

### Channelized E1 Controller Example

The following example configures a Cisco 7500 series router to acknowledge an E1 line. For an example of configuring circuits refer to the next section; circuits are configured in the same way, whether the line is E1 or T1.

```
controller e1 3/0
 channel-group 0 timeslots 1
 channel-group 8 timeslots 5-15, 20-30
 channel-group 12 timeslots 2
 channel-group 29 timeslots 31
```

### Channelized T1 Controller and Interface Examples

The following example applies only to a Cisco 7500 series router. It configures the router to acknowledge a T1 line and its circuits. Four different circuits (and their corresponding serial interfaces) are defined for the second CxCT1 attached to the MIP in slot 4.

```
controller t1 4/1
 framing esf
 linecode b8zs
 channel-group 0 timeslots 1
 channel-group 8 timeslots 5,7,12-15, 20 speed 64
 channel-group 12 timeslots 2
 channel-group 23 timeslots 24
```

The following example configures circuit 0 for Point-to-Point (PPP) encapsulation:

```
interface serial 4/1:0
 ip address 131.108.13.1 255.255.255.0
 encapsulation ppp
```

The following example configures circuit 8 for IP routing and disables IP route cache:

```
interface serial 4/1:8
 ip address 131.108.1.1 255.255.255.0
 no ip route-cache
```

The following example configures circuit 12 for Frame Relay encapsulation and subinterface support:

```
interface serial 4/1:12
 encapsulation frame-relay
!
interface serial 4/1:12.1
 ip address 1.1.1.1 255.0.0.0
!
interface serial 4/1:12.2
 ip address 2.2.2.2 255.0.0.0
```

The following example configures circuit 23 for IP routing and enables autonomous switching:

```
interface serial 4/1:23
 ip address 3.3.3.3 255.0.0.0
 ip route-cache cbus
```

### Interface Shutdown Examples

The following example shuts down a T1 circuit number 23 running on a Cisco 7500 series router:

```
interface serial 4/0:23
 shutdown
```

The following example shuts down the entire T1 line physically connected to a Cisco 7500 series router:

```
controller t1 4/0
 shutdown
```

CHAPTER 14

# Synchronous Serial Port Setup Commands

This chapter describes the commands available to configure synchronous serial interfaces for dial-up solutions on your router. For information about configuring synchronous serial interfaces for dial-up solutions, see Chapter 13, "Configuring Synchronous Serial Ports."

## BANDWIDTH

To communicate the bandwidth value of an interface to the higher-level protocols, use the **bandwidth** interface configuration command. Use the **no** form of this command to restore the default values.

**bandwidth** *kilobits*
**no bandwidth**

| *Syntax* | *Description* |
|---|---|
| *kilobits* | Intended bandwidth in kilobits per second. |

### *Default*

Default bandwidth values are set during startup and can be displayed with the EXEC command **show interfaces.**

### *Command Mode*

Interface configuration

*Usage Guidelines*

This command first appeared in Cisco IOS Release 10.0.

The **bandwidth** command sets an informational parameter to communicate the current bandwidth to the higher-level protocols.

IGRP uses the minimum path bandwidth to determine a routing metric. The TCP protocol adjusts initial retransmission parameters based on the apparent bandwidth of the outgoing interface.

At higher bandwidths, the value you configure with the **bandwidth** command is not what is displayed by the **show interface** command. The value shown is that used in IGRP updates and also used in computing load.

**NOTES**

This is a routing parameter only; it does not affect the physical interface.

*Example*

The following example sets the full bandwidth for DS3 transmissions:

```
interface serial 0
 bandwidth 44736
```

### CLOCK RATE

Use the **clock rate** interface configuration command to configure the clock rate for the hardware connections on serial interfaces such as network interface modules (NIMs) and interface processors to an acceptable bit rate. Use the **no** form of this command to remove the clock rate if you change the interface from a DCE to a DTE device. Using the **no** form of this command on a DCE interface sets the clock rate to the hardware-dependent default value.

**clock rate** *bps*
**no clock rate**

| *Syntax* | *Description* |
|---|---|
| *bps* | Desired clock rate in bits per second: 1200, 2400, 4800, 9600, 19200, 38400, 56000, 64000, 72000, 125000, 148000, 250000, 500000, 800000, 1000000, 1300000, 2000000, 4000000, or 8000000.<br><br>For the synchronous serial port adapters (PA-8T-V35, PA-8T-X21, PA-8T-232, and PA-4T+), a nonstandard clock rate can be used. You can enter any value from 300 to 8000000 bps. The clock rate you enter is rounded (adjusted), if necessary, to the nearest value your hardware can support, except for the following standard rates: 1200, 2400, 4800, 9600, 14400, 19200, 28800, 38400, 56000, 64000, 128000, or 2015232. |

### *Default*

No clock rate is configured.

### *Command Mode*

Interface configuration

### *Usage Guidelines*

This command first appeared in Cisco IOS Release 10.0.

This command was modified in Cisco IOS Release 11.3 to include nonstandard clock rates for the PA-8T-V35, PA-8T-X21, PA-8T-232, and PA-4T+ synchronous serial port adapters.

**Cable Length**

Be aware that the fastest speeds might not work if your cable is too long, and that speeds faster than 148,000 bits per second are too fast for EIA/TIA-232 signaling. It is recommended that you only use the synchronous serial EIA/TIA-232 signal at speeds up to 64,000 bits per second. To permit a faster speed, use EIA/TIA-449 or V.35.

**Synchronous Serial Port Adapters**

For the synchronous serial port adapters (PA-8T-V35, PA-8T-X21, PA-8T-232, and PA-4T+) on Cisco 7200 series routers, on second-generation Versatile Interface Processors (VIP2s) in Cisco 7500 series routers, and on Cisco 7000 series routers with RSP7000 and 7000 Series Chassis Interface (RSP7000CI), the clock rate you enter is rounded (if needed) to the nearest value that your hardware can support. To display the clock rate value for the port adapter, use the **show running-configuration** command.

If you plan to netboot your router over a synchronous serial port adapter interface and have a boot image prior to Cisco IOS Release 11.1(9)CA that does not support nonstandard (rounded) clock rates for the port adapters, you must use one of the following standard clock rates:

1200, 2400, 4800, 9600, 19200, 38400, 56000, 64000

### *Examples*

The following example sets the clock rate on the first serial interface to 64,000 bits per second:

```
interface serial 0
 clock rate 64000
```

The following example sets the clock rate on a synchronous serial port adapter in slot 5, port 0 to 1234567. In this example, the clock rate is adjusted to 1151526 bps.

```
interface serial 5/0
 clock rate 1234567
%Clockrate rounded to nearest value that your hardware can support.
%Use Exec Command 'show running-config' to see the value rounded to.
```

The following example configures serial interface 5/0 with a clock rate that is rounded to the nearest value that is supported by the hardware:

```
Router# configure terminal
Enter configuration commands, one per line.  End with CNTL/Z.
Router(config)# interface serial 5/0
Router(config-if)# clock rate 1234567
%Clockrate rounded to nearest value that your hardware can support.
%Use Exec Command 'show running-config' to see the value rounded to.
Router(config-if)# exit
Router(config)#
```

The following example shows how to determine the exact clock rate that the serial interface was rounded to using the **show running-config** command. This example shows only the relevant information displayed by the **show running-config** command; other information was omitted.

```
Router# show running-config
Building configuration...
...
!
interface Serial5/0
 no ip address
 clockrate 1151526
!
...
```

## CLOCK SOURCE (INTERFACE)

To control which clock a G.703 E1 interface will use to clock its transmitted data, use the **clock source** interface configuration command. Use the **no** form of this command to restore the default value.

**clock source {line | internal}**
**no clock source**

| *Syntax* | *Description* |
|---|---|
| **line** | Specifies that the interface will clock its transmitted data from a clock recovered from the line's receive data stream (default). |
| **internal** | Specifies that the interface will clock its transmitted data from its internal clock. |

### *Default*

By default, the clock source is the line's receive data stream.

### *Command Mode*

Interface configuration

### *Usage Guidelines*

This command first appeared in Cisco IOS Release 10.3.

This command applies to a Cisco 4000 router or Cisco 7000 series routers with RSP7000 and Cisco 7500 series router. A G.703-E1 interface can clock its transmitted data from either its internal clock or from a clock recovered from the line's receive data stream.

*Example*

The following example specifies the G.703-E1 interface to clock its transmitted data from its internal clock:

```
clock source internal
```

## COMPRESS

To configure software compression for Link Access Procedure, Balanced (LAPB), and High-Level Data Link Control (HDLC) encapsulations, use the **compress** interface configuration command. To disable compression, use the **no** form of this command.

**compress [predictor | stac]**
**no compress [predictor | stac]**

| *Syntax* | *Description* |
|---|---|
| **predictor** | (Optional) Specifies that a predictor compression algorithm will be used. |
| **stac** | (Optional) Specifies that a Stacker (LZS) compression algorithm will be used. |

*Default*

Compression is disabled.

*Command Mode*

Interface configuration

*Usage Guidelines*

This command first appeared in Cisco IOS Release 10.0 (as **compress predictor**). The command, **compress predictor stac** first appeared in Cisco IOS Release 10.3.

**Point-to-Point Compression**

You can configure point-to-point software compression for all LAPB, PPP, and HDLC encapsulations. Compression reduces the size of frames via lossless data compression. The compression algorithm used is a predictor algorithm (the RAND compression algorithm), which uses a compression dictionary to predict what the next character in the frame will be.

**HDLC Encapsulations**

For HDLC encapsulations, you can specify a Stacker compression algorithm by using the **stac** keyword. PPP and LAPB encapsulations support both predictor and Stacker compression algorithms.

### System Performance

Compression is performed in software and may significantly affect system performance. It is recommended that you disable compression if CPU load exceeds 65 percent. To display the CPU load, use the **show process cpu** EXEC command.

If the majority of your traffic is already compressed files, it is recommended that you not use compression. If the files are already compressed, the additional processing time spent in attempting unsuccessfully to compress them again will slow system performance.

**NOTES**

The best performance data compression algorithms adjust their compression methodology as they identify patterns in the data. To prevent data loss and support this adjustment process, the compression algorithm is run over LAPB to ensure that everything is sent in order, with no missing data and no duplicate data.

### Public Data Network Connections

Compression requires that both ends of the serial link be configured to use compression. You should never enable compression for connections to a public data network.

Table 14–1 provides general guidelines for deciding which compression type to select for LAPB encapsulations.

**Table 14–1** *Compression Guidelines for LAPB Encapsulations*

| Compression Type To Use | Situation |
|---|---|
| Predictor | The bottleneck is caused by the load on the router or access server. |
| Stacker | The bottleneck is the result of line bandwidth. |
| None | Most files are already compressed. |

Stacker compression for LAPB encapsulations reaches its performance ceiling on T1 lines; it is not recommended for faster lines because the added processing slows their performance. Stacker compression processing might be slower on other systems than on the Cisco 4500 routers.

When using predictor compression, you can adjust the MTU for the serial interface and the LAPB maximum bits per frame (N1) parameter—as shown in the first example—to avoid informational diagnostics regarding excessive MTU or N1 sizes. However, you should not change those parameters when you use Stacker compression.

## *Examples*

The following example enables predictor compression on serial interface 0 for a LAPB link:

```
interface serial 0
 encapsulation lapb
```

```
compress predictor
mtu 1509
lapb n1 12072
```

The following example enables Stacker compression on serial interface 0 for a LAPB link. This example does not set the MTU size and the maximum bits per frame (N1); it is recommended that you not change those LAPB parameters for Stacker compression:

```
interface serial 0
 encapsulation lapb
 compress predictor
```

### *Related Commands*

Search online to find documentation for related commands.

**encapsulation lapb**
**encapsulation x25**
**show compress**
**show processes**

## crc4

To enable generation of CRC4 on the G.703 E1 port adapter on the FSIP, use the **crc4** interface configuration command. To disable this feature, use the **no** form of this command.

**crc4**
**no crc4**

### *Syntax Description*

This command has no arguments or keywords.

### *Default*

Disabled

### *Command Mode*

Interface configuration

### *Usage Guidelines*

This command applies to a Cisco 4000 router or Cisco 7000 series and Cisco 7500 series router. It is useful for checking data integrity while operating in framed mode. CRC4 provides additional protection for a frame alignment signal under noisy conditions. Refer to CCITT Recommendation G.704 for a definition of CRC4.

This command does not apply to the Cisco 7200 series.

### Example

The following example enables CRC4 generation on the G.703 E1 port adapter on the FSIP:

```
crc4
```

## CRC BITS 5

To enable generation of CRC5 (per ITU Recommendation G.704 and G.703) to improve data integrity, use the **crc bits** 5 interface configuration command. To disable this feature, use the **no** form of this command.

**crc bits** 5
**no crc bits** 5

### Syntax Description

This command has no arguments or keywords.

### Default

Disabled

### Command Mode

Interface configuration

### Usage Guidelines

This command first appeared in Cisco IOS Release 11.1 CA.

This command is available for the JT2 6.3-MHz serial port adapter (PA-2JT2) on second-generation Versatile Interface Processor (VIP2) in Cisco 7500 series routers and in Cisco 7000 series routers with the 7000 Series Route Switch Processor (RSP7000) and 7000 Series Chassis Interface (RSP7000CI).

This command is useful for checking data integrity while operating in framed mode. CRC5 provides additional protection for a frame alignment signal under noisy conditions. For data transmission at JT2 (6.312 Mbps), the G.704 standard suggests 5 bits CRC. Refer to ITU Recommendation G.704 for a definition of CRC5.

You can also use the **crc bits** 5 command to set the CRC size for the HDLC controllers.

### Example

The following example enables CRC 5 generation on the PA-2JT2 port adapter and also sets the CRC size to 32 bits:

```
interface Serial 0/0
 crc 32
 crc bits 5
```

## DCE-TERMINAL-TIMING ENABLE

When running the line at high speeds and long distances, use the **dce-terminal-timing enable** interface configuration command to prevent phase shifting of the data with respect to the clock. If SCTE is not available from the DTE, use **no** form of this command, which causes the DCE to use its own clock rather than SCTE from the DTE.

**dce-terminal-timing enable**
**no dce-terminal-timing enable**

### *Syntax Description*

This command has no keywords or arguments.

### *Default*

DCE uses its own clock.

### *Command Mode*

Interface configuration

### *Usage Guidelines*

This command first appeared in Cisco IOS Release 10.0.

On the Cisco 4000 platform, you can specify the serial Network Interface Module timing signal configuration. When the board is operating as a DCE and the DTE provides terminal timing (SCTE or TT), the **dce-terminal-timing enable** command causes the DCE to use SCTE from the DTE.

### *Example*

The following example prevents phase shifting of the data with respect to the clock:

```
interface serial 0
 dce-terminal-timing enable
```

## DESCRIPTION (INTERFACE)

To add a description to an interface configuration, use the **description** interface configuration command. Use the **no** form of this command to remove the description.

**description** *string*
**no description**

| *Syntax* | *Description* |
|---|---|
| *string* | Comment or a description to help you remember what is attached to this interface. |

### Default

No description is added.

### Command Mode

Interface configuration

### Usage Guidelines

The **description** command is meant solely as a comment to be put in the configuration to help you remember what certain interfaces are used for. The description appears in the output of the following EXEC commands: **show startup-config**, **show interfaces**, and **show running-config**.

### Example

The following example shows how to add a description for a T1 interface:

```
interface serial 0
 description Fractional T1 line to Mountain View -- 128 Kb/s
```

### Related Commands

Search online to find documentation for related commands.

**show interfaces**
**show running-config**
**show startup-config**

## DTE-INVERT-TXC

On the Cisco 4000 series, you can specify the serial Network Processor Module timing signal configuration. When the board is operating as a DTE, the **dte-invert-txc** command inverts the TXC clock signal it gets from the DCE that the DTE uses to transmit data. Use the **no** form of this command if the DCE accepts SCTE from the DTE.

**dte-invert-txc**
**no dte-invert-txc**

### Syntax Description

This command has no arguments or keywords.

### Default

Disabled

### Command Mode

Interface configuration

### Usage Guidelines

This command first appeared in Cisco IOS Release 10.0.

Use this command if the DCE cannot receive SCTE from the DTE, the data is running at high speeds, and the transmission line is long. This prevents phase shifting of the data with respect to the clock.

If the DCE accepts SCTE from the DTE, use **no dte-invert-txc**.

### Example

The following example inverts the TXC on serial interface 0:

```
interface serial 0
 dte-invert-txc
```

## ENCAPSULATION

To set the encapsulation method used by a serial interface, use the **encapsulation** interface configuration command.

**encapsulation** *encapsulation-type*

| Syntax | Description |
|---|---|
| *encapsulation-type* | Encapsulation type; one of the following keywords:<br>**hdlc**—High-Level Data Link Control (HDLC) protocol for serial interface. This encapsulation method provides the synchronous framing and error-detection functions of HDLC without windowing or retransmission. This is the default.<br>**ppp**—Point-to-Point Protocol (PPP) (for serial interface). |

### Default

The default depends on the type of interface. For example, synchronous serial interface defaults to HDLC.

### Command Mode

Interface configuration

### Usage Guidelines

This command first appeared in Cisco IOS Release 10.0.

To use PPP, the router or access server must be configured with an IP routing protocol or with the **ip host-routing** command.

### Examples

The following example resets HDLC serial encapsulation on serial interface 1:

```
interface serial 1
 encapsulation hdlc
```

The following example enables PPP encapsulation on serial interface 0:

```
interface serial 0
 encapsulation ppp
```

### Related Commands

Search online to find documentation for related commands.

**keepalive**

**ppp**

**ppp authentication**

## IGNORE-DCD

Use the **ignore-dcd** interface configuration command to configure the serial interface to monitor the DSR signal (rather than the DCD signal) as the line up/down indicator. Use the **no** form of this command to restore the default behavior.

**ignore-dcd**
**no ignore-dcd**

### Syntax Description

This command has no arguments or keywords.

### Default

The serial interface, operating in DTE mode, monitors the DCD signal as the line up/down indicator.

### Command Mode

Interface configuration

### Usage Guidelines

This command first appeared in Cisco IOS Release 11.0.

This command applies to Quad Serial NIM interfaces on the Cisco 4000 series routers and Hitachi-based serial interfaces on the Cisco 2500 and 3000 series routers.

**Serial Interfaces in DTE Mode**

When the serial interface is operating in DTE mode, it monitors the Data Carrier Detect (DCD) signal as the line up/down indicator. By default, the attached DCE device sends the DCD signal. When the DTE interface detects the DCD signal, it changes the state of the interface to up.

**SDLC Multidrop Environments**

In some configurations, such as an SDLC multidrop environment, the DCE device sends the Data Set Ready (DSR) signal rather than the DCD signal, which prevents the interface from coming up. Use this command to tell the interface to monitor the DSR signal instead of the DCD signal as the line up/down indicator.

### *Example*

The following example configures serial interface 0 to monitor the DSR signal as the line up/down indicator:

```
interface serial 0
 ignore-dcd
```

## INVERT TXCLOCK

Use the **invert txclock** interface configuration command to invert the transmit clock signal. To return the transmit clock signal to its initial state, use the **no** form of this command.

**invert txclock**
**no invert txclock**

### *Syntax Description*

This command has no arguments or keywords.

### *Default*

Transmit clock signal is not inverted.

### *Command Mode*

Interface configuration

### *Usage Guidelines*

This command first appeared in Cisco IOS Release 10.0.

This command was modified in Cisco IOS Release 11.3 to change the command from **invert-transmit-clock** to **invert txclock**.

Delays between the SCTE clock and data transmission indicate that the transmit clock signal might not be appropriate for the interface rate and length of cable being used. Different ends of the wire can have variances that differ slightly. The **invert txclock** command compensates for these variances. This command replaces the **invert data** command.

This command applies only to the Cisco 7000 series routers equipped with the Cisco 7000 Series Route Switch Processor (RSP7000) and 7000 Series Chassis Interface (RSP7000CI), Cisco 7200 series, and Cisco 7500 series routers.

Systems that use long cables or cables that are not transmitting the TxC signal (transmit echoed clock line, also known as TXCE or SCTE clock) can experience high error rates when operating at the higher transmission speeds. For example, if a PA-8T synchronous serial port adapter is reporting a high number of error packets, a phase shift might be the problem. Inverting the clock might correct this shift.

When a PA-8T or PA-4T+ port adapter interface is DTE, the **invert txclock** command inverts the TxC signal it received from the remote DCE. When the PA-8T or PA-4T+ port adapter interface is DCE, this command changes the signal back to its original phase.

### *Example*

In the following example, the clock signal on serial interface 3/0 is inverted:

```
interface serial 3/0
 invert txclock
```

## NRZI-ENCODING

Use the **nrzi-encoding** interface configuration command to enable nonreturn-to-zero inverted (NRZI) line-coding format. Use the **no** form of this command to disable this capability.

**nrzi-encoding**
**no nrzi-encoding**
**nrzi-encoding [mark]** (Cisco 7000 series routers with RSP7000, Cisco 7200 series routers, and Cisco 7500 series routers)

| *Syntax* | *Description* |
|---|---|
| **mark** | (Optional) Specifies that NRZI mark encoding is required on the PA-8T and PA-4T+ synchronous serial port adapters on the Cisco 7000 series routers with RSP7000, Cisco 7200 and 7500 series routers. If mark is not specified, NRZI space encoding is used. |

### *Default*

Disabled

### *Command Mode*

Interface configuration

### *Usage Guidelines*

This command first appeared in Cisco IOS Release 10.0.

This command was modified in Cisco IOS Release 11.3 to include the **mark** keyword.

All FSIP, PA-8T, and PA-4T+ interface types support nonreturn-to-zero (NRZ) and nonreturn-to-zero inverted (NRZI) format. This is a line-coding format that is required for serial connections in some environments. NRZ encoding is most common. NRZI encoding is used primarily with EIA/TIA-232 connections in IBM environments.

### *Examples*

In the following example, serial interface 1 is configured for NRZI encoding:

```
interface serial 1
 nrzi-encoding
```

In the following example, serial interface 3/1/0 is configured for NRZI mark encoding:

```
interface serial 3/1/0
 nrzi-encoding mark
```

## PULSE-TIME

To enable pulsing DTR signal intervals on the serial interfaces, use the **pulse-time** interface configuration command. Use the **no** form of this command to restore the default interval.

**pulse-time** *seconds*
**no pulse-time**

| *Syntax* | *Description* |
|---|---|
| *seconds* | Integer that specifies the DTR signal interval in seconds. |

### *Default*

0 seconds

### *Command Mode*

Interface configuration

### *Usage Guidelines*

This command first appeared in Cisco IOS Release 10.0.

When the serial line protocol goes down (for example, because of loss of synchronization) the interface hardware is reset and the DTR signal is held inactive for at least the specified interval. This function is useful for handling encrypting or other similar devices that use the toggling of the DTR signal to resynchronize.

### *Example*

The following example enables DTR pulse signals for three seconds on serial interface 2:

```
interface serial 2
 pulse-time 3
```

### TIMESLOT

To enable framed mode serial interface on a G.703 E1 port adapter on an FSIP, use the **timeslot** interface configuration command. To restore the default, use the **no** form of this command or set the start slot to 0.

**timeslot** *start-slot* – *stop-slot*
**no timeslot**

| *Syntax* | *Description* |
|---|---|
| *start-slot* | The first subframe in the major frame. Range is 1 to 31 and must be less than or equal to *stop-slot*. |
| *stop-slot* | The last subframe in the major frame. Range is 1 to 31 and must be greater than or equal to *start-slot*. |

#### *Default*

A G.703 E1 interface is configured for unframed mode.

#### *Command Mode*

Interface configuration

#### *Usage Guidelines*

This command first appeared in Cisco IOS Release 10.3.

This command applies to a Cisco 4000 router or Cisco 7000 series and Cisco 7500 series router. G.703 E1 interfaces have two modes of operation: framed and unframed. When in framed mode, the range from *start-slot* to *stop-slot* gives the number of 64-Kbps slots in use. There are 32 64-Kbps slots available.

#### *Example*

The following example enables framed mode on a serial interface on a G.703 E1 port adapter:

```
timeslot 1-3
```

#### *Related Commands*

Search online to find documentation for related commands.

**ts16**

### TRANSMIT-CLOCK-INTERNAL

When a DTE does not return a transmit clock, use the **transmit-clock-internal** interface command to enable the internally generated clock on a serial interface on a Cisco 7000 series, Cisco 7200 series, or Cisco 7500 series. Use the **no** form of this command to disable the feature.

**transmit-clock-internal**
**no transmit-clock-internal**

*Syntax Description*

This command has no keywords or arguments.

*Default*

Disabled

*Command Mode*

Interface configuration

*Usage Guidelines*

This command first appeared in Cisco IOS Release 10.0.

*Example*

In the following example, the internally generated clock is enabled on serial interface 3/0 on a Cisco 7000 series or Cisco 7200 series router:

```
interface serial 3/0
 transmit-clock-internal
```

### TRANSMITTER-DELAY

To specify a minimum dead-time after transmitting a packet, use the **transmitter-delay** interface configuration command. The **no** form of this command restores the default.

**transmitter-delay** {*delay*}
**no transmitter-delay**

| *Syntax* | *Description* |
|---|---|
| *delay* | On the FSIP, HSSI, and on the IGS router, the minimum number of HDLC flags to be sent between successive packets. On all other serial interfaces and routers, approximate number of microseconds of minimum delay after transmitting a packet. The valid range is 0 to 131071. |

*Default*

0 flags or microseconds

*Command Mode*

Interface configuration

*Usage Guidelines*

This command first appeared in Cisco IOS Release 10.0.

This command is especially useful for serial interfaces that can send back-to-back data packets over serial interfaces faster than some hosts can receive them.

The transmitter delay feature is implemented for the following Token Ring cards: CSC-R16, CSC-R16M, CSC-1R, CSC-2R, and CSC-CTR. For the first four cards, the command syntax is the same as the existing command and specifies the number of milliseconds to delay between sending frames that are generated by the router. Transmitter delay for the CSC-CTR uses the same syntax but specifies a relative time interval to delay between transmission of all frames.

### *Example*

The following example specifies a delay of 300 microseconds on serial interface 0:

```
interface serial 0
 transmitter-delay 300
```

## TS16

To control the use of timeslot 16 for data on a G.703 E1 interface, use the **ts16** interface configuration command. To restore the default, use the **no** form of this command.

**ts16**
**no ts16**

### *Syntax Description*

This command has no arguments or keywords.

### *Default*

Timeslot 16 is used for signaling.

### *Command Mode*

Interface configuration

### *Usage Guidelines*

This command first appeared in Cisco IOS Release 10.3.

This command applies to a Cisco 4000 router or Cisco 7000 series and Cisco 7500 series router. By default, timeslot 16 is used for signaling. Use this command to configure timeslot 16 to be used for data. When in framed mode, in order to get all possible subframes or timeslots, you must use the **ts16** command.

### *Example*

The following example configures timeslot 16 to be used for data on a G.703 E1 interface:

```
ts16
```

### *Related Commands*

Search online to find documentation for related commands.

**timeslot**

# CHAPTER 15

# Configuring Channelized E1 and Channelized T1

Channelized T1 and channelized E1 can be configured for ISDN PRI, synchronous serial, and asynchronous serial communications.

Channelized T1 and channelized E1 are supported by corresponding controllers. Each T1 or E1 controller has one physical network termination, but it can have many virtual interfaces, depending on the configuration.

This chapter describes how to configure channelized E1 and channelized T1 for ISDN PRI and for two types of signaling to support analog calls over digital lines. It provides three main configuration sections:

- Configuring ISDN PRI
- Configuring Robbed-Bit Signaling for Analog Calls over T1 Lines (Cisco AS5200)
- Configuring Channel-Associated Signaling for Analog Calls over E1 Lines (Cisco AS5200)

In addition, this chapter describes how to run interface loopback diagnostics on channelized E1 and channelized T1 (see the section "Troubleshooting Channelized E1 and Channelized T1," later in this chapter).

For hardware technical descriptions, and for information about installing the controllers and interfaces, refer to the hardware installation and maintenance publication for your particular product.

For a complete description of the channelized E1/T1 commands in this chapter, see Chapter 16, "Channelized E1 and Channelized T1 Setup Commands."

## BACKGROUND INFORMATION

This section presents background information about signaling and about the use of channelized E1/T1 on the Cisco AS5200.

### About In-Band and Out-of-Band Signaling

The terms *in-band* and *out-of-band* indicate whether various signals—used to set up, control, and terminate calls—travel in the same channel (or band) with users' voice calls or data, or whether those signals travel a separate channel (or band).

ISDN, which uses the D channel for signaling and the B channels for user data, fits into the out-of-band signaling category.

Robbed-bit signaling, which uses bits from specified frames in the user data channel for signaling, fits into the in-band signaling category.

Channel-associated signaling, which uses E1 timeslot 16 (the D channel) for signaling, fits into the out-of-band signaling category.

### About Channelized E1 and T1 on the Cisco AS5200

On a Cisco AS5200, you can allocate the available channels for channelized E1 or T1 in the following ways:

- All channels can be configured to support ISDN PRI.
- If you are not running ISDN PRI, all channels can be configured to support robbed-bit signaling (also known as *channel-associated signaling*), which enables a Cisco AS5200 modem to receive and transmit analog calls.
- All channels can be configured in a single channel group.
- Mix and match channels supporting ISDN PRI and channel grouping.
- Mix and match channels supporting ISDN PRI, robbed-bit signaling, and channel grouping across the same T1 line. For example, on the same channelized T1 you can configure the **pri-group timeslots 1-10** command, **channel-group 11 timeslots 11-16** command, and **cas-group 17 timeslots 17-23 type e&m-fgb** command. This is a rare configuration because it requires you to align the correct range of timeslots on both ends of the connection.

See the "PRI Groups and Channel Groups on the Same Channelized T1 Controller Example," "Robbed-Bit Signaling Examples," and the "ISDN Channel-Associated Signaling Examples" sections at the end of this chapter for concrete illustrations.

## Configuring ISDN PRI

This section describes tasks that are required to get ISDN PRI up and running. This section does not address routing issues, dialer configuration, or dial backup. For information about those topics, see the chapters in Part V, "Dial-on-Demand Routing."

ISDN PRI is supported on the Cisco 7200 series and 7500 series routers using T1 or E1 versions of the Multichannel Interface Processor (MIP) card, on the Cisco 4000 series channelized E1/T1/PRI network processor module (NPM), and on the Cisco AS5200. Channelized T1 ISDN PRI offers

23 B channels and 1 D channel. Channelized E1 ISDN PRI offers 30 B channels and 1 D channel. Channel 24 is the D channel for T1, and channel 16 is the D channel for E1.

For a complete description of the commands mentioned in this chapter, see Chapter 16.

Perform the tasks in the following sections to configure ISDN PRI:

- Request PRI Line and Switch Configuration from a Telco Service Provider
- Configure Channelized E1 ISDN PRI
- Configure Channelized T1 ISDN PRI
- Configure the Serial Interface
- Configure NSF Call-by-Call Support
- Perform Configuration Self-Tests (optional)
- Monitor and Maintain ISDN PRI Interfaces (optional)

ISDN PRI examples are found at the end of the chapter.

**NOTES**

After the ISDN PRI interface and lines are operational, configure the D channel interface for DDR. The DDR configuration specifies the packets that can trigger outgoing calls, specifies whether to place or receive calls, and provides the protocol, address, and phone number to use.

For DDR configuration information, see Part V.

## Request PRI Line and Switch Configuration from a Telco Service Provider

Before configuring ISDN PRI on your Cisco router, you need to order a correctly provisioned ISDN PRI line from your telecommunications service provider.

This process varies dramatically from provider to provider on a national and international basis. However, some general guidelines follow:

- On a PRI, ask for the channels to be called in descending order.
- Ask for delivery of calling line identification. Providers sometimes call this *CLI* or *Automatic Number Identification* (ANI).
- If the router is to be attached to an ISDN bus (to which other ISDN devices might be attached), ask for point-to-multipoint service (subaddressing is required) and a voice-and-data line.

When you order ISDN service, request the PRI switch configuration attributes displayed in Table 15–1.

**Table 15–1** *PRI Switch Configuration Attributes to Request from Service Vendor*

| Attribute | Value |
|---|---|
| Line format | Extended Superframe Format (ESF) |
| Line coding | Binary 8-zero substitution (B8ZS) |
| Call type | 23 incoming channels and 23 outgoing channels |
| Speed | 64 Kbps |
| Call-by-call capability | Enabled |
| Channels | 23 B+D |
| Trunk selection sequence | Descending from 23 to 1 |
| B + D glare | Yield |
| Directory numbers | Only 1 directory number assigned by service provider |
| ISDN call speed outside local exchange | Speed set to 56 Kbps outside local exchange |
| SPIDs required? | None |

## Configure Channelized E1 ISDN PRI

To configure ISDN PRI on a channelized E1 controller, perform the following tasks, beginning in global configuration mode:

| Task | Command |
|---|---|
| Select a service provider switch type that accommodates PRI. (See Table 15–2 for a list of supported switch type keywords.) | **isdn switch-type** *switch-type* |
| Define the controller location in the Cisco7200 or Cisco 7500 series by slot and port number.<br>or<br>Define the controller location in the Cisco 4000 series or the Cisco AS5200 universal access server by unit number.* | **controller e1** *slot/port*<br><br>**controller e1** *number* |
| Define the framing characteristics as cyclic redundancy check 4 (CRC4). | **framing crc4** |
| Define the line code as high-density bipolar 3 (HDB3). | **linecode hdb3** |
| Configure ISDN PRI. | **pri-group** [**timeslots** *range*] |

* Controller numbers range 0 through 2 on the Cisco 4000 series and 1 to 2 on the Cisco AS5200.

**NOTES**

Any router configured for ISDN support must be connected to the same switch type on all its ISDN interfaces.

If you do not specify the timeslots, the specified controller is configured for 30 B channels and one D channel. The B channel numbers range 1 to 31; channel 16 is the D channel for E1. Corresponding serial interfaces numbers range 0 to 30. In commands, the D channel is **interface serial** *controller-number*:15. For example, **interface serial 0:15**.

**Table 15–2** *ISDN Service Provider PRI Switch Types*

| Keywords by Area | Switch Type |
|---|---|
| none | No switch defined |
| **Europe** | |
| primary-net5 | European ISDN PRI switches; covers the Euro-ISDN E-DSS1 signaling system and is ETSI-compliant. |
| **Japan** | |
| primary-ntt | Japanese ISDN PRI switches |
| **North America** | |
| primary-4ess | AT&T 4ESS switch type for the U.S. |
| primary-5ess | AT&T 5ESS switch type for the U.S. |
| primary-dms100 | NT DMS-100 switch type for the U.S. |

## Configure Channelized T1 ISDN PRI

To configure ISDN PRI on a channelized T1 controller, perform the following tasks beginning in global configuration mode:

| Task | Command |
|---|---|
| Select a service provider switch type that accommodates PRI. (Refer to Table 15–2 for a list of supported PRI switch type keywords.) | **isdn switch-type** *switch-type* |
| Specify a T1 controller on a Cisco 7500<br>or<br>Specify a T1 controller on a Cisco 4000.* | **controller t1** *slot/port*<br>or<br>**controller t1** *number* |
| Define the framing characteristics as Extended Superframe Format (ESF). | **framing esf** |

| Task | Command |
|---|---|
| Define the line code as binary 8 zero substitution (B8ZS). | **linecode b8zs** |
| Configure ISDN PRI.<br>If you do not specify the timeslots, this controller is configured for 23 B channels and 1 D channel. | **pri-group** [**timeslots** *range*][†] |

[*] Controller numbers range 0 through 2 on the Cisco 4000 series and 1 to 2 on the Cisco AS5200.
[†] On channelized T1, timeslots range 1 to 24. You can specify a range or timeslots (for example, **pri-group timeslots 12-24**) if other timeslots are used for non-PRI channel groups.

**NOTES**

Any router configured for ISDN support must be connected to the same switch type on all its ISDN interfaces.

If you do not specify the timeslots, the specified controller is configured for 24 B channels and one D channel. The B channel numbers range 1 to 24; channel 24 is the D channel for T1. Corresponding serial interfaces numbers range 0 to 23. In commands, the D channel is **interface serial** *controller-number*:23—for example, **interface serial 0:23.**

## Configure the Serial Interface

When you configure ISDN PRI on the channelized E1 or channelized T1 controller, in effect you create a serial interface that corresponds to the PRI group timeslots. This interface is a logical entity associated with the specific controller. After you create the serial interface by configuring the controller, you must configure the D channel serial interface. The configuration applies to all the PRI B channels (timeslots).

To configure the D channel serial interface, complete the tasks in the following sections:

- Specify an IP Address for the Interface
- Configure Encapsulation
- Configure Network Addressing
- Configure ISDN Calling Number Identification
- Configure Inclusion of the Sending Complete Information Element

### *Specify an IP Address for the Interface*

To configure the D channel serial interface created for ISDN PRI, complete the following tasks beginning in global configuration mode:

When you configure the D channel, its configuration is applied to all the individual B channels.

| Task | | Command |
|---|---|---|
| **Step 1** | Specify D channel on the serial interface for channelized T1. | **interface serial** *slot/port*:**23**<br>**interface serial** *number*:**23** |
| | Specify D channel on the serial interface for channelized E1. | **interface serial** *slot/port*:**15**<br>**interface serial** *number*:**15** |
| **Step 2** | Specify an IP address for the interface. | **ip address** *ip-address* |

### Configure Encapsulation

PPP encapsulation is configured for most ISDN communication. However, the router might require a different encapsulation for traffic sent over a Frame Relay or X.25 network, or the router might need to communicate with devices that require a different encapsulation protocol.

Configuring encapsulation is described in the following sections:

- Configure PPP Encapsulation
- Configure Encapsulation for Frame Relay or X.25 Networks
- Configure Encapsulation for Combinet Compatibility

In addition, the router can be configured for automatic detection of encapsulation type on incoming calls. To configure this feature, complete the tasks in the following section:

- Configure Automatic Detection of Encapsulation Type of Incoming Calls

#### Configure PPP Encapsulation

Each ISDN B channel is treated as a serial line and supports HDLC and PPP encapsulation. The default serial encapsulation is HDLC. To configure PPP encapsulation, perform the following task in interface configuration mode:

| Task | Command |
|---|---|
| Configure PPP encapsulation. | **encapsulation ppp** |

#### Configure Encapsulation for Frame Relay or X.25 Networks

If traffic from this ISDN interface crosses a Frame Relay or X.25 network, the appropriate addressing and encapsulation tasks must be completed as required for Frame Relay or X.25 networks.

#### Configure Encapsulation for Combinet Compatibility

Historically, Combinet devices supported only the Combinet Proprietary Protocol (CPP) for negotiating connections over ISDN B channels. To enable Cisco routers to communicate with those Combinet bridges, the Cisco IOS software supports a new CPP encapsulation type.

To enable routers to communicate over ISDN interfaces with Combinet bridges that support only CPP, perform the following tasks in interface configuration mode:

| Task | Command |
|---|---|
| Specify CPP encapsulation. | **encapsulation cpp** |
| Enable CPP callback acceptance. | **cpp callback accept** |
| Enable CPP authentication. | **cpp authentication** |

Now most Combinet devices support PPP. Cisco routers can communicate over ISDN with these devices by using PPP encapsulation, which supports both routing and fast switching.

Combinet devices support only IP, IPX, and bridging. For AppleTalk, Cisco routers automatically perform half-bridging with Combinet devices. For more information about half-bridging, see the section "Configure PPP Half-Bridging," in Chapter 25, "Configuring Media-Independent PPP and Multilink PPP."

Cisco routers can also half-bridge IP and IPX with Combinet devices that support only CPP. To configure this feature, you only need to set up the addressing with the ISDN interface as part of the remote subnet; no additional commands are required.

### *Configure Automatic Detection of Encapsulation Type of Incoming Calls*

You can enable a serial or ISDN interface to accept calls and dynamically change the encapsulation in effect on the interface when the remote device does not signal the call type. For example, if an ISDN call does not identify the call type in the Lower Layer Compatibility fields and is using an encapsulation that is different from the one configured on the interface, the interface can change its encapsulation type at that time.

This feature enables interoperation with ISDN terminal adapters that use V.120 encapsulation but do not signal V.120 in the call setup message. An ISDN interface that by default answers a call as synchronous serial with PPP encapsulation can change its encapsulation and answer such calls.

Automatic detection is attempted for the first 10 seconds after the link is established or the first five packets exchanged over the link, whichever is first.

To enable automatic detection of encapsulation type, perform the following task in interface configuration mode:

| Task | Command |
|---|---|
| Enable automatic detection of encapsulation type on the specified interface. | **autodetect encapsulation** *encapsulation-type* |

You can specify one or more encapsulations to detect. Cisco IOS software currently supports automatic detection of PPP and V.120 encapsulations.

### *Configure Network Addressing*

When you configure networking, you specify how to reach the remote recipient. To configure network addressing, complete the following tasks beginning in interface configuration mode:

| Task | | Command |
|---|---|---|
| **Step 1** | Define the remote recipient's protocol address, host name, and dialing string; optionally, provide the ISDN subaddress; set the dialer speed to 56 or 64 Kbps, as needed.<br>or<br>(Australia) Use the **spc** keyword that enables ISDN semipermanent connections. | **dialer map** *protocol next-hop-address* **name** *hostname* **speed 56\|64** *dial-string*[*:isdn-subaddress*]<br><br>**dialer map** *protocol next-hop-address* **name** *hostname* **spc** [**speed 56 \| 64**] [**broadcast**] *dial-string*[*:isdn-subaddress*] |
| **Step 2** | Assign the interface to a dialer group to control access to the interface. | **dialer-group** *group-number* |
| **Step 3** | Associate the dialer group number with an access list number. | **dialer-list** *dialer-group* **list** *access-list-number* |
| **Step 4** | Define an access list permitting or denying access to specified protocols, sources, or destinations. | **access-list** *access-list-number* {**deny \| permit**} *protocol source address source-mask destination destination-mask* |

Australian networks allow semipermanent connections between customer routers with PRIs and the TS-014 ISDN PRI switches in the exchange. Semipermanent connections are offered at better pricing than leased lines.

Packets that are permitted by the access list specified in Step 4 are considered interesting and cause the router to place a call to the destination protocol address that is identified in both Step 1 and Step 4.

**NOTES**

The access list reference in Step 4 of this task list is an example of the access list commands allowed by different protocols. Some protocols might require a different command form or might require multiple commands.

For more information about defining outgoing call numbers, see Chapter 40, "Configuring Legacy DDR Spokes," Chapter 42, "Configuring Legacy DDR Hubs," Chapter 44, "Configuring Peer-to-Peer DDR with Dialer Profiles," and Chapter 48, "Configuring Dial Backup with Dialer Profiles."

### *Configure ISDN Calling Number Identification*

A router might need to supply the ISDN network with a billing number for outgoing calls. Some networks offer better pricing on calls in which the number is presented. When configured, the calling number information is included in the outgoing Setup message.

To configure the interface to identify the billing number, perform the following task in interface configuration mode:

| Task | Command |
|---|---|
| Specify the calling party number. | **isdn calling-number** *calling-number* |

This command can be used with all ISDN PRI switch types.

### *Configure Inclusion of the Sending Complete Information Element*

In some geographic locations, such as Hong Kong and Taiwan, ISDN switches require that the Sending Complete information element be included in the outgoing Setup message to indicate that the entire number is included. This information element is not required in other locations.

To configure the interface to include the Sending Complete information element in the outgoing call Setup message, complete the following task in interface configuration mode:

| Task | Command |
|---|---|
| Include the Sending Complete information element in the outgoing call Setup message. | **isdn sending-complete** |

### Configure NSF Call-by-Call Support

Network-Specific Facilities (NSF) are used to request a particular service from the network or to provide an indication of the service being provided. Call-by-call support means that a B channel can be used for any service; its use is not restricted to a certain preconfigured service, such as incoming 800 calls or outgoing 800 calls. This specific NSF call-by-call service supports outgoing calls configured as voice calls.

This NSF call-by-call support feature is vendor-specific; only routers connected to AT&T Primary-4ESS switches need to configure this feature. This feature is supported on channelized T1.

To enable the router for NSF call-by-call support and, optionally, to place outgoing voice calls, complete the following steps:

**Step 1** Configure the controller for ISDN PRI.

**Step 2** Configure the D channel interface to place outgoing calls, using the **dialer map** command with a dialing-plan keyword. You can enter a **dialer map** command for each dialing plan to be supported.

**Step 3** Define the dialer map class for that dialing plan.

To define the dialer map class for the dialing plan, complete the following tasks beginning in global configuration mode:

| Task | | Command |
|---|---|---|
| **Step 1** | Specify the dialer map class, using the dialing-plan keyword as the classname. | **map-class dialer** *classname* |
| **Step 2** | (Optional) Enable voice calls. | **dialer voice-call** |
| **Step 3** | Configure the specific dialer map class to make outgoing calls. | **dialer outgoing** *classname* |

**NOTES**

To set the called-party type to international, the dialed number must be prefaced by 011.

Table 15–3 lists the NSF dialing plans and supported services offered on AT&T Primary-4ESS switches.

**Table 15–3** *NSF Supported Services on AT&T Primary-4ESS Switches*

| NSF Dialing Plan | Data | Voice | International |
|---|---|---|---|
| Software Defined Network (SDN)* | Yes | Yes | GSDN (Global SDN) |
| MEGACOMM | No | Yes | Yes |
| ACCUNET | Yes | Yes | Yes |

* The dialing plan terminology in this table is defined and used by AT&T.

## Perform Configuration Self-Tests

To test the router's ISDN configuration, it is suggested that you perform the following tasks:

| Task | Command |
|---|---|
| Check Layer 1 (physical layer) of the PRI over T1. | **show controllers t1** *slot/port* |
| Check Layer 1 (physical layer) of the PRI over E1. | **show controllers e1** *slot/port* |
| Check Layer 2 (data link layer). | **debug q921** |
| Check Layer 3 (network layer). | **debug isdn events**<br>debug q931<br>**debug dialer**<br>**show dialer** |

### Monitor and Maintain ISDN PRI Interfaces

Use the following commands to monitor and maintain ISDN interfaces:

| Task | Command |
|---|---|
| Display information about the physical attributes of the ISDN PRI over T1 B and D channels. | **show interfaces serial** *slot/port* **bchannel** *channel-number* (Cisco 7500 series )<br><br>**show interfaces serial** *number* **bchannel** *channel-number* (Cisco 4000 series) |
| Display information about the physical attributes of the ISDN PRI over E1 B and D channels. | **show interfaces serial** *slot/port* **bchannel** *channel-number* (Cisco 7500 series)<br><br>**show interfaces serial** *number* **bchannel** *channel-number* (Cisco 4000 series) |
| Display information about the T1 links supported on the ISDN PRI B and D channels. | **show controllers t1** [*slot/port*] (Cisco 7500 series)<br><br>**show controller t1** *number* (Cisco 4000 series) |
| Display information about the E1 links supported on the ISDN PRI B and D channels. | **show controllers e1** [*slot/port*] (Cisco 7500 series)<br><br>**show controllers e1** *number* (Cisco 4000 series) |
| Display information about current calls, history, memory, services, status of PRI channels, or Layer 2 or Layer 3 timers. (The **service** keyword is available for PRI only.) | **show isdn** {**active** \| **history** \| **memory** \| **services** \| **status** [*dsl* \| **serial** *number*] \| **timers**} |
| Obtain general diagnostic information about the specified interface. | **show dialer** [**interface** *type number*] |

## Configuring Robbed-Bit Signaling for Analog Calls over T1 Lines

The Cisco AS5200 supports robbed-bit signaling for receiving and transmitting analog calls on T1 lines. Robbed-bit signaling emulates older analog trunk and line in-band signaling methods that are transmitted in many networks.

In countries that support T1 framing (such as the United States and Canada), many networks send supervisory and signaling information to each other by removing the 8th bit of each timeslot of the 6th and 12th frame for superframe (SF) framing. For networks supporting extended superframe (ESF) framing, the 6th, 12th, 18th, and 24th frames are affected. This is done to support channel banks in the network that convert various battery and ground operations on analog lines into signaling bits that are forwarded over digital lines.

Robbed-bit signaling configured on the Cisco AS5200 enables the integrated modems in the access server to answer and transmit analog calls. To support analog signaling over T1 lines on the Cisco AS5200, robbed-bit signaling must be enabled.

**NOTES**

The signal type configured on the access server must match the signal type offered by your telco provider. Ask your telco provider which signal type to configure on each T1 controller.

The Cisco AS5200 has two controllers—controller T1 1 and controller T1 0—that must be configured individually.

To configure robbed-bit signaling support for calls made and received, perform the following tasks beginning in global configuration mode:

| Task | | Command |
|---|---|---|
| **Step 1** | Enable the T1 0 controller, and enter controller configuration mode. | **controller t1 0** |
| **Step 2** | If the channelized T1 line connects to a smart jack instead of a CSU, set pulse equalization (use parameter values specified by your telco service provider). | **cablelength long** *dbgain-value dbloss-value* |
| **Step 3** | Set the framing to match your telco service provider's offering, which in most cases is *esf*. | **framing esf** |
| **Step 4** | Set the line code type to match your telco service provider's offering, which in most cases is *b8zs*. | **linecode b8zs** |
| **Step 5** | Configure one T1 line to serve as the primary or most stable clock source line. | **clock source line primary** |
| **Step 6** | Configure channels to accept voice calls.<br>This step creates interfaces that you can configure. | **cas-group** *channel-number* **timeslots** *range* **type** *signal-type* |
| **Step 7** | Set the facilities data link exchange standard for the CSU, as specified by your telco service provider. | **fdl** {**att** \| **ansi**} |

If you want to configure robbed-bit signaling on the other T1 controller, repeat Steps 1 through 7, making sure in Step 5 to select T1 controller 1's line as the secondary clock source.

If you want to configure ISDN on the other controller, see the "Configuring ISDN PRI" section of this chapter. If you want to configure channel groupings on the other controller, see Chapter 13, "Configuring Synchronous Serial Ports"; specify the channel groupings when you specify the interface.

## Configuring Channel-Associated Signaling for Analog Calls over E1 Lines

The Cisco AS5200 Universal Access Server now supports channel-associated signaling for channelized E1 lines, which are commonly deployed in networks in Latin America, Asia, and Europe. Channel-associated signaling is configured to support channel banks in the network that convert various battery and ground operations on analog lines into signaling bits, which are forwarded over digital lines.

Channel-associated signaling is call signaling that is configured on an E1 controller and enables the access server to send or receive analog calls. The signaling uses the16th channel (timeslot); thus, channel-associated signaling fits in the out-of-band signaling category.

Once channel-associated signaling is configured on a single E1 controller, up to 30 remote users can simultaneously dial in to the Cisco AS5200 through networks running the R2 protocol. The R2 protocol is an international signaling standard for analog connections. Because R2 signaling is not supported in the Cisco AS5200, an E1-to-E1 converter is required. Refer to Figure 15–1.

Because the Cisco AS5200 has two physical E1 ports on its dual E1 PRI board, up to 60 simultaneous connections can be made through one dual E1 PRI board.

*Figure 15–1 Remote PC Accessing Network Resources through the Cisco AS5200.*

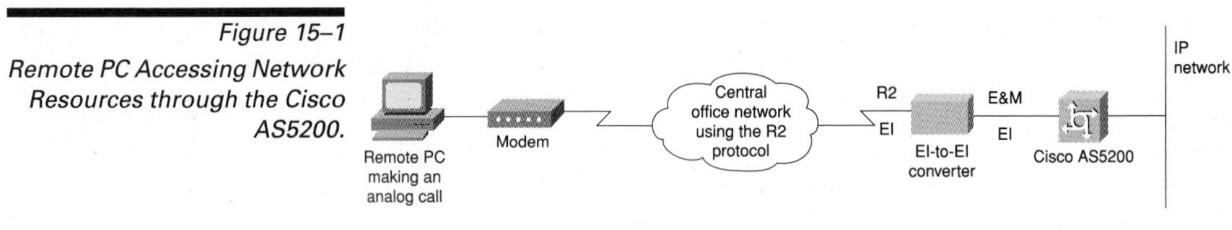


**Notes**

For information on how to configure an Anadigicom E1-to-E1 converter, refer to the documentation that came with the converter.

### Prerequisites

The dual E1 PRI card must be installed in the Cisco AS5200 before you attempt to configure channel-associated signaling.

### Channel-Associated Signaling Configuration Tasks

To configure the Cisco AS5200's E1 controllers, perform the following tasks, beginning in global configuration mode. If you do not specify the timeslots, channel-associated signaling is configured on all 30 B channels and one D channel on the specified controller.

| Task | | Command |
|---|---|---|
| **Step 1** | Define the controller location in the Cisco AS5200 by unit number, ranging from 1 to 2. | **controller e1** *number* |
| **Step 2** | Configure channel-associated signaling and the R2 signaling protocol on a specified number of timeslots. | **cas-group** *channel-number* **timeslots** *range* **type** *signal-type* |
| **Step 3** | Define the framing characteristics as cyclic redundancy check 4 (CRC4). | **framing crc4** |
| **Step 4** | Define the line code as high-density bipolar 3 (HDB3). | **linecode hdb3** |
| **Step 5** | Specify one E1 line to serve as the primary or most stable clock source line. | **clock source line primary*** |

* Specify the other E1 line as the secondary clock source with the **clock source line secondary** command.

## TROUBLESHOOTING CHANNELIZED E1 AND CHANNELIZED T1

When troubleshooting channelized T1 or E1, you must first determine if the problem is with a particular channel group or with the T1 or E1 line.

If the problem is with a single channel group, you have a potential interface problem. If the problem is with the T1 or E1 line, or with all channel groups, you have a potential controller problem.

The following sections describe how to determine whether the problem affects an interface or a controller.

### Troubleshooting Channelized E1 and T1 Controllers

When you troubleshoot E1 or T1 controllers, first check that the configuration is correct. The framing type and line code should match to what the service provider has specified. Then check channel-group and PRI-group configurations, especially to verify that the timeslots and speeds are what the service provider has specified.

At this point, the **show controller t1** or **show controller e1** commands should be used to check for T1 or E1 errors. Use the command several times to determine if error counters are increasing, or if the line status is continually changing. If this is occurring, you need to work with the service provider.

**NOTES**

Cisco routers do not have CSU capability and do not react to any remote loopback codes at the T1 or E1 level.

#### *Running Controller Loopback Diagnostic Tests*

Controller loopback tests are available for channelized T1 controllers and for channelized E1 controllers.

### *Channelized T1 Controller Loopbacks*

For the T1 controller, two loopbacks are available for testing:

- Local loopback
- Remote loopback

**Local Loopback:** The local loopback loops the controller both toward the router and toward the line. Because the loopback is done internally to the router, the controller should transition to the UP state within approximately 10 seconds, and no further T1 errors should be detected.

All channel groups will be looped back; if the encapsulation on that channel group supports loopbacks (for example, HDLC and PPP), you can test that channel group by pinging the interface address. For example, if you have assigned an IP address to the serial interface defined for a channel group, you can ping that IP address.

To place the controller into local loopback, perform the following task in controller configuration mode:

| Task | Command |
|---|---|
| Loop the T1 controller toward the router and toward the line. | **loopback local** (controller) |

To test a channel group, perform the following task in EXEC mode:

| | |
|---|---|
| Ping the interface address. | **ping** *protocol protocol-address* |

Check errors by performing the following task in EXEC mode:

| | |
|---|---|
| Check errors. | **show controller t1** |

If any errors occur, or the controller fails to change to the UP state, contact the Cisco Technical Assistance Center (TAC).

Since the controller local loopback is bidirectional, the service provider can test the line integrity using a T1 BERT test set.

**Remote Loopback:** The second T1 controller loopback is a remote loopback. This loopback can be used only if the *entire* T1 goes to a remote CSU. This is not the case with 99.9% of channelized T1. When the **loopback remote** controller command is executed, an inband CSU loop-up code will be sent over the entire T1, which will attempt to loop up the remote CSU. To place the controller in remote loopback, perform the following task in controller configuration mode:

| Task | Command |
|---|---|
| Place the T1 controller in remote loopback. | **loopback remote** (controller) |

**NOTES**

If controller loopbacks are used, they will disrupt service for all channel groups on that interface.

### *Channelized E1 Controller Loopback*

For the E1 controller, only the local loopback is available. Local loopback operates the same as the local loopback on the T1 controller, forming a bidirectional loopback, both toward the router and toward the line. To place the E1 controller in local loopback, perform the following task in controller configuration mode:

| Task | Command |
|---|---|
| Place the E1 controller in local loopback toward the router and toward the line. | **loopback** (controller) |

All channel groups will be looped back; if the encapsulation on that channel group supports loopbacks (for example, HDLC and PPP), you can test that channel group by pinging the interface address. For example, if you have assigned an IP address to the serial interface defined for a channel group, you can ping that IP address.

To place the controller into local loopback, perform the following task in controller configuration mode:

| Task | Command |
|---|---|
| Loop the T1 controller toward the router and toward the line. | **loopback local** (controller) |

To test a channel group, perform the following task in EXEC mode:

| | |
|---|---|
| Ping the interface address. | **ping** *protocol protocol-address* |

Check errors if any by performing the following task in EXEC mode:

| | |
|---|---|
| Check errors. | **show controller t1** |

If any errors occur, it is most likely a hardware problem; contact the Cisco TAC. In addition, you can ask the service provider to test the line by using a T1 BERT test set.

### Troubleshooting Channelized E1/T1 Channel Groups

Each channelized T1 or channelized E1 channel group is treated as a separate serial interface. To troubleshoot channel groups, first verify configurations and check everything that is normally checked for serial interfaces. You can verify that the timeslots and speed are correct for the channel group by checking for CRC errors and aborts on the incoming line.

**NOTES**

None of the Cisco channelized interfaces will react to any loop codes. To loop a channelized interface requires that the configuration command be entered manually.

Two loopbacks are available for channel groups:

- Interface local loopback
- Interface remote loopback

#### *Interface Local Loopback*

Interface local loopback is a bidirectional loopback, which will loopback toward the router and toward the line. The entire set of timeslots for the channel group are looped back. The service provider can use a BERT test set to test the link from the central office to your local router, or the remote router can test using pings to their local interface (which will go from the remote site, looped back at your local site, and return to the interface on the remote site).

To place the serial interface (channel group) into local loopback, perform the following task in interface configuration mode:

| Task | Command |
|---|---|
| Place the serial interface (channel group) in local loopback. | **loopback local** |

#### *Interface Remote Loopback*

Remote loopback is the ability to put the remote DDS CSU/DSU in loopback. It will work only with channel groups that have a single DS0 (1 timeslot), and with equipment that works with a latched CSU loopback as specified in AT&T specification TR-TSY-000476, "OTGR Network Maintenance Access and Testing." To place the serial interface (channel group) in remote loopback, perform the following task in interface configuration mode:

| Task | Command |
|---|---|
| Place the serial interface (channel group) in remote loopback. | **loopback remote** (interface) |

Using the **loopback remote** interface command sends a latched CSU loopback command to the remote CSU/DSU. The router must detect the response code, at which time the remote loopback is verified.

## CHANNELIZED E1 AND CHANNELIZED T1 CONFIGURATION EXAMPLES

This section contains the following groups of examples:

- ISDN PRI Examples
- PRI Groups and Channel Groups on the Same Channelized T1 Controller Example
- Robbed-Bit Signaling Examples
- ISDN Channel-Associated Signaling Examples

### ISDN PRI Examples

This section contains the following ISDN PRI examples:

- NSF Call-by-Call Support Example
- PRI on a Cisco AS5200 Examples

#### *NSF Call-by-Call Support Example*

The following example configures Network-Specific Facility (NSF), needed for an AT&T 4ESS switch when it is configured for Call-by-Call selection. The PRI 4ESS switch expects some AT&T-specific information when placing outgoing ISDN PRI voice calls; the options are accunet, sdn, and megacom.

This example shows both the controller and interface commands required to make the ISDN interface operational and the DDR commands, such as the **dialer map**, **dialer-group**, and map-class dialer commands, that are needed to configure the ISDN interface to make outgoing calls.

```
! The following lines configure the channelized T1 controller; all timeslots are
! configured for ISDN PRI.
!
controller t1 1/1
 framing esf
 linecode b8zs
 pri-group timeslots 1-23
 isdn switchtype primary-4ess
!
! The following lines configure the D channel for DDR. This configuration applies
! to all B channels on the ISDN PRI interface.
!
interface serial 1/1:23
 description Will mark outgoing calls from AT&T type calls.
 ip address 7.1.1.1 255.255.255.0
 encapsulation ppp
 dialer map ip 7.1.1.2 name tommyjohn class sdnplan 14193460913
 dialer map ip 7.1.1.3 name angus class megaplan 14182616900
 dialer map ip 7.1.1.4 name angus class accuplan 14193453730
```

```
dialer-group 1
 ppp authentication chap

map-class dialer sdnplan
 dialer outgoing sdn

map-class dialer megaplan
 dialer voice-call
 dialer outgoing mega

map-class dialer accuplan
 dialer outgoing accu
```

### PRI on a Cisco AS5200 Examples

The following example configures ISDN PRI on the appropriate interfaces for IP dial-in on channelized T1:

```
! T1 PRI controller configuration

controller T1 0
 framing esf
 linecode b8zs
 clock source line primary
 pri-group timeslots 1-24
!
controller T1 1
 framing esf
 linecode b8zs
 clock source line secondary
 pri-group timeslots 1-24
!
interface Serial0:23
 isdn incoming-voice modem
 dialer rotary-group 1
!
interface Serial1:23
 isdn incoming-voice modem
 dialer rotary-group 1
!
interface Loopback0
 ip address 172.16.254.254 255.255.255.0
!
interface Ethernet0
 ip address 172.16.1.1 255.255.255.0
!
interface Group-Async1
 ip unnumbered Loopback0
 ip tcp header-compression passive
 encapsulation ppp
 async mode interactive
 peer default ip address pool default
 dialer-group 1
 ppp authentication chap pap default
```

```
 group-range 1 48
!
interface Dialer1
 ip unnumbered Loopback0
 encapsulation ppp
 peer default ip address pool default
 ip local pool default 172.16.254.1 172.16.254.48
 dialer in-band
 dialer-group 1
 dialer idle-timeout 3600
 ppp multilink
 ppp authentication chap pap default
```

The following example configures ISDN PRI on the appropriate interfaces for IP dial-in on channelized E1:

```
! E1 PRI controller configuration

controller E1 0
  framing crc4
 linecode hdb3
 clock source line primary
 pri-group timeslots 1-31
!
controller E1 1
 framing crc4
 linecode hdb3
 clock source line secondary
 pri-group timeslots 1-31

interface serial0:15
 isdn incoming-voice modem
 dialer rotary-group 1
!
interface serial1:15
 isdn incoming-voice modem
 dialer rotary-group 1
!
interface loopback0
 ip address 172.16.254.254 255.255.255.0
!
interface ethernet0
 ip address 172.16.1.1 255.255.255.0
!
!The following block of commands configures DDR for all the ISDN PRI interfaces
!configured above. The dialer-group and dialer rotary-group commands tie the
!interface configuration blocks to the DDR configuration.
!
interface dialer1
 ip unnumbered loopback0
 encapsulation ppp
 peer default ip address pool default
 ip local pool default 172.16.254.1 172.16.254.60
 dialer in-band
 dialer-group 1
```

```
dialer idle-timeout 3600
ppp multilink
ppp authentication chap pap default
```

## PRI Groups and Channel Groups on the Same Channelized T1 Controller Example

The following example shows a channelized T1 controller configured for PRI groups and for channel groups. The **pri-group** command and the **channel-group** command cannot have overlapping timeslots; note the correct timeslot configuration in the following example:

```
controller t1 0
channel-group 0 timeslot 1-6
channel-group 1 timeslot 7
channel-group 2 timeslot 8
channel-group 3 timeslot 9-11
pri-group timeslot 12-24
```

The same type of configuration also applies to channelized E1.

## Robbed-Bit Signaling Examples

This section provides sample configurations for the Cisco AS5200's T1 controllers. You can configure the 24 channels of a channelized T1 to support ISDN PRI, robbed-bit signaling, channel grouping, or a combination of all three. It provides the following sections:

- Allocating All Channels for Robbed-Bit Signaling Example
- Mixing and Matching Channels Example

### *Allocating All Channels for Robbed-Bit Signaling Example*

The following example configures all 24 channels to support robbed-bit signaling feature group B on a Cisco AS5200:

```
controller T1 0
 cas-group 1 timeslots 1-24 type e&m-fgb
```

### *Mixing and Matching Channels Example*

The following example shows you how to configure all 24 channels to support a combination of ISDN PRI, robbed-bit signaling, and channel grouping. The range of timeslots that you allocate must match the timeslot allocations that your central office chooses to use. This is a rare configuration due to the complexity of aligning the correct range of timeslots on both ends of the connection.

The following configuration creates serial interfaces 0 to 9, which correspond to ISDN PRI timeslots 1 to 10 (shown as serial 1:0 through serial 1:9). The serial line 1:23 is the D channel, which carries the analog signal bits that dial a modem's phone number and determine if a modem is busy or available. The D channel is automatically created and assigned to timeslot 24.

```
controller T1 0
! ISDN PRI is configured on timeslots 1 through 10.
 pri-group timeslots 1-10
! Channelized T1 data is transmitted over timeslots 11 through 16.
 channel-group 11 timeslots 11-16
```

```
! The channel-associated signal ear and mouth feature group B is configured on
! virtual signal group 17 for timeslots 17 to 23, which are used for incoming
! and outgoing analog calls.
 cas-group 17 timeslots 17-23 type e&m-fgb
```

There is no specific interface, such as the serial interface shown in the earlier examples, that corresponds to the timeslot range.

## ISDN Channel-Associated Signaling Examples

This section provides channelized E1 sample configurations for the Cisco AS5200. You can configure the 30 available channels with channel-associated signaling, channel grouping, or a combination of the two.

- Allocating All Channels for Channel-Associated Signaling
- Mixing and Matching Channels Example

### *Allocating All Channels for Channel-Associated Signaling*

The following interactive example configures channels (also known as timeslots) 1-30 with ear and mouth channel signaling and feature group B support on a Cisco AS5200; it also shows that the router displays informative messages about each timeslot. Signaling messages are transmitted in the 16th timeslot; therefore, that timeslot is not brought up.

```
Router#
%SYS-5-CONFIG_I: Configured from console by console
Router# configure terminal
Enter configuration commands, one per line.  End with CNTL/Z.
Router(config)# controller e1 0
Router(config-controller)# cas-group 1 timeslots 1-31 type e&m-fgb
Router(config-controller)#
%DSX0-5-RBSLINEUP: RBS of controller 0 timeslot 1 is up
%DSX0-5-RBSLINEUP: RBS of controller 0 timeslot 2 is up
%DSX0-5-RBSLINEUP: RBS of controller 0 timeslot 3 is up
%DSX0-5-RBSLINEUP: RBS of controller 0 timeslot 4 is up
%DSX0-5-RBSLINEUP: RBS of controller 0 timeslot 5 is up
%DSX0-5-RBSLINEUP: RBS of controller 0 timeslot 6 is up
%DSX0-5-RBSLINEUP: RBS of controller 0 timeslot 7 is up
%DSX0-5-RBSLINEUP: RBS of controller 0 timeslot 8 is up
%DSX0-5-RBSLINEUP: RBS of controller 0 timeslot 9 is up
%DSX0-5-RBSLINEUP: RBS of controller 0 timeslot 10 is up
%DSX0-5-RBSLINEUP: RBS of controller 0 timeslot 11 is up
%DSX0-5-RBSLINEUP: RBS of controller 0 timeslot 12 is up
%DSX0-5-RBSLINEUP: RBS of controller 0 timeslot 13 is up
%DSX0-5-RBSLINEUP: RBS of controller 0 timeslot 14 is up
%DSX0-5-RBSLINEUP: RBS of controller 0 timeslot 15 is up
%DSX0-5-RBSLINEUP: RBS of controller 0 timeslot 17 is up
%DSX0-5-RBSLINEUP: RBS of controller 0 timeslot 18 is up
%DSX0-5-RBSLINEUP: RBS of controller 0 timeslot 19 is up
%DSX0-5-RBSLINEUP: RBS of controller 0 timeslot 20 is up
%DSX0-5-RBSLINEUP: RBS of controller 0 timeslot 21 is up
%DSX0-5-RBSLINEUP: RBS of controller 0 timeslot 22 is up
%DSX0-5-RBSLINEUP: RBS of controller 0 timeslot 23 is up
```

```
%DSX0-5-RBSLINEUP: RBS of controller 0 timeslot 24 is up
%DSX0-5-RBSLINEUP: RBS of controller 0 timeslot 25 is up
%DSX0-5-RBSLINEUP: RBS of controller 0 timeslot 26 is up
%DSX0-5-RBSLINEUP: RBS of controller 0 timeslot 27 is up
%DSX0-5-RBSLINEUP: RBS of controller 0 timeslot 28 is up
%DSX0-5-RBSLINEUP: RBS of controller 0 timeslot 29 is up
%DSX0-5-RBSLINEUP: RBS of controller 0 timeslot 30 is up
%DSX0-5-RBSLINEUP: RBS of controller 0 timeslot 31 is up
```

### *Mixing and Matching Channels*

The following interactive example shows you how to configure an E1 controller to support a combination of channel-associated signaling and channel grouping. The range of timeslots that you allocate must match the timeslot allocations that your central office chooses to use. This is a rare configuration because of the complexity of aligning the correct range of timeslots on both ends of the connection.

Timeslots 1 through 15 are assigned to channel group 1. In turn, these timeslots are assigned to serial interface 0 and virtual channel group 1 (shown as serial 0:1).

```
AS5200(config)# controller e1 0
Router(config-controller)# channel-group 1 timeslots 1-15
Router(config-controller)#
%LINEPROTO-5-UPDOWN: Line protocol on Interface Serial0:1, changed state to down
%LINK-3-UPDOWN: Interface Serial0:1, changed state to up
%LINEPROTO-5-UPDOWN: Line protocol on Interface Serial0:1, changed state to up
```

Timeslots 17 to 31 are configured with channel-associated signaling.

```
Router(config-controller)# cas-group 2 timeslots 17-31 type e&m-fgb
%LINEPROTO-5-UPDOWN: Line protocol on Interface Serial0:1, changed state to down
Router(config-controller)#
%DSX0-5-RBSLINEUP: RBS of controller 0 timeslot 17 is up
%DSX0-5-RBSLINEUP: RBS of controller 0 timeslot 18 is up
%DSX0-5-RBSLINEUP: RBS of controller 0 timeslot 19 is up
%DSX0-5-RBSLINEUP: RBS of controller 0 timeslot 20 is up
%DSX0-5-RBSLINEUP: RBS of controller 0 timeslot 21 is up
%DSX0-5-RBSLINEUP: RBS of controller 0 timeslot 22 is up
%DSX0-5-RBSLINEUP: RBS of controller 0 timeslot 23 is up
%DSX0-5-RBSLINEUP: RBS of controller 0 timeslot 24 is up
%DSX0-5-RBSLINEUP: RBS of controller 0 timeslot 25 is up
%DSX0-5-RBSLINEUP: RBS of controller 0 timeslot 26 is up
%DSX0-5-RBSLINEUP: RBS of controller 0 timeslot 27 is up
%DSX0-5-RBSLINEUP: RBS of controller 0 timeslot 28 is up
%DSX0-5-RBSLINEUP: RBS of controller 0 timeslot 29 is up
%DSX0-5-RBSLINEUP: RBS of controller 0 timeslot 30 is up
%DSX0-5-RBSLINEUP: RBS of controller 0 timeslot 31 is up
Router(config-controller)#
```

# CHAPTER 16

# Channelized E1 and Channelized T1 Setup Commands

This chapter describes commands needed to configure channelized E1 and channelized T1 for the following:

- ISDN PRI on any platform that supports PRI
- Robbed-bit (in-band) signaling for analog calls over digital T1 lines
- Channel-associated (out-of-band) signaling over digital E1 lines on the AS5200 access servers

In Cisco IOS Release 11.3, all commands supported on the Cisco 7500 series are also supported on the Cisco 7000 series.

## AUTODETECT ENCAPSULATION

To enable automatic detection of the encapsulation types in operation over a point-to-point link to a specified serial or ISDN interface, use the **autodetect encapsulation** interface configuration command. To disable automatic, dynamic detection of the encapsulation types in operation on a link, use the **no** form of this command.

**autodetect encapsulation** *encapsulation-type*
**no autodetect encapsulation**

| *Syntax* | *Description* |
|---|---|
| *encapsulation-type* | One or both of the encapsulation keywords **v120** and **ppp**. |

### *Default*

Disabled

### *Command Mode*

Interface configuration

### *Usage Guidelines*

This command first appeared in Release 11.2.

At least one encapsulation type is required in the command, but you can specify additional encapsulation types.

Use this command to enable the specified serial or ISDN interface to accept calls and dynamically change the encapsulation in effect on the interface when the remote device does not signal the call type. For example, if an ISDN call does not identify the call type in the Lower Layer Compatibility fields and is using an encapsulation that is different from the one configured on the interface, the interface can change its encapsulation type dynamically.

This command enables interoperation with ISDN terminal adapters that use V.120 encapsulation but do not signal V.120 in the call setup message. An ISDN interface that by default answers a call as synchronous serial with PPP encapsulation can change its encapsulation and answer such calls.

Automatic detection is attempted for the first 10 seconds after the link is established or the first five packets exchanged over the link, whichever is first.

### *Related Commands*

Search online to find documentation for related commands.

**encapsulation**

## CAS-GROUP (CONTROLLER E1)

To configure an E1 controller on a Cisco AS5200 with channel-associated signaling (also known as *robbed-bit signaling*), use the **cas-group** controller configuration command. Use the **no** form of this command to disable channel-associated signaling for one or more timeslots.

**cas-group** *channel* **timeslots** *range* **type** *signal*
**no cas-group** *channel* **timeslots** *range* **type** *signal*

| *Syntax* | *Description* |
|---|---|
| *channel* | Single channel group number, in the range 0 to 30. |
| **timeslots** *range* | One or more ranges of timeslot values, in the range 1 to 31. You can specify timeslot ranges (for example, 1–31), individual timeslots separated by commas (for example 1, 3, 5), or a combination of the two (for example 1–3, 8, 17–31). The 16th timeslot is not specified in the command line, because it is reserved for transmitting the channel signaling. |
| **type** *signal* | Specifies the type of channel-associated signaling. Choose one of the following signal types to configure:<br>• **e&m-fgb**—Specifies ear and mouth channel signaling with feature group b support. |

- **e&m-fgd**—Specifies ear and mouth channel signaling with feature group d support.
- **fxs-loopstart**— Specifies foreign exchange system loopstart signaling support.
- **fxs-groundstart**—Specifies foreign exchange system ground-start signaling support.
- **sas-loopstart**—Specifies specific access station loopstart signaling support.
- **sas-groundstart**—Specifies specific access station ground-start signaling support.

### *Default*

No channel-associated signaling is configured on the controller.

### *Command Mode*

Controller configuration

### *Usage Guidelines*

This command first appeared in Cisco IOS Release 11.2.

Use this command to configure support for incoming and outgoing call signals (such as on-hook and off-hook) on each E1 controller.

If you specify the timeslot range 1–31 at the router prompt, the system software automatically uses the 16th timeslot to transmit the channel-associated signaling.

### *Example*

The following example configures timeslots 1–30 with ear and mouth channel signaling with feature group b support on a Cisco AS5200. Because the signaling is transmitted through the 16th timeslot, this timeslot is not brought up or displayed in the output.

```
Router# configure terminal
Enter configuration commands, one per line.  End with CNTL/Z.
Router(config)# controller e1 0
Router(config-controller)# cas-group 1 timeslots 1-31 type e&m-fgb
Router(config-controller)#
%DSX0-5-RBSLINEUP: RBS of controller 0 timeslot 1 is up
%DSX0-5-RBSLINEUP: RBS of controller 0 timeslot 2 is up
%DSX0-5-RBSLINEUP: RBS of controller 0 timeslot 3 is up
%DSX0-5-RBSLINEUP: RBS of controller 0 timeslot 4 is up
%DSX0-5-RBSLINEUP: RBS of controller 0 timeslot 5 is up
%DSX0-5-RBSLINEUP: RBS of controller 0 timeslot 6 is up
%DSX0-5-RBSLINEUP: RBS of controller 0 timeslot 7 is up
%DSX0-5-RBSLINEUP: RBS of controller 0 timeslot 8 is up
%DSX0-5-RBSLINEUP: RBS of controller 0 timeslot 9 is up
%DSX0-5-RBSLINEUP: RBS of controller 0 timeslot 10 is up
%DSX0-5-RBSLINEUP: RBS of controller 0 timeslot 11 is up
%DSX0-5-RBSLINEUP: RBS of controller 0 timeslot 12 is up
```

```
%DSX0-5-RBSLINEUP: RBS of controller 0 timeslot 13 is up
%DSX0-5-RBSLINEUP: RBS of controller 0 timeslot 14 is up
%DSX0-5-RBSLINEUP: RBS of controller 0 timeslot 15 is up
%DSX0-5-RBSLINEUP: RBS of controller 0 timeslot 17 is up
%DSX0-5-RBSLINEUP: RBS of controller 0 timeslot 18 is up
%DSX0-5-RBSLINEUP: RBS of controller 0 timeslot 19 is up
%DSX0-5-RBSLINEUP: RBS of controller 0 timeslot 20 is up
%DSX0-5-RBSLINEUP: RBS of controller 0 timeslot 21 is up
%DSX0-5-RBSLINEUP: RBS of controller 0 timeslot 22 is up
%DSX0-5-RBSLINEUP: RBS of controller 0 timeslot 23 is up
%DSX0-5-RBSLINEUP: RBS of controller 0 timeslot 24 is up
%DSX0-5-RBSLINEUP: RBS of controller 0 timeslot 25 is up
%DSX0-5-RBSLINEUP: RBS of controller 0 timeslot 26 is up
%DSX0-5-RBSLINEUP: RBS of controller 0 timeslot 27 is up
%DSX0-5-RBSLINEUP: RBS of controller 0 timeslot 28 is up
%DSX0-5-RBSLINEUP: RBS of controller 0 timeslot 29 is up
%DSX0-5-RBSLINEUP: RBS of controller 0 timeslot 30 is up
%DSX0-5-RBSLINEUP: RBS of controller 0 timeslot 31 is up
```

## CAS-GROUP (CONTROLLER T1)

To configure channelized T1 timeslots with channel-associated signaling (also known as *robbed-bit signaling*), which enables a Cisco AS5200 modem to receive and transmit analog calls, use the **cas-group** controller configuration command. Use the **no** form of this command to disable channel-associated signaling for one or more timeslots.

**cas-group** *channel* **timeslots** *range* **type** *signal*
**no cas-group** *channel* **timeslots** *range* **type** *signal*

| *Syntax* | *Description* |
|---|---|
| *channel* | Single channel group number, in the range 0 to 23. |
| **timeslots** *range* | One or more ranges of timeslot values, in the range 1 to 24. You can specify timeslot ranges (for example, 1–24), individual timeslots separated by commas (for example 1, 3, 5), or a combination of the two (for example 1–3, 8, 15–23). The 24th timeslot is not specified in the command line, because it is reserved for transmitting the channel signaling. |
| **type** *signal* | Type of channel-associated signaling. Choose one of the following signal types:<br>• **e&m-fgb**—Specifies ear and mouth channel signaling with feature group b support.<br>• **e&m-fgd**—Specifies ear and mouth channel signaling with feature group d support.<br>• **fxs-loopstart**—Specifies foreign exchange system loopstart signaling support.<br>• **fxs-groundstart**—Specifies foreign exchange system ground-start signaling support.<br>• **sas-loopstart**—Specifies specific access station loopstart signaling support.<br>• **sas-groundstart**—Specifies specific access station ground-start signaling support. |

### Default

No channelized T1 robbed-bit signaling is configured.

### Command Mode

Controller configuration

### Usage Guidelines

This command first appeared in Cisco IOS Release 11.2.

Use this command to enable a Cisco AS5200 modem to receive and transmit incoming and outgoing call signaling (such as on-hook and off-hook) through each T1 controller that is configured for a channelized T1 line.

Switched 56 digital calls are not supported in this feature.

### Example

The following example configures all 24 channels with ear and mouth channel signaling with feature group b support on a Cisco AS5200:

```
AS5200(config)# controller T1 0
AS5200(config-controller)# cas-group 1 timeslots 1-24 type e&m-fgb
AS5200(config-controller)#
%DSX0-5-RBSLINEUP: RBS of controller 1 timeslot 1 is up
%DSX0-5-RBSLINEUP: RBS of controller 1 timeslot 2 is up
%DSX0-5-RBSLINEUP: RBS of controller 1 timeslot 3 is up
%DSX0-5-RBSLINEUP: RBS of controller 1 timeslot 4 is up
%DSX0-5-RBSLINEUP: RBS of controller 1 timeslot 5 is up
%DSX0-5-RBSLINEUP: RBS of controller 1 timeslot 6 is up
%DSX0-5-RBSLINEUP: RBS of controller 1 timeslot 7 is up
%DSX0-5-RBSLINEUP: RBS of controller 1 timeslot 8 is up
%DSX0-5-RBSLINEUP: RBS of controller 1 timeslot 9 is up
%DSX0-5-RBSLINEUP: RBS of controller 1 timeslot 10 is up
%DSX0-5-RBSLINEUP: RBS of controller 1 timeslot 11 is up
%DSX0-5-RBSLINEUP: RBS of controller 1 timeslot 12 is up
%DSX0-5-RBSLINEUP: RBS of controller 1 timeslot 13 is up
%DSX0-5-RBSLINEUP: RBS of controller 1 timeslot 14 is up
%DSX0-5-RBSLINEUP: RBS of controller 1 timeslot 15 is up
%DSX0-5-RBSLINEUP: RBS of controller 1 timeslot 16 is up
%DSX0-5-RBSLINEUP: RBS of controller 1 timeslot 17 is up
%DSX0-5-RBSLINEUP: RBS of controller 1 timeslot 18 is up
%DSX0-5-RBSLINEUP: RBS of controller 1 timeslot 19 is up
%DSX0-5-RBSLINEUP: RBS of controller 1 timeslot 20 is up
%DSX0-5-RBSLINEUP: RBS of controller 1 timeslot 21 is up
%DSX0-5-RBSLINEUP: RBS of controller 1 timeslot 22 is up
%DSX0-5-RBSLINEUP: RBS of controller 1 timeslot 23 is up
%DSX0-5-RBSLINEUP: RBS of controller 1 timeslot 24 is up
```

### CHANNEL-GROUP

Use the **channel-group** controller configuration command to define the timeslots that belong to each T1 or E1 circuit.

**channel-group** *number* **timeslots** *range* [**speed** {**48** | **56** | **64**}]

| *Syntax* | *Description* |
|---|---|
| *number* | Channel group number. When configuring a T1 data line, channel group numbers can be values from 0 to 23. When configuring an E1 data line, channel group numbers can be values from 0 to 30. |
| **timeslots** *range* | One or more timeslots or ranges of timeslots belonging to the channel group. The first timeslot is numbered 1. For a T1 controller, the timeslot range is from 1 to 24. For an E1 controller, the timeslot range is from 1 to 31. |
| **speed** {**48** \| **56** \| **64**} | (Optional) Line speed (in kilobits per second) of the T1 or E1 link. |

#### *Default*

The default line speed when configuring a T1 controller is 56 Kbps.

The default line speed when configuring an E1 controller is 64 Kbps.

#### *Command Mode*

Controller configuration

#### *Usage Guidelines*

Use this command in configurations where the router or access server must communicate with a T1 or E1 fractional data line. The channel group number may be arbitrarily assigned and must be unique for the controller. The timeslot range must match the timeslots assigned to the channel group. The service provider defines the timeslots that comprise a channel group.

#### *Example*

In the following example, three channel groups are defined. Channel group 0 consists of a single timeslot, channel group 8 consists of 7 timeslots and runs at a speed of 64 Kbps per timeslot, and channel group 12 consists of a single timeslot.

```
channel-group 0 timeslots 1
channel-group 8 timeslots 5,7,12-15,20 speed 64
channel-group 12 timeslots 2
```

### *Related Commands*

Search online to find documentation for related commands.

**framing**
**linecode**

## CLEAR CONTROLLER

Use the **clear controller** EXEC command to reset the T1 or E1 controller.

**clear controller** {**t1** | **e1**} *slot/port* (Cisco 7200 series and Cisco 7500 series)
**clear controller** {**t1** | **e1**} *number* (Cisco 4000 series)

| *Syntax* | *Description* |
|---|---|
| *slot/port* | Backplane slot number and port number on the interface. See your hardware installation manual for the specific slot and port numbers. |
| *number* | Network interface module (NIM) number, in the range 0 through 2. |

### *Command Mode*

EXEC

### *Examples*

The following example resets the T1 controller at slot 4, port 0 on a Cisco 7500 series router:

```
clear controller t1 4/0
```

The following example resets the E1 controller at NIM 0 on a Cisco 4000 series router:

```
clear controller e1 0
```

### *Related Commands*

Search online to find documentation for related commands.

**controller e1**
**controller t1**

## CLOCK SOURCE (CONTROLLER)

Use the **clock source** controller configuration command to set the E1 line clock source for the Cisco AS5200.

**clock source line** {**primary** | **secondary**}
**no clock source line** {**primary** | **secondary**} |

| *Syntax* | *Description* |
|---|---|
| **line** | E1 line from which the clocking is taken. |
| **primary** | Primary TDM clock source. |
| **secondary** | Secondary TDM clock source. |

### Default

Primary TDM clock source is taken from the E1 controller 0 on the Cisco AS5200.

Secondary TDM clock source is taken from the E1 controller 1 on the Cisco AS5200.

### Command Mode

Controller configuration

### Usage Guidelines

This command first appeared in Cisco IOS Release 11.1.

Configure the **clock source line primary** command on the controller that takes the most reliable clocking from an E1 line. Configure the **clock source line secondary** command on the controller that has the next best-known clocking. With this configuration, the primary line clocking is backed up to the secondary line if the primary clocking shuts down.

### Examples

The following example configures the Cisco AS5200 to use the E1 controller 0 as the primary clocking source and the E1 controller 1 as the secondary clocking source:

```
controller e1 0
 framing esf
 linecode hdb3
 pri-group timeslots 1-23
 clock source line primary
!
controller e1 1
 framing esf
 linecode hdb3
 pri-group timeslots 1-23
 clock source line secondary
```

### Related Commands

Search online to find documentation for related commands.

**framing**
**linecode**

## CLOCK SOURCE (CISCO AS5200)

To select the clock source for the time-division multiplexing (TDM) bus in a Cisco AS5200 access server, use the **clock source** interface configuration command. The **no** form of this command configures the clock source to its default setting.

**clock source {line {primary | secondary} | internal}**
**no clock source line {primary | secondary}**

| *Syntax* | *Description* |
|---|---|
| **line** | Clock source on the active line. |
| **primary** | Primary TDM clock source. |
| **secondary** | Secondary TDM clock source. |
| **internal** | Free-running clock (also known as internal clock) as the clock source. |

### *Defaults*

Primary TDM clock source from the T1 0 controller

Secondary TDM clock source from the T1 1 controller

### *Command Mode*

Interface configuration

### *Usage Guidelines*

To use the clocking coming in from a T1 line, configure the **clock source line primary** command on the T1 interface that has the most reliable clocking. Configure the **clock source line secondary** command on the T1 interface that has the next best-known clocking. With this configuration, the primary line clocking is backed up to the secondary line if the primary clocking shuts down.

### *Example*

The following example configures the Cisco AS5200 access server to use T1 controller 0 as the primary clock source and T1 controller 1 as the secondary clock source:

```
controller t1 0
 clock source line primary
controller t1 1
 clock source line secondary
```

## CONTROLLER

To configure a T1 or E1 controller and enter controller configuration mode, use the **controller** global configuration command.

**controller** {**t1** | **e1**} *slot/port* (on the Cisco 7200 and Cisco 7500 series)
**controller** {**t1** | **e1**} *number* (on the Cisco AS5200 and Cisco 4000 series)

| *Syntax* | *Description* |
|---|---|
| **t1** | T1 controller. |
| **e1** | E1 controller. |

| | |
|---|---|
| *slot/port* | Backplane slot number and port number on the interface. See your hardware installation manual for the specific values and slot numbers. |
| *number* | Network processor module (NPM) number, in the range 0 through 2. |

### *Default*

No T1 or E1 controller is configured.

### *Command Mode*

Global configuration

### *Usage Guidelines*

This command first appeared in Release 10.0; the **e1** keyword was added in Release 10.3.

This command is used in configurations where the router or access server is intended to communicate with a T1 or E1 fractional data line. Additional parameters for the T1 or E1 line must be configured for the controller before the T1 or E1 circuits can be configured by means of the **interface** global configuration command.

This command is used on a Cisco 7500 series or Cisco 4000 series router.

This command does not apply to the Cisco 7200 series.

### *Example*

In the following example, the MIP in slot 4, port 0 of a Cisco 7500 is configured as a T1 controller:

```
controller t1 4/0
```

In the following example, NIM 0 of a Cisco 4000 is configured as a T1 controller:

```
controller t1 0
```

### *Related Commands*

Search online to find documentation for related commands.

**channel-group**
**clear controller lex**
**clear controller t1**
**clock source** (controller)
**framing**
**linecode**
**show controllers e1**
**show controller t1**

## CPP AUTHENTICATION

To enable negotiation of authentication with a router or bridge that supports the Combinet Proprietary Protocol (CPP) and that is calling in to this router, use the **cpp authentication** interface configuration command. To disable negotiation of CPP authentication, use the **no** form of this command.

**cpp authentication**
**no cpp authentication**

### Syntax Description

This command has no arguments or keywords.

### Default

Disabled

### Command Mode

Interface configuration

### Usage Guidelines

This command first appeared in Release 11.2.

Use this command for authenticating the device that is calling in to this router.

Use this command to communicate over an ISDN interface with Combinet devices that do not support Point-to-Point Protocol (PPP) but do support the Combinet Proprietary Protocol (CPP).

Currently, most Combinet devices *do* support PPP. Cisco routers can communicate over ISDN with these devices by using PPP encapsulation, which supports both routing and fast switching.

This command is supported on ISDN and dialer interfaces.

This command uses names and passwords from the **username password** command. It does not support the Terminal Access Controller Access Control System (TACACS).

### Example

The following example configures a Primary Rate Interface to communicate with a Combinet bridge that does not support PPP:

```
controller t1 1/1
 framing esf
 linecode b8zs
 pri-group timeslots 1-23
 isdn switchtype primary-4ess

interface Serial1/1:23
 encapsulation cpp
 cpp callback accept
 cpp authentication
```

### Related Commands

Search online to find documentation for related commands.

**cpp callback accept**

**encapsulation cpp**
**username password**

## CPP CALLBACK ACCEPT

To enable the router to accept callback from a Combinet router or bridge that supports the Combinet Proprietary Protocol (CPP), use the **cpp callback accept** interface configuration command.

**cpp callback accept**

### *Syntax Description*

This command has no arguments or keywords.

### *Default*

Disabled

### *Command Mode*

Interface configuration

### *Usage Guidelines*

Use this command to communicate over an ISDN interface with Combinet devices that do not support PPP but do support CPP.

Currently, most Combinet devices *do* support PPP. Cisco routers can communicate over ISDN with these devices by using PPP encapsulation, which supports both routing and fast switching.

This command is supported on ISDN and dialer interfaces.

### *Example*

The following example configures the PRI interface serial1/1:23 to communicate with a Combinet router or bridge that does not support PPP:

```
controller t1 1/1
 framing esf
 linecode b8zs
 pri-group timeslots 1-23
 isdn switchtype primary-4ess
!
interface Serial1/1:23
 encapsulation cpp
 cpp callback accept
 cpp authentication
```

### *Related Commands*

Search online to find documentation for related commands.

**cpp authentication**
**encapsulation cpp**

## DESCRIPTION (CONTROLLER)

To add a description to an E1 or T1 controller, use the **description** controller configuration command. Use the **no** form of this command to remove the description.

**description** *string*
**no description**

| *Syntax* | *Description* |
|---|---|
| *string* | Comment or a description to help you remember what is attached to the controller. |

### *Default*

No description is added.

### *Command Mode*

Controller configuration

### *Usage Guidelines*

The **description** command is meant solely as a comment to be put in the configuration to help you remember what certain E1 or T1 controllers are used for. The description affects the MIP interfaces only and appears in the output of the **show controllers e1, show controllers t1,** and **show running-config** EXEC commands.

### *Example*

The following example describes a 3174 controller:

```
controller t1
 description 3174 Controller for test lab
```

### *Related Commands*

Search online to find documentation for related commands.

**show controllers e1**
**show controller t1**
**show running-config**

## DESCRIPTION (INTERFACE)

To add a description to an interface configuration, use the **description** interface configuration command. Use the **no** form of this command to remove the description.

**description** *string*
**no description**

| *Syntax* | *Description* |
| --- | --- |
| *string* | Comment or a description to help you remember what is attached to this interface. |

### *Default*

No description is added.

### *Command Mode*

Interface configuration

### *Usage Guidelines*

The **description** command is meant solely as a comment to be put in the configuration to help you remember what certain interfaces are used for. The description appears in the output of the following EXEC commands: **show startup-config show interfaces,** and **show running-config.**

### *Example*

The following example shows how to add a description for a T1 interface:

```
interface serial 0
description Fractional T1 line to Mountain View -- 128 Kbps
```

### *Related Commands*

Search online to find documentation for related commands.

**show interfaces**
**show running-config**
**show startup-config**

## DIALER OUTGOING

To configure the dialer map class for an NSF dialing plan to support outgoing calls, use the **dialer outgoing** map-class dialer configuration command.

**dialer outgoing** *classname*

### *Default*

This command is disabled; no classname is provided.

| *Syntax* | *Description* |
| --- | --- |
| *classname* | Keyword for a specified AT&T Primary-4ESS NSF dialing plan; the following keywords are supported: **sdn, megacomm,** and **accunet.** |

### Command Mode

Map-class dialer configuration

### Usage Guidelines

This command first appeared in Cisco IOS Release 11.0.

Use this command only to define a dialer map class for an NSF call-by-call service offered by AT&T on Primary-4ESS ISDN switches. This command is not used for other vendors and switch types.

### Example

The following partial example shows a class called SDN to support the Software Defined Network (SDN) dialing plan. For a more complete example using all the related commands, see the **map-class dialer** command.

```
dialer outgoing sdn
```

### Related Commands

Search online to find documentation for related commands.

**dialer map class**
**map-class dialer**
**dialer voice-call**

## DIALER VOICE-CALL

To configure the dialer map class for an NSF dialing plan to support outgoing voice calls, use the **dialer voice-call** map-class dialer command.

**dialer voice-call**

### Syntax Description

This command has no arguments and keywords.

### Default

This command is disabled.

### Command Mode

Map-class dialer configuration

### Usage Guidelines

This command first appeared in Cisco IOS Release 11.0.

### *Example*

The following partial example defines a dialer map class to support the SDN dialing plan and to support outgoing voice calls. For a more complete example using all the related commands, see the **map-class dialer** command.

```
map-class dialer sdnplan
dialer voice-call
dialer outgoing sdn
```

### *Related Commands*

Search online to find documentation for related commands.

**dialer map class**
**map-class dialer**
**dialer outgoing**

## ENCAPSULATION CPP

To enable encapsulation for communication with routers or bridges using the Combinet Proprietary Protocol (CPP), use the **encapsulation cpp** interface configuration command.

**encapsulation cpp**

### *Syntax Description*

This command has no arguments or keywords.

### *Default*

Disabled

### *Command Mode*

Interface configuration

### *Usage Guidelines*

Use this command to communicate over an ISDN interface with Combinet devices that do not support PPP but do support CPP.

Currently, most Combinet devices *do* support PPP. Cisco routers can communicate over ISDN with these devices by using PPP encapsulation, which supports both routing and fast switching.

Combinet devices support only IP, IPX, and bridging. For AppleTalk, Cisco routers automatically perform half-bridging with Combinet devices.

This command is supported on ISDN BRIs and Primary Rate Interfaces (PRIs) only.

### *Example*

The following example configures PRI interface serial 1/1:23 to communicate with a Combinet router or bridge that does not support PPP:

```
contoller t1 1/1
 framing esf
```

```
 linecode b8zs
 pri-group timeslots 1-23
 isdn switchtype primary-4ess
!
interface Serial1/1:23
 encapsulation cpp
 cpp callback accept
 cpp authentication
```

### *Related Commands*

Search online to find documentation for related commands.

**cpp authentication**
**cpp callback accept**

## FRAMING

Use the **framing** controller configuration command to select the frame type for the T1 or E1 data line.

**framing** {**sf** | **esf**} (for T1 lines)
**framing** {**crc4** | **no-crc4**} [**australia**] (for E1 lines)

| *Syntax* | *Description* |
|---|---|
| **sf** | Specifies Super Frame as the T1 frame type. |
| **esf** | Specifies Extended Super Frame as the T1 frame type. |
| **crc4** | Specifies CRC4 frame as the E1 frame type. |
| **no-crc4** | Specifies no CRC4 frame as the E1 frame type. |
| **australia** | (Optional) Specifies the E1 frame type used in Australia. |

### *Defaults*

Super Frame is the default on a T1 line.

CRC4 frame is the default on an E1 line.

### *Command Mode*

Controller configuration

### *Usage Guidelines*

Use this command in configurations where the router or access server is intended to communicate with T1 or E1 fractional data line. The service provider determines which framing type—either **sf**, **esf**, or **crc4**—is required for your T1/E1 circuit.

### *Example*

The following example selects Extended Super Frame as the T1 frame type:

```
framing esf
```

### *Related Commands*

Search online to find documentation for related commands.

**channel-group**
**linecode**

## INTERFACE SERIAL

To specify a serial interface created on a channelized E1 or channelized T1 controller (for ISDN PRI, channel-associated signaling, or robbed-bit signaling), use the **interface serial** global configuration command.

**interface serial** *slot/port:timeslot* (on the Cisco 7200 and Cisco 7500 series)
**interface serial** *number:timeslot* (on the Cisco AS5200 and Cisco 4000 series)

| *Syntax* | *Description* |
|---|---|
| *slot/port* | Slot number and port number where the channelized E1 or T1 controller is located. |
| *number* | Channelized E1 or T1 controller number. |
| *timeslots* | For ISDN, the D channel timeslot, which is **:23** channel for channelized T1 and the **:15** for channelized E1. PRI timeslots are in the range 0 to 23 for channelized T1 and in the range 0 to 30 for channelized E1.<br>For channel-associated signaling or robbed-bit signaling, the channel group number.<br>The colon (:) is required.<br>On a dual port card, it is possible to run channelized on one port and primary rate on the other port. |

### *Default*

None

### *Command Mode*

Global configuration

### *Usage Guidelines*

This command first appeared prior to Release 10.0.

The D channel is always the **:23** channel for T1 and the **:15** for E1.

### *Examples*

The following example configures channel groups on timeslots 1 to 11 and ISDN PRI on timeslots 12 to 24 of T1 controller 0. Then the example configures the first two channel groups as serial interfaces 0:0 and 0:1.

```
controller t1 0
channel-group 0 timeslot 1-6
channel-group 1 timeslot 7
channel-group 2 timeslot 8
channel-group 3 timeslot 9-11
pri-group timeslots 12-24
!
interface serial 0:0
ip address 131.108.13.2 255.255.255.0
encapsulation ppp
!
interface serial 0:1
ip address 131.108.13.3 255.255.255.0
encapsulation ppp
```

The following example configures ISDN PRI on T1 controller 4/1 and then configures the D channel on the resulting serial interface 4/1:23:

```
controller t1 4/1
framing crc4
linecode hdb3
pri-group timeslots 1-24

interface serial 4/1:23
ip address 131.108.13.1 255.255.255.0
encapsulation ppp
```

### *Related Commands*

Search online to find documentation for related commands.

**circuit**
**controller**
**show interfaces**
**show interfaces serial bchannel**

## ISDN ANSWER1, ISDN ANSWER2

To have the router verify a called-party number or subaddress number in the incoming setup message for ISDN PRI calls, if the number is delivered by the switch, use the **isdn answer1** interface configuration command. To remove the verification request, use the **no** form of this command.

**isdn answer1** [*called-party-number*][*:subaddress*]
**no isdn answer1** [*called-party-number*][*:subaddress*]

To have the router verify an *additional* called-party number or subaddress number in the incoming setup message for ISDN PRI calls, if the number is delivered by the switch, use the **isdn answer2** interface configuration command. To remove this second verification request, use the **no** form of this command.

**isdn answer2** [*called-party-number*][*:subaddress*]
**no isdn answer2** [*called-party-number*][*:subaddress*]

| *Syntax* | *Description* |
|---|---|
| *called-party-number* | (Optional) Telephone number of the called party. At least one value—*called-party-number* or *subaddress*—must be specified. |
| *:subaddress* | (Optional) Subaddress number, 20 or fewer characters long, used for ISDN multipoint connections. At least one value—*called-party-number* or *subaddress*—must be specified.<br>Use the colon (:) when you configure both the called-party number and the subaddress, or when you configure only the subaddress. |

### *Default*

The router does not verify the called-party or subaddress number.

### *Command Mode*

Interface configuration

### *Usage Guidelines*

If you do not specify the **isdn answer1** or **isdn answer2** command, all calls are processed and/or accepted. If you specify the **isdn answer1** or **isdn answer2** command, the router must verify the incoming called-party number and the subaddress before processing and/or accepting the call. The verification proceeds from right to left for the called-party number; it also proceeds from right to left for the subaddress number.

You can configure just the called-party number or just the subaddress. In such a case, only that part is verified. To configure a subaddress only, include the colon (:) before the subaddress number.

You can declare a digit a "don't care" digit by entering it as an *x* or X. In such a case, any incoming digit is allowed.

### *Examples*

In the following partial configuration example, 5552222 is the called-party number and 1234 is the subaddress:

```
interface serial 4/1:0
 isdn answer1 5552222:1234
```

In the following partial configuration example, only the subaddress is configured:

```
interface serial 4/1:0
 isdn answer1 :1234
```

## ISDN CALLER

To configure ISDN caller ID screening, use the **isdn caller** interface configuration command. To disable this feature, use the **no** form of this command.

**isdn caller** *number*
**no isdn caller** *number*

| *Syntax* | *Description* |
|---|---|
| *number* | Telephone number for which to screen. Specify an *x* or *X* to represent a single "don't-care" character. The maximum length of each number is 25 characters. |

*Default*

Disabled

*Command Mode*

Interface configuration

*Usage Guidelines*

This command first appeared in Release 11.2 F.

This command configures the router to accept calls from the specified number.

Caller ID screening is available on Cisco 7200 and 7500 series, Cisco 4000 series, Cisco 3000 series, and Cisco 2500 series routers that have one or more BRIs.

The maximum length of each number is 25 characters. You can specify up to 64 numbers per interface.

**NOTES**

Caller ID screening requires a local switch that is capable of delivering the caller ID to the router. If you enable caller ID screening but do not have such a switch, no calls are allowed in.

*Examples*

The following example configures the router to accept a call with a delivered caller ID equal to 4155551234:

```
isdn caller 4155551234
```

The following example configures the router to accept a call with a delivered caller ID having 41555512 and any numbers in the last two positions:

```
isdn caller 41555512xx
```

*Related Commands*

Search online to find documentation for related commands.

**show dialer**

### ISDN CALLING-NUMBER

To configure an ISDN PRI serial interface to present a billing number of the device making the outgoing call, use the **isdn calling-number** interface configuration command. To remove a previously configured calling number, use the **no** form of this command.

**isdn calling-number** *calling-number*
**no isdn calling number**

| *Syntax* | *Description* |
|---|---|
| *calling-number* | Number of the device making the outgoing call; only one entry is allowed, and it is limited to 16 digits. |

### *Default*

No calling number is presented.

### *Command Mode*

Interface configuration

### *Usage Guidelines*

This command first appeared in Cisco IOS Release 10.3.

An interface can have only one ISDN calling-number entry.

This command is intended for use when the network offers better pricing on calls in which devices present the calling number (that is, the billing number). The calling number information is included in the outgoing Setup message.

**NOTES**

This command can be used with all ISDN PRI switches.

### *Example*

In the following example, the T1 controller is configured and then the D channel interface is configured to present the billing number 4233570925 when it makes outgoing calls:

```
controller t1 1/1
 framing esf
 linecode b8zs
 pri-group timeslots 1-23
 isdn switchtype primary-4ess
!
interface serial 1/1:23
 ip address 7.1.1.1 255.255.255.0
 encapsulation ppp
 isdn calling-number 4233570925
 dialer map ip 7.1.1.2 name dallas 14193460913
```

### *Related Commands*

Search online to find documentation for related commands.

**interface serial**

## ISDN FAST-ROLLOVER-DELAY

To specify the time delay between successive attempts to dial out to a number, use the **isdn fast-rollover-delay** interface configuration command.

**isdn fast-rollover-delay** *seconds*

| *Syntax* | *Description* |
|---|---|
| *seconds* | Number of seconds to delay before dialing the next dialer map after receiving an ISDN message indicating the current call will not succeed. |

### *Default*

This command is disabled by default. If enabled, the default value of the timer is 0 seconds.

### *Command Mode*

Interface configuration

### *Usage Guidelines*

This command first appeared in Cisco IOS Release 11.1.

This command provides a timer separate from the dialer wait-for-carrier timer to control the amount of time that elapses before calls are redialed. This delay is provided to allow the old call to be torn down completely before the new call is attempted.

When using PPP callback, this command specifies the time delay before the callback is done. This command is necessary on some ISDN switches because the new call may be attempted before the old call is completely torn down. This causes the callback to fail.

Use this command when *all* the following conditions are true:

- You are dialing in to a BRI that has two phone numbers configured, one for each B channel.
- You have a dialer map for each phone number.
- The first call succeeds, but the second call fails with no channel available.

If this has occurred, set **isdn fast-rollover-delay** to 5 seconds and try again.

A delay of 5 seconds should cover most cases. Configure sufficient delay to make sure the ISDN RELEASE_COMPLETE message has been sent or received before making the fast rollover call. Use the **debug isdn q931** command to display this information.

### *Example*

The following partial example sets the fast-rollover delay that is suggested when all the conditions specified above are true.

```
isdn fast-rollover-delay 5
```

### *Related Commands*

Search online to find documentation for related commands.

**dialer map**
**dialer wait-for-carrier**
**ppp callback**

## ISDN INCOMING-VOICE DATA

To answer incoming voice calls at a configured rate (overriding the incoming data rate in the call), use the **isdn incoming-voice data** interface configuration command.

**isdn incoming-voice data** [**56** | **64**]

| *Syntax* | *Description* |
|---|---|
| 56 | Answers all voice calls at 56 Kbps. |
| 64 | Answers all voice calls at 64 Kbps. |

### *Default*

None

### *Command Mode*

Interface configuration

### *Usage Guidelines*

When used without a keyword, this command checks the bearer capacity.

If this command is used, the dialing side must dial at 56 Kbps.

Ordinarily, a data device ignores incoming voice calls, but the tariff structure for data and voice calls might make it less expensive to do "data over voice" calls.

### *Example*

The following partial example for channelized T1 configures the D channel (hence, all B channels) to answer all incoming voice calls at 56 Kbps:

```
interface serial 0:23
 isdn incoming-voice data 56
```

## ISDN NOT-END-TO-END

For incoming calls, to override the speed that the network reports it will use to deliver the call data, use the **isdn not-end-to-end** interface configuration command.

**isdn not-end-to-end** {**56** | **64**}

| *Syntax* | *Description* |
|---|---|
| 56 | Answers all voice calls at 56 Kbps. |
| 64 | Answers all voice calls at 64 Kbps. |

### *Default*

The default line speed is 64 Kbps.

### *Command Mode*

Interface configuration

### *Usage Guidelines*

This command might be needed to handle incoming calls properly. Although a call might originate at a speed of 56 Kbps, the network or internetworking networks might improperly deliver the call to the user at a speed of 64 Kbps. This creates a speed mismatch and causes the data to be garbled. Enabling this command makes the router look more closely at the information elements of the incoming call to determine a speed.

A speed mismatch can occur when the source and destination ISDN ports do not belong to the same network.

### *Example*

In the following example, the line speed for incoming calls is set to 56 Kbps:

```
isdn not-end-to-end 56
```

## ISDN SENDING-COMPLETE

To specify that the Sending Complete information element (IE) is included in the outgoing SETUP message, use the **isdn sending-complete** interface configuration command.

**isdn sending-complete**

### *Syntax Description*

This command has no arguments or keywords.

### *Default*

This command is disabled by default.

### *Command Mode*

Interface configuration

### *Usage Guidelines*

Some switches in some countries want a Sending Complete information element to be included in the outgoing SETUP message to indicate that the entire number is included. The Sending Complete IE is needed for Hong Kong and Taiwan, and the **isdn sending-complete** command forces it to be sent.

### Example

```
interface serial 0:15
 description connected to PBX 61886
 ip address 7.1.1.1 255.255.255.0
 encapsulation ppp
 isdn sending-complete
 dialer idle-timeout 20
 dialer map ip 7.1.1.2 name rudder 61884
 dialer map ip 7.1.1.3 name goodie 61885
 dialer-group 1
 ppp authentication chap
```

## ISDN SWITCH-TYPE

To specify the central office switch type on the ISDN interface, use the **isdn switch-type** global configuration command.

**isdn switch-type** *switch-type*

| *Syntax* | *Description* |
|---|---|
| *switch-type* | Service provider switch type; see Table 16–1 for a list of supported switches. |

### Default

The switch type defaults to **none**, which disables the switch on the ISDN interface.

### Command Mode

Global configuration

### Usage Guidelines

To disable the switch on the ISDN interface, specify **isdn switch-type none**.

Table 16–1 lists supported PRI switch types by geographic area.

**Table 16–1** *ISDN Service Provider PRI Switch Types*

| Keywords by Area | Switch Type |
|---|---|
| none | No switch defined |
| **Europe** | |
| primary-net5 | European ISDN PRI switches; covers the Euro-ISDN E-DSS1 signaling system and is ETSI-compliant. |
| **Japan** | |
| primary-ntt | Japanese ISDN PRI switches |
| **North America** | |
| primary-4ess | AT&T 4ESS switch type for the U.S. |

**Table 16–1** *ISDN Service Provider PRI Switch Types, Continued*

| Keywords by Area | Switch Type |
|---|---|
| primary-5ess | AT&T 5ESS switch type for the U.S. |
| primary-dms100 | NT DMS-100 switch type for the U.S. |

### *Example*

The following example configures the French VN3 ISDN switch type:

```
isdn switch-type vn3
```

## LINECODE

Use the **linecode** controller configuration command to select the line-code type for the T1 or E1 line.

**linecode** {**ami** | **b8zs** | **hdb3**}

| *Syntax* | *Description* |
|---|---|
| **ami** | Specifies alternate mark inversion (AMI) as the line-code type. Valid for T1 or E1 controllers; the default for T1 lines. |
| **b8zs** | Specifies B8ZS as the line-code type. Valid for T1 controller only. |
| **hdb3** | Specifies high-density bipolar 3 (hdb3) as the line-code type. Valid for E1 controller only; the default for E1 lines. |

### *Defaults*

AMI is the default for T1 lines.

High-density bipolar 3 is the default for E1 lines.

### *Command Mode*

Controller configuration

### *Usage Guidelines*

Use this command in configurations where the router or access server must communicate with T1 fractional data lines. The T1 service provider determines which line-code type—either **ami** or **b8zs**—is required for your T1 circuit. Likewise, the E1 service provider determines which line-code type—either **ami** or **hdb3**—is required for your E1 circuit.

### *Example*

The following example specifies B8ZS as the line-code type:

```
linecode b8zs
```

### LOOPBACK (CONTROLLER)

To loop an entire E1 line (including all channel groups defined on the controller) toward the line and back toward the router or access server, use the **loopback** controller configuration command. To remove the loop, use the **no** form of this command.

**loopback**
**no loopback**

#### *Syntax Description*

This command has no arguments or keywords.

#### *Default*

Disabled

#### *Command Mode*

Controller configuration

#### *Usage Guidelines*

This command first appeared in Cisco IOS Release 11.1.

This command is useful for testing the DCE device (CSU/DSU) itself.

To show interfaces currently in loopback operation, use the **show interfaces loopback** EXEC command.

#### *Example*

The following example configures the loopback test on the E1 line:

```
controller e1 0
 loopback
```

### LOOPBACK LOCAL (CONTROLLER)

To loop an entire T1 line (including all channel groups defined on the controller) toward the line and the router or access server, use the **loopback local** controller configuration command. To remove the loop, use the **no** form of this command.

**loopback local**
**no loopback local**

#### *Syntax Description*

This command has no arguments or keywords.

#### *Default*

Disabled

### *Command Mode*

Controller configuration

### *Usage Guidelines*

This command first appeared in Cisco IOS Release 11.1.

This command is useful for testing the DCE device (CSU/DSU) itself.

To show interfaces currently in loopback operation, use the **show interfaces loopback** EXEC command.

### *Example*

The following example configures the loopback test on the T1 line:

```
controller t1 0
 loopback local
```

## LOOPBACK LOCAL (INTERFACE)

To loop a channelized T1 or channelized E1 channel group, use the **loopback local** interface configuration command. To remove the loop, use the **no** form of this command.

**loopback local**
**no loopback local**

### *Syntax Description*

This command has no arguments or keywords.

### *Default*

Disabled

### *Command Mode*

Interface configuration

### *Usage Guidelines*

This command first appeared in Cisco IOS Release 11.1.

This command is useful for looping a single channel group in a channelized environment without disrupting the other channel groups.

To show interfaces currently in loopback operation, use the **show interfaces loopback** EXEC command.

### *Example*

The following example configures the loopback test on the T1 line:

```
interface serial 1/0:22
 loopback local
```

### *Related Commands*

Search online to find documentation for related commands.

**show interfaces loopback**

## LOOPBACK REMOTE (CONTROLLER)

To loop packets from a MIP through the CSU/DSU, over a dedicated T1 link, to the remote CSU at the single destination for this T1 link and back, use the **loopback remote** controller configuration command. To remove the loop, use the **no** form of this command.

**loopback remote**
**no loopback remote**

### *Syntax Description*

This command has no arguments or keywords.

### *Default*

Disabled

### *Command Mode*

Controller configuration

### *Usage Guidelines*

This command first appeared in Cisco IOS Release 11.1.

This command applies only when the device supports the remote function. It is used for testing the data communication channels.

For MIP cards, this controller configuration command applies if *only one* destination exists at the remote end of the cloud, the entire T1 line is dedicated to it, and the device at the remote end is a CSU (not a CSU/DSU). This is an uncommon case; MIPs are not usually used in this way.

To show interfaces currently in loopback operation, use the **show interfaces loopback** EXEC command.

### *Example*

The following example configures a remote loopback test:

```
interface serial 0
 loopback remote
```

### *Related Commands*

Search online to find documentation for related commands.

**show interfaces loopback**

### LOOPBACK REMOTE (INTERFACE)

To loop packets through a CSU/DSU, over a DS-3 link or a channelized T1 link, to the remote CSU/DSU and back, use the **loopback remote** interface configuration command. To remove the loop, use the **no** form of this command.

**loopback remote**
**no loopback remote**

#### *Default*

This command is disabled.

#### *Command Mode*

Interface configuration

#### *Usage Guidelines*

This command first appeared in Cisco IOS Release 11.1.

This command applies only when the remote CSU/DSU device supports the function. It is used for testing the data communication channels. The loopback usually is performed at the line port, rather than the DTE port, of the remote CSU/DSU.

For a multiport interface processor (MIP) connected to a network via a channelized T1 link, the **loopback remote** interface configuration command applies if the remote interface is served by a DDS line (56 Kbps or 64 Kbps) and the device at the remote end is a CSU/DSU. In addition, the CSU/DSU at the remote end *must* react to latched DDS CSU loopback codes. Destinations that are served by other types of lines or that have CSU/DSUs that do not react to latched DDS CSU codes cannot participate in an interface remote loopback. Latched DDS CSU loopback code requirements are described in AT&T specification TR-TSY-000476, "OTGR Network Maintenance Access and Testing."

To show interfaces currently in loopback operation, use the **show interfaces loopback** EXEC command.

#### *Example*

The following example configures a remote loopback test:

```
interface serial 0
 loopback remote
```

#### *Related Commands*

Search online to find documentation for related commands.

**show interfaces loopback**

### MAP-CLASS DIALER

To define a class of shared configuration parameters for outgoing calls from an ISDN interface, use the **map-class dialer** global configuration command.

**map-class dialer** *classname*

| *Syntax* | *Description* |
|---|---|
| *classname* | Unique class identifier. |

#### *Default*

Disabled; no class name is provided.

#### *Command Mode*

Global configuration

#### *Usage Guidelines*

This command first appeared in Cisco IOS Release 11.0.

The *classname* in the **map-class dialer** command used to specify the class must be the same as a *classname* used in a **dialer map** command.

This command is used to define classes of calls for PPP callback for DDR, for ISDN Advice of Charge, and for NSF call-by-call dialing plans.

For NSF call-by-call support on ISDN Primary-4ESS switches only, use one of the dialing-plan keywords listed in Table 16–2.

**Table 16–2** *NSF Keywords and Supported Services*

| Keyword | NSF Dialing Plan | Data | Voice | International |
|---|---|---|---|---|
| **sdnplan** | SDN | Yes | Yes | GSDN (Global SDN) |
| **megaplan** | MEGACOMM | No | Yes | Yes |
| **accuplan** | ACCUNET | Yes | Yes | Yes |

#### *Example*

The following example configures the PPP callback server on an ISDN BRI interface on a router in Atlanta. The callback server requires an enable timeout and a map class to be defined.

```
interface BRI0
 ip address 7.1.1.7 255.255.255.0
 encapsulation ppp
 dialer callback-secure
 dialer enable-timeout 2
 dialer map ip 7.1.1.8 name atlanta class dial1 81012345678901
```

```
 dialer-group 1
 ppp callback accept
 ppp authentication chap
!
map-class dialer dial1
 dialer callback-server username
```

In the following example, the ISDN switch type is set to Primary-4ESS, ISDN PRI is configured on T1 controller 1/0, and the D channel is configured for dialer map classes that reference the NSF dialing plans. Finally, the **map-class dialer** command uses a dialing plan keyword, and the **dialer outgoing** command refers to the same plan.

```
isdn switch-type primary-4ess
!
!
controller T1 1/0
 framing esf
 linecode b8zs
 pri-group timeslots 1-24
!
interface Serial1/0:23
 description This is the DMS D-channel 415-390-9503
 ip address 6.1.1.3 255.255.255.0
 encapsulation ppp
 no keepalive
 dialer map ip 6.1.1.1 name tommyjohn class sdnplan 14085770715
 dialer map ip 6.1.1.2 name angus class megaplan 14085773775
 dialer map ip 6.1.1.4 name angus class accuplan 14085773778
 dialer-group 1
 ppp authentication chap
!
map-class dialer sdnplan
 dialer outgoing sdn
!
map-class dialer megaplan
 dialer voice-call
 dialer outgoing mega
!
map-class dialer accuplan
 dialer outgoing accu
```

### *Related Commands*

Search online to find documentation for related commands.

**dialer map class**
**map-class dialer**
**dialer outgoing**

## PRI-GROUP

To specify ISDN Primary Rate Interface (PRI) on a channelized T1 or channelized E1 controller, use the **pri-group** controller configuration command. Use the **no** form of this command to remove the ISDN PRI configuration.

**pri-group** [**timeslots** *range*]
**no pri-group**

| *Syntax* | *Description* |
|---|---|
| **timeslots** *range* | (Optional) Specifies a single range of values from 1 to 23 for channelized T1 and from 1 to 31 for channelized E1. |

### *Default*

This command is disabled.

### *Command Mode*

Controller configuration

### *Usage Guidelines*

Before you enter the **pri-group** command, you must specify an ISDN PRI switch type and an E1 or T1 controller.

### *Examples*

The following example configures ISDN PRI on all timeslots of the T1 controller in slot 1 port 0 on a Cisco 7200 series router:

```
isdn switch-type primary-4ess
controllers t1 1/0
 framing esf
 linecode b8zs
 pri-group timeslots 1-24
```

The following example configures E1 controller 0 on a Cisco 4000 series router for ISDN PRI on all timeslots:

```
isdn switch-type primary-net5
controllers e1 0/0
 framing esf
 linecode b8zs
 pri-group timeslots 1-31
```

### *Related Commands*

Search online to find documentation for related commands.

**controllers e1**
**controllers t1**
**framing**
**isdn switch-type**
**linecode b8zs**

## SHOW CONTROLLERS E1

Use the **show controllers e1** privileged EXEC command to display information about the E1 links supported by the Network Processor Module (NPM) (Cisco 4000) or MultiChannel Interface Processor (MIP) (Cisco 7500 series).

**show controllers e1** [*slot/port*] (on the Cisco 7500 series)
**show controller e1** *number* (on the Cisco 4000 series)

| *Syntax* | *Description* |
|---|---|
| *slot/port* | Backplane slot number and port number on the interface. See your hardware installation manual for the specific slot and port numbers. |
| *number* | Network processor module (NPM) number, in the range 0 through 2. |

### *Command Mode*

Privileged EXEC

### *Usage Guidelines*

The NPM or MIP can query the port adapters to determine their current status. Issue a **show controllers e1** command to display statistics about the E1 link.

If you specify a slot and port number, each 15-minute period will be displayed.

This command displays controller status that is specific to the controller hardware. The information displayed is generally useful for diagnostic tasks performed by technical support personnel only.

### *Sample Displays*

The following is sample output from the **show controllers e1** command on the Cisco 7500 series:

```
Router# show controllers e1

e1 0/0 is up.
  Applique type is Channelized E1 - unbalanced
  Framing is CRC4, Line Code is HDB3
  No alarms detected.
  Data in current interval (725 seconds elapsed):
     0 Line Code Violations, 0 Path Code Violations
     0 Slip Secs, 0 Fr Loss Secs, 0 Line Err Secs, 0 Degraded Mins
     0 Errored Secs, 0 Bursty Err Secs, 0 Severely Err Secs, 0 Unavail Secs
  Total Data (last 24 hours)
     0 Line Code Violations, 0 Path Code Violations,
     0 Slip Secs, 0 Fr Loss Secs, 0 Line Err Secs, 0 Degraded Mins,
     0 Errored Secs, 0 Bursty Err Secs, 0 Severely Err Secs, 0 Unavail Secs
```

Following is an example of the **show controllers e1** display including the board identifier type:

```
Router# show controllers e1

E1 4/1 is up.
```

```
No alarms detected.
Framing is CRC4, Line Code is hdb3
Data in current interval (0 seconds elapsed):
   0 Line Code Violations, 0 Path Code Violations 0 Slip Secs, 0 Fr Loss Secs,
   0 Line Err Secs, 0 Degraded Mins 0 Errored Secs, 0 Bursty Err Secs,
   0 Severely Err Secs, 0 Unavail Secs
Total Data (last 79 15 minute intervals):
   0 Line Code Violations, 0 Path Code Violations, 0 Slip Secs, 0 Fr Loss Secs,
   0 Line Err Secs, 0 Degraded Mins, 0 Errored Secs, 0 Bursty Err Secs,
   0 Severely Err Secs, 0 Unavail Secs
```

Table 16–3 describes the **show controllers e1** display fields.

**Table 16–3** *Show Controllers E1 Field Descriptions*

| Field | Description |
|---|---|
| e1 0/0 is up. | The E1 controller 0 in slot 0 is operating. The controller's state can be up, down, or administratively down. Loopback conditions are shown by (Locally Looped) or (Remotely Looped). |
| Applique type | The applique type is shown and will indicate balanced or unbalanced. |
| Framing is | Shows the current framing type. |
| Linecode is | Shows the current linecode type. |
| No alarms detected. | Any alarms detected by the controller are displayed here. Possible alarms are as follows:<br>• Transmitter is sending remote alarm.<br>• Transmitter is sending AIS.<br>• Receiver has loss of signal.<br>• Receiver is getting AIS.<br>• Receiver has loss of frame.<br>• Receiver has remote alarm.<br>• Receiver has no alarms. |
| Data in current interval (725 seconds elapsed) | Shows the current accumulation period, which rolls into the 24-hour accumulation every 15 minutes. Accumulation period is from 1 to 900 seconds. The oldest 15-minute period falls off the back of the 24-hour accumulation buffer. |
| Line Code Violations | Indicates the occurrence of either a Bipolar Violation (BPV) or Excessive Zeros (EXZ) error event. |
| Path Code Violations | Indicates a frame synchronization bit error in the D4 and E1-noCRC formats, or a CRC error in the ESF and E1-CRC formats. |

**Table 16–3** *Show Controllers E1 Field Descriptions, Continued*

| Field | Description |
|---|---|
| Slip Secs | Indicates the replication or deletion of the payload bits of a DS1 frame. A slip might be performed when there is a difference between the timing of a synchronous receiving terminal and the received signal. |
| Fr Loss Secs | Indicates the number of seconds an Out Of Frame (OOF) error is detected. |
| Line Err Secs | Line Errored Seconds (LES) is a second in which one or more Line Code Violation errors are detected. |
| Degraded Mins | A Degraded Minute is one in which the estimated error rate exceeds 1E-6 but does not exceed 1E-3. |
| Errored Secs | In ESF and E1 CRC links, an Errored Second is a second in which one of the following are detected: one or more Path Code Violations; one or more Out of Frame defects; one or more Controlled Slip events; a detected AIS defect.<br>For SF and E1 no-CRC links, the presence of Bipolar Violations also triggers an Errored Second. |
| Bursty Err Secs | A second with fewer than 320 and more than 1 Path Coding Violation error, no Severely Errored Frame defects, and no detected incoming AIS defects. Controlled slips are not included in this parameter. |
| Severely Err Secs | For ESF signals, a second with one of the following errors: 320 or more Path Code Violation errors; one or more Out of Frame defects; a detected AIS defect.<br>For E1-CRC signals, a second with one of the following errors: 832 or more Path Code Violation errors; one or more Out of Frame defects.<br>For E1-nonCRC signals, a second with 2048 Line Code Violations or more.<br>For D4 signals, a count of 1-second intervals with Framing Errors, or an Out of Frame defect, or 1544 Line Code Violations. |
| Unavail Secs | A count of the total number of seconds on the interface. |

### SHOW CONTROLLERS T1

To display information about the T1 links, use the **show controllers t1** privileged EXEC command.

**show controllers t1** [*slot/port*] (Cisco 7500 series)
**show controller t1** *number* (Cisco 4000 series)

| *Syntax* | *Description* |
|---|---|
| *slot/port* | Backplane slot number and port number on the interface. See your hardware installation manual for the specific slot and port numbers. |
| *number* | Network processor module (NPM) number, in the range 0 through 2. |

#### *Command Mode*

EXEC

#### *Usage Guidelines*

This command displays controller status that is specific to the controller hardware. The information displayed is generally useful for diagnostic tasks performed by technical support personnel only.

The NPM or MIP can query the port adapters to determine their current status. Issue a **show controller t1** command to display statistics about the T1 link.

If you specify a slot and port number, each 15-minute period will be displayed.

#### *Sample Display*

The following is sample output from the **show controller t1** command on the Cisco 7500 series:

```
Router# show controllers t1

T1 4/1 is up.
  No alarms detected.
  Framing is ESF, Line Code is AMI, Clock Source is line
  Data in current interval (0 seconds elapsed):
     0 Line Code Violations, 0 Path Code Violations 0 Slip Secs, 0 Fr Loss Secs,
     0 Line Err Secs, 0 Degraded Mins 0 Errored Secs, 0 Bursty Err Secs,
     0 Severely Err Secs, 0 Unavail Secs
  Total Data (last 79 15 minute intervals):
     0 Line Code Violations, 0 Path Code Violations, 0 Slip Secs, 0 Fr Loss Secs,
     0 Line Err Secs, 0 Degraded Mins, 0 Errored Secs, 0 Bursty Err Secs,
     0 Severely Err Secs, 0 Unavail Secs
```

Table 16–4 describes the **show controllers t1** display fields.

**Table 16–4** *Show Controller T1 Field Descriptions*

| Field | Description |
|---|---|
| T1 0/0 is up. | The T1 controller 0 in slot 0 is operating. The controller's state can be up, down, administratively down. Loopback conditions are shown by (Locally Looped) or (Remotely Looped). |
| No alarm detected. | Any alarms detected by the controller are displayed here. Possible alarms are as follows:<br>• Transmitter is sending remote alarm.<br>• Transmitter is sending AIS.<br>• Receiver has loss of signal.<br>• Receiver is getting AIS.<br>• Receiver has loss of frame.<br>• Receiver has remote alarm.<br>• Receiver has no alarms. |
| Data in current interval (725 seconds elapsed) | Shows the current accumulation period, which rolls into the 24-hour accumulation every 15 minutes. Accumulation period is from 1 to 900 seconds. The oldest 15-minute period falls off the back of the 24-hour accumulation buffer. |
| Line Code Violations | Indicates the occurrence of either a Bipolar Violation (BPV) or Excessive Zeros (EXZ) error event. |
| Path Code Violations | Indicates a frame synchronization bit error in the D4 and E1-noCRC formats, or a CRC error in the ESF and E1-CRC formats. |
| Slip Secs | Indicates the replication or deletion of the payload bits of a DS1 frame. A slip may be performed when there is a difference between the timing of a synchronous receiving terminal and the received signal. |
| Fr Loss Secs | Indicates the number of seconds an Out Of Frame (OOF) error is detected. |
| Line Err Secs | Line Errored Seconds (LES) is a second in which one or more Line Code Violation errors are detected. |
| Degraded Mins | A Degraded Minute is one in which the estimated error rate exceeds 1E-6 but does not exceed 1E-3. |

**Table 16–4** *Show Controller T1 Field Descriptions, Continued*

| Field | Description |
|---|---|
| Errored Secs | In ESF and E1-CRC links, an Errored Second is a second in which one of the following are detected: one or more Path Code Violations; one or more Out of Frame defects; one or more Controlled Slip events; a detected AIS defect.<br>For D4 and E1-noCRC links, the presence of Bipolar Violations also triggers an Errored Second. |
| Bursty Err Secs | A second with fewer than 320 and more than 1 Path Coding Violation error, no Severely Errored Frame defects, and no detected incoming AIS defects. Controlled slips are not included in this parameter. |
| Severely Err Secs | For ESF signals, a second with one of the following errors: 320 or more Path Code Violation errors; one or more Out of Frame defects; a detected AIS defect.<br>For E1-CRC signals, a second with one of the following errors: 832 or more Path Code Violation errors; one or more Out of Frame defects.<br>For E1-noCRC signals, a second with 2048 Line Code Violations or more.<br>For D4 signals, a count of 1-second intervals with Framing Errors, or an Out of Frame defect, or 1544 Line Code Violations. |
| Unavail Secs | A count of the total number of seconds on the interface. |

## SHOW INTERFACES SERIAL BCHANNEL

To display information about the physical attributes of the ISDN PRI over channelized E1 or channelized T1 B and D channels, use the **show interfaces serial bchannel** EXEC command.

**show interfaces serial** *slot/port* **bchannel** *channel-number*
**show interfaces serial** *number* **bchannel** *channel-number*

| *Syntax* | *Description* |
|---|---|
| *slot/port* | Backplane slot number and port number on the interface. See your hardware installation manual for the specific slot and port numbers. |
| *number* | Network processor module (NPM) number, in the range 0 through 2. |
| *channel-number* | E1 Channel number in the range 1 to 31 or T1 channel number in the range 1 to 23. |

### *Command Mode*

EXEC

### *Usage Guidelines*

This command first appeared in Cisco IOS Release 11.2 F.

## SHOW ISDN

To display the information about memory, Layer 2 and Layer 3 timers, and the status of PRI channels, use the **show isdn** global configuration command.

**show isdn** {**active** | **history** | **memory** | **services** | **status** [*dsl* | **serial** *number*] | **timers**}

| *Syntax* | *Description* |
|---|---|
| **active** | Displays current call information, including called number, the time until the call is disconnected, AOC charging units used during the call, and whether the AOC information is provided during calls or at the end of calls. |
| **history** | Displays historic and current call information, including the called number, the time until the call is disconnected, AOC charging time units used during the call, and whether the AOC information is provided during calls or at the end of calls. |
| **memory** | Displays memory pool statistics. This keyword is for use by technical development staff only. |
| **services** | Displays the status of PRI channels. |
| **status** [*dsl* \| **serial** *number*] | Displays the status of all ISDN interfaces or, optionally, a specific digital signal link (DSL) or a specific ISDN PRI interface (created and configured as a serial interface). Values of *dsl* range 0 to 15. |
| **timers** | Displays the values of Layer 2 and Layer 3 timers. |

### *Command Mode*

Global configuration

### *Usage Guidelines*

This command first appeared in Cisco IOS Release 11.1.

### *Sample Displays*

The following is sample output from the **show isdn active** command:

```
Router# show isdn active

--------------------------------------------------------------------------------
                                ISDN ACTIVE CALLS
--------------------------------------------------------------------------------
History Table MaxLength = 320 entries
History Retain Timer = 15 Minutes
```

```
--------------------------------------------------------------------------------
Call Calling        Called         Duration  Remote    Time until   Recorded Charges
Type Number         Number         Seconds   Name      Disconnect   Units/Currency
--------------------------------------------------------------------------------
Out                9876543222       Active(10)  idacom               11       u(E)
Out                9876543210       Active(34)  idacom 115           5        u(D)
--------------------------------------------------------------------------------
```

The following is sample output from the **show isdn history** command:

```
Router# show isdn history

--------------------------------------------------------------------------------
                              ISDN CALL HISTORY
--------------------------------------------------------------------------------
History Table MaxLength = 320 entries
History Retain Timer = 15 Minutes
--------------------------------------------------------------------------------
Call Calling        Called         Duration  Remote    Time until   Recorded Charges
Type Number         Number         Seconds   Name      Disconnect   Units/Currency
--------------------------------------------------------------------------------
Out                47887654        240       blackcanary             5        u(D)
In    67893                        90        delorean
Out                56745678        Active(90)  blackcanary  240      13       u(D)
--------------------------------------------------------------------------------
```

Table 16–5 describes the fields in the **show isdn active** and **show isdn history** output displays.

**Table 16–5** *Show ISDN Active and Show ISDN History Field Descriptions*

| Field | Description |
|---|---|
| History Table MaxLength | Maximum number of entries that can be retained in the Call History table. |
| History Retain Timer | Maximum number of seconds any entry can be retained in Call History table. |
| Call Type | Type of call: incoming or outgoing. |
| Calling Number | For incoming calls, the number from which the call was received. |
| Called Number | For outgoing calls, the number to which the call was placed. |
| Duration Seconds | Number of seconds the call lasted. Indicates whether the call is still active, and how many seconds it has lasted so far. |
| Remote Name | Name of the host placing the call or the host called. |
| Time until Disconnect | Number of seconds before the call is configured to disconnect because of the static idle timer for the map class or the interface. |
| Recorded Charges Units/Currency | For outgoing calls, number of ISDN AOC charging units used or the currency cost of the call. |

The following sample display shows the output of the **show isdn service** command when PRI is configured on a T1 controller:

```
Router# show isdn service

PRI Channel Statistics:
ISDN Se1/0:23, Channel (1-31)
  Activated dsl 0
  State (0=Idle 1=Propose 2=Busy 3=Reserved 4=Restart 5=Maint)
  0 0 0 0 0 0 0 0 0 0 0 0 0 0 0 0 0 0 0 0 0 0 0 0 3 3 3 3 3 3 3
  Channel (1-31) Service (0=Inservice 1=Maint 2=Outofservice)
  0 0 0 0 0 0 0 0 0 0 0 0 0 0 0 0 0 0 0 0 0 0 0 2 0 0 0 0 0 0 0
```

Table 16–6 describes the fields in the sample output of the **show isdn service** command.

**Table 16–6** *Show ISDN Service Field Descriptions*

| Field | Description |
|---|---|
| ISDN Se1/0:23 | ISDN PRI interface corresponding to serial interface 1/0:23. |
| Channel (1-31) | Channel range "1-31" is a standard format for both T1 and E1 outputs, but the state value shown identifies whether the channel is used. |
| Activated dsl 0 | The digital signal link (DSL) value is 0. |
| State (0=Idle 1=Propose 2=Busy 3=Reserved 4=Restart 5=Maint) | Current state of each channel. Channels 24 through 31 are marked as reserved when the output is from T1. |
| Channel (1-31) Service (0=Inservice 1=Maint 2=Outofservice) | Service state assigned to each channel. Channel 24 is marked as out of service.* |

* If channel 24 (marked as out of service) is configured as the NFAS primary D channel, NFAS will roll over to the backup D channel if one is configured. If channel 24 is a B channel, calls will not be accepted to it.

The following shows sample output from the **show isdn status** command for PRI interfaces configured on two different ports of the same controller. This example shows one active call:

```
Router# show isdn status

The current ISDN Switchtype = primary-5ess
ISDN Serial1/0:23 interface
    Layer 1 Status:
        ACTIVE
    Layer 2 Status:
        TEI = 0, State = MULTIPLE_FRAME_ESTABLISHED
    Layer 3 Status:
        0 Active Layer 3 Call(s)
    Activated dsl 0 CCBs = 0
    Number of active calls = 0
    Number of available B-channels = 23
ISDN Serial1/1:23 interface
    Layer 1 Status:
```

```
        ACTIVE
    Layer 2 Status:
        TEI = 0, State = MULTIPLE_FRAME_ESTABLISHED
    Layer 3 Status:
        1 Active Layer 3 Call(s)
    Activated dsl 1 CCBs = 1
        CCB:callid=8001, callref=0, sapi=0, ces=0, B-chan=23
    Number of active calls = 1
    Number of available B-channels = 22
    Total Allocated ISDN CCBs = 1
```

Table 16–7 describes significant fields in the output of the **show isdn status** command.

**Table 16–7** *Show ISDN Status Field Descriptions*

| **Field** | **Description** |
|---|---|
| ISDN Switchtype = primary-5ess | PRI switch type the router is connected to. |
| ISDN Serial1/0:23 interface | Serial slot, port, and timeslot numbers that define the PRI interface location. |
| **Layer 1 Status** | |
| ACTIVE | Status of ISDN Layer 1. |
| **Layer 2 Status** | |
| TEI = 65,<br>State = MULTIPLE_FRAME_ESTABLISHED | Status of ISDN Layer 2. Terminal endpoint identifier number and multiframe structure state. |
| **Layer 3 Status:** | |
| 1 Active Layer 3 Call(s) | Number of active calls. |
| Activated dsl 1 CCBs = | Number of the Digital Signal Link activated. Number of call control blocks in use. |
| CCB:callid=8001, callref=0, sapi=0, ces=1, B-chan=23 | Call control block information about the active call. |
| Number of active calls = | Number of active calls. |
| Number of available B-channels = | Number of B channels that are not being used. |
| Total Allocated ISDN CCBs = | Number of ISDN call control blocks that are allocated. |

# CHAPTER 17

# Configuring ISDN Special Signaling

This chapter describes features that either depend on special signaling services offered by an ISDN network service provider or overcome an inability to deliver certain signals.

For a complete description of the ISDN signaling commands in this chapter, see Chapter 18, "Special ISDN Signaling Commands."

This following sections of this chapter describe how to configure special signaling features of ISDN:

- Configuring ISDN AOC
- Configuring ISDN NFAS
- Configuring ISDN Semipermanent Connections
- Configuring ISDN BRI for Leased-Line Service
- Configuring Automatic Detection of Encapsulation Type
- Configuring Encapsulation for Combinet Compatibility

ISDN signaling configuration examples can be found at the end of this chapter. A troubleshooting section can also be found later in this chapter.

## CONFIGURING ISDN AOC

ISDN Advice of Charge (AOC) allows users to obtain charging information for all calls during the call (AOC-D) or at the end of the call (AOC-E) or both.

Users must have subscribed through their local ISDN network to receive the AOC information from the switch. No router configuration changes are required to retrieve this call-charging information.

The ISDN AOC feature also supports, for the AOC-D service, an optional configurable short-hold mode that provides a dynamic idle timeout by measuring the call-charging period, based on the frequency of the AOC-D or the AOC-E message from the network. The short-hold mode allows users to track call costs and to control and possibly reduce tariff charges. The short-hold mode idle time will do the following:

- Disconnect a call just prior to the beginning of a new charging period if the call has been idle for at least the configured minimum idle time.
- Maintain the call to the end of the current charging period past the configured idle timeout if the time left in the charging period is longer.

Incoming calls are disconnected using the static dialer idle timeout value.

The AOC-D and AOC-E messages are part of the Facility Information Element (IE) message. Its contents can be verified with the **debug q931** command. Call accounting information from AOC-D and AOC-E messages is stored in SNMP MIB objects.

ISDN AOC is provided for ISDN PRI NET5 and ISDN BRI NET3 switch types only. AOC information at call setup is not supported.

### ISDN AOC Terminology

**AOC-D message**—ISDN Advice of Charge information sent during a call. The message is sent periodically by the network to subscribers of AOC during-call services.

**AOC-E message**—ISDN Advice of Charge information sent at the end of a call. The message is sent periodically by the network to subscribers of AOC end-of-call services.

**Short-hold mode**—Configurable option for outgoing calls that causes the dialer idle timeout to be at the end of the current charging period, after a specified minimum idle time has elapsed. If the link has been idle less than the specified minimum time, the call stays connected into another charging period.

### Configure Short-Hold Mode

No configuration is required to enable ISDN AOC.

However, you can configure the optional short-hold minimum idle timeout period for outgoing calls; the default minimum idle timeout is 120 seconds. If the short-hold option is not configured, the router default is to use the static dialer idle timeout. If the short-hold idle timeout has been configured but no charging information is available from the network, the static dialer idle timeout applies.

To configure an ISDN interface and provide the AOC short-hold mode option on an ISDN interface, complete the following steps:

**Step 1** Configure the ISDN BRI or PRI interface—as described in Chapter 11, "Setting Up ISDN Basic Rate Service,"or section, "Configuring ISDN PRI," of Chapter 15, "Configuring Channelized E1 and Channelized T1"—using the relevant keyword in the **isdn switch-type** command:

- BRI interface—**basic-net3**
- PRI interface—**primary-net5**

**Step 2** Configure Dialer Profiles or legacy DDR for outgoing calls, as described in the chapters found in Part V, "Dial-on-Demand Routing," making sure to do the following:

- Configure the static line-idle timeout to be used for incoming calls.
- For each destination, use the **dialer map** command with the **class** keyword (legacy DDR) or a **dialer string class** command (Dialer Profiles) to identify the dialer map class to be used for outgoing calls to the destination.

**Step 3** Configure each specified dialer map class, providing a dialer idle timeout, or ISDN short-hold timeout, or both for outgoing calls, as described in this chapter.

To configure a dialer map class with timers, complete the following tasks beginning in global configuration mode:

| Task | | Command |
|---|---|---|
| **Step 1** | Specify the dialer map class. | **map-class dialer** *class-name* |
| **Step 2** | (Optional) Specify a static idle timeout for the map class to override the static line-idle timeout configured on the BRI interface. | **dialer idle-timeout** *seconds* |
| **Step 3** | Specify a dialer ISDN short-hold timeout for the map class. | **dialer isdn short-hold** *seconds* |

### Monitor ISDN AOC Call Information

Use the following command to monitor ISDN AOC call information:

| Task | Command |
|---|---|
| Display information about active calls, call history, memory, Layer 2 or Layer 3 timers, or status of PRI channels. The **history** keyword displays AOC charging time units used during the call and indicates whether the AOC information is provided during calls or at the end of calls.<br>(The service keyword is available for PRI only.) | **show isdn** {**active** \| **history** \| **memory** \| **service** \| **status** \| **timers**} |

## CONFIGURING ISDN NFAS

ISDN Non-Facility Associated Signaling (NFAS) allows a single D channel to control multiple PRI interfaces. A backup D channel can also be configured for use when the primary NFAS D channel fails.

Use of a single D channel to control multiple PRI interfaces can free one B channel on each interface to carry other traffic.

Once the channelized T1 controllers are configured for ISDN PRI, only the NFAS primary D channel must be configured; its configuration is distributed to all members of the associated NFAS group.

### ISDN NFAS Prerequisites

The router must connect to an AT&T 4ESS ISDN PRI switch. It must also have a channelized T1 controller and, as a result, be ISDN PRI capable.

In addition, the router's channelized T1 controllers must be configured for ISDN, as described in the section "Configuring ISDN PRI," of Chapter 15.

### ISDN NFAS Terminology

The following terms are used in this description of ISDN NFAS:

**24 B channel interface**—PRI channel group configured to have no NFAS D channel; all its channels are B channels.

**NFAS group**—PRI channel group (the group of interfaces) under control of a single D channel. The channel group can include all the ISDN channels on multiple T1 controllers.

**NFAS member**—PRI interface in an NFAS group. For example, an NFAS group might include serial interfaces 1/0:23, 1/1:23, and 2/0:23 if T1 controllers 1/0, 1/1, and 2/0 are configured for NFAS.

### ISDN NFAS Configuration Task List

To configure NFAS on channelized T1 controllers configured for ISDN, complete the tasks in the following section:

- Configure NFAS on PRI Groups

You can also take a channel or interface out of service, if necessary, and monitor NFAS groups and ISDN service. To do so, complete the tasks in the following sections:

- Take a Channel or Interface Out of Service
- Monitor NFAS Groups
- Monitor ISDN Service

See section "NFAS Primary and Backup D Channels Example" later in this chapter for a complete ISDN, NFAS, and DDR configuration.

#### *Configure NFAS on PRI Groups*

When configuring NFAS, you use an extended version of the ISDN **pri-group** command to specify the following for specified channelized T1 controllers configured for ISDN:

- The range of PRI timeslots to be under the control of the D channel (timeslot 24).
- The function to be performed by timeslot 24 (primary D channel, backup, or none); the latter specifies its use as a B channel.
- The group identifier number for the interface under this D channel's control.

To configure ISDN NFAS, complete the following tasks in controller configuration mode:

| Task | Command |
|---|---|
| On one channelized T1 controller, configure the NFAS primary D channel. | **pri-group timeslots 1-24 nfas_d primary nfas_interface** *number* **nfas_group** *number* |
| On a different channelized T1 controller, configure the NFAS backup D channel to be used if the primary D channel fails. | **pri-group timeslots 1-24 nfas_d backup nfas_interface** *number* **nfas_group** *number* |
| On other channelized T1 controllers, configure a 24 B channel interface, if desired. (Optional) | **pri-group timeslots 1-24 nfas_d none nfas_interface** *number* **nfas_group** *number* |

For an example of configuring three T1 controllers for the NFAS primary D channel, the backup D channel, and 24 B channels, along with the DDR configuration for the PRI interface, see section "NFAS Primary and Backup D Channels Example" later in this chapter.

When a backup NFAS D channel is configured and the primary NFAS D channel fails, rollover to the backup D channel is automatic and all connected calls stay connected.

### Take a Channel or Interface Out of Service

You can take a specified channel or an entire PRI interface out of service or put it into one of the other states that is passed into the switch. To do so, complete one of the following tasks in interface configuration mode:

| Task | Command |
|---|---|
| Take an individual B channel out of service or set it to a different state. | **isdn service dsl** *number* **b_channel** *number* **state** *state-value* |
| Set the entire PRI interface to the specified state. | **isdn service dsl** *number* **b_channel 0 state** *state-value* |

These are the supported state values:

- 0—In service
- 1—Maintenance
- 2—Out of service

### Monitor NFAS Groups

To monitor NFAS groups, complete the following task in EXEC mode:

| Task | Command |
|---|---|
| Display information about members of an NFAS group. | **show isdn nfas group** *number* |

### *Monitor ISDN Service*

To display information about ISDN channel service states, complete the following task in EXEC mode:

| Task | Command |
|---|---|
| Display information about ISDN channels and the service states. | **show isdn service** |

## Configuring ISDN Semipermanent Connections

German networks allow semipermanent connections between customer routers with BRIs and the 1TR6 basic rate switches in the exchange. Australian networks allow semipermanent connections between ISDN PRIs and the TS-014 primary rate switches in the exchange. Semipermanent connections are offered at better pricing than leased lines.

Configuring BRIs for semipermanent connection requires only that you use a keyword that indicates semipermanent connections when you are setting up network addressing as described in the previous section of this chapter.

To configure a BRI for semipermanent connections, complete the following tasks:

**Step 1** Set up the ISDN lines and ports as described in Chapter 11 or in the section "Configuring ISDN PRI" of Chapter 15.

**Step 2** Configure dial-on-demand routing on a selected interface, as described in the chapters found in Part V.

When you get to the DDR network addressing step, complete the following task in interface configuration mode:

| Task | Command |
|---|---|
| Define the remote recipient's protocol address, host name, and dialing string; indicate semipermanent connections; optionally, provide the ISDN subaddress; set the dialer speed to 56 or 64 Kbps, as needed. | **dialer map** *protocol next-hop-address* **name** *hostname* **spc** [**speed 56 \| 64**] [**broadcast**] *dial-string*[*:isdn-subaddress*] |

## Configuring ISDN BRI for Leased-Line Service

To configure ISDN BRI for leased-line service, perform the tasks in one of the following sections as needed and available locally:

- Configure Leased-Line Service at Normal Speeds (available in Japan and Germany)
- Configure Leased-Line Service at 128 Kbps (available only in Japan)

**NOTES**

Once an ISDN BRI interface is configured for access over leased lines, it is no longer a dialer interface, and signaling over the D channel no longer applies. Although the interface is called **interface bri** *n*, it is configured as a synchronous serial interface having the default HDLC encapsulation. However, the Cisco IOS commands that set the physical characteristics of a serial interface (such as the pulse time) do not apply to this interface.

## Configure Leased-Line Service at Normal Speeds

This service is offered in Japan and Germany, and no call setup or tear-down is involved. Data is placed on the ISDN interface similar to the way data is placed on a leased line connected to a serial port.

To configure the BRI to use the ISDN connection as a leased-line service, complete the following tasks in global configuration mode:

| Task | Command |
|---|---|
| Configure the BRI switch type, as specified by the local service provider. | **isdn switch-type** *type* |
| Specify the BRI interface number. | **isdn leased-line bri** *number* |

To disable leased-line service if you no longer want to support it on a specified ISDN BRI, complete the following task in global configuration mode:

| Task | Command |
|---|---|
| Remove leased-line configuration from a specified ISDN BRI interface. | **no isdn leased-line bri** *number* |

## Configure Leased-Line Service at 128 Kbps

Beginning in Cisco IOS Release 11.2, leased-line service at 128 Kbps via ISDN BRI is supported. This service combines two B channels into a single pipe.

This feature requires one or more ISDN BRI hardware interfaces that support channel aggregation and service provider support for ISDN channel aggregation at 128 Kbps. At the time of Release 11.2, service providers offered support for ISDN channel aggregation at 128 Kbps only in Japan.

**NOTES**

This feature is not supported on the Cisco 2500 series because its BRI hardware does not support channel aggregation.

To enable leased-line service at 128 Kbps on a specified ISDN BRI, complete the following tasks in global configuration mode:

| Task | Command |
|---|---|
| Select the service provider switch type. | **isdn switch-type** *switch-type* |
| Configure a specified BRI for access over leased lines. | **isdn leased-line bri** *number* **128** |

To complete the configuration of the interface, see Chapter 13, "Configuring Synchronous Serial Ports."

To remove the leased-line service configuration from a specified ISDN BRI, complete the following task in global configuration mode:

| Task | Command |
|---|---|
| Remove leased-line configuration from a specified ISDN BRI interface. | **no isdn leased-line bri** *number* |

## CONFIGURING AUTOMATIC DETECTION OF ENCAPSULATION TYPE

You can enable a serial or ISDN interface to accept calls and dynamically change the encapsulation in effect on the interface when the remote device does not signal the call type. For example, if an ISDN call does not identify the call type in the lower-layer compatibility fields and is using an encapsulation that is different from the one configured on the interface, the interface can change its encapsulation type dynamically.

This feature enables interoperation with ISDN terminal adapters that use V.120 encapsulation but do not signal V.120 in the call setup message. An ISDN interface that by default answers a call as synchronous serial with PPP encapsulation can change its encapsulation and answer such calls.

Automatic detection is attempted for the first 10 seconds after the link is established or the first five packets exchanged over the link, whichever is first.

To enable automatic detection of encapsulation type, perform the following task in interface configuration mode:

| Task | Command |
|---|---|
| Enable automatic detection of encapsulation type on the specified interface. | **autodetect encapsulation** *encapsulation-type* |

You can specify one or more encapsulations to detect. Cisco IOS software currently supports automatic detection of PPP and V.120 encapsulations.

## Configuring Encapsulation for Combinet Compatibility

Historically, Combinet devices supported only the Combinet Packet Protocol (CPP) for negotiating connections over ISDN B channels. To enable Cisco routers to communicate with those Combinet bridges, the Cisco IOS supports a new CPP encapsulation type.

To enable routers to communicate over ISDN interfaces with Combinet bridges that support only CPP, perform the following tasks in interface configuration mode:

| Task | Command |
|---|---|
| Specify CPP encapsulation. | **encapsulation cpp** |
| Enable CPP callback acceptance. | **cpp callback accept** |
| Enable CPP authentication. | **cpp authentication** |

Now most Combinet devices support PPP. Cisco routers can communicate over ISDN with these devices by using PPP encapsulation, which supports both routing and fast switching.

Combinet devices support only IP, IPX, and bridging. For AppleTalk, Cisco routers automatically perform half-bridging with Combinet devices. For more information about half-bridging, see the section "Configuring PPP Half-Bridging on Serial Interfaces" of Chapter 25, "Configuring Media-Independent PPP and Multilink PPP."

Cisco routers can also half-bridge IP and IPX with Combinet devices that support only CPP. To configure this feature, you only need to set up the addressing with the ISDN interface as part of the remote subnet; no additional commands are required.

## Troubleshooting ISDN

You can troubleshoot ISDN by using the following commands:

| Task | Command |
|---|---|
| Display the values of timers. | **debug dialer** |
| Display link layer information for all interfaces or, optionally, for a single BRI interface.<br>or<br>Display link layer information for a single PRI interface. | **debug isdn q921** [**interface bri** *number*]<br><br><br>**debug isdn q921 interface serial** *slot/controller-number*:**23** |
| Display the content of call-control messages and information elements, in particular the Facility IE message for all interfaces or, optionally, for a single BRI interface.<br>or<br>Display the content of call-control messages and information elements, in particular the Facility IE message for a single PRI interface. | **debug isdn q931** [**interface bri** *number*]<br><br><br><br><br>**debug isdn q931 interface serial** *slot/controller-number*:**23** |

## ISDN Signaling Configuration Examples

This section provides the following configuration examples:

- ISDN AOC Configuration Examples
- ISDN NFAS Configuration Examples
- ISDN BRI Leased-Line Configuration Examples

### ISDN AOC Configuration Examples

This section provides the following ISDN Advice of Charge configuration examples:

- Using Legacy DDR for ISDN PRI AOC Configuration Example
- Using Dialer Profiles for ISDN BRI AOC Configuration Example

#### *Using Legacy DDR for ISDN PRI AOC Configuration Example*

This example shows ISDN PRI configured on an E1 controller. Legacy DDR is configured on the ISDN D channel (serial interface 0:15) and propagates to all ISDN B channels. A static dialer idle-timeout is configured for all incoming calls on the B channels, but the map classes are configured independently of it. Map classes Kappa and Beta use AOC charging unit duration to calculate the timeout for the call. A short-hold idle timer is set so that if the line is idle for 10 or more seconds, the call is disconnected when the current charging period ends. Map class Iota uses a static idle timeout.

```
version 11.2
service timestamps debug datetime msec
service timestamps log datetime msec
!
hostname A
```

```
!
username c2503isdn password 7 1511021F0725
username B password 7 110A1016141D29
username C password 7 1511021F072508
isdn switch-type primary-net5
!
controller E1 0
 pri-group timeslots 1-31
!
interface Serial 0:15
 ip address 10.0.0.35 255.0.0.0
 encapsulation ppp
 dialer idle-timeout 150
 dialer map ip 10.0.0.33 name c2503isdn class Iota 06966600050
 dialer map ip 10.0.0.40 name B class Beta 778578
 dialer map ip 10.0.0.45 name C class Kappa 778579
 dialer-group 1
 ppp authentication chap
!
map-class dialer Kappa
 dialer idle-timeout 300
 dialer isdn short-hold 120
!
map-class dialer Iota
 dialer idle-timeout 300
!
map-class dialer Beta
 dialer idle-timeout 300
 dialer isdn short-hold 90
!
dialer-list 1 protocol ip permit
```

### *Using Dialer Profiles for ISDN BRI AOC Configuration Example*

This example shows ISDN BRI configured as a member of two dialer pools for Dialer Profiles.

```
version 11.2
service timestamps debug datetime msec
service timestamps log datetime msec
!
hostname delorean
!
username spanky password 7 0705344245
username delorean password 7 1511021F0725
isdn switch-type basic-net3
!
interface BRI0
 description Connected to NTT 81012345678901
 no ip address
 dialer pool-member 1 max-link 1
 dialer pool-member 2 max-link
 encapsulation ppp
 no fair-queue
!
interface Dialer1
```

```
 ip address 7.1.1.8 255.255.255.0
 encapsulation ppp
 dialer remote-name spanky
 dialer string 81012345678902 class Omega
 dialer pool 1
 dialer-group 1
 ppp authentication chap
!
interface Dialer2
 ip address 8.1.1.8 255.255.255.0
 encapsulation ppp
 dialer remote-name dmsisdn
 dialer string 81012345678902 class Omega
 dialer string 14153909503 class Gamma
 dialer pool 2
 dialer-group 1
 ppp authentication chap
!
map-class dialer Omega
 dialer idle-timeout 60
 dialer isdn short-hold 150
!
map-class dialer Gamma
 dialer isdn short-hold 60
!
dialer-list 1 protocol ip permit
```

## ISDN NFAS Configuration Examples

This section provides the following configuration examples:

- NFAS Primary and Backup D Channels Example
- PRI Interface Service State Example

### NFAS Primary and Backup D Channels Example

The following example configures ISDN PRI and NFAS on three T1 controllers of a Cisco 7500 series router. The NFAS primary D channel is configured on the 1/0 controller, and the NFAS backup D channel is configured on the 1/1 controller. No NFAS D channel is configured on the 2/0 controller; it is configured for 24 B channels.

Once the NFAS primary D channel is configured, it is the only interface you see and have to configure; DDR configuration for the primary D channel—which is distributed to all B channels—is also included in this example.

```
isdn switch-type primary-4ess
!
! NFAS primary D channel on the channelized T1 controller in 1/0
controller t1 1/0
 framing esf
linecode b8zs
 pri-group timeslots 1-24 nfas_d primary nfas_interface 0 nfas_group 1
!
```

```
! NFAS backup D channel on the channelized T1 controller in 1/1
controller t1 1/1
 framing esf
linecode b8zs
 pri-group timeslots 1-24 nfas_d backup nfas_interface 1 nfas_group 1
!
! NFAS 24 B channels on the channelized T1 controller in 2/0
controller t1 2/0
 framing esf
linecode b8zs
 pri-group timeslots 1-24 nfas_d none nfas_interface 2 nfas_group 1
!
! NFAS primary D channel interface configuration for PPP and DDR. This
! configuration is distributed to all the B channels in NFAS group 1 on the
! three channelized T1 controllers.
!
interface Serial 1/0:23
 ip address 1.1.1.2 255.255.255.0
 no ip mroute-cache
 encapsulation ppp
 dialer map ip 1.1.1.1 name flyboy 567898
 dialer map ip 1.1.1.3 name flyboy 101112345678
 dialer map ip 1.1.1.4 name flyboy 01112345678
 dialer-group 1
 no fair-queue
 no cdp enable
 ppp authentication chap
```

### *PRI Interface Service State Example*

The following example puts the entire PRI interface back in service after it previously had been taken out of service:

```
isdn service dsl 0 b-channel 0 state 0
```

## ISDN BRI Leased-Line Configuration Examples

The following example configures the BRI 0 interface for leased-line access at 128 Kbps. Because of the leased-line—not dialed—environment, configuration of ISDN called and calling numbers are not needed and not used. The BRI 0 interface is henceforth treated as a synchronous serial interface, with the default HDLC encapsulation.

```
isdn leased-line bri 0 128
```

The following example configures the BRI 0 interface for PPP encapsulation:

```
interface bri 0
 ip address 1.1.1.2 255.255.255.0
 encapsulation ppp
 bandwidth 128
```

# CHAPTER 18

# Special ISDN Signaling Commands

This chapter describes the commands available to configure special ISDN signaling for dial-up solutions on your router. These signaling features are supported:

- ISDN Advice of Charge (AOC)
- ISDN Non-Facility Associated Signaling (NFAS)
- ISDN semipermanent connections
- Automatic detection of encapsulation type
- Encapsulation for Combinet compatibility

For information about configuring ISDN special signaling features, see Chapter 17, "Configuring ISDN Special Signaling."

## AUTODETECT ENCAPSULATION

To enable automatic detection of the encapsulation types in operation over a point-to-point link to a specified serial or ISDN interface, use the **autodetect encapsulation** interface configuration command. To disable automatic, dynamic detection of the encapsulation types in operation on a link, use the **no** form of this command.

**autodetect encapsulation** *encapsulation-type*
**no autodetect encapsulation**

| *Syntax* | *Description* |
|---|---|
| *encapsulation-type* | One or both of the encapsulation keywords **v120** and **ppp**. |

### *Default*

Disabled

### *Command Mode*

Interface configuration

### *Usage Guidelines*

This command first appeared in Cisco IOS Release 11.2.

At least one encapsulation type is required in the command, but you can specify additional encapsulation types.

Use this command to enable the specified serial or ISDN interface to accept calls and dynamically change the encapsulation in effect on the interface when the remote device does not signal the call type. For example, if an ISDN call does not identify the call type in the Lower Layer Compatibility fields and is using an encapsulation that is different from the one configured on the interface, the interface can change its encapsulation type dynamically.

This command enables interoperation with ISDN terminal adapters that use V.120 encapsulation but do not signal V.120 in the call setup message. An ISDN interface that by default answers a call as synchronous serial with PPP encapsulation can change its encapsulation and answer such calls.

Automatic detection is attempted for the first 10 seconds after the link is established or the first five packets exchanged over the link, whichever is first.

### *Example*

The following command line enables automatic detection of V.120 encapsulation.

```
autodetect encapsulation v120
```

### *Related Commands*

Search online to find documentation for related commands.

**encapsulation**

## CPP AUTHENTICATION

To enable negotiation of authentication with a router or bridge that supports the Combinet Proprietary Protocol (CPP) and that is calling in to this router, use the **cpp authentication** interface configuration command. To disable negotiation of CPP authentication, use the **no** form of this command.

**cpp authentication**
**no cpp authentication**

### *Syntax Description*

This command has no arguments or keywords.

*Default*

Disabled

*Command Mode*

Interface configuration

*Usage Guidelines*

This command first appeared in Cisco IOS Release 11.2.

Use this command for authenticating the device that is calling in to this router.

Use this command to communicate over an ISDN interface with Combinet devices that do not support Point-to-Point Protocol (PPP) but do support the Combinet Proprietary Protocol (CPP).

Currently, most Combinet devices *do* support PPP. Cisco routers can communicate over ISDN with these devices by using PPP encapsulation, which supports both routing and fast switching.

This command is supported on ISDN and dialer interfaces.

This command uses names and passwords from the **username password** command. It does not support the Terminal Access Controller Access Control System (TACACS).

*Example*

The following example configures a Basic Rate Interface (BRI) to communicate with a Combinet bridge that does not support PPP:

```
interface bri 0
 encapsulation cpp
 cpp callback accept
 cpp authentication
```

*Related Commands*

Search online to find documentation for related commands.

**cpp callback accept**
**encapsulation cpp**
**username password**

### CPP CALLBACK ACCEPT

To enable the router to accept callback from a Combinet router or bridge that supports the Combinet Proprietary Protocol (CPP), use the **cpp callback accept** interface configuration command.

**cpp callback accept**

*Syntax Description*

This command has no arguments or keywords.

### Default

Disabled

### Command Mode

Interface configuration

### Usage Guidelines

This command first appeared in Cisco IOS Release 11.2.

Use this command to communicate over an ISDN interface with Combinet devices that do not support PPP but do support CPP.

Currently, most Combinet devices *do* support PPP. Cisco routers can communicate over ISDN with these devices by using PPP encapsulation, which supports both routing and fast switching.

This command is supported on ISDN and dialer interfaces.

### Example

The following example configures BRI 0 to communicate with a Combinet router or bridge that does not support PPP:

```
interface bri 0
encapsulation cpp
cpp callback accept
cpp authentication
```

### Related Commands

Search online to find documentation for related commands.

**cpp authentication**
**encapsulation cpp**

## DIALER ISDN SHORT-HOLD

To configure the router to disconnect a call at the end of the current charging period if the line has been idle for at least the specified minimum period, use the **dialer isdn short-hold** map-class dialer configuration command. To reset the ISDN short-hold timer to the default period, use the **no** form of the command.

**dialer isdn short-hold** *seconds*
**no dialer isdn short-hold**

| Syntax | Description |
| --- | --- |
| *seconds* | Minimum number of seconds of idle time on the line. Default is 120 seconds. |

### *Default*

Disabled; the router uses a static idle timeout. When this command is enabled, the default short-hold timeout is 120 seconds.

### *Command Mode*

Map-class dialer configuration

### *Usage Guidelines*

This command first appeared in Cisco IOS Release 11.3.

This command is used for configuring ISDN Advice of Charge (AOC) on Cisco routers.

Use the **dialer isdn short-hold** command if you subscribe to an ISDN AOC during-call service provided by the local ISDN network and want to use this option. The router uses the frequency at which the network sends the AOC-D message to determine the charging period. If the line has been idle for the short-hold timeout, the call disconnects at the end of the charging period. If the line has not been idle for at least that long, the call is maintained into the next charging period.

### *Example*

The following partial example configures the dialer map class *Deutschland* with a static idle timeout for outgoing calls. The static idle timer is to be used if for any reason the network does not provide charging information. It also configures a short-hold timeout to allow the router to determine dynamically whether to disconnect or continue the call at the end of the charging period.

```
dialer map-class Deutschland
 dialer idle-timeout 150
 dialer isdn short-hold 120
```

### *Related Commands*

Search online to find documentation for related commands.

**dialer idle-timeout (map-class dialer configuration)**
**dialer map** (AOC) (with the **class** keyword)
**dialer string (dialer profiles)**
**map-class dialer**

## DIALER MAP (AOC)

To configure an ISDN interface to place a call to multiple sites, to authenticate calls from multiple sites, and to identify the class name that configures the ISDN AOC short-hold idle timeout, use the following form of the **dialer map** interface configuration command:

**dialer map** *protocol next-hop-address* [**name** *hostname*] [**spc**] [**speed 56 | 64**] [**broadcast**]
 **class** *class-name* [*dial-string*[*:isdn-subaddress*]]
**no dialer map** *protocol next-hop-address* [**name** *hostname*] [**spc**] [**speed 56 | 64**]
[**broadcast**]
 **class** *class-name* [*dial-string*[*:isdn-subaddress*]]

| *Syntax* | *Description* |
|---|---|
| *protocol* | Protocol keywords; one of the following: **appletalk**, **bridge**, **clns**, **decnet**, **ip**, **ipx**, **novell**, **snapshot**, **vines**, and **xns**. |
| *next-hop-address* | Protocol address used to match against addresses to which packets are destined. This argument is not used with the **bridge** protocol keyword. |
| **name** *hostname* | (Optional) Case-sensitive name or ID of the remote device (usually the host name). For routers with ISDN interfaces, if calling line identification—sometimes called *CLI*, but also known as *caller ID* and *automatic number identification* (ANI)—is provided, the *hostname* field can contain the number that the calling line ID provides. |
| **spc** | (Optional) Specifies a semipermanent connection between customer equipment and the exchange; used only in Germany to configure connections between an ISDN BRI and a 1TR6 ISDN switch type. |
| **speed 56 \| 64** | (Optional) Line speed in kilobits per second to use. Used for ISDN only. The default speed is 64 Kbps. |
| **broadcast** | (Optional) Indicates that broadcasts should be forwarded to this protocol address. |
| **class** *class-name* | Name of the class that configures the ISDN AOC static dialer timeout period or the short-hold timeout period or both. |
| *dial-string*[:*isdn-subaddress*] | (Optional) Telephone number and optional ISDN subaddress used for ISDN multipoint connections that are sent to the dialing device when it recognizes packets with the specified next hop address that matches the access lists defined. The dial string and ISDN subaddress, if used, must be the last item in the command line. |

#### *Defaults*

No dialer map is configured. The default speed is 64 Kbps. No default class name is provided.

#### *Command Mode*

Interface configuration

#### *Usage Guidelines*

A simple version of the **dialer map** command first appeared in Cisco IOS Release 9.1. This version of the **dialer map** command for AOC first appeared in Cisco IOS Release 11.3.

This form of the **dialer map** command is used for configuring ISDN Advice of Charge (AOC) on Cisco routers.

For ISDN interfaces, use the **dialer map** command with the **name** keyword in configurations in which remote sites are calling a central site, but the central site is not calling the remote site. With this command, the local device will authenticate the remote site using CHAP or PAP, which will transmit the remote site's host name to the central site. The central site will then use this name to authenticate the caller, and will use the next hop address to transmit packets to the remote site. Because there is no dialer string specified, the central site cannot call the remote router.

For ISDN interfaces only, you can specify an optional speed parameter for **dialer map** commands if you also specify a dial string. This option informs the ISDN software whether it should place a call at 56 or 64 Kbps. If you omit the ISDN speed parameter, the default is 64 Kbps.

For routers with ISDN interfaces, if calling line identification (CLI)—also known as *caller ID* and *ANI*—is provided, the *hostname* field may contain the number that calling line ID provides.

Use the **dialer map** command with the **class** keyword for outgoing calls when the network provides ISDN Advice of Charge (AOC) information. Use the **map-class dialer** global command to identify the class name, the **dialer idle-timeout** map-class command to define a static idle timeout period for outgoing calls to the class, and the **dialer isdn short-hold** map-class command to define the minimum idle time to wait before disconnecting calls at the end of the charging period.

### Example

In the following legacy DDR example, a BRI interface is configured with dialer map classes to use for outgoing calls and a dialer idle timeout period to use for all incoming calls. All of the map classes are configured with dialer idle timeout periods that override the interface static dialer idle timeout for outgoing calls. Two map classes are also configured for an ISDN AOC short-hold idle timeout.

```
hostname A
!
username c2503isdn password 7 1511021F0725
username B password 7 110A1016141D29
username C password 7 1511021F072508
isdn switch-type basic-net3
!
interface bri 0
 ip address 10.0.0.35 255.0.0.0
 encapsulation ppp
 dialer idle-timeout 150
 dialer map ip 10.0.0.33 name c2503isdn class Iota 06966600050
 dialer map ip 10.0.0.40 name B class Beta 778578
 dialer map ip 10.0.0.45 name C class Kappa 778579
 ppp authentication chap
!
map-class dialer Kappa
 dialer idle-timeout 300
 dialer isdn short-hold 10
!
map-class dialer Iota
 dialer idle-timeout 300
!
```

```
map-class dialer Beta
 dialer idle-timeout 300
 dialer isdn short-hold 10
```

*Related Commands*

Search online to find documentation for related commands.

**dialer isdn short-hold**
**map-class dialer**
**ppp authentication chap**
**username**

## DIALER MAP (SPC)

To set up network addressing on an ISDN BRI interface to support semipermanent connections (if the ISDN switch supports such connections), use the following form of the **dialer map** interface configuration command:

**dialer map** *protocol next-hop-address* [**name** *hostname*] **spc** [**speed 56 | 64**] [**broadcast**] *dial-string*[*:isdn-subaddress*]
**no dialer map** *protocol next-hop-address* [**name** *hostname*] **spc** [**speed 56 | 64**] [**broadcast**] *dial-string*[*:isdn-subaddress*]

| *Syntax* | *Description* |
|---|---|
| *protocol* | Protocol keywords; one of the following: **appletalk**, **bridge**, **clns**, **decnet**, **ip**, **ipx**, **novell**, **snapshot**, **vines**, and **xns**. |
| *next-hop-address* | Protocol address used to match against addresses to which packets are destined. This argument is not used with the **bridge** protocol keyword. |
| **name** *hostname* | (Optional) Case-sensitive name or ID of the remote device (usually the host name). For routers with ISDN interfaces, if calling line identification—sometimes called *CLI*, but also known as *caller ID* and *automatic number identification* (ANI)—is provided, the *hostname* field can contain the number that the calling line ID provides. |
| **spc** | (Optional) Specifies a semipermanent connection between customer equipment and the exchange; used only in Germany to configure connections between an ISDN BRI and a 1TR6 ISDN switch type. |
| **speed 56 \| 64** | (Optional) Line speed in kilobits per second to use. Used for ISDN only. The default speed is 64 Kbps. |

| | |
|---|---|
| **broadcast** | (Optional) Indicates that broadcasts should be forwarded to this protocol address. |
| *dial-string*[:*isdn-subaddress*] | (Optional) Telephone number and optional ISDN subaddress used for ISDN multipoint connections that are sent to the dialing device when it recognizes packets with the specified next hop address that matches the access lists defined. The dial string and ISDN subaddress, if used, must be the last item in the command line. |

### Defaults

No dialer map is configured. The default speed is 64 Kbps. No default class name is provided.

### Command Mode

Interface configuration

### Usage Guidelines

A simple version of the **dialer map** command first appeared in Cisco IOS Release 9.1 for synchronous serial interfaces using V.25*bis* dialing.

For ISDN interfaces, use the **dialer map** command with the **name** keyword in configurations in which remote sites are calling a central site, but the central site is not calling the remote site.With this command, the local device will authenticate the remote site using CHAP or PAP, which will transmit the remote site's host name to the central site. The central site will then use this name to authenticate the caller, and will use the next hop address to transmit packets to the remote site. If no dialer string specified, the central site cannot call the remote router.

For ISDN interfaces only, you can specify an optional speed parameter for **dialer map** commands if you also specify a dial string. This option informs the ISDN software whether it should place a call at 56 or 64 Kbps. If you omit the ISDN speed parameter, the default is 64 Kbps.

For routers with ISDN interfaces, if calling line identification (CLI)—also known as *caller ID* and *ANI*—is provided, the *hostname* field may contain the number that calling line ID provides.

### Example

In the following example, the interface is configured for semipermanent connections in Germany; the IP address and the phone number are provided.

```
dialer map ip 192.36.48.2 spc 49302345655:3789
```

### Related Commands

Search online to find documentation for related commands.

**dialer isdn short-hold**
**map-class dialer**

**ppp authentication chap**
**username**

## ENCAPSULATION CPP

To enable encapsulation for communication with routers or bridges using the Combinet Proprietary Protocol (CPP), use the **encapsulation cpp** interface configuration command.

**encapsulation cpp**

### *Syntax Description*

This command has no keywords or arguments.

### *Default*

Disabled

### *Command Mode*

Interface configuration

### *Usage Guidelines*

This command first appeared in Cisco IOS Release 11.2.

Use this command to communicate over an ISDN interface with Combinet devices that do not support PPP but do support CPP.

Currently, most Combinet devices *do* support PPP. Cisco routers can communicate over ISDN with these devices by using PPP encapsulation, which supports both routing and fast switching.

Combinet devices support only IP, IPX, and bridging. For AppleTalk, Cisco routers automatically perform half-bridging with Combinet devices.

This command is supported on ISDN BRIs and Primary Rate Interfaces (PRIs) only.

### *Example*

The following example configures BRI 0 to communicate with a Combinet router or bridge that does not support PPP:

```
interface bri 0
 encapsulation cpp
 cpp callback accept
 cpp authentication
```

### *Related Commands*

Search online to find documentation for related commands.

**cpp authentication**
**cpp callback accept**

## ISDN LEASED-LINE BRI 128

To configure an ISDN BRI for leased-line service at 128 Kbps, use the **isdn leased-line bri 128** global configuration command.

**isdn leased-line bri** *number* **128**

| *Syntax* | *Description* |
|---|---|
| *number* | BRI interface number. |

### *Default*

Disabled

### *Command Mode*

Global configuration

### *Usage Guidelines*

This command first appeared in Cisco IOS Release 11.2 F.

Use this command to aggregate two B channels into a single pipe at a speed of 128 Kbps. This service is available only for ISDN BRI.

When you use an ISDN BRI interface for access over leased lines, configure the ISDN BRI as a synchronous serial interface. Do not configure ISDN calling and called numbers.

### *Examples*

The following example configures the BRI 0 interface for leased-line access at 128 Kbps in Japan. Because of the leased-line—not dialed—environment, configuration of ISDN called and calling numbers is not needed and not used. The BRI 0 interface is henceforth treated as a synchronous serial interface, with the default HDLC encapsulation.

```
isdn leased-line bri 0 128
```

The following example configures the BRI 0 interface for PPP encapsulation:

```
interface bri 0
 ip address 1.1.1.2 255.255.255.0
 encapsulation ppp
 bandwidth 128
```

### *Related Commands*

Search online to find documentation for related commands.

**isdn switch-type**

### ISDN SERVICE

To take an individual B channel or an entire PRI interface out of service or set it to a different channel service state that is passed in to the switch, use the **isdn service** interface configuration command.

**isdn service dsl** *number* **b_channel** *number* **state** *state-value*

| *Syntax* | *Description* |
|---|---|
| **dsl** *number* | Digital subscriber loop number; displayed with the **show isdn status** command. |
| **b_channel** *number* | B channel or range of B channels to be set with the passed-in state value. The **b_channel 0** keyword sets the entire PRI interface to a specified state value. B channel numbers range from 1 to 24. |
| **state** *state-value* | Desired channel service state to be set on the channels. The following channel service state values are supported:<br>0—In service<br>1—Maintenance<br>2—Out of service |

#### *Default*

Disabled

#### *Command Mode*

Interface configuration

#### *Usage Guidelines*

This command first appeared in Cisco IOS Release 11.3.

This command is used to configure the ISDN NFAS feature on Cisco routers.

Use the **b_channel 0** keyword to set the entire PRI interface to the specified state value.

Use the **show isdn status** command to display the digital subscriber loop (DSL) value. Use the **show isdn service** command to display the service states that were set by the **isdn service** command.

#### *Examples*

The following example sets the entire PRI interface to maintenance state; the digital signal link value was displayed and then used in the command:

```
isdn service dsl 3 b_channel 0 state 1
```

The following example puts B channel 11 out of service; the DSL value was displayed and then used in the command:

```
isdn service dsl 3 b_channel 11 state 2
```

### *Related Commands*

Search online to find documentation for related commands.

**show isdn service**
**show isdn status**

## PRI-GROUP TIMESLOTS NFAS_D

To configure NFAS and specify the channels to be controlled by the primary NFAS D channel, use the **pri-group timeslots nfas_d** controller configuration command.

> **pri-group timeslots** *range* **nfas_d [primary | backup | none] nfas_interface** *number* **nfas_group** *number*

| *Syntax* | *Description* |
|---|---|
| *range* | Channels in the range 1 to 24. A range of channels is shown with a hyphen (-). |
| **primary** | (Optional) Function of channel 24: the primary NFAS D channel. |
| **backup** | (Optional) Function of channel 24: the backup NFAS D channel. |
| **none** | (Optional) Function of channel 24: B channel. |
| **nfas_interface** *number* | Value in the range 0 to 9 assigned by the service provider to ensure unique identification of a PRI interface. The 0 interface number should be assigned to the primary NFAS D channel. |
| **nfas_group** *number* | Group identifier unique on the router. Multiple NFAS groups can exist on the router. |

### *Default*

Disabled

### *Command Mode*

Controller configuration

### *Usage Guidelines*

This command first appeared in Cisco IOS Release 11.3.

This command is used to configure the ISDN NFAS feature on Cisco routers.

The primary and backup D channels should be configured on separate T1 controllers. The router's other T1 controllers can be configured for 24 B channels.

Once this command is in use, all configuration changes made to the primary D channel propagate to all the NFAS group members. The primary D channel interface is the only interface shown after the configuration is written to memory.

### *Example*

The following example configures T1 controller 1/0 for PRI and for the NFAS primary D channel. This primary D channel controls all the B channels in NFAS group 1.

```
controller t1 1/0
 framing esf
 linecode b8zs
 pri-group timeslots 1-24 nfas_d primary nfas_interface 0 nfas_group 1
```

### *Related Command*

Search online to find documentation for related commands.

**show isdn nfas group**

## SHOW ISDN

To display the information about memory, Layer 2 and Layer 3 timers, and the status of PRI channels, use the **show isdn** global configuration command.

**show isdn** {**active** | **history** | **memory** | **services** | **status** [*dsl* | *interface-type number*] | **timers**}

| *Syntax* | *Description* |
|---|---|
| **active** | Displays current call information, including called number, the time until the call is disconnected, AOC charging units used during the call, and whether the AOC information is provided during calls or at the end of calls. |
| **history** | Displays historic and current call information, including the called number, the time until the call is disconnected, AOC charging time units used during the call, and whether the AOC information is provided during calls or at the end of calls. |
| **memory** | Displays memory pool statistics. This keyword is for use by technical development staff only. |
| **services** | Displays the status of PRI channels. |
| **status** [*dsl*\| *interface-type number*] | Displays the status of all ISDN interfaces or, optionally, a specific digital signal link (DSL) or a specific ISDN interface. Values of *dsl* range from 0 to 15. *Interface-type* can be **bri** or **serial.** |
| **timers** | Displays the values of Layer 2 and Layer 3 timers. |

### *Command Mode*

Global configuration

### *Usage Guidelines*

This command first appeared in Cisco IOS Release 11.2.

### *Sample Displays*

The following is sample output from the **show isdn active** command:

```
Router# show isdn active

------------------------------------------------------------------------------
                            ISDN ACTIVE CALLS
------------------------------------------------------------------------------
History Table MaxLength = 320 entries
History Retain Timer = 15 Minutes
------------------------------------------------------------------------------
Call Calling     Called        Duration  Remote    Time until   Recorded Charges
Type Number      Number        Seconds   Name      Disconnect   Units/Currency
------------------------------------------------------------------------------
Out             9876543222      Active(10)  idacom                 11      u(E)
Out             9876543210      Active(34)  idacom 115             5       u(D)
------------------------------------------------------------------------------
```

The following is sample output from the **show isdn history** command:

```
Router# show isdn history

------------------------------------------------------------------------------
                            ISDN CALL HISTORY
------------------------------------------------------------------------------
History Table MaxLength = 320 entries
History Retain Timer = 15 Minutes
------------------------------------------------------------------------------
Call Calling     Called        Duration  Remote    Time until   Recorded Charges
Type Number      Number        Seconds   Name      Disconnect   Units/Currency
------------------------------------------------------------------------------
Out             47887654       240       blackcanary              5       u(D)
In     67893                   90        delorean
Out             56745678       Active(90)  blackcanary  240       13      u(D)
------------------------------------------------------------------------------
```

Table 18–1 describes the fields in the **show isdn active** and **show isdn history** output displays.

**Table 18–1** *Show ISDN Active and Show ISDN History Field Descriptions*

| Field | Description |
|---|---|
| History Table MaxLength | Maximum number of entries that can be retained in the Call History table. |
| History Retain Timer | Maximum number of seconds any entry can be retained in Call History table. |
| Call Type | Type of call: incoming or outgoing. |

**Table 18–1** *Show ISDN Active and Show ISDN History Field Descriptions, Continued*

| Field | Description |
|---|---|
| Calling Number | For incoming calls, the number from which the call was received. |
| Called Number | For outgoing calls, the number to which the call was placed. |
| Duration Seconds | Number of seconds the call lasted. Indicates whether the call is still active, and how many seconds it has lasted so far. |
| Remote Name | Name of the host placing the call or the host called. |
| Time until Disconnect | Number of seconds before the call is configured to disconnect because of the static idle timer for the map class or the interface. |
| Recorded Charges Units/Currency | For outgoing calls, number of ISDN AOC charging units used or the currency cost of the call. |

## SHOW ISDN NFAS GROUP

To display all the members of a specified NFAS group or all NFAS groups, use the **show isdn nfas group** privileged EXEC command.

**show isdn nfas group** [*number*]

| *Syntax* | *Description* |
|---|---|
| *number* | (Optional) Identifier number of a specific NFAS group. |

### *Command Mode*

Privileged EXEC

### *Usage Guidelines*

This command first appeared in Cisco IOS Release 11.3.

### *Sample Displays*

The following is sample output from the **show isdn nfas group** command:

```
Router# show isdn nfas group 1

ISDN NFAS GROUP 1 ENTRIES:

The primary D is Serial1/0:23.
The backup D is Serial1/1:23.
The NFAS member is Serial2/0:23.

There are 3 total nfas members.
There are 93 total available B channels.
The primary D-channel is DSL 0 in state INITIALIZED.
The backup D-channel is DSL 1 in state INITIALIZED.
The current active layer 2 DSL is 1.
```

The following three examples show the D channel state changes when rollover occurs from the primary NFAS D channel to the backup D channel. The first example shows the output with the primary D channel in service and the backup D channel in standby.

```
Router# show isdn nfas group 0

ISDN NFAS GROUP 0 ENTRIES:

The primary D is Serial1/0:23.
The backup D is Serial1/1:23.
The NFAS member is Serial2/0:23.

There are 3 total nfas members.
There are 70 total available B channels.
The primary D-channel is DSL 0 in state IN SERVICE.
The backup D-channel is DSL 1 in state STANDBY.
The current active layer 2 DSL is 0.
```

The second example shows the output in the middle of rollover. The configured primary D channel is in maintenance busy state and the backup D channel is waiting.

```
Router# show isdn nfas group 0

ISDN NFAS GROUP 0 ENTRIES:

The primary D is Serial1/0:23.
The backup D is Serial1/1:23.
The NFAS member is Serial2/0:23.

There are 3 total nfas members.
There are 70 total available B channels.
The primary D-channel is DSL 0 in state MAINTENANCE BUSY.
The backup D-channel is DSL 1 in state WAIT.
The current active layer 2 DSL is 1.
```

The third example shows the output when rollover is complete. The configured primary D channel is now in standby and the backup D channel is in service.

```
Router# show isdn nfas group 0

ISDN NFAS GROUP 0 ENTRIES:

The primary D is Serial1/0:23.
The backup D is Serial1/1:23.
The NFAS member is Serial2/0:23.

There are 3 total nfas members.
There are 70 total available B channels.
The primary D-channel is DSL 0 in state STANDBY.
The backup D-channel is DSL 1 in state IN SERVICE.
The current active layer 2 DSL is 1.
```

Table 18–2 describes the fields in the sample output.

### *Related Commands*

Search online to find documentation for related commands.

**pri-group timeslots nfas_d**

Table 18–2 *Show ISDN NFAS Group Field Descriptions*

| Field | Description |
|---|---|
| The primary D is Serial1/0:23. | Identifies the primary D channel. |
| The backup D is Serial1/1:23. | Identifies the backup D channel. |
| The NFAS member is Serial2/0:23. | Identifies the NFAS group. |
| There are 3 total nfas members. | Number of member interfaces in the group. |
| There are 70 total available B channels. | Number of B channels in this NFAS group. |
| The primary D channel is DSL 0 in state STANDBY. | Service state of the NFAS primary D channel; this D channel is in service. |
| The backup D channel is DSL 1 in state IN SERVICE. | Service state of the NFAS backup D channel; this D channel is in service. The states are In service, Standby, Out of service, Maintenance, Wait, Initialized, and Busy. |
| The current active layer 2 DSL is 1. | Digital subscriber loop (DSL) identifier assigned by the service provider. If both D channels are out of service, the value displayed in this line is –1. |

## SHOW ISDN SERVICE

To display the state and the service status of each ISDN channel, use the **show isdn service** privileged EXEC command.

**show isdn service**

### *Syntax Description*

This command has no arguments or keywords.

### *Command Mode*

Privileged EXEC

### *Usage Guidelines*

This command first appeared in Cisco IOS Release 11.3.

### *Sample Display*

The following sample display shows the output of the **show isdn service** command when PRI is configured on a T1 controller:

```
Router# show isdn service

PRI Channel Statistics:
```

```
ISDN Se1/0:23, Channel (1-31)
  Activated dsl 0
  State (0=Idle 1=Propose 2=Busy 3=Reserved 4=Restart 5=Maint)
  0 0 0 0 0 0 0 0 0 0 0 0 0 0 0 0 0 0 0 0 0 0 0 3 3 3 3 3 3 3 3
  Channel (1-31) Service (0=Inservice 1=Maint 2=Outofservice)
  0 0 0 0 0 0 0 0 0 0 0 0 0 0 0 0 0 0 0 0 0 0 0 2 0 0 0 0 0 0 0
```

Table 18–3 describes the fields in this sample output.

**Table 18–3** *Show ISDN Service Field Descriptions*

| Field | Description |
|---|---|
| ISDN Se1/0:23 | ISDN PRI interface corresponding to serial interface 1/0:23. |
| Channel (1-31) | Channel range "1-31" is a standard format for both T1 and E1 outputs, but the state value shown identifies whether the channel is used. |
| Activated dsl 0 | The digital signal link (DSL) value is 0. |
| State (0=Idle 1=Propose 2=Busy 3=Reserved 4=Restart 5=Maint) | Current state of each channel. Channels 24 through 31 are marked as reserved when the output is from T1. |
| Channel (1-31) Service (0=Inservice 1=Maint 2=Outofservice) | Service state assigned to each channel. Channel 24 is marked as out of service.* |

* If channel 24 (marked as out of service) is configured as the NFAS primary D channel, NFAS will roll over to the backup D channel if one is configured. If channel 24 is a B channel, calls will not be accepted to it.

### *Related Commands*

Search online to find documentation for related commands.

**isdn service**

## PART 3

# Dial-In Terminal Service and Remote Node Configuration

# CHAPTER 19

# Configuring Dial-In Terminal Services

This chapter describes how to configure support for asynchronous character stream calls running Telnet, rlogin, local-area transport (LAT), XRemote, or TN3270, and includes the following sections:

- Terminal Service Connections Overview
- Configuring Support for Telnet and rlogin Calls
- Configuring Support for Local Area Transport Calls
- Configuring Support for TN3270 Calls
- Configuring Support for XRemote Calls

Inbound asynchronous character stream calls are routed to virtual terminal lines and virtual asynchronous interfaces, which are used to terminate incoming character steams that do not share a physical connection with the access server or router (such as a physical interface). A virtual asynchronous interface is the place where inbound Telnet, LAT, V.120, TN3270, and PAD calls or sessions terminate on the router. Virtual terminal lines are used for attaching to the router in a nonphysical way.

For a complete description of the commands in this chapter, see Chapter 20, "Dial-In Terminal Service Commands."

## TERMINAL SERVICE CONNECTIONS OVERVIEW

Configuring support for terminal service connections means to enable network devices running the same protocol (such as LAT or TCP) to connect across a LAN or WAN through network and terminal-emulation software such as Telnet, rlogin, TN3270, LAT, and NetWare Asynchronous Services Interface (NASI).

### Terminal Services

Terminal services permit asynchronous devices to be connected to a LAN or WAN through network and terminal-emulation software including Telnet, rlogin, NASI, Digital's LAT protocol, and IBM TN3270. (See Figure 19–1.)

Access services permit terminals to connect with remote hosts using virtual terminal protocols, including Telnet, NASI, LAT, TN3270, rlogin, and X.25 packet assembler/disassembler (PAD). You can use a router that supports access services to function as a terminal server to provide terminal access to devices on the network.

A host can also connect directly to an access server. In IBM environments, TN3270 allows a standard ASCII terminal to emulate a 3278 terminal and access an IBM host across an IP network.

In Digital environments, LAT support provides a terminal with connections to VMS hosts. X.25 PAD allows terminals to connect directly to an X.25 host over an X.25 network through the router. X.25 PAD eliminates the need for a separate PAD device. This connection requires use of one of the synchronous serial interfaces on the router supporting access services.

Figure 19–1 shows some of the terminal connection services available on your router.

*Figure 19–1*
*Terminal Connection Services.*

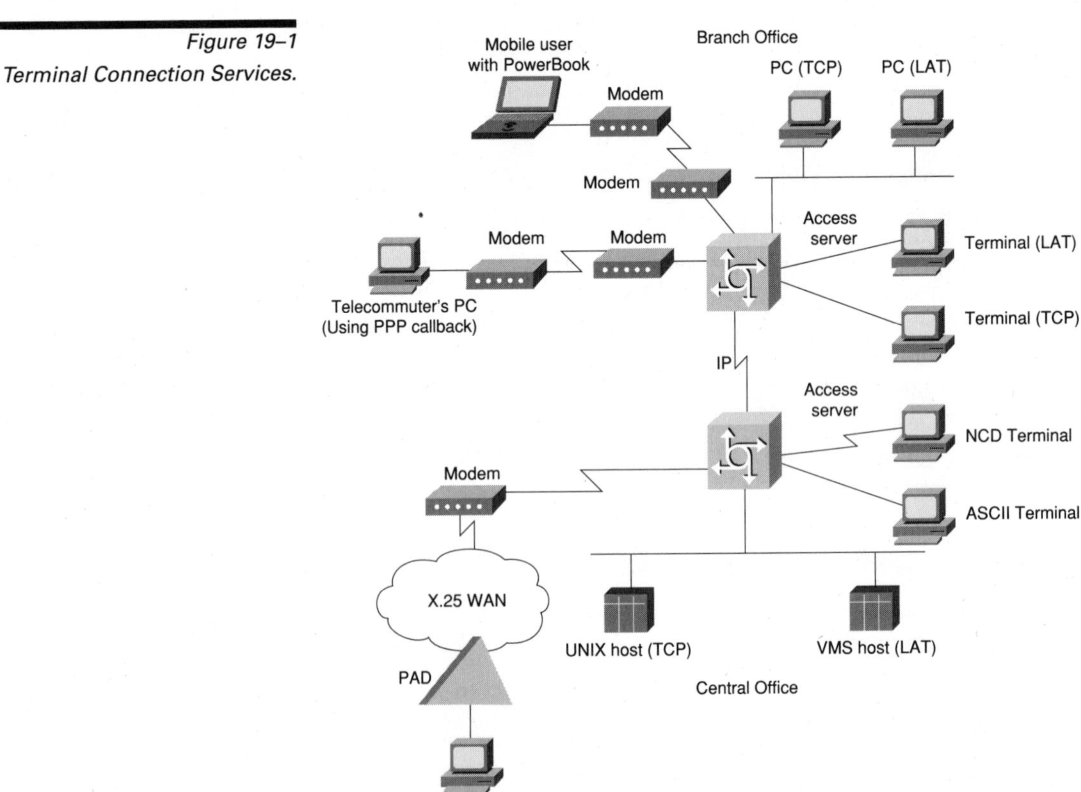

### Supported Protocols

The following protocols are supported for dial-in terminal services:

- Telnet and rlogin—Of all protocol suites, Transmission Control Protocol/Internet Protocol (TCP/IP) is the most widely implemented on networks of all media types. TCP/IP is today's standard for internetworking and is supported by most computer vendors, including all UNIX-based workstation manufacturers. TCP/IP includes Telnet and rlogin.
- NASI—Configuring the Cisco IOS software as a NASI server enables NASI clients to connect through your router to network resources.
- LAT—Digital Equipment Corporation's proprietary terminal connection protocol used with Digital minicomputers.
- TN3270—IBM 3278 terminal emulation provides TN3270-based connectivity to IBM hosts over serial lines.
- Terminal or remote node services using protocol translation—Connecting devices running dissimilar protocols (such as LAT-to-TCP or TCP-to-LAT) and converting one virtual terminal protocol into another protocol.

## Configuring Support for Telnet and rlogin Calls

This section describes the configuration access server and router lines to support Telnet and rlogin connections and includes the following sections:

- Cisco's Implementation of Telnet and UNIX rlogin
- Configure Telnet and UNIX rlogin
- Make Telnet and UNIX rlogin Connections
- Monitor TCP/IP Connections
- Telnet and rlogin Configuration Examples

### Cisco's Implementation of Telnet and UNIX rlogin

Telnet and rlogin are protocols that enable TCP/IP connections to a host. Telnet, a virtual terminal protocol that is part of the TCP/IP protocol suite, is the more widely used protocol. The rlogin protocol is a remote login service developed for the BSD UNIX system. It provides better control and output suppression than Telnet, but can only be used when the host (typically, a UNIX system) supports rlogin. The Cisco IOS implementation of rlogin does not subscribe to the rlogin "trusted host" model. That is, a user cannot automatically log on to a UNIX system from the router, but must provide a user ID and a password for each connection.

Telnet allows a user at one site to establish a TCP connection to a login server at another site, then passes the keystrokes from one system to the other. Telnet can accept either an IP address or a domain name as the remote system address. In short, Telnet offers three main services:

- Network virtual terminal connection
- Option negotiation
- Symmetric connection

The Cisco Systems implementation of Telnet supports the following Telnet options:

- Remote echo
- Binary transmission
- Suppress go ahead
- Timing mark
- Terminal type
- Send location
- Terminal speed
- Remote flow control
- X display location

### Configure Telnet and UNIX rlogin

To configure support for Telnet or rlogin calls, perform the following tasks. Unless specified otherwise, all commands are entered in line configuration mode:

| Task | | Command |
|---|---|---|
| **Step 1** | Negotiate speeds on reverse Telnet lines. | **telnet speed** *default-speed maximum-speed* |
| **Step 2** | Cause Telnet to refuse to negotiate full duplex, remote echo requests on incoming connections. | **telnet refuse-negotiations** |
| **Step 3** | Set line to send a RETURN (CR) as a CR followed by a NULL instead of a CR followed by a LINE FEED (LF). | **telnet transparent** |
| **Step 4** | Set line to send a Telnet Synchronize signal when it receives a Telnet Break signal. | **telnet sync-on-break** |
| **Step 5** | Set the line to cause the system to generate a hardware Break signal on the RS-232 line that is associated with a reverse Telnet connection, when a Telnet Interrupt-Process command is received on that connection. | **telnet break-on-ip** |

| Task | | Command |
|---|---|---|
| **Step 6** | In global configuration mode, optimize the line by setting the number of characters output before the interrupt executes. | **ip tcp chunk-size** *number* |
| **Step 7** | In interface configuration mode, assign an IP address to the service provided on a TCP port. | **ip alias** *ip-address tcp-port* |
| **Step 8** | In global configuration mode, define a message that the router displays whenever a Telnet or rlogin connection to the specified host fails. | **busy-message** *hostname d message d* |
| **Step 9** | In global configuration mode, define a message that the router displays whenever a Telnet or rlogin connection to the specified host succeeds. | **login-string** *hostname d message* [%*sec***p**] [%*sec***w**] [%**b**] *d* |
| **Step 10** | Set up a line to notify a user who has multiple, concurrent Telnet connections when output is pending on a connection other than the current one. | **notify** |
| **Step 11** | Define a "line-in-use" message to indicate that the line is currently busy. | **refuse-message** *d message d* |

The **telnet speed** command sets the line speed to match line speeds on remote systems in reverse Telnet, host machines hooked to an access server or router to access the network, or a group of console lines hooked up to the access server or router when disparate line speeds are in use at the local and remote ends of the connection. Line speed negotiation adheres to the Remote Flow Control option, defined in RFC 1080.

When the **telnet refuse-negotiations** command is set, it suppresses negotiation of the Telnet Remote Echo and Suppress Go Ahead options.

The **telnet transparent** command is useful for coping with different interpretations of end-of-line handling in the Telnet protocol specification.

The **telnet sync-on-break** command sets the line to cause a reverse Telnet line to send a Telnet Synchronize signal when it receives a Telnet Break signal. The Telnet Synchronize signal clears the data path but still interprets incoming commands.

Issue the **telnet break-on-ip** command to control the translation of Telnet Interrupt-Process commands into X.25 Break indications, and to work around the following situations:

- Several user Telnet programs send a Telnet Interrupt-Process command, but cannot send a Telnet Break signal.
- Some Telnet programs implement a Break signal that sends a Telnet Interrupt-Process command.
- Some RS-232 hardware devices use a hardware Break signal for various purposes.

When used with a correctly operating host, Cisco IOS software implements the Telnet Synchronize and Abort Output signals, which can stop output within one packet's worth of data from the time the user types the interrupt character. Issue the **ip tcp chunk-size** command to configure a faster response to user interrupt characters. Changing the number of characters output, or chunk size, affects neither the size of the packet used nor the TCP window size, either of which would cause serious efficiency problems for the remote host as well as for the access server or router. Instead, the Telnet status is checked after the number of characters specified, causing only a relatively minor performance loss.

Use the **ip alias** command to configure connections to an IP address to act identically to connections made to the server's primary IP address on the TCP port. A user trying to connect is connected to the first free line in a rotary group using the Telnet protocol.

With the **login-string** commands options, you can set a pause, prevent a user from issuing commands during a pause, send a Break character, and use a percent sign (%) in the login string. The **busy-message** command and **login-string** command are only useful with two-step protocol translation sessions. For more information about protocol translation, see Chapter 21, "Configuring Protocol Translation and Virtual Asynchronous Devices."

For actual sample configurations on how to configure Telnet and rlogin, see the section "Telnet and rlogin Configuration Examples," later in this chapter.

### Make Telnet and UNIX rlogin Connections

Telnet and rlogin are protocols that enable TCP/IP connections to a host.

Telnet, a virtual terminal protocol that is part of the TCP/IP protocol suite, is the more widely used protocol.

The rlogin protocol is a remote login service developed for the BSD UNIX system. It provides better control and output suppression than Telnet, but can only be used when the host (typically, a UNIX system) supports rlogin. The Cisco IOS implementation of rlogin does not subscribe to the rlogin "trusted host" model. That is, a user cannot automatically log on to a UNIX system from the router, but must provide a user ID and a password for each connection.

To provide Telnet and rlogin connection capabilities, perform the following tasks in EXEC mode:

| Task | | Command |
|---|---|---|
| **Step 1** | Log on to a host that supports Telnet. | **connect** *host* [*port*] [*keyword*]<br>or<br>**telnet** *host* [*port*] [*keyword*] |
| **Step 2** | Display a list of available hosts. | **show hosts** |
| **Step 3** | Display the status of all TCP connections. | **show tcp** |
| **Step 4** | Log off the host by entering the default escape sequence.* | **Ctrl^** |
| **Step 5** | Log off the host by entering a special escape sequence.* These special Telnet sequences map generic terminal control functions to operating system-specific functions. | Choose from the following list of escape sequences, according to your task:<br>• Use **Ctrl^ b** if your task is to break<br>• Use **Ctrl^ c** if your task is to interrupt a process (IP)<br>• Use **Ctrl^ h** if your task is to erase a character (EC)<br>• Use **Ctrl^ o** if your task is to abort an output display (AO)<br>• Use **Ctrl^ t** if your task is to confirm you are at the host (AYT)<br>• Use **Ctrl^ u** if your task is to erase a line (EL) |
| **Step 6** | List the available Telnet commands at any time during the active Telnet session.* | **Ctrl-^ ?** |
| **Step 7** | Log on to a host that supports rlogin. | **rlogin** *host* [**debug**] [**/user** *username*] |
| **Step 8** | Exit a Telnet or rlogin session. | **exit**<br>or<br>**logout** |

* Press and hold the **Ctrl** and **Shift** keys while pressing the 6 key. You can enter the command character as you hold down **Ctrl** or with **Ctrl** released; you can enter the command characters as either uppercase or lowercase letters.

With the Cisco IOS implementation of TCP/IP, you are not required to enter the **connect** or **telnet** commands to establish a Telnet connection. You can just enter the learned host name—as long as the host name is different from a command word for the router. Telnet must be the default (you can make it the default with the **transport preferred** command). Use the **show hosts** EXEC command to display a list of the available hosts. Use the **show tcp** EXEC command to display the status of all TCP connections. The Cisco IOS software assigns a logical name to each connection, and several commands use these names to identify connections. The logical name is the same as the host name, unless that name is already in use, or you change the connection name with the **name-connection** EXEC command. If the name is already in use, the Cisco IOS software assigns a null name to the connection. For an example of making a Telnet connection, see the section "Telnet and rlogin Configuration Examples," later in this chapter.

After the **rlogin** command is issued, you can have several concurrent rlogin connections open and switch between them. To open a new connection, exit the current connection by entering the escape sequence (**Ctrl-Shift-6** then **x** [**Ctrl^x**] by default) to return to the system command prompt, then open a new connection. For an example of making a rlogin connection or switching between connections, see the section "rlogin Example," or the section "Switch between Telnet and rlogin Sessions Examples," later this chapter.

**NOTES**

Cisco recommends that you use Encrypted Kerberized Telnet whenever you establish a Telnet session to a router or access server, which protects the device's integrity.

### Monitor TCP/IP Connections

To display the status of a TCP connection or view a summary of the TCP connection end points in the system, perform the following tasks in user EXEC mode:

| Task | Command |
|---|---|
| Display the status of a TCP connection. | **show tcp** [*line-number*] |
| Display a summary of the TCP connection endpoints in the system. | **show tcp brief** [**all**] |

### Telnet and rlogin Configuration Examples

The following examples are provided:

- Telnet Connection Examples
- rlogin Example
- Switch between Telnet and rlogin Sessions Examples
- List Supported Telnet Commands Example

### *Telnet Connection Examples*

The following example routes packets from the source system host1 to kl.sri.com, then to 10.1.0.11, and finally back to host1:

```
router> connect host1 /route:kl.sri.com 10.1.0.11 host1
```

The following example connects to a host with logical name host1:

```
router> host1
```

### *rlogin Example*

The following example makes an rlogin connection to a host at address 108.33.21.2 and enables the message mode for debugging:

```
router> rlogin 108.33.21.2 debug
```

### *Switch between Telnet and rlogin Sessions Examples*

You can switch between sessions by escaping one session and resuming a previously opened session. The following example shows how to escape out of a connection to the host host1 and to resume connection 2. You escape out of the current session and return to the EXEC prompt by entering the command sequence **Ctrl-Shift-6** then **x**. Resume the connection with the **resume** [connection] [keyword] command.

```
host1% ^^X
router> resume 2
```

You can omit the command name and simply enter the connection number to resume that connection. The following example illustrates how to resume connection 3:

```
router> 3
```

To list all the open sessions associated with the current terminal line, use the **where** command.

### *List Supported Telnet Commands Example*

At any time during an active Telnet session, you can list the Telnet commands by pressing the escape sequence keys (by default **Ctrl-Shift-6**) followed by a question mark at the system prompt:

**Ctrl-^ ?**

A sample of this list follows:

```
router> ^^?
```

**NOTES**

In screen output examples that show two caret (^^) symbols together, the first caret represents the Control key and the second caret represents the keystroke sequence Shift-6. The double caret combination (^^) means hold down the **Control** key while you press the **Shift** and the **6** key.

```
[Special telnet escape help]
^^B  sends telnet BREAK
^^C  sends telnet IP
```

```
^^H  sends telnet EC
^^O  sends telnet AO
^^T  sends telnet AYT
^^U  sends telnet EL
```

## CONFIGURING SUPPORT FOR LOCAL AREA TRANSPORT CALLS

The Digital Equipment Corporation (Digital) Local Area Transport (LAT) protocol is the one used most often to connect to Digital hosts. LAT is a Digital-proprietary protocol. Cisco provides LAT technology licensed from Digital. This section describes how to configure the LAT transmission protocol.

The following sections are provided:

- Cisco's Implementation of the LAT Protocol
- LAT Configuration Task List
- Make LAT Connections
- Monitor and Maintain LAT Connections
- LAT Configuration Examples
- LAT Connection Examples

### Cisco's Implementation of the LAT Protocol

The LAT protocol allows a user to establish a LAT connection to a host at another site, then pass the keystrokes from one system to the other. A user can establish a LAT connection through a router to a LAT host simply by entering the host name. The Cisco IOS software supports the LAT 5.2 specification.

Unlike the Transmission Control Protocol/Internet Protocol (TCP/IP), LAT was designed to be used on LANs and it cannot be routed because it does not have a routing layer. However, a bridge or combined bridge and router, such as a Cisco router, can be used to carry LAT traffic across a WAN. Protocol translation can be used to carry LAT traffic over a WAN by first translating LAT to X.25 or Telnet, as shown in Figure 19–2.

The following sections describe Cisco's implementation of LAT in more detail:

- LAT Functionality
- LAT Services
- LAT Groups
- LAT Sessions and Connection Support
- Connect a VMS Host Using LAT
- Port Names when Configuring a LAT Printer
- Additional LAT Capability

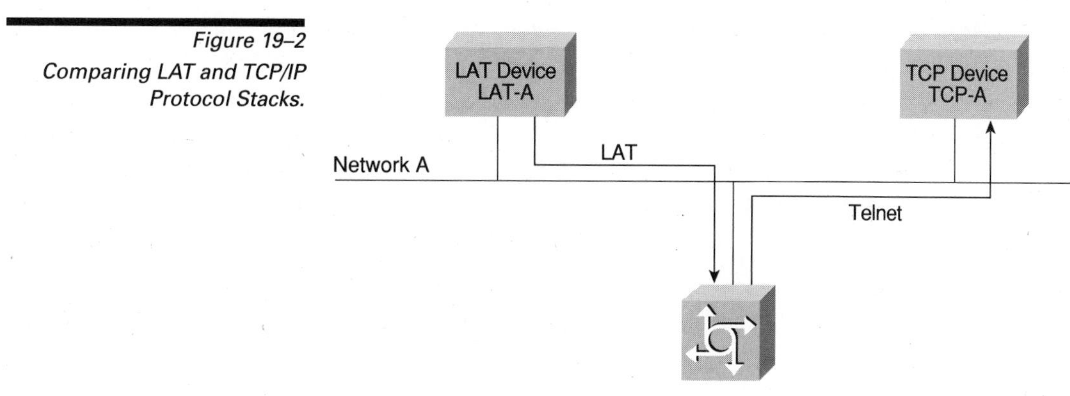


*Figure 19–2*
*Comparing LAT and TCP/IP Protocol Stacks.*

### LAT Functionality

The LAT protocol is asymmetrical; it has master and slave functionality. First, the LAT master starts a LAT circuit by sending a circuit start message, and then a LAT slave responds with its own circuit start message. From 1 to 255 LAT sessions can then be multiplexed on a circuit.

In a typical setup, where the user's terminal is connected to a router, the router acts as the master, and the target VMS host acts as the slave.

For example, the following command results in the device *router1* acting as the master (or server) and the target VMS host, *wheel*, acting as the slave (or host).

```
router1> lat wheel
```

A router can also act as a slave. This happens if the user connects from one access server to another. For example, the following command results in *router1* acting as the master (server) and *router2* acting as the slave (host).

```
router1> lat router2
```

In a LAT host-initiated connection, the VMS system always acts as the LAT slave. For example, a print job originating from a VMS system initiates or triggers the router to which the printer is connected to act as the LAT master. In short, the master-slave relationship also applies to host-initiated sessions from a LAT slave.

### LAT Services

Resources such as modems, computers, and application software are viewed in a LAT network as *services* that, potentially, any user in the network can use. A LAT node can offer one or more such LAT services, and more than one LAT node can offer the same LAT service.

A LAT node that offers one or more services, collectively called *advertised services*, broadcasts its services in the form of Ethernet multicast messages, called LAT *service announcements*. Conversely, a LAT node can listen for LAT service announcements on the network. These messages are cached in a dynamic table of known LAT services, collectively called *learned services*.

The Cisco IOS software supports both learned and advertised LAT services; therefore, it also supports incoming and outgoing LAT sessions. The services rating of its advertised nodes are determined dynamically but can also be set statically.

To establish outgoing connections to a LAT service, the Cisco IOS software searches for the service in the learned services cache. If one or more nodes are offering the same service, the node with the highest rating is chosen. For example, a LAT connection to a service offered by a VAX cluster connects to the node in that cluster with the smallest load and thus the highest service rating. This is how load balancing works in relation to a group of nodes offering the same service.

To establish an incoming connection, a LAT session connects from another LAT node to the service advertised by the local LAT node.

### LAT Groups

Because potentially any user can access any of the services on a LAT network, a LAT server manager uses the concept of *group codes* to allow or restrict access to the services.

When both the router and the LAT host share a common group code, a connection can be established between the two. If the default group codes have not been changed on either side, a user on any router can connect to any learned service on the network.

However, if you define groups for access servers or routers and LAT hosts, you can partition these services into logical subnetworks. You can organize the groups so that users on one device view one set of services, and users on another device (or another line on the same device) view a different set. You might also design a plan that correlates group numbers with organizational groups, such as departments. The section, "LAT Configuration Task List," later in this chapter describes how to enter group code lists in your configuration file.

A LAT host node's services cannot be accessed individually; access is granted, per node, on an all-or-none basis.

### LAT Sessions and Connection Support

A LAT session is a two-way logical connection between a LAT service and the router. All this is transparent to the user at a console connected to a LAT session; to the user it appears that connection has been made directly to the desired device or application program. There is no inherent upper limit to the number of LAT sessions you can create from an asynchronous terminal to the router.

When a host print job connects to a router, this is called a *host-initiated connection*. The Cisco IOS software maintains a queue of hosts requesting connection by sending periodic status messages to the requesting host.

You can establish host-initiated connections by specifying a port number or by defining a service. These same services are used for connections from other access servers or routers.

**NOTES**

If a connection request is received that specifies a service and a destination port number, the port number is used to determine the line number for connection purposes. This allows a user to connect to a specified port simply by specifying any service on the server and a port number. (Earlier versions of the Cisco IOS software ignored the service name on inbound connections.)

### *Connect a VMS Host Using LAT*

The process of connecting to a VMS host is slightly different if you are connecting to a VMS host running VMS Version 5.4 or earlier than when connecting to a VMS host running VMS Version 5.5 or later software.

#### *VMS Version 5.4 or Earlier System*

If a host-initiated connection is received that specifies a destination port number that corresponds to a virtual port on the router, a virtual EXEC process will be created for the user to log in with. This process can be used, in conjunction with the Digital **set host/dte** command on VMS, to connect to a router named router1 from a VMS host node, as shown in the following example:

```
$lcp :==$latcp
$lcp create port lta300:
$lcp set port lta300:/service=able /node=router1
$set host/dte lta300:
```

#### *VMS Version 5.5 or Later System*

To connect to a VMS host running VMS Version 5.5 or later, you must turn on the VMS LAT host's outgoing connections and use the Digital **set host/lat** command, as shown in the following example:

```
$lcp :== $latcp
$lcp set node/connection =outgoing
$set host/lat able
```

### *Port Names when Configuring a LAT Printer*

When you configure a LAT printer, the LAT port name is the line number without the "TTY." For example, if you configure terminal line 10, named ABLE, to be a LAT printer port, you must use the OpenVMS command to associate an arbitrary LAT device to a LAT port name as follows:

```
$lcp :== $lcp
$lcp create port lta300:
$lcp set port/node=ABLE/port=10 lta300:
```

The LAT port name is the line number without the "TTY," regardless of whether the format of the TTY line number is decimal or octal.

### *Additional LAT Capability*

The Cisco IOS software fully supports the LAT protocol suite, and provides the following features:

- High-speed buffering—Handles a full screen of data (2000 characters) at full speed without requiring additional flow control.

- Protocol transparency—Handles connections transparently. The user needs no protocol information to establish a connection.
- Simplified configuration management—Uses logical names for LAT group codes to simplify the network structure.
- Maintenance Operation Protocol (MOP)—Supports Digital's protocol to support the request ID message, periodic system ID messages, and the remote console carrier functions for Ethernet interfaces.

## LAT Configuration Task List

The Cisco IOS software LAT protocol is supplied with a default configuration and does not require additional configuration for you to use it. The software does provide commands for customizing the LAT software for your environment, if desired.

Perform the tasks in the following sections to enable LAT and customize LAT for your particular network environment:

- Configure Basic LAT Services
- Enable Inbound Services
- Control Service Announcements and Service Solicitation
- Configure Traffic Timers
- Optimize Performance
- Define Access Lists
- Enable Remote LAT Modification

### *Configure Basic LAT Services*

To enable basic LAT services, perform the following tasks in global configuration mode:

| Task | | Command |
|---|---|---|
| **Step 1** | In interface configuration mode, enable the LAT protocol. LAT is disabled by default. | **lat enabled** |
| **Step 2** | Give the router a LAT node name that is different than the host name. | **lat node** *node-name* |
| **Step 3** | (Optional) In line configuration mode, define the group list for an outgoing connection on a specified line. | **lat out-group** {*groupname* \| *number* \| *range* \| **all**} |

| Task | | Command |
|---|---|---|
| **Step 4** | (Optional) Specify logical names for group lists. | **lat group-list** *groupname* {*number* \| *range* \| **all**} [**enabled** \| **disabled**] |
| **Step 5** | (Optional) Specify groups to be advertised. | **lat service-group** {*groupname* \| *number* \| *range* \| **all**} [**enabled** \| **disabled**] |
| **Step 6** | (Optional) In line configuration mode, enable remote LAT modification of line characteristics. | **lat remote-modification** |

Use the **lat out-group** command to define the list of services to which a user can connect. Do this by defining the group code lists used for connections from specific lines. You can limit the connection choices for an individual line by defining the group code lists for an outgoing connection. When a user initiates a connection with a LAT host, the user's line must share a common group number with the remote LAT host before a connection can be made.

Use the **lat group-list** command to specify a name for group lists to simplify the task of entering individual group codes. A name makes it easier to refer to a long list of group code numbers. To display the defined groups, use the **show lat groups** command.

Use the **lat service-group** command to specify a group code mask to use when advertising all services for a node. You can enter more than one group code by listing the numbers. You can also enter both a group code name and group codes.

Use the **lat remote-modification** line configuration command to configure a LAT line so that a remote LAT node can change the operating characteristics of the line.

### *Enable Inbound Services*

Just as LAT services are offered by host computers, they also can be offered by access servers and routers, as they implement both the host and server portions of the LAT protocol. This allows connections from either hosts or local access servers or routers. When a host connects to a local device, this is called a *host-initiated connection.*

The tasks described in this section define support for host-initiated connections. This support includes refining the list of services that the router will support. An incoming session can be to either a port or a service. The port name is the terminal line number, as reported by the EXEC command **show users all**. Perform any of the following optional tasks in global configuration mode:

| Task | Command |
|---|---|
| Set the LAT password for a service. | **lat service** *service-name* **password** *password* |
| Set the LAT service ID for a specific service. | **lat service** *service-name* **ident** *identification* |

| Task | Command |
|---|---|
| Specify a static service rating for a specific service. | **lat service** *service-name* **rating** *static-rating* |
| Configure a LAT rotary group. | **lat service** *service-name* **rotary** *group* |
| Associate a command with a specific service for auto-execution. | **lat service** *service-name* **autocommand** *command* |
| Enable inbound connections to a specific service. | **lat service** *service-name* **enabled** |

Use the **show lat advertised** EXEC command to display LAT services offered to other systems on the network.

A service must be specifically enabled, but not all of the attributes in the previous task table are necessary in a particular environment.

### *Control Service Announcements and Service Solicitation*

You can configure the Cisco IOS software to support the service responder feature that is part of the LAT Version 5.2 specification.

Specifically, the DECserver90L+, which has less memory than other DEC servers, does not maintain a cache of learned services. Instead, the DECserver90L+ solicits information about services as they are needed.

LAT Version 5.2 nodes can respond for themselves, but LAT Version 5.1 nodes, for example VMS Version 5.4 or earlier nodes, cannot. Instead, a LAT Version 5.2 node configured as a service responder can respond in proxy for those LAT Version 5.1 nodes.

The Cisco IOS software can be configured as a LAT service responder. Of course, if all your nodes are LAT Version 5.2 nodes, you do not need to enable the service responder features.

To control service announcements and service solicitations, perform the following tasks in global configuration mode:

| Task | | Command |
|---|---|---|
| Step 1 | Enable a proxy node to respond to solicit-information multicast messages. | **lat service-responder** |
| Step 2 | Disable periodic broadcasts of service advertisements. | **no lat service-announcements** |
| Step 3 | Adjust the time between service announcements. | **lat service-timer** *interval* |

Use the **lat service-responder** command to configure the Cisco IOS software to respond to solicit-information requests addressed to LAT Version 5.1 nodes. This function allows nodes that do not cache service advertisements to interoperate with nodes that do not respond to solicit requests. Figure 19–3 shows how a router can act as a proxy for LAT servers.

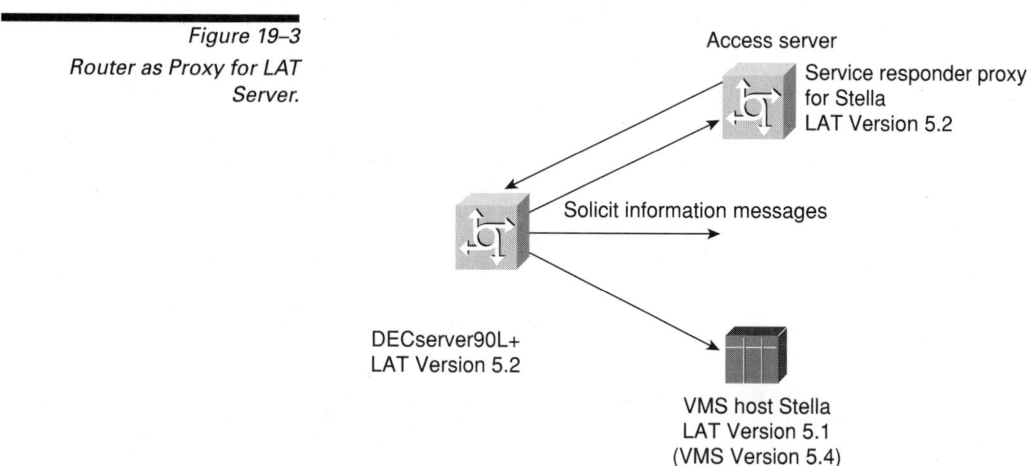


*Figure 19–3*
*Router as Proxy for LAT Server.*

The DECserver90L+ broadcasts a solicit-information request in search of service "Stella's" address. The VMS host, Stella, is unable to respond to the request because it is running LAT Version 5.1. The access server is running LAT Version 5.2 with service responder enabled and informs the DECserver90L+ of Stella's address.

Use the **no lat service-announcements** command to disable periodic broadcasts of service announcements. If service announcements are enabled, the LAT node will periodically broadcast service advertisements. If service announcements are disabled, the LAT node will not send service announcements, so a remote node requiring connection to the local node has to use solicit-information messages to look up node information. Only disable service announcements if all of the nodes on the LAN support the service responder feature.

Use the **lat service-timer** command to adjust the time between LAT service advertisements for services offered. This is useful in large networks with many LAT services and limited bandwidth.

### Configure Traffic Timers

You can customize the environment for transmitting LAT messages. The Cisco IOS implementation of LAT allows you to set the following features:

- The number of retransmissions before declaring a system unreachable
- The interval of time LAT waits before sending a keepalive message on an idle connection
- The interval of time LAT waits between transmission of messages

These features affect all LAT connection types. Perform the following tasks in global configuration mode:

| Task | Command |
|---|---|
| Set the message retransmit limit. | **lat retransmit-limit** *number* |
| Set the keepalive timer. | **lat ka-timer** *seconds* |
| Set the virtual-circuit timer. | **lat vc-timer** *milliseconds* |

### Optimize Performance

To optimize performance for your LAT environment, perform one or more of the following optional tasks beginning in global configuration mode:

| Task | Command |
|---|---|
| Set the maximum number of sessions on a LAT virtual circuit. The maximum (and default) number of sessions is 255. | **lat vc-sessions** *number* |
| Allow a LAT host node to receive more than one message at a time. | **lat host-buffers** *receive-buffers* |
| Allow a LAT server node to receive more than one message at a time. | **lat server-buffers r***eceive-buffers* |
| Specify the delay acknowledgment for incoming LAT slave connections, where *number* is milliseconds. | **lat host-delay** *number* |

Use the **lat host-buffers** command to set the number of messages received by a host at one time. Increasing this number can enhance performance. Before LAT Version 5.2, LAT allowed only one outstanding message at one time on a virtual circuit. This restriction could limit the performance of the Cisco IOS software processing a large number of messages because only one Ethernet packet of data could be in transit at a time. During virtual circuit startup, each side communicates to the other how many outstanding messages it is willing to accept.

Use the **lat server-buffers** command to set the number of messages received by a server at one time. Increasing this number can enhance performance. Before LAT Version 5.2, LAT allowed only one outstanding message on a virtual circuit at a time. This restriction limited the performance of Cisco IOS software when it processed a large number of messages, because only one Ethernet packet of data could be in transit at a time. With LAT Version 5.2, nodes can indicate that they are willing to receive more than one message at a time. During virtual circuit startup, each side communicates to the other how many outstanding messages it is willing to accept.

Use the **lat host-delay** command to set a user-defined delay for the acknowledgment for incoming LAT slave connections. This is useful in situations where you need to control the delay. For example, if data is being transferred between a Digital server (using LAT) and a UNIX host (using Telnet) via a protocol translator, the protocol translator imposes the LAT delay on the Telnet as well as the LAT service, where Telnet may time out due to the LAT restriction.

### *Define Access Lists*

Because LAT groups were not intended to implement security or access control, the Cisco IOS software supports *access lists* to provide these functions. An access list is a sequential collection of permit and deny conditions that serve to restrict access to or from LAT nodes on a specific terminal line. Each access list statement defines a permit or deny condition and a matching criterion for the node name.

When a LAT connection is attempted (either incoming or outgoing), the node name of the destination service (*not* the service name) is compared against the regular expression. If they match, the connection is permitted or denied as specified.

Perform the following tasks to define access lists and conditions:

| Task | | Command |
|---|---|---|
| **Step 1** | Enter global configuration mode. | **configure terminal** |
| **Step 2** | Specify an access condition. | **lat access-list** *number* {**permit** \| **deny**} n*odename* |
| **Step 3** | Enter line configuration mode. | **line** *line-number* |
| **Step 4** | Restrict incoming and outgoing connections between a particular terminal line or group of lines and the node names in an access list. | **access-class** *access-list-number* {**in** \| **out**} |

### *Enable Remote LAT Modification*

You can configure a LAT line so that a remote LAT node can change the operating characteristics of the line. To enable remote LAT modification, perform the following task in line configuration mode:

| Task | Command |
|---|---|
| Enable remote LAT modification of line characteristics. | **lat remote-modification** |

### Make LAT Connections

The Digital Equipment Corporation (Digital) LAT protocol is most often used to connect routers to Digital hosts. LAT is a Digital-proprietary protocol, and the Cisco IOS software uses LAT technology licensed from Digital to allow the following LAT services:

- Make a LAT connection
- Define a group code list for outgoing LAT connections
- Switch between LAT sessions
- Use digital commands on the server
- Exit a LAT session

For actual LAT connection examples, see the section "LAT Connection Examples," later in this chapter.

To enable specific LAT connections or services, perform one or more of the following tasks in EXEC mode:

| Task | Command |
|---|---|
| Connect to a LAT host.* | **lat** *name* [**node** *nodename* \| **port** *portname* \| **/debug**] |
| (Optional) Define a temporary list of services to which you or another user can connect by defining the group code lists used for connections from specific lines. | **terminal lat out-group** {*groupname* \| *number* \| *range*} |
| (Optional) List available LAT services. | **show lat services** |
| (Optional) List the subset of Digital commands that the Cisco IOS software supports. | **help** |
| (Optional) Exit a LAT session by logging off the remote system. Then, terminate the active LAT session. | **exit** |

* You can quit the connection by pressing **Ctrl-C** or complete the connection by entering the password for a given service.

You can also set your preferred connection protocol to any available connection protocol supported in the Cisco IOS software. Your preferred connection protocol is also referred to in the Cisco IOS software as a "preferred transport type." If your preferred connection protocol is set to **lat**, you can use the **connect** command in place of the **lat** command. To configure a preferred connection protocol, use the **transport preferred** command. When your preferred connection protocol is set to **none** or to another protocol, you must use the **lat** command to connect to a LAT host.

To specify a temporary list of services to which you or another user can connect, you must define the group code lists used for connections from specific lines. You limit the connection choices for an individual line by defining the group code lists for an outgoing connection. To define a group code list, use the **terminal lat out-group** command. When a user initiates a connection with a LAT host, the user's line must share a common group number with the remote LAT host before a connection can be made. The group code range *must be* a subset of the line's configured group code range.

You can have several concurrent LAT sessions open and switch between them. To open a subsequent session, first enter the escape sequence (**Ctrl-Shift-6** then **x** [**Ctrl^x**] by default) to suspend the current session. Then open a new session. To list the available LAT services, issue the **show lat services** EXEC command.

## Monitor and Maintain LAT Connections

To monitor and maintain LAT connections, perform one or more of the following tasks in EXEC mode:

| Task | Command |
|---|---|
| Delete an entry from the queue. | **clear entry** *number* |
| Display queued host-initiated connections. | **show entry** |
| Display LAT services offered to other LAT systems. | **show lat advertised** |
| Display defined LAT groups. | **show lat groups** |
| Display information about LAT nodes. | **show lat nodes** |
| Display information about LAT learned services. | **show lat services** |
| Display active LAT sessions. | **show lat sessions** [*line-number*] |
| Display traffic and resource utilization statistics. | **show lat traffic** |
| Display information about LAT nodes. Information is displayed in the same way as in the Digital interface. | **show node** [**all** \| *node-name*] [**counters** \| **status** \| **summary**] |
| Display LAT learned services. | **show service** [*service-name*] |

## LAT Configuration Examples

This section contains the following LAT examples:

- Establishing Basic LAT Service Example
- Establishing a LAT Service with Selected Group Codes Example
- Displaying the LAT Services on the Same LAN Example
- Establishing an Outbound LAT Session Example
- Logically Partitioning LAT Services by the Terminal Line Example
- Configuring LAT Rotary Groups Example
- LAT Access List Example
- Associating a Rotary Group with a Service Example
- LAT Connection Examples

### *Establishing Basic LAT Service Example*

The following example establishes the LAT service *ABLE* for your router. Subsequently, your router advertises ABLE (with default group code 0) on the LAN. Other LAT nodes can connect to you using LAT service ABLE, provided the group codes on the LAT nodes and the group codes for ABLE intersect. By default, most LAT nodes, such as OpenVMS Version 5.5 hosts, have user group code set to 0, so you have default access to ABLE.

```
! Create LAT service with password protection and
! identification string using the following global configuration commands
 lat service ABLE password secret
 lat service ABLE ident Welcome to my machine
```

### *Establishing a LAT Service with Selected Group Codes Example*

The following example establishes the LAT service ABLE from your router with selected group codes 1, 4 through 7, and 167. This limits inbound access to those LAT nodes that have group codes that intersect with those for LAT service ABLE.

```
! Establish a LAT group list
 lat group-list HUBS 1 4-7 167
!
! Enable LAT group list for the service-group
 lat service-group HUBS enabled
!
! Create LAT service with password protection and
! identification string
 lat service ABLE password secret
 lat service ABLE ident Welcome to my machine
```

### *Displaying the LAT Services on the Same LAN Example*

The following example demonstrates how you can check which LAT services are on the same LAN as your router. Note that your router's own LAT service ABLE is also listed, with the "Interface" column listing the interface as "Local."

```
able> show lat services

Service Name        Rating    Interface       Node (Address)
CAD                  16       Ethernet0       WANDER
ABLE                 16       Local
CERTIFY              33       Ethernet0       STELLA
```

### Establishing an Outbound LAT Session Example

The following example establishes a LAT session to remote LAT service *HELLO* using an interactive session:

```
able> lat HELLO
```

### Logically Partitioning LAT Services by the Terminal Line Example

The following example illustrates how LAT services are logically partitioned by terminal line. At the example site, lines 1 through 7 go to the shop floor, lines 8 through 11 go to the Quality Assurance department, and lines 12 through 16 go to a common area.

```
! Define LAT groupnames
 lat group-list DEFAULT 0
 lat group-list FLOOR 3
 lat group-list QA 4

line 1 7
 lat out-group FLOOR enabled
 lat out-group DEFAULT disabled
line 8 11
 lat out-group QA enabled
 lat out-group DEFAULT disabled
 line 12 16
lat out-group DEFAULT QA FLOOR enabled
```

### Configuring LAT Rotary Groups Example

The following example illustrates how to configure a range of lines for rotary connections, then establishes the LAT service named Modems for rotary connection:

```
! Establish rotary groups
line 3 7
 rotary 1
!
! Establish modem rotary service
!
 lat service Modems rotary 1
 lat service Modems enabled
```

### LAT Access List Example

The following example illustrates incoming permit conditions for all IP hosts and LAT nodes with specific characters in their names and a deny condition for X.25 connections to a printer. Outgoing connections, however, are less restricted.

```
! Permit all IP hosts, LAT nodes beginning with "VMS" and no X.25
! connections to the printer on line 5
!
```

```
access-list 1 permit 0.0.0.0 255.255.255.255
lat access-list 1 permit ^VMS.*
x29 access-list 1 deny .*
!
line 5
 access-class 1 in
!
! Meanwhile, permit outgoing connections to various places on all the
! other lines.
!
! Permit IP access within cisco
access-list 2 permit 172.30.0.0 0.0.255.255
!
! Permit LAT access to the Stella/blue complexes.
lat access-list 2 permit ^STELLA$
lat access-list 2 permit ^BLUE$
!
! Permit X25 connections to infonet hosts only.
x29 access-list 2 permit ^31370
!
line 0 99
 access-class 2 out
```

The following example illustrates how to define access lists that permit all connections, thereby conforming to software behavior prior to Software Release 9.0. Keep in mind that the value supplied for the *list* argument in both variations of the **access-class** commands is used for *all* protocols supported by the Cisco IOS software. If you are already using an IP access list, it will be necessary to define LAT (and possibly X.25) access lists permitting connections to everything, to emulate the behavior of earlier software versions.

```
access-list 1 permit 172.30.0.0 0.0.255.255
access-list 1 permit 172.30.0.0 0.0.255.255
!
line 1 40
 access-class 1 out
! define LAT access list that permits all connections
 lat access-list 1 permit .*
```

### Associating a Rotary Group with a Service Example

The following example defines a service that communicates with a specific line and defines a rotary with only that line specified. Establish rotary groups using line configuration commands and the **rotary** line configuration command.

```
hostname ciscots
! Service name for the access server as a whole
lat service ciscopt enable
! Set up some lines with unique service names
line 1
 rotary 1
 lat service ciscopt1 rotary 1
 lat service ciscopt1 enable
!
line 2
```

```
rotary 2
lat service ciscopt2 rotary 2
lat service ciscopt2 enable
```

### *LAT Connection Examples*

The following example establishes a LAT connection from the router named router to host eng2:

```
router> lat eng2
Trying ENG2...Open
         ENG2 - VAX/VMS V5.2
Username: JSmith
Password: <password>
    Welcome to VAX/VMS version V5.2 on node ENG2
    Last interactive login on Friday,  1-APR-1994 19:46
```

The system informs you of its progress by displaying the messages "Trying <system>..." and then "Open." If the connection attempt is not successful, you receive a failure message.

The following example establishes a LAT connection from the router named router to our-modems and specifies port 24, which is a special modem:

```
router> lat our-modems port 24
```

The following example establishes a LAT connection from the router named router to our-modems and specifies a node named eng:

```
router> lat our-modems node eng
```

The following example uses the LAT session debugging capability:

```
router> lat Eng2 /debug
Trying ENG2...Open
         ENG2 - VAX/VMS V5.2
 Username: JSmith
 Password: <password>
    Welcome to VAX/VMS version V5.2 on node ENG2
    Last interactive login on Tuesday, 5-APR-1994 19:02
[Set Flow out off, Flow in on, Format 8:none, Speed 9600/9600]
[Set Flow out off, Flow in on, Format 8:none, Speed 9600/9600]
$ set ter/speed=2400
[Set Flow out off, Flow in on, Format 8:none, Speed 2400/2400]
```

A variety of LAT events are reported, including all requests by the remote system to set local line parameters. The messages within brackets ([ ]) are the messages produced by the remote system setting the line characteristics as the operating system defaults.

The following example defines a group code list for the outgoing group 4 LAT connection:

```
router> terminal lat out-group 4, 6-189
```

## CONFIGURING SUPPORT FOR TN3270 CALLS

IBM 3270 display terminals are among the computing community's most widely implemented and emulated terminals for host-based computing. Information in this section describes the TN3270 terminal emulation environment and how to use and create files that allow terminals connected to the access server or router to be used for TN3270 operation. This section does not describe how to configure a TN3270 server.

The following sections are provided:

- Cisco's Implementation of TN3270
- Configure TN3270
- Map TN3270 Characters
- Make TN3270 Connections
- TN3270 Configuration Examples

## Cisco's Implementation of TN3270

TN3270 terminal emulation software allows any terminal to be used as an IBM 3270-type terminal. Users with non-3270 terminals can take advantage of the emulation capabilities to perform the functions of an IBM 3270-type terminal. The Cisco IOS software supports emulation of the following terminal types:

- IBM 3278-2 terminal with an 80-by-24 display
- IBM 3278-2 terminal with a 24-by-80 display
- IBM 3278-3 terminal with a 32-by-80 display
- IBM 3278-4 terminal with a 48-by-80 display
- IBM 3278-5 terminal with a 27-by-132 display

True IBM 3270-type terminals use a character format referred to as extended binary-coded decimal interchange code (EBCDIC). EBCDIC consists of 8-bit coded characters and was originally developed by IBM. Emulation is made possible by the *termcap* protocol. Termcap functions translate the keyboard and terminal characteristics for ASCII-type terminals into those required for an IBM host.

Formally, a termcap is a two-part terminal-handling mechanism. It consists of a database and a subroutine library. The database describes the capabilities of each supported terminal, and the subroutine library allows programs to query the database and to make use of the values it contains.

The Cisco IOS software includes a default termcap entry for Digital VT100 terminal emulation. More samples are available directly from Cisco at http://www.cisco.com/warp/public/494/1.html. (This URL is subject to change without notice.)

TN3270 emulation capability allows users to access an IBM host without using a special IBM server or a UNIX host acting as a server (see Figure 19–4). The IBM host must directly support TCP/IP or have a front-end processor that supports TCP/IP.

A two-step translation method connects IBM hosts from LAT, TCP, and X.25/PAD environments. See Chapter 21 for more information about two-step translations. In general, TN3270 support allows outgoing TN3270 connections only. In other words, LAT, TCP, and X.25/PAD users must first establish a connection with the access server or router, then use the TN3270 facility from the Cisco IOS software to make a connection to the IBM host.

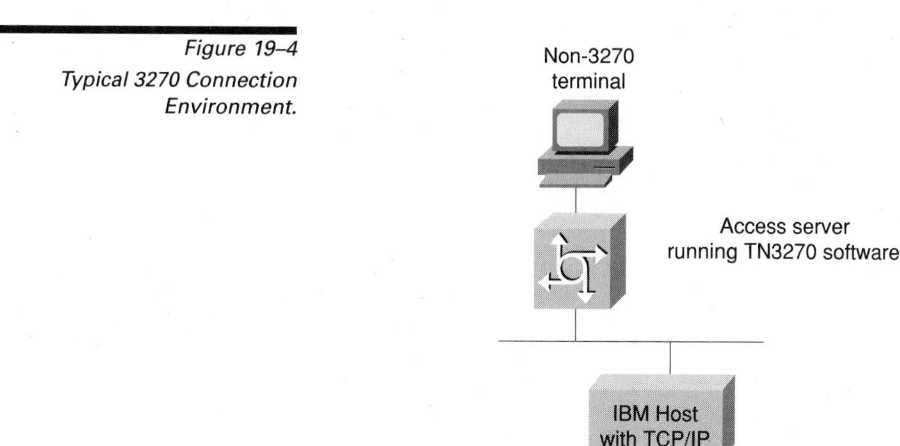


*Figure 19–4*
*Typical 3270 Connection Environment.*

### Keymaps and TTYcaps

Figure 19–5 shows how the keymapping and TTYcap functionality in the Cisco IOS software help IBM hosts and non-IBM terminals to communicate.

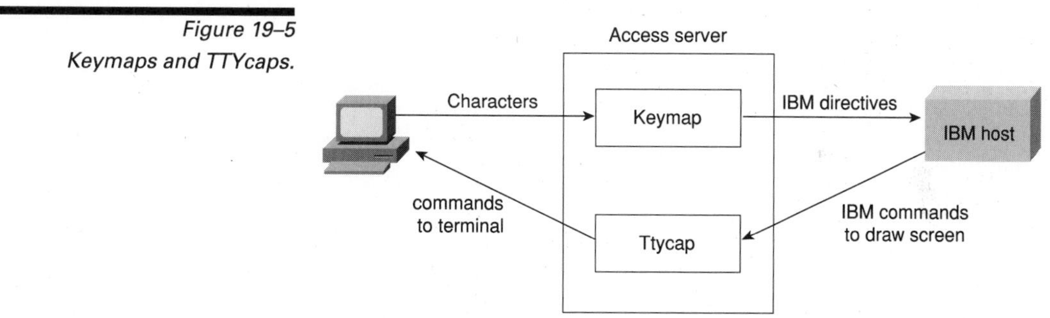


*Figure 19–5*
*Keymaps and TTYcaps.*

Keymaps and TTYcaps have the following functionality:

- Keymapping—Terminals send a key sequence for every key used to send packets to an IBM host. The keymapping function in the Cisco IOS software identifies special sequences and converts them to directives to the IBM host. A minimal level of keymapping is supported by default. Several keys can convert to the same IBM directives.
- TTYcap—IBM sends commands to the terminal, including cursor position, clear screen, and so forth. The TTYcap functionality in the Cisco IOS software changes IBM directives into the terminal language. By default, protocol translation on access servers and routers conforms to the ANSI terminal standard, which is VT*xxx* terminal compatible.

### *Startup Sequence Priorities*

At system startup, the Cisco IOS software uses the following decision sequence when selecting a terminal emulation file, also called a *TTYcap*:

1. Use a user-supplied terminal emulation filename.
2. Use a terminal emulation filename specified using line configuration commands.
3. Use a default terminal emulation filename supplied by the administrator.
4. Use the default VT100 emulation.

Figure 19–6 illustrates the decision process used by the Cisco IOS software to choose a TTYcap for a specific TN3270 session.

*Figure 19–6*
*Decision Diagram for Cisco IOS Software TTYcap Selection Process.*

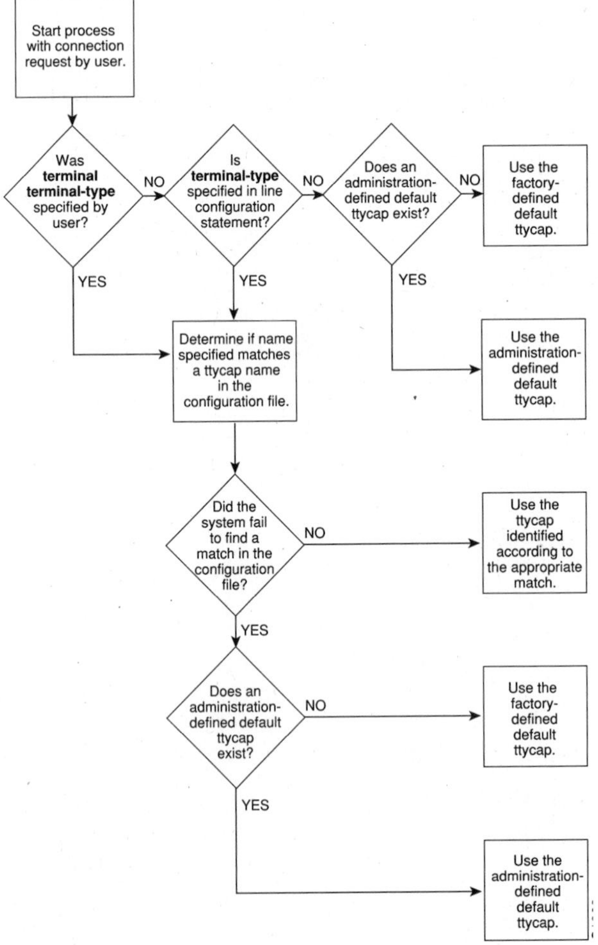

At system startup, the Cisco IOS software uses the following decision sequence when selecting a keyboard map file, also called a *keymap*:

1. Use a user-supplied keyboard map filename.
2. Use a keyboard map filename specified using line configuration commands.
3. Use a user-supplied terminal emulation filename.
4. Use a terminal emulation filename specified using line configuration commands.
5. Use the default keyboard map filename supplied by the administrator.
6. Use the default VT100 emulation.

The software uses the following criteria to determine the file to use:

- If a filename is specified by the user but fails to match any name in the configuration file, the access server or router adopts the default specified by the administrator. If one has not been specifically defined, the factory-default emulation file is adopted.
- If a filename is specified for line configuration that does not match any name in the configuration file, the access server or router adopts the default specified by the administrator. If one has not been specifically defined, the factory-default VT100 emulation file is used.

Figure 19–7 illustrates the decision process used by the Cisco IOS software to choose a keymap for a specific TN3270 session. When one of the first four priority checks fails (that is, the name specified does not match any name in the configuration file), the same rules listed for the terminal emulation file apply.

### Use the Default Terminal Emulation File to Connect

By default, an ASCII terminal and keyboard connected to the Cisco device emulate a Digital VT100 terminal type.

To connect to an IBM host, enter the **tn3270** command from EXEC mode. This command will make the connection using the terminal emulation file selected using the startup sequence priorities outlined in section, "Startup Sequence Priorities," found earlier in this chapter.

See the section "Configure TN3270," for more information about making connections.

### Copy a Sample Terminal Emulation File

If the default file does not work for your terminal and keyboard type or the host that you connect to, you might be able to find a file that will work from the growing list of sample terminal emulation files created by Cisco engineers and customers. You can obtain the TN3270 examples from Cisco Systems Cisco Connection Online (CCO). Numerous emulation files are listed in here, which allow various terminal types to emulate an IBM 3270-type terminal.

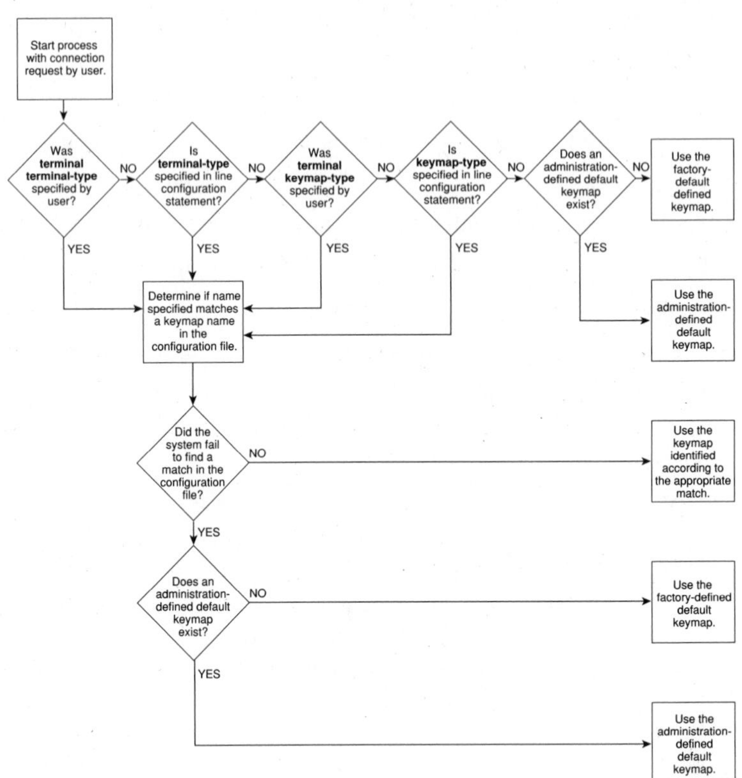


*Figure 19–7*
*Cisco IOS Software Keymap Selection Process.*

**Step 1** Obtain a sample configuration file from the following URL. The TN3270 Keymap Examples document appears. (Note that this URL is subject to change without notice.)

```
http://www.cisco.com/warp/public/494/1.html

TN3270 Keymap Examples
!!!!!!!!!!!!!!!!!!!!!!!!!!!!!!!!!!!!!!!!!!!!!!!!!!!!!!!!!!!!!!!!!!!!!!!!
!
! TN3270 examples file
! For use with the TN3270 on the cisco terminal server
! If you have requests for additions, contact tac@cisco.com
! If you have contributions, send them to remaker@cisco.com
!
!!!!!!!!!!!!!!!!!!!!!!!!!!!!!!!!!!!!!!!!!!!!!!!!!!!!!!!!!!!!!!!!!!!!!!!!
!
! Example of a ttycap for a televideo 925
! Taken from standard TTYCAP from BSD Unix
!
ttycap televideo \
v8¦vi¦tvi925¦925¦televideo model 925:\
        :hs:am:bs:co#80:li#24:cm=\E=%+ %+ :cl=\E*:cd=\Ey:ce=\Et:\
```

```
:al=\EE:dl=\ER:im=:ei=:ic=\EQ:dc=\EW:mr=\EG4:mk=\EG1:md=\EG4:me=\EG0:\
        :ho=^^:nd=^L:bt=\EI:pt:so=\EG4:se=\EG0:sg#1:us=\EG8:ue=\EG0:ug#1:\
        :up=^K:do=^V:kb=^H:ku=^K:kd=^V:kl=^H:kr=^L:kh=^^:ma=^V^J^L :\
        :k1=^A@\r:k2=^AA\r:k3=^AB\r:k4=^AC\r:k5=^AD\r:k6=^AE\r:k7=^AF\r:\
        :k8=^AG\r:k9=^AH\r:k0=^AI\r:ko=ic,dc,al,dl,cl,ce,cd,bt:\
        :ts=\Ef:fs=\Eg:ds=\Eh:sr=\Ej:xn:ti=\EG0:to=\EG0:\
        :is=\El\E"^M\E3^M        \E1        \E1        \E1        \E1
\E1        \E1        \E1        \E1        \E1^M
!
! Example of a keymap for a 925
! Borrowed from MAP3270 of the BSD TN3270
!
...
```

**Step 2** Use a text editor or word-processing application to copy the sample terminal emulation file into the configuration file.

**Step 3** Load the configuration file onto the host or network.

These steps add new terminal emulation capability to the configuration file. Each time the system is started up, or booted, the settings in the file will be used as the default for terminal emulation.

## Configure TN3270

To connect to an IBM host and configure TN3270, perform the following tasks. Unless specified otherwise, all configuration is performed in global configuration mode.

| Task | | Command |
|---|---|---|
| **Step 1** | Create a custom terminal emulation file, or TTYcap. | **ttycap** *ttycap-name termcap-entry* |
| **Step 2** | Create a custom keyboard emulation file, or keymap. | **keymap** *keymap-name keymap-entry* |
| **Step 3** | In line configuration mode, specify the type of terminal connected to the line. | **terminal-type** *terminal-name* |
| **Step 4** | In line configuration mode, specify the keyboard map for a terminal connected to the line. | **keymap-type** *keymap-name* |
| **Step 5** | (Optional) In EXEC mode, display a list of the available TTYcap files. | **show ttycap** [*ttycap-name* \| **all**] |
| **Step 6** | (Optional) In EXEC mode, display a list of the available keymap files. | **show keymap** [*keymap-name* \| **all**] |
| **Step 7** | (Optional) Enable TN3270 extended features. | **tn3270 datastream** [**extended** \| **normal**] |

| Task | Command |
|---|---|
| **Step 8** (Optional) Enable null processing. | **tn3270 null-processing** [3270 \| 7171] |
| **Step 9** (Optional) Specify a resent whenever a 3278-x terminal keyboard locks up. | **tn3270 reset-required** |

To use a custom emulation file, you must load the emulation settings into the system configuration file. This establishes the settings in the file as the terminal and keyboard defaults and provides several ways in which the emulation settings can be used within the system, as follows. You can:

- Provide default settings for all terminals in the network or terminals on a specific host.
- Set up your system to boot, or load, a specific configuration file using configuration commands.
- Temporarily override default settings using terminal EXEC commands.
- Use the local **terminal terminal-type** and **terminal keyboard-type** EXEC command to load in the files.
- Configure line-specific emulation types for terminal negotiations with a remote host.

If you intend to use an alternate TTYcap and keymap, you must assign the following two characteristics:

- Terminal type
- Keymap type

The terminal and keymap type information is used by the Cisco IOS software when negotiating connections with hosts. Use the **terminal-type** and **keymap-type** line configuration commands to assign TTYcap and keymap line characters. You must assign the terminal and keyboard type to the line if you intend to use alternate TTYcap and keymap files.

Use the **tn3270 datastream** command to cause an "-E" to be appended to the terminal type string sent to the IBM host. This addition allows you to use the extended TN3270 features.

If a user enters data, uses an arrow key to move the cursor to the right on the screen, and then enters more data, the intervening spaces are filled in with NULLs. To specify how NULLs are handled: enter the command **tn3270 null-processing** either with the argument **3270**, where NULLs are compressed out of the string (as on a real 3278-x terminal), or use the argument **7171**, where NULLs are converted to spaces as on a 7171 controller.

On a 3278-x terminal, the keyboard is locked and further input is not permitted after an input error (due to field overflow, invalid entry, and so on), until the user presses the RESET key. Most TN3270 implementations leave the keyboard unlocked and remove any error message on the next key input after the error. Use the **tn3270 reset-required** command to enable a reset in these situations.

### Map TN3270 Characters

To control the mapping of extended binary coded decimal interchange code (EBCDIC) and ASCII characters, perform one or more of the following optional tasks:

| Task | Command |
|---|---|
| In global configuration mode, create character mappings by configuring a two-way binding between EBCDIC and ASCII characters. | **tn3270 character-map** *ebcdic-in-hex ascii-in-hex* |
| In global configuration mode, reset character mappings to their default settings. | **no tn3270 character-map** {**all** \| *ebcdic-in-hex*} [*ascii-in-hex*] |
| In EXEC mode, display character mappings. | **show tn3270 character-map** {**all** \| *ebcdic-in-hex*} |
| In EXEC mode, display the hexadecimal value of an ASCII character.* | **show tn3270 ascii-hexval** |
| In line configuration mode, temporarily configure the Cisco IOS software to use the 8-bit mask. | **tn3270 8bit display** |
| In line configuration mode, temporarily configure the Cisco IOS software to use the 8-bit mask if you use a file transfer protocol such as Kermit in 8-bit mode. | **tn3270 8bit transparent-mode** |

* After you enter the **show tn3270 ascii-hexval** command, enter the ASCII character whose hexadecimal value you want to display.

When you create character mappings between extended EBCDIC or extended ASCII characters, you must configure the Cisco IOS software for the correct data character bit length. The default mask used for TN3270 connections is a 7-bit mask. In certain situations, you must use an 8-bit display. When an 8-bit mask has been set by the line configuration command **data-character-bits** {7 | 8} or the EXEC command **terminal data-character-bits** {7 | 8}, you can temporarily configure the software to use the 8-bit mask by issuing the **tn3270 8bit display** line configuration command.

When you use a file transfer protocol such as Kermit in 8-bit mode or you use 8-bit graphics, which rely on transparent mode, use the **tn3270 8bit transparent-mode** line configuration command to configure the software for the 8-bit mask.

### Make TN3270 Connections

You use TN3270 terminal emulation to connect to an IBM 3278-type host. Your system administrator must configure a default terminal emulation file that permits the terminal to communicate with the host. See the section "Configure TN3270," earlier in this chapter for information on how to specify alternate terminal emulations.

Unlike Telnet and LAT connections, you *must* enter the **tn3270** command to make a connection to an IBM 3278 host. To begin a TN3270 session, perform the following task in EXEC mode:

| Task | Command |
|---|---|
| Begin a TN3270 connection. | **tn3270** *host* |

To terminate an active TN3270 session, enter the escape sequence (**Ctrl-Shift-6** then **x** [**Ctrl^x**] by default) and enter the **disconnect** command at the EXEC prompt. You can also log off the remote system by issuing the command specific to that system (such as **exit, logout, quit, close,** or **disconnect**).

For an example of setting TN3270 connections, see the following section "TN3270 Configuration Examples."

## TN3270 Configuration Examples

This section provides the following examples to help you define custom terminal and keyboard emulation files and to configure your system to use those files:

- Custom Terminal Emulation File Example
- Custom Keyboard Emulation File Example
- Line Specification for a Custom Emulation Example
- Character Mapping Examples
- TN3270 Connection Example

### *Custom Terminal Emulation File Example*

The following example allows a Televideo 925™ terminal to emulate an IBM 3270-type terminal. The file is part of the global **ttycap** command and is included in the system configuration file. Notice that a carriage return (^M) indicates the last character in the file.

```
ttycap ttycap1 \
v8 ¦ vi ¦ tvi925 ¦ 925 ¦ televideo model 925:\
        :so=\EG4:se=\EG0:\
        :hs:am:bs:co#80:li#24:cm=\E=%+ %+ :cl=\E*:cd=\Ey:ce=\Et:\
        :al=\EE:dl=\ER:im=:ei=:ic=\EQ:dc=\EW:\
        :ho=^^:nd=^L:bt=\EI:pt:so=\EG4:se=\EG0:sg#1:us=\EG8:ue=\EG0:ug#1:\
        :up=^K:do=^V:kb=^H:ku=^K:kd=^V:kl=^H:kr=^L:kh=^^:ma=^V^J^L :\
        :k1=^A@\r:k2=^AA\r:k3=^AB\r:k4=^AC\r:k5=^AD\r:k6=^AE\r:k7=^AF\r:\
        :k8=^AG\r:k9=^AH\r:k0=^AI\r:ko=ic,dc,al,dl,cl,ce,cd,bt:\
        :md=\E(:me=\E):ti=\E):te=\E(:\
        :ts=\Ef:fs=\Eg:ds=\Eh:sr=\Ej:xn:\
        :is=\El\E"^M\E3^M      \E1         \E1         \E1         \E1         \E\
1        \E1         \E1         \E1         \E1^M
```

### Custom Keyboard Emulation File Example

The following example allows a keyboard to emulate an asynchronous connection to an IBM 7171™ keyboard. The file is part of the **keymap** global configuration command and is included in the system configuration file.

```
keymap ibm7171 \
vt100av ¦ vt100 ¦ vt100nam ¦ pt100 ¦ vt102 ¦ vt125{ \
enter = '^m';\
erase = '^?'; reset = '^g'; clear = '^z'  ¦  '\EOM';\
nl = '^j'; tab = '^i'; btab = '^b';\
left = '\EOD'; right = '\EOC'; up = '\EOA'; down = '\EOB';\
home = '^h'; delete = '^d'; eeof = '^e'  ¦  '\E^?'; einp = '^w'; insrt = '\EOn';\
pfk1 = '\EOP'  ¦  '\E1'; pfk2 = '\EOQ'  ¦  '\E2'; pfk3 = '\EOR'  ¦  '\E3';\
pfk4 = '\EOw'  ¦  '\E4'; pfk5 = '\EOx'  ¦  '\E5'; pfk6 = '\EOy'  ¦  '\E6';\
pfk7 = '\EOt'  ¦  '\E7'; pfk8 = '\EOu'  ¦  '\E8'; pfk9 = '\EOv'  ¦  '\E9';\
pfk10 = '\EOq'  ¦  '\E0'; pfk11 = '\EOr'  ¦  '\E-';\
pfk12 = '\EOs'  ¦  '\E='; pfk13 = '\EOp\EOP'  ¦  '^f13';\
pfk14 = '\EOp\EOQ'  ¦  '^f14'; pfk15 = '\EOp\EOR'  ¦  '^f15';\
pfk16 = '\EOp\EOw'  ¦  '^f16'; pfk17 = '\EOp\EOx'  ¦  '^f17';\
pfk18 = '\EOp\EOy'  ¦  '^f18'; pfk19 = '\EOp\EOt'  ¦  '^f19';\
pfk20 = '\EOp\EOu'  ¦  '^f20'; pfk21 = '\EOp\EOv'  ¦  '^f21';\
pfk22 = '\EOp\EOq'  ¦  '^f22'; pfk23 = '\EOp\EOr'  ¦  '^f23';\
pfk24 = '\EOp\EOs'  ¦  '^f24';\
pa1 = '^p1'  ¦  '\EOS';\
pa2 = '^p2'  ¦  '\EOm';\
pa3 = '^p3'  ¦  '\EOl';\
}
```

### Line Specification for a Custom Emulation Example

The following example sets up a line with specific terminal and keyboard characteristics that are used during negotiation with a host upon connection. The line configuration commands in the example must follow the global **ttycap** and **keymap** global configuration commands containing the emulation settings to be used.

```
line 3
 terminal-type ttycap1
 keymap-type ibm7171
```

### Character Mapping Examples

The following example shows the configuration of the EBCDIC and ASCII character mappings listed in Table 19–1:

```
tn3270 character-map 0x81 0x78
tn3270 character-map 0x82 0x79
tn3270 character-map 0x83 0x7A
```

**Table 19–1** *Sample EBCDIC, ASCII Character Mapping*

| EBCDIC | ASCII |
|---|---|
| a | x |

**Table 19–1** *Sample EBCDIC, ASCII Character Mapping, Continued*

| EBCDIC | ASCII |
|---|---|
| b | y |
| c | z |

The following example displays all nonstandard character mappings:

```
router# show tn3270 character-map all

EBCDIC 0x81 <=> 0x78 ASCII
EBCDIC 0x82 <=> 0x79 ASCII
EBCDIC 0x83 <=> 0x7A ASCII
```

The following example shows the standard key mapping for the letter d and c:

```
router# show tn3270 character-map 83

EBCDIC 0x83 <=> 0x63 ASCII = `c´
EBCDIC 0x84 <=> 0x64 ASCII = `d´
```

The following example unmaps a specific key, first with optional *ascii-in-hex* argument, then without the argument:

```
router# configure terminal

Enter configuration commands, one per line. End with CNTL/Z.
router(config)# no tn3270 character-map 0x80 0x78
router(config)# ^Z

router# show tn3270 character-map all

EBCDIC 0x82 <=> 0x79 ASCII
EBCDIC 0x83 <=> 0x7A ASCII

router# config term

Enter configuration commands, one per line.  End with CNTL/Z.
router(config)# no tn3270 character-map 0x82
router(config)# ^Z
router# show t3270 character-map all
EBCDIC 0x82 <=> 0x79 ASCII
```

The following example displays character mappings, then removes all mappings with the **all** keyword:

```
router# show tn3270 character-map all

EBCDIC 0x81 <=> 0x78 ASCII
EBCDIC 0x82 <=> 0x79 ASCII
EBCDIC 0x83 <=> 0x7A ASCII

router# configure terminal

Enter configuration commands, one per line.  End with CNTL/Z.
router(config)# no tn3270 character-map all
```

```
router(config)# ^Z

router# show tn3270 character-map all
```

### *TN3270 Connection Example*

The following example establishes a terminal session with an IBM host named finance:

```
router> tn3270 finance
```

To terminate an active TN3270 session, log out of the remote system by issuing the command specific to that system (such as **exit, logout, quit,** or **close**). You can also enter the escape sequence (**Ctrl-Shift-6** then **x** [**Ctrl^x**] by default) and enter the **disconnect** command at the EXEC prompt. Because the **disconnect** command can "hang" a port, it is recommended that you avoid using it routinely when you exit a session.

## CONFIGURING SUPPORT FOR XREMOTE CALLS

The following section describe the X Window system and how to configure the Cisco IOS software to support XRemote connections:

- Cisco's Implementation of XRemote
- Configure XRemote
- Select Fonts for X Terminal Applications
- XRemote Connections
- Establish XRemote Sessions between Servers
- Monitor XRemote Connections
- XRemote Configuration Example
- XRemote Connection Examples

### Cisco's Implementation of XRemote

The X Window System, also called X, is a network-based graphics window system originally developed for workstations running UNIX. Cisco Systems, Inc. has developed an XRemote application that allows the XRemote capabilities of X terminals to run on an access server or router.

Previous window systems for terminals were *kernel-based* and therefore were closely linked to the operating system running on the workstation itself. They typically only ran on discrete systems, such as a single workstation. The X Window System is not part of any operating system, but instead, is composed of application programs. Thus, the X Window System enables flexible, graphics-based network computing across a wide range of operating systems and hardware platforms.

### *X and the Client/Server Model*

The underlying architecture of the X Window System is based on a *client/server* model. The system is split into two parts: *clients* and *display servers*. Clients are application programs that perform specific tasks, and display servers provide specific display capabilities and track user input. These two parts can reside on the same computer or can be separated over a network. In an X terminal environment, such as in NCD terminal implementations, the display server resides on the display station and the client resides on a host computer.

Because the X Windows System employs this client/server partitioning and is independent of both the hardware and operating environment, X terminal users can access different types of computers to simultaneously access several applications and resources in a multivendor environment. A user at an X terminal can run and display a calendar program on a VAX, a spreadsheet program on a PC, and a compiler on a workstation concurrently.

### *How XRemote Works*

XRemote is a protocol developed specifically to optimize support for the X Windows System over a serial communications link. Its compression and decompression algorithms are designed to handle bitmapped displays and windowing systems.

There are two basic parts to XRemote:

- Server-side helper process
- Client-side helper process

These two helper processes communicate with each other using the XRemote protocol. The client-side helper communicates with X clients using the standard X protocol. The server-side helper communicates with the server using the standard X Window System. The server-side helper might operate as part of the X server or it might be external and accessed across the network; for example, the server-side helper can operate in an access server or router at your house or work site. If the server-side helper is in the X terminal, it must have XRemote PROMs installed.

XRemote enables a user of a display station to run the X Window System via 9600-baud (and faster) modem connections with performance that is superior to using conventional serial protocols, such as Serial Line Internet Protocol (SLIP). An X display station must either implement XRemote or be connected to a network configuration that includes an access server or router.

### *Connection Capability*

The Cisco implementation of XRemote is fully compatible with the NCD XRemote protocol. Figure 19–8 illustrates an XRemote connection between an X terminal and an access server. In Figure 19–8, the server-side helper runs on the X terminal, and the client-side helper runs on the access server.

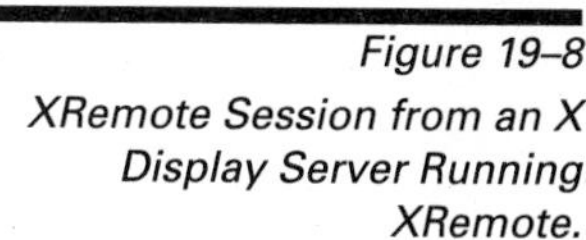
*Figure 19–8*
*XRemote Session from an X Display Server Running XRemote.*

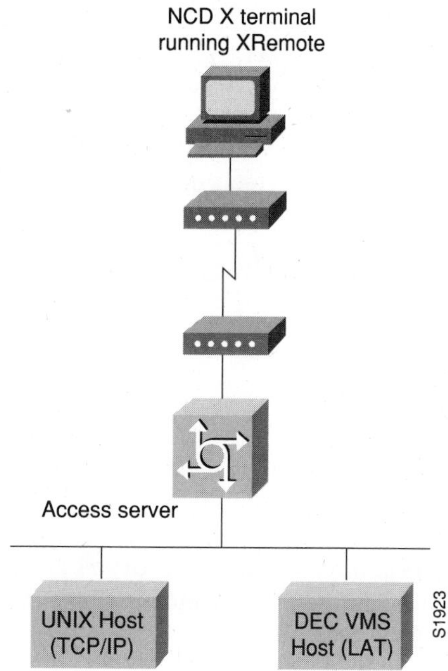


### *Remote Access to Fonts*

Remote access to fonts is provided in three ways:

- Using the industry-standard protocol for transporting X traffic over Transmission Control Protocol/Internet Protocol (TCP/IP) networks
- Using the Digital Equipment Corporation protocol for transporting X traffic over local-area transport (LAT) networks
- Using the Internet standard Trivial File Transfer Protocol (TFTP) for TCP/IP networks

A single XRemote user can use any combination of TCP/IP and LAT client connections and any combination of TFTP and LAT font access.

## Configure XRemote

To allow host connections using the NCD's XRemote feature and the access server or router, perform the following tasks. Unless specified otherwise, all commands in this task table are issued from global configuration mode.

| Task* | | Command |
|---|---|---|
| **Step 1** | Verify that a modem is externally or internally connected with your access server or router. | |

| Task[*] | | Command |
|---|---|---|
| Step 2 | Define a specific TFTP font server as the source for fonts. | **xremote tftp host** *hostname* |
| Step 3 | Set the buffer size used for loading font files. | **xremote tftp buffersize** *buffersize* |
| Step 4 | Increase the number of times that the font loader tries to load the fonts.[†] | **xremote tftp retries** *retries* |
| Step 5 | (Optional) In EXEC mode, display current XRemote connections and monitor traffic. | **show xremote** |
| Step 6 | (Optional) In EXEC mode, display XRemote traffic and line statistics. | **show xremote line** *number* |

[*] The X Server for the X terminal and the network and serial parameters for the X terminal must be configured as described in the publications for the specific X terminal you are using. In general, the X terminal configuration determines the mode of operation for the terminal, the source of font information, and the source of remote configuration information (when applicable).
[†] This feature is particularly useful when the font servers are known to be heavily loaded.

In general, you can use any modem that provides acceptable performance for your application. The following guidelines apply to an XRemote operation using a modem (refer to the user manual for your modem for specific connection procedures):

- Attach cables and set up your modem for use with XRemote (access over asynchronous lines only), or cable the X terminal directly to the access server or router.
- Disable any error correction and compression features of the modem. Because XRemote implements its own compression and error correction, the modem's compression and error correction actually impair performance.
- If you must use a flow control mechanism, hardware flow control (such as RTS/CTS or DTR/DSR) is recommended. Software flow control (such as XON/XOFF) is discouraged.
- The modem should incur minimal delays in round-trip transmissions, even when transmitting small packets, and should be transparent to the data stream.
- The modem should provide true full-duplex transmission at 9600 baud or faster. Half-duplex modems are not suitable for use with XRemote.

Refer to Chapter, 5, "Configuring Modem Support and Asynchronous Devices," for more information about configuring modems.

When the X terminal requests that a font file be loaded, the Cisco IOS software must first load the font file into an internal buffer before passing it to the X terminal. The default value for this buffer is 70,000 bytes, which is adequate for most font files, but the size can be increased as necessary for nonstandard font files using the **xremote tftp buffersize** global configuration command. This task can be performed for both TFTP and LAT font access.

## Select Fonts for X Terminal Applications

The NCD terminal contains a small set of built-in fonts in local ROM. You should use these fonts because loading fonts over a serial line can increase application startup time. The default for an NCD terminal is to use built-in fonts, unless you log in using DECwindows over LAT. When using DECwindows over LAT, the standard DECwindows fonts are used automatically.

Perform the following two tasks to select fonts:

- Access Nonresident Fonts Using TFTP
- Select DECwindows Fonts

### *Access Nonresident Fonts Using TFTP*

When an X terminal application requests a font that is not stored in the terminal's ROM, the X terminal makes a request for a font file from the access server or router. The Cisco IOS software uses the Trivial File Transfer Protocol (TFTP) to load the font from the font server, and then passes the font to the X terminal using the XRemote protocol. The process of loading fonts from the access server or router to the X terminal can take 30 to 45 seconds, depending on the size of the font file.

An X server can display only the fonts it finds in the directories in its font path. The X server's default font path includes only the built-in fonts. To access fonts stored on a host, you must add the host's font directories to the X server's font path. To do this, use the UNIX command **xset** with the **fp+** argument to add fonts to the end of the server's font path.

For example, to allow your display station to access the 100 dots per inch (dpi) fonts found in the standard font directory, run the following command at the host system prompt:

```
host_prompt% xset fp+ /usr/lib/x11/ncd/fonts/100dpi
```

### *Select DECwindows Fonts*

Downloading of fonts occurs automatically when you initiate a remote DECwindows login session using the EXEC **xremote lat** command. Instead of relying on TFTP to download the fonts, the fonts are read in via the LAT protocol.

If you want to use DECwindows fonts while running standard X applications on a UNIX host, you need to use the UNIX **xset** command or an application that issues an XSetFontPath request to set a font path. You might want to do this if you are primarily a TCP/IP user but also run some DECwindows applications.

Execute **xset**, or the application to issue an XSetFontPath request, to set the following path:

```
/LAT/SERVICE
```

In this path, *SERVICE* is a LAT service name with DECwindows support; case is not significant.

When the Cisco IOS software sees a request for font files in that directory, it uses LAT rather than TFTP to access the specified service.

### XRemote Connections

You use the XRemote protocol with an X display station and a modem to connect to remote hosts via TCP/IP and LAT. This section outlines the steps for starting XRemote in several typical environments and for exiting XRemote sessions. It contains the following sections:

- Connect Through Automatic Session Startup with an XDMCP Server
- Connect Through Automatic Session Startup with a DECwindows Login via LAT
- Connect Through Manual XRemote Session Startup
- Establish XRemote Sessions between Servers
- Exit XRemote Sessions

When possible, use the automated processes. Make sure that your system administrator has already configured a path for loading fonts.

You can run the XRemote protocols between two servers. This is useful if you use an X display server that does not support XRemote, or if an X display station is connected to a LAN and you want to use the LAN rather than a dial-in link to connect to a server. (Note that XRemote is faster when the X display station connects to a server over a dial-in link.) See the section "Establish XRemote Sessions between Servers," for more informaiton.

For an example of making an XRemote connection, see the section "XRemote Connection Examples."

#### Connect Through Automatic Session Startup with an XDMCP Server

If your host computer supports a server for XDMCP (such as the xdm program included in X11R4 or later), you can use automatic session startup to make an XRemote session connection. To do so, perform the following task in EXEC mode:

| Task | Command |
|---|---|
| Create a connection with XRemote and an XDMCP server. | **xremote xdm** [*hostname*] |

This command sends an XDMCP session startup request to the host computer. If you do not specify a host name, a broadcast message is sent to all hosts. The first host to respond by starting up a session is used.

The server and X terminal stay in XRemote mode until either the display manager terminates the session, or a reset request is received from the X terminal.

#### Connect Through Automatic Session Startup with a DECwindows Login via LAT

If your host computer supports DECwindows login sessions, you can use automatic session startup to make an XRemote session connection. If the system administrator at the remote host configures support for DECwindows over LAT, perform the following task in EXEC mode to initiate the connection:

| Task | Command |
|---|---|
| Create a connection with XRemote and DECwindows over LAT. | **xremote lat** *service* |

After you issue this command, expect the following to occur:

- The XRemote font server loads several initial fonts for the DECwindows login display.
- The terminal displays the Digital logo and DECwindows login box.

Log on to the system. Upon completion of login, more fonts are loaded, and the remote session begins.

**NOTES**

Because of heavy font usage, DECwindows applications can take longer than expected to start when you use XRemote. After the application starts, performance and access times should be normal.

### *Connect Through Manual XRemote Session Startup*

If you do not use a host computer that supports XDMCP or LAT, you must use manual session startup. To use manual session startup, perform the following tasks in EXEC mode:

1. Enable XRemote Manually
2. Connect to the Remote Host Computer
3. Set the Location of the X Display
4. Start Client Applications
5. Return to the EXEC Prompt
6. Re-enable XRemote Manually

The following sections describe these tasks.

#### *Enable XRemote Manually*

To prepare the XRemote server for manual startup, perform the following task in EXEC mode:

| Task | Command |
|---|---|
| Prepare the XRemote server for manual startup. | **xremote** |

After you issue this command, instructions prompt you through the process of manually enabling XRemote.

**NOTES**

In manual operation, the server and X terminal remain in XRemote mode until all clients disconnect or the server receives a reset request from the X terminal. A session might terminate during startup because you invoked transient X clients that set some parameters and then disconnected (such as **xset** or **xmodmap** parameters). There must always be one session open or the connection is reset.

### *Connect to the Remote Host Computer*

To connect to a host, perform one of the following tasks in EXEC mode:

| Task | Command |
|---|---|
| Prepare the server for XRemote manual startup. | **telnet**<br>or<br>**lat**<br>or<br>**rlogin** |

After entering the command, you can log on as usual.

### *Set the Location of the X Display*

At this point, you are logged in to the remote host computer.

**NOTES**

If you are using a version of Telnet on the remote host that supports the "X Display Location" option (RFC 1096), skip this step and go on to section, "Start Client Applications."

Inform the host computer of your X display location that the server provided when you enabled XRemote manually.

For most versions of the UNIX operating system, the X display location is set by using the **setenv** command to set the Display environment variable. Refer to your UNIX system's online X(1) manual page for more information.

On VAX/VMS systems, use the **SET DISPLAY** command to set the X display location. For more information, refer to the *VMS DCL Dictionary.*

**NOTES**

To set the location of the X display for VAX/VMS client systems, you must install either the TCP/IP transport from Digital or a third-party TCP/IP transport. Contact your VAX/VMS system administrator for the appropriate TCP/IP transport name.

#### *Start Client Applications*

Now you can start your client applications for your host operating system, as specified in the documentation for the client applications.

The server accepts the X connection attempt from the client application and places the client in a dormant state.

#### *Return to the EXEC Prompt*

If it is possible to log off the host computer and keep your X clients running in the background, you can do so now. This conserves resources on both the host and the server that would otherwise be inaccessible until you exited from the XRemote state.

If you cannot log off the host computer and keep your clients running, escape back to the access server's EXEC prompt using the escape sequence (**Ctrl-Shift-6** then **x** [**Ctrl^x**] by default).

#### *Re-enable XRemote Manually*

To begin a manual remote session again, refer to section, "Enable XRemote Manually," found earlier in this chapter. If the X clients connected successfully, the session is put into XRemote mode, and the clients complete their startup.

If no clients are found, you see the following message:

```
No X clients waiting - check that your display is darkstar:2018
```

Check your hosts to determine whether an error has occurred when the session started. The most likely causes are that there is an improperly specified display location, or the host computer did not recognize the name of your server.

### *Establish XRemote Sessions between Servers*

If you are on an X display server that does not support XRemote, you can still run the XRemote protocols. An X display server (such as a PCX, MacX, or UNIX workstation) connected to an Ethernet network can dial out through an access server on a conventional modem to access an X client program on a host residing on another network. The access server provides the server-side helper process.

To run XRemote, connect to one of the XRemote ports.

**NOTES**

The NCD helper process does not support X display devices that use a maximum request and response size larger than 64 Kb.

Find out from your administrator whether the connection from your X display server is configured as an individual line or a rotary connection.

- To connect to an individual line, use Telnet to connect from the X display server to port 9000 plus the decimal value of the line number.
- To make a rotary connection, use Telnet to connect from the X display server to port 10000 plus the decimal value of the line number.

For information about how to configure individual lines and rotary connections, see Chapter 5.

Figure 19–9 illustrates a configuration in which a display server is not running XRemote. In this configuration, the server-side XRemote helper is running on Access Server 1, and the client-side XRemote helper is running on Access Server 2.

*Figure 19–9*
*XRemote Session between Servers.*

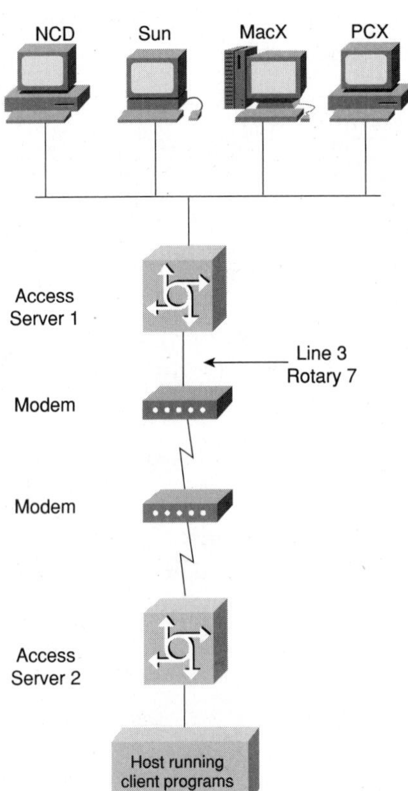

### *Exit XRemote Sessions*

When you exit XRemote, you must quit all active X connections, usually with a command supported by your X client system. Usually, when you quit the last connection (all client processes are stopped), XRemote closes and you return to the EXEC prompt. Check your X client system documentation for specific information about exiting an XRemote session.

## Monitor XRemote Connections

To list XRemote connections and monitor XRemote traffic through the router, perform one of the following tasks in user EXEC mode:

| Task | Command |
|---|---|
| List XRemote connections and monitor XRemote traffic through the router or access server. | **show xremote** |
| List XRemote connections and monitor XRemote traffic for specific lines on an XRemote server. | **show xremote line** *number* |

## XRemote Configuration Example

The following example illustrates how to specify IBM-1 as the host name of the TFTP font server, specify 7 retry attempts at accessing the server, and reduce the buffer size to 20,000 bytes.

```
xremote tftp host IBM-1
xremote tftp retries 7
xremote tftp buffersize 20000
```

## XRemote Connection Examples

Use the examples in this section to understand how to make the following XRemote connections:

- Connect through Automatic Session Startup with XDMCP Server Example
- Connect through Automatic Session Startup with DECwindows Login via LAT Example
- Enable XRemote Manually Example
- Connect an X Display Terminal Example
- Make XRemote Connections between Servers Examples

### *Connect through Automatic Session Startup with XDMCP Server Example*

The following example starts a session with a remote host named star:

```
router> xremote xdm star
```

### *Connect through Automatic Session Startup with DECwindows Login via LAT Example*

The following example begins connection with a LAT service named WHIRL:

```
router> xremote lat WHIRL
```

### *Enable XRemote Manually Example*

The following example illustrates how a successful manual XRemote session begins:

```
dialup> xremote
XRemote enabled; your display is dialup:2006
Start your clients and type XRemote again
```

The system replies with a message informing you of your X display location. Use this information to tell the host the location of your X display server.

If no clients are found, you see the following message:

```
No X clients waiting - check that your display is darkstar:2006
```

Check your hosts to determine whether an error has occurred when the session started. The most likely causes are that there is an improperly specified display location or the host computer did not recognize the name of your server.

### *Connect an X Display Terminal Example*

The following example shows how to make a connection from an X display terminal through a server to a host running client programs:

**Step 1** Enter the **xremote** command at the EXEC prompt.

```
dialup> xremote
```

**Step 2** Read and follow the instruction from the host.

```
XRemote enabled; your display is dialup:2006
Start your clients and type XRemote again
```

**Step 3** Connect to the client.

```
dialup> telnet eureka
Trying EUREKA.NOWHERE.COM (252.122.1.55)... Open

SunOS UNIX (eureka)
```

**Step 4** Log on at the prompt.

```
login: deal
Password:
Last login: Fri Apr 1 17:17:46 from dialup.nowhere.com
SunOS Release (SERVER+FDDI+DBE.patched) #14: Fri Apr 8 10:37:29 PDT 1994
```

**Step 5** At the client prompt, enter the display name from Step 2 in this procedure and the **xterm** command.

```
eureka% setenv DISPLAY dialup:2006
eureka% xterm &
[1] 15439
```

**Step 6** Disconnect from the client.

```
eureka% logout

[Connection to EUREKA closed by foreign host]
```

**Step 7** Begin the XRemote session.

```
dialup> xremote
Entering XRemote
```

The server and X terminal stay in XRemote mode until either the display manager terminates the session, or a reset request is received from the X terminal.

```
Connection closed by foreign host.
eureka%
```

### *Make XRemote Connections between Servers Examples*

This section provides two examples of XRemote connections between servers.

The following example shows how an XRemote connection is established for a configuration such as the one shown in Figure 19–9 in section, "Establish XRemote Sessions between Servers," found earlier in this chapter. This example assumes that the administrator has set the display environment variable to identify and match the user's X display terminal.

**Step 1** From the PCX, MacX, or UNIX machine in Figure 19–9, the user connects to port 9003 on Access Server 1. If your administrator has configured a rotary number 7, the user connects to port 10007. For more information about rotary groups, see Chapter 5.

Access Server 1 connects the user to a modem.

The modem calls Access Server 2.

**Step 2** Enter the **xremote** command at the Access Server 2 prompt.

**Step 3** Connect to the remote host from Access Server 2 using the **telnet** command.

**Step 4** Start the X client program that runs on the remote host and displays on the X display server (PCX, MacX, or UNIX host).

**Step 5** Escape from the remote host back to the Access Server 2, or log out if clients were run in the background, and enter the **xremote** command again at the Access Server 2 prompt.

The following example shows the steps to make an XRemote connection between servers. The number 9016 in the first line of the display indicates a connection to individual line 16. If the administrator had configured a rotary connection, the user would enter 10000 plus the number of the rotary (instead of 9016).

**Step 1** Enter the **telnet** command to make the connection.

```
space% telnet golden-road 9016
Trying 192.31.7.84 ...
Connected to golden-road.cisco.com.
Escape character is '^]'.
```

**Step 2** Supply the password for TACACS verification.

```
User Access Verification
```

```
Password:<password>
Password OK

 --- Outbound XRemote service ---
Enter X server name or IP address: innerspace
Enter display number [0]:

 Connecting to tty16... please start up XRemote on the remote system
```

**Step 3** Dial in to the remote system using the modem, and then log in.

```
atdt 13125554141
DIALING
RING
CONNECT 14400

User Access Verification
Username: deal
Password:
  Welcome to the cisco dial-up access server.
```

**Step 4** Enter the **xremote** command at the EXEC prompt, then follow the instructions from the host.

```
dialup> xremote
XRemote enabled; your display is dialup:2006
Start your clients and type XRemote again
```

**Step 5** Connect to the client.

```
dialup> telnet sparks
Trying SPARKS.NOWHERE.COM (252.122.1.55)... Open

SunOS UNIX (sparks)

login: deal
Password: <password>
Last login: Fri Apr 1 17:17:46 from dialup.nowhere.com
SunOS Release (SERVER+FDDI+DBE.patched) #14: Fri Apr 8 10:37:29 PDT 1994
```

**Step 6** At the client prompt, enter the display name from step 4 and the **xterm** command.

```
sparks% setenv DISPLAY dialup:2006
sparks% xterm &
[1] 15439
Disconnect from the client.
sparks% logout

[Connection to SPARKS closed by foreign host]
Begin the XRemote session.
dialup> xremote
Entering XRemote
```

When the connection is closed by the foreign host, the Xterm window appears on the local workstation screen.

```
Connection closed by foreign host.
sparks%
```

CHAPTER 20

# Dial-In Terminal Service Commands

The commands described in this chapter are used to configure support for asynchronous character stream calls running the protocols Telnet, rlogin, LAT, XRemote, and TN3270.

**NOTES**

Although the commands found in this chapter continue to perform their normal functions in the current release, support for these commands will cease in future releases.

For configuration information and examples, see Chapter 19, "Configuring Dial-In Terminal Services."

This chapter provides command reference documentation for the following types of dial-in terminal service calls:

- Telnet calls
- LAT calls
- TN3270 calls
- XRemote calls

Telnet is a simple remote terminal protocol that is part of the Internet Protocol (IP) suite. Telnet allows a user at one site to establish a TCP connection to a login server at another site; then, Telnet passes the keystrokes from one system to the other. Telnet can accept either an IP address or a domain name as the remote system address.

The Digital Equipment Corporation (Digital) Local Area Transport (LAT) protocol is the protocol used most often to connect to Digital hosts. LAT is a Digital-proprietary protocol. Cisco provides LAT technology licensed from Digital.

TN3270 terminal emulation software allows any terminal to be used as an IBM 3270-type terminal. Users with non-3270 terminals can take advantage of the emulation capabilities to perform the functions of an IBM 3270-type terminal. Specifically, the Cisco IOS software supports emulation of an IBM 3278-2 terminal providing an 80-by-24 display.

XRemote is a protocol developed specifically to optimize support for the X Window System over a serial communications link. Its compression and decompression algorithms are designed to handle bit-mapped displays and windowing systems.

### ACCESS-CLASS

To define restrictions on incoming and outgoing connections, use the **access-class** line configuration command. To remove the access-list number, use the **no** form of this command.

**access-class** *access-list-number* {**in** | **out**}

**no access-class** *number*

| *Syntax* | *Description* |
|---|---|
| *access-list-number* | Specifies an integer between 1 and 199 that defines the access list. |
| **in** | Controls which nodes can make LAT connections into the server. |
| **out** | Defines the access checks made on outgoing connections. (A user who types a node name at the system prompt to initiate a LAT connection is making an outgoing connection.) |

#### *Default*

Disabled

#### *Command Mode*

Line configuration

#### *Usage Guidelines*

This command first appeared in Cisco IOS Release 10.0.

This command defines access list numbers that will then be used with the **lat access-list** command to specify the access conditions.

The value supplied for the *access-list-number* argument is used for all protocols supported by the Cisco IOS software. If you are already using an IP access list, you must define LAT (and possibly X.25) access lists permitting connections to everything, to emulate the behavior of previous software versions.

When both IP and LAT connections are allowed from a terminal line and an IP access list is applied to that line with the **access-class** line command, you must also create a LAT access list with the same number if you want to allow any LAT connections from that terminal. You can specify only one incoming and one outgoing access list number for each terminal line. When checking LAT access lists, if the specified list does not exist, the system denies all LAT connections.

### Example

The following example configures an incoming access class on virtual terminal line 4:

```
line vty 4
 access-class 4 in
```

### Related Commands

Search online to find documentation for related commands.

**lat access-list**

## BUSY-MESSAGE



To create a "host failed" message that displays when a connection fails, use the **busy-message** global configuration command. Use the **no** form of this command to disable the "host failed" message from displaying on the specified host.

**busy-message** *hostname d message d*

**no busy-message** *hostname*

| *Syntax* | *Description* |
|---|---|
| *hostname* | Name of the host that cannot be reached. |
| *d* | Delimiting character of your choice—a pound sign (#) for example. You cannot use the delimiting character in the message. |
| *message* | Message text. |

### Default

No message is displayed.

### Command Mode

Global configuration

### Usage Guidelines

This command first appeared in Cisco IOS Release 10.0.

This command applies only to Telnet connections.

Follow the **busy-message** command with one or more blank spaces and a delimiting character of your choice. Then enter one or more lines of text, terminating the message with the second occurrence of the delimiting character.

Defining a "host failed" message for a host prevents all Cisco IOS software-initiated user messages, including the initial message that indicates the connection is "Trying..." The **busy-message** command can be used in the **autocommand** command to suppress these messages.

*Example*

The following example sets a message that will be displayed on the terminal whenever an attempt to connect to the host named *dross* fails. The pound sign (#) is used as a delimiting character.

```
busy-message dross #
Cannot connect to host. Contact the computer center.
#
```

### CLEAR ENTRY

To delete an entry from the list of queued host-initiated connections, enter the **clear entry** EXEC command at the system prompt.

**clear entry** *number*

| *Syntax* | *Description* |
|---|---|
| *number* | An entry number obtained from the **show entry** EXEC command. |

*Command Mode*

EXEC

*Usage Guidelines*

This command first appeared in Cisco IOS Release 10.0.

*Example*

The following example deletes pending entry number 3 from the queue:

```
router# clear entry 3
```

*Related Commands*

Search online to find documentation for related commands.

**show entry**

### CONNECT

To log on to a host that supports Telnet, rlogin, or LAT, use the **connect** EXEC command.

**connect** *host* [*port*] [*keyword*]

| *Syntax* | *Description* |
|---|---|
| *host* | A host name or an IP address. |
| *port* | (Optional) A decimal TCP port number; the default is the Telnet router port (decimal 23) on the host. |
| *keyword* | (Optional) One of the options listed in Table 20–1. |

**Table 20–1** *Telnet Connection Options*

| Option | Description |
|---|---|
| **/debug** | Enables Telnet debugging mode. |
| **/encrypt kerberos** | Enables an encrypted Telnet session. This keyword is available only if you have the Kerberized Telnet subsystem.<br>If you authenticate using Kerberos Credentials, the use of this keyword initiates an encryption negotiation with the remote server. If the encryption negotiation fails, the Telnet connection will be reset. If the encryption negotiation is successful, the Telnet connection will be established, and the Telnet session will continue in encrypted mode (all Telnet traffic for the session will be encrypted). |
| **/line** | Enables Telnet line mode. In this mode, the Cisco IOS software sends no data to the host until you press **Return**. You can edit the line using the standard Cisco IOS software command editing characters. The **/line** keyword is a local switch; the remote router is not notified of the mode change. |
| **/noecho** | Disables local echo. |
| **/route** *path* | Specifies loose source routing. The *path* argument is a list of host names or IP addresses that specify network nodes and ends with the final destination. |
| **/source-interface** | Specifies the source interface. |
| **/stream** | Turns on *stream* processing, which enables a raw TCP stream with no Telnet control sequences. A stream connection does not process Telnet options and can be appropriate for connections to ports running UUCP and other non-Telnet protocols. |
| *port-number* | Port number. |
| **bgp** | Border Gateway Protocol. |
| **chargen** | Character generator. |
| **cmd** *rcmd* | Remote commands. |
| **daytime** | Daytime. |
| **discard** | Discard. |
| **domain** | Domain Naming Service. |
| **echo** | Echo. |
| **exec** | EXEC. |
| **finger** | Finger. |

Part III Command Reference

**Table 20–1** *Telnet Connection Options, Continued*

| Option | Description |
|---|---|
| **ftp** | File Transfer Protocol. |
| **ftp-data** | FTP data connections (used infrequently). |
| **gopher** | Gopher. |
| **hostname** | Network Information Center (NIC) host name server. |
| **ident** | Ident Protocol. |
| **irc** | Internet Relay Chat. |
| **klogin** | Kerberos login. |
| **kshell** | Kerberos shell. |
| **login** | Login (rlogin). |
| **lpd** | Printer service. |
| **nntp** | Network News Transport Protocol. |
| **node** | Connect to a specific LAT node. |
| **pop2** | Post Office Protocol v2. |
| **pop3** | Post Office Protocol v3. |
| **port** | Destination LAT port name. |
| **smtp** | Simple Mail Transport Protocol. |
| **sunrpc** | Sun Remote Procedure Call. |
| **syslog** | Syslog. |
| **tacacs** | Specify TACACS security. |
| **talk** | Talk. |
| **telnet** | Telnet. |
| **time** | Time. |
| **uucp** | UNIX-to-UNIX Copy Program. |
| **whois** | Nickname. |
| **www** | World Wide Web (HTTP). |

### *Command Mode*

EXEC

### *Usage Guidelines*

This command first appeared in a release prior to Cisco IOS Release 10.0.

With the Cisco IOS software implementation of TCP/IP, you are not required to enter the **connect**, **telnet**, **lat**, or **rlogin** commands to establish a terminal connection. You can just enter the learned host name—as long as the host name is different from a command word in the Cisco IOS software.

To display a list of the available hosts, enter the following command:

**show hosts**

To display the status of all TCP connections, enter the following command:

**show tcp**

The Cisco IOS software assigns a logical name to each connection, and several commands use these names to identify connections. The logical name is the same as the host name, unless that name is already in use, or you change the connection name with the EXEC command **name-connection**. If the name is already in use, the Cisco IOS software assigns a null name to the connection.



### *Examples*

The following example establishes an encrypted Telnet session from a router to a remote host named *host1*:

```
router> connect host1 /encrypt kerberos
```

The following example routes packets from the source system host1 to kl.sri.com, then to 10.1.0.11, and finally back to host1:

```
router> connect host1 /route:kl.sri.com 10.1.0.11 host1
```

The following example connects to a host with logical name *host1*:

```
router> host1
```

### *Related Commands*

Search online to find documentation for related commands.

**lat**
**telnet**

## DISCONNECT

To disconnect a line, use the **disconnect** EXEC command.

**disconnect** [*connection*]

| *Syntax* | *Description* |
|---|---|
| *connection* | (Optional) Number of the line or name of the active network connection to be disconnected. |

### *Command Mode*

EXEC

### *Usage Guidelines*

This command first appeared in a release prior to Cisco IOS Release 10.0.

Do not disconnect a line to end a session. Instead, log off the host, so the Cisco IOS software can clear the connection. Then end the session. If you cannot log out of an active session, disconnect the line.

### *Example*

In the following example, the user disconnects from the device Slab to return back to the router.

```
Slab% disconnect
  Connection closed by remote host

router#
```

### *Related Commands*

Search online to find documentation for related commands.

**login** (EXEC)

## IP ALIAS

To assign an IP address to the service provided on a TCP port, use the **ip alias** interface configuration command. Use the **no** form of this command to remove the specified address for the router.

**ip alias** *ip-address tcp-port*
**no ip alias** *ip-address*

| *Syntax* | *Description* |
|---|---|
| *ip-address* | Specifies the IP address for the service. |
| *tcp-port* | Specifies the number of the TCP port. |

### *Default*

None

### *Command Mode*

Interface configuration

### *Usage Guidelines*

This command first appeared in Cisco IOS Release 10.0.

A user attempting to establish a connection is connected to the first free line in a rotary group using the Telnet protocol.

The IP address must be on the same network or subnet as the router's main address, and must not be used by another host on that network or subnet. Connecting to the IP address has the same effect as connecting to the router's main address, using *tcp-port* as the TCP port.

You can use the **ip alias** command to assign multiple IP addresses to the router. For example, in addition to the primary alias address, you can specify addresses that correspond to lines or rotary groups. Using the **ip alias** command in this way makes the process of connecting to a specific rotary group transparent to the user.

When asynchronous mode is implemented, the Cisco IOS software creates the appropriate IP aliases, which map the asynchronous addresses for the lines to which they are connected. This process is automatic and does not require configuration.

### *Example*

The following example configures connections to IP address 172.30.42.42 to act identically to connections made to the server's primary IP address on TCP port 3001. In other words, a user is connected to the first free line on port 1 of the rotary group that uses the Telnet protocol.

```
ip alias 172.30.42.42 3001
```

## IP TCP CHUNK-SIZE

To enable a faster response to user interrupt characters, use the **ip tcp chunk-size** global configuration command.

**ip tcp chunk-size** *number*

| *Syntax* | *Description* |
|---|---|
| *number* | The number of characters output before the interrupt executes. The suggested value is 80, which will typically abort output within a line or two of where the user types the interrupt character. For efficiency reasons, values of less than 50 are not recommended. |

### *Command Mode*

Global configuration

### Usage Guidelines

This command first appeared in Cisco IOS Release 10.0.

When used with a correctly operating host, the Cisco IOS software implements the Telnet Synchronize and Abort Output signals, which can stop output within one packet's worth of data from the time the user types the interrupt character.

Changing the chunk size (the number of characters output before the interrupt executes) affects neither the size of the packet used nor the TCP window size, either of which would cause serious efficiency problems for the remote host as well as for the router. Instead, the Telnet status is checked after the number of characters specified, causing only a relatively minor performance loss.

### Example

The following example allows a router to execute an interrupt after an output of 100 characters, when an interrupt character or sequence is entered (Ctrl-C, for example):

```
ip tcp chunk-size 100
```

## KEYMAP

To define specific characteristics of keyboard mappings, use the **keymap** global configuration command. To remove the named keymap from the current image of the configuration file, use the **no** form of this command.

**keymap** *keymap-name keymap-entry*
**no keymap** *keymap-name*

| *Syntax* | *Description* |
|---|---|
| *keymap-name* | Name of the file containing the keyboard mappings. The name can be up to 32 characters long and must be unique. |
| *keymap-entry* | Commands that define the keymap. |

### Default

VT100 keyboard emulation

### Command Mode

Global configuration

### Usage Guidelines

This command first appeared in Cisco IOS Release 10.0.

The **keymap** command maps individual keys on a non-3270 keyboard to perform the function defined for the 3270 keyboard. Use the EXEC command **show keymap** to test for the availability of a keymap.

The guidelines for creating a keymap file follow.

Do not name a ttycap entry filename *default* or the Cisco IOS software will adopt the newly defined entry as the default.

### *The Keymap Entry Structure*

A keymap is a keyboard map file. A keymap consists of an entry for a keyboard. The first part of a keymap lists the names of the keyboards that use that entry. These names will often be the same as in the ttycaps (terminal emulation) file, and often the terminals from various ttycap entries will use the same keymap entry. For example, both 925 and 925vb (for 925 with visual bells) terminals would probably use the same keymap entry. There are other circumstances in which it is necessary to specify a keyboard name as the name of the entry (for example, if a user requires a custom key layout).

After the names, which are separated by vertical bars (|), comes a left brace ({), the text that forms the definitions, and a right brace (}), as follows:

```
ciscodefault{
clear = '^z';\
flinp = '^x';\
enter = '^m';\
delete = '^d' ¦ '^?';\
synch = '^r';\
ebcdic_xx='string'
reshow = '^v';\
eeof = '^e';\
tab = '^i';\
btab = '^b';\
nl = '^n';\
left = '^h';\
right = '^l';\
up = '^k';\
down = '^j';\
einp = '^w';\
reset = '^t';\
ferase = '^u';\
insrt = '\E ';\
pa1 = '^p1'; pa2 = '^p2'; pa3 = '^p3';\
pfk1 = '\E1'; pfk2 = '\E2'; pfk3 = '\E3'; pfk4 = '\E4';\
pfk5 = '\E5'; pfk6 = '\E6'; pfk7 = '\E7'; pfk8 = '\E8';\
pfk9 = '\E9'; pfk10 = '\E0'; pfk11 = '\E-'; pfk12 = '\E=';\
pfk13 = '\E!'; pfk14 = '\E@'; pfk15 = '\E#'; pfk16 = '\E$';\
pfk17 = '\E%'; pfk18 = '\E'; pfk19 = '\E&'; pfk20 = '\E*';\
pfk21 = '\E('; pfk22 = '\E)'; pfk23 = '\E_'; pfk24 = '\E+';\
}
```

Each definition consists of a reserved keyword, which identifies the 3270 function, followed by an equal sign (=), followed by the various ways to generate this particular function, followed by a semi-colon (;), as follows:

```
pa1 = '^p1'; pa2 = '^p2'; pa3 = '^p3';\
```

Part III Command Reference

Each alternative way to generate the function is a sequence of ASCII characters enclosed inside single quotes (''); the alternatives are separated by vertical bars (|), as follows:

```
delete = '^d' ¦ '^?';\
```

Inside the single quotes, a few characters are special. A caret (^) specifies that the next character is a control (Ctrl) character. The two-character string caret-a (^a) represents Ctrl-a. The caret-A sequence (^A) generates the same code as caret-a (^a). To generate Delete (or DEL), enter the caret-question mark (^?) sequence.

**NOTES**

The Ctrl-caret combination (Ctrl-^), used to generate a hexadecimal 1E, is represented as two caret symbols in sequence (^^)—not as a caret-backslash-caret combination (^\^).

In addition to the caret, a letter can be preceded by a backslash (\). Because this has little effect for most characters, its use is usually not recommended. In the case of a single quote ('), the backslash prevents that single quote from terminating the string. In the case of a caret (^), the backslash prevents the caret from having its special meaning. To include the backslash in the string, place two backslashes (\\) in the keymap. Table 20–2 lists other supported special characters.

**Table 20–2** *Special Characters Supported by TN3270 Keymap Capability*

| Character | Description |
|---|---|
| \E | Escape character |
| \n | Newline |
| \t | Tab |
| \r | Carriage return |

It is not necessary for each character in a string to be enclosed within single quotes. For example, \E\E\E means three escape characters.

To enter a keymap, provide a unique name for it and explicitly define all special keys you intend to include in it within curly brackets. Also, except for the last line, each line must be terminated with a backslash symbol (\). The last line ends with the closing curly brackets (}) symbol and an end-of-line character.

### *Keymap Restrictions*

When emulating IBM-style 3270 terminals, a mapping must be performed between sequences of keys pressed at a user's (ASCII) keyboard and the keys available on a 3270-type keyboard. For example, a 3270-type keyboard has a key labeled EEOF that erases the contents of the current field from the location of the cursor to the end. To accomplish this function, the terminal user and a program emulating a 3270-type keyboard must agree on what keys will be typed to invoke the function. The requirements for these sequences follow:

- The first character of the sequence must be outside of the standard ASCII printable characters.
- No sequence can be a complete subset of another sequence (although sequences can share partial elements).

Following are examples of acceptable keymap entries:

```
pfk1 = '\E1';
pfk2 = '\E2';
```

Following are examples of unacceptable keymap entries:

```
pfk1 = '\E1';
pfk11 = '\E11';
```



In the acceptable example, the keymap entry for *pfk1* is not completely included in the keymap entry for *pfk2*. By contrast, in the unacceptable, or conflicting, keymap pair, the sequence used to represent *pfk1* is a complete subset of the sequence used to represent *pfk11*. Refer to the keymap entry provided later in this section for an example of how various keys can be represented to avoid this kind of conflict.

Table 20–3 lists 3270 key names that are supported in this keymap. Note that some of the keys do not really exist on a 3270-type keyboard. An unsupported function will cause the Cisco IOS software to send a (possibly visual) bell sequence to the user's terminal.

**Table 20–3** *3270 Key Names Supported by Default Keymap*

| 3270 Key Name | Functional Description |
|---|---|
| LPRT* | Local print |
| DP | Duplicate character |
| FM | Field mark character |
| CURSEL | Cursor select |
| CENTSIGN | EBCDIC cent sign |
| RESHOW | Redisplay the screen |
| EINP | Erase input |
| EEOF | Erase end of field |
| DELETE | Delete character |
| INSRT | Toggle insert mode |
| TAB | Field tab |
| BTAB | Field back tab |

**Table 20–3** *3270 Key Names Supported by Default Keymap, Continued*

| 3270 Key Name | Functional Description |
|---|---|
| COLTAB | Column tab |
| COLBAK | Column back tab |
| INDENT | Indent one tab stop |
| UNDENT | Undent one tab stop |
| NL | New line |
| HOME | Home the cursor |
| UP | Up cursor |
| DOWN | Down cursor |
| RIGHT | Right cursor |
| LEFT | Left cursor |
| SETTAB | Set a column tab |
| DELTAB | Delete a column tab |
| SETMRG | Set left margin |
| SETHOM | Set home position |
| CLRTAB | Clear all column tabs |
| APLON* | Apl on |
| APLOFF* | Apl off |
| APLEND* | Treat input as ASCII |
| PCON* | Xon/xoff on |
| PCOFF* | Xon/xoff off |
| DISC | Disconnect (suspend) |
| INIT* | New terminal type |
| ALTK* | Alternate keyboard dvorak |
| FLINP | Flush input |
| ERASE | Erase last character |
| WERASE | Erase last word |
| FERASE | Erase field |

**Table 20–3** *3270 Key Names Supported by Default Keymap, Continued*

| 3270 Key Name | Functional Description |
|---|---|
| SYNCH | We are in synch with the user |
| RESET | Reset key-unlock, keyboard |
| MASTER_RESET | Reset, unlock, and redisplay |
| XOFF | Please hold output |
| XON* | Please give me output |
| WORDTAB | Tab to beginning of next word |
| WORDBACKTAB | Tab to beginning of current/last word |
| WORDEND | Tab to end of current/next word |
| FIELDEND | Tab to last nonblank of current/next unprotected (writable) field |
| PA1 | Program attention 1 |
| PA2 | Program attention 2 |
| PA3 | Program attention 3 |
| CLEAR | Local clear of the 3270 screen |
| TREQ | Test request |
| ENTER | Enter key |
| PFK1 to PFK30 | Program function key 1 program function key 30 |

* Not supported by Cisco's TN3270 implementation.

Table 20–4 illustrates the proper keys used to emulate each 3270 function when using default key mappings.

**Table 20–4** *Keys Used to Emulate Each 3270 Function with Default Keymap*

| Key Types | IBM 3270 Key | Default Keys |
|---|---|---|
| Cursor Movement Keys | New Line | Ctrl-n or Home |
| | Tab | Ctrl-i |
| | Back Tab | Ctrl-b |
| | Cursor Left | Ctrl-h |
| | Cursor Right | Ctrl-l |
| | Cursor Up | Ctrl-k |
| | Cursor Down | Ctrl-j or LINE FEED |

**Table 20–4** *Keys Used to Emulate Each 3270 Function with Default Keymap, Continued*

| Key Types | IBM 3270 Key | Default Keys |
|---|---|---|
| Edit Control Keys | Delete Char | Ctrl-d or RUB |
| | Erase EOF | Ctrl-e |
| | Erase Input | Ctrl-w |
| | Insert Mode | ESC-Space* |
| | End Insert | ESC-Space |
| Program Function Keys | PF1 | ESC 1 |
| | PF2 | ESC 2 |
| | ... | ... |
| | PF10 | ESC 0 |
| | PF11 | ESC - |
| | PF12 | ESC = |
| | PF13 | ESC ! |
| | PF14 | ESC @ |
| | ... | ... |
| | PF24 | ESC + |
| Program Attention Keys | PA1 | Ctrl-p 1 |
| | PA2 | Ctrl-p 2 |
| | PA3 | Ctrl-p 3 |
| Local Control Keys | Reset After Error | Ctrl-r |
| | Purge Input Buffer | Ctrl-x |
| | Keyboard Unlock | Ctrl-t |
| | Redisplay Screen | Ctrl-v |
| Other Keys | Enter | Return |
| | Clear | Ctrl-z |
| | Erase current field | Ctrl-u |

* ESC refers to the Escape key.

### *Example*

The following example is the default entry used by the TN3270 emulation software when it is unable to locate a valid keymap in the active configuration image. Table 20–3 lists the key names supported by the default Cisco TN3270 keymap.

```
ciscodefault{
clear = '^z';\
flinp = '^x';\
enter = '^m';\
delete = '^d' ¦ '^?';\
synch = '^r';\
reshow = '^v';\
ebcdic_xx='string'
eeof = '^e';\
tab = '^i';\
btab = '^b';\
nl = '^n';\
left = '^h';\
right = '^l';\
up = '^k';\
down = '^j';\
einp = '^w';\
reset = '^t';\
ferase = '^u';\
insrt = '\E ';\
pa1 = '^p1'; pa2 = '^p2'; pa3 = '^p3';\
pfk1 = '\E1'; pfk2 = '\E2'; pfk3 = '\E3'; pfk4 = '\E4';\
pfk5 = '\E5'; pfk6 = '\E6'; pfk7 = '\E7'; pfk8 = '\E8';\
pfk9 = '\E9'; pfk10 = '\E0'; pfk11 = '\E-'; pfk12 = '\E=';\
pfk13 = '\E!'; pfk14 = '\E@'; pfk15 = '\E#'; pfk16 = '\E$';\
pfk17 = '\E%'; pfk18 = '\E'; pfk19 = '\E&'; pfk20 = '\E*';\
pfk21 = '\E('; pfk22 = '\E)'; pfk23 = '\E_'; pfk24 = '\E+';\
}
```

The following keymap statement maps the "|" character to send EBCDIC 0x6A:

```
ebcdic_6f='¦'
```

### *Related Commands*

Search online to find documentation for related commands.

**keymap-type**
**show keymap**
**terminal-type**

Part III Command Reference

## KEYMAP-TYPE

To specify the keyboard map for a terminal connected to the line, use the **keymap-type** line configuration command. To reset the keyboard type for the line to the default, use the **no** form of this command.

**keymap-type** *keymap-name*
**no keymap-type**

| *Syntax* | *Description* |
|---|---|
| *keymap-name* | Name of a keymap defined within the configuration file of the router. The TN3270 terminal-type negotiations use the specified keymap type when setting up a connection with the remote host. |

### *Default*

VT100

### *Command Mode*

Line configuration

### *Usage Guidelines*

This command first appeared in Cisco IOS Release 10.0.

This command must follow the corresponding **keymap** global configuration entry in the configuration file. The TN3270 terminal-type negotiations use the specified keymap type when setting up a connection with the remote host.

Setting the keyboard to a different keymap requires that a keymap be defined with the Cisco IOS software's configuration either by obtaining a configuration file over the network that includes the keymap definition or by defining the keyboard mapping using the global configuration command **keymap**.

Use the EXEC command **show keymap** to test for the availability of a keymap.

### *Example*

The following example sets the keyboard mapping to a keymap named *vt100map*:

```
line 3
 keymap-type vt100map
```

### *Related Commands*

Search online to find documentation for related commands.

**keymap**
**show keymap**
**ttycap**

### LAT

To connect to a LAT host, use the **lat** EXEC command.

**lat** *name* [**node** *nodename* | **port** *portname* | **/debug**]

| *Syntax* | *Description* |
|---|---|
| *name* | LAT-learned service name. |
| **node** *nodename* | (Optional) Specifies a connection to a particular LAT node that offers a service. If you do not include the node name option, the node with the highest rating offering the service is used. Use the **show lat nodes** EXEC command to display information about all known LAT nodes. |
| **port** *portname* | (Optional) Specifies a destination LAT port name. This keyword is ignored in most time-sharing systems but is used by routers and network access servers offering *reverse LAT* services. Reverse LAT involves connecting to one router from another, so that the target router runs the host portion of the protocol. Enter the port name in the format of the remote system as the *portname* argument. |
| **/debug** | (Optional) Enables a switch to display parameter changes and other special messages. |



#### *Command Mode*

EXEC

#### *Usage Guidelines*

This command first appeared in Cisco IOS Release 11.0.

After entering the **lat** command, you can quit the connection by pressing Ctrl-C, or complete the connection by entering the password for a given service.

You can have several concurrent LAT sessions open and switch back and forth between them. To open a subsequent session, first enter the escape sequence (**Ctrl-Shift-6** then **x** [Ctrl^x] by default) to suspend the current session. Then open a new session.

To list the available LAT services, use the **show lat services** EXEC command.

You can temporarily define the list of services to which you or another user can connect. To do so, use the **terminal lat out-group** command to define the group code lists used for connections from specific lines.

To exit a session, log off the remote system. Then terminate an active LAT session by entering **exit.**

If your preferred transport is set to **lat,** you can use the **connect** command in place of the **lat** command. When your preferred transport is set to **none** or to another protocol, you must use the **lat** command to connect to a LAT host.

### *Examples*

The following example establishes a LAT connection from the router named *Router_A* to host *eng2*:

```
Router_A> lat eng2
Trying ENG2...Open
         ENG2 - VAX/VMS V5.2
Username: JSmith
Password:
    Welcome to VAX/VMS version V5.2 on node ENG2
    Last interactive login on Friday,  1-APR-1994 19:46
```

The system informs you of its progress by displaying the messages "Trying <system>..." and then "Open." If the connection attempt is not successful, you receive a failure message.

The following example establishes a LAT connection from the router named *Router_B* to something named *our-modems* and specifies port 24, which is a special modem:

```
Router_B> lat our-modems port 24
```

The following example establishes a LAT connection from the router named *Router_C* to something named *our-modems* and specifies a node named *eng*:

```
Router_C> lat our-modems node eng
```

The following example uses the LAT session debugging capability:

```
Router_D> lat Eng2 /debug
Trying ENG2...Open
        ENG2 - VAX/VMS V5.2
 Username: JSmith
 Password:
    Welcome to VAX/VMS version V5.2 on node ENG2
    Last interactive login on Tuesday, 5-APR-1994 19:02
[Set Flow out off, Flow in on, Format 8:none, Speed 9600/9600]
[Set Flow out off, Flow in on, Format 8:none, Speed 9600/9600]
$ set ter/speed=2400
[Set Flow out off, Flow in on, Format 8:none, Speed 2400/2400]
```

A variety of LAT events are reported, including all requests by the remote system to set local line parameters. The messages within brackets ([ ]) are the messages produced by the remote system setting line characteristics to operating system defaults.

### *Related Commands*

Search online to find documentation for related commands.

**connect**
**show lat services**
**terminal lat**

### LAT ACCESS-LIST

To specify access conditions to nodes on the LAT network, use the **lat access-list** global configuration command. To remove a specified access list number, use the **no** form of this command.

**lat access-list** *number* {**permit** | **deny**} *nodename*
**no lat access-list** *number*

| *Syntax* | *Description* |
|---|---|
| *number* | Specifies a number between 1 and 199 assigned to the line using the **access-class** line configuration command. |
| **permit** | Allows any matching node name to access the line. |
| **deny** | Denies access to any matching node name. |
| *nodename* | Specifies the name of the LAT node, with or without regular expression pattern matching characters, with which to compare for access. The UNIX-style regular expression characters allow for pattern matching of characters and character strings in the node name. |

#### *Default*

No access conditions defined

#### *Command Mode*

Global configuration

#### *Usage Guidelines*

This command first appeared in Cisco IOS Release 10.0.

Regular expressions are case-sensitive. Because LAT node names are always in all capital letters, make sure you use only all capital-letter regular expressions.

Table 20–5 and Table 20–6 summarize pattern- and character-matching symbols and their uses. A more complete description of the pattern-matching characters is found in Appendix C, "Regular Expressions."

**Table 20–5** *Pattern Matching*

| **Character** | **Description** |
|---|---|
| \0 | Replaces the entire original address. |
| \1..9 | Replaces the strings that match the first through ninth parenthesized part of X.121 address. |
| * | Matches 0 or more sequences of the regular expressions. |

**Table 20–5** *Pattern Matching, Continued*

| Character | Description |
|---|---|
| + | Matches 1 or more sequences of the regular expressions. |
| ? | Matches the regular expression of the null string. |

**Table 20–6** *Character Matching*

| Character | Description |
|---|---|
| ^ | Matches the null string at the beginning of the input string. |
| $ | Matches the null string at the end of the input string. |
| *char* | Matches *char*. |
| . | Matches any single character. |

### *Examples*

The following example permits all packets destined for any LAT node named *WHEEL*:

```
lat access-list 1 permit WHEEL
```

The following example denies all packets destined for any LAT node name beginning with the *BLDG1-* prefix:

```
lat access-list 2 deny ^BLDG1-
```

### *Related Commands*

Search online to find documentation for related commands.

access-class

## LAT ENABLED

To enable LAT, use the **lat enabled** interface configuration command. To disable LAT, use the **no** form of this command.

**lat enabled**
**no lat enabled**

### *Syntax Description*

This command has no arguments or keywords.

### *Default*

Enabled

### Command Mode

Interface configuration

### Usage Guidelines

This command first appeared in Cisco IOS Release 10.0.

### Examples

The following example enables LAT on Ethernet interface 0:

```
interface ethernet 0
 lat enabled
```

The following example disables LAT on the same Ethernet interface:

```
interface ethernet 0
 no lat enabled
```



## LAT GROUP-LIST

Use the **lat group-list** global configuration command to allow a name to be assigned to the group list. A group list is any combination of group names, numbers, or ranges. To remove the specified group list, use the **no** form of this command.

**lat group-list** *groupname* {*number* | *range* | **all**} [**enabled** | **disabled**]
**no lat group-list** *groupname* {*number* | *range* | **all**} [**enabled** | **disabled**]

| *Syntax* | *Description* |
|---|---|
| *groupname* | Specifies a group code name. |
| *number* | Specifies a group code number. You can enter both a group code name and group code numbers. |
| *range* | Specifies a hyphenated range of numbers. |
| **all** | Specifies the range from 0 to 255. |
| **enabled** | (Optional) Allows incremental changes to the list; that is, you can add a group code without retyping the entire command. |
| **disabled** | (Optional) Allows selective removal of a group code from the list. |

### Default

No group names are assigned to the list.

### Command Mode

Global configuration

### *Usage Guidelines*

This command first appeared in Cisco IOS Release 11.1.

Specifying a name for a group list simplifies the task of entering individual group codes. In other words, a name makes it easier to refer to a long list of group code numbers. The group list must already exist. Use the EXEC command **show lat groups** to see a list of existing groups.

### *Examples*

The following example creates the new group named *stockroom* and defines it to include the group numbers 71 and 99:

```
lat group-list stockroom 71 99
```

The following example adds group code 101 to the group named *stockroom*:

```
lat group-list stockroom 101 enabled
```

The following example deletes the group named *Bldg-2*:

```
no lat group-list Bldg-2
```

### *Related Commands*

Search online to find documentation for related commands.

**lat out-group**
**lat service-group**

## LAT HOST-BUFFERS

To set the number of receive buffers that will be negotiated when the router is acting as a LAT host, use the **lat host-buffers** global configuration command. To return to the default of one receive buffer, use the **no** form of this command.

**lat host-buffers** *receive-buffers*
**no lat host-buffers** *receive-buffers*

| *Syntax* | *Description* |
|---|---|
| *receive-buffers* | An integer that specifies the number of receive buffers that will be negotiated. The argument can be any number between 1 and 128. |

### *Default*

One receive buffer

### *Command Mode*

Global configuration

*Usage Guidelines*

This command first appeared in Cisco IOS Release 10.0.

Before LAT Version 5.2, LAT allowed only one outstanding message at a time on a virtual circuit. This could limit the performance of large routers. For example, only one Ethernet packet of data could be in transit at a time. With LAT Version 5.2, nodes can indicate that they are willing to receive more than one message at a time. During virtual circuit startup, each side communicates to the other how many outstanding messages it is willing to accept.

*Example*

The following example enables LAT and configures the LAT host to negotiate 100 receive buffers:

```
lat enabled
lat host-buffers 100
```



*Related Commands*

Search online to find documentation for related commands.

**lat server-buffers**

### LAT HOST-DELAY

To set the delayed acknowledgment for incoming LAT slave connections, use the **lat host-delay** global configuration command. To restore the default, use the **no** form of this command.

**lat host-delay** *number*
**no host-delay**

| *Syntax* | *Description* |
|---|---|
| *number* | The delay in milliseconds. |

*Default*

Disabled

*Command Mode*

Global configuration

*Usage Guidelines*

This command first appeared in Cisco IOS Release 10.3.

*Example*

The following example sets the acknowledgment for incoming LAT slave connections to 100 milliseconds:

```
lat host-delay 100
```

### LAT KA-TIMER

To set the rate of the keepalive timer, use the **lat ka-timer** global configuration command. To restore the default, use the **no** form of this command.

**lat ka-timer** *seconds*
**no lat ka-timer**

| *Syntax* | *Description* |
|---|---|
| *seconds* | The timer rate in seconds. |

#### *Default*

20 seconds

#### *Command Mode*

Global configuration

#### *Usage Guidelines*

This command first appeared in Cisco IOS Release 10.0.

The keepalive timer sets the rate that messages are sent in the absence of actual traffic between the router and the remote node. The server uses keepalive messages to detect when communication with a remote node is disrupted or when the remote node has crashed.

#### *Example*

The following example sets the keepalive timer rate to 5 seconds:

```
lat ka-timer 5
```

### LAT NODE

To change the LAT node name without changing the system host name, use the **lat node** global configuration command.

**lat node** *node-name*

| *Syntax* | *Description* |
|---|---|
| *node-name* | Name of the LAT node. |

#### *Default*

No default LAT node name

#### *Command Mode*

Global configuration

### *Usage Guidelines*

This command first appeared in Cisco IOS Release 10.0.

This command allows you to give the server a node name that is different from the host name. Use the EXEC command **show entry** to determine which LAT hosts have queue entries for printers on the servers. Use the EXEC command **clear entry** to delete entries from the queue.

### *Example*

The following example specifies the LAT node name as *DEC2*:

```
lat node DEC2
```

### *Related Commands*

Search online to find documentation for related commands.

**clear entry**
**hostname**
**show entry**



## LAT OUT-GROUP

To define a group list for a line's outgoing user-initiated connections, use the **lat out-group** line configuration command. Use the **lat out-group 0** command to return to the default value.

**lat out-group** {*groupname number range* | **all**}

| *Syntax* | *Description* |
|---|---|
| *groupname* | Group code name. |
| *number* | Group code number. You can also enter both a group code name and group code numbers. |
| *range* | Hyphenated range of numbers. |
| **all** | Range from 0 to 255. |

### *Default*

The default group code number is 0.

### *Command Mode*

Line configuration

### *Usage Guidelines*

This command first appeared in Cisco IOS Release 10.0.

You can have values for one, two, or all three arguments. If the keyword **all** is specified, no arguments can be used. You can enter the arguments *groupname*, *number*, and *range* in any order.

Use the EXEC command **show lat** to display group numbers. If the host node and router do not share a common group number, the host's services will not be displayed.

### *Example*

The following example defines the services for lines 1 through 7, 10 through 17, and 20 through 24. Access to systems on the first set of lines is limited to groups 12 and 18 through 23; the second set is limited to group 12; the third set is limited to group codes 12, 18 through 23, and 44. All other lines use the default of group zero.

```
line 1 7
 lat out-group 12 18-23
line 10 17
 lat out-group 12
line 20 24
 lat out-group 12 18-23 44
```

### *Related Commands*

Search online to find documentation for related commands.

**lat group-list**
**terminal lat out-group**

## LAT REMOTE-MODIFICATION

To enable remote LAT modification of a line's characteristics (for example, baud rate), use the **lat remote-modification** line configuration command. To disable remote LAT modification of line characteristics, use the **no** form of this command.

**lat remote-modification**
**no lat remote-modification**

### *Syntax Description*

This command has no arguments or keywords.

### *Default*

Remote modification is disabled.

### *Command Mode*

Line configuration

### *Usage Guidelines*

This command first appeared in Cisco IOS Release 10.0.

Enabling the line for remote modification allows the remote LAT node to change the line's characteristics (for example, baud rate, parity, and so forth).

### *Example*

The following example enables remote LAT modification on line 4:

```
line 4
 lat remote-modification
```

### *Related Commands*

Search online to find documentation for related commands.

**terminal lat remote-modification**



## LAT RETRANSMIT-LIMIT

To set the number of times that LAT retransmits a message before declaring the remote system unreachable, use the **lat retransmit-limit** global configuration command. To restore the default retry value, use the **no** form of this command.

**lat retransmit-limit** *number*
**no lat retransmit-limit**

| *Syntax* | *Description* |
|---|---|
| *number* | Number of retries; any number between 4 and 255. |

### *Default*

8 retries

### *Command Mode*

Global configuration

### *Usage Guidelines*

This command first appeared in Cisco IOS Release 10.0.

Assigning larger values to the number of tries increases the robustness of the LAT service at the cost of longer delays when communications are disrupted. Because LAT generally retransmits messages once per second, the value is approximately the number of seconds that LAT connections will survive connection disruption.

If you bridge LAT, the retransmission limit should be set to at least 20 tries for LAT sessions to survive a worst-case spanning-tree reconfiguration, because bridging spanning-tree reconfiguration can take up to 15 seconds.

### *Example*

The following example sets the retransmission limit to 30 tries, enough time to sustain the downtime incurred when the system must reconfigure a spanning-tree topology:

```
lat retransmit-limit 30
```

## LAT SERVER-BUFFERS

To set the number of receive buffers that will be negotiated when the router is acting as a LAT server, use the **lat server-buffers** global configuration command. To return to the default of one receive buffer, use the **no** form of this command.

**lat server-buffers** *receive-buffers*
**no lat server-buffers** *receive-buffers*

| *Syntax* | *Description* |
| --- | --- |
| *receive-buffers* | Integer that specifies the number of receive buffers that will be negotiated. The argument can be any number between 1 and 128. |

### *Default*

1 receive buffer

### *Command Mode*

Global configuration

### *Usage Guidelines*

This command first appeared in Cisco IOS Release 10.0.

Before LAT Version 5.2, LAT allowed only one outstanding message on a virtual circuit at a time. This could limit the performance of large routers because only one Ethernet packet of data could be in transit at a time. With LAT Version 5.2, nodes can indicate that they are willing to receive more than one message at a time. During virtual circuit startup, each side communicates to the other how many outstanding messages it is willing to accept.

### *Example*

The following example enables LAT and configures the server to negotiate 25 receive buffers:

```
lat enabled
lat server-buffers 25
```

### *Related Commands*

Search online to find documentation for related commands.

**lat host-buffers**

### LAT SERVICE-ANNOUNCEMENTS

To reenable LAT broadcast service announcements, use the **lat service-announcements** global configuration command. To disable the sending of LAT service announcements, use the **no** form of this command.

**lat service-announcements**
**no lat service-announcements**

#### *Syntax Description*

This command has no arguments or keywords.

#### *Default*

Enabled

#### *Command Mode*

Global configuration

#### *Usage Guidelines*

This command first appeared in Cisco IOS Release 10.0.

If this command is enabled, the LAT code will periodically broadcast service advertisements. If the command is disabled, the LAT code will not send service announcements, so solicit-information messages will have to be used to look up node information.

**NOTES**

You should only disable service announcements if all of the nodes on the local-area network (LAN) support the service responder feature.

#### *Example*

The following example reenables the sending of broadcast service announcements:

```
lat service-announcements
```

#### *Related Commands*

Search online to find documentation for related commands.

**lat service-responder**

### LAT SERVICE AUTOCOMMAND

To associate a command with a service, use the **lat service autocommand** global configuration command. To remove the specified autocommand, use the **no** form of this command.

**lat service** *service-name* **autocommand** *command*
**no lat service** *service-name* **autocommand** *command*

| *Syntax* | *Description* |
|---|---|
| *service-name* | Name of the service. |
| *command* | Command to be associated with the service. |

#### *Default*

No commands are automatically associated with a service.

#### *Command Mode*

Global configuration

#### *Usage Guidelines*

This command first appeared in Cisco IOS Release 10.0.

When an inbound connection is received for the specified service, the command associated with the service is automatically executed instead of the user receiving a virtual terminal session.

Authentication is bypassed for these services; only the LAT password is checked.

**NOTES**

Do not use this option with the **rotary** keyword.

#### *Example*

The following example associates the command **telnet ramana** to the service *RAMANA*:

```
lat service RAMANA autocommand telnet ramana
```

### LAT SERVICE ENABLED

To enable inbound connections to the specified service and enable the advertisement of this service to routers on the network, use the **lat service enabled** global configuration command. To delete the named service, use the **no** form of this command.

**lat service** *service-name* **enabled**
**no lat service** *service-name* **enabled**

| *Syntax* | *Description* |
|---|---|
| *service-name* | Name of the service. |

#### *Default*

No services enabled

#### *Command Mode*

Global configuration

#### *Usage Guidelines*

This command first appeared in Cisco IOS Release 10.0.

In the simplest form, this command creates a service that gives connecting users access to a VTY port on the server.

Use the **enabled** keyword after commands that define a service so that users do not connect to a service before all the parameters are set.

Deleting a service does not disconnect existing connections.

#### *Example*

The following example enables inbound connections to the service *WHEEL*:

```
lat service WHEEL enabled
```

### LAT SERVICE-GROUP

To specify a group code mask to use when advertising all services for this node and to control incoming services, use the **lat service-group** global configuration command. To remove the group code mask specified, use the **no** form of this command.

**lat service-group** {*groupname* | *number* | *range* | **all**} [**enabled** | **disabled**]
**no lat service-group** {*groupname* | *number* | *range* | **all**} [**enabled** | **disabled**]

| *Syntax* | *Description* |
|---|---|
| *groupname* | Specifies a group code name. |
| *number* | Specifies a group code number. |
| *range* | Specifies a hyphenated range of numbers between 0 and 255. |
| **all** | Specifies the range from 0 to 255. |
| **enabled** | (Optional) Allows incremental changes to the list; that is, you can add a group code without retyping the entire command. |
| **disabled** | (Optional) Allows selective removal of a group code from the list. |

### *Default*

If no service group is specified, the Cisco IOS software defaults to advertising to group 0.

### *Command Mode*

Global configuration

### *Usage Guidelines*

This command first appeared in Cisco IOS Release 10.0.

When this command is written to nonvolatile memory (using the EXEC **write memory** command), the system looks for an exact match on a group code name. If it finds one, it uses that name in the command. Otherwise, it writes out a list of numbers, using the range syntax whenever possible.

### *Examples*

The following example specifies groups 100 through 103, then defines *engineering* as the group code list to advertise:

```
lat group-list engineering 100-103
lat service-group engineering enabled
```

The following example specifies the groups 1, 5, 20 through 36, and 52:

```
lat service-group 1 5 20-36 52
```

You can enter the following command to add group 99:

```
lat service-group 99 enabled
```

### *Related Commands*

Search online to find documentation for related commands.

**lat group-list**

## LAT SERVICE IDENT

To set the LAT service identification for a specified service, use the **lat service ident** global configuration command. To remove the identification, use the **no** form of this command.

**lat service** *service-name* **ident** *identification*
**no lat service** *service-name* **ident**

| *Syntax* | *Description* |
|---|---|
| *service-name* | Name of the service. |
| *identification* | Descriptive name (text only) that identifies the service. |

### *Default*

No LAT service identification is set for specific services.

### *Command Mode*

Global configuration

### *Usage Guidelines*

This command first appeared in Cisco IOS Release 10.0.

The identification is advertised to other servers on the network and is displayed along with the list of name services on the LAN.

### *Example*

The following example specifies the identification "Welcome to Gateway-A" on service *STELLA*:

```
lat service STELLA ident Welcome to Gateway-A
```



## LAT SERVICE PASSWORD

To set up a LAT password for a service, use the **lat service password** global configuration command. To remove the password, use the **no** form of this command.

**lat service** *service-name* **password** *password*
**no lat service** *service-name* **password**

| *Syntax* | *Description* |
|---|---|
| *service-name* | Name of the service. |
| *password* | Password used to gain access to the service. |

### *Default*

No default LAT service passwords

### *Command Mode*

Global configuration

### *Usage Guidelines*

This command first appeared in Cisco IOS Release 10.0.

The connecting user will be required to enter the password to complete the connection.

The password is obtained through the LAT password mechanism.

### *Example*

The following example specifies a service named *BLUE* and the password *secret*:

```
lat service BLUE password secret
```

### LAT SERVICE RATING

To set a static service rating for the specified service, use the **lat service rating** global configuration command. To remove the service rating, use the **no** form of this command.

**lat service** *service-name* **rating** *static-rating*
**no lat service** *service-name* **rating**

| *Syntax* | *Description* |
|---|---|
| *service-name* | Name of the service. |
| *static-rating* | Static service rating. The rating must be in the range of 1 to 255. |

#### *Default*

Dynamic rating

#### *Command Mode*

Global configuration

#### *Usage Guidelines*

This command first appeared in Cisco IOS Release 10.0.

If this command is not entered, the Cisco IOS software calculates a dynamic rating based on the number of free ports that can handle connections to the service. Setting a static rating overrides this calculation and causes the specified value to be used.

#### *Example*

The following example specifies a service rating of 84 on the service *WHEEL*:

```
lat service WHEEL rating 84
```

### LAT SERVICE-RESPONDER

To configure a node to act as proxy for other nodes when a solicit-information multicast message is received, use the **lat service-responder** global configuration command. To remove any proxy definition setup using the **lat service-responder** command, use the **no** form of this command.

**lat service-responder**
**no lat service responder**

#### *Syntax Description*

This command has no arguments or keywords.

#### *Default*

Disabled

### *Command Mode*

Global configuration

### *Usage Guidelines*

This command first appeared in Cisco IOS Release 10.0.

The Cisco IOS software can be configured to support the service responder feature that is part of the latest LAT Version 5.2 specification.

Specifically, the DECserver90L+, which has less memory than other DECservers, does not maintain a cache of learned services. Instead, the DECserver90L+ solicits information about services as they are needed.

LAT Version 5.2 nodes can respond for themselves; LAT Version 5.1 nodes, for example VMS Version 5.4 or earlier nodes, cannot. Instead, a LAT Version 5.2 node configured as a service responder can respond in proxy for those LAT Version 5.1 nodes.

The Cisco IOS software can be configured as a LAT service responder. If all your nodes are LAT Version 5.2 nodes, you do not need to enable the service responder features.

### *Example*

The following example configures a node to act as a proxy for a node when a solicit-information multicast message is received. The node configured with this command will respond to solicit messages.

```
lat service-responder
```

### *Related Commands*

Search online to find documentation for related commands.

**lat service-announcements**

## LAT SERVICE ROTARY

To associate a rotary group with a service, use the **lat service rotary** global configuration command. To remove the association, use the **no** form of this command.

**lat service** *service-name* **rotary** *group*
**no lat service** *service-name* **rotary**

| *Syntax* | *Description* |
|---|---|
| *service-name* | Name of the service. |
| *group* | Rotary group number. |

### *Default*

Disabled

### Command Mode

Global configuration

### Usage Guidelines

This command first appeared in Cisco IOS Release 10.0.

Establish rotary groups using the **rotary** line configuration command.

When an inbound connection is received for this service, the router establishes a reverse LAT connection to a terminal in that rotary group.

If the rotary option is not set, the connection will be to a virtual terminal session on the router.

### Example

The following example creates a service called *MODEM* to establish a rotary group:

```
lat services MODEM rotary 1
```

### Related Commands

Search online to find documentation for related commands.

**rotary**

## LAT SERVICE-TIMER

To adjust the time between LAT service advertisements, use the **lat service-timer** global configuration command.

**lat service-timer** *interval*

| *Syntax* | *Description* |
|---|---|
| *interval* | Number of seconds between service announcements. Note that the granularity offered by this command is 10-second intervals, and the *interval* value is rounded up. |

### Default

20 seconds

### Command Mode

Global configuration

### Usage Guidelines

This command first appeared in Cisco IOS Release 11.1.

This command adjusts the time, in seconds, between LAT service announcements for services offered by the router. This is useful in large networks with many LAT services and limited bandwidth.

### *Example*

The following example sets the interval between LAT service advertisements to 11, and illustrates the rough granularity of the **lat service-timer** command:

```
! The time between LAT service advertisements is set to 11. Because the
! granularity is in ten-second intervals, the actual time between advertisement
! is 20 seconds.
lat service-timer 11
! 20 seconds between updates
lat service-timer 19
! 120 seconds between updates
lat service-timer 120
```



## LAT VC-SESSIONS

To set the maximum number of sessions to be multiplexed onto a single LAT virtual circuit, use the **lat vc-sessions** global configuration command. To remove a prior session's definition, use the **no** form of this command.

**lat vc-sessions** *number*
**no lat vc-sessions** *number*

| *Syntax* | *Description* |
|---|---|
| *number* | Specifies the number of sessions that will be multiplexed onto a single LAT virtual circuit. This number cannot be greater than 255. |

### *Default*

255 sessions per virtual circuit

### *Command Mode*

Global configuration

### *Usage Guidelines*

This command first appeared in Cisco IOS Release 10.0.

Setting the number of sessions to a smaller number can increase throughput if there are many sessions on one host, especially with routers with many physical ports. It can also increase overhead if there is little traffic but a large number of sessions to the same host.

### *Example*

The following example sets the maximum number of sessions to be multiplexed onto a single LAT virtual circuit at 100:

```
lat vc-sessions 100
```

## LAT VC-TIMER

To set the interval of time LAT waits before sending any traffic, use the **lat vc-timer** global configuration command. To remove a timer definition, use the **no** form of this command.

**lat vc-timer** *milliseconds*
**no lat vc-timer** *milliseconds*

| *Syntax* | *Description* |
|---|---|
| *milliseconds* | Timer value. Specifies the amount of time LAT will wait before sending traffic. Acceptable values are between 10 and 1000 milliseconds. |

### *Default*

80 milliseconds

### *Command Mode*

Global configuration

### *Usage Guidelines*

This command first appeared in Cisco IOS Release 10.0.

Smaller timer values increase the overhead on both the router and the host. However, you can use smaller values to correct buffer overflows, which happen when the router receives more data than it can buffer during a virtual circuit timer interval.

Larger values increase the need for buffering and can cause noticeable echoing delay. However, increased values can reduce traffic. In environments with slow bridging, retransmissions can be reduced if you increase the value to at least three times the worst-case, round-trip interval.

### *Example*

The following example sets the time between transmitting messages to 500 milliseconds:

```
lat vc-timer 500
```

## LOCK

To set up a temporary password on a line, use the **lock** EXEC command.

**lock**

### Syntax Description

This command has no arguments or keywords.

### Command Mode

EXEC

### Usage Guidelines

This command first appeared in a release prior to Cisco IOS Release 10.0.

You can prevent access to your session while keeping your connection open by setting up a temporary password. To lock access to the terminal, follow this procedure:

**Step 1** Issue the **lock** command.

When you issue this command, the system prompts you for a password.

**Step 2** Enter a password, which can be any arbitrary string.

The screen clears and displays the message "Locked."

**Step 3** To regain access to your sessions, reenter the password.

The Cisco IOS software honors session timeouts on locked lines. You must clear the line to remove this feature. The system administrator must set the line up to allow use of the temporary locking feature by using the **lockable** line configuration command.

### Example

The following command locks access to the terminal line to which the user is connected. Only this user can access the session:

```
router(config-line)# lockable
router(config-line)# Ctrl-z
router# copy running-config startup-config
Building configuration...
OK
router# lock
Password:
Again:
                    Locked

Password:
router#
```

### Related Commands

Search online to find documentation for related commands.

**lockable**
**login** (EXEC)

## LOGIN (EXEC)

To change a login username, use the **login** EXEC command.

**login**

### *Syntax Description*

This command has no arguments or keywords.

### *Command Mode*

EXEC

### *Usage Guidelines*

This command first appeared in a release prior to Cisco IOS Release 10.0.

You can change a login username if you must match outgoing access list requirements or other login prompt requirements.

When you enter this command, the Cisco IOS software prompts you for a username and password. Enter the new username and the original password. If the username does not match, but the password does, the Cisco IOS software updates the session to the new username with which the **login** command attempt was made.

If no username and password prompts appear when you enter this command, the network administrator did not specify that a username and password be required at login time. If both the username and password are entered correctly, the session becomes associated with the specified username.

When you access a system using TACACS security with this command, you can enter your login name or specify a TACACS server by using the following command when the "Username:" prompt appears:

*user @tacacs-server*

The TACACS server must be one of those defined in a Cisco IOS software configuration file.

If you do not specify a host, the Cisco IOS software tries each of the TACACS servers in the list until it receives a response.

If you do specify a host that does not respond, no other TACACS server is queried. The Cisco IOS software will deny access or function according to the action specified by the **tacacs-server last-resort** command, if one is configured.

If you specified a TACACS server host with the *user @tacacs-server* argument, the TACACS server specified will be used for all subsequent authentication or notification queries, with the possible exception of SLIP address queries.

### *Example*

The following example shows how login usernames and passwords can be changed. In this example, a user currently logged on under the username user1 attempts to change that login name to user2. After entering the **login** command, the user enters the new username, but enters an incorrect password. Because the password does not match the original password, the system rejects the attempt to change the username.

```
router> login
Username: user2
Password:
% Access denied
Still logged in as "user1"
```

Next, the user attempts the login change again, with the user name user2, but enters the correct (original) password. This time the password matches the current login information, the login username is changed to user2, and the user is allowed access to the EXEC at the user-level.

```
router> login
Username: user2
Password:
router>
```



### *Related Commands*

Search online to find documentation for related commands.

**lock**
**lockable**

## LOGIN (LINE)

To enable password checking at login, use the **login** line configuration command. Use the **no** form of this command to disable password checking and allow connections without a password.

**login** [**local** | **tacacs**]
**no login**

| *Syntax* | *Description* |
|---|---|
| **local** | (Optional) Selects local password checking. Authentication is based on the username specified with the **username** global configuration command. |
| **tacacs** | (Optional) Selects the TACACS-style user ID and password-checking mechanism. |

### *Default*

Virtual terminals require a password. If you do not set a password for a virtual terminal, it responds to attempted connections by displaying an error message and closing the connection.

### *Command Mode*

Line configuration

### *Usage Guidelines*

This command first appeared in Cisco IOS Release 10.0.

If you specify the **login** command without the **local** or **tacacs** option, authentication is based on the password specified with the **password** line configuration command.

**NOTES**

This command cannot be used with AAA/TACACS+. Use the **login authentication** command instead.

*Examples*

The following example sets the password letmein on virtual terminal line 4:

```
line vty 4
password letmein
login
```

The following example enables the TACACS-style user ID and password-checking mechanism:

```
line 0
password mypassword
login tacacs
```

*Related Commands*

Search online to find documentation for related commands.

**enable password**
**password**
**username**

### LOGIN-STRING

To define a string of characters that the Cisco IOS software sends to a host after a successful Telnet connection, use the **login-string** global configuration command. Use the **no** form of this command to remove the login string.

**login-string** *hostname d message* [%*sec***p**] [%*sec***w**] [%**b**] [%**m**] *d*
**no login-string** *hostname*

| *Syntax* | *Description* |
|---|---|
| *hostname* | Specifies the name of the host. |
| *d* | Sets a delimiting character of your choice—a pound sign (#) for example. You cannot use the delimiting character in the busy message. |
| *message* | Specifies the login string. |
| %*sec***p** | (Optional) Sets a pause in seconds. To insert pauses into the login string, embed a percent sign (%) followed by the number of seconds to pause and the letter "p." |
| %*sec***w** | (Optional) Prevents users from issuing commands or keystrokes during a pause. |

| *Syntax* | *Description* |
|---|---|
| %b | (Optional) Sends a Break character. |
| %m | (Optional) Supports TN3270 terminals. Sends only CR and no LINE FEED. |

### *Default*

No login strings are defined.

### *Command Mode*

Global configuration

### *Usage Guidelines*

This command first appeared in Cisco IOS Release 10.0.

Follow this command with one or more blank spaces and a delimiting character of your choice. Then enter one or more lines of text, terminating the message with the second occurrence of the delimiting character. To use a percent sign in the login string, precede it with another percent sign; that is, type the characters "%%." The options can be used anywhere within the message string.

This command applies only to rlogin and Telnet sessions.

### *Example*

In the following example, the value *%5p* causes a 5-second pause:

```
login-string office #ATDT 555-1234
%5p hello
#
```

## NOTIFY

To enable terminal notification about pending output from other Telnet connections, use the **notify** line configuration command. Use the **no** form of this command to end notification.

**notify**
**no notify**

### *Syntax Description*

This command has no arguments or keywords.

### *Default*

Disabled

### *Command Mode*

Line configuration

### *Usage Guidelines*

This command first appeared in Cisco IOS Release 10.0.

This command sets a line to inform a user who has multiple, concurrent Telnet connections when output is pending on a connection other than the current one.

### *Example*

The following example sets up notification of pending output from connections on virtual terminal lines 0 to 4:

```
line vty 0 4
 notify
```

### *Related Commands*

Search online to find documentation for related commands.

**terminal notify**

## RESUME (SWITCHING SESSIONS)

To switch to another open Telnet, rlogin, LAT, or PAD session, use the **resume** EXEC command.

**resume** [*connection*] [*keyword*] [**/set** *parameter:value*]

| *Syntax* | *Description* |
|---|---|
| *connection* | (Optional) The name or number of the connection; the default is the most recent connection. |
| *keyword* | (Optional) One of the options listed in Table 20–7. |
| **/set** *parameter:value* | (Optional) Sets PAD parameters for the Cisco IOS software (see Table 20–7). |

**Table 20–7** *Telnet and rlogin Resume Options*

| Option | Description |
|---|---|
| **/debug** | Displays parameter changes and messages. In the Cisco IOS software, this option displays informational messages whenever the remote host changes an X.3 parameter, or sends an X.29 control packet. |
| **/echo** | Performs local echo. |
| **/line** | Enables line-mode editing. |
| **/nodebug** | Cancels printing of parameter changes and messages. |
| **/noecho** | Disables local echo. |
| **/noline*** | Disables line mode and enables character-at-a-time mode, which is the default. |
| **/nostream** | Disables stream processing. |

**Table 20–7** *Telnet and rlogin Resume Options, Continued*

| Option | Description |
|---|---|
| /set *parameter: value* | Sets X.3 connection options. See Chapter 23, "Configuring the Cisco PAD Facility for X.25 Connections," for a list of these connection options. |
| /stream | Enables stream processing. |

* **/noline** is the default keyword.

### *Command Mode*

EXEC



### *Usage Guidelines*

This command first appeared in a release prior to Cisco IOS Release 10.0.

You can have several concurrent sessions open and switch back and forth between them. The number of sessions that can be open is defined by the **session-limit** command.

You can switch between sessions by escaping one session and resuming a previously opened session, as follows:

**Step 1** Escape out of the current session by pressing the escape sequence (**Ctrl-Shift-6** then **x** [Ctrl^x] by default) and return to the EXEC prompt.

**Step 2** Enter the **where** command, to list the open sessions. All open sessions associated with the current terminal line are displayed.

**Step 3** Enter the **resume** command and the session number to make the connection.

You also can resume the previous session by pressing the **Return** key.

The **Ctrl^x**, **where**, and **resume** commands are available with all supported connection protocols.

### *Examples*

The following example shows how to escape out of a connection and to resume connection 2:

```
Swift% ^^X
router> resume 2
```

You can omit the command name and simply enter the connection number to resume that connection. The following example illustrates how to resume connection 3:

```
router> 3
```

### *Related Commands*

Search online to find documentation for related commands.

**show sessions**
**where**

## RLOGIN

To log on to a UNIX host using rlogin, use the **rlogin** EXEC command.

**rlogin** *host* [**debug**] [**/user** *username*]

### *Syntax Description*

| *Syntax* | *Description* |
|---|---|
| *host* | Specifies the host name or IP address. |
| **debug** | (Optional) Enables debugging output from the rlogin protocol. |
| **/user** *username* | (Optional) Specifies a remote username in the initial exchange with the remote host. The rlogin protocol will not present you with the "login:" prompt. |

### *Command Mode*

EXEC

### *Usage Guidelines*

This command first appeared in Cisco IOS Release 10.0.

You can have several concurrent rlogin connections open and switch back and forth between them. To open a new connection, suspend the current connection by pressing the escape sequence (**Ctrl-Shift-6** then **x** [**Ctrl^x**] by default) to return to the EXEC prompt, then open a new connection. A user cannot automatically log on to a UNIX system from the router, but must provide a user ID and a password for each connection.

If your preferred transport is set to **rlogin,** you can use the **connect** command in place of the **rlogin** command. When your preferred transport is set to **none** or to another protocol, you must use the **rlogin** command to connect to a host.

To terminate an active rlogin session, issue the appropriate command from the following list at the UNIX prompt of the device to which you are connecting:

**close**
**disconnect**
**exit**
**logout**
**quit**

### *Example*

The following example makes an rlogin connection to a host at address 108.33.21.2 and enables the message mode for debugging:

```
router> rlogin 108.33.21.2 debug
```

### *Related Commands*

Search online to find documentation for related commands.

**connect**
**telnet**

## RLOGIN TRUSTED-REMOTEUSER-SOURCE LOCAL

To configure the router to use the current user's name (as discovered during IOS authentication on the router) as the rlogin username on the remote host, use the **rlogin trusted-remoteuser-source local** global configuration command. Use the **no** form of this command to restore the default rlogin behavior of prompting the user for the remote username.

**rlogin trusted-remoteuser-source local**
**no rlogin trusted-remoteuser-source local**



### *Syntax Description*

This command has no additional options.

### *Command Mode*

EXEC

### *Usage Guidelines*

This command first appeared in Cisco IOS Release 11.1

The current username is only used if the **rlogin** *host* **/user** *username* command is not enabled. If the current username is not known, rlogin falls back to providing the "login:" prompt to discover a remote username.

Configuring the remote host to consider the Cisco router a "trusted" host should be considered a security hole.

### *Examples*

After you issue the **rlogin trusted-remoteuser-source local** command, you will not be prompted for a username. The first response you see is the password prompt from the remote system. For example, when this command is not enabled, you must enter your username twice (once at initial system login and once for the **rlogin** command).

```
User Access Verification

Username: gmcmilla
Password:

router> rlogin puli
Trying puli.cisco.com (170.69.3.154)... Open
login: gmcmilla
Password:
Login incorrect
```

After you issue the **rlogin trusted-remoteuser-source local** command, you no longer have to specify the username after the **rlogin** command. The username is automatically copied from the router's user ID.

```
router> enable
Password:
router# configure terminal
Enter configuration commands, one per line.  End with CNTL/Z.
router(config)# rlogin trusted-remoteuser-source local
router(config)# ^Z

router# rlogin puli
Trying puli.cisco.com (170.69.3.154)... Open
Password:
Login incorrect
```

The following example uses the **/user root** option as an override.

```
router# rlogin puli /user root
Trying puli.cisco.com (170.69.3.154)... Open
Password:
Login incorrect
login:
```

### *Related Commands*

Search online to find documentation for related commands.

**connect**
**telnet**

## SHOW ENTRY

To display the list of queued host-initiated connections to a router, use the **show entry** EXEC command. You can also use this command to determine which LAT hosts have queue entries for printers on routers.

**show entry**

### *Syntax Description*

This command has no arguments or keywords.

### *Command Mode*

EXEC

### *Usage Guidelines*

This command first appeared in Cisco IOS Release 11.1.

### *Sample Display*

The following is sample output from the **show entry** command. The display shows that two LAT connections are waiting for access to port 5. The list is ordered so that the lower numbered entry has been waiting longer, and will get to use the line next.

```
sloth# show entry

1 waiting 0:02:22 for port 5 from LAT node BLUE
2 waiting 0:00:32 for port 5 from LAT node STELLA
```

Table 20–8 describes the fields in the first line of output shown in the display.

**Table 20–8** *Show Entry Field Descriptions*

| Field | Description |
|---|---|
| 1 | Number assigned to the queued connection attempt. |
| waiting 0:02:22 | Interval (hours:minutes:seconds) during which the connection attempt has been waiting. |
| for port 5 | Port for which the connection attempt is waiting. |
| from LAT node BLUE | Name of the user (BLUE) attempting to make the connection. |



## SHOW KEYMAP

Use the **show keymap** EXEC command to test for the availability of a keymap after a connection on a router takes place.

**show keymap** [*keymap-name* | **all**]

| *Syntax* | *Description* |
|---|---|
| *keymap-name* | (Optional) Name of the keymap. |
| **all** | (Optional) Lists the names of all defined keymaps. The name of the default keymap is not listed. |

### *Command Mode*

EXEC

### *Usage Guidelines*

This command first appeared in Cisco IOS Release 10.0.

The Cisco IOS software searches for the specified keymap in its active configuration image and lists the complete entry if found. If the keymap is not found, an appropriate "not found" message appears.

If you do not use any arguments with the **show keymap** command, then the keymap currently used for the terminal is displayed.

### *Sample Display*

The following is sample output from the **show keymap** command:

```
router# show keymap
ciscodefault { clear = '^z'; flinp = '^x'; enter = '^m';\
      delete = '^d' ¦ '^?';\
      synch = '^r'; reshow = '^v'; eeof = '^e'; tab = '^i';\
      btab = '^b'; nl = '^n'; left = '^h'; right = '^l';\
      up = '^k'; down = '^j'; einp = '^w'; reset = '^t';\
      xoff = '^s'; xon = '^q'; escape = '^c'; ferase = '^u';\
      insrt = '\E ';\
      pa1 = '^p1'; pa2 = '^p2'; pa3 = '^p3';\
      pfk1 = '\E1'; pfk2 = '\E2'; pfk3 = '\E3'; pfk4 = '\E4';\
      pfk5 = '\E5'; pfk6 = '\E6'; pfk7 = '\E7'; pfk8 = '\E8';\
      pfk9 = '\E9'; pfk10 = '\E0'; pfk11 = '\E-'; pfk12 = '\E=';\
      pfk13 = '\E!'; pfk14 = '\E@'; pfk15 = '\E#'; pfk16 = '\E$';\
      pfk17 = '\E%'; pfk18 = '\E\^'; pfk19 = '\E&'; pfk20 = '\E*';\
      pfk21 = '\E('; pfk22 = '\E)'; pfk23 = '\E_'; pfk24 = '\E+';\
}
```

## SHOW LAT ADVERTISED

To display the LAT services a router offers to other systems running LAT on the network, use the **show lat advertised** EXEC command.

**show lat advertised**

### *Syntax Description*

This command has no arguments or keywords.

### *Command Mode*

EXEC

### *Usage Guidelines*

This command first appeared in Cisco IOS Release 10.0.

Advertised services are created with the **lat service** commands. The display includes the service rating, rotary group, if present, and whether or not the service is enabled for incoming connections.

### *Sample Display*

The following is sample output from the **show lat advertised** command:

```
router# show lat advertised
Service Name          Rating      Rotary  Flags
BEAR-CAT             4(Dynamic)    None   Enabled
  Autocommand: telnet bear-cat
MODEMS               0(Dynamic)      12   Enabled
  Ident: SpaceBlazer modem services
RECLUSE              4(Dynamic)    None   Enabled
  Ident: white recluse...
```

The display shows output from a router, *sloth*, which has three services defined: BEAR-CAT, MODEMS, and RECLUSE:

Table 20–9 describes significant fields shown in the display.

**Table 20–9** *Show LAT Advertised Field Descriptions*

| Field | Description |
|---|---|
| Service Name | Lists the LAT service name. |
| Rating | Lists the static service rating set, if any. |
| Rotary | Lists the associated rotary service. |
| Flags | Lists whether or not a service is enabled. |
| Autocommand | Defines the autocommand associated with the service. |
| Ident | Lists the advertised identification for the service. |



### SHOW LAT GROUPS

To display the groups that were defined in the Cisco IOS software with the **lat group-list** command, use the **show lat groups** EXEC command.

**show lat groups**

#### *Syntax Description*

This command has no arguments or keywords.

#### *Command Mode*

EXEC

#### *Usage Guidelines*

This command first appeared in Cisco IOS Release 10.0.

#### *Sample Display*

The following is sample output from the **show lat groups** command:

```
sloth# show lat groups

Group Name          Len    Groups
cafeteria           3       13  15  23
engineering         7       55
manufacturing       10      70  71  72
```

Table 20–10 describes only the significant fields shown in the previous display.

**Table 20–10** *Show LAT Groups Field Descriptions*

| Field | Description |
|---|---|
| Group Name | Assigned group name. |
| Len | Size of internal data structure used to contain the group code map. |
| Groups | Group codes associated with the learned group. |

### *Related Commands*

Search online to find documentation for related commands.

**lat group-list**

## SHOW LAT NODES

To display information about all known LAT nodes, use the **show lat nodes** EXEC command.

**show lat nodes**

### *Syntax Description*

This command has no arguments or keywords.

### *Command Mode*

EXEC

### *Usage Guidelines*

This command first appeared in Cisco IOS Release 10.0.

### *Sample Display*

The following is sample output from the **show lat nodes** command:

```
router# show lat nodes

Node "CHAOS", usage -1, Interface Ethernet0, Address 0000.0c01.0509
  Timer 89,  sequence 188,  changes 131,  flags 0x0, protocol 5.1
  Facility 0,  Product code 0,  Product version 0
  Recv 0/0/0,  Xmit 0/0/0,  0 Dups, 0 ReXmit
  Bad messages: 0,  Bad slots: 0,  Solicits accepted: 0
  Solicits rejected: 0,  Multiple nodes: 0
  Groups:   0
  Service classes:   1
Node "CONFUSED", usage -1, Local
  Timer 99,  sequence 4,  changes 151,  flags 0x0, protocol 5.2
  Facility 0,  Product code 0,  Product version 0
  Recv 0/0/0,  Xmit 0/0/0,  0 Dups, 0 ReXmit
```

```
    Bad messages: 0,  Bad slots: 0,  Solicits accepted: 0
    Solicits rejected: 0,  Multiple nodes: 0
    Groups:   0
    Service classes:   1
  Node "EMAN-cs", usage -1, Interface Ethernet0, Address 0000.0cff.c9ed
    Timer 99,  sequence 9,  changes 159,  flags 0x0, protocol 5.1
    Facility 0,  Product code 0,  Product version 0
    Recv 0/0/0,  Xmit 0/0/0,  0 Dups, 0 ReXmit
    Bad messages: 0,  Bad slots: 0,  Solicits accepted: 0
    Solicits rejected: 0,  Multiple nodes: 0
    Groups:   0
    Service classes:   1
  Node "TARMAC", usage -1, Interface Ethernet0, Address 0000.0c02.c7c1
    Timer -10351,  sequence 1,  changes 131,  flags 0x40, protocol 5.2
    Facility 0,  Product code 0,  Product version 0
    Recv 0/0/0,  Xmit 0/0/0,  0 Dups, 0 ReXmit
    Bad messages: 0,  Bad slots: 0,  Solicits accepted: 0
    Solicits rejected: 0,  Multiple nodes: 0
    Groups:   0
    Service classes:   1
```

Table 20–11 describes significant fields shown in the display.

**Table 20–11** *Show LAT Nodes Field Descriptions*

| Field | Description |
|---|---|
| Node | The node name as reported by the host computer. |
| usage | The number of virtual circuits currently active to this node. |
| Interface | Node interface type and number. |
| Address | The MAC address of the node's Ethernet interface. |
| Timer | The number of seconds remaining until this node's service advertisement message will time out; this value is set to three times the nodes multicast timer value whenever a new service advertisement message is received. |
| sequence | The sequence number received in the last service advertisement message received. Nodes increment their sequence number when the contents of the service advertisement change. |
| changes | The internal representation of what changed in the multicast message the last time the sequence number changed. |
| flags | The internal representation of various state information about the node. |
| protocol | The LAT protocol version used by the node. |
| Facility | The remote facility number. |
| Product code | The remote product code. |

**Table 20–11** *Show LAT Nodes Field Descriptions, Continued*

| Field | Description |
|---|---|
| Product version | The remote product version. |
| Recv and Xmit | The number of messages, slots, and bytes received or transmitted to the node. The number of messages is the number of LAT virtual circuit messages. Each virtual circuit message contains some number of slots, which contain actual terminal data or control information. Bytes is the number of data bytes (input or output characters) exchanged. |
| Dups | The number of duplicate virtual circuit messages received. |
| ReXmit | The number of virtual circuit messages retransmitted. |
| Bad messages | The number of bad messages received. |
| Bad slots | The number of bad slots received. |
| Solicits accepted | The number of solicit-information requests accepted. |
| Solicits rejected | The number of solicit-information requests rejected. |
| Multiple nodes | The total of multiple nodes seen. |
| Groups | The list of group codes advertised by the node's service advertisement message. |
| Service classes | The number of service classes. |

## SHOW LAT SERVICES

To display information about learned LAT services in the Cisco IOS software, use the **show lat services** user EXEC command.

**show lat services** [*service-name*]

| *Syntax* | *Description* |
|---|---|
| *service-name* | (Optional) Name of a specific LAT service. |

### *Command Mode*

User EXEC

### *Usage Guidelines*

This command first appeared in Cisco IOS Release 11.2.

### *Sample Display*

The following is sample output from the **show lat services** command:

```
router# show lat services

Service Name     Rating   Interface  Node (Address)
ABCDEFGHIJ            5   Ethernet0  CONFUSED (0000.0c00.391f)
GLAD                 84   Ethernet0  BLUE (aa00.0400.9205)
  Ident: Welcome to Big Blue Gateway
WHEEL                83   Ethernet0  WHEEL (aa00.0400.9005)
ZXYW                  5   Ethernet0  CONFUSED (0000.0c00.391f)
```

Table 20–12 describes significant fields shown in this display.

**Table 20–12** *Show LAT Services Field Descriptions*

| Field | Description |
|---|---|
| Service Name | LAT service name. |
| Rating | Rating of the service. If a single service is provided by more than one host, the Cisco IOS software connects to the one with the highest rating. |
| Interface | Interface type. |
| Node | Connection address. |
| (Address) | Advertised identification for the service. |



### *Related Commands*

Search online to find documentation for related commands.

**show lat sessions**
**show service**

## SHOW LAT SESSIONS

To display active LAT sessions, use the **show lat sessions** user EXEC command.

**show lat sessions** [*line-number*]

| *Syntax* | *Description* |
|---|---|
| *line-number* | (Optional) Shows an active LAT session on a specific line. |

### *Command Mode*

User EXEC

### *Usage Guidelines*

This command first appeared in Cisco IOS Release 11.2.

### *Sample Displays*

The following is sample output from the **show lat sessions** command. In this example, information about all active LAT sessions is displayed. The output is divided into three sections for each session (in this case two sessions): TTY data, session data, and remote node data.

```
router> show lat sessions

tty0, connection 1 to service TERM1
TTY data:
  Name "0", Local usage 1/0, Remote usage disabled
  Flags: Local Connects, Enabled
  Type flags: none
  Config flags: -FlowOut, -FlowIn, Parameter Info
  Flow control ^S/^Q in ^S/^Q out,  Mode Normal, Parity None, databits 8
  Groups:   0
Session data:
  Name TERM1, Remote Id 1, Local Id 1
  Remote credits 2, Local credits 0, Advertised Credits 2
  Flags: none
  Max Data Slot 255, Max Attn Slot 255, Stop Reason 0
Remote Node data:
Node "TERM1", Address 0000.0C00.291F, usage 1
  Timer 59,  sequence 5,  changes 159,  flags 0x0, protocol 5.1
  Recv 56/22/83,  Xmit 41/23/14,  0 Dups, 0 ReXmit
  Groups:   0
tty10, connection 1 to service ENG2
TTY data:
  Name "10", Local usage 1/0, Remote usage disabled
  Flags: Local Connects, Enabled
  Type flags: none
  Config flags: -FlowOut, +FlowIn, Set Parameters, 0x40000000
  Flow control ^S/^Q in ^S/^Q out,  Mode Normal, Parity None, databits 8
  Groups:   0
Session data:
  Name ENG2, Remote Id 1, Local Id 1
  Remote credits 1, Local credits 0, Advertised Credits 2
  Flags: none
  Max Data Slot 255, Max Attn Slot 255, Stop Reason 0
Remote Node data:
Node "ENG2", Address AA00.0400.34DC, usage 1
  Timer 179,  sequence 60,  changes 255,  flags 0x0, protocol 5.1
  Recv 58/29/186,  Xmit 50/36/21,  0 Dups, 0 ReXmit
  Groups:   0
```

The following sample output displays information about active LAT sessions on one line (line 10). The output is divided into three sections: TTY data, session data, and remote node data.

```
router# show lat sessions 10

tty10, connection 1 to service ENG2
TTY data:
  Name "10", Local usage 1/0, Remote usage disabled
  Flags: Local Connects, Enabled
  Type flags: none
  Config flags: -FlowOut, +FlowIn, Set Parameters, 0x40000000
```

```
  Flow control ^S/^Q in ^S/^Q out,  Mode Normal, Parity None, databits 8
  Groups:   0
Session data:
  Name ENG2, Remote Id 1, Local Id 1
  Remote credits 1, Local credits 0, Advertised Credits 2
  Flags: none
  Max Data Slot 255, Max Attn Slot 255, Stop Reason 0
Remote Node data:
Node "ENG2", Address AA00.0400.34DC, usage 1
  Timer 189,  sequence 61,  changes 247,  flags 0x0, protocol 5.1
  Recv 60/29/186,  Xmit 52/36/21,  0 Dups, 0 ReXmit
  Groups:   0
```

Table 20–13 describes the screen output for the preceding two examples.



**Table 20–13** *Show LAT Sessions Status Display Field Descriptions*

| Field | Description |
|---|---|
| **TTY data** | Summary of the LAT-oriented terminal-line-specific data. |
| Name | Name used for this port as a port identification string. The name is reported to remote systems, which can display it in some operating-system-dependent manner. This value is also used for targets of host-initiated connections. Currently, this value is hard-wired to be the line number of the associated terminal line. |
| Local/Remote usage | Current status of the terminal. The number is reported as current/maximum, where current is the current number of sessions of a given type, and maximum is the maximum number of sessions allowed (or zero if there is no maximum). If a terminal is being used for outgoing sessions, the local usage is equal to the number of current LAT sessions. If the terminal is being used for incoming sessions, local usage is disabled, and the remote count and maximum is one. |
| Flags | Current state of the line, and whether there are any queued host-initiated connections. |
| Type flags | Report flags not used in the current software release. |
| Config flags | Current port state as reflected by the most recent configuration message exchange. |
| Flow control | Lists set flow control characters. |
| Groups | Group code list currently in use for the line. |
| **Session data** | Reports various parameters about the connection. |
| Name | For the outbound connection, the name of the remote service to which it is connected. For inbound connections, this field is currently unused. |

**Table 20–13** *Show LAT Sessions Status Display Field Descriptions, Continued*

| Field | Description |
|---|---|
| Remote/Local ID | Slot IDs being used to uniquely identify the session multiplexed over the underlying LAT virtual circuit. |
| Remote/Local/ Advertised Credits | Number of flow control credits that the Cisco IOS software will be sending to the host as soon as possible. The advertised credits are the number of credits that have already been sent. |
| Flags | Transient conditions in the LAT-state machine dealing with the current connection status. |
| Max Data Slot | Maximum number of characters that can be sent in a single data slot. |
| Max Attn Slot | Maximum amount of data that can be sent in an attention message. Current LAT implementations only sends 1-byte attention messages (attention messages are used to flush buffered output). A nonzero value means that remote data flushing can be used; a zero means that it cannot. |
| Stop Reason | Reason the session was stopped, if it was stopped but not deleted. This value is usually zero, indicating that the session has not yet been stopped. If a session persists for a long time with a nonzero stop reason, there is probably a problem in the local LAT software. |
| **Remote Node data** | Reports information about the remote node. The data includes the same fields as those from the **show lat nodes** output. |
| Node | Node name as reported by the host computer. |
| Address | MAC address of the node's Ethernet interface. |
| usage | Number of virtual circuits currently active to the node. |
| Timer | Number of seconds remaining until the node's service advertisement message will time out; this value is set to three times greater than the node's multicast timer value whenever a new service advertisement message is received. |
| sequence | Sequence number received in the last service advertisement message. Nodes increment their sequence number when the contents of the service advertisement change. |
| changes | Internal representation of what changed in the multicast message the last time the sequence number changed. |
| flags | Internal representation of various state information about the node. |
| protocol | LAT protocol version used by the node. |

**Table 20–13** *Show LAT Sessions Status Display Field Descriptions, Continued*

| Field | Description |
|---|---|
| Recv and Xmit | Number of messages, slots, and bytes received or transmitted to the node. The number of messages is the number of LAT virtual circuit messages. Each virtual circuit message contains some number of slots, which contain actual terminal data or control information. |
| Dups | Number of duplicate virtual circuit messages received. |
| ReXmit | Number of virtual circuit messages retransmitted. |
| Groups | Group codes advertised by the node's service advertisement message. |



### *Related Commands*

Search online to find documentation for related commands.

**show lat services**
**show service**

## SHOW LAT TRAFFIC

Use the **show lat traffic** EXEC command to display information about traffic and resource utilization statistics on all active lines.

**show lat traffic**

### *Syntax Description*

This command has no arguments or keywords.

### *Command Mode*

EXEC

### *Usage Guidelines*

This command first appeared in Cisco IOS Release 10.0.

### *Sample Display*

The following is sample output from the **show lat traffic** command:

```
router# show lat traffic
Local host statistics:
  0/100 circuits, 0/500 sessions, 1/500 services
  100 sessions/circuit, circuit timer 80, keep-alive timer 5
Recv:   335535 messages (2478 duplicates),  161722 slots,  1950146 bytes
        0 bad circuit messages,  3458 service messages (52 used)
Xmit:   182376 messages (2761 retransmit),  146490 slots,  36085 bytes
        1 circuit timeouts
Total:  23 circuits created,  38 sessions
```

Table 20–14 describes significant fields shown in the display.

**Table 20–14** *Show LAT Traffic Field Descriptions*

| Field | Description |
|---|---|
| **Local host statistics** | Information about the router. |
| circuits | Current number and maximum support number of virtual circuits. |
| sessions | Current and maximum number of sessions. |
| services | Current number of known remote services, and the maximum supported. |
| sessions/circuit | Number of sessions per virtual circuit supported by the software. |
| circuit timer | Value of the virtual circuit timer parameter defined by the **lat vc-timer** global configuration command. |
| keep-alive timer | Value defined by the **lat ka-timer** global configuration command. |
| **Recv** | Statistics about local node receive totals. |
| messages | Total count of virtual circuit messages received. |
| duplicates | Number of duplicate virtual circuit messages received. |
| slots | Number of slots received. |
| bytes | Number of data bytes received. |
| bad circuit messages | Count of invalid messages received. |
| service messages | Number of service advertisement multicast messages received. |
| used | Number of multicast messages that caused the local node information to be updated. |
| **Xmit** | Various transmission totals. |
| messages | Total number of virtual circuit messages transmitted. |
| retransmit | Number of virtual circuit messages retransmitted due to the lack of an acknowledgment. |
| slots | Number of data and control slots transmitted. |
| bytes | Count of user data bytes transmitted. |

**Table 20–14** *Show LAT Traffic Field Descriptions, Continued*

| Field | Description |
|---|---|
| circuit timeouts | Count of times that a virtual circuit timed out because the remote node stopped responding (due to a node failure or communications failure). |
| **Total** | Count of virtual circuits and sessions that have existed since the router booted or rebooted. |



## SHOW NODE

To display information about LAT nodes, use the **show node** EXEC command. The **show node** command with no further parameters shows a one-line summary of all known nodes. The **show node** command displays three different sets of information about a node: the node counters, the node status, or a one-line summary of the node status.

**show node** [**all** | *node-name*] [**counters** | **status** | **summary**]

| *Syntax* | *Description* |
|---|---|
| **all** | (Optional) Specifies all nodes. |
| *node-name* | (Optional) Indicates the name of the node for which status is required. |
| **counters** | (Optional) Specifies the various node counters. |
| **status** | (Optional) Specifies detailed node status. This is the default if a node name is specified. |
| **summary** | (Optional) Specifies a status summary for the node. This is the default if no node name is specified. |

### *Command Mode*

EXEC

### *Usage Guidelines*

This command first appeared in Cisco IOS Release 10.0.

Entering the **show node** command with no arguments is the same as entering **show node all summary.**

You can enter the **show node** command with either a specific node name or the keyword **all**, but not both.

You can enter the **show node** command with only one of the keywords **counters, status,** or **summary.** If you enter **show node** and two of these keywords without specifying a node name, the first keyword is treated as a node name, causing an error. If you enter **show node** *node-name* and two of these keywords, the second keyword will be treated as ambiguous.

The **show node** command with a *node-name* argument but no **counters, status,** or **summary** keyword defaults to **show node** *node-name* **status.**

### *Sample Display with No Keywords*

The following is sample output from the **show node** command with no further parameters (the same as **show node all summary**):

```
router> show node

Node Name       Status       Identification
CHAOS           Reachable
MUDDY-RIVER     Reachable
TARMAC          Reachable
WHEEL           Reachable    Welcome to VAX/VMS V5.4-2
```

Table 20–15 describes significant fields shown in the display.

**Table 20–15** *Show Node Field Descriptions*

| **Field** | **Description** |
|---|---|
| Node Name | Lists the names of the nodes. |
| Status | Indicates whether the node is reachable or not. |
| Identification | Identification string for the node. |

### *Sample Display with a Node Name*

The following is sample output from the **show node** output that defaults to **show node chaos status.** It results in a display of the detailed status of node chaos.

```
router> show node chaos

Node: CHAOS        Address: 00-00-0C-01-05-09
LAT Protocol: V5.1    Data Link Frame Size: 1500
Identification:
Node Groups: 0
Service Name  Status      Rating   Identification
CHAOS         Available   80
```

Table 20–16 describes significant fields shown in the display.

**Table 20–16** *Show Node Field Descriptions*

| **Field** | **Description** |
|---|---|
| Node | Lists the node name as reported by the host computer. |
| Address | Identifies the MAC address of the node's Ethernet interface. |
| LAT protocol | Lists the version of the LAT protocol used by the node. |
| Data Link Frame Size | Lists the size of the largest packet that can be sent to the LAT host. |

**Table 20–16** *Show Node Field Descriptions, Continued*

| **Field** | **Description** |
|---|---|
| Identification | Lists the identification string for the node. |
| Node Groups | Lists the group code list that is advertised by the remote node, which comes from the remote node's service advertisement. |
| Service Name | Lists the LAT service name. |
| Status | Indicates whether or not the node is currently available on the network. |
| Rating | Indicates the rating of the service: An integer from 0 to 255, with the highest number being the preferred service. Used for load balancing. |



### *Sample Display with the Counters Keyword*

The following is sample output for the counter information for a specific node:

```
router> show node tarmac counters

Node: tarmac
Seconds Since Zeroed: 100 Multiple Node Addresses: 0
Messages Received: 0 Duplicates Received: 0
Messages Transmitted: 0 Messages Re-transmitted: 0
Slots Received: 0 Illegal Messages Received: 0
Slots Transmitted: 0 Illegal Slots Received: 0
Bytes Received: 0 Solicitations Accepted: 0
Bytes Transmitted: 0 Solicitations Rejected: 0
```

### *Additional Sample Displays*

In the following example, the keyword **status** is treated as the node name:

```
router> show node status counters

Local -710- Node STATUS not known
```

In the following example, the second keyword **counters** is treated as ambiguous:

```
router> show node lager status counters

Local -702- Keyword "COUNTERS" not known or ambiguous
```

## SHOW SERVICE

Use the **show service** EXEC command to display specific LAT learned services.

**show service** [*service-name*]

| *Syntax* | *Description* |
|---|---|
| *service-name* | (Optional) The name of a specific LAT service. |

### Command Mode

EXEC

### Usage Guidelines

This command first appeared in Cisco IOS Release 10.0.

The **show service** command without a service name displays a list of known LAT learned services. When entered with the *service-name* argument, it displays a more-detailed status of the named service. If no LAT learned service by the specified name is known, then a lookup is done for an IP host of that name.

### Sample Displays

The following is sample output from the **show service** command:

```
router> show service

Service Name  Status      Identification
BLUE          Available   Welcome to VAX/VMS V5.4
CHAOS         Available
MRL12         Available
MUDDY-RIVER   Available
STELLA-BLUE   Available   Welcome to VAX/VMS V5.4
```

The following display shows sample **show service** output for a specific service:

```
router> show service blue

Service BLUE - Available
Node Name    Status     Rating    Identification
BLUE         reachable 84         Welcome to VAX/VMS V5.4
```

Table 20–17 describes significant fields shown in the two previous displays.

**Table 20–17** *Show Service Field Descriptions*

| Field | Description |
|---|---|
| Service | Name of the service. |
| Node Name | Name of the nodes advertising the service. |
| Status | Status of the service: Available or Unknown when command is entered without a service name. Available, Unknown, Initializing, or Unreachable when command is entered with a service name. |
| Rating | Rating of the service: An integer from 0 to 255, with the highest number being the preferred service. Used for load balancing. |
| Identification | Identification string. |

## SHOW SESSIONS

To display information about open LAT, Telnet, or rlogin connections, use the **show sessions** user EXEC command.

**show sessions**

### *Command Mode*

User EXEC

### *Usage Guidelines*

This command first appeared in a release prior to Cisco IOS Release 10.0.

This command displays the host name, address, number of unread bytes for the user to receive, idle time, and connection name.

### *Sample Display*

The following is sample output from the **show sessions** command:

```
sloth# show sessions

Conn Host                 Address          Byte    Idle  Conn Name
   1 MATHOM               192.31.7.21         0       0  MATHOM
*  2 CHAFF                131.108.12.19       0       0  CHAFF
```

The asterisk (*) indicates the current terminal session.

Table 20–18 describes significant fields shown in the display.

**Table 20–18** *Show Sessions Field Descriptions*

| Field | Description |
|---|---|
| Conn | Name or address of the remote host to which the connection is made. |
| Host | Remote host to which the router is connected through a Telnet session. |
| Address | IP address of the remote host. |
| Byte | Number of unread bytes displayed for the user to receive. |
| Idle | Interval (in minutes) since data was last sent on the line. |
| Conn Name | Assigned name of the connection. |

### *Related Commands*

Search online to find documentation for related commands.

**resume**
**where**

### SHOW TCP

To display the status of a TCP connection, use the **show tcp** user EXEC command.

**show tcp** [*line-number*]

| *Syntax* | *Description* |
|---|---|
| *line-number* | (Optional) Displays (in octal) the status of the TCP connections for a particular line. |

#### *Command Mode*

User EXEC

#### *Usage Guidelines*

This command first appeared in a release prior to Cisco IOS Release 10.0.

#### *Sample Displays*

The following is sample output from the **show tcp** command:

```
router# show tcp

tty0, connection 1 to host cider
Connection state is ESTAB, I/O status: 1, unread input bytes: 0
Local host: 171.69.232.17, Local port: 11184
Foreign host: 171.69.1.137, Foreign port: 23

Enqueued packets for retransmit: 0, input: 0, saved: 0

Event Timers (current time is 67341276):
Timer:          Retrans   TimeWait    AckHold    SendWnd  KeepAlive
Starts:              30          0         32          0          0
Wakeups:              1          0         14          0          0
Next:                 0          0          0          0          0

iss:   67317172  snduna:   67317228  sndnxt:   67317228     sndwnd:    4096
irs: 1064896000  rcvnxt: 1064897597  rcvwnd:        2144  delrcvwnd:       0

SRTT: 317 ms, RTTO: 900 ms, RTV: 133 ms, KRTT: 0 ms
minRTT: 4 ms, maxRTT: 300 ms, ACK hold: 300 ms
Flags: idle user, retransmission timeout

Datagrams (max data segment is 536 bytes):
Rcvd: 41 (out of order: 0), with data: 34, total data bytes: 1596
Sent: 57 (retransmit: 1), with data: 35, total data bytes: 55
```

Table 20–19 describes the following lines of output shown in the display:

**Table 20–19** *Show TCP Field Descriptions—First Section of Output*

| Field | Description |
|---|---|
| tty0 | Line number. |
| connection 1 | Number identifying the TCP connection. |
| to host cider | Name of the remote host to which the connection is made. |
| Connection state is ESTAB | A connection progresses through a series of states. The states include the following:<br>• LISTEN—Waiting for a connection request from any remote TCP port.<br>• SYNSENT—Waiting for a matching connection request after having sent a connection request.<br>• SYNRCVD—Waiting for a confirming connection request acknowledgment after having both received and sent a connection request.<br>• ESTAB—Indicates an open connection; data received can be delivered to the user. This is the normal state for the data transfer phase.<br>• FINWAIT1—Waiting for a connection termination request from the remote TCP host or an acknowledgment of the connection termination request previously sent.<br>• FINWAIT2—Received an acknowledgment of the connection termination request that was sent.<br>• CLOSEWAIT—Received a connection request.<br>• CLOSING—Sent and received a connection termination request acknowledgment from the remote TCP host.<br>• LASTACK—Received a connection termination request from the remote TCP host and the local user.<br>• TIMEWAIT—Waiting for enough time to pass to be certain the remote TCP host has received the acknowledgment of its connection termination request.<br>• CLOSED—Indicates no connection state at all.<br>For more information about connection states, see RFC 793, *Transmission Control Protocol Functional Specification.* |
| I/O status: 1 | Number describing the internal status of the connection. |
| unread input bytes: 0 | Number of bytes that the lower-level TCP processes have read, but the higher-level TCP processes have not yet processed. |

**Table 20–19** *Show TCP Field Descriptions—First Section of Output, Continued*

| Field | Description |
|---|---|
| Local host: 171.69.232.17 | IP address of the network router. |
| Local port: 11184 | Local port number derived from the following equation: *line-number* + (512 * *random-number*). The line number uses the lower nine bits; the other bits are random. |
| Foreign host: 171.69.1.137 | IP address of the remote host to which the TCP connection was made. |
| Foreign port: 23 | Port number for the remote host. |
| Enqueued packets for retransmit: 0 | Number of packets waiting on the retransmit queue. These are packets on this TCP connection that have been sent but not yet acknowledged by the remote TCP host. |
| input: 0 | Number of packets waiting on the input queue to be read by the user. |
| saved: 0 | Number of received out-of-order packets waiting for all packets comprising the message to be received before they enter the input queue. For example, if packets 1, 2, 4, 5, and 6 have been received, packets 1 and 2 would enter the input queue, and packets 4, 5, and 6 would enter the saved queue. |

The following line of output shows the current time according to the system clock of the local host.

```
Event Timers (current time is 67341276):
```

The following lines of output display the number of times that various local TCP timeout values were reached during a connection. In this example, the Cisco IOS software retransmitted once because it received no response from the remote host, and it transmitted an ACK-only segment 14 times because there was no data segment on which to piggyback. Table 20–20 describes the fields in the following lines of output:

```
Timer:         Retrans   TimeWait    AckHold    SendWnd  KeepAlive
Starts:             30          0         32          0          0
Wakeups:             1          0         14          0          0
Next:                0          0          0          0          0
```

**Table 20–20** *Show TCP Field Descriptions—Second Section of Output*

| Field | Description |
|---|---|
| Timer | Names of the timers in the display. |
| Retrans | Determines how long a transmitted frame can remain unacknowledged before the Cisco IOS software polls for an acknowledgment. |

**Table 20–20** *Show TCP Field Descriptions—Second Section of Output, Continued*

| Field | Description |
|---|---|
| TimeWait | Determines how long the local TCP connection waits to be sure that the remote TCP host has received the acknowledgment of its connection termination request. |
| AckHold | Number of times the system failed to piggyback data required on a TCP acknowledgment. Such piggybacking can significantly reduce network traffic. |
| SendWnd | Timers for sending "zero window probes." Essentially, this field reflects how often users overload the remote host with data and how long it takes users to send it. For most normal Cisco IOS software applications, this value should be zero. |
| KeepAlive | Determines the frequency (in seconds) at which the Cisco IOS software sends messages to itself (Ethernet and Token Ring) or to the other end (serial) to ensure that a network interface is alive. The **keepalive** interface configuration command is used to set this timer. |
| Starts | Number of times the timer was started during this connection. |
| Wakeups | Number of times the timer has expired. |
| Next | Time that the timer expires. |



The following lines of output display the sequence numbers that TCP uses to ensure sequenced, reliable transport of data. The router and remote host each use these sequence numbers for flow control and to acknowledge receipt of datagrams. Table 20–21 describes the fields in this output.

```
iss:    67317172  snduna:    67317228  sndnxt:    67317228     sndwnd:   4096
irs: 1064896000  rcvnxt: 1064897597  rcvwnd:         2144  delrcvwnd:      0
```

**Table 20–21** *Show TCP Field Descriptions—Sequence Numbers*

| Field | Description |
|---|---|
| iss: 67317172 | Initial send sequence number. |
| snduna: 67317228 | Last send sequence number that the Cisco IOS software has sent but for which it has not received an acknowledgment. |
| sndnxt: 67317228 | Sequence number that the Cisco IOS software will send next. |
| sndwnd: 4096 | TCP window size of the remote host. |
| irs: 1064896000 | Initial receive sequence number. |
| rcvnxt: 1064897597 | Last receive sequence number that the Cisco IOS software has acknowledged. |

**Table 20–21** *Show TCP Field Descriptions—Sequence Numbers, Continued*

| Field | Description |
|---|---|
| rcvwnd: 2144 | The Cisco IOS software's TCP window size. |
| delrcvwnd: 0 | Delayed receive window—data that the Cisco IOS software has read from the connection, but has not yet subtracted from the receive window advertised to the remote host. The value in this field gradually increases until it is larger than a full-sized packet, at which point it is cleared and applied to the rcvwnd field. |

The following lines of output show the values that the Cisco IOS uses to keep track of transmission times so that TCP can adjust to the network it is using. Table 20–22 describes the fields in this output.

```
SRTT: 317 ms, RTTO: 900 ms, RTV: 133 ms, KRTT: 0 ms
minRTT: 4 ms, maxRTT: 300 ms, ACK hold: 300 ms
Flags: higher precedence, idle user, retransmission timeout
```

**Table 20–22** *Show TCP Field Descriptions—Line Beginning with RTTO*

| Field | Descriptions |
|---|---|
| SRTT: 317 ms | Round-trip time estimate. |
| RTTO: 900 ms | Round-trip timeout. |
| RTV: 133 ms | Variance of the round-trip time. |
| KRTT: 0 ms | New round-trip timeout (using the Karn algorithm). This field separately tracks the round-trip time of packets that have been retransmitted. |
| minRTT: 4 ms | Smallest recorded round-trip timeout (hard wire value used for calculation). |
| maxRTT: 300 ms | Largest recorded round-trip timeout. |
| ACK hold: 300 ms | Time the Cisco IOS software will delay an acknowledgment so that it can piggyback data on it. |
| Flags | The following is a list of possible flags that describe your type of connection.<br>• Idle user—The connection is idle because the user has suspended the connection.<br>• Retransmission timeout—The connection will be dropped if retransmission continues to be unsuccessful.<br>• Passive open—The connection was accepted by the router that issued the **show tcp** command. |

**Table 20–22** *Show TCP Field Descriptions—Line Beginning with RTTO, Continued*

| Field | Descriptions |
|---|---|
| | • Active—The connection was initiated by the router.<br>• Keepalive running—TCP is searching for inactive clients.<br>• Alias—The connection was made to an alias.<br>• Timing out—The connection will soon be suspended due to excessive retransmissions.<br>• Nagle—The local router is using the Nagle algorithm to maximize packet size (see RFC 896).<br>• Net output pending—The Nagle algorithm is holding small packets from the TCP output queue and waiting to put them into the network once the packet size is optimized.<br>• Always push—The router sets the push bit when sending data packets.<br>• Sync listen—The connection to the router is synchronized with the application.<br>• Path mtu discovery—The connection is using path mtu discovery to determine its MSS. |



For more information about these fields, refer to the article "Round Trip Time Estimation," by P. Karn and C. Partridge, ACM SIGCOMM-87, August 1987.

Table 20–23 describes the fields in the following lines of output from the **show tcp** command:

```
Datagrams (max data segment is 536 bytes):
Rcvd: 41 (out of order: 0), with data: 34, total data bytes: 1596
Sent: 57 (retransmit: 1), with data: 35, total data bytes: 55
```

**Table 20–23** *Show TCP Field Descriptions—Last Section of Output*

| Field | Description |
|---|---|
| Datagrams | Datagrams sent and received on the line. |
| Rcvd: 41(out of order: 0) | Number of datagrams the local host has received during this connection (and the number of these datagrams that were out of order). |
| with data: 34 | Number of datagrams that contained data. |
| total data bytes: 1596 | Total number of bytes of data in the transmitted datagrams. |
| Sent: 57(and retransmitted: 1) | Number of datagrams the local host sent during this connection (and the number of these datagrams that had to be retransmitted). |

**Table 20–23** *Show TCP Field Descriptions—Last Section of Output, Continued*

| Field | Description |
|---|---|
| with data: 35 | Number of transmitted datagrams that contained data. |
| total data bytes: 55 | Total number of bytes of data in the transmitted datagrams. |

### *Related Commands*

Search online to find documentation for related commands.

**show tcp brief**

## SHOW TCP BRIEF

To view a summary of the TCP connection endpoints in the system, use the **show tcp brief** user EXEC command.

**show tcp brief** [*all*]

| *Syntax* | *Description* |
|---|---|
| *all* | (Optional) Shows the status for all endpoints. Endpoints in the LISTEN state are usually not shown. |

### *Command Mode*

User EXEC

### *Usage Guidelines*

This command first appeared in Cisco IOS Release 11.2.

### *Sample Display*

The following example is the output from the **show tcp brief** command after a user has connected to the router using Telnet:

```
router# show tcp brief

TCB       Local Address           Foreign Address        (state)
609789AC  Router.cisco.com.23     cider.cisco.com.3733   ESTAB
```

Table 20–24 describes the fields shown in the example.

**Table 20–24** *Show TCP Brief Fields Descriptions*

| Field | Description |
|---|---|
| TCB: `609789AC` | An internal identifier for the endpoint. |
| Local Address: `Router.cisco.com.23` | The local IP address and port. |

**Table 20–24** *Show TCP Brief Fields Descriptions, Continued*

| Field | Description |
|---|---|
| Foreign Address: `cider.cisco.com.3733` | The foreign IP address and port. |
| (state): `ESTAB` | The state of the connection. (See Table 20–25 for a description of connection states.) |

### *Related Commands*

Search online to find documentation for related commands.

**show tcp**



## SHOW TN3270 ASCII-HEXVAL

To determine ASCII-hexadecimal character mappings, use the **show tn3270 ascii-hexval** EXEC command.

**show tn3270 ascii-hexval**

### *Syntax Description*

This command has no arguments or keywords.

### *Command Mode*

EXEC

### *Usage Guidelines*

This command first appeared in Cisco IOS Release 10.3.

Use the **show tn3270 ascii-hexval** command to display the hexadecimal value of a character on your keyboard. After entering the **show tn3270 ascii-hexval** command, you are prompted to press a key. The hexadecimal value of the ASCII character is displayed. This command is useful for users who do not know the ASCII codes associated with various keys or do not have manuals for their terminals.

### *Sample Display*

The following is sample output from the **show tn3270 ascii-hexval** command:

```
router> show tn3270 ascii-hexval

Press key> 7 - hexadecimal value is 0x37.
chaff> show tn3270 ascii-hexval
Press key> f - hexadecimal value is 0x66.

tarmac> show tn3270 ascii-hexval
Press key> not printable - hexadecimal value is 0xD.
```

### *Related Commands*

Search online to find documentation for related commands.

**show tn3270 character-map**
**tn3270 character-map**

## SHOW TN3270 CHARACTER-MAP

To display character mappings between ASCII and EBCDIC, use the **show tn3270 character-map** EXEC command.

**show tn3270 character-map** {**all** | *ebcdic-in-hex*}

| *Syntax* | *Description* |
|---|---|
| **all** | Displays all nonstandard character mappings. |
| *ebcdic-in-hex* | Displays the ASCII mapping for a specific EBCDIC character. |

### *Command Mode*

EXEC

### *Usage Guidelines*

This command first appeared in Cisco IOS Release 11.1.

### *Sample Display*

The following is sample output from the **show tn3270 character-map** command:

```
router# show tn3270 character-map all

EBCDIC 0x81 <=> 0x78 ASCII
EBCDIC 0x82 <=> 0x79 ASCII
EBCDIC 0x83 <=> 0x7A ASCII
```

### *Related Commands*

Search online to find documentation for related commands.

**show tn3270 ascii-hexval**
**tn3270 character-map**

## SHOW TTYCAP

To test for the availability of a ttycap after a connection on a router takes place, use the **show ttycap** EXEC command.

**show ttycap** [*ttycap-name* | **all**]

| *Syntax* | *Description* |
|---|---|
| *ttycap-name* | (Optional) Name of a ttycap. |
| **all** | (Optional) Lists the names of all defined ttycaps. The name of the default ttycap is not listed. |

### *Command Mode*

EXEC

### *Usage Guidelines*

This command first appeared in Cisco IOS Release 10.0.

The Cisco IOS software searches for the specified ttycap in its active configuration image, and lists the complete entry if found. If it is not found, an appropriate "not found" message appears.

If you do not include any arguments with the **show ttycap** command, then the current keymap used for the terminal is displayed.

### *Sample Display*

The following is sample output from the **show ttycap** command:

```
router# show ttycap

d0¦vt100¦vt100-am¦vt100am¦dec vt100:do=^J:co#80:li#24:\
cl=50^[[;H^[[2J:bs:am:cm=5^[[%i%d;%dH:nd=2^[[C:up=2^[[A:\
ce=3^[[K:so=2^[[7m:se=2^[[m:us=2^[[4m:ue=2^[[m:md=2^[[1m:\
me=2^[[m:ho=^[[H:xn:sc=^[7:rc=^[8:cs=^[[%i%d;%dr:

router# show ttycap all

ttycap3    d0¦vt100¦vt100-am¦vt100am¦dec vt100
ttycap2    dl¦vt200¦vt220¦vt200-js¦vt220-js¦dec vt200 series with jump scroll
ttycap1    ku¦h19-u¦h19u¦heathkit with underscore cursor

router# show ttycap ttycap1

ttycap1  ku¦h19-u¦h19u¦heathkit with underscore cursor:\:vs@:ve@:tc=h19-b:\
        :al=1*\EL:am:le=^H:bs:cd=\EJ:ce=\EK:cl=\EE:cm=\EY%+ %+\
        :co#80:dc=\EN:\:dl=1*\EM:do=\EB:ei=\EO:ho=\EH\
        :im=\E@:li#24:mi:nd=\EC:as=\EF:ae=\EG:\
        :ms:pt:sr=\EI:se=\Eq:so=\Ep:up=\EA:vs=\Ex4:ve=\Ey4:\
        :kb=^h:ku=\EA:kd=\EB:kl=\ED:kr=\EC:kh=\EH:kn#8:ke=\E>:ks=\E=:\
        :k1=\ES:k2=\ET:k3=\EU:k4=\EV:k5=\EW:\
        :l6=blue:l7=red:l8=white:k6=\EP:k7=\EQ:k8=\ER:\
        :es:hs:ts=\Ej\Ex5\Ex1\EY8%+ \Eo:fs=\Ek\Ey5:ds=\Ey1:
```

## SHOW XREMOTE

To display XRemote connections and monitor XRemote traffic through the router, use the **show xremote** EXEC command.

**show xremote**

Part III *Command Reference*

### *Syntax Description*

This command has no arguments or keywords.

### *Command Mode*

EXEC

### *Usage Guidelines*

This command first appeared in Cisco IOS Release 10.0.

The **show xremote** command displays XRemote parameters applied to the entire system, as well as statistics that are pulled for all active XRemote connections.

### *Sample Display*

The following is sample output from the **show xremote** command when XRemote is enabled and XRemote sessions are active:

```
router# show xremote
XRemote server-wide parameters:
  Font buffersize:     72000                Font retries: 3
  Font memory errors:  0
TFTP font load statistics for host 172.16.1.111:
  Bytes read:          2697239              Files read: 258
  Network errors:      4                    File errors: 0
LAT font load statistics for service WHEEL, incarnation 5:
 Bytes read            182401               Files read: 14
 Protocol errors:      0                    Insufficient memory: 0
XRemote statistics for tty2:
  Current clients:     9                    Total clients: 17
  Requesting client:   5                    Current request size: 0
  Replying client:     6                    Current reply size: 0
  XDM state:           10                   Next timeout: 172460
  Retransmit counter:  0                    Local UDP port: 53616
  Keepalive dormancy:  180                  Session id: 94
  Unread input:        0                    Unwritten output: 0
  Input buffer size:   1024                 Output buffer size: 108
  Protocol version:    2                    Line state: Connected
  Transmit packets:    50768                Receive packets: 49444
  Transmit errors:     0                    Receive errors: 37
  Retransmissions:     403                  Receive out of sequence: 76
  Round trip time:     383                  Retransmit interval: 766
  Transmit window:     7                    Receive window: 7
  Transmit next:       6                    Receive next: 3
  Transmit unacked:    6                    Receive unacked: 0
Connection 0 - TCP connection from 172.16.1.55  [Display Manager]
    Client state:        CS_ACTIVE          Byte order: MSBfirst
    Unread input:        0                  Unwritten output: 0
    Input buffer size:   1024               Output buffer size: 1024
 Connection 1 - LAT connection from WHEEL
```

```
Client state:       CS_ACTIVE         Byte order: LSBfirst
Unread input:       0                 Unwritten output: 0
Input buffer size:  1024              Output buffer size: 1024
```

Table 20–25 describes the significant fields shown in the display.

**Table 20–25** *Show XRemote Field Descriptions*

| Field | Description |
|---|---|
| **XRemote server-wide parameters** | This section displays XRemote parameters that apply to the protocol translator. |
| Font buffer size | XRemote font buffer size that was specified with the **xremote tftp buffersize** global configuration command. |
| Font retries | Number of retries the font loader (host) will attempt before declaring an error condition. |
| Font memory errors | Number of font memory error conditions that have been declared for the protocol translator. |
| **TFTP font load statistics for host 172.16.1.111** | This section displays XRemote statistics for fonts that have been loaded from a TFTP font server at the IP address shown. |
| Bytes read | Number of bytes the host read in order to load the fonts. |
| Files read | Number of files the host read in order to load the fonts. |
| **XRemote statistics for tty2** | This section displays XRemote for the specified line. |
| Current clients | Number of clients using this line for active XRemote sessions. |
| Total clients | Includes the number of clients using this line for active XRemote sessions. |
| Requesting client | Number of clients requesting XRemote service. |
| Retransmit counter | Number of times that XRemote connection requests were retransmitted. |
| Local UDP port | Number assigned to the local UDP port. |
| Keepalive dormancy | Amount of time between keepalive messages. |

## SHOW XREMOTE LINE

To list XRemote connections and monitor XRemote traffic, use the **show xremote line** EXEC command.

**show xremote line** *number*

| *Syntax* | *Description* |
|---|---|
| *number* | A decimal value representing the number of virtual terminal lines about which to display information. |

### *Command Mode*

EXEC

### *Usage Guidelines*

This command first appeared in Cisco IOS Release 10.0.

### *Sample Display*

The following is sample output from the **show xremote line** command (line 3 is specified) when XRemote is enabled and XRemote sessions are active. Only information specific to an individual terminal line is provided.

```
router# show xremote line 3

Xremote statistics for tty3:
  Current clients:     11                   Total clients: 19
  Requesting client:   10                   Current request size: 0
  Replying client:     10                   Current reply size: 0
  XDM state:           10                   Next timeout: 173304
  Retransmit counter:  0                    Local UDP port: 28384
  Keepalive dormancy:  180                  Session id: 29
  Unread input:        0                    Unwritten output: 0
  Input buffer size:   1024                 Output buffer size: 108
  Protocol version:    2                    Line state: Connected
  Transmit packets:    28875                Receive packets: 18644
  Transmit errors:     0                    Receive errors: 13
  Retransmissions:     53                   Receive out of sequence: 41
  Round trip time:     384                  Retransmit interval: 768
  Transmit window:     7                    Receive window: 7
  Transmit next:       2                    Receive next: 7
  Transmit unacked:    2                    Receive unacked: 0

  Connection 0 - TCP connection from 172.16.1.27  [Display Manager]
    Client state:        CS_ACTIVE          Byte order: MSBfirst
    Unread input:        0                  Unwritten output: 0
    Input buffer size:   1024               Output buffer size: 1024

  Connection 1 - TCP connection from 172.16.1.27
    Client state:        CS_ACTIVE          Byte order: MSBfirst
    Unread input:        0                  Unwritten output: 0
    Input buffer size:   1024               Output buffer size: 1024

  Connection 2 - TCP connection from 172.16.1.27
    Client state:        CS_ACTIVE          Byte order: MSBfirst
    Unread input:        0                  Unwritten output: 0
    Input buffer size:   1024               Output buffer size: 1024
```

See Table 20–25 in the **show xremote** command description earlier in this chapter for **show xremote line** output field descriptions.

### TELNET

To log on to a host that supports Telnet, use the **telnet** EXEC command.

**telnet** *host* [*port*] [*keyword*]

| *Syntax* | *Description* |
|---|---|
| *host* | A host name or an IP address. |
| *port* | (Optional) A decimal TCP port number; the default is the Telnet router port (decimal 23) on the host. |
| *keyword* | (Optional) One of the options listed in Table 20–26. |



**Table 20–26** *Telnet Connection Options*

| Option | Description |
|---|---|
| **/debug** | Enables Telnet debugging mode. |
| **/encrypt kerberos** | Enables an encrypted Telnet session. This keyword is available only if you have the Kerberized Telnet subsystem.<br>If you authenticate using Kerberos Credentials, the use of this keyword initiates an encryption negotiation with the remote server. If the encryption negotiation fails, the Telnet connection will be reset. If the encryption negotiation is successful, the Telnet connection will be established, and the Telnet session will continue in encrypted mode (all Telnet traffic for the session will be encrypted). |
| **/line** | Enables Telnet line mode. In this mode, the Cisco IOS software sends no data to the host until you press **Return**. You can edit the line using the standard Cisco IOS software command-editing characters. The **/line** keyword is a local switch; the remote router is not notified of the mode change. |
| **/noecho** | Disables local echo. |
| **/route** *path* | Specifies loose source routing. The *path* argument is a list of host names or IP addresses that specify network nodes and ends with the final destination. |
| **/source-interface** | Specifies the source interface. |
| **/stream** | Turns on *stream* processing, which enables a raw TCP stream with no Telnet control sequences. A stream connection does not process Telnet options and can be appropriate for connections to ports running UUCP and other non-Telnet protocols. |

**Table 20–26** *Telnet Connection Options, Continued*

| Option | Description |
|---|---|
| *port-number* | Port number. |
| **bgp** | Border Gateway Protocol. |
| **chargen** | Character generator. |
| **cmd** *rcmd* | Remote commands. |
| **daytime** | Daytime. |
| **discard** | Discard. |
| **domain** | Domain Name Service. |
| **echo** | Echo. |
| **exec** | EXEC. |
| **finger** | Finger |
| **ftp** | File Transfer Protocol. |
| **ftp-data** | FTP data connections (used infrequently). |
| **gopher** | Gopher. |
| **hostname** | NIC host name server. |
| **ident** | Ident Protocol. |
| **irc** | Internet Relay Chat |
| **klogin** | Kerberos login. |
| **kshell** | Kerberos shell. |
| **login** | Login (rlogin). |
| **lpd** | Printer service. |
| **nntp** | Network News Transport Protocol. |
| **node** | Connect to a specific LAT node |
| **pop2** | Post Office Protocol v2. |
| **pop3** | Post Office Protocol v3. |
| **port** | Destination LAT port name. |
| **smtp** | Simple Mail Transport Protocol. |
| **sunrpc** | Sun Remote Procedure Call. |

**Table 20–26** *Telnet Connection Options, Continued*

| Option | Description |
|---|---|
| syslog | Syslog. |
| tacacs | Specify TACACS security. |
| talk | Talk. |
| telnet | Telnet. |
| time | Time. |
| uucp | UNIX-to-UNIX Copy Program. |
| whois | Nickname. |
| www | World Wide Web (HTTP). |



### *Command Mode*

EXEC

### *Usage Guidelines*

This command first appeared in a release prior to Cisco IOS Release 10.0.

With the Cisco IOS implementation of TCP/IP, you are not required to enter the **connect** or **telnet** commands to establish a Telnet connection. You can just enter the learned host name—as long as the following conditions are met:

- The host name is different from a command word for the router
- The preferred transport protocol is set to telnet

To display a list of the available hosts, use the **show hosts** command. To display the status of all TCP connections, use the **show tcp** command.

The Cisco IOS software assigns a logical name to each connection, and several commands use these names to identify connections. The logical name is the same as the host name, unless that name is already in use, or you change the connection name with the **name-connection** EXEC command. If the name is already in use, the Cisco IOS software assigns a null name to the connection.

The Telnet software supports special Telnet commands in the form of Telnet sequences that map generic terminal control functions to operating system-specific functions. To issue a special Telnet command, enter the escape sequence and then a command character. The default escape sequence is Ctrl-^ (press and hold the Control and Shift keys and the 6 key). You can enter the command character as you hold down Ctrl or with Ctrl released; you can use either uppercase or lowercase letters. Table 20–27 lists the special Telnet escape sequences.

**Table 20–27** *Special Telnet Escape Sequences*

| **Task** | **Escape Sequence*** |
|---|---|
| Break | Ctrl-^ b |
| Interrupt Process (IP) | Ctrl-^ c |
| Erase Character (EC) | Ctrl-^ h |
| Abort Output (AO) | Ctrl-^ o |
| Are You There? (AYT) | Ctrl-^ t |
| Erase Line (EL) | Ctrl-^ u |

* The caret (^) symbol refers to Shift-6 on your keyboard.

At any time during an active Telnet session, you can list the Telnet commands by pressing the escape sequence keys followed by a question mark at the system prompt:

**Ctrl-^ ?**

A sample of this list follows. In this sample output, the first caret (^) symbol represents the Control key, while the second caret represents Shift-6 on your keyboard:

```
router> ^^?
[Special telnet escape help]
^^B  sends telnet BREAK
^^C  sends telnet IP
^^H  sends telnet EC
^^O  sends telnet AO
^^T  sends telnet AYT
^^U  sends telnet EL
```

You can have several concurrent Telnet sessions open and switch back and forth between them. To open a subsequent session, first suspend the current connection by pressing the escape sequence (**Ctrl-Shift-6** then **x** [**Ctrl^x**] by default) to return to the system command prompt. Then open a new connection with the **telnet** command.

To terminate an active Telnet session, issue any of the following commands at the prompt of the device to which you are connecting:

**close**
**disconnect**
**exit**
**logout**
**quit**

### *Examples*

The following example establishes an encrypted Telnet session from a router to a remote host named *host1:*

```
router> telnet host1 /encrypt kerberos
```

The following example routes packets from the source system host1 to kl.sri.com, then to 10.1.0.11, and finally back to *host1*:

```
router> telnet host1 /route:kl.sri.com 10.1.0.11 host1
```

The following example connects to a host with logical name *host1*:

```
router> host1
```

### *Related Commands*

Search online to find documentation for related commands.

**connect**
**rlogin**



## TELNET BREAK-ON-IP

To cause the system to generate a hardware BREAK signal on the RS-232 line that is associated with a reverse Telnet connection when a Telnet Interrupt-Process command is received on that connection, use the **telnet break-on-ip** line configuration command.

**telnet break-on-ip**

### *Syntax Description*

This command has no arguments or keywords.

### *Default*

No hardware Break signal is generated when an Interrupt-Process command is received.

### *Command Mode*

Line configuration

### *Usage Guidelines*

This command first appeared in Cisco IOS Release 10.0.

This command causes the system to generate a hardware BREAK signal on the RS-232 line that is associated with a reverse Telnet connection. It is useful when a Telnet Interrupt-Process command is received on that connection because it can control the translation of Telnet Interrupt-Process commands into X.25 BREAK indications. It is also a useful workaround in the following situations:

- Several user Telnet programs send an Interrupt-Process command, but cannot send a Telnet BREAK signal.
- Some Telnet programs implement a BREAK signal that sends an Interrupt-Process command.
- Some RS-232 hardware devices use a hardware BREAK signal for various purposes.

A hardware BREAK signal is generated when a Telnet BREAK command is received.

### *Example*

In the following example, line 5 is configured with the **telnet break-on-ip** command. The location text notes that this refers to the high-speed modem. The **telnet transparent** command sets end-of-line handling.

```
line 5
 location high-speed modem
 telnet transparent
 telnet break-on-ip
```

### *Related Commands*

Search online to find documentation for related commands.

**connect**
**telnet** (EXEC)
**telnet transparent**
**terminal telnet break-on-ip**

## TELNET REFUSE-NEGOTIATIONS

To set a line using Telnet to refuse to negotiate full duplex, remote echo requests on incoming connections, use the **telnet refuse-negotiations** line configuration command.

**telnet refuse-negotiations**

### *Syntax Description*

This command has no arguments or keywords.

### *Command Mode*

Line configuration

### *Usage Guidelines*

This command first appeared in Cisco IOS Release 10.0.

Use this command on reverse Telnet connections to allow the Cisco IOS software to refuse full-duplex, remote echo option connection requests from the other end. This command suppresses negotiation of the Telnet Remote Echo and Suppress Go Ahead options.

This command does not apply to protocol translation configurations. It is intended for applications wherein the router is functioning as a terminal server to allow terminal connections to remote devices through the asynchronous terminal ports of the router. Terminal server connections are those where the user types a command similar to the following to access network resources:

```
telnet access-server 2005
```

where access-server is the host name of the Cisco router functioning as a terminal server, and 2005 is the port number on the router to which the remote terminal is connected.

### Example

The following example shows how to set line 5 to refuse full-duplex, remote echo requests:

```
line 5
 telnet refuse-negotiations
```

### Related Commands

Search online to find documentation for related commands.

**connect**
**telnet** (EXEC)
**terminal telnet refuse-negotiations**



## TELNET SPEED

To allow the Cisco IOS software to negotiate transmission speed of the line to a connected device, use the **telnet speed** line configuration command.

**telnet speed** *default-speed maximum-speed*

| *Syntax* | *Description* |
|---|---|
| *default-speed* | Line speed (in bps) that the Cisco IOS software will use if the device on the other end of the connection has not specified a speed. |
| *maximum-speed* | Maximum speed (in bps) that the device on the port will use. |

### Command Mode

Line configuration

### Usage Guidelines

This command first appeared in Cisco IOS Release 10.0.

Negotiates speeds on reverse Telnet lines. You can match line speeds on remote systems in reverse Telnet, on host machines hooked up to a router used to access the network, or on a group of console lines hooked up to the router, when disparate line speeds are in use at the local and remote ends of the connection. Line speed negotiation adheres to the Remote Flow Control option, defined in RFC 1080.

### Example

The following example allows a router to negotiate a bit rate on the line using the Telnet option. If no speed is negotiated, the line will run at 2400 bits per second. If the remote host requests a speed of greater than 9600 bps, then 9600 will be used.

```
line 5
 telnet speed 2400 9600
```

### Related Commands

Search online to find documentation for related commands.

**connect**
**telnet** (EXEC)
**terminal telnet speed**

## TELNET SYNC-ON-BREAK

To configure the Cisco IOS software to cause an incoming connection to send a Telnet Synchronize signal when it receives a Telnet BREAK signal, use the **telnet sync-on-break** line configuration command.

**telnet sync-on-break**

### Syntax Description

This command has no arguments or keywords.

### Command Mode

Line configuration

### Usage Guidelines

This command first appeared in Cisco IOS Release 10.0.

This command causes a reverse Telnet line to send a Telnet Synchronize signal when it receives a Telnet BREAK signal. This option is used very rarely to ensure the ordering of BREAK reception with respect to data characters sent after the BREAK.

### Example

In the following example, line 8 is configured with the **telnet sync-on-break** command:

```
line aux 0
 telnet sync-on-break
```

### Related Commands

Search online to find documentation for related commands.

**connect**
**telnet** (EXEC)
**terminal telnet sync-on-break**

## TELNET TRANSPARENT

To configure the Cisco IOS software to send a CARRIAGE RETURN (CR) as a CR followed by a NULL instead of a CR followed by a LINE FEED (LF), use the **telnet transparent** line configuration command.

**telnet transparent**

*Syntax Description*

This command has no arguments or keywords.

*Default*

CARRIAGE RETURN followed by a LINE FEED

*Command Mode*

Line configuration

*Usage Guidelines*

This command first appeared in Cisco IOS Release 10.0.

This command is useful for coping with different interpretations of end-of-line handling in the Telnet protocol specification.

*Example*

The following example causes the Cisco IOS software, when sending a CR, to send a CR followed by a NULL character:

```
line 7
 telnet transparent
```

*Related Commands*

Search online to find documentation for related commands.

**connect**
**telnet** (EXEC)
**terminal telnet transparent**



## TERMINAL LAT

To temporarily define the list of services to which you or another user can connect, use the **terminal lat** EXEC command.

**terminal lat remote-modification**
**terminal lat out-group** *group_number* [*start-end*] {**disabled | enabled**}

| *Syntax* | *Description* |
|---|---|
| **remote-modification** | Sets the line to be remotely modifiable. |
| **out-group** | Defines a group list for outgoing user-initiated connections. |
| *group_number* [*start-end*] | Number of the group that has access to the system through the specified line. This number is identified by the system administrator. You also can specify a range of group numbers. Separate the beginning and end of the range with a hyphen. |

| *Syntax* | *Description* |
|---|---|
| **disabled** | Incrementally removes specified groups from list. |
| **enabled** | Incrementally adds specified groups to list. |

*Command Mode*

EXEC

*Usage Guidelines*

This command first appeared in Cisco IOS Release 11.2.

To temporarily define the list of services to which you or another user can connect, you define the group code lists used for connections from specific lines. You limit the connection choices for an individual line by defining the group code lists for an outgoing connection. When a user initiates a connection with a LAT host, the user's line must share a common group number with the remote LAT host before a connection can be made.

The group code range entered in this command must fall within the group code range already configured for the line.

*Example*

The following example defines a group code list for the outgoing group 4:

```
router> terminal lat out-group 4, 6-189
```

*Related Commands*

Search online to find documentation for related commands.

**connect**
**lat**

### TERMINAL TRANSPORT PREFERRED

To specify the preferred protocol to use for the current session when a command does not specify one, use the **terminal transport preferred** EXEC command.

**terminal transport preferred {all | lat | mop | nasi | none | pad | rlogin | telnet}**

| *Syntax* | *Description* |
|---|---|
| **all** | Specifies all recognized protocols. |
| **lat** | Specifies the LAT protocol. |
| **mop** | Specifies the Maintenance Operation Protocol (MOP). |
| **nasi** | Specifies the NetWare Asynchronous Services Interface (NASI) protocol. |

| *Syntax* | *Description* |
|---|---|
| **none** | Prevents any protocol selection on the line. The router default is that any unrecognized command is a host name. If the preferred protocol is set to none, the router will not attempt any connections if the command is not recognized. |
| **pad** | Specifies X.3 PAD, which is used most often to connect a server product to X.25 hosts. |
| **rlogin** | Specifies UNIX rlogin. |
| **telnet** | Specifies the TCP/IP Telnet protocol. |

*Default*

**lat** (if lat is not supported, **telnet**)



*Command Mode*

EXEC

*Usage Guidelines*

The **terminal transport** [**none** | **telnet**] command first appeared in a release prior to Cisco IOS Release 10.0. The entire command first appeared in Cisco IOS Release 11.2.

*Example*

The following example configures the console so that it does not connect when an unrecognized command is entered:

```
router> terminal transport preferred none
```

*Related Commands*

Search online to find documentation for related commands.

**transport preferred**

## TN3270

To begin a TN3270 session, use the **tn3270** EXEC command.

**tn3270** *host*

| *Syntax* | *Description* |
|---|---|
| *host* | Name or IP address of a specific host on a network that can be reached by the router. The default terminal emulation mode allows access using a VT100 emulation. |

*Default*

None

*Command Mode*

EXEC

*Usage Guidelines*

This command first appeared in Cisco IOS Release 11.1.

Unlike Telnet and LAT connections, you *must* enter the command **tn3270** to make a connection to an IBM TN3278 host.

To terminate an active TN3270 session, enter the escape sequence (**Ctrl-Shift-6** then **x** [**Ctrl^x**] by default) and enter the **disconnect** command at the EXEC prompt. Or log off the remote system by issuing the command specific to that system (such as **exit, logout, quit, close,** or **disconnect**).

*Example*

The following example establishes a terminal session with an IBM TN3270 host named finance:

```
router> tn3270 finance
```

## TN3270 8BIT DISPLAY

To configure the Cisco IOS software to use the mask set by the **data-character-bits** {7 | 8} line configuration command or the **terminal data-character bits** {7 | 8} EXEC command, use the **tn3270 8bit display** line configuration command. To restore the default 7-bit mask used for TN3270 connections, use the **no** form of this command.

**tn3270 8bit display**
**no tn3270 8bit display**

*Syntax Description*

This command has no arguments or keywords.

*Default*

Disabled

*Command Mode*

Line configuration

*Usage Guidelines*

This command first appeared in Cisco IOS Release 10.0.

Use the **tn3270-character-map** command to map between extended EBCDIC or extended ASCII characters.

### *Example*

The following example configures the Cisco IOS software to use the mask set by the **data-character-bits** line configuration and EXEC commands on line 5:

```
line 5
 tn3270 8bit display
```

### *Related Commands*

Search online to find documentation for related commands.

**data-character-bits**
**terminal data-character-bits**



## TN3270 8BIT TRANSPARENT-MODE

To configure the Cisco IOS software to use the mask set by the **data-character-bits** {7 | 8} line configuration command or the **terminal data-character bits** {7 | 8} EXEC command, use the **tn3270 8bit display** line configuration command. To restore the default 7-bit mask used for TN3270 connections, use the **no** form of this command.

**tn3270 8bit transparent-mode**
**no tn3270 8bit transparent-mode**

### *Syntax Description*

This command has no arguments or keywords.

### *Default*

Disabled

### *Command Mode*

Line configuration

### *Usage Guidelines*

This command first appeared in Cisco IOS Release 10.0.

This command is needed if you are using a file transfer protocol such as Kermit in 8-bit mode or you are using 8-bit graphics, both of which rely on transparent mode.

### *Example*

The following example configures the software to use the mask set by the **data-character-bits** line configuration and EXEC commands on line 5:

```
line 5
 tn3270 8bit transparent-mode
```

### *Related Commands*

Search online to find documentation for related commands.

**data-character-bits**
**terminal data-character-bits**

## TN3270 CHARACTER-MAP

To convert incoming EBCDIC characters into ASCII characters, use the **tn3270 character-map** global configuration command. To restore default character mappings, use the **no** form of this command.

**tn3270 character-map** *ebcdic-in-hex ascii-in-hex*
**no tn3270 character-map** {**all** | *ebcdic-in-hex*} [*ascii-in-hex*]

| *Syntax* | *Description* |
|---|---|
| *ebcdic-in-hex* | Hexadecimal value of an EBCDIC character. |
| *ascii-in-hex* | Hexadecimal value of an ASCII character. |
| **all** | Indicates all character mappings. |

### *Default*

Disabled

### *Command Mode*

Global configuration

### *Usage Guidelines*

This command first appeared in Cisco IOS Release 10.0.

Use this command to print international characters that are EBCDIC characters not normally printed, including umlauts (¨) and tildes (~). The command first restores default mapping for both EBCDIC and ASCII characters. In the **no** form of the command, the **all** keyword resets all character mappings to Cisco defaults.

Table 20–28 shows the default character mappings between ASCII and EBCDIC in decimal and hexadecimal format.

To convert outgoing ASCII characters into EBCDIC characters, use the **keymap** command to modify the keymap structure with the tag *ebcdic_xx=string*, where *xx* is a hexadecimal value and *string* is the sequence of characters that send the ESCDIC character.

**Table 20–28** *Default ASCII, EBCDIC Character Mappings*

| Character | ASCII Decimal | ASCII Hexadecimal | EBCDIC Decimal | EBCDIC Hexadecimal |
|---|---|---|---|---|
| ! | 33 | 0x21 | 90 | 0x5a |
| " | 34 | 0x22 | 127 | 0x7f |
| # | 35 | 0x23 | 123 | 0x7b |
| $ | 36 | 0x24 | 91 | 0x5b |
| % | 37 | 0x25 | 108 | 0x6c |
| & | 38 | 0x26 | 80 | 0x50 |
| ' | 39 | 0x27 | 125 | 0x7d |
| ( | 40 | 0x28 | 77 | 0x4d |
| ) | 41 | 0x29 | 93 | 0x5d |
| * | 42 | 0x2a | 92 | 0x5c |
| + | 43 | 0x2b | 78 | 0x4e |
| , | 44 | 0x2c | 107 | 0x6b |
| - | 45 | 0x2d | 96 | 0x60 |
| . | 46 | 0x2e | 75 | 0x4b |
| / | 47 | 0x2f | 97 | 0x61 |
| 0 | 48 | 0x30 | 240 | 0xf0 |
| 1 | 49 | 0x31 | 241 | 0xf1 |
| 2 | 50 | 0x32 | 242 | 0xf2 |
| 3 | 51 | 0x33 | 243 | 0xf3 |
| 4 | 52 | 0x34 | 244 | 0xf4 |
| 5 | 53 | 0x35 | 245 | 0xf5 |
| 6 | 54 | 0x36 | 246 | 0xf6 |
| 7 | 55 | 0x37 | 247 | 0xf7 |
| 8 | 56 | 0x38 | 248 | 0xf8 |
| 9 | 57 | 0x39 | 249 | 0xf9 |
| : | 58 | 0x3a | 122 | 0x7a |
| ; | 59 | 0x3b | 94 | 0x5e |

**Table 20–28** *Default ASCII, EBCDIC Character Mappings, Continued*

| Character | ASCII Decimal | ASCII Hexadecimal | EBCDIC Decimal | EBCDIC Hexadecimal |
|---|---|---|---|---|
| < | 60 | 0x3c | 76 | 0x4c |
| = | 61 | 0x3d | 126 | 0x7e |
| > | 62 | 0x3e | 110 | 0x6e |
| ? | 63 | 0x3f | 111 | 0x6f |
| @ | 64 | 0x40 | 124 | 0x7c |
| A | 65 | 0x41 | 193 | 0xc1 |
| B | 66 | 0x42 | 194 | 0xc2 |
| C | 67 | 0x43 | 195 | 0xc3 |
| D | 68 | 0x44 | 196 | 0xc4 |
| E | 69 | 0x45 | 197 | 0xc5 |
| F | 70 | 0x46 | 198 | 0xc6 |
| G | 71 | 0x47 | 199 | 0xc7 |
| H | 72 | 0x48 | 200 | 0xc8 |
| I | 73 | 0x49 | 201 | 0xc9 |
| J | 74 | 0x4a | 209 | 0xd1 |
| K | 75 | 0x4b | 210 | 0xd2 |
| L | 76 | 0x4c | 211 | 0xd3 |
| M | 77 | 0x4d | 212 | 0xd4 |
| N | 78 | 0x4e | 213 | 0xd5 |
| O | 79 | 0x4f | 214 | 0xd6 |
| P | 80 | 0x50 | 215 | 0xd7 |
| Q | 81 | 0x51 | 216 | 0xd8 |
| R | 82 | 0x52 | 217 | 0xd9 |
| S | 83 | 0x53 | 226 | 0xe2 |
| T | 84 | 0x54 | 227 | 0xe3 |
| U | 85 | 0x55 | 228 | 0xe4 |
| V | 86 | 0x56 | 229 | 0xe5 |

**Table 20–28** *Default ASCII, EBCDIC Character Mappings, Continued*

| Character | ASCII Decimal | ASCII Hexadecimal | EBCDIC Decimal | EBCDIC Hexadecimal |
|---|---|---|---|---|
| W | 87 | 0x57 | 230 | 0xe6 |
| X | 88 | 0x58 | 231 | 0xe7 |
| Y | 89 | 0x59 | 232 | 0xe8 |
| Z | 90 | 0x5a | 233 | 0xe9 |
| [ | 91 | 0x5b | 173 | 0xad |
| \ | 92 | 0x5c | 224 | 0xe0 |
| ] | 93 | 0x5d | 189 | 0xbd |
| ^ | 94 | 0x5e | 95 | 0x5f |
| _ | 95 | 0x5f | 109 | 0x6d |
| ` | 96 | 0x60 | 121 | 0x79 |
| a | 97 | 0x61 | 129 | 0x81 |
| b | 98 | 0x62 | 130 | 0x82 |
| c | 99 | 0x63 | 131 | 0x83 |
| d | 100 | 0x64 | 132 | 0x84 |
| e | 101 | 0x65 | 133 | 0x85 |
| f | 102 | 0x66 | 134 | 0x86 |
| g | 103 | 0x67 | 135 | 0x87 |
| h | 104 | 0x68 | 136 | 0x88 |
| i | 105 | 0x69 | 137 | 0x89 |
| j | 106 | 0x6a | 145 | 0x91 |
| k | 107 | 0x6b | 146 | 0x92 |
| l | 108 | 0x6c | 147 | 0x93 |
| m | 109 | 0x6d | 148 | 0x94 |
| n | 110 | 0x6e | 149 | 0x95 |
| o | 111 | 0x6f | 150 | 0x96 |
| p | 112 | 0x70 | 151 | 0x97 |
| q | 113 | 0x71 | 152 | 0x98 |

**Table 20–28** *Default ASCII, EBCDIC Character Mappings, Continued*

| Character | ASCII Decimal | ASCII Hexadecimal | EBCDIC Decimal | EBCDIC Hexadecimal |
|---|---|---|---|---|
| r | 114 | 0x72 | 153 | 0x99 |
| s | 115 | 0x73 | 162 | 0xa2 |
| t | 116 | 0x74 | 163 | 0xa3 |
| u | 117 | 0x75 | 164 | 0xa4 |
| v | 118 | 0x76 | 165 | 0xa5 |
| w | 119 | 0x77 | 166 | 0xa6 |
| x | 120 | 0x78 | 167 | 0xa7 |
| y | 121 | 0x79 | 168 | 0xa8 |
| z | 122 | 0x7a | 169 | 0xa9 |
| { | 123 | 0x7b | 192 | 0xc0 |
| \| | 124 | 0x7c | 79 | 0x4f |
| } | 125 | 0x7d | 208 | 0xd0 |
| ~ | 126 | 0x7e | 161 | 0xa1 |

### *Example*

The following example creates a two-way binding between an EBCDIC character and an ASCII character:

```
tn3270 character-map 0x81 0x78
```

### *Related Commands*

Search online to find documentation for related commands.

**show tn3270 ascii-hexval**
**show tn3270 character-map**

## TN3270 DATASTREAM

Use the **tn3270 datastream extended** global configuration command to enable the TN3270 extended datastream. Use the **no** form of this command to return to the normal TN3270 datastream.

**tn3270 datastream [extended | normal]**
**no tn3270 datastream**

| *Syntax* | *Description* |
|---|---|
| **extended** | Extended datastream. |
| **normal** | Normal datastream. |

*Default*

Normal datastream

*Command Mode*

Global configuration



*Usage Guidelines*

This command first appeared in Cisco IOS Release 10.3.

This command causes an "-E" to be appended to the terminal type string sent to the IBM host. This allows you to use the extended TN3270 features.

*Example*

The following example shows the supported tn3270 datastream options:

```
router(config)# tn3270 datastream ?
  extended  Use extended TN3270 datastream
  normal    Use normal TN3270 datastream
```

### TN3270 NULL-PROCESSING

Use the **tn3270 null-processing** global configuration command to specify how NULLs are handled. Use the **no** form of the command to return to 7171 NULL processing.

**tn3270 null-processing** [3270 | 7171]
**no tn3270 null-processing** [3270 | 7171]

| *Syntax* | *Description* |
|---|---|
| 3270 | (Optional) NULLs are compressed out of the string, as on a 3278-x terminal. |
| 7171 | (Optional) NULLs are converted to spaces, as on a 7171 controller. |

*Default*

7171 NULL processing

*Command Mode*

Global configuration

### *Usage Guidelines*

This command first appeared in Cisco IOS Release 10.3.

If a user enters data, uses an arrow key to move the cursor to the right on the screen, and then enters more data, the intervening spaces are filled with NULLs. To specify how NULLs are handled, enter the command **tn3270 null-processing** either with the argument **3270**, where NULLs are compressed out of the string (as on a real 3278-x terminal) or the argument **7171**, where NULLs are converted to spaces as on a 7171 controller. Enter this command in global configuration.

### *Example*

This example shows the two available null-processing methods:

```
router(config)# tn3270 null-processing ?
  3270  Use 3270-style null processing
  7171  Use 7171-style null processing
```

## TN3270 OPTIMIZE-CURSOR-MOVE

To increase performance between a remote user and a TN3270 host by limiting cursor movement information that is sent to user terminals, issue the **tn3270 optimize-cursor-move** global configuration command. To ensure that all cursor movement information is sent between the user's terminal and the TN3270 host, use the **no** form of the command.

**tn3270 optimize-cursor-move**
**no tn3270 optimize-cursor-move**

### *Syntax Description*

This command has no arguments or keywords.

### *Default*

Cursor movement escape strings are sent to the terminal.

### *Command Mode*

Global configuration

### *Usage Guidelines*

This command first appeared in Cisco IOS Release 11.2.

Issuing this command increases the speed of information transfer between users and TN3270 hosts through an access server.

If you do not issue this command, virtually every byte of information between the user's terminal and the TN3270 host is prepended and trailed by cursor-movement strings.

### *Example*

The following example disables status messages to users who are connected to 3278 terminals:

```
router(config)# tn3270 optimize-cursor-move
```

### *Related Commands*

Search online to find documentation for related commands.

**tn3270 status-message**

## TN3270 RESET-REQUIRED

To lock a terminal after input error until the user resets the terminal, use the **tn3270 reset-required** global configuration command. Use the **no** form of the command to return to the default of no reset required.

**tn3270 reset-required**
**no tn3270 reset-required**



### *Syntax Description*

This command has no arguments or keywords.

### *Default*

No reset is required.

### *Command Mode*

Global configuration

### *Usage Guidelines*

This command first appeared in Cisco IOS Release 10.3.

On a 3278-x terminal, the keyboard is locked and further input is not permitted after input error (due to field overflow, invalid entry, and so on), until the user presses the RESET key. Most TN3270 implementations leave the keyboard unlocked and remove any error message on the next key input after the error. Use this command to lock the keyboard until the user performs a reset.

## TN3270 STATUS-MESSAGE

To re-enable the display of status messages after they have been disabled, use the **tn3270 status-message** global configuration command. To save bandwidth on asynchronous lines by not displaying status messages, use the **no** form of this command.

**tn3270 status-message**
**no tn3270 status-message**

### *Syntax Description*

This command has no arguments or keywords.

### *Default*

Status messages appear.

### *Command Mode*

Global configuration

### *Usage Guidelines*

This command first appeared in Cisco IOS Release 11.2.

Status messages appear on the user's console by default. These messages include "System Locked," "Field error," and "System UnLocked" messages, among others. These messages are sent back to the user's terminal via the TTY line on the access server.

Disabling status messages saves bandwidth on asynchronous lines, which have very low bandwidth.

### *Example*

The following example disables status messages to users who are connected to 3270 terminals:

```
router(config)# no tn3270 status-message
```

### *Related Commands*

Search online to find documentation for related commands.

**tn3270 optimize-cursor-move**

## TN3270 TYPEAHEAD

To buffer keyboard data when a 3278 server is in locked mode, use the **tn3270 typeahead** global configuration command. To disable the typeahead function, use the **no** form of this command.

**tn3270 typeahead**
**no tn3270 typeahead**

### *Syntax Description*

This command has no arguments or keywords.

### *Default*

No typeahead

### *Command Mode*

Global configuration

### *Usage Guidelines*

This command first appeared in Cisco IOS Release 11.2.

When typeahead is enabled, the TN3270 client implementation in the Cisco IOS software permits you (the user) to continue typing while the system is trying to obtain a response from the TN3270 server. Information you type while a "System Locked" message appears on the terminal is stored in a buffer. After the "System Locked" message disappears, the information is then used as though it were just typed.

### *Example*

The following example saves user information when "System Locked" messages appear on the screen:

```
router(config)# tn3270 typeahead
```

### *Related Commands*

Search online to find documentation for related commands.

**tn3270 reset-required**



## TTYCAP

To define characteristics of a terminal emulation file, use the **ttycap** global configuration command. To delete any named ttycap entry from the configuration file, use the **no** form of this command.

**ttycap** *ttycap-name termcap-entry*
**no ttycap** *ttycap-name*

| *Syntax* | *Description* |
|---|---|
| *ttycap-name* | Name of a file. It can be up to 32 characters long and must be unique. |
| *termcap-entry* | Commands that define the ttycap. Consists of two parts (see the "Usage Guidelines" section of this command for details). |

### *Default*

VT100 terminal emulation

### *Command Mode*

Global configuration

### *Usage Guidelines*

This command first appeared in Cisco IOS Release 10.3.

Use the EXEC command **show ttycap** to test for the availability of a ttycap.

**NOTES**

Do not type a ttycap entry filename "default," or the Cisco IOS software will adopt the newly defined entry as the default.

The *termcap-entry* consists of two parts: a *name* portion and a *capabilities* portion:

- The *name* portion is a series of names that can be used to refer to a specific terminal type. Generally, these names should represent commonly recognized terminal names (such as VT100 and VT200). Multiple names can be used. Each name is separated by a vertical bar symbol (|). The series is terminated by a colon symbol (:).

  The following example illustrates a name specification for a VT100 termcap.

  ```
  d0¦vt100¦vt100-am¦vt100am¦dec vt100:
  ```

- The *capabilities* portion of the termcap-entry consists of a sequence of termcap capabilities. These capabilities can include boolean flags, string sequences, or numeric sequences. Each individual capability is terminated using a colon symbol (:).

  A *Boolean flag* can be set to true by including the two-character capability name in the termcap entry. The absence of any supported flag results in the flag being set to false.

  The following is an example of a backspace Boolean flag:

  ```
  bs:
  ```

A *string sequence* is a two-character capability name followed by an equal sign (=) and the character sequence.

The following example illustrates the capability for homing the cursor:

```
ho=\E[H:
```

The sequence \E represents the ESC character.

Control characters can be represented in *string sequences* by entering a two-character sequence starting with a caret symbol (^), followed by the character to be used as a control character.

The following example illustrates the definition of a control character.

```
bc=^h:
```

In this example, the backspace is entered into the *termcap-entry* as the string sequence as the characters "^h."

A *numeric sequence* is a two-character capability name followed by a number symbol (#) and the number.

The following example represents the number of columns on a screen.

```
co#80:
```

Use the backslash symbol ( \ ) to extend the definition to multiple lines. The end of the ttycap *termcap-entry* is specified by a colon terminating a line followed by an end-of-line character and no backslash.

For the definitions of supported Boolean-flag ttycap capabilities, see Table 20–29. For the definitions of supported string-sequence ttycap capabilities, see Table 20–30. For the definitions of supported number-sequence ttycap capabilities, see Table 20–31. For the definitions of supported color-sequence ttycap capabilities, see Table 20–32.

**Table 20–29** *Definitions of ttycap Capabilities: Boolean Flags*

| Boolean Flag | Description |
|---|---|
| am | Automatic margin |
| bs | Terminal can backspace with bs |
| ms | Safe to move in standout modes |
| nc | No currently working carriage return |
| xn | NEWLINE ignored after 80 columns (Concept) |
| xs | Standout not erased by overwriting (Hewlett-Packard) |

**Table 20–30** *Definitions of ttycap Capabilities: String Sequences*

| String Sequence | Description |
|---|---|
| AL | Add line below with cursor sequence |
| bc | Backspace if not ^h |
| bt | Backtab sequence |
| ce | Clear to end of line |
| cl | Clear screen, cursor to upper left |
| cm | Move cursor to row # and col # |
| cr | Carriage return sequence |
| cs | Change scrolling region |
| DL | Delete the line the cursor is on |
| ei | End insert mode |
| ho | Home, move cursor to upper left |
| ic | Character insert |
| im | Begin insert mode |
| is | Initialization string (typically tab stop initialization) |
| ll | Move cursor to lower-left corner |

**Table 20–30** *Definitions of ttycap Capabilities: String Sequences, Continued*

| String Sequence | Description |
|---|---|
| md | Turn on bold (extra bright) character attribute |
| me | Turn off all character attributes |
| nd | Nondestructive space |
| nl | Newline sequence |
| pc | Pad character if not NULL |
| rc | Restore cursor position |
| rs | Resets terminal to known starting state |
| sc | Save cursor position |
| se | End standout mode (highlight) |
| so | Start standout mode (highlight) |
| ta | Tab |
| te | End programs that use cursor motion |
| ti | Initialization for programs that use cursor motion |
| uc | Underline character at cursor |
| ue | End underline mode |
| up | Move cursor up |
| us | Begin underline mode |
| vb | Visual bell |
| vs | Visual cursor |
| ve | Normal cursor |

**Table 20–31** *Definitions of ttycap Capabilities: Number Sequences*

| Number Sequence | Description |
|---|---|
| li | Lines on the screen |
| co | Columns on the screen |

**Table 20–31** *Definitions of ttycap Capabilities: Number Sequences, Continued*

| Number Sequence | Description |
|---|---|
| sg | Standout glitch, number of spaces printed when entering or leaving standout display mode |
| ug | Underline glitch, number of spaces printed when entering or leaving underline mode |

**Table 20–32** *Definitions of ttycap Capabilities: Color Sequences*

| Color Sequence | Description |
|---|---|
| x0 | Black |
| x1 | Blue |
| x2 | Red or orange |
| x3 | Pink or purple |
| x4 | Green, which is the default color. |
| x5 | Turquoise |
| x6 | Yellow |
| x7 | Gray or white |



The ttycap database uses these color sequences to translate IBM directives into screen-drawing commands. These color sequences control only foreground terminal colors. They do not control background color, which is configured to black by default.

### *Example*

The following is an example of a ttycap file. See Chapter 19 for more examples.

```
ttycap ttycap1\
d0¦vt100¦vt100-am¦vt100am¦dec vt100:do=^J:co#80:li#24:\
cl=50^[[;H^[[2J:bs:am:cm=5^[[%i%d;%dH:nd=2^[[C:up=2^[[A:\
ce=3^[[K:so=2^[[7m:se=2^[[m:us=2^[[4m:ue=2^[[m:md=2^[[1m:\
me=2^[[m:ho=^[[H:xn:sc=^[7:rc=^[8:cs=^[[%i%d;%dr:
```

### *Related Commands*

Search online to find documentation for related commands.

**keymap-type**
**terminal-type**

### TUNNEL

To set up a network layer connection to a router, use the **tunnel** user EXEC command.

**tunnel** *host*

| *Syntax* | *Description* |
|---|---|
| *host* | Name or IP address of a specific host on a network that can be reached by the router. |

#### *Command Mode*

User EXEC

#### *Usage Guidelines*

This command first appeared in a release prior to Cisco IOS Release 10.0.

If you are a mobile user, it is often impractical to dial in to your "home" router from a remote site. The asynchronous mobility feature allows you to dial in to different routers elsewhere on the internetwork while experiencing the same server environment that you would if you were connecting directly to your home router.

This asynchronous host mobility is accomplished by packet tunneling, a technique by which raw data from the dial-in user is encapsulated and transported directly to the host site where your home router performs the actual protocol processing.

You enable asynchronous mobility by entering the **tunnel** command to set up a network layer connection to a specified host. From a router other than a Cisco router, however, you need to use the Telnet protocol.

After a connection is established, you receive an authentication dialog or prompt from your home router and can proceed as if you are connected directly to it. When communications are complete, the network connection can be closed and terminated from either end of the connection.

#### *Example*

The following example establishes a network layer connection with an IBM host named mktg:

```
router> tunnel mktg
```

### WHERE

To list the open sessions, use the **where** EXEC command.

**where**

#### *Syntax Description*

This command has no arguments or keywords.

### *Command Mode*

EXEC

### *Usage Guidelines*

This command first appeared in a release prior to Cisco IOS Release 10.0.

The **where** command displays all open sessions associated with the current terminal line.

The **Ctrl^x**, **where**, and **resume** commands are available with all supported connection protocols.

### *Example*

The following is sample output from the **where** command:

```
router# where
Conn Host                    Address             Byte     Idle   Conn Name
   1 MATHOM                  192.31.7.21            0        0   MATHOM
*  2 CHAFF                   131.108.12.19          0        0   CHAFF
```

The asterisk (*) indicates the current terminal session.

Table 20–33 describes significant fields shown in the display.

**Table 20–33** *Where Field Descriptions*

| Field | Description |
|---|---|
| Conn | Name or address of the remote host to which the connection is made. |
| Host | Remote host to which the router is connected through a Telnet session. |
| Address | IP address of the remote host. |
| Byte | Number of unread bytes for the user to see on the connection. |
| Idle | Interval (in minutes) since data was last sent on the line. |
| Conn Name | Assigned name of the connection. |

### *Related Commands*

Search online to find documentation for related commands.

**resume**
**show sessions**

## XREMOTE

To prepare the router for manual startup and initiate an XRemote connection, use the **xremote** EXEC command. This command begins the instructions that prompt you through the connection.

**xremote**

### *Syntax Description*

This command has no arguments or keywords.

### *Default*

Disabled

### *Command Mode*

EXEC

### *Usage Guidelines*

This command first appeared in Cisco IOS Release 11.1.

If you do not use a host computer that supports XDMCP or LAT, you must use manual session startup. Manual session startup involves the following steps:

1. Enable XRemote manually on the router's port.
2. Connect to the host computer by using a **telnet, lat,** or **rlogin** command, then log on as usual.
3. Set the location of the X display.
4. Start client applications.
5. Return to the EXEC prompt.
6. Enter the **xremote** command to enable XRemote manually again on the server port.

**NOTES**

In manual operation, the server and X terminal remain in XRemote mode until all clients disconnect or the access server receives a reset request from the X terminal. A session might terminate during startup because you invoked transient X clients that set some parameters (such as**xset** or **xmodmap**) and then disconnected. There must always be one session open or the connection resets.

### *Examples*

The following example starts a manual XRemote session:

```
dialup> xremote
XRemote enabled; your display is dialup:2006
Start your clients and type XRemote again
```

The router replies with a message informing you of your X display location. Use this information to tell the XRemote host the location of your X display server. If no clients are found, you see the following message:

```
No X clients waiting - check that your display is darkstar:2006
```

The following example shows a connection from an X display terminal through a router to a host running client programs:

```
dialup> xremote

XRemote enabled; your display is dialup:2006
Start your clients and type XRemote again

dialup> telnet eureka
Trying EUREKA.NOWHERE.COM (252.122.1.55)... Open

SunOS UNIX (eureka)

login: deal
Password:

Last login: Fri Apr 1 17:17:46 from dialup.nowhere.com
SunOS Release (SERVER+FDDI+DBE.patched) #14: Fri Apr 8 10:37:29 PDT 1994

eureka% setenv DISPLAY dialup:2006
eureka% xterm &
[1] 15439

eureka% logout

[Connection to EUREKA closed by foreign host]

dialup> xremote
Entering XRemote
```

The following example shows how an XRemote connection is established for a configuration like the one shown in Figure 20–1. This example assumes that the administrator has set the user's display environment variable to identify the user's X display terminal.

1. From the PCX, MacX, or UNIX machine in Figure 20–1, the user connects to port 9003 on AccessServer1. If your administrator has configured a rotary number 7, the user connects to port 10007.
2. AccessServer1 connects the user to a modem.
3. The modem calls AccessServer2.
4. The user enters **xremote** at the AccessServer2 prompt.
5. The user connects to the host from AccessServer2 using the **telnet** command.
6. The user starts the X client program that will run on the host and display on the X display server (PCX, MacX, or UNIX host).
7. The user escapes from the host back to the AccessServer2, or logs out if clients were run in the background, and enters **xremote** command at the AccessServer2 prompt.
8. You can use the master indexes or search online to find documentation of related commands.

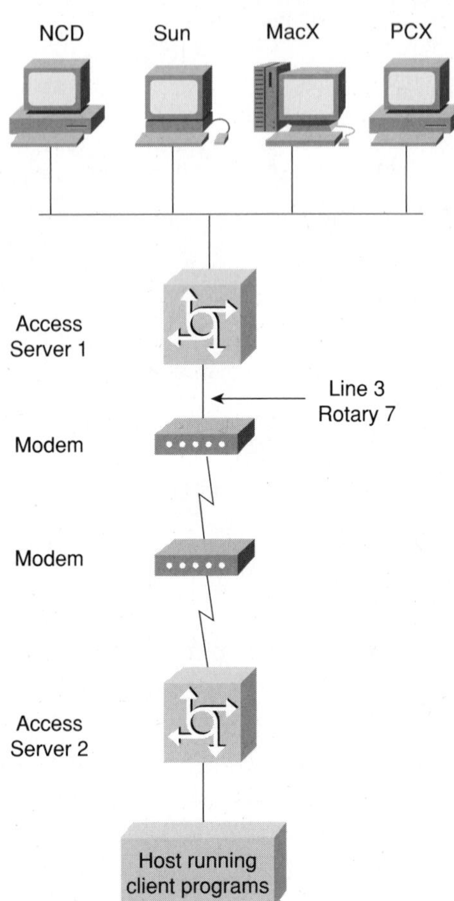


*Figure 20–1*
*XRemote Session Between Servers.*

The following example shows how to make an XRemote connection between servers. The number 9016 in the first line of the display indicates a connection to individual line 16. If the administrator had configured a rotary connection, the user enters 10000 plus the number of the rotary instead of 9016.

```
router% telnet golden-road 9016

Trying 192.31.7.84 ...
Connected to golden-road.cisco.com.
Escape character is '^]'.

User Access Verification

Password:
Password OK

 --- Outbound XRemote service ---
```

```
Enter X server name or IP address: innerspace
Enter display number [0]:

 Connecting to tty16... please start up XRemote on the remote system

atdt 13125554141
DIALING
RING
CONNECT 14400

User Access Verification
Username: deal
Password:
  Welcome to the cisco dial-up access server.

dialup> xremote
XRemote enabled; your display is dialup:2006
Start your clients and type XRemote again

dialup> telnet sparks
Trying SPARKS.NOWHERE.COM (252.122.1.55)... Open

SunOS UNIX (sparks)

login: deal
Password:
Last login: Fri Apr 1 17:17:46 from dialup.nowhere.com
SunOS Release (SERVER+FDDI+DBE.patched) #14: Fri Apr 8 10:37:29 PDT 1994

sparks% setenv DISPLAY dialup:2006
sparks% xterm &
[1] 15439

sparks% logout

[Connection to SPARKS closed by foreign host]

dialup> xremote
Entering XRemote
```



### *Related Commands*

Search online to find documentation for related commands.

**xremote lat**
**xremote xdm**

## XREMOTE LAT

To initiate a DECwindow session over a LAT connection, use the **xremote lat** EXEC command.

**xremote lat** *service*

| *Syntax* | *Description* |
|---|---|
| *service* | Name of the desired LAT service. |

### Command Mode

EXEC

### Usage Guidelines

This command first appeared in Cisco IOS Release 11.2.

If your host computer supports DECwindows login sessions, you can use automatic session startup to make an XRemote session connection. Once the system administrator at the remote host configures support for DECwindows over LAT, use the **xremote lat** EXEC command to initiate the connection. After you issue this command, the following events occur:

- The XRemote font server down-line loads several initial fonts for the DECwindows login display.
- The terminal displays the DIGITAL logo and DECwindows login box.

Log on to the host. Upon completion of login, more fonts are loaded, and the remote session begins.

**NOTES**

Because of heavy font usage, DECwindows applications can take longer than expected to start when using XRemote. Once the application starts, performance and access times should be as expected.

To exit XRemote sessions, you must quit all active X connections, usually with a command supported by your X client system. Usually, when you quit the last connection (when all client processes are stopped), XRemote closes and you return to the EXEC prompt. However, your X client system determines how the session closes.

### Example

The following example begins connection with a LAT service named service1:

```
router> xremote lat service1
```

### Related Commands

Search online to find documentation for related commands.

**xremote**
**xremote xdm**

## XREMOTE TFTP BUFFERSIZE

To change the buffer size used for loading font files, use the **xremote tftp buffersize** global configuration command. To restore the buffer size to the default value, use the **no** form of this command.

**xremote tftp buffersize** *buffersize*
**no xremote tftp buffersize**

| *Syntax* | *Description* |
|---|---|
| *buffersize* | (Optional) Buffer size in bytes. This is a decimal number in the range from 4096 to 70,000 bytes. The default is 70,000. |

### *Default*

70,000 bytes

### *Command Mode*

Global configuration

### *Usage Guidelines*

This command first appeared in Cisco IOS Release 10.0.

When the X terminal requests that a font file be loaded, the Cisco IOS software must first load the font file into an internal buffer before passing it to the X terminal. The default value of 70,000 bytes is adequate for most font files, but the size can be increased as necessary for nonstandard font files.

The buffer size can be set as low as 4,096 bytes and as large as the available memory on the router will allow. If you are using LAT font access, you should not lower the buffer size below the default, because the font directory for all of the LAT fonts (created internally) requires 70,000 bytes.

This command applies to both TFTP and LAT font access.

### *Example*

The following example sets the buffer size to 20,000 bytes:

```
xremote tftp buffersize 20000
```

## XREMOTE TFTP HOST

To add a specific TFTP font server as a source of fonts for the terminal, use the **xremote tftp host** global configuration command. To remove a font server from the list, use the **no** form of this command.

**xremote tftp host** *hostname*
**no xremote tftp host** *hostname*

| *Syntax* | *Description* |
|---|---|
| *hostname* | IP address or name of the host containing fonts. |

*Default*

No TFTP font server is specified.

*Command Mode*

Global configuration

*Usage Guidelines*

This command first appeared in Cisco IOS Release 10.0.

Each time a new host name is entered, the list in the Cisco IOS software is updated. Font servers are queried in the order of their definition when the X terminal requests a font.

*Examples*

The following example sets the host IBM-1 as an XRemote TFTP font server:

```
xremote tftp host IBM-1
```

The following example sets the host with IP address 10.0.0.7 as an XRemote TFTP font server:

```
xremote tftp host 10.0.0.7
```

### XREMOTE TFTP RETRIES

To specify the number of retries the font loader will attempt before declaring an error condition, use the **xremote tftp retries** global configuration command. To restore the default retries number, use the **no** form of this command.

**xremote tftp retries** *retries*
**no xremote tftp retries**

| *Syntax* | *Description* |
|---|---|
| *retries* | (Optional) Number of retries. Acceptable values are decimal numbers in the range from 1 to 15. |

*Default*

3 retries

*Command Mode*

Global configuration

*Usage Guidelines*

This command first appeared in Cisco IOS Release 10.0.

Under certain conditions, you might need to increase the number of retries, particularly if the font servers are known to be heavily loaded.

*Example*

The following example sets the font loader retries to 5:

```
xremote tftp retries 5
```

### XREMOTE XDM



To activate automatic session startup for an XRemote connection, use the **xremote xdm** EXEC command.

**xremote xdm** [*hostname*]

| *Syntax* | *Description* |
|---|---|
| *hostname* | (Optional) Host computer name or IP address. |

*Command Mode*

EXEC

*Usage Guidelines*

This command first appeared in Cisco IOS Release 11.2.

If your host computer supports a server running XDMCP (such as the *xdm* program included in X11R4 or later), you can use automatic session startup to make an XRemote session connection. To do so, use the **xremote xdm** EXEC command.

This command sends an X Display Manager Control Protocol (XDMCP) session startup request to the host computer. If you do not specify a host name or IP address, a broadcast message is sent to all hosts. The first host to respond by starting up a session is used.

The XRemote (the host) server and X terminal stay in XRemote mode until either the display manager terminates the session or the XRemote server receives a reset request from the X terminal.

To exit XRemote sessions, you must quit all active X connections, usually with a command supported by your X client system. Usually, when you quit the last connection (all client processes are stopped), XRemote closes and you return to the EXEC prompt. However, your remote X client system determines how the session closes.

To terminate a session, disconnect from the device on the network using the command specific to that device. Then, exit from the EXEC by using the **exit** command.

### Example

The following example starts a session with a remote host named host1:

```
router> xremote xdm host1
```

### Related Commands

Search online to find documentation for related commands.

**xremote**
**xremote lat**

CHAPTER 21

# Configuring Protocol Translation and Virtual Asynchronous Devices

This chapter describes the configuration of protocol translation and virtual asynchronous connections using Cisco IOS software. The protocol translation facility assumes that you understand how to use the configuration software. Before using this chapter, you should be familiar with the configuration of the protocols for which you want to translate: X.25, Telnet, LAT, TN3270, ARA, PPP, SLIP, and XRemote.

For a complete description of the commands in this chapter, see Chapter 22, "Protocol Translation and Virtual Asynchronous Device Commands."

**NOTES**

Telnet is a remote terminal protocol that is part of the Transmission Control Protocol/Internet Protocol (TCP/IP) suite. The descriptions and examples in the following sections use the term TCP as a reference to Telnet functionality.

The following sections describe the process of tunneling and protocol translation, as well as the two-step and one-step translation methods:

- Cisco's Implementation of Protocol Translation
- Configuring Protocol Translation
- Changing the Number of Supported Translation Sessions
- Configuring Tunneling of SLIP, PPP, or ARA
- Creating X.29 Access Lists
- Creating an X.29 Profile Script
- Defining X.25 Host Names
- Increasing or Decreasing the Number of Virtual Terminal Lines

- Enabling Asynchronous Functions on VTY Lines
- Monitoring and Maintaining Virtual Interfaces
- Monitoring Protocol Translation Connections
- Virtual Template for Protocol Translation Examples
- Protocol Translation Application Examples
- Protocol Translation Session Examples

The X.3 packet assembler/disassembler (PAD) parameters are described in Appendix B, "X.3 PAD Parameters."

## Cisco's Implementation of Protocol Translation

This section describes the additional tasks required to perform protocol translation from one host to another host or to a router. Specifically, it contains the following sections:

- Definition of Protocol Translation
- Definition of Tunneling
- Whether To Use One-Step or Two-Step Protocol Translation
- One-Step Protocol Translation
- Two-Step Protocol Translation
- Tunnel SLIP, PPP, and ARA
- Set Up Virtual Templates for Protocol Translation
- Enable Mobile Remote Node Connections

### Definition of Protocol Translation

The protocol translation feature provides transparent protocol translation between systems running different protocols. It enables terminal users on one network to access hosts on another network, despite differences in the native protocol stacks associated with the originating device and the targeted host.

Protocol translation is a resourceful facility for many business applications. Figure 21–1, for example, shows a remote PC dialing through an IP network and connecting to an X.25 host. The PC's TCP packets undergo a TCP-to-X.25 protocol translation by the Cisco 4700-M router.

### Definition of Tunneling

Unlike other protocols, such as LAT, X.25, and TCP, which are actually translated when you use one-step protocol translation, SLIP, PPP, and ARA are not translated to the destination protocol. Instead, they are carried inside a LAT, X.25, or TCP tunnel specific to the device on the remote network. However, the protocol translation facility is used to enable tunneling of SLIP, PPP, or ARA.

Figure 21–2 shows a typical tunneling scenario.

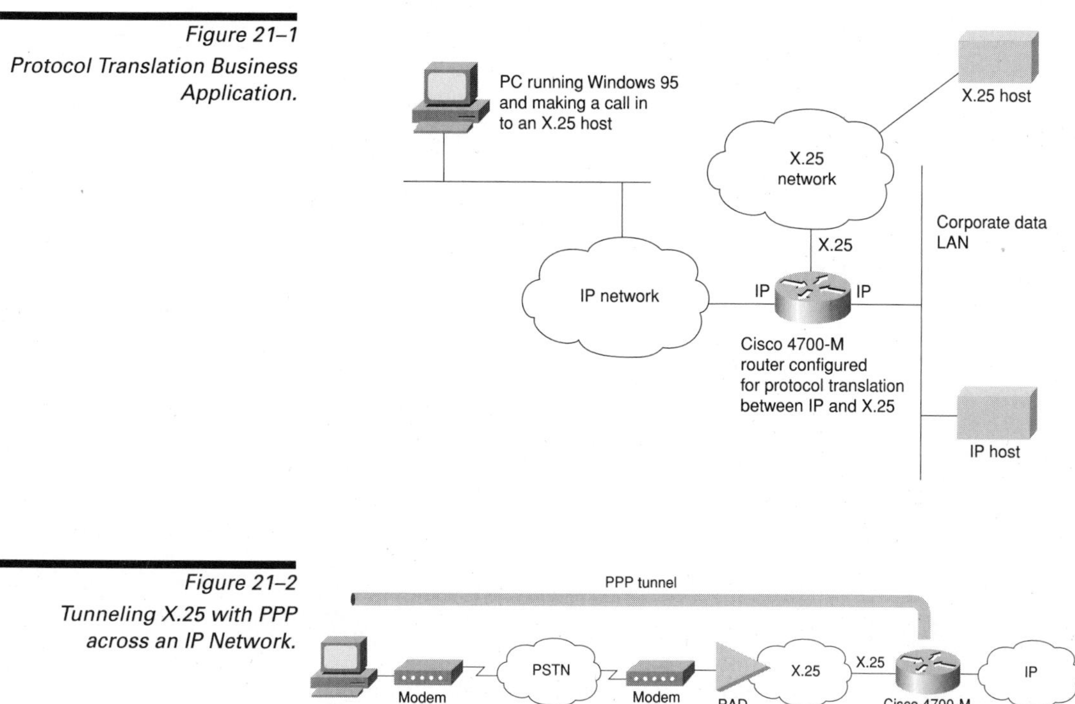


*Figure 21–1*
*Protocol Translation Business Application.*

*Figure 21–2*
*Tunneling X.25 with PPP across an IP Network.*

You can also tunnel IPX PPP over X.25, TCP, or LAT to an IPX network when tunneling PPP on virtual terminal (VTY) lines.

## Whether To Use One-Step or Two-Step Protocol Translation

The Cisco IOS software supports virtual terminal connections in both directions between the protocols in the following list. You can configure the router to translate automatically between them. This is called *one-step translation*, which is the most popular translation method.

- X.25 and local-area transport (LAT)
- X.25 and Telnet sessions using the Transmission Control Protocol (TCP)
- LAT and TCP/Telnet

On outgoing connections, you can also use the one-step protocol translation facility to tunnel SLIP- or PPP-to-IP and -IPX networks or ARA-to-AppleTalk networks across X.25, LAT, or IP (on outgoing connections only).

Cisco IOS software supports limited connections in both directions between the protocols listed in the following list. Connecting between these protocols requires that you first connect to a router, then to the host to which you want to connect. This is called *two-step translation*, which is the least popular translation method.

- XRemote to SLIP/PPP and X.25 PAD environments (XRemote must use the two-step method)
- LAT, X.25, SLIP/PPP, and TCP (Telnet) to TN3270 (TN3270 must use the two-step method)

### One-Step Protocol Translation

Use the one-step method when network users repeatedly log on to the same remote network hosts through a router. This connection is more efficient and enables the device to have more knowledge of the protocols in use because the router acts as a network connection rather than as a terminal. The one-step method provides transparent protocol conversion. When connecting to the remote network host, the user enters the connection command to the remote network host but does not need to specify protocol translation. The network administrator has already created a configuration that defines a connection and the protocols to be translated. The user performs only one step to connect with the host.

When you make a one-step connection to the router, the Cisco IOS software determines which host the connection is for and which protocol that host is using. It then establishes a new network connection using the protocol required by that host.

A disadvantage of the one-step protocol translation method is that the initiating computer or user does not know that two networking protocols are being used. This means that parameters of the foreign network protocols cannot be changed after connections are established. The exception to this limitation is any set of parameters common to both networking protocols. Any parameter common to both can be changed from the first host to the final destination.

To configure the one-step method of protocol translation, set up the following protocols and connection options in the configuration file:

- The incoming connection—The configuration includes the protocol to be used—LAT, X.25, or TCP/IP (Telnet)—the address, and any options such as reverse charging or binary mode that are supported for the incoming connection.
- The outgoing connection—The outgoing connection is defined in the same way as the incoming connection, except that SLIP, PPP (including IP and IPX on PPP sessions), and ARA are also supported.
- The connection features global options—You can specify additional features for the connection to allow, for example, incoming call addresses to match access list conditions or limit the number of users that can make the connection.

See the section "Configuring Protocol Translation," later in this chapter for configuration tasks.

### Two-Step Protocol Translation

Use two-step protocol translation for one-time connections or when you use the router as a general-purpose gateway between two types of networks (for example, X.25 PDN and TCP/IP). As with the one-step method, Cisco recommends that you configure virtual templates for this feature.

**NOTES**

You must use the two-step method for translations of TN3270 and XRemote.

---

With the two-step connection process, you can modify the parameters of either network connection, even while a session is in process. This process is similar to connecting a group of terminal lines from a PAD to a group of terminal lines from a TCP server. The difference is that you do not encounter the wiring complexity, unreliability, management problems, and performance bottlenecks that occur when two devices are connected via asynchronous serial lines.

See the section "Configuring Protocol Translation," later in this chapter for configuration tasks.

### Tunnel SLIP, PPP, and ARA

Unlike other protocols, such as LAT, X.25, and TCP, which are actually translated when you use one-step protocol translation, SLIP, PPP, and ARA are not translated to the destination protocol. Instead, they are carried inside a LAT, X.25, or TCP tunnel specific to the device on the remote network. However, you use the protocol translation facility to enable tunneling of SLIP, PPP, or ARA.

You can also tunnel IPX–PPP over X.25, TCP, or LAT, to an IPX network when tunneling PPP on virtual terminal (VTY) lines.

See the section "Configuring Tunneling of SLIP, PPP, or ARA," later in this chapter for configuration tasks.

#### *One-Step Tunneling of SLIP, PPP, and ARA*

To use one-step protocol translation to tunnel SLIP, PPP (or IPX–PPP), or ARA, you do not need to enter any preliminary commands. Just use the **translate** command with the **slip** or **ppp** keywords for one-step SLIP or PPP connections or **autocommand arap** for one-step ARA connections. Because ARA does not use addressing, you must specify the **autocommand** keyword, then specify the string **arap** to tunnel ARA to an AppleTalk network.

If you are tunneling PPP, SLIP, or ARA across X.25, you must also set up your X.3 profile correctly using the **x29 profile** command, as described in section, "Configure One-Step Tunneling of SLIP or PPP," found later in this chapter.

#### *Two-Step Tunneling of PPP and SLIP*

To tunnel SLIP or PPP across an X.25 WAN to an IP network using the two-step protocol translation method, use the **vty-async** command, which enables you to run PPP and SLIP on VTY lines.

Normally, PPP and SLIP function only on physical asynchronous interfaces. The **vty-async** command enables you to run PPP and SLIP on VTY lines, which permits you to tunnel from an incoming protocol to SLIP or PPP and then to an IP network (or IPX–PPP to an IPX network).

If you make a PAD connection to a router running protocol translation and then issue the **ppp** *definitions* command to connect across an X.25 network, you also must set up your X.3 profile using the **pad** [/**profile** *name*] command.

### Two-Step Tunneling of ARA

To tunnel ARA using the two-step method, you configure ARA on one or more VTY lines and then configure automatic protocol startup. After a user connects to the VTY line and receives an EXEC prompt, ARA starts up automatically on the outgoing VTY line.

## Set Up Virtual Templates for Protocol Translation

The Cisco IOS software simplifies the process of configuring protocol translation to tunnel PPP or SLIP across X.25, TCP, and LAT networks. It does so by providing virtual interface templates that you can configure independently and apply to any protocol translation session. You can configure virtual interface templates for one-step and two-step protocol translation.

A virtual interface template is an interface that exists just inside the router (it is not a physical interface). You can configure virtual interface templates just as you do regular asynchronous serial interfaces. You then apply these virtual interface templates for one-step and two-step protocol translation (the process is described in detail in the later section, "Configuring Protocol Translation"). After a user dials in through a virtual terminal (VTY) line and a tunnel connection is established, the router clones the attributes of the virtual interface template onto a *virtual access interface*. This virtual access interface is a temporary interface that supports the asynchronous protocol configuration specified in the virtual interface template. This virtual access interface is created dynamically and lasts only as long as the tunnel session is active.

Before virtual templates were implemented, you enabled asynchronous protocol functions on VTY lines by creating virtual *asynchronous* interfaces rather than virtual *access* interfaces. (For one-step translation, you did so by specifying **ppp** or **slip** as outgoing options in the **translate** command. For two-step translation, you did so by specifying the **vty-async** command.) The differences between virtual asynchronous interfaces and virtual access interfaces are as follows:

- Virtual asynchronous interfaces are allocated permanently, whereas virtual access interfaces are created dynamically when a user calls in, and are closed down when the connection drops.
- Virtual asynchronous interfaces were unconfigurable. That is, you could create a virtual asynchronous interface, but you could not configure it using interface configuration commands. However, virtual access interfaces are fully configurable via the virtual interface template. All attributes of the virtual interface template are cloned onto the virtual access interface when a call comes in.

Virtual access interfaces replace virtual asynchronous interfaces for both one-step and two-step translation.

You can configure up to 25 virtual interface templates and have up to 300 virtual access interfaces per router (300 is the hardware limit on the router, based on the number of IDBs).

**NOTES**

You can configure only a single virtual interface template when tunneling PPP or SLIP using two-step protocol translation.

Figure 21–3 shows a typical network diagram for a tunnel session from a PC across an X.25 network, through a router set up with a virtual interface template for protocol translation, and to a corporate intranet.

*Figure 21–3*
*PPP Tunnel Session across an X.25 Network.*

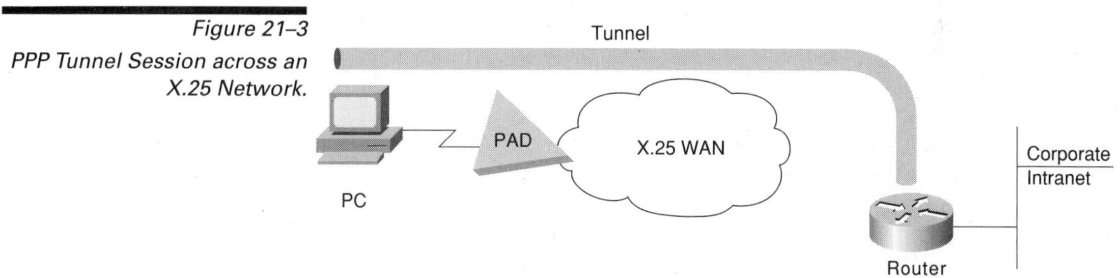


Figure 21–4 shows a typical network diagram for a tunnel session from a PC across a TCP or LAT WAN, through a router set up with a virtual interface template for protocol translation, and to a corporate intranet.

*Figure 21–4*
*PPP Tunnel Session across a TCP or LAT WAN.*

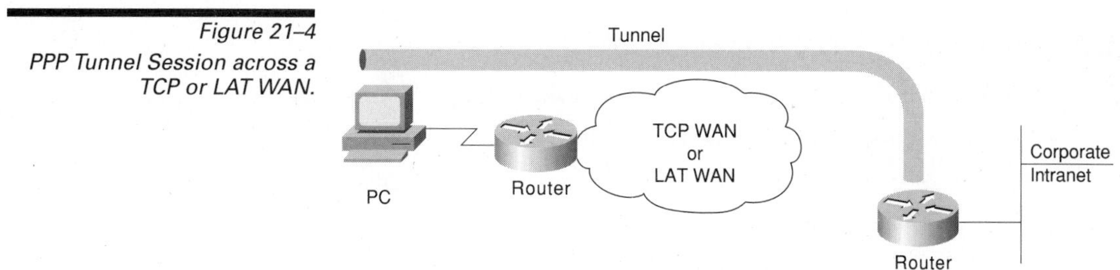


The virtual interface template service for protocol translation provides the following benefits:

- Allows customized configurations to be predefined in one location, then applied dynamically to any protocol translation session, whether one-step or two-step, for easier maintenance.

- Simplifies the **translate** command syntax by reducing the number of options required within each command.
- Makes virtual asynchronous interfaces configurable for both one-step and two-step protocol translation.

### Enable Mobile Remote Node Connections

If you are a mobile user, dialing in to your "home" router from a remote site is often impractical. The asynchronous mobility feature enables you to dial in to different routers elsewhere on the internetwork while experiencing the same server environment that you would if you were connecting directly to your home router.

This asynchronous host mobility is accomplished by *packet tunneling*, a technique by which raw data from the dial-in user is encapsulated and transported directly to the host site where your home router performs the actual protocol processing.

Asynchronous mobility requires setting up a network layer connection between two Cisco routers—the home and remote router. To do so, perform the following task in user EXEC mode:

| Task | Command |
|---|---|
| Set up a network layer connection to a router by specifying its Internet name or address. | **tunnel** *host* |

From a router other than a Cisco router, you must use Telnet.

After a connection is established, you receive an authentication dialog or prompt from your home router, and can proceed as if you are connected directly to that router. When communications are complete, the network connection can be closed and terminated from either end of the connection.

The home router must be configured correctly to accept the tunnel connection.

## CONFIGURING PROTOCOL TRANSLATION

To configure protocol translation, perform the tasks in the following sections:

- Configure One-Step Protocol Translation
- Configure a Virtual Template for One-Step Protocol Translation
- Configure Two-Step Protocol Translation
- Configure a Virtual Template for Two-Step Protocol Translation

### Configure One-Step Protocol Translation

To create one-step protocol translation connection specifications, perform the following task in global configuration mode:

| Task | Command |
|---|---|
| Create the connection specifications for one-step protocol translation. | **translate** *protocol incoming-address* [*in-options*] *protocol outgoing-address* [*out-options*] [*global-options*] |

For incoming PAD connections, the router uses a default PAD profile to set the remote X.3 PAD parameters unless a profile script is defined in the **translate** command. To override the default PAD profile the router uses, you must create a PAD profile script using the **x29 profile** global configuration command. In the following example, *default* is the name of the default PAD profile script and *parameter:value* is the X.3 PAD parameter number and value separated by a colon.

```
x29 profile default parameter:value [parameter:value]
```

## Configure a Virtual Template for One-Step Protocol Translation

To configure a virtual interface template to enable tunneling of PPP or SLIP across an X.25, TCP, or LAT WAN, first create and configure a virtual interface template, then apply it as the single outgoing option to the **translate** command.

**NOTES**

Virtual interface templates in general support all commands available on any serial interface, because virtual templates are used for purposes other than protocol translation. However, a virtual access interface—which clones the configuration of the corresponding virtual interface template when created for protocol translation—supports only asynchronous protocol commands.

To enable tunneling of PPP or SLIP across an X.25, TCP, or LAT WAN by using one-step protocol translation, complete the following tasks beginning in global configuration mode:

| Task | | Command |
|---|---|---|
| **Step 1** | Create a virtual interface template, and enter interface configuration mode. | **interface virtual-template** *number* |
| **Step 2** | Assign an IP address to the virtual interface template. | **ip unnumbered ethernet** 0* |
| **Step 3** | Enable encapsulation on the virtual interface template. | **encapsulation** {**ppp** \| **slip**}† |
| **Step 4** | Assign an IP address to the device connecting to the virtual access interface (such as the PC in ). | peer default ip address {*ip-address* \| dhcp \| pool [*pool-name*]} |
| **Step 5** | Exit back to global configuration mode. | exit |

| Task | Command |
|---|---|
| **Step 6** Assign the virtual interface template to a protocol translation session. | **translate** {**lat** \| **tcp** \| **x25**} *incoming-address* [*in-options*] **virtual-template** *number* [*global-options*] |

* You can also assign a specific IP address by using the **ip address** *address* command, though assigning the IP address of the Ethernet 0 interface as shown is most common.

† Virtual interface templates use PPP encapsulation by default, so you need not specify **encapsulation ppp**. However, to use SLIP encapsulation, you must explicitly specify **encapsulation slip**.

Rather than specifying outgoing translation options in the **translate** command, configure these options as interface configuration commands under the virtual interface template, then apply the virtual interface template to the **translate** command. Table 21–1 maps outgoing **translate** command options to interface commands you can configure in the virtual interface template.

**Table 21–1** *Mapping Outgoing Translate Command Options to Interface Commands*

| Translate Command Options | Corresponding Interface Configuration Command |
|---|---|
| **ip-pool** | **peer default ip address** {**ip-address** \| **dhcp** \| **pool** [*poolname*]} |
| **header-compression** | **ip tcp header compression** [**on** \| **off** \| **passive**] |
| **routing** | **ip routing** or **ipx routing** |
| **mtu** | **mtu** |
| **keepalive** | **keepalive** |
| **authentication** {**chap** \| **pap**} | **ppp authentication** {**chap** \| **pap**} |
| **ppp use-tacacs** | **ppp use-tacacs** |
| **ipx loopback** | **ipx ppp-client loopback** *number* |

## Configure Two-Step Protocol Translation

To translate using the two-step method, perform the following task beginning in global configuration mode. The first step is required only if you are tunneling SLIP or PPP using the two-step protocol translation facility:

| Task | Command |
|---|---|
| **Step 1** Establish an incoming connection to the router running protocol translation. | **connect**<br>**lat**<br>**pad**<br>**telnet**<br>**tunnel** |

| Task | | Command |
|---|---|---|
| **Step 2** | Establish the outgoing connection from the router supporting protocol translation to another network host. | **connect**<br>**lat**<br>**pad**<br>**telnet**<br>**tunnel**<br>**ppp**<br>**slip** |

The Cisco IOS software supports the two-step method in both directions for protocols other than PPP and SLIP (for example, from Telnet to PAD, and vice versa). PPP and SLIP are supported on outgoing connections only.

### Configure a Virtual Template for Two-Step Protocol Translation

If you are tunneling PPP or SLIP using two-step protocol translation with virtual interface templates, you still use the **vty-async** command, just as before implementation of virtual templates. However, virtual asynchronous interfaces are not created as they were before virtual interface templates. Virtual access interfaces are created dynamically when a tunnel connection is established.

To create and configure a virtual interface template and apply it to a two-step protocol translation session, complete the following tasks beginning in global configuration mode:

| Task | | Command |
|---|---|---|
| **Step 1** | Create a virtual interface template, and enter interface configuration mode. | **interface virtual-template** *number* |
| **Step 2** | Assign an IP address to the virtual interface template. | **ip unnumbered ethernet 0**[*] |
| **Step 3** | Enable encapsulation on the virtual interface template. | **encapsulation** {**ppp** \| **slip**}[†] |
| **Step 4** | Assign an IP address to the device connecting to the virtual access interface (such as the PC in ). | peer default ip address {*ip-address* \| dhcp \| pool [*pool-name*]} |
| **Step 5** | Exit back to global configuration mode. | exit |
| **Step 6** | Create a virtual asynchronous interface. | vty-async |
| **Step 7** | Apply the virtual template to the virtual asynchronous interface. | vty-async virtual-template *number* |

[*] You can also assign a specific IP address by using the **ip address** *address* command, though assigning the IP address of the Ethernet0 interface as shown is most common.

[†] Virtual interface templates use PPP encapsulation by default, so you need not specify **encapsulation ppp**. However, to use SLIP encapsulation, you must explicitly specify **encapsulation slip**.

Other asynchronous configuration commands can be added to the virtual template configuration. It is recommended that you include security on your virtual interface template. For example, you can enter the **ppp authentication chap** command.

## Changing the Number of Supported Translation Sessions

Because each protocol translation session uses a virtual terminal (VTY) line, you need to increase the number of VTY lines to increase the number of protocol translation sessions. That is, if your router has 10 VTY lines, you can have up to 10 protocol translation sessions. The default number of VTY lines is 5 (lines 0 through 4). To increase the number of lines, and thus the maximum number of protocol translation sessions, perform the following tasks, as appropriate, beginning in global configuration mode:

| Task | Command |
|---|---|
| Increase the number of virtual terminal lines, and thus, the maximum number of protocol translation sessions. | **line vty** *number* |
| Decrease the number of virtual terminal lines, and thus, the maximum number of protocol translation sessions. | **no line vty** *number* |

Protocol translation is a CPU-intensive task. Increasing the number of protocol translation sessions while routing is enabled can impact available memory. The amount of memory available depends on the platform type, the amount of DRAM available, the activity of each translation session, and the speed of the link. If you are using the maximum number of sessions and have problems with memory, you might need to decrease the number of protocol translation sessions.

## Configuring Tunneling of SLIP, PPP, or ARA

This section describes how to perform the following tasks:

- Configure One-Step Tunneling of SLIP or PPP
- Configure One-Step Tunneling of ARA
- Configure Two-Step Tunneling of SLIP or PPP
- Enable Dynamic Address Assignment for Outgoing PPP and SLIP on VTY Lines

You can also enable IPX over tunneled PPP sessions.

### Configure One-Step Tunneling of SLIP or PPP

To tunnel SLIP or PPP using the one-step protocol translation facility, perform the following task in global configuration mode:

| Task | Command |
|---|---|
| (Optional) If you are tunneling PPP over X.25, create an X.3 Profile so that the router will interoperate with the PAD. | **x29 profile** *name parameter:value* [*parameter:value*] |
| Create the connection specifications for one-step protocol translation. | **translate** *protocol incoming-address* [*in-options*] *protocol* *outgoing-address* [*out-options*] [*global-options*] |

If you are configuring PPP over X.25 and do not know which X.3 profile parameters to use, try the following (these parameters do not function in all cases; they are simply a place from which to start):

> 1:0, 2:0, 3:2, 4:1, 5:0, 6:0, 7:21, 8:0, 9:0, 10:0, 11:14, 12:0, 13:0, 14:0, 15:0, 16:127, 17:24, 18:18, 19:0, 20:0, 21:0, 22:0

For more information about creating an X.29 profile script, see section, "Creating an X.29 Profile Script," found later in this chapter. For an example of configuring PPP over X.25, see section, "Tunneling PPP over X.25 Example," found later in this chapter.

You can configure an outgoing session for IPX–PPP. To do so, issue the **ipx loopback** *number* option for the outgoing session.

To tunnel SLIP or PPP across X.25, LAT, or Telnet using the one-step method, you do not need to enter any additional commands, as you do when you tunnel SLIP or PPP using the two-step method. The **translate** command enables asynchronous protocol features on one VTY line at a time.

PPP and SLIP, including IPX–PPP, can be tunnelled on outgoing connections only.

## Configure One-Step Tunneling of ARA

To tunnel ARA using the one-step protocol translation facility, perform the following tasks, beginning in global configuration mode. The first four steps are required. The next seven steps (5 through 11) are optional:

| Task | | Command |
|---|---|---|
| **Step 1** | Turn on AppleTalk routing. | **appletalk routing** |
| **Step 2** | Use the protocol translation facility to enable an ARA tunnel across a remote network. | **translate** *protocol incoming-address* [*in-options*] **autocommand arap** |
| **Step 3** | Enter line configuration mode. | **line vty** *line-number* [*ending-line-number*] |
| **Step 4** | Enable ARA on one or more lines. | **arap enable** |
| **Step 5** | Set one or more dedicated ARA lines. | **arap dedicated** |

| Task | | Command |
|---|---|---|
| **Step 6** | Set the session time limit. | **arap timelimit** [*minutes*] |
| **Step 7** | Set the disconnect warning time. | **arap warningtime** [*minutes*] |
| **Step 8** | Disallow guests. | **arap noguest** |
| **Step 9** | Require manual password entry. | **arap require-manual-password** |
| **Step 10** | Limit the zones the Macintosh user sees. | **arap zonelist** *zone-access-list-number* |
| **Step 11** | Control access to networks. | **arap net-access-list** *net-access-list number* |

## Configure Two-Step Tunneling of SLIP or PPP

To tunnel SLIP or PPP using the two-step protocol translation facility, perform the following tasks, beginning in global configuration mode:

| Task | | Command |
|---|---|---|
| **Step 1** | Enable tunneling of PPP and SLIP using two-step protocol translation. | **vty-async** |
| **Step 2** | Exit from global configuration mode into EXEC mode. | **exit** |
| **Step 3** | Establish an incoming connection to the router running protocol translation. | **connect**<br>**lat**<br>**pad**<br>**telnet**<br>**tunnel** |
| **Step 4** | Establish the outgoing connection from the router supporting protocol translation to another network host. | **connect**<br>**slip**<br>**ppp**<br>**tunnel** |

If you want to configure IPX over your PPP sessions on VTY lines, see Chapter 27, "Configuring Asynchronous PPP and SLIP."

## Enable Dynamic Address Assignment for Outgoing PPP and SLIP on VTY Lines

You can specify IP addresses dynamically from a Dynamic Host Configuration Protocol (DHCP) proxy client or a local IP address pool on outgoing PPP and SLIP sessions on VTY lines.

### Assign IP Addresses Using DHCP

The Dynamic Host Control Protocol (DHCP) client-proxy feature manages a pool of IP addresses available to PPP or SLIP dial-in clients without a known IP address. This allows a finite number of IP addresses to be reused quickly and efficiently by many clients. Additional benefits include the ability to maintain sessions, such as Telnet, even when a modem line fails. When the client is auto-dialed back in to the access server or router, the session can be resumed because the same IP address is reissued to the client by the access server or router.

A DHCP proxy client is a Cisco access server or router configured to arbitrate DHCP calls between a DHCP server and a DHCP client.

To assign IP addresses using DHCP, perform the following tasks in global configuration mode:

| Task | | Command |
|---|---|---|
| **Step 1** | Specify that the router use the DHCP client-proxy. | **ip address-pool dhcp-proxy-client** |
| **Step 2** | Specify DHCP pooling for the SLIP or PPP client on the outgoing session. | **translate** *protocol incoming-address* [*in-options*] {**slip** \| **ppp**} **ip-pool** |

The name argument is the name of the DHCP proxy client specified with the **ip address-pool dhcp-proxy-client** command.

### Assign IP Addresses Using Local IP Address Pooling

You can make temporary IP addresses available for outgoing PPP and SLIP clients on outgoing sessions. To do so, you must first specify that the Cisco IOS software use a local IP address pool on all asynchronous interfaces and create one or more local IP address pools. You then assign local pooling as part of the **translate** command. To assign IP addresses dynamically on a virtual asynchronous connection, perform the following task beginning in global configuration mode:

| Task | | Command |
|---|---|---|
| **Step 1** | Specify that the router use a local IP address pool on all asynchronous interfaces. | **ip address-pool local** |
| **Step 2** | Create one or more local IP address pools. | **ip local-pool** *name begin-ip-address-range* [*end-ip-address-range*] |
| **Step 3** | Specify local pooling for the SLIP or PPP client on the outgoing session. | **translate** *protocol incoming-address* [*in-options*] **slip** \| **ppp ip-pool** [**scope-name** *name*] |

The **scope-name** option takes the name of any local IP address pool that has been defined using the **ip local-pool** command.

## Creating X.29 Access Lists

Cisco IOS software provides access lists to limit access to a router from certain X.25 hosts. Access lists take advantage of the message field defined by "Recommendation X.29," which describes procedures for exchanging data between two PADs or between a PAD and a DTE device.

To define X.29 access lists, perform the following tasks:

1. Create an access list.
2. Apply an access list to a virtual line or include it in a **translate** command.

These tasks are described in the following sections.

When configuring protocol translation, you can specify an access list number with each **translate** command. In the case of translation sessions that result from incoming PAD connections, the corresponding X.29 access list is used.

### Create an Access List

To specify the access conditions, perform the following task in global configuration mode:

| Task | Command |
|---|---|
| Restrict incoming and outgoing connections between a particular virtual terminal line (into a router) and the addresses in an access list. | **x29 access-list** *access-list-number* {**permit** \| **deny**} *regular-expression* |

An access list can contain any number of lines. The lists are processed in the order in which you type the entries. The first match causes the permit or deny condition. If an X.121 address does not match any of the entries in the access list, access is denied.

### Apply an Access List to a Virtual Line

To apply an access list to a virtual line, perform the following task in line configuration mode:

| Task | Command |
|---|---|
| Restrict incoming and outgoing connections between a particular virtual terminal line (into a router) and the addresses in an access list. | **access-class** *number* **in** |

The access list number is used for incoming TCP access and incoming PAD access. For TCP access, the access server or router using protocol translation uses the defined IP access lists. For incoming PAD connections, the same X.29 access list is used. If you want to have access restrictions on only one of the protocols, you can create an access list that permits all addresses for the other protocol.

**NOTES**

For an example of including an access list in a **translate** command, see section, "Tunneling PPP over X.25 Example," found near the end of this chapter.

## CREATING AN X.29 PROFILE SCRIPT

You can create an X.29 profile script for the **translate** command to use. An X.29 profile script uses X.3 PAD parameters. When an X.25 connection is established, the Cisco IOS software configured for protocol translation functions similar to an X.29 SET PARAMETER packet, which contains the parameters and values set by this command.

To create an X.29 profile script, perform the following global configuration task:

| Task | Command |
|---|---|
| Create an X.29 profile script. | **x29 profile** {**default** \| *name*} *parameter:value* [*parameter:value*] |

For incoming PAD connections, the router running protocol translation uses a default PAD profile to set the remote X.3 PAD parameters, unless a profile script is defined in the **translate** command. To override the default PAD profile the router uses, you must create a PAD profile script named *default* by using the **x29 profile** {**default** | *name*} *parameter:value* [*parameter:value*] global configuration command, where *default* is the name of the default PAD profile script and *parameter:value* is the X.3 PAD parameter number and value separated by a colon. For more information about X.3 PAD parameters, see Appendix B.

You can also create an X.29 profile script when connecting to a PAD using the **pad** [**/profile** *name*] EXEC command, which is described in Chapter 24, "PAD and X.25 Connection Setup Commands."

## DEFINING X.25 HOST NAMES

This section describes how to define symbolic host names. This means that instead of remembering a long numeric address for an X.25 host, you can refer to the X.25 host using a symbolic host name. To define a symbolic host name, perform the following task in global configuration mode:

| Task | Command |
|---|---|
| Define a symbolic host name. | **x25 host** *name x.121-address* [**cud** *call-user-data*] |

## Increasing or Decreasing the Number of Virtual Terminal Lines

Because each protocol translation session uses a virtual terminal (VTY) line, you need to increase the number of VTY lines to increase the number of protocol translation sessions. That is, if your router has 10 VTY lines, you can have up to 10 protocol translation sessions. The default number of VTY lines is 5 (lines 0 through 4). To increase the number of lines, and thus the maximum number of protocol translation sessions, perform the following tasks, as appropriate, beginning in global configuration mode:

| Task | Command |
|---|---|
| Increase the number of virtual terminal lines, and thus, the maximum number of protocol translation sessions. | **line vty** *number* |
| Decrease the number of virtual terminal lines, and thus, the maximum number of protocol translation sessions. | **no line vty** *number* |

Protocol translation is a CPU-intensive task. Increasing the number of protocol translation sessions while routing is enabled can impact available memory. The amount of memory available depends on the platform type, the amount of DRAM available, the activity of each translation session, and the speed of the link. If you are using the maximum number of sessions and have problems with memory, you might need to decrease the number of protocol translation sessions.

The maximum number of protocol translation sessions for each platform can be increased to the number specified in Table 21–2. One VTY line is required for each protocol translation session.

**Table 21–2** *Maximum Number of Protocol Translation Sessions by Platform*

| Platform | Default Number of VTY Lines | Total Number of Lines* | Maximum vty Lines with PT Option |
|---|---|---|---|
| Cisco 1000 running Cisco IOS software | 5 | 6 | 5 |
| Cisco 2500 series (8 asynchronous ports) | 5 | 200 | 190 |
| Cisco 2500 series (16 asynchronous ports) | 5 | 200 | 182 |
| Cisco 3000 series | 5 | 200 | 198 |
| Cisco 3640 | 5 | 1002 | 872 |
| Cisco 3620 | 5 | 1002 | 936 |
| Cisco 4000 series | 5 | 200 | 198 |
| Cisco 4500 series | 5 | 1002 | 1000 |
| Cisco 4700 series | 5 | 1002 | 1000 |

**Table 21–2** *Maximum Number of Protocol Translation Sessions by Platform, Continued*

| Platform | Default Number of VTY Lines | Total Number of Lines* | Maximum vty Lines with PT Option |
|---|---|---|---|
| Cisco AS5200 | 5 | 200 | 182 |
| Cisco 7000 series | 5 | 120 | 118 |
| Cisco 7200 series | 5 | 1002 | 1000 |
| Cisco 7000 series with RSP | 5 | 1002 | 1000 |

* Maximum number of VTYs + (TTYs + AUX + CON lines).

## Enabling Asynchronous Functions on VTY Lines

Using Cisco IOS software, you can configure asynchronous protocol features, such as PPP and SLIP, on VTY lines. PPP and SLIP normally function only on asynchronous interfaces, not on VTY lines. When you configure a VTY line to support asynchronous protocol features, you are creating *virtual asynchronous interfaces* on the VTY lines. One practical benefit of virtual asynchronous interfaces is the ability to tunnel PPP and SLIP across X.25, TCP, or LAT networks on VTY lines. You tunnel PPP and SLIP using the protocol translation facility.

Perform the tasks in the following sections to configure and use virtual asynchronous interfaces. The first task is required; the remaining tasks are optional.

- Create Virtual Asynchronous Interfaces
- Enable Protocol Translation of PPP and SLIP on Virtual Asynchronous Interfaces
- Enable Dynamic Routing on Virtual Asynchronous Interfaces
- Enable TCP/IP Header Compression on Virtual Asynchronous Interfaces
- Enable Keepalive Updates on Virtual Asynchronous Interfaces
- Set an MTU on Virtual Asynchronous Interfaces
- Enable PPP Authentication on Virtual Asynchronous Interfaces
- Enable PPP Authentication via TACACS on Virtual Asynchronous Interfaces

**Notes**

These tasks enable PPP and SLIP on a virtual asynchronous interface on a global basis on the router. To configure SLIP or PPP on a per-VTY basis, use the **translate** command.

### Create Virtual Asynchronous Interfaces

To create a virtual asynchronous interface, perform the following task in global configuration mode:

| Task | Command |
|---|---|
| Configure all virtual terminal lines to support asynchronous protocol features. | **vty-async** |

### Enable Protocol Translation of PPP and SLIP on Virtual Asynchronous Interfaces

One practical benefit of enabling virtual asynchronous interfaces is the ability to tunnel PPP and SLIP over X.25, thus extending remote node capability into the X.25 area. You can also tunnel PPP and SLIP over Telnet or LAT on virtual terminal lines. You can tunnel PPP and SLIP over X.25, LAT, or Telnet, but you do so by using the protocol translation feature in the Cisco IOS software.

To tunnel incoming dial-up SLIP or PPP connections over X.25, LAT, or TCP to an IP network, you can use one-step protocol translation or two-step protocol translation, as follows:

- If you are tunneling SLIP or PPP using the one-step method, you do not need to enter the **vty-async** command. Using the **translate** command with the SLIP or PPP keywords for one-step connections automatically enables asynchronous protocol functions on a per-VTY basis.
- If you are tunneling SLIP or PPP using the two-step method, you must first enter the **vty-async** command on a global basis. Next, you perform a two-step connection process.

### Enable IPX–PPP over X.25 to an IPX Network on VTY Lines

You can enable IPX–PPP on VTYs, which permits clients to log in to a VTY on a router, invoke a PPP session at the EXEC prompt to a host, and run IPX to the host.

For example, in Figure 21–5, the client Terminal on the X.25 network logs in to the VTY line on the access server, which is configured for IPX–PPP. When the user connects to the access server and the EXEC prompt appears, the user issues the PPP command to connect to the IPX host. The VTY is configured to run IPX, so when the PPP session is established from the access server, the terminal can access the IPX host using an IPX application.

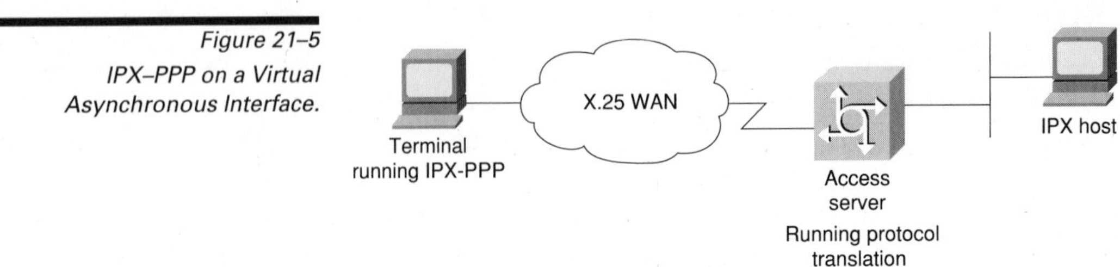


*Figure 21–5 IPX–PPP on a Virtual Asynchronous Interface.*

To enable IPX to run over your PPP sessions on VTY lines, perform the following tasks, beginning in global configuration mode:

| Task | | Command |
|---|---|---|
| **Step 1** | Enable IPX routing. | **ipx routing** [*node*] |
| **Step 2** | Create a loopback interface. | **interface loopback** *number* |
| **Step 3** | Enable a virtual IPX network on the loopback interface. | **ipx network** *network*[*] |
| **Step 4** | Enable IPX–PPP on VTY lines by assigning the VTY to the loopback interface configured for IPX. | **vty-async ipx ppp-client loopback** *number* |

[*] Every loopback interface must have a *unique* IPX network number.

## Enable Dynamic Routing on Virtual Asynchronous Interfaces

To route IP packets using the IGRP, RIP, and OSPF routing protocols on virtual asynchronous interfaces, perform the following task in global configuration mode:

| Task | Command |
|---|---|
| Enable dynamic routing of IP packets on all virtual terminal lines. | **vty-async dynamic-routing** |

When you make a connection, you must specify the **routing** *keyword* on the SLIP or PPP command line.

**NOTES**

The **vty-async dynamic routing** command is similar to the **async dynamic routing** command, except that the **async dynamic routing** command is used for physical asynchronous interfaces, and the **vty-async dynamic-routing** command is used on virtual terminal lines configured for asynchronous protocol functionality.

## Enable TCP/IP Header Compression on Virtual Asynchronous Interfaces

You can compress the headers on TCP/IP packets on virtual asynchronous interfaces to reduce their size and increase performance. This feature only compresses the TCP header, so it has no effect on UDP packets or other protocol headers. The TCP header compression technique, described fully in RFC 1144, is supported on virtual asynchronous interfaces using PPP and SLIP encapsulation. You must enable compression on both ends of the connection.

Optionally, you can specify outgoing packets to be compressed only if TCP incoming packets on the same virtual terminal line are compressed. If you do not specify this option, the Cisco IOS software will compress all traffic. The default is no compression. This option is valid for SLIP.

To compress the headers of outgoing TCP packets on virtual asynchronous interfaces, perform the following task in global configuration mode:

| Task | Command |
|---|---|
| Enable header compression on IP packets on all virtual terminal lines. | **vty-async header-compression** [**passive**] |

### Enable Keepalive Updates on Virtual Asynchronous Interfaces

Keepalive updates are enabled on all virtual asynchronous interfaces by default. To change the keepalive timer or disable it on virtual asynchronous interfaces, perform the following task in global configuration mode:

| Task | Command |
|---|---|
| Specify the frequency with which the Cisco IOS software sends keepalive messages to the other end of an asynchronous serial link. | **vty-async keepalive** [*seconds*] |

The default interval is 10 seconds. It is adjustable in 1-second increments from 0 to 32,767 seconds. To turn off keepalive updates, set the value to 0. A connection is declared down after three update intervals have passed without receiving a keepalive packet.

Virtual terminal lines have very low bandwidth. When adjusting the keepalive timer, large packets can delay the smaller keepalive packets long enough to cause the session to disconnect. You might need to experiment to determine the best value.

### Set an MTU on Virtual Asynchronous Interfaces

The maximum transmission unit (MTU) refers to the size of an IP packet. You might want to change to a smaller MTU size for IP packets transmitted on a virtual asynchronous interface for any of the following reasons:

- The SLIP or PPP application at the other end only supports packets up to a certain size.
- You want to ensure a shorter delay by using smaller packets.
- The host Telnet echoing takes longer than 0.2 seconds.

  For example, at 9600 baud, a 1500-byte packet takes about 1.5 seconds to transmit. This delay would indicate that you want an MTU size of about 200 (1.5 seconds / 0.2 seconds = 7.5 and 1500-byte packet / 7.5 = 200-byte packet).

To specify the maximum IP packet size, perform the following task in interface configuration mode:

| Task | Command |
|---|---|
| Specify the size of the largest IP packet that the virtual asynchronous interface can support. | **vty-async mtu** *bytes* |

The default MTU size is 1,500 bytes. Possible values are 64 bytes to 1,000,000 bytes.

The TCP protocol running on the remote device can have a different MTU size than the MTU size configured on your router. Because the Cisco IOS software performs IP fragmentation of packets larger than the specified MTU, do not change the MTU size unless the SLIP or PPP implementation running on the host at the other end of the asynchronous line supports reassembly of IP fragments.

## Enable PPP Authentication on Virtual Asynchronous Interfaces

You can enable Challenge Handshake Authentication Protocol (CHAP) or Password Authentication Protocol (PAP) for authentication of PPP on VTY lines set up for asynchronous protocol features.

**NOTES**

Passwords cannot contain spaces or underscores. A user with a password containing spaces or underscores will not be able to log in to a TTY or VTY line.

### *Enable CHAP*

Access control using Challenge Handshake Authentication Protocol (CHAP) is available on all virtual asynchronous interfaces configured for PPP encapsulation. The authentication feature reduces the risk of security violations on your router.

When CHAP is enabled, a remote device (such as a PC, workstation, or router) attempting to connect to the local router is requested, or "challenged," to respond.

The challenge consists of an ID, a random number, and either the host name of the local router or the name of the user on the remote device. This challenge is transmitted to the remote device.

The required response consists of two parts:

- An encrypted version of the ID, a secret password (or secret), and the random number
- Either the host name of the remote device or the name of the user on the remote device

When the local router receives the challenge response, it verifies the secret by looking up the name given in the response and performing the same encryption operation. The secret passwords must be identical on the remote device and the local router.

By transmitting this response, the secret is never transmitted, thus preventing other devices from stealing it and gaining illegal access to the system. Without the proper response, the remote device cannot connect to the local router.

CHAP transactions occur only when a link is established. The local router does not request a password during the rest of the session. (The local router can, however, respond to such requests from other devices during a session.)

To use CHAP on virtual asynchronous interfaces for PPP, perform the following task in global configuration mode:

| Task | Command |
|---|---|
| Enable CHAP on all virtual asynchronous interfaces. | **vty-async ppp authentication chap** |

CHAP is specified in RFC 1334. It is an additional authentication phase of the PPP Link Control Protocol.

Once you have enabled CHAP, the local router requires a response from the remote devices. If the remote device does not support CHAP, no traffic is passed to that device.

### *Enable PAP*

Access control using the Password Authentication Protocol (PAP) is available on all virtual asynchronous interfaces configured for PPP encapsulation. The authentication feature reduces the risk of security violations on your router.

To use PAP, perform the following task in interface configuration mode:

| Task | Command |
|---|---|
| Enable PAP on all virtual asynchronous interfaces. | **vty-async ppp authentication pap** |

## Enable PPP Authentication via TACACS on Virtual Asynchronous Interfaces

Access control using the Terminal Access Controller Access Control System (TACACS) is available on all virtual asynchronous interfaces configured for PPP encapsulation. The authentication feature reduces the risk of security violations on your router.

To use TACACS with either CHAP or PAP, perform the following task in global configuration mode:

| Task | Command |
|---|---|
| Enable TACACS on all virtual asynchronous interfaces. | **vty-async ppp use-tacacs** |

### Mobile Remote Node Example

The following example establishes a network layer connection with an IBM host named `mktg`:

```
Router> tunnel mktg
```

## MONITORING AND MAINTAINING VIRTUAL INTERFACES

This section describes how to perform the following optional tasks:

- Monitor and Maintain a Virtual Access Interface
- Display a Virtual Asynchronous Interface

### Monitor and Maintain a Virtual Access Interface

When a virtual interface template is applied to a protocol translation session, a virtual access interface is created dynamically. This is the only way a virtual access interface can be created; it cannot be created directly. However, a virtual access interface can be cleared and displayed.

To display or clear a specific virtual access interface, perform the relevant task(s):

| Task | Command |
|---|---|
| Identify the number associated with the virtual access interface, so you can display statistics about the interface or clear the interface. | **show users** [**all**] |
| Display the configuration of the virtual access interface. | **show interface virtual-access** *number* |
| Tear down the virtual access interface and free the memory for other dial-in uses. | **clear interface virtual-access** *number* |

### Display a Virtual Asynchronous Interface

When the configuration of a virtual interface template is cloned to a VTY line configured as a virtual access interface for two-step protocol translation, you can view information about the VTY line by performing the following tasks:

| Task | Command |
|---|---|
| Display statistics about a VTY line. | **show line** *number* |
| Display interfaces about a virtual asynchronous interface (an asynchronous interface created on a VTY line). | **show interfaces vty** *number* |

## Monitoring Protocol Translation Connections

This section describes how to log significant VTY-asynchronous authentication information, such as the X.121 calling address, Call User Data (CUD), and the IP address assigned to a VTY asynchronous connection. Depending on how you configure the logging information to be displayed, you can direct this authentication information to the console, an internal buffer, or a UNIX syslog server. This authentication information can be used to associate an incoming PAD VTY-asynchronous connection with an IP address.

**Notes**

By default, the Cisco IOS software displays all messages to the console terminal.

This section describes how to perform the following tasks:

- Log VTY-Async Authentication Information to the Console Terminal
- Log VTY-Async Authentication Information to a Buffer
- Log VTY-Async Authentication Information to a UNIX Syslog Server

### Log VTY-Async Authentication Information to the Console Terminal

To log significant VTY-asynchronous authentication information to the console terminal, perform the following task in global configuration mode:

| Task | Command |
|---|---|
| Log significant VTY-asynchronous authentication information. | **service pt-vty-logging** |

### Log VTY-Async Authentication Information to a Buffer

To log significant VTY-asynchronous authentication information to a buffer, perform the following tasks in global configuration mode:

| Task | Command |
|---|---|
| Log significant VTY-asynchronous authentication information. | **service pt-vty-logging** |
| Direct the authentication log information to a buffer. | **logging buffered** [*size*] |

### Log VTY-Async Authentication Information to a UNIX Syslog Server

To log significant VTY-asynchronous authentication information to a UNIX syslog server, perform the following tasks in global configuration mode:

| Task | Command |
|---|---|
| Log significant VTY-asynchronous authentication information. | **service pt-vty-logging** |
| Direct the authentication log information to a UNIX syslog server. | **logging** *host* |

## VIRTUAL TEMPLATE FOR PROTOCOL TRANSLATION EXAMPLES

This section shows examples of configuring tunneling of PPP and SLIP using one-step and two-step protocol translation in the following sections:

- One-Step Examples
- Two-Step Examples

### One-Step Examples

The following examples show how to configure a virtual template and apply them in one-step protocol translation sessions.

#### *Tunneling PPP across X.25 Example*

In the following example, the virtual interface template specifies a peer IP address of 172.18.2.131, which is the IP address of the PC in Figure 21–6. The virtual interface template explicitly specifies PPP encapsulation. The translation is from X.25 to PPP, which enables tunneling of PPP across an X.25 network, as shown in Figure 21–6.

```
interface virtual-template 1
 ip unnumbered Ethernet0
 ! static address of 172.18.2.131 for the PC dialing in to the corporate intranet
 peer default ip address 172.18.2.131
 encapsulation ppp
!
! X.121 address of 5555678 is the number the PAD dials to connect through the router
translate x25 5555678 virtual-template 1
```

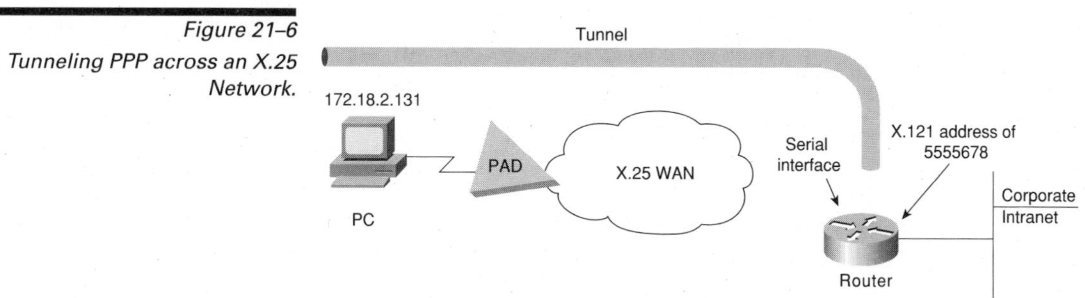


*Figure 21–6 Tunneling PPP across an X.25 Network.*

### Tunneling SLIP across X.25 Example

The virtual template interface in this example uses SLIP encapsulation, instead of the PPP encapsulation.

```
interface Virtual-Template5
 ip unnumbered Ethernet0
 encapsulation slip
 peer default ip address 172.22.2.130
!
translate x25 5555000 virtual-template 5
```

### Tunneling PPP across X.25, and Specifying CHAP and Access List Security Example

The virtual template interface in this example uses PPP encapsulation, although it is not explicitly specified. It also uses CHAP authentication and an X.29 access list.

```
x29 access-list 1 permit ^5555
!
interface Virtual-Template1
 ip unnumbered Ethernet0
 peer default ip address 172.16.2.129
 ppp authentication chap
!
translate x25 5555667 virtual-template 1 access-class 1
```

### Tunneling PPP with Header Compression On Example

The following example uses TCP header compression when tunneling PPP across X.25:

```
interface Virtual-Template1
 ip unnumbered Ethernet0
 ip tcp header-compression passive
 peer default ip address 172.16.2.128
!
translate x25 5555676 virtual-template 1
```

### Tunneling IPX-PPP across X.25 Example

The following example shows how to tunnel IPX–PPP across the X.25 network. It creates an internal IPX network number on a loopback interface, then assigns that loopback interface to the virtual interface template.

```
ipx routing 0000.0c07.b509
!
interface loopback0
 ipx network 544
 ipx sap-interval 2000
!
interface Virtual-Template1
 ip unnumbered Ethernet0
 ipx ppp-client Loopback0
 peer default ip address 172.16.2.127
!
translate x25 5555766 virtual-template 1
```

### Two-Step Examples

The following examples show how to create and configure virtual interface templates and apply them in two-step protocol translation sessions.

#### Two-Step Tunneling of PPP with Dynamic Routing and Header Compression Example

The virtual template interface in the following example uses the default encapsulation of PPP. It does not specify a peer default IP address because it is using two-step translation.

```
vty-async
vty-async virtual-template 1
vty-async dynamic-routing
vty-async header-compression
!
interface Virtual-Template1
 ip unnumbered Ethernet0
 no peer default ip address
```

After the user connects to the router (in this example, named *waffler*), they invoke the **ppp** command to complete the two-step connection:

```
waffler> ppp /routing /compressed 172.16.2.31
Entering PPP routing mode.
Async interface address is unnumbered (Ethernet0)
Your IP address is 172.16.2.31. MTU is 1500 bytes
```

#### Two-Step Tunneling of PPP with Dynamic Routing, TACACS, and CHAP Example

The virtual template interface in the following example uses the default encapsulation of PPP and applies CHAP authentication with TACACS+:

```
aaa authentication ppp default tacacs+
!
vty-async
vty-async dynamic-routing
vty-async virtual-template 1
!
interface Ethernet0
 ip address 10.11.12.2 255.255.255.0
!
interface Virtual-Template1
 ip unnumbered Ethernet0
 no peer default ip address
 ppp authentication chap
```

## Protocol Translation Application Examples

This section provides protocol translation examples for the following scenarios:

- Assign Addresses Dynamically for PPP Example
- Basic Configuration Example

- Central Site Protocol Translation Example
- Decreasing the Number of Translation Sessions Example
- Increasing the Number of Translation Sessions Example
- LAT-to-LAT over an IP WAN Example
- LAT-to-LAT over Frame Relay or SMDS Example
- LAT-to-LAT Translation over a WAN Example
- LAT-to-LAT over an X.25 Translation Example
- LAT-to-TCP Translation over a WAN Example
- LAT-to-TCP over an X.25 Example
- LAT-to-X.25 Host Example
- Local IP Address Pool Example
- Local LAT-to-TCP Translation Example
- Local LAT-to-TCP Example
- Stand-alone LAT-to-TCP Translation Example
- Tunneling SLIP inside TCP Example
- Tunneling PPP over X.25 Example
- X.25 PAD-to-LAT Example
- X.25 PAD-to-TCP Example
- X.29 Access List Example
- X.3 Profile Example

**NOTES**

In the application illustrations throughout the remainder of this chapter, source and destination device icons used to illustrate the flow of translated information are shown with black type in outlined shapes. Other elements in the environment are shown with reverse type on solid black shapes.

### Assign Addresses Dynamically for PPP Example

The following example shows how to configure the Cisco IOS software to assign an IP address dynamically to a PPP client using the one-step protocol translation facility:

```
! enable DHCP proxy-client status on the router
ip address-pool dhcp-proxy-client
! specify rockjaw as the DHCP server on the network.
ip dhcp-server rockjaw
translate x25 5467835 ppp ip-pool keepalive 0
```

## Basic Configuration Example

The following examples illustrate the basic global configuration commands and interface configuration commands for setting up Router-A (connected to Network A) and Router-B (connected to Network B), as illustrated in Figure 21–7. See Chapter 19, "Configuring Dial-In Terminal Services," for more information about LAT.

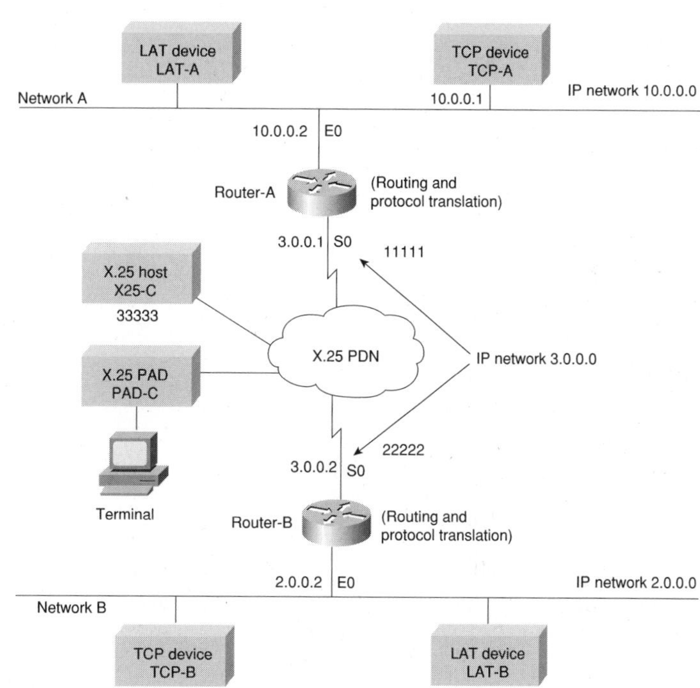


*Figure 21–7 Diagram Showing Routers with Protocol Translation.*

**NOTES**

The examples that follow focus on creating configurations that support one-step protocol translation. These connections can also be made using the two-step protocol translation method.

### *Configuration for Router-A*

The following partial configuration for Router-A outlines a baseline configuration for a router's Ethernet and serial interfaces and configures support for IP, LAT, and X.25:

```
interface ethernet 0
 ip address 10.0.0.2 255.255.0.0
 !
 ! Enable LAT on interface
 lat enabled
 !
```

```
interface serial 0
 encapsulation X.25
 x25 address 11111
 !
 ! The following parameters may depend on your network
 x25 facility packetsize 512 512
 x25 facility windowsize 7 7
 !
 ! IP address and MAP command needed only if routing IP
 ip address 10.3.0.1 255.255.0.0
 x25 map ip 10.4.0.2 22222 broadcast
 !
! Set up IP routing
router igrp 100
 network 10.0.0.0
 network 10.3.0.0
 !
 ! Advertise as available for connections via LAT
 ! Use this name (router-A) if connecting via 2-step method
 ! (for connecting directly to a specific router)
 lat service router-A enable
 !
 ! Set up some IP host names/addresses
 ip host router-A 10.0.0.2 3.0.0.1
 ip host TCP-A 10.0.0.1
 ip host TCP-B 10.2.0.1
 ip host router-B 10.3.0.2 2.0.0.2
```

### *Configuration for Router-B*

The following partial configuration for Router-B outlines a baseline configuration for a router's Ethernet and serial interfaces and configures support for IP, LAT, and X.25:

```
interface ethernet 0
 ip address 10.2.0.2 255.255.0.0
 !
 ! enable LAT on interface
 lat enabled
 !
interface serial 0
 encapsulation X.25
 x25 address 22222
 ! The following parameters may depend on your network
 x25 facility packetsize 512 512
 x25 facility windowsize 7 7
 !
 ! IP address and MAP command needed only if routing IP
 ip address 10.3.0.2 255.255.0.0
 x25 map ip 10.3.0.2 11111 broadcast
 !
 ! Set up IP routing
router igrp 100
 network 10.2.0.0
 network 10.3.0.0
 !
```

```
! advertise as available for connections via LAT
! Use this name (router-B) if connecting via 2-step method
! (for connecting directly to a specific router)
lat service router-B enable
!
! Set up some IP host names/addresses
ip host router-A 10.3.0.1 10.0.0.2
ip host TCP-A 10.0.0.1
ip host TCP-B 10.2.0.1
ip host router-B 10.2.0.2 10.3.0.2
```

**NOTES**

You can specify IP host names used to identify specific hosts by explicitly using the ip host global configuration command or by using Domain Name System (DNS) facilities.

### Central Site Protocol Translation Example

To support this application, a router with an image that supports protocol translation is directly connected back-to-back to another router (see Figure 21–8). This second device acts as an X.25 switch, by sending X.25 packets to Router-B while concurrently routing and bridging other protocols.

The following example illustrates how to configure a router to support translating protocols over an X.25 network among multiple sites.

Router-C is configured to act as an X.25 switch to send X.25 packets to Router-A while concurrently routing and bridging other protocols.

The following example also illustrates how to use the **translate** global configuration command to translate LAT and TCP over X.25 WAN media. In this configuration, Router-A can translate LAT or TCP traffic into X.25 packets for transmission over an X.25 PDN network. Packets are then translated back to LAT or TCP on the other side of the WAN.

```
interface ethernet 0
 ip address 10.0.0.2 255.255.0.0
 !
 ! enable LAT on interface if concurrently routing (8.3 feature)
 lat enable
 !
interface serial 0
 encapsulation X.25
 ! note that this is subaddress 3 of 11111
 x25 address 111113
 ! The following parameters may depend on your network
 x25 facility packetsize 512 512
 x25 facility windowsize 7 7
 no ip address

 ! "Other" Central Site Cisco router Configuration
 !
 ! Interface to WAN
interface serial 0
```

```
 x25 address 11111
 x25 route ^111113 interface serial 1
 ip address ....
 ! Interface to router-A
interface serial 1
 x25 route .* interface serial 0
 no ip address

 ! Translate Configuration for router-A
 !
 no ip routing
 ! Note subaddress of subaddress 11111(3(3))
translate x25 1111133 tcp tcpdevice
translate lat TCP-B x25 3333301
translate lat lat-device tcp tcp-device
! etc...any translate commands needed by application
```

*Figure 21–8 Central Site Protocol Translation Example.*

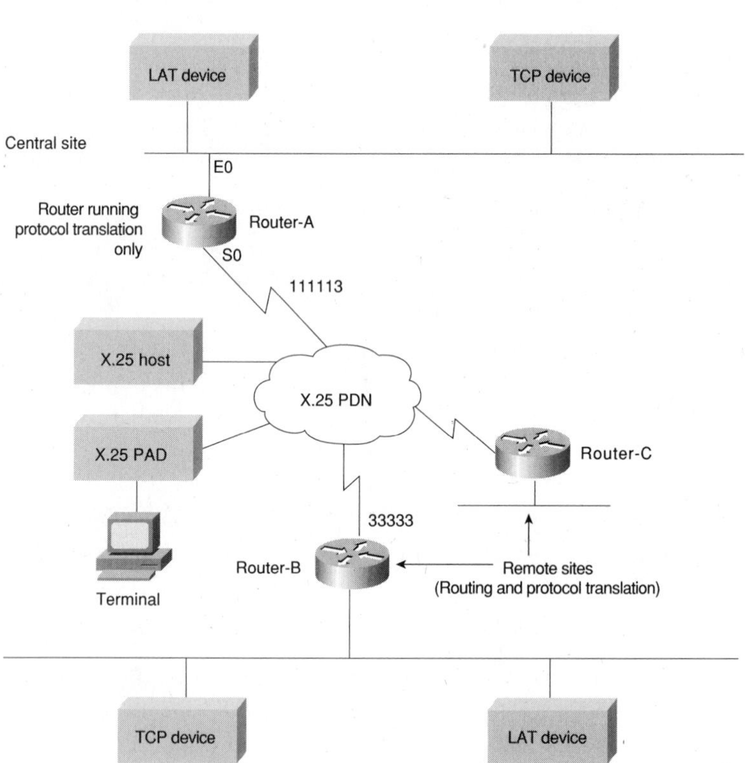


## Decreasing the Number of Translation Sessions Example

The following example sets the number of protocol translation sessions to 10, whether routing is turned on or off:

```
no line vty 10
```

### Increasing the Number of Translation Sessions Example

The following example sets the number of protocol translation sessions to 120, whether routing is turned on or off:

```
line vty 119
```

### LAT-to-LAT over an IP WAN Example

The Cisco IOS software can be used to connect LAT devices over a WAN backbone that only allows routable protocols (see Figure 21–9). This configuration exists when LAT networks are either isolated or on their own internetwork.

With the protocol translation, LAT traffic can be translated to TCP and then routed on the WAN as TCP traffic. The LAT connections stay local between the LAT device and the router running the protocol translation option. Thus, connections are not susceptible to delays on the WAN. Thi reduces the amount of traffic on the WAN because only the data from specific LAT sessions is forwarded on the WAN rather than all the LAT protocol status information packets.

*Figure 21–9*
*LAT-to-LAT over an IP WAN.*

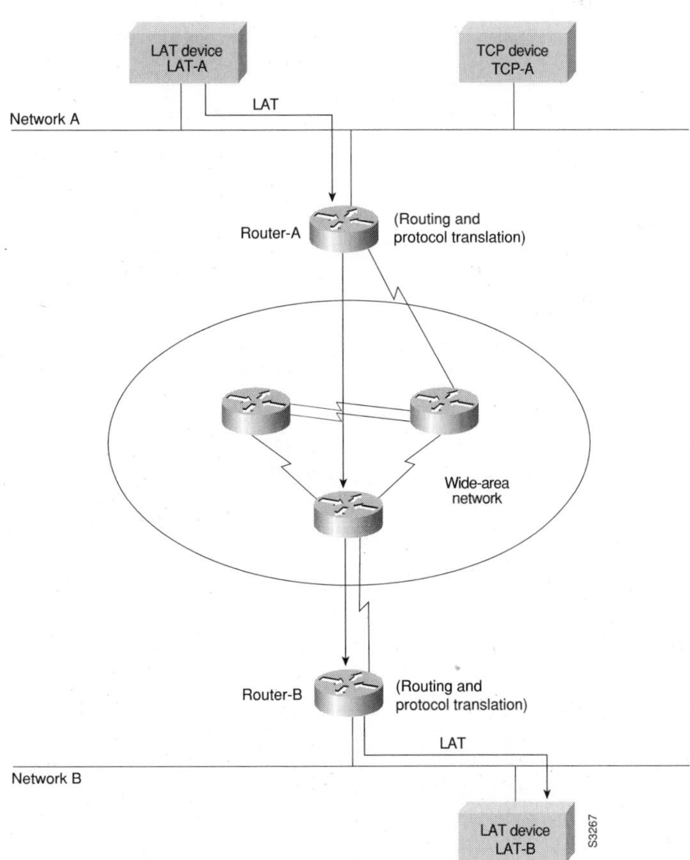

The following example illustrates how to use the **translate** global configuration command to translate from LAT to LAT when an IP WAN is used. In this configuration, Router-B with the protocol translation option routes encapsulated packets translated from LAT to TCP over the WAN. Router-A translates packets back to LAT on the other side of the WAN. Sample translation configurations for both Router-A and Router-B are shown, but these examples do not include specifics of configuration for devices in the WAN. These examples are essentially the same configurations for protocol translation as those in the following Frame Relay example.

```
! Translate LAT to TCP/Telnet for router-A, which is on Network A
translate lat DISTANT-LAT tcp router-A
! Translate TCP to LAT for router-B, which is on Network B
translate tcp router  B lat LAT-B
```

**NOTES**

You can use the same name (for example, "LAT-B") in the **translate** command for both Router-A and Router-B, because each router operates independently. However, this symmetry is not required. The key is the common IP name in both **translate** commands.

### LAT-to-LAT over Frame Relay or SMDS Example

To transport LAT traffic over a Frame Relay or an SMDS network, LAT must first be translated to TCP. The TCP traffic is routed over the Frame Relay network and then translated back to LAT on Router-B on Network B (see Figure 21–10).

**NOTES**

The interface configurations for a Frame Relay or an SMDS implementation differ from the specifications at the beginning of this chapter.

The following example illustrates how to use **translate** global configuration command to translate from LAT to LAT when the WAN uses Frame Relay or SMDS. In this configuration, the Cisco IOS software routes encapsulated packets translated from LAT to TCP over the Frame Relay or SMDS network. Packets are then translated back to LAT on the other side of the Frame Relay or SMDS network.

```
! Translate LAT to TCP/Telnet on router-A, which is on Network A
translate lat DISTANT-LAT tcp router-A
! Translate TCP to LAT on router-B, which is on Network B
translate tcp router-B lat LAT-B
```

**NOTES**

You can use the same name (for example, "LAT-B") in the **translate** command for both Router-A and Router-B because each router operates independently. However, this symmetry is not required. The key is the common IP name used in both **translate** commands.

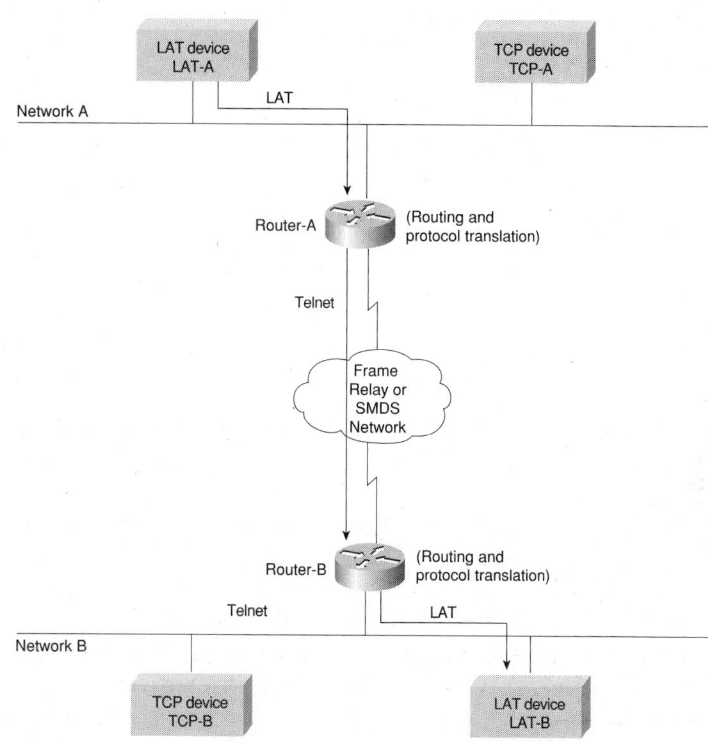


*Figure 21–10*
*LAT-to-LAT over Frame Relay or SMDS.*

## LAT-to-LAT Translation over a WAN Example

In Figure 21–11, LAT can be transported to a remote LAT device by translating the packets to TCP format and using Telnet to send them across the WAN. The configuration files for Router-A and Router-B follow the figure. The logical name *CS-B1* is the name given to device *CS-B*.

### *Configuration for Router-A*

```
interface ethernet 0
 ip address 192.168.32.16 255.255.0.0
!
! enable LAT on this interface
 lat enabled
!
translate lat distant-LAT tcp TS-B1
```

### *Configuration for Router-B*

```
interface ethernet 0
 ip address 192.168.38.42 255.255.0.0
!
! enable LAT on this interface
 lat enabled
!
translate lat TS-B1 lat LAT-B
```

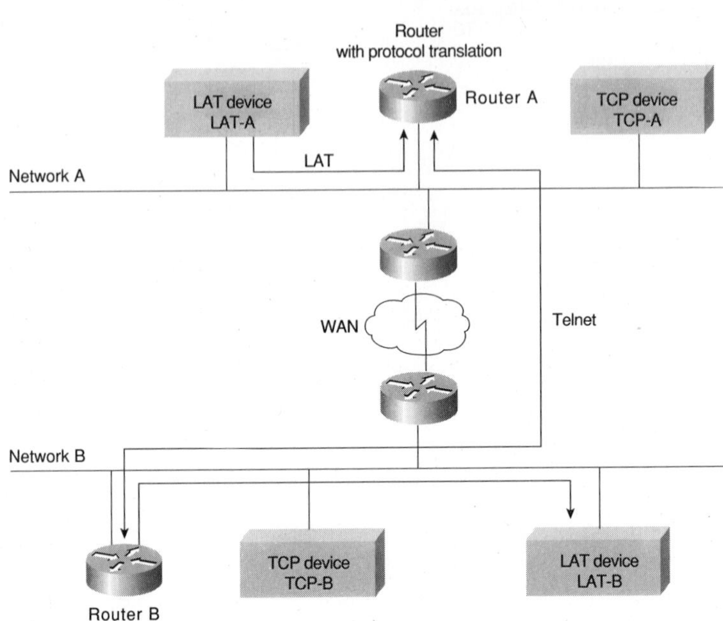


*Figure 21–11*
*LAT-to-LAT Translation over a WAN.*

## LAT-to-LAT over an X.25 Translation Example

Protocol translation provides transparent connectivity between LAT devices on different networks via an X.25 PDN. In Figure 21–12, which illustrates this application, the LAT device on Network A (LAT-A) first makes a virtual connection to Router-A on Network A using the LAT protocol. Router-A then translates the LAT packets into X.25 packets and sends them through the X.25 network to Router-B on Network B. Router-B translates the X.25 packets back to LAT packets and establishes a virtual connection to the LAT device on Network B (LAT-B). These handoffs are handled transparently when the Cisco IOS software is configured for one-step protocol translation.

The following two examples illustrate how to use the **translate** global configuration command to translate from LAT to X.25 and from X.25 back to LAT to allow connection service to a LAT device on Network B from a LAT device on Network A. This requires two separate configurations, one for each LAT device.

```
! Translate LAT to X.25 on router-A, which is on Network A
translate lat DISTANT-LAT x25 2222201

! Translate X.25 to LAT on router-B, which is on Network B
translate x25 2222201 lat LAT-B
```

In the first **translate** command, *DISTANT-LAT* defines a LAT service name for Router-A. When a user on device LAT-A attempts to connect to TCP-B, the target specified in the **connect** command is DISTANT-LAT.

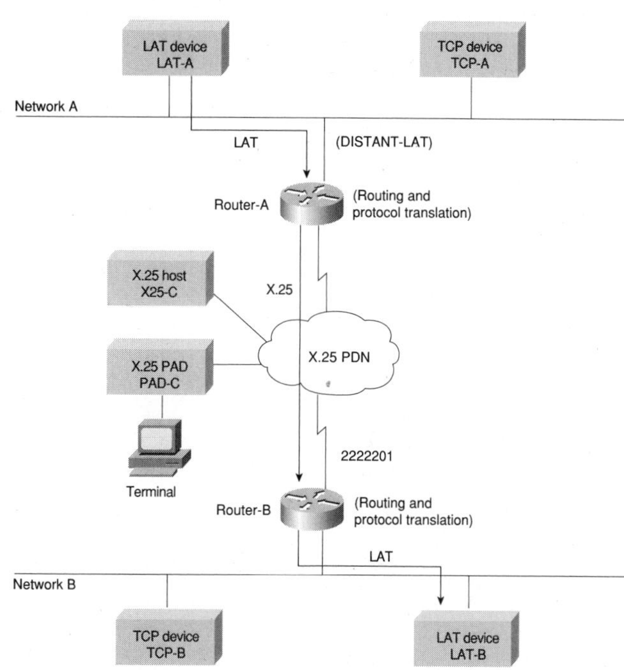


*Figure 21–12*
*LAT-to-LAT via an X.25 PDN.*

In the **translate** command for Router-B, the name of the LAT service on the target host (LAT-B) is LAT-B. Router-B translates the incoming X.25 packets from 2222201 to LAT and then transparently relays these packets to LAT-B.

The following is an example of a connection request. In this configuration example, when the user enters this command, a connection attempt from LAT-A on Network A to TCP-B on Network B is attempted.

```
local> connect DISTANT-LAT
```

To configure Router-B to send information back from LAT-B to LAT-A, use commands symmetrical to the prior configuration (this path is not shown in Figure 21–12):

```
! Translate LAT to X.25 on router-B, which is on Network B
translate lat FAR-LAT x25 1111103
! Translate X.25 to LAT on router-A, which is on Network A
translate x25 1111103 lat LAT-A
```

**NOTES**

You can use the same name (for example, "LAT-B") in the **translate** command for both Router-A and Router-B because each router with the protocol translation option operates independently. However, this symmetry is not required. The key is the common X.121 address used in both **translate** commands. If you prefer to have unique service names, set the names in each router to be the same.

### LAT-to-TCP Translation over a WAN Example

Figure 21–13 shows a configuration that allows translation of LAT to TCP and transmission across an IP-based WAN. The configuration file for Router-A follows the figure. The logical LAT service name *distant-TCP* is given to device *TCP-B*.

Configuration for Access Server A

```
interface ethernet 0
 ip address 192.168.38.42 255.255.0.0
!
! enable LAT on this interface
 lat enabled
!
translate lat distant-TCP tcp TCP-B
```

*Figure 21–13*
*LAT-to-TCP Translation over a WAN.*

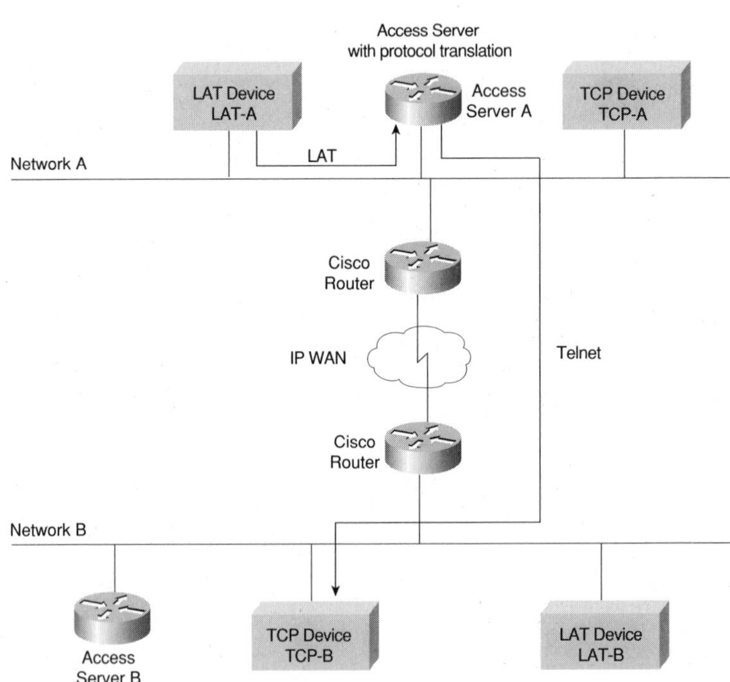


### LAT-to-TCP over an X.25 Example

You can use protocol translation to provide transparent connectivity between LAT and TCP devices on different networks via an X.25 PDN. In Figure 21–14, which illustrates this application, the LAT device on Network A is communicating with the TCP device on Network B. There are two ways to provide this connectivity: The LAT traffic from Network A can be translated into either X.25 packets or TCP/IP packets to be sent out on the X.25 PDN.

If the traffic is translated from LAT directly into X.25 frames by Router-A, then Router-B on Network B translates incoming packets intended for device TCP-B into TCP. If Router-A converts LAT to TCP, then the TCP traffic is being encapsulated in X.25 and sent on the X.25 network. Router-B on Network B strips off the encapsulation and routes the TCP packet. In this case, protocol translation is not needed on Router-B.

If the traffic is translated to TCP by Router-A, the packets are encapsulated within X.25 frames. In general, translating the traffic directly to X.25 is more efficient in this application because no encapsulation is necessary. X.25 packets have only 5 bytes of header information; TCP over X.25 has 45 bytes of header information.

*Figure 21–14*
*LAT-to-TCP via X.25.*

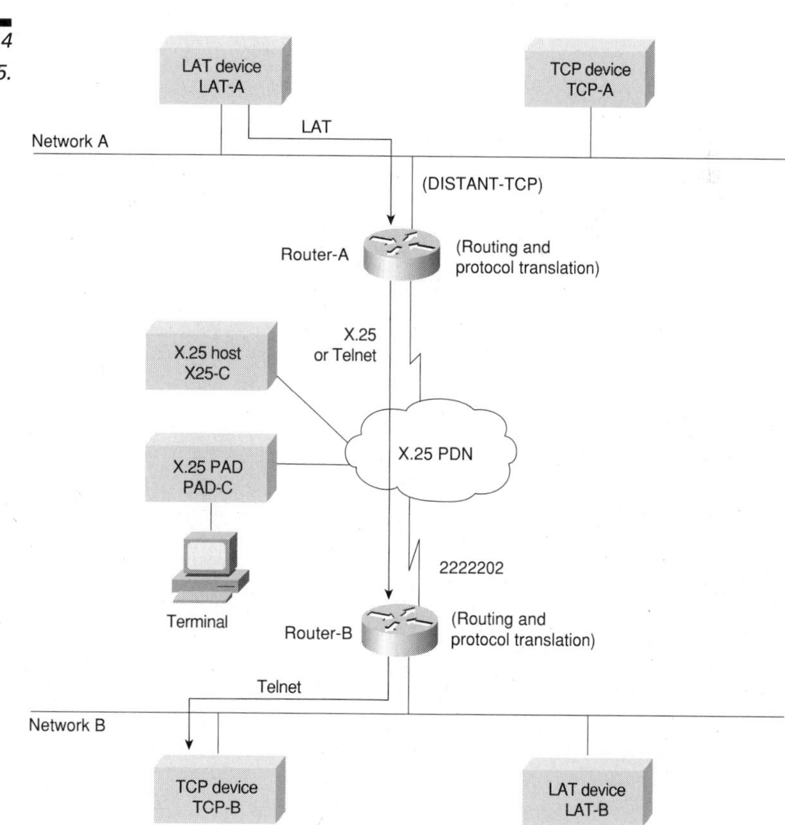


The following examples illustrate how to use the **translate** global configuration command to translate from LAT to X.25 (on Router-A) and from X.25 to TCP (on Router-B), thus allowing connection service to a TCP device on Network B (TCP-B) from a LAT device on Network A (LAT-A). You must configure Router-A and Router-B separately.

```
! Translate LAT to X.25 on router-A, which is on Network A
translate lat DISTANT-TCP x25 2222202
```

```
! Translate X.25 to TCP on router-B, which is on Network B
translate x25 2222202 tcp TCP-B
```

In the **translate** command for Router-A, *DISTANT-TCP* defines a LAT service name for Router-A. When a user on device LAT-A attempts to connect to LAT-B, the target specified in the **connect** command is DISTANT-TCP.

In the **translate** command for Router-B, the TCP service on the target host is TCP-B. Router-B translates the incoming X.25 packets from 2222202 to TCP packets and transparently relays these packets to TCP-B.

The following is an example of a connection request. In this configuration example, when the user enters this command, a connection attempt from LAT-A on Network A to LAT-B on Network B is attempted.

```
local> connect DISTANT-TCP
```

**NOTES**

You can use the same name (for example, "TCP-B") in the **translate** command for both Router-A and Router-B, because each router operates independently. However, this symmetry is not required. The key is the common X.121 address used in both **translate** commands. If you prefer to have unique service names, set the names in each router to be the same.

## LAT-to-X.25 Host Example

Protocol translation permits LAT devices to communicate with X.25 hosts through an X.25 PDN. In the application illustrated in Figure 21–15, LAT-A is a LAT device that is communicating with X25-C, an X.25 host. The LAT traffic from LAT-A is translated to X.25.

The following example illustrates how to use the **translate** global configuration command to translate from LAT to X.25. It is applied to Router-A. This example sets up reverse charging for connections, which causes the router with the protocol translation option to instruct the PDN to charge the destination for the connection. It is essentially a collect call. The reversal of charges must be prearranged with the PDN and destination location (on an administrative basis), or the call will not be accepted.

```
! Translate LAT to X.25 host, with reverse charging
translate lat X25-C x25 33333 reverse
!
! Specify optional X.25 hostname
x25 host X25-C 33333
```

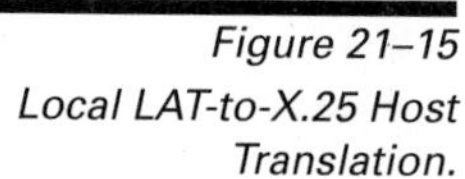

*Figure 21–15*
*Local LAT-to-X.25 Host Translation.*

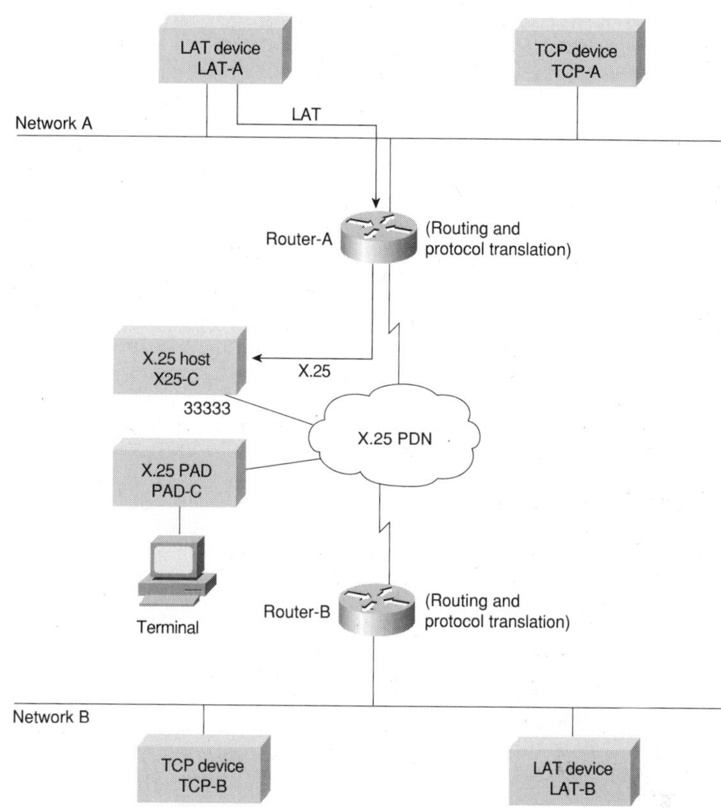


## Local IP Address Pool Example

The following example shows how to select the IP pooling mechanism and how to create a pool of local IP addresses that are used when a client dials in on an asynchronous line. The address pool is named *group1* and consists of interfaces 0 through 5.

```
! tell the server to use a local pool
ip address-pool local
! define the ip address pool
ip local-pool group1 192.168.35.1 192.168.35.5
translate x25 5467835 ppp ip-pool scope-name group1
```

## Local LAT-to-TCP Translation Example

Figure 21–16 shows a simple LAT-to-TCP translation across an Ethernet network. Its Cisco IOS configuration file follows the figure. The name *TCPA* is the logical name given to the device *TCP-A*.

*Figure 21–16*
*Local LAT-to-TCP Translation.*

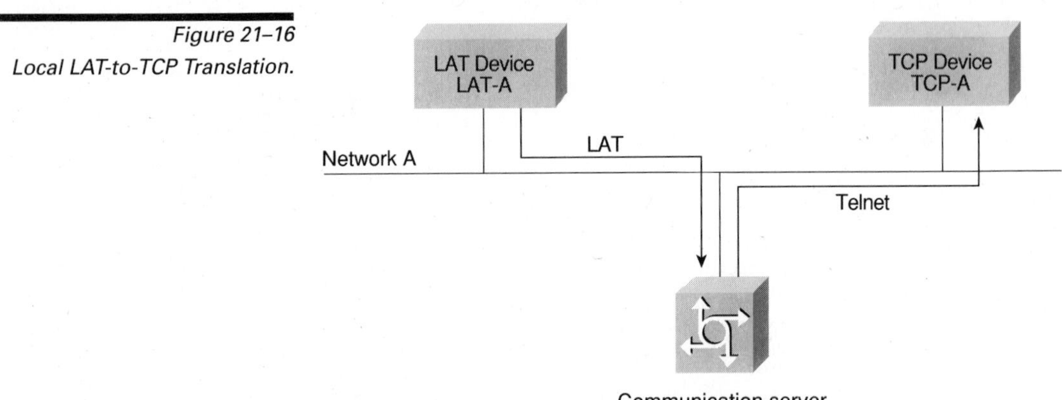


*Configuration for the Access Server*

```
interface ethernet 0
 ip address 192.168.38.42 255.255.0.0
!
! enable LAT on this interface
 lat enabled
!
translate lat TCPA tcp TCP-A
```

## Local LAT-to-TCP Example

The Cisco IOS software running protocol translation can translate between LAT and Telnet traffic to allow communication among resources in these protocol environments. In Figure 21–17, the LAT device on Network A (LAT-A) is shown connecting to a device running Telnet (TCP-A).

This is only a partial example. The commands in this example are only part of the complete configuration file for an individual device

The following example configures Router-A to translate from LAT to TCP:

```
! Translate LAT connections to TCP for connectivity to TCP-A
translate lat TCP-A tcp TCP-A
! Optional additional commands
lat service TCP-A ident Protocol Translation to TCP-A
```

In the last command, the text string "Protocol Translation to TCP-A" is an identification string for the LAT service named *TCP-A*. This string is sent to other routers on the local network.

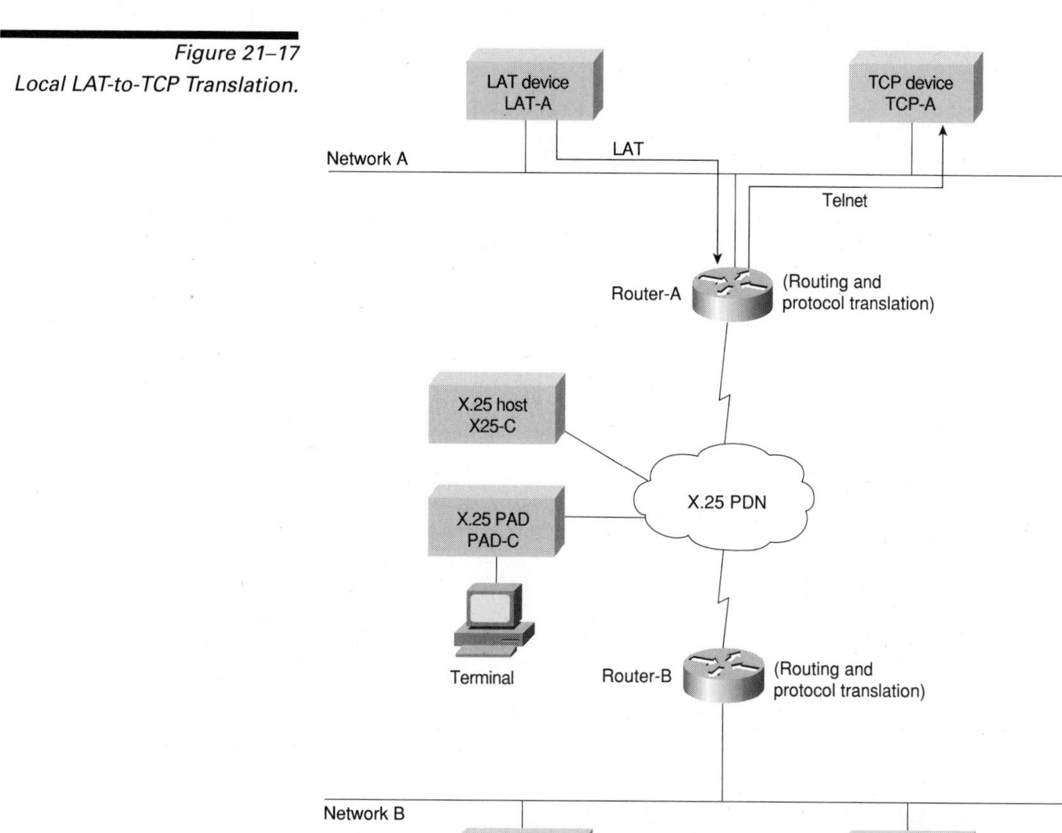


*Figure 21–17*
*Local LAT-to-TCP Translation.*

## Stand-Alone LAT-to-TCP Translation Example

If you need a large number of local LAT-to-TCP translation sessions, you can set up Router-A to use only an Ethernet port. This application allows 100 concurrent translation sessions. In the applications illustrated in Figure 21–18, any other router that supports protocol translation can be used to interconnect network segments performing bridging or routing.

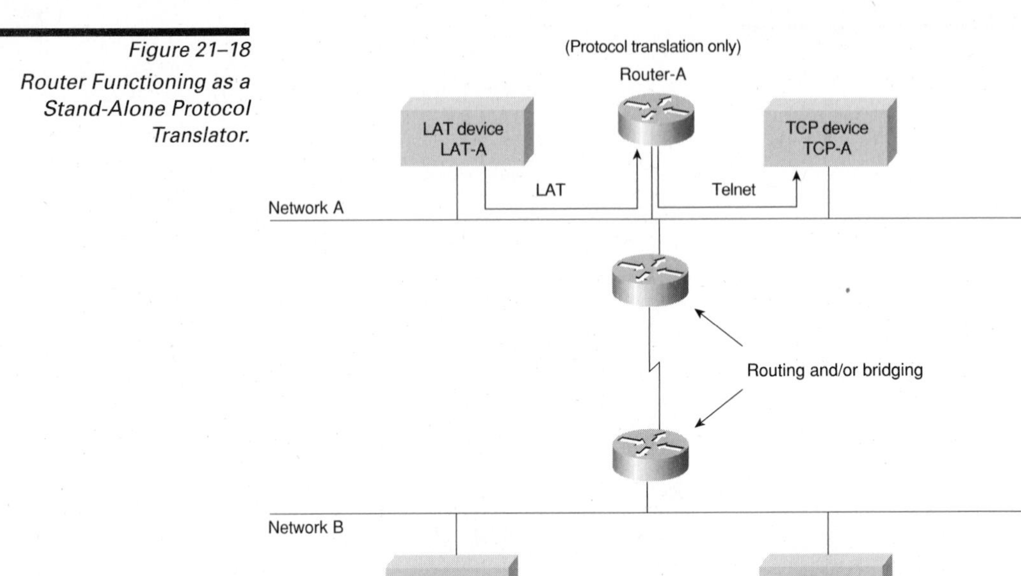


*Figure 21–18*
*Router Functioning as a Stand-Alone Protocol Translator.*

### *Configuration for Router-A*

```
! Translation Configuration for router-A only
!
interface ethernet 0
 ip address 10.0.0.2 255.255.0.0
 !
 ! enable LAT on this interface
 lat enabled
 !
interface serial 0
 shutdown
 no ip routing
 default-gateway 10.0.0.100
!
translate lat TCP-A tcp TCP-A
translate lat TCP-B tcp TCP-B
translate tcp LAT-A lat lat-z
! etc...translate commands as required
```

## Tunneling SLIP inside TCP Example

Protocol translation enables you to tunnel from TCP to SLIP in order to allow communication among resources in these protocol environments. In Figure 21–19, the PC running SLIP is connecting to a TCP/IP network and making a connection with the device IP host. This example enables routing and turns on header compression.

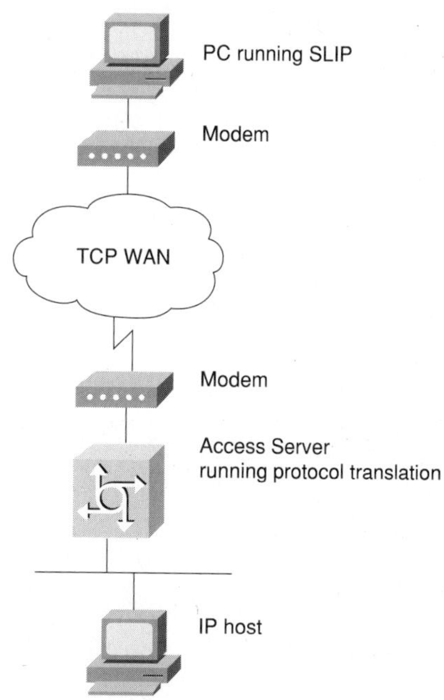


*Figure 21–19*
*Tunneling SLIP inside TCP Example.*

The following configuration tunnels SLIP inside of TCP packets from the SLIP client with IP address 10.2.0.5 to the router. It then establishes a protocol translation session to IP host. Routing and header compression are enabled for the SLIP session.

```
translate tcp 10.0.0.1 slip 10.2.0.5 routing header-compression passive
```

The device IP host on a different network attached to the router can be accessed by the SLIP client because routing has been enabled on the interface in the router where the SLIP session is established.

This is only a partial example. The commands in this example would be only part of the complete configuration file for an individual router.

## Tunneling PPP over X.25 Example

Cisco IOS software can tunnel PPP traffic across an X.25 WAN to allow communication among resources in these protocol environments. In Figure 21–20, the PC establishes a dial-up PPP session through an X.25 network using CHAP authentication.

The following configuration tunnels PPP over X.25 from the PPP client to the virtual asynchronous interface with IP address 10.0.0.4. Routing and CHAP authentication are enabled for the PPP session. The X.121 address of the X.25 host is 31370054065. An X.29 profile script named *x25-ppp* is created using the following X.3 PAD parameters:

1:0, 2:0, 3:2, 4:1, 5:0, 6:0, 7:21, 8:0, 9:0, 10:0, 11:14, 12:0, 13:0, 14:0, 15:0, 16:127, 17:24, 18:18, 19:0, 20:0, 21:0, 22:0

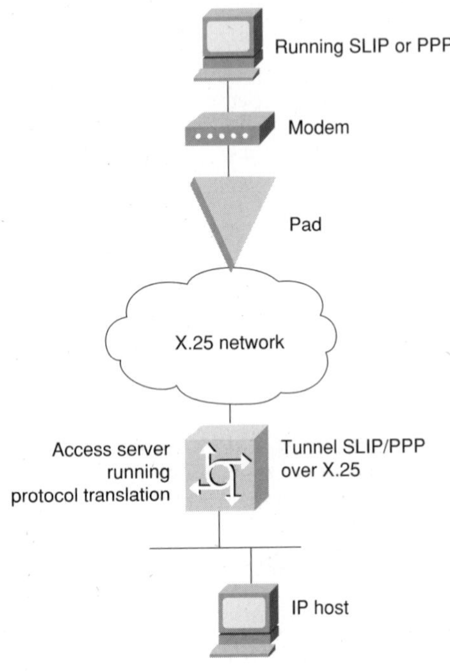


*Figure 21–20*
*Tunneling PPP in X.25.*

For more information about X.3 PAD parameters, see Appendix B. If you were performing a two-step connection, you would specify these X.3 PAD parameters using the **pad** [**/profile** *name*] command.

With the router connected to the IP host, the PC running PPP can now communicate with the IP host.

```
2509# config term
2509(config)# X29 profile x25-ppp 1:0  2:0  3:2  4:1  5:0  6:0  7:21  8:0  9:0
              10:0  11:14  12:0  13:0  14:0  15:0  16:127  17:24 18:18
2509(config)# translate x25 31370054065 profile x25-ppp ppp 10.0.0.4 routing
              authentication chap
```

This is only a partial example. The commands in this example are only a part of the complete configuration file for an individual router.

## X.25 PAD-to-LAT Example

Protocol translation permits terminals connected to X.25 PADs to communicate with LAT devices on a remote LAN (see Figure 21–21). X.25 PAD terminals make a call using an X.121 address, which is translated to a LAT node. To the PAD terminal user, the connection appears to be a direct connection to a host on the X.25 PDN. The Cisco IOS software also supports X.29 access lists, which allow you to restrict LAN resources (LAT or TCP) available to the PAD user.

*Figure 21–21*
*X.25 PAD-to-LAT Translation.*

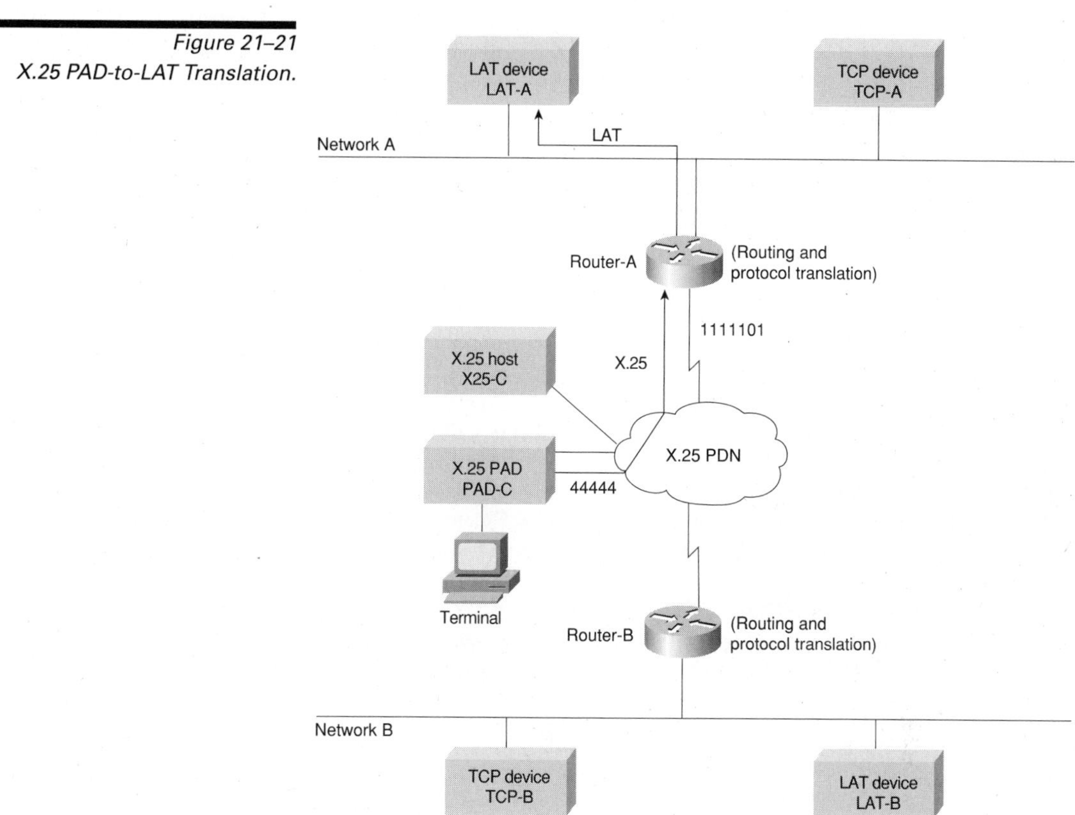


The following example illustrates how to use the **translate** global configuration command to translate from an X.25 PAD to a LAT device on Network A. It is applied to Router-A. The configuration example includes an access list that limits remote LAT access through Router-A to connections from PAD-C.

```
! Define X25 access list to only allow pad-c
x29 access-list 1 permit ^44444
x29 access-list 1 deny .*
!
! Set up translation
translate x25 1111101 lat LAT-A access-class 1
```

This configuration example typifies the use of access lists in the Cisco IOS software. The first two lines define the scope of *access-list 1*. The first line specifies that access list 1 will permit all calls from X.121 address 44444. The caret symbol (^) specifies that the first number 4 is the beginning of the address number. See Appendix C, "Regular Expressions," for details concerning the use of special characters in defining X.121 addresses. The second line of the definition explicitly denies calls from any other number.

This access list is then applied to all incoming traffic on the serial port for Router-A (X.121 address 1111101) with the third configuration line in the example. However, it applies only to the **translate** command at the end of this example. This **translate** command specifies that incoming X.25 packets on the serial line (with address 1111101) be translated to LAT and sent to LAT-A if they pass the restrictions of the access list.

If you define multiple X.25 **translate** commands, each must contain a unique X.121 address. Also, the ITU-T protocol that transfers packets must match the X.121 addresses. This is specified in the protocol identification field of call-user data. This field specifies whether a packet is routed, translated, or handled as a virtual terminal connection.

**NOTES**

The X.121 address 1111101 used in this example can be a subaddress of the address 11111 originally assigned to this serial port on Router-A at the beginning of the configuration example section. However, that is not a requirement. The number to use in the **translate** command is negotiated (administratively) between your network management personnel and the PDN service provider. The X.121 address in the **translate** command represents the X.121 address of the calling device. That number might or might not be the number (or a subaddress of the number) administratively assigned to the router with the protocol translation option. It is up to you and the PDN to agree on a number to be used, because it is possible that the PDN can be configured to place calls that are intended for a destination on a given line that does not match the number assigned by you in the configuration file. Refer to the *1984 CCITT Red Book* specifications for more information concerning X.121 addresses.

## X.25 PAD-to-TCP Example

Making a translated connection from an X.25 PAD to a TCP device (as in Figure 21–22) is analogous to the preceding X.25 PAD-to-LAT example. Instead of translating to LAT, the configuration for Router-A includes a statement to translate to TCP (Telnet). Note that a router with the protocol translation software option can include statements supporting both translations (X.25 PAD-to-LAT and X.25 PAD-to-TCP). Different users on the same PAD can talk to X.25, LAT, or TCP devices.

The following example illustrates how to use the **translate** global configuration command to translate from an X.25 PAD to a TCP device on Network A. It is applied to Router-A.

```
! Set up translation
translate x25 2222 tcp TCP-A
```

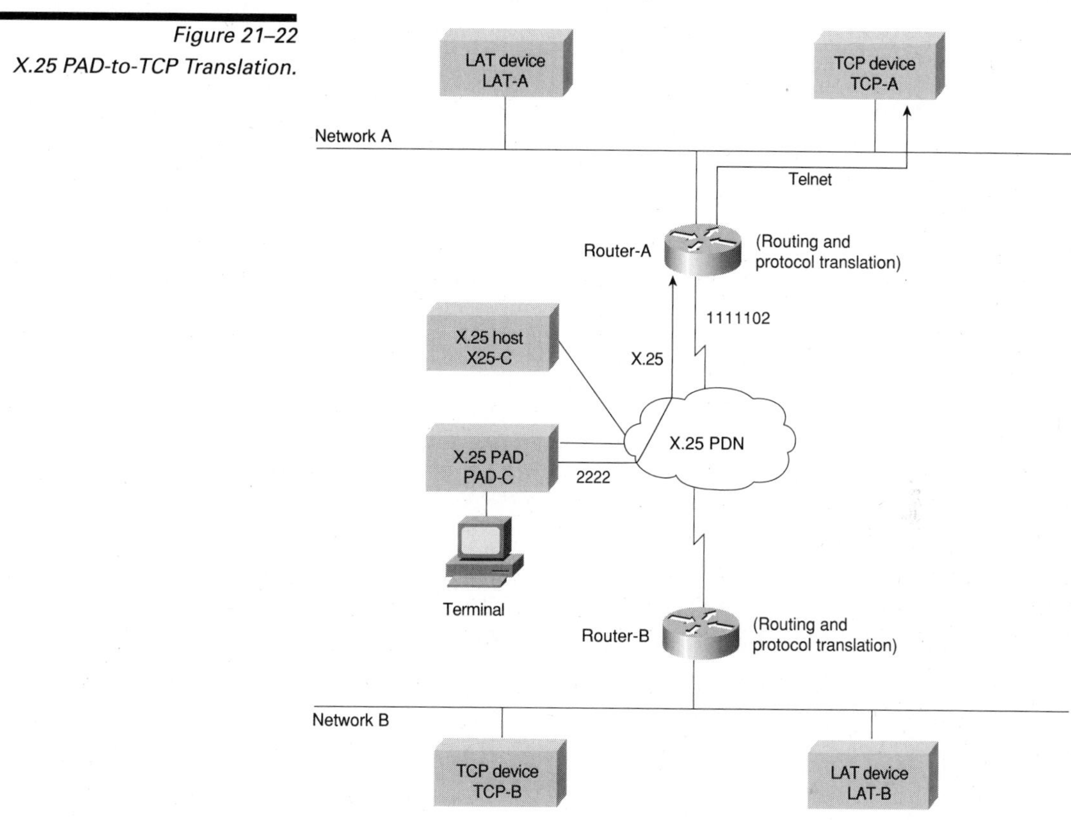


*Figure 21–22*
*X.25 PAD-to-TCP Translation.*

## X.29 Access List Example

The following example illustrates an X.29 access list. Incoming permit conditions are set for all IP hosts and LAT nodes that have specific characters in their names. All X.25 connections to a printer are denied. Outgoing connections are restricted.

```
!Permit all IP hosts and LAT nodes beginning with "VMS".
!Deny X.25 connections to the printer on line 5.
!
access-list 1 permit 0.0.0.0 255.255.255.255
lat access-list 1 permit ^VMS.*
x29 access-list 1 deny .*
!
line vty 5
 access-class 1 in
 !
 !Permit outgoing connections for other lines.
 !
 !Permit IP access with the network 172.16
 access-list 2 permit 172.16.0.0 0.0.255.255
 !
```

```
 !Permit LAT access to the prasad/gopala complexes.
 lat access-list 2 permit ^prasad$
 lat access-list 2 permit ^gopala$
 !
 !Permit X.25 connections to Infonet hosts only.
 x29 access-list 2 permit ^31370
 !
line vty 0 16
 access-class 2 out
 !
translate tcp 172.16.1.26 x25 5551234 access-class 2
```

### X.3 Profile Example

The following profile script turns local edit mode on when the connection is made and establishes local echo and line termination upon receipt of a Return character. The name *linemode* is used with the **translate** command to affect use of this script.

```
x29 profile linemode 2:1 3:2 15:1
translate tcp 172.16.1.26 x25 55551234 profile linemode
```

The X.3 PAD parameters are described in Appendix B.

## Protocol Translation Session Examples

This section illustrates how to make connections for protocol translation using the one-step and two-step methods:

- Using the One-Step Method for TCP-to-X.25 Host Connections Example
- Using Two-Step Protocol Translation for TCP-to-PAD Connections Examples
- Monitoring Protocol Translation Connections Example
- Changing Parameters and Settings Dynamically Example

### Using the One-Step Method for TCP-to-X.25 Host Connections Example

This example illustrates one-step protocol translation featuring a UNIX workstation user making a connection to a remote X.25 host named *host1* over an X.25 PDN. The router automatically converts the Telnet connection request to an X.25 connection request and transmits the request as specified in the system configuration.

A connection is established by entering the **telnet** EXEC command at the UNIX workstation system prompt, as follows:

```
unix% telnet host1
```

**Notes**

This example implicitly assumes that the name *host1* is known to the UNIX host (obtained via DNS, IEN116, or a static table) and is mapped to the IP address used in a **translate** command.

The router accepts the Telnet connection and immediately forms an outgoing connection with remote *host1* as defined in a **translate** command.

Next, *host1* sets several X.3 parameters, including local echo. Since the Telnet connection is already set to local echo (at the UNIX host), no changes are made on the TCP connection.

The *host1* connection prompts for a user name, then *host1* sets the X.3 parameters to cause remote echo (the same process as setting X.3 PAD parameter 2:0), and prompts for a password. The Cisco IOS software converts this to a Telnet option request on the UNIX host, which then stops the local echo mode.

At this point, the user is connected to the PAD application, and the application will set the X.3 PAD parameters (although they can always be overridden by the user). When the user is finished with the connection, he enters the escape character to exit back to the host connection, then enters the appropriate command to close the connection.

The *host1* host immediately closes the X.25 connection. The Cisco IOS software then drops the TCP connection, leaving the user back at the UNIX system prompt. Use the Two-Step Method for TCP-to-PAD Connections.

To use the two-step method, perform the following steps:

**Step 1** Connect directly from a terminal or workstation to a router.

For example, you might make the following connection requests at a UNIX workstation as a first step to logging in to a database called *Information Place* on an X.25 PDN:

```
unix% telnet orion
```

If the router named *orion* is accessible, it returns a login message and you enter your login name and password.

**Step 2** Connect from the router to *Information Place*, which is on an X.25 host. You connect to an X.25 host using the **pad** EXEC command followed by the service address:

```
orion> pad 71330
```

Once the connection is established, the router immediately sets the PAD to single character mode with local echoing, because this is the behavior the router expects. The PAD responds with its login messages and a prompt for a password:

```
Trying 71330...Open
Welcome to the Information Place
Password:
```

Because the password should not echo on your terminal, the PAD requests remote echoing so that characters will be exchanged between the PAD and the router, but not echoed locally or displayed. After the password is verified, the PAD again requests local echoing from the router, which it does from then on.

To complete this sample session, log off, which returns you to the router system EXEC prompt. From there, execute the EXEC **quit** command and the router drops the network connection to the PAD.

### Using Two-Step Protocol Translation for TCP-to-PAD Connections Examples

The following example shows a connection from a local UNIX host (host1) to a router (router1) as the first step in a two-step translation process:

```
host1% telnet router1
```

The following example shows a connection from router1 to a host named ibm3278 as the second step in a two-step translation process:

```
Tasmania> tn3270 ibm3278
ibm3278%
```

In the following example, you connect directly from a terminal or workstation on a TCP/IP network to a router, and then to a database called Information Place on an X.25 packet data network. The database has a service address of 71330.

**Step 1** Make the following connection requests at a UNIX workstation as a first step to logging in to the database Information Place:

```
unix% telnet router1
```

If the router named router1 is accessible, it returns a login message and you enter your login name and password.

**Step 2** Connect from the router to the database Information Place, which is on an X.25 host. You connect to an X.25 host using the **pad** EXEC command followed by the service address:

```
router1> pad 71330
```

Once the connection is established, the router immediately sets the PAD to single-character mode with local echoing, because these are the settings that the router expects. The PAD responds with its login messages and a prompt for a password.

```
Trying 71330...Open
Welcome to the Information Place
Password:
```

Because the password should not echo on your terminal, the PAD requests remote echoing so that characters will be exchanged between the PAD and the router, but not echoed locally or displayed. After the password is verified, the PAD again requests local echoing from the router.

**Step 3** Complete this sample session by logging off, which returns you to the router system EXEC prompt.

**Step 4** Execute the **quit** EXEC command, and the router drops the network connection to the PAD.

### Changing Parameters and Settings Dynamically Example

The following example illustrates how to make a dynamic change during a protocol translation session. In this example, you need to edit information on remote host *Information Place*. Suppose that you need to change the X.3 PAD parameters that define the editing characters from the default **Delete** key setting to the **Ctrl-D** sequence.

**Step 1** Enter the escape sequence to return to the system EXEC prompt:

`Ctrl ^ x`

**Step 2** Enter the **resume** command with the **/set** keyword and the desired X.3 parameters. X.3 parameter 16 sets the Delete function. ASCII character 4 is the Ctrl-D sequence.

router > **resume /set 16:4**

The session resumes with the new settings, but the information is not displayed correctly. You might want to set the **/debug** switch to check that your parameter setting has not been changed by the host PAD.

**Step 3** Enter the escape sequence to return to the system EXEC prompt, then enter the **resume** command with the **/debug** switch.

router> **resume /debug**

The **/debug** switch provides helpful information about the connection.

You can also set a packet dispatch character or sequence using the **terminal dispatch-character** command. The following example shows how to set ESC (ASCII character 27) as a dispatch character:

```
router> terminal dispatch-character 27
```

To return to the PAD connection, enter the following:

```
router> resume
```

### Monitoring Protocol Translation Connections Example

The following example shows how to log significant VTY-asynchronous authentication information, such as the X.121 calling address, Call User Data (CUD), and the IP address assigned to a VTY asynchronous connection to a UNIX syslog server named *alice*:

```
service pt-vty-logging
logging alice
```

# CHAPTER 22

# Protocol Translation and Virtual Asynchronous Device Commands

Protocol translation provides transparent translation between systems running different protocols. The Cisco IOS software supports two-way virtual terminal protocol translation between nodes running X.25, LAT, and Telnet.

This chapter describes the commands that you use to configure protocol translation.

For protocol translation configuration information and examples, see Chapter 21, "Configuring Protocol Translation and Virtual Asynchronous Devices."

## SERVICE PT-VTY-LOGGING

To log the X.121 calling address, Call User Data (CUD), and the IP address assigned to a VTY asynchronous connection, use the **service pt-vty-logging** global configuration command. Use the **no** form of this command to disable this function.

**service pt-vty-logging**
**no service pt-vty-logging**

### *Syntax Description*

This command has no arguments or keywords.

### *Default*

This feature is disabled.

### *Command Mode*

Global configuration

### *Usage Guidelines*

This command first appeared in Cisco IOS Release 11.2.

This command permits you to log the X.121 calling address, Call User Data (CUD), and the IP address assigned to a VTY asynchronous connection and direct this information to the console, an internal buffer, or a UNIX syslog server, depending on the logging configuration command you use. This authentication information can be used to associate an incoming PAD VTY-asynchronous connection with an IP address.

**NOTES**

By default, the Cisco IOS software displays all messages to the console terminal.

### *Example*

The following example enables you to log the X.121 calling address, Call User Data (CUD), and the IP address assigned to a VTY asynchronous connection and save this information to a syslog server:

```
service pt-vty-logging
```

The following is sample output resulting from the **service pt-vty-logging** command:

```
01:24:31: PAD18: call from 00011890 on LCI 10 PID 1 0 0 0 CUD "xyz"
```

Table 22–1describes the fields shown in the output.

**Table 22–1** *Service PT-VTY-Logging Field Descriptions*

| Field | Description |
|---|---|
| 01:24:31: | Time stamp. |
| PAD18: | Active VTY line number using the PAD connection. |
| 00011890 | The source/calling address. |
| on LCI 10 | Incoming call is initiated on Logical Channel 10. |
| PID 1 0 0 0 | The PAD Protocol Identifier is “01000000.” |
| CUD “xyz” | Call User Data “xyz.” If no CUD is available, this field will appear as follows: `CUD ""` |

### *Related Commands*

Search online to find documentation for related commands.

**logging**
**logging buffered**

## SHOW INTERFACES VIRTUAL-ACCESS

Use the **show interfaces virtual-access** EXEC command to display information about virtual access interfaces.

**show interfaces virtual-access** *number*

| *Syntax* | *Description* |
|---|---|
| *number* | Number of the virtual terminal (VTY) line on which the virtual access interface has been created. |

### *Command Mode*

EXEC

### *Usage Guidelines*

This command first appeared in Cisco IOS Release 11.3.

To identify the number of the VTY line on which the virtual access interface was created, issue the **show users** EXEC command (covered later in this chapter).

### *Sample Display*

The following is sample output from the **show interfaces virtual-access** command:

```
router# show interface virtual-access 2

Virtual-Access2 is up, line protocol is up
  Hardware is Virtual Access interface
  Interface is unnumbered. Using address of Ethernet0 (10.0.21.14)
  MTU 1500 bytes, BW 9 Kbit, DLY 100000 usec, rely 255/255, load 1/255
  Encapsulation PPP, loopback not set, keepalive not set
  DTR is pulsed for 0 seconds on reset
  LCP Open
  Open: IPCP
  Last input 00:00:06, output 00:00:05, output hang never
  Last clearing of "show interface" counters 00:14:58
  Input queue: 1/75/0 (size/max/drops); Total output drops: 0
  Queueing strategy: weighted fair
  Output queue: 0/64/0 (size/threshold/drops)
     Conversations  0/1 (active/max active)
     Reserved Conversations 0/0 (allocated/max allocated)
  5 minute input rate 0 bits/sec, 0 packets/sec
  5 minute output rate 0 bits/sec, 0 packets/sec
     4 packets input, 76 bytes, 0 no buffer
     Received 0 broadcasts, 0 runts, 0 giants
     0 input errors, 0 CRC, 0 frame, 0 overrun, 0 ignored, 0 abort
     8 packets output, 330 bytes, 0 underruns
     0 output errors, 0 collisions, 0 interface resets
     0 output buffer failures, 0 output buffers swapped out
     0 carrier transitions
```

Table 22–2 describes the fields shown in this sample display.

**Table 22–2** *Show Interfaces Virtual-Access Field Descriptions*

| Field | Description |
|---|---|
| Virtual-Access ... is {up \| down \| administratively down} | Indicates whether the interface is currently active (whether carrier detect is present), inactive, or has been taken down by an administrator. |
| line protocol is {up \| down \| administratively down} | Indicates whether the software processes that handle the line protocol think the line is usable (that is, whether keepalives are successful). |
| Hardware is Virtual Access interface | Type of interface. In this case, the interface is a dynamically created virtual access interface existing on a VTY line. |
| Internet address \| interface is unnumbered | IP address, or IP unnumbered for the line. If unnumbered, the output lists the interface and IP address to which the line is assigned (Ethernet0 at 10.0.21.14 in this example). |
| MTU | Maximum transmission unit for packets on the virtual access interface. |
| BW | Bandwidth of the virtual access interface in kilobits per second. |
| DLY | Delay of the virtual access interface in microseconds. |
| rely | Reliability of the virtual access interface as a fraction of 255 (255/255 is 100% reliability), calculated as an exponential average over five minutes. |
| load | Load on the virtual access interface as a fraction of 255 (255/255 is completely saturated), calculated as an exponential average over five minutes. The calculation uses the value from the **bandwidth** interface configuration command. |
| Encapsulation | Encapsulation method assigned to the virtual access interface. |
| loopback | Test in which signals are sent and then directed back toward the source at some point along the communication path. Used to test network interface usability. |
| keepalive | Interval set for keepalive packets on the interface. If keepalives have not been enabled, the message is "keepalive not set." |
| DTR | Data Terminal Ready. An RS232-C circuit that is activated to let the DCE know when the DTE is ready to send and receive data. |

**Table 22–2** *Show Interfaces Virtual-Access Field Descriptions, Continued*

| Field | Description |
|---|---|
| LCP open \| closed \| req sent | Link control protocol (for PPP only; not for SLIP). LCP must come to the open state before any useful traffic can cross the link. |
| Open IPCP \| IPXCP \| ATCP | IPCP is IP control protocol for PPP, IPXCP is IPX control protocol for PPP, ATCP is AppleTalk control protocol for PPP. Network control protocols (NCPs) for the PPP suite. The NCP is negotiated after the LCP opens. The NCP must come into the open state before useful traffic can cross the link. |
| Last input | Number of hours, minutes, and seconds since the last packet was successfully received by a virtual access interface. Useful for knowing when a dead interface failed. |
| output | Number of hours, minutes, and seconds since the last packet was successfully transmitted by a virtual access interface. |
| output hang | Number of hours, minutes, and seconds (or never) since the virtual access interface was last reset because of a transmission that took too long. When the number of hours in any of the "last" fields exceeds 24 hours, the number of days and hours is printed. If that field overflows, asterisks are printed. |
| Last clearing | Time at which the counters that measure cumulative statistics (such as number of bytes transmitted and received) shown in this report were last reset to zero. Note that variables that might affect routing (for example, load and reliability) are not cleared when the counters are cleared.<br>*** indicates the elapsed time is too large to be displayed. 0:00:00 indicates the counters were cleared more than $2^{31}$ms (and less than $2^{32}$ms) ago. |
| Input queue, drops | Number of packets in input queues. Each number is followed by a slash, the maximum size of the queue, and the number of packets dropped due to a full queue. |
| Queueing strategy | Type of queueing selected to prioritize network traffic. The options are first-come, first-served (FCFS) queueing, weighted fair queueing, priority queueing, and custom queueing. |
| Output queue | Number of packets in output queues. Each number is followed by a slash, the maximum size of the queue, and the number of packets dropped due to a full queue. |

**Table 22–2** *Show Interfaces Virtual-Access Field Descriptions, Continued*

| Field | Description |
|---|---|
| Conversations | Number of weighted fair queueing conversations. |
| Reserved Conversations | Number of reserved weighted fair queueing conversations. The example shows the number of allocated conversations divided by the number of maximum allocated conversations. In this case, there have been 0 reserved conversations. |
| Five minute input rate, Five minute output rate | Average number of bits and packets transmitted per second in the last five minutes. |
| packets input | Total number of error-free packets received by the system. |
| bytes | Total number of bytes, including data and MAC encapsulation, in the error-free packets received by the system. |
| no buffer | Number of received packets discarded because there was no buffer space in the main system. Compare with ignored count. Broadcast storms on Ethernets and bursts of noise on serial lines are often responsible for no input buffer events. |
| broadcasts | Total number of broadcast or multicast packets received by the virtual access interface. |
| runts | Number of packets that are discarded because they are smaller than the medium's minimum packet size. |
| giants | Number of packets that are discarded because they exceed the medium's maximum packet size. |
| input errors | Total number of no buffer, runts, giants, CRCs, frame, overrun, ignored, and abort counts. Other input-related errors can also increment the count, so that this sum might not balance with the other counts. |
| CRC | Cyclic redundancy checksum generated by the originating LAN station or far-end device does not match the checksum calculated from data received. On a LAN, this often indicates noise or transmission problems on the LAN interface or the LAN bus. A high number of CRCs is usually the result of collisions or a station transmitting bad data. On a serial link, CRCs often indicate noise, gain hits, or other transmission problems on the data link. |

**Table 22–2** *Show Interfaces Virtual-Access Field Descriptions, Continued*

| Field | Description |
|---|---|
| frame | Number of packets received incorrectly having a CRC error and a noninteger number of octets. On a serial line, this is usually the result of noise or other transmission problems. |
| overrun | Number of times the serial receiver hardware was unable to hand received data to a hardware buffer because the input rate exceeded the receiver's ability to handle the data. |
| ignored | Number of received packets ignored by the virtual access interface because the interface hardware ran low on internal buffers. These buffers are different than the system buffers mentioned previously in the buffer description. Broadcast storms and bursts of noise can cause the ignored count to be incremented. |
| abort | Illegal sequence of one bits on a virtual access interface. This usually indicates a clocking problem between the virtual access interface and the data link equipment. |
| packets output | Total number of messages transmitted by the system. |
| bytes | Total number of bytes, including data and MAC encapsulation, transmitted by the system. |
| underruns | Number of times that the far-end transmitter has been running faster than the near-end communication server's receiver can handle. This might never be reported on some virtual access interfaces. |
| output errors | Sum of all errors that prevented the final transmission of datagrams out of the virtual access interface being examined. Note that this might not balance with the sum of the enumerated output errors, as some datagrams might have more than one error, and others might have errors that do not fall into any of the tabulated categories. |
| collisions | Number of packets colliding. |

**Table 22–2** *Show Interfaces Virtual-Access Field Descriptions, Continued*

| Field | Description |
|---|---|
| interface resets | Number of times a virtual access interface has been completely reset. This can happen if packets queued for transmission were not sent within several seconds. This can be caused by a malfunctioning modem that is not supplying the transmit clock signal, or by a cable problem. If the system notices that the carrier detect line of a virtual access interface is up, but the line protocol is down, it periodically resets the interface in an effort to restart it. Interface resets can also occur when a virtual access interface is looped back or shut down. |
| restarts | Number of times the controller was restarted because of errors. |
| carrier transitions | Number of times the carrier detect (CD) signal of a virtual access interface has changed state. Indicates modem or line problems if the CD line changes state often. If data carrier detect (DCD) goes down and comes up, the carrier transition counter increments two times. |
| output buffer failures | Number of outgoing packets dropped from the output buffer. |
| output buffers swapped out | Number of times the output buffer was swapped out. |

## SHOW TRANSLATE

To view translation sessions that have been configured, use the **show translate** global configuration command:

**show translate**

### *Syntax Description*

This command has no arguments or keywords.

### *Command Mode*

Privileged EXEC

### *Usage Guidelines*

This command first appeared in Cisco IOS Release 10.3.

The display from this command shows each translation session set up on the router. It shows the incoming device and virtual terminal protocol as well as the outgoing device and protocol.

### *Sample Display*

The **show translate** output in this sample display is based on the following translation command configured:

```
translate x25 3131415912345 ppp ip-pool scope-name cardinal keepalive 0
```

If the previous **translate** command is enabled, the following output is created by the **show translation** command:

```
router# show translate

Translate From: x25 3131415912345
          To:    PPP ip-pool scope-name cardinal keepalive 0
          1/1 users active, 1 peak, 1 total, 0 failures
```

Table 22–3 describes fields shown in the display.

**Table 22–3** *Show Translate Field Descriptions*

| Field | Description |
|---|---|
| Translate From: x25 3131415912345 | Protocol (X.25) and address (3131415912345) of the incoming device. |
| To: PPP | The virtual terminal protocol (PPP). |
| ip-pool | Obtain an IP address from a DHCP proxy client or a local pool. |
| scope-name cardinal | Specific local scope name (cardinal) from which to obtain an IP address. |
| keepalive 0 | Indicates that keepalive updates have been disabled for the current translation session. |
| 1/1 users active | Number of users active over the total number of users. |
| 1 peak | Maximum number of translate sessions up at any given time. |
| 1 total | Total number of translation sessions. |
| 0 failures | Number of failed translation attempts resulting from this configuration. |

The **show translate** output in this sample display is based on the following translation command configured:

```
translate x25 31301234 PPP 192.168.14.23  ipx-client Loopback0
```

If the previous **translate** command is enabled, the following output is created by the **show translation** command:

```
router# show translate

Translate From: x25 31301234
          To:    PPP 192.168.14.23  ipx-client Loopback0
          1/1 users active, 1 peak, 1 total, 0 failures
```

Table 22–4 describes fields shown in the display.

**Table 22–4** *Show Translate Field Descriptions*

| Field | Description |
|---|---|
| Translate From: x25 31301234 | Protocol (X.25) and address (31301234) of the incoming device. |
| To: PPP 192.168.14.23 | The virtual terminal protocol (PPP) and IP address of the outgoing device. |
| ipx-client loopback0 | Indicates that loopback interface 0 has been configured in client mode. |
| 1/1 users active | Number of users active over the total number of users. |
| 1 peak | Maximum number of translate sessions up at any given time. |
| 1 total | Total number of translation sessions. |
| 0 failures | Number of failed translation attempts resulting from this configuration. |

## SHOW USERS (VIRTUAL ACCESS INTERFACES)

To display information about the active lines on the router, use the **show users** user EXEC command.

**show users** [**all**]

*Syntax* *Description*

**all** (Optional) Specifies that all lines be displayed, regardless of whether anyone is using them.

### *Command Mode*

User EXEC

### *Usage Guidelines*

This command first appeared in Cisco IOS Release 11.2.

This command displays the line number, connection name, idle time, hosts (including virtual access interfaces), and terminal location.

### *Sample Display*

The following is sample output from the **show users** command. You can use it to identify an active virtual access interface:

```
router> show users

Line          User      Host(s)                      Idle     Location
```

```
*  0 con 0              idle                   01:58
  10 vty 0              Virtual-Access2         0       1212321
```

The asterisk (*) indicates the current terminal session.

Table 22–5 describes significant fields shown in the displays.

**Table 22–5** *Show Users Field Descriptions*

| Field | Description |
|---|---|
| Line | Contains three subfields.<br>• The first subfield (0, 10, and Vi2 in the sample output) is the absolute line number.<br>The second subfield (con and vty) indicates the type of line. Possible values follow:<br>con—Console<br>aux—Auxiliary port<br>tty—Asynchronous terminal port<br>vty—Virtual terminal<br>• The third subfield (0 in the sample output) indicates the relative line number within the type. |
| User | User connected to the line. If no user is listed in this field, no one is using the line. |
| Host(s) | Host to which the user is connected (outgoing connection). A value of `idle` means that there is no outgoing connection to a host. The value of `Virtual-Access2` in the example refers to virtual access interface number 2. The value of `Virtual PPP (PT)` is the virtual access interface referred to by the previous line. |
| Idle | Interval (in minutes) since the user has entered something. |
| Location | Either the hard-wired location for the line or, if there is an incoming connection, the host from which incoming connection originated. In the example, 1212321 refers to the X.121 address of an X.25 host. |



### TRANSLATE LAT

When receiving a LAT connection request to a service name, the Cisco router can automatically translate the request to another outgoing protocol connection type. To set this up, use the **translate** global configuration command.

**translate lat** *incoming-service-name* [*in-option*] *protocol outgoing-address* [*out-options*] [*global-options*]

| *Syntax* | *Description* |
|---|---|
| *incoming-service-name* | A LAT service name. When used on the incoming portion, *service-name* is the name of the service that users specify when trying to make a translated connection. This name can match the name of final destination resource, but this is not required. Can be useful when making remote translated connections. |
| *in-option* | (Optional) Incoming connection request option:<br>• **unadvertised**—Prevents service advertisements from being broadcast to the network. This can be useful, for example, when you define translations for many printers, and you do not want these services advertised to other LAT terminal servers. (VMS systems will be able to connect to the service even though it is not advertised.) |
| *protocol outgoing-address* | A protocol name followed by an IP address or host name. The host name is translated to an IP address during configuration, unless you use the tcp **host-name** option, which allows load balancing by dynamically resolving an IP address from a host name. These arguments can have the following values:<br>• **x25** *X.121-address*—X.25 and an X.121 address. The X.121 address must conform to specifications provided in the *CCITT 1984 Red Book*. This number generally consists of a portion that is administered by the PDN and a portion that is locally assigned. You must be sure that the numbers that you assign agree with the addresses assigned to you by the X.25 service provider. The X.121 addresses will generally be subaddresses of the X.121 address for the X.25 network interface. Typically, the interface address will be a 12-digit number. Any additional digits are interpreted as a subaddress. The PDN still routes these calls to the interface, and the Cisco IOS software itself is responsible for dealing with the extra digits appropriately.<br>• **tcp** *ip-address*—TCP/IP Telnet and a standard IP address or host name. The argument *ip-address* is a standard, four-part dotted decimal IP address or the name of an IP host that can be resolved by the Domain Name System (DNS) or explicit specification in an ip host command.<br>• **slip** *ip-address*—The argument *ip-address* is a standard, four-part dotted decimal IP address or the name of an IP host that can be resolved by the Domain Name System (DNS).<br>• **ppp** *ip-address*—The argument *ip-address* is a standard, four-part dotted decimal IP address or the name of an IP host that can be resolved by the Domain Name System (DNS). |

| *Syntax* | *Description* |
|---|---|
| | • **autocommand**—Enables you to specify a string for an outgoing connection. The string executes upon connection to a host. If you want to enable ARA on an outgoing connection, you need to specify **autocommand arap.**<br>The **autocommand** option is necessary for ARA, because ARA does not use addressing, and **autocommand** permits you to invoke the **arap** string.<br>If the string following **autocommand** has one or more spaces as part of the string, you must place quotation marks (" ") around the string. For example, if you specify **autocommand tn3270 abracadabra**, you must enclose **tn3270 abracadabra** in quotes.<br>The **autocommand** option applies only to outgoing connections.<br>You can issue any EXEC command and any switch or host name as an argument to the autocommand option. |
| *out-options* | (Optional) Incoming and outgoing connection request options. These arguments can have the following values:<br>X.25 translation options:<br>• **cud** *c-u-data*—Sends the specified Call User Data (CUD) text (*c-u-data*) as part of an outgoing call request after the protocol identification bytes.<br>• **no-reverse**—Specifies that outgoing calls are not to use reverse charging, when the interface default is that all outgoing calls are reverse charged.<br>• **profile** *profile*—Sets the X.3 PAD parameters as defined in the profile created by the **x29 profile** command.<br>• **reverse**—Provides reverse charging for X.25 on a per-call rather than a per-interface basis. Requests reverse charges on a specified X.121 address, even if the serial interface is not configured to request reverse charge calls. This is an outgoing option only.<br>Telnet TCP translation option:<br>• **port** *number*—For incoming connections, number of the port to match. The default is port 23 (any port). For outgoing connections, number of the port to use. The default is port 23 (Telnet).<br>SLIP and PPP translation options:<br>• **ip-pool**—Obtain an IP address from a DHCP proxy client or a local pool. If the **scope-name** option is not specified, the address is obtained from a DHCP proxy client. If the **scope-name** option is specified, the IP address is obtained from the specified local pool.<br>• **scope-name**—Specific local scope name from which to obtain an IP address. Can specify a range of IP addresses. |

| *Syntax* | *Description* |
|---|---|
| | • **header-compression** [**passive**]—Implements header compression on IP packets only. The option **passive** for SLIP connections permits compression on outgoing packets only if incoming TCP packets on the same virtual asynchronous interface are compressed. The default (without the **passive** option) permits compression on all traffic.<br>• **routing**—Permits routing updates between connections. This option is required if the destination device is not on a subnet connected to one of the interfaces on the router.<br>• **mtu** *bytes*—Permits you to change the maximum transmission unit (MTU) of packets that the virtual asynchronous interface supports. The default MTU is 1,500 bytes on a virtual asynchronous interface. The acceptable range is 64 to 1,000,000 bytes.<br>More PPP translation options:<br>• *keepalive number-of-seconds*—Permits you to specify the interval at which keepalive packets are sent on SLIP and PPP virtual asynchronous interfaces. By default, keepalive packets are enabled and are sent every 10 seconds. To shut off keepalive packets, use a value of 0. The active keepalive interval is 1 through 32767 seconds. When you do not change from the default of 10, the keepalive interval does not appear in **show running-config** or **show translate** output.<br>• **authentication** {**chap** \| **pap**}—Use CHAP or PAP authentication for PPP on virtual asynchronous interfaces. If you specify both options, order is significant; the system will try to use the first authentication type, then the second.<br>• **ppp use-tacacs**—Enables TACACS authentication for CHAP or PAP on virtual asynchronous interfaces (for PPP only; TACACS authentication is not supported for SLIP).<br>• **ipx loopback** *number*—Permits clients running IPX–PPP over X.25 to connect through virtual terminal (VTY) lines on the router. The **loopback** *number* option specifies the loopback interface to be created. A loopback interface must have been created and configured with a Novell IPX network number before IPX–PPP can work on the VTY line. The VTY line is assigned to the loopback interface. |
| *global-options* | (Optional) Translation options that can be used by any connection type. It can be one or more of the following:<br>• **access-class** *number*—Allows the incoming call to be used by source hosts that match the access list parameters. The argument *number* is the number (integer) previously assigned to an access list. The standard access list is 1-99. |

*Syntax* *Description*

- **max-users** *number*—Limits the number of simultaneous users of the translation to *number* (an integer you specify).
- **local**—Allows Telnet protocol negotiations to *not* be translated.
- **rotor**—Provides a basic load sharing of the IP destinations.
- **login**—Requires that the user log in before the outgoing connection is made. This type of login is specified on the VTY lines with the **login** command.
- **quiet**—Suppresses printing of user-information messages.



### Default

No default translation parameters

### Command Mode

Global configuration

### Usage Guidelines

This command first appeared in Cisco IOS Release 10.0.

Table 22–6 provides a visual aid for the **translate lat** command. You define protocol translation connections by supplying a protocol keyword and the address, host name, or service name, followed by optional features. Global options apply to most connection types, but there are exceptions.

**Table 22–6** *Translate LAT Command Options*

| | Incoming Address | Options | Outgoing Protocol | Options | Global Options |
|---|---|---|---|---|---|
| translate lat | *incoming-address* | [*in-options*] | *protocol outgoing-address* | [*out-options*] | [*global-options*] |
| | lat *service-name* | unadvertised | x25 *x.121-address* | cud *c-u-data* | access-class *number* |
| | | | | no-reverse | max-users *number* |
| | | | | profile *profile* | local |
| | | | | reverse | login |
| | | | tcp *ip-address* | port *number* | quiet |
| | | | | host-name *name* | |

**Table 22–6** *Translate LAT Command Options, Continued*

| | Incoming Address | Options | Outgoing Protocol | Options | Global Options |
|---|---|---|---|---|---|
| | | | | **multibyte-IAC** | |
| | | | **slip** *ip-address* | **ip-pool** [**scope-name** *name*] | |
| | | | | **headercompression** [**passive**] | |
| | | | | **routing** | |
| | | | | **keepalive** *number-of-seconds* | |
| | | | | **mtu** *bytes* | |
| | | | **ppp** *ip-address* | **ip-pool** [**scope-name** *name*] | |
| | | | | **headercompression** [**passive**] | |
| | | | | **routing** | |
| | | | | **keepalive** *number-of-seconds* | |
| | | | | **mtu** *bytes* | |
| | | | | **authentication** {**pap** \| **chap**} | |
| | | | | **ppp use-tacacs** | |
| | | | | **ipx loopback** *number* | |
| | | | **autocommand** [**arap** \| *exec-string*] | | |

### *Examples*

The following example illustrates incoming LAT to outgoing TCP translations. The **unadvertised** keyword prevents broadcast of service advertisements to other servers. Outgoing translated packets are transmitted to IP host rubble, TCP port 4005.

```
translate lat pt-printer1 unadvertised tcp rubble port 4005
               incoming         option        outgoing    option
```

The following example translates LAT on an incoming line to SLIP on an outgoing line. It uses header compression only if incoming TCP packets on the same interface are compressed.

```
translate lat rudolph slip 10.0.0.4 header-compression
          incoming    outgoing     option
```

The following example first shows the command to disable keepalive packets on a PPP line, then shows sample output from the **show translate** command when keepalive packets have been turned off on the line.

```
translate lat ramble ppp 172.21.2.2 keepalive 0
.
.
router# show translate

Translate From: LAT ramble
          To:    PPP 172.21.2.2 keepalive 0
          0/0 users active, 0 peak, 0 total, 0 failures
```

*Related Commands*

Search online to find documentation for related commands.

**show translate**
**translate tcp**
**translate x25**
**x29 access-list**
**x29 profile**



## TRANSLATE LAT (VIRTUAL ACCESS INTERFACES)

When receiving a LAT connection request to a service name, the Cisco router can automatically translate the request to another outgoing protocol connection type. To set this up, use the **translate lat** global configuration command.

The command syntax that follows shows how to apply a virtual interface template in place of outgoing **translate** options. If you are using virtual templates for protocol translation, all outgoing options are defined in the virtual interface template. Table 22–7 lists all outgoing options and their corresponding interface configuration commands.

**translate lat** *incoming-service-name* [**unadvertised**] **virtual-template** *number* [*global-options*]

| *Syntax* | *Description* |
|---|---|
| *incoming-service-name* | A LAT service name. When used on the incoming portion of the **translate lat** command, *service-name* is the name of the service that users specify when trying to make a translated connection. This name can match the name of the final destination resource, but this match is not required. Such matches can be useful when making remote translated connections. |

| *Syntax* | *Description* |
|---|---|
| **unadvertised** | (Optional) The only incoming connection request option for LAT—Prevents service advertisements from being broadcast to the network. This can be useful, for example, when you define translations for many printers, and you do not want these services advertised to other LAT terminal servers. (VMS systems will be able to connect to the service even though it is not advertised.) |
| **virtual-template** *number* | Applies the virtual interface template specified by *number* in place of outgoing options. |
| *global-options* | (Optional) Translation options that can be used by any connection type. It can be one or more of the following:<br>• **access-class** *number*—Allows the incoming call to be used by source hosts that match the access list parameters. The argument *number* is the number (integer) previously assigned to an access list. The standard access list is 1 to 99.<br>• **max-users** *number*—Limits the number of simultaneous users of the translation to *number* (an integer you specify).<br>• **local**—Allows Telnet protocol negotiations to *not* be translated.<br>• **rotor**—Provides a basic load sharing of the IP destinations.<br>• **login**—Requires that the user log in before the outgoing connection is made. This type of login is specified on the VTY lines with the **login** command.<br>• **quiet**—Suppresses printing of user-information messages. |

### *Default*

No default translation parameters

### *Command Mode*

Global configuration

### *Usage Guidelines*

This command first appeared before Cisco IOS Release 10.0.

You define the protocol translation connections by choosing a protocol keyword and supplying the appropriate address, host name, or service name. The protocol connection information is followed by optional features for that connection, as appropriate. For example, the **binary** option is only appropriate with TCP/IP connections. The global options, in general, apply to all the connection types, but there are exceptions.

Rather than specifying outgoing translation options in the **translate** command, configure these options as interface configuration commands under the virtual interface template, then apply the virtual interface template to the **translate** command. Table 22–7 maps outgoing **translate** command options to interface commands you can configure in the virtual interface template.

**Table 22–7** *Mapping Outgoing Translate Command Options to Interface Commands*

| Translate Command Options | Corresponding Interface Configuration Command |
|---|---|
| **ip-pool** | **peer default ip address** {**ip-address** \| **dhcp** \| **pool** [*poolname*]} |
| **header-compression** | **ip tcp header compression** [**on** \| **off** \| **passive**] |
| **routing** | **ip routing** or **ipx routing** |
| **mtu** | **mtu** |
| **keepalive** | **keepalive** |
| **authentication** {**chap** \| **pap**} | **ppp authentication** {**chap** \| **pap**} |
| **ppp use-tacacs** | **ppp use-tacacs** |
| **ipx loopback** | **ipx ppp-client loopback** *number* |



### *Example*

The following example configures PPP tunneling from a PC across a LAT network. The remote PC is given the IP address 10.12.118.12 when it dials in. The **unadvertised** keyword prevents broadcast of service advertisements to other servers.

```
interface Virtual-Template1
 ip unnumbered Ethernet0
 peer default ip address 10.12.118.12
 ppp authentication chap
!
translate lat pt-printer1 unadvertised virtual-template 1
            incoming         option         outgoing
```

### *Related Commands*

Search online to find documentation for related commands.

**show translate**
**translate tcp**
**translate x25**
**x29 access-list**
**x29 profile**

### TRANSLATE TCP

When receiving a TCP connection request to a particular destination address or host name, the Cisco router can automatically translate the request to another outgoing protocol connection type. To set this up, use the **translate** global configuration command.

**translate tcp** *incoming-address* [*in-options*] *protocol outgoing-address* [*out-options*] [*global-options*]

| *Syntax* | *Description* |
|---|---|
| *incoming-address* | TCP/IP Telnet and a standard IP address or host name. The argument *ip-address* is a standard, four-part dotted decimal IP address or the name of an IP host that can be resolved by the Domain Name System (DNS) or explicit specification in an **ip host** command. |
| *in-options* | (Optional) Incoming connection request options. These arguments can have the following values: |

Telnet TCP translation options:

- **binary**—Negotiates Telnet binary mode on the Telnet connection. (This was the default in previous versions of the protocol translation software and is set automatically when you enter at **translate** command in the old format.)
- **port** *number*—For incoming connections, number of the port to match. The default is port 23 (any port). For outgoing connections, number of the port to use. The default is port 23 (Telnet).
- **printer**—Supports LAT and X.25 printing over a TCP network among multiple sites. Causes the protocol translation software to delay the completion of an incoming Telnet connection until after the outgoing protocol connection (to LAT or X.25) has been successfully established. An unsuccessful outgoing connection attempt results in the TCP connection to the router being refused, rather than being accepted and then closed, which is the default behavior. Note that using this option will force the global option *quiet* to be applied to the translation.
- **stream**—Performs stream processing, which enables a raw TCP stream with no Telnet control sequences. A stream connection does not process or generate any Telnet options, and prevents Telnet processing of the data stream as well. This option might be useful for connections to ports running UUCP or other non-Telnet protocols, or to ports connected to printers. For ports connected to printers using Telnet, the stream option prevents some of usual problems associated with using Telnet for printers, such as "strange" things happening to bare carriage returns or line feeds and echoing of data back to VMS systems.

| *Syntax* | *Description* |
|---|---|
| *protocol outgoing-address* | Name of a protocol followed by a service name, IP address, or host name. The host name is translated to an IP address during configuration. These arguments can have the following values:<br>• **lat** *service-name*—LAT and a LAT service name. You must learn the service name, through LAT service advertisements, before you can use it.<br>• **x25** *X.121-address*—X.25 and an X.121 address. The X.121 address must conform to specifications provided in the *CCITT 1984 Red Book*. This number generally consists of a portion that is administered by the PDN and a portion that is locally assigned. You must be sure that the numbers that you assign agree with the addresses assigned to you by the X.25 service provider. The X.121 addresses will generally be subaddresses of the X.121 address for the X.25 network interface.<br>• **slip** *ip-address*—The argument *ip-address* is a standard, four-part dotted decimal IP address or the name of an IP host that can be resolved by the Domain Name System (DNS). The **slip** argument applies only to outgoing connections; SLIP is not supported on incoming protocol translation connections.<br>• **ppp** *ip-address*—The argument *ip-address* is a standard, four-part dotted decimal IP address or the name of an IP host that can be resolved by the Domain Name System (DNS). The **ppp** argument applies only to outgoing connections; PPP is not supported for incoming protocol translation connections.<br>• **autocommand**—Enables you to specify a string for an outgoing connection. The string executes upon connection to a host. If you want to enable ARA on an outgoing connection, you need to specify **autocommand arap.**<br>The **autocommand** option is necessary for ARA, because ARA does not use addressing, and **autocommand** permits you to invoke the **arap** string.<br>If the string following **autocommand** has one or more spaces as part of the string, you must place quotation marks (" ") around the string. For example, if you specify **autocommand tn3270 abracadabra**, you must enclose **tn3270 abracadabra** in quotes.<br>The **autocommand** option applies only to outgoing connections.<br>You can issue any EXEC command and any switch or host name as an argument to the **autocommand** option. |
| *out-options* | (Optional) Outgoing connection request options. These arguments can have the following values:<br>LAT translation options: |

Part III Command Reference

| *Syntax* | *Description* |
|---|---|
| | • **node** *node-name*—Connects to the specified node (*node-name*) that offers a service. By default, the connection is made to the highest-rated node that offers the service.<br>• **port** *port-name*—Destination LAT port name (*port-name*) in the format of the remote system. This parameter is usually ignored in most timesharing systems, but is used by terminal servers that offer reverse-LAT services.<br>X.25 translation options:<br>• **cud** *c-u-data*—Sends the specified Call User Data (CUD) text (*c-u-data*) as part of an outgoing call request after the protocol identification bytes.<br>• **no-reverse**—Specifies that outgoing calls are not to use reverse charging, when the interface default is that all outgoing calls are reverse charged.<br>• **profile** *profile*—Sets the X.3 PAD parameters as defined in the profile created by the **x29 profile** command.<br>• **reverse**—Provides reverse charging for X.25 on a per-call rather than a per-interface basis. Requests reverse charges on a specified X.121 address, even if the serial interface is not configured to request reverse charge calls. This is an outgoing option only.<br>SLIP and PPP translation options:<br>• **ip-pool**—Obtain an IP address from a DHCP proxy client or a local pool. If the **scope-name** option is not specified, the address is obtained from a DHCP proxy client. If the **scope-name** option is specified, the IP address is obtained from the specified local pool.<br>• **scope-name**—Specific local scope name from which to obtain an IP address. Can specify a range of IP addresses.<br>• **header-compression** [**passive**]—Implements header compression on IP packets only. The option **passive** for SLIP connections permits compression on outgoing packets only if incoming TCP packets on the same virtual asynchronous interface are compressed. The default (without the **passive** option) permits compression on all traffic.<br>• **routing**—Permits routing updates between connections. This option is required if the destination device is not on a subnet connected to one of the interfaces on the router.<br>• **mtu** *bytes*—Permits you to change the maximum transmission unit (MTU) of packets that the virtual asynchronous interface supports. The default MTU is 1,500 bytes on a virtual asynchronous interface. The acceptable range is 64 to 1,000,000 bytes. |

| *Syntax* | *Description* |
|---|---|
| | More PPP translation options:<br>• **keepalive** *number-of-seconds*—Permits you to specify the interval at which keepalive packets are sent on SLIP and PPP virtual asynchronous interfaces. By default, keepalive packets are enabled and are sent every 10 seconds. To shut off keepalive packets, use a value of 0. The active keepalive interval is 1 to 32,767 seconds. When you do not change from the default of 10, the keepalive interval does not appear in **show running-config** or **show translate** output.<br>• **authentication** {**chap** \| **pap**}—Use CHAP or PAP authentication for PPP on virtual asynchronous interfaces. If you specify both options, order is significant; the system will try to use the first authentication type, then the second.<br>• **ppp use-tacacs**—Enables TACACS authentication for CHAP or PAP on virtual asynchronous interfaces (for PPP only; TACACS authentication is not supported for SLIP).<br>• **ipx loopback** *number*—Permits clients running IPX–PPP over X.25 to connect through virtual terminal (VTY) lines on the router. The **loopback** *number* option specifies the loopback interface to be created. A loopback interface must have been created and configured with a Novell IPX network number before IPX–PPP can work on the VTY line. The VTY line is assigned to the loopback interface. |
| *global-options* | (Optional) Translation options that can be used by any connection type. It can be one or more of the following:<br>• **access-class** *number*—Allows the incoming call to be used by source hosts that match the access list parameters. The argument *number* is the number (integer) previously assigned to an access list. The standard access list is 1-99.<br>• **max-users** *number*—Limits the number of simultaneous users of the translation to *number* (an integer you specify).<br>• **local**—Allows Telnet protocol negotiations to *not* be translated.<br>• **rotor**—Provides a basic load sharing of the IP destinations.<br>• **login**—Requires that the user log in before the outgoing connection is made. This type of login is specified on the VTY lines with the **login** command.<br>• **quiet**—Suppresses printing of user-information messages. |



### *Default*

No default translation parameters

### *Command Mode*

Global configuration

### *Usage Guidelines*

This command first appeared in Cisco IOS Release 11.2.

Table 22–8 provides a visual aid for understanding how to use the **translate tcp** command. As the table illustrates, you define the protocol translation connections by choosing a protocol keyword and supplying the appropriate address, host name, or service name. The protocol connection information is followed by optional features for that connection, as appropriate. For example, the **binary** option is only appropriate with TCP/IP connections. The global options, in general, apply to all the connection types, but there are exceptions.

**Table 22–8** *Translate TCP Command Options*

| | Incoming Protocol | Options | Outgoing Protocol | Options | Global Options |
|---|---|---|---|---|---|
| **translate** | *protocol incoming-address* | [*in-options*] | *protocol outgoing-address* | [*out-options*] | [*global-options*] |
| | **tcp** *ip-address* \| *host_name* | **port** *number* | **lat** *service-name* | **node** *node-name* | **access-class** *number* |
| | | **binary** | | **port** *port-name* | **max-users** *number* |
| | | **stream** | **x25** *x.121-address* | **cud** *c-u-data* | **local** |
| | | **printer** | | **no-reverse** | **login** |
| | | | | **profile** *profile* | **quiet** |
| | | | | **reverse** | |
| | | | **slip** *ip-address* | **ip-pool** [**scope-name** *name*] | |
| | | | | **headercompression** [**passive**] | |
| | | | | **routing** | |
| | | | | **keepalive** *number-of-seconds* | |
| | | | | **mtu** *bytes* | |
| | | | **ppp** *ip-address* | **ip-pool** | |

**Table 22–8** *Translate TCP Command Options, Continued*

| | Incoming Protocol | Options | Outgoing Protocol | Options | Global Options |
|---|---|---|---|---|---|
| | | | | **headercompression** [**passive**] | |
| | | | | **routing** | |
| | | | | **keepalive** *number-of-seconds* | |
| | | | | **mtu** *bytes* | |
| | | | | **authentication** {**pap** \| **chap**} | |
| | | | | **ppp use-tacacs** | |
| | | | | **ipx loopback** *number* | |
| | | | **autocommand** [**arap** \| *exec-string*] | | |



### *Examples*

The following example illustrates the use of the TCP incoming protocol option **printer** for an incoming TCP connection:

```
translate tcp 172.19.32.250 printer x25 5678
          incoming          option  outgoing
```

The following example permits clients running IPX/PPP to connect through the device's VTY lines to a server running PPP:

```
interface loopback0
  no ip address
  ipx network 544
  ipx sap-interval 2000
!
translate tcp 172.21.14.67 port 1234 ppp 10.0.0.2 ipx loopback0
!         incoming                   outgoing    option
```

### *Related Commands*

Search online to find documentation for related commands.

**show translate**
**translate lat**
**translate x25**
**x29 access-list**
**x29 profile**

### TRANSLATE TCP (VIRTUAL ACCESS INTERFACES)

When receiving a TCP connection request to a particular destination address or host name, the Cisco router can automatically translate the request to another outgoing protocol connection type. To set this up, use the **translate tcp** global configuration command.

The command syntax that follows shows how to apply a virtual interface template in place of outgoing **translate** options. If you are using virtual templates for protocol translation, all outgoing options are defined in the virtual interface template.

**translate tcp** *incoming-address* [*in-options*] **virtual-template** *number* [*global-options*]

| *Syntax* | *Description* |
|---|---|
| *incoming-address* | TCP/IP Telnet and a standard IP address or host name. The argument *ip-address* is a standard, four-part dotted decimal IP address or the name of an IP host that can be resolved by the Domain Name System (DNS) or explicit specification in an **ip host** command. |
| *in-options* | (Optional) Incoming connection request options. These arguments can have the following values:<br>• **binary**—Negotiates Telnet binary mode on the Telnet connection. (This was the default in previous versions of the Cisco IOS software and is set automatically when you enter at **translate** command in the old format.)<br>• **port** *number*—For incoming connections, enter the number of the port to match. The default is port 23 (any port). For outgoing connections, enter the number of the port to use. The default is port 23 (Telnet).<br>• **printer**—Supports LAT and X.25 printing over a TCP network among multiple sites. This option causes the Cisco IOS software to delay the completion of an incoming Telnet connection until after the outgoing protocol connection (to LAT or X.25) has been successfully established. An unsuccessful outgoing connection attempt results in the TCP connection to the router being refused, rather than being accepted and then closed, which is the default behavior. Note that using this option will force the global option **quiet** to be applied to the translation.<br>• **stream**—Performs stream processing, which enables a raw TCP stream with no Telnet control sequences. A stream connection does not process or generate any Telnet options, and prevents Telnet processing of the data stream as well. This option might be useful for connections to ports running UUCP or other non-Telnet protocols, or to ports connected to printers. For ports connected to printers using Telnet, the stream option prevents some of the usual problems associated with using Telnet for printers, such as "strange" things happening to bare carriage returns or line feeds and echoing of data back to VMS systems. |

| *Syntax* | *Description* |
|---|---|
| **virtual-template** *number* | Applies the virtual interface template specified by *number* in place of outgoing options. |
| *global-options* | (Optional) Translation options that can be used by any connection type. It can be one or more of the following:<br>• **access-class** *number*—Allows the incoming call to be used by source hosts that match the access list parameters. The argument *number* is an integer value previously assigned to an access list. The standard access list range is from 1 to 99.<br>• **local**—Allows Telnet protocol negotiations to *not* be translated.<br>• **login**—Requires that the user log in before the outgoing connection is made. This type of login is specified on the VTY lines with the **login** command.<br>• **max-users** *number*—Maximum number of simultaneous users of the translation.<br>• **quiet**—Suppresses printing of user-information messages.<br>• **rotor**—Provides a basic load sharing of the IP destinations. |



### Default

No default translation parameters

### Command Mode

Global configuration

### Usage Guidelines

This command first appeared before Cisco IOS Release 10.0.

You define the protocol translation connections by choosing a protocol keyword and supplying the appropriate address, host name, or service name. The protocol connection information is followed by optional features for that connection, as appropriate. For example, the **binary** option is only appropriate with TCP/IP connections. The global options, in general, apply to all the connection types, but there are exceptions.

### Example

The following example illustrates the use of the TCP incoming option **printer** for an incoming TCP connection:

```
interface Virtual-Template1
 ip unnumbered Ethernet0
 peer default ip address 10.12.108.1
 ppp authentication chap
```

```
translate tcp 172.19.32.250 printer Virtual-Template1
          incoming          option  outgoing
```

*Related Commands*

Search online to find documentation for related commands.

**show translate**
**translate lat**
**translate x25**
**x29 access-list**
**x29 profile**

## TRANSLATE X25

When receiving an X.25 connection request to a particular destination address, the Cisco router can automatically translate the request to another outgoing protocol connection type. To set this up, use the **translate** global configuration command.

**translate x25** *incoming-address* [*in-options*] *protocol outgoing-address* [*out-options*] [*global-options*]

| *Syntax* | *Description* |
|---|---|
| *incoming-address* | X.25 and an X.121 address. The X.121 address must conform to specifications provided in the *CCITT 1984 Red Book*. This number generally consists of a portion that is administered by the PDN and a portion that is locally assigned. You must be sure that the numbers that you assign agree with the addresses assigned to you by the X.25 service provider. The X.121 addresses will generally be subaddresses of the X.121 address for the X.25 network interface. Typically, the interface address will be a 12-digit number. Any additional digits are interpreted as a subaddress. The PDN still routes these calls to the interface, and the Cisco IOS software itself is responsible for dealing with the extra digits appropriately. Do not use the same address on the interface and for translation. |
| *in-options* | (Optional) Incoming connection request options. These arguments can have the following values:<br>• **accept-reverse**—Accepts reverse charged calls on an X.121 address even if the serial interface is not configured to accept reverse charged calls. This is an incoming option only.<br>• **cud** *c-u-data*—Sends the specified Call User Data (CUD) text (*c-u-data*) as part of an outgoing call request after the protocol identification bytes. |

| *Syntax* | *Description* |
|---|---|
| | • **idle** *minutes*—Specifies the number of minutes the VC is idle. This option enables the protocol translation function to clear a switched virtual circuit (SVC) after a set period of inactivity, where *minutes* is the number of minutes in the period. Calls either originated or terminated are cleared. The maximum value of *minutes* is 255. The default value of *minutes* is zero.<br>• **printer**—Supports LAT and TCP printing over an X.25 network among multiple sites. Provides an "interlock mechanism" between the acceptance of an incoming X.25 connection and the opening of an outgoing LAT or TCP connection. The option causes the Cisco IOS software to delay the call confirmation of an incoming X.25 call request until the outgoing protocol connection (to TCP or LAT) has been successfully established. An unsuccessful outgoing connection attempt to the router results in the incoming X.25 connection being refused, rather than being confirmed and then cleared, which is the default behavior. Note that using this option will force the global option **quiet** to be applied to the translation.<br>• **profile** *profile*—Sets the X.3 PAD parameters as defined in the profile created by the **x29 profile** command. |
| *protocol outgoing-address* | Name of a protocol followed by a service name, IP address, or host name. The host name is translated to an IP address during configuration, unless you use the TCP **host-name** option, which allows load balancing by dynamically resolving an IP address from a host name. These arguments can have the following values:<br>• **lat** *service-name*—LAT and a LAT service name. You must learn the service name, through LAT service advertisements, before you can use it.<br>• **tcp** *ip-address*—TCP/IP Telnet and a standard IP address or host name. The argument *ip-address* is a standard, four-part dotted decimal IP address or the name of an IP host that can be resolved by the Domain Name System (DNS) or explicit specification in an **ip host** command.<br>• **slip** *ip-address*—The argument *ip-address* is a standard, four-part dotted decimal IP address or the name of an IP host that can be resolved by the Domain Name System (DNS). The **slip** argument applies only to outgoing connections; SLIP is not supported on incoming protocol translation connections. |

| *Syntax* | *Description* |
| --- | --- |
| | • **ppp** *ip-address*—The argument *ip-address* is a standard, four-part dotted decimal IP address or the name of an IP host that can be resolved by the Domain Name System (DNS). The **ppp** argument applies only to outgoing connections; PPP is not supported for incoming protocol translation connections.<br>• **autocommand**—Enables you to specify a string for an outgoing connection. The string executes upon connection to a host. If you want to enable ARA on an outgoing connection, you need to specify the **autocommand arap** string.<br>The **autocommand** option is necessary for ARA, because ARA does not use addressing, and **autocommand** permits you to invoke the **arap** string.<br>If the string following **autocommand** has one or more spaces as part of the string, you must place quotation marks (" ") around the string. For example, if you specify **autocommand tn3270 abracadabra**, you must enclose the **tn3270 abracadabra** string in quotes.<br>The **autocommand** option applies only to outgoing connections.<br>You can issue any EXEC command and any switch or host name as an argument to the **autocommand** option. |
| *out-options* | (Optional) Outgoing connection request options. These arguments can have the following values:<br>• **use-map**—Applies **x25 map pad** command entry options (such as CUD and idle) and facilities (such as packet in, packet out, win in, and win out) to the outgoing protocol translation call. This application occurs when the protocol translation function searches the X.25 map PAD entries and finds a matching X.121 destination address. The X.25 map facilities applied to the outgoing translation can be viewed with the **show translation** command throughout the duration of the translation session.<br>LAT translation options:<br>• **node** *node-name*—Connects to the specified node (*node-name*) that offers a service. By default, the connection is made to the highest-rated node that offers the service.<br>• **port** *port-name*—Destination LAT port name (*port-name*) in the format of the remote system. This parameter is usually ignored in most timesharing systems but is used by terminal servers that offer reverse-LAT services. |

| *Syntax* | *Description* |
|---|---|

Telnet TCP translation options:

- **port** *number*—For incoming connections, number of the port to match. The default is port 23 (any port). For outgoing connections, number of the port to use. The default is port 23 (Telnet).

SLIP and PPP translation options:

- **ip-pool**—Obtain an IP address from a DHCP proxy client or a local pool. If the **scope-name** option is not specified, the address is obtained from a DHCP proxy client. If the **scope-name** option is specified, the IP address is obtained from the specified local pool.
- **scope-name**—Specific local scope name from which to obtain an IP address. This option can specify a range of IP addresses.
- **header-compression** [**passive**]—Implements header compression on IP packets only. The option **passive** for SLIP connections permits compression on outgoing packets only if incoming TCP packets on the same virtual asynchronous interface are compressed. The default (without the **passive** option) permits compression on all traffic.
- **routing**—Permits routing updates between connections. This option is required if the destination device is not on a subnet connected to one of the interfaces on the router.
- **mtu** *bytes*—Permits you to change the maximum transmission unit (MTU) of packets that the virtual asynchronous interface supports. The default MTU is 1,500 bytes on a virtual asynchronous interface. The acceptable range is 64 to 1,000,000 bytes.

PPP translation options:

- **keepalive** *number-of-seconds*—Permits you to specify the interval at which keepalive packets are sent on SLIP and PPP virtual asynchronous interfaces. By default, keepalive packets are enabled and are sent every 10 seconds. To shut off keepalive packets, use a value of 0. The active keepalive interval is 1 to 32767 seconds. When you do not change from the default of 10, the keepalive interval does not appear in the **show running-config** or **show translate** command output.
- **authentication** {**chap** | **pap**}—Use CHAP or PAP authentication for PPP on virtual asynchronous interfaces. If you specify both options, order is significant; the system will try to use the first authentication type, then the second.
- **ppp use-tacacs**—Enables TACACS authentication for CHAP or PAP on virtual asynchronous interfaces (for PPP only; TACACS authentication is not supported for SLIP).

| *Syntax* | *Description* |
|---|---|
| | • **ipx loopback** *number*—Specifies the loopback interface to be created and permits clients running IPX-PPP over X.25 to connect through virtual terminal (VTY) lines on the router. A loopback interface must have been created and configured with a Novell IPX network number before IPX-PPP can work on the VTY line. The VTY line is assigned to the loopback interface. |
| *global-options* | (Optional) Translation options that can be used by any connection type. It can be one or more of the following:<br>• **access-class** *number*—Allows the incoming call to be used by source hosts that match the access list parameters. The argument *number* is the number (integer) previously assigned to an access list. The standard access list is 1 to 99.<br>• **max-users** *number*—Limits the number of simultaneous users of the translation to *number* (an integer you specify).<br>• **local**—Prevents Telnet protocol negotiations from being translated.<br>• **login**—Requires that the user log in before the outgoing connection is made. This type of login is specified on the VTY lines with the **login** command.<br>• **rotor**—Provides a basic load sharing of the IP destinations.<br>• **quiet**—Suppresses printing of user-information messages.<br>• **swap**—Allows X.3 parameters to be set on the router by the host originating the X.25 call or by an X.29 profile. This configuration enables incoming and outgoing X.25 connections to be swapped so that the device is treated like a PAD when it accepts a call. By default, the router functions like a PAD for calls that it initiates, and like an X.25 host for calls it accepts. The **swap** keyword allows connections from an X.25 host that wants to connect to the router, and then treats it like a PAD. For X.25-to-TCP translations only. |

| *Syntax* | *Description* |
|---|---|
| | • **pvc** *number* {[**interface serial** *number*] [**packetsize** *in-size out-size*] [**windowsize** *in-size out-size*]}—Specifies that the incoming or outgoing connection is actually a permanent virtual circuit (PVC). Only one session is allowed per PVC, where:<br>*number* —Specifies the virtual-circuit channel number of the incoming connection, which must be less than the virtual circuits assigned to the switched virtual circuits (SVC).<br>**interface serial** *number*—Specifies a PVC interface on which to set up the PVC connection.<br>**packetsize** *in-size out-size*—Specifies the input packet size (*in-size*) and output packet size (*out-size*) for the PVC. Following are valid packet size values:<br>16, 32, 64, 128, 256, 512, 1024, 2048, or 4096<br>**windowsize** *in-size out-size*—Specifies the packet count for input windows (*in-size*) and output windows (*out-size*) for the outgoing translation. Values of *in-size* and *out-size* range 1 to 127 and must not be greater than the value set for the **x25 modulo** command. You must specify the same value for *in-size* and *out-size.* |



### *Default*

No default translation parameters

### *Command Mode*

Global configuration

### *Usage Guidelines*

This command first appeared in Cisco IOS Release 10.0.

Table 22–9 provides a visual aid for understanding how the command syntax flows for the **translate x25** command. In the table, follow the steps horizontally (from left to right). As you travel from step to step, you can choose from a vertical list of options at each step. As the table illustrates, you define the protocol translation connections by choosing a protocol keyword and supplying the appropriate address or service name. The protocol connection information is followed by optional features for that connection, as appropriate. The global options, in general, apply to all the connection types, but there are exceptions. The **swap** keyword, for example, is for X.25 to TCP translations only. See the examples for more explanations on how to enter this command.

To use virtual templates with incoming X.25 translation, see the **translate x.25 (virtual access interfaces)** command.

**Table 22–9** *Sequence of Steps for Translating a Protocol*

| | Incoming Address Step 1 | Incoming Options Step 2 | Protocol Outgoing Address Step 3 | Outgoing Options Step 4 | Global Options Step 5 |
|---|---|---|---|---|---|
| translate x25 | x.21 address | idle *minutes* | lat *service-name* | use-map | access-class *number* |
| | | cud *c-u-data* | tcp *ip-address* | node *node-name* | max-users *number* |
| | | profile *profile* | slip *ip-address* | port *port-name* | local |
| | | accept-reverse | ppp *ip-address* | port *number* | login |
| | | printer | autocommand [arap \| *exec-string*] | host-name *name* | quiet |
| | | *idle minutes* | | multibyte-iac | swap |
| | | | | ip-pool [scope-name *name*] | pvc [*number* \| interface *serial-number*] packetsize *in-size out-size* windowsize *in-size out-size* |
| | | | | headercompression [passive] | |
| | | | | routing | |
| | | | | keepalive *number-of-seconds* | |
| | | | | mtu *bytes* | |
| | | | | ip-pool | |
| | | | | headercompression [passive] | |
| | | | | routing | |
| | | | | keepalive *number-of-seconds* | |

**Table 22–9** *Sequence of Steps for Translating a Protocol, Continued*

| | Incoming Address Step 1 | Incoming Options Step 2 | Protocol Outgoing Address Step 3 | Outgoing Options Step 4 | Global Options Step 5 |
|---|---|---|---|---|---|
| | | | | **mtu** *bytes* | |
| | | | | **authentication {pap \| chap}** | |
| | | | | **ppp use-tacacs** | |
| | | | | **ipx loopback** *number* | |



### *Examples*

The following example illustrates a simple X.25-to-TCP **translate x25** command. Packets coming in X.25 address 652365123 arrive via PVC 1 and are translated to TCP packets and transmitted out IP address 172.16.1.1.

```
translate x25 652365123 pvc 1 tcp 172.16.1.1
!         incoming       option outgoing
```

The following example illustrates a more complex configuration that calls an X.29 profile and swaps the default PAD operation of the router to that of an X.25 host. The name of the profile is *fullpackets*.

```
x29 profile fullpackets 2:0 3:0 4:100 7:21
translate x25 217536124 profile fullpackets tcp rubble port 4006 swap
!         incoming      option              outgoing   option    global
```

The following example illustrates the use of the X.25 incoming protocol option **printer** for an incoming X.25 connection:

```
translate x25 55555 printer tcp 172.16.1.1
!         incoming   option  outgoing
```

The following example translates X.25 packets to PPP. It enables routing updates between the two connections:

```
translate x25 12345678 ppp 10.0.0.2 routing
!         incoming     outgoing    option
```

The following example permits clients running ARA to connect through the devices' VTY lines to an AppleTalk network:

```
appletalk routing
translate x25 12345678 autocommand arap
!         incoming     outgoing
  arap enable
  arap dedicated
  arap timelimit 45
  arap warningtime 5
  arap noguest
```

```
arap require-manual-password
arap net-access-list 614
```

The following example specifies IP pooling from a DHCP server named *ludicrous*. It then specifies that incoming TCP traffic be translated to SLIP. The DHCP server will dynamically assign IP addresses on the outgoing sessions.

```
ip address-pool dhcp-proxy-client
ip dhcp-server ludicrous
translate x25 5467835 ppp ip-pool scope-name ludicrous
```

The following example specifies a local IP pool named *scandal* with IP addresses ranging from 172.18.10.10 to 172.18.10.110. It then specifies that incoming X.25 traffic be translated to PPP. The local IP pool *scandal* will be used to dynamically assign IP addresses on the outgoing sessions.

```
ip-pool scandal 172.18.10.10 172.18.10.110
translate x25 1234567 ppp ip-pool scope-name scandal
```

X.25 calls are cleared if they are idle for the configured time, as shown in the following example:

```
translate x25 1234 idle 2 lat shazam
```

### *Related Commands*

Search online to find documentation for related commands.

**show translate**
**translate lat**
**translate tcp**
**x29 access-list**
**x29 profile**

## TRANSLATE X25 (VIRTUAL ACCESS INTERFACES)

When receiving a X.25 connection request to a particular destination address, the Cisco router can automatically translate the request to another outgoing protocol connection type. To set up this feature, use the **translate x25** global configuration command.

The command syntax that follows shows how to apply a virtual interface template in place of outgoing **translate x25** options. If you are using virtual templates for protocol translation, all outgoing options are defined in the virtual interface template. Table 22–10 lists all outgoing options and their corresponding interface configuration commands.

**translate x25** *incoming-address* [*in-options*] **virtual-template** *number* [*global-options*]

| *Syntax* | *Description* |
|---|---|
| *incoming-address* | X.25 and an X.121 address. The X.121 address must conform to specifications provided in the *CCITT 1984 Red Book*. This number generally consists of a portion that is administered by the PDN and a portion that is locally assigned. You must be sure that the numbers that you assign agree with the addresses assigned to you by the X.25 service provider. The X.121 addresses will generally be subaddresses of the X.121 address for the X.25 network interface. Typically, the interface address will be a 12-digit number. Any additional digits are interpreted as a subaddress. The PDN still routes these calls to the interface, and the Cisco IOS software is responsible for appropriately dealing with the extra digits. Do not use the same address on the interface and for translation. |
| *in-options* | (Optional) Incoming connection request options. These arguments can have the following values:<br>• **accept-reverse**—Accepts reverse charged calls on an X.121 address even if the serial interface is not configured to accept reverse charged calls. This is an incoming option only.<br>• **cud** *c-u-data*—Sends the specified Call User Data (CUD) text (*c-u-data*) as part of an outgoing call request after the protocol identification bytes.<br>• **printer**—Supports LAT and TCP printing over an X.25 network among multiple sites. Provides an "interlock mechanism" between the acceptance of an incoming X.25 connection and the opening of an outgoing LAT or TCP connection. The option causes the Cisco IOS software to delay the call confirmation of an incoming X.25 call request until the outgoing protocol connection (to TCP or LAT) has been successfully established. An unsuccessful outgoing connection attempt to the router results in the incoming X.25 connection being refused, rather than being confirmed and then cleared, which is the default behavior. Note that using this option will force the global option **quiet** to be applied to the translation.<br>• **profile** *profile*—Sets the X.3 PAD parameters as defined in the profile created by the **x29 profile** command.<br>• **pvc** *number*—Specifies that the incoming connection (identified by the argument *number*) is actually a permanent virtual circuit (PVC). |
| **virtual-template** *number* | Apply the virtual interface template specified by *number* in place of outgoing options. |

| *Syntax* | *Description* |
| --- | --- |
| *global-options* | (Optional) Translation options that can be used by any connection type. It can be one or more of the following:<br>• **access-class** *number*—Allows the incoming call to be used by source hosts that match the access list parameters. The argument *number* is an integer in the range 1 to 99 that was previously assigned to an access list.<br>• **max-users** *number*—Limits the number of simultaneous users of the translation to *number* (an integer you specify).<br>• **local**—Allows Telnet protocol negotiations to *not* be translated.<br>• **login**—Requires that the user log in before the outgoing connection is made. This type of login is specified on the VTY lines with the **login** command.<br>• **rotor**—Provides a basic load sharing of the IP destinations.<br>• **quiet**—Suppresses printing of user-information messages.<br>• **swap**—Allows X.3 parameters to be set on the router by the host originating the X.25 call, or by an X.29 profile. This allows incoming and outgoing X.25 connections to be swapped so that the device is treated like a PAD when it accepts a call. By default, the router functions like a PAD for calls that it initiates, and like an X.25 host for calls it accepts. The **swap** keyword allows connections from an X.25 host that wants to connect to the router, and then treats it like a PAD. For X.25-to-TCP translations only. |

### *Default*

No default translation parameters

### *Command Mode*

Global configuration

### *Usage Guidelines*

This command first appeared before Cisco IOS Release 10.0.

You define the protocol translation connections by choosing a protocol keyword and supplying the appropriate address or service name. The protocol connection information is followed by optional features for that connection, as appropriate. The global options, in general, apply to all the connection types, but there are exceptions. The **swap** keyword, for example, is for X.25 to TCP translations only. See the example for more explanations on how to enter this command.

Rather than specifying outgoing translation options in the **translate** command, configure these options as interface configuration commands under the virtual interface template, then apply the virtual interface template to the **translate** command. Table 22–10 maps outgoing **translate** command options to interface commands you can configure in the virtual interface template.

**Table 22–10** *Mapping Outgoing Translate Command Options to Interface Commands*

| Translate Command Options | Corresponding Interface Configuration Command |
|---|---|
| **ip-pool** | **peer default ip address** {**ip-address** \| **dhcp** \| **pool** [*poolname*]} |
| **header-compression** | **ip tcp header compression** [**on** \| **off** \| **passive**] |
| **routing** | **ip routing** or **ipx routing** |
| **mtu** | **mtu** |
| **keepalive** | **keepalive** |
| **authentication** {**chap** \| **pap**} | **ppp authentication** {**chap** \| **pap**} |
| **ppp use-tacacs** | **ppp use-tacacs** |
| **ipx loopback** | **ipx ppp-client loopback** *number* |



### *Example*

The following example shows a virtual template with PPP encapsulation specified by default (not explicit). It also specifies CHAP authentication and an X.29 access list.

```
x29 access-list 1 permit ^5555
!
interface Virtual-Template1
 ip unnumbered Ethernet0
 peer default ip address 172.16.2.129
 ppp authentication chap
!
translate x25 5555667 virtual-template 1 access-class 1
```

### *Related Commands*

Search online to find documentation for related commands.

**interface virtual-template**
**show translate**
**translate lat**
**translate tcp**
**x29 access-list**
**x29 profile**

### VTY-ASYNC

To configure all virtual terminal lines on a router to support asynchronous protocol features, use the **vty-async** global configuration command. Use the **no** form of this command to disable asynchronous protocol features on virtual terminal lines.

**vty-async**
**no vty-async**

#### *Syntax Description*

This command has no arguments or keywords.

#### *Default*

Asynchronous protocol features are not enabled by default on virtual terminal lines.

#### *Command Mode*

Global configuration

#### *Usage Guidelines*

This command first appeared in Cisco IOS Release 10.3.

The **vty-async** command extends asynchronous protocol features from physical asynchronous interfaces to virtual terminal lines. Normally, SLIP and PPP can function only on asynchronous interfaces, not on virtual terminal lines. However, extending asynchronous functionality to virtual terminal lines permits you to run SLIP and PPP on these *virtual asynchronous interfaces*. One practical benefit is the ability to tunnel SLIP and PPP over X.25 PAD, thus extending remote node capability into the X.25 area. You can also tunnel SLIP and PPP over Telnet or LAT on virtual terminal lines. To tunnel SLIP and PPP over X.25, LAT, or Telnet, you use the protocol translation feature in the Cisco IOS software.

To tunnel SLIP or PPP inside X.25, LAT, or Telnet, you can use two-step protocol translation or one-step protocol translation, as follows:

- If you are tunnelling SLIP or PPP using the two-step method, you need to first enter the **vty-async** command. Next, you perform two-step translation.
- If you are tunnelling SLIP or PPP using the one-step method, you do not need to enter the **vty-async** command. You only need to issue the **translate** command with the SLIP or PPP keywords, because the **translate** command automatically enables asynchronous protocol features on virtual terminal lines.

#### *Example*

The following example enables asynchronous protocol features on virtual terminal lines:

```
vty-async
```

### Related Commands

Search online to find documentation for related commands.

**ppp**
**slip**
**translate**

## VTY-ASYNC DYNAMIC-ROUTING

To enable dynamic routing on all virtual asynchronous interfaces, use the **vty-async dynamic-routing** global configuration command. Use the **no** form of this command to disable asynchronous protocol features on virtual terminal lines and, therefore, disable routing on virtual terminal lines.

**vty-async dynamic-routing**
**no vty-async**



### Syntax Description

This command has no arguments or keywords.

### Default

Dynamic routing is not enabled on virtual asynchronous interfaces.

### Command Mode

Global configuration

### Usage Guidelines

This command first appeared in Cisco IOS Release 10.3.

This feature enables IP routing on virtual asynchronous interfaces. When you issue this command and a user later makes a connection to another host using SLIP or PPP, the user must specify **/routing** on the SLIP or PPP command line.

If you had not previously entered the **vty-async** command, the **vty-async dynamic-routing** command creates virtual asynchronous interfaces, then enables dynamic routing on them.

### Example

The following example enables dynamic routing on virtual asynchronous interfaces:

```
vty-async dynamic-routing
```

### Related Commands

Search online to find documentation for related commands.

**async dynamic routing**

## VTY-ASYNC HEADER-COMPRESSION

To compress the headers of all TCP packets on virtual asynchronous interfaces, use the **vty-async header-compression** global configuration command. Use the **no** form of this command to disable virtual asynchronous interfaces and header compression.

**vty-async header-compression [passive]**
**no vty-async**

| *Syntax* | *Description* |
| --- | --- |
| **passive** | (Optional) Specifies that outgoing packets to be compressed only if TCP incoming packets on the same virtual asynchronous interface are compressed. For SLIP, if you do not specify this option, the Cisco IOS software will compress all traffic. The default is no compression. For PPP, the Cisco IOS software always negotiates header compression. |

### *Default*

Header compression is not enabled on virtual asynchronous interfaces.

### *Command Mode*

Global Configuration

### *Usage Guidelines*

This command first appeared in Cisco IOS Release 10.3.

This feature compresses the headers on TCP/IP packets on virtual asynchronous connections to reduce the size of the packets and to increase performance.This feature only compresses the TCP header, so it has no effect on UDP packets or other protocol headers. The TCP header compression technique, described fully in RFC 1144, is supported on virtual asynchronous interfaces using SLIP or PPP encapsulation. You must enable compression on both ends of a connection.

### *Example*

The following example compresses outgoing TCP packets on virtual asynchronous interfaces only if incoming TCP packets are compressed:

```
vty-async header-compression passive
```

### *Related Commands*

Search online to find documentation for related commands.

**async dynamic routing**

### VTY-ASYNC IPX PPP-CLIENT LOOPBACK

To enable IPX–PPP on virtual terminal (VTY) lines, use the **vty-async ipx ppp-client loopback** global configuration command. Use the **no** form of this command to disable IPX–PPP sessions on VTYs.

**vty-async ipx ppp-client loopback** *number*
**no vty-async**

| *Syntax* | *Description* |
|---|---|
| *number* | Number of the loopback interface configured for IPX to which the VTY lines are assigned. |



#### *Default*

IPX over PPP is not enabled on VTY lines.

#### *Command Mode*

Global configuration

#### *Usage Guidelines*

This command first appeared in Cisco IOS Release 11.0.

This command enables users to log in to the router from a device running a virtual terminal protocol, then issue the PPP command at the EXEC prompt to connect to a remote device.

A loopback interface must already have been defined and an IPX network number must have been assigned to the loopback interface before the **vty-async ipx ppp-client loopback** command will permit IPX–PPP on VTY lines.

#### *Example*

The following example enables IPX over PPP on VTY lines:

```
ipx routing ramana
interface loopback0
 ipx network 12345
vty-async ipx ppp-client loopback0
```

#### *Related Commands*

Search online to find documentation for related commands.

**interface loopback**
**ipx network**

### VTY-ASYNC KEEPALIVE

To change the frequency of keepalive packets on all virtual asynchronous interfaces, use the **vty-async keepalive** global configuration command. Use the **no vty-async** command to disable asynchronous protocol features on virtual terminal lines, or the **vty-async keepalive 0** command to disable keepalive packets on virtual terminal lines.

**vty-async keepalive** *seconds*
**no vty-async**
**vty-async keepalive 0**

| *Syntax* | *Description* |
| --- | --- |
| *seconds* | The frequency, in seconds, with which the Cisco IOS software sends keepalive messages to the other end of a virtual asynchronous interface. To disable keepalive packets, use a value of 0. The active keepalive interval is 1 to 32767 seconds. The default is 10 seconds. |

#### *Default*

10 seconds

#### *Command Mode*

Global configuration

#### *Usage Guidelines*

This command first appeared in Cisco IOS Release 10.3.

Use this command to change the frequency of keepalive updates on virtual asynchronous interfaces from the default of 10, or to disable keepalive updates. If you do not change from the default of 10, the keepalive interval does not appear in **show running-config** or **show translate** output.

A connection is declared down after three update intervals have passed without receiving a keepalive packet.

#### *Examples*

In the following example, the keepalive interval is set to 30 seconds.

```
vty-async keepalive 30
```

In the following example, the keepalive interval is set to 0 (off), and the sample output for **show running-config** is shown.

```
vty-async keepalive 0

router# show running-config
no vty-async keepalive
```

### Related Commands

Search online to find documentation for related commands.

**keepalive**

## VTY-ASYNC MTU

To set the maximum transmission unit (MTU) size on virtual asynchronous interfaces, use the **vty-async mtu** global configuration command. Use the **no** form of this command to disable asynchronous protocol features on virtual terminal lines.

**vty-async mtu** *bytes*
**no vty-async**

| *Syntax* | *Description* |
|---|---|
| *bytes* | MTU size of IP packets that the virtual asynchronous interface can support. The default MTU is 1,500 bytes, the minimum MTU is 64 bytes, and the maximum is 1,000,000 bytes. |



### Default

1,500 bytes

### Command Mode

Global configuration

### Usage Guidelines

This command first appeared in Cisco IOS Release 10.3.

Use this command to modify the maximum transmission unit (MTU) for packets on a virtual asynchronous interfaces. You might want to change to a smaller MTU size for IP packets transmitted on a virtual terminal line configured for asynchronous functions for any of the following reasons:

- The SLIP or PPP application at the other end only supports packets up to a certain size.
- You want to ensure a shorter delay by using smaller packets.
- The host echoing takes longer than 0.2 second.

Do not change the MTU size unless the SLIP or PPP implementation running on the host at the other end of the virtual asynchronous interface supports reassembly of IP fragments. Because each fragment occupies a spot in the output queue, it might also be necessary to increase the size of the SLIP or PPP hold queue if your MTU size is such that you might have a high amount of packet fragments in the output queue.

### Example

The following example sets the MTU for IP packets to 256 bytes:

```
vty-async mtu 256
```

### *Related Commands*

Search online to find documentation for related commands.

**mtu**

## VTY-ASYNC PPP AUTHENTICATION

To enable PPP authentication on virtual asynchronous interfaces, use the **vty-async ppp authentication** {**chap** | **pap**} global configuration command. Use the **no** form of this command to disable PPP authentication.

**vty-async ppp authentication** {**chap** | **pap**}
**no vty-async ppp authentication** {**chap** | **pap**}

| *Syntax* | *Description* |
|---|---|
| **chap** | Enable CHAP on all virtual asynchronous interfaces. |
| **pap** | Enable PAP on all virtual asynchronous interfaces. |

### *Default*

No CHAP or PAP authentication for PPP.

### *Command Mode*

Global configuration

### *Usage Guidelines*

This command first appeared in Cisco IOS Release 10.3.

This command configures the virtual asynchronous interface to either authenticate CHAP or PAP while running PPP. After you have enabled CHAP or PAP, the local router requires a password from remote devices. If the remote device does not support CHAP or PAP, no traffic will be passed to that device.

### *Example*

The following example enables CHAP authentication for PPP sessions on virtual asynchronous interfaces:

```
vty-async ppp authentication chap
```

### *Related Commands*

Search online to find documentation for related commands.

**ppp authentication chap**
**ppp authentication pap**
**ppp use-tacacs**
**vty-async**
**vty-async ppp use-tacacs**

## VTY-ASYNC PPP USE-TACACS

To enable TACACS authentication for PPP on virtual asynchronous interfaces, use the **vty-async ppp use-tacacs** global configuration command. Use the **no** form of this command to disable TACACS authentication on virtual asynchronous interfaces.

**vty-async ppp use-tacacs**
**no vty-async ppp use-tacacs**

### *Syntax Description*

This command has no arguments or keywords.

### *Default*

TACACS for PPP is disabled.

### *Command Mode*

Global configuration

### *Usage Guidelines*

This command first appeared in Cisco IOS Release 10.3.

This command requires the extended TACACS server.

After you have enabled TACACS, the local router requires a password from remote devices.

This feature is useful when integrating TACACS with other authentication systems that require a clear-text version of a user's password. Such systems include one-time password systems and token card systems.

If the username and password are contained in the CHAP password, then the CHAP secret is not used by the router. Because most PPP clients require that a secret be specified, you can use any arbitrary string; the Cisco IOS software ignores it.

You cannot enable TACACS authentication for SLIP on asynchronous or virtual asynchronous interfaces.

### *Example*

The following example enables TACACS authentication for PPP sessions:

```
vty-async ppp use-tacacs
```

### *Related Commands*

Search online to find documentation for related commands.

**ppp use-tacacs**
**vty-async ppp authentication**

### VTY-ASYNC VIRTUAL-TEMPLATE

To configure virtual terminal (VTY) lines to support asynchronous protocol functions based on the definition of a virtual interface template, use the **vty-async virtual-template** global configuration command. Use the **no** form of this command to disable virtual interface templates for asynchronous functions on virtual terminal lines.

**vty-async virtual-template** *number*
**no vty-async**

| *Syntax* | *Description* |
|---|---|
| *number* | The virtual interface number. |

#### *Default*

Asynchronous protocol features are not enabled by default on virtual terminal lines.

#### *Command Mode*

Global configuration

#### *Usage Guidelines*

The **vty-async** command first appeared in Cisco IOS Release 10.3. The **vty-async virtual-template** command first appeared in Cisco IOS Release 11.3.

The **vty-async virtual-template** command enables you to support tunneling of SLIP or PPP across X.25, TCP, or LAT networks by using two-step protocol translation.

Before issuing the **vty-async virtual-template** command, create and configure a virtual interface template by using the **interface virtual-template** command. Configure this virtual interface as a regular asynchronous serial interface. That is, assign the virtual interface template the IP address of the Ethernet interface, and configure addressing, just as on an asynchronous interface. You can also enter commands in interface configuration mode that compress TCP headers or configure CHAP authentication for PPP.

After creating a virtual interface template, apply it by issuing the **vty-async virtual-template** command. When a user dials in through a VTY line, the router creates a virtual access interface, which is a temporary interface that supports the asynchronous protocol configuration specified in the virtual interface template. This virtual access interface is created dynamically, and is freed up as soon as the connection drops.

Before virtual templates were implemented, you could use the **vty-async** command to extend asynchronous protocol functions from physical asynchronous interfaces to VTY lines. However, in doing so, you created a virtual asynchronous interface, rather than the virtual access interface. The difference is that the virtual asynchronous interfaces are allocated permanently, whereas the virtual access interfaces are created dynamically when a user calls in and closed down when the connection drops.

You can have up to 25 virtual templates interfaces, but you can apply only one template to vty-async interfaces on a router. There can be up to 300 virtual access interfaces on a router.

### *Example*

The following example enables asynchronous protocol features on virtual terminal lines:

```
vty-async
vty-async Virtual-Template 1
vty-async dynamic-routing
vty-async header-compression
!
interface Virtual-Template1
 ip unnumbered Ethernet0
 encapsulation ppp
 no peer default ip address
 ppp authentication chap
```

### *Related Commands*

Search online to find documentation for related commands.

**ppp**
**slip**
**translate lat**
**translate tcp**
**translate x25**
**interface virtual-template**



## X25 HOST

Use the **x25 host** global configuration command to define a static host name-to-address mapping. Use the **no** form of this command to remove the host name.

**x25 host** *name x.121-address* [**cud** *call-user-data*]
**no x25 host** *name*

| *Syntax* | *Description* |
|---|---|
| *name* | Host name. |
| *x.121-address* | X.121 address. |
| **cud** *call-user-data* | (Optional) Specifies the Call User Data (CUD) field in the X.25 Call Request packet. |

### *Default*

No static address mapping is defined.

### *Command Mode*

Global configuration

### *Usage Guidelines*

This command first appeared in Cisco IOS Release 10.0.

This command permits you to map an X.121 address to an easily recognizable name. You can later use this host name instead of the X.121 address when you issue the **translate** command for X.25.

### *Examples*

The following example specifies a static address mapping:

```
x25 host Willard 4085551212
```

The following example removes a static address mapping:

```
no x25 host Willard
```

The following example specifies static address mapping from the X.121 address 12345678 to the host name *masala*. It then uses the name *masala* in the **translate** command in place of the X.121 address when translating from the X.25 host to the PPP host with address 10.0.0.2.

```
x25 host masala 12345678
translate x25 masala ppp 10.0.0.2 routing
```

### *Related Commands*

Search online to find documentation for related commands.

**translate**

## X29 ACCESS-LIST

To limit access to the access server from certain X.25 hosts, use the **x29 access-list** global configuration command. To delete an entire access list, use the **no** form of this command.

**x29 access-list** *access-list-number* {**permit** | **deny**} *rx121-address*
**no x29 access-list** *access-list-number*

| *Syntax* | *Description* |
|---|---|
| *access-list-number* | Number of the access list. It can be a value between 1 and 199. |
| **deny** | Denies access and clears call requests immediately. |

| *Syntax* | *Description* |
|---|---|
| **permit** | Permits access to the router. |
| *x121-address* | If applied as an inbound access class, specifies the X.121 address that can or cannot have access (with or without regular expression pattern-matching characters). The X.121 address is the source address of the incoming packet.<br>If applied as an outbound access class, then the address specifies a destination to where connections are allowed. |

### *Default*

No access lists are defined.

### *Command Mode*

Global configuration

### *Usage Guidelines*

This command first appeared in Cisco IOS Release 10.0.

An access list can contain any number of access list items. The list items are processed in the order in which you entered them, with the first match causing the permit or deny condition. If an X.121 address does not match any of the regular expressions in the access list, access will be denied.

Access lists take advantage of the message field defined by Recommendation X.29, which describes procedures for exchanging data between two PADs or a PAD and a DTE device.

The UNIX-style regular expression characters allow for pattern matching of characters and character strings in the address. Various pattern-matching constructions are available that will allow many addresses to be matched by a single regular expression. See Appendix B, "X.3 PAD Parameters," and Appendix C, "Regular Expressions," for more information.

### *Example*

The following example permits connections to hosts with addresses beginning with the string 31370:

```
x29 access-list 2 permit ^31370
```

## X29 PROFILE

To create a PAD profile script for use by the **translate** command, use the **x29 profile** global configuration command.

**x29 profile** {**default** | *name*} *parameter:value* [*parameter:value*]

Part III Command Reference

| *Syntax* | *Description* |
|---|---|
| **default** | Specifies default profile script. |
| *name* | Name of the PAD profile script. |
| *parameter:value* | X.3 PAD parameter number and value separated by a colon. You can specify multiple parameter-value pairs. |

### *Default*

The default PAD profile script is used. The default for inbound connections is:

```
2:0, 4:1, 15:0, 7:21
```

### *Command Mode*

Global configuration

### *Usage Guidelines*

This command first appeared in Cisco IOS Release 10.0.

When an X.25 connection is established, the router acts as if an X.29 SET PARAMETER packet had been sent containing the parameters and values set by the **x29 profile** command and sets the access server accordingly.

For incoming PAD connections, the Protocol Translator uses a default PAD profile to set the remote X.3 PAD parameters unless a profile script is defined with the **translate** command.

### *Examples*

The following profile script turns local edit mode on when the connection is made and establishes local echo and line termination upon receipt of a Return. The name *linemode* is used with the **translate** global configuration command to effect use of this script.

```
x29 profile linemode 2:1 3:2 15:1
```

To override the default PAD profile, create a PAD profile script named "default" by using the following command:

```
x29 profile default 2:1 4:1, 15:0, 4:0
```

### *Related Commands*

Search online to find documentation for related commands.

**translate**

# CHAPTER 23

# Configuring the Cisco PAD Facility for X.25 Connections

This chapter describes the configuration of the internal packet assembler/disassembler (PAD) facility to make connections with remote devices over the X.25 protocol.

The following sections are provided in this chapter:

- Network Scenarios Using PADs
- Configuring PAD Connections Using the Standard X.28 User Interface
- Configuring PAD Connections Using Cisco's Legacy PAD User Interface
- Enabling PAD Calls to an X.25 Host over an IP Network
- Configuring PAD Subaddressing

For a complete description of the commands in this chapter, see Chapter 24, "PAD and X.25 Connection Setup Commands."

For a complete description of each X.3 parameter supported by the standard X.28 mode or Cisco's traditional PAD user interface, see Appendix B, "X.3 PAD Parameters."

## NETWORK SCENARIOS USING PADS

PADs are configured to enable X.25 connections between network devices. A PAD is a device that receives a character stream from one or more terminals, assembles the character stream into packets, and sends the data packets out to a host. A PAD can also do the reverse. It can take data packets from a network host and translate them into a character stream that can be understood by the terminals. A PAD is defined by CCITT Recommendations X.3, X.28, and X.29.

Figure 23–1 shows a remote X.25 user placing a call through an X.25 switched network, to the internal PAD application on a Cisco 4700-M router, and to an X.25 host located inside a corporate data center.

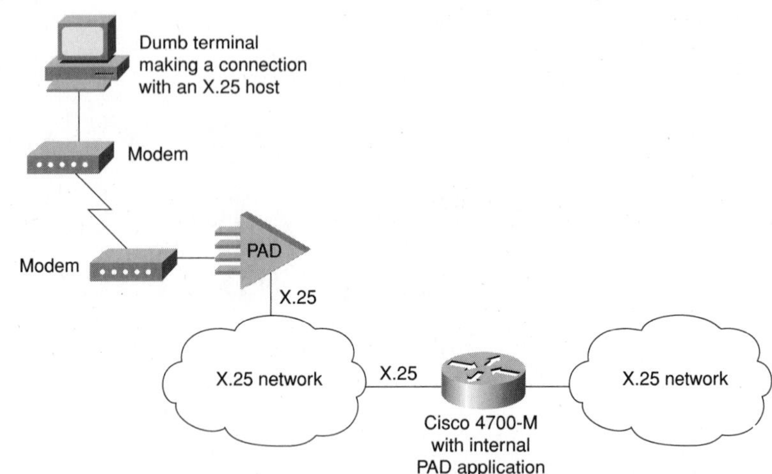


*Figure 23–1 Standard X.25 Connection between a Dumb Terminal and an X.25 Host.*

PADs can also be configured to work with a protocol translation application. Figure 23–2 shows an example of a remote PC placing an analog modem call to an IP network, connecting to a Cisco 4700-M router, allowing its IP packets to undergo an IP-to-X.25 protocol translation, which in turn communicates with an internal PAD device and establishes a connection with an X.25 host.

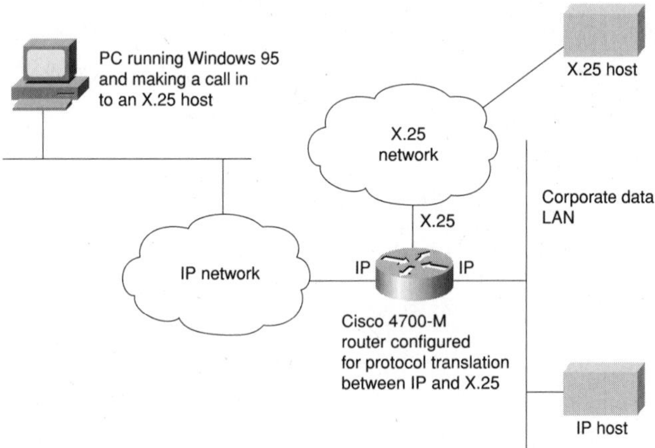


*Figure 23–2 PC Dialing In to an X.25 Host Using Protocol Translation.*

## CONFIGURING PAD CONNECTIONS USING THE STANDARD X.28 USER INTERFACE

The following sections describe how to use the X.28 standard user interface to make PAD connections:

- X.28 Description
- Business Applications for X.28 Emulation

- X.28 Configuration Task List
- Set X.3 PAD Parameters for X.25 Connections
- X.28 Emulation Examples

## X.28 Description

X.28 emulation is the standard user interface between data terminal equipment (DTE) and a packet assembler/disassembler (PAD). The Cisco IOS software provides an X.28 user emulation mode, which enables you to interact with and control the PAD. During this exchange of control information, messages or commands sent from the terminal to the PAD are called PAD command signals. Messages sent from the PAD to the terminal are called PAD service signals. These signals and any transmitted data take the form of encoded character streams as defined by International Alphabet Number 5.

For asynchronous devices such as terminals or modems to access an X.25 network host, the device's packets must be assembled or disassembled by a PAD device. Using standard X.28 commands from the PAD, calls can be made into an X.25 network, X.3 PAD parameters can be set, or calls can be reset. X.3 is the ITU-T recommendation that defines various PAD parameters used in X.25 networks. There are 22 available X.3 PAD parameters to configure. X.3 PAD parameters are internal variables that define the operation of a PAD. For example, parameter number 9 is the crpad parameter. It determines the number of bytes to add after a carriage return. X.3 parameters can also be set by a remote X.25 host using X.29 (see Figure 23–3).

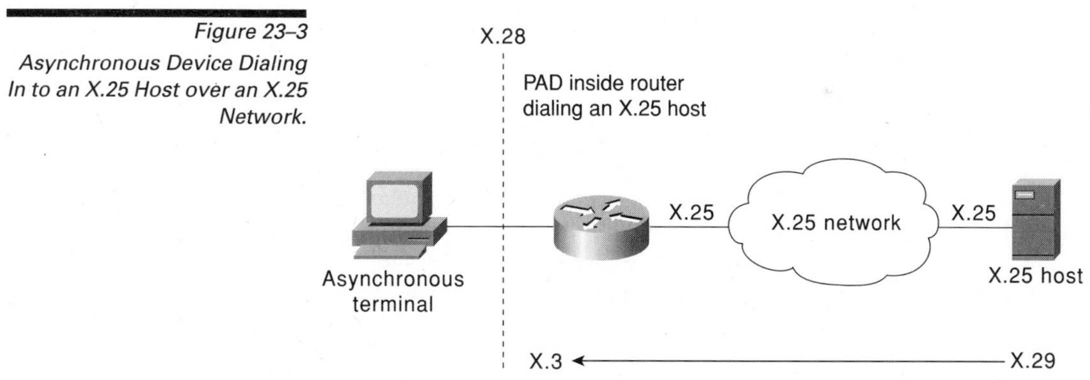


*Figure 23–3 Asynchronous Device Dialing In to an X.25 Host over an X.25 Network.*

**NOTES**

Most Cisco routers have internal PAD devices.

### Business Applications for X.28 Emulation

Cisco's new X.28 PAD implementation enables users to access X.25 networks or set PAD parameters using the X.28 standard user interface. This standard interface is common in many European countries and adheres to the X.25 International Telecommunication Union Telecommunication (ITU-T) standards.

The new X.28 interface is designed for asynchronous devices that require X.25 transport to access a remote or native asynchronous or synchronous host application. For example, dial-up users can use the X.28 interface to access a remote X.25 host. Banks implement Cisco routers to support back office applications, ATM, point of sales authorization devices, and alarm systems. These alarm devices are connected asynchronously to the same Cisco router and report alarm conditions to a remote alarm host for the dispatch of police. Cisco's X.28 PAD calls can be transported over a public packet network, a private X.25 network, the Internet, a private IP-based network, or a Frame Relay network. With this new service, Cisco now offers the flexibility to use the X.28 interface either directly or over a Cisco IOS application service such as protocol translation. The protocol translation VTY asynchronous application enables users to bidirectionally access an X.25 application with the PAD service or protocols such as Digital Equipment Corporation (DEC), local-area transport (LAT), and transmission control protocol (TCP).

## X.28 Configuration Task List

The following optional tasks are described in this section:

- Set Access and Display Options
- Enter PAD Command Signals for X.25 Connections
- Set X.3 PAD Parameters for X.25 Connections

X.28 mode can be manually invoked with the **x28** EXEC command, or it can be automatically invoked with the **autocommand** line configuration command. The **autocommand** command can be assigned to a particular line, range of lines, or user ID. When a user connects to the line using the autocommand feature, the user enters X.28 mode. If the **noescape** option is used with the autocommand feature, users cannot return to EXEC mode.

The default X.28 router prompt is an asterisk (*). Once you enter this mode, the standard X.28 user interface is available. From this interface, you can configure or use the PAD inside a Cisco router with X.3 parameters (see the section "Set X.3 PAD Parameters for X.25 Connections"), or you can access an X.25 network (see the section "Enter PAD Command Signals for X.25 Connections").

### *Set Access and Display Options*

To enter X.28 mode and set different access and display parameters, perform any of the following tasks beginning in EXEC mode:

| Task | | Command |
|---|---|---|
| **Step 1** | Specify a character string to use to exit X.28 mode and return to EXEC mode.* | **x28 escape** *character-string* |
| **Step 2** | Specify the network user identification data to be placed in the call user data area of the call request packet.† | **x28 nuicud** |

| Task | | Command |
|---|---|---|
| **Step 3** | Specify using a user-configured profile of X.3 parameters.‡ | **x28 profile** *file-name* |
| **Step 4** | Reverse the charges of all calls dialed from the local router. The address of the destination device is charged for the call. | **x28 reverse** |
| **Step 5** | Display detailed information about the X.25 call connection (for example, address of the remote DTE device and the facility block used). | **x28 verbose** |

* If the **x28 noescape** command is configured, a user cannot return to EXEC mode.
† Upon entering the **x28 nuicud** command, the network user identification (NUI) data will not be placed in the NUI facility of the call request. Instead it will be placed in the call user data field. If you configure the **x28 nuicud** command, reverse charging set by the **x28 reverse** command is disabled.
‡ Profiles are created with the **x29 profile** EXEC command.

See section "X.28 Emulation Examples" for actual sample X.28 configurations.

### *Enter PAD Command Signals for X.25 Connections*

Many X.25-related functions can be performed from the PAD in X.28 mode. Table 23–1 lists the available PAD command signals that can be issued. However, only the following two most common tasks are described in this section:

- Connect to a Remote X.25 Device
- Clear a Connection to a Remote X.25 Device

In X.28 mode, you can set PAD command signals using standard or extended command syntax. For example, you can enter the **clr** command or **clear** command to clear a virtual call. A command specified with standard command syntax is merely an abbreviated version of the extended syntax version. Both syntaxes have the same functionality.

**Table 23–1** *Available PAD Command Signals*

| Standard Syntax | Extended Syntax | Description |
|---|---|---|
| break | | Simulate an asynchronous break. |
| call | | Place a virtual call to a remote device. |
| *command-signal* | | Specify a call request without using a standard X.28 command, which is entered with the following syntax: *facilities-x121-address*D*call-user-data*. The dash (-) and "D" are required keywords. |
| clr | clear | Clear a virtual call. |
| help | iclear | Display help information. |
| iclr | iclear | Request the remote device to clear the call. |

**Table 23–1** *Available PAD Command Signals, Continued*

| Standard Syntax | Extended Syntax | Description |
|---|---|---|
| int | interrupt | Send an Interrupt Packet. |
| par?<br>par | parameter read | Show the current values of local parameters. |
| prof | profile *file-name* | Load a standard or named profile. |
| reset | | Reset the call. |
| rpar? | rread | Show the current values of remote parameters. |
| rset? | rsetread | Set and then read values of remote parameters. |
| set | | Change the values of local parameters. (See section "Set X.3 PAD Parameters for X.25 Connections.") |
| set? | setread | Change and then read the values of parameters. |
| stat | status | Request status of a connection. |
| selection pad | | Set up a virtual call. |

### *Connect to a Remote X.25 Device*

To call an X.25 device using a local PAD signal command, perform the following steps beginning in EXEC mode:

| Task | Command |
|---|---|
| **Step 1** Enter X.28 mode. An asterisk prompt will appear. | **x28** |
| **Step 2** Dial the address of the remote interface. | **call** *address* |

**NOTES**

In X.28 mode, you can perform the same functions as the Cisco proprietary **pad** command. However, X.28 mode adds additional functionality such as setting X.3 PAD parameters with industry standard X.28 commands.

See section "X.28 Emulation Examples" for a sample connection to a remote X.25 device.

### *Clear a Connection to a Remote X.25 Device*

Once you connect to a remote X.25 device, you can clear the connection by performing the following steps beginning in EXEC mode:

| Task | | Command |
|---|---|---|
| **Step 1** | From the remote host, escape back to the local router. | **Ctrl-p** |
| **Step 2** | Clear the virtual call. | **clr** |

See the section "X.28 Emulation Examples," for a sample of how to clear a connection to a remote X.25 device.

## Set X.3 PAD Parameters for X.25 Connections

To set an X.3 PAD parameter from a local terminal, perform the following steps beginning in EXEC mode:

| Task | | Command |
|---|---|---|
| **Step 1** | Enter X.28 mode. | **x28** |
| **Step 2** | Display the current X.3 PAD parameters. | **par** |
| **Step 3** | Change the value of a parameter. | **set** *parameter-number*: *new-value* |
| **Step 4** | Verify that the new PAD parameter was set correctly. | **par** |

See the section "X.28 Emulation Examples" for an example of how to set X.3 parameters for X.25 connections.

## X.28 Emulation Examples

The following examples are provided:

- PAD Signal Examples
- Set X.3 PAD Parameters Examples
- X.25 PAD Parameter Profile Example
- Network User Identification Data Relocation Example
- X.25 Reverse Charge Call Example
- X.25 Call Detail Display Example

### PAD Signal Examples

The following examples show two ways to make a call to a remote X.25 host over a serial line. The remote host's interface address is 123456. In the first example, router-A calls router-B using the **pad 123456** EXEC command. The second example shows router-A calling router-B using the **call 123456** PAD signal command in X.28 mode. Both commands accomplish the same goal.

```
router-A# pad 123456
Trying 123456...Open

router-B> exit

[Connection to 123456 closed by foreign host]

router-A# x28

* call 123456
COM

router-B>
```

The following examples show two ways to clear a connection with a remote X.25 host. The first example shows router-A disconnecting from router-B using the **disconnect** command in EXEC mode. The second example shows router-B disconnecting from router-A using the **clr** command in X.28 mode.

```
router-A# pad 123456
Trying 123456...Open

router-B> <Enter the escape sequence (for example, press Shift-Ctrl-^-x).>

router-A# disconnect
Closing connection to 123456 [confirm]
router-A#

router-A# x28

* call 123456
COM

router-B> <Press Ctrl-p>
* clr

CLR CONF

*
```

### Set X.3 PAD Parameters Examples

The following example configures parameter 9 from 0 to 1, which adds one byte after the carriage return. This setting is performed from a local terminal using the **set** *parameter-number: new-value* PAD command signal.

```
router-A# x28
```

```
* par
   PAR 1:1 2:1 3:126 4:0 5:1 6:2 7:2 8:0 9:0 10:0 11:14 12:1 13:0 14:0 15:0 16:127 17:24
18:18 19:2 20:0 21:0 22:0

* set 9:1

* par
   PAR 1:1 2:1 3:126 4:0 5:1 6:2 7:2 8:0 9:1 10:0 11:14 12:1 13:0 14:0 15:0 16:127 17:24
18:18 19:2 20:0 21:0 22:0

*
```

The following example shows how to change a local X.3 PAD parameter from a remote X.25 host using X.29 messages, which is a secure way to enable a remote host to gain control of local PAD. The local device is router-A. The remote host is router-B. The parameters listed in the ParamsIn field are incoming parameters, which are sent by the remote PAD. The parameters listed in the ParamsOut field are parameters sent by the local PAD.

```
router-A# pad 123456
Trying 123456...Open

router-B> x3 2:0
router-B>
router-A# show x25 pad

tty0, connection 1 to host 123456

Total input: 12, control 3, bytes 35. Queued: 0 of 7 (0 bytes).
Total output: 10, control 3, bytes 64.
Flags: 1,   State: 3,   Last error: 1
 ParamsIn:  1:0, 2:0, 3:0, 4:0, 5:0, 6:0, 7:0,
    8:0, 9:0, 10:0, 11:0, 12:0, 13:0, 14:0, 15:0,
    16:0, 17:0, 18:0, 19:0, 20:0, 21:0, 22:0,
 ParamsOut:  1:1, 2:0, 3:2, 4:1, 5:1, 6:0, 7:21,
    8:0, 9:1, 10:0, 11:14, 12:1, 13:0, 14:0, 15:0,
    16:127, 17:21, 18:18, 19:0, 20:0, 21:0, 22:0,
router-A#
```

### *X.25 PAD Parameter Profile Example*

The following example modifies and loads an existing X.25 PAD parameter profile. It accesses the existing PAD profile *ppp*, changes its padding parameter (specified as 9) to a value of 2, and displays the new parameters using the **par** command in X.28 mode.

```
router-A# configure terminal
Enter configuration commands, one per line.  End with CNTL/Z.
router-A(config)# x29 profile ppp 9:2
router-A(config)# end
router-A#
%SYS-5-CONFIG_I: Configured from console by console
router-A# x28 profile ppp

* par
```

```
    PAR 1:1 2:1 3:126 4:0 5:1 6:2 7:2 8:0 9:2 10:0 11:14 12:1 13:0 14:0 15:0 16:127 17:24
18:18 19:2 20:0 21:0 22:0
```

### Network User Identification Data Relocation Example

The following example sends an authentication message to a remote X.25 host using the **x28 nuicud** command in X.28 mode followed by the **Ncisc-123456** X.28 command. The network identifier is *N*. The network user password is *cisc*. The destination address of the remote device is *123456*. The ASCII representation of the user password appears in the call user data field, not in the data packet.

```
router-A# debug x25 event
X.25 special event debugging is on
router-A# x28 nuicud

* Ncisc-123456
COM

router-B>
02:02:58: Serial1: X.25 O P1 Call (16) 8 lci 20
02:02:58:   From(3): 222 To(3): 123456
02:02:58:   Facilities: (0)
02:02:58:   Call User Data (8): 0x01000000xxxxxxxx (pad)
02:02:58: Serial1; X.25 I P2 Call Confirm (5) 8 lci 20
02:02:58:   From(0):  To(0):
02:02:58:   Facilities: (0)
```

### X.25 Reverse Charge Call Example

The charges for all outgoing calls made from the local router can be reversed to the destination device using the **x28 reverse** command. To reverse the charges for only one outgoing call, use the **R-** *address* command, which is the standard X.28 reverse charge facility command.

```
router-A# x28 reverse

* exit

router-A# x28

* R-123456
COM
```

### X.25 Call Detail Display Example

Each time a call is made to a remote device, you can specify that detailed information be displayed about the call and the destination device by entering the **x28 verbose** command. The following example shows reverse charging configured and call user data represented as *userdata*:

```
router# x28 verbose

* R-111*userdata

Called DTE Address : 3001
Facility Block     : R
Call User Data     :userdata
COM
```

## CONFIGURING PAD CONNECTIONS USING CISCO'S LEGACY PAD USER INTERFACE

The following sections describe X.3 PAD connection tasks:

- Make a PAD Connection
- Switch between Connections
- Exit a PAD Session
- Monitor X.25 PAD Connections
- Set X.3 PAD Parameters
- PAD Session Examples

### Make a PAD Connection

To display information about packet transmission and X.3 PAD parameter settings and log on to a PAD, perform the following tasks in EXEC mode:

| Task | | Command |
|---|---|---|
| **Step 1** | Display information about packet transmission and X.3 PAD parameter settings. | **show x25 pad** |
| **Step 2** | Log on to a PAD. | **pad** {*x121-address* \| *hostname*} [**/cud** *text*] [**/debug**] [**/profile** *name*] [**/reverse**] |

You can exit a connection and return to the user EXEC prompt at any point.

To open a new connection, first exit the current connection by typing the escape sequence (**Ctrl-Shift-6** then **x** [**Ctrl^x**] by default) to return to the EXEC prompt, then open the new connection.

### Switch between Connections

You can have several concurrent sessions open and switch between them. The number of sessions that can be open is defined by the **session-limit** command (see Chapter 5, "Configuring Modem Support and Asynchronous Devices," and Chapter 6, "Modem Support and Asynchronous Device Commands").

To switch between sessions by escaping one session and resuming a previously opened session, perform the following tasks:

| Task | | Command |
|---|---|---|
| **Step 1** | Escape the current connection, if you have one open, and return to EXEC mode. | **Ctrl-Shift-6** then **x** (**Ctrl^x**) by default |

| Task | | Command |
|---|---|---|
| **Step 2** | From EXEC mode, list the open sessions. All open sessions associated with the current terminal line are displayed. | **where** |
| **Step 3** | Make the connection. | **resume** [*connection*] [*keyword*] |

The **Ctrl^x**, **where**, and **resume** commands are available with all supported connection protocols.

### Exit a PAD Session

To exit a PAD session, enter the escape sequence (**Ctrl-Shift-6** then **x** [**Ctrl^x**] by default) and enter the **disconnect** command at the EXEC prompt. You can also log off the remote system by issuing the command specific to that system (such as **exit, logout, quit, close,** or **disconnect**).

### Monitor X.25 PAD Connections

To display information about current open connections, perform the following task in user EXEC mode:

| Task | Command |
|---|---|
| Display information about X.25 PAD connections that are currently open. | **show x25 pad** |

The information includes packet transmissions, X.3 parameter settings, and the current status of virtual circuits.

### Set X.3 PAD Parameters

To set X.3 PAD parameters, perform the following task in EXEC mode:

| Task | Command |
|---|---|
| Set X.3 PAD parameters. | **resume** [*connection*] [**/set** *parameter:value*]<br>or<br>**x3** *parameter:value* |

The parameters are numbered from 1 through 18. See Appendix B for more information.

An example of setting X.3 PAD parameters follows in the next section.

### PAD Session Examples

The following example starts a PAD session:

```
router> pad 123456789
Trying 123456789...Open
router2>
```

The following example illustrates how to reset the outgoing connection default for local echo mode on a router. The **/set** switch sets the X.3 parameters defined by parameter number and value, separated by a colon.

```
router> resume 3 /set 2:1
```

The following are examples of **show x25 vc** command output for PAD over CMNS, PAD to PAD over X25, and PAD over XOT connections:

```
router# show x25 vc
SVC 1,  State: D1,  Interface: Ethernet0
  Started 00:01:48, last input 00:01:48, output 00:01:48

  Line: 0   con 0    Location: console Host: 2193330
   connected to 2193330 PAD <--> CMNS Ethernet0 00e0.b0e3.0d62

  Window size input: 2, output: 2
  Packet size input: 128, output: 128
  PS: 2  PR: 3  ACK: 3  Remote PR: 2  RCNT: 0  RNR: no
  P/D state timeouts: 0  timer (secs): 0
  data bytes 54/19 packets 2/3 Resets 0/0 RNRs 0/0 REJs 0/0 INTs 0/0

SVC 1024,  State: D1,  Interface: Serial1
  Started 00:00:07, last input 00:00:26, output 00:00:26

  Line: 0   con 0    Location: console Host: 2194443
  2191111 connected to 2194443 PAD <--> X25

  Window size input: 5, output: 5
  Packet size input: 128, output: 128
  PS: 0  PR: 0  ACK: 0  Remote PR: 0  RCNT: 0  RNR: no
  P/D state timeouts: 0  timer (secs): 0
  data bytes 0/0 packets 0/0 Resets 0/0 RNRs 0/0 REJs 0/0 INTs 0/0

SVC 1,  State: D1,  Interface: [172.21.9.7,1998/172.21.9.11,11000]
  Started 00:06:48, last input 00:06:43, output 00:06:43

  Line: 0   con 0    Location: console Host: 219444001
  219111 connected to 219444001 PAD <--> XOT 172.21.9.7,1998

  Window size input: 2, output: 2
  Packet size input: 128, output: 128
  PS: 5  PR: 4  ACK: 4  Remote PR: 5  RCNT: 0  RNR: no
  P/D state timeouts: 0  timer (secs): 0
  data bytes
```

The following is example output for the **show x25 pad** command:

```
router# show x25 pad

tty0 (console), connection 1 to host 2194440

Total input: 75, control 2, bytes 3168. Input Queued: 0 of 7 (0 bytes).
Total output: 50, control 2, bytes 52. Output Queued: 0 of 5.
```

```
Flags: 1,    State: 3,    Last error: 1
 ParamsIn:  1:0, 2:0, 3:0, 4:0, 5:0, 6:0, 7:0,
    8:0, 9:0, 10:0, 11:0, 12:0, 13:0, 14:0, 15:0,
    16:0, 17:0, 18:0, 19:0, 20:0, 21:0, 22:0,
 ParamsOut:  1:1, 2:0, 3:2, 4:1, 5:1, 6:0, 7:21,
    8:0, 9:0, 10:0, 11:14, 12:1, 13:0, 14:0, 15:0,
    16:127, 17:21, 18:18, 19:0, 20:0, 21:0, 22:0,

tty18, Incoming PAD connection
Total input: 2, control 2, bytes 54. Input Queued: 0 of 7 (0 bytes).
Total output: 1, control 2, bytes 9. Output Queued: 0 of 5.
Flags: 1,    State: 3,    Last error: 1
 ParamsIn:  1:1, 2:0, 3:2, 4:1, 5:0, 6:0, 7:21,
    8:0, 9:0, 10:0, 11:14, 12:0, 13:0, 14:0, 15:0,
    16:127, 17:21, 18:18, 19:0, 20:0, 21:0, 22:0,
 ParamsOut:  1:1, 2:1, 3:2, 4:1, 5:0, 6:0, 7:4,
    8:0, 9:0, 10:0, 11:14, 12:0, 13:0, 14:0, 15:0,
    16:127, 17:21, 18:18, 19:0, 20:0, 21:0, 22:0,
```

## Enabling PAD Calls to an X.25 Host over an IP Network

PAD calls can be made to destinations that are not reachable over physical X.25 interfaces, but instead over TCP tunnels. PAD calls originating from a router on an IP link can reach an X.25 device. This feature is also known as PAD over XOT. The **service pad to-xot** command and **service pad from-xot** global configuration commands enable the PAD over XOT feature. Figure 23–4 shows PAD calls originating from a router in an IP network reaching a X.25 device.

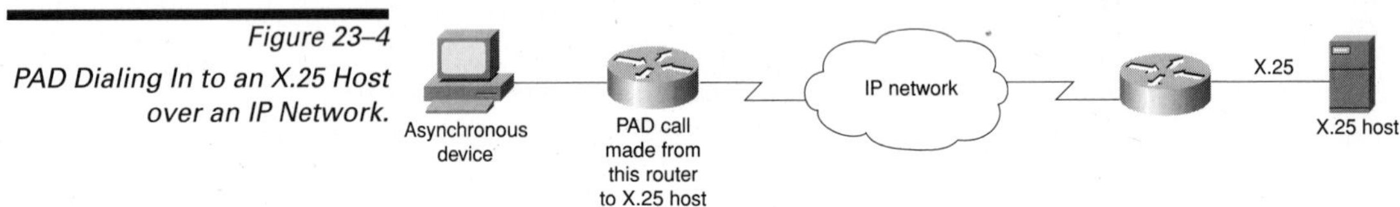


*Figure 23–4*
*PAD Dialing In to an X.25 Host over an IP Network.*

To allow PAD connections over XOT on the router, perform the following tasks beginning in privileged EXEC mode:

| Task | | Command |
|---|---|---|
| **Step 1** | Enter global configuration mode. | **configure terminal** |
| **Step 2** | Specify outgoing PAD calls over XOT or incoming XOT to PAD connections. | **service pad [from-xot] [to-xot]** |
| **Step 3** | Depending on your application, specify an X.121 address for the host name of the router or an X.25 route pointing out over XOT.* | **x25 host** *name x121-address* or **x25 route** *x121-address* **xot** *x121-address* |

* The X.121 address of the **x25 host** command serves as a source address or sink address for PAD over XOT connections that do not have an interface. Protocol translation can also be used with incoming PAD calls over XOT, which is configured with the **translate x25** command.

## PAD XOT Examples

This section provides the following PAD over XOT configuration examples:

- Accept XOT to PAD Connections Example
- Accept XOT to Protocol Translation Example
- Initiate a PAD Call over an XOT Connection Example

### *Accept XOT to PAD Connections Example*

The following example enables connections from XOT to a local PAD. Because XOT is a TCP connection, the connection is not tied to an X.25 interface. An X.25 address must be configured for the host name of the router that is accepting the call. In this case, the router answers and clears an incoming PAD call through address 1234.

```
service pad from-xot
x25 host router-A 1234
```

### *Accept XOT to Protocol Translation Example*

The following example accepts an incoming PAD call over XOT to address 12345. The router then translates the call and makes a TCP connection to the device called *puli*.

```
service pad from-xot
translate x25 12345 tcp puli
```

### *Initiate a PAD Call over an XOT Connection Example*

The following example enables outgoing PAD to XOT connections from an asynchronous line or virtual terminal line. A route pointing out over XOT must be configured on the routing table to make a PAD call. This route can also be used for switching.

```
service pad to-xot
x25 route 1111 xot 2.2.2.2.
```

## Configuring PAD Subaddressing

In situations where the X.121 calling address is not sufficient to identify the source of the call, you can append a specified value to the calling address using the PAD subaddressing feature. PAD subaddressing allows you to create unique X.121 calling addresses by including either a physical port number or a value specified for a line as a subaddress to the X.121 calling address.

PAD subaddressing enables an X.25 host application to uniquely identify the source of an X.121 call. For example, in some bank security alarm applications, the central alarm host identifies the physical location of the alarm units from subaddressing information contained in the Call Request packet.

## Prerequisites

Before you can configure PAD subaddressing, you need to configure your router or access server to support X.25.

## Configuration Tasks

To configure PAD subaddressing, you need to perform the following tasks:

- Identify the Line(s)
- Configure PAD Subaddressing

### *Identify the Line(s)*

To identify the line(s) whose information will be appended to the X.121 calling address as the subaddress (and start the line configuration command mode), perform the following task in global configuration mode:

| Task | Command |
|---|---|
| Identify the line(s) to be appended to the X.121 address as the subaddress. | **line** [**aux** \| **console** \| **tty** \| **vty**] *line-number* [*ending-line-number*] |

### *Configure PAD Subaddressing*

To create a unique X.121 calling address by adding either a physical port number or a numeric value for a line as a subaddress to the X.121 calling address, perform the following task in line configuration mode:

| Task | Command |
|---|---|
| Configure PAD subaddressing. | **x25 subaddress** {**line** \| *number*} |

## Configuration Examples

The following example shows how to configure subaddressing on vty lines 10 through 20 by appending the line number as a subaddress to the X.121 calling address:

```
line vty 10 20
x25 subaddress line
```

The following example shows how to configure subaddressing on the first five tty lines by appending the value "09" as a subaddress to the X.121 calling address of the X.28 connection originating on these lines:

```
line 1 5
x25 subaddress 9
autocommand x28
```

You can use the output from the **debug x25 event** and the **show line** commands to display information about PAD subaddressing. Once you have configured PAD subaddressing, the output from both of these commands changes to reflect the additional subaddress information.

The following example shows **debug x25 event** output, where the X.25 address is 12345 and the subaddress for tty line 3 is 09.

```
router# debug x25 event

Serial1: X.25 O P1 Call (14) 8 lci 1024
  From(7): 1234509 To(4): 6789
  Facilities: (0)
  Call User Data (4): 0x01000000 (pad)
Serial1: X.25 I P2 Call Confirm (5) 8 lci 1024
  From (0): to (0):
  Facilities: (0)
  PAD3: Call completed
```

The following example shows sample **show line** output for a router called enkidu, where line 18 has been configured for PAD subaddressing.

```
router# show line 18

Tty Typ     Tx/Rx     A Modem  Roty AccO AccI  Uses  Noise  Overruns
 18 VTY               -    -      -    -    -     1      0       0/0

Line 18, Location: "enkidu", Type: " "
Length: 48 lines, Width: 80 columns
Baud rate: (TX/RX) is 9600/9600
Status: Ready, Connected, Active, No Exit Banner
Capabilities: Line usable as async interface, PAD Sub-addressing used
Modem state: Ready
```

CHAPTER 24

# PAD and X.25 Connection Setup Commands

This chapter describes the commands used for configuring an internal packet assembler/disassembler (PAD) application to make connections with remote devices using the X.25 protocol.

You can configure an internal PAD in the following ways:

- Use the **x28** EXEC command to access and use the X.28 standard interface. After the **x28** command is issued, you enter X.28 mode and the router prompt changes to an asterisk (*). From this mode, you can set X.3 PAD parameters.
- Issue the **pad** EXEC command, which is Cisco's proprietary interface. Use the **resume** EXEC command or **x3** EXEC command to set X.3 parameters.

For configuration tasks and examples, see Chapter 23, "Configuring the Cisco PAD Facility for X.25 Connections."

## PAD

To log on to a PAD, use the **pad** user EXEC command.

**pad** {*x121-address* | *hostname*} [**/cud** *text*] [**/debug**] [**/profile** *name*] [**/reverse**] [**/use-map**]

| *Syntax* | *Description* |
|---|---|
| *x121-address* | Specifies the X.121 address of the X.25 host. |
| *hostname* | Specifies the X.25 host name if the host-to-address mapping has been set with the **X.25 host** command. |
| **/cud** *text* | (Optional) Includes the specified *text* in the call user data field of the outgoing Call Request Packet. |
| **/debug** | (Optional) Displays the informational level of logging messages whenever the remote host changes an X.3 parameter setting or sends any other X.29 control packet. |

| | |
|---|---|
| **/profile** *name* | (Optional) Sets X.3 PAD parameters for the *name* script. This is the same as issuing the **x29 profile** global configuration command when translating X.25. |
| **/reverse** | (Optional) Causes reverse charge calls to be accepted on a per-call (rather than a per-interface) basis. |
| **/use-map** | (Optional) Applies **x25 map pad** command entry options (such as CUD and idle) and facilities (such as packet in, packet out, win in, and win out) to the outgoing PAD call. This function occurs only if a matching X.121 destination address exists in a **x25 map pad** command entry. |

### *Command Mode*

User EXEC

### *Usage Guidelines*

This command first appeared in Cisco IOS Release 11.2.

The **pad** command supports one-word connections. You do not have to enter the **pad** command; just entering the address is enough to start the connection. A PAD can also be accessed and X.3 parameters configured with the **x28** EXEC command, which uses the standard X.28 user interface.

You can have several PAD connections open at the same time and switch between them. You also can exit a connection and return to the user EXEC prompt at any point. To open a new connection, first exit the current connection by entering the escape sequence (**Ctrl-Shift-6** then **x** [**Ctrl^x**] by default) to return to the EXEC prompt, then open the new connection.

If the **/use-map** option is selected on the outgoing **pad** command, the **x25 map pad** command entries are searched for a matching X.121 destination address. If a match is found, the **x25 map pad** command entry options (such as CUD and idle) and facilities (such as packet in, packet out, win in, and win out) are applied to the outgoing PAD call.

To display information about packet transmission and X.3 PAD parameter settings, enter the **show x25 pad** command.

To exit a session, simply log off the remote system. Then, terminate the active session by entering the **exit** command.

### *Examples*

The following example starts a PAD session:

```
router> pad 123456789
Trying 123456789...Open
router>
```

You can also access a PAD using standard X.28 commands. The following example enters X.28 mode with the **x28** EXEC command and configures a PAD with the **set** X.3 parameter command. The **set** command sets the idle time delay to 40 seconds.

```
router# x28
* set 4:40
```

The following example uses the **/use-map** option to configure a larger window and packet size than the default specified on the interface, and it sets the VC idle time to 2 seconds. Notice that the map values are used rather than the interface default values.

```
Router-A(config-if)# x25 map pad 2194441 cud gmcmilla windowsize 7 7 packetsize 1024 1024
idle 2
Router-A(config-if)# end
Router-A#
%SYS-5-CONFIG_I: Configured from console by console.
Router-A# pad 2194441 /cud gmcmillla /use-map
Trying 2194441....Open

06:31:12: pad_open_connection: found a matching x25 map pad
06:31:12: Serial1: X.25 O R1 Call (22) 8 lci 1024
06:31:12:   From(7): 2191111 To(7): 2194441
06:31:12:   Facilities: (6)
06:31:12:     Packet sizes: 1024 1024
06:31:12:     Window sizes: 7 7
06:31:12:   Call User Data (12): 0x01000000 (pad)
06:31:12: Serial1: X.25 I R1 Call Confirm (5) 8 lci 1024
06:31:12:   From(0):  To(0):
06:31:12:   Facilities: (0)
06:31:12: PAD0: Call completed
```



### *Related Commands*

Search online to find documentation for related commands.

**translate x25**

## RESUME (SETTING X.3 PAD PARAMETERS)

To set X.3 parameters, use the **resume** EXEC command as follows:

**resume** [*connection*] [**/set** *parameter:value*]

| *Syntax* | *Description* |
|---|---|
| connection | (Optional) The name or number of the connection; the default is the most recent connection. |
| **/set** *parameter:value* | (Optional) Sets the X.3 connection options and PAD parameters for the Cisco IOS software. Refer to Table 24–1 for PAD parameters.<br><br>See Chapter 23 for a list of these connection options. |

**Table 24–1** *PAD Parameters*

| Parameter | Action | Value | Description |
|---|---|---|---|
| 1 | Escape from data transfer | | Not supported. |
| 2 | Local echo mode | 0 | No local echo (incoming PAD connection default). |
| | | 1 | Local echo on (outgoing connection default). |
| 3 | Data forward character | 0 | None—full packet. |
| | | 1 | Forward packet on receipt of an alphanumeric character. |
| | | 2 | Forward packet on receipt of a RETURN (outgoing connection default). |
| | | 4 | Forward packet on receipt of ESCAPE, BEL, ENQ, or ACK. |
| | | 8 | Forward packet on receipt of DEL, CAN, or DC2. |
| | | 16 | Forward packet on receipt of ETX or EOT. |
| | | 32 | Forward packet on receipt of HT, LT, VT, or FF. |
| | | 64 | All other characters in the ASCII chart. |
| 4 | Idle timer | 0 | No timer. |
| | | 1-255 | Delay value in twentieths of a second (default for both connection types is 1). |
| 5 | Device control | | Transmits flow-control characters during data transfer to the terminal, which controls the terminal and data flow. |
| 6 | PAD service signals | | Not supported. |
| 7 | Receipt of break | 0 | Ignore the Break signal. |
| | | 1 | Transmit an INTERRUPT packet to notify the remote host or another PAD that the Break signal was generated. |
| | | 2 | Transmit a RESET packet to reset the virtual circuit. |
| | | 4 | Transmit an X.29 break indication to the remote host, or to a PAD (outgoing connection default). |
| | | 8 | Escape from data transfer mode. |
| | | 16 | Discard output to the terminal by setting parameter 8 to a value of 1. |
| | | 21 | Combination of values 1, 4, and 16 (incoming connection default). |

**Table 24–1** *PAD Parameters, Continued*

| Parameter | Action | Value | Description |
|---|---|---|---|
| 8 | Discard output | 0 | Normal data delivery to the terminal (outgoing connection default). |
| | | 1 | Discard all output to the terminal; set by parameter 7. |
| 9 | Return padding | | Determines if PAD can provide padding (insert filler characters) upon receipt of a Return character from the terminal. |
| 10 | Line folding | | Not supported. |
| 11 | Baud rate | 10 | 50 baud. |
| | | 5 | 75 baud. |
| | | 9 | 100 baud. |
| | | 0 | 110 baud. |
| | | 1 | 134.5 baud. |
| | | 6 | 150 baud. |
| | | 8 | 200 baud. |
| | | 2 | 300 baud. |
| | | 4 | 600* baud. |
| | | 3 | 1200 baud. |
| | | 7 | 1800 baud. |
| | | 11 | 75/1200† baud. |
| | | 12 | 2400 baud. |
| | | 13 | 4800 baud. |
| | | 14 | 9600 baud. |
| | | 15 | 19200 baud. |
| | | 16 | 48000 baud. |
| | | 17 | 56000 baud. |
| | | 18 | 64000 baud. |
| 12 | Input flow control | | Determines whether or not the terminal can transmit ASCII XON/XOFF (transmission on and off) characters to PAD during the data transfer mode. |

**Table 24–1** *PAD Parameters, Continued*

| Parameter | Action | Value | Description |
|---|---|---|---|
| 13 | Line feed insertion | 0<br>1<br>2<br>4 | Do not insert (outgoing connection default).<br>Insert after transmitting RETURN to the terminal.<br>Insert after echoing RETURN to the terminal.<br>Insert after echoing RETURN to the remote host. |
| 14 | Line feed padding | | Determines if PAD can provide padding (insert filler characters) upon receipt of a LINE FEED character from the terminal. |
| 15 | Local editing | 0<br>1 | Disables editing capabilities.<br>Enables editing capabilities. |
| 16 | Character delete | 0-127 | Select one ASCII character. Default is ASCII 127 (Del). |
| 17 | Line delete | 0-127 | Select one ASCII character. Default is ASCII 21 (Ctrl-U). |
| 18 | Line display | 0-127 | Select one ASCII character. Default is ASCII 18 (Ctrl-R). |
| 19 | Editing PAD service signals | | Not supported. |
| 20 | Echo mask | | Not supported. |
| 21 | Parity treatment | | Not supported. |
| 22 | Page wait | | Not supported. |

* 600 is the beginning of values that are PAD-type dependent.
† 75 is from PAD; is to PAD.

### *Default*

For outgoing connections, the X.3 parameters default to the following:

```
2:1, 3:2, 4:1, 7:4, 16:127, 17:21, 18:19
```

All other parameters default to zero, but can be changed using the **/set** switch option with either the **resume** command or the **x3** command.

For incoming PAD connections, the software sends an X.29 SET PARAMETER packet to set only the following parameters:

```
2:0, 4:1, 7:21, 15:0
```

*Command Mode*

EXEC

*Usage Guidelines*

This command first appeared in a release prior to Cisco IOS Release 10.0.

The **resume** [*connection*] command first appeared in Cisco IOS Release 9.1.

The **/set** switch sets the X.3 parameters defined by parameter number and value, separated by a colon. You set one or more X.3 PAD parameters, as follows:

**Step 1** Escape out of the current session by pressing the escape sequence (**Ctrl-Shift-6** then **x** [**Ctrl^x**] by default) and return to the EXEC prompt.

**Step 2** Issue the **where** command, to list the open sessions. All open sessions associated with the current terminal line are displayed.

**Step 3** Enter the **resume** command, followed by the parameter, a colon, and then the value to be set.



*Example*

The following example specifies that local echo mode be turned on for a connection to the device Swift (which is session number 3). As shown in Table 24–1, "local echo on" uses the parameter 2 and the value 1 (represented as 2:1 in this example):

```
Swift% ^^X
router> resume 3 /set 2:1
Swift%
```

## SERVICE PAD

To enable all packet assembler/disassembler (PAD) commands and connections between PAD devices and access servers, use the **service pad** global configuration command. Use the **no** form of this command to not accept incoming and outgoing PAD connections.

**service pad [cmns] [from-xot | to-xot]**
**no service pad [cmns] [from-xot | to-xot]**

| *Syntax* | *Description* |
|---|---|
| **cmns** | (Optional) Specifies sending and receiving PAD calls over CMNS. |
| **from-xot** | (Optional) Accept XOT to PAD connections. |
| **to-xot** | (Optional) Allow outgoing PAD calls over XOT. |

*Default*

All PAD commands and associated connections are enabled. PAD services over XOT or CMNS are not enabled.

### *Command Mode*

Global configuration

### *Usage Guidelines*

The **service pad** command first appeared in Cisco IOS Release 10.0. The options **cmns, from-xot,** and **to-xot** first appeared in Cisco IOS Release 11.3.

The options **from-xot** and **to-xot** enable PAD calls to destinations that are not reachable over physical X.25 interfaces, but instead over TCP tunnels. This feature is known as PAD over XOT (X.25 over TCP).

### *Examples*

If the **service pad** command is disabled, the EXEC **pad** command and all PAD-related configurations, such as X.29, are unrecognized, as shown in the following example:

```
router(config)# no service pad
router(config)# x29 ?
% Unrecognized command
router(config)# exit
router# pad ?
% Unrecognized command
```

If the **service pad** command is enabled, the EXEC **pad** command and access to an X.29 configuration are granted, as shown in the following example:

```
router# config terminal
Enter configuration commands, one per line. End with CNTL/Z.
router(config)# service pad
router(config)# x29 ?
access-list        Define an X.29 access list
inviteclear-time   Wait for response to X.29 Invite Clear message
profile            Create an X.3 profile
router# pad ?
WORD   X121 address or name of a remote system
```

### *Related Commands*

Search online to find documentation for related commands.

**x29 access-list**
**x29 profile**

## SHOW X25 PAD

To display information about current open connections, including packet transmissions, X.3 parameter settings, and the current status of virtual circuits, use the **show x25 pad** user EXEC command.

**show x25 pad**

### *Syntax Description*

This command has no arguments or keywords.

### Command Mode

User EXEC

### Usage Guidelines

This command first appeared in Cisco IOS Release 11.2.

### Sample Display

The following is sample output from the **show x25 pad** command:

```
router# show x25 pad

tty2, Incoming PAD connection
Total input: 61, control 6, bytes 129. Queued: 0 of 7 (0 bytes).
Total output: 65, control 6, bytes 696.
Flags: 1,   State: 3,   Last error: 1
 ParamsIn:  1:1, 2:0, 3:2, 4:1, 5:1, 6:0, 7:21,
    8:0, 9:0, 10:0, 11:14, 12:0, 13:0, 14:0, 15:1,
    16:127, 17:21, 18:18, 19:0, 20:0, 21:0, 22:0,
 ParamsOut:  1:1, 2:1, 3:2, 4:1, 5:0, 6:0, 7:4,
    8:0, 9:0, 10:0, 11:14, 12:0, 13:0, 14:0, 15:0,
    16:127, 17:21, 18:18, 19:0, 20:0, 21:0, 22:0,
 LCI: 1,  State: D1,  Interface: Serial0
 Started 0:11:10, last input 0:00:16, output 0:00:16
 Connected to 313700540651
 Window size input: 7, output: 7
 Packet size input: 512, output: 512
 PS: 1  PR: 5  ACK: 5  Remote PR: 1  RCNT: 0  RNR: FALSE
 Retransmits: 0  Timer (secs): 0  Reassembly (bytes): 0
 Held Fragments/Packets: 0/0
 Bytes 696/129 Packets 65/61 Resets 0/0 RNRs 0/0 REJs 0/0 INTs 0/0
```

Table 24–2 describes significant fields shown in the output in the display.

**Table 24–2** *Show X.25 Pad Field Descriptions*

| Field | Description |
|---|---|
| Total input/output | Number of packets received or sent for the connection. |
| control | Number of packets with Qbit set (X.29 control packets). |
| bytes | Number of bytes in each direction. |
| Queued | Number of unread packets waiting for the connection. |
| Waiting to send | Local data packet bit not sent (part of a line). |
| Flags, State, Last error | Displays data for detecting errors and tracing initialization status. Only useful to your Cisco-certified technical support personnel. |
| ParamsIn | Parameters read from the PAD at the start of the connection. |

**Table 24–2** *Show X.25 Pad Field Descriptions, Continued*

| Field | Description |
|---|---|
| ParamsOut | Active X.3 parameters. |
| LCI, State, Interface | Status of the X.25 virtual circuit associated with the PAD connection. This is the same display that the **show x25 vc** command shows. |

## WHERE

To list the open sessions, use the **where** EXEC command.

**where**

### *Syntax Description*

This command has no arguments or keywords.

### *Command Mode*

EXEC

### *Usage Guidelines*

This command first appeared in a release prior to Cisco IOS Release 10.0.

The **where** command displays all open sessions associated with the current terminal line.

The **Ctrl^x, where,** and **resume** commands are available with all supported connection protocols.

### *Example*

The following is sample output from the **where** command:

```
router# where
Conn Host                 Address          Byte    Idle  Conn Name
   1 MATHOM               192.31.7.21         0       0  MATHOM
*  2 CHAFF                131.108.12.19       0       0  CHAFF
```

The asterisk (*) indicates the current terminal session.

Table 24–3 describes significant fields shown in the display.

**Table 24–3** *Show X.25 Pad Field Descriptions*

| Field | Description |
|---|---|
| Conn | Name or address of the remote host to which the connection is made. |
| Host | Remote host to which the router is connected through a Telnet session. |
| Address | IP address of the remote host. |
| Byte | Number of unread bytes for the user to see on the connection. |

**Table 24–3** *Show X.25 Pad Field Descriptions, Continued*

| Field | Description |
|---|---|
| Idle | Interval (in minutes) since data was last sent on the line. |
| Conn Name | Assigned name of the connection. |

### *Related Commands*

Search online to find documentation for related commands.

**resume**
**show sessions**



## x3

To set X.3 PAD parameters, use the **x3** EXEC command.

**x3** *parameter:value*

| *Syntax* | *Description* |
|---|---|
| *parameter:value* | Sets the PAD parameters. (Refer to Table 24–1.) |

### *Default Values*

For outgoing connections, the X.3 parameters default to the following:

```
2:1, 3:2, 4:1, 7:4, 16:127, 17:21, 18:19
```

All other parameters default to zero, but can be changed using the **/set** switch keyword with either the **resume** command or the **x3** command.

For incoming PAD connections, the software sends an X.29 SET PARAMETER packet to set only the following parameters:

```
2:0, 4:1, 7:21, 15:0
```

For a complete description of the X.3 PAD parameters, see Appendix B, "X.3 PAD Parameters."

### *Command Mode*

EXEC

### *Usage Guidelines*

This command first appeared in Cisco IOS Release 11.2.

You can have several PAD connections open at the same time and switch between them. You can also exit a connection and return to the user EXEC prompt at any point.

To open a new connection, first suspend the current connection by pressing the escape sequence (**Ctrl-Shift-6** then **x** [**Ctrl^x**] by default) to return to the system command prompt, then open the new connection with the **pad** command.

You can have several concurrent sessions open and switch back and forth between them. The number of PAD sessions that can be open is defined by the **session-limit** command.

To switch between sessions, you must escape one session and resume a previously opened session. Use the **Ctrl^x**, **where**, and **resume** commands, which are available with all supported connection protocols, to do this.

You can issue any of the following commands to terminate a terminal session:

**exit**
**quit**
**logout**

To display information about packet transmission and X.3 PAD parameter settings, use the **show x25 pad** command.

### *Example*

The following example shows how to change a local X.3 PAD parameter from a remote X.25 host using X.29 messages, which is a secure way to enable a remote host to gain control of local PAD. The local device is Router-A. The remote host is Router-B. The parameters listed in the ParamsIn field are incoming parameters, which are sent by the remote PAD. The parameters listed in the ParamsOut field are parameters sent by the local PAD.

```
Router-A# pad 123456
Trying 123456...Open

Router-B> x3 2:0
Router-B>
Router-A# show x25 pad

tty0, connection 1 to host 123456

Total input: 12, control 3, bytes 35. Queued: 0 of 7 (0 bytes).
Total output: 10, control 3, bytes 64.
Flags: 1,    State: 3,    Last error: 1
 ParamsIn:  1:0, 2:0, 3:0, 4:0, 5:0, 6:0, 7:0,
    8:0, 9:0, 10:0, 11:0, 12:0, 13:0, 14:0, 15:0,
    16:0, 17:0, 18:0, 19:0, 20:0, 21:0, 22:0,
 ParamsOut:  1:1, 2:0, 3:2, 4:1, 5:1, 6:0, 7:21,
    8:0, 9:1, 10:0, 11:14, 12:1, 13:0, 14:0, 15:0,
    16:127, 17:21, 18:18, 19:0, 20:0, 21:0, 22:0,
Router-A#
```

### *Related Commands*

Search online to find documentation for related commands.

**resume**

## x25 SUBADDRESS

To append either a physical port number or a value specified for a line as a subaddress to the X.121 calling address, use the **x25 subaddress** line configuration command. Use the **no** form of this command to disable subaddressing.

**x25 subaddress** {**line** | *number*}
**no x25 subaddress** {**line** | *number*}

| *Syntax* | *Description* |
|---|---|
| **line** | The physical port number for the indicated line will be appended to the X.121 address as the subaddress. |
| *number* | Numeric variable assigned to a specific line. |



### *Command Mode*

Line configuration

### *Usage Guidelines*

This command first appeared in Cisco IOS Release 11.2F.

Use the **x25 subaddress** line command to create a unique X.121 calling address by adding either a physical port number or a numeric value for a line as a subaddress to the X.121 calling address.

### *Examples*

The following example shows how to configure subaddressing on vty lines 10 through 20 by appending the line number as a subaddress to the X.121 calling address:

```
line vty 10 20
x25 subaddress line
```

The following example shows how to configure subaddressing on the first five tty lines by appending the value "09" as a subaddress to the X.121 calling address of an X.28 connection originating on these lines:

```
line 1 5
x25 subaddress 9
autocommand x28
```

### *Related Command*

Search online to find documentation for related commands.

**line**

## x28

To enter X.28 mode and access an X.25 network or set X.3 PAD parameters, use the **x28** EXEC command.

**x28** [**escape** *character-string*] [**noescape**] [**nuicud**] [**profile** *file-name*] [**reverse**] [**verbose**]
**no x28** [**escape** *character-string*] [**noescape**] [**nuicud**] [**profile** *file-name*] [**reverse**] [**verbose**]

| *Syntax* | *Description* |
|---|---|
| **escape** *character-string* | (Optional) Specifies a character string to use to exit X.28 mode and return to EXEC mode. The character string can be any string of alphanumeric characters. The **Ctrl** key can be used in conjunction with the character string. |
| **noescape** | (Optional) Specifies that no escape character string is defined (user cannot return to EXEC mode). On the console line, the **noescape** option is ignored, and the default escape sequence is used (**exit** command). |
| **nuicud** | (Optional) Specifies the network user identification (NUI) data to not be placed in the network user identification facility of the call request. Instead, it is placed in the call user data (CUD) area of the call request packet. |
| **profile** *file-name* | (Optional) Specifies using a user-configured profile of X.3 parameters. A profile is created with the **x29 profile** EXEC command. |
| **reverse** | (Optional) Specifies reverse charges for outgoing calls made from the local router to the destination device. |
| **verbose** | (Optional) Displays optional service signals such as the called DTE address, facility block, and CUD. |

### *Default*

It is disabled. X.28 mode uses standard X.28 command syntax.

### *Command Mode*

EXEC

### *Usage Guidelines*

This command first appeared in Cisco IOS Release 11.2 F.

If both the **escape** and **noescape** options are not set, the default escape sequence is used (**exit** command).

X.28 mode is identified with an asterisk (*) router prompt. After you enter this mode, the standard X.28 user interface (with the exception of the escape sequence) is available. From this interface, you can configure a PAD device using X.3 parameters, or you can access an X.25 network.

In X.28 mode, you can set PAD command signals using standard or extended command syntax. For example, you can enter the **clr** command or **clear** command to clear a virtual call. A command specified with standard command syntax is merely an abbreviated version of the extended syntax version.

Table 24–4 lists the commands available in both standard and extended command syntax.

**Table 24–4** *Available PAD Command Signals*

| Standard Syntax | Extended Syntax | Description |
|---|---|---|
| break | | Simulate an asynchronous break. |
| call | | Place a virtual call to a remote device. |
| clr | clear | Clear a virtual call. |
| *command-signal*[*] | | Specifies a call request without using a standard X.28 command, which is entered with the following syntax: *facilities-x121-address*D*call-user-data* |
| help | | Display help information (see Table 24–5). |
| iclr | iclear | Request the remote device to clear the call. |
| int | interrupt | Send an Interrupt Packet. |
| par? par | parameter read | Show the current values of local parameters (see Table 24–5). |
| prof | profile *file-name* | Load a standard or a named profile. |
| reset | | Reset the call. |
| rpar? | rread | Show the current values of remote parameters. |
| rset? | rsetread | Set and then read the values of remote parameters. |
| set | | Change the values of local parameters (see Table 24–5). |
| set? | setread | Change and then read values of parameters. |
| stat | status | Request the status of a connection. |
| selection pad | | Set up a virtual call. |

[*] Here is an example of issuing a call request command: the **R,G23,P2-234234Duser1** command.

Table 24–5 lists the different types of parameters you can set using the **set** *parameter-number*: *new-value* PAD command signal from X.28 mode.

**NOTES**

Abbreviated X.121 addresses are not supported. Such addresses start with a period, are alphanumeric, and are mapped to a full X.121 address by the PAD.

**Table 24–5** *Supported X.3 PAD Parameters*

| Parameter Number | Parameter Name | Description |
|---|---|---|
| 1 | Escape from data transfer | PAD recall using a character. Minimum value: 0; maximum value: 126; default: 1. |
| 2 | Local echo mode | Minimum value: 0; maximum value: 1; default: 1. |
| 3 | Data forward character | Selection of data forwarding characters. Minimum value: 0; maximum value: 255; default: 126. |
| 4 | Idle timer | Selection of idle timer delay. Minimum value: 0; maximum value: 255; default: 0. |
| 5 | Device control | Ancillary device control. Minimum value: 0; maximum value: 2; default: 1. |
| 6 | PAD service signals | Control of PAD service signals. Minimum value: 0; maximum value: 255; default: 2. |
| 7 | Action upon receipt of a BREAK signal | Operation on receipt of break signal. Minimum value: 0; maximum value: 31; default: 2. |
| 8 | Discard option | Minimum value: 0; maximum value: 1; default: 0. |
| 9 | Return Padding | Bytes to add after the carriage return. Minimum value: 0; maximum value: 255; default:2. |
| 10* | Line folding | Not supported. |
| 11 | Baud rate | Binary speed of start-stop mode DTE. Minimum value: 0; maximum value: 18; default: 14. |
| 12 | Input flow control | Flow control of the PAD. Minimum value: 0; maximum value: 1; default: 1. |
| 13 | LINE FEED insertion | Linefeed insertion after carriage return. Minimum value: 0; maximum value: 7; default: 0. |
| 14 | LINE FEED Padding | Minimum value: 0; maximum value: 255; default: 0. |
| 15 | Local editing | Minimum value: 0; maximum value: 1; default: 0. |
| 16 | Character delete | Minimum value: 0; maximum value: 127; default: 127. |
| 17 | Line delete | Minimum value: 0; maximum value: 127; default: 24. |

**Table 24–5** *Supported X.3 PAD Parameters, Continued*

| Parameter Number | Parameter Name | Description |
|---|---|---|
| 18 | Line display | Minimum value: 0; maximum value: 127; default: 18. |
| 19 | Editing PAD service signals | Minimum value: 0; maximum value: 126; default: 2. |
| 20 | Echo mask | Minimum value: 0; maximum value: 255; default: 0. |
| 21* | Parity treatment | Not supported. |
| 22* | Page wait | Not supported. |

* These parameters are not supported in Cisco IOS Release 11.2 or 11.3.



Table 24–6 lists the options for the X.28 **help** command.

**Table 24–6** *Help Command Options*

| Command | Description |
|---|---|
| **help** | Describes the **help** PAD command. |
| **help command** | Displays the list of available PAD command signals. |
| **help parameter** | Displays the list of available X.3 PAD parameters. |
| **help parameter** *number* | Displays the specified X.3 PAD parameter and its current value. |
| **help list** | Lists the available help subjects. |
| **help profiles** | Lists available profiles. |
| **help profile** *name* | Shows the specified parameter's name and current value. |
| **help** *any-PAD-command* | Describes the specified PAD command signal. |

You can issue call requests from X.28 mode without using standard X.28 commands. To do this, use the following command syntax:

*facilities-x121-address*D*call-user-data*

| | |
|---|---|
| *facilities-* | Applies X.25 facilities to the outgoing call. The hyphen is mandatory. |
| *x121-address* | Specifies the address of the remote X.25 device. |
| D | Facility request code that specifies call user data for the outgoing call. |
| *call-user-data* | Specifies the data that accompanies the call request packet sent to the remote X.25 device. |

The following rules apply to all call requests parsed in X.28 mode:

- When an X.121 address specified using standard command syntax is followed by an optional call user data field, the call is placed to the X.121 address.
- While using standard command syntax, one or more facility request codes can be entered, followed by the code value. Additional facility request codes and values can also be entered; separate each entry with a comma, followed by a dash. An X.121 address and optional call user data can follow this entry.
- If an X.28 command is not entered, a call request is assumed.
- Ensure that the call request begins with a facility code letter, and that it contains a dash (-) followed by a string of digits (the X.121 address). The call request can be optionally terminated by an asterisk (*), a "P," or a "D," followed by some data.
- While using extended command syntax, the **call** command uses the facility codes and X.121 address as its operand.
- If facility codes are entered without an X.121 address, remember the codes for the next call. When a call is completed, forget the facility codes until they are once again set.

Table 24–7 shows examples of parsed call requests.

**Table 24–7** *Sample X.28 Call Requests*

| Command | Description |
|---|---|
| 123456789 | Calls this X.121 address. |
| 123456789*userdata | Calls this X.121 address, with specified data. |
| 123456789Puserdata | Calls this X.121 address, with specified data. |
| 123456789Duserdata | Calls this X.121 address, with specified data. |
| Nabcd-123456789 | Calls this X.121 address, with NUI set to abcd. |
| Nabcd,R-123456789 | Calls 123456789 with NUI of abcd, and with reverse charging. |

### *Examples*

The following example places a virtual call using the **call** PAD command signal in X.28 mode:

```
router# x28
* call 123456
```

The following example enters X.28 mode with the **x28** EXEC command and configures a PAD with the **set** X.3 parameter command. The **set** command sets the idle time delay to 40 seconds.

```
router# x28
* set 4:40
```

### *Related Commands*

Search online to find documentation for related commands.

**pad**

CHAPTER 25

# Configuring Media-Independent PPP and Multilink PPP

This chapter describes the configuration of the Point-to-Point Protocol (PPP) and Multilink PPP features that can be configured on any interface. This chapter also describes address pooling for point-to-point links, which is available on all asynchronous serial, synchronous serial, and ISDN interfaces.

See Chapter 27, "Configuring Asynchronous PPP and SLIP," for information about PPP features and requirements that apply only to asynchronous lines and interfaces.

For a complete description of the PPP commands in this chapter, see Chapter 26, "Media-Independent PPP and Multilink PPP Commands."

## IMPLEMENTATION INFORMATION

PPP, described in RFC 1661, encapsulates network layer protocol information over point-to-point links. You can configure PPP on the following types of physical interfaces:

- Asynchronous serial
- HSSI
- ISDN
- Synchronous serial

By enabling PPP encapsulation on physical interfaces, PPP can also be in effect on calls placed by the dialer interfaces that use the physical interfaces.

The current implementation of PPP supports option 3, authentication using CHAP or PAP, option 4, Link Quality Monitoring, and option 5, Magic Number configuration options. The software always sends option 5 and negotiates for options 3 and 4 if so configured. All other options are rejected.

Magic Number support is available on all serial interfaces. PPP always attempts to negotiate for Magic Numbers, which are used to detect looped-back lines. Depending on how the **down-when-looped** command is configured, the router might shut down a link if it detects a loop.

The software provides the Challenge Handshake Authentication Protocol (CHAP) and Password Authentication Protocol (PAP) on serial interfaces running PPP encapsulation.

With Cisco IOS Release 11.2 F, Cisco now supports fast switching of incoming and outgoing DECnet and CLNS packets over PPP.

## PPP Configuration Task List

To configure PPP on a serial interface (including ISDN), perform the task (in interface configuration mode) covered in the following section:

- Enabling PPP Encapsulation

You can also complete the tasks in the following sections; these tasks are optional but offer a variety of uses and enhancements for PPP on your systems and networks:

- Enabling CHAP or PAP Authentication
- Enabling Link Quality Monitoring (LQM)
- Configuring Compression of PPP Data
- Configuring IP Address Pooling
- Configuring PPP Reliable Link
- Disabling or Re-enabling Peer Neighbor Routes
- Configuring PPP Half-Bridging
- Configuring Multilink PPP
- Configuring MLP Interleaving and Queuing for Real-Time Traffic
- Monitoring and Maintaining PPP and MLP Interfaces

See sections "PPP Configuration Examples" and "MLP Interleaving and Queuing for Real-Time Traffic Examples," at the end of this chapter.

## Enabling PPP Encapsulation

You can enable PPP on serial lines to encapsulate IP and other network protocol datagrams. To do so, perform the following task in interface configuration mode:

| Task | Command |
|---|---|
| Enable PPP encapsulation. | **encapsulation ppp** |

PPP echo requests are used as keepalives to minimize disruptions to the end users of your network. The **no keepalive command** can be used to disable echo requests.

## ENABLING CHAP OR PAP AUTHENTICATION

The Point-to-Point Protocol (PPP) with Challenge Handshake Authentication Protocol (CHAP) authentication or Password Authentication Protocol (PAP) is often used to inform the central site about which remote routers are connected to it.

With this authentication information, if the router or access server receives another packet for a destination to which it is already connected, it does not place an additional call. However, if the router or access server is using rotaries, it sends the packet out the correct port.

CHAP and PAP were originally specified in RFC 1334, and CHAP is updated in RFC 1994. These protocols are supported on synchronous and asynchronous serial interfaces. When using CHAP or PAP authentication, each router or access server identifies itself by a *name*. This identification process prevents a router from placing another call to a router to which it is already connected, and also prevents unauthorized access.

Access control using Challenge Handshake Authentication Protocol (CHAP) or Password Authentication Protocol (PAP) is available on all serial interfaces that use PPP encapsulation. The authentication feature reduces the risk of security violations on your router or access server. You can configure either CHAP or PAP for the interface.

**NOTES**

To use CHAP or PAP, you must be running PPP encapsulation.

When CHAP is enabled on an interface and a remote device attempts to connect to it, the local router or access server sends a CHAP packet to the remote device. The CHAP packet requests or "challenges" the remote device to respond. The challenge packet consists of an ID, a random number, and the host name of the local router.

The required response consists of two parts:

- An encrypted version of the ID, a secret password (or *secret*), and the random number
- Either the host name of the remote device or the name of the user on the remote device

When the local router or access server receives the response, it verifies the secret by performing the same encryption operation as indicated in the response and looking up the required host name or username. The secret passwords must be identical on the remote device and the local router.

By transmitting this response, the secret is never transmitted in clear text, preventing other devices from stealing it and gaining illegal access to the system. Without the proper response, the remote device cannot connect to the local router.

CHAP transactions occur only at the time a link is established. The local router or access server does not request a password during the rest of the call. (The local device can, however, respond to such requests from other devices during a call.)

When PAP is enabled, the remote router attempting to connect to the local router or access server is required to send an authentication request. If the username and password specified in the authentication request are accepted, the Cisco IOS software sends an authentication acknowledgment.

After you have enabled CHAP or PAP, the local router or access server requires authentication from remote devices. If the remote device does not support the enabled protocol, no traffic will be passed to that device.

To use CHAP or PAP, you must perform the following tasks:

**Step 1** Enable PPP encapsulation.

**Step 2** Enable CHAP or PAP on the interface.

**Step 3** For CHAP, configure host name authentication and the secret or password for each remote system with which authentication is required.

To enable PPP encapsulation, perform the following task in interface configuration mode:

| **Task** | **Command** |
|---|---|
| Enable PPP on an interface. | **encapsulation ppp** |

To enable CHAP or PAP authentication on an interface configured for PPP encapsulation, perform the following task in interface configuration mode:

| **Task** | **Command** |
|---|---|
| Define the authentication methods supported and the order in which they are used. | **ppp authentication** {**chap** \| **chap pap** \| **pap chap** \| **pap**} [**if-needed**] [*list-name* \| **default**] [**callin**] |

The **ppp authentication chap** optional keyword **if-needed** can be used only with TACACS or extended TACACS.

With authentication, authorization, and accounting (AAA) configured on the router and list names defined for AAA, the optional keyword *list-name* can be used with AAA/TACACS+.

**CAUTION**

If you use a *list-name* that has not been configured with the **aaa authentication ppp** command, you disable PPP on the line.

Add a **username** entry for each remote system from which the local router or access server requires authentication.

To specify the password to be used in CHAP or PAP caller identification, perform the following task in global configuration mode:

| Task | Command |
|---|---|
| Configure identification. | **username** *name* **password** *secret* |

Make sure this password does not include spaces or underscores.

To configure Terminal Access Controller Access Control System (TACACS) on a specific interface as an alternative to global host authentication, perform the following task in interface configuration mode:

| Task | Command |
|---|---|
| Configure TACACS. | **ppp use-tacacs** [**single-line**]<br>or<br>**aaa authentication ppp** |

Use the **ppp use-tacacs** command with TACACS and Extended TACACS. Use the **aaa authentication ppp** command with AAA/TACACS+.

For an example of CHAP, see section "CHAP with an Encrypted Password Examples" near the end of this chapter. CHAP is specified in RFC 1994, "PPP Challenge Handshake Authentication Protocol (CHAP)."

## Enabling Link Quality Monitoring (LQM)

Link Quality Monitoring (LQM) is available on all serial interfaces running PPP. LQM will monitor the link quality, and if the quality drops below a configured percentage, the router shuts down the link. The percentages are calculated for both the incoming and outgoing directions. The outgoing quality is calculated by comparing the total number of packets and bytes sent with the total number of packets and bytes received by the destination node. The incoming quality is calculated by comparing the total number of packets and bytes received with the total number of packets and bytes sent by the destination peer.

When LQM is enabled, Link Quality Reports (LQRs) are sent, in place of keepalives, every keepalive period. All incoming keepalives are responded to properly. If LQM is not configured, keepalives are sent every keepalive period and all incoming LQRs are responded to with an LQR.

LQR is specified in RFC 1989, "PPP Link Quality Monitoring," by William A. Simpson of Computer Systems Consulting Services.

To enable LQM on the interface, perform the following task in interface configuration mode:

| Task | Command |
|---|---|
| Enable LQM on the interface. | **ppp quality** *percentage* |

The *percentage* argument specifies the link quality threshold. That percentage must be maintained, or the link is deemed to be of poor quality and taken down.

## Configuring Compression of PPP Data

You can configure point-to-point software compression on serial interfaces that use PPP encapsulation. Compression reduces the size of a PPP frame via lossless data compression. PPP encapsulations support both predictor and Stacker compression algorithms.

If the majority of your traffic is already compressed files, do not use compression.

Most routers support software compression only, but in the Cisco 7000 series, hardware compression and distributed compression are also available, depending on the interface processor and compression service adapter hardware installed in the router.

To configure compression, complete the tasks in one of the following sections:

- Software Compression
- Hardware-Dependent Compression

### Software Compression

Software compression is available on all router platforms. Software compression is performed by the router's main processor.

Compression is performed in software and might significantly affect system performance. Cisco recommends that you disable compression if the router CPU load exceeds 65 percent. To display the CPU load, use the **show process cpu** EXEC command.

To configure compression over PPP, perform the following tasks in interface configuration mode:

| Task | | Command |
|---|---|---|
| **Step 1** | Enable encapsulation of a single protocol on the serial line. | **encapsulation ppp** |
| **Step 2** | Enable compression. | **ppp compress [predictor \| stac]** |

### Hardware-Dependent Compression

When you configure Stacker compression on Cisco 7000 series routers with RSP7000, on Cisco 7200 series routers, and on Cisco 7500 series routers, there are three methods of compression: hardware compression, distributed compression, and software compression.

Hardware and distributed compression are available on routers that have the SA-Comp/1 and SA-Comp/4 data compression service adapters (CSAs). CSAs are available on Cisco 7200 series routers, on Cisco 7500 series routers with second-generation Versatile Interface Processors (VIP2s), and on Cisco 7000 series routers with the 7000 Series Route Switch Processor (RSP7000) and 7000 Series Chassis Interface (RSP7000CI). CSAs require VIP2 model VIP2-40.

To configure hardware or distributed compression over PPP, perform the following tasks in interface configuration mode:

| Task | | Command |
|---|---|---|
| **Step 1** | Enable encapsulation of a single protocol on the serial line. | **encapsulation ppp** |
| **Step 2** | Enable compression. | **compress stac** [**distributed** \| **software**] (Cisco 7000 series with RSP7000 and Cisco 7500 series)<br>or<br>**compress stac** [**csa** *slot* \| **software**] (Cisco 7200 series) |

Specifying the **compress stac** command with no options causes the router to use the fastest available compression method:

- If the router contains a compression service adapter (CSA), compression is performed in the CSA hardware (hardware compression).
- If the CSA is not available, compression is performed in the software installed on the VIP2 (distributed compression).
- If the VIP2 is not available, compression is performed in the router's main processor (software compression).

Using hardware compression in the CSA frees the router's main processor for other tasks. You can also configure the router to use the VIP2 to perform compression by using the **distributed** option, or to use the router's main processor by using the **software** option. If the VIP2 is not available, compression is performed in the router's main processor.

When compression is performed in software installed in the router's main processor, it might significantly affect system performance. It is recommended that you disable compression in the router's main processor if the router CPU load exceeds 40 percent. To display the CPU load, use the **show process cpu** EXEC command.

Specifying the **compress stac** command with no options causes the router to use the fastest available compression method.

## Configuring IP Address Pooling

Point-to-point interfaces must be able to provide a remote node with its IP address through the IP Control Protocol (IPCP) address negotiation process. The IP address can be obtained from a variety of sources. The address can be configured through the command line, entered with an EXEC-level command or provided by TACACS+, DHCP, or from a locally administered pool.

IP address pooling uses a pool of IP addresses from which an incoming interface can provide an IP address to a remote node through the IP Control Protocol (IPCP) address negotiation process. IP address pooling also enhances configuration flexibility by allowing multiple types of pooling to be active simultaneously.

See Chapter 27 for additional information about address pooling on asynchronous interfaces and about SLIP.

### Peer Address Allocation

A peer IP address can be allocated to an interface through several methods:

- Dialer map lookup—This method is used only if the peer requests an IP address, no other peer IP address has been assigned, and the interface is a member of a dialer group.
- PPP or SLIP EXEC command—An asynchronous dial-up user can enter a peer IP address or host name when PPP or SLIP is invoked from the command line. The address is used for the current session and then discarded.
- IPCP negotiation—If the peer presents a peer IP address during IPCP address negotiation and no other peer address is assigned, the presented address is acknowledged and used in the current session.
- Default IP address—The **peer default ip address** command and the **member peer default ip address** command can be used to define default peer IP addresses.
- TACACS+ assigned IP address—During the authorization phase of IPCP address negotiation, TACACS+ can return an IP address that the user being authenticated on a dial-up interface can use. This address overrides any default IP address and prevents pooling from taking place.
- DHCP retrieved IP address—If configured, the routers acts as a proxy client for the dial-up user and retrieves an IP address from a DHCP server. That address is returned to the DHCP server when the timer expires or when the interface goes down.
- Local address pool—The local address pool contains a set of contiguous IP addresses (a maximum of 256 addresses) stored in two queues. The *free* queue contains addresses available to be assigned and the *used* queue contains addresses that are in use. Addresses are stored to the free queue in first-in first-out (FIFO) order to minimize the chance the address will be reused and to allow a peer to reconnect using the same address that it used in the last connection. If the address is available, it is assigned; if not, another address from the free queue is assigned.
- Chat script—(Asynchronous serial interfaces only) The IP address in the dialer map command entry that started the script is assigned to the interface and overrides any previously assigned peer IP address.
- VTY/Protocol translation—The translate command can define the peer IP address for a VTY (pseudo asynchronous interface).

  The pool configured for the interface is used, unless TACACS+ returns a pool name as part of AAA. If no pool is associated with a given interface, the global pool named *default* is used.

### Precedence Rules

The following precedence rules of peer IP address support determine which address is used. Precedence is listed from most likely to least likely:

1. AAA/TACACS+ provided address or addresses from the pool named by AAA/TACACS+
2. An address from a local IP address pool or DHCP (typically not allocated unless no other address exists)
3. Dialer map lookup address (not done unless no other address exists)
4. Address from an EXEC-level PPP or SLIP command or from a chat script
5. Configured address from the **peer default ip address** command or address from the protocol **translate** command
6. Peer-provided address from IPCP negotiation (not accepted unless no other address exists)

### Interfaces Affected

Address pooling is available on all asynchronous serial, synchronous serial, ISDN BRI, and ISDN PRI interfaces running the Point-to-Point Protocol (PPP).

### Choose the IP Address Assignment Method

The IP address pooling feature now allows configuration of a global default address pooling mechanism, per-interface configuration of the address pooling mechanism, and per-interface configuration of a specific address or pool name.

You can define the type of IP address pooling mechanism used on router interfaces in one or both of the following ways:

- Define the Global Default Address Pooling Mechanism
- Configure Per-Interface IP Address Assignment, as needed

### Define the Global Default Address Pooling Mechanism

The global default mechanism applies to all point-to-point interfaces that support PPP encapsulation and that have not otherwise been configured for IP address pooling. You can define the global default mechanism to be either DHCP or local address pooling.

To configure the global default mechanism for IP address pooling, perform the tasks in one of following sections:

- Define DHCP as the Global Default Mechanism
- Define Local Address Pooling as the Global Default Mechanism

After you have defined a global default mechanism, you can disable it on a specific interface by configuring the interface for some other pooling mechanism. You can define a local pool other than the default pool for the interface or you can configure the interface with a specific IP address to be used for dial-in peers.

### *Define DHCP as the Global Default Mechanism*

The Dynamic Host Configuration Protocol (DHCP) specifies the following components:

- A DHCP server—A host-based DHCP server configured to accept and process requests for temporary IP addresses.
- A DHCP proxy-client—A Cisco access server configured to arbitrate DHCP calls between the DHCP server and the DHCP client. The DHCP client-proxy feature manages a pool of IP addresses available to dial-in clients without a known IP address.

To enable DHCP as the global default mechanism, complete the following tasks in global configuration mode:

| Task | | Command |
|---|---|---|
| **Step 1** | Specify DHCP client-proxy as the global default mechanism. | **ip address-pool dhcp-proxy-client** |
| **Step 2** | (Optional) Specify the IP address of a DHCP server for the proxy client to use. | **ip dhcp-server** [*ip-address* \| *name*] |

In Step 2, you can provide as few as 1 or as many as 10 DHCP servers for the proxy-client (the Cisco router or access server) to use. DHCP servers provide temporary IP addresses.

### *Define Local Address Pooling as the Global Default Mechanism*

To specify that the global default mechanism to use is local pooling, complete the following tasks in global configuration mode:

| Task | | Command |
|---|---|---|
| **Step 1** | Specify local pooling as the global default mechanism. | **ip address-pool local** |
| **Step 2** | Create one or more local IP address pools. | **ip local pool** {**default** \| *poolname*} *low-ip-address* [*high-ip-address*] |

If no other pool is defined, the local pool called *default* is used.

## Configure Per-Interface IP Address Assignment

After you have defined a global default mechanism for assigning IP addresses to dial-in peers, you can then configure the few interfaces for which it is important to have a nondefault configuration. You can do any of the following;

- Define a nondefault address pool for use by a specific interface.
- Define DHCP on an interface even if you have defined local pooling as the global default mechanism.

- Specify one IP address to be assigned to all dial-in peers on an interface.
- Make temporary IP addresses available on a per-interface basis to asynchronous clients using Serial Line Internet Protocol (SLIP) or Point-to-Point Protocol (PPP).

To define a nondefault address pool for use on an interface, perform the following tasks beginning in global configuration mode:

| Task | Command |
|---|---|
| Create one or more local IP address pools. | **ip local pool** *poolname* {*low-ip-address* [*high-ip-address*]} |
| Specify the interface and enter interface configuration mode. | **interface** *type number* |
| Specify the pool for the interface to use. | **peer default ip address pool** *poolname* |

To define DHCP as the IP address mechanism for an interface, complete the following tasks beginning in global configuration mode:

| Task | Command |
|---|---|
| Specify the interface and enter interface configuration mode. | **interface** *type number* |
| Specify DHCP as the IP address mechanism on this interface. | **peer default ip address pool dhcp** |

To define a specific IP address to be assigned to all dial-in peers on an interface, complete the following tasks beginning in global configuration mode:

| Task | Command |
|---|---|
| Specify the interface and enter interface configuration mode. | **interface** *type number* |
| Specify the IP address to assign. | **peer default ip address** *ip-address* |

## Configuring PPP Reliable Link

PPP reliable link is Cisco's implementation of RFC 1663, "PPP Reliable Transmission," which defines a method of negotiating and using Numbered Mode LAPB to provide a reliable serial link. Numbered Mode LAPB provides retransmission of errored packets across the serial link.

Although LAPB protocol overhead consumes some bandwidth, this can be offset by the use of PPP compression over the reliable link. PPP compression is separately configurable and is not required for use of a reliable link.

PPP reliable link is available only on synchronous serial interfaces, including ISDN BRI and ISDN PRI interfaces. PPP reliable link cannot be used over V.120.

To configure PPP reliable link on a specified interface, complete the following task in interface configuration mode:

| Task | Command |
|---|---|
| Enable PPP reliable link. | **ppp reliable-link** |

Having reliable link enabled does not guarantee that all connections through the specified interface will in fact use reliable link. It only guarantees that the router will attempt to negotiate reliable link on this interface.

### Restrictions

PPP reliable link does not work with Multilink PPP.

PPP reliable link is not available on asynchronous serial interfaces, including ISDN BRI and ISDN PRI interfaces. PPP reliable link cannot be used over V.120.

### Troubleshooting

You can troubleshoot PPP reliable link by using the **debug lapb** command and the **debug ppp negotiations, debug ppp errors**, and **debug ppp packets** commands. You can determine whether LAPB has been established on a connection by using the **show interface** command.

## Disabling or Re-enabling Peer Neighbor Routes

The Cisco IOS software automatically creates neighbor routes by default; that is, it automatically sets up a route to the peer address on a point-to-point interface when the PPP IPCP negotiation is completed.

To disable this default behavior or to re-enable it once it has been disabled, complete the following tasks in interface configuration mode:

| Task | Command |
|---|---|
| Disable creation of neighbor routes. | **no peer neighbor-route** |
| Re-enable creation of neighbor routes. | **peer neighbor-route** |

**NOTES**

If entered on a dialer or async-group interface, this command affects all member interfaces.

## CONFIGURING PPP HALF-BRIDGING

For situations in which a routed network needs connectivity to a remote bridged Ethernet network, a serial or ISDN interface can be configured to function as a PPP half-bridge. The line to the remote bridge functions as a virtual Ethernet interface, and the router's serial or ISDN interface functions as a node on the same Ethernet subnetwork as the remote network.

The bridge sends bridge packets to the PPP half-bridge, which converts them to routed packets and forwards them to other router processes. Likewise, the PPP half-bridge converts routed packets to Ethernet bridge packets and sends them to the bridge on the same Ethernet subnetwork.

**NOTES**

An interface cannot function as both a half-bridge and a bridge.

Figure 25–1 shows a router with a serial interface configured as a PPP half-bridge. The interface functions as a node on the Ethernet subnetwork with the bridge. Note that the serial interface has an IP address on the same Ethernet subnetwork as the bridge.

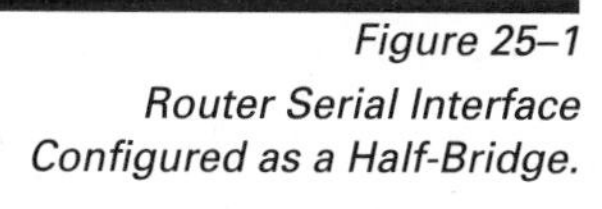

*Figure 25–1 Router Serial Interface Configured as a Half-Bridge.*

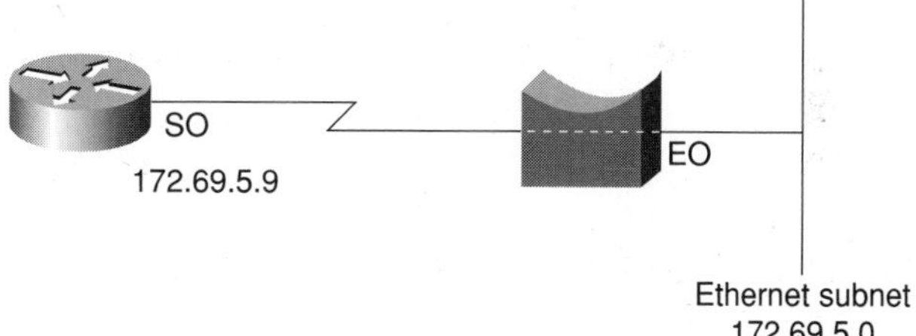


**NOTES**

The Cisco IOS software supports no more than one PPP half-bridge per Ethernet subnetwork.

To configure a serial interface to function as a half-bridge, compete the following tasks beginning in global configuration mode:

| Task | | Command |
|---|---|---|
| **Step 1** | Specify the interface (and enter interface configuration mode). | **interface serial** *number* |
| **Step 2** | Enable PPP half-bridging for one or more routed protocols: AppleTalk, IP, or IPX. | **ppp bridge appletalk**<br>**ppp bridge ip**<br>**ppp bridge ipx** [**novell-ether** \| **arpa** \| **sap** \| **snap**] |
| **Step 3** | Provide a protocol address on the same subnetwork as the remote network. | **ip address** *n.n.n.n*<br>**appletalk address** *network.node*<br>**appletalk cable-range** *cable-range network.node*<br>**ipx network** *network* |

**NOTES**

You must enter the **ppp bridge** command either when the interface is shut down or before you provide a protocol address for the interface.

## CONFIGURING MULTILINK PPP

The Multilink Point-to-Point Protocol (PPP) feature provides load balancing functionality over multiple WAN links, while providing multivendor interoperability, packet fragmentation and proper sequencing, and load calculation on both inbound and outbound traffic. Cisco's implementation of Multilink PPP supports the fragmentation and packet sequencing specifications in RFC 1717.

Multilink PPP allows packets to be fragmented and the fragments to be sent at the same time over multiple point-to-point links to the same remote address. The multiple links come up in response to a dialer load threshold that you define. The load can be calculated on inbound traffic, outbound traffic, or on either, as needed for the traffic between the specific sites. MLP provides bandwidth on demand and reduces transmission latency across WAN links.

Multilink PPP is designed to work over single or multiple interfaces of the following types that are configured to support both dial-on-demand rotary groups and PPP encapsulation:

- Asynchronous serial interfaces
- Basic Rate Interfaces (BRIs)
- Primary Rate Interfaces (PRIs)

### Configure Multilink PPP on Asynchronous Interfaces

To configure Multilink PPP on asynchronous interfaces, you configure the asynchronous interfaces to support DDR and PPP encapsulation, then you configure a dialer interface to support PPP encapsulation, bandwidth on demand, and Multilink PPP.

To configure an asynchronous interface to support DDR and PPP encapsulation, complete the following tasks beginning in global configuration mode:

| Task | | Command |
|---|---|---|
| **Step 1** | Specify an asynchronous interface. | **interface async** *number* |
| **Step 2** | Specify no IP address for the interface. | **no ip address** |
| **Step 3** | Enable PPP encapsulation. | **encapsulation ppp** |
| **Step 4** | Enable DDR on the interface. | **dialer in-band** |
| **Step 5** | Include the interface in a specific dialer rotary group. | **dialer rotary-group** *number* |

Repeat this step for additional asynchronous interfaces, as needed.

At some point, adding more asynchronous interfaces does not improve performance, With the default MTU size, Multilink PPP should support three asynchronous interfaces using V.34 modems. However, packets might be dropped occasionally if the MTU is small or large bursts of short frames occur.

To configure a dialer interface to support PPP encapsulation and Multilink PPP, complete the following tasks beginning in global configuration mode:

| Task | | Command |
|---|---|---|
| **Step 1** | Define a dialer rotary group. | **interface dialer** *number* |
| **Step 2** | Specify no IP address for the interface. | **no ip address** |
| **Step 3** | Enable PPP encapsulation. | **encapsulation ppp** |
| **Step 4** | Enable DDR on the interface. | **dialer in-band** |
| **Step 5** | Configure bandwidth on demand by specifying the maximum load before the dialer places another call to a destination. | **dialer load-threshold** *load* [**inbound** \| **outbound** \| **either**] |
| **Step 6** | Enable Multilink PPP. | **ppp multilink** |

## Configure Multilink PPP on a Single ISDN BRI Interface

To enable Multilink PPP on a single Integrated Services Digital Network (ISDN) BRI interface, you are not required to define a dialer rotary group separately because ISDN interfaces are dialer rotary groups by default.

To enable PPP on an ISDN BRI interface, perform the following tasks beginning in global configuration mode:

| Task | | Command |
|---|---|---|
| **Step 1** | Specify an interface. | **interface bri** *number* |
| **Step 2** | Provide an appropriate protocol address for the interface. | **ip address** *ip-address mask* |
| **Step 3** | Enable PPP encapsulation. | **encapsulation ppp** |
| **Step 4** | (Optional) Specify a dialer idle timeout. | **dialer idle-timeout** *seconds* |
| **Step 5** | Specify the dialer load threshold for bringing up additional WAN links. | **dialer load-threshold** *load* |
| **Step 6** | Configure the ISDN interface to call the remote site. | **dialer map** *protocol next-hop-address* [**name** *hostname*] [**spc**] [**speed 56 \| 64**] [**broadcast**] [*dial-string*[*:isdn-subaddress*]] |
| **Step 7** | Control access to this interface by adding it to a dialer access group. | **dialer-group** *group-number* |
| **Step 8** | (Optional) Enable PPP authentication. | **ppp authentication pap** |
| **Step 9** | Enable Multilink PPP on the dialer rotary group. | **ppp multilink** |

If you do not use PPP authentication procedures (Step 8), your telephone service must pass caller ID information.

The load threshold number is required. For an example of configuring Multilink PPP on a single ISDN BRI interface, see the section "Multilink PPP on One ISDN Interface Example," later in this chapter.

When Multilink PPP is configured and you want a multilink bundle to be connected indefinitely, use the **dialer idle-timeout** command to set a very high idle timer. (The **dialer-load threshold 1** command no longer keeps a multilink bundle of *n* links connected indefinitely, and the **dialer-load threshold 2** command no longer keeps a multilink bundle of two links connected indefinitely.)

### Configure Multilink PPP on Multiple ISDN BRI Interfaces

To enable Multilink PPP on multiple ISDN BRI interfaces, you set up a dialer rotary interface and configure it for Multilink PPP and then you configure the BRIs separately and add them each to the same rotary group.

To set up the dialer rotary interface for the BRI interfaces, perform the following tasks beginning in global configuration mode:

| Task | | Command |
|---|---|---|
| **Step 1** | Specify the dialer rotary interface. | **interface dialer** *number* |

| Task | | Command |
|---|---|---|
| **Step 2** | Specify the protocol address for the dialer rotary interface. | **ip address** *address mask* |
| **Step 3** | Enable PPP encapsulation. | **encapsulation ppp** |
| **Step 4** | Specify in-band dialing. | **dialer in-band** |
| **Step 5** | (Optional) Specify the dialer idle timeout period, using the same timeout period as the individual BRI interfaces. | **dialer idle-timeout** *seconds* |
| **Step 6** | Map the next-hop protocol address and name to the dial string needed to reach it. | **dialer map** *protocol next-hop-address* [**name** *hostname*] [**spc**] [**speed 56** \| **64**] [**broadcast**] [*dial-string*[*:isdn-subaddress*]] |
| **Step 7** | Specify the dialer load threshold, using the same threshold as the individual BRI interfaces. | **dialer load-threshold** *load* |
| **Step 8** | Control access to this interface by adding it to a dialer access group. | **dialer-group** *group-number* |
| **Step 9** | (Optional) Enable PPP Challenge Handshake Authentication Protocol (CHAP) authentication. | **ppp authentication chap** |
| **Step 10** | Enable Multilink PPP. | **ppp multilink** |

If you do not use PPP authentication procedures (Step 10), your telephone service must pass caller ID information.

To configure each of the BRIs to belong to the same rotary group, perform the following tasks beginning in global configuration mode:

| Task | | Command |
|---|---|---|
| **Step 1** | Specify one of the BRI interfaces. | **interface bri** *number* |
| **Step 2** | Specify that it does not have an individual protocol address. | **no ip address** |
| **Step 3** | Enable PPP encapsulation. | **encapsulation ppp** |
| **Step 4** | Set the dialer idle timeout period, using the same timeout for each of the BRI interfaces you configure. | **dialer idle-timeout** *seconds* |
| **Step 5** | Add the interface to the rotary group. | **dialer rotary-group** *group-number* |

| Task | | Command |
|---|---|---|
| **Step 6** | Specify the dialer load threshold for bringing up additional WAN links. | **dialer load-threshold** *load* |

Repeat Steps 1 through 6 for each BRI you want to belong to the same dialer rotary group.

For an example of configuring Multilink PPP on multiple ISDN BRI interfaces, see the section "Multiple ISDN Interfaces Configured for Multilink PPP Example," later in this chapter.

When Multilink PPP is configured and you want a multilink bundle to be connected indefinitely, use the **dialer idle-timeout** command to set a very high idle timer. (The **dialer load-threshold 1** command no longer keeps a multilink bundle of *n* links connected indefinitely and the **dialer load-threshold 2** command no longer keeps a multilink bundle of two links connected indefinitely.)

## Configuring MLP Interleaving and Queuing for Real-Time Traffic

Interleaving on Multilink PPP allows large packets to be multilink encapsulated and fragmented into a small enough size to satisfy the delay requirements of real-time traffic; small real-time packets are not multilink encapsulated and are transmitted between fragments of the large packets. The interleaving feature also provides a special transmit queue for the smaller, delay-sensitive packets, enabling them to be transmitted earlier than other flows.

Weighted fair-queuing on Multilink PPP works on the packet level, not at the level of multilink fragments. Thus, if a small real-time packet gets queued behind a larger best-effort packet and no special queue has been reserved for real-time packets, the small packet will be scheduled for transmission only after all the fragments of the larger packet are scheduled for transmission.

Weighted fair-queuing is now supported on all interfaces that support Multilink PPP, including Multilink PPP virtual access interfaces and virtual interface templates. Weighted fair-queuing is enabled by default.

Fair-queuing on Multilink PPP overcomes a prior restriction. Previously, fair-queuing was not allowed on virtual access interfaces and virtual interface templates. Interleaving provides the delay bounds for delay-sensitive voice packets on a slow link that is used for other best-effort traffic.

### Restrictions

Interleaving applies only to interfaces that can configure a multilink bundle interface. These include virtual templates, dialer interfaces, and ISDN BRI or PRI interfaces.

Multilink and fair-queuing are not supported when a multilink bundle is offloaded to a different system using Multichassis Multilink PPP. Thus, interleaving is not supported in Multichassis Multilink PPP (MMP) networking designs.

### MLP Interleaving Configuration Tasks

Multilink PPP support for interleaving can be configured on virtual templates, dialer interfaces, and ISDN BRI or PRI interfaces. To configure interleaving, complete the following tasks:

**Step 1** Configure the dialer interface, BRI interface, PRI interface, or virtual template.

**Step 2** Configure Multilink PPP and interleaving on the interface or template.

**NOTES**

Fair-queueing, which is enabled by default, must remain enabled on the interface.

To configure Multilink PPP and interleaving on a configured and operational interface or virtual interface template, perform the following tasks in interface configuration mode:

| Task | Command |
|---|---|
| **Step 1** Enable Multilink PPP. | **ppp multilink** |
| **Step 2** Enable real-time packet interleaving. | **ppp multilink interleave** |
| **Step 3** Optionally, configure a maximum fragment delay. | **ppp multilink fragment-delay** *milliseconds* |
| **Step 4** Reserve a special queue for real-time packet flows to specified destination UDP ports, allowing real-time traffic to have higher priority than other flows. | **ip rtp reserve** *lowest-UDP-port range-of-ports* [*maximum-bandwidth*] |
| **Step 5** For virtual templates only, apply the virtual template to the multilink bundle.* | **multilink virtual-template 1** |

* This step is not used for ISDN or dialer interfaces.

Interleaving statistics can be displayed by using the **show interfaces** command, specifying the particular interface on which interleaving is enabled. Interleaving data is displayed only if there are interleaves. For example, the following line shows interleaves:

```
Output queue: 315/64/164974/31191 (size/threshold/drops/interleaves)
```

## MONITORING AND MAINTAINING PPP AND MLP INTERFACES

To monitor and maintain virtual interfaces, perform the following task:

| Task | Command |
|---|---|
| Display MLP and MMP bundle information. | **show ppp multilink** |

## PPP Configuration Examples

The examples provided in this section show various PPP configurations as follows:

- CHAP with an Encrypted Password Examples
- PPP Reliable Link Examples
- Multilink PPP Examples

### CHAP with an Encrypted Password Examples

The following configuration examples enable CHAP on serial interface 0 of three devices.

#### *Configuration of Router yyy*

```
hostname yyy
interface serial 0
 encapsulation ppp
 ppp authentication chap
username xxx password secretxy
username zzz password secretzy
```

#### *Configuration of Router xxx*

```
hostname xxx
interface serial 0
 encapsulation ppp
 ppp authentication chap

username yyy password secretxy
username zzz password secretxz
```

#### *Configuration of Router zzz*

```
hostname zzz
interface serial 0
encapsulation ppp
ppp authentication chap
username xxx password secretxz
username yyy password secretzy
```

When you look at the configuration file, the passwords will be encrypted and the display will look similar to the following:

```
hostname xxx
interface serial 0
 encapsulation ppp
 ppp authentication chap
username yyy password 7 121F0A18
username zzz password 7 1329A055
```

### PPP Reliable Link Examples

The following example enables PPP reliable link and Stac compression on BRI 0:

```
interface BRI0
 description Enables stac compression on BRI 0
```

```
ip address 172.1.1.1 255.255.255.0
encapsulation ppp
dialer map ip 172.1.1.2 name baseball 14195386368
compress stac
ppp authentication chap
dialer-group 1
ppp reliable-link
```

The following example shows output of the **show interface** command when PPP reliable link is enabled. The LAPB output lines indicate that PPP reliable link is provided over LAPB.

```
Router# show interface serial 0
Serial0 is up, line protocol is up
  Hardware is HD64570
  Description: connects to enkidu s 0
  Internet address is 172.21.10.10/8
  MTU 1500 bytes, BW 1544 Kbit, DLY 20000 usec, rely 255/255, load 1/255
  Encapsulation PPP, loopback not set
  LCP Open
  Open: IPCP, CDP
  LAPB DTE, state CONNECT, modulo 8, k 7, N1 12048, N2 20
      T1 3000, T2 0, interface outage (partial T3) 0, T4 0, PPP over LAPB
      VS 1, VR 1, tx NR 1, Remote VR 1, Retransmissions 0
      Queues: U/S frames 0, I frames 0, unack. 0, reTx 0
      IFRAMEs 1017/1017 RNRs 0/0 REJs 0/0 SABM/Es 1/1 FRMRs 0/0 DISCs 0/0
  Last input 00:00:18, output 00:00:08, output hang never
  Last clearing of "show interface" counters never
  Input queue: 0/75/0 (size/max/drops); Total output drops: 0
  Queueing strategy: weighted fair
  Output queue: 0/64/0 (size/threshold/drops)
     Conversations  0/1 (active/max active)
     Reserved Conversations 0/0 (allocated/max allocated)
  5 minute input rate 3000 bits/sec, 4 packets/sec
  5 minute output rate 3000 bits/sec, 7 packets/sec
     1365 packets input, 107665 bytes, 0 no buffer
     Received 0 broadcasts, 0 runts, 0 giants, 0 throttles
     0 input errors, 0 CRC, 0 frame, 0 overrun, 0 ignored, 0 abort
     2064 packets output, 109207 bytes, 0 underruns
     0 output errors, 0 collisions, 4 interface resets
     0 output buffer failures, 0 output buffers swapped out
     4 carrier transitions
     DCD=up  DSR=up  DTR=up  RTS=up  CTS=up
```

## Multilink PPP Examples

The following examples configure Multilink PPP. The first example configures it on one BRI interface, and the second configures multiple BRIs to belong to the same dialer rotary group, which is then configured for Multilink PPP.

### *Multilink PPP on One ISDN Interface Example*

The following example enables Multilink PPP on the BRI interface 0. Because an ISDN interface is a rotary group by default, when one BRI is configured, no dialer rotary group configuration is required.

```
interface bri 0
 description connected to ntt 81012345678902
 ip address 171.1.1.7 255.255.255.0
 encapsulation ppp
 dialer idle-timeout 30
 dialer load-threshold 40 either
 dialer map ip 171.1.1.8 name atlanta 81012345678901
 dialer-group 1
 ppp authentication pap
 ppp multilink
```

### *Multilink PPP on Multiple ISDN Interfaces Example*

The following example configures multiple ISDN BRIs to belong to the same dialer rotary group for Multilink PPP. The **dialer rotary-group** command is used to assign each of the ISDN BRIs to that dialer rotary group.

```
interface BRI0
 no ip address
 encapsulation ppp
 dialer idle-timeout 500
 dialer rotary-group 0
 dialer load-threshold 30 either
!
interface BRI1
 no ip address
 encapsulation ppp
 dialer idle-timeout 500
 dialer rotary-group 0
 dialer load-threshold 30 either
!
interface BRI2
 no ip address
 encapsulation ppp
 dialer idle-timeout 500
 dialer rotary-group 0
 dialer load-threshold 30 either
!
interface Dialer0
 ip address 99.0.0.2 255.0.0.0
 encapsulation ppp
 dialer in-band
 dialer idle-timeout 500
 dialer map ip 99.0.0.1 name atlanta broadcast 81012345678901
 dialer load-threshold 30 either
 dialer-group 1
 ppp authentication chap
 ppp multilink
```

## MLP Interleaving and Queuing for Real-Time Traffic Examples

The following example defines a virtual interface template that enables Multilink PPP interleaving and a maximum real-time traffic delay of 20 milliseconds, and then applies that virtual template to the multilink PPP bundle:

```
interface virtual-template 1
 ip unnumbered ethernet 0
 ppp multilink
 ppp multilink interleave
 ppp multilink fragment-delay 20
 ip rtp interleave 32768 20 1000
multilink virtual-template 1
```

The following example enables Multilink PPP interleaving on a dialer interface that controls a rotary group of BRI interfaces. This configuration permits IP packets to trigger calls.

```
interface BRI 0
 description connected into a rotary group
 encapsulation ppp
 dialer rotary-group 1
!
interface BRI 1
 no ip address
 encapsulation ppp
 dialer rotary-group 1
!
interface BRI 2
 encapsulation ppp
 dialer rotary-group 1
!
interface BRI 3
 no ip address
 encapsulation ppp
 dialer rotary-group 1
!
interface BRI 4
 encapsulation ppp
 dialer rotary-group 1
!
interface Dialer 0
 description Dialer group controlling the BRIs
 ip address 8.1.1.1 255.255.255.0
 encapsulation ppp
 dialer map ip 8.1.1.2 name angus 14802616900
 dialer-group 1
 ppp authentication chap
! Enables Multilink PPP interleaving on the dialer interface and reserves
! a special queue.
 ppp multilink
 ppp multilink interleave
 ip rtp reserve 32768 20 1000
! Keeps fragments of large packets small enough to ensure delay of 20 ms or less.
 ppp multilink fragment-delay 20
dialer-list 1 protocol ip permit
```

# CHAPTER 26

# Media-Independent PPP and Multilink PPP Commands

This chapter describes the commands available to configure the Point-to-Point Protocol (PPP) for dial-up wide-area networking on your router.

For information about configuring PPP on Cisco routers, see Chapter 25, "Configuring Media-Independent PPP and Multilink PPP." For information about configuring PPP on asynchronous links, see Chapter 27, "Configuring Asynchronous PPP and SLIP." For PPP commands for asynchronous links, see Chapter 28, "Asynchronous PPP and SLIP Commands." For more information about PPP, see RFC 1661. For more information about MLP, see RFC 1717. For more information about PAP, see RFC 1334. For more information about CHAP, see RFC 1994.

## COMPRESS

To configure software compression for Point-to-Point Protocol (PPP) encapsulation, use the **ppp compress** interface configuration command. To disable compression, use the **no** form of this command.

**compress** [**predictor** | **stac**]
**no compress** [**predictor** | **stac**]

| *Syntax* | *Description* |
|---|---|
| **predictor** | (Optional) Specifies that a predictor compression algorithm will be used. |
| **stac** | (Optional) Specifies that a Stacker (LZS) compression algorithm will be used. |

### *Default*

PPP compression is disabled.

### *Command Mode*

Interface configuration

### *Usage Guidelines*

This command first appeared in Cisco IOS Release 11.2.

Compression reduces the size of frames via lossless data compression. The compression algorithm used is a predictor algorithm (the RAND compression algorithm), which uses a compression dictionary to predict what the next character in the frame will be.

PPP encapsulation supports both predictor and Stacker compression algorithms.

Compression is performed in software and may significantly affect system performance. We recommend that you disable compression if CPU load exceeds 65 percent. To display the CPU load, use the **show process cpu** EXEC command.

Compression requires that both ends of the point-to-point link be configured to use compression. You should never enable compression for connections to a public data network.

If the majority of your traffic is already compressed files, it is recommended that you not use compression. If the files are already compressed, the additional processing time spent in attempting unsuccessfully to compress them again will slow system performance.

### *Example*

The following example enables predictor compression on serial interface 0:

```
interface serial 0
 encapsulation ppp
 compress predictor
```

### *Related Commands*

Search online to find documentation for related commands.

**encapsulation ppp**
**show compress**

## ENCAPSULATION PPP

To set the Point-to-Point Protocol (PPP) as the encapsulation method used by a serial or ISDN interface, use the **encapsulation ppp** interface configuration command.

**encapsulation ppp**

### *Syntax Description*

This command has no arguments or keywords.

### *Default*

HDLC on synchronous serial interfaces

### *Command Mode*

Interface configuration

### *Usage Guidelines*

This command first appeared in a release prior to Cisco IOS Release 10.0.

To use PPP encapsulation, the router must be configured with an IP routing protocol.

### *Example*

The following example enables PPP encapsulation on serial interface 0:

```
interface serial 0
 encapsulation ppp
```

### *Related Commands*

Search online to find documentation for related commands.

**keepalive**

**ppp**

**ppp authentication**



## IP ADDRESS-POOL

To enable an address pooling mechanism used to supply IP addresses to dial-in asynchronous, synchronous, or ISDN point-to-point interfaces, use the **ip address-pool** global configuration command. To disable IP address pooling globally on all interfaces with the default configuration, use the **no** form of the command.

**ip address-pool [dhcp-proxy-client | local]**
**no ip address-pool**

| *Syntax* | *Description* |
|---|---|
| **dhcp-proxy-client** | (Optional) Uses the router as the proxy client between a third-party Dynamic Host Configuration Protocol (DHCP) server and peers connecting to the router. |
| **local** | (Optional) Uses the local address pool named *default*. |

### *Default*

IP address pooling is disabled.

### *Command Mode*

Global configuration

### *Usage Guidelines*

The global default mechanism applies to all interfaces that have been left in the default setting of the **peer default ip address pool** command.

If any **peer default ip address** command other than **peer default ip address pool** (the default) is configured, then the interface uses that mechanism and not the global default mechanism. Thus, all interfaces can be independently configured or left unconfigured so that the global default mechanism settings apply. This flexibility minimizes the configuration effort on the part of the administrator.

### *Examples*

The following example specifies the DHCP proxy-client mechanism as the global default mechanism for assigning peer IP addresses:

```
ip address-pool dhcp-proxy-client
```

The following example specifies a local IP address pool called *default* as the global default mechanism for all interfaces that have been left in their default setting:

```
ip address-pool local
```

### *Related Commands*

Search online to find documentation for related commands.

**encapsulation ppp**
**encapsulation slip**
**ip dhcp-server**
**ip local pool**
**member peer default ip address**
**peer default ip address**
**peer default ip address pool**
**ppp**
**show dhcp**
**show ip local pool**
**slip**

## IP DHCP-SERVER

To specify which Dynamic Host Configuration Protocol (DHCP) servers to use on your network, to specify the IP address of one or more DHCP servers available on the network, use the **ip dhcp-server** global configuration command. Use the **no** form of the command to remove a DHCP server's IP address.

**ip dhcp-server** [*ip-address* | *name*]
**no ip dhcp-server** [*ip-address* | *name*]

| *Syntax* | *Description* |
|---|---|
| *ip-address* | (Optional) IP address of a DHCP server. |
| *name* | (Optional) Name of a DHCP server. |

### *Default*

The IP limited broadcast address of 255.255.255.255 is used for transactions if no DHCP server is specified. This allows automatic detection of DHCP servers.

### *Command Mode*

Global configuration



### *Usage Guidelines*

A DHCP server temporarily allocates network addresses to clients through the access server on an as-needed basis. While the client is active, the address is automatically renewed in a minimum of 20-minute increments. When the user terminates the session, the interface connection is terminated so that network resources can be quickly reused. You can specify up to 10 servers on the network.

In normal situations, if a user's SLIP/PPP session fails (for example if a modem line disconnects), the allocated address will be reserved temporarily to preserve the same IP address for the client when dialed back in to the server. This way, the session that was accidentally terminated can often be resumed.

To use the DHCP proxy-client feature, enable your access server to be a proxy client on asynchronous interfaces by using the **ip address-pool dhcp-proxy-client** command. If you wish to specify which DHCP servers are used on your network, use the **ip dhcp-server** command to define up to ten specific DHCP servers.

**NOTES**

To facilitate transmission, configure intermediary routers (or access servers with router functionality) to use an IP helper address whenever the DHCP server is not on the local LAN and the access server is using broadcasts to interact with the DHCP server.

The **ip address-pool dhcp-proxy-client** command initializes proxy-client status to all interfaces defined as asynchronous on the access server. To selectively disable proxy-client status on a single asynchronous interface, use the **no peer default ip address** interface command.

### *Example*

The following command specifies a DHCP server with the IP address of 129.12.13.81:

```
ip dhcp-server 129.12.13.81
```

### *Related Commands*

Search online to find documentation for related commands.

**ip address-pool dhcp-proxy-client**
**ip helper address**
**peer default ip address pool**
**show dhcp**

## IP LOCAL POOL

To configure a local pool of IP addresses to be used when a remote peer connects to a point-to-point interface, use the **ip local pool** global configuration command. To delete an address pool, use the **no** form of this command.

**ip local pool** {**default** | *pool-name low-ip-address* [*high-ip-address*]}
**no ip local pool** {**default** | *poolname*}

| *Syntax* | *Description* |
|---|---|
| **default** | Default local address pool that is used if no other pool is named. |
| *pool-name* | Name of a specific local address pool. |
| *low-ip-address* | Lowest IP address in the pool. |
| *high-ip-address* | (Optional) Highest IP address in the pool. If this value is omitted, only the *low-ip-address* IP address is included in the local pool. The maximum number of IP addresses per pool is 256. |

### *Default*

No address pools are configured.

### *Command Mode*

Global configuration

### *Usage Guidelines*

Use the **ip local pool** command to create one or more local address pools from which IP addresses are assigned when a peer connects. The **default** address pool is then used on all point-to-point interfaces after the **ip address-pool local** global configuration command is issued. To use a specific, named address pool on an interface, use the **peer default ip address pool** interface configuration command.

These pools can also be used with the **translate** commands for one-step vty-async connections and in certain AAA/TACACS+ authorization functions. See Chapter 21, "Configuring Protocol Translation and Virtual Asynchronous Devices," for more information. Pools can be displayed with the **show ip local pool** command.

*Example*

The following command creates a local IP address pool by the name of quark, which contains all local IP addresses from 172.16.23.0 to 172.16.23.255:

```
ip local pool quark 172.16.23.0 172.16.23.255
```

*Related Commands*

Search online to find documentation for related commands.

**ip address-pool**
**show ip local pool**



## IP RTP RESERVE

To reserve a special queue for a set of Real-Time Transport Protocol (RTP) packet flows belonging to a range of UDP destination ports, use the **ip rtp reserve** interface configuration command. To disable the special queue for real-time traffic, use the **no** form of the command.

**ip rtp reserve** *lowest-udp-port range-of-ports* [*maximum-bandwidth*]
**no rtp reserve**

| *Syntax* | *Description* |
|---|---|
| *lowest-udp-port* | Lowest UDP port number to which the packets are sent. |
| *range-of-ports* | Number, which when added to the lowest-UDP-port value yields the highest UDP port value. |
| *maximum-bandwidth* | (Optional) Bandwidth, in kilobits per second, reserved for the RTP packets to be sent to the specified UDP ports. |

*Default*

This function is disabled by default. No default values are provided for the arguments.

*Command Mode*

Interface configuration

*Usage Guidelines*

This command first appeared in Release 11.3.

If the bandwidth needed for RTP packet flows exceeds the maximum bandwidth specified, the reserved queue degrades to a best-effort queue.

This command helps in improving the delay bounds of voice streams by giving them a higher priority.

### *Example*

The following example reserves a unique queue for traffic to destination UDP ports in the range 32768 to 32788 and reserves 1,000-Kbps bandwidth for that traffic:

```
ip rtp reserve 32768 20 1000
```

### *Related Commands*

Search online to find documentation for related commands.

**ppp multilink**
**ppp multilink fragment-delay**
**ppp multilink interleave**

## MULTILINK VIRTUAL-TEMPLATE

To specify a virtual template from which the specified Multilink PPP bundle interface can clone its interface parameters, use the **multilink virtual-template** global configuration command.

**multilink virtual-template** *number*

| *Syntax* | *Description* |
|---|---|
| *number* | Number of the virtual template; an integer in the range 1 through 9. |

### *Default*

Disabled. No template number is defined.

### *Command Mode*

Global configuration

### *Usage Guidelines*

This command first appeared in Cisco IOS Release 11.2.

MLP virtual templates require that an IP address be defined for the remote client.

### *Example*

The following example specifies an MLP virtual template to be used and then defines the template to be applied to an MLP bundle interface:

```
multilink virtual-template 1
ip local pool default 2.2.2.2
interface virtual-template 1
 ip unnumbered ethernet 0
 encapsulation ppp
 ppp multilink
 ppp authentication chap
```

*Related Commands*

Search online to find documentation for related commands.

**interface virtual-template**
**ip local pool**

### PEER DEFAULT IP ADDRESS

Use the **peer default ip address** interface configuration command to specify an IP address, an address from a specific IP address pool, or an address from the DHCP mechanism to be returned to a remote peer connecting to this interface. Use the **no** form of the command to disable a prior peer IP address pooling configuration on an interface.

**peer default ip address** {*ip-address* | **dhcp** | **pool** [*pool-name*]}
**no peer default ip address**

| *Syntax* | *Description* |
|---|---|
| *ip-address* | Specific IP address to be assigned to a remote peer dialing in to the interface. To prevent duplicate IP addresses from being assigned on more than one interface, this command argument cannot be applied to a dialer rotary group nor to an ISDN interface. |
| **dhcp** | Retrieve an IP address from the DHCP server. |
| **pool** | Use the global default mechanism as defined by the **ip address-pool** command unless the optional *pool-name* argument is supplied. This is the default. |
| *pool-name* | (Optional) Name of a local address pool created using the **ip local pool** command. Retrieve an address from this pool regardless of the global default mechanism setting. |

*Default*

**pool**

*Command Mode*

Interface configuration

*Usage Guidelines*

This command applies to point-to-point interfaces that support the PPP or SLIP encapsulation.

This command allows an administrator to configure all possible address pooling mechanisms on an interface-by-interface basis.

The **peer default ip address** command can override the global default mechanism defined by the **ip address-pool** command on an interface-by-interface basis.

- For all interfaces not configured with a peer default IP address mechanism (equivalent to selecting the **peer default ip address pool** command), the router uses the global default mechanism that is defined by the **ip address-pool** command.
- If you select the **peer default ip address pool** *pool-name* form of this command, then the router uses the locally configured pool on this interface and does not follow the global default mechanism.
- If you select the **peer default ip address** *ip-address* `form of this` command, the specified IP address is assigned to any peer connecting to this interface, and any global default mechanism is overridden for this interface.
- If you select the **peer default ip address dhcp** form of this command, the DHCP proxy-client mechanism is used by default on this interface and any global default mechanism is overridden for this interface.

### *Examples*

The following command specifies that this interface will use a local IP address pool called pool3:

```
peer default ip address pool pool3
```

The following command specifies that this interface will use the IP address 172.140.34.21:

```
peer default ip address 172.140.34.21
```

The following command re-enables the global default mechanism to be used on this interface:

```
peer default ip address pool
```

### *Related Commands*

Search online to find documentation for related commands.

**encapsulation ppp**
**encapsulation slip**
**ip address-pool**
**ip dhcp-server**
**ip local pool**
**ppp**
**slip**
**show dhcp**

## PEER NEIGHBOR-ROUTE

To re-enable the creation of peer neighbor routes on an interface once this default behavior has been disabled, use the **peer neighbor-route** interface configuration command. To disable the default behavior of creating a neighbor route for the peer on a point-to-point interface, use the **no** form of this command.

**peer neighbor-route**
**no peer neighbor-route**

### *Syntax Description*

This command has no keywords and arguments.

### *Default*

Creation of a route to the peer address on any point-to-point interface when the PPP IPCP negotiation is completed

### *Command Mode*

Interface configuration

### *Usage Guidelines*

This command first appeared in Cisco IOS Release 11.2.

Use the **no** form of this command only if the default behavior creates problems in your network environment.

If you enter this command on a dialer interface or an async-group interface, it affects all member interfaces.

### *Example*

The following example re-enables the default behavior on an interface.

```
peer neighbor-route
```

## PPP AUTHENTICATION

To specify the order in which the CHAP or PAP protocols are requested on the interface, use the **ppp authentication** interface configuration command. Use the **no** form of the command to disable this authentication.

**ppp authentication** {**chap** | **chap pap** | **pap chap** | **pap**} [**if-needed**] [*list-name* | **default**] [**callin**]
**no ppp authentication**

| *Syntax* | *Description* |
|---|---|
| **chap** | Enables CHAP on a serial interface. |
| **pap** | Enables PAP on a serial interface. |
| **chap pap** | Enables both CHAP and PAP, and performs CHAP authentication before PAP. |
| **pap chap** | Enables both CHAP and PAP, and performs PAP authentication before CHAP. |

| | |
|---|---|
| **if-needed** | (Optional) Used with TACACS and XTACACS. Do not perform CHAP or PAP authentication if the user has already provided authentication. This option is available only on asynchronous interfaces. |
| *list-name* | (Optional) Used with AAA/TACACS+. Specifies the name of a list of TACACS+ methods of authentication to use. If no list name is specified, the system uses the default. Lists are created with the **aaa authentication ppp** command. |
| **default** | (Optional) Used with AAA/TACACS+. Created with the **aaa authentication ppp** command. |
| **callin** | Specifies authentication on incoming (received) calls only. |

### *Default*

PPP authentication is not enabled.

### *Command Mode*

Interface configuration

### *Usage Guidelines*

This command first appeared in a release prior to Cisco IOS Release 11.1.

Once you have enabled CHAP or PAP authentication or both, the local router requires the remote device to prove its identity before allowing data traffic to flow.

- PAP authentication requires the remote device to send a name and password to be checked against a matching entry in the local username database or in the remote TACACS/TACACS+ database.
- CHAP authentication sends a challenge to the remote device. The remote device must encrypt the challenge value with a shared secret and return the encrypted value and its name to the local router in a response message. The local router uses the remote device's name to look up the appropriate secret in the local username or remote TACACS/TACACS+ database. It uses the looked-up secret to encrypt the original challenge and verify that the encrypted values match.

You may enable PAP or CHAP or both, in either order. If both methods are enabled, then the first method specified will be requested during link negotiation. If the peer suggests using the second method or simply refuses the first method, then the second method will be tried. Some remote devices support CHAP only and some PAP only. The order in which you specify the methods will be based on your concerns about the remote device's ability to correctly negotiate the appropriate method as well as your concern about data line security. PAP usernames and passwords are sent as "clear-text" strings and can be intercepted and reused. CHAP has eliminated most of the known security holes.

Enabling or disabling PPP authentication does not affect the local router's willingness to authenticate itself to the remote device.

**CAUTION**

If you use a *list-name* that has not been configured with the **aaa authentication ppp** command, you disable PPP on this line.

### *Example*

The following example enables CHAP on asynchronous interface 4, and uses the authentication list *MIS-access*:

```
interface async 4
 encapsulation ppp
 ppp authentication chap MIS-access
```

### *Related Commands*

Search online to find documentation for related commands.

**aaa authentication ppp**
**aaa new-model**
**autoselect**
**dialer map**
**encapsulation ppp**
**ppp use-tacacs**
**username password**

## PPP BRIDGE APPLETALK

To enable half-bridging of AppleTalk packets across a serial interface, use the **ppp bridge appletalk** interface configuration command.

**ppp bridge appletalk**

### *Syntax Description*

This command has no arguments or keywords.

### *Default*

Disabled

### *Command Mode*

Interface configuration

### *Usage Guidelines*

This command first appeared in Cisco IOS Release 11.2.

When you configure a serial or ISDN interface for half-bridging, you configure it to function as a node on an Ethernet subnetwork. It communicates with a bridge on the subnetwork by sending and receiving bridge packets. The serial or ISDN interface converts bridge packets to routed packets and forwards them, as needed.

The serial interface must be configured with an AppleTalk address for communication on the Ethernet subnetwork, and the AppleTalk address must have the same AppleTalk cable range as the bridge.

You cannot configure a serial interface for both half-bridging and for transparent bridging.

No more than one half-bridge should be on any subnetwork.

### *Example*

The following example configures serial interface 0 for half-bridging of AppleTalk. The remote bridge and other Ethernet nodes must be on the same network.

```
interface serial 0
 ppp bridge appletalk
 appletalk cable-range 301-301
 appletalk zone remote-lan
```

### *Related Commands*

Search online to find documentation for related commands.

**appletalk cable-range**
**appletalk zone**
**ppp bridge ip**
**ppp bridge ipx**

## PPP BRIDGE IP

To enable half-bridging of IP packets across a serial interface, use the **ppp bridge ip** interface configuration command.

**ppp bridge ip**

### *Syntax Description*

This command has no arguments or keywords.

### *Default*

Disabled

### *Command Mode*

Interface configuration

### *Usage Guidelines*

This command first appeared in Cisco IOS Release 11.2.

When you configure a serial or ISDN interface for half-bridging, you configure it to function as a node on an Ethernet subnetwork. It communicates with a bridge on the subnetwork by sending and receiving bridge packets. The serial interface converts bridge packets to routed packets and forwards them, as needed.

The interface must be configured with an IP address for communication on the Ethernet subnetwork, and the IP address must be on the same subnetwork as the bridge.

You cannot configure a serial interface for both half-bridging and for transparent bridging.

No more than one half-bridge should be on any subnetwork.



### *Example*

The following example configures serial interface 0 for half-bridging of IP. The remote bridge and other Ethernet nodes must be on the same subnetwork.

```
interface serial 0
 ip address 172.69.5.8
 ppp bridge ip
```

### *Related Commands*

Search online to find documentation for related commands.

**ip address**
**ppp bridge appletalk**
**ppp bridge ipx**

## PPP BRIDGE IPX

To enable half-bridging of IPX packets across a serial interface, use the **ppp bridge ipx** interface configuration command.

**ppp bridge ipx [novell-ether | arpa | sap | snap]**

| *Syntax* | *Description* |
|---|---|
| **novell-ether** | Use Novell's Ethernet_802.3 encapsulation. This is the default. |
| **arpa** | Use Novell's Ethernet_II encapsulation. |
| **sap** | Use Novell's Ethernet_802.2 encapsulation. |
| **snap** | Use Novell Ethernet_Snap encapsulation. |

### *Default*

Default encapsulation is **novell-ether**.

### *Command Mode*

Interface configuration

### *Usage Guidelines*

This command first appeared in Cisco IOS Release 11.2.

When you configure a serial interface for half-bridging, you configure it to function as a node on an Ethernet subnetwork. It communicates with a bridge on the subnetwork by sending and receiving bridge packets. The serial interface converts bridge packets to routed packets and forwards them as needed.

The serial interface must be configured with an IPX address for communication on the Ethernet subnetwork, and the IPX address must be on the same subnetwork as the bridge.

You cannot configure a serial interface for both half-bridging and for transparent bridging.

No more than one half-bridge should be on any subnetwork.

### *Example*

The following example configures serial interface 0 for half-bridging of IPX. The remote bridge and other Ethernet nodes must be on the same subnetwork.

```
interface serial 0
 ppp bridge ipx
 ipx network 1800
```

### *Related Commands*

Search online to find documentation for related commands.

**ipx network**
**ppp bridge appletalk**
**ppp bridge ip**

## PPP CHAP HOSTNAME

Use the **ppp chap hostname** interface configuration command to create a pool of dial-up routers that all appear to be the same host when authenticating with CHAP. To disable this function, use the **no** form of the command.

**ppp chap hostname** *hostname*
**no ppp chap hostname** *hostname*

| *Syntax* | *Description* |
|---|---|
| *hostname* | Name to be sent in the CHAP challenge. |

### *Default*

Disabled. The router name is sent in any CHAP challenges.

### Command Mode

Interface configuration

### Usage Guidelines

This command first appeared in Cisco IOS Release 11.2.

Currently, a router dialing a pool of access routers requires a username entry for each possible router in the pool because each router challenges with its host name. If a router is added to the dial-up rotary pool, all connecting routers must be updated. The **ppp chap hostname** command allows you to specify a common alias for all routers in a rotary to use so that only one username must be configured on the dialing routers.

This command is normally used with local CHAP authentication (when authenticating to the peer), but it will also be used for remote CHAP authentication.

### Example

The commands in the following example identify the dialer interface 0 as the dialer rotary group leader and specifies ppp as the method of encapsulation used by all member interfaces. Authentication is by CHAP on received calls only. The username *ISPCorp* will be sent in all CHAP challenges and responses.

```
interface dialer 0
 encapsulation ppp
 ppp authentication chap callin
 ppp chap hostnmae ISPCorp
```

### Related Commands

Search online to find documentation for related commands.

**aaa authentication ppp**
**ppp authentication**
**ppp chap password**
**ppp pap**

## PPP CHAP PASSWORD

To configure a common CHAP secret to be used in responses to challenges from an unknown remote peer in a collection of routers that do not support this command (such as routers running older Cisco IOS software images), use the **ppp chap password** interface configuration command. To disable this function, use the **no** form of this command.

**ppp chap password** *secret*
**no ppp chap password** *secret*

| *Syntax* | *Description* |
|---|---|
| *secret* | Secret used to compute the response value for any CHAP challenge from an unknown peer. |

Part III Command Reference

### *Default*

Disabled

### *Command Mode*

Interface configuration

### *Usage Guidelines*

This command first appeared in Cisco IOS Release 11.2.

This command allows you to replace several username and password configuration commands with a single copy of this command on any dialer interface or asynchronous group interface.

This command is used for remote CHAP authentication only (when authenticating to the peer) and does not affect local CHAP authentication.

### *Example*

The following example configures interface BRI 0 for PPP encapsulation. If a CHAP challenge is received from a peer whose name is not found in the global list of usernames, the encrypted secret 7 1234567891 is decrypted and used to create a CHAP response value.

```
interface bri0
 encapsulation ppp
 ppp chap password 7 1234567891
```

### *Related Commands*

Search online to find documentation for related commands.

**aaa authentication ppp**
**ppp authentication**
**ppp chap hostname**
**ppp pap**

## PPP MAX-BAD-AUTH

To configure a point-to-point interface not to reset itself immediately after an authentication failure but instead to allow a specified number of authentication retries, use the **ppp max-bad-auth** interface configuration command. To reset to the default of immediate reset, use the **no** form of this command.

**ppp max-bad-auth** *number*
**no ppp max-bad-auth**

| *Syntax* | *Description* |
|---|---|
| *number* | Number of retries after which the interface is to reset itself. Default is 0. |

### Default

0

### Command Mode

Interface configuration

### Usage Guidelines

This command applies to any serial interface (asynchronous serial, synchronous serial, or ISDN) on which PPP encapsulation is enabled.

### Example

This command first appeared in Cisco IOS Release 11.2.

The following example sets BRI interface 0 to allow two additional retries after an initial authentication failure (for a total of three failed authentication attempts):

```
interface bri 0
 encapsulation ppp
 ppp authentication chap
 ppp max-bad-auth 3
```

### Related Commands

Search online to find documentation for related commands.

**encapsulation ppp**



## PPP MULTILINK

To enable Multilink PPP on an interface, use the **ppp multilink** interface configuration command. To disable Multilink PPP, use the **no** form of this command.

**ppp multilink**
**no ppp multilink**

### Syntax Description

This command has no arguments or keywords.

### Default

Disabled

### Command Mode

Interface configuration

### *Usage Guidelines*

This command first appeared in Cisco IOS Release 11.1.

Multilink PPP is designed to work over single or multiple interfaces that are configured to support both dial-on-demand rotary groups and PPP encapsulation. This command applies asynchronous serial interfaces, ISDN Basic Rate Interfaces (BRIs), and ISDN Primary Rate Interfaces (PRIs).

PPP compression is allowed with MLP.

Multilink PPP and PPP reliable link do not work together.

The **dialer load-threshold** command is used to enable a rotary group to bring up additional links and to add them to a multilink bundle.

When multilink PPP is configured, **dialer-load threshold 1** command no longer keeps a multilink bundle of *n* links connected indefinitely, and the **dialer-load threshold 2** command no longer keeps a multilink bundle of 2 links connected indefinitely. If you want a multilink bundle to be connected indefinitely, you must set a very high idle timer.

### *Example*

The following partial example configures a dialer for Multilink PPP; it does not show the configuration of the physical interfaces.

```
interface Dialer0
 ip address 99.0.0.2 255.0.0.0
 encapsulation ppp
 dialer in-band
 dialer idle-timeout 500
 dialer map ip 99.0.0.1 name atlanta broadcast 81012345678901
 dialer load-threshold 30 either
 dialer-group 1
 ppp authentication chap
 ppp multilink
```

### *Related Commands*

Search online to find documentation for related commands.

**dialer-group**
**dialer idle-timeout**
**dialer load-threshold**
**encapsulation ppp**
**ppp authentication**
**compress**

## PPP MULTILINK FRAGMENT-DELAY

To configure a maximum delay allowed for transmission of a packet fragment on a Multilink PPP bundle, use the **ppp multilink fragment-delay** interface configuration command. To reset the maximum delay to the default value, use the **no** form of the command.

**ppp multilink fragment-delay** *milliseconds*
**no ppp multilink fragment-delay**

| *Syntax* | *Description* |
|---|---|
| *milliseconds* | Maximum delay, in milliseconds, allowed for any packet fragment. Default is 30 milliseconds. |

### *Default*

This command is disabled by default.

Default delay is 30 milliseconds.

### *Command Mode*

Interface configuration

### *Usage Guidelines*

This command first appeared in Cisco IOS Release 11.3.

The **ppp multilink fragment-delay** command applies only to interfaces that can configure a bundle interface. These include virtual templates, dialer interfaces, and ISDN BRI or PRI interfaces.

Multilink PPP chooses a fragment size based on the maximum delay allowed. If real-time traffic requires a certain maximum bound on delay, using this command to set that maximum delay can ensure that a real-time packet will get interleaved within the fragments of a large packet.

### *Example*

In the following example, a voice stream is required to have a maximum bound on delay of 20 milliseconds:

```
ppp multilink fragment-delay 20
```

### *Related Commands*

Search online to find documentation for related commands.

**ip rtp reserve**
**ppp multilink**
**ppp multilink interleave**

## PPP MULTILINK INTERLEAVE

To enable interleaving of Real-Time Transport Protocol (RTP) packets among the fragments of larger packets on a Multilink PPP bundle, use the **ppp multilink interleave** interface configuration command. To disable interleaving, use the **no** form of the command.

**ppp multilink interleave**
**no ppp multilink interleave**

### Syntax Description

This command has no arguments and keywords.

### Default

This function is disabled by default.

### Command Mode

Interface configuration

### Usage Guidelines

This command first appeared in Release 11.3.

The **ppp multilink interleave** command applies only to interfaces that can configure a bundle interface. These include virtual templates, dialer interfaces, and ISDN BRI or PRI interfaces.

### Example

The following example defines a virtual interface template that enables Multilink PPP interleaving and a maximum real-time traffic delay of 20 milliseconds, and then applies that virtual template to the Multilink PPP bundle:

```
interface virtual-template 1
 ip unnumbered ethernet 0
 ppp multilink
 ppp multilink interleave
 ppp multilink fragment-delay 20

multilink virtual-template 1
```

### Related Commands

Search online to find documentation for related commands.

**ip rtp reserve**
**ppp multilink**
**ppp multilink fragment-delay**

## PPP PAP SENT-USERNAME

To enable remote PAP support for an interface and use the **sent-username** and **password** elements in the PAP authentication request packet to the peer, use the **ppp pap sent-username** interface configuration command. Use the **no** form of this command to disable remote PAP support.

**ppp pap sent-username** *username* **password** *password*
**no ppp pap sent-username**

| *Syntax* | *Description* |
| --- | --- |
| *username* | Username sent in the PAP authentication request. |
| **password** | Password sent in the PAP authentication request. |
| *password* | Must contain from 1 to 25 uppercase and lowercase alphanumeric characters; cannot contain spaces or underscores. |

### *Default*

Remote PAP support disabled

### *Command Mode*

Interface configuration

### *Usage Guidelines*

This command first appeared in Cisco IOS Release 11.2.

Use this command to enable remote PAP support (for example, to respond to the peer's request to authenticate with PAP) and to specify the parameters to be used when sending the PAP Authentication Request.

### *Example*

The following example configures dialer interface 0 as the dialer rotary group leader and enables PPP encapsulation on the interface. Authentication is by CHAP or PAP on received calls only. *ISP-Corp* is the username sent to the peer if the peer requires the router to authenticate with PAP.

```
interface dialer0
 encapsulation ppp
 ppp authentication chap pap callin
 ppp chap hostname ISPCorp
 ppp pap sent username ISPCorp password 7 fjhfeu
 ppp pap sent-username ISPCorp password 7 1123659238
```

### *Related Commands*

Search online to find documentation for related commands.

**aaa authentication ppp**
**ppp authentication**
**ppp chap hostname**
**ppp chap password**
**ppp use-tacacs**

## PPP QUALITY

To enable Link Quality Monitoring (LQM) on a serial interface, use the **ppp quality** interface configuration command. Use the **no** form of this command to disable LQM.

**ppp quality** *percentage*
**no ppp quality**

| *Syntax* | *Description* |
|---|---|
| *percentage* | Specifies the link quality threshold. Range is 1 to 100. |

### *Default*

Disabled

### *Command Mode*

Interface configuration

### *Usage Guidelines*

This command first appeared in a release prior to Cisco IOS Release 10.0.

The percentages are calculated for both incoming and outgoing directions. The outgoing quality is calculated by comparing the total number of packets and bytes sent to the total number of packets and bytes received by the destination node. The incoming quality is calculated by comparing the total number of packets and bytes received to the total number of packets and bytes sent by the destination node.

If the link quality percentage is not maintained, the link is deemed to be of poor quality and is taken down. LQM implements a time lag so that the link does not bounce up and down.

### *Example*

The following example enables LQM on serial interface 2:

```
interface serial 2
 encapsulation ppp
 ppp quality 80
```

### *Related Commands*

Search online to find documentation for related commands.

**encapsulation ppp**
**keepalive**

## PPP RELIABLE-LINK

To enable LAPB Numbered Mode negotiation for a reliable serial link, use the **ppp reliable-link** interface configuration command. To disable negotiation for a PPP reliable link on a specified interface, use the **no** form of the command.

**ppp reliable-link**
**no ppp reliable-link**

### *Syntax Description*

This command has no arguments and keywords.

### *Default*

Disabled

### *Command Mode*

Interface configuration

### *Usage Guidelines*

This command first appeared in Cisco IOS Release 11.0.

Enabling LAPB Numbered Mode negotiation as a means of providing a reliable link does not guarantee that all connections through the specified interface will in fact use reliable link. It only guarantees that the router will attempt to negotiate reliable link on this interface.

PPP reliable link can be used with PPP compression over the link, but it does not require PPP compression.

PPP reliable link does not work with Multilink PPP.

You can use the **show interface** command to determine whether LAPB has been established on the link. You can troubleshoot PPP reliable link by using the **debug lapb** command and the **debug ppp negotiations**, **debug ppp errors**, and **debug ppp packets** commands.

### *Example*

The following example enables PPP reliable link and predictor compression on interface BRI 0:

```
interface bri 0
 description Enables predictor compression on BRI 0
 ip address 170.1.1.1 255.255.255.0
 encapsulation ppp
 dialer map ip 170.1.1.2 name starbuck 14195291357
 compress predictor
 ppp authentication chap
 dialer-group 1
 ppp reliable-link
```

### *Related Commands*

Search online to find documentation for related commands.

**debug lapb**
**debug ppp**
**compress**
**show interface**

## SHOW DHCP

To display the current DHCP settings on point-to-point interfaces, use the **show dhcp** privileged EXEC command.

**show dhcp** {**server** | **lease** [**interface async** [*number*]]}

| *Syntax* | *Description* |
|---|---|
| **server** | Show known DHCP servers. |
| **lease** | Show DHCP addresses leased from a server. |
| **interface async** [*number*] | (Optional) Specify asynchronous interfaces and, optionally, a specific interface number. |

### *Command Mode*

Privileged EXEC

### *Usage Guidelines*

If you omit the optional argument, the **show dhcp** command displays information about all interfaces.

You can use this command on any point-to-point type of interface (for example, serial, ISDN, or asynchronous) that uses DHCP for temporary IP address allocation.

### *Sample Display*

```
Router# show dhcp server

IP address pooling for Point to Point clients is: DHCP Proxy Client
DHCP Proxy Client Status:
   DHCP server: ANY (255.255.255.255)
    Leases:   0
    Offers:   0      Requests: 0     Acks: 0     Naks: 0
    Declines: 0      Releases: 0     Bad:  0
```

Table 26–1 describes the fields shown in the display.

**Table 26–1** *Show DHCP Field Descriptions*

| Field | Description |
|---|---|
| Leases | Number of current leased IP addresses. |
| Offers | Number of offers for an IP address sent to a proxy-client from the server. |
| Requests | Number of requests for an IP address to the server. |
| Acks | Number of 'acknowledge' messages sent by the server to the proxy-client. |
| Naks | Number of 'not acknowledge' messages sent by the server to the proxy-client. |

**Table 26–1** *Show DHCP Field Descriptions, Continued*

| Field | Description |
|---|---|
| Declines | Number of offers from the server that are declined by the proxy-client. |
| Releases | Number of times IP addresses have been relinquished gracefully by the client. |
| Bad | Number of bad packets received from wrong length, wrong field type, and so on. |

### *Related Commands*

Search online to find documentation for related commands.

**ip address-pool**
**ip dhcp-server**
**peer default ip address**



## SHOW IP LOCAL POOL

To display statistics for any defined IP address pools, use the **show ip local pool** command.

**show ip local pool** [*name*]

| *Syntax* | *Description* |
|---|---|
| *name* | (Optional) Name of a specific IP address pool. |

### *Command Mode*

Privileged EXEC

### *Usage Guidelines*

If you omit the variable *name*, the software will display a generic list of all defined address pools and the IP addresses that belong to them. If you specify a name, the software displays more detailed information for that pool.

### *Sample Display*

```
Router# show ip local pool

Scope     Begin            End              Free InUse
 Dialin    172.30.228.11    172.30.228.26    16   0
Available addresses:
   172.30.228.12
   172.30.228.13
   172.30.228.14
   172.30.228.15
   172.30.228.16
   172.30.228.17
   172.30.228.18
   172.30.228.19
```

```
         172.30.228.20
         172.30.228.21
         172.30.228.22
         172.30.228.23
         172.30.228.24
         172.30.228.25
         172.30.228.26
         172.30.228.11          Async5

      Inuse addresses:
           None
```

Table 26–2 describes the fields shown in the display.

**Table 26–2** *Show IP Local Pool Field Descriptions*

| Field | Description |
|---|---|
| Scope | The type of access. |
| Begin | The first IP address in the defined range of addresses in this pool. |
| End | The last IP address in the defined range of addresses in this pool. |
| Free | The number of addresses currently available. |
| InUse | The number of addresses currently in use. |

### *Related Commands*

Search online to find documentation for related commands.

**ip address-pool**
**ip local pool**

## SHOW PPP MULTILINK

To display bundle information for the Multilink PPP bundles, use the **show ppp multilink** EXEC command.

**show ppp multilink**

### *Syntax Description*

This command has no arguments or keywords.

### *Command Mode*

EXEC

### *Usage Guidelines*

This command first appeared in Cisco IOS Release 11.2.

### *Sample Displays*

The following is the output when no bundles are on a system.

```
impulse# show ppp multilink

No active bundles
```

The following is sample output when a single Multilink PPP bundle (named rudder) is on a system:

```
systema# show ppp multilink

Bundle rudder, 3 members, first link is BRI0: B-channel 1
0 lost fragments, 8 reordered, 0 unassigned, sequence 0x1E/0x1E rcvd/sent
```

The following is sample output when two active bundles are on a system. Subsequent bundles would be displayed below the previous bundle.

```
impulse# show ppp multilink

Bundle rudder, 3 members, first link is BRI0: B-Channel 1
  0 lost fragments, 8 reordered, 0 unassigned, sequence 0x1E/0x1E rcvd/sent
Bundle dallas, 4 members, first link is BRI2: B-Channel 1
  0 lost fragments, 28 reordered, 0 unassigned, sequence 0x12E/0x12E rcvd/sent
```

The following example shows output when a stack group has been created. On stack group member *systema* on stackgroup *stackq*, Multilink PPP bundle *hansolo* has bundle interface *Virtual-Access4*. Two child interfaces are joined to this bundle interface. The first is a local PRI channel (serial 0:4), and the second is an interface from stack group member *systemb*.

```
systema# show ppp multilink

Bundle hansolo 2 members, Master link is Virtual-Access4
0 lost fragments, 0 reordered, 0 unassigned, 100/255 load
0 discarded,  0 lost received, sequence 40/66 rcvd/sent
members 2
 Serial0:4
 systemb:Virtual-Access6    (1.1.1.1)
```

## SHOW QUEUING VIRTUAL-ACCESS

To display information about interleaving, use the **show queuing virtual-access** EXEC command.

**show queuing virtual-access** *number*

| *Syntax* | *Description* |
|---|---|
| *number* | Virtual access interface number. |

### *Command Mode*

EXEC

### *Usage Guidelines*

This command was first added in Cisco Release 11.3.

### *Sample Display*

The following is sample output of the **show queuing virtual-access** command:

```
Router# show queuing virtual-access 1

    Input queue: 0/75/0 (size/max/drops); Total output drops: 164974
    Queueing strategy: weighted fair
    Output queue: 315/64/164974/31191 (size/threshold/drops/interleaves)
       Conversations  5/8 (active/max active)
       Reserved Conversations 2/2 (allocated/max allocated)

    (depth/weight/discards/interleaves) 64/4096/38669/0
    Conversation 36, linktype: ip, length: 52
    source: 140.3.3.201, destination: 225.1.2.3, id: 0x0001, ttl: 254,
    TOS: 0 prot: 17, source port 6789, destination port 2345

    (depth/weight/discards/interleaves) 64/4096/0/0
    Conversation 2, linktype: ip, length: 52
    source: 140.3.3.201, destination: 225.1.2.4, id: 0x0001, ttl: 254,
    TOS: 0 prot: 17, source port 5432, destination port 9870
```

Table 26–3 describes significant fields in the **show queuing virtual-access** command output.

**Table 26–3** *Show Queuing Virtual-Access Command Output*

| **Field** | **Description** |
|---|---|
| Input queue: size, max, drops | Input queue used for virtual access interface 1, with the current size, the maximum size, and the number of dropped packets. |
| Total output drops | Number of output packets dropped. |
| Output queue: size/threshold/drops/interleaves | Output queue counters. Maximum number of packets allowed in the queue, number in the queue, the number of packets dropped due to a full queue, and the number of real-time packets interleaved among fragments of larger packets. |
| Conversations (active/max active) | Fair queue conversation statistics: number of conversations currently active and the maximum that have been active. |
| Reserved conversations (allocated, max allocated) | Reserved conversations in the weighted fair queue. (current/maxumim number allocated). Reserved conversations get the highest priority. |
| (depth/weight/discards/interleaves) 64/4096/38669/0 | Depth of the queue, weight assigned to each packet in the queue, number of packets discarded in the queue so far, and the number of interleaves. |

**Table 26–3** *Show Queuing Virtual-Access Command Output, Continued*

| Field | Description |
|---|---|
| Conversation 36, linktype: ip, length: 52 | Conversation identifier, protocol used on the link (IP), and the number of bytes. |
| source: 140.3.3.201, destination: 225.1.2.3, | Source IP address and destination IP address. |
| id: 0x0001 | Protocol ID, identifying IP. |
| ttl: 254 | Time to live, in seconds. |
| TOS: 0 | Type of service. |
| prot: 17 | Protocol field in IP. The value 17 indicates UDP. |
| source port 5432 | Source TCP/UDP port. |
| destination port 9870 | Destination TCP/UDP port. |



## USERNAME

To specify the password to be used in the PPP Challenge Handshake Authentication Protocol (CHAP) caller identification and Password Authentication Protocol (PAP), use the **username** global configuration command.

**username** *name* **password** *secret*

| *Syntax* | *Description* |
|---|---|
| *name* | Host name, server name, user ID, or command name. |
| **password** | An encrypted password for this username. |
| *secret* | For CHAP authentication: specifies the secret password for the local router or access server or the remote device. The secret is encrypted when it is stored on the local router or access server, preventing the secret from being stolen. The secret password can consist of any string of up to 11 printable ASCII characters, but cannot include spaces or underscores. There is no limit to the number of username-password combinations that can be specified, allowing any number of remote devices to be authenticated. |

### *Default*

No password is predefined.

### *Command Mode*

Global configuration

### *Usage Guidelines*

This command first appeared in a release prior to Cisco IOS Release 11.1.

Add a *name* entry for each remote system that the local router or access server requires authentication from.

The **username** command is required as part of the configuration for authentication protocols, such as CHAP and PAP. For each remote system that the local router or access server communicates with from which it requires authentication, you add a **username** entry.

**NOTES**

To enable the local router or access server to respond to remote CHAP challenges, one **username** *name* entry must be the same as the **hostname** *name* entry that has already been assigned to your device.

If no secret is specified and **debug serial-interface** is enabled, an error is displayed when a link is established, and the authentication protocol challenge is not implemented. Debugging information about authentication protocols is available via the **debug serial-interface** and **debug serial-packet** commands.

### *Examples*

The following example configuration enables CHAP on serial interface 0. It also defines a password for local server *Adam* and remote server *Eve*.

```
hostname Adam
interface serial 0
 encapsulation ppp
 ppp authentication chap
username Eve password theirsystem
```

When you look at your configuration file, the passwords will be encrypted and the display will look similar to the following:

```
hostname Adam
interface serial 0
 encapsulation ppp
 ppp authentication chap
username Eve password 7 121F0A18
```

### *Related Commands*

Search online to find documentation for related commands.

**hostname**

# CHAPTER 27

# Configuring Asynchronous PPP and SLIP

This chapter describes the configuration of PPP or SLIP encapsulation over asynchronous lines for connection-oriented protocols such as IP, IPX, and AppleTalk. For a complete description of the PPP and SLIP commands in this chapter, see Chapter 28, "Asynchronous PPP and SLIP Commands."

## CISCO'S IMPLEMENTATION OF PPP AND SLIP

Serial Line Internet Protocol (SLIP) and Point-to-Point Protocol (PPP) define methods of sending Internet Protocol (IP) packets over standard asynchronous serial lines with minimum line speeds of 1200 baud.

Using SLIP or PPP encapsulation over asynchronous lines is an inexpensive way to connect PCs to a network. PPP and SLIP over asynchronous dial-up modems allow a home computer to be connected to a network without the cost of a leased line. Dial-up PPP and SLIP links can also be used for remote sites that need only occasional remote-node or backup connectivity. Both public-domain and vendor-supported PPP and SLIP implementations are available for a variety of computer applications.

The Cisco IOS software concentrates a large number of SLIP or PPP PC or workstation client hosts onto a network interface that allows the PCs to communicate with any host on the network. The Cisco IOS software can support any combination of SLIP or PPP lines and lines dedicated to normal asynchronous devices, such as terminals and modems. Refer to RFC 1055 for more information about SLIP, and RFCs 1331 and 1332 for more information about PPP.

SLIP is an older protocol. PPP is a newer, more robust protocol than SLIP, and it contains functions that can detect or prevent misconfiguration. PPP also provides greater built-in security mechanisms.

**NOTES**

Most asynchronous serial links have very low bandwidth. Take care to configure your system so the links will not be overloaded. Consider using default routes and filtering routing updates to prevent them from being sent on these asynchronous lines.

Figure 27–1 illustrates a typical asynchronous SLIP or PPP remote-node configuration.

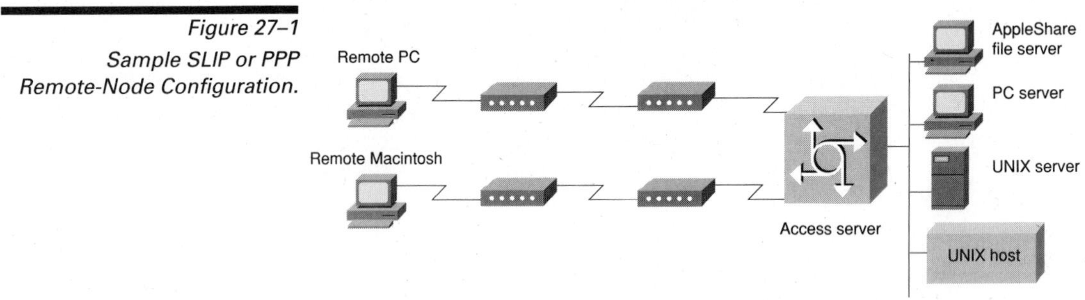


*Figure 27–1 Sample SLIP or PPP Remote-Node Configuration.*

## Responding to BOOTP Requests

The BOOTP protocol allows a client machine to discover its own IP address, the address of the router, and the name of a file to be loaded into memory and executed. There are typically two phases to using BOOTP: first, the client's address is determined and the boot file is selected; then the file is transferred, typically using TFTP.

PPP and SLIP clients can send BOOTP requests to the Cisco IOS software, and the Cisco IOS software responds with information about the network. For example, the client can send a BOOTP request to find out what its IP address is and where the boot file is located, and the Cisco IOS software responds with the information.

BOOTP supports the extended BOOTP requests specified in RFC 1084 and works for both PPP and SLIP encapsulation.

BOOTP compares to Reverse Address Resolution Protocol (RARP) as follows: RARP is an older protocol that allows a client to determine its IP address if it knows its hardware address. However, RARP is a hardware link protocol, so it can be implemented only on hosts that have special kernel or driver modifications that allow access to these raw packets. BOOTP does not require kernel modifications.

## Asynchronous Network Connections and Routing

Line configuration commands configure a connection to a terminal or a modem. Interface configuration (**async**) commands, described in this chapter, configure a line as an asynchronous network interface over which networking functions are performed.

The Cisco IOS software also supports IP routing connections for communication that requires connecting one network to another.

The Cisco IOS software supports protocol translation for PPP and SLIP between other network devices running Telnet, LAT, or X.25. For example, you can send IP packets across a public X.25 PAD network using SLIP or PPP encapsulation when SLIP or PPP protocol translation is enabled. For more information, see Chapter 21, "Configuring Protocol Translation and Virtual Asynchronous Devices."

If asynchronous dynamic routing is enabled, you can enable routing at the user level by using the **routing** keyword with the **slip** or **ppp** EXEC command.

Asynchronous interfaces offer both dedicated and dynamic address assignment, configurable hold queues and IP packet sizes, extended BOOTP requests, and permit and deny conditions for controlling access to lines. Figure 27–2 shows a sample asynchronous routing configuration.

*Figure 27–2*
*Sample Asynchronous Routing Configuration.*

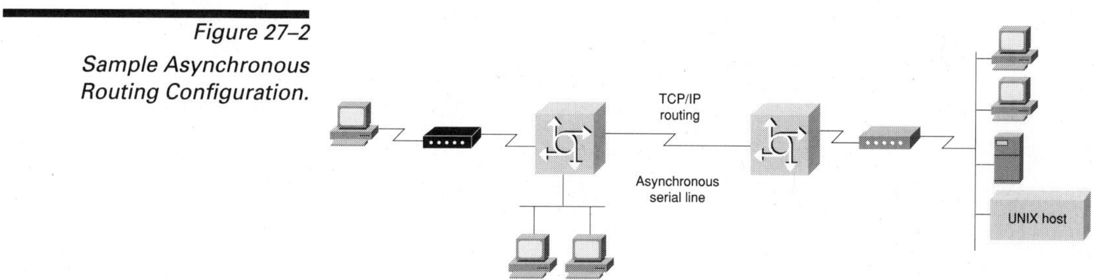


## Asynchronous Interfaces and Broadcasts

The Cisco IOS software recognize a variety of IP broadcast addresses. When a router receives an IP packet from an asynchronous client, it rebroadcasts the packet onto the network without changing the IP header.

The Cisco IOS software receives the SLIP or PPP client broadcasts and responds to BOOTP requests with the current IP address assigned to the asynchronous interface from which the request was received. This facility allows the asynchronous client software to automatically learn its own IP address.

## Asynchronous PPP and SLIP Task List

The following tasks are covered in the upcoming sections:

- Configuring Network-Layer Protocols over PPP and SLIP
- Configuring Asynchronous Host Mobility
- Making Additional Remote-Node Connections
- Configuring Remote Access to NetBEUI Services
- Configuring Performance Parameters

## CONFIGURING NETWORK-LAYER PROTOCOLS OVER PPP AND SLIP

You can configure network-layer protocols, such as AppleTalk, IP, and IPX, over PPP and SLIP. SLIP supports only IP, but PPP supports each of these protocols. Refer to the sections that follow to configure these protocols over PPP and SLIP.

### Configure IP–PPP

To enable IP–PPP (IPCP) on a synchronous or asynchronous interface, perform the following tasks, beginning in interface configuration mode:

| Task | | Command |
|---|---|---|
| **Step 1** | Configure IP routing on the interface.<br>or<br>Configure IP unnumbered routing on a serial interface. | **ip address** *ip-address mask*<br>or<br>**ip unnumbered** *type number* |
| **Step 2** | Enable PPP encapsulation on the serial interface. | **encapsulation ppp** |
| **Step 3** | Enable interactive mode on an asynchronous interface. | **async mode interactive** |

### Configure IPX–PPP

You can configure IPX to run over PPP (IPXCP) on synchronous serial and asynchronous serial interfaces using one of two methods.

The first method associates an asynchronous interface with a loopback interface configured to run IPX. It permits you to configure IPX–PPP on asynchronous interfaces only.

The second method permits you to configure IPX–PPP on asynchronous and synchronous serial interfaces. However, it requires that you specify a dedicated IPX network number for each interface, which can require a substantial number of network numbers for a large number of interfaces.

You can also configure IPX to run on vtys configured for PPP. See the section "Enable IPX–PPP over X.25 to an IPX Network on vty Lines," later in this chapter.

#### *IPX-PPP—Associating Asynchronous Interfaces with Loopback Interfaces*

To permit IPX client connections to an asynchronous interface, the interface must be associated with a loopback interface configured to run IPX. To permit such connections, perform the following tasks, beginning in global configuration mode:

| Task | | Command |
|---|---|---|
| **Step 1** | Enable IPX routing. | **ipx routing** [*node*] |
| **Step 2** | Create a loopback interface, which is a virtual interface, existing only inside the router. | **interface loopback** *number* |

| Task | | Command |
|---|---|---|
| **Step 3** | Enable IPX routing on the loopback interface. | **ipx network** *network*[*] |
| **Step 4** | Exit to global configuration mode. | **exit** |
| **Step 5** | Enter interface configuration mode for the asynchronous interface. | **interface async** *number* |
| **Step 6** | Configure IP unnumbered routing on the interface. | **ip unnumbered** *type number* |
| **Step 7** | Enable PPP encapsulation on the interface. | **encapsulation ppp** |
| **Step 8** | Enable interactive mode on an asynchronous interface. | **async mode interactive** |
| **Step 9** | Assign the asynchronous interface to the loopback interface configured for IPX. | **ipx ppp-client Loopback** *number* |
| **Step 10** | Turn off SAP updates to optimize bandwidth on asynchronous interfaces. | **ipx sap-interval 0** |

[*] Every interface must have a unique IPX network number.

If you are configuring IPX–PPP on asynchronous interfaces, you should filter routing updates on the interface. Most asynchronous serial links have very low bandwidth, and routing updates take up a great deal of bandwidth. Step 10 in the previous task table uses the **ipx sap-interval 0** to filter SAP updates.

### *IPX–PPP—Using Dedicated IPX Network Numbers for Each Interface*

To enable IPX–PPP, perform the following tasks starting in global configuration mode. The first five tasks are required. The last task is optional:

| Task | | Command |
|---|---|---|
| **Step 1** | Enable IPX routing. | **ipx routing** [*node*] |
| **Step 2** | Create a loopback interface, which is a virtual interface, existing only inside the router. | **interface loopback** *number* |
| **Step 3** | Enable PPP encapsulation on the interface. | **encapsulation ppp** |
| **Step 4** | Enable interactive mode on an asynchronous interface. | **async mode interactive** |
| **Step 5** | Enable IPX routing on the interface. | **ipx network** *network*[*] |
| **Step 6** | Turn off SAP updates to optimize bandwidth on asynchronous interfaces. | **ipx sap-interval 0** |

[*] Every interface must have a unique ipx network number.

If you are configuring IPX–PPP on asynchronous interfaces, you should filter routing updates on the interface. Most asynchronous serial links have very low bandwidth, and routing updates take up a great deal of bandwidth.

### Enable IPX–PPP over X.25 to an IPX Network on vty Lines

You can enable IPX–PPP on virtual terminal lines (vtys), which permits clients to log in to a vty on a router, invoke a PPP session at the EXEC prompt to a host, and run IPX to the host.

For example, in Figure 27–3, the client terminal on the X.25 network logs in to the access server via a vty line, which is configured for IPX–PPP. When the user connects to the access server and the EXEC prompt appears, the user issues the PPP command to connect to the IPX host. The vty is configured to run IPX, so when the PPP session is established from the access server, the terminal can access the IPX host using an IPX application.

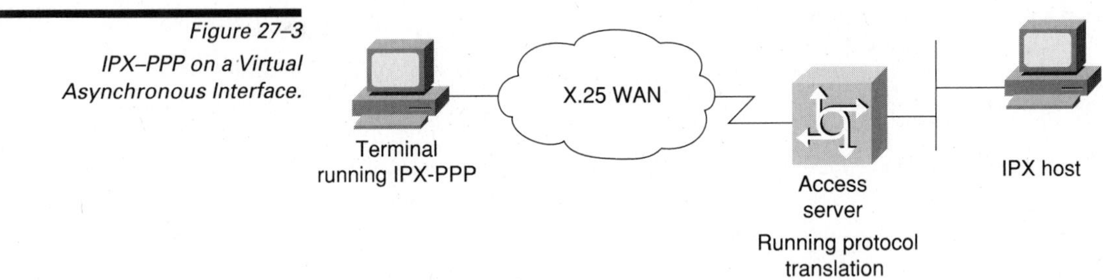


*Figure 27–3*
*IPX–PPP on a Virtual Asynchronous Interface.*

To enable IPX to run over your PPP sessions on vty lines, perform the following tasks, beginning in global configuration mode:

| Task | | Command |
|---|---|---|
| **Step 1** | Enable IPX routing. | **ipx routing** [*node*] |
| **Step 2** | Create a loopback interface. | **interface loopback** *number* |
| **Step 3** | Enable a virtual IPX network on the loopback interface. | **ipx network** *network*[*] |
| **Step 4** | Enable IPX–PPP on vty lines by assigning the vty to the loopback interface configured for IPX. | **vty-async ipx ppp-client loopback** *number* |

[*] Every loopback interface must have a unique IPX network number.

## Configure AppleTalk–PPP

You can configure an asynchronous interface so that users can access AppleTalk zones by dialing in to the router via PPP through this interface. Users accessing the network can run AppleTalk and IP natively on a remote Macintosh, access any available AppleTalk zones from Chooser, use networked peripherals, and share files with other Macintosh users. This feature is also referred to as ATCP.

You create a virtual network that exists only for accessing an AppleTalk internet through the server. To create a new AppleTalk zone, issue the **appletalk virtual-net** command and use a new zone name; this network number is then the only one associated with this zone. To add network numbers to an existing AppleTalk zone, use this existing zone name in the command; this network number is then added to the existing zone.

Routing is not supported on these interfaces.

To enable ATCP for PPP, perform the following tasks in interface configuration (asynchronous) mode:

| Task | | Command |
|---|---|---|
| **Step 1** | Define encapsulation as PPP on this interface. | **encapsulation ppp** |
| **Step 2** | Create an internal network on the server. | **appletalk virtual-net** *network-number zone-name* |
| **Step 3** | Enable client-mode on this interface. | **appletalk client-mode** |

### Configure IP–SLIP

To enable IP–SLIP on a synchronous or asynchronous interface, perform the following tasks, beginning in interface configuration mode:

| Task | | Command |
|---|---|---|
| **Step 1** | Configure IP routing on the interface.<br>or<br>Configure IP unnumbered routing on a serial interface. | **ip address** *ip-address mask*<br>or<br>**ip unnumbered** *type number* |
| **Step 2** | Enable SLIP encapsulation on the serial interface. | **encapsulation slip** |
| **Step 3** | Enable interactive mode on an asynchronous interface. | **async mode interactive** |

## Configuring Asynchronous Host Mobility

Increasingly, remote users are accessing networks through dial-up telephone connections. In contrast to local users who can connect directly into the network, remote users must first dial in to an access server.

The access server supports a packet tunneling strategy that extends the internetwork—in effect creating a virtual private link for the mobile user. When a user activates asynchronous host mobility, the access server on which the remote user dials in to becomes a remote point-of-presence (POP) for the user's home network. Once logged in, users experience a server environment identical to the one that they experience when they connect directly to the "home" access server.

Once the network layer connection is made, data packets are tunneled at the physical and/or data link layer instead of at the protocol layer. In this way, raw data bytes from dial-in users are transported directly to the "home" access server, which processes the protocols.

Figure 27–4 illustrates the implementation of asynchronous host mobility on an extended internetwork. A mobile user connects to an access server on the internetwork and, by activating asynchronous host mobility, is connected to a "home" access server configured with the appropriate username. The user sees an authentication dialog or prompt from the "home" system and can proceed as if he or she were connected directly to that device.

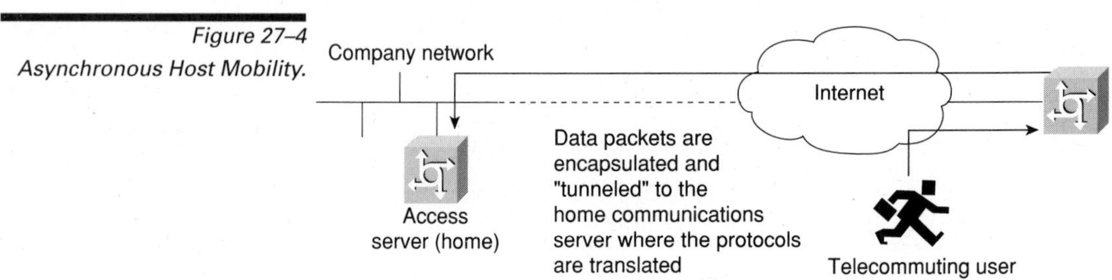


*Figure 27–4 Asynchronous Host Mobility.*

The remote user implements asynchronous host mobility by executing the **tunnel** command in the User EXEC mode. The **tunnel** command sets up a network layer connection to the specified destination. The access server accepts the connection, attaches it to a virtual terminal (vty), and runs a command parser capable of running the normal dial-in services. After the connection is established, data is transferred between the modem and network connection with a minimum of interpretations. When communications are complete, the network connection can be closed and terminated from either end.

## Making Additional Remote-Node Connections

This section describes how to connect devices across telephone lines by using the Point-to-Point Protocol (PPP) and Serial Line Internet Protocol (SLIP).

This section contains the following sections:

- PPP Connections
- SLIP Connections

### PPP Connections

When you connect from a remote-node computer, through an asynchronous port on an access server to the EXEC facility, and you want to connect from the access server to a device on the network, perform the following task in EXEC mode:

| Task | Command |
|---|---|
| Create a PPP connection. | **ppp /default** \| {{*remote-ip-address* \| *remote-name*} [**@***tacacs-server*] [**/routing**]} |

If you specify an address for the TACACS server using **/default** or *tacacs-server*, the address must be the first parameter in the command after you type **ppp**. If you do not specify an address or enter **/default**, you are prompted for an IP address or host name. You can enter **/default** at this point.

For example, in Figure 27–5, if you are working at home on the device *ntpc* and want to connect to Server 1 using PPP, you could dial in to the access server. When you connect to the EXEC prompt on the access server, type the **ppp** command to connect with the device.

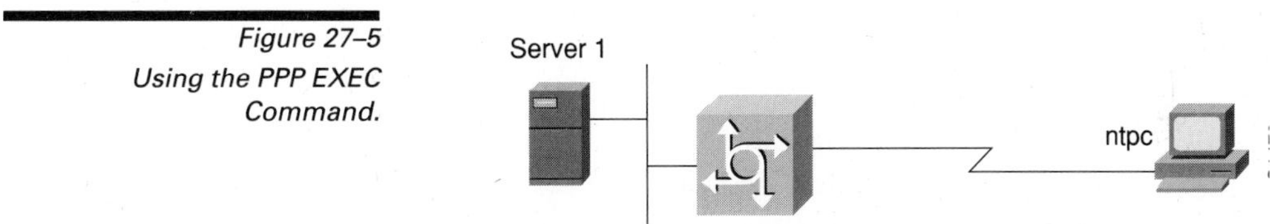

*Figure 27–5 Using the PPP EXEC Command.*

To terminate a session, disconnect from the device on the network using the command specific to that device. Then, exit from the EXEC by using the **exit** command.

### SLIP Connections

To make a serial connection to a remote host by using SLIP, perform the following task in EXEC mode:

| Task | Command |
|---|---|
| Create a SLIP connection. | **slip /default** \| {*remote-ip-address* \| *remote-name*} [**@***tacacs-server*] [**/routing**]} [**/compressed**] |

Your system administrator can configure SLIP to expect a specific address or to provide one for you. It is also possible to set up SLIP in a mode that compresses packets for more efficient use of bandwidth on the line.

If you specify an address for the TACACS server using **/default** or *tacacs-server*, the address must be the first parameter in the command after you type **slip**. If you do not specify an address or enter **/default**, you are prompted for an IP address or host name. You can enter **/default** at this point.

If you do not use the *tacacs-server* argument to specify a TACACS server for SLIP address authentication, the TACACS server specified at login (if any) is used for the SLIP address query.

To optimize bandwidth on a line, SLIP enables compression of the SLIP packets using Van Jacobson TCP header compression as defined in RFC 1144.

To terminate a session, disconnect from the device on the network using the command specific to that device. Then, exit from EXEC mode by using the **exit** command.

## Configuring Remote Access to NetBEUI Services

NetBIOS Extended User Interface (NetBEUI) is a simple networking protocol developed by IBM for use by PCs in a LAN environment. It is an extension of IBM's original Network Basic Input/Output System (NetBIOS). NetBEUI uses a broadcast-based name to 802.x address translation mechanism. Because NetBEUI has no network layer, it is a nonroutable protocol.

The NetBIOS Frames Control Protocol (NBFCP) enables packets from a NetBEUI application to be transferred via a PPP connection. For this release, NetBEUI/PPP is supported in the access server and Cisco enterprise images only.

Using the Cisco IOS implementation, remote NetBEUI users can have access to LAN-based NetBEUI services. The PPP link becomes the ramp for the remote node to access NetBIOS services on the LAN (see Figure 27–6). An LLC2 connection is set up between the remote access client and router, and a second LLC2 connection is set up between the router and the remote access (NetBEUI) server.

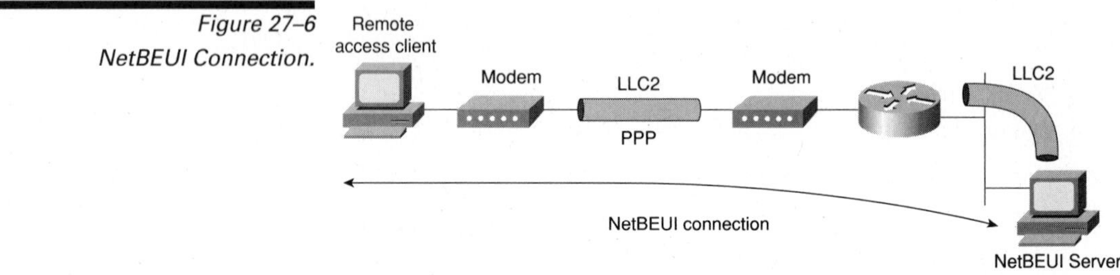


*Figure 27–6*
*NetBEUI Connection.*

By supporting NetBEUI remote clients over PPP, Cisco routers function as a native NetBEUI dial-in router for remote NetBEUI clients. Thus, you can offer remote access to a NetBEUI network through asynchronous or ISDN connections.

To enable a remote access client using a NetBEUI application to connect with the remote router providing NetBEUI services, you must configure interfaces on the remote access client side and the remote router side. Perform the following task, beginning in interface configuration mode:

| Task | Command |
|---|---|
| Enable NetBEUI's NetBIOS Frames Protocol on each side of a NetBEUI connection. | **netbios nbf** |

To view NetBEUI connection information, perform the following task in EXEC mode:

| Task | Command |
|---|---|
| View NetBEUI connection information. | **show nbf sessions** |

## Configuring Performance Parameters

To tune IP performance, complete the tasks in the following sections:

- Compress TCP Packet Headers
- Set the TCP Connection Attempt Time
- Compress IPX Packet Headers over PPP
- Enable Fast Switching
- Control Route Cache Invalidation

### Compress TCP Packet Headers

You can compress the headers of your TCP/IP packets to reduce their size and thereby increase performance. Header compression is particularly useful on networks with a large percentage of small packets, such as those supporting many Telnet connections. This feature only compresses the TCP header, so it has no effect on UDP packets or other protocol headers. The TCP header compression technique, described fully in RFC 1144, is supported on serial lines using HDLC or PPP encapsulation. You must enable compression on both ends of a serial connection.

You can optionally specify outgoing packets to be compressed only if TCP incoming packets on the same interface are compressed. If you do not specify this option, the Cisco IOS software will compress all traffic. The default is no compression.

You can also specify the total number of header compression connections that can exist on an interface. You should configure one connection for each TCP connection through the specified interface.

To enable compression, perform either of the following optional tasks in interface configuration mode:

| Task | Command |
|---|---|
| Enable TCP header compression. | **ip tcp header-compression** [passive] |
| Specify the total number of header compression connections that can exist on an interface. | **ip tcp compression-connections** *number* |

**NOTES**

When compression is enabled, fast switching is disabled. Fast processors can handle several fast interfaces, such as T1s, that are running header compression. However, you should think carefully about your network's traffic characteristics before compressing TCP headers. You might want to use the monitoring commands to help compare network utilization before and after enabling header compression.

## Set the TCP Connection Attempt Time

You can set the amount of time that the Cisco IOS software will wait to attempt to establish a TCP connection. In previous versions of the Cisco IOS software, the system would wait a fixed 30 seconds when attempting to do so. This amount of time is not sufficient in networks that have dial-up asynchronous connections, such as a network consisting of dial-on-demand links that are implemented over modems, because it will affect your ability to Telnet over the link (from the router) if the link must be brought up.

Because the connection attempt time is a host parameter, it does not pertain to traffic going through the router, just to traffic originated at it.

To set the TCP connection attempt time, perform the following task in global configuration mode:

| Task | Command |
|---|---|
| Set the amount of time the Cisco IOS software will wait to attempt to establish a TCP connection. | **ip tcp synwait-time** *seconds* |

## Compress IPX Packet Headers over PPP

The Cisco IOS software permits compression of IPX packet headers over various WAN media. There are two protocols for IPX compression on point-to-point links.

- CIPX, known also as Telebit style compression
- Shiva compression, which is proprietary

Cisco routers support IPX Header Compression (CIPX) on all point-to-point Novell interfaces over various WAN media.

CIPX is described in RFC 1553, "Compressing IPX Headers Over WAN Media." The CIPX algorithm is based on the same concepts as Van Jacobson's TCP/IP header compression algorithm. CIPX operates over PPP WAN links using either the IPXCP or IPXWAN communications protocols.

CIPX compresses all IPX headers and IPX/NCP headers for Novell packets with the following Network Control Program (NCP) packet types:

- 0x2222—NCP request from workstation
- 0x3333—NCP replies from file server

In this version of software, CIPX is configurable only for PPP links.

CIPX header compression can reduce header information from 30 bytes down to as little as 1 byte in size. This reduction can save bandwidth and reduce costs associated with IPX routing over WAN links that are configured to use IPXCP or IPXWAN.

Consider the following issues before implementing CIPX:

- CIPX is supported on all point-to-point IPX interfaces using PPP or IPXWAN processing (or both).
- CIPX needs to be negotiated for both directions of the link, because it uses the reverse direction of the link for communicating decompression problems back to the originating peer. In other words, all peer routers must have CIPX enabled.

To configure CIPX, perform the following task in global configuration mode:

| Task | Command |
|---|---|
| Compress IPX packet headers in a PPP session. | **ipx compression cipx** *number-of-slots* |

**NOTES**

It is recommended that you keep a slot value of 16. Because slots are maintained in the router buffer, a larger number can impact buffer space for other operations.

### Enable Fast Switching

Fast switching involves the use of a high-speed switching cache for IP routing. With fast switching, destination IP addresses are stored in the high-speed cache so that some time-consuming table look-ups can be avoided. The Cisco IOS software generally offers better packet transfer performance when fast switching is enabled.

To enable or disable fast switching, perform the following tasks in interface configuration mode:

| Task | Command |
|---|---|
| Enable fast switching (use of a high-speed route cache for IP routing). | **ip route-cache** |
| Disable fast switching and enable load balancing on a per-packet basis. | **no ip route-cache** |

### Control Route Cache Invalidation

The high-speed route cache used by IP fast switching is invalidated when the IP routing table changes. By default, the invalidation of the cache is delayed slightly to avoid excessive CPU load while the routing table is changing.

To control route cache invalidation, perform the following tasks in global configuration mode as needed for your network:

| Task | Command |
|---|---|
| Allow immediate invalidation of the cache. | **no ip cache-invalidate-delay** |
| Delay invalidation of the cache. | **ip cache-invalidate-delay** [*minimum maximum quiet threshold*] |

**NOTES**

This task normally should not be necessary. It should be performed only under the guidance of technical staff. Incorrect configuration can seriously degrade the performance of your router.

## PPP AND SLIP CONNECTION EXAMPLES

The following example shows a line that is in asynchronous mode using PPP encapsulation (see Figure 27–7). The name of the PC is ntpc. Assuming that the name ntpc is in the Domain Naming System (DNS), the access server can match a real IP address. The PC must be running a terminal emulator program.

```
router> ppp ntpc@server1
```

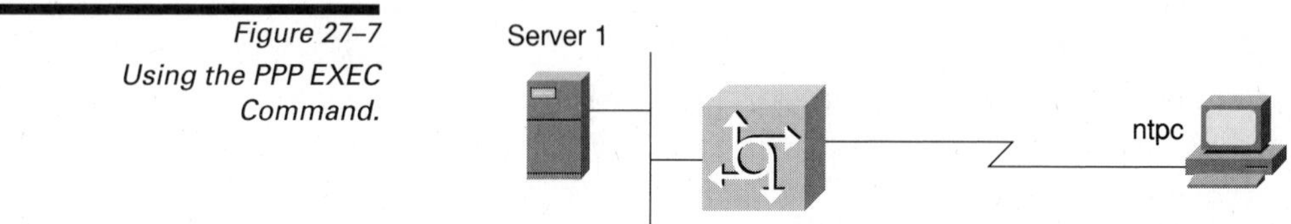


*Figure 27–7 Using the PPP EXEC Command.*

The following example illustrates how to make a connection when the system administrator defines a default IP address by including the **peer default ip address** command in interface configuration mode.

**NOTES**

The **peer default ip address** command replaces the **async default ip address** command.

Once a correct password is entered, you are placed in SLIP mode, and the IP address appears.

```
router> slip
Password:
Entering SLIP mode.
Your IP address is 192.31.7.28, MTU is 1524 bytes
```

The following example illustrates the prompts displayed and the response required when dynamic addressing is used to assign the SLIP address:

```
router> slip
IP address or hostname? 192.31.6.15
Password:
Entering SLIP mode
Your IP address is 192.31.6.15, MTU is 1524 bytes
```

In the preceding example, the address 192.31.6.15 has been assigned as the default. Password verification is still required before SLIP mode can be enabled.

```
router> slip default
Password:
Entering SLIP mode
Your IP address is 192.31.6.15, MTU is 1524 bytes
```

The following example illustrates the implementation of header compression on the interface with the IP address 128.66.2.1:

```
router> slip 128.66.2.1 /compressed
Password:
Entering SLIP mode.
Interface IP address is 128.66.2.1, MTU is 1500 bytes.
Header compression will match your system.
```

In the preceding example, the interface is configured for **ip tcp header-compression passive**, which permitted the user to enter the **/compressed** keyword at the EXEC mode prompt. The message "Header compression will match your system" indicates that the user specified compression. If the line was configured for **ip tcp header-compression on**, this line would read "Header compression is On."

The following example specifies a TACACS server named *parlance* for address authentication:

```
router> slip 1.0.0.1@parlance
Password:
Entering SLIP mode.
Interface IP address is 1.0.0.1, MTU is 1500 bytes
Header compression will match your system.
```

# CHAPTER 28

# Asynchronous PPP and SLIP Commands

Point-to-Point Protocol (PPP) and Serial Line Internet Protocol (SLIP) define methods of sending IP packets over standard EIA/TIA-232 asynchronous serial lines with minimum line speeds of 1200 baud. This chapter describes the commands used to configure your router to enable PPP and SLIP on asynchronous interfaces.

Using PPP or SLIP encapsulation over asynchronous lines is an inexpensive way of connecting PCs to a network. PPP and SLIP over asynchronous dial-up modems allow a home computer to be connected to a network without the cost of a leased line. Dial-up PPP and SLIP links can also be used for remote sites that need only occasional remote-node or backup connectivity. Both public-domain and vendor-supported PPP and SLIP implementations are available for a variety of computer applications.

**NOTES**

Although the commands found in this chapter continue to perform their normal functions in the current release, support for these commands will cease in future releases.

Use the commands in this chapter to configure PPP and SLIP on your router. For configuration information and examples, see Chapter 27, "Configuring Asynchronous PPP and SLIP."

### ASYNC MODE DEDICATED

To place a line into dedicated asynchronous mode using SLIP or PPP encapsulation, use the **async mode dedicated** interface configuration command. To return the line to interactive mode, use the **no** form of this command.

**async mode dedicated**
**no async mode dedicated**

*Syntax Description*

This command has no arguments or keywords.

### Default

Asynchronous mode is disabled.

### Command Mode

Interface configuration

### Usage Guidelines

This command first appeared in Cisco IOS Release 10.0.

With dedicated asynchronous network mode, the interface will use either SLIP or PPP encapsulation, depending on which encapsulation method is configured for the interface. An EXEC prompt does not appear, and the router is not available for normal interactive use.

If you configure a line for dedicated mode, you will not be able to use the **async dynamic address** command, because there is no user prompt.

### Example

The following example assigns an IP address to an asynchronous line and places the line into network mode. Setting the stop bits to 1 enhances performance.

```
interface async 4
 async default ip address 172.31.7.51
 async mode dedicated
 encapsulation slip

line 20
 location Joe's computer
 stopbits 1
 speed 115200
```

### Related Commands

Search online to find documentation for related commands.

**async mode interactive**

## ASYNC MODE INTERACTIVE

To return a line that has been placed into dedicated asynchronous network mode to interactive mode, thereby enabling the **slip** and **ppp** EXEC commands, use the **async mode interactive** interface configuration command. To prevent users from implementing SLIP and PPP at the EXEC level, use the **no** form of this command.

**async mode interactive**
**no async mode interactive**

### Syntax Description

This command has no arguments or keywords.

### *Default*

Asynchronous mode is disabled.

### *Command Mode*

Interface configuration

### *Usage Guidelines*

This command first appeared in Cisco IOS Release 10.0.

Interactive mode enables the **slip** and **ppp** EXEC commands. In dedicated mode, there is no user EXEC level. The user does not enter any commands, and a connection is automatically established when the user logs in, according to the configuration.



### *Example*

The following example places async interface 6 into interactive asynchronous mode:

```
interface async 6
 async default ip address 172.31.7.51
 async mode interactive
 ip unnumbered ethernet 0
```

### *Related Commands*

Search online to find documentation for related commands.

**async mode dedicated**

## AUTOSELECT

To configure a line to start an ARA, PPP, or SLIP session, use the **autoselect** line configuration command. Use the **no** form of this command to disable this function on a line.

**autoselect** {**arap** | **ppp** | **slip** | **during-login**}
**no autoselect**

| *Syntax* | *Description* |
|---|---|
| **arap** | Configures the Cisco IOS software to allow an ARA session to start up automatically. |
| **ppp** | Configures the Cisco IOS software to allow a PPP session to start up automatically. |
| **slip** | Configures the Cisco IOS software to allow a SLIP session to start up automatically. |
| **during-login** | The username and/or password prompt is displayed without pressing the Return key. After the user logs in, the autoselect function begins. |

### *Default*

ARA session

### *Command Mode*

Line configuration

### *Usage Guidelines*

This command first appeared in Cisco IOS Release 10.3. The **no autoselect** command and the **during-login** command first appeared in Cisco IOS Release 11.0.

This command eliminates the need for users to enter an EXEC command to start an ARA, PPP, or SLIP session.

**NOTES**

SLIP does not support authentication. For PPP and ARAP, you must enable authentication.

The **autoselect** command configures the Cisco IOS software to identify the type of connection being requested. For example, when a user on a Macintosh running ARA selects the Connect button, the Cisco IOS software automatically starts an ARAP session. If, on the other hand, the user is running SLIP or PPP and uses the **autoselect ppp** or **autoselect slip** command, the Cisco IOS software automatically starts a PPP or SLIP session, respectively. This command is used on lines making different types of connections.

A line that does not have **autoselect** configured views an attempt to open a connection as noise. The router does not respond, and the user client times out.

**NOTES**

After the modem connection is established, a Return is required to evoke a response, such as to get the username prompt. You might need to update your scripts to include this requirement. Additionally, the activation character should be set to the default and the exec-character-bits set to 7. If you change these defaults, the application cannot recognize the activation request.

### *Examples*

The following example enables ARA on a line:

```
line 3
 arap enable
 autoselect arap
```

The following example enables PPP on a line:

```
line 7
 autoselect ppp
```

The following example enables ARA on a line and allows logins from users with a modified CCL script and an unmodified script to log in:

```
line 3
 arap enable
 autoselect arap
 autoselect during-login
 arap noguest if-needed
```

### *Related Commands*

Search online to find documentation for related commands.

**arap use-tacacs**
**ppp authentication chap**
**ppp authentication pap**
**ppp use-tacacs**



## ENCAPSULATION

To configure SLIP or PPP encapsulation as the default on an asynchronous interface, use the **encapsulation** interface configuration command. To disable encapsulation, use the **no** form of this command.

**encapsulation** {**slip** | **ppp**}
**no encapsulation** {**slip** | **ppp**}

| Syntax | Description |
|---|---|
| **slip** | Specifies SLIP encapsulation for an interface configured for dedicated asynchronous mode or DDR. |
| **ppp** | Specifies PPP encapsulation for an interface configured for dedicated asynchronous mode or dial-on-demand routing (DDR). |

### *Default*

SLIP encapsulation is enabled by default.

### *Command Mode*

Interface configuration

### *Usage Guidelines*

This command first appeared in Cisco IOS Release 10.3.

On lines configured for interactive use, encapsulation is selected by the user when he or she establishes a connection with the **slip** or **ppp** EXEC command.

IP Control Protocol (IPCP) is the part of PPP that brings up and configures IP links. After devices at both ends of a connection communicate and bring up PPP, they bring up the control protocol for each network protocol that they intend to run over the PPP link such as IP or IPX. If you have problems passing IP packets and the **show interface** command shows that line is up, use the **negotiations** command to see if and where the negotiations are failing. You might have different versions of software running, or different versions of PPP, in which case you might need to upgrade your software or turn off PPP option negotiations. All IPCP options as listed in RFC 1332 are supported on asynchronous lines. Only Option 2, TCP/IP header compression, is supported on synchronous interfaces.

PPP echo requests are used as keepalive packets to detect line failure. The **no keepalive** command can be used to disable echo requests.

In order to use SLIP or PPP, the Cisco IOS software must be configured with an IP routing protocol or with the **ip host-routing** command. This configuration is done automatically if you are using old-style **slip address** commands. However, you must configure it manually if you configure SLIP or PPP via the **interface async** command.

**NOTES**

Disable software flow control on SLIP and PPP lines.

### *Example*

In the following example, async interface 1 is configured for PPP encapsulation.

```
router# config
Configuring from terminal, memory, or network [terminal]?
Enter configuration commands, one per line. End with CNTL/Z.
router(config)# interface async 1
router(config-if)# encapsulation ppp
```

### *Related Commands*

Search online to find documentation for related commands.

**keepalive**

## IP ACCESS-GROUP

To configure an access list to be used for packets transmitted to and from the asynchronous host, use the **ip access-group** interface configuration command. To disable control over packets transmitted to or from an asynchronous host, use the **no** form of this command.

**ip access-group** *access-list-number* {in | out}
**no ip access-group** *access-list-number*

| *Syntax* | *Description* |
|---|---|
| *access-list-number* | Assigned IP access list number. |
| **in** | Defines access control on packets transmitted *from* the asynchronous host. |
| **out** | Defines access control on packets being sent *to* the asynchronous host. |

### *Default*

Disabled

### *Command Mode*

Interface configuration

### *Usage Guidelines*

This command first appeared in Cisco IOS Release 10.0.

With this command in effect, the IP destination address of each packet is run through the access list for acceptability then dropped or passed.

### *Example*

The following example assumes that users are restricted to certain servers designated as SLIP or PPP servers, but that normal terminal users can access anything on the local network:

```
! access list for normal connections
access-list 1 permit 172.16.0.0 0.0.255.255
!
! access list for SLIP packets.
access-list 2 permit 172.16.42.55
access-list 2 permit 172.16.111.1
access-list 2 permit 172.16.55.99
!
! Specify the access list
interface async 6
 async dynamic address
 ip access-group 1 out
 ip access-group 2 in
```

## IP ADDRESS

To set IP addresses for an interface, use the **ip address** interface configuration command. To remove the specified addresses, use the **no** form of this command.

**ip address** *address mask* [**secondary**]
**no ip address** *address mask* [**secondary**]

| *Syntax* | *Description* |
|---|---|
| *address* | IP address. |
| *mask* | Network mask for the associated IP network. |
| **secondary** | (Optional) Specifies additional IP addresses. |

### *Default*

No IP addresses are specified.

### *Command Mode*

Interface configuration

### *Usage Guidelines*

This command first appeared in Cisco IOS Release 10.0.

The subnet mask must be the same for all interfaces connected to subnets of the same network. Hosts can determine subnet masks using the Internet Control Message Protocol (ICMP) *Mask Request* message. The Cisco IOS software responds to this request with an ICMP *Mask Reply* message.

You can disable IP processing on a particular interface by removing its IP address with the **no ip address** interface configuration command. If the router detects another host using one of its IP addresses, it will print an error message on the console.

### *Example*

In the example that follows, 172.16.1.27 is the primary address and 192.168.7.17 and 192.168.8.17 are secondary addresses for async interface 1:

```
interface async 1
 ip address 172.16.1.27 255.255.255.0
 ip address 192.168.7.17 255.255.255.0 secondary
 ip address 192.168.8.17 255.255.255.0 secondary
```

## IP TCP HEADER-COMPRESSION

To configure TCP header compression on the asynchronous link, use the **ip tcp header-compression** interface configuration command. To disable header compression, use the **no** form of this command.

**ip tcp header-compression [on | off | passive]**
**no ip tcp header-compression**

| *Syntax* | *Description* |
|---|---|
| **on** | (Optional) Turns header compression on. |
| **off** | (Optional) Turns header compression off. |
| **passive** | (Optional) On SLIP lines, prevents transmission of compressed packets until a compressed packet arrives from the asynchronous link, unless a user specifies SLIP on the command line. For PPP, this option functions the same as the **on** option. |



### *Default*

Header compression is on.

### *Command Mode*

Interface configuration

### *Usage Guidelines*

This command first appeared in Cisco IOS Release 10.0.

Header compression data areas are initialized to handle up to 16 simultaneous TCP connections. Currently, you cannot change this number. You can only turn header compression on or off or use the **passive** keyword.

On lines configured for PPP encapsulation, the keywords **passive** and **on** cause the same behavior because, before attempting header compression, PPP automatically negotiates whether compression is available at each end of the connection.

There are two ways to implement header compression when the line is configured for **ip tcp header-compression passive:**

- The user enters the **/compressed** option with the **slip** EXEC commands to force the line into compressed mode. This overrides the passive setting and causes the interface to behave as if header compression is enabled.
- The user enters **slip** or **slip default**, and the connecting system sends compressed packets to the server. The server detects the use of compression by the connecting system and automatically enters compressed mode.

If a line is configured for passive header compression and you use the **slip** or **ppp** EXEC command to enter asynchronous mode, you will see that the interface is set to match the compression status used by the host at the other end of the asynchronous line.

```
router> slip 10.0.0.1
Password:
Entering SLIP mode.
Interface IP address is 10.0.0.1, MTU is 1500 bytes
Header compression will match your system.
```

The message "Header compression will match your system" indicates that the interface is set to match the compression status used by the host at the other end of the asynchronous line. If the line was configured to have header compression on, this line would read "Header compression is On."

### Example

The following example enables Van Jacobson TCP header compression. The **passive** keyword prevents transmission of compressed packets until a compressed packet arrives from the IP link. Notice that asynchronous routing and dynamic addressing are also enabled.

```
interface async 6
 async dynamic routing
 async dynamic address
 ip tcp header-compression passive
```

### Related Commands

Search online to find documentation for related commands.

**ppp**
**slip**
**slip default**
**slip /compressed**

## IP UNNUMBERED

To conserve network resources, use the **ip unnumbered** interface configuration command. To disable unnumbered interfaces, use the **no** form of this command.

**ip unnumbered** *type number*
**no ip unnumbered**

| Syntax | Description |
|---|---|
| *type* | Interface type. |
| *number* | Interface number. |

### Default

Disabled

### Command Mode

Interface configuration

### Usage Guidelines

This command first appeared in Cisco IOS Release 10.0.

You must use either the **ip address** or **ip unnumbered** command to provide the local address for an interface.

Unnumbered interfaces do not have an address. Network resources are conserved because fewer network numbers are used and routing tables are smaller.

Whenever the unnumbered interface generates a packet (for example, a routing update), it uses the address of the specified interface as the source address of the IP packet. It also uses the address of the specified interface to determine which routing processes are sending updates over the unnumbered interface. Restrictions include the following:

- You cannot use the **ping** command to determine whether the interface is up, because the interface has no address. SNMP can be used to remotely monitor interface status.
- You cannot netboot an executable image over an unnumbered serial interface.
- The arguments *type* and *number* must be another interface in the network server that has an IP address, not another unnumbered interface.



### *Example*

The following example configures async interface 6 as unnumbered:

```
interface async 6
 ip unnumbered ethernet 0
```

### *Related Commands*

Search online to find documentation for related commands.

**ip address**

## IPX COMPRESSION CIPX

To enable compression of IPX packet headers in a PPP session, use the **ipx compression cipx** interface configuration command. To disable compression of IPX packet headers in a PPP session, use the **no** form of this command.

**ipx compression cipx** *number-of-slots*
**no ipx compression cipx**

| *Syntax* | *Description* |
|---|---|
| *number-of-slots* | Number of stored IPX headers allowed. The range is from 10 to 256. The default is 16.<br>A slot is similar to a table entry for a complete IPX header. When a packet is received, the receiver stores the complete IPX header in a slot and tells the destination which slot it used. As subsequent CIPX packets are sent, the receiver uses the slot number field to determine which complete IPX header to associate with the CIPX packet before passing the packet up to IPX. |

### *Default*

No compression of IPX packets during a PPP session

### Command Mode

Interface configuration

### Usage Guidelines

This command first appeared in Cisco IOS Release 11.1.

This interface configuration command enables IPX header compression on PPP links.

### Example

The following example enables IPX header compression for PPP:

```
encapsulation ppp
ipx compression cipx 128
```

### Related Commands

Search online to find documentation for related commands.

**show ipx compression**

## IPX PPP-CLIENT

To enable a non-routing IPX client to connect to an asynchronous interface, the interface must be associated with a loopback interface configured to run IPX. To permit such connections, use the **ipx ppp-client** interface configuration command. To disable a non-routing IPX client, use the **no** form of this command.

**ipx ppp-client loopback** *number*
**no ipx ppp-client loopback** *number*

| *Syntax* | *Description* |
|---|---|
| **loopback** | Loopback interface configured with a unique IPX network number. |
| *number* | Number of the loopback interface. |

### Default

IPX client connections are not permitted over PPP.

### Command Mode

Interface configuration

### Usage Guidelines

This command first appeared in Cisco IOS Release 11.1.

This command enables IPX clients to log in to the router from a device running a virtual terminal protocol, then issue the PPP command at the EXEC prompt to connect to a remote device.

You must first configure a loopback interface with a unique IPX network number. The loopback interface is then assigned to an asynchronous interface, which permits IPX clients to connect to the asynchronous interface.

### *Example*

The following example configures IPX to run over PPP on asynchronous interface 3:

```
ipx routing 0000.0c07.b509
interface loopback0
 no ip address
 ipx network 544
 ipx sap-interval 2000
interface ethernet0
 ip address 172.21.14.64
 ipx network AC150E00
 ipx encapsulation SAP
interface async 3
 ip unnumbered ethernet0
 encapsulation ppp
 async mode interactive
 async default ip address 172.18.1.128
 ipx ppp-client loopback0
 ipx sap-interval 0
```

### *Related Commands*

Search online to find documentation for related commands.

**interface loopback**
**ipx network**



## PEER DEFAULT IP ADDRESS

Use the **peer default ip address** interface configuration command to specify an IP address, an address from a specific IP address pool, or an address from the DHCP mechanism to be returned to a remote peer connecting to this interface. This command sets the address used on the remote (PC) side. Use the **no** form of this command to disable a prior peer IP address pooling configuration on an interface.

To remove the default address from your configuration, use the **no** form of this command also.

**peer default ip address** {**ip-address** | **dhcp** | **pool** [*poolname*]}
**no peer default ip address**

| *Syntax* | *Description* |
|---|---|
| **ip-address** | Specific IP address to be assigned to a remote peer dialing in to this interface. To prevent the assignment of duplicate IP addresses on two or more interfaces, this form of the command cannot be applied to a dialer rotary group nor to an ISDN interface. |
| **dhcp** | Retrieve an IP address from the DHCP server. |

| | |
|---|---|
| **pool** | Use the Global Default Mechanism as defined by the **ip address-pool** command unless the optional *poolname* is supplied. |
| *poolname* | (Optional) Name of a local address pool created using the **ip local pool** command. The router retrieves an address from this pool regardless of the Global Default Mechanism setting. |

### *Default*

**pool**

### *Command Mode*

Interface configuration

### *Usage Guidelines*

This command first appeared in Cisco IOS Release 11.0.

This command applies to point-to-point interfaces that support the PPP or SLIP encapsulation.

**NOTES**

This command replaces the **async default ip address** command.

This command allows an administrator to configure all possible address pooling mechanisms on a interface-by-interface basis. The **peer default ip address** command can be used to override the Global Default Mechanism defined by the **ip address-pool** command on an interface-by-interface basis.

For all interfaces not configured with a peer default IP address mechanism (equivalent to selecting the **peer default ip address pool** command), the router uses the Global Default Mechanism that is defined by the **ip address-pool** command.

If you select the **peer default ip address pool** *poolname* command, then the router uses the locally configured pool on this interface and does not follow the Global Default Mechanism.

If you select the **peer default ip address** *ip-address* form of this command, the specified IP address is assigned to any peer connecting to this interface, and any Global Default Mechanism is overridden for this interface.

If you select the **peer default ip address dhcp** form of this command, the DHCP proxy-client mechanism is used by default on this interface, and any Global Default Mechanism is overridden for this interface.

### *Example*

The following example specifies address 192.31.7.51 for async interface 6:

```
line 20
 speed 115200
```

```
interface async 6
 peer default ip address 192.31.7.51
```

### *Related Commands*

Search online to find documentation for related commands.

**async dynamic address**

## PPP

To start an asynchronous connection using PPP, use the **ppp** EXEC command.

**ppp** {**/default** | {*remote-ip-address* | *remote-name*} [**@***tacacs-server*]} [**/routing**]

| *Syntax* | *Description* |
|---|---|
| **/default** | (Optional) Makes a PPP connection when a default address has been configured. |
| *remote-ip-address* | IP address of the client workstation or PC. This parameter can only be specified if the line is set for dynamic addresses using the **async address dynamic** line configuration command. |
| *remote-name* | Name of the client workstation or PC. This parameter can be specified if the line is set for dynamic addresses using the **async address dynamic** line configuration command. |
| *@tacacs-server* | (Optional) IP address or IP host name of the TACACS server to which the user's TACACS authentication request is sent. |
| **/routing** | (Optional) Indicates that the remote system is a router and that routing messages should be exchanged over the link. The line must be configured for asynchronous routing using PPP encapsulation. |

### *Command Mode*

EXEC

### *Usage Guidelines*

This command first appeared in a release prior to Cisco IOS Release 10.0.

When you connect from a remote-node computer to an EXEC session on the access server and want to connect from the access server to a device on the network, issue the **ppp** command.

If you specify an address for the TACACS server (either **/default** or *tacacs-server*), the address must be the first parameter in the command after you type **ppp**. If you do not specify an address or enter **default**, you are prompted for an IP address or host name. You can enter **default** at this point.

To terminate a session, disconnect from the device on the network using the command specific to that device. Then, exit from the EXEC by using the **exit** command.

### *Example*

The following example shows a line that is in asynchronous mode using PPP encapsulation (see Figure 28–1). The PC's name is ntpc—assuming that the name ntpc is in the Domain Naming System (DNS) so that it can be resolved to a real IP address). The PC must be running a terminal emulator program.

```
router> ppp ntpc@server1
```

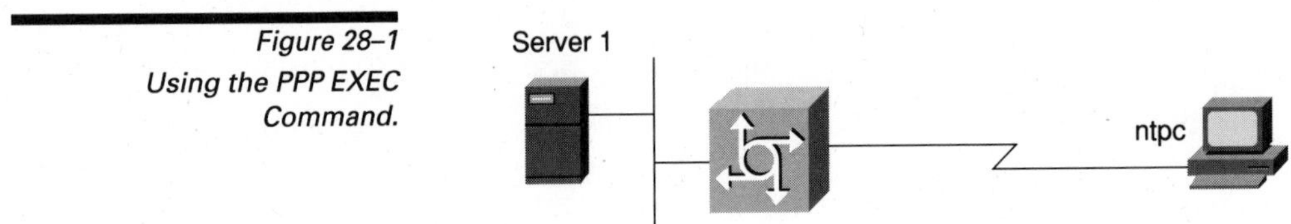


*Figure 28–1 Using the PPP EXEC Command.*

## SERVICE OLD-SLIP-PROMPTS

To provide backward compatibility for client software scripts expecting SLIP and PPP dialogs to be formatted with software release 9.1 or earlier, use the **service old-slip-prompts** global configuration command. Use the **no** form of this command to disable this function.

**service old-slip-prompts**
**no service old-slip-prompts**

### *Syntax Description*

This command has no arguments or keywords.

### *Default*

The prompts and information transmitted by SLIP and PPP are formatted with the current release of Cisco IOS software.

### *Command Mode*

Global configuration

### *Usage Guidelines*

This command first appeared in Cisco IOS Release 11.1.

### *Example*

The following example shows the output of a SLIP command after **service old-slip-prompts** is enabled:

```
router# configure terminal
Enter configuration commands, one per line.  End with CNTL/Z.
router(config)# service old-slip-prompts
router(config)# exit
```

```
router# slip
IP address or hostname: 2.2.2.2
Entering SLIP mode.
Your IP address is 2.2.2.2. MTU is 1500 bytes
```

## SHOW IPX COMPRESSION

To show the current status and statistics of IPX header compression during PPP sessions, use the **show ipx compression** EXEC command.

**show ipx compression detail** *int-spec*

| *Syntax* | *Description* |
|---|---|
| **detail** | Shows detailed link-state database information for NLSP. |
| *int-spec* | Interface type, as listed in Table 28–1. |

**Table 28–1** *Interface Specifications for Show IPX Compression Command*

| Keyword | Description |
|---|---|
| Async | Asynchronous interface. |
| Ethernet | Ethernet IEEE 802.3 interface. |
| Null | Null interface. |
| Serial | WAN serial interface. |

### *Command Mode*

EXEC

### *Usage Guidelines*

This command first appeared in Cisco IOS Release 11.1.

### *Related Commands*

Search online to find documentation for related commands.

**ipx compression cipx**
**show ipx interface**

## SLIP

To start a serial connection to a remote host by using SLIP, use the **slip** EXEC command.

**slip** [**/default**] {*remote-ip-address* | *remote-name*} [**@***tacacs-server*] [**/routing**]} [**/compressed**]

| *Syntax* | *Description* |
|---|---|
| **/default** | (Optional) Makes a SLIP connection when a default address has been configured. |
| *remote-ip-address* | IP address of the client workstation or PC. |
| *remote-name* | Name of the client workstation or PC. |
| @*tacacs-server* | (Optional) IP address or IP host name of the TACACS server to which your TACACS authentication request is sent. |
| **/routing** | (Optional) Indicates that the remote system is a router. Line must be configured for asynchronous routing using SLIP encapsulation. |
| **/compressed** | (Optional) Indicates that IP header compression should be negotiated. |

### *Command Mode*

EXEC

### *Usage Guidelines*

This command first appeared in a release prior to Cisco IOS Release 10.0.

When you connect from a remote-node computer to the EXEC facility on a router and want to connect from the router to a device on the network, issue the **slip** command.

If you specify an address for the TACACS server by using **/default** or *tacacs-server*, the address must be the first parameter in the command after you enter **slip**. If you do not specify an address or enter **/default**, you are prompted for an IP address or host name. You can enter **/default** at this point.

If you do not use the *tacacs-server* argument to specify a TACACS server for SLIP address authentication, the TACACS server specified at login (if any) is used for the SLIP address query.

To optimize bandwidth on a line, SLIP enables compression of the SLIP packets using Van Jacobson TCP header compression as defined in RFC 1144.

Your system administrator must configure the system with the **ip tcp header-compression passive** command for the **/compressed** command option to be valid in EXEC mode. The **ip tcp header-compression** command forces header compression on or off. The default is to not compress the packets. The configuration file must have header compression on, and the **slip /compressed** EXEC command must be entered for header compression to occur.

To terminate a session initiated with the slip command, disconnect from the device on the network using the command specific to that device. Then, exit from the EXEC by using the **exit** command.

### *Examples*

The following example makes a connection when a default IP address is assigned. Once a correct password is entered, you are placed in SLIP mode, and the IP address is displayed.

```
router> slip
Password:
```

```
Entering SLIP mode.
Your IP address is 192.31.7.28, MTU is 1524 bytes
```

The following example illustrates the prompts displayed and the response required when you use dynamic addressing to assign the SLIP address:

```
router> slip
IP address or hostname? 192.31.6.15
Password:
Entering SLIP mode
Your IP address is 192.31.6.15, MTU is 1524 bytes
```

In the preceding example, the address 192.31.6.15 has been assigned as the default. Password verification is still required before SLIP mode can be enabled.

```
router> slip /default
Password:
Entering SLIP mode
Your IP address is 192.31.6.15, MTU is 1524 bytes
```

The following example illustrates the implementation of header compression on the interface with the IP address 128.66.2.1:

```
router> slip 128.66.2.1 /compressed
Password:
Entering SLIP mode.
Interface IP address is 128.66.2.1, MTU is 1500 bytes.
Header compression will match your system.
```

In the preceding example, the interface is configured for **ip tcp header-compression passive**, which permits the user to enter the **/compressed** keyword at the EXEC mode prompt. The message "Header compression will match your system" indicates that the user specified compression. If the line was configured for **ip tcp header-compression on**, this line would read "Header compression is On."

The following example specifies a TACACS server named server1 for address authentication:

```
router> slip 1.0.0.1@server1
Password:
Entering SLIP mode.
Interface IP address is 1.0.0.1, MTU is 1500 bytes
Header compression will match your system.
```

# CHAPTER 29

# Configuring V.120 Access

The V-series recommendations are ITU-T standards dealing with data communications over telephone networks. V.120 allows for reliable transport of synchronous, asynchronous, or bit transparent data over ISDN bearer channels.

Cisco provides three V.120 support features for terminal adapters that do not send the low-layer compatibility fields or bearer capability V.120 information:

- Answer all incoming calls as V.120—static configuration used when all remote users have asynchronous terminals and need to connect with a vty on the router.
- Automatically detect V.120 encapsulation—encapsulation dynamically detected and set.
- Enable V.120 Support for Asynchronous Access over ISDN.

For terminal adapters that send the low-layer compatibility or bearer capability V.120 information, mixed V.120 and ISDN calls are supported. No special configuration is required. For a complete description of the commands mentioned in this chapter, see Chapter 30, "V.120 Access Commands."

## CONFIGURING ANSWERING OF ALL INCOMING CALLS AS V.120

This V.120 support feature allows users to connect using an asynchronous terminal over ISDN terminal adapters with V.120 support to a vty on the router, much like a direct asynchronous connection. Beginning with Cisco IOS Release 11.1, this feature supports incoming calls only.

When all the remote users have asynchronous terminals and call in to a router through an ISDN terminal adapter that uses V.120 encapsulation but does not send the low-layer compatibility or bearer capability V.120 information, you can configure the interface to answer all calls as V.120. Such calls are connected with an available vty on the router.

To configure an ISDN BRI or PRI interface to answer all incoming calls as V.120, complete the following tasks beginning in global configuration mode:

| Task | Command |
|---|---|
| Specify the ISDN BRI interface.<br>or<br>Specify the ISDN PRI D channel. | **interface bri** *number* (Cisco 4000 series)<br>**interface bri** *slot:number* (Cisco 7200 series)<br>**interface serial e1** *controller-number*:**15**<br>**interface serial t1** *controller-number*:**23** |
| Configure the interface to answer all calls as V.120. | **isdn all-incoming-calls-v120** |

## Configuring Automatic Detection of Encapsulation Type

If an ISDN call does not identify the call type in the lower-layer compatibility fields and is using an encapsulation that is different from the one configured on the interface, the interface can change its encapsulation type dynamically.

This feature enables interoperation with ISDN terminal adapters that use V.120 encapsulation but do not signal V.120 in the call setup message. An ISDN interface that by default answers a call as synchronous serial with PPP encapsulation can change its encapsulation and answer such calls.

Automatic detection is attempted for the first 10 seconds after the link is established or the first five packets exchanged over the link, whichever is first.

To enable automatic detection of V.120 encapsulation, perform the following task in interface configuration mode:

| Task | Command |
|---|---|
| Enable automatic detection of encapsulation type on the specified interface. | **autodetect encapsulation v120** |

You can specify one or more encapsulations to detect. Cisco IOS software currently supports automatic detection of PPP and V.120 encapsulations.

## Enabling V.120 Support for Asynchronous Access over ISDN

You can optionally configure a router to support asynchronous access over ISDN by globally enabling PPP on vty lines. Asynchronous access is then supported over ISDN from the ISDN terminal to the vty session on the router.

To enable asynchronous protocol features on vty lines, perform the following task in global configuration mode:

| Task | Command |
|---|---|
| Configure all vty lines to support asynchronous protocol features | **vty-async** |

This task enables PPP on vty lines on a global basis on the router. If you prefer instead to configure PPP on a per-vty basis, use the **translate** command, found in Chapter 22, "Protocol Translation and Virtual Asynchronous Device Commands."

## V.120 Configuration Example

The following example configures BRI 0 to call and receive calls from two sites, to use Point-to-Point Protocol (PPP) encapsulation on outgoing calls, and to use Challenge Handshake Authentication Protocol (CHAP) authentication on incoming calls. This example also enables BRI 0 to configure itself dynamically to answer calls that use V.120 but that do not signal V.120 in the call setup message.

```
interface bri 0
 encapsulation ppp
 autodetect encapsulation v120
 no keepalive
 dialer map ip 131.108.36.10 name EB1 234
 dialer map ip 131.108 36.9 name EB2 456
 dialer-group 1
 isdn spid1 0146334600
 isdn spid2 0146334610
 isdn T200 1000
 ppp authentication chap
```

CHAPTER 30

# V.120 Access Commands

This chapter describes the commands used to configure ISDN interfaces for use with terminal adapters that use V.120 signaling but that might not send the Low-Level Compatibility message. To configure an ISDN interface for V.120 access, see Chapter 29, "Configuring V.120 Access."

## AUTODETECT ENCAPSULATION V120

To enable an ISDN interface to detect the encapsulation type used in incoming calls and to configure itself dynamically, use the **autodetect encapsulation v120** interface configuration command.

**autodetect encapsulation** v120

### *Syntax Description*

This command has no arguments or keywords.

### *Default*

Disabled

### *Command Mode*

Interface configuration

### *Usage Guidelines*

This command first appeared in Cisco IOS Release 11.2.

Use this command to enable interoperation with ISDN terminal adapters that use V.120 encapsulation but do not signal V.120 in the call Setup message. An ISDN interface that by default answers a call as synchronous serial with PPP encapsulation can change its encapsulation and answer such calls.

### Example

The following example configures BRI 0 to call and receive calls from two sites, use Point-to-Point Protocol (PPP) encapsulation on outgoing calls, and use Challenge Handshake Authentication Protocol (CHAP) authentication on incoming calls. This example also enables BRI 0 to configure itself dynamically to answer calls that use V.120 but that do not signal V.120.

```
interface bri 0
 encapsulation ppp
 autodetect encapsulation v120
 no keepalive
 dialer map ip 131.108.36.10 name EB1 234
 dialer map ip 131.108 36.9 name EB2 456
 dialer-group 1
 isdn spid1 0146334600
 isdn spid2 0146334610
 isdn T200 1000
 ppp authentication chap
```

### Related Commands

Search online to find documentation for related commands.

**encapsulation ppp**

## ISDN ALL-INCOMING-CALLS-V120

To configure an ISDN BRI or PRI interface to answer all incoming calls as V.120 when the terminal adapter uses V.120 signaling but does not send the Lower-Layer Compatibility field in Setup messages, use the **isdn all-incoming-calls-v120** interface configuration command.

**isdn all-incoming-calls-v120**

### Syntax Description

This command has no arguments or keywords.

### Default

By default, ISDN interfaces answer calls as synchronous serial with PPP encapsulation.

### Command Mode

Interface configuration

### Usage Guidelines

This command first appeared in Cisco IOS Release 11.2.

Use this command only when you want *all* incoming calls to be answered as V.120. If you want the interface to automatically detect whether the incoming call uses V.120 or PPP encapsulation, use the **autodetect encapsulation** command.

This command applies only when the incoming call originates on an asynchronous device and needs to terminate in an available VTY on the router.

### *Example*

The following partial example shows that BRI 0 is configured to answer all calls as V.120:

```
interface bri 0
 isdn all-incoming-calls-v120
```

### *Related Commands*

Search online to find documentation for related commands.

**autodetect encapsulation**

CHAPTER 31

# Configuring AppleTalk Remote Access

This chapter describes the configuration of your router to act as an AppleTalk Remote Access (ARA) server. It does not describe how to configure or use the client Macintosh. Refer to the Apple Computer, Inc. *Apple Remote Access Client User's Guide* for information about how to set up and use the ARA software on your Macintosh.

For a complete description of the commands in this chapter, see Chapter 32, "AppleTalk Remote Access Commands."

## AppleTalk Remote Access

The Cisco implementation of ARA gives Macintosh users direct access to information and resources in remote AppleTalk networks over standard telephone lines. For example, if you have a PowerBook at home and need to get a file from your Macintosh at the office, ARA software can make the connection between your home and office computers over telephone lines.

You can configure your router to act as an ARA server by enabling AppleTalk and ARA protocol on physical terminal (TTY) or virtual terminal (VTY) lines. Configuring your router to act as an ARA server allows remote Macintosh users to dial in, become a network node, and connect to devices on other networks. ARA protocol support is transparent to the Macintosh end user. Macintosh users can also use Serial Line Internet Protocol (SLIP) to access remote IP network resources and Point-to-Point Protocol (PPP) to access both AppleTalk and IP resources.

The following Macintosh and Cisco IOS software support is required for ARA connectivity:

- Macintosh running ARA software and a connection control language (CCL) script
- Router configured as an ARA server

Figure 31–1 shows how your router can act as an ARA server between remote Macintosh computers (in Figure 31–1, a Power Macintosh and a PowerBook) and devices on another network.

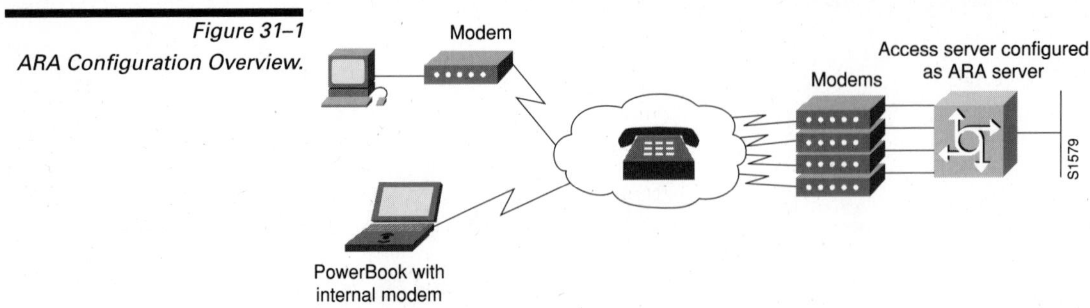


*Figure 31–1 ARA Configuration Overview.*

## ARA Configuration Task List

The following upcoming sections describe how to set up the Cisco IOS software to act as an ARA server:

- Connecting Cables
- Configuring the Line and the Modem
- Configuring ARA Required Tasks

The following tasks (sections) are optional:

- Configuring ARA Optional Tasks
- Configuring ARA Security
- Connecting to an AppleTalk Network from a Client Running a Different Virtual Terminal Protocol

To enable asynchronous callback to ARA clients, see section "Calling Back ARA Clients," found in Chapter 65, "Configuring Asynchronous Callback."

To enable remote clients running PPP to dial in and access AppleTalk resources on a network, you must configure AppleTalk over PPP (referred to as ATCP). To configure ATCP, see the section "Configure AppleTalk–PPP," later in Chapter 27, "Configuring Asynchronous PPP and SLIP."

## Connecting Cables

Figure 31–2 shows how to connect a Macintosh using internal and external modems.

Use the MMOD version of the RJ-45-to-DB-25 adapter (labeled "Modem" if the adapter is from Cisco) to connect a "rolled" RJ-45 cable from the router to the modem. Use a high-speed modem cable with hardware flow control to connect a modem to your Macintosh (refer to the user documentation for your modem for more specific information).

For more information about connecting cables, refer to the installation and configuration or product user guide that came with your router.

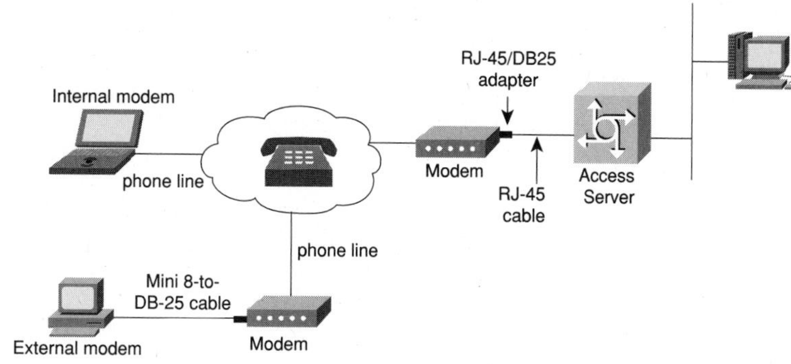


*Figure 31–2 ARA Server Cabling and Connections.*

## CONFIGURING THE LINE AND THE MODEM

Configure the line as follows:

**Step 1** Specify the maximum common line speed for the modem and the access server. The access server supports 4x compression of data, so you can typically use the speeds shown in the following list:

- 115,200 bps for use with modems that support a transmission rate of 28,800
- 57,600 bps for use with modems that support a transmission rate of 14,400
- 38,400 bps for use with modems that support a transmission rate of 9,600

**NOTES**

Refer to your modem guide to ensure that the modem can support these maximum line speeds.

**Step 2** Set hardware flow control—Use the **flowcontrol hardware** command to enable hardware flow control.

**NOTES**

The Cisco IOS software does not support modems that do not support hardware flow control.

**Step 3** Specify your modem control parameters—Use the **modem inout** command to configure the line for both incoming and outgoing calls, or use the **modem dialin** command to configure the line for incoming calls only.

**Step 4** Configure security on your dial-in lines—Use the **aaa new-model** command to enable the authentication, authorization, and accounting (AAA) process on the router, the **aaa authentication arap** command to create an authentication list, and **arap authentication** command to apply the authentication list to a line or set of lines configured for ARA.

For more information about configuring lines and modem control, see Chapter 5, "Configuring Modem Support and Asynchronous Devices."

**NOTES**

The **autobaud** command is not supported with ARA and should never be used.

## CONFIGURING ARA REQUIRED TASKS

To allow ARA connections to pass through the access server or router, perform the following tasks beginning in global configuration mode:

| Task | | Command |
|---|---|---|
| **Step 1** | Enable AppleTalk. | **appletalk routing** |
| **Step 2** | Create a new network or zone for ARA clients when they dial in. The *network-number* argument must be a unique network number. | **arap network** [*network-number*] [*zone-name*] |
| **Step 3** | In interface configuration mode, ensure that a new internal network is advertised by enabling the Routing Table Maintenance Protocol (RTMP). | **appletalk send-rtmps** |
| **Step 4** | Configure an AppleTalk interface using the discovery mode in the Cisco IOS software. To do so, an interface on the router must be connected to a network that has at least one other router configured for AppleTalk. | |
| **Step 5** | Return to global configuration mode and turn on AppleTalk routing. | **appletalk routing** |
| **Step 6** | Enter line configuration mode. | **line** [**tty** \| **aux** \| **vty**] *line-number* [*ending-line-number*] |
| **Step 7** | Enable ARA on a line. | **arap enable** |

If you discover that the AppleTalk network already exists when you get to Step 4, the zone and cable range must match the existing configuration. To identify existing cable ranges and zone names, configure the Cisco IOS software for discovery mode. You must manually configure an AppleTalk interface on a segment for which there are no AppleTalk routers.

## CONFIGURING ARA OPTIONAL TASKS

Refer to this section after you have configured AppleTalk routing, created an internal ARA network or zone, and enabled ARA. At this point, you can enable optional tasks. Though optional, the tasks in this section *might* be required for your network environment.

To configure the Cisco IOS software to allow an ARA session to start automatically, perform the following tasks beginning in global configuration mode:

| Task | | Command |
|---|---|---|
| **Step 1** | Configure a line to automatically start an ARA session. | **autoselect** {**arap** \| **ppp** \| **slip** \| **during-login**} |
| **Step 2** | Enter line configuration mode. | **line x** (x = the line you want to configure is Step 3) |
| **Step 3** | Enter line configuration mode and dedicate a line to function only as an ARA connection. | **arap dedicated** |
| **Step 4** | Set the maximum length of an ARA session for a line.The default is to have unlimited length connections. | **arap timelimit** [*minutes*] |
| **Step 5** | Set when a disconnect warning message is displayed, in number of minutes before the line is disconnected. This command is valid only when a session time limit is set. | **arap warningtime** [*minutes*] |

The autoselect command permits the router to start an ARA session automatically when it detects the start character for an ARAP packet. The Cisco IOS software detects either a Return character, which is the start character for an EXEC session, or the Start character for the ARA protocol. By issuing the **autoselect** command with the **during-login** argument, you can display the username or password prompt without pressing the Return key. While the username or password prompts are displayed, you can choose to answer these prompts or to start sending packets from an autoselected protocol.

For information about using ARA with TACACS, Extended TACACS, and AAA/TACACS+, refer to the section "Configuring ARA Security," later in this chapter.

**NOTES**

When you use the autoselect function, the activation character should be set to the default, Return, and exec-character-bits to 7. If you change these defaults, the application cannot recognize the activation request.

To customize the AppleTalk configuration even further, you can perform the following additional tasks:

- Disable Checksum Generation and Verification
- Configure MacIP

## Configuring ARA Security

The following three types of security can be used with ARA:

- ARA Server Security, including required manual password entry, limited network visibility, and no guest access
- Local or Remote Security Database, including username and password authentication and access lists
- TACACS and TACACS+ Security for ARA, including TACACS, TACACS+/AAA, and Kerberos

The following sections describe these tasks.

### ARA Server Security

This section describes the following security features that are specific to the ARA protocol:

- Require Manual Password Entry
- Limit Network Visibility
- Disallow Guests

#### *Require Manual Password Entry*

You can control access by requiring users to enter their password manually at the time they log in. To force manual password entry, perform the following task in line configuration mode:

| Task | Command |
|---|---|
| Require manual password entry. | **arap require-manual-password** |

#### *Limit Network Visibility*

You can control Macintosh access to zones and networks by using **arap** commands to reference access control lists configured using AppleTalk **access-list** commands.

To control which zones the Macintosh user can see, perform the following task in line configuration mode:

| Task | Command |
|---|---|
| Limit the zones the Macintosh user sees. | **arap zonelist** *zone-access-list-number* |

To control traffic from the Macintosh to networks, perform the following task in line configuration mode:

| Task | Command |
|---|---|
| Control access to networks. | **arap net-access-list** *net-access-list-number* |

### *Disallow Guests*

A guest is a person who connects to the network without having to give a name or a password. To prohibit Macintosh guests from logging in through the router, perform the following task in line configuration mode. Use the optional **if-needed** argument to allow users to log in as guests if they are already authenticated with a username or password.

| Task | Command |
|---|---|
| Prohibit guests from logging in to the ARA network. | **arap noguest** [**if-needed**] |

**CAUTION**

Do not use the **arap noguest** command if you are using modified CCL scripts and the **login tacacs** command.

## Local or Remote Security Database

To prevent unauthenticated users from accessing your network resources, you configure a username and password database. This database can be local on the router or can be stored on a remote security server (a PC or UNIX computer set up with a security database). Perform the tasks in the following sections to configure the Cisco IOS software to support either local or remote authentication:

- Configure Local Username Authentication
- Enable Remote TACACS or TACACS+ Server Authentication

### *Configure Local Username Authentication*

To configure internal username authentication, perform the following task in global configuration mode. Enter this information for each supported user.

| Task | Command |
|---|---|
| Specify a username and password. | **username** *name* **password** *password* |

When users try to log in to the access server, username and password prompts require them to authenticate themselves before they can have access to the router or the network.

### Enable Remote TACACS or TACACS+ Server Authentication

To enable the Cisco IOS software to use a remote TACACS or TACACS+ authentication database, perform the following tasks in global configuration mode:

| Task | Command |
| --- | --- |
| Specify the IP address or the host name of the remote TACACS+ server host. This host is typically a UNIX system running TACACS+ software. | **tacacs-server host** {*hostname* \| *ip-address*} |
| Specify a shared secret text string used between the router and the TACACS+ server. The router and TACACS+ server use this text string to encrypt passwords and exchange responses. | **tacacs-server key** *shared-secret-text-string* |

After you specify these commands in the Cisco IOS software, you must populate the remote username database to all users to whom you want to provide network access. When users try to log in to the router, username and password prompts require them to authenticate themselves before they can have access to the router or the network.

## TACACS and TACACS+ Security for ARA

You can prevent unauthenticated users from accessing your network resources using the following security mechanisms:

- TACACS and AAA/TACACS+ user authentication, with username and password information stored on a TACACS or TACACS+ server
- Kerberos, which is configured through the AAA facility

Perform the tasks in the following sections to configure TACACS and TACACS+ security to authenticate clients that are using ARA to dial in:

- Enable Standard and Extended TACACS for ARA Authentication.
- Enable AAA/TACACS+ for ARA Authentication.
- Modify Scripts To Support a Standard EXEC Security Dialog—This is only necessary if you are running Standard TACACS on both your router and your TACACS server.

### Enable Standard and Extended TACACS for ARA Authentication

To use Extended TACACS, you must already have set up an Extended TACACS server using the Cisco Extended TACACS server software, available from the ftp.cisco.com directory. Refer to the

README in this directory for more information. There are two authentication methods used with standard TACACS:

- You issue the **arap use-tacacs** command. The remote user logs in by entering the appropriate username at the ARA username prompt and password at the password prompt.
- You issue the **arap use-tacacs** command and the **single-line** keyword. The remote user logs in by entering *username*password* at the ARA username prompt, and **arap** at the password prompt.

**NOTES**

The **arap use-tacacs** command provides TACACS security without having to modify CCL scripts and respond to dialog boxes. The use of scripts is still a supported feature, and is described in the section "Modify Scripts to Support a Standard EXEC Security Dialog," later in this chapter.

To configure the router to authenticate using TACACS, perform one of the following tasks in line configuration mode:

| Task | Command |
|---|---|
| Enable TACACS under ARA. | **arap use-tacacs** [**single-line**] |
| Enable login authentication using TACACS. | **login tacacs** |

For an example of enabling TACACS for ARA authentication, see the section "ARA Configuration Examples," later in this chapter.

### Enable AAA/TACACS+ for ARA Authentication

To enable TACACS+ authentication for ARA sessions, perform the following tasks, beginning in global configuration mode:

| Task | | Command |
|---|---|---|
| **Step 1** | Enable the authentication, authorization, and accounting (AAA) function in the Cisco IOS software. | **aaa new-model** |
| **Step 2** | Create an authentication list that you later apply to lines configured for ARA sessions or log in to the router. | **aaa authentication arap \| login** {**default** \| *list-name*} *method1* [...[*method4*]} |
| **Step 3** | Enter line configuration mode. | **line** [**tty**] *line-number* [*ending-line-number*] |

| Task | | Command |
|---|---|---|
| **Step 4** | Apply an ARA authentication list to lines configured for ARA. | **arap authentication** {**default** \| *list-name*} |
| **Step 5** | Apply a login authentication list to lines that users can log in to. | **login authentication** {**default** \| *list-name*} |

### *Modify Scripts To Support a Standard EXEC Security Dialog*

This section describes how to modify your CCL script to work with TACACS security and how to configure a line to use a TACACS server for user authentication.

**CAUTION**

Because of the underlying structure of the ARA protocol, modem-layer error control is disabled during the exchange of username and password. This makes the exchange highly susceptible to line noise, especially at higher baud rates enabled by V.34 modems. For this reason, Cisco does not recommend the use of modified scripts and encourages users to either upgrade to later versions of TACACS or use the **arap use-tacacs single-line** command.

If you are currently using modified CCL scripts and want to migrate to nonmodified scripts, see the section "Configure Modified and Unmodified Scripts Example," near the end of this chapter for information on how to use both in the same environment.

For several popular modems, Cisco provides CCL files that you can use as examples to modify your CCL scripts to support TACACS security. This section explains how to use the CCL files provided by Cisco with TACACS security.

Cisco recommends using the ARA Modem Toolkit provided through the AppleTalk Programmers and Developers Association (APDA); it provides both syntax checking and a script tester.

The Macintosh client uses ARA CCL scripts to establish point-to-point links with the modem to the AppleTalk network. When the connection has been established, the script ends and ARA is activated. TACACS authentication occurs after the connection is established and the ARA script ends, but before the ARAP protocol becomes active.

Insert TACACS logic just before the end of a script. The CCL TACACS logic performs the following user authentication tasks:

1. When the "Username:" prompt is received from the router, the TACACS server queries the user for a username, as shown in Figure 31–3.

*Figure 31–3*
*TACACS Login Screen on the Macintosh Computer.*

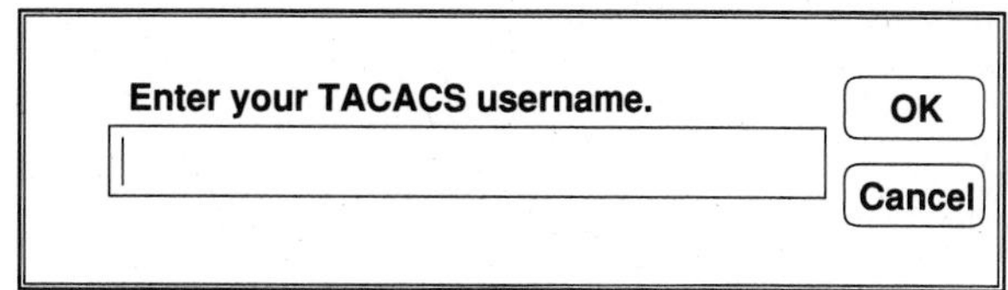


2. When the "Password:" prompt is received from the router, the TACACS server queries the user for a password, as shown in Figure 31–4.

*Figure 31–4*
*TACACS Password Screen on the Macintosh Computer.*

Enter your TACACS password.
OK
Cancel

3. After a successful login, indicated by an EXEC prompt, the **arap** EXEC command is executed.
4. The script ends and ARA is activated on the client.

CCL scripts control logical flow by jumping to labels. The labels are the numbers 1 through 128 and are not necessarily in sequential order in script files. The TACACS logic in the Cisco IOS software CCL files has label numbers from 100 through 127. In most environments, you can copy the complete TACACS logic from a sample file.

To create a new TACACS CCL file, perform the following steps:

**Step 1** Copy the TACACS logic from a sample CCL script into the new CCL script.

In most cases, you can insert the TACACS logic at the appropriate place in your CCL script. The one case that requires extra attention is when the original CCL script has labels that conflict with the logic in the new file. The labels must be resolved on a case-by-case basis, usually by changing the label numbers used in the original CCL script. Be sure to read the manual that comes with the Modem Toolkit before beginning.

**Step 2** Locate the logical end of the CCL script and insert the command **jump 100**.

You can locate the logical end of the script by following its flow. Most scripts have the following basic structure:

- Initialize the modem.
- Dial the number.
- Exit.

The characteristic logical end of the script is as follows:

```
@label N
! N is any integer between 1 and 128
if ANSWER N+1
! If we're answering the phone, jump directly
! to the label N+1
pause 30
! We're not answering the phone, therefore we
! must be calling. Wait three seconds for the
! modems to sync up.
@label N+1
exit 0
! quit and start up ARA
```

It is common in this case to replace "pause 30" with "jump 100." In fact, this is usually the only change made to the logic of the original CCL script.

See Chapter 5 for information about configuring a line to support your modem.

### Enable Kerberos Security for ARA Authentication

You can use Kerberos as an authentication method within ARA sessions. To do so, you configure Kerberos using the AAA/TACACS+ facility in the Cisco IOS software. Perform the following tasks in global configuration mode to enable Kerberos security:

| Task | Command |
|---|---|
| Define the name of the Kerberos realm in which the router is located. | **kerberos local realm** {*kerberos-realm*} |
| Define the DNS domain of the Kerberos realm in which the router is located. | **kerberos realm** {*dns-domain* \| *dns-host*} *kerberos-realm* |
| Display the contents of your credentials cache. | **show kerberos creds** |
| Delete the contents of your credentials cache. | **clear kerberos creds** |

### Use Access Lists To Control Access to AppleTalk Networks

An access list is a list of AppleTalk network numbers or zones that is maintained by the Cisco IOS software and used to control access to or from specific zones or networks.

## Connecting to an AppleTalk Network from a Client Running a Different Virtual Terminal Protocol

ARA can run on any point-to-point link, such as a Public Switched Telephone Network (PSTN) or an X.25 WAN. This permits remote Macintosh users to dial in to a remote network and access AppleTalk services (such as file sharing and printing). For example, you can enable a Macintosh client on the remote side of an X.25 WAN to connect to an AppleTalk network through the router.

To do so, you configure a virtual terminal (VTY) line on the router so that the client sees one of two scenarios:

- A client clicks **Connect** in an ARA application dialog box and connects to a VTY line on the router. ARA automatically starts up on the outgoing VTY line, and the client is connected to the AppleTalk network. This section describes how to configure the Cisco IOS software for this process.
- A client clicks **Connect** in an ARA application dialog box and connects directly through the router to the AppleTalk network. This process is described in the section "Configuring Tunneling of SLIP, PPP, or ARA," in Chapter 21, "Configuring Protocol Translation and Virtual Asynchronous Devices."

To enable ARA on VTY lines and enable clients running different virtual terminal protocols to connect to an AppleTalk network through the router, perform the following tasks, beginning in global configuration mode. The first four steps are required. The next eight steps (Steps 5 through 12) are optional. Step 5, Configure automatic protocol startup, dedicates the line to ARA.

| Task | Command |
|---|---|
| **Step 1** Turn on AppleTalk routing. | **appletalk routing** |
| **Step 2** Create an internal AppleTalk network. | **arap network** [*network-number*] [*zone-name*] |
| **Step 3** Enter line configuration mode. | **line vty** *line-number* [*ending-line-number*] |
| **Step 4** Enable ARA on a line. | **arap enable** |
| **Step 5** Configure automatic protocol startup. | **autocommand arap** |
| **Step 6** Set a dedicated ARA line. | **arap dedicated** |
| **Step 7** Set the session time limit. | **arap timelimit** [*minutes*] |
| **Step 8** Set the disconnect warning time. | **arap warningtime** [*minutes*] |
| **Step 9** Disallow guests. | **arap noguest** |
| **Step 10** Require manual password entry. | **arap require-manual-password** |
| **Step 11** Limit the zones the Macintosh user sees. | **arap zonelist** *zone-access-list-number* |
| **Step 12** Control access to networks. | **arap net-access-list** *net-access-list number* |

## Monitoring an ARA Server

To display information about a running ARA connection, perform the following task in privileged EXEC mode (reached by entering the **enable** command and a password):

| Task | Command |
|---|---|
| Display information about a running ARA connection. | **show arap** [*line-number*] |

The **show arap** command with no arguments displays a summary of ARA traffic since the router was last booted. The **show arap** command with a specified line number displays information about the connection on that line.

## Monitoring the AppleTalk Network

The Cisco IOS software provides several commands that you can use to monitor an AppleTalk network. In addition, you can use Apple Computer's Inter•Poll, a tool used to verify that a device is configured and operating properly. Use the commands described in this section to monitor an AppleTalk network using both Cisco IOS software commands and Inter•Poll.

To monitor the AppleTalk network, perform one or more of the following tasks:

| Task | Command |
|---|---|
| List the entries in the AppleTalk ARP table. | **show appletalk arp** |
| Display AppleTalk-related interface settings. | **show appletalk interface** [**brief**] [*type number*] |
| Display the status of all known MacIP clients. | **show appletalk macip-clients** |
| Display the status of MacIP servers. | **show appletalk macip-servers** |
| Display statistics about MacIP traffic. | **show appletalk macip-traffic** |
| Display the statistics about AppleTalk protocol traffic, including MacIP traffic. | **show appletalk traffic** |
| Display the contents of the zone information table. | **show appletalk zone** [*zone-name*] |

## Making ARA Connections

If you are a Macintosh user, you can use AppleTalk Remote Access (ARA) to connect to an AppleTalk network through a Cisco access server. The Cisco IOS Release 10.2 and later software support ARA 2.0 and ARA 1.0 so that you can remotely dial in through asynchronous network devices using ARA to access AppleTalk services (such as file sharing and printing) elsewhere on the network. For example, you can dial in from an X.25 network and connect to an AppleTalk network through a router. To enable ARA and dial-in access, configure a virtual terminal (VTY) line on the router. You can also configure ARA on TTY lines.

Because there are no user commands for connecting to the network from your Macintosh client, the process is not described in this book. To start a connection in most ARA client packages, you click the **Connect** button from within the client software.

## ARA Configuration Examples

This section contains the following examples of ARA configuration:

- Extended AppleTalk Network Configuration Example
- Extended Network in Discovery Mode Configuration Example

- ARA Configuration Example
- Connect to an AppleTalk Network over a Foreign Protocol Example
- Cable Range Expansion Example
- TACACS Username Authentication Configuration Examples
- Enable TACACS for ARA Authentication Examples
- Dedicated ARA Line Configuration Example
- Configure a Multiuse Line Example
- Configure Modified and Unmodified Scripts Example
- Configure an ARA Server Example
- Telebit T-3000 Modem Setup Example

### Extended AppleTalk Network Configuration Example

The following example configures the interface for an extended AppleTalk network. It defines the zones Orange and Brown. The cable range of one allows compatibility with nonextended AppleTalk networks.

```
appletalk routing
interface ethernet 0
 appletalk cable-range 1-1
 appletalk zone Orange
 appletalk zone Brown
```

### Extended Network in Discovery Mode Configuration Example

The following example configures an extended network in discovery mode. In Figure 31–5, access server A provides the zone and network number information to the interface when it starts.

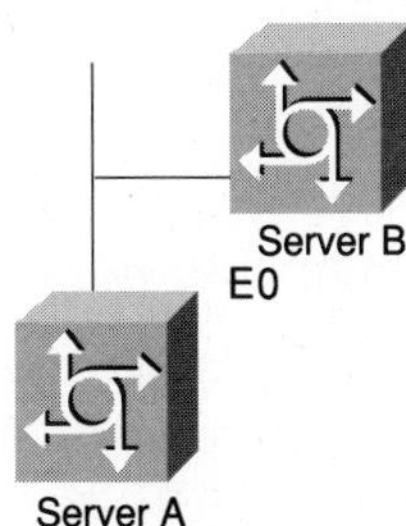


*Figure 31–5*
*Discovery Mode.*

Use the following commands to configure this extended network in discovery mode:

```
appletalk routing
interface ethernet 0
 appletalk cable-range 0-0 0.0
```

### ARA Configuration Example

The following example configures the router for ARA support, as described in the comments (lines beginning with an exclamation point [!]).

```
! Enable AppleTalk on the router
appletalk routing
!
interface Ethernet 0
 ip address 172.30.1.1 255.255.255.0
!
! On interface Ethernet 0, assign network number 103 to the physical cable and
! assign zone name "Marketing Lab" to the interface. Assign a zone name if
! you are creating a new AppleTalk internet. If the internet already exists,
! the zone and cable range must match exactly, or you can leave the cable
! range at 0 to enter discovery mode. The suggested AppleTalk
! address for the interface in this example is 103.1
interface Ethernet 0
 appletalk cable-range 103-103 103.1
 appletalk zone Marketing Lab
! Configure a username and password for the router.
username jake password sesame
! On lines 4 through 8, InOut modems are specified, the lines are configured
! to automatically start an EXEC session or enable AppleTalk, AppleTalk Remote
! Access Protocol is enabled, the modem speed is specified as 38400 bps, and
! hardware flow control is enabled.
line 4 8
 modem InOut
 autoselect
 arap enabled
 speed 38400
 flowcontrol hardware
```

**NOTES**

You must set your terminal emulator to match the speed that you set for the line.

### Connect to an AppleTalk Network over a Foreign Protocol Example

The following example enables a Macintosh client running ARA on a remote network to connect across an X.25 network, through the router, to an AppleTalk network. In this example, VTY lines 0 through 19 are configured for ARA.

```
appletalk routing
line vty 0 19
 arap enable
 autocommand arap
 arap dedicated
 arap timelimit 45
 arap warningtime 5
 arap noguest
 arap require-manual-password
 arap net-access-list 611
```

The Macintosh client connects to any VTY line from 0 through 19. When the EXEC prompt appears, ARA begins automatically on the line (because of the **autocommand arap** command). The VTY lines 0 through 19 are dedicated to ARA dial-in clients, and those clients have a 45-minute time limit. Five minutes before the line is disconnected, a warning message appears, indicating that the session will be disconnected in five minutes. Guest access is denied, and manual password entry is required. The AppleTalk access list 611 has been applied to the VTY lines, meaning that access to other networks through these VTY lines has been limited.

### Cable Range Expansion Example

In the following example, the cable range is changed, and the zone name is re-entered.

The initial configuration is as follows:

```
appletalk cable-range 100-103
appletalk zone Twilight Zone
```

The cable range is expanded as follows:

```
appletalk cable-range 100-109
```

At this point, you must re-enter the zone name as follows:

```
appletalk zone Twilight Zone
```

### TACACS Username Authentication Configuration Examples

In the following example for TACACS and Extended TACACS, line 1 is configured for ARA and username authentication is performed on a TACACS server:

```
line 1
 login tacacs
 arap enable
```

In the following example of AAA/TACACS+, line 1 is configured for ARA and username authentication is performed on a TACACS server:

```
line 1
 login authentication
 arap authentication
```

### Enable TACACS for ARA Authentication Examples

The following example shows regular TACACS enabled for ARA authentication:

```
line 3
 arap use-tacacs
```

The following example shows AAA/TACACS+ enabled for ARA authentication:

```
line 3
 aaa authentication arap
```

### Dedicated ARA Line Configuration Example

In the following example, line 2 is configured as a dedicated ARA line, user authentication information is configured on the ARA server, and guests are not allowed to make ARA sessions:

```
username jsmith password woof
line 2
```

```
arap dedicated
arap noguest
```

### Configure a Multiuse Line Example

In the following configuration, ARA is enabled on lines 2 through 16, username authentication is configured on the ARA server, and the lines are configured to automatically start an ARA session when an ARA user on a Macintosh attempts a connection:

```
username jsmith password woof
line 2 16
 autoselect
 arap enabled
 arap noguest
```

### Configure Modified and Unmodified Scripts Example

If you are currently using modified CCL scripts and want to migrate to nonmodified scripts, you can set your system to accept logins using both modified (CCL) and unmodified scripts by entering the following commands in line configuration mode:

```
autoselect arap
autoselect during-login
arap noguest if-needed
```

### Configure an ARA Server Example

The following example shows how to set up ARA functionality.

Log in to the router, use the **enable** command to enter your password if one is set, use the **configure** command to enter configuration mode, and add the following commands to your configuration:

```
appletalk routing
arap network 104 ARAP Dialin Zone
interface ethernet 0
 appletalk cable-range 0-0 0.0
! puts router in discovery mode
line 5 6
 modem inout
 speed 38400
 arap enabled
 autoselect
```

If you already know the cable-range and the zone names you need, include the information in the configuration file. If you do not know this information, perform the following steps to use the discovery mode to allow the Cisco IOS software to learn about the AppleTalk network:

**Step 1** Permit the Cisco IOS software to monitor the line for a few minutes.

**Step 2** Log in and enter configuration mode.

**Step 3** Show the configuration again (using the **show startup-config** command).

**Step 4** Note the **appletalk cable-range** and **appletalk zone** variables.

**Step 5** Manually add the information in those two entries and add any user accounts.

```
appletalk cable-range 105-105 105.222
appletalk zone Marketing Lab
username arauser password arapasswd
! Add as many users as you need
```

**Step 6** Save the configuration.

**Step 7** Show the configuration again (using the **show startup-config** command) to make sure the configuration is correct.

### Telebit T-3000 Modem Setup Example

The following example describes how to set up a Telebit T-3000 modem that attaches to a router, which supports hardware flow control. The Macintosh will use a CCL script to configure the attached modem.

**NOTES**

When you configure modems for ARA, turn off MNP4 error correction because it can cause connection failures for ARA 1.0 clients. For dedicated ARA lines, it is sufficient to turn off error correction completely in the modem; for multiuse lines it is preferable to leave all forms of non-MNP4 error correction enabled so that users of other protocols can achieve error-corrected connections. This restriction does not apply to installations that only receive calls from ARAP 2.0 clients.

Start with the modem at factory defaults. (The preferred configuration for hardware flow control is AT&F9.) Use the direct command if you have a terminal attached to the modem, or use the T/D Reset sequence described in the Telebit T-3000 manual to reset the modem to the &F9 defaults.

Attach a hardware flow control-capable cable between the modem and the device with which you are configuring the modem. (At this point, the modem is in hardware flow control mode, with auto-baud-rate-recognition, and can detect your speed between 300 and 38,400 bps at 8-N-1. However, the modem must receive the flow control signals from the device to which you have the modem attached.)

Send the modem the following commands:

```
ATS51=6 E0 Q1 S0=2 &D3 &R3 S58=2 &W
```

This sequence directs the modem to perform the following tasks:

- Lock your DTE interface speed to 38,400 bps.
- Turn "command echo" off.
- Do not send any result codes.
- Auto-answer on the second ring (Germany requires this, but elsewhere you can set it to answer on the first ring with "s0=1".)
- When DTR is toggled, reset to the settings in NVRAM.
- CTS is always enabled if hardware flow control is disabled.

- Use full-duplex RTS/CTS flow control.
- Write these settings to NVRAM.

At this point, if you press the Return key or enter characters, no characters appear on your screen because the result codes are turned off. You can determine whether the modem is working by getting a list of its configuration registers using the following command:

```
AT&V
```

After the modem is configured, connect it to the router with a modem-to-RJ45 adapter and an RJ-45 cable to the lines(s) that you plan to use.

The following Cisco IOS commands are compatible with the Telebit 3000 settings described in this section:

```
line 1 8
 arap enable
 autoselect
 no escape-character
 flowcontrol hardware
 modem dialin
 speed 38400
```

# CHAPTER 32

# AppleTalk Remote Access Commands

This chapter describes the commands used to configure your router to act as an AppleTalk Remote Access (ARA) server. The Cisco implementation of ARA gives remote Macintosh users direct access to information and resources on the network. Macintosh users can connect to another Macintosh computer or AppleTalk network over standard telephone lines. For example, if you have a PowerBook at home and need to get a file from your Macintosh at the office, ARA software can make the connection between your home computer and office computer.

This chapter does not describe how to configure or use the client Macintosh. Refer to the Apple Computer, Inc. *Apple Remote Access Client User's Guide* for information about how to use ARA software on your Macintosh. For ARA configuration tasks and examples, see Chapter 31, "Configuring AppleTalk Remote Access."

This chapter also does not describe how to configure AppleTalk routing, AppleTalk access lists, or other AppleTalk routing functions.

## ARAP AUTHENTICATION

To enable TACACS+ authentication for ARA on a line, use the **arap authentication** line configuration command. Use the **no** form of the command to disable authentication for an ARA line.

**arap authentication** {**default** | *list-name*}
**no arap authentication** {**default** | *list-name*}

| *Syntax* | *Description* |
|---|---|
| **default** | Use the default list created with the **aaa authentication arap** command. |
| *list-name* | Use the indicated list created with the **aaa authentication arap** command. |

### *Default*

ARAP authentication uses the default set with the **aaa authentication arap** command. If no default is set, the local user database is checked.

### *Command Mode*

Line configuration

### *Usage Guideline*

This command first appeared in Cisco IOS Release 10.3.

This command is a per-line command used with TACACS+, and specifies the name of a list of AAA authentication processes to try at login. If no list is specified, the default list is used (whether or not it is specified in the command line). Defaults and lists are created with the **aaa authentication arap** command. Entering the **no** version of **arap authentication** has the same effect as entering the command with the **default** argument.

Before issuing this command, create a list of authentication processes by using the global configuration **aaa authentication arap** command.

**NOTES**

If you use a *list-name* that is not configured using the **aaa authentication arap** command, you will disable ARAP on this line.

### *Example*

The following example specifies that the TACACS+ authentication list called MIS-access is to be used on ARA line 7:

```
line 7
 arap authentication MIS-access
```

### *Related Command*

Search online to find documentation for related commands.

**aaa authentication arap**

## ARAP DEDICATED

To configure a line to be used only as an ARA connection, use the **arap dedicated** line configuration command. Use the **no** form of the command to return the line to interactive mode.

**arap dedicated**
**no arap dedicated**

### *Syntax Description*

This command has no arguments or keywords.

*Default*

Disabled

*Command Mode*

Line configuration

*Usage Guidelines*

This command first appeared in Cisco IOS Release 10.0.

*Example*

The following example configures line 3 to be used only for ARA connections:

```
line 3
 arap dedicated
```



## ARAP ENABLE

To enable ARA for a line, use the **arap enable** line configuration command. Use the **no** form of this command to disable ARA.

**arap enable**
**no arap enable**

*Syntax Description*

This command has no arguments or keywords.

*Default*

Disabled

*Command Mode*

Line configuration

*Usage Guidelines*

This command first appeared in Cisco IOS Release 10.0.

*Example*

The following example enables ARA on a line:

```
line 3
 arap enable
```

*Related Commands*

Search online to find documentation for related commands.

**appletalk routing**
**autoselect**

## ARAP NET-ACCESS-LIST

To control Macintosh access to networks, use the **arap net-access-list** line configuration command. Use the **no** form of this command to return to the default setting.

**arap net-access-list** *net-access-list-number*
**no arap net-access-list** *net-access-list-number*

| *Syntax* | *Description* |
|---|---|
| *net-access-list-number* | One of the list values configured using the AppleTalk **access-list cable-range, access-list includes, access-list network, access-list other-access,** and **access-list within** commands. |

### *Default*

Disabled. The Macintosh has access to all networks.

### *Command Mode*

Line configuration

### *Usage Guidelines*

This command first appeared in Cisco IOS Release 10.0.

You can use the **arap net-access-list** command to apply access lists defined by the **access-list cable-range, access-list includes, access-list network, access-list other-access,** and **access-list within** commands.

You cannot use the **arap net-access-list** command to apply access lists defined by the **access-list zone** and **access-list additional-zones** commands.

### *Example*

In the following example, ARA is enabled on line 3 and the Macintosh will have access to the AppleTalk access list numbered 650:

```
line 3
 arap enable
 arap net-access-list 650
```

### *Related Commands*

Search online to find documentation for related commands.

**arap zonelist**

### ARAP NETWORK

To create a new network/zone and cause it to be advertised, use the **arap network** global configuration command. Use the **no** form of this command to prevent a new network/zone from being advertised.

**arap network** [*network-number*] [*zone-name*]
**no arap network**

| *Syntax* | *Description* |
|---|---|
| *network-number* | (Optional) AppleTalk network number. The network number must be unique on your AppleTalk network. This network is where all ARAP users appear when they dial in to the network. |
| *zone-name* | (Optional) AppleTalk zone name. |

*Default*

A new network or zone is not created.

*Command Mode*

Global configuration

*Usage Guidelines*

This command first appeared in Cisco IOS Release 10.0.

This is a required command. ARAP does not run without it in Cisco IOS Release 10.2 and above.

*Example*

The following example creates a new network/zone:

```
arap network 400 test zone
```

### ARAP NOGUEST

To prevent Macintosh guests from logging in to the router, use the **arap noguest** line configuration command. Use the **no** form of this command to remove this restriction.

**arap noguest [if-needed]**
**no arap noguest**

| *Syntax* | *Description* |
|---|---|
| **if-needed** | (Optional) Does not authenticate if the user already provided authentication. This allows users to log in as guests if they have already been authenticated through a username and/or password. |

*Default*

Disabled

*Command Mode*

Line configuration

*Usage Guidelines*

This command first appeared in Cisco IOS Release 10.0.

A guest is a person who connects to the network without having to give a name or a password.

**NOTES**

You should not use the **arap noguest** command if you are using modified (CCL) scripts and the **login tacacs** command.

*Example*

The following example prohibits guests from logging in to the router:

```
line 3
 arap enable
 arap noguest
```

### ARAP REQUIRE-MANUAL-PASSWORD

To require users to enter their password manually at the time they log in, use the **arap require-manual-password** line configuration command.

**arap require-manual-password**

*Syntax Description*

This command has no arguments or keywords.

*Default*

Disabled

*Command Mode*

Line configuration

*Usage Guidelines*

This command first appeared in Cisco IOS Release 11.1.

This command only works for ARAP 2.0 connections.

### *Example*

The following example forces users to enter their passwords manually at the time they log in, rather than use a saved password:

```
arap require-manual-password
```

### *Related Commands*

Search online to find documentation for related commands.

**enable password**
**login** (line configuration)
**password**



## ARAP TIMELIMIT

To set the maximum length of an ARA session for a line, use the **arap timelimit** line configuration command. Use the **no** form of this command to return to the default of unlimited session length.

**arap timelimit** [*minutes*]
**no arap timelimit**

| *Syntax* | *Description* |
|---|---|
| *minutes* | (Optional) Maximum length of time (in minutes) for a session. |

### *Default*

Unlimited session length

### *Command Mode*

Line configuration

### *Usage Guidelines*

This command first appeared in Cisco IOS Release 10.0.

After the specified length of time, the session will be terminated.

### *Example*

The following example specifies a maximum length of 20 minutes for ARA sessions:

```
line 3
 arap enable
 arap timelimit 20
```

### *Related Commands*

Search online to find documentation for related commands.

**arap warningtime**

### ARAP USE-TACACS

To enable TACACS for ARAP authentication, use the **arap use-tacacs** line configuration command. Use the **no** form of this command to disable TACACS for ARAP authentication.

**arap use-tacacs [single-line]**
**no arap use-tacacs**

| *Syntax* | *Description* |
| --- | --- |
| **single-line** | (Optional) Accepts the username and password in the username field. If you are using an older version of TACACS (before Extended TACACS), you must use this keyword. |

#### *Default*

Disabled

#### *Command Mode*

Line configuration

#### *Usage Guidelines*

This command first appeared in Cisco IOS Release 10.0.

This is a per-line command. Use this command only when you have set up an extended TACACS server. This command requires the new Cisco extended TACACS server.

**NOTES**

This command cannot be used with AAA/TACACS+. Use the **arap authentication** command instead.

The command specifies that if a username and password are specified in the username, separated by an asterisk (*), then a standard TACACS login query is performed using that username and password. If the username does not contain an asterisk, then normal ARAP authentication is performed using TACACS.

This feature is useful when integrating TACACS with other authentication systems that require a clear text version of the user's password. Such systems include one-time password systems, token card systems, and others.

**NOTES**

Normal ARAP authentications prevent the clear-text password from being transmitted over the link. When you use the **single-line** keyword, passwords cross the link in the clear, exposing them to anyone looking for such information.

Due to the two-way nature of the ARAP authentication, the ARA application requires that a password value be entered in the Password field in the ARA dialog box. This secondary password must be "arap." First enter the username and password in the form *username*password* in the Name field of the dialog box, then enter **arap** in the Password field.

### *Example*

The following example enables TACACS for ARAP authentication:

```
line 3
 arap use-tacacs
```

### *Related Commands*

Search online to find documentation for related commands.

**arap enable**
**arap noguest**
**autoselect**
**tacacs-server extended**
**tacacs-server host**



## ARAP WARNINGTIME

To set when a disconnect warning message is displayed, use the **arap warningtime** line configuration command. Use the **no** form of this command to disable this function.

**arap warningtime** [*minutes*]
**no arap warningtime**

| *Syntax* | *Description* |
|---|---|
| *minutes* | (Optional) Amount of time, in minutes, before the configured session time limit. At the configured amount of time before a session is to be disconnected, the router sends a message to the Macintosh client, which causes a warning message to appear on the user's screen. |

### *Default*

Disabled

### *Command Mode*

Line configuration

### *Usage Guidelines*

This command first appeared in Cisco IOS Release 10.0.

This command can only be used if a session time limit has been configured on the line.

### *Example*

The following example shows a line configured for 20-minute ARA sessions, with a warning 17 minutes after the session is started:

```
line 3
 arap enable
 arap dedicated
 arap timelimit 20
 arap warningtime 3
```

### *Related Commands*

Search online to find documentation for related commands.

**arap timelimit**

## ARAP ZONELIST

To control what zones the Macintosh client sees, use the **arap zonelist** line configuration command. Use the **no** form of this command to disable the default setting.

**arap zonelist** *zone-access-list-number*
**no arap zonelist** *zone-access-list-number*

**CAUTION**

Hiding a zone from a user is not the same as preventing them from sending and receiving packets from the networks that make up that zone. For true security, an **arap net-access-list** command must be issued to prevent traffic to and from those networks.

| *Syntax* | *Description* |
|---|---|
| *zone-access-list-number* | One of the *list* values configured using the AppleTalk **access-list zone** or **access-list additional-zones** commands. |

### *Default*

Disabled. The Macintosh will see all defined zones.

### *Command Mode*

Line configuration

### *Usage Guidelines*

This command first appeared in Cisco IOS Release 10.0.

You can use the **arap zonelist** command to apply access lists defined by the **access-list zone** and **access-list additional-zones** command.

You cannot use the **arap zonelist** command to apply access lists defined by the **access-list network** command.

### *Example*

In the following example, ARA is enabled on line 3, and the Macintosh will see only zones permitted by access list 650.

```
line 3
 arap enable
 arap zonelist 650
```

### *Related Commands*

Search online to find documentation for related commands.

**arap net-access-list**



## SHOW ARAP

To display information about a running ARAP connection, use the **show arap** user EXEC command.

**show arap** [*line-number*]

| *Syntax* | *Description* |
|---|---|
| *line-number* | (Optional) Number of the line on which an ARAP connection is established and active. |

### *Command Mode*

EXEC

### *Usage Guidelines*

This command first appeared in Cisco IOS Release 10.0.

Use the **show arap** command with no arguments to display a summary of the ARAP traffic since the router was last booted.

### *Sample Displays*

The following is sample output from the **show arap** command:

```
router# show arap

Statistics are cumulative since last reboot
Total ARAP connections: 2
Total Appletalk packets output: 157824
Total Appletalk packets input: 12465
```

These fields refer to the sum of all of the ARA connections since the box was last reloaded.

The following example results in a display of information about ARA activity on a specific line (line 3):

```
router# show arap 3

Active for 23 minutes
"Unlimited time left" or "22 minutes left"
"Doing smartbuffering" or "Smartbuffering disabled"
Appletalk packets output: 157824
Appletalk packets input: 12465
Appletalk packets overflowed: 1642
Appletalk packets dropped: 586
V42bis compression efficiency (incoming/outgoing): {percentage/percentage}
MNP4 packets received: 864
MNP4 packets sent: 1068
MNP4 garbled packets received: 4
MNP4 out of order packets received: 0
MNP4 packets resent: 0
MNP4 nobuffers: 0
```

Table 32–1 describes the fields shown in the display.

**Table 32–1** *Show ARAP Field Descriptions*

| **Field** | **Description** |
|---|---|
| Active for *integer* minutes | Number of minutes since ARAP started on the line. |
| Unlimited time left or *integer* minutes left | Remaining time limit on the line, if applicable on the line. |
| Doing smartbuffering or Smartbuffering disabled | Obsolete. Always says "Doing smartbuffering." |
| Appletalk packets output: | Number of AppleTalk packets that have been received from the Macintosh and out to the network during this connection. |
| Appletalk packets input: | Number of AppleTalk packets that have been received from the network and sent to the Macintosh during this connection. |
| Appletalk packets overflowed: | Number of packets from the network that have been dropped because the link to the Macintosh was congested. |
| Appletalk packets dropped: | Number of packets from the network that have been dropped because it was unnecessary to pass them (frequently RTMP). |

**Table 32–1** *Show ARAP Field Descriptions, Continued*

| Field | Description |
|---|---|
| V42bis compression efficiency (incoming/outgoing): | Performance of the v42bis protocol underneath ARA, expressed as percentage of incoming/percentage outgoing. If the efficiency is low, a network user is probably copying already compressed files across the link. Generally, low efficiency means slow performance. |
| MNP4 packets received: | Number of link-level packets that have been received from the Macintosh. |
| MNP4 packets sent: | How many link-level packets have been sent to the Macintosh. |
| MNP4 garbled packets received: | Number of garbled packets that have been received from the Macintosh. |
| MNP4 out of order packets received: | Number of out-of-order packets that have been received from the Macintosh. |
| MNP4 packets resent: | Number of times packets have been resent.* |
| MNP4 nobuffers: | How many times MNP4 has run out of buffers. This field should be zero. |

* *Each of these fields indicates line noise. The higher the value, the higher the noise.*

**PART 4**

# Dial Authentication

CHAPTER 33

# Configuring Authentication

Using the AAA facility, you can authenticate users with either a local or a remote security database. For more information about what a local and remote security database are, see Chapter 34, "Local versus Remote Server Authentication."

Whether you maintain a local or remote security database, or use TACACS+ or RADIUS authentication and authorization, the process of configuring the access server for these different databases and protocols is similar. The basic process of configuring the Cisco IOS software for authentication requires the following tasks:

1. Securing Access to Privileged EXEC and Configuration Mode
2. Enabling Communication between the Access Server and the Security Server
3. Configuring Authentication on a TACACS+ Server
4. Enabling AAA Globally on the Access Server
5. Defining Authentication Method Lists
    - Issue the aaa authentication Command
    - Specify Protocol or Login Authentication
    - Identify a List Name
    - Specify the Authentication Method
    - Populate the Local Username Database if Necessary
6. Applying Authentication Method Lists to Lines and Interfaces
    - Apply login lists to VTY lines and the console port
    - Apply authentication lists to asynchronous or ISDN *interfaces* configured for PPP
    - Apply authentication lists asynchronous (TTY) *lines* configured for ARA

## SECURING ACCESS TO PRIVILEGED EXEC AND CONFIGURATION MODE

The first thing you secure is access to privileged EXEC (enable) mode. Enable mode provides access to configuration mode, which enables any type of configuration change to the access server. To secure Privileged EXEC mode, use one of the commands listed in Table 33–1:

**Table 33–1** *Commands Used to Secure Access to Privileged EXEC Mode*

| Task | Command |
|---|---|
| Requires that network administrators enter a password to access privileged EXEC mode. Do not provide access to non-administrators. | **enable password** *password* |
| Specifies a secret password that is encrypted, so that the password cannot be read when crossing a network. After you issue this command, the encryption cannot be reversed. The encrypted version of the password appears in output of the **show running-config** and **show startup-config** commands. The enable secret password has precedence over the enable password. Do not enter the same password as the enable password. If the two passwords are the same, the enable secret password is not a secret, because the enable password appears in output of **show running-config** and **show startup-config** commands. | **enable secret** *password* |

**CAUTION**

If you use the **enable secret** command and specify an encryption type, you *must* enter the *encrypted version* of a specific password. Do not enter the cleartext version of the password after specifying an encryption type. You must comply with the following procedure when you specify an encryption type or you will be locked irretrievably out of privileged EXEC (enable) mode. The only way to regain access to privileged EXEC mode will be to erase the contents of NVRAM, erase your entire configuration, and reconfigure the router.

To enter an encryption type with the **enable secret** command, perform the following steps:

**Step 1** From within global configuration mode, enter the **enable secret** command, followed by the cleartext password that you will use to gain access to privileged EXEC mode. Do not specify an encryption type.

**Step 2** Exit from global configuration mode and enter the command **show running-config** to view the encrypted version of the password. The following example illustrates these first two steps:

```
router(config)# enable secret mypassword
router(config)# exit
router# show running-config
Building configuration...
```

```
Current configuration:
!
version 11.1
! some of the configuration skipped
enable secret 5 $1$h7dd$VTNs4.BAfQMUU0Lrvw6570
! the rest of the configuration skipped
```

**Step 3** At this point, select and copy the encrypted password following `enable secret 5` in the configuration output, which is `$1$h7dd$VTNs4.BAfQMUU0Lrvw6570`.

**Step 4** Enter global configuration mode and enter the **enable secret** command, followed by the encryption type (5 is the only valid encryption type for **enable secret**), then paste in the encrypted version of the password, as shown in the following example:

```
router(config)# enable secret 5 $1$h7dd$VTNs4.BAfQMUU0Lrvw6570
```

**Step 5** Exit from global configuration mode and copy the running configuration to NVRAM.

```
router(config)# exit
router# copy running-config startup-config
```

You can also specify additional protection for privileged EXEC mode, including the following:

- Privilege levels for Cisco IOS commands
- Privileged EXEC passwords for different privilege levels
- Privilege levels for specific lines on the access server
- Encrypt passwords using **service password-encryption**

## Enabling Communication between the Access Server and the Security Server

This section describes the Cisco IOS software commands that enable the access server to communicate with a security server. This process is similar for communicating with TACACS+ and RADIUS servers, and the following sections describe the process.

If you are using local authentication, refer to the section "Enabling AAA Globally on the Access Server," later in this chapter.

If you are using a remote security server for authentication and authorization, you must configure the security server before performing the tasks described in this chapter. The section "Comprehensive Security Examples," later in this chapter shows some typical TACACS+ and RADIUS server entries corresponding to the access server security configurations.

### Communicating with a TACACS+ Server

To enable communication between the TACACS+ security (database) server and the access server, issue the commands listed in Table 33–2 in global configuration mode.

**Table 33–2** *Commands for Communicating with a TACACS+Server*

| Task | Command |
|---|---|
| Specifies the IP address or the host name of the remote TACACS+ server host. This host is typically a UNIX system running TACACS+ software. | **tacacs-server host** {*hostname* \| *ip-address*} |
| Specifies a shared secret text string used between the access server and the TACACS+ server. The access server and TACACS+ server use this text string to encrypt passwords and exchange responses. | **tacacs-server key** *shared-secret-text-string* |

For example, to enable the remote TACACS+ server to communicate with the access server, enter the commands as follows:

```
router# configure terminal
router(config)# tacacs-server host alcatraz
router(config)# tacacs-server key abra2cad
```

The host name of the TACACS+ server in the previous example is alcatraz. The key (**abra2cad**) in the previous example is the encryption key shared between the TACACS+ server and the access server.

## Communicating with a RADIUS Server

To enable communication between the RADIUS security (database) server and the access server, issue the commands listed in Table 33–3 in global configuration mode.

**Table 33–3** *RADIUS Server Commands*

| Task | Command |
|---|---|
| Specifies the IP address or the host name of the remote RADIUS server host. This host is normally a UNIX system running RADIUS software. | **radius-server host** {*hostname* \| *ip-address*} |
| Specifies a shared secret text string used between the router and the RADIUS server. The router and RADIUS server use this text string to encrypt passwords and exchange responses. | **radius-server key** *shared-secret-text-string* |

For example, to enable the remote RADIUS server to communicate with the access server, enter the commands as follows:

```
router# configure terminal
router(config)# radius-server host alcatraz
router(config)# radius-server key abra2cad
```

The host name of the RADIUS server in the previous example is alcatraz. The key (**abra2cad**) in the previous example is the encryption key shared between the RADIUS server and the access server.

You can use any of the following optional commands to interact with the RADIUS server host:

- **radius-server retransmit** *number*

  This command specifies the number of times that the router transmits each RADIUS request to the server before the router gives up.

- **radius-server timeout** *seconds*

  This command specifies the number of seconds that an access server waits for a reply to a RADIUS request before the access server retransmits the request. The default is five seconds. If the RADIUS server's response is slow (because of support for a large number of users or large network latency), increase the timeout value.

## CONFIGURING AUTHENTICATION ON A TACACS+ SERVER

On most TACACS+ security servers, there are three ways to authenticate a user for login:

- Include a cleartext (DES) password for a user or for a group the user is a member of (each user can belong to only one group). Note that AppleTalk Remote Access Protocol (ARAP), Challenge Handshake Authentication Protocol (CHAP), and global user authentication must be specified in cleartext.

  The following is the configuration for global authentication:

  ```
  user = pierre {
                  global = cleartext "pierre global password"
  }
  ```

  To assign different passwords for ARAP, CHAP, and a normal login, you must enter a string for each user that specifies the security protocols, whether the password is cleartext, and if it authentication is performed via a DES card. The following example shows a user (carol), who has authentication configured for ARAP, CHAP, and login. Her ARAP and CHAP passwords, "arap password" and "chap password," are shown in cleartext. Her login password has been encrypted.

  ```
  user = carol {
          arap  = cleartext "arap password"
          chap  = cleartext "chap password"
          login = des XQj4892fjk
  }
  ```

- Use password (5) files instead of entering the password into the configuration file directly.

  The default authentication is to deny authentication. You can change this at the top level of the configuration file to have the default use passwd(5) file, by issuing the following command:

  ```
  default authentication = /etc/passwd
  ```

- Authenticate using an s/key. If you have built and linked in an s/key library and compiled TACACS+ to use the s/key, you can specify that a user be authenticated via the s/key, as shown in the following example:

  ```
  user= fred {
  login = skey
  }
  ```

On the access server, you configure authentication on all lines including the VTY and console lines by entering the following commands, beginning in privileged EXEC mode:

```
router# configure terminal
router(config)# aaa new-model
router(config)# aaa authentication login default tacacs+ enable
```

**CAUTION**

When you issue the **aaa authentication login default tacacs+ enable** command, you are specifying that if your TACACS+ server fails to respond (because it is set up incorrectly), you can log in to the access server by using your enable password. If you do not have an enable password set on the router, you will not be able to log in to it until you have a functioning TACACS+ daemon configured with usernames and passwords. The enable password in this case is a last-resort authentication method. You also can specify **none** as the last-resort method, which means that no authentication is required if all other methods failed.

## Enabling AAA Globally on the Access Server

To use the authentication, authorization, and accounting (AAA) security facility in the Cisco IOS software, you must issue the **aaa new-model** command from global configuration mode.

When you issue the **aaa new-model** command, all lines on the access server receive the implicit **login authentication default** method list, and all interfaces with Point-to-Point Protocol (PPP) enabled have an implicit **ppp authentication pap default** method list applied.

**CAUTION**

If you intend to authenticate users via a security server, make sure you do not inadvertently lock yourself out of the access server ports after you issue the **aaa new-model** command. Enter line configuration mode and issue the **aaa authentication login default tacacs+ enable** global configuration command. This command specifies that if your TACACS+ (or RADIUS) server is not functioning properly, you can enter your enable password to log in to the access server. In general, make sure you have a last-resort access method before you are certain that your security server is set up and functioning properly. For more information about the **aaa authentication** command, see the section "Defining Authentication Method Lists," later in this chapter.

**NOTES**

Cisco recommends that you use CHAP authentication with PPP, rather than Password Authentication Protocol (PAP). CHAP passwords are encrypted when they cross the network, whereas PAP passwords are cleartext when they cross the network. The Cisco IOS software selects PAP as the default, so you must manually select CHAP. The process for specifying CHAP is described in the section "Applying Authentication Method Lists," later in this chapter.

For example, enter the following commands to enable AAA in the Cisco IOS software:

```
router# configure terminal
router(config)# aaa new-model
```

## Defining Authentication Method Lists

After you enable AAA globally on the access server, you need to define authentication method lists, which you then apply to lines and interfaces. These authentication method lists are security profiles that indicate the protocol (ARAP or PPP) or login and authentication method (TACACS+, RADIUS, or local authentication).

To define an authentication method list, perform the following steps, which are described in this section:

1. Issue the **aaa authentication** command.
2. Specify protocol (ARAP or PPP) or login authentication.
3. Identify a list name or **default.** A list name is any alphanumeric string you choose. You assign different authentication methods to different named lists.
4. Specify the authentication method. You can specify multiple methods, such as **tacacs+**, followed by **local** in case a TACACS+ server is not available on the network.
5. Populate the local username database if you specified **local** as the authentication method (or one of the authentication methods). To use a local username database, you must issue the **username** global configuration command. See the section "Populate the Local Username Database if Necessary," a little later in this chapter.

After you define these authentication method lists, you apply them to one of the following:

- Lines—VTY lines or the console port for login and asynchronous lines (in most cases) for ARA
- Interfaces—Asynchronous or ISDN interfaces configured for PPP

See the section "Applying Authentication Method Lists," later in this chapter for information on how to apply these lists.

### Issue the aaa authentication Command

To define an authentication method list, start by issuing the **aaa authentication** global configuration command, as shown in the following example:

```
router# configure terminal
router(config)# aaa authentication
```

### Specify Protocol or Login Authentication

After you issue **aaa authentication**, you must specify one of the following dial-in protocols as applicable for your network:

- If you are enabling dial-in PPP access, specify **ppp**
- If you are enabling dial-in ARA access, specify **arap**
- If you are enabling users to connect to the EXEC facility, specify **login**

You can specify only one dial-in protocol per authentication method list. However, you can create multiple authentication method lists with each of these options. You must give each list a different name, as described in the next section, "Identify a List Name."

If you specify the **ppp** option, the default authentication method for PPP is PAP. For greater security, specify CHAP. The full command is **aaa authentication ppp chap**. If you specify the **arap** option, the authentication method built in to ARA is used. The full command is **aaa authentication arap**.

For example, if you specify PPP authentication, the configuration thus far looks like this:

```
router# configure terminal
router(config)# aaa authentication ppp
```

### Identify a List Name

A list name identifies each authentication list. You can choose either to use the keyword **default**, or choose any other name that describes the authentication list. For example, you might give it the name isdn-radius if you intend to apply it to interfaces configured for ISDN and RADIUS authentication. The list name can be any alphanumeric string. Use **default** as the list name for most lines and interfaces, and use different names on an exception basis.

You can create different authentication method lists and apply them to lines and interfaces selectively. You can even create a named authentication method list that you do not apply to a line or interface, but which you intend to apply at some later point, such as when you deploy a new login method for users.

After you define a list name, you must identify additional security attributes (such as local authentication versus TACACS+ or RADIUS).

In the following example, the default authentication method list for PPP dial-in clients uses the local security database:

```
router# configure terminal
router(config)# aaa authentication ppp default
```

In the following example, the PPP authentication method list name is insecure:

```
router# configure terminal
router(config)# aaa authentication ppp insecure
```

In the following example, the ARA authentication method list name is callback (because asynchronous callback is used on the access server):

```
router# configure terminal
router(config)# aaa authentication arap callback
```

In the following example, the login authentication method list name is deveng:

```
router# configure terminal
router(config)# aaa authentication login deveng
```

### Specify the Authentication Method

After you identify a list name, you must specify an authentication method. An authentication method identifies how users are authenticated. For example, will users be authenticated by a local security database resident on the access server (local method)? Will they be authenticated by a remote security database, such as a TACACS+ or RADIUS daemon? Will guest access to an AppleTalk network be permitted?

Authentication methods are defined with optional keywords in the **aaa authentication** command. The available authentication methods for PPP are described in Table 33–4. The available authentication methods for ARA are described in Table 33–5.

**Table 33–4** *PPP Authentication Methods*

| Authentication Methods for PPP | Purpose |
|---|---|
| if-needed | Authenticates only if not already authenticated. No duplicate authentication. |
| krb5 | Specifies Kerberos 5 authentication. |
| local | Uses the local username database in the access server. Defined with the **username** global configuration command. |
| none | No authentication is required. Do not prompt for a username or password. |
| radius | Use RADIUS authentication as defined on a RADIUS security server. |
| tacacs+ | Use TACACS+ authentication as defined on a TACACS+ security server. |

**TIMESAVER**

If you are not sure whether you should use TACACS+ or RADIUS, here are some comparisons: TACACS+ encrypts the entire payload of packets passed across the network, whereas RADIUS only encrypts the password when it crosses the network. TACACS+ can query the security server multiple times, whereas a RADIUS server gives one response only and is therefore not as flexible regarding per-user authentication and authorization attempts. Moreover, RADIUS does not support authentication of ARA.

**Table 33–5** *ARA Authentication Mode*

| Authentication Methods for ARA | Purpose |
|---|---|
| auth-guest | Allows guests to log in only if they have already been authenticated at the EXEC. |
| guest | Allows guests to log in. |
| line | Uses the line (login) password for authentication. |
| local | Uses the local username database in the access server for authentication. This database is defined with the **username** global configuration command. |
| tacacs+ | Use TACACS+ authentication as defined on a TACACS+ security server. |

**NOTES**

RADIUS does not support ARA. If you want to authenticate Macintosh users with RADIUS, you must configure AppleTalk to run over PPP, which is referred to as ATCP.

You can specify multiple authentication methods for each authentication list. The following example authentication method list for PPP first queries a TACACS+ server, then a RADIUS server, then the local security database. Multiple authentication methods can be useful if you have multiple types of security servers on the network and one or more types of security servers do not respond:

```
router(config)# aaa authentication ppp testbed tacacs+ radius local
```

If you specify more than one authentication method and the first method (TACACS+ in the previous example) is not available, the Cisco IOS software attempts to authenticate using the next method (such as RADIUS). If in the previous example the RADIUS server has no information about the user, or if no RADIUS server can be found, the user is authenticated using the local username database that was populated with the **username** command.

However, if authentication *fails* using the first method listed, the Cisco IOS software does *not* permit access. It does not attempt to authenticate using the subsequent security methods if the user entered the incorrect password.

## Populate the Local Username Database if Necessary

If you specify **local** as the security method, you must specify username profiles for each user who might log in. An example of specifying local authentication is as follows:

```
router(config)# aaa authentication login deveng local
```

This command specifies that any time a user attempts to log in to a line on an access server, the Cisco IOS software checks the username database. To create a local username database, define username profiles using the **username** global configuration command.

The following example shows how to use the **username** command for a user gmcmilla with password n1vriti:

```
router(config)# username gmcmilla password n1vriti
```

The **show running-config** command shows the encrypted version of the password, as follows:

```
router# show running-config
Building configuration...

Current configuration:
!
version 11.1
! most of config omitted
username gmcmilla password 7 0215055500070C294D
```

**NOTES**

The Cisco IOS software adds the encryption type of 7 automatically for passwords. If you were to manually enter the number 7 to represent an encryption type, you must follow the 7 with the *encrypted* version of the password. If you specify the number 7, then enter a cleartext password, the user will not have access to the line, interface, or the network they are trying to access, and you must reconfigure the user's authentication profile.

## AUTHENTICATION METHOD LIST EXAMPLES

This section shows some examples of authentication lists.

### *Authentication Method List Examples for Users Logging In to the Access Server*

The following example creates a local authentication list for users logging in to any line on the access server.

```
router(config)# aaa authentication login default local
```

The following example specifies login authentication using RADIUS (the RADIUS daemon is polled for authentication profiles):

```
router(config)# aaa authentication login default radius
```

The following example specifies login authentication using TACACS+ (the TACACS+ daemon is polled for authentication profiles):

```
router(config)# aaa authentication login default tacacs+
```

### *Authentication List Examples for Dial-In Users Using ARA to Access Network Resources*

The following example creates a local authentication list for Macintosh users dialing in to an AppleTalk network through the access server.

```
router(config)# aaa authentication arap default local
```

The following example specifies that Macintosh users dialing in to an AppleTalk network through the access server be authenticated by a TACACS+ daemon:

```
router(config)# aaa authentication arap default tacacs+
```

The following example creates an authentication method list that does the following:

- Enables guest access if the guest has been authenticated at the EXEC facility.
- Queries a TACACS+ daemon for authentication.
- Polls the line (login) authentication password if the TACACS+ server has no information about the user or if no TACACS+ server on the network responds.
- Uses the local security database if there is no line password.

```
aaa authentication arap default auth-guest tacacs+ line local
```

### Authentication Method List Examples for Users Dialing In Using PPP

The following example creates a TACACS+ authentication list for users connecting to interfaces (such as ISDN BRI or asynchronous interfaces) configured for dial-in using PPP. The name of the list is marketing. This example specifies that a remote TACACS+ daemon be used as the security database. If this security database is not available, the Cisco IOS software then polls the RADIUS daemon. Users are not authenticated if they are already authenticated on a TTY line.

```
aaa authentication ppp marketing if-needed tacacs+ radius
```

In this example, **default** can be substituted for **marketing** if the administrator wants this list to be the default list.

## APPLYING AUTHENTICATION METHOD LISTS

As described previously in the section "Defining Authentication Method Lists," the **aaa authentication** global configuration command creates authentication method lists or profiles. You apply these authentication method lists to lines or interfaces by issuing the **login authentication**, **arap authentication**, or **ppp authentication** command, as described in Table 33–6.

**Table 33–6** *Line and Interface Authentication Method Lists*

| Interface and Line Command | Action | Port to Which List is Applied | Corresponding Global Configuration Command |
|---|---|---|---|
| login authentication | Logs directly in to the access server | Console Port or VTY lines | aaa authentication login |
| arap authentication | Uses ARA to access AppleTalk network resources | TTY line | aaa authentication arap |
| ppp authentication* | Uses PPP to access IP or IPX network resources | Interface (asynchronous, ISDN, or other WAN) | aaa authentication ppp |

* If you issued the **ppp authentication** command, you must specify either CHAP or PAP authentication. PAP is enabled by default, but Cisco recommends that you use CHAP because CHAP is more secure.

You can create more than one authentication list or profile for login and protocol authentication and apply them to different lines or interfaces. The following examples show the line or interface authentication commands that correspond to the **aaa authentication** global configuration command.

### Login Authentication Examples

The following example shows the default login authentication list applied to the console port and the default virtual terminal (VTY) lines on the access server:

```
aaa authentication login default local
line console 0
```

```
login authentication default
line vty 0 4
login authentication default
```

In the following example, the login authentication list named rtp2-office, which uses RADIUS authentication, is created. It is applied to all 40 lines on a Cisco 2509 access server, including the console (CTY) port, the 8 physical asynchronous (TTY) lines, the auxiliary (AUX) port, and 30 virtual terminal (VTY) lines:

```
aaa authentication login rtp2-office radius
line 0 39
 login authentication rtp2-office
```

The following sample output shows lines and their status on the access server:

```
2509#show line
 Tty Typ      Tx/Rx       A Modem  Roty AccO AccI  Uses    Noise   Overruns
 *  0 CTY                 -   -      -    -    -      0        0        0/0
 *  1 TTY  57600/57600    - inout    -    -    -      0        0        0/0
...
I   8 TTY 115200/115200   - inout    -    -    -      0        0        0/0
    9 AUX  38400/38400    -   -      -    -    -      0        0        0/0
   10 VTY                 -   -      -    -    -      0        0        0/0
...
   39 VTY                 -   -      -    -    -      0        0        0/0
```

### ARA Authentication Example

In the following example, the ARA authentication list bldg-d-list is created, then applied to lines 1 through 16 (the physical asynchronous lines) on a Cisco 2511 access server:

```
aaa authentication arap bldg-d-list auth-guest tacacs+
line 1 16
 arap authentication bldg-d-list
```

### PPP Authentication Example

The following example creates the PPP authentication list marketing, which uses TACACS+, then RADIUS authentication. The list marketing requires authentication only if the user has not already been authenticated on another line. It is then applied to asynchronous lines 1 through 48 on a Cisco AS5200 access server and uses CHAP authentication, instead of the default of PAP:

```
aaa authentication ppp marketing if-needed tacacs+ radius
line 1 48
 ppp authentication chap marketing
```

## Comprehensive Security Examples

This series of examples shows complete security configuration components of a configuration file on an access server. Each of these examples shows authentication and authorization.

### Simple Local Security Example

This sample configuration uses AAA to configure default authentication using a local security database on the access server. All lines and interfaces have the default authentication lists applied. Users dellain, gmcmilla, and scottyin have been assigned privilege level 7, which prevents them from issuing the **ppp arap**, and **slip** commands, because these commands have been assigned to privilege level 8.

```
aaa new-model
aaa authentication login default local
aaa authentication arap default local
aaa authentication ppp default local
aaa authorization exec local
aaa authorization network local
aaa authorization
!
username dellain privilege exec level 7 privilege network level 8 password 7 095E470B1110
username gmcmilla privilege network level 7 password 7 0215055500070C294D
username scottyin privilege network level 7 password 7 095E4F10140A1916
!
privilege exec level 8 ppp
privilege exec level 8 arap
privilege exec level 8 slip
!
interface Group-Async1
 ppp authentication chap default
 group-range 1 16
!
line console 0
 login authentication default
!
line 1 16
 arap authentication default
!
```

With this configuration, the sign-on dialog from a remote PC appears as follows:

```
atdt5551234
CONNECT 14400/ARQ/V32/LAPM/V42BIS
User Access Verification
Username: dellain
Password:
Router> enable
Password:
Router#
```

## TACACS+ Security Example for Login, PPP, and ARA

The following example shows how to create and apply the following authentication lists:

- A TACACS+ server named dog-house is polled for authentication information (so you do not need to define a local username database). The shared key between the access server and the TACACS+ security server is shepard4:
- A login authentication list named rtp2-office is created, then applied to the console port.
- A PPP authentication list named marketing is created, then applied to group async interface 0, which includes asynchronous interfaces 1 to 16.
- An ARA list named park-central-office is created and applied to lines 1 to 16.

**NOTES**

The authentication method lists in this example use names other than default. However, you generally specify **default** as the list name for most lines and interfaces, and apply different named lists on an exception basis. These names are used only for illustrative purposes.

```
hostname router
!
tacacs-server host dog-house
tacacs-server key shepard4
!
aaa authentication login rtp2-office tacacs+
aaa authentication ppp marketing if-needed tacacs+
aaa authentication arap park-central-office tacacs+
!
line console0
 login authentication rtp2-office
!
interface group-async0
 ppp authentication chap marketing
 group-range 1 16
!
line 1 16
 arap authentication park-central-office
!
```

## RADIUS Example for Login and PPP

The following example shows how to create the following authentication lists:

- A RADIUS server named spike is polled for authentication information (so you do not need to define a local username database). The shared key between the access server and the RADIUS security server is BaBe218.
- A login authentication list named fly is created, then applied to all lines that users can log in to, except the console port. In this example, the console port is physically secure and does not need password protection. The access server is locked in a closet and secured behind a deadbolt lock.
- A PPP authentication list maaaa is created, then applied to group async interface 658, which includes asynchronous interfaces 1 to 16. CHAP authentication is used, because it is more secure than PAP.

```
radius-server host spike
radius-server key BaBe218
!
privilege exec level 14 configure
privilege exec level 14 reload
privilege exec level 8 arap
privilege exec level 8 ppp
!
aaa authentication login fly radius
```

```
aaa authentication ppp maaaa if-needed radius
aaa authorization network radius
aaa authorization exec radius
!
line 1 39
 login authentication fly
!
interface group-async658
 ppp authentication chap maaaa
 group-range 1 16
!
```

# CHAPTER 34

# Local Versus Remote Server Authentication

This chapter describes the differences between local and remote security databases and the basic authentication process for each. Remote security databases described in this chapter include Terminal Access Controller Access Control System (TACACS+) with Cisco proprietary enhancements and Remote Access Dial-In User Service (RADIUS).

Generally, the size of the network and type of corporate security policies and control determines whether you use a local or remote security database.

**NOTES**

This chapter does not provide an exhaustive security overview. For example, it does not describe how to configure TACACS, Extended TACACS, Kerberos, or access lists. It presents the most commonly used security mechanisms to prevent unauthenticated and unauthorized access to network resources through Cisco access servers.

Specifically, this chapter describes the following:

- Assumptions
- Local Security Database
- Remote Security Database

## ASSUMPTIONS

This chapter assumes the following:

- You know which network protocols you will allow access to your network. For example, you know if you will be allowing clients to dial in using modems to access IP, IPX, or AppleTalk networks, or whether clients will be using ISDN to access any of these networks.

- You are not an advanced user of the Cisco authentication, authorization, and accounting (AAA) security facility.

## Local Security Database

If you have one or two access servers providing access to your network, you probably want to store username and password security information on the Cisco access server itself. This is referred to as local authentication. A remote security server is not used. (See Figure 34–1.)

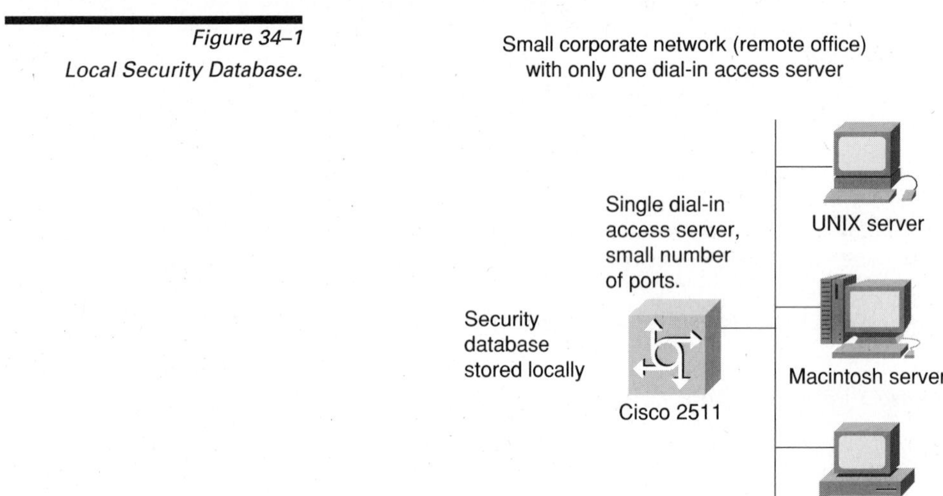


*Figure 34–1*
*Local Security Database.*

A local security database configured on the access server is useful if you have very few access servers providing network access. A local security database does not require a separate (and costly) security server.

## Remote Security Database

As your network or demand for dial access grows, you need a centralized security database that provides username and password information to each of the access servers on the network. This centralized security database resides in a security server, which allows you to more easily manage your security solution. (See Figure 34–2.)

An example of a remote security database server is the CiscoSecure product from Cisco Systems, Inc. CiscoSecure is a UNIX security daemon solution, with which the administrator creates a database that defines the network users and their privileges. CiscoSecure uses a central database that stores user and group profiles with authentication and authorization information.

The Cisco access server exchanges user authentication information with a TACACS+ or RADIUS database on the security server by transmitting encrypted TACACS+ or RADIUS packets across the network.

*Figure 34–2*
*Remote Security Database.*

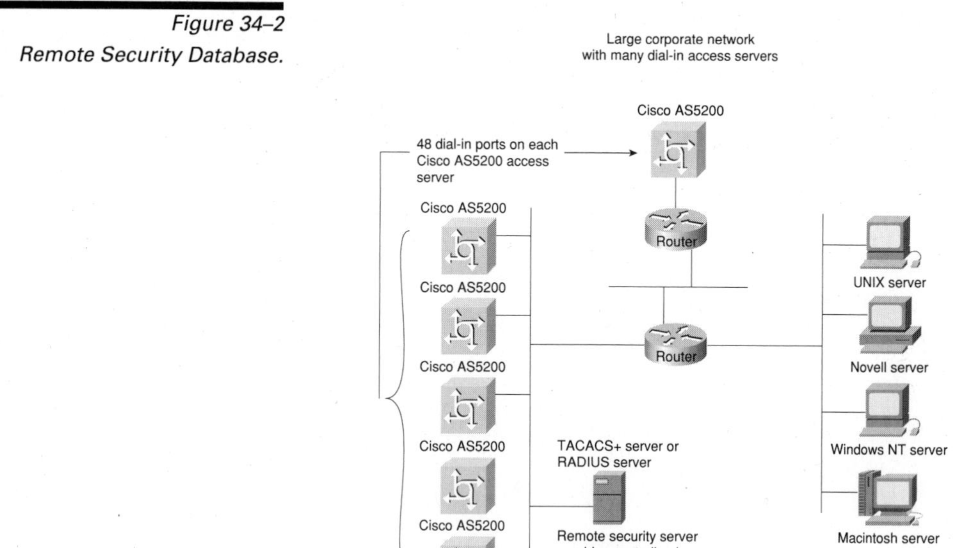


A remote, centralized security database is useful when you have a large number of access servers providing network access. It prevents having to update each access server with new or changed authentication and authorization information for potentially hundreds of thousands of dial-in network users. A centralized security database also helps establish consistent remote access policies throughout a corporation.

For more information about security databases and how to configure authentication, see Chapter 33, "Configuring Authentication."

CHAPTER 35

# Dial Authentication Commands

## LOGIN AUTHENTICATION

To enable AAA/TACACS+ authentication for logins, use the **login authentication** line configuration command. Use the **no** form of the command to return to the default.

**login authentication** [**default** | *list-name*]
**no login authentication** [**default** | *list-name*]

| *Syntax* | *Description* |
|---|---|
| **default** | Uses the default list created with the **aaa authentication login** command. |
| *list-name* | Uses the list specified. |

### *Default*

Login authentication uses the default set with **aaa authentication login** command. If no default is set, the local user database is checked. No authentication is performed on the console.

### *Command Mode*

Line configuration

### *Usage Guidelines*

This command first appeared in Cisco IOS Release 10.3.

This command is a per-line command used with AAA authentication and specifies a list of TACACS+ authentication processes that are tried at login. If no list is specified, the default list is used (whether or not it is specified in the command line). Defaults and lists are created with the **aaa authentication login** command. Note that entering the **no** version of **login authentication** has the same effect as entering the command with the **default** argument.

Before issuing this command, create a list of authentication processes with the **aaa authentication login** global configuration command.

**CAUTION**

If you use a *list-name* that has not been configured with the **aaa authentication login** command, you will disable logins on this line.

### *Examples*

The following example specifies that the default AAA authentication is to be used on line 4:

```
line 4
 login authentication default
```

The following example specifies that the AAA authentication list called MIS-access is to be used on line 7:

```
line 7
 login authentication MIS-access
```

### *Related Commands*

Search online to find documentation for related commands.

**aaa authentication login**

**PART 5**

# Dial-on-Demand Routing

CHAPTER 36

# Deciding and Preparing to Configure DDR

This chapter presents the decisions and preparations leading to a DDR configuration and shows where some advanced features fit into the DDR configuration steps. It distinguishes between the topology decisions and the implementation of the decisions. In the implementation phase, it distinguishes the DDR-independent decisions from the DDR-dependent decisions.

This chapter provides the following information:

- Decision Flowchart

  A flowchart of topology and implementation decisions you will need to make before you configure DDR

- Topology Decisions, DDR-Independent Implementation Decisions, and DDR-Dependent Implementation Decisions

  References to sources of detailed information for the configuration steps associated with each decision

- Global and Interface Preparations for DDR

  Brief description indicating which preparations are global and which are interface-specific.

- Preparations for Routing or Bridging over DDR

  A description of the required steps to be completed for bridging or routing over DDR.

For a complete description of the global dialer commands in this chapter, see Chapter 37, "DDR Preparation Commands."

## DECISION FLOWCHART

This section provides a flowchart of the decisions to be made before and while you configure DDR and notes to the flowchart.

Figure 36–1 presents the entire decision flowchart. The decision phases are shown in separate boxes. Numbers in parentheses refer to notes, which are located on the next page.

*Figure 36–1 Decisions and Implementation Flow to DDR.*

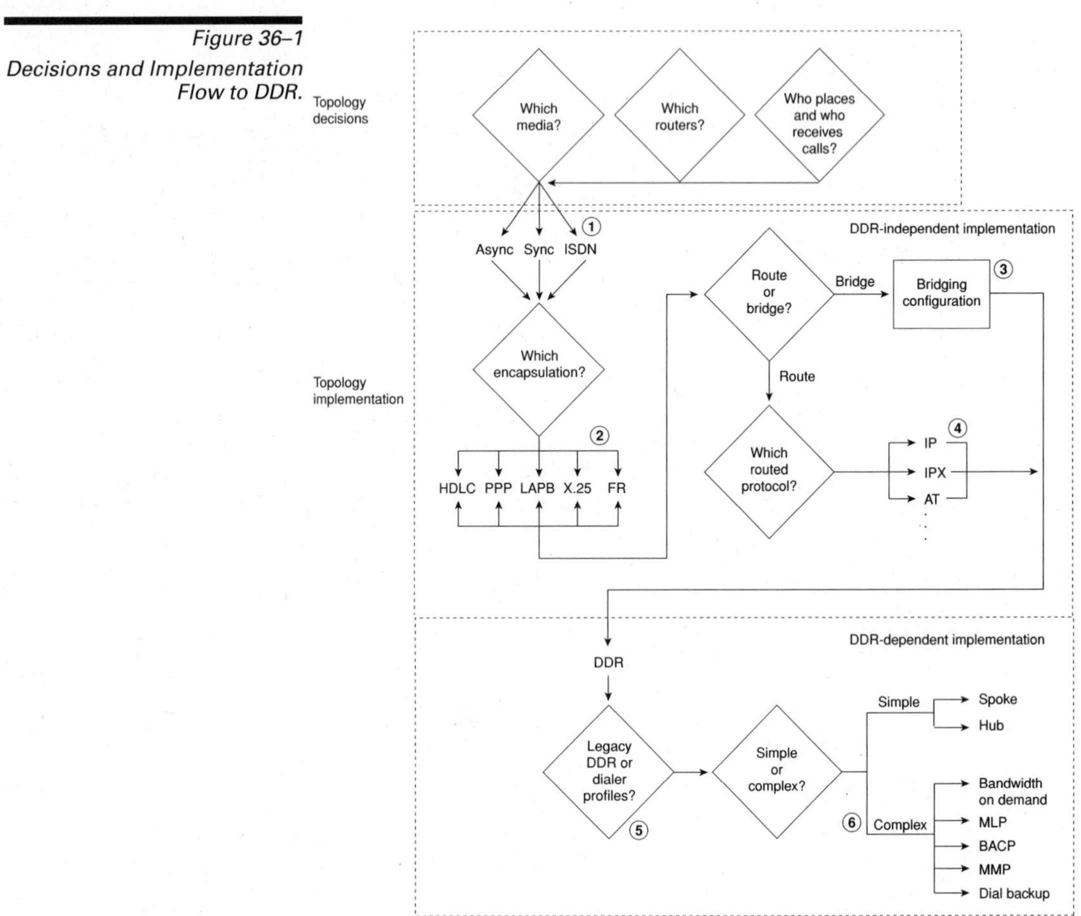


**Notes to the Flowchart.** The DDR chapters do not provide complete configuration information for most of the items in the following list. However, detailed information is available in other chapters. The numbers in this list correspond to the circled numbers in the flowchart.

1. Configuration of the dial port and interface. The port, line, and interface are expected to be configured and operational before you configure DDR. See the relevant chapters in Part II, "Dial-In Port Setup."
2. Encapsulation; including encapsulation for other wide-area networks. See Chapter 25, "Configuring Media-Independent PPP and Multilink PPP," for PPP encapsulation.
3. Bridging configurations.

4. Routed protocols to be supported. See the protocol-specific chapters in this book.
5. Dialer Profiles and Legacy DDR are described in various chapters of this part of the book, Part V, "Dial-on-Demand Routing."
6. Complex DDR configurations. See Chapter 25, as well as Part VIII, "Large-Scale Dial Solutions," and Part IX, "Cost-Control Solutions."

The DDR chapters provide complete configuration information about the simple spoke-and-hub DDR configurations, about the Dialer Profiles implementation of DDR, and about preparations required for configuring asynchronous interfaces for DDR.

## Topology Decisions

Topology decisions determine which routers will use DDR, which media and interfaces each one will use for DDR, and how each interface will function when using DDR. For example, if you choose a hub-and-spoke topology, one router will communicate with multiple routers. You must decide whether that router will use one interface or multiple interfaces for DDR, and whether it will receive calls only (forcing the spokes to initiate and bear the cost of calls). If it will use multiple interfaces, you must decide whether they will be of different types or the same type.

## DDR-Independent Implementation Decisions

DDR-independent implementation decisions include:

- Using a specific interface or combination of interfaces for DDR.

  For complete configuration steps for the various media and interfaces, see the chapters in Part II.

- Using nondefault encapsulations.

  The default encapsulation is HDLC. However, PPP is widely used for situations in which authentication is desired, especially situations in which an interface will receive calls from multiple sites. Detailed PPP encapsulation requirements are described in Chapter 25 and in Chapter 27, "Configuring Asynchronous PPP and SLIP."

  If you decide to send dial-on-demand traffic over Frame Relay, X.25, or LAPB networks, the interface must be configured with the appropriate encapsulation.

- Routing or bridging the DDR traffic.

  Legacy DDR supports bridging to only one destination, but Dialer Profiles supports bridging to multiple destinations.

  If you decide to bridge traffic over a dial-on-demand connection, configure the interface for transparent bridging.

- Supporting one or more specific routed protocols, if you decide to route traffic.

  Depending on the protocol, you do need to control access by entering access lists and decide how to support network addressing on an interface to be configured for DDR. You might also need to spoof keepalive or other packets.

## DDR-Dependent Implementation Decisions

You must decide whether to implement Legacy DDR or the newer Dialer Profiles; both are documented in this part of the book. You must also decide whether a simple DDR configuration meets your business needs or whether to add on other features.

### Dialer Profiles

The Dialer Profiles implementation of DDR is based on a separation between logical and physical interface configuration. Dialer Profiles also allows the logical and physical configurations to be bound together dynamically on a per-call basis.

Dialer Profiles is advantageous when you want to share an interface (ISDN, asynchronous, or synchronous serial) to place or receive calls, when you want to change any configuration on a per-user basis (except encapsulation in the first phase of Dialer Profiles), when you want to bridge to many destinations, and for avoiding the split-horizon problem.

Most routed protocols are supported; however, Frame Relay, ISO CLNS, and LAPB are not supported.

If you decide to configure Dialer Profiles, you must disable validation of source addresses for the routed protocols you support.

For detailed Dialer Profiles information, see Chapter 44, "Configuring Peer-to-Peer DDR with Dialer Profiles."

### Legacy DDR

Legacy DDR is powerful and comprehensive, but its limitations affect scaling and extensibility. Legacy DDR is based on a static binding between the per-destination call specification and the physical interface configuration.

However, Legacy DDR also has many strengths. It supports Frame Relay, ISO CLNS, LAPB, snapshot routing, and all routed protocols that are supported on Cisco routers. By default, Legacy DDR supports fast switching.

For information about simple Legacy DDR spoke configurations, see Chapter 40, "Configuring Legacy DDR Spokes." For information about simple Legacy DDR hub configurations, see Chapter 42, "Configuring Legacy DDR Hubs."

### Simple or Complex DDR Configuration

You must also decide whether to implement a simple DDR configuration—whether it is a simple point-to-point (spoke-to-spoke) layout or a simple hub-and-spoke layout—or to add on features that make the implementation more complex. Add-on features include dial backup, bandwidth on demand, application of the Bandwidth Allocation Control Protocol (BACP), Multilink PPP, and many others.

For information about add-on features, see the chapters in Part VIII and Part IX of this book.

## GLOBAL AND INTERFACE PREPARATIONS FOR DDR

Some preparations are global in nature, and some depend on the type of interface you will configure for DDR.

### Global Preparations

After you have made the required global decision whether to bridge or to route a specified protocol over a dial-on-demand link, you can make the following preparations:

- If you choose to bridge the protocol, decide whether to allow bridge packet access by Ethernet type codes or to permit all bridge packets across the link. Allowing access by Ethernet type codes requires you to define a bridging access list in global configuration mode.

  Allowing all bridge packets to trigger calls across a dial-on-demand link to a single destination is a DDR-dependent task addressed in the section "Configure Dialer Access Lists To Trigger Outgoing Calls," found in both Chapter 40 and Chapter 42.

  Bridging to multiple destinations requires Dialer Profiles.

- If you choose to route the protocol
    - Define one or more access lists for the selected routed protocol to determine which packets should be permitted or denied access to the dial-on-demand link.

      Allowing those packets to trigger calls across a dial-on-demand link is a DDR-dependent task addressed in the section "Configure Dialer Access Lists to Trigger Outgoing Calls," found in both Chapter 40 and Chapter 42.
    - Define an appropriate dialer list for the protocol.
    - Disable validation of source addresses, if you decide to configure Dialer Profiles.

### Preparations Depending on the Selected Interface Type

The steps shown in this chapter assume that you have also completed the required preparatory steps for the type of interface you will configure for DDR:

- The interface is installed, the cable is connected as needed, and operational.
- Chat scripts are ready, as needed, for any asynchronous interfaces and modem scripts have been assigned to the relevant asynchronous lines.
- Asynchronous lines and modems are configured and operational, as needed.
- Any ISDN line that will be used for DDR is properly provisioned and running.
- You have decided which interfaces and how many interfaces are to be configured for DDR, and what functions each interface is to perform.

## Preparations for Routing or Bridging over DDR

The following tasks are DDR-independent and can be completed before you configure DDR. Minimal tasks required for each item are presented in this chapter.

Complete the following minimal tasks for the global decisions you have made:

- Prepare for Transparent Bridging over DDR
- Prepare for Routing over DDR

### Prepare for Transparent Bridging over DDR

To prepare for transparent bridging over DDR, complete the tasks in the following sections:

- Define the Protocols To Bridge
- Specify the Bridging Protocol
- Control Bridging Access

#### *Define the Protocols To Bridge*

IP packets are routed by default unless they are explicitly bridged; all others are bridged by default unless they are explicitly routed. To bridge IP packets, complete the following task in global configuration mode:

| Task | Command |
|---|---|
| Disable IP routing. | **no ip routing** |

If you choose *not* to bridge another protocol supported on your network, use the relevant command to enable routing of that protocol.

#### *Specify the Bridging Protocol*

You must specify the type of spanning tree bridging protocol to use and also identify a bridge group. To specify the spanning tree protocol and a bridge group number, complete the following task in global configuration mode:

| Task | Command |
|---|---|
| Define the type of spanning tree protocol and identify a bridge group. | **bridge** *bridge-group* **protocol** {**ieee** \| **dec**} |

The bridge-group number is used when you configure the interface and assign it to a bridge group. Packets are bridged only among members of the same bridge group.

### *Control Bridging Access*

You can control access by defining any transparent bridge packet as *interesting*, or you can use the finer granularity of controlling access by Ethernet type codes.

To control access by Ethernet type codes, complete the following tasks in global configuration mode:

| Task | Command |
|---|---|
| Identify interesting packets by Ethernet type codes (access list numbers must be in the range 200–299). | **access-list** *access-list-number* {**permit** \| **deny**} *type-code* [*mask*] |
| Define a dialer list for the specified access list. | **dialer-list** *dialer-group* **protocol bridge list** *access-list-number* |

Packets with a specified Ethernet type code can trigger outgoing calls. Spanning tree bridge protocol data units (BPDUs) are always treated as *uninteresting* and cannot trigger calls.

To identify all transparent bridge packets as interesting, complete the following task in global configuration mode:

| Task | Command |
|---|---|
| Define a dialer list that treats all transparent bridge packets as interesting. | **dialer-list** *dialer-group* **protocol bridge permit** |

## Prepare for Routing over DDR

DDR supports the following routed protocols: AppleTalk, Banyan VINES, DECnet, IP, Novell IPX, ISO CLNS, and XNS.

To prepare for routing a protocol over DDR, perform the tasks in the relevant section:

- Configure the Protocol for Routing and Access Control
- Associate the Protocol Access List with a Dialer Group

### *Configure the Protocol for Routing and Access Control*

This section specifies the minimal steps required to configure a protocol for routing over DDR. For more options and more detailed descriptions, refer to the relevant protocol chapter.

#### *Configure IP Routing*

IP routing is enabled by default on Cisco routers; thus no preparation is required simply to enable it. You might, however, need to decide your addressing strategy and complete other global preparations for routing IP in your networks. To use dynamic routing where multiple remote sites communicate with each other through a central site, you might need to disable the IP split-horizon feature.

At a minimum, you must complete the following tasks.

- Disable validation of source addresses.
- Configure one or more IP access lists before you refer to the access lists in DDR **dialer-list** commands to specify which packets can trigger outgoing calls.

To disable validation of source addresses, complete the following tasks beginning in global configuration mode:

| Task | Command |
|---|---|
| Specify the routing protocol; RIP, for example. | **router rip** |
| Disable validation of source addresses. | **no validate-update-source** |
| Specify the IP address. | **network** *number* |

To configure IP access lists, perform one of the following tasks in global configuration mode:

| Task | Command |
|---|---|
| Specify an IP standard access list. | **access-list** *access-list-number* {**deny** \| **permit**} *source* [*source-mask*] |
| or | |
| Specify an IP extended access list. | **access-list** *access-list-number* {**deny** \| **permit**} *protocol source source-mask destination destination-mask* [*operator operand*] |

You can now also use simplified IP access lists that use the abbreviation *any* instead of the numeric forms of source and destination addresses and masks. Other forms of IP access lists are also available.

For an example of configuring DDR for IP, see Chapter 40 or Chapter 42.

You can configure IP routing on DDR asynchronous, synchronous serial, and ISDN interfaces, as well as dialer rotary groups.

### *Configure Novell IPX Routing*

To configure routing of IPX over DDR, you must complete both global and interface-specific tasks:

**Step 1** Enable IPX routing globally.

**Step 2** Enable IPX watchdog spoofing, or enable SPX keepalive spoofing on the interface.

To enable IPX routing, complete the following task in global configuration mode:

| Task | Command |
|---|---|
| Enable IPX routing. | **ipx routing** [*node*] |

To enable IPX watchdog spoofing on the interface, complete the following task in interface configuration mode:

| Task | Command |
|---|---|
| Enable IPX watchdog spoofing. | **ipx watchdog-spoof** |

To enable SPX keepalive spoofing, perform the following tasks in interface configuration mode:

| Task | Command |
|---|---|
| Enable SPX keepalive spoofing. | **ipx spx-spoof** |
| Set the idle time after which SPX spoofing begins. | **ipx spx-idle-time** *delay-in-seconds* |

You can configure IPX routing on DDR asynchronous, synchronous serial, and ISDN interfaces, as well as dialer rotary groups.

### *Configure AppleTalk Routing*

You must enable AppleTalk routing and then specify AppleTalk access lists. After you specify AppleTalk access lists, define dialer lists. Use the **dialer-list protocol** command to define permit or deny conditions for the entire protocol; for a finer granularity, use the **dialer-list protocol** command with the **list** keyword.

You can configure AppleTalk routing on DDR asynchronous, synchronous serial, and ISDN interfaces, as well as dialer rotary groups.

See Chapter 40 or Chapter 42 for more information and examples.

### *Configure Banyan VINES Routing*

To configure DDR for Banyan VINES, perform one of the following tasks in global configuration mode:

| Task | Command |
|---|---|
| Specify a VINES standard access list. | **vines access-list** *access-list-number* {**permit** \| **deny**} *source source-mask1* |
| or<br>Specify a VINES extended access list. | **vines access-list** *access-list-number* {**permit** \| **deny**} *source source-mask* [*destination*] [*destination-mask*] |

After you specify VINES standard or extended access lists, define DDR dialer lists. Use the **dialer-list protocol** command to define permit or deny conditions for the entire protocol; for a finer granularity, use the **dialer-list protocol** command with the **list** keyword. See Chapter 40 or Chapter 42 for more information and examples.

You can configure Banyan VINES on DDR asynchronous, synchronous serial, and ISDN interfaces, as well as dialer rotary groups.

**NOTES**

The Banyan VINES "neighbor" command is not supported for LAPB and X.25 encapsulations.

### *Configure DECnet Routing*

To configure DDR for DECnet, perform one of the following tasks in global configuration mode:

| Task | Command |
|---|---|
| Specify a DECnet standard access list. | **access-list** *access-list-number* {**permit** \| **deny**} *source source-mask1* |
| or<br>Specify a DEcnet extended access list. | **access-list** *access-list-number* {**permit** \| **deny**} *source source-mask* [*destination*] [*destination-mask*] |

After you specify DECnet standard or extended access lists, define DDR dialer lists. Use the **dialer-list protocol** command to define permit or deny conditions for the entire protocol; for a finer granularity, use the **dialer-list protocol** command with the **list** keyword. See Chapter 40 or Chapter 42 for more information and examples.

You classify DECnet control packets, including hello packets and routing updates, using one or more of the following commands: **dialer-list protocol decnet_router-L1 permit, dialer-list protocol decnet_router-L2 permit**, and **dialer-list protocol decnet_node permit.**

You can configure DECnet on DDR asynchronous, synchronous serial, and ISDN interfaces, as well as dialer rotary groups.

### *Configure ISO CLNS Routing*

To configure ISO CLNS for DDR, perform the following tasks, beginning in global configuration mode:

| Task | | Command |
|---|---|---|
| **Step 1** | Specify one or more CLNS filters, repeating this command as needed to build the filter list associated with the filter name. | **clns filter-set** *name* [**permit** \| **deny**] *template* |
| **Step 2** | Specify the interface to apply the filter to. | **interface** *type number* |
| **Step 3** | Filter CLNS traffic going out of the interface, on the basis of the filter specified and named in Step 1. | **clns access-group** *name* **out** |

After you complete these CLNS-specific steps, define a dialer list for CLNS. Use the **dialer-list protocol** command to define permit or deny conditions for the entire protocol; for a finer granularity, use the **dialer-list protocol** command with the **list** keyword. Use the *access-group* argument with this command, because ISO CLNS uses access groups but does not use access lists. See Chapter 40 or Chapter 42 for more information and examples.

You classify CLNS control packets, including hello packets and routing updates, using the **dialer-list protocol clns_is permit** and/or **dialer-list protocol clns_es permit** command.

You can configure ISO CLNS on DDR asynchronous, synchronous serial, and ISDN interfaces, as well as dialer rotary groups.

### *Configure XNS Routing*

You must enable XNS routing and then define an access list.

To define an XNS access list, perform one of the following tasks in global configuration mode:

| Task | Command |
|---|---|
| Specify a standard XNS access list. | **access-list** *access-list-number* {**deny** \| **permit**} *source-network*[*.source-address* [*source-address-mask*]] |

| Task | Command |
|---|---|
| or | [*destination-network*[*.destination-address* [*destination-address-mask*]]] |
| Specify an extended XNS access list. | **access-list** *access-list-number* {**deny** \| **permit**} *protocol* [*source-network*[*.source-host* [*source-network-mask.*]*source-host-mask*] *source-socket* [*destination-network* [*.destination-host* [*destination-network-mask.destination-host-mask*] *destination-socket*[**/pep**]]] |

After you specify an XNS access list, define a DDR dialer list. Use the **dialer-list protocol** command to define permit or deny conditions for the entire protocol; for a finer granularity, use the **dialer-list protocol** command with the **list** keyword. See Chapter 40 or Chapter 42 for more information and examples.

You can configure XNS on DDR asynchronous, synchronous serial, and ISDN interfaces, as well as dialer rotary groups.

### *Associate the Protocol Access List with a Dialer Group*

DDR supports the following routed protocols: AppleTalk, Banyan VINES, DECnet, IP, Novell IPX, ISO CLNS, and XNS.

You can permit or deny access by protocol, or you can specify an access list for more refined control. To associate a protocol or access list with a dialer group, perform the following task in global configuration mode:

| Task | Command |
|---|---|
| Associate a protocol access list number or access group name with the dialer group. | **dialer-list** *dialer-group* **protocol** *protocol-name* {**permit** \| **deny** \| **list** *access-list-number* \| *access-group*} |

**NOTES**

For a given protocol and a given dialer group, only one access list can be specified in the **dialer-list** command.

For the **dialer-list protocol list** command form, acceptable access list numbers are:

- Banyan VINES, DECnet, IP, and XNS standard and extended access list numbers
- Novell IPX standard, extended, and SAP access list numbers
- AppleTalk access lists numbers
- Bridge type codes

CHAPTER 37

# DDR Preparation Commands

This chapter describes the commands required to configure global dialer lists required for preparing the router to bridge or route over a dial-on-demand link.

For preparation tasks and examples, see Chapter 36, "Deciding and Preparing To Configure DDR."

## DIALER-LIST PROTOCOL

To define a DDR dialer list to control dialing by protocol or by a combination of a protocol and a previously defined access list, use the **dialer-list protocol** global configuration command. To delete a dialer list, use the **no** form of this command.

**dialer-list** *dialer-group* **protocol** *protocol-name* {**permit** | **deny** | **list** *access-list-number* | *access-group*}
**no dialer-list** *dialer-group* [**protocol** *protocol-name* [**list** *access-list-number* | *access-group*]]

| *Syntax* | *Description* |
|---|---|
| *dialer-group* | Number of a dialer access group identified in any **dialer-group** interface configuration command. |
| *protocol-name* | One of the following protocol keywords: **appletalk**, **bridge**, **clns**, **clns_es**, **clns_is**, **decnet**, **decnet_router-L1**, **decnet_router-L2**, **decnet_node**, **ip**, **ipx**, **vines**, or **xns**. |
| **permit** | Permits access to an entire protocol. |
| **deny** | Denies access to an entire protocol. |
| **list** | Specifies that an access list will be used for defining a granularity finer than an entire protocol. |

| | |
|---|---|
| *access-list-number* | Access list numbers specified in any DECnet, Banyan VINES, IP, Novell IPX, or XNS standard or extended access lists, including Novell IPX extended service access point (SAP) access lists and bridging types. See Table 37–1 for the supported access list types and numbers. |
| *access-group* | Filter list name used in the **clns filter-set** and **clns access-group** commands. |

### *Default*

No dialer lists are defined.

### *Command Mode*

Global configuration

### *Usage Guidelines*

This command first appeared in Cisco IOS Release 10.0. The **list** command and *access-list-number* and *access-group* arguments first appeared in Cisco IOS Release 10.3.

The various **no** forms of this command have the following effects:

- The **no dialer-list 1** command deletes all lists configured with list 1, regardless of the keyword previously used (**permit, deny, protocol,** or **list**).
- The **no dialer-list 1 protocol** *protocol-name* command deletes all lists configured with list 1 and protocol *protocol-name.*
- The **no dialer-list 1 protocol** *protocol-name* **list** *access-list-number* command deletes the specified list.

The **dialer-list protocol** form of this command permits or denies access to an entire protocol. The **dialer-list protocol list** form of this command provides a finer permission granularity and also supports protocols that were not previously supported.

The **dialer-list protocol list** form of this command applies protocol access lists to dialer access groups to control dialing using DDR. The dialer access groups are defined with the **dialer-group** command.

lists the access list types and numbers that the **dialer-list protocol list** command supports. The table does not include ISO CLNS because that protocol uses filter names instead of predefined access list numbers.

**Table 37–1** *Dialer-List Supported Access List Types and Numbers*

| Access List Type | Access List Number Range (decimal) |
|---|---|
| AppleTalk | 600–699 |
| Banyan VINES (standard) | 1–100 |
| Banyan VINES (extended) | 101–200 |
| DECnet | 300–399 |
| IP (standard) | 1–99 |
| IP (extended) | 100–199 |
| Novell IPX (standard) | 800–899 |
| Novell IPX (extended) | 900–999 |
| Transparent Bridging | 200–299 |
| XNS | 500–599 |

### *Examples*

Dialing occurs when an interesting packet (one that matches access list specifications) needs to be output on an interface. Using the standard access list method, packets can be classified as interesting or uninteresting. In the following example, IGRP TCP/IP routing protocol updates are not classified as interesting and do not initiate calls:

```
access-list 101 deny igrp 0.0.0.0 255.255.255.255 255.255.255.255 0.0.0.0
```

The following example classifies all other IP packets as interesting and permits them to initiate calls:

```
access-list 101 permit ip 0.0.0.0 255.255.255.255 0.0.0.0 255.255.255.255
```

Then the following command places list 101 into dialer access group 1:

```
dialer-list 1 protocol ip list 101
```

In the following example, DECnet access lists allow any DECnet packets with source area 10 and destination area 20 to trigger calls:

```
access-list 301 permit 10.0 0.1023 10.0 0.1023
access-list 301 permit 10.0 0.1023 20.0 0.1023
```

Then the following command places access list 301 into dialer access group 1:

```
dialer-list 1 protocol decnet list 301
```

In the following example, both IP and VINES access lists are defined. The IP access lists define IGRP packets as uninteresting, but permits all other IP packets to trigger calls. The VINES access lists do not allow Routing Table Protocol (RTP) routing updates to trigger calls, but allow any other data packets to trigger calls.

```
access-list 101 deny igrp 0.0.0.0 255.255.255.255 0.0.0.0 255.255.255.255
access-list 101 permit ip 0.0.0.0 255.255.255.255 0.0.0.0 255.255.255.255
!
vines access-list 107 deny RTP 00000000:0000 FFFFFFFF:FFFF 00000000:0000 FFFFFFFF:FFFF
vines access-list 107 permit IP 00000000:0000 FFFFFFFF:FFFF 00000000:0000 FFFFFFFF:FFFF
```

Then the following two commands place the IP and VINES access lists into dialer access group 1:

```
dialer-list 1 protocol ip list 101
dialer-list 1 protocol vines list 107
```

In the following example, a Connectionless Network Service (CLNS) filter is defined and then the filter is placed in dialer access group 1:

```
clns filter-set ddrline permit 47.0004.0001....
!
dialer-list 1 protocol clns list ddrline
```

### *Related Commands*

Search online to find documentation for related commands.

**access-list**
**clns filter-set**
**dialer-group**
**vines access-list**

# CHAPTER 38

# Preparing for Asynchronous DDR

This chapter describes the preparations to be completed before you configure an asynchronous interface for DDR.

Complete the preparations in the following sections:

- Configuring the Line
- Creating Chat Scripts
- Specifying Chat Scripts To Use on a Line

For a complete description of the global and line configuration commands in this chapter, see Chapter 39, "Asynchronous DDR Preparation Commands."

## CONFIGURING THE LINE

Before you configure an asynchronous interface to support DDR, configure the line as follows:

- Specify line speed.
- Set flow control on the line, if any.
- Specify the type of modem used on the line.

For detailed information about these tasks, see Chapter 5, "Configuring Modem Support and Asynchronous Devices."

You may also need to configure the asynchronous interface for remote-node access using PPP. See Chapter 27, "Configuring Asynchronous PPP and SLIP," for information.

## CREATING CHAT SCRIPTS

You must create one or more chat scripts before you configure the asynchronous interface.

A chat script is a one-line command that is used on an asynchronous interface to send commands for modem dialing and for logging on to remote systems. Chat scripts indicate the possible responses to expect and the information to send in each case. You can create a different chat script for each type of modem in use on the router and for each system the router might need to log in to.

Chat scripts are required for dialing out on the asynchronous interface on the router's auxiliary port, but are also used on other asynchronous interfaces on access servers.

To create a chat script, perform the following task in global configuration mode:

| Task | Command |
|---|---|
| Create a script that will place a call on a modem or log on to a remote system or both. | **chat-script** *script-name expect send* |

It is recommended that you write one chat script (a "dialer" chat script) for placing a call and another one (a "login" chat script) to log on to remote systems, where required.

For an example of how to use chat scripts, see the section "Using Chat Scripts Example," later in this chapter, as well as Chapter 5.

For information about the recommended chat script naming convention, see the **chat-script** command in Chapter 39.

Adhering to the recommended naming convention allows you to specify a range of chat scripts by using partial names in UNIX-style regular expressions. The regular expressions are used to match patterns and select chat scripts to use. This method is particularly useful for dialer rotary groups on an interface that dials multiple destinations. Regular expressions are described in Appendix C, "Regular Expressions."

## SPECIFYING CHAT SCRIPTS TO USE ON A LINE

After a chat script has been defined, it must be applied to a line or an interface before it can be used. To specify a chat script for a line, perform the following task in line configuration mode:

| Task | Command |
|---|---|
| Specify a modem script for a line. | **script dialer** *regexp* |

A maximum of one **script dialer** command can be configured per line. The chat script naming convention described in Appendix A, "Configuring Modem Support and Chat Scripts," allows you to specify a chat script by the type of the modem attached to that line as follows:

```
script dialer modem-type*
```

It is recommended that one chat script (a "dialer" chat script) be written for placing a call and another chat script (a "system" or "login" chat script) be written to log in to remote systems, where required.

You can also assign chat scripts to asynchronous interfaces for purposes other than DDR. For more information, see Chapter 5.

## LEGACY DDR CONFIGURATION EXAMPLES

The examples provided in this section show various DDR configurations as follows:

- Using Chat Scripts Example
- Writing and Implementing Chat Scripts Examples
- Chat Scripts and Dialer Mapping Example
- System Login Scripts and Modem Scripts Example
- Set Up Point-to-Point DDR without Authentication Example
- Set Up Point-to-Point DDR with Authentication Example

### Using Chat Scripts Example

Figure 38–1 shows the following configuration:

- The configuration is on Router A.
- The modem chat script *dial* is used to dial out to Router B's modem.
- The system login chat script *login* is used to log in to Router B.
- The phone number is the number of the modem attached to Router B.
- The IP address in the **dialer map** command is the address of Router B.

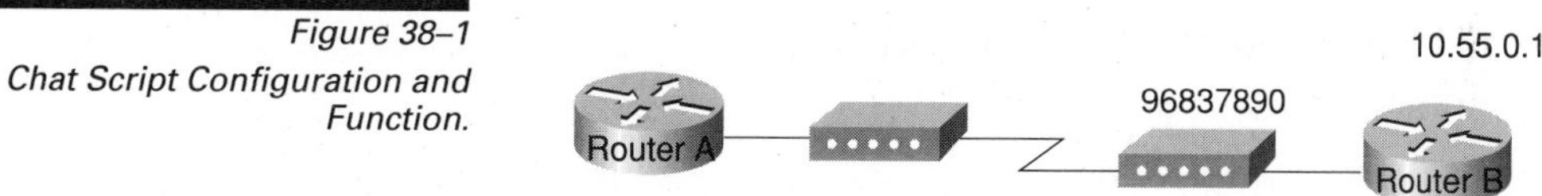


*Figure 38–1 Chat Script Configuration and Function.*

```
chat-script dial ABORT ERROR "" "AT Z" OK "ATDT \T" TIMEOUT 30 CONNECT \c
chat-script login ABORT invalid TIMEOUT 15  name: billw word: wewpass ">"
"slip default"
interface async 10
dialer in-band
dialer map ip 10.55.0.1 modem-script dial system-script login 96837890
```

### Writing and Implementing Chat Scripts Examples

In the following example chat script, a pair of empty quotation marks (" ") means *expect anything* and \r means *send a return*:

```
" " \r "name:" "myname" "ord":" "mypassword" ">" "slip default"
```

The following example shows a configuration in which, when there is traffic, a random line will be used. The dialer code will try to find a script that matches both the modem script *.*-v32* and the system script *cisco*. If there is no match for both the modem script and the system script, you will see a "no matching chat script found" message.

```
interface dialer 1
! v.32 rotaries are in rotary 1
dialer rotary-group 1
! Use v.32 generic script
dialer map ip 1.0.0.1 modem-script .*-v32 system-script cisco 1234
```

The following example shows line chat scripts being specified for lines connected to Telebit and US Robotics modems:

```
! Some lines have telebit modems
line 1 6
 modem chat-script telebit.*
! Some lines have US robotics modems
line 7 12
 modem chat-script usr.*
```

### Chat Scripts and Dialer Mapping Example

The following example shows a modem chat script called *dial* and a system login chat script called *login*. The **dialer in-band** command enables DDR on asynchronous interface 10, and the **dialer map** command dials 96837890 after finding the specified dialing and the system login scripts.

```
chat-script dial ABORT ERROR "" "AT Z" OK "ATDT \T" TIMEOUT 30 CONNECT \c
chat-script login ABORT invalid TIMEOUT 15  name: myname word: mypassword ">"
                "slip default"
interface async 10
 dialer in-band
 dialer map ip 10.55.0.1 modem-script dial system-script login 96837890
```

When a packet is received for 10.55.0.1, the first thing that happens is that the modem script is implemented. Table 38–1 shows the functions that are implemented with each *expect-send* pair in the modem script called *dial*.

**Table 38–1** *Example Modem Script Execution*

| Expect and Send Pair | Implementation |
|---|---|
| ABORT ERROR | End the script execution if the text "ERROR" is found. (You can have as many active abort entries as you like.) |
| " " "AT Z" | Without expecting anything, send an "AT Z" command to the modem. (Note the use of quotation marks to allow a space in the send string.) |
| OK "ATDT \T" | Wait to see "OK." Send "ATDT 96837890." |
| TIMEOUT 30 | Wait up to 30 seconds for next expect string. |
| CONNECT \c | Expect "connect," but do not send anything. (Note that \c is effectively nothing; " " would have indicated nothing followed by a carriage return.) |

After the modem script is successfully executed, the system login script is executed. Table 38–2 shows the functions that are executed with each *expect-send* pair in the system script called *login*.

**Table 38–2** *Example System Script Execution*

| Expect and Send Pair | Implementation |
|---|---|
| ABORT invalid | End the script execution if the message "invalid username or password" is displayed. |
| TIMEOUT 15 | Wait up to 15 seconds. |
| name: myname | Look for "name:" and send "billw." (Using just "name:" will help avoid any capitalization issues.) |
| word: mypassword | Wait for "word:" and send the password. |
| ">" "slip default" | Wait for the *ts* prompt and put the line into SLIP mode with its default address. |

## System Login Scripts and Modem Scripts Example

The following example shows the use of chat scripts implemented with the **system-script** and **modem-script** options of the **dialer map** command.

If there is traffic for IP address 1.2.3.4, the router will dial the 91800 number using the *usrobotics-v32* script, matching the regular expression in the modem chat script. Then the router will run the *unix-slip* chat script as the system script to log in.

If there is traffic for 4.3.2.1, the router will dial 8899 using *usrobotics-v32*, matching both the modem script and modem chat script regular expressions. The router will then log in using the *cisco-compressed* script.

```
! Script for dialing a usr v.32 modem:
chat-script usrobotics-v32 ABORT ERROR "" "AT Z" OK "ATDT \T" TIMEOUT 30 CONNECT \c
!
! Script for logging into a unix system and starting up slip:
chat-script unix-slip ABORT invalid TIMEOUT 15  name: billw word: wewpass ">"
                "slip default"
!
! Script for logging into a cisco comm server and starting up TCP header
! compression
chat-script cisco-compressed...
!
line 15
 modem chat-script usrobotics-*
!
interface async 15
 dialer map ip 1.2.3.4 system-script unix-slip 918005551212
 dialer map ip 4.3.2.1 modem-script *-v32 system-script cisco-compressed 8899
```

## Set Up Point-to-Point DDR without Authentication Example

This example shows chat scripts used in a configuration that sets up two-way reciprocal dial-on-demand routing (DDR) without authentication; the client and server have dial-in access to each other.

### *Remote Configuration*

The following example configuration is performed on the remote side of the connection:

```
interface ethernet 0
 ip address 172.30.44.1 255.255.255.0
!
interface async 7
 ip address 172.30.45.2 255.255.255.0
 async mode dedicated
 peer default ip address 172.30.45.1
 encapsulation ppp
 dialer in-band
 dialer string 1234
 dialer-group 1
!
ip route 172.30.43.0 255.255.255.0 async 7
 ip default-network 172.30.0.0
 chat-script generic ABORT BUSY ABORT NO ## AT OK ATDT\T TIMEOUT 30 CONNECT
 dialer-list 1 protocol ip permit
!
line 7
 no exec
 modem InOut
 speed 38400
 flowcontrol hardware
 modem chat-script generic
```

### *Local Configuration*

The following example configuration is performed on the local side of the connection:

```
interface ethernet 0
 ip address 172.30.43.1 255.255.255.0
!
interface async 7
 async mode dedicated
 peer default ip address 172.30.45.2
 encapsulation ppp
 dialer in-band
 dialer string 1235
 dialer rotary-group 1
!
interface async 8
 async mode dedicated
 peer default ip address 172.30.45.2
 dialer rotary-group 1
!
ip route 172.30.44.0 255.255.255.0 async 7
 ip address 172.30.45.2 255.255.255.0
```

```
 encapsulation ppp
 ppp authentication chap
 dialer in-band
 dialer map ip 172.30.45.2 name remote 4321
 dialer load-threshold 80
!
ip route 172.30.44.0 255.255.255.0 128.150.45.2
 chat-script generic ABORT BUSY ABORT NO ## AT OK ATDT\T TIMEOUT 30 CONNECT
 dialer-list 1 protocol ip permit
!
route igrp 109
network 172.30.0.0
redistribute static
passive-interface async 7
!
line 7
 modem InOut
 speed 38400
 flowcontrol hardware
 modem chat-script generic
```

## Set Up Point-to-Point DDR with Authentication Example

This example shows chat scripts used in a configuration that sets up two-way dial-on-demand routing (DDR) with authentication; the client and server have dial-in access to each other. This configuration is demonstrated in the following two subsections.

### *Remote Configuration*

The following example configuration is performed on the remote side of the connection. It provides authentication by identifying a password that must be provided on each end of the connection.

```
username local password secret1
username remote password secret2
interface ethernet 0
 ip address 172.30.44.1 255.255.255.0
!
interface async 7
 ip address 172.30.45.2 255.255.255.0
 async mode dedicated
 peer default ip address 172.30.45.1
 encapsulation ppp
 dialer in-band
 dialer string 1234
 dialer-group 1
!
ip route 172.30.43.0 255.255.255.0 async 7
 ip default-network 172.30.0.0
 chat-script generic ABORT BUSY ABORT NO ## AT OK ATDT\T TIMEOUT 30 CONNECT
 dialer-list 1 protocol ip permit
!
line 7
 no exec
 modem InOut
```

```
speed 38400
flowcontrol hardware
modem chat-script generic
```

## *Local Configuration*

The following example configuration is performed on the local side of the connection. As with the remote side configuration, it provides authentication by identifying a password for each end of the connection.

```
username remote password secret1
username local password secret2
!
interface ethernet 0
 ip address 172.30.43.1 255.255.255.0
!
interface async 7
 async mode dedicated
 peer default ip address 172.30.45.2
 dialer rotary-group 1
!
interface async 8
 async mode dedicated
 peer default ip address 172.30.45.2
 dialer rotary-group 1
!
interface dialer 1
 ip address 172.30.45.2 255.255.255.0
 encapsulation ppp
 ppp authentication chap
 dialer in-band
 dialer map ip 172.30.45.2 name remote 4321
 dialer load-threshold 80
!
ip route 172.30.44.0 255.255.255.0 172.30.45.2
 chat-script generic ABORT BUSY ABORT NO ## AT OK ATDT\T TIMEOUT 30 CONNECT
!
 route igrp 109
 network 172.30.0.0
 redistribute static
 passive-interface async 7
!
line 7
 modem InOut
 speed 38400
 flowcontrol hardware
 modem chat-script generic
```

CHAPTER 39

# Asynchronous DDR Preparation Commands

This chapter describes the commands required in the preparation steps to be completed before you configure DDR on asynchronous serial interfaces on the router.

For the preparation tasks and configuration examples, see Chapter 38, "Preparing for Asynchronous DDR."

## CHAT-SCRIPT

To create a script that will place a call over a modem, use the **chat-script** global configuration command. To disable the specified chat script, use the **no** form of this command.

**chat-script** *script-name expect-send*
**no chat-script** *script-name expect-send*

| *Syntax* | *Description* |
|---|---|
| *script-name* | Name of the chat script. |
| *expect-send* | Pairs of information elements: an item to expect and an item to send in response. |

### *Default*

No chat scripts are defined.

### *Command Mode*

Global configuration

### Usage Guidelines

This command first appeared in Cisco IOS Release 10.0.

Chat scripts are used in dial-on-demand routing (DDR) to give commands to dial a modem and commands to log on to remote systems. The defined script will be used to place a call over a modem.

Some characteristics of chat scripts are as follows:

- Chat scripts are case-sensitive.
- You can have any number of ABORT sequences active at once.
- When a chat script starts, the default timeout is 5 seconds. Changes to the timeout persist until the next time you change them in the script.
- A string within quotation marks is treated as a single entity.

It is recommended that one chat script (a "modem" chat script) be written for placing a call and another chat script (a "system" or "login" chat script) be written to log on to remote systems, where required.

### Suggested Chat Script Naming Conventions

A suggested chat script naming convention is as follows:
*vendor-type-modulation*

If you follow this convention, the syntax of the **chat-script** command becomes the following:
**chat-script** *vendor-type-modulation expect-send*

For example, if you have a Telebit T3000 modem that uses V.32*bis* modulation, you would name your chat script as follows:

```
telebit-t3000-v32bis
```

The **chat-script** command could become the following:

```
chat-script telebit-t3000-v32bis ABORT ERROR ABORT BUSY ABORT "NO ANSWER" "" "AT H" OK "AT
DT \T" DIALING \c TIMEOUT 30 CONNECT \c
```

For example, you could have script names like the following:

- telebit-tb-b103
- telebit-tb-v21
- telebit-tb-v22
- codex-326x-b103
- codex-326x-v21
- codex-326x-v22
- codex-326x-v22bis
- codex-326x-v32
- codex-326x-v32bis

- usr-courier-v22bis
- usr-courier-hst
- usr-courier-v32
- usr-courier-v32bis

Adhering to this naming convention allows you to use partial chat script names with regular expressions to specify a range of chat scripts that can be used. This capability is particularly useful for dialer rotary groups and is explained further in the next section.

Chat scripts are in the form *expect-send*, where the send string following the hyphen (-) is executed if the preceding expect string fails. Each send string is followed by a return unless it ends with the escape sequence \c. The sequence ^*x* is translated into the appropriate control character, and the sequence \x is translated into *x* if \x is not one of the special sequences listed in Table 39–1.

### *Escape Sequences*

The escape sequences used in chat scripts are listed in Table 39–1.

**Table 39–1** *Chat Script Escape Sequences*

| Escape Sequence | Description |
|---|---|
| " " | Expect a null string. |
| EOT | Send an end-of-transmission character. |
| BREAK | Cause a BREAK. This sequence is sometimes simulated with line speed changes and null characters. May not work on all systems. |
| \c | Suppress newline at the end of the send string. |
| \d | Delay for 2 seconds. |
| \K | Insert a BREAK. |
| \n | Send a newline or linefeed character. |
| \p | Pause for 1/4 second. |
| \r | Send a return. |
| \s | Send a space character. |
| \t | Send a table character. |
| \\ | Send a backslash (\) character. |
| \T | Replaced by phone number. |
| \q | Reserved, not yet used. |

### *Expect-Send Pairs*

Sample supported *expect-send* pairs are described in Table 39–2.

**Table 39–2** *Sample Supported Expect-Send Pairs*

| Expect and Send Pair | Function |
|---|---|
| ABORT *string* | Designates a string whose presence in the input indicates that the chat script has failed. |
| TIMEOUT *time* | Sets the time to wait for input, in seconds. The default is 5 seconds. |

For example, if a modem reports BUSY when the number dialed is busy, you can indicate that you want the attempt stopped at this point by including ABORT BUSY in your chat script.

### *Alternate Handlers*

If you use the *expect-send* pair ABORT SINK instead of ABORT ERROR, the system terminates abnormally when it encounters SINK instead of ERROR.

### *Missed Characters*

After the connection is established and you press the Return key, you must often press Return a second time before the prompt appears.

You might include the following as part of your chat script:

```
ssword:-/r-ssword
```

This part of the script specifies that, after the connection is established, you want **ssword** to be displayed. If it is not displayed, you must press Return again after the timeout passes.

### *Example*

The following example shows the **chat-script** command being used to create a chat script named *t3000*:

```
chat-script t3000 ABORT ERROR ABORT BUSY ABORT "NO ANSWER" "" "AT H" OK "AT DT \T" DIALING
\c TIMEOUT 30 CONNECT \c
```

### *Related Commands*

Search online to find documentation for related commands.

**dialer map**
**script dialer**

### SCRIPT DIALER

To specify a default modem chat script, use the **script dialer** line configuration command. Use the **no** form of this command to disable this feature.

**script dialer** *regexp*
**no script dialer**

| *Syntax* | *Description* |
|---|---|
| *regexp* | Specifies the set of modem scripts that might be executed. The first script that matches the argument *regexp* will be used. |

#### *Default*

No chat script is defined.

#### *Command Mode*

Line configuration

#### *Usage Guidelines*

This command first appeared in Cisco IOS Release 10.3.

This command is used by DDR modules to provide modem dialing commands and commands to log in to remote systems.

The argument *regexp* is used to specify the name of the modem script that is to be executed. The first script that matches the argument in this command and the **dialer map** command will be used. For more information about regular expressions, see Appendix C, "Regular Expressions."

If you adhere to the naming convention recommended for chat scripts (see the **chat-script** command), the modem lines (the argument *regexp* in the **script dialer** command) will be set to one of the following regular expressions to match patterns, depending on the kind of modem you have:

- **codex-.***
- **telebit-.***
- **usr-.***
- **xyz-.***

In the **dialer map** command, you can specify the modulation but leave the type of modem unspecified, as in *.*-v32bis*.

#### *Example*

The following example shows line chat scripts being specified for lines connected to Telebit and U.S. Robotics modems:

```
! Some lines have telebit modems
line 1 6
```

```
dialer script telebit.*
!
! Some lines have US robotics modems
line 7 12
dialer script usr.*
```

### *Related Commands*

Search online to find documentation for related commands.

**chat-script**
**dialer map modem-script system-script**
**dialer map name modem-script system-script**
**script activation**
**script connection**
**script reset**
**script startup**
**start-chat**

CHAPTER 40

# Configuring Legacy DDR Spokes

This chapter describes the configuration of legacy dial-on-demand routing on interfaces functioning as a *spoke* in a hub-and-spoke network topology. This chapter considers a spoke interface to be any interface that calls or receives calls from exactly one other router, and considers a hub interface to be an interface that calls or receives calls from more than one router: all the spokes in the network.

This chapter also describes the DDR-independent tasks required to bridge protocols or to route protocols over DDR. Most of these tasks are global in scope and can be completed before you begin to configure DDR.

For configuration tasks for the central hub interface in a hub-and-spoke network topology, see Chapter 42,"Configuring Legacy DDR Hubs." For a complete description of the commands mentioned in this chapter, see Chapter 41, "Legacy DDR Spokes Commands." For information about the Dialer Profiles implementation of DDR, see Chapter 44, "Configuring Peer-to-Peer DDR with Dialer Profiles."

## Configuration Task Flow

Before you configure DDR, make sure you have completed the preparations for bridging or routing as described in Chapter 36, "Deciding and Preparing To Configure DDR." That chapter provides information about the minimal requirements.

When you configure DDR on a spoke interface in a hub-and-spoke topology, you perform the following general steps:

**Step 1** Specify the interface that will place calls to or receive calls from a single site. (See Chapter 42 for information about configuring an interface to place calls to or receive calls from multiple sites.)

**Step 2** Enable DDR on the interface. This step is not required for some interfaces; for example, ISDN interfaces and passive interfaces that receive only from DTR-dialing interfaces.

**Step 3** Configure the interface to receive calls only, if applicable. Receiving calls from multiple sites requires each inbound call to be authenticated.

**Step 4** Configure the interface to place calls only, if applicable.

**Step 5** Configure the interface to place and receive calls, if applicable.

**Step 6** If the interface will place calls, specify access control for:

- Transparent bridging—Assign the interface to a bridge group, and define dialer lists associated with the bridging access lists. The interface switches between members of the same bridge group, and dialer lists specify which packets can trigger calls.

  or

- Routed protocols—Define dialer lists associated with the protocol access lists to specify which packets can trigger calls.

**Step 7** Customize the interface settings (timers, interface priority, hold queues, bandwidth on demand, and disabling fast switching) as needed.

When you have configured the interface and it is operational, you can monitor its performance and its connections as described in section, "Monitoring DDR Connections," later in this chapter.

You can also enhance DDR by configuring Multilink PPP and configuring PPP callback. The PPP configuration tasks are described in Chapter 25, "Configuring Media-Independent PPP and Multilink PPP."

See the section "Legacy DDR Spoke Configuration Examples," later in this chapter for examples of how to configure DDR on your network.

## DDR Configuration Task List

To configure DDR on an interface, complete the tasks in the following sections. The first five bulleted items are required. The remaining tasks are not absolutely required, but might be necessary in your networking environment.

- Specifying the Interface
- Enabling DDR on the Interface
- Configuring the Interface to Place Calls
  or
  Configuring the Interface to Receive Calls
  or
  Configuring the Interface to Place and Receive Calls
- Defining the Traffic to Be Authenticated

- Configuring Access Control for Outgoing Calls, if applicable
- Customizing the Interface Settings, as needed
- Configuring To Send Traffic over Frame Relay, X.25, or LAPB Networks, if needed

You can also monitor DDR connections. See section, "Monitoring DDR Connections," for commands and other information.

For examples of Legacy DDR on a point-to-point connection, see section, "Legacy DDR Spoke Configuration Examples."

## SPECIFYING THE INTERFACE

The steps shown in this section assume that you have completed any preparatory steps required for the relevant interface. For example, if you intend to use an asynchronous interface, it assumes that you have completed the modem support and line configuration steps and the chat script creation steps. If you intend to use an ISDN interface, it assumes that you have the ISDN line properly provisioned and running.

You can configure any asynchronous, synchronous serial, ISDN, or dialer interface for Legacy DDR.

**NOTES**

When you specify an interface, make sure to use the interface numbering scheme supported on the network interface module or other port hardware on the router. On the Cisco 7200 series, for example, you specify an interface by indicating its type, slot number, and port number.

To specify an interface to configure for DDR, complete the following task(s) in global configuration mode:

| Task | Command |
|---|---|
| Specify an interface to configure for DDR.<br>or | **interface async** *number*<br>**interface serial** *number*<br>**interface bri** *number* |
| Specify an ISDN PRI D channel (T1).<br>Specify an ISDN PRI D channel (E1) | **interface serial** *slot/port*:**23**<br>**interface serial** *slot/port*:**15** |
| or | |
| Specify a logical interface to function as a dialer rotary group leader. | **interface dialer** *number* |

Dialer interfaces are logical or virtual entities, but they use physical interfaces to place or receive calls.

### ENABLING DDR ON THE INTERFACE

This step is required for asynchronous or synchronous serial interfaces but not for ISDN interfaces. The software automatically configures ISDN interfaces to be dialer type ISDN.

This step is not required for ISDN interfaces (BRI interfaces and ISDN PRI D channels) and for *purely passive* interfaces that will receive calls only from interfaces that use DTR dialing.

Enabling DDR on an interface usually requires you to specify the type of dialer to be used. This step is not required for ISDN interfaces because the software automatically configures ISDN interfaces to be dialer type ISDN.

To enable DDR by specifying the dialer type, perform one of the following tasks in global configuration mode:

| Task | Command |
|---|---|
| Enable DDR and configure the specified serial interface to use DTR dialing—for interfaces with non-V.25*bis* modems using EIA Data Terminal Ready (DTR) signaling. | **dialer dtr** |
| or | |
| Enable DDR and configure the specified serial interface to use in-band dialing—for asynchronous interfaces or interfaces using V.25*bis* modems. | **dialer in-band** [**no-parity** \| **odd-parity**] |

**NOTES**

An interface configured with the **dialer in-band** command can both place and receive calls. A serial interface configured for DTR dialing can place calls only; it cannot accept them.

You can optionally specify parity if the modem on this interface uses the V.25*bis* command set. The 1984 version of the V.25*bis* specification states that characters must have odd parity. However, the default for the **dialer in-band** command is no parity.

For an example of configuring an interface to support DTR dialing, see the section "DTR Dialing Example," later in this chapter.

To receive calls from an interface that is using DTR dialing, an interface can be configured for in-band dialing or not configured for anything but encapsulation, depending on the desired behavior. If you expect the receiving interface to terminate a call when no traffic is received for some time, you must configure in-band dialing (along with access lists and a dummy dialer string). If the receiving interface is purely passive, no additional configuration is necessary.

**NOTES**

You can configure an interface or dialer rotary group to both place and receive calls. If the interface is calling and being called by a single site, just enable DDR and specify a dial string.

## CONFIGURING THE INTERFACE TO PLACE CALLS

To configure an interface to place calls to one site only, complete the tasks in one of the following sections:

- Specify the Dial String for Synchronous Serial Interfaces
- Specify Chat Scripts and Dial Strings for Asynchronous Serial Interfaces

### Specify the Dial String for Synchronous Serial Interfaces

If you want to call only one remote system per synchronous serial interface, use the **dialer string** command. Dialers pass the string you have defined to the external DCE. ISDN devices call the number specified in the string.

To specify the telephone number call on a serial interface (asynchronous or synchronous), perform the following task in interface configuration mode:

| Task | Command |
|---|---|
| Specify the number to dial. | **dialer string** *dial-string*[:*isdn-subaddress*] |

Dialers pass the string (telephone number) to the external DCE, which dials the number; ISDN devices themselves call the specified number.

### Specify Chat Scripts and Dial Strings for Asynchronous Serial Interfaces

The modem chat script becomes the default chat script for an interface. This means that it becomes the default chat script for the **dialer string** and **dialer map** commands presented in this section.

To place a call to a single site on an asynchronous line for which either a modem dialing script has not been assigned or for which a system script login must be specified, perform the following task in interface configuration mode:

| Task | Command |
|---|---|
| Specify chat scripts and a dial string. | **dialer map** *protocol next-hop-address* [**modem-script** *modem-regexp*] [**system-script** *system-regexp*] *dial-string* [:*isdn-subaddress*] |

## Configuring the Interface to Receive Calls

If you enable DDR on an interface by using the **dialer in-band** command, the interface can receive calls. No additional configuration steps are required simply to receive calls. Parity is not required for receiving calls only. An interface configured with the **dialer in-band** command can terminate calls when the line is idle for some configurable time.

You cannot set up an ISDN interface only to receive calls from a single site, but you can set it up to receive and place calls to a single site.

To receive calls from an interface that is using DTR dialing, an interface can be configured for in-band dialing or not configured for anything but encapsulation, depending on the desired behavior. If you expect the receiving interface to terminate a call when no traffic is received for some time, you must configure in-band dialing (along with access lists and a dummy dialer string). If the receiving interface is purely passive, no additional configuration is necessary.

Authentication is not required when traffic comes from only one site. However, you can configure authentication for security. See the section "Defining the Traffic to Be Authenticated." If you want to receive calls *only*, do not provide a dial string in the **dialer map** command shown in that section.

## Configuring the Interface to Place and Receive Calls

If you enable DDR on an interface by using the **dialer in-band** command, the interface can receive calls. To enable it to place calls to one site, you must define the dialing destination.

To define the dialing destination, complete the following task in interface configuration mode:

| Task | Command |
|---|---|
| Specify the number to dial one site. | **dialer string** *dial-string*[:*isdn-subaddress*] |

**Notes**

Use the **dialer map** command instead of the **dialer string** command if you want to authenticate calls received. See the section "Defining the Traffic to Be Authenticated," for more information.

When a dialer string is configured but PPP Challenge Handshake Authentication Protocol (CHAP) is not configured on the interface, the Cisco IOS software recognizes each incoming call as coming from the configured dialer string. That is, if your outgoing calls go to only one number and you don't authenticate incoming calls, it is assumed that all incoming calls come from that number. (If you received calls from multiple sites, you would need to authenticate the calls.)

Authentication is not required when traffic comes from only one site. However, you can configure authentication for an extra measure of security. See the section "Defining the Traffic to Be Authenticated," for more information. If you want to receive and place calls, use the **dialer map** command.

### DEFINING THE TRAFFIC TO BE AUTHENTICATED

Authentication can be done through CHAP or PAP. In addition, the interface must be configured to map a host's protocol address to the name to use for authenticating the remote host.

To enable CHAP or PAP on an interface and authenticate sites that are calling in, perform the following tasks in interface configuration mode:

| Task | | Command |
|---|---|---|
| **Step 1** | Configure an interface for PPP encapsulation. | **encapsulation ppp** |
| **Step 2** | Enable CHAP.<br>or<br>Enable PAP. | **ppp authentication chap** [**if-needed**]<br>or<br>**ppp authentication pap** [**if-needed**] |
| **Step 3** | Map the protocol address to a host name. | **dialer map** *protocol next-hop-address* **name** *hostname* [**modem-script** *modem-regexp*] [**system-script** *system-regexp*] [*dial-string*[*:isdn-subaddress*]] |

If the dial string is not provided in Step 3, the interface will be able to receive calls from the host but will not be able to place calls to the host.

### CONFIGURING ACCESS CONTROL FOR OUTGOING CALLS

Protocol access lists and dialer access lists are central to the operation of DDR. In general, access lists are used as the screening criteria for determining when to initiate DDR calls. All packets are tested against the dialer access list. Packets that match a permit entry are deemed *interesting*. Packets that do not match a permit entry or that do match a deny entry are deemed *uninteresting*. When a packet is found to be interesting, either the dialer idle timer is reset (if the line is active) or a connection is attempted (if the line is available but not active). If a tested packet is deemed *uninteresting*, it will be forwarded if it is intended for a destination known to be on a specific interface and the link is active. However, such a packet will not initiate a DDR call and will not reset the idle timer.

#### Configure Access Control for Bridging

You can control access by defining any transparent bridge packet as *interesting*, or you can use the finer granularity of controlling access by Ethernet type codes. To control access for DDR bridging, complete *one* of the following tasks in global configuration mode:

- Control Bridging Access by Ethernet Type Codes
- Permit All Bridge Packets to Trigger Calls
- Assign the Interface to a Bridge Group

**NOTES**

Spanning tree bridge protocol data units (BPDUs) are always treated as *uninteresting*.

### Control Bridging Access by Ethernet Type Codes

To control access by Ethernet type codes, complete the following task in global configuration mode:

| Task | Command |
|---|---|
| Identify interesting packets by Ethernet type codes (access list numbers must be in the range 200–299). | **access-list** *access-list-number* {**permit** \| **deny**} *type-code* [*mask*] |

To enable packets with a specified Ethernet type code to trigger outgoing calls, complete the following task in interface configuration mode:

| Task | Command |
|---|---|
| Define a dialer list for the specified access list. | **dialer-list** *dialer-group* **protocol bridge list** *access-list-number* |

### Permit All Bridge Packets to Trigger Calls

To identify all transparent bridge packets as interesting, complete the following task in interface configuration mode when you are configuring DDR:

| Task | Command |
|---|---|
| Define a dialer list that treats all transparent bridge packets as interesting. | **dialer-list** *dialer-group* **protocol bridge permit** |

### Assign the Interface to a Bridge Group

Packets are bridged only among interfaces that belong to the same bridge group. To assign an interface to a bridge group, complete the following task in interface configuration mode:

| Task | Command |
|---|---|
| Assign the specified interface to a bridge group. | **bridge-group** *bridge-group* |

### Configure Access Control for Routing

Before you perform the tasks outlined in this section, configure access lists for the protocols you intend to route over DDR as described briefly in Chapter 36.

An interface can be associated only with a single dialer access group; multiple dialer access group assignments are not allowed. To specify the dialer access group to which you want to assign an access list, perform the following task in interface configuration mode:

| Task | Command |
|---|---|
| Specify the number of the dialer access group to which the specific interface belongs. | **dialer-group** *group-number* |

## CUSTOMIZING THE INTERFACE SETTINGS

Perform the tasks in the following sections as needed to customize DDR in your network:

- Configure Timers on the DDR Interface
- Set Dialer Interface Priority
- Configure a Dialer Hold Queue
- Configure Bandwidth on Demand
- Disable and Re-Enable DDR Fast Switching

### Configure Timers on the DDR Interface

Perform the tasks in the following sections as needed to set the timers:

- Set Line-Idle Time
- Set Idle Time for Busy Interfaces
- Set Line-Down Time
- Set Carrier-Wait Time

#### *Set Line-Idle Time*

To specify the amount of time a line will stay idle before it is disconnected, perform the following task in interface configuration mode:

| Task | Command |
|---|---|
| Set line-idle time. | **dialer idle-timeout** *seconds* |

### Set Idle Time for Busy Interfaces

The dialer fast idle timer is activated if there is contention for a line. Contention occurs when a line is in use, a packet for a different next hop address is received, and the busy line is required to send the competing packet.

If the line has been idle for the configured amount of time, the current call is disconnected immediately and the new call is placed. If the line has not yet been idle as long as the fast idle timeout period, the packet is dropped because there is no way to get through to the destination. (After the packet is dropped, the fast idle timer remains active and the current call is disconnected as soon as it has been idle for as long as the fast idle timeout). If, in the meantime, another packet is transmitted to the currently connected destination, and it is classified as interesting, the fast-idle timer is restarted.

To specify the amount of time a line for which there is contention will stay idle before the line is disconnected and the competing call is placed, perform the following task in interface configuration mode:

| Task | Command |
|---|---|
| Set idle time for high traffic lines. | **dialer fast-idle** *seconds* |

This command applies both to inbound and outbound calls.

#### *Set Line-Down Time*

To set the length of time the interface stays down before it is available to dial again after a line is disconnected or fails, perform the following task in interface configuration mode:

| Task | Command |
|---|---|
| Set the interface downtime. | **dialer enable-timeout** *seconds* |

This command applies both to inbound and outbound calls.

#### *Set Carrier-Wait Time*

To set the length of time an interface waits for the telephone service (carrier), perform the following task in interface configuration mode:

| Task | Command |
|---|---|
| Set the length of time the interface waits for the carrier to come up when a call is placed. | **dialer wait-for-carrier-time** *seconds* |

For asynchronous interfaces, this command sets the total time to wait for a call to connect. This time is set to allow for running the chat script.

### Set Dialer Interface Priority

Interface priority indicates which interface in a dialer rotary group will get used first for outgoing calls. You might give one interface a higher priority if it is attached to a faster, more reliable modem. In this way, the higher-priority interface will be used as often as possible.

To assign priority to an interface in a dialer rotary group, perform the following task in interface configuration mode:

| Task | Command |
|---|---|
| Set the interface priority in the dialer rotary group. | **dialer priority** *number* |

The range of values for *number* is 0 through 255. Zero is the default value and lowest priority; 255 is the highest priority. This command applies to outgoing calls only.

### Configure a Dialer Hold Queue

Sometimes packets destined for a remote router are discarded because no connection exists. Establishing a connection using an analog modem can take time, during which packets are discarded. However, configuring a dialer hold queue will allow *interesting* outgoing packets to be queued and sent as soon as the modem connection is established.

A dialer hold queue can be configured on any type of dialer, including in-band synchronous, asynchronous, DTR, and ISDN dialers. Also, *hunt group leaders* can be configured with a dialer hold queue. If a hunt group leader (of a rotary dialing group) is configured with a hold queue, all members of the group will be configured with a dialer hold queue and no individual member's hold queue can be altered.

To establish a dialer hold queue, perform the following task in interface configuration mode:

| Task | Command |
|---|---|
| Create a dialer hold queue and specify the number of packets to be held in it. | **dialer hold-queue** *packets* |

As many as 100 packets can be held in an outgoing dialer hold queue.

### Configure Bandwidth on Demand

You can configure a dialer rotary group to use additional bandwidth by placing additional calls to a single destination if the load for the interface exceeds a specified weighted value. Parallel communication links are established based on traffic load. The number of parallel links that can be established to one location is not limited.

To set the dialer load threshold for bandwidth on demand, perform the following task in interface configuration mode:

| Task | Command |
|---|---|
| Configure the dialer rotary group to place additional calls to a single destination, as indicated by interface load. | **dialer load-threshold** *load* |

Once multiple links are established, they are still governed by the load threshold. If the total load on all the links falls below the threshold, an idle link will be torn down.

### Disable and Re-Enable DDR Fast Switching

Fast switching is enabled by default on all DDR interfaces. When fast switching is enabled or disabled on an ISDN D channel, it is enabled or disabled on all B channels. When fast switching is enabled or disabled on a dialer interface, it is enabled or disabled on all rotary group members but cannot be enabled or disabled on the serial interfaces individually.

Fast switching can be disabled and re-enabled on a protocol-by-protocol basis. To disable fast switching and re-enable it, complete one of the following protocol-specific tasks:

| Task | Command |
|---|---|
| Disable IP fast switching over a DDR interface. | **no ip route-cache** |
| Re-enable IP fast switching over a DDR interface. | **ip route cache** |
| Disable distributed IP fast switching over a DDR interface. This feature works in Cisco 7500 routers with a Versatile Interface Processor (VIP) card. | **no ip route-cache distributed** |
| Enable distributed IP fast switching over a DDR interface. This feature works in Cisco 7500 routers with a Versatile Interface Processor (VIP) card. | **ip route-cache distributed** |
| Disable IPX fast switching over a DDR interface. | **no ipx route-cache** |
| Re-enable IPX fast switching over a DDR interface. | **ipx route-cache** |

## Configuring to Send Traffic over Frame Relay, X.25, or LAPB Networks

An interface configured for DDR can send traffic over networks that require LAPB, X.25, or Frame Relay encapsulation. To configure an interface for those networks, complete the tasks in the following sections:

- Configure the Interface for Sending Traffic over a Frame Relay Network
- Configure the Interface for Sending Traffic over an X.25 Network
- Configure the Interface for Sending Traffic over a LAPB Network

## Configure the Interface for Sending Traffic over a Frame Relay Network

Access to Frame Relay networks is now available through dial-up connections as well as leased lines. Dial-up connectivity allows Frame Relay networks to be extended to sites that do not generate enough traffic to justify leased lines and also allows a Frame Relay network to back up another network or point-to-point line.

DDR over Frame Relay is supported for synchronous serial and ISDN interfaces and for rotary groups, and is available for in-band, DTR, and ISDN dialers.

Frame Relay supports multiple PVC connections over the same serial interface or ISDN B channel, but only one *physical* interface can be used (dialed, connected, and active) in a rotary group or with ISDN.

### *Configuration Restrictions*

The following restrictions apply to DDR used over Frame Relay:

- Frame Relay is not available for asynchronous dialers.
- Like HDLC, LAPB, and X.25, Frame Relay does not provide authentication. However, ISDN dialers can offer some authentication through the caller ID feature.
- Only one ISDN B channel can be dialed at any one time. When configuring a rotary group, you can use only one serial interface.

Frame Relay subinterfaces work the same on dial-up connections as they do on leased lines.

### *Configuration Overview*

No new commands are required to support DDR over Frame Relay. In general, you configure Frame Relay and configure DDR. Complete the following steps to configure an interface for DDR over Frame Relay:

- Specify the interface.
- Specify the protocol identifiers for the interface.

  For example, enter the IP address and mask, the IPX network number, and the AppleTalk cable range and zone.
- Configure Frame Relay.

  As a minimum, you must enable Frame Relay encapsulation and decide whether you need to do static or dynamic address mapping. If you decide to do dynamic mapping, you do not need to enter a command because Inverse ARP is enabled by default. If you decide to do static mapping, you must enter Frame Relay mapping commands.

You can then configure various options as needed for your Frame Relay network topology.

- Configure DDR.

  At a minimum, you must decide and configure the interface for outgoing calls only, incoming calls only, or both outgoing and incoming calls.

  You can also configure DDR for your routed protocols (as specified in the section "Preparations for Routing or Bridging over DDR," of Chapter 36) and for snapshot routing (as specified in Chapter 69, "Configuring Snapshot Routing"). You can also customize DDR interfaces on your router or access server (as described in the section "Customizing the Interface Settings," later in this chapter).

For examples of configuring various interfaces for DDR over Frame Relay, see section, "Frame Relay Support Examples," later in this chapter.

### Configure the Interface for Sending Traffic over an X.25 Network

X.25 interfaces can now be configured to support DDR. Synchronous serial and ISDN interfaces on our routers and access servers can be configured for X.25 addresses, X.25 encapsulation, and mapping of protocol addresses to a remote host's X.25 address. In-band, DTR, and ISDN dialers can be configured to support X.25 encapsulation, but rotary groups cannot. On ISDN dialers configured for X.25 encapsulation, only one B channel can be used.

To configure an interface to support X.25, perform the following X.25-specific tasks in interface configuration mode and also complete the DDR configuration of the interface:

| Task | | Command |
|---|---|---|
| **Step 1** | Configure the interface to use X.25 encapsulation. | **encapsulation x25** [**dte** \| **dce**] [**ietf**] |
| **Step 2** | Assign an X.25 address to the interface. | **x25 address** *x.121-address* |
| **Step 3** | Set up the LAN protocols-to-remote host address mapping. | **x25 map** *protocol address* [*protocol2 address2* [...[*protocol9 address9*]]] *x.121-address* [*option*] |

The order of DDR and X.25 configuration tasks is not critical; you can configure DDR before or after X.25, and you can even mix the DDR and X.25 commands.

For an example of configuring an interface for X.25 encapsulation and then completing the DDR configuration, see the section "X.25 Support Example," later in this chapter.

### Configure the Interface for Sending Traffic over a LAPB Network

Dial-on-demand routing over serial lines now supports Link Access Procedure, Balanced (LAPB) encapsulation, in addition to the previously supported PPP, HDLC, and X.25 encapsulations.

LAPB encapsulation is supported on synchronous serial, ISDN, and dialer rotary group interfaces, but not on asynchronous dialers.

Because the default encapsulation is HDLC, you must explicitly configure LAPB encapsulation. To configure an interface to support LAPB encapsulation, perform the following task in interface configuration mode and also complete the DDR configuration of the interface:

| Task | Command |
|---|---|
| Specify LAPB encapsulation. | **encapsulation lapb** [**dte** \| **dce**] [**multi** \| *protocol*] |

For an example of configuring an interface for DDR over LAPB, see the section "LAPB Support Example," later in this chapter.

## Monitoring DDR Connections

To monitor DDR connections, perform the following tasks in privileged EXEC mode:

| Task | Command |
|---|---|
| Display general diagnostics about the DDR interface. | **show dialer** [**interface** *type number*] |
| Display current dialer maps, next-hop protocol addresses, usernames, and the interfaces on which they are configured. | **show dialer map** |
| Display information about the ISDN interface. | **show interfaces bri 0** |
| Display status about the IPX interface. | **show ipx interface** [*type number*] |
| Display information about the IPX packets transmitted by the router or access server, including watchdog counters. | **show ipx traffic** |
| Display information about the AppleTalk packets transmitted by the router or access server. | **show appletalk traffic** |
| Display information about the Banyan VINES packets transmitted by the router or access server. | **show vines traffic** |
| Display information about the DECnet packets transmitted by the router or access server. | **show decnet traffic** |
| Display information about the XNS packets transmitted by the router or access server. | **show xns traffic** |
| Clear the values of the general diagnostic statistics. | **clear dialer** |

## Legacy DDR Spoke Configuration Examples

The examples provided in this section show various DDR configurations as follows:

- Transparent Bridging over DDR Examples
- Configuring DDR in an IP Environment Example
- Set Up Two-Way DDR for Novell IPX Example
- AppleTalk Configuration Example
- DECnet Configuration Example
- ISO CLNS Configuration Example
- XNS Configuration Example
- Dialing a Single Site Example
- DTR Dialing Example
- Set Up Hub-and-Spoke DDR for Asynchronous Interfaces and Authentication Example
- Set Up Two-Way Reciprocal Client/Server DDR without Authentication Example
- Frame Relay Support Examples
- X.25 Support Example
- LAPB Support Example

### Transparent Bridging over DDR Examples

The following two examples differ only in the packets that cause calls to be placed. The first example specifies by protocol (any bridge packet is permitted to cause a call to be made); the second example allows a finer granularity by specifying the Ethernet type codes of bridge packets.

The first example configures the serial 1 interface for DDR bridging. Any bridge packet is permitted to cause a call to be placed.

```
no ip routing
!
interface Serial1
 no ip address
 encapsulation ppp
 dialer in-band
 dialer enable-timeout 3
 dialer map bridge name urk broadcast 8985
 dialer hold-queue 10
 dialer-group 1
 ppp authentication chap
 bridge-group 1
 pulse-time 1
!
dialer-list 1 protocol bridge permit
bridge 1 protocol ieee
bridge 1 hello 10
```

The second example also configures the serial 1 interface for DDR bridging. However, this example includes an **access-list** command that specifies the Ethernet type codes that can cause calls to be placed and a **dialer list protocol list** command that refers to the specified access list.

```
no ip routing
!
interface Serial1
 no ip address
 encapsulation ppp
 dialer in-band
 dialer enable-timeout 3
 dialer map bridge name urk broadcast 8985
 dialer hold-queue 10
 dialer-group 1
 ppp authentication chap
 bridge-group 1
 pulse-time 1
!
access-list 200 permit 0x0800 0xFFF8
!
dialer-list 1 protocol bridge list 200
bridge 1 protocol ieee
bridge 1 hello 10
```

## Configuring DDR in an IP Environment Example

The following example illustrates how to use DDR on a synchronous interface in an IP environment. You could use the same configuration on an asynchronous serial interface by changing *interface serial 1* to specify an asynchronous interface (for example, *interface async 0*).

```
interface serial 1
ip address 131.108.126.1 255.255.255.0
dialer in-band
! The next command sets the dialer idle time-out to 10 minutes
dialer idle-timeout 600
! The next command inserts the phone number
dialer string 5551234
! The next command gives the modem enough time to recognize that
! DTR has dropped so the modem disconnects the call
pulse-time 1
! The next command adds this interface to the dialer access group defined with
! the dialer-list command
dialer-group 1
!
! The first access list statement, below, specifies that IGRP updates are not
! interesting packets. The second access-list statement specifies that all
! other IP traffic such as Ping, Telnet, or any other IP packet are interesting
! packets. The dialer-list command then creates dialer access group 1 and
! states that access list 101 is to be used to classify packets as interesting
! or uninteresting. The ip route commands
! specify that there is a route to network 131.108.29.0 and to network
! 131.108.1.0 via 131.108.126.2. This means that several destination networks
! are available through a router that is dialed from interface async 1.
!
```

```
access-list 101 deny igrp 0.0.0.0 255.255.255.255 255.255.255.255 0.0.0.0
access-list 101 permit ip 0.0.0.0 255.255.255.255 0.0.0.0 255.255.255.255
dialer-list 1 list 101
ip route 131.108.29.0 131.108.126.2
ip route 131.108.1.0 131.108.126.2
ip local pool dialin 101.102.126.2 101.102.126.254
```

With many modems, the **pulse-time** command must be used so that DTR is dropped for sufficient time to allow the modem to disconnect.

The **redistribute static** command can be used to advertise static route information for DDR applications. Without this command, static routes to the hosts or network that the router can access with DDR will not be advertised to other routers with which the router is communicating. This behavior can block communication because some routes will not be known.

## Set Up Two-Way DDR for Novell IPX Example

You can set dial-on-demand routing (DDR) for Novell IPX so that both the client and server have dial-in access to each other. This configuration is demonstrated in the following two subsections.

### *Remote Configuration*

The following example configuration is performed on the remote side of the connection:

```
username local password secret
ipx routing
!
interface ethernet 0
 ipx network 40
!
interface async
 ip unnumbered e0
 encapsulation ppp
 async mode dedicated
 async dynamic routing
 ipx network 45
 ipx watchdog-spoof
 dialer in-band
 dialer map ipx 45.0000.0cff.d016 broadcast name local 1212
 dialer-group 1
 ppp authentication chap
!
access-list 901 deny 0 FFFFFFFF 452
access-list 901 deny 0 FFFFFFFF 453
access-list 901 deny 0 FFFFFFFF 457
access-list 901 deny 0 FFFFFFFF 0 FFFFFFFF 452
access-list 901 deny 0 FFFFFFFF 0 FFFFFFFF 453
access-list 901 deny 0 FFFFFFFF 0 FFFFFFFF 457
access-list 901 permit 0
ipx route 41 45.0000.0cff.d016
ipx route 50 45.0000.0cff.d016
ipx sap 4 SERVER 50.0000.0000.0001 451 2
chat-script generic ABORT BUSY ABORT NO ## AT OK ATDT\T TIMEOUT 30 CONNECT
!
```

```
dialer-list 1 list 901
!
line 7
 modem InOut
 speed 38400
 flowcontrol hardware
 modem chat-script generic
```

### *Local Configuration*

The following example configuration is performed on the local side of the connection:

```
username remote password secret
ipx routing
!
interface ethernet 0
 ipx network 41
!
interface async
 ip unnumbered e0
 encapsulation ppp
 async mode dedicated
 async dynamic routing
 ipx network 45
 ipx watchdog-spoof
 dialer in-band
 dialer map ipx 45.0000.0cff.d016 broadcast name remote 8888
 dialer-group 1
 ppp authentication chap
!
access-list 901 deny 0 FFFFFFFF 452
access-list 901 deny 0 FFFFFFFF 453
access-list 901 deny 0 FFFFFFFF 457
access-list 901 deny 0 FFFFFFFF 0 FFFFFFFF 452
access-list 901 deny 0 FFFFFFFF 0 FFFFFFFF 453
access-list 901 deny 0 FFFFFFFF 0 FFFFFFFF 457
access-list 901 permit 0
ipx route 40 45.0000.0cff.d016
chat-script generic ABORT BUSY ABORT NO ## AT OK ATDT\T TIMEOUT 30 CONNECT
!
dialer-list 1 list 901
!
line 7
 modem InOut
 speed 38400
 flowcontrol hardware
 modem chat-script generic
```

## AppleTalk Configuration Example

The following example configures DDR for AppleTalk access using an ISDN BRI. Two access lists are defined: one for IP and IGRP, and one for AppleTalk. AppleTalk packets from network 2141 only (except broadcast packets) can initiate calls.

```
interface BRI0
 ip address 130.1.20.107 255.255.255.0
 encapsulation ppp
```

```
 appletalk cable-range 2141-2141 2141.65
 appletalk zone SCruz-Eng
 no appletalk send-rtmps
 dialer map ip 130.1.20.106 broadcast 1879
 dialer map appletalk 2141.66 broadcast 1879
 dialer-group 1
!
access-list 101 deny   igrp 0.0.0.0 255.255.255.255 255.255.255.255 0.0.0.0
access-list 101 permit ip 0.0.0.0 255.255.255.255 0.0.0.0 255.255.255.255
access-list 601 permit cable-range 2141-2141 broadcast-deny
access-list 601 deny other-access
!
dialer-list 1 list 101
dialer-list 1 list 601
```

## DECnet Configuration Example

The following example configures DDR for DECnet:

```
decnet routing 10.19
!
username RouterB password 7 030752180531
!
interface serial 0
 no ip address
 decnet cost 10
 encapsulation ppp
 dialer in-band
 dialer map decnet 10.151 name RouterB broadcast 4155551212
 dialer-group 1
 ppp authentication chap
 pulse-time 1
!
access-list 301 permit 10.0 0.1023 0.0 63.1023
!
dialer-list 1 protocol decnet list 301
```

## ISO CLNS Configuration Example

The following example configures DDR for ISO CLNS:

```
username RouterB password 7 111C140B0E
clns net 47.0004.0001.0000.0c00.2222.00
clns routing
clns filter-set ddrline permit 47.0004.0001....
!
interface serial 0
 no ip address
 encapsulation ppp
 dialer in-band
 dialer map clns 47.0004.0001.0000.0c00.1111.00 name RouterB broadcast 1212
 dialer-group 1
 ppp authentication chap
 clns enable
 pulse-time 1
```

```
!
clns route default serial 0
dialer-list 1 protocol clns list ddrline
```

## XNS Configuration Example

The following example configures DDR for XNS. The access lists deny broadcast traffic to any host on any network, but allow all other traffic.

```
xns routing 0000.0c01.d8dd

username RouterB password 7 111B210A0F

interface serial 0
 no ip address
 encapsulation ppp
 xns network 10
 dialer in-band
 dialer map xns 10.0000.0c01.d877 name RouterB broadcast 4155551212
 dialer-group 1
 ppp authentication chap
 pulse-time 1
!
access-list 400 deny -1 -1.ffff.ffff.ffff 0000.0000.0000
access-list 400 permit -1 10
!
dialer-list 1 protocol xns list 400
```

## Dialing a Single Site Example

Assume that your configuration is as shown in Figure 40–1 and your router receives a packet with a next hop address of 1.1.1.1.

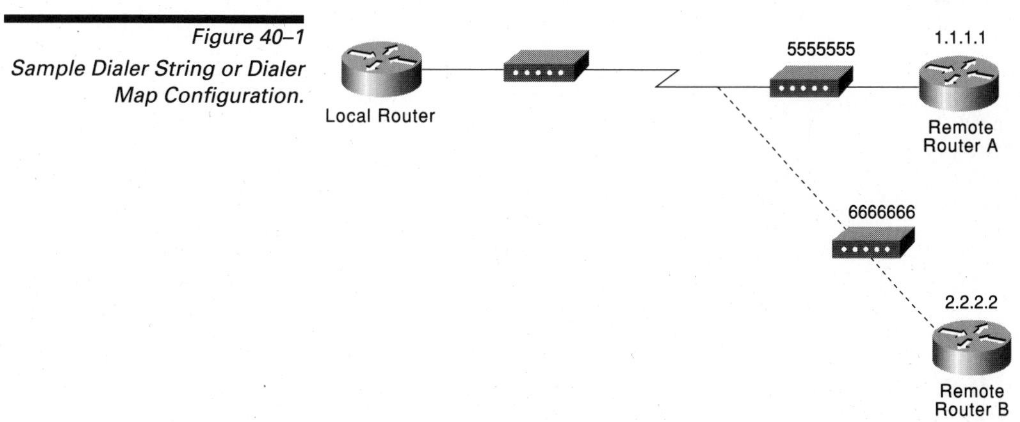


*Figure 40–1 Sample Dialer String or Dialer Map Configuration.*

If the single site called by the DDR spoke interface on your router has the phone number *5555555*, it will send the packet to that site, assuming that the next hop address 1.1.1.1 indicates the same remote device as phone number *5555555*. The **dialer string** command is used to specify the string (telephone number) to be called.

```
interface serial 1
 dialer in-band
 dialer string 5555555
```

### DTR Dialing Example

In the following example, Router A and Router B are connected to a public switched telephone network (PSTN). Router A is configured for DTR dialing. Remote Router B is configured for in-band dialing so it can disconnect an idle call (see Figure 40–2).

*Figure 40–2*
*DTR Dialing Through a PSTN.*

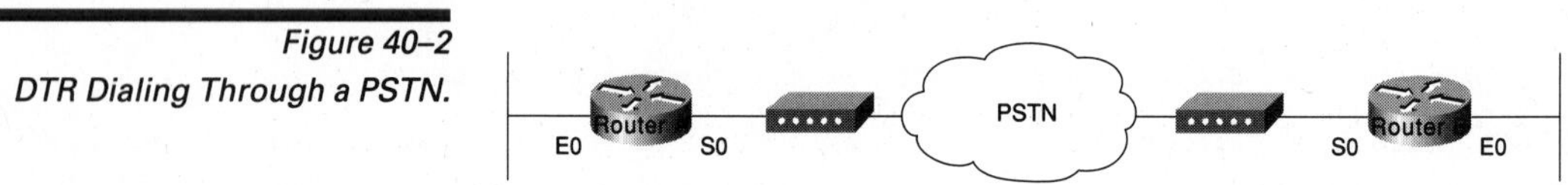


*Router A*

```
interface serial 0
 ip address 131.108.170.19 255.255.255.0
 dialer dtr
 dialer-group 1
!
access-list 101 deny igrp 0.0.0.0 255.255.255.255 0.0.0.0 255.255.255.255
access-list 101 permit ip 0.0.0.0 255.255.255.255 0.0.0.0 255.255.255.255
!
dialer-list 1 list 101
```

*Router B*

```
interface serial 0
 ip address 131.108.170.20 255.255.255.0
 dialer in-band
 dialer string 9876543
 pulse-time 1
!
access-list 101 deny igrp 0.0.0.0 255.255.255.255 0.0.0.0 255.255.255.255
access-list 101 permit ip 0.0.0.0 255.255.255.255 0.0.0.0 255.255.255.255
!
dialer-list 1 list 101
```

### Set Up Hub-and-Spoke DDR for Asynchronous Interfaces and Authentication Example

You can set up dial-on-demand routing (DDR) to provide service to multiple remote sites. In a hub-and-spoke configuration, you can use a generic configuration script to set up each remote connection. Figure 40–3 illustrates a typical hub-and-spoke configuration.

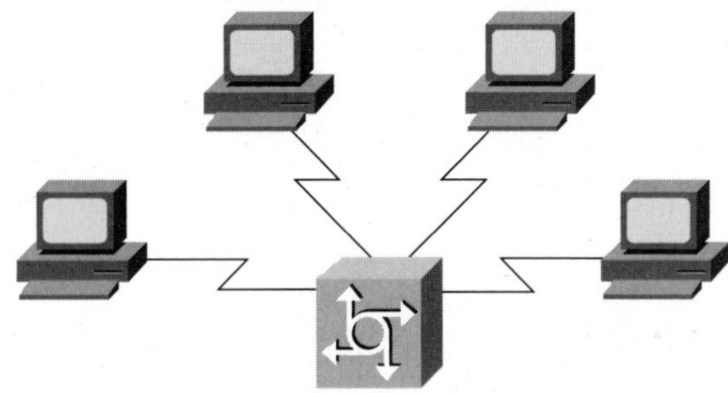

*Figure 40–3 Hub-and-Spoke DDR Configuration.*

This configuration is demonstrated in the following two subsections.

### Spoke Configuration

In the following example, configuration is performed on the spoke side of the connection. (A different "spoke" password must be specified for each remote client.) It provides authentication by identifying a password that must be provided on each end of the connection.

```
interface ethernet 0
 ip address 172.30.44.1 255.255.255.0
!
interface async 7
 async mode dedicated
 async default ip address 128.150.45.1
 ip address 1172.30.45.2 255.255.255.0
 encapsulation ppp
 ppp authentication chap
 dialer in-band
 dialer map ip 172.30.45.1 name hub system-script hub 1234
 dialer map ip 172.30.45.255 name hub system-script hub 1234
 dialer-group 1
!
ip route 172.30.43.0 255.255.255.0 172.30.45.1
ip default-network 172.30.0.0
chat-script generic ABORT BUSY ABORT NO ## AT OK ATDT\T TIMEOUT 30 CONNECT
chat-script hub "" "" name: spoke1 word: <spoke1-passwd> PPP
dialer-list 1 protocol ip permit
!
username hub password <spoke1-passwd>
!
router igrp 109
 network 172.30.0.0
 passive-interface async 7
!
line 7
 modem InOut
 speed 38400
 flowcontrol hardware
 modem chat-script generic
```

### Hub Router Configuration

In the following example, configuration is performed on the local side of the connection—the hub router. It configures the server for communication with three clients and provides authentication by identifying a unique password for each "spoke" in the hub-and-spoke configuration.

```
interface ethernet 0
 ip address 172.30.43.1 255.255.255.0
!
interface async 7
 async mode interactive
 async dynamic address
 dialer rotary-group 1
!
interface async 8
 async mode interactive
 async dynamic address
 dialer rotary-group 1
!
interface dialer 1
 ip address 172.30.45.2 255.255.255.0
 no ip split-horizon
 encapsulation ppp
 ppp authentication chap
 dialer in-band
 dialer map ip 172.30.45.2 name spoke1 3333
 dialer map ip 172.30.45.2 name spoke2 4444
 dialer map ip 172.30.45.2 name spoke3 5555
 dialer map ip 172.30.45.255 name spoke1 3333
 dialer map ip 172.30.45.255 name spoke2 4444
 dialer map ip 172.30.45.255 name spoke3 5555
 dialer-group 1
!
ip route 172.30.44.0 255.255.255.0 172.30.45.2
ip route 172.30.44.0 255.255.255.0 172.30.45.3
ip route 172.30.44.0 255.255.255.0 172.30.45.4
dialer-list 1 list 101
 access-list 101 deny igrp 0.0.0.0 255.255.255.255 0.0.0.0 255.255.255.255
 access-list 101 permit ip 0.0.0.0 255.255.255.255 0.0.0.0 255.255.255.255
 chat-script generic ABORT BUSY ABORT NO ## AT OK ATDT\T TIMEOUT 30 CONNECT
!
username spoke1 password <spoke1-passwd>
username spoke2 password <spoke2-passwd>
username spoke3 password <spoke3-passwd>
username spoke1 autocommand ppp 172.30.45.2
username spoke2 autocommand ppp 172.30.45.3
username spoke3 autocommand ppp 172.30.45.4
!
router igrp 109
 network 172.30.0.0
 redistribute static
!
line 7
 login tacacs
```

```
modem InOut
speed 38400
flowcontrol hardware
modem chat-script generic
```

## Set Up Two-Way Reciprocal Client/Server DDR without Authentication Example

You can set up two-way reciprocal dial-on-demand routing (DDR) without authentication in which both the client and server have dial-in access to each other. This configuration is demonstrated in the following two subsections.

### Remote Configuration

The following example configuration is performed on the remote side of the connection:

```
interface ethernet 0
 ip address 172.30.44.1 255.255.255.0
!
interface async 7
 ip address 172.30.45.2 255.255.255.0
 async mode dedicated
 async default ip address 172.30.45.1
 encap ppp
 dialer in-band
 dialer string 1234
 dialer-group 1
!
ip route 172.30.43.0 255.255.255.0 async 7
 ip default-network 172.30.0.0
 chat-script generic ABORT BUSY ABORT NO ## AT OK ATDT\T TIMEOUT 30 CONNECT
 dialer-list 1 protocol ip permit
!
line 7
 no exec
 modem InOut
 speed 38400
 flowcontrol hardware
 modem chat-script generic
```

### Local Configuration

The following example configuration is performed on the local side of the connection:

```
interface ethernet 0
 ip address 172.30.43.1 255.255.255.0
!
interface async 7
 async mode dedicated
 async default ip address 172.30.45.2
 encapsulation ppp
 dialer in-band
 dialer string 1235
 dialer rotary-group 1
!
interface async 8
 async mode dedicated
```

```
 async default ip address 172.30.45.2
 dialer rotary-group 1
!
ip route 172.30.44.0 255.255.255.0 async 7
 ip address 172.30.45.2 255.255.255.0
 encapsulation ppp
 ppp authentication chap
 dialer in-band
 dialer map ip 172.30.45.2 name remote 4321
 dialer load-threshold 80
!
ip route 172.30.44.0 255.255.255.0 128.150.45.2
 chat-script generic ABORT BUSY ABORT NO ## AT OK ATDT\T TIMEOUT 30 CONNECT
 dialer-list 1 protocol ip permit
!
route igrp 109
network 172.30.0.0
redistribute static
passive-interface async 7
!
line 7
 modem InOut
 speed 38400
 flowcontrol hardware
 modem chat-script generic
```

## Frame Relay Support Examples

The examples in this section present various combinations of interfaces, Frame Relay features, and DDR features.

### *Frame Relay Access with In-Band Dialing (V.25bis) and Static Mapping Example*

In the following example, a router is configured for IP over Frame Relay using in-band dialing. A Frame Relay static map is used to associate the next-hop protocol address to the DLCI. The dialer string allows dialing to only one destination.

```
interface Serial0
 ip address 1.1.1.1 255.255.255.0
 encapsulation frame-relay
 frame-relay map ip 1.1.1.2 100 broadcast
 dialer in-band
 dialer string 4155551212
 dialer-group 1
!
access-list 101 deny igrp any host 255.255.255.255
access-list 101 permit ip any any
!
dialer-list 1 protocol ip list 101
```

### *Frame Relay Access with ISDN Dialing and DDR Dynamic Maps Example*

The following example shows a BRI interface configured for Frame Relay and for IP, IPX, and AppleTalk routing. No static maps are defined because this setup relies on Frame Relay local management interface (LMI) signaling and Inverse ARP to determine the network addresses-to-DLCI mappings dynamically. (Because Frame Relay Inverse ARP is enabled by default, no command is required.)

```
interface BRI0
 ip address 1.1.1.1 255.255.255.0
 ipx network 100
 appletalk cable-range 100-100 100.1
 appletalk zone ISDN
 no appletalk send-rtmps
 encapsulation frame-relay IETF
 dialer map ip 1.1.1.2 broadcast 4155551212
 dialer map apple 100.2 broadcast 4155551212
 dialer map ipx 100.0000.0c05.33ed broadcast 4085551234
 dialer-group 1
!
access-list 101 deny igrp any host 255.255.255.255
access-list 101 permit ip any any
access-list 901 deny -1 FFFFFFFF 452
access-list 901 deny -1 FFFFFFFF 453
access-list 901 deny -1 FFFFFFFF 457
access-list 901 deny -1 FFFFFFFF 0 FFFFFFFF 452
access-list 901 deny -1 FFFFFFFF 0 FFFFFFFF 453
access-list 901 deny -1 FFFFFFFF 0 FFFFFFFF 457
access-list 901 permit -1
access-list 601 permit cable-range 100-100 broadcast-deny
access-list 601 deny other-access
!
dialer-list 1 protocol ip list 101
dialer-list 1 protocol novell list 901
dialer-list 1 protocol apple list 601
```

## X.25 Support Example

In the following example, a router is configured to support X.25 and DTR dialing:

```
interface serial 0
 ip address 131.108.170.19 255.255.255.0
 encapsulation x25
 x25 address 12345
 x25 map ip 131.108.171.20 67890 broadcast
 dialer dtr
 dialer-group 1
!
access-list 101 deny igrp 0.0.0.0 255.255.255.255 0.0.0.0 255.255.255.255
access-list 101 permit ip 0.0.0.0 255.255.255.255 0.0.0.0 255.255.255.255
!
dialer-list 1 list 101
```

## LAPB Support Example

In the following example, the router is configured for LAPB encapsulation and in-band dialing:

```
interface serial 0
 ip address 131.108.170.19 255.255.255.0
 encapsulation lapb
```

```
 dialer in-band
 dialer string 4155551212
 dialer-group 1
!
access-list 101 deny igrp 0.0.0.0 255.255.255.255 0.0.0.0 255.255.255.255
access-list 101 permit ip 0.0.0.0 255.255.255.255 0.0.0.0 255.255.255.255
!
dialer-list 1 protocol ip list 101
```

# CHAPTER 41

# Legacy DDR Spokes Commands

This chapter lists legacy dial-on-demand routing (DDR) commands that are used for configuring the "spoke" router in a hub-and-spoke network topology, explains the command syntax, and provides usage guidelines. A spoke router in a hub-and-spoke network configuration dials only one remote location: the network hub.

For information about configuring network spokes for legacy DDR and for configuration examples, see Chapter 40, "Configuring Legacy DDR Spokes."

## CLEAR DIALER

To clear the values of dialer statistics for one or more serial interfaces or Basic Rate Interfaces (BRIs) configured for DDR, use the **clear dialer** privileged EXEC command.

**clear dialer** [**interface** *type number*]
**clear dialer** [**interface serial** *slot/port*] (Cisco 7500 series)

| *Syntax* | *Description* |
|---|---|
| **interface** | (Optional) Indicates that one interface will be specified. |
| *type* | (Optional) Interface type, either **async**, **serial**, or **bri**. |
| *number* | (Optional) Interface number. |
| *slot/port* | Backplane slot number and port number on the interface. See your hardware installation manual for the specific slot and port numbers. |

### *Command Mode*

Privileged EXEC

### *Usage Guidelines*

This command first appeared in Cisco IOS Release 11.0.

If the **interface** keyword and the arguments are not used, dialer statistics are cleared on all interfaces.

### *Example*

The following example clears the dialer statistics on serial interface 1:

```
clear dialer interface serial 1
```

## DIALER DTR

To enable DDR on an interface and specify that the serial line is connected by non-V.25*bis* modems using Electronic Industries Association (EIA) signaling only—specifically, the data terminal ready (DTR) signal—use the **dialer dtr** interface configuration command. To disable dial-on-demand routing (DDR) for the interface, use the **no** form of this command.

**dialer dtr**
**no dialer dtr**

### *Syntax Description*

This command has no arguments or keywords.

### *Default*

DTR dialing is disabled.

### *Command Mode*

Interface configuration

### *Usage Guidelines*

This command first appeared in Cisco IOS Release 10.0.

A serial interface configured for DTR dialing can place calls only; it cannot accept them.

When a local interface is configured for DTR dialing, the remote interface (that will be receiving the calls) can be configured for in-band dialing or not configured for anything but encapsulation, depending on the desired behavior. If the remote interface is expected to terminate a call when no traffic is transmitted for some time, it must be configured for in-band dialing (along with access lists and a dummy dialer string). If the remote interface is purely passive, no configuration is necessary.

Rotary groups cannot be configured for DTR dialing.

The **dialer map** and **dialer string** commands have no effect on DTR dialers.

### *Example*

The following example enables DDR and specifies DTR dialing on an interface:

```
dialer dtr
```

### *Related Commands*

Search online to find documentation for related commands.

**dialer in-band**
**dialer string (legacy DDR)**

## DIALER IN-BAND

To specify that dial-on-demand routing (DDR) is to be supported, use the **dialer in-band** interface configuration command. To disable DDR for the interface, use the **no** form of this command.

**dialer in-band** [**no-parity** | **odd-parity**]
**no dialer in-band**

| *Syntax* | *Description* |
|---|---|
| **no-parity** | (Optional) Indicates that no parity is to be applied to the dialer string that is sent out to the modem on synchronous interfaces. |
| **odd-parity** | (Optional) Indicates that the dialed number has odd parity (7-bit ASCII characters with the eighth bit as the parity bit) on synchronous interfaces. |

### *Default*

Disabled. By default, no parity is applied to the dialer string.

### *Command Mode*

Interface configuration

### *Usage Guidelines*

This command first appeared in Cisco IOS Release 10.0.

The **dialer in-band** command specifies that chat scripts will be used on asynchronous interfaces and V.25*bis* will be used on synchronous interfaces. The parity keywords do not apply to asynchronous interfaces.

The parity setting applies to the dialer string that is sent out to the modem. If you do not specify a parity, or if you specify no parity, no parity is applied to the output number. If odd parity is configured, the dialed number will have odd parity (7-bit ASCII characters with the eighth bit as the parity bit.)

If an interface only accepts calls and does not place calls, the **dialer in-band** interface configuration command is the only command needed to configure it. If an interface is configured in this manner, with no dialer rotary groups, the idle timer never disconnects the line. It is up to the remote end (the end that placed the call) to disconnect the line based on idle time.

### Example

The following example specifies DDR for asynchronous interface 1:

```
interface async 1
 dialer in-band
```

### Related Commands

Search online to find documentation for related commands.

**dialer string (legacy DDR)**

## DIALER STRING (LEGACY DDR)

To specify the destination string (telephone number) to be called for interfaces calling a single site, use the **dialer string** interface configuration command. To delete the dialer string specified for the interface, use the **no** form of this command.

**dialer string** *dial-string*[*:isdn-subaddress*]
**no dialer string**

| *Syntax* | *Description* |
|---|---|
| *dial-string* | String of characters to be sent to a DCE device. |
| *:isdn-subaddress* | (Optional) ISDN subaddress. |

### Default

No strings are predefined.

### Command Mode

Interface configuration

### Usage Guidelines

This command first appeared in Cisco IOS Release 10.0.

To use this command on an asynchronous interface, you must define a modem chat script for the associated line by using the **script dialer** command. A script must be used to implement dialing.

Dialers configured as **in-band** pass the string to the external dialing device. Specify one **dialer string** command per interface.

In general, you include a **dialer string** command if you intend to use a specific interface to initiate a DDR call.

**NOTES**

If a **dialer string** command is specified without a **dialer-group** command with access lists defined, dialing is never initiated. If the **debug dialer** command is enabled, an error message is displayed indicating that dialing never will occur.

The string of characters specified for the *dial-string* argument is the default number used under the following conditions:

- A **dialer map** command is not included in the interface configuration.
- The next hop address specified in a packet is not included in any of the **dialer map** interface configuration commands recorded—assuming that the destination address passes any access lists specified for DDR with the **dialer-list** command.

### *ITU-T V.25bis Options*

On synchronous interfaces, depending on the type of modem you are using, International Telecommunication Union Telecommunication (ITU-T) Standardization Sector V.25*bis* options might be supported as *dial-string* parameters of the **dialer string** command. Supported options are listed in Table 41–1. The functions of the parameters are nation-specific, and they may have different implementations in your country. These options apply only if you have enabled DDR with the **dialer in-band** command. Refer to the operation manual for your modem for a list of supported options.

**NOTES**

The ITU-T carries out the functions of the former Consultative Committee for International Telegraph and Telephone (CCITT).

**Table 41–1** *ITU-T V.25bis OptionsITU-T V.25bis Options*

| Option | Description |
|---|---|
| : | Wait tone. |
| < | Pause.<br>Usage and duration of this parameter vary by country. |
| = | Separator 3.<br>For national use. |
| > | Separator 4.<br>For national use. |

**Table 41–1** *ITU-T V.25bis OptionsITU-T V.25bis Options, Continued*

| Option | Description |
|---|---|
| P | Dialing to be continued in pulse mode.<br>Optionally accepted parameter. |
| T | Tone. Dialing to be continued in Dual Tone Multifrequency (DTMF) mode.<br>Optionally accepted parameter. |
| & | Flash. (The flash duration varies by country.)<br>Optionally accepted parameter. |

### *Example*

The following example specifies a DDR telephone number to be tone-dialed on asynchronous interface 1 using the **dialer string** command:

```
interface async 1
dialer string T14085553434
```

### *Related Commands*

Search online to find documentation for related commands.

**dialer in-band**
**script dialer**

# Chapter 42

# Configuring Legacy DDR Hubs

This chapter describes the configuration of legacy dial-on-demand routing on interfaces functioning as the hub in a hub-and-spoke network topology. This chapter considers a *hub* interface to be any interface that calls or receives calls from more than one other router and a *spoke* interface to be an interface that calls or receives calls from exactly one router.

For configuration tasks for the spoke interfaces in a hub-and-spoke network topology, see Chapter 40, "Configuring Legacy DDR Spokes." For a complete description of the DDR commands mentioned in this chapter, see Chapter 43, "Legacy DDR Hub Commands." For information about the Dialer Profiles implementation of DDR, see Chapter 44, "Configuring Peer-to-Peer DDR with Dialer Profiles."

## DDR Issues

A DDR configuration applies to a specified router interface but serves to meet the communication needs of the network. The router configured for DDR has a function to serve in preserving communications and ensuring that routes are known to other routers at both ends of the dial link. Thus, these issues are important:

- Types and number of router interfaces to be configured for dial-on-demand routing
- Function of each specific interface—to place calls, or receive calls, or both—and the number of sites connecting to the interface
- Identity and characteristics of the router at the other end of each connection—phone number, host name, next-hop network protocol addresses, type of signaling used or required, ability to place or receive calls, other requirements
- Types of packets that will be allowed to trigger outgoing calls—if the interface places calls

- End of the connection which will control the communication: initiating calls, and terminating calls when the line is idle
- Method for authenticating other routers—if the interface receives calls from multiple sites
- Passing routing information across the dial link

## Configuration Task Flow

Before you configure DDR, make sure you have completed the preparations for bridging or routing as described in Chapter 36, "Deciding and Preparing To Configure DDR." That chapter provides information about the minimal requirements.

When you configure DDR on a hub interface in a hub-and-spoke topology, you perform the following general steps:

**Step 1** Specify the interface that will place calls to or receive calls from multiple sites. (See Chapter 40 for information about configuring an interface to place calls to or receive calls from one site only.)

**Step 2** Enable DDR on the interface. This step is not required for some interfaces; for example, ISDN interfaces and passive interfaces that receive only from DTR-dialing interfaces.

**Step 3** Configure the interface to receive calls only, if applicable. Receiving calls from multiple sites requires each inbound call to be authenticated.

**Step 4** Configure the interface to place calls only, if applicable.

**Step 5** Configure the interface to place and receive calls, if applicable.

**Step 6** If the interface will place calls, specify access control for:

- Transparent bridging—Assign the interface to a bridge group, and define dialer lists associated with the bridging access lists. The interface switches between members of the same bridge group, and dialer lists specify which packets can trigger calls.

  or

- Routed protocols—Define dialer lists associated with the protocol access lists to specify which packets can trigger calls.

**Step 7** Customize the interface settings (timers, interface priority, hold queues, bandwidth on demand, and disabling fast switching) as needed.

When you have configured the interface and it is operational, you can monitor its performance and its connections as described in section, "Monitoring DDR Connections," found later in this chapter.

You can also enhance DDR by configuring Multilink PPP and configuring PPP callback. The PPP configuration tasks are described in Chapter 25, "Configuring Media-Independent PPP and Multilink PPP."

See section "Legacy DDR Hub Configuration Examples," found later in this chapter for examples of how to configure DDR on your network.

## DDR Configuration Task List

To configure DDR on an interface, complete the tasks in the following sections. The first five bulleted items are required. The remaining tasks are not absolutely required, but might be necessary in your networking environment.

- Specifying the Interface
- Enabling DDR on the Interface
- Configuring the Interface To Place Calls Only
  or
  Configuring the Interface To Receive Calls Only
  or
  Configuring the Interface To Place and Receive Calls
- Configuring Access Control for Outgoing Calls, if applicable
- Customizing the Interface Settings, as needed
- Configuring To Send Traffic over Frame Relay, X.25, or LAPB Networks, if needed

You can also monitor DDR connections. See section "Monitoring DDR Connections" for commands and other information.

## Specifying the Interface

You can configure any asynchronous, synchronous serial, ISDN, or dialer interface for Legacy DDR.

**NOTES**

When you specify an interface, make sure to use the interface numbering scheme supported on the network interface module or other port hardware on the router. On the Cisco 7200 series, for example, you specify an interface by indicating its type, slot number, and port number.

To specify an interface to configure for DDR, complete the following task(s) in global configuration mode:

| Task | Command |
|---|---|
| Specify an interface to configure for DDR.<br>or | **interface async** *number*<br>**interface serial** *number*<br>**interface bri** *number* |
| Specify an ISDN PRI D channel (T1).<br>Specify an ISDN PRI D channel (E1). | **interface serial** *slot/port*:**23**<br>**interface serial** *slot/port*:**15** |
| or | |
| Specify a logical interface to function as a dialer rotary group leader. | **interface dialer** *number* |

Dialer interfaces are logical or virtual entities, but they use physical interfaces to place or receive calls.

## Enabling DDR on the Interface

This step is required for asynchronous serial, synchronous serial, and logical dialer interfaces.

This step is not required for ISDN interfaces (BRI interfaces and ISDN PRI D channels) and for *purely passive* interfaces that will receive calls only from interfaces that use DTR dialing.

Enabling DDR on an interface usually requires you to specify the type of dialer to be used. This step is not required for ISDN interfaces because the software automatically configures ISDN interfaces to be dialer type ISDN.

To enable DDR on the interface, complete the following task in interface configuration mode:

| Task | Command |
|---|---|
| Enable DDR on an asynchronous interface or a synchronous serial interface using V.25*bis* modems. | **dialer in-band** [**no-parity** \| **odd-parity**] |

You can optionally specify parity if the modem on this interface uses the V.25*bis* command set. The 1984 version of the V.25*bis* specification states that characters must have odd parity. However, the default for the **dialer in-band** command is no parity.

## Configuring the Interface To Place Calls Only

To configure an interface to place calls to multiple destinations, complete the following tasks. The first task is required for all interface types. The second task is required only if you specified a dialer interface.

- Define the Dialing Destination
- Specify a Physical Interface To Use and Assign it to a Dialer Rotary Group

### Define the Dialing Destination

For calling multiple sites, an interface or dialer rotary group must be configured to map each next-hop protocol address to the dial string (some form of a telephone number) used to reach it.

To define each dialing destination, perform one of the following tasks in interface configuration mode:

| Task | Command |
|---|---|
| Define a dialing destination for a synchronous serial interface or a dialer interface. | **dialer map** *protocol next-hop-address dial-string*[:*isdn-subaddress*] |
| Define a dialing destination for an ISDN interface (including an ISDN PRI D channel). | **dialer map** *protocol next-hop-address* [**spc**] [**speed 56** \| **64**] [**broadcast**] [*dial-string*[:*isdn-subaddress*]] |
| Define a dialing destination for an asynchronous interface.<br>If a modem dialing chat script has not been assigned to the line or a system login chat script must be specified, define both a dialing destination and the chat scripts to use. | **dialer map** *protocol next-hop-address* [**modem-script** *modem-regexp*] [**system-script** *system-regexp*] *dial-string*[:*isdn-subaddress*] |

Repeat this step as many times as needed to ensure that all dialing destinations are reachable via some next-hop address and dialed number.

If you intend to send traffic over other types of networks, see the appropriate section: "Configure the Interface for Sending Traffic over a Frame Relay Network," "Configure the Interface for Sending Traffic over an X.25 Network," or "Configure the Interface for Sending Traffic over a LAPB Network."

### Specify a Physical Interface To Use and Assign it to a Dialer Rotary Group

This section applies only if you specified a dialer interface to configure for DDR.

To assign a physical interface to a dialer rotary group, perform the following tasks starting in global configuration mode:

| Task | Command |
|---|---|
| **Step 1** Specify a physical interface to use. | **interface serial** *number*<br>**interface async** *number* |

| Task | | Command |
|---|---|---|
| **Step 2** | Assign the specified physical interface to a dialer rotary group. | **dialer rotary-group** *number* |

Repeat these two steps for each physical interface to be used by the dialer interface.

An ISDN BRI is a rotary group of B channels. An ISDN interface can be part of a rotary group comprising other interfaces (synchronous, asynchronous, ISDN BRI, or ISDN PRI). However, Cisco supports at most one level of recursion; that is, a rotary of rotaries is acceptable, but a rotary of rotaries of rotaries is not supported.

Interfaces in a dialer rotary group do not have individual addresses; when the interface is being used for dialing, it inherits the parameters configured for the dialer interface. However, if the individual interface is configured with an address and it is subsequently used to establish a connection from the user EXEC level, the individual interface address again applies.

**NOTES**

When you look at your configuration file, commands will not appear in the order in which you entered them. You will also see interface configuration commands that you did not enter, because each interface assigned to a dialer rotary group inherits the parameters of the dialer interface in the dialer rotary group.

Figure 42–1 illustrates how dialer interfaces work. In this configuration, serial interfaces 1, 2, and 3 are assigned to dialer rotary group 1 and thereby take on the parameters configured for dialer interface 1. When it is used for dialing, the IP address of serial interface 2 is the same as the address of the dialer interface, 131.108.1.1.

*Figure 42–1 Sample Dialer Interface Configuration.*

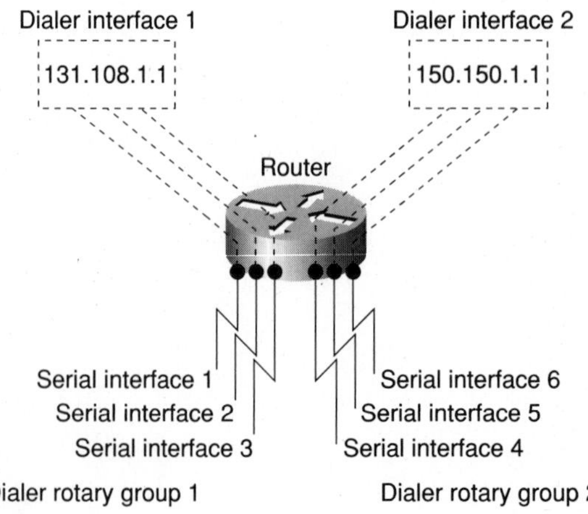

### CONFIGURING THE INTERFACE TO RECEIVE CALLS ONLY

Once DDR is enabled on an asynchronous serial, synchronous serial, and ISDN interface, the interface can receive calls from multiple sites using one line or multiple lines.

However, interfaces that receive calls from multiple sites require authentication of the remote sites. In addition, dialer interfaces require at least one physical interface to be specified and added to the dialer rotary group. Complete the tasks in the following sections:

- Configure the Interface for TACACS+

  or

- Configure the Interface for PPP Authentication
- Specify Physical Interfaces and Assign them to the Dialer Rotary Group

#### Configure the Interface for TACACS+

To configure Terminal Access Controller Access Control System (TACACS) as an alternative to host authentication, perform the following task in interface configuration mode:

| Task | Command |
|---|---|
| Configure TACACS. | **ppp use-tacacs** [**single-line**]<br>or<br>**aaa authentication ppp** |

Use the **ppp use-tacacs** command with TACACS and Extended TACACS. Use the **aaa authentication ppp** command with Authentication, Authorization, and Accounting (AAA)/TACACS+.

#### Configure the Interface for PPP Authentication

This section specifies the minimum required configuration for PPP CHAP or PAP authentication. For more detailed information, see Chapter 25.

To use CHAP or PAP authentication, perform the following tasks beginning in interface configuration mode:

(After you have enabled one of these protocols, the local router or access server requires authentication of the remote devices that are calling. If the remote device does not support the enabled authentication protocol, no traffic will be passed to that device.)

**Step 1** For CHAP, configure host name authentication and the secret or password for each remote system with which authentication is required.

**Step 2** Map the protocol address to the name of the host calling in.

To enable PPP encapsulation, perform the following tasks in interface configuration mode:

| Task | | Command |
|---|---|---|
| **Step 1** | Enable PPP on an interface. | **encapsulation ppp** |
| **Step 2** | Enable CHAP on an interface.<br>or<br>Enable PAP on an interface. | **ppp authentication chap** [**if-needed**]<br><br>**ppp authentication pap** |
| **Step 3** | For any host calling in to the local router or access server, map its host name (case-sensitive) to the next-hop address used to reach it.<br>Repeat this step for each host calling in to this interface. | **dialer map** *protocol next-hop-address* **name** *hostname* |
| **Step 4** | Return to global configuration mode. | **exit** |
| **Step 5** | Specify the password to be used in CHAP caller identification.<br>Repeat this step to add a username entry for each remote system from which the local router or access server requires authentication. | **username** *hostname* **password** *secret* |

### Specify Physical Interfaces and Assign them to the Dialer Rotary Group

To assign a physical interface to a dialer rotary group, perform the following tasks starting in global configuration mode:

| Task | | Command |
|---|---|---|
| **Step 1** | Specify a physical interface to use. | **interface serial** *number*<br>**interface async** *number* |
| **Step 2** | Assign the specified physical interface to a dialer rotary group. | **dialer rotary-group** *number* |

Repeat these two steps for each physical interface to be used by the dialer interface.

## Configuring the Interface To Place and Receive Calls

You can configure a physical interface or dialer interface to both place and receive calls. For placing calls, the interface must be configured to map each next-hop address to the telephone number to dial. For receiving calls from multiple sites, the interface must be configured to authenticate callers.

Figure 42–2 shows a configuration in which the central site is placing and receiving calls from multiple sites. In this configuration, multiple sites are calling in to a central site, and the central site might be calling one or more of the remote sites.

*Figure 42–2*
*Hub-and-Spoke Configuration Using Dial-on-Demand Routing (DDR).*

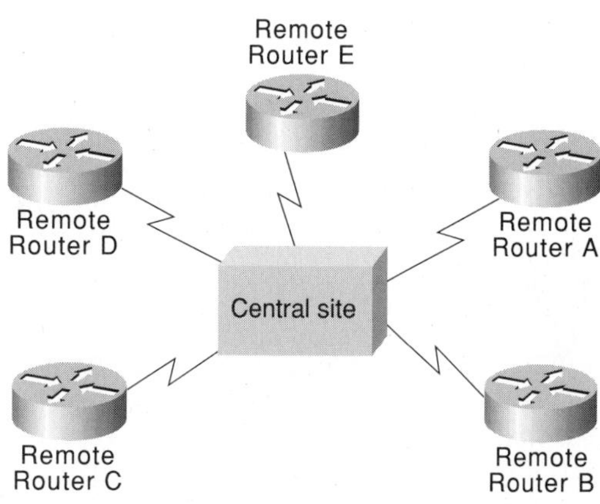


To configure a single line, multiple lines, or a dialer interface to place calls to and receive calls from multiple sites, perform the following tasks in interface configuration mode:

**Step 1** Define One or More Dialing Destinations

**Step 2** Define the Traffic To Be Authenticated

If you intend to send traffic over other types of networks, see the appropriate section: "Configure the Interface for Sending Traffic over a Frame Relay Network," "Configure the Interface for Sending Traffic over an X.25 Network," or "Configure the Interface for Sending Traffic over a LAPB Network."

### Define One or More Dialing Destinations

For calling multiple sites, an interface or dialer rotary group must be configured to map each next-hop protocol address to the dial string (some form of a telephone number) used to reach it.

To define each dialing destination, perform one of the following tasks in interface configuration mode:

Repeat this step as many times as needed to ensure that all dialing destinations are reachable via some next-hop address and dialed number.

| Task | Command |
|---|---|
| Define only one dialing destination (used to configure one phone number on multiple lines only). | **dialer string** *dial-string*[:*isdn-subaddress*] |
| Define one of several dialing destinations for a synchronous serial interface or a dialer interface. | **dialer map** *protocol next-hop-address dial-string*[:*isdn-subaddress*] |
| Define one of several dialing destinations for an ISDN interface (including an ISDN PRI D channel). | **dialer map** *protocol next-hop-address* [**spc**] [**speed 56** \| **64**] [**broadcast**] [*dial-string*[:*isdn-subaddress*]] |
| Define one of several dialing destinations for an asynchronous interface.<br>If a modem dialing chat script has not been assigned to the line or a system login chat script must be specified, define both a dialing destination and the chat scripts to use. | **dialer map** *protocol next-hop-address* [**modem-script** *modem-regexp*] [**system-script** *system-regexp*] *dial-string*[:*isdn-subaddress*] |

### Define the Traffic To Be Authenticated

Calls from the multiple sites must be authenticated. Authentication can be done through CHAP or PAP. In addition, the interface must be configured to map a host's protocol address to the name to use for authenticating the remote host.

To enable CHAP or PAP on an interface and authenticate sites that are calling in, perform the following tasks in interface configuration mode:

| Task | | Command |
|---|---|---|
| **Step 1** | Configure an interface for PPP encapsulation. | **encapsulation ppp** |
| **Step 2** | Enable CHAP.<br>or<br>Enable PAP. | **ppp authentication chap** [**if-needed**]<br>or<br>**ppp authentication pap** [**if-needed**] |
| **Step 3** | Map the protocol address to a host name. | **dialer map** *protocol next-hop-address* **name** *hostname* [**modem-script** *modem-regexp*] [**system-script** *system-regexp*] [*dial-string*[:*isdn-subaddress*]] |

If the dial string is not used in Step 3, the interface will be able to receive calls from the host, but will not be able to place calls to the host.

Repeat Step 3 for each site from which the router will receive calls.

## CONFIGURING ACCESS CONTROL FOR OUTGOING CALLS

Protocol access lists and dialer access lists are central to the operation of DDR. In general, access lists are used as the screening criteria for determining when to initiate DDR calls. All packets are tested against the dialer access list. Packets that match a permit entry are deemed *interesting* or *packets of interest*. Packets that do not match a permit entry or that do match a deny entry are deemed *uninteresting*. When a packet is found to be interesting, either the dialer idle timer is reset (if the line is active) or a connection is attempted (assuming the line is available but not active). If a tested packet is deemed *uninteresting*, it will be forwarded if it is intended for a destination known to be on a specific interface and the link is active. However, such a packet will not initiate a DDR call and will not reset the idle timer.

### Configure Access Control for Bridging

When you completed preparations for bridging over DDR, you entered global access lists to specify the protocol packets to be permitted or denied, and global dialer lists to specify which access list to use and which dialer group would place the outgoing calls.

Now you must tie those global lists to an interface configured for DDR. You accomplish that by assigning selected interfaces to a bridge group. Because packets are bridged only among interfaces that belong to the same bridge group, you need to assign this interface and others to the same bridge group.

To assign an interface to a bridge group, complete the following task in interface configuration mode:

| Task | Command |
|---|---|
| Assign the specified interface to a bridge group. | **bridge-group** *bridge-group* |

For examples of bridging over DDR, see the section "Transparent Bridging over DDR Examples," later in this chapter.

### Configure Access Control for Routing

Before you perform the tasks outlined in this section, you should have completed the preparations for routing a protocol over DDR as described briefly in Chapter 36.

An interface can be associated only with a single dialer access group; multiple dialer access group assignments are not allowed. To specify the dialer access group to which you want to assign an access list, perform the following task in interface configuration mode:

| Task | Command |
| --- | --- |
| Specify the number of the dialer access group to which the specific interface belongs. | **dialer-group** *group-number* |

## CUSTOMIZING THE INTERFACE SETTINGS

Perform the tasks in the following sections as needed to customize DDR in your network:

- Configure Timers on the DDR Interface
- Set Dialer Interface Priority
- Configure a Dialer Hold Queue
- Configure Bandwidth on Demand
- Disable and Re-Enable DDR Fast Switching

### Configure Timers on the DDR Interface

Perform the tasks in the following sections as needed to configure DDR interface timers:

- Set Line-Idle Time
- Set Idle Time for Busy Interfaces
- Set Line-Down Time
- Set Carrier-Wait Time

#### *Set Line-Idle Time*

To specify the amount of time a line will stay idle before it is disconnected, perform the following task in interface configuration mode:

| Task | Command |
| --- | --- |
| Set line-idle time. | **dialer idle-timeout** *seconds* |

#### *Set Idle Time for Busy Interfaces*

The dialer fast-idle timer is activated if there is contention for a line. Contention occurs when a line is in use, a packet for a different next-hop address is received, and the busy line is required to send the competing packet.

If the line has been idle for the configured amount of time, the current call is disconnected immediately and the new call is placed. If the line has not yet been idle as long as the fast-idle timeout period, the packet is dropped because there is no way to get through to the destination. (After the packet is dropped, the fast-idle timer remains active and the current call is disconnected as soon as it has been idle for as long as the fast-idle timeout). If, in the meantime, another packet is transmitted to the currently connected destination, and it is classified as interesting, the fast-idle timer is restarted.

To specify the amount of time a line for which there is contention will stay idle before the line is disconnected and the competing call is placed, perform the following task in interface configuration mode:

| Task | Command |
|---|---|
| Set idle time for high traffic lines. | **dialer fast-idle** *seconds* |

This command applies both to inbound and outbound calls.

### *Set Line-Down Time*

To set the length of time the interface stays down before it is available to dial again after a line is disconnected or fails, perform the following task in interface configuration mode:

| Task | Command |
|---|---|
| Set the interface downtime. | **dialer enable-timeout** *seconds* |

This command applies both to inbound and outbound calls.

### *Set Carrier-Wait Time*

To set the length of time an interface waits for the telephone service (carrier), perform the following task in interface configuration mode:

| Task | Command |
|---|---|
| Set the length of time the interface waits for the carrier to come up when a call is placed. | **dialer wait-for-carrier-time** *seconds* |

For asynchronous interfaces, this command sets the total time to wait for a call to connect. This time is set to allow for running the chat script.

## Set Dialer Interface Priority

You can assign dialer priority to an interface. Priority indicates which interface in a dialer rotary group will get used first. Perform the following task in interface configuration mode:

| Task | Command |
|---|---|
| Specify which dialer interfaces will be used first. | **dialer priority** *number* |

For example, you might give one interface in a dialer rotary group higher priority than another if it is attached to faster, more reliable modem. In this way, the higher-priority interface will be used as often as possible.

The range of values for *number* is 0 to 255. Zero is the default value and lowest priority; 255 is the highest priority. This command applies to outgoing calls only.

### Configure a Dialer Hold Queue

Sometimes packets destined for a remote router are discarded because no connection exists. Establishing a connection using an analog modem can take time, during which packets are discarded. However, configuring a dialer hold queue will allow *interesting* outgoing packets to be queued and sent as soon as the modem connection is established.

A dialer hold queue can be configured on any type of dialer, including in-band synchronous, asynchronous, DTR, and ISDN dialers. Also, *hunt group leaders* can be configured with a dialer hold queue. If a hunt group leader (of a rotary dialing group) is configured with a hold queue, all members of the group will be configured with a dialer hold queue and no individual member's hold queue can be altered.

To establish a dialer hold queue, perform the following task in interface configuration mode:

| Task | Command |
|---|---|
| Create a dialer hold queue and specify the number of packets to be held in it. | **dialer hold-queue** *packets* |

As many as 100 packets can be held in an outgoing dialer hold queue.

### Configure Bandwidth on Demand

You can configure a dialer rotary group to use additional bandwidth by placing additional calls to a single destination if the load for the interface exceeds a specified weighted value. Parallel communication links are established based on traffic load. The number of parallel links that can be established to one location is not limited.

To set the dialer load threshold for bandwidth on demand, perform the following task in interface configuration mode:

Once multiple links are established, they are still governed by the load threshold. If the total load falls below the threshold, an idle link will be torn down.

| Task | Command |
|---|---|
| Configure the dialer rotary group to place additional calls to a destination, as indicated by interface load. | **dialer load-threshold** *load* |

### Disable and Re-Enable DDR Fast Switching

Fast switching is enabled by default on all DDR interfaces. When fast switching is enabled or disabled on an ISDN D channel, it is enabled or disabled on all B channels. When fast switching is enabled or disabled on a dialer interface, it is enabled or disabled on all rotary group members but cannot be enabled or disabled on the serial interfaces individually.

Fast switching can be disabled and re-enabled on a protocol-by-protocol basis. To disable fast switching and re-enable it, complete one of the following protocol-specific tasks:

| Task | Command |
|---|---|
| Disable IP fast switching over a DDR interface. | **no ip route-cache** |
| Re-enable IP fast switching over a DDR interface. | **ip route cache** |
| Disable distributed IP fast switching over a DDR interface. This feature works in Cisco 7500 routers with a Versatile Interface Processor (VIP) card. | **no ip route-cache distributed** |
| Enable distributed IP fast switching over a DDR interface. This feature works in Cisco 7500 routers with a Versatile Interface Processor (VIP) card. | **ip route-cache distributed** |
| Disable IPX fast switching over a DDR interface. | **no ipx route-cache** |
| Re-enable IPX fast switching over a DDR interface. | **ipx route-cache** |

## Configuring To Send Traffic over Frame Relay, X.25, or LAPB Networks

An interface configured for DDR can send traffic over networks that require LAPB, X.25, or Frame Relay encapsulation. To configure an interface for those networks, complete the tasks in the following sections:

- Configure the Interface for Sending Traffic over a Frame Relay Network
- Configure the Interface for Sending Traffic over an X.25 Network
- Configure the Interface for Sending Traffic over a LAPB Network

### Configure the Interface for Sending Traffic over a Frame Relay Network

Access to Frame Relay networks is now available through dial-up connections as well as leased lines. Dial-up connectivity allows Frame Relay networks to be extended to sites that do not generate enough traffic to justify leased lines and also allows a Frame Relay network to back up another network or point-to-point line.

DDR over Frame Relay is supported for synchronous serial and ISDN interfaces and for rotary groups, and is available for in-band, DTR, and ISDN dialers.

Frame Relay supports multiple PVC connections over the same serial interface or ISDN B channel, but only one *physical* interface can be used (dialed, connected, and active) in a rotary group or with ISDN.

### Configuration Restrictions

The following restrictions apply to DDR used over Frame Relay:

- Frame Relay is not available for asynchronous dialers.
- Like HDLC, LAPB, and X.25, Frame Relay does not provide authentication. However, ISDN dialers can offer some authentication through the caller ID feature.
- Only one ISDN B channel can be dialed at any one time. When configuring a rotary group, you can use only one serial interface.

**NOTES**

Frame Relay subinterfaces work the same on dial-up connections as they do on leased lines.

### Configuration Overview

No new commands are required to support DDR over Frame Relay. In general, you configure Frame Relay and configure DDR. In general, complete the following steps to configure an interface for DDR over Frame Relay:

- Specify the interface.
- Specify the protocol identifiers for the interface.

  For example, enter the IP address and mask, the IPX network number, and the AppleTalk cable range and zone.
- Configure Frame Relay.

  As a minimum, you must enable Frame Relay encapsulation and decide whether you need to do static or dynamic address mapping. If you decide to do dynamic mapping, you do not need to enter a command because Inverse ARP is enabled by default. If you decide to do static mapping, you must enter Frame Relay mapping commands.

  You can then configure various options as needed for your Frame Relay network topology.
- Configure DDR.

  At a minimum, you must decide and configure the interface for outgoing calls only, incoming calls only, or both outgoing and incoming calls.

You can also configure DDR for your routed protocols (as specified in Chapter 36) and for snapshot routing (as specified in Chapter 69, "Configuring Snapshot Routing"). You can also customize DDR on your router or access server (as described in the section "Customizing the Interface Settings," later in this chapter).

For examples of configuring various interfaces for DDR over Frame Relay, see the section "Frame Relay Support Examples," later in this chapter.

## Configure the Interface for Sending Traffic over an X.25 Network

X.25 interfaces can now be configured to support DDR. Synchronous serial and ISDN interfaces on our routers and access servers can be configured for X.25 addresses, X.25 encapsulation, and mapping of protocol addresses to a remote host's X.25 address. In-band, DTR, and ISDN dialers can be configured to support X.25 encapsulation, but rotary groups cannot. On ISDN dialers configured for X.25 encapsulation, only one B channel can be used.

To configure an interface to support X.25, perform the following X.25-specific tasks in interface configuration mode and also complete the DDR configuration of the interface:

| Task | | Command |
|---|---|---|
| **Step 1** | Configure the interface to use X.25 encapsulation. | **encapsulation x25** [**dte** \| **dce**] [**ietf**] |
| **Step 2** | Assign an X.25 address to the interface. | **x25 address** *x.121-address* |
| **Step 3** | Set up the LAN protocols-to-remote host address mapping. | **x25 map** *protocol address* [*protocol2 address2* [...[*protocol9 address9*]]] *x.121-address* [*option*] |

The order of DDR and X.25 configuration tasks is not critical; you can configure DDR before or after X.25, and you can even mix the DDR and X.25 commands.

For an example of configuring an interface for X.25 encapsulation and then completing the DDR configuration, see the section "X.25 Support Configuration Example," later in this chapter.

## Configure the Interface for Sending Traffic over a LAPB Network

Dial-on-demand routing over serial lines now supports Link Access Procedure, Balanced (LAPB) encapsulation, in addition to the previously supported PPP, HDLC, and X.25 encapsulations.

LAPB encapsulation is supported on synchronous serial, ISDN, and dialer rotary group interfaces, but not on asynchronous dialers.

Because the default encapsulation is HDLC, you must explicitly configure LAPB encapsulation. To configure an interface to support LAPB encapsulation, perform the following task in interface configuration mode and also complete the DDR configuration of the interface:

| Task | Command |
|---|---|
| Specify LAPB encapsulation. | **encapsulation lapb** [**dte** \| **dce**] [**multi** \| *protocol*] |

For an example of configuring an interface for DDR over LAPB, see the section "X.25 Support Configuration Example," later in this chapter.

## Monitoring DDR Connections

To monitor DDR connections and snapshot routing, perform the following tasks in privileged EXEC mode:

| Task | Command |
|---|---|
| Display general diagnostics about the DDR interface. | **show dialer** [**interface** *type number*] |
| Display current dialer maps, next-hop protocol addresses, user names, and the interfaces on which they are configured. | **show dialer map** |
| Display information about the ISDN interface. | **show interfaces bri 0** |
| Display status about the IPX interface. | **show ipx interface** [*type number*] |
| Display information about the IPX packets transmitted by the router or access server, including watchdog counters. | **show ipx traffic** |
| Display information about the AppleTalk packets transmitted by the router or access server. | **show appletalk traffic** |
| Display information about the Banyan VINES packets transmitted by the router or access server. | **show vines traffic** |
| Display information about the DECnet packets transmitted by the router or access server. | **show decnet traffic** |
| Display information about the XNS packets transmitted by the router or access server. | **show xns traffic** |
| Clear the values of the general diagnostic statistics. | **clear dialer** |

## Legacy DDR Hub Configuration Examples

The examples provided in this section show various DDR configurations as follows:

- Transparent Bridging over DDR Examples
- Configuring DDR in an IP Environment Example
- AppleTalk Configuration Example
- Banyan VINES Configuration Example
- DECnet Configuration Example
- ISO CLNS Configuration Example
- XNS Configuration Example
- Set Up Hub-and-Spoke DDR for Asynchronous Interfaces and Authentication Example
- Dialing a Single Site or Multiple Sites Example
- Configuring Multiple Destinations Example
- Configuring Dialer Interfaces and Dialer Rotary Groups Example
- DDR Using Dialer Interface and PPP Encapsulation Example
- Set Up Two-Way DDR with Authentication Example
- Frame Relay Support Examples
- X.25 Support Configuration Example
- LAPB Support Configuration Example

### Transparent Bridging over DDR Examples

The following two examples differ only in the packets that cause calls to be placed. The first example specifies by protocol (any bridge packet is permitted to cause a call to be made); the second example allows a finer granularity by specifying the Ethernet type codes of bridge packets.

The first example configures serial interface 1 for DDR bridging. Any bridge packet is permitted to cause a call to be placed.

```
no ip routing
!
interface Serial1
 no ip address
 encapsulation ppp
 dialer in-band
 dialer enable-timeout 3
 dialer map bridge name urk broadcast 8985
 dialer hold-queue 10
 dialer-group 1
 ppp authentication chap
 bridge-group 1
 pulse-time 1
!
```

```
dialer-list 1 protocol bridge permit
bridge 1 protocol ieee
bridge 1 hello 10
```

The second example also configures the serial interface 1 for DDR bridging. However, this example includes an **access-list** command that specifies the Ethernet type codes that can cause calls to be placed and a **dialer list protocol list** command that refers to the specified access list.

```
no ip routing
!
interface Serial1
 no ip address
 encapsulation ppp
 dialer in-band
 dialer enable-timeout 3
 dialer map bridge name urk broadcast 8985
 dialer hold-queue 10
 dialer-group 1
 ppp authentication chap
 bridge-group 1
 pulse-time 1
!
access-list 200 permit 0x0800 0xFFF8
!
dialer-list 1 protocol bridge list 200
bridge 1 protocol ieee
bridge 1 hello 10
```

## Configuring DDR in an IP Environment Example

The following example illustrates how to configure DDR to call one site from a synchronous serial interface in an IP environment. You could use the same configuration on an asynchronous serial interface by changing **interface serial 1** to specify an asynchronous interface (for example, **interface async** 0).

```
interface serial 1
 ip address 131.108.126.1 255.255.255.0
 dialer in-band
 dialer idle-timeout 600
 dialer string 5551234
 pulse-time 1
! The next command adds this interface to the dialer access group defined with
! the dialer-list command
 dialer-group 1
!
!The first access list statement, below, specifies that IGRP updates are not
!interesting packets. The second access-list statement specifies that all
!other IP traffic such as Ping, Telnet, or any other IP packet is interesting.
!The dialer-list command then creates dialer access group 1 and states that
!access list 101 is to be used to classify packets as interesting or
!uninteresting. The ip route commands specify that there is a route to network
!131.108.29.0 and to network 131.108.1.0 via 131.108.126.2. This means that
!several destination networks are available through a router that is dialed
!from interface serial 1.
```

```
!
access-list 101 deny igrp 0.0.0.0 255.255.255.255 255.255.255.255 0.0.0.0
access-list 101 permit ip 0.0.0.0 255.255.255.255 0.0.0.0 255.255.255.255
dialer-list 1 list 101
ip route 131.108.29.0 131.108.126.2
ip route 131.108.1.0 131.108.126.2
ip local pool dialin 101.102.126.2 101.102.126.254
```

With many modems, the **pulse-time** command must be used so that DTR is dropped for sufficient time to allow the modem to disconnect.

### AppleTalk Configuration Example

In the following example, DDR is configured for AppleTalk access using an ISDN BRI. Two access lists are defined: one for IP and IGRP, and one for AppleTalk. AppleTalk packets from network 2141 only (except broadcast packets) can initiate calls.

```
interface BRI0
 ip address 130.1.20.107 255.255.255.0
 encapsulation ppp
 appletalk cable-range 2141-2141 2141.65
 appletalk zone SCruz-Eng
 no appletalk send-rtmps
 dialer map ip 130.1.20.106 broadcast 1879
 dialer map appletalk 2141.66 broadcast 1879
 dialer-group 1
!
access-list 101 deny   igrp 0.0.0.0 255.255.255.255 255.255.255.255 0.0.0.0
access-list 101 permit ip 0.0.0.0 255.255.255.255 0.0.0.0 255.255.255.255
access-list 601 permit cable-range 2141-2141 broadcast-deny
access-list 601 deny other-access
!
dialer-list 1 list 101
dialer-list 1 list 601
```

### Banyan VINES Configuration Example

In the following example, a router is configured for VINES and IP DDR with in-band dialing. The VINES access list does not allow RTP routing updates to place a call, but any other data packet is interesting.

```
vines routing BBBBBBBB:0001
!
hostname RouterA
!
username RouterB password 7 030752180500
username RouterC password 7 00071A150754
!
interface serial 0
 ip address 131.108.170.19 255.255.255.0
 encapsulation ppp
 vines metrics 10
 vines neighbor AAAAAAAA:0001 0
```

```
 dialer in-band
 dialer map ip 131.108.170.151 name RouterB broadcast 4155551234
 dialer map vines AAAAAAAA:0001 name RouterC broadcast 4155551212
 dialer-group 1
 ppp authentication chap
 pulse-time 1
!
access-list 101 deny igrp 0.0.0.0 255.255.255.255 0.0.0.0 255.255.255.255
access-list 101 permit ip 0.0.0.0 255.255.255.255 0.0.0.0 255.255.255.255
!
vines access-list 107 deny RTP 00000000:0000 FFFFFFFF:FFFF 00000000:0000 FFFFFFFF:FFFF
vines access-list 107 permit IP 00000000:0000 FFFFFFFF:FFFF 00000000:0000 FFFFFFFF:FFFF
!
dialer-list 1 protocol ip list 101
dialer-list 1 protocol vines list 107
```

## DECnet Configuration Example

In the following example, a router is configured for DECnet DDR with in-band dialing:

```
decnet routing 10.19
!
username RouterB password 7 030752180531
!
interface serial 0
 no ip address
 decnet cost 10
 encapsulation ppp
 dialer in-band
 dialer map decnet 10.151 name RouterB broadcast 4155551212
 dialer-group 1
 ppp authentication chap
 pulse-time 1
!
access-list 301 permit 10.0 0.1023 0.0 63.1023
!
dialer-list 1 protocol decnet list 301
```

## ISO CLNS Configuration Example

In the following example, a router is configured for CLNS DDR with in-band dialing:

```
username RouterB password 7 111C140B0E
clns net 47.0004.0001.0000.0c00.2222.00
clns routing
clns filter-set ddrline permit 47.0004.0001....
!
interface serial 0
 no ip address
 encapsulation ppp
 dialer in-band
 dialer map clns 47.0004.0001.0000.0c00.1111.00 name RouterB broadcast 1212
 dialer-group 1
 ppp authentication chap
 clns enable
```

```
 pulse-time 1
!
clns route default serial 0
dialer-list 1 protocol clns list ddrline
```

## XNS Configuration Example

In the following example, a router is configured for XNS DDR with in-band dialing. The access lists deny broadcast traffic to any host on any network, but allow all other traffic.

```
xns routing 0000.0c01.d8dd
username RouterB password 7 111B210A0F
interface serial 0
 no ip address
 encapsulation ppp
 xns network 10
 dialer in-band
 dialer map xns 10.0000.0c01.d877 name RouterB broadcast 4155551212
 dialer-group 1
 ppp authentication chap
 pulse-time 1
access-list 400 deny -1 -1.ffff.ffff.ffff 0000.0000.0000
access-list 400 permit -1 10
dialer-list 1 protocol xns list 400
```

## Set Up Hub-and-Spoke DDR for Asynchronous Interfaces and Authentication Example

You can set up dial-on-demand routing (DDR) to provide service to multiple remote sites. In a hub-and-spoke configuration, you can use a generic configuration script to set up each remote connection. Figure 42–3 illustrates a typical hub-and-spoke configuration.

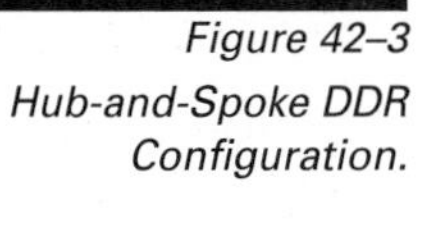

*Figure 42–3 Hub-and-Spoke DDR Configuration.*

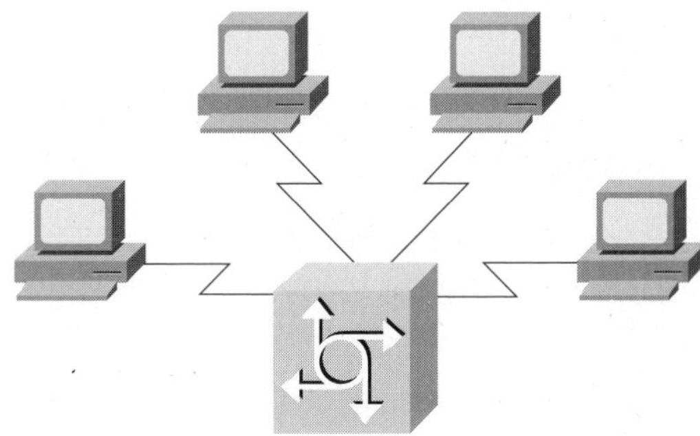

This configuration is demonstrated in the following two subsections.

### *Spoke Router*

In the following example, configuration is performed on the spoke side of the connection. (A different "spoke" password must be specified for each remote client.) It provides authentication by identifying a password that must be provided on each end of the connection.

```
interface ethernet 0
 ip address 172.30.44.1 255.255.255.0
!
interface async 7
 async mode dedicated
 async default ip address 128.150.45.1
 ip address 1172.30.45.2 255.255.255.0
 encapsulation ppp
 ppp authentication chap
 dialer in-band
 dialer map ip 172.30.45.1 name hub system-script hub 1234
 dialer map ip 172.30.45.255 name hub system-script hub 1234
 dialer-group 1
!
ip route 172.30.43.0 255.255.255.0 172.30.45.1
 ip default-network 172.30.0.0
 chat-script generic ABORT BUSY ABORT NO ## AT OK ATDT\T TIMEOUT 30 CONNECT
 chat-script hub "" "" name: spoke1 word" <spoke1-passwd> PPP
 dialer-list 1 protocol ip permit
!
username hub password <spoke1-passwd>
!
router igrp 109
 network 172.30.0.0
 passive-interface async 7
!
line 7
 modem InOut
 speed 38400
 flowcontrol hardware
modem chat-script generic
```

### *Hub Router Configuration*

In the following example, configuration is performed on the local side of the connection—the hub router. It configures the router for communication with three clients and provides authentication by identifying a unique password for each "spoke" in the hub-and-spoke configuration.

```
interface ethernet 0
 ip address 172.30.43.1 255.255.255.0
!
interface async 7
 async mode interactive
 async dynamic address
 dialer rotary-group 1
!
interface async 8
 async mode interactive
 async dynamic address
```

```
 dialer rotary-group 1
!
interface dialer 1
 ip address 172.30.45.2 255.255.255.0
 no ip split-horizon
encapsulation ppp
  ppp authentication chap
 dialer in-band
 dialer map ip 172.30.45.2 name spoke1 3333
 dialer map ip 172.30.45.2 name spoke2 4444
 dialer map ip 172.30.45.2 name spoke3 5555
 dialer map ip 172.30.45.255 name spoke1 3333
 dialer map ip 172.30.45.255 name spoke2 4444
 dialer map ip 172.30.45.255 name spoke3 5555
 dialer-group 1
!
ip route 172.30.44.0 255.255.255.0 172.30.45.2
ip route 172.30.44.0 255.255.255.0 172.30.45.3
ip route 172.30.44.0 255.255.255.0 172.30.45.4
 dialer-list 1 protocol ip list 101
 access-list 101 deny igrp 0.0.0.0 255.255.255.255 0.0.0.0 255.255.255.255
 access-list 101 permit ip 0.0.0.0 255.255.255.255 0.0.0.0 255.255.255.255
 chat-script generic ABORT BUSY ABORT NO ## AT OK ATDT\T TIMEOUT 30 CONNECT
!
username spoke1 password <spoke1-passwd>
username spoke2 password <spoke2-passwd>
username spoke3 password <spoke3-passwd>
username spoke1 autocommand ppp 172.30.45.2
username spoke2 autocommand ppp 172.30.45.3
username spoke3 autocommand ppp 172.30.45.4
!
router igrp 109
 network 172.30.0.0
 redistribute static
!
line 7
 login tacacs
 modem InOut
 speed 38400
 flowcontrol hardware
 modem chat-script generic
```

The **redistribute static** command can be used to advertise static route information for DDR applications. Without this command, static routes to the hosts or network that the router can access with DDR will not be advertised to other routers with which the router is communicating. This behavior can block communication because some routes will not be known.

## Dialing a Single Site or Multiple Sites Example

Assume that your configuration is as shown in Figure 42–4 and your router receives a packet with a next-hop address of 1.1.1.1.

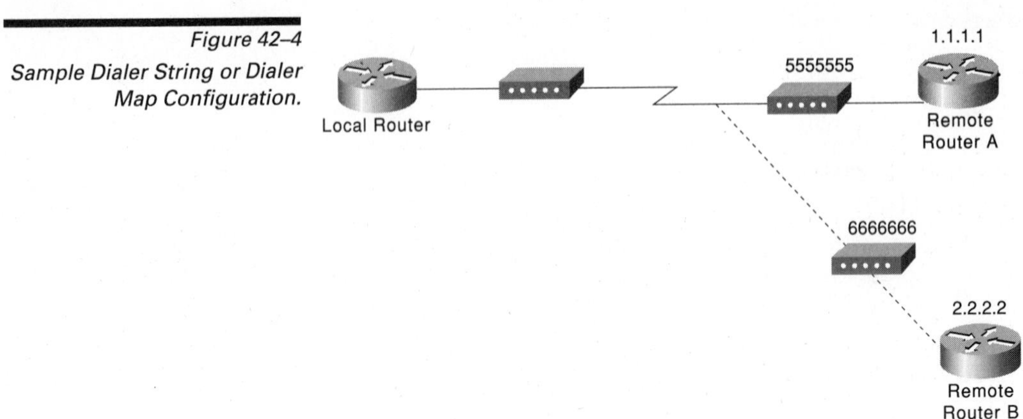


*Figure 42–4 Sample Dialer String or Dialer Map Configuration.*

If the interface on your router is configured to call a single site with phone number 5555555, it will send the packet to that site, assuming that the next-hop address 1.1.1.1 indicates the same remote device as phone number 5555555. The **dialer string** command is used to specify the string (telephone number) to be called.

```
interface serial 1
 dialer in-band
 dialer string 5555555
```

If the interface is configured to dial multiple sites, the interface or dialer rotary group must be configured so that the correct phone number, 5555555, is mapped to the address 1.1.1.1. If this mapping is not configured, the interface or dialer rotary group does not know what phone number to call to deliver the packet to its correct destination, which is the address 1.1.1.1. In this way, a packet with a destination of 2.2.2.2 will not be sent to 5555555. The **dialer map** command is used to map next-hop addresses to phone numbers.

```
interface serial 1
 dialer in-band
 dialer map ip 1.1.1.1 5555555
 dialer map ip 2.2.2.2 6666666
```

## Configuring Multiple Destinations Example

The following example demonstrates how to specify multiple destination numbers to dial for outgoing calls:

```
interface serial 1
 ip address 131.108.126.1 255.255.255.0
 dialer in-band
 dialer wait-for-carrier-time 100
 pulse-time 1
 dialer-group 1
 dialer map ip 131.108.126.10 5558899
 dialer map ip 131.108.126.15 5555555
!
```

```
access-list 101 deny igrp 0.0.0.0 255.255.255.255 255.255.255.255 0.0.0.0
access-list 101 permit ip 0.0.0.0 255.255.255.255 0.0.0.0 255.255.255.255
dialer-list 1 protocol ip list 101
```

As in section, "Configuring DDR in an IP Environment Example," a pulse time is assigned and a dialer access group specified.

The first **dialer map** command specifies that the number 555-8899 is to be dialed for IP packets with a *next-hop-address* value of 131.108.126.10. The second **dialer map** then specifies that the number 5555555 will be called when an IP packet with a *next-hop-address* value of 131.108.126.15 is detected.

## Configuring Dialer Interfaces and Dialer Rotary Groups Example

The following configuration places serial interfaces 1 and 2 into dialer rotary group 1, defined by the **interface dialer 1** command:

```
!PPP encapsulation is enabled for interface dialer 1.
interface dialer 1
 encapsulation ppp
 dialer in-band
 ip address 131.108.2.1 255.255.255.0
 ip address 131.126.2.1 255.255.255.0 secondary
!The first dialer map command allows remote site YYY and the central site to
!call each other. The second dialer map command, with no dialer string, allows
!remote site ZZZ to call the central site but the central site cannot call
!remote site ZZZ (no phone number).
!
 dialer map ip 131.108.2.5 name YYY 1415553434
 dialer map ip 131.126.2.55 name ZZZ
!
!The DTR pulse signals for three seconds on the interfaces in dialer group 1.
!This holds the DTR low so the modem can recognize that DTR has been dropped.
 pulse-time 3

!Serial interfaces 1 and 2 are placed in dialer rotary group 1. All the
!interface configuration commands (the encapsulation and dialer map commands
!shown earlier in this example) that applied to interface dialer 1 also apply
!to these interfaces.
interface serial 1
 dialer rotary-group 1
interface serial 2
 dialer rotary-group 1
```

## DDR Using Dialer Interface and PPP Encapsulation Example

The following example shows a configuration for XXX, the local router shown in Figure 42–5. In this example, remote Routers YYY and ZZZ can call Router XXX. Router XXX has dialing information only for Router YYY and cannot call Router ZZZ.

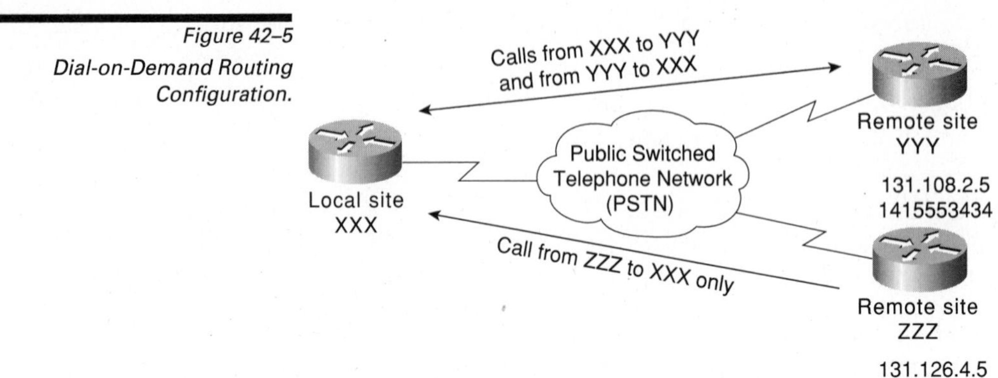


*Figure 42-5*
*Dial-on-Demand Routing Configuration.*

*Router XXX*

```
username YYY password theirsystem
username ZZZ password thatsystem

!Create a dialer interface with PPP encapsulation and CHAP authentication.
interface dialer 1
 ip address 131.108.2.1 255.255.255.0
 ip address 131.126.4.1 255.255.255.0 secondary
 encapsulation ppp
 ppp authentication chap
 dialer in-band
 dialer group 1
!The first dialer map command indicates that calls between the remote site
!YYY and the central site will be placed at either end. The second dialer
!map command, with no dialer string, indicates that remote site ZZZ will call
!the central site but the central site will not call out.
 dialer map ip 131.108.2.5 name YYY 1415553434
 dialer map ip 131.126.4.5 name ZZZ
!The DTR pulse holds the DTR low for three seconds, so the modem can recognize
!that DTR has been dropped.
 pulse-time 3
!
!Place asynchronous serial interfaces 1 and 2 in dialer group 1.
!The interface commands applied to dialer group 1 (for example,
!PPP encapsulation and CHAP) apply to these interfaces.
!
interface async 1
 dialer rotary-group 1
interface async 2
 dialer rotary-group 1
```

## Set Up Two-Way DDR with Authentication Example

You can set up two-way dial-on-demand routing (DDR) with authentication in which both the client and server have dial-in access to each other. This configuration is demonstrated in the following two subsections.

### *Remote Configuration*

The following example configuration is performed on the remote side of the connection. It provides authentication by identifying a password that must be provided on each end of the connection.

```
username local password secret1
username remote password secret2
!
interface ethernet 0
 ip address 172.30.44.1 255.255.255.0
!
interface async 7
 ip address 172.30.45.2 255.255.255.0
 async mode dedicated
 async default ip address 172.30.45.1
 encapsulation ppp
 dialer in-band
 dialer string 1234
 dialer-group 1
!
ip route 172.30.43.0 255.255.255.0 async 7
ip default-network 172.30.0.0
chat-script generic ABORT BUSY ABORT NO ## AT OK ATDT\T TIMEOUT 30 CONNECT
dialer-list 1 protocol ip permit
!
line 7
 no exec
 modem InOut
 speed 38400
 flowcontrol hardware
 modem chat-script generic
```

### *Local Configuration*

The following example configuration is performed on the local side of the connection. As with the remote side configuration, it provides authentication by identifying a password for each end of the connection.

```
username remote password secret1
username local password secret2
!
interface ethernet 0
 ip address 172.30.43.1 255.255.255.0
!
interface async 7
 async mode dedicated
 async default ip address 172.30.45.2
 dialer rotary-group 1
!
interface async 8
 async mode dedicated
 async default ip address 172.30.45.2
 dialer rotary-group 1
!
interface dialer 1
```

```
 ip address 172.30.45.2 255.255.255.0
 encapsulation ppp
 ppp authentication chap
 dialer in-band
 dialer map ip 172.30.45.2 name remote 4321
 dialer load-threshold 80
!
ip route 172.30.44.0 255.255.255.0 172.30.45.2
 chat-script generic ABORT BUSY ABORT NO ## AT OK ATDT\T TIMEOUT 30 CONNECT
!
router igrp 109
 network 172.30.0.0
 redistribute static
 passive-interface async 7
!
line 7
 modem InOut
 speed 38400
 flowcontrol hardware
 modem chat-script generic
```

## Frame Relay Support Examples

The examples in this section present various combinations of interfaces, Frame Relay features, and DDR features.

### *Frame Relay Access with In-Band Dialing and Static Mapping Example*

In the following example, a router is configured for IP over Frame Relay using in-band dialing. A Frame Relay static map is used to associate the next-hop protocol address to the DLCI. The dialer string allows dialing to only one destination.

```
interface Serial0
 ip address 1.1.1.1 255.255.255.0
 encapsulation frame-relay
 frame-relay map ip 1.1.1.2 100 broadcast
 dialer in-band
 dialer string 4155551212
 dialer-group 1
!
access-list 101 deny igrp any host 255.255.255.255
access-list 101 permit ip any any
!
dialer-list 1 protocol ip list 101
```

### *Frame Relay Access with ISDN Dialing and DDR Dynamic Maps Example*

The following example shows a BRI interface configured for Frame Relay and for IP, IPX, and AppleTalk routing. No static maps are defined because this setup relies on Frame Relay local management interface (LMI) signaling and Inverse ARP to determine the network addresses-to-DLCI mappings dynamically. (Because Frame Relay Inverse ARP is enabled by default, no command is required.)

```
interface BRI0
 ip address 1.1.1.1 255.255.255.0
 ipx network 100
 appletalk cable-range 100-100 100.1
 appletalk zone ISDN
 no appletalk send-rtmps
 encapsulation frame-relay IETF
 dialer map ip 1.1.1.2 broadcast 4155551212
 dialer map apple 100.2 broadcast 4155551212
 dialer map ipx 100.0000.0c05.33ed broadcast 4085551234
 dialer-group 1
!
access-list 101 deny igrp any host 255.255.255.255
access-list 101 permit ip any any
access-list 901 deny -1 FFFFFFFF 452
access-list 901 deny -1 FFFFFFFF 453
access-list 901 deny -1 FFFFFFFF 457
access-list 901 deny -1 FFFFFFFF 0 FFFFFFFF 452
access-list 901 deny -1 FFFFFFFF 0 FFFFFFFF 453
access-list 901 deny -1 FFFFFFFF 0 FFFFFFFF 457
access-list 901 permit -1
access-list 601 permit cable-range 100-100 broadcast-deny
access-list 601 deny other-access
!
dialer-list 1 protocol ip list 101
dialer-list 1 protocol novell list 901
dialer-list 1 protocol apple list 601
```

### *Frame Relay Access with ISDN Dialing and Subinterfaces Example*

The following example shows a BRI interface configured for Frame Relay and for IP, IPX, and AppleTalk routing. Two logical subnets are used; a point-to-point subinterface and a multipoint subinterface are configured. Frame Relay Annex A (LMI type Q933a) and Inverse ARP are used for dynamic routing.

```
interface BRI0
 no ip address
 encapsulation frame-relay
 dialer string 4155551212
 dialer-group 1
 frame-relay lmi-type q933a
!
interface BRI0.1 multipoint
 ip address 1.1.100.1 255.255.255.0
 ipx network 100
 appletalk cable-range 100-100 100.1
 appletalk zone ISDN
 no appletalk send-rtmps
 frame-relay interface-dlci 100
 frame-relay interface-dlci 110
 frame-relay interface-dlci 120
!
interface BRI0.2 point-to-point
 ip address 1.1.200.1 255.255.255.0
```

```
 ipx network 200
 appletalk cable-range 200-200 200.1
 appletalk zone ISDN
 no appletalk send-rtmps
 frame-relay interface-dlci 200 broadcast IETF
!
access-list 101 deny igrp any host 255.255.255.255
access-list 101 permit ip any any
access-list 901 deny -1 FFFFFFFF 452
access-list 901 deny -1 FFFFFFFF 453
access-list 901 deny -1 FFFFFFFF 457
access-list 901 deny -1 FFFFFFFF 0 FFFFFFFF 452
access-list 901 deny -1 FFFFFFFF 0 FFFFFFFF 453
access-list 901 deny -1 FFFFFFFF 0 FFFFFFFF 457
access-list 901 permit -1
access-list 601 permit cable-range 100-100 broadcast-deny
access-list 601 permit cable-range 200-200 broadcast-deny
access-list 601 deny other-access

dialer-list 1 protocol ip list 101
dialer-list 1 protocol novell list 901
dialer-list 1 protocol apple list 601
```

## X.25 Support Configuration Example

In the following example, a router is configured to support X.25 and DTR dialing:

```
interface serial 0
 ip address 131.108.170.19 255.255.255.0
 encapsulation x25
 x25 address 12345
 x25 map ip 131.108.171.20 67890 broadcast
 dialer dtr
 dialer-group 1
!
access-list 101 deny igrp 0.0.0.0 255.255.255.255 0.0.0.0 255.255.255.255
access-list 101 permit ip 0.0.0.0 255.255.255.255 0.0.0.0 255.255.255.255
!
dialer-list 1 protocol ip list 101
```

## LAPB Support Configuration Example

In the following example, the router is configured for LAPB encapsulation and in-band dialing:

```
interface serial 0
 ip address 131.108.170.19 255.255.255.0
 encapsulation lapb
 dialer in-band
 dialer string 4155551212
 dialer-group 1
!
access-list 101 deny igrp 0.0.0.0 255.255.255.255 0.0.0.0 255.255.255.255
access-list 101 permit ip 0.0.0.0 255.255.255.255 0.0.0.0 255.255.255.255
!
dialer-list 1 protocol ip list 101
```

# CHAPTER 43

# Legacy DDR Hub Commands

This chapter describes the commands required to configure interfaces on the router functioning as the hub in a hub-and-spoke network topology.

For configuration tasks and examples, see Chapter 42, "Configuring Legacy DDR Hubs."

## CLEAR DIALER

To clear the values of dialer statistics for one or more serial interfaces or Basic Rate Interfaces (BRIs) configured for DDR, use the **clear dialer** privileged EXEC command.

**clear dialer** [**interface** *type number*
**clear dialer** [**interface serial** *slot/port*] (Cisco 7500 series)

| *Syntax* | *Description* |
|---|---|
| **interface** | (Optional) Indicates that one interface will be specified. |
| *type* | (Optional) Interface type, either **async**, **serial**, or **bri**. |
| *number* | (Optional) Interface number. |
| *slot/port* | Backplane slot number and port number on the interface. See your hardware installation manual for the specific slot and port numbers. |

### *Command Mode*

Privileged EXEC

### *Usage Guidelines*

This command first appeared in Cisco IOS Release 11.0.

If the **interface** keyword and the arguments are not used, dialer statistics are cleared on all interfaces.

### *Example*

The following example clears the dialer statistics on serial interface 1:

```
clear dialer interface serial 1
```

## DIALER DTR

To enable DDR on an interface and specify that the serial line is connected by non-V.25*bis* modems using Electronic Industries Association (EIA) signaling only—specifically, the data terminal ready (DTR) signal—use the **dialer dtr** interface configuration command. To disable dial-on-demand routing (DDR) for the interface, use the **no** form of this command.

**dialer dtr**
**no dialer dtr**

### *Syntax Description*

This command has no keywords or arguments.

### *Default*

DTR dialing is disabled.

### *Command Mode*

Interface configuration

### *Usage Guidelines*

This command first appeared in Cisco IOS Release 10.0.

A serial interface configured for DTR dialing can place calls only; it cannot accept them.

When a local interface is configured for DTR dialing, the remote interface (that will be receiving the calls) can be configured for in-band dialing or not configured for anything but encapsulation, depending on the desired behavior. If the remote interface is expected to terminate a call when no traffic is transmitted for some time, it must be configured for in-band dialing (along with access lists and a dummy dialer string). If the remote interface is purely passive, no configuration is necessary.

Rotary groups cannot be configured for DTR dialing.

The **dialer map** and **dialer string** commands have no effect on DTR dialers.

### *Example*

The following example enables DDR and specifies DTR dialing on an interface:

```
dialer dtr
```

### *Related Commands*

Search online to find documentation for related commands.

**dialer in-band**
**dialer map**
**dialer string**

## DIALER ENABLE-TIMEOUT

To set the length of time an interface stays down after a call has completed or failed and before it is available to dial again, use the **dialer enable-timeout** interface configuration command. To return to the default value, use the **no** form of this command.

**dialer enable-timeout** *seconds*
**no dialer enable-timeout**

| *Syntax* | *Description* |
|---|---|
| *seconds* | Time in seconds that the Cisco IOS software waits before the next call can occur on the specific interface. Acceptable values are positive, nonzero integers.<br>This value must be greater than the serial pulse interval for this interface, set via the **pulse-time** command. |

### *Default*

15 seconds

### *Command Mode*

Interface configuration

### *Usage Guidelines*

This command first appeared in Cisco IOS Release 10.0.

This command applies to inbound and outbound calls.

If your phone lines are often busy or down, you might want to enforce a certain period of time before the system repeats an attempt to make a connection with a remote site. Configuring this timeout can prevent outgoing lines and switching equipment from being needlessly overloaded.

### *Example*

The following example specifies a waiting period of 30 seconds on asynchronous interface 1:

```
interface async 1
 dialer enable-timeout 30
```

### DIALER FAST-IDLE (INTERFACE CONFIGURATION)

To specify the amount of time that a line for which there is contention will stay idle before it is disconnected and the competing call is placed, use the **dialer fast-idle** interface configuration command. To return to the default value, use the **no** form of this command.

**dialer fast-idle** *seconds*
**no dialer fast-idle**

| *Syntax* | *Description* |
|---|---|
| *seconds* | Idle time, in seconds, that must occur on an interface before the line is disconnected. Acceptable values are positive, nonzero integers. |

#### *Default*

20 seconds

#### *Command Mode*

Interface configuration

#### *Usage Guidelines*

This command first appeared in Cisco IOS Release 10.0.

The dialer fast-idle timer is activated if there is contention for a line. The dialer fast-idle timer is activated if a line is busy, a packet for a different next-hop address is received, and the busy line is required to send the competing packet.

If the line becomes idle for configured length of time, the current call is disconnected immediately and the new call is placed.

If the line has not yet been idle as long as the fast-idle timeout period, the packet is dropped because there is no way to get through to the destination. After the packet is dropped, the fast-idle timer remains active and the current call is disconnected as soon as it has been idle for as long as the fast-idle timeout.

The fast-idle timer will be restarted if, in the meanwhile, another packet is transmitted to the currently connected destination and it is classified as *interesting*.

This command applies to inbound and outbound calls.

Combining this command with the **dialer idle-timeout** command allows you to configure lines to stay up for a longer period of time when there is no contention, but to be reused more quickly when there are not enough lines for the current demand.

#### *Example*

The following example specifies a fast-idle timeout of 35 seconds on asynchronous interface 1:

```
interface async 1
dialer fast-idle 35
```

### *Related Commands*

Search online to find documentation for related commands.

**dialer idle-timeout (interface configuration)**
**dialer map**

## DIALER-GROUP

To control access by configuring an interface to belong to a specific dialing group, use the **dialer-group** interface configuration command. To remove an interface from the specified dialer access group, use the **no** form of this command.

**dialer-group** *group-number*
**no dialer-group**

| *Syntax* | *Description* |
|---|---|
| *group-number* | Number of the dialer access group to which the specific interface belongs. This access group is defined with the **dialer-list** command. Acceptable values are nonzero, positive integers between 1 and 10. |

### *Default*

No access is predefined.

### *Command Mode*

Interface configuration

### *Usage Guidelines*

This command first appeared in Cisco IOS Release 10.0.

An interface can be associated with a single dialer access group only; multiple **dialer-group** assignment is not allowed. A second dialer access group assignment will override the first. A dialer access group is defined with the **dialer-group** command. The **dialer-list** command associates an access list with a dialer access group.

Packets that match the dialer group specified trigger a connection request.

### *Example*

The following example specifies dialer access group number 1.

The destination address of the packet is evaluated against the access list specified in the associated **dialer-list** command. If it passes, either a call is initiated (if no connection has already been established) or the idle timer is reset (if a call is currently connected).

```
interface async 1
 dialer-group 1
access-list 101 deny igrp 0.0.0.0 255.255.255.255 255.255.255.255 0.0.0.0
```

```
access-list 101 permit ip 0.0.0.0 255.255.255.255 0.0.0.0 255.255.255.255
dialer-list 1 protocol ip list 101
```

### *Related Commands*

Search online to find documentation for related commands.

**dialer-list**

## DIALER HOLD-QUEUE

To allow *interesting* outgoing packets to be queued until a modem connection is established, use the **dialer hold-queue** interface configuration command. To disable the hold queue, use the **no** form of this command.

**dialer hold-queue** *packets*
**no dialer hold-queue** [*packets*]

| *Syntax* | *Description* |
|---|---|
| *packets* | Number of packets, in the range 0 to 100, to hold in the queue. This argument is optional with the **no** form of the command. |

### *Default*

The outgoing packet queue is disabled.

### *Command Mode*

Interface configuration

### *Usage Guidelines*

This command first appeared in Cisco IOS Release 10.0.

A dialer hold queue can be configured on any type of dialer, including in-band synchronous, asynchronous, data terminal ready (DTR), and Integrated Services Digital Network (ISDN) dialers. Rotary groups can be configured with a dialer hold queue. If a rotary group is configured with a hold queue, all members of the group will be configured with a dialer hold queue and no individual member's hold queue can be altered.

If no hold queue is configured, packets are dropped during the time required to establish a connection.

### *Example*

The following command configures a dialer hold queue to hold 10 packets:

```
dialer hold-queue 10
```

### *Related Commands*

Search online to find documentation for related commands.

**dialer-group**

## DIALER IDLE-TIMEOUT (INTERFACE CONFIGURATION)

To specify the idle time before the line is disconnected, use the **dialer idle-timeout** interface configuration command. To reset the idle timeout to the default, use the **no** form of this command.

**dialer idle-timeout** *seconds*
**no dialer idle-timeout**

| *Syntax* | *Description* |
|---|---|
| *seconds* | Idle time, in seconds, that must occur on the interface before the line is disconnected. Acceptable values are positive, nonzero integers. |

### *Default*

120 seconds

### *Command Mode*

Interface configuration

### *Usage Guidelines*

This command first appeared in Cisco IOS Release 10.0.

This command is used on lines for which there is no contention. When contention occurs, the **dialer fast-idle** command is activated. For example, when a busy line is requested to send another packet to a different destination than it is currently connected to, line contention occurs and the **dialer fast-idle** command is activated.

This command applies to inbound and outbound calls. For example, if a receiving system needs to make outgoing calls, you might configure it with a short-idle timeout.

Only packets that match the dialer group reset the idle timer.

Use the **dialer idle-timeout** command to set a very high idle timer when multilink PPP is configured and you want a multilink bundle to be connected indefinitely. (The **dialer-load threshold 1** command no longer keeps a multilink bundle of *n* links connected indefinitely, and the **dialer-load threshold 2** command no longer keeps a multilink bundle of 2 links connected indefinitely.)

### *Example*

The following example specifies of an idle timeout of 3 minutes (180 seconds) on asynchronous interface 1:

```
interface async 1
 dialer idle-timeout 180
```

*Related Commands*

Search online to find documentation for related commands.

**dialer fast-idle (interface configuration)**
**dialer-group**

## DIALER IN-BAND

To specify that dial-on-demand routing (DDR) is to be supported, use the **dialer in-band** interface configuration command. To disable DDR for the interface, use the **no** form of this command.

**dialer in-band** [**no-parity** | **odd-parity**]
**no dialer in-band**

| *Syntax* | *Description* |
|---|---|
| **no-parity** | (Optional) Indicates that no parity is to be applied to the dialer string that is sent out to the modem on synchronous interfaces. |
| **odd-parity** | (Optional) Indicates that the dialed number has odd parity (7-bit ASCII characters with the eighth bit as the parity bit) on synchronous interfaces. |

*Default*

Disabled. By default, no parity is applied to the dialer string.

*Command Mode*

Interface configuration

*Usage Guidelines*

This command first appeared in Cisco IOS Release 10.0.

The **dialer in-band** command specifies that chat scripts will be used on asynchronous interfaces and V.25*bis* will be used on synchronous interfaces. The parity keywords do not apply to asynchronous interfaces.

The parity setting applies to the dialer string that is sent out to the modem. If you do not specify a parity, or if you specify no parity, no parity is applied to the output number. If odd parity is configured, the dialed number will have odd parity (7-bit ASCII characters with the eighth bit as the parity bit.)

If an interface only accepts calls and does not place calls, the **dialer in-band** interface configuration command is the only command needed to configure it. If an interface is configured in this manner, with no dialer rotary groups, the idle timer never disconnects the line. It is up to the remote end (the end that placed the call) to disconnect the line based on idle time.

### *Example*

The following example specifies DDR for asynchronous interface 1:

```
interface async 1
 dialer in-band
```

### *Related Commands*

Search online to find documentation for related commands.

**dialer map**
**dialer string**

## DIALER-LIST

To define a DDR dialer list to control dialing by protocol or by a combination of protocol and access list, use the **dialer-list** global configuration command. To delete a dialer list, use the **no** form of this command.

**dialer-list** *dialer-group* **protocol** *protocol-name* {**permit** | **deny** | **list** *access-list-number* | *access-group*}

**no dialer-list** *dialer-group* [**protocol** *protocol-name* [**list** *access-list-number* | *access-group*]]

| *Syntax* | *Description* |
|---|---|
| *dialer-group* | Number of a dialer access group identified in any **dialer-group** interface configuration command. |
| *protocol-name* | One of the following protocol keywords: **appletalk**, **bridge**, **clns**, **clns_es**, **clns_is**, **decnet**, **decnet_router-L1**, **decnet_router-L2**, **decnet_node**, **ip**, **ipx**, **vines**, or **xns**. |
| **permit** | Permits access to an entire protocol. |
| **deny** | Denies access to an entire protocol. |
| **list** | Specifies that an access list will be used for defining a granularity finer than an entire protocol. |
| *access-list-number* | Access list numbers specified in any DECnet, Banyan VINES, IP, Novell IPX, or XNS standard or extended access lists, including Novell IPX extended service access point (SAP) access lists and bridging types. See for the supported access list types and numbers. |
| *access-group* | Filter list name used in the **clns filter-set** and **clns access-group** commands. |

### *Default*

No dialer lists are defined.

### *Command Mode*

Global configuration

### *Usage Guidelines*

This command first appeared in Cisco IOS Release 10.0. The **list** command and *access-list-number* and *access-group* arguments first appeared in Cisco IOS Release 10.3.

The various **no** forms of this command have the following effects:

- The **no dialer-list 1** command deletes all lists configured with list 1, regardless of the keyword previously used (**permit, deny, protocol,** or **list**).
- The **no dialer-list 1 protocol** *protocol-name* command deletes all lists configured with list 1 and protocol *protocol-name.*
- The **no dialer-list 1 protocol** *protocol-name* **list** *access-list-number* command deletes the specified list.

The **dialer-list protocol** form of this command permits or denies access to an entire protocol. The **dialer-list protocol list** form of this command provides a finer permission granularity and also supports protocols that were not previously supported.

The **dialer-list protocol list** form of this command applies protocol access lists to dialer access groups to control dialing using DDR. The dialer access groups are defined with the **dialer-group** command.

The **dialer-list protocol list** command should be used for all protocols.

Table 43–1 lists the access list types and numbers that the **dialer-list protocol list** command supports. The table does not include ISO CLNS because that protocol uses filter names instead of predefined access list numbers.

**Table 43–1** *Dialer-List Supported Access List Types and Numbers*

| **Access List Type** | **Access List Number Range (decimal)** |
|---|---|
| AppleTalk | 600–699 |
| Banyan VINES (standard) | 1–100 |
| Banyan VINES (extended) | 101–200 |
| DECnet | 300–399 |
| IP (standard) | 1–99 |
| IP (extended) | 100–199 |

**Table 43–1** *Dialer-List Supported Access List Types and Numbers, Continued*

| Access List Type | Access List Number Range (decimal) |
|---|---|
| Novell IPX (standard) | 800–899 |
| Novell IPX (extended) | 900–999 |
| Transparent Bridging | 200–299 |
| XNS | 500–599 |

### *Examples*

Dialing occurs when an interesting packet (one that matches access list specifications) needs to be output on an interface. Using the standard access list method, packets can be classified as interesting or uninteresting. In the following example, IGRP TCP/IP routing protocol updates are not classified as interesting and do not initiate calls:

```
access-list 101 deny igrp 0.0.0.0 255.255.255.255 255.255.255.255 0.0.0.0
```

The following example classifies all other IP packets as interesting and permits them to initiate calls:

```
access-list 101 permit ip 0.0.0.0 255.255.255.255 0.0.0.0 255.255.255.255
```

Then the following command places list 101 into dialer access group 1:

```
dialer-list 1 protocol ip list 101
```

In the following example, DECnet access lists allow any DECnet packets with source area 10 and destination area 20 to trigger calls:

```
access-list 301 permit 10.0 0.1023 10.0 0.1023
access-list 301 permit 10.0 0.1023 20.0 0.1023
```

Then the following command places list 301 into dialer access group 1:

```
dialer-list 1 protocol decnet list 301
```

In the following example, both IP and VINES access lists are defined. The IP access lists define IGRP packets as uninteresting but permits all other IP packets to trigger calls. The VINES access lists do not allow Routing Table Protocol (RTP) routing updates to trigger calls but allow any other data packets to trigger calls.

```
access-list 101 deny igrp 0.0.0.0 255.255.255.255 0.0.0.0 255.255.255.255
access-list 101 permit ip 0.0.0.0 255.255.255.255 0.0.0.0 255.255.255.255
!
vines access-list 107 deny RTP 00000000:0000 FFFFFFFF:FFFF 00000000:0000 FFFFFFFF:FFFF
vines access-list 107 permit IP 00000000:0000 FFFFFFFF:FFFF 00000000:0000 FFFFFFFF:FFFF
```

Then the following two commands place the IP and VINES access lists into dialer access group 1:

```
dialer-list 1 protocol ip list 101
dialer-list 1 protocol vines list 107
```

In the following example, a Connectionless Network Service (CLNS) filter is defined and then the filter is placed in dialer access group 1:

```
clns filter-set ddrline permit 47.0004.0001....
!
dialer-list 1 protocol clns list ddrline
```

### *Related Commands*

Search online to find documentation for related commands.

**access-list**
**clns filter-set**
**dialer-group**
**vines access-list**

## DIALER LOAD-THRESHOLD

To configure bandwidth on demand by setting the maximum load before the dialer places another call to a destination, use the **dialer load-threshold** interface command. To disable the setting, use the **no** form of this command.

**dialer load-threshold** *load* [**outbound** | **inbound** | **either**]
**no dialer load-threshold**

| *Syntax* | *Description* |
|---|---|
| *load* | Interface load used to determine whether to initiate another call or to drop a link to the destination. This argument represents a utilization percentage; it is a number between 1 and 255, where 255 is 100%. |
| **outbound** | (Optional) Calculates the actual load using outbound data only. |
| **inbound** | (Optional) Calculates the actual load using inbound data only. |
| **either** | (Optional) Sets the maximum calculated load as the larger of the outbound and inbound loads. |

### *Default*

No maximum load is predefined.

### *Command Mode*

Interface configuration

### *Usage Guidelines*

This command first appeared in Cisco IOS Release 10.0. The **list** command and *access-list-number* and *access-group* arguments first appeared in Cisco IOS Release 10.3.

This command applies to dialer rotary groups only.

When the cumulative load of all UP links (a number *n*) exceeds the load threshold, the dialer adds an extra link; and when the cumulative load of all UP links minus one (*n* - 1) is at or below load threshold, then the dialer can bring down that one link. The dialer will make additional calls or drop links as necessary but will never interrupt an existing call to another destination.

The argument *load* is the calculated weighted average load value for the interface; 1 is unloaded, and 255 is fully loaded. The load is calculated by the system dynamically, based on bandwidth. You must set the bandwidth for an interface in kilobits per second, using the **bandwidth** command.

The load calculation determines how much of the total bandwidth you are using. A *load* value of 255 means that you are using one hundred percent of the bandwidth. The load number is required.

See Chapter 14, "Synchronous Serial Port Setup Commands," for a description of the **bandwidth** command.

When multilink PPP is configured, the **dialer-load threshold 1** command no longer keeps a multilink bundle of *n* links connected indefinitely and the **dialer-load threshold 2** command no longer keeps a multilink bundle of 2 links connected indefinitely. If you want a multilink bundle to be connected indefinitely, you must set a very high idle timer.

### *Example*

In the following example, if the load to a particular destination on an interface in dialer rotary group 5 exceeds interface load 200, the dialer will initiate another call to the destination:

```
interface dialer 5
 dialer load-threshold 200
```

### *Related Commands*

Search online to find documentation for related commands.

**bandwidth**
**interface dialer**
**dialer rotary-group**

## DIALER MAP

To configure a serial interface or Integrated Services Digital Network (ISDN) interface to call one or multiple sites or to receive calls from multiple sites, use a form of the **dialer map** interface configuration command; all options are shown in the first form of the command. To delete a particular dialer map entry, use a **no** form of this command.

**dialer map** *protocol next-hop-address* [**name** *hostname*] [**spc**] [**speed 56** | **64**] [**broadcast**] [**modem-script** *modem-regexp*] [**system-script** *system-regexp*] [*dial-string*[*:isdn-subaddress*]]

**no dialer map** *protocol next-hop-address* [**name** *hostname*] [**spc**] [**speed 56** | **64**] [**broadcast**] [**modem-script** *modem-regexp*] [**system-script** *system-regexp*] [*dial-string*[*:isdn-subaddress*]]

To configure a serial interface or ISDN interface to place a call to multiple sites and to authenticate calls from multiple sites, use the second form of the **dialer map** command:

**dialer map** *protocol next-hop-address* [**name** *hostname*] [**spc**] [**speed 56 | 64**] [**broadcast**] [*dial-string*[*:isdn-subaddress*]]

**no dialer map** *protocol next-hop-address* [**name** *hostname*] [**spc**] [**speed 56 | 64**] [**broadcast**] [*dial-string*[*:isdn-subaddress*]]

To configure a serial interface or ISDN interface to support bridging, use the third form of the command:

**dialer map bridge** [**name** *hostname*] [**spc**] [**broadcast**] [*dial-string*[*:isdn-subaddress*]]

**no dialer map bridge** [**name** *hostname*] [**spc**] [**broadcast**] [*dial-string*[*:isdn-subaddress*]]

To configure an asynchronous interface to place a call to a single site that requires a system script or that has no assigned modem script, or to multiple sites on a single line, on multiple lines, or on a dialer rotary group, use the fourth form of the **dialer map** command:

**dialer map** *protocol next-hop-address* [**name** *hostname*] [**broadcast**] [**modem-script** *modem-regexp*] [system-script *system-regexp*] [*dial-string*]

no **dialer map** *protocol next-hop-address* [**name** *hostname*] [**broadcast**] [**modem-script** *modem-regexp*] [**system-script** *system-regexp*] [*dial-string*]

| *Syntax* | *Description* |
|---|---|
| *protocol* | Protocol keywords; one of the following: **appletalk**, **bridge**, **clns**, **decnet**, **ip**, **ipx**, **novell**, **snapshot**, **vines**, and **xns**. |
| *next-hop-address* | Protocol address used to match against addresses to which packets are destined. This argument is not used with the **bridge** protocol keyword. |
| **name** | (Optional) Indicates the remote system with which the local router or access server communicates. Used for authenticating the remote system on incoming calls. |
| *hostname* | (Optional) Case-sensitive name or ID of the remote device (usually the host name). For routers with ISDN interfaces, if calling line identification—sometimes called *CLI*, but also known as *caller ID* and *automatic number identification* (ANI)—is provided, the *hostname* field can contain the number that the calling line ID provides. |
| **spc** | (Optional) Specifies a semipermanent connection between customer equipment and the exchange; used only in Germany for circuits between an ISDN BRI and a 1TR6 ISDN switch and in Australia for circuits between an ISDN PRI and a TS-014 switch. |
| **speed 56 \| 64** | (Optional) Keyword and value indicating the line speed in kilobits per second to use. Used for ISDN only. The default speed is 64 Kbps. |

| | |
|---|---|
| **broadcast** | (Optional) Indicates that broadcasts should be forwarded to this protocol address. |
| **modem-script** | (Optional) Indicates the modem script to be used for the connection (for asynchronous interfaces). |
| *modem-regexp* | (Optional) Regular expression to which a modem script will be matched (for asynchronous interfaces). |
| **system-script** | (Optional) Indicates the system script to be used for the connection (for asynchronous interfaces). |
| *system-regexp* | (Optional) Regular expression to which a system script will be matched (for asynchronous interfaces). |
| *dial-string*[*:isdn-subaddress*] | (Optional) Telephone number sent to the dialing device when it recognizes packets with the specified next-hop address that matches the access lists defined, and the optional subaddress number used for ISDN multipoint connections.<br>*The dial string and ISDN subaddress, if used, must be the last item in the command line.* |

### Defaults

No dialer map is configured. The default speed is 64 Kbps. No scripts are defined for placing calls.

### Command Mode

Interface configuration

### Usage Guidelines for Synchronous Interfaces

This command first appeared in Cisco IOS Release 10.0.

Use the **dialer map** command with the **name** keyword but without the dial string in configurations in which remote sites are calling a central site, but the central site is not calling the remote site. With this command, the local device will authenticate the remote site using Challenge Handshake Authentication Protocol (CHAP) or Password Authentication Protocol (PAP), which will transmit the remote site's host name to the central site. The central site will then use this name to authenticate the caller and will use the next-hop address to transmit packets to the remote site. Because there is no dialer string specified, the central site cannot call the remote router.

### Usage Guidelines for ISDN Interfaces

Use the **dialer map** command with the **name** keyword in configurations in which remote sites are calling a central site, but the central site is not calling the remote site. With this command, the local device will authenticate the remote site using CHAP or PAP, which will transmit the remote site's host name to the central site. The central site will then use this name to authenticate the caller and will use the next-hop address to transmit packets to the remote site. Because there is no dialer string specified, the central site cannot call the remote router.

For ISDN interfaces only, you can specify an optional speed parameter for **dialer map** commands if you also specify a dial string. This option informs the ISDN software whether it should place a call at 56 or 64 Kbps. If you omit the ISDN speed parameter, the default is 64 Kbps.

For routers with ISDN interfaces, if calling line identification (CLI)—also known as *caller ID* and *ANI*—is provided, the *hostname* field may contain the number that calling line ID provides.

### *Usage Guidelines for Asynchronous Interfaces*

Specify chat scripts for a physical interface that is not part of a dialer rotary group if no chat script is specified for the line, or if an additional (system) chat script is required to log on to the remote system.

Configure a **dialer map** command for each remote destination for that interface.

You do not need to specify a system script under the following conditions:

- The modem script can be used to dial in and log on to the remote system.
- You are calling a system that does not require a login script—that is, a system that answers and immediately goes into protocol mode.

If you adhere to the chat script naming convention suggested in the description of the **chat-script** command, use the form [**modem-script** **modulation-type*] in the **dialer map** command; for example, *.*-v32bis*. This form allows you to specify the modulation type that is best for the system you are calling and allows the modem type for the line to be specified by the **script dialer** command.

The period (.) is a wildcard that matches any character, and the asterisk (*) indicates that the preceding character can be duplicated multiple times. For more information about regular expressions, see Appendix C, "Regular Expressions."

If a modem script is specified in the **dialer map** interface configuration command and a modem script specified in the **script dialer** line configuration command, the first chat script that matches both is used. If no script matches both, an error message is logged and the connection is not established. If there is no modem chat script specified for the line, the first chat script (that is, the one specified in the **chat-script** global configuration command) that matches the modem script's regular expression is used. If there is a system script specified in the **dialer map** interface configuration command, the first chat script to match the regular expression is used.

The **modem-script** and **system-script** keywords and corresponding arguments are optional. They are ignored on synchronous interfaces.

If you have named your chat script according to the type of modem and modulation (for example, *codex-v32* or *telebit v32*), your regular expression could be **codex-.*** in the **script dialer** line configuration command, and ***-v32bis** in the modem script specified in the **dialer map** command for a system that you wish to connect to using V.32*bis* modulation.

The modem lines (specified by the argument *regexp* in the **script dialer** line configuration command) would be set to one of the following regular expressions to match patterns, depending on the kind of modem you have:

- **codex-.***
- **telebit-.***
- **usr-.***

With an interface configured for Challenge Handshake Authentication Protocol (CHAP) or Password Authentication Protocol (PAP) and configured with the **name** *hostname* keyword and argument pair, the local device authenticates the remote site using CHAP, which transmits the remote site's host name to the central site. The central site then uses this name to authenticate the caller and uses the next-hop address to transmit packets to the remote site. Because no dialer string is specified, the central site cannot call the remote router.

For routers with ISDN interfaces, if calling line identification (CLI)—also known as *caller ID* and *ANI*—is provided, the *hostname* field can contain the number that calling line ID provides.

### *Examples*

In the following example, the dialer speed is set at 56 Kbps to call a remote site at 131.108.2.5:

```
interface async 1
encapsulation ppp
ppp authentication chap
dialer map ip 131.108.2.5 speed 56
```

The following example shows a dialing chat script and a login chat script. The **dialer in-band** command enables DDR on asynchronous interface 10, and the **dialer map** command looks for the specified dialing and the login scripts and then uses those scripts to dial 96837890.

```
chat-script dial ABORT ERROR "" "AT Z" OK "ATDT \T" TIMEOUT 30 CONNECT \c
chat-script login ABORT invalid TIMEOUT 15 name: billw word: wewpass ">"
                "slip default"
interface async 10
dialer in-band
dialer map ip 10.55.0.1 modem-script dial system-script login 96837890
```

In the following example, the remote site is calling the central site, and the central site is calling the remote site. The central router can use the name ZZZ to authenticate the remote router when they connect and also can use the dialer string 14155553434 to call the remote router if it is not currently connected.

```
interface async 1
dialer map ip 131.108.2.5 name ZZZ 14155553434
```

In the following example, a remote site is calling a central site, but the central site is not calling the remote site. The local device will authenticate the site that is calling in using CHAP. CHAP will cause the remote site's name, YYY, to be transmitted to the site it is calling. The central site will then use this name to authenticate the remote site.

```
interface async 1
encapsulation ppp
ppp authentication chap
dialer map ip 131.108.2.5 name YYY
```

### *Related Commands*

Search online to find documentation for related commands.

**chat-script**
**ppp authentication chap**
**ppp authentication pap**
**username**

## DIALER PRIORITY

To set the priority of an interface in a dialer rotary group, use the **dialer priority** interface configuration command. Use the **no** form of the command to revert to the default setting.

**dialer priority** *number*
**no dialer priority**

| *Syntax* | *Description* |
|---|---|
| *number* | Priority of an interface in a dialer rotary group; the highest number indicates the highest priority. This is a number from 0 through 255. The default value is 0, the lowest priority. |

### *Default*

No priority is predefined. When priority is defined, the default value is 0.

### *Command Mode*

Interface configuration

### *Usage Guidelines*

This command first appeared in Cisco IOS Release 10.0.

This command is meaningful only for interfaces that are part of dialer rotary groups.

The value 0 indicates the lowest priority, and 255 indicates the highest priority. The **dialer priority** command controls which interfaces within a dialer rotary group will be used first. Higher priority interfaces (configured with higher *n* value) are used first.

The **dialer priority** command gives you the ability to tell the dialer rotary group which free interface (and, by extension for asynchronous interfaces, which modem) to use first. This command applies to outgoing calls only.

For example, a router or access server might have a selection of many modems, some of which are better performers than others. You might have a 19.2-Kbps, two 4800-Bps, three 1200-Bps, and one 300-bps modem on interfaces in one dialer rotary group. You do not want the router or access server to make the call on the 300-baud modem if any of the faster modems are free. You want to use the highest-performance modems first, and the slowest modems last.

*Example*

In the following example, asynchronous interface 3 will be used after interfaces with higher priority and before interfaces with lower priority:

```
interface async 3
 dialer priority 5
```

*Related Commands*

Search online for documentation for related commands.

**interface dialer**
**dialer rotary-group**

## DIALER ROTARY-GROUP

To include a specified interface in a dialer rotary group, use the **dialer rotary-group** interface configuration command.

**dialer rotary-group** *number*

| *Syntax* | *Description* |
| --- | --- |
| *number* | Number of the previously defined dialer interface in whose rotary group this interface is to be included. This is a number from 0 to 255. The dialer interface is defined by the **interface dialer** command. |

*Default*

No interfaces are included in a dialer rotary group.

*Command Mode*

Interface configuration

*Usage Guidelines*

This command first appeared in Cisco IOS Release 10.0.

*Example*

The following example places asynchronous interfaces 1 and 2 into dialer rotary group 1, defined by the **interface dialer 1** command:

```
hostname central-site
! PPP encapsulation is enabled for interface dialer 1.
interface dialer 1
 encapsulation ppp
 dialer in-band
 ip address 131.108.2.1 255.255.255.0
 ip address 131.126.4.1 255.255.255.0 secondary
!
```

```
! The first dialer map command allows the central site and remote site YYY
! to call each other and allows the central site to authenticate site YYY
! when it calls in. The second dialer map command, with no dialer string,
! allows the central site to authenticate remote site ZZZ when it calls in, but
! the central site cannot call remote site ZZZ (no phone number).
 dialer map ip 131.108.2.5 name YYY 14155553434
 dialer map ip 131.126.4.5 name ZZZ
!
! The DTR pulse signals for three seconds on the interfaces in dialer
! group 1. This holds the DTR low so the modem can recognize that DTR has been
! dropped.
pulse-time 3
!
! Interfaces async 1 and async 2 are placed in dialer rotary group 1.
! All of the interface configuration commands (the encapsulation and dialer
! map commands shown earlier in this example) applied to interface
! dialer 1 apply to the physical interfaces assigned to the dialer group.
!
interface async 1
 dialer rotary-group 1
interface async 2
 dialer rotary-group 1
```

*Related Commands*

Search online to find documentation for related commands.

**interface dialer**

### DIALER ROTOR

To specify the method for identifying the outbound line to be used for ISDN or asynchronous DDR calls, use the **dialer rotor** interface configuration command.

**dialer rotor {priority | best}**

| *Syntax* | *Description* |
|---|---|
| **priority** | Selects the first outbound line with the highest priority; this is the selection criterion that was previously used. |
| **best** | Selects the outbound line with the most recent success. If that line also has the most recent failure, then it will try the line with the least recent failure. If that line also has the most recent failure, it will then try an as-of-yet untried outbound line. |

*Default*

Disabled

*Command Mode*

Interface Configuration

### *Usage Guidelines*

This command first appeared in Cisco IOS Release 10.0.

This command allows the router to skip outbound ISDN BRI and asynchronous lines that have problems. This command would not be useful for ISDN PRI, unless your local telephone service provider has problems keeping your lines properly configured.

### *Related Command*

Search online to find documentation for related commands.

**dialer priority**

## DIALER STRING

To specify the string (telephone number) to be called for interfaces calling a single site, use the **dialer string** interface configuration command. To delete the dialer string specified for the interface, use the **no** form of this command.

**dialer string** *dial-string*[:*isdn-subaddress*]

**no dialer string**

| *Syntax* | *Description* |
|---|---|
| *dial-string* | String of characters to be sent to a DCE device. |
| *:isdn-subaddress* | (Optional) ISDN subaddress. |

### *Default*

No strings are predefined.

### *Command Mode*

Interface configuration

### *Usage Guidelines*

This command first appeared in Cisco IOS Release 10.0.

To use this command on an asynchronous interface, you must define a modem chat script for the associated line by using the **script dialer** command. A script must be used to implement dialing.

Dialers configured as **in-band** pass the string to the external dialing device. Specify one **dialer string** command per interface.

To specify multiple strings, use the **dialer map** command. In general, you include a **dialer string** or **dialer map** command if you intend to use a specific interface to initiate a DDR call.

**NOTES**

If a **dialer string** command is specified without a **dialer-group** command with access lists defined, dialing is never initiated. If the **debug dialer** command is enabled, an error message is displayed indicating that dialing never will occur.

The string of characters specified for the *dial-string* argument is the default number used under the following conditions:

- A **dialer map** command is not included in the interface configuration.
- The next-hop address specified in a packet is not included in any of the **dialer map** interface configuration commands recorded—assuming that the destination address passes any access lists specified for DDR with the **dialer-list** command.

### *ITU-T V.25bis Options*

On synchronous interfaces, depending on the type of modem you are using, International Telecommunication Union Telecommunication (ITU-T) Standardization Sector V.25*bis* options might be supported as *dial-string* parameters of the **dialer string** command. Supported options are listed in Table 43–2. The functions of the parameters are nation-specific, and they may have different implementations in your country. These options apply only if you have enabled DDR with the **dialer in-band** command. Refer to the operation manual for your modem for a list of supported options.

**NOTES**

The ITU-T carries out the functions of the former Consultative Committee for International Telegraph and Telephone (CCITT).

**Table 43–2** *ITU-T V.25bis Options*

| Option | Description |
|---|---|
| : | Wait tone. |
| < | Pause.<br>Usage and duration of this parameter vary by country. |
| = | Separator 3.<br>For national use. |
| > | Separator 4.<br>For national use. |
| P | Dialing to be continued in pulse mode.<br>Optionally accepted parameter. |

**Table 43–2** *ITU-T V.25bis Options, Continued*

| Option | Description |
|---|---|
| T | Tone. Dialing to be continued in Dual Tone Multifrequency (DTMF) mode.<br>Optionally accepted parameter. |
| & | Flash. (The flash duration varies by country.)<br>Optionally accepted parameter. |

### *Example*

The following example specifies a DDR telephone number to be tone-dialed on interface *async 1* using the **dialer string** command:

```
interface async 1
 dialer string T14085553434
```

### *Related Commands*

Search online to find documentation for related commands.

**dialer-group**
**dialer in-band**
**dialer map**
**script dialer**

## DIALER WAIT-FOR-CARRIER-TIME (INTERFACE CONFIGURATION)

To specify the length of time the interface waits for a carrier, use the **dialer wait-for-carrier-time** interface configuration command. To reset the carrier wait time value to the default, use the **no** form of this command.

**dialer wait-for-carrier-time** *seconds*
**no dialer wait-for-carrier-time**

| *Syntax* | *Description* |
|---|---|
| *seconds* | Number of seconds that the interface waits for the carrier to come up when a call is placed. Acceptable values are positive, nonzero integers. |

### *Default*

30 seconds

### *Command Mode*

Interface configuration

### Usage Guidelines

This command first appeared in Cisco IOS Release 10.0.

On asynchronous interfaces, the **dialer wait-for-carrier-time** command sets the total time allowed for the chat script to run.

If a carrier signal is not detected in this amount of time, the interface is disabled until the enable timeout occurs (configured with the **dialer enable-timeout** command).

### Example

The following example specifies a carrier wait time of 45 seconds on asynchronous interface 1:

```
interface async 1
 dialer wait-for-carrier-time 45
```

### Related Command

Search online to find documentation for related commands.

**dialer enable-timeout**

## INTERFACE DIALER

To define a dialer rotary group, use the **interface dialer** global configuration command.

**interface dialer** *number*

| *Syntax* | *Description* |
| --- | --- |
| *number* | Number of the dialer rotary group. It can be number in the range 0 through 255. |

### Default

No dialer rotary groups are predefined.

### Command Mode

Global configuration

### Usage Guidelines

This command first appeared in Cisco IOS Release 10.0.

Dialer rotary groups allow you to apply a single interface configuration to a set of physical interfaces. This allows a group of interfaces to be used as a pool of interfaces for calling many destinations.

Once the interface configuration is propagated to a set of interfaces, those interfaces can be used to place calls using the standard DDR criteria. When multiple destinations are configured, any of these interfaces can be used for outgoing calls.

Dialer rotary groups are useful in environments that require multiple calling destinations. Only the rotary group needs to be configured with the **dialer map** commands. The only configuration required for the interfaces is the **dialer rotary-group** command indicating that each interface is part of a dialer rotary group.

Although a dialer rotary group is configured as an interface, it is not a physical interface. Instead, it represents a group of interfaces. Interface configuration commands entered after the **interface dialer** command will be applied to all physical interfaces assigned to specified rotary groups. Individual interfaces in a dialer rotary group do not have individual addresses. The dialer interface has a protocol address, and that address is used by all interfaces in the dialer rotary group.

### *Example*

The following example identifies interface dialer 1 as the dialer rotary group leader. Interface dialer 1 is not a physical interface, but represents a group of interfaces. The interface configuration commands that follow apply to all interfaces included in this group.

```
interface dialer 1
 encapsulation ppp
 authentication chap
 dialer in-band
 ip address 1.2.3.4
 dialer map ip 1.2.2.5 name YYY 14155553434
 dialer map ip 1.3.2.6 name ZZZ
```

## SHOW DIALER

To display general diagnostic information for interfaces configured for DDR, use the **show dialer** EXEC command.

**show dialer** [**interface** *type number*]

| *Syntax* | *Description* |
|---|---|
| **interface** | (Optional) Displays information for the interface specified by the arguments *type* and *number*. |
| *type* | (Optional) Interface type. |
| *number* | (Optional) Interface number. |

### *Command Mode*

EXEC

### *Usage Guidelines*

This command first appeared in Cisco IOS Release 10.0.

If you enter the **show dialer interface** command for the D channel of an ISDN BRI or PRI, the command output also displays the B channels. That is, the command **show dialer interface bri 0** displays information of interfaces bri 0, bri 0:1, and bri 0:2. The command **show dialer interface serial 0:23** (for a channelized T1 line configured for ISDN PRI) displays information for serial interfaces 0:23, 0:0, 0:1, and so forth to 0:22.

If you have defined a dialer group that consists of the interfaces serial 0, serial 1, and bri 2, the command **show dialer interface dialer 1** displays information for interfaces bri 0, bri 0:1, bri 0:2, serial 1, and serial 0.

### *Sample Displays*

The following is sample output from the **show dialer** command for a BRI interface when dialer profiles are configured:

```
impulse# show dialer interface bri 0

BRI0 - dialer type = ISDN

Dial String      Successes   Failures    Last called   Last status

0 incoming call(s) have been screened.

BRI0: B-Channel 1
Idle timer (120 secs), Fast idle timer (20 secs)
Wait for carrier (30 secs), Re-enable (15 secs)

Dialer state is data link layer up

Dial reason: ip (s=6.1.1.8, d=6.1.1.1)

Interface bound to profile Dialer0

Time until disconnect 102 secs
Current call connected 00:00:19
Connected to 5773872 (wolfman)

BRI0: B-Channel 2
Idle timer (120 secs), Fast idle timer (20 secs)
Wait for carrier (30 secs), Re-enable (15 secs)
Dialer state is idle
```

Table 43–3 describes significant fields shown in the display.

**Table 43–3** *Show Dialer Interface BRI Field Descriptions*

| Field | Description |
|---|---|
| BRI0 - dialer type = ISDN | ISDN dialer. |
| Dial String | Dial strings of logged calls (telephone numbers). On ISDN BRI interfaces, if you have specified a subaddress number in the **dialer string,** this number is included in the dial string after a colon. |

**Table 43–3** *Show Dialer Interface BRI Field Descriptions, Continued*

| Field | Description |
|---|---|
| Successes | Successful connections (even if no data is passed). |
| Failures | Failed connections; call not successfully completed. |
| Last called | Time that last call occurred to specific dial string. |
| Last status | Status of last call to specific dial string (successful or failed). |
| 0 incoming call(s) have been screened. | Number of calls subjected to Dialer Profiles screening to determine how the call is to be treated. |
| BRI0: B-Channel 1 | Header indicating the following data is for B channel 1. |
| Idle timer (120 secs), Fast idle timer (20 secs) | Settings (in seconds) for the idle timer and the fast-idle timer. |
| Wait for carrier (30 secs), Re-enable (15 secs) | Settings (in seconds) for the wait-for-carrier timer and the re-enable timer. |
| Dialer state is data link layer up | The message "data link layer up" suggests that the dialer came up properly; if it says anything else, then dialer did not come up properly. The message "physical layer up" means the line protocol (LCP) came up but the NCP did not come up. The **show interfaces** command also provides the similar information. |
| Dial reason: ip (s=6.1.1.8, d=6.1.1.1) | What initiated the dial, namely an IP packet, plus source and destination address in the packet. |
| Interface bound to profile Dialer0 | Dialer profile that is bound to this interface or B channel. |
| Time until disconnect | Time until line is configured to disconnect. |
| Current call connected | Time at which the current call was connected. |
| Connected to | Dial string to which line is currently connected. |



The following is sample output from the **show dialer** command for an asynchronous interface:

```
Router# show dialer interface async 1

Async1 - dialer type = IN-BAND NO-PARITY
Idle timer (900 secs), Fast idle timer (20 secs)
Wait for carrier (30 secs), Re-enable (15 secs)
```

```
Time until disconnect 838 secs
Current call connected 0:02:16
Connected to 8986

 Dial String       Successes   Failures    Last called   Last status
 8986                      0          0     never                      Default
 8986                      8          3     0:02:16      Success       Default
```

Table 43–4 describes significant fields shown in the display.

**Table 43–4** *Show Dialer Interface Async Field Descriptions for In-Band Dialers*

| Field | Description |
|---|---|
| Async 1 | Name of an asynchronous interface. |
| dialer type = IN-BAND | Indicates that DDR is enabled. |
| Idle timer (900 secs) | Idle timeout specification (in seconds). |
| Fast idle timer (20 secs) | Fast-idle timer specification (in seconds). |
| Wait for carrier (30 secs) | Wait for carrier timer specification (in seconds). |
| Re-enable (15 secs) | Enable timeout specification (in seconds). |
| Time until disconnected | Time until line is configured to disconnect. |
| Current call connected | Time at which the current call was connected. |
| Connected to | Dial string to which line is currently connected. |
| Dial String | Dial strings of logged calls (telephone numbers). On ISDN BRI interfaces, if you have specified a subaddress number in the **dialer string** or **dialer map** command, this number is included in the dial string after a colon. |
| Successes | Successful connections (even if no data is passed). |
| Failures | Failed connections; call not successfully completed. |
| Last called | Time that last call occurred to specific dial string. |
| Last status | Status of last call to specific dial string (successful or failed). |
| Default | If the DDR facility is using the dial string specified with the **dialer string** command, the word *Default* is appended to the Last status entry. |

When the **show dialer** EXEC command is issued for a synchronous serial interface configured for DTR dialing, output similar to the following is displayed:

```
Serial 0 - dialer type = DTR SYNC
Idle timer (120 secs), Fst idle timer (20 secs)
```

```
Wait for carrier (30 secs), Re-enable (15 secs)

 Dial String     Successes    Failures    Last called    Last status
 ----                    1           0      1:04:47      Success      DTR dialer
 8986                    0           0      never                     Default
```

Table 43–5 describes additional fields shown in the display.

**Table 43–5** *Show Dialer Field Descriptions for DTR Dialers*

| Field | Description |
|---|---|
| DTR SYNC | Indicates that DDR is enabled and that DTR dialing is enabled on this synchronous interface. |
| Last status: Success | Indicates that the last call was successful and that DTR dialing was used. |
| DTR dialer | Phrase appended to the Last status entry to indicate that this is a DTR dialer. |

If an interface is connected to a destination, a display is provided that indicates the idle time before the line is disconnected. (The value decrements each second.) Then the duration of the current connection is shown. The following shows an example of this display; it appears after the third line in the **show dialer** display:

```
Time until disconnect 596 secs
Current call connected 0:00:25
```

After a call disconnects, the system displays the time remaining before it can dial again. The following is an example of this display; it appears after the third line in the **show dialer** display:

```
Time until interface enabled 8 secs
```

If the **show dialer** command is issued for an interface on which DDR is not enabled, the system displays an error message. The following is a sample error message:

```
Async 1 - Dialing not enabled on this interface.
```

If an interface is configured for DDR, the **show interfaces** command displays the following message:

```
Async1 is up, line protocol is up (spoofing)
Hardware is Async Serial
```

The word *spoofing* indicates that the line really is not up, but the dialer is forcing the line to masquerade as "up" so that upper level protocols will continue to operate as expected. Spoofing is a state added to allow DDR to work. The interface "dials on demand" in response to packets being routed to it. But because no packets are routed to down interfaces, the interface must pretend to be up (spoof) so packets will be routed to it when it is not connected. Spoofing is the normal idle state on a dial-on-demand interface.

If caller ID screening is configured on an ISDN BRI, the **show dialer** command display includes a line similar to the following:

```
1 incoming call(s) have been screened.
```

This line reports the number of calls that have been screened.

## SHOW DIALER MAP

To display the current dialer maps, next-hop protocol addresses, user names, and interfaces on which they are configured, use the **show dialer map** privileged EXEC command.

**show dialer map**

### *Syntax Description*

This command has no arguments and keywords.

### *Command Mode*

Privileged EXEC

### *Usage Guidelines*

This command first appeared in Cisco IOS Release 11.2.

### *Sample Display*

The following is sample output from the **show dialer map** command. The dialer maps are grouped by network address. When multiple dialer maps exist for the same network address, the dialer maps differ only by phone number. In this output, the dialer maps marked "BAP" are temporary dialer maps the PPP Bandwidth Allocation Control Protocol (BACP) creates when a peer calls from a different phone number than is configured or when a peer calls from a number that does not appear in an existing map. The temporary dialer maps allows PPP BACP to make outgoing calls to the peers.

```
bap_peer# show dialer map

Static dialer map ip 6.1.1.1 name peer_1 on Dialer1
Static dialer map ip 6.1.1.2 name peer_2 on Dialer1
BAP dialer map ip 6.1.1.2 name peer_2 on Dialer1
Dynamic dialer map ip 6.1.1.3 name peer_3 on Dialer1
BAP dialer map ip 6.1.1.3 name peer_3 on Dialer1
```

### *Related Commands*

Search online to find documentation for related commands.

**dialer map**

CHAPTER 44

# Configuring Peer-to-Peer DDR with Dialer Profiles

This chapter describes configuration of the Cisco IOS software for the Dialer Profiles implementation of dial-on-demand routing (DDR).

For information about preparations for configuring Dialer Profiles, see Chapter 36, "Deciding and Preparing to Configure DDR." The Dialer Profiles feature is contrasted with legacy DDR. For information about legacy DDR, see the other chapters in this part, Part V, "Dial-on-Demand Routing." For information about dial backup using Dialer Profiles, see Chapter 48, "Configuring Dial Backup with Dialer Profiles." For a complete description of the Dialer Profiles commands in this chapter, see Chapter 45, "Peer-to-Peer DDR with Dialer Profiles Commands."

## RESTRICTIONS

Dialer Profiles supports most routed protocols. However, Frame Relay, ISO CLNS, and LAPB are not supported.

## BACKGROUND ABOUT DIALER INTERFACES AND DIALER PROFILES

Dialer profiles allow the configuration of physical interfaces to be separated from the logical configuration required for a call, and they also allow the logical and physical configurations to be bound together dynamically on a per-call basis.

A *dialer profile* consists of the following elements:

- A *dialer interface* (a logical entity) configuration including one or more dial strings (each of which is used to reach one destination subnetwork)
- A *dialer map class* that defines all the characteristics for any call to the specified dial string
- An ordered *dialer pool* of physical interfaces to be used by the dialer interface

All calls going to or from the same destination subnetwork use the same dialer profile.

A dialer interface configuration includes all settings needed to reach a specific destination subnetwork (and any networks reached through it). Multiple dial strings can be specified for the same dialer interface, each dial string being associated with a different dialer map class. The dialer map class defines all the characteristics for any call to the specified dial string. For example, the map class for one destination might specify a 56-Kbps ISDN speed; the map class for a different destination might specify a 64-Kbps ISDN speed.

Each dialer interface uses a dialer pool, a pool of physical interfaces ordered on the basis of the priority assigned to each physical interface. A physical interface can belong to multiple dialer pools, contention being resolved by priority. ISDN BRI and PRI interfaces can set a limit on the minimum and maximum number of B channels reserved by any dialer pools. A channel reserved by a dialer pool remains idle until traffic is directed to the pool.

When dialer profiles are used to configure DDR, a physical interface has no configuration settings except encapsulation and the dialer pools to which the interface belongs.

**NOTES**

The preceding paragraph has one exception: commands that apply before authentication is complete must be configured on the physical (or BRI or PRI) interface and not on the dialer profile. Dialer profiles do not copy PPP authentication commands (or LCP commands) to the physical interface.

---

Figure 44–1 shows a typical application of dialer profiles. Router A has dialer interface 1 for dial-on-demand routing with subnetwork 1.1.1.0, and dialer interface 2 for dial-on-demand routing with subnetwork 2.2.2.0. The IP address for dialer interface 1 is its address as a node in network 1.1.1.0; at the same time, that IP address serves as the IP address of the physical interfaces used by the dialer interface 1. Similarly, the IP address for dialer interface 2 is its address as a node in network 2.2.2.0.

A dialer interface uses only one dialer pool. A physical interface, however, can be a member of one or many dialer pools, and a dialer pool can have several physical interfaces as members.

Figure 44–2 illustrates the relations among the concepts of dialer interface, dialer pool, and physical interfaces. Dialer interface 0 uses dialer pool 2. Physical interface BRI 1 belongs to dialer pool 2 and has a specific priority in the pool. Physical interface BRI 2 also belongs to dialer pool 2. Because contention is resolved on the basis of priority levels of the physical interfaces in the pool, BRI 1 and BRI 2 have to be assigned different priorities in the pool. Perhaps BRI 1 is assigned priority 100 and BRI 2 is assigned priority 50 in dialer pool 2 (a priority of 50 is higher than a priority of 100). BRI 2 has a higher priority in the pool, and its calls will be placed first.

*Figure 44–1 Typical Dialer Profiles Application.*

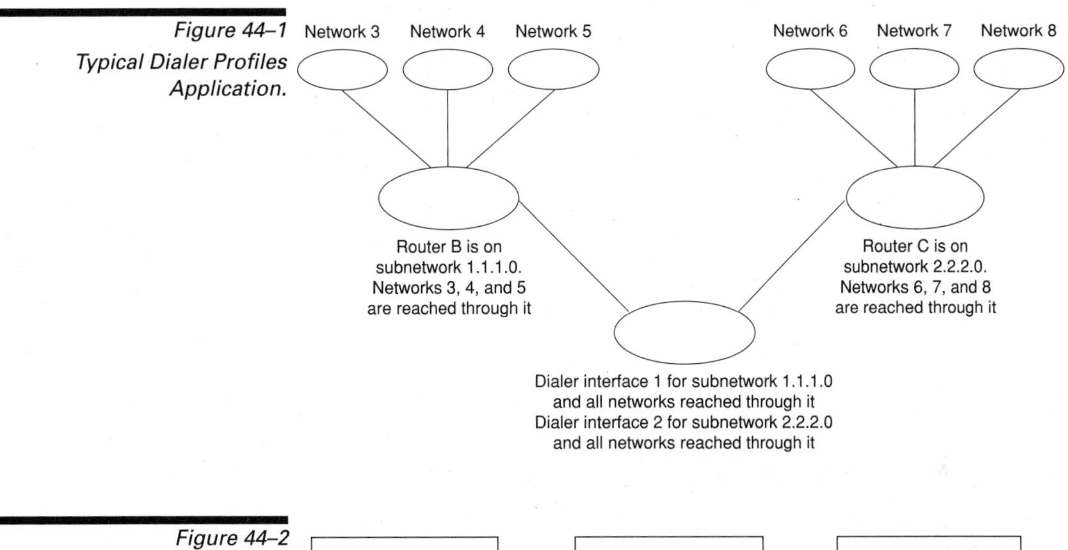


*Figure 44–2 Relations among Dialer Interfaces, Dialer Pools, and Physical Interfaces.*

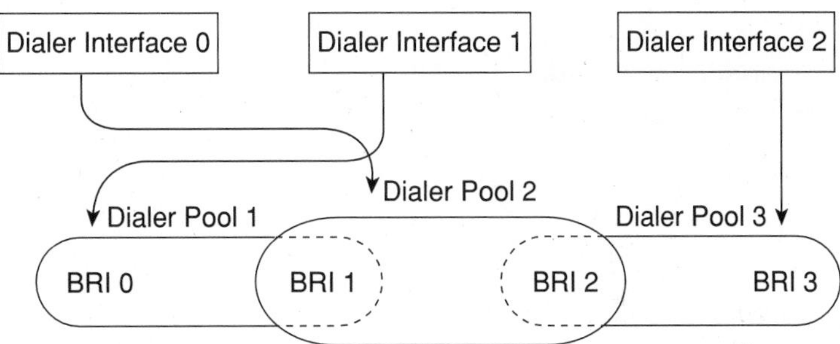


## DIALER PROFILES CONFIGURATION TASK LIST

To configure dialer profiles, perform the tasks in the following section:

- Configuring a Dialer Profile

The following tasks can be configured whether you use legacy DDR or Dialer Profiles. Perform these tasks as needed for your network:

- Configuring Dialer Profiles for Routed Protocols
- Configuring Dialer Profiles for Transparent Bridging

See the section "Dialer Profiles Configuration Examples," for comprehensive configuration examples.

## CONFIGURING A DIALER PROFILE

To configure a dialer profile, perform the tasks in the following sections. The first and last are required. Map-class configuration is optional.

- Configure a Dialer Interface
- Configure a Map Class
- Configure the Physical Interfaces

### Configure a Dialer Interface

Any number of dialer interfaces can be created for a router. Each dialer interface is the complete configuration for a destination subnetwork and any networks reached through it. The router on the destination subnetwork sends traffic on to the appropriate shadowed networks.

To configure a dialer interface, complete the following tasks beginning in global configuration mode:

| Task | | Command |
|---|---|---|
| **Step 1** | Create a dialer interface. | **interface dialer** *number* |
| **Step 2** | Specify the IP address and mask of the dialer interface as a node in the destination network to be called. | **ip address** *address mask* |
| **Step 3** | Specify PPP encapsulation. | **encapsulation ppp** |
| **Step 4** | Specify the remote router CHAP authentication name. | **dialer remote-name** *name* |
| **Step 5** | Specify the remote destination to call and the map class that defines characteristics for calls to this destination. | **dialer string** *string* **class** *class-name* |
| **Step 6** | Specify the dialing pool to use for calls to this destination. | **dialer pool** *number* |
| **Step 7** | Assign the dialer interface to a dialer group. | **dialer-group** *number* |
| **Step 8** | Specify an access list by list number or by protocol and list number to define the "interesting" packets that can trigger a call. | **dialer-list** *dialer-group* **protocol** *protocol-name* {**permit** \| **deny** \| **list** *access-list-number*} |

### Configure a Map Class

Map-class configuration is optional but allows you to specify different characteristics for different types of calls on a per-call-destination basis. For example, you can specify higher priority and a lower wait-for-carrier time for an ISDN-calls map class than for a modem-calls map class. You can also specify a different speed for some ISDN calls than for other ISDN calls.

A specific map class is tied to a specific call destination by the use of the map-class name in the **dialer-string** command with the **class** keyword.

To specify a map class and define its characteristics, complete the following tasks beginning in global configuration mode:

| Task | Command |
|---|---|
| Specify a map class and enter map-class configuration mode. | **map-class dialer** class-*name* |
| Specify the fast-idle timer value. | **dialer fast-idle** *seconds* |
| Specify the idle time before the calls in this map class are disconnected. | **dialer idle-timeout** *seconds* |
| Specify the length of time to wait for a carrier when dialing out to the dial string associated with the map class. | **dialer wait-for-carrier-time** *seconds* |
| For ISDN only, specify the bit rate used on the B channel associated with a specified map class or specify that an ISDN semipermanent connection is to be used for calls associated with this map. | **dialer isdn** [**speed** *speed*] [**spc**] |

### Configure the Physical Interfaces

To configure a physical interface, complete the following tasks beginning in global configuration mode:

| Task | | Command |
|---|---|---|
| **Step 1** | Specify the physical interface. | **interface** *type number* |
| **Step 2** | Enable PPP encapsulation. | **encapsulation ppp** |
| **Step 3** | Specify PPP CHAP authentication, if you also want to receive calls on this interface. | **ppp authentication chap** |

| Task | | Command |
|---|---|---|
| **Step 4** | Put the interface in a dialing pool and, optionally, assign the interface a priority. | **dialer pool-member** *number* [**priority** *priority*] |
| | For ISDN interfaces, you can also optionally specify the minimum number of channels reserved and maximum number of channels that can be for this dialing pool. | **dialer pool-member** *number* [**priority** *priority*] [**min-link** *minimum*] [**max-link** *maximum*]* |
| **Step 5** | (Optional) Repeat Step 4 if you want to put the interface in additional dialing pools. | **dialer pool-member** *number* [**priority** *priority*] or **dialer pool-member** *number* [**priority** *priority*] [**min-link** *minimum*] [**max-link** *maximum*] |

* When you specify a min-link number, that number of channels is reserved for that dialer pool; the channels remain idle when no calls are active.

Repeat this procedure for additional physical interfaces that you want to use with Dialer Profiles.

## CONFIGURING DIALER PROFILES FOR ROUTED PROTOCOLS

Both legacy DDR and Dialer Profiles support the following routed protocols: AppleTalk, Banyan VINES, DECnet, IP, Novell IPX, and XNS.

To configure Dialer Profiles for a routed protocol, perform the tasks in the relevant section:

- Configure Dialer Profiles for AppleTalk
- Configure Dialer Profiles for Banyan VINES
- Configure Dialer Profiles for DECnet
- Configure Dialer Profiles for IP
- Configure Dialer Profiles for Novell IPX
- Configure XNS over DDR

### Configure Dialer Profiles for AppleTalk

To configure Dialer Profiles for AppleTalk, you specify AppleTalk access lists and then configure the dialer interface for Dialer Profiles, defining the dialer list to be used. Use the **dialer-list protocol** command to define permit or deny conditions for the entire protocol; for a finer granularity, use the **dialer-list protocol** command with the **list** keyword. See the section "Configure a Dialer Interface," earlier in this chapter for more information about defining dialer lists.

### Configure Dialer Profiles for Banyan VINES

To configure DDR for Banyan VINES, perform one of the following tasks in global configuration mode:

| Task | Command |
|---|---|
| Specify a VINES standard access list. | **vines access-list** *access-list-number* {**permit** \| **deny**} *source source-mask1* |
| or<br>Specify a VINES extended access list. | **vines access-list** *access-list-number* {**permit** \| **deny**} *source source-mask* [*destination*] [*destination-mask*] |

After you specify VINES standard or extended access lists, configure the dialer interface for Dialer Profiles, defining the dialer list to be used. Use the **dialer-list protocol** command to define permit or deny conditions for the entire protocol; for a finer granularity, use the **dialer-list protocol** command with the **list** keyword. See the section "Configure a Dialer Interface," earlier in this chapter for more information about defining dialer lists.

**NOTES**

The Banyan VINES **neighbor** command is not supported for LAPB and X.25 encapsulations.

### Configure Dialer Profiles for DECnet

To configure DDR for DECnet, perform one of the following tasks in global configuration mode:

| Task | Command |
|---|---|
| Specify a DECnet standard access list. | **access-list** *access-list-number* {**permit** \| **deny**} *source source-mask1* |
| or<br>Specify a DECnet extended access list. | **access-list** *access-list-number* {**permit** \| **deny**} *source source-mask* [*destination*] [*destination-mask*] |

After you specify DECnet standard or extended access lists, configure the dialer interface for Dialer Profiles, defining the dialer list to be used. Use the **dialer-list protocol** command to define permit or deny conditions for the entire protocol; for a finer granularity, use the **dialer-list protocol** command with the **list** keyword. See the section "Configure a Dialer Interface," earlier in this chapter for more information about defining dialer lists.

You classify DECnet control packets, including hello packets and routing updates, using one or more of the following commands: **dialer-list protocol decnet_router-L1 permit**, **dialer-list protocol decnet_router-L2 permit**, and **dialer-list protocol decnet_node permit**.

### Configure Dialer Profiles for IP

To configure DDR for IP, perform one of the following tasks in global configuration mode:

| Task | Command |
|---|---|
| Specify an IP standard access list.<br><br>or | **access-list** *access-list-number* {**deny** \| **permit**} *source* [*source-mask*] |
| Specify an IP extended access list. | **access-list** *access-list-number* {**deny** \| **permit**} *protocol source source-mask destination destination-mask* [*operator operand*] |

You can now also use simplified IP access lists that use the abbreviation *any* instead of the numeric forms of source and destination addresses and masks. Other forms of IP access lists are also available.

To use dynamic routing where multiple remote sites communicate with each other through a central site, you might need to disable the IP split-horizon feature. Split horizon applies to RIP, IGRP, and Enhanced IGRP.

### Configure Dialer Profiles for Novell IPX

On DDR links for Novell IPX, the link may come up often even when all client sessions are idle because the server sends watchdog or keepalive packets to all the clients approximately every 5 minutes. You can configure a local router or access server to idle out the DDR link and respond to the watchdog packets on behalf of the clients.

To modify the Dialer Profiles dialer interface configuration for Novell IPX, perform the following tasks in interface configuration mode:

| Task | Command |
|---|---|
| Disable fast switching for IPX. | **no ipx route-cache** |
| Enable IPX watchdog spoofing.<br>or<br>Enable SPX keepalive spoofing. | **ipx watchdog-spoof**<br><br>**ipx spx-spoof** |
| Set the idle time after which SPX keepalive spoofing begins. | **ipx spx-idle-time** *delay-in-seconds* |

### Configure XNS over DDR

To configure XNS over DDR, perform one of the following tasks in global configuration mode:

| Task | Command |
|---|---|
| Specify a standard XNS access list. | **access-list** *access-list-number* {**deny** \| **permit**} *source-network*[*.source-address* [*source-address-mask*]] [*destination-network*[*.destination-address* [*destination-address-mask*]]] |
| or | |
| Specify an extended XNS access list. | **access-list** *access-list-number* {**deny** \| **permit**} *protocol* [*source-network*[*.source-host* [*source-network-mask.*]*source-host-mask*] *source-socket* [*destination-network* [*.destination-host* [*destination-network-mask.destination-host-mask*] *destination-socket*[**/pep**]]] |

After you specify an XNS access list, configure the dialer interface for Dialer Profiles, defining the dialer list to be used. Use the **dialer-list protocol** command to define permit or deny conditions for the entire protocol; for a finer granularity, use the **dialer-list protocol** command with the **list** keyword. See the section "Configure a Dialer Interface," earlier in this chapter for more information about defining dialer lists.

## Configuring Dialer Profiles for Transparent Bridging

The Cisco IOS software supports transparent bridging over both legacy DDR and Dialer Profiles, and it provides you some flexibility in controlling access and configuring the interface.

To configure Dialer Profiles for bridging, complete the tasks in the following sections:

- Define the Protocols to Bridge
- Specify the Bridging Protocol
- Control Access for Bridging
- Configure an Interface for Bridging

### Define the Protocols to Bridge

IP packets are routed by default unless they are explicitly bridged; all others are bridged by default unless they are explicitly routed. To bridge IP packets, complete the following task in global configuration mode:

| Task | Command |
|---|---|
| Disable IP routing. | **no ip routing** |

If you choose *not* to bridge another protocol, use the relevant command to enable routing of that protocol.

### Specify the Bridging Protocol

You must specify the type of spanning tree bridging protocol to use and also identify a bridge group. To specify the spanning tree protocol and a bridge group number, complete the following task in global configuration mode:

| Task | Command |
|---|---|
| Define the type of spanning tree protocol and identify a bridge group. | **bridge** *bridge-group* **protocol** {**ieee** \| **dec**} |

The *bridge-group* number is used when you configure the interface and assign it to a bridge group. Packets are bridged only among members of the same bridge group.

### Control Access for Bridging

You can control access by defining any transparent bridge packet as *interesting*, or you can use the finer granularity of controlling access by Ethernet type codes. To control access for DDR bridging, complete *one* of the following tasks in global configuration mode:

- Permit All Bridge Packets
- Control Bridging Access by Ethernet Type Codes

**NOTES**

Spanning tree bridge protocol data units (BPDUs) are always treated as *uninteresting*.

#### *Permit All Bridge Packets*

To identify all transparent bridge packets as interesting, complete the following task in global configuration mode:

| Task | Command |
|---|---|
| Define a dialer list that treats all transparent bridge packets as interesting. | **dialer-list** *dialer-group* **protocol bridge permit** |

#### *Control Bridging Access by Ethernet Type Codes*

To control access by Ethernet type codes, complete the following tasks in global configuration mode:

### Configure an Interface for Bridging

You can configure serial interfaces or ISDN interfaces for DDR bridging. To configure an interface for DDR bridging, complete all the tasks in the following sections:

| Task | Command |
| --- | --- |
| Identify interesting packets by Ethernet type codes (access list numbers must be in the range 200–299). | **access-list** *access-list-number* {**permit** \| **deny**} *type-code* [*mask*] |
| Define a dialer list for the specified access list. | **dialer-list** *dialer-group* **protocol bridge list** *access-list-number* |

- Specify the Interface
- Configure the Destination
- Assign the Interface to a Bridge Group

### *Specify the Interface*

To specify the interface and enter interface configuration mode, complete the following task, starting in global configuration mode:

| Task | Command |
| --- | --- |
| Specify the serial or ISDN interface and enter interface configuration mode. | **interface** *type number* |

### *Configure the Destination*

You can configure the destination by specifying either of the following:

- A dial string—for unauthenticated calls to a single site
- A dialer bridge map—when you want to use authentication.

To configure the destination for bridging over a specified interface, complete the following task in interface configuration mode:

| Task | Command |
| --- | --- |
| Configure the dial string to call. | **dialer string** *dial-string* |

**NOTES**

You can define only one dialer bridge map for the interface. If you enter a different bridge map, the previous one is replaced immediately.

### Assign the Interface to a Bridge Group

Packets are bridged only among interfaces that belong to the same bridge group. To assign an interface to a bridge group, complete the following task in interface configuration mode:

| Task | Command |
|---|---|
| Assign the specified interface to a bridge group. | **bridge-group** *bridge-group* |

## MONITORING AND MAINTAINING DIALER PROFILES CONNECTIONS

To monitor DDR dialer profile connections, perform the following tasks in privileged EXEC mode:

| Task | Command |
|---|---|
| Display information for the interfaces configured for DDR dialer profiles. | **show dialer interface** |
| Display information about the ISDN interface. | **show interfaces bri 0** |
| Display status about the IPX interface. | **show ipx interface** [*type number*] |
| Display information about the IPX packets transmitted by the router or access server, including watchdog counters. | **show ipx traffic** |
| Display information about the AppleTalk packets transmitted by the router or access server. | **show appletalk traffic** |
| Display information about the Banyan VINES packets transmitted by the router or access server. | **show vines traffic** |
| Display information about the DECnet packets transmitted by the router or access server. | **show decnet traffic** |
| Display information about the XNS packets transmitted by the router or access server. | **show xns traffic** |
| Clear the values of the general diagnostic statistics. | **clear dialer** |

## DIALER PROFILES CONFIGURATION EXAMPLES

This section provides two comprehensive configuration examples:

- Dialer Profile for Central Site with Multiple Remote Sites Example
- Dialer Profile for ISDN BRI Backing Up Two Leased Lines Example

### Dialer Profile for Central Site with Multiple Remote Sites Example

This central site can place or receive calls from three remote sites over four ISDN BRI lines. Each remote site is on a different IP subnet and has different bandwidth requirements. Therefore three dialer interfaces and three dialer pools are defined.

```
! This is a Dialer Profile for reaching remote subnetwork 1.1.1.1.
interface Dialer1
 ip address 1.1.1.1 255.255.255.0
 encapsulation ppp
 dialer remote-name Smalluser
 dialer string 4540
 dialer pool 3
 dialer-group 1

! This is a Dialer Profile for reaching remote subnetwork 2.2.2.2.
interface Dialer2
 ip address 2.2.2.2 255.255.255.0
 encapsulation ppp
 dialer remote-name Mediumuser
 dialer string 5264540 class Eng
 dialer load-threshold 50 either
 dialer pool 1
 dialer-group 2

! This is a Dialer Profile for reaching remote subnetwork 3.3.3.3.
interface Dialer3
 ip address 3.3.3.3 255.255.255.0
 encapsulation ppp
 dialer remote-name Poweruser
 dialer string 4156884540 class Eng
 dialer hold-queue 10
 dialer load-threshold 80
 dialer pool 2
 dialer-group 2

! This map class ensures that these calls use an ISDN speed of 56 Kbps.
map-class dialer Eng
 isdn speed 56

interface BRI0
 encapsulation PPP
! BRI 0 has a higher priority than BRI 1 in dialer pool 1.
 dialer pool-member 1 priority 100
 ppp authentication chap

interface BRI1
 encapsulation ppp
 dialer pool-member 1 priority 50
 dialer pool-member 2 priority 50
! BRI 1 has a reserved channel in dialer pool 3; the channel remains inactive
! until BRI 1 uses it to place calls.
 dialer pool-member 3 min-link 1
 ppp authentication chap
```

```
interface BRI2
 encapsulation ppp
! BRI 2 has a higher priority than BRI 1 in dialer pool 2.
 dialer pool-member 2 priority 100
 ppp authentication chap

interface BRI3
 encapsulation ppp
! BRI 3 has the highest priority in dialer pool 2.
 dialer pool-member 2 priority 150
 ppp authentication chap
```

## Dialer Profile for ISDN BRI Backing Up Two Leased Lines Example

The following example shows the configuration of a site that backs up two leased lines using one BRI. Two dialer interfaces are defined. Each serial (leased-line) interface is configured to use one of the dialer interfaces as a backup. Both of the dialer interfaces use BRI 0, and BRI 0 1s a member of the two dialer pools. Thus, BRI 0 can back up two different serial interfaces and can make calls to two different sites.

```
interface dialer0
 ip unnumbered loopback0
 encapsulation ppp
 dialer remote-name Remote0
 dialer pool 1
 dialer string 5551212
 dialer-group 1

interface dialer1
 ip unnumbered loopback0
 encapsulation ppp
 dialer remote-name Remote1
 dialer pool 2
 dialer string 5551234
 dialer-group 1

interface bri 0
 encapsulation PPP
 dialer pool-member 1
 dialer pool-member 2
 ppp authentication chap

interface serial 0
 ip unnumbered loopback0
 backup interface dialer0
 backup delay 5 10

interface serial 1
 ip unnumbered loopback0
 backup interface dialer1
 backup delay 5 10
```

# CHAPTER 45

# Peer-to-Peer DDR with Dialer Profiles Commands

This chapter lists commands for the Dialer Profiles implementation of dial-on-demand routing (DDR), explains the command syntax, and provides usage guidelines.

For information about configuring Dialer Profiles DDR and for configuration examples, see Chapter 44, "Configuring Peer-to-Peer DDR with Dialer Profiles."

## DIALER FAST-IDLE (MAP-CLASS DIALER CONFIGURATION)

To specify the fast-idle timer value to use when placing a call to any telephone number associated with a specified class, use the **dialer fast-idle** map-class dialer configuration command. To reset the dialer fast-idle timer to the default, use the **no** form of this command.

**dialer fast-idle** *seconds*
**no dialer fast-idle**

| *Syntax* | *Description* |
|---|---|
| *seconds* | Number of seconds to wait before placing a different call. |

### *Default*

Defaults to the fast-idle timer value set for the interface

### *Command Mode*

Map-class dialer

### Usage Guidelines

This command first appeared in Cisco IOS Release 10.0.

The **dialer string class** command defines the map class associated with the dial string and interface.

This fast-idle timer is associated only with the map class, not the entire interface.

### Example

```
dialer string 4156884540 class Eng

! This map-class ensures that these calls use an ISDN speed of 56 Kbps and a
! fast-idle time of 10 seconds.
map-class dialer Eng
 isdn speed 56
 dialer fast-idle 10
 dialer wait-for-carrier-time 30
```

### Related Command

Search online to find documentation for related commands.

**dialer fast-idle (interface)**
**dialer string (dialer profiles)**
**map-class dialer**

## DIALER-GROUP

To control access by configuring an interface to belong to a specific dialing group, use the **dialer-group** interface configuration command. To remove an interface from the specified dialer access group, use the **no** form of this command.

**dialer-group** *group-number*
**no dialer-group**

| *Syntax* | *Description* |
|---|---|
| *group-number* | Number of the dialer access group to which the specific interface belongs. This access group is defined with the **dialer-list** command. Acceptable values are nonzero, positive integers between 1 and 10. |

### Default

No access is predefined.

### Command Mode

Interface configuration

### *Usage Guidelines*

This command first appeared in Cisco IOS Release 10.0.

An interface can be associated with a single dialer access group only; multiple **dialer-group** assignment is not allowed. A second dialer access group assignment will override the first. A dialer access group is defined with the **dialer-group** command. The **dialer-list** command associates an access list with a dialer access group.

Packets that match the dialer group specified trigger a connection request.

### *Example*

The following example specifies dialer access group number 1.

The destination address of the packet is evaluated against the access list specified in the associated **dialer-list** command. If it passes, either a call is initiated (if no connection has already been established) or the idle timer is reset (if a call is currently connected).

```
interface async 1
 dialer-group 1
access-list 101 deny igrp 0.0.0.0 255.255.255.255 255.255.255.255 0.0.0.0
access-list 101 permit ip 0.0.0.0 255.255.255.255 0.0.0.0 255.255.255.255
dialer-list 1 list 101
```

## DIALER IDLE-TIMEOUT (MAP-CLASS DIALER CONFIGURATION)

To specify the idle time before the calls in this map class are disconnected, use the **dialer idle-timeout** map-class dialer configuration command. To reset the idle timeout to the default, use the **no** form of this command.

**dialer idle-timeout** *seconds*
**no dialer idle-timeout**

| *Syntax* | *Description* |
|---|---|
| *seconds* | Idle time, in seconds, that must occur on an interface associated with a map class before calls are disconnected. Acceptable values are positive, nonzero integers. |

### *Default*

Defaults to a value set for the interface

### *Command Mode*

Map-class configuration

### *Usage Guidelines*

The **dialer string class** command defines the map class associated with the dial string and interface.

### *Example*

The following example sets a dialer idle-timeout interval of 180 seconds:

```
dialer idle-timeout 180
```

### *Related Command*

Search online to find documentation for related commands.

**dialer string (dialer profiles)**

## DIALER ISDN

To specify the bit rate used on the B channel associated with a specified map class and to specify whether to set up semipermanent connections for this map class, use the **dialer isdn** map-class configuration command.

**dialer isdn** [**speed** *speed*] [**spc**]
**no dialer isdn** [**speed** *speed*] [**spc**]

| *Syntax* | *Description* |
|---|---|
| **speed** *speed* | (Optional) Bit rate, in kilobytes per second (Kbps), used on the ISDN B channel. Values are **56** and **64**. Default is 64. |
| **spc** | (Optional) Specifies that an ISDN semipermanent connection is to be used for calls associated with this map class. |

### *Default*

Bit rate is 64 Kbps. Semipermanent connections are not set up.

### *Command Mode*

Map-class dialer configuration

### *Usage Guidelines*

This command first appeared in Cisco IOS Release 11.2.

This command is valid for ISDN interfaces only.

### *Example*

The following example configures a speed of 56 Kbps and no semipermanent connections for the *Eng* map class:

```
dialer string 4156884540 class Eng

! This map-class ensures that these calls use an ISDN speed of 56 Kbps and that
! no semipermanent connection is set up.
map-class dialer Eng
dialer isdn speed 56
```

*Related Command*

Search online to find documentation for related commands.

**dialer string** (**dialer profiles**)

### DIALER-LIST PROTOCOL

To define a DDR dialer list to control dialing by protocol or by a combination of protocol and access list, use the **dialer-list protocol** global configuration command. To delete a dialer list, use the **no** form of this command.

**dialer-list** *dialer-group* **protocol** *protocol-name* {**permit** | **deny** | **list** *access-list-number* | *access-group*}

**no dialer-list** *dialer-group* [**protocol** *protocol-name* [**list** *access-list-number* | *access-group*]]

| *Syntax* | *Description* |
|---|---|
| *dialer-group* | Number of a dialer access group identified in any **dialer-group** interface configuration command. |
| *protocol-name* | One of the following protocol keywords: **appletalk**, **bridge**, **clns**, **clns_es**, **clns_is**, **decnet**, **decnet_router-L1**, **decnet_router-L2**, **decnet_node**, **ip**, **ipx**, **vines**, or **xns**. |
| **permit** | Permits access to an entire protocol. |
| **deny** | Denies access to an entire protocol. |
| **list** | Specifies that an access list will be used for defining a granularity finer than an entire protocol. |
| *access-list-number* | Access list numbers specified in any DECnet, Banyan VINES, IP, Novell IPX, or XNS standard or extended access lists, including Novell IPX extended service access point (SAP) access lists and bridging types. See Table 45–1 for the supported access list types and numbers. |
| *access-group* | Filter list name used in the **clns filter-set** and **clns access-group** commands. |

*Default*

No dialer lists are defined.

*Command Mode*

Global configuration

*Usage Guidelines*

This command first appeared in Cisco IOS Release 10.0. The **list** keyword and *access-list-number* and *access-group* arguments first appeared in Cisco IOS Release 10.3.

The various **no** forms of this command have the following effects:

- The **no dialer-list 1** command deletes all lists configured with list 1, regardless of the keyword previously used (**permit, deny, protocol,** or **list**).
- The **no dialer-list 1 protocol** *protocol-name* command deletes all lists configured with list 1 and protocol *protocol-name.*
- The **no dialer-list 1 protocol** *protocol-name* **list** *access-list-number* command deletes the specified list.

The **dialer-list protocol** form of this command permits or denies access to an entire protocol. The **dialer-list protocol list** form of this command provides a finer permission granularity and also supports protocols that were not previously supported.

The **dialer-list protocol list** form of this command applies protocol access lists to dialer access groups in order to control dialing using DDR. The dialer access groups are defined with the **dialer-group** command.

Although the **dialer-list list** command is still supported for IP, IPX, DECnet, AppleTalk, XNS, and bridging, the new **dialer-list protocol list** command should be used for all protocols. The **dialer-list protocol list** command is supported for all those protocols and also for Banyan VINES and International Organization for Standardization (ISO) Connectionless Network Service (CLNS).

Table 45–1 lists the access list types and numbers that the **dialer-list protocol list** command supports. The table does not include ISO CLNS because that protocol uses filter names instead of predefined access list numbers.

**Table 45–1** *Dialer-List Supported Access List Types and Numbers*

| Access List Type | Access List Number Range (decimal) |
|---|---|
| AppleTalk | 600–699 |
| Banyan VINES (standard) | 1–100 |
| Banyan VINES (extended) | 101–200 |
| DECnet | 300–399 |
| IP (standard) | 1–99 |
| IP (extended) | 100–199 |
| Novell IPX (standard) | 800–899 |
| Novell IPX (extended) | 900–999 |
| Transparent Bridging | 200–299 |
| XNS | 500–599 |

### *Examples*

Dialing occurs when an interesting packet (one that matches access list specifications) needs to be output on an interface. Using the standard access list method, packets can be classified as interesting or uninteresting. In the following example, IGRP TCP/IP routing protocol updates are not classified as interesting and do not initiate calls:

```
access-list 101 deny igrp 0.0.0.0 255.255.255.255 255.255.255.255 0.0.0.0
```

The following example classifies all other IP packets as interesting and permits them to initiate calls:

```
access-list 101 permit ip 0.0.0.0 255.255.255.255 0.0.0.0 255.255.255.255
```

Then the following command places list 101 into dialer access group 1:

```
dialer-list 1 protocol ip list 101
```

In the following example, DECnet access lists allow any DECnet packets with source area 10 and destination area 20 to trigger calls:

```
access-list 301 permit 10.0 0.1023 10.0 0.1023
access-list 301 permit 10.0 0.1023 20.0 0.1023
```

Then the following command places list 301 into dialer access group 1:

```
dialer-list 1 protocol decnet list 301
```

In the following example, both IP and VINES access lists are defined. The IP access lists define IGRP packets as uninteresting but permit all other IP packets to trigger calls. The VINES access lists do not allow Routing Table Protocol (RTP) routing updates to trigger calls but allow any other data packets to trigger calls.

```
access-list 101 deny igrp 0.0.0.0 255.255.255.255 0.0.0.0 255.255.255.255
access-list 101 permit ip 0.0.0.0 255.255.255.255 0.0.0.0 255.255.255.255
!
vines access-list 107 deny RTP 00000000:0000 FFFFFFFF:FFFF 00000000:0000 FFFFFFFF:FFFF
vines access-list 107 permit IP 00000000:0000 FFFFFFFF:FFFF 00000000:0000 FFFFFFFF:FFFF
```

Then the following two commands place the IP and VINES access lists into dialer access group 1:

```
dialer-list 1 protocol ip list 101
dialer-list 1 protocol vines list 107
```

In the following example, a Connectionless Network Service (CLNS) filter is defined and then the filter is placed in dialer access group 1:

```
clns filter-set ddrline permit 47.0004.0001....
!
dialer-list 1 protocol clns list ddrline
```

### *Related Commands*

Search online to find documentation for related commands.

**access-list**
**clns filter-set**
**dialer-group**
**vines access-list**

### DIALER MAX-LINK

To specify, for a dialer profile, the maximum number of links to a remote destination that can be up at any one time, use the **dialer max-link** interface configuration command.

**dialer max-link** *number*

| *Syntax* | *Description* |
|---|---|
| *number* | Maximum number of links, in the range 1 to 255. Default is 255 links. |

#### *Default*

255 links

#### *Command Mode*

Interface configuration

#### *Usage Guidelines*

This command first appeared in Cisco IOS Release 11.2.

This command applies to dialer interfaces only.

This command is used mainly to set the maximum number of links below the maximum possible.

#### *Example*

The following example sets a maximum of six links:

```
dialer max-link 6
```

#### *Related Commands*

Search online to find documentation for related commands.

**dialer isdn**
**dialer string (dialer profiles)**

### DIALER POOL

To specify, for a dialer interface, which dialing pool to use to connect to a specific destination subnetwork, use the **dialer pool** interface configuration command.

**dialer pool** *number*

| *Syntax* | *Description* |
|---|---|
| *number* | Dialing pool number, in the range 1 through 255. |

### *Default*

Disabled. No default number is specified.

### *Command Mode*

Interface configuration

### *Usage Guidelines*

This command first appeared in Cisco IOS Release 11.2.

This command applies to dialer interfaces only.

### *Examples*

The following example shows a dialer interface configuration that is linked to the physical interface configuration shown for BRI 1 in the **dialer pool-member** command section. Dialer interface 1 uses dialer pool 3, of which BRI 1 is a member.

```
! This is a dialer profile for reaching remote subnetwork 1.1.1.1.
interface Dialer1
 ip address 1.1.1.1 255.255.255.0
 encapsulation ppp
 dialer remote-name Smalluser
 dialer string 4540
 dialer pool 3
 dialer-group 1
```

The following example might accompany the previous dialer profile configuration example. Physical interface BRI 1 has a reserved channel in dialer pool 3. That channel is inactive until BRI 1 uses it to place calls.

```
interface BRI1
 encapsulation ppp
 dialer pool-member 1 priority 50
 dialer pool-member 2 priority 50
!BRI 1 has a reserved channel in dialer pool 3; the channel remains inactive
!until BRI 1 uses it to place calls.
 dialer pool-member 3 min-link 1
 ppp authentication chap
```

### *Related Commands*

Search online to find documentation for related commands.

**dialer pool-member**
**dialer remote-name**

## DIALER POOL-MEMBER

To configure a physical interface to be a member of a Dialer Profiles dialing pool, use the **dialer pool-member** interface configuration command.

**dialer pool-member** *number* [**priority** *priority*] [**min-link** *minimum*] [**max-link** *maximum*]

| *Syntax* | *Description* |
|---|---|
| *number* | Dialing pool number, in the range 1 to 255. |
| **priority** *priority* | (Optional) Priority of this interface within the dialing pool, in the range 0 (lowest) to 255 (highest). Interfaces with the highest priority are selected first for dialing out. Default is 0. |
| **min-link** *minimum* | (Optional) Minimum number of B channels on this interface that are reserved for this dialing pool, in the range 0 to 255. Default is 0. A reserved channel is inactive until the specified interface uses it to place calls. Applies to ISDN interfaces only. |
| **max-link** *maximum* | (Optional) Maximum number of B channels on this interface that can be used by this dialing pool, in the range 0 to 255. Default is 255. Applies to ISDN interfaces only. |

### *Defaults*

Disabled. When enabled, no default dialing pool number is assigned; the default value of *priority* and *minimum* is 0; the default value of *maximum* is 255.

### *Command Mode*

Interface configuration

### *Usage Guidelines*

This command first appeared in Cisco IOS Release 11.2.

This command applies to asynchronous serial, synchronous serial, BRI, and PRI *physical* interfaces only. It does not apply to dialer interfaces.

The common number used in the **dialer pool** command and in the **dialer pool-member** command links the physical interface and dialer interface configurations together.

The min-link keyword and value are used primarily for dial backup.

### *Examples*

This following example shows the configuration of one ISDN BRI interface to be a member of dialer pool 2 with priority 100:

```
interface BRI2
 encapsulation ppp
 dialer pool-member 2 priority 100
 ppp authentication chap
```

In the following example, BRI physical interface configuration BRI 1 has a reserved channel in dialer pool 3. That channel is inactive until BRI 1 uses it to place calls.

```
interface BRI1
 encapsulation ppp
 dialer pool-member 1 priority 50
```

```
 dialer pool-member 2 priority 50
!BRI 1 has a reserved channel in dialer pool 3; the channel remains inactive
!until BRI 1 uses it to place calls.
 dialer pool-member 3 min-link 1
 ppp authentication chap
```

### *Related Commands*

Search online to find documentation for related commands.

**dialer pool**

## DIALER REMOTE-NAME

To specify, for a dialer interface, the authentication name of the remote router on the destination subnetwork, use the **dialer remote-name** interface configuration command.

**dialer remote-name** *username*

| *Syntax* | *Description* |
|---|---|
| *username* | Case-sensitive character string identifying the remote device; maximum length is 255 characters. |

### *Default*

Disabled. No default username is specified.

### *Command Mode*

Interface configuration

### *Usage Guidelines*

This command first appeared in Cisco IOS Release 11.2.

This command applies only to dialer interfaces.

When using CHAP or PAP authentication, *username* is the name of the remote device that is authenticating.

### *Example*

The following partial example sets the name of the remote host to dallas.

```
dialer remote-name dallas
```

### *Related Commands*

Search online to find documentation for related commands.

**ppp authentication chap**
**ppp authentication pap**

### DIALER STRING (DIALER PROFILES)

To specify the string (telephone number) to be used when placing a call from an interface, use the **dialer string** interface configuration command. To delete the telephone number specified for the interface, use the **no** form of this command.

**dialer string** *dial-string* [**class** *class-name*]
**no dialer string**

| *Syntax* | *Description* |
|---|---|
| *dial-string* | Telephone number to be sent to a DCE device. |
| **class** *class-name* | (Optional) Dialer map class associated with this telephone number. |

#### *Default*

No telephone numbers and class names are predefined.

#### *Command Mode*

Interface configuration

#### *Usage Guidelines*

This command first appeared in Cisco IOS Release 11.2.

When you use Dialer Profiles for DDR, use the **dialer string class** form of this command to define a map class for a specific dialer profile.

Dialer Profiles make it unnecessary to use dialer maps to configure DDR.

**NOTES**

If a **dialer string** command is specified without a **dialer-group** command with access lists defined, dialing is never initiated. If the **debug dialer** command is enabled, an error message is displayed indicating that dialing never will occur.

#### *Example*

The following example specifies that the dial string 4159991234 be used in calls to destinations defined by the map class sf:

```
dialer string 4159991234 class sf
```

#### *Related Commands*

Search online to find documentation for related commands.

**dialer remote-name**
**interface dialer**

### DIALER WAIT-FOR-CARRIER-TIME (MAP-CLASS DIALER CONFIGURATION)

To specify the length of time to wait for a carrier when dialing out to the dial string associated with a specified map class, use the **dialer wait-for-carrier-time** map-class dialer configuration command. To reset the carrier-wait-time value to the default, use the **no** form of this command.

**dialer wait-for-carrier-time** *seconds*
**no dialer wait-for-carrier-time**

| *Syntax* | *Description* |
|---|---|
| *seconds* | Number of seconds that the interface waits for the carrier to come up when a call is placed. Acceptable values are positive, nonzero integers. The default is 30 seconds. |

#### *Default*

30 seconds

#### *Command Mode*

Map-class dialer configuration

#### *Usage Guidelines*

This command first appeared in Cisco IOS Release 10.0.

You can define different dialer map classes with different wait-for-carrier times to suit the different types of lines and interfaces. For example, you must define a longer wait time for a map class used by serial interfaces than for one used by ISDN interfaces.

#### *Example*

The following example specifies a carrier wait time of 20 seconds for the *Eng* class on the *Dialer2* interface:

```
interface Dialer2
 ip address 2.2.2.2 255.255.255.0
 encapsulation ppp
 dialer remote-name Mediumuser
 dialer string 5264540 class Eng
 dialer wait-for-carrier-time 20
 dialer load-threshold 50 either
 dialer pool 1
 dialer-group 2
```

#### *Related Commands*

Search online to find documentation for related commands.

**dialer string (dialer profiles)**

### INTERFACE DIALER

To define a dialer rotary group, use the **interface dialer** global configuration command.

**interface dialer** *number*

| *Syntax* | *Description* |
|---|---|
| *number* | Number of the dialer rotary group. It can be in the range 0 to 255. |

#### *Default*

No dialer rotary groups are predefined.

#### *Command Mode*

Global configuration

#### *Usage Guidelines*

This command first appeared in Cisco IOS Release 10.0.

Dialer rotary groups allow you to apply a single interface configuration to a set of physical interfaces. This allows a group of interfaces to be used as a pool of interfaces for calling many destinations.

Once the interface configuration is propagated to a set of interfaces, those interfaces can be used to place calls using the standard DDR criteria. When multiple destinations are configured, any of these interfaces can be used for outgoing calls.

Dialer rotary groups are useful in environments that require multiple calling destinations. Only the rotary group needs to be configured with the **dialer map** commands. The only configuration required for the interfaces is the **dialer rotary-group** command indicating that each interface is part of a dialer rotary group.

Although a dialer rotary group is configured as an interface, it is not a physical interface. Instead, it represents a group of interfaces. Interface configuration commands entered after the **interface dialer** command will be applied to all physical interfaces assigned to specified rotary groups. Individual interfaces in a dialer rotary group do not have individual addresses. The dialer interface has a protocol address, and that address is used by all interfaces in the dialer rotary group.

#### *Example*

The following example identifies interface dialer 1 as the dialer rotary group leader. Interface dialer 1 is not a physical interface but represents a group of interfaces. The interface configuration commands that follow apply to all interfaces included in this group.

```
interface dialer 1
 encapsulation ppp
 authentication chap
 dialer in-band
 ip address 1.2.3.4
```

```
dialer map ip 1.2.2.5 name YYY 14155553434
dialer map ip 1.3.2.6 name ZZZ
```

## MAP-CLASS DIALER

To define a class of shared configuration parameters associated with the **dialer map** command, use the **map-class dialer** global configuration command.

**map-class dialer** *classname*

| *Syntax* | *Description* |
|---|---|
| *classname* | Unique class identifier. |

### *Default*

Disabled; no class name is provided.

### *Command Mode*

Global configuration

### *Usage Guidelines*

The *classname* must be the same as the *classname* in the **dialer map** command.

### *Example*

The following example configures a map class called "hawaii" and sets an ISDN speed of 56 Kbps for the class.

```
map-class dialer hawaii
 isdn speed 56
```

### *Related Commands*

Search online to find documentation for related commands.

**dialer map**

## SHOW DIALER

To display general diagnostic information for interfaces configured for DDR, use the **show dialer** EXEC command.

**show dialer** [**interface** *type number*]

| *Syntax* | *Description* |
|---|---|
| **interface** | (Optional) Displays information for the interface specified by the arguments *type* and *number.* |

| *Syntax* | *Description* |
|---|---|
| *type* | (Optional) Interface type. |
| *number* | (Optional) Interface number. |

### Command Mode

EXEC

### Usage Guidelines

This command first appeared in Cisco IOS Release 10.0.

### Sample Displays

If you enter the **show dialer interface** command for the D channel of an ISDN BRI or PRI, the command output also displays the B channels. That is, the command **show dialer interface bri 0** displays information for interfaces bri 0, bri 0:1, and bri 0:2. The command **show dialer interface serial 0:23** (for a channelized T1 line configured for ISDN PRI) displays information for serial interfaces 0:23, 0:0, 0:1, and so forth, to 0:22.

If you have defined a dialer group that consists of the interfaces serial 0, serial 1, and bri 2, the command **show dialer interface dialer 1** displays information for interfaces bri 0, bri 0:1, bri 0:2, serial 1, and serial 0.

The following is sample output from the **show dialer** command for a BRI interface when dialer profiles are configured:

```
impulse# show dialer interface bri 0

BRI0 - dialer type = ISDN

Dial String      Successes   Failures    Last called   Last status

0 incoming call(s) have been screened.

BRI0: B-Channel 1
Idle timer (120 secs), Fast idle timer (20 secs)
Wait for carrier (30 secs), Re-enable (15 secs)

Dialer state is data link layer up

Dial reason: ip (s=6.1.1.8, d=6.1.1.1)

Interface bound to profile Dialer0

Time until disconnect 102 secs
Current call connected 00:00:19
Connected to 5773872 (wolfman)

BRI0: B-Channel 2
Idle timer (120 secs), Fast idle timer (20 secs)
```

```
Wait for carrier (30 secs), Re-enable (15 secs)
Dialer state is idle
```

Table 45–2 describes significant fields shown in the display.

**Table 45–2** *Show Dialer Interface BRI Field Descriptions*

| Field | Description |
|---|---|
| BRI0 - dialer type = ISDN | ISDN dialer. |
| Dial String | Dial strings of logged calls (telephone numbers). On ISDN BRI interfaces, if you have specified a subaddress number in the **dialer string**, this number is included in the dial string after a colon. |
| Successes | Successful connections (even if no data is passed). |
| Failures | Failed connections; call not successfully completed. |
| Last called | Time that last call occurred to specific dial string. |
| Last status | Status of last call to specific dial string (successful or failed). |
| 0 incoming call(s) have been screened. | Number of calls subjected to Dialer Profiles screening to determine how the call is to be treated. |
| BRI0: B-Channel 1 | Header indicating the following data is for B channel 1. |
| Idle timer (120 secs), Fast idle timer (20 secs) | Settings (in seconds) for the idle timer and the fast-idle timer. |
| Wait for carrier (30 secs), Re-enable (15 secs) | Settings (in seconds) for the wait for carrier timer and the re-enable timer. |
| Dialer state is data link layer up | The message "data link layer up" suggests that the dialer came up properly; if it says anything else, then dialer did not come up properly. The message "physical layer up" means the line protocol (LCP) came up, but the NCP did not come up. The **show interfaces** command also provides similar information. |
| Dial reason: ip (s=6.1.1.8, d=6.1.1.1) | What initiated the dial, namely an IP packet, plus source and destination address in the packet. |
| Interface bound to profile Dialer0 | Dialer profile that is bound to this interface or B channel. |
| Time until disconnect | Time until line is configured to disconnect. |
| Current call connected | Time at which the current call was connected. |
| Connected to | Dial string to which line is currently connected. |

The following is sample output from the **show dialer** command for an asynchronous interface:

```
Router# show dialer interface async 1

Async1 - dialer type = IN-BAND NO-PARITY
Idle timer (900 secs), Fast idle timer (20 secs)
Wait for carrier (30 secs), Re-enable (15 secs)
Time until disconnect 838 secs
Current call connected 0:02:16
Connected to 8986

 Dial String      Successes   Failures    Last called   Last status
 8986                     0          0     never                      Default
 8986                     8          3     0:02:16       Success      Default
```

Table 45–3 describes significant fields shown in the display.

**Table 45–3** *Show Dialer Interface Async Field Descriptions for In-Band Dialers*

| Field | Description |
|---|---|
| Async 1 | Name of an asynchronous interface. |
| dialer type = IN-BAND | Indicates that DDR is enabled. |
| Idle timer (900 secs) | Idle timeout specification (in seconds). |
| Fast idle timer (20 secs) | Fast-idle timer specification (in seconds). |
| Wait for carrier (30 secs) | Wait for carrier timer specification (in seconds). |
| Re-enable (15 secs) | Enable timeout specification (in seconds). |
| Time until disconnected | Time until line is configured to disconnect. |
| Current call connected | Time at which the current call was connected. |
| Connected to | Dial string to which line is currently connected. |
| Dial String | Dial strings of logged calls (telephone numbers). On ISDN BRI interfaces, if you have specified a subaddress number in the **dialer string** or **dialer map** command, this number is included in the dial string after a colon. |
| Successes | Successful connections (even if no data is passed). |
| Failures | Failed connections; call not successfully completed. |
| Last called | Time that last call occurred to specific dial string. |
| Last status | Status of last call to specific dial string (successful or failed). |
| Default | If the DDR facility is using the dial string specified with the **dialer string** command, the word *Default* is appended to the Last status entry. |

When the **show dialer** EXEC command is issued for a synchronous serial interface configured for DTR dialing, output similar to the following is displayed:

```
Serial 0 - dialer type = DTR SYNC
Idle timer (120 secs), Fst idle timer (20 secs)
Wait for carrier (30 secs), Re-enable (15 secs)

  Dial String    Successes    Failures    Last called   Last status
  ----                   1           0      1:04:47     Success      DTR dialer
  8986                   0           0      never                    Default
```

Table 45–4 describes additional fields shown in the display.

**Table 45–4** *Show Dialer Field Descriptions for DTR Dialers*

| Field | Description |
|---|---|
| DTR SYNC | Indicates that DDR is enabled and that DTR dialing is enabled on this synchronous interface. |
| Last status: Success | Indicates that the last call was successful and that DTR dialing was used. |
| DTR dialer | Phrase appended to the Last status entry to indicate that this is a DTR dialer. |

If an interface is connected to a destination, a display is provided that indicates the idle time before the line is disconnected. (The value decrements each second.) Then the duration of the current connection is shown. The following shows an example of this display; it appears after the third line in the **show dialer** display:

```
Time until disconnect 596 secs
Current call connected 0:00:25
```

After a call disconnects, the system displays the time remaining before being it can dial again. The following is an example of this display; it appears after the third line in the **show dialer** display:

```
Time until interface enabled 8 secs
```

If the **show dialer** command is issued for an interface on which DDR is not enabled, the system displays an error message. The following is a sample error message:

```
Async 1 - Dialing not enabled on this interface.
```

If an interface is configured for DDR, the **show interfaces** command displays the following message:

```
Async1 is up, line protocol is up (spoofing)
Hardware is Async Serial
```

The word *spoofing* indicates that the line really is not up, but the dialer is forcing the line to masquerade as "up" so that upper-level protocols will continue to operate as expected. Spoofing is a state added to allow DDR to work. The interface "dials on demand" in response to packets being routed to it. But because no packets are routed to down interfaces, the interface must pretend to be up (spoof) so packets will be routed to it when it is not connected. Spoofing is the normal idle state on a dial-on-demand interface.

If caller ID screening is configured on an ISDN BRI, the **show dialer** command display includes a line similar to the following:

```
1 incoming call(s) have been screened.
```

This line reports the number of calls that have been screened.

**PART 6**

# Dial Backup

# CHAPTER 46

# Configuring Dial Backup for Serial Lines

A backup interface is an interface that stays idle until certain circumstances occur; then it is activated. A backup interface for a serial interface can be an ISDN interface or a different serial interface. A backup interface can be configured to be activated when any of the following three circumstances occurs:

- The primary line goes down.
- The load on the primary line reaches a certain threshold.
- The load on the primary line exceeds a specified threshold.

To configure a dial backup to a serial interface, you must configure the interface to use the dial backup interface, specify the conditions in which the backup interface will be activated, and then configure the dial backup interface for DDR. The DDR configuration specifies the conditions and destinations for dial calls. The serial interface (often called the *primary* interface) might be configured for DDR or for Frame Relay or X.25 over a leased line, but the backup tasks are the same in all three cases.

To configure a backup interface for an interface, complete the following general steps:

- Specify the interface and configure it as needed (for DDR, Frame Relay, or X.25). You can also specify and configure a Frame Relay subinterface.

  See Chapter 13, "Configuring Synchronous Serial Ports," and the chapters in Part V, "Dial-on-Demand Routing," for details.

- Configure the primary interface or subinterface by specifying the dial backup interface and the conditions for activating the backup interface, as described in this chapter.
- Configure the backup interface for DDR, as described in the chapters found in Part V.

  See Chapter 40, "Configuring Legacy DDR Spokes" (for point-to-point Legacy DDR connections), or Chapter 42, "Configuring Legacy DDR Hubs" (for point-to-multipoint

Legacy DDR connections). If you have configured Dialer Profiles instead of Legacy DDR, see Chapter 48, "Configuring Dial Backup with Dialer Profiles," for backup information.

This chapter describes how to configure the primary interface to use the dial backup interface.

## Prerequisite

For a backup serial interface, an external data communications equipment (DCE) device, such as a modem attached to a circuit-switched service, must be connected to the backup serial interface. The external device must be capable of responding to a DTR Active signal by automatically dialing the preconfigured telephone number of the remote site.

## Dial Backup for Serial Interfaces Configuration Task List

You must decide whether to activate the backup interface when the primary line goes down, when the traffic load on the primary line exceeds the defined threshold, or both. The tasks you perform depend on your decision. Perform the tasks in the following sections as needed to configure dial backup:

- Specifying the Backup Interface
- Defining the Traffic Load Threshold
- Defining Backup Line Delays

Then configure the backup interface for DDR, so that calls are placed as needed. See the chapters found in Part V for more information.

For simple configuration examples, see the section "Dial Backup for Serial Interfaces Configuration Examples," later in this chapter.

## Specifying the Backup Interface

To specify a backup interface for a primary serial interface or subinterface, perform the following task in interface configuration mode:

| Task | Command |
|---|---|
| Select a backup interface. | **backup interface** *type number*<br>or<br>**backup interface** *type slot/port*<br>(For the Cisco 7500 series)<br>or<br>**backup interface** *type slot/port-adapter/port* (Cisco 7200 series) |

**NOTES**

When you use a Basic Rate Interface (BRI) for a dial backup, neither of the B channels can be used while the interface is in a standby mode. In addition, when a BRI is used as a backup interface and the BRI is configured for Legacy DDR, only one B channel is usable. Once the backup is initiated over one B channel, the second B channel is unavailable. When the backup interface is configured for Dialer Profiles, both B channels can be used.

When configured for Legacy DDR, the backup interface can back up only one interface. For examples of selecting a backup line, see the section "Dial Backup Using an Asynchronous Interface Example," and the section "Dial Backup Using DDR and ISDN Example," later in this chapter.

## Defining the Traffic Load Threshold

You can configure dial backup to activate the secondary line based on the traffic load on the primary line. The software monitors the traffic load and computes a 5-minute moving average. If this average exceeds the value you set for the line, the secondary line is activated and, depending upon how the line is configured, some or all of the traffic will flow onto the secondary dial-up line.

To define how much traffic should be handled at one time on an interface, perform the following task in interface configuration mode:

| Task | Command |
| --- | --- |
| Define the traffic load threshold as a percentage of the primary line's available bandwidth. | **backup load** {*enable-threshold* \| **never**} {*disable-load* \| **never**} |

## Defining Backup Line Delays

You can configure a value that defines how much time should elapse before a secondary line status changes after a primary line status has changed. This means that you can define two delays:

- A delay that applies after the primary line goes *down* but before the secondary line is activated
- A delay that applies after the primary line comes *up* but before the secondary line is deactivated

To define these delays, perform the following task in interface configuration mode:

| Task | Command |
| --- | --- |
| Define backup line delays. | **backup delay** {*enable-delay* \| **never**} {*disable-delay* \| **never**} |

For examples of how to define backup line delays, see section, "Dial Backup Using an Asynchronous Interface Example," and section, "Dial Backup Using DDR and ISDN Example," later in this chapter.

## DIAL BACKUP FOR SERIAL INTERFACES CONFIGURATION EXAMPLES

The following sections present examples of backup interfaces configured to be activated in three different circumstances:

- The primary line goes down.
- The load on the primary line reaches a certain threshold.
- The load on the primary line exceeds a specified threshold.

### Dial Backup Using an Asynchronous Interface Example

The following is an example for dial backup using interface async 1, which is configured for DDR:

```
interface serial 0
 ip address 172.30.3.4 255.255.255.0
 backup interface async1
 backup delay 10 10
!
interface async 1
 ip address 172.30.3.5 255.255.255.0
 dialer in-band
 dialer string 5551212
 dialer-group 1
 async dynamic routing
!
dialer-list 1 protocol ip permit
!
chat-script sillyman "" "atdt 5551212" TIMEOUT 60 "CONNECT"
!
line 1
 modem chat-script sillyman
 modem inout
 speed 9600
```

### Dial Backup Using DDR and ISDN Example

The following example uses an ISDN interface to back up a serial interface.

**NOTES**

When you use a BRI interface for dial backup, neither of the B channels can be used while the interface is in standby mode.

---

Interface BRI 0 is configured to make outgoing calls to one number. This is a legacy DDR spoke example.

```
interface serial 1
 backup delay 0 0
 backup interface bri 0
 ip address 1.2.3.4 255.255.255.0
!
interface bri 0
 ip address 1.2.3.5 255.255.255.0
 dialer string 5551212
 dialer-group 1
!
dialer-list 1 protocol ip permit
```

**NOTES**

Dialing will occur only after a packet is received to be output on BRI 0. We recommend using the **dialer-list** command with the **protocol** and **permit** keywords specified to control access for dial backup. Using this form of access control specifies that all packets are interesting.

## Dial Backup Service When the Primary Line Goes Down Examples

The following example configures serial 1 as a backup line that becomes active only when the primary line (serial 0) goes down. The backup line will not be activated because of load on the primary line.

```
interface serial 0
 backup interface serial 1
 backup delay 30 60
```

The backup line is configured to activate 30 seconds after the primary line goes down and to remain on for 60 seconds after the primary line is reactivated.

The same example on the Cisco 7500 would be as follows:

```
interface serial 1/1
 backup interface serial 2/0
 backup delay 30 60
```

## Dial Backup Service When the Primary Line Reaches Threshold Examples

The following example configures the secondary line (serial 1) to be activated only when the load of the primary line reaches a certain threshold:

```
interface serial 0
 backup interface serial 1
 backup load 75 5
```

In this case, the secondary line will not be activated when the primary goes down. The secondary line will be activated when the load on the primary line is greater than 75 percent of the primary's bandwidth. The secondary line will then be brought down when the aggregate load between the primary and secondary lines fits within 5 percent of the primary bandwidth.

The same example on the Cisco 7500 would be as follows:

```
interface serial 1/1
 backup interface serial 2/2
 backup load 75 5
```

### Dial Backup Service When the Primary Line Exceeds Threshold Examples

The following example configures the secondary line to activate once the traffic threshold on the primary line exceeds 25 percent:

```
interface serial 0
 backup interface serial 1
 backup load 25 5
 backup delay 10 60
```

Once the aggregate load of the primary and the secondary lines return to within 5 percent of the primary bandwidth, the secondary line is deactivated. The secondary line waits 10 seconds after the primary goes down before activating and remains active for 60 seconds after the primary returns and becomes active again.

The same example on the Cisco 7500 is as follows:

```
interface serial 1/0
 backup interface serial 2/0
 backup load 25 5
 backup delay 10 60
```

# CHAPTER 47

# Dial Backup for Serial Lines Commands

This chapter describes the commands used to configure a primary serial interface for using a specific dial backup interface, whether the primary interface is configured for DDR, for Frame Relay, or X.25 over a leased line.

The backup interface in each of these cases must be configured for DDR. The DDR configuration specifies the conditions in which the backup interface makes dial calls.

In Cisco IOS Release 11.3, all commands supported on the Cisco 7500 series are supported on the Cisco 7000 series.

For configuration tasks and examples, see Chapter 46, "Configuring Dial Backup for Serial Lines." For information about configuring the specific backup interface for DDR, see Chapter 40, "Configuring Legacy DDR Spokes" (for point-to-point DDR connections), or Chapter 42, "Configuring Legacy DDR Hubs" (for point-to-multipoint DDR connections).

## BACKUP DELAY

To define how much time should elapse before a secondary line status changes after a primary line status has changed, use the **backup delay** interface configuration command. To return to the default so that as soon as the primary fails the secondary is immediately brought up without delay, use the **no** form of this command.

**backup delay** {*enable-delay* | **never**} {*disable-delay* | **never**}
**no backup delay** {*enable-delay* | **never**} {*disable-delay* | **never**}

| *Syntax* | *Description* |
|---|---|
| *enable-delay* | Number of seconds that elapse after the primary line goes down before the Cisco IOS software activates the secondary line. |

| | |
|---|---|
| *disable-delay* | Number of seconds that elapse after the primary line comes up before the Cisco IOS software deactivates the secondary line. |
| **never** | Prevents the secondary line from being activated or deactivated. |

### Default

0 seconds

### Command Mode

Interface configuration

### Usage Guidelines

This command first appeared in Cisco IOS Release 10.0.

For environments in which there are spurious signal disruptions that may appear as intermittent lost carrier signals, we recommend that you enable some delay before activating and deactivating a secondary line.

### Example

The following example sets a 10-second delay on deactivating the secondary line (serial interface 0); however, the line is activated immediately:

```
interface serial 0
 backup delay 0 10
```

## BACKUP INTERFACE

To configure an interface as a secondary or dial backup, use the **backup interface** interface configuration command. To disable this feature, use the **no** form of this command.

**backup interface** *type number*
**no backup interface** *type number*

**backup interface** *slot/port* (for the Cisco 7200 series and Cisco 7500 series)
**no backup interface** *slot/port*

| *Syntax* | *Description* |
|---|---|
| *type number* | Interface type and port number to use as the backup interface. |
| *slot/port* | Backplane slot number and port number on the interface. See your hardware installation manual for the specific slot and port numbers. |

### Default

Disabled

### Command Mode

Interface configuration

### Usage Guidelines

This command first appeared in Cisco IOS Release 11.0.

The interface you define with this command can back up only one other interface.

**NOTES**

Routers support only serial and ISDN backup interfaces. Access servers support both asynchronous and serial backup interfaces.

### Examples

The following example sets serial 1 as the backup line to serial 0:

```
interface serial 0
 backup interface serial 1
```

The following example on the Cisco 7200 sets serial 2 as the backup line to serial 1:

```
interface serial 1/1
 backup interface serial 2/2
```

## BACKUP LOAD

To set a traffic load threshold for dial backup service, use the **backup load** interface configuration command. To return to the default value, use the **no** form of this command.

**backup load** {*enable-threshold* | **never**} {*disable-load* | **never**}
**no backup load** {*enable-threshold* | **never**} {*disable-load* | **never**}

| Syntax | Description |
|---|---|
| *enable-threshold* | Percentage of the primary line's available bandwidth that the traffic load must exceed to enable dial backup. |
| *disable-load* | Percentage of the primary line's available bandwidth that the traffic load must be less than to disable dial backup. |
| **never** | Sets the secondary line never to be activated due to traffic load. |

### Default

No threshold is predefined.

### Command Mode

Interface configuration

### *Usage Guidelines*

This command first appeared in Cisco IOS Release 10.0.

When the transmitted or received load on the primary line is greater than the value assigned to the *enable-threshold* argument, the secondary line is enabled.

The secondary line is disabled when one of the following conditions occurs:

- The transmitted load on the primary line plus the transmitted load on the secondary line is less than the value entered for the *disable-load* argument.
- The received load on the primary line plus the received load on the secondary line is less than the value entered for the *disable-load* argument.

If the **never** keyword is used instead of an *enable-threshold* value, the secondary line is never activated because of traffic load. If the **never** keyword is used instead of a *disable-load* argument, the secondary line is never activated because of traffic load.

### *Example*

The following example sets the traffic load threshold to 60 percent of the primary line serial 0. When that load is exceeded, the secondary line is activated, and will not be deactivated until the combined load is less than 5 percent of the primary bandwidth.

```
interface serial 0
 backup load 60 5
 backup interface serial 1
```

CHAPTER 48

# Configuring Dial Backup with Dialer Profiles

Dialer interfaces can be configured as the logical intermediary between one or more physical interfaces and another physical interface that is to function as backup.

Dialer interfaces can be configured to use a specific dialing pool; in turn, physical interfaces can be configured to belong to the same dialing pool.

To configure a dialer interface and a specific physical interface to function as backup to other physical interfaces, perform the tasks in the following sections:

- Configuring a Dialer Interface
- Configuring a Physical Interface To Function as Backup
- Configuring Interfaces To Use a Backup Interface

See section, "Dialer Profile for ISDN BRI Backing Up Two Leased Lines Example," for a comprehensive backup example using Dialer Profiles. In this example, one BRI functions as backup to two serial lines and can make calls to two different destinations. For a complete description of the dial backup commands in this chapter, see Chapter 49, "Dialer Profiles Backup Commands."

## CONFIGURING A DIALER INTERFACE

To configure the dialer interface that will be used as an intermediary between a physical interface that will function as backup interface and the interfaces that will use the backup, perform the following tasks beginning in global configuration mode:

| Task | | Command |
|---|---|---|
| **Step 1** | Create a dialer interface. | **interface dialer** *number* |
| **Step 2** | Specify IP unnumbered loopback. | **ip unnumbered loopback0** |
| **Step 3** | Specify PPP encapsulation. | **encapsulation ppp** |
| **Step 4** | Specify the remote router's CHAP authentication name. | **dialer remote-name** *name* |
| **Step 5** | Specify the remote destination to call. | **dialer string** *string* |
| **Step 6** | Specify the dialing pool to use for calls to this destination. | **dialer pool** *number* |
| **Step 7** | Assign the dialer interface to a dialer group. | **dialer-group** *number* |

### Configuring a Physical Interface to Function as Backup

To configure the physical interface that is to function as backup, perform the following tasks beginning in global configuration mode:

| Task | | Command |
|---|---|---|
| **Step 1** | Specify the interface. | **interface** *type number* |
| **Step 2** | Specify PPP encapsulation. | **encapsulation ppp** |
| **Step 3** | Make the interface a member of the dialing pool that the dialer interface will use; make sure the *number* arguments have the same value. | **dialer pool-member** *number* |
| **Step 4** | Specify CHAP authentication. | **ppp authentication chap** |

### Configuring Interfaces to Use a Backup Interface

To configure one or more interfaces to use a backup interface, perform the following tasks beginning in global configuration mode:

| Task | | Command |
|---|---|---|
| **Step 1** | Specify the interface to be backed up. | **interface** *type number* |
| **Step 2** | Specify IP unnumbered loopback. | **ip unnumbered loopback0** |
| **Step 3** | Specify the backup interface. | **backup interface dialer** *number* |

| Task | | Command |
|---|---|---|
| **Step 4** | Specify delay between the physical interface going down and the backup being enabled, and between the physical interface coming back up and the backup being disabled. | **backup delay** *enable-delay disable-delay* |

## Dialer Profile for ISDN BRI Backing Up Two Leased Lines Example

The following example shows the configuration of a site that backs up two leased lines using one BRI. Two dialer interfaces are defined. Each serial (leased-line) interface is configured to use one of the dialer interfaces as a backup. Both of the dialer interfaces use dialer pool 1, which has physical interface BRI 0 as a member. Thus, physical interface BRI 0 can back up two different serial interfaces and can make calls to two different sites.

```
interface dialer0
 ip unnumbered loopback0
 encapsulation ppp
 dialer remote-name Remote0
 dialer pool 1
 dialer string 5551212
 dialer-group 1

interface dialer1
 ip unnumbered loopback0
 encapsulation ppp
 dialer remote-name Remote1
 dialer pool 1
 dialer string 5551234
 dialer-group 1

interface bri 0
 encapsulation PPP
 dialer pool-member 1
 ppp authentication chap

interface serial 0
 ip unnumbered loopback0
 backup interface dialer 0
 backup delay 5 10

interface serial 1
 ip unnumbered loopback0
 backup interface dialer1
 backup delay 5 10
```

CHAPTER 49

# Dialer Profiles Backup Commands

This chapter describes the commands used to configure Dialer Profiles for backing up physical interfaces.

Dialer interfaces can be configured as the logical intermediary between one or more physical interfaces and another physical interface that is to function as backup.

Dialer interfaces can be configured to use a specific dialing pool; in turn, physical interfaces can be configured to belong to the same dialing pool.

The advantage of using Dialer Profiles for backing up physical interfaces is that it enables ISDN B channels to be used independently, which allows a single BRI to back up two serial interfaces.

For dialer profiles backup configuration tasks and examples, see Chapter 48, "Configuring Dial Backup with Dialer Profiles."

## BACKUP INTERFACE DIALER

To configure a dialer interface as a secondary or dial backup, use the **backup interface dialer** interface configuration command. To disable this feature, use the **no** form of this command.

**backup interface dialer** *number*
**no backup interface dialer** *number*

| *Syntax* | *Description* |
|---|---|
| *number* | Dialer interface number to use as the backup interface. |

### *Default*

Disabled

### *Command Mode*

Interface configuration

### *Usage Guidelines*

This command first appeared in Cisco IOS Release 11.2.

Multiple dialer interfaces can use the same dialer pool, which might have a single ISDN interface as a member. Thus, that ISDN interface can back up different serial interfaces and can make calls to different sites.

### *Example*

The following example shows the configuration of a site that backs up two leased lines using one BRI. Two dialer interfaces are defined. Each serial (leased-line) interface is configured to use one of the dialer interfaces as a backup. Both of the dialer interfaces use dialer pool 1, which has BRI 0 as a member. Thus, BRI 0 can back up two different serial interfaces and can make calls to two different sites.

```
interface dialer0
 ip unnumbered loopback0
 encapsulation ppp
 dialer remote-name Remote0
 dialer pool 1
 dialer string 5551212
 dialer-group 1

interface dialer1
 ip unnumbered loopback0
 encapsulation ppp
 dialer remote-name Remote1
 dialer pool 1
 dialer string 5551234
 dialer-group 1

interface bri 0
 encapsulation PPP
 dialer pool-member 1
 ppp authentication chap

interface serial 0
 ip unnumbered loopback0
 backup interface dialer 0
 backup delay 5 10

interface serial 1
 ip unnumbered loopback0
 backup interface dialer1
 backup delay 5 10
```

## BACKUP LOAD

To set a traffic load threshold for dial backup service, use the **backup load** interface configuration command. To return to the default value, use the **no** form of this command.

**backup load** {*enable-threshold* | **never**} {*disable-load* | **never**}
**no backup load** {*enable-threshold* | **never**} {*disable-load* | **never**}

| *Syntax* | *Description* |
|---|---|
| *enable-threshold* | Percentage of the primary line's available bandwidth that the traffic load must exceed to enable dial backup. |
| *disable-load* | Percentage of the primary line's available bandwidth that the traffic load must be less than to disable dial backup. |
| **never** | Sets the secondary line never to be activated due to traffic load. |

### *Default*

No threshold is predefined.

### *Command Mode*

Interface configuration

### *Usage Guidelines*

This command first appeared in Cisco IOS Release 10.0.

When the transmitted or received load on the primary line is greater than the value assigned to the *enable-threshold* argument, the secondary line is enabled.

The secondary line is disabled when one of the following conditions occurs:

- The transmitted load on the primary line plus the transmitted load on the secondary line is less than the value entered for the *disable-load* argument.
- The received load on the primary line plus the received load on the secondary line is less than the value entered for the *disable-load* argument.

If the **never** keyword is used instead of an *enable-threshold* value, the secondary line is never activated because of traffic load. If the **never** keyword is used instead of a *disable-load* argument, the secondary line is never activated because of traffic load.

### *Example*

The following example sets the traffic load threshold to 60 percent of the primary line serial 0. When that load is exceeded, the secondary line is activated and will not be deactivated until the combined load is less than 5 percent of the primary bandwidth.

```
interface serial 0
 backup load 60 5
 backup interface serial 1
```

PART 7

# Dial-Out Modem Pooling

CHAPTER 50

# Establishing a Reverse Telnet Session to a Modem

This chapter describes how to communicate with the modem by establishing a reverse Telnet session from an access server's or router's asynchronous line to a modem.

**NOTES**

This process is sometimes referred to as *direct Telnet*. The term reverse Telnet means that you are initiating a Telnet session out the asynchronous line, instead of accepting a connection into the line (which is a *forward* connection).

To establish a reverse Telnet session to a modem, determine the IP address of your LAN (Ethernet) interface, then enter a Telnet command to port 2000 + *n* on the access server, where *n* is the line number to which the modem is connected. For example, to connect to the modem attached to line 1, enter the following command from an EXEC session on the access server:

```
router# telnet 172.16.1.10 2001
Trying 172.16.1.10, 2001 ... Open
```

This example enables you to communicate with the modem on line 1 using the **AT** (attention) command set defined by the modem vendor.

**TIMESAVER**

Use the **ip host** configuration command to simplify reverse Telnet sessions with modems. The **ip host** command maps an IP address of a port to a device name.

If you are unable to connect to the modem, check the following:

1. Issue the **show users** EXEC command. It should not indicate the line is in use.
2. Verify that the line is configured for **modem inout**.

3. Issue the **show line** EXEC command. The output should contain the following two lines:

```
Modem state: Idle
Modem hardware state: CTS noDSR  DTR RTS
```

4. Check to see if the virtual terminal connections to lines in the access server require passwords.
5. Check to see if the speed between the modem and the access server are the same. They are likely to be different. If they are different, switch off the modem, then switch it back on. This should match the speed of the modem with the speed of the access server.

### Testing the Modem Connection

After you make a reverse Telnet connection to the modem, you need to test the connection. Send the modem the **AT** command to request its attention. It should respond with OK. For example:

```
at
OK
```

If the modem does not reply to the **AT** command, check the following:

1. Look at the output of the **show line 1** command. If it displays "no CTS" for the modem hardware state, the modem is not connected or powered on, and is waiting for data; or the modem might not be configured for hardware flow control.
2. Check your cabling and the modem configuration (echo or result codes might be off). Enter the appropriate AT modem command to view the modem configuration, or enter the command **at&f** to return to factory defaults. Refer to your modem documentation to learn the appropriate AT command to view your modem configuration.

### Suspending and Terminating Telnet Sessions

The reverse Telnet session must be terminated before the line can accept incoming calls. If you do not terminate the session, it will be indicated in the output of the **show users** command when it returns a modem state of ready if the line is still in use. If the line is no longer in use, the output of the **show line** *value* command will return a state of idle.

Terminating the Telnet session requires first suspending it, then disconnecting it. To suspend a Telnet session, enter the escape sequence **Ctrl-Shift-6 x** (press **Control-Shift-6**, let go, then press **x**). Enter the **disconnect** EXEC command to terminate the Telnet session.

**Notes**

Ensure that you can reliably issue the escape sequence to suspend a Telnet session. Some terminal emulator packages have difficulty sending the **Ctrl-Shift-6 x** sequence. Refer to your terminal emulator documentation for more information about escape sequences.

To suspend and then disconnect a Telnet session, perform the following steps:

**Step 1** Suspend the Telnet session by entering **Ctrl-Shift-6 x**:

```
- suspend keystroke -
router#
```

**Step 2** Enter the **where** EXEC command to check for open sessions:

```
router# where
Conn Host                    Address              Byte  Idle Conn Name
*  1 172.16.1.10             172.16.1.10             0     0  172.16.1.10
   2 172.16.1.11             172.16.1.11             0    12  modem2
```

**Step 3** After suspending a session with one modem, you can connect to another modem (then suspend it):

```
router# telnet modem2
Trying modem2 (172.16.1.11, 2002) ... Open

- suspend keystroke -
router#
```

**Step 4** To disconnect (completely close) a session, issue the **disconnect** EXEC command:

```
router# disconnect line 1
Closing connection to 172.16.1.10 [confirm] y
router# disconnect line 2
Closing connection to 172.16.1.11 [confirm] y
router#
```

**NOTES**

Before attempting to allow inbound connections, make sure you close all open connections to the modems attached to the access server. If you have a modem port in use, the modem will not accept a call properly.

CHAPTER 51

# Configuring Support for NASI Clients to Access Network Resources

This chapter describes how to allow your router to function as a NetWare Asynchronous Services Interface (NASI) server. For a complete description of the NASI commands in this chapter, see Chapter 52, "NASI Commands."

## GENERAL NASI CONCEPTS

A NASI server enables a NASI client to connect to asynchronous network resources (such as modems) without having these resources located on the client's desktop, as shown in Figure 51–1.

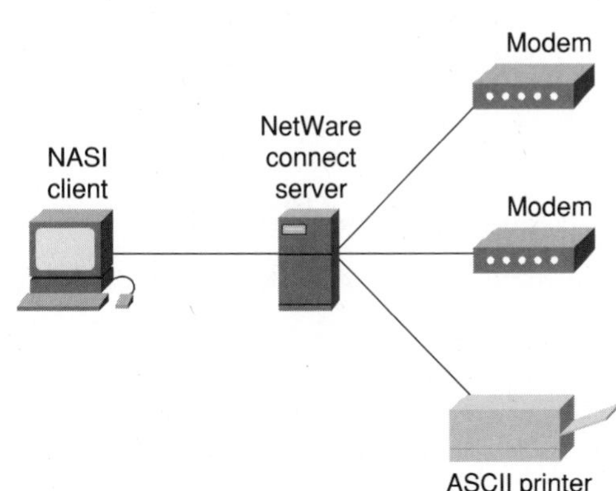


*Figure 51–1 NASI Setup in a NetWare Environment.*

You can configure the Cisco IOS software to enable NASI clients to connect to asynchronous resources attached to your router. The NASI client can connect to any port on the router other than the console port to access network resources. (See Figure 51–2.) The NASI clients are connected to the Ethernet interface 0 on the router. When the user on the NASI client uses the Windows or DOS application to connect to the router, a list of available tty and vty lines appears, beginning with tty1. The user selects the desired outgoing tty or vty port. You also can configure TACACS+ security on the router so that after the user selects a tty or vty port, a username and password prompt appear for authentication, authorization, and accounting (AAA) purposes.

*Figure 51–2*
*NASI Clients Accessing Asynchronous Resources through an Access Server.*

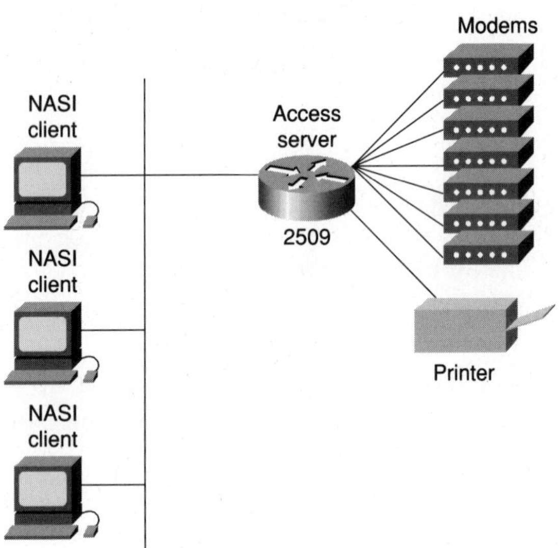


**NOTES**

The Cisco IOS implementation of NASI functions best with NASI client software version 2.0 and later.

The NASI client can be on a local LAN or can also be on a remote LAN. If it is on a remote LAN, the following two requirements must be met:

- A router routing IPX forwards NetWare Connect Server SAP advertisements from the remote LAN to the LAN to which the local router is connected.
- The same router routing IPX spoofs Get Nearest Server (GNS) replies for the GNS requests that the client sends out.

The fact that you can connect to many different ports on the router means that you can provide access to more than one asynchronous device. When the user accesses the vty line, the user can connect to the user EXEC facility and issue a Telnet or NASI command to access a remote network (see

Figure 51–3). Only the first available vty line appears in the list of available ports on the router (and it is titled *RCONSOLE*).

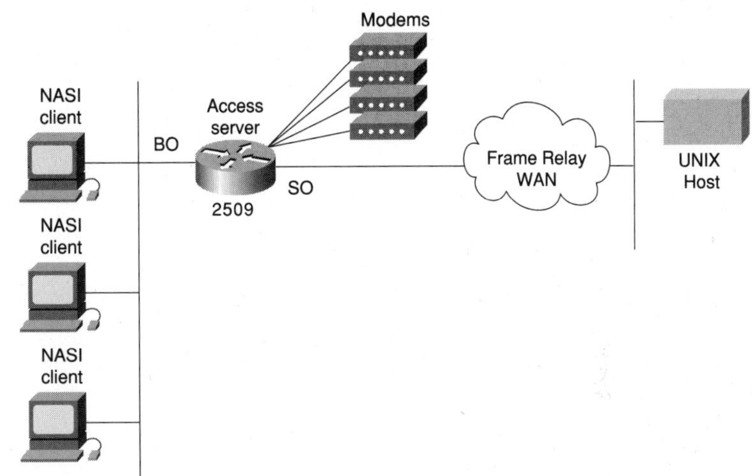


*Figure 51–3*
*NASI Clients Gaining Access to IP Hosts on a Remote Network.*

## CONFIGURING NASI

To configure your router as a NASI server, perform the following tasks, beginning in global configuration mode:

| Task | | Command |
|---|---|---|
| **Step 1** | Enable IPX routing on the router. | **ipx routing** |
| **Step 2** | Define an internal IPX network number. | **ipx internal-network** |
| **Step 3** | Enter interface configuration mode. | **interface** *type number* |
| **Step 4** | Enable IPX routing on an interface. | **ipx network** [*network* \| **unnumbered**] |
| **Step 5** | Exit to global configuration mode. | **exit** |
| **Step 6** | Enable NASI. | **ipx nasi-server enable** |
| **Step 7** | Configure TACACS+ security on all lines on the router (optional). | **aaa authentication nasi** {*list-name* \| **default**} {**methods list**} |
| **Step 8** | Enter line configuration mode. | **line** [**aux** \| **tty** \| **vty**] *line-number* [*ending-line-number*] |
| **Step 9** | Configure TACACS+ security on a per-line basis (optional). | **login authentication nasi** {*list-name* \| **default**} |

You also can configure SAP filters to filter SAP updates and access lists to filter NASI traffic between interfaces on the router.

**NOTES**

If a NASI server is already on the LAN segment connected to the router, the router cannot respond to Get Next Server (GNS) requests for NASI services.

If you have configured NetWare asynchronous services interface (NASI) on your router, you can use IPX client applications to make IPX dial-out connections to a shared pool of asynchronous devices. For example, a NASI client on the LAN can connect to a serial (synchronous or asynchronous) port on the router, which provides access to remote modems, printers, and networks. The command the user issues depends on the application being used to connect to the NASI server.

NASI relies on Sequenced Packet Exchange (SPX).

# CHAPTER 52

# NASI Commands

This chapter describes the commands used to enable your router to function as a NetWare Asynchronous Services Interface (NASI) server. A NASI server enables a NASI client to connect to asynchronous network resources (such as modems) without having these resources located on the client's desktop.

For configuration tasks and examples, see Chapter 51, "Configuring Support for NASI Clients To Access Network Resources."

## IPX NASI-SERVER ENABLE

To enable NetWare Asynchronous Services Interface (NASI) clients to connect to asynchronous devices attached to your router, use the **ipx nasi-server enable** global configuration command. To prevent NASI clients from connecting through a router, use the **no** form of this command.

**ipx nasi-server enable**
**no ipx nasi-server enable**

### *Syntax Description*

This command has no arguments or keywords.

### *Default*

NASI is not enabled.

### *Command Mode*

Global configuration

### *Usage Guidelines*

This command first appeared in Cisco IOS Release 11.1.

When you issue this command, NASI clients can connect to any port on the router other than the console port to access network resources. When the user on the NASI client uses the Windows or DOS application to connect to the router, a list of available tty and vty lines appears, beginning with tty1. The user selects the desired outgoing tty or vty port.

You can configure TACACS+ security on the router so that after the user selects a tty or vty port, a username and password prompt appear for authentication, authorization, and accounting purposes.

### *Example*

The following example shows a minimum configuration to enable NASI client dial-in access with TACACS+ authentication:

```
ipx routing
ipx internal-network ncs001
interface ethernet 0
  ipx network 1
ipx nasi-server enable
! enable TACACS+ authentication for NASI clients using the list name swami
aaa authentication nasi swami tacacs+
line 1 8
  modem inout
```

### *Related Commands*

Search online to find documentation for related commands.

**aaa authentication nasi**
**nasi authentication**
**show ipx nasi connections**
**show ipx spx-protocol**

## SHOW IPX NASI CONNECTIONS

To show the status of NetWare Asynchronous Services Interface (NASI) connections, use the **show ipx nasi connections** EXEC command.

**show ipx nasi connections**

### *Syntax Description*

This command has no arguments or keywords.

### *Command Mode*

EXEC

### *Usage Guidelines*

This command first appeared in Cisco IOS Release 11.1.

### *Sample Displays*

The following is sample output from the **show ipx nasi connections** command:

```
router# show ipx nasi connections

NASI Remote: A001500::0020.afe5.3ec5:626C   Local: ACBB::0000.0000.0001:2010
  flags 0

NASI Remote: A001500::0020.afe5.3ec5:6E6C   Local: ACBB::0000.0000.0001:20D0
  flags 0
   Connected to line 2  incount 0  outcount 0  OVF 0
```

The following sample display shows an incoming NASI connection on tty line 2:

```
router# show users
    Line      User      Host(s)                 Idle Location
*  0 con 0              idle                       1
   2 tty 2  chris       incoming                   1 A001500.0020.afe5.3ec5
```

Table 52–1 describes fields from the **show ipx nasi connections** sample display.

**Table 52–1** *Show IPX NASI Connections Field Descriptions*

| Field | Description |
|---|---|
| NASI Remote | •*xxxxxxxx::yyyyyyyyy:zzzz* is the address for the remote NASI client connected to the router.<br>•*xxxx* is the IPX network number.<br>•*yyyyyyy* is the IPX host node (MAC address) for the client.<br>•*zzzz* is the SPX connection number. |
| Local | *xxxxxxxx::yyyyyyyyyy:zzzz* is the local address associated to this connection on the router end of the link. |
| flags | A status bit that is used internally to allow and close connections. |
| Connected to line 2 | Appears only when the connection is associated with a tty port. Indicates that this NASI connection is attached to tty 2. |
| incount 0 | Data from the remote client. |
| outcount 0 | Data to be sent to the remote client. |
| OVF 0 | Refers to the number of times data could not be written to the tty line, because the buffers were full. Ideally, this counter should stay at 0. |

### *Related Commands*

Search online to find documentation for related commands.

**ipx nasi-server enable**
**show ipx spx-protocol**

## SHOW IPX SPX-PROTOCOL

To view the status of the SPX protocol stack and related counters, use the **show ipx spx-protocol** command.

**show ipx spx-protocol**

### *Syntax Description*

This command has no arguments or keywords.

### *Command Mode*

EXEC

### *Usage Guidelines*

This command first appeared in Cisco IOS Release 11.1.

### *Sample Display*

The following is sample output from the **show ipx spx-protocol** command:

```
router> show ipx spx-protocol
Next wake time:

SPX socket: 1D90
  state: 0  Connections: 2

   SPX Remote: A001500::0000.c047.ed5a:3A80   Local: ACBB::0000.0000.0001:2010
   state 1  flags 1
   Queue counts:  inq 0,  outQ 0,  unackedQ 0
   Sequence: 34,  Ack: 34,  local-alloc: 39,  remote-alloc: 35
   Abort Timer fires in 24 secs
   Verify Watchdog Timer fires in 3 secs

   SPX Remote: A001500::0000.c047.ed5a:C980   Local: ACBB::0000.0000.0001:2900
   state 1  flags 1
   Queue counts:  inq 0,  outQ 0,  unackedQ 0
   Sequence: 111,  Ack: 55,  local-alloc: 60,  remote-alloc: 112
   Abort Timer fires in 27 secs
   Verify Watchdog Timer fires in 0 secs
```

Table 52–2 describes significant fields from this sample display.

**Table 52–2** *Show IPX SPX-Protocol Field Descriptions*

| Field | Description |
|---|---|
| SPX socket: | IPX/SPX socket number. |
| state | Internal state. |
| connections: | Number of open connections for this IPX/SPX socket. |
| SPX Remote: *xxxxxxx::yyyy:zzzz* | The SPX client address for each SPX connection on this IPX/SPX socket, where *xxxx* is the client IPX network number, *yyyy* is the client IPX MAC address, and *zzzz* is the client SPX connection number. |
| SPX Local *xxxxxxx::yyyy:zzzz* | The local SPX address, where *xxxx* is local IPX network number, *yyyy* is the local IPX MAC address, and *zzzz* is the local SPX connection number. |
| state | Internal state. |
| flags | A status bit that is used internally to allow and close connections. |
| Queue counts | inQ, outQ, and unackedQ, as specified in the following three rows. |
| inq | Number of SPX packets available for the SPX application to read. |
| outQ | Number of SPX packets that must be sent to the remote client. |
| unackedQ | Number of SPX packets sent, but no packet was received by the client, so far. |
| Sequence: | SPX sequence number. Represents the sequence number of next packet of data to be sent by the router. |
| Ack: | SPX acknowledgment number. Represents the sequence number of the client's packet that the router has received, so far. |
| local-alloc: | Maximum packet sequence number that is acceptable from the client. This is a method of imposing flow control on the NASI client. |
| remote-alloc: | Maximum packet sequence number that the NASI client can accept from the router. This is the NASI client's way of imposing flow control on the router. |

**Table 52–2** *Show IPX SPX-Protocol Field Descriptions, Continued*

| Field | Description |
|---|---|
| Purge Timer | Time in seconds until this SPX connection is closed and deleted from the list. |
| Abort Timer | Time in seconds until this SPX connection is closed and deleted if a watchdog packet is not received. |
| Verify Watchdog Timer fires in X secs | Indicates the time when you last sent a watchdog packet to the client. |

### *Related Commands*

Search online to find documentation for related commands.

**aaa authentication nasi**
**ipx nasi-server enable**
**nasi authentication**
**show ipx nasi connections**

# CHAPTER 53

# Configuring Dial-Out

The Cisco DialOut feature enables local users to send faxes or connect to service provider services outside the LAN by using modems attached or internal to a network access server. This feature extends the functionality of Telnet by enabling users to control the activity of these modems from their desktop computers using standard communications software.

The Cisco DialOut feature has two components:

- Telnet Extensions for Dialout—Network access server component
- The DialOut Utility—Client/desktop component

Both components are required, and neither can function as a stand-alone feature.

The Telnet Extensions for DialOut uses reverse Telnet to access modems attached to the network access server. This component enables the network access server to interface with the client/desktop component of the Cisco DialOut feature and to return Carrier Detect signals to the communications software so that the software can determine when to start dialing a particular number.

Telnet extensions allow the communications software running on the client's desktop computer to control modem settings, such as baud rate, parity, bit size, and stop bits.

To enable this feature, you only need to configure the access server or router for reverse Telnet and configure the appropriate lines to send and receive calls.

The client/desktop component of the Cisco DialOut feature must be installed on the client workstation before this feature can be used.

**PART 8**

# Large-Scale Dial Solutions

# CHAPTER 54

# Configuring Virtual Template Interfaces

Beginning with Cisco IOS Release 11.2, virtual template interfaces can be configured independently of any physical interface and applied dynamically, as needed, to create virtual access interfaces. When a user dials in, a predefined configuration template is used to configure a virtual access interface; when the user is done, the virtual access interface goes down and the resources are freed for other dial-in uses.

The Virtual Template Interface Service feature provides a generic service that can be used to apply predefined interface configurations (virtual template interfaces) in creating and freeing virtual access interfaces dynamically, as needed.

This feature is supported on all platforms that support Multilink PPP, Virtual Profiles, PPP over ATM, VPDN, or protocol translation.

For a complete description of the commands mentioned in this chapter, see Chapter 55, "Virtual Template Interface Commands."

## BACKGROUND INFORMATION

A virtual template interface is a logical entity—a configuration for a serial interface but not tied to a physical interface—that can be applied dynamically as needed. Virtual access interfaces are virtual interfaces that are created, configured dynamically (for example, by applying [*cloning*] a virtual template interface), used, and then freed when no longer needed.

### Limitations

The following template and virtual interface limitations apply:

- Although a system can have as many as 25 virtual template interfaces, one template for each virtual access application is a more realistic limit.
- When in use, each virtual access interface cloned from a template requires the same amount of memory as a serial interface. Cisco routers support a maximum of 300 virtual interfaces.
- Virtual access interfaces are not directly configurable by users, except by configuring a virtual template interface or including a user's configuration information (through Virtual Profiles or Per-User Configuration) on an AAA server. However, information about an in-use virtual access interface can be displayed, and the virtual access interface can be cleared.
- Virtual interface templates provide no *direct* value to users; they must be applied to or associated with a virtual access feature by use of a command with the **virtual-template** keyword.

  For example, the **interface virtual-template** command creates the virtual template interface, and the **multilink virtual-template** command applies the virtual template to a Multilink stack group. The **virtual-profile virtual-template** command specifies that a virtual template interface will be used as a source of configuration information for virtual profiles.

### Intended Users and Benefits

The virtual template interface service is intended primarily for customers with large numbers of dial-in users and provides the following benefits:

- For easier maintenance, allows customized configurations to be predefined and then applied dynamically when the specific need arises.
- For scalability, allows interface configuration to be separated from physical interfaces. Virtual interfaces can share characteristics, no matter what specific type of interface the user called on.
- For consistency and configuration ease, allows the same predefined template to be used for all users dialing in for a specific application.
- For efficient router operation, frees the virtual access interface memory for another dial-in use when the user's call ends.

### Virtual Template Interfaces and Virtual Access Interface Configuration

Virtual template interfaces are one possible source of configuration information for a virtual access interface.

Each virtual access interface can clone from only one template. But some applications can take configuration information from multiple sources; for example, Virtual Profiles can take configuration information from a virtual template interface, or from a user's interface-specific configuration information stored on an AAA server, or from a user's network protocol configuration stored on an AAA server, or all three. The result of using template and AAA configuration sources is a virtual access interface uniquely configured for a specific dial-in user.

Figure 54–1 illustrates that a router can create a virtual access interface by first using the information from a virtual template interface (if any is defined for the application) and then using the information in a per-user configuration (if AAA is configured on the router and Virtual Profiles or Per-User Configuration or both are defined for the specific user).

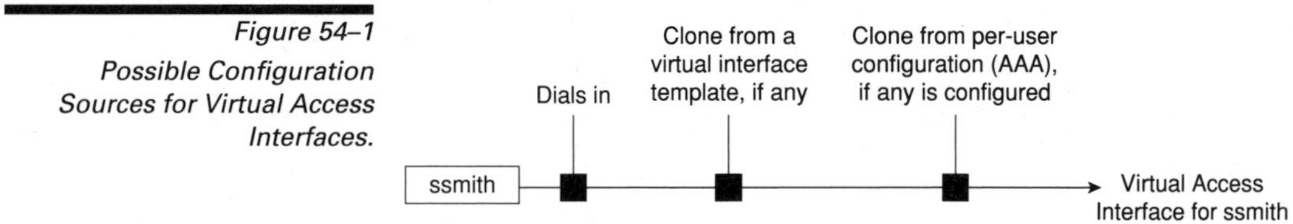


*Figure 54–1 Possible Configuration Sources for Virtual Access Interfaces.*

## Features That Apply Virtual Template Interfaces

The following features apply virtual template interfaces to create virtual access interfaces dynamically. The Cisco IOS software releases in which they were introduced are also listed:

- Virtual Profiles—Release 11.2 F
- Virtual Private Dial-Up Networks—Release 11.2
- Multilink PPP (MLP)—Release 11.1
- Multichassis Multilink PPP (MMP)—Release 11.2
- Virtual Templates for Protocol Translation—Release 11.2 F
- PPP over ATM—Release 11.2 F

To create and configure a virtual template interface, compete the tasks in this chapter. To apply a virtual template interface, refer to the specific feature that applies the virtual template interface.

## Prerequisites

All prerequisites depend on the feature that is applying a virtual template interface to create a virtual access interface. Virtual template interfaces themselves have no other prerequisites.

The order in which you create virtual template interfaces and virtual profiles, and configure the features that use the templates and profiles, is not important. They must exist, however, before someone calling in can use them.

## Terminology

The following new or uncommon terms are used in this chapter:

**cloning**—Creating and configuring a virtual access interface by applying a specific virtual template interface. The template is the source of the generic user information and router-dependent information. The result of cloning is a virtual access interface configured with all the commands in the template.

**virtual access interface**—Instance of a unique virtual interface that is created dynamically and exists temporarily. Virtual access interfaces can be created and configured differently by different applications, such as virtual profiles and virtual private dial-up networks.

**virtual profile**—Unique virtual access interface created dynamically when certain users call in, and torn down dynamically when the call disconnects. A specific user's virtual profile can be configured by a virtual template interface, user-specific interface configuration stored on an AAA server, or both a virtual template interface and user-specific interface configuration from AAA.

Configuration of a virtual access interface begins with a virtual template interface (if any), followed by application of user-specific configuration for the particular user's dial-in session (if any).

**virtual template interface**—Generic configuration of an interface for a certain purpose or configuration common to certain users, plus router-dependent information. The template takes the form of a list of Cisco IOS interface commands to be applied to a virtual access interface as needed.

## Creating and Configuring a Virtual Template Interface

To create and configure a virtual template interface, complete the following tasks beginning in global configuration mode:

| Task | | Command |
|---|---|---|
| **Step 1** | Create a virtual template interface, and enter interface configuration mode. | **interface virtual-template** *number* |
| **Step 2** | Enable IP without assigning a specific IP address on the LAN. | **ip unnumbered ethernet 0** |
| **Step 3** | Enable PPP encapsulation on the virtual template interface. | **encapsulation ppp** |

Optionally, other PPP configuration commands can be added to the virtual template configuration. For example, you can add the **ppp authentication chap** command.

All configuration commands that apply to serial interfaces can also be applied to virtual template interfaces, except **shutdown** and **dialer** commands.

For virtual template interface examples, see the section "Virtual Template Interface Configuration Examples."

## Monitoring and Maintaining a Virtual Access Interface

When a virtual template Interface or a user's configuration on an AAA server or both are applied dynamically, a virtual access interface is created. Although a virtual access interface cannot be created and configured directly, it can be displayed and cleared.

To display or clear a specific virtual access interface, perform the relevant task in EXEC mode:

| Task | Command |
|---|---|
| Display the configuration of the virtual access interface. | **show interface virtual-access** *number* **configuration** |
| Tear down the virtual access interface and free the memory for other dial-in uses. | **clear interface virtual-access** *number* |

## Virtual Template Interface Configuration Examples

The following example enables virtual profiles (configured only by virtual template) on straightforward PPP (no MLP), and configures a virtual template interface that can be cloned on a virtual access interface for dial-in users:

```
virtual-profile virtual-template 1

interface virtual-template 1
 ip unnumbered ethernet 0
 encapsulation ppp
 ppp authentication chap
```

The following two examples configure a virtual template interface and then display the configuration of a virtual access interface when the template interface has been applied. The first example uses a named IPX access list.

```
interface virtual-template 1
 ip unnumbered Ethernet0
 ipx ppp-client Loopback2
 no cdp enable
 ppp authentication chap
```

This example displays the configuration of the active virtual access interface that was configured by virtual-template 1, defined in the preceding example:

```
Router# show interface virtual-access 1 configuration

Virtual-Access1 is a L2F link interface
interface Virtual-Access1 configuration...
ip unnumbered Ethernet0
ipx ppp-client Loopback2
no cdp enable
ppp authentication chap
```

CHAPTER 55

# Virtual Template Interface Commands

The Virtual Template Interface Service feature provides a generic service that can be used to apply predefined configurations (virtual template interfaces) in dynamically creating and freeing virtual access interfaces as needed. This feature is supported on all platforms that support Multilink PPP.

For virtual template interface configuration tasks and examples, see Chapter 54, "Configuring Virtual Template Interfaces."

## CLEAR INTERFACE VIRTUAL-ACCESS

To tear down the virtual access interface and free the memory for other dial-in uses, use the **clear interface virtual-access** EXEC command.

**clear interface virtual-access** *number*

| *Syntax* | *Description* |
|---|---|
| *number* | Number used to identify the virtual access interface. |

### *Command Mode*

EXEC

### *Usage Guidelines*

This command first appeared in Cisco IOS Release 11.2 F.

This command does not free the memory for uses unrelated to dial-in access.

### Example

The following example clears a specified virtual access interface. You can use the **show interfaces virtual-access** command to display the interface numbers before you clear any specific one.

```
clear interface virtual access 1
```

### Related Commands

Search online to find documentation for related commands.

**interface virtual-template**

## INTERFACE VIRTUAL-TEMPLATE

To create a virtual template interface that can be configured and applied dynamically in creating virtual access interfaces, use the **interface virtual-template** global configuration command.

**interface virtual-template** *number*

| *Syntax* | *Description* |
|---|---|
| *number* | Number used to identify the virtual template interface. |

### Default

Disabled. No virtual template number is defined.

### Command Mode

Global configuration

### Usage Guidelines

This command first appeared in Cisco IOS Release 11.2 F.

A virtual template interface is used to provide the configuration for dynamically created virtual access interfaces. It is created by users and can be saved in nonvolatile RAM (NVRAM).

Once the virtual template interface is created, it can be configured in the same way as a serial interface.

Virtual template interfaces can be created and applied by various applications such as Virtual Profiles, virtual private dialup networks (VPDN), PPP over ATM, protocol translation, and Multichassis Multilink PPP (MMP).

### Example

The following example creates and configures virtual template interface 1:

```
interface virtual-template 1
 ip unnumbered ethernet 0
 ppp multilink
 ppp authentication chap
```

## SHOW INTERFACES VIRTUAL-ACCESS

To display status, traffic data, and configuration information about a specified virtual access interface, use the **show interfaces virtual-access** EXEC command.

**show interfaces virtual-access** *number* [**configuration**]

| *Syntax* | *Description* |
|---|---|
| *number* | Number of the virtual access interface. |
| **configuration** | (Optional) Restricts output to configuration information. |

### *Command Mode*

EXEC

### *Usage Guidelines*

This command first appeared in Cisco IOS Release 11.2 F.

### *Sample Display*

The following is sample output of the **show interfaces virtual-access** EXEC command.

```
Router# show interfaces virtual-access 1

Virtual-Access1 is up, line protocol is up
  Hardware is Virtual Access interface
  Interface is unnumbered.  Using address of Ethernet0 (172.21.114.132)
  MTU 1500 bytes, BW 64 Kbit, DLY 100000 usec, rely 255/255, load 1/255
  Encapsulation PPP, loopback not set, keepalive set (10 sec)
  DTR is pulsed for 5 seconds on reset
  LCP Open, multilink Closed
  Open: IPCP, CDP
  Last input 5d04h, output never, output hang never
  Last clearing of "show interface" counters 00:06:42
  Queueing strategy: fifo
  Output queue 0/40, 0 drops; input queue 0/75, 0 drops
  5 minute input rate 0 bits/sec, 0 packets/sec
  5 minute output rate 0 bits/sec, 0 packets/sec
     76 packets input, 3658 bytes, 0 no buffer
     Received 0 broadcasts, 0 runts, 0 giants
     0 input errors, 0 CRC, 0 frame, 0 overrun, 0 ignored, 0 abort
     141 packets output, 2909 bytes, 0 underruns
     0 output errors, 0 collisions, 0 interface resets
     0 output buffer failures, 0 output buffers swapped out
     0 carrier transitions
```

Table 55–1 describes the fields in this output that are most significant to virtual access interfaces.

**Table 55–1** *Show Interfaces Virtual-Access Field Descriptions*

| Field | Description |
|---|---|
| Virtual-Access1 is up, line protocol is up | Virtual access interface is up, and the line can be used. |
| Hardware is Virtual Access interface | Hardware used for the incoming calls is not a static characteristic of virtual access interfaces. |
| Interface is unnumbered. Using address of Ethernet0 | Virtual template interface cloned on this interface included the **ip unnumbered ethernet** 0 command. |
| Encapsulation PPP | Virtual template interface cloned on this interface included the **encapsulation ppp** command. |
| LCP Open, multilink Closed | Link Control Protocol has established a connection and the Opened state is in effect, but no Multilink PPP connection is established. |
| Open: IPCP, CDP | Internet Protocol Control Protocol has reached the Opened state. |

## SHOW IP INTERFACE VIRTUAL-ACCESS

To display network layer IP information about a specified virtual access interface, use the **show ip interface virtual-access** EXEC command.

**show ip interface virtual-access** *number*

| *Syntax* | *Description* |
|---|---|
| *number* | Number of the virtual access interface. |

### *Command Mode*

EXEC

### *Usage Guidelines*

This command first appeared in Cisco IOS Release 11.2 F.

### *Sample Display*

The following is output from the **show ip interface virtual-access** command. This virtual access interface has been configured with a virtual template interface that applies the **ip unnumbered ethernet** 0 command.

```
Router# show ip interface virtual-access 1

Virtual-Access1 is up, line protocol is up
```

```
Interface is unnumbered. Using address of Ethernet0 (172.21.114.132)
Broadcast address is 255.255.255.255
Peer address is 20.0.0.1
MTU is 1500 bytes
Helper address is not set
Directed broadcast forwarding is enabled
Outgoing access list is not set
Inbound  access list is Virtual-Access1#0
Proxy ARP is enabled
Security level is default
Split horizon is enabled
ICMP redirects are always sent
ICMP unreachables are always sent
ICMP mask replies are never sent
IP fast switching is disabled
```

Table 55–2 describes only the output fields that are significant to virtual access interfaces and not described in other IP commands.

**Table 55–2** *Show Interfaces Virtual-Access Field Descriptions*

| Field | Description |
|---|---|
| Virtual-Access1 is up, line protocol is up | Virtual access interface is up, and the upper layers consider the line usable. |
| Interface is unnumbered. Using address of Ethernet0 (172.21.114.132) | **ip unnumbered ethernet 0** command was included in the virtual template interface cloned on this interface. |

CHAPTER 56

# Configuring Multichassis Multilink PPP

Prior to Release 11.2, Cisco IOS supported Multilink PPP. Beginning with Release 11.2, Cisco IOS software also supports Multichassis Multilink PPP (MMP).

Multilink PPP provides the capability of splitting and recombining packets to a single end-system across a logical pipe (also called a *bundle*) formed by multiple links. Multilink PPP provides bandwidth on demand and reduces transmission latency across WAN links.

MMP, on the other hand, provides the additional capability for links to terminate at multiple routers with different remote addresses. MMP can also handle both analog and digital traffic.

This feature is intended for situations with large pools of dial-in users, where a single chassis cannot provide enough dial-in ports. This feature allows companies to provide a single dial-up number to its users and to apply the same solution to analog and digital calls. This feature allows Internet service providers, for example, to allocate a single ISDN rotary number to several ISDN PRIs across several routers. For a complete description of the MMP commands in this chapter, see Chapter 57, "Multichassis Multilink PPP Commands."

MMP is supported on the Cisco 7500, 4500, and 2500 series platforms and on synchronous serial, asynchronous serial, ISDN BRI, ISDN PRI, and dialer interfaces.

MMP does not require reconfiguration of telephone company switches.

## Understanding Multichassis Multilink PPP

Routers or access servers are configured to belong to groups of peers, called *stack groups*. All members of the stack group are peers; stack groups do not need a permanent lead router. Any stack group member can answer calls coming from a single access number, which is usually an ISDN PRI hunt group. Calls can come in from remote user devices, such as routers, modems, ISDN terminal adapters, or PC cards.

Once a connection is established with one member of a stack group, that member owns the call. If a second call comes in from the same client and a different router answers the call, the router establishes a tunnel and forwards all packets belonging to the call to the router that owns the call. Establishing a tunnel and forwarding calls through it to the router that owns the call is sometimes called *projecting the PPP link to the call-master.*

If a more powerful router is available, it can be configured as a member of the stack group and the other stack group members can establish tunnels and forward all calls to it. In such a case, the other stack group members are just answering calls and forwarding traffic to the more powerful *offload* router.

**NOTES**

High-latency WAN lines between stack group members can make stack group operation inefficient.

MMP call handling, bidding, and Layer 2 forwarding operations in the stack group proceed as follows, as shown in Figure 56–1:

1. When the first call comes in to the stack group, Router A answers.
2. In the bidding, Router A wins because it already has the call. Router A becomes the *call-master* for that session with the remote device. (Router A might also be called the *host to the master bundle interface.*)
3. When the remote device that initiated the call needs more bandwidth, it makes a second Multilink PPP call to the group.
4. When the second call comes in, Router D answers it and informs the stack group. Router A wins the bidding because it already is handling the session with that remote device.
5. Router D establishes a tunnel to Router A and forwards the raw PPP data to Router A.
6. Router A reassembles and resequences the packets.
7. If more calls come in to Router D and they, too, belong to Router A, the tunnel between A and D enlarges to handle the added traffic. Router D does not establish an additional tunnel to A.
8. If more calls come in and are answered by any other router, that router also establishes a tunnel to A and forwards the raw PPP data.
9. The reassembled data is passed on the corporate network as if it had all come through one physical link.

In contrast to the previous figure, Figure 56–2 features an offload router. Access servers that belong to a stack group answer calls, establish tunnels, and forward calls to a Cisco 4700 router that wins the bidding and is the call-master for all the calls. The Cisco 4700 reassembles and resequences all the packets coming in through the stack group.

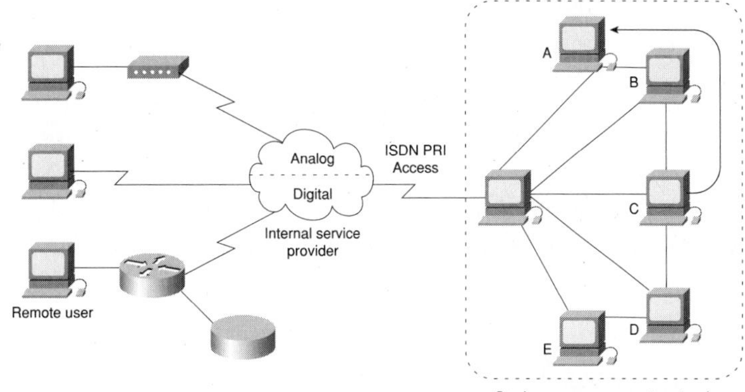


*Figure 56–1*
*Typical Multichassis Multilink PPP Scenario.*

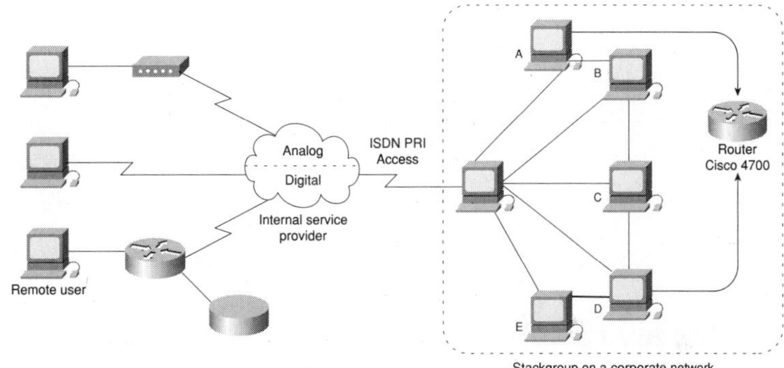


*Figure 56–2*
*Multichassis Multilink PPP with an Offload Router as a Stack Group Member.*

**NOTES**

You can build stack groups using different access server, switching, and router platforms. However, universal access servers such as the Cisco AS5200 should not be combined with ISDN-only access servers such as the 4*x*00 platform. Because calls from the central office are allocated in an arbitrary way, this combination could result in an analog call being delivered to a digital-only access server, which would not be able to handle the call.

## REQUIREMENTS

MMP support on a group of routers requires that each router be configured to support the following:

- Multilink PPP
- Stack Group Bidding Protocol (SGBP)
- Virtual template used for cloning interface configuration to support MMP

## CONFIGURING MULTICHASSIS MULTILINK PPP

To configure MMP, perform the tasks in the following sections, in the order listed:

- Configure the Stack Group and Identify Members
- Configure a Virtual Template and Create a Virtual Template Interface

### Configure the Stack Group and Identify Members

To configure the stack group on the router, complete the following tasks beginning in global configuration mode:

| Task | | Command |
|---|---|---|
| **Step 1** | Create the stack group and assign this router to it. | **sgbp group** *group-name* |
| **Step 2** | Specify a peer member of the stack group.<br>Repeat this step for each additional stack group peer. | **sgbp member** *peer-name* [*peer-ip-address*] |

**NOTES**

Only one stack group can be configured per access server or router.

### Configure a Virtual Template and Create a Virtual Template Interface

You need to configure a virtual template for MMP when asynchronous or synchronous serial interfaces are used, but dialers are not defined. When dialers are configured on the physical interfaces, do not specify a virtual template interface.

To configure a virtual template for any non-dialer interfaces, perform the following tasks beginning in global configuration mode:

| Task | | Command |
|---|---|---|
| **Step 1** | Define a virtual template for the stack group.<br><br>This step is not required if ISDN interfaces or other dialers are configured and used by the physical interfaces. | **multilink virtual-template** *number* |
| **Step 2** | Specify an IP address pool by using any pooling mechanism—for example, IP local pooling or DHCP pooling. | **ip local pool default** *ip-address* |

| Task | | Command |
|---|---|---|
| **Step 3** | Create a virtual template interface, and enter interface configuration mode.<br><br>This step is not required if ISDN interfaces or other dialers are configured and used by the physical interfaces. | **interface virtual-template** *number* |
| **Step 4** | Specify unnumbered IP. | **ip unnumbered ethernet 0** |
| **Step 5** | Enable PPP encapsulation on the virtual template interface. | **encapsulation ppp** |
| **Step 6** | Enable Multilink PPP on the virtual template interface. | **ppp multilink** |
| **Step 7** | Enable PPP authentication on the virtual template interface. | **ppp authentication chap** |

If dialers are or will be configured on the physical interfaces, the **ip unnumbered** command, mentioned in Step 4, will be used in configuring the dialer interface. For examples that show MMP configured with and without dialers, see the section "MMP Configuration Examples," at the end of this chapter.

**NOTES**

Never define a specific IP address on the virtual template because projected virtual access interfaces are always cloned from the virtual template interface. If a subsequent PPP link also gets projected to a stack member with a virtual access interface already cloned and active, we will have identical IP addresses on the two virtual interfaces. IP will erroneously route between them.

For more information about address pooling, see Chapter 25, "Configuring Media-Independent PPP and Multilink PPP."

## MONITORING AND MAINTAINING MMP VIRTUAL INTERFACES

To monitor and maintain virtual interfaces, you can perform any of the following tasks in EXEC mode:

| Task | Command |
|---|---|
| Display MLP and MMP bundle information. | **show ppp multilink** |
| Display the status of the stack group members. | **show sgbp** |
| Display the current seed bid value. | **show sgbp queries** |

## MMP Configuration Examples

The examples in this section show MMP configuration without and with dialers.

### Multichassis Multilink PPP Using PRI but no Dialers Example

The following example shows the configuration of MMP when no dialers are involved. Comments in the configuration discuss the commands. Variations are shown for a Cisco AS5200 access server or Cisco 4000 series router, and for an E1 controller.

```
sgbp group stackq
sgbp member systemb 1.1.1.2
sgbp member systemc 1.1.1.3

username stackq password therock
! First make sure the multilink virtual template number is defined globally on
¡ each router that is a member of the stack group.
multilink virtual-template 1

! If you have not configured any dialer interfaces for the physical interfaces in
! question (PRI, BRI, async, sync serial), you can define a virtual template.

interface virtual-template 1
 ip unnumbered e0
 ppp authentication chap
 ppp multilink

! Never define a specific IP address on the virtual template because projected
! virtual access interfaces are always cloned from the virtual template interface.
! If a subsequent PPP link also gets projected to a stack member with a virtual
! access interface already cloned and active, we will have identical IP addresses
! on the two virtual interfaces. IP will erroneously route between them.

! On an AS5200 or 4XXX platform:

! On a TI controller
!
controller T1 0
 framing esf
 linecode b8zs
 pri-group timeslots 1-24
!
interface Serial 0:23
 no ip address
 encapsulation ppp
 no ip route-cache
 ppp authentication chap
 ppp multilink
!
! On an E1 Controller
!
controller E1 0
 framing crc4
 linecode hdb3
 pri-group timeslots 1-31
interface Serial 0:15
```

```
no ip address
encapsulation ppp
no ip route-cache
ppp authentication chap
ppp multilink
```

## Multichassis Multilink PPP with Dialers Examples

When dialers are configured on the physical interfaces and when the interface itself is a dialer, do not specify a virtual template interface. For dialers, you only need to define the stack group name, common password, and its members across all the stack members. No virtual template interface is defined at all.

Only the PPP commands in dialer interface configuration are applied to the bundle interface. Subsequent projected PPP links are also cloned with the PPP commands from the dialer interface.

This section includes the following examples:

- MMP with Explicitly Defined Dialer Example
- MMP with ISDN PRI but no Explicitly Defined Dialer Example

### *MMP with Explicitly Defined Dialer Example*

The following example includes a dialer that is explicitly specified by the **interface dialer** command and configured by the commands that immediately follow:

```
sgbp group stackq
sgbp member systemb 1.1.1.2
sgbp member systemc 1.1.1.3

username stackq password therock

interface dialer 1
 ip unnumbered e0
 dialer map .....
 encapsulation ppp
 ppp authentication chap
 dialer-group 1
 ppp multilink
!
! on a T1 controller
!
controller T1 0
 framing esf
 linecode b8zs
 pri-group timeslots 1-24

interface Serial0:23
 no ip address
 encapsulation ppp
 dialer in-band
 dialer rotary 1
 dialer-group 1
!
! or on an E1 Controller
!
controller E1 0
 framing crc4
```

```
 linecode hdb3
 pri-group timeslots 1-31

interface Serial0:15
 no ip address
 encapsulation ppp
 no ip route-cache
 ppp authentication chap
 ppp multilink
```

### MMP with ISDN PRI but no Explicitly Defined Dialer Example

ISDN PRIs and BRIs by default are dialer interfaces. That is, a PRI configured without an explicit **interface dialer** command is *still* a dialer interface. The following example configures ISDN PRI. The D channel configuration on serial interface 0:23 is applied to all the B channels. MMP is enabled, but no virtual interface template needs to be defined.

```
sgbp group stackq
sgbp member systemb 1.1.1.2
sgbp member systemc 1.1.1.3

username stackq password therock

isdn switch-type primary-4ess
controller t1 0
 framing esf
 linecode b8zs
 pri-group timeslots 1-23
!
interface Serial0:23
 ip unnumbered e0
 dialer map .....
 encap ppp
 ppp authentication chap
 dialer-group 1
 dialer rot 1
!
ppp multilink
```

### Multichassis Multilink PPP with Offload Server Example

The following example shows a virtual template interface for a system being configured as an offload server (via the **sgbp seed-bid offload** command). All other stack group members must be defined with **sgbp seed-bid default** command (or if you do not enter any **sgbp seed-bid** command, it defaults to this).

```
multilink virtual-template 1
 sgbp group stackq
 sgbp member systemb 1.1.1.2
 sgbp member systemc 1.1.1.3
 sgbp seed-bid offload
 username stackq password therock

interface virtual-template 1
 ip unnumbered e0
 ppp authentication chap
 ppp multilink
```

CHAPTER 57

# Multichassis Multilink PPP Commands

This chapter describes the commands used to configure Multichassis Multilink PPP (MMP). For information about configuring MMP, see Chapter 56, "Configuring Multichassis Multilink PPP."

## SGBP GROUP

To define a named stack group and make this router a member of that stack group, use the **sgbp group** global configuration command.

**sgbp group** *name*

| *Syntax* | *Description* |
|---|---|
| *name* | Name of the stack group the system belongs to. |

### *Default*

Disabled. No stack group name is provided.

### *Command Mode*

Global configuration

### *Usage Guidelines*

This command first appeared in Cisco IOS Release 11.2.

Define the same stack group name across all the stack members.

### *Example*

In the following example, this system is made a member of the stack group named *stackq*:

```
sgbp group stackq
```

### Related Commands

Search online to find documentation for related commands.

**sgbp member**
**sgbp seed-bid**

## SGBP MEMBER

To specify the host name and IP address of a router or access server that is a peer member of a stack group, use the **sgbp member** global configuration command.

**sgbp member** *peer-name* [*peer-ip-address*]

| *Syntax* | *Description* |
|---|---|
| *peer-name* | Host name of the peer member. |
| *peer-ip-address* | (Optional) IP address of the peer member. If the domain name system (DNS) can perform a lookup on the *peer-name* value, the IP address is not required. Otherwise, it must be specified. |

### Default

Disabled. When enabled, names and IP addresses of peer routers or access servers in the stack group are not provided.

### Command Mode

Global configuration

### Usage Guidelines

This command first appeared in Cisco IOS Release 11.2.

Use this command to specify the names of peer hosts (other hosts, not the one being configured) in the specified stack group after you have entered the **sgbp group** command.

### Example

The following example configures the current router to recognize the three routers (*yoda*, *han*, and *darth*) as peer members of the *starfleet* stack group:

```
sgbp group starfleet
sgbp member yoda 10.69.5.2
sgbp member han 172.16.6.3
sgbp member darth 192.165.15.4
```

### Related Commands

Search online to find documentation for related commands.

**sgbp group**
**sgbp seed-bid**

### SGBP PPP-FORWARD

To enable forwarding of PPP calls—in addition to Multilink PPP calls—to the winner of the SGBP bid, use the **sgbp ppp-forward** global configuration command.

**sgbp ppp-forward**

#### *Syntax Description*

This command has no arguments and keywords.

#### *Default*

This command is disabled by default.

#### *Command Mode*

Global configuration

#### *Usage Guidelines*

This command first appeared in Cisco IOS Release 11.3.

When this command is enabled, both PPP and PPP multilink calls are projected to the winner of the SGBP bid. By default, only Multilink PPP calls are forwarded.

#### *Example*

The following partial example enables forwarding of PPP calls, as well as MLP calls, to the winner of the SGBP bidding:

```
sgbp ppp-forward
```

#### *Related Commands*

Search online to find documentation for related commands.

**sgbp member**
**sgbp seed-bid**

### SGBP SEED-BID

To set the bidding level that a stack group member can bid with for a bundle, use the **sgbp seed-bid** global configuration command.

**sgbp seed-bid** {**default** | **offload** | **forward-only** | *bid*}

| *Syntax* | *Description* |
|---|---|
| **default** | If set across all members of a stack group, indicates that the member that receives the first call for a certain user always wins the bid and hosts the master bundle interface. All subsequent calls to the same user received by another stack group member will *project* to this stackgroup member. This is the default. |

| | |
|---|---|
| **offload** | Indicates that this router is a relatively higher powered stack group member that is to function as an offload server, and host the master bundle interface. |
| **forward-only** | Indicates that this router or access server is to forward calls to another system and never wins the bid to host a master interface. This router or access server should hang up—instead of answering a call—if all the offload servers are down. |
| *bid* | Bid level, an integer in the range 0 through 9999. |

### *Default*

The **default** keyword; no bid-level integer value is set.

### *Command Mode*

Global configuration

### *Usage Guidelines*

This command first appeared in Cisco IOS Release 11.2.

In the case of equivalent stack group members stacked to receive calls in a rotary group across multiple PRIs, use **sgbp seed-bid default** *across all stack members*. The stack member that receives the first call for a certain user always wins the bid and hosts the master bundle interface. All subsequent calls to the same user received by another stack member will project to this stack member. If the multiple calls come in concurrently over multiple stack members, the SGBP tie-breaking mechanism will break the tie.

To leverage the relative higher power of one stack member over another, you can set the designated stack member (of higher CPU power) as offload server with **sgbp seed-bid offload**. The bid that is sent is the precalibrated per-platform bid approximating the CPU power, minus the *bundle load*. In this case, the offload server hosts the master bundle. All calls from other stack members get projected to this stack member. One or more offload servers can be defined—if the bids are equal, the SGBP tie-breaking mechanism will break the tie.

The interfaces that received the calls are projected to the master bundle interface and are considered children of the master bundle interface for the call. See the output of **show ppp multilink** for an example of master bundle interface (shown as "Master link") and the children of it.

You can also manually designate bid values with the **sgbp seed-bid** command. This value overrides the **default** or **offload** setting. The bid sent out is the user-configured value minus the *bundle load*. The *bundle load* is defined as the number of active bundles on the stack member. In effect, the more current active bundles on a router, the lower its bid for an additional bundle.

If you have assorted or exactly the same platforms and for some reason want to designate one or more as offload servers, you can *manually* set the bid value to be significantly higher than the rest. For example, you might use **sgbp seed-bid 9999**. To determine the initial bid value associated with your particular platform, use the **show sgbp** command. This method allows you to manually designate the bid values when you have assorted platforms and want to designate one or more platforms as offload servers; for example, one Cisco 4700 (given the highest seed-bid), two Cisco 4000s, and one Cisco 7000.

To check the bid value currently assigned on the system, use the **show sgbp queries** command.

### *Related Commands*

Search online to find documentation for related commands.

**sgbp group**
**sgbp member**
**show sgbp queries**

## SHOW SGBP

To display the status of the stack group members, use the **show sgbp** EXEC command.

**show sgbp**

### *Syntax Description*

This command has no keywords or arguments.

### *Command Mode*

EXEC

### *Usage Guidelines*

This command first appeared in Cisco IOS Release 11.2.

### *Sample Display*

The following is sample output from the **show sgbp** command:

```
systema# show sgbp

Group Name: stack State: 0 Ref: 0xC07B060
  Member Name: systemb State: ACTIVE  Id: 1
  Ref: 0xC14256F
  Address: 1.1.1.1 Tcb: 0x60B34538

  Member Name: systemc State: ACTIVE  Id: 2
  Ref: 0xA24256D
  Address: 1.1.1.2 Tcb: 0x60B34439

  Member Name: systemd State: IDLE Id: 3
  Ref: 0x0
  Address: 1.1.1.3 Tcb: 0x0
```

Table 57–1 describes the fields in the **show sgbp** command output display.

**Table 57–1** *Show SGBP Command Output Field Description*

| Field | Description |
|---|---|
| Group Name | Name of the stack group. |
| State | Status of the group or its member. The values are 0 for the stack group itself, and either ACTIVE or IDLE for each of the members of the group. |
| Member Name | Name of a specific host defined as a member of this stack group. |
| Id | Identifier used for each member of the group; typically the final digit of the host's IP address on the network they share. |
| Address | IP address of the stack group member. |

## SHOW SGBP QUERIES

To display the current seed bid value, use the **show sgbp queries** EXEC command.

**show sgbp queries**

### *Syntax Description*

This command has no arguments or keywords.

### *Command Mode*

EXEC

### *Usage Guidelines*

This command first appeared in Cisco IOS Release 11.2.

### *Sample Display*

The following example shows a bid of 50 from this system. Peers queried the system for the bid, the bid was accepted, and a connection was opened from a peer in the stack group:

```
systema# show sgbp queries

Seed bid: default, 50

Bundle: book State: Query_from_peers OurBid: 50
1.1.1.2         State: Open_from_peer   Bid: 050 Retry: 0
```

Table 57–2 describes the fields in the **show sgbp queries** command sample display output.

**Table 57–2** *Show SGBP Queries Command Output Field Descriptions*

| Field | Description |
|---|---|
| Seed bid | The initial bid; in this case, the default 50. |
| Bundle | Name of the MMP bundle. |
| State | Activity that occurred. In this case, a peer queried this system for its bid for the specified bundle. |
| OurBid | What this system bid for the bundle. It bid 50. |
| 1.1.1.2 | The peer's IP address. |
| State Bid Retry | Activity that occurred on the bid. In this case, the stack group peer 1.1.1.2 accepted this system's bid of 50 for the bundle and opened a connection with this system. Since the peer opened a connection, no retry was needed. |

# CHAPTER 58

# Configuring Virtual Profiles

Virtual Profiles is a unique Point-to-Point Protocol (PPP) application that can create and configure a virtual access interface dynamically when a dial-in call is received, and tear down the interface dynamically when the call ends. Virtual Profiles works with straightforward PPP and with Multilink PPP (MLP).

The configuration information for a Virtual Profiles virtual access interface can come from a virtual template interface, or from user-specific configuration stored on an authentication, authorization, and accounting (AAA) server, or both.

The user-specific AAA configuration used by Virtual Profiles is *interface* configuration and is downloaded during LCP negotiations. Another feature, called Per-User Configuration, also uses configuration information gained from an AAA server. However, Per-User Configuration uses *network* configuration (such as access lists and route filters) downloaded during NCP negotiations.

Two rules govern virtual access interface configuration by Virtual Profiles virtual template interfaces and AAA configurations:

- Each virtual access application can have at most one template to clone from but can have multiple AAA configurations to clone from (Virtual Profiles AAA information and AAA Per-User Configuration, which in turn might include configuration for multiple protocols).
- When Virtual Profiles is configured by virtual template, its template has higher priority than any other virtual template.

See the section "How Virtual Profiles Work—Four Configuration Cases," for a description of the possible configuration sequences for configuration by virtual template or AAA or both. See the section, "Interoperability with Other Cisco Dial Features," for a description of the possible configuration sequences that depend on the presence or absence by MLP or another virtual access feature that clones a virtual template interface.

This feature runs on all Cisco IOS platforms that support MLP.

For a complete description of the commands mentioned in this chapter, see Chapter 59, "Virtual Profiles Commands."

## BACKGROUND INFORMATION

This section presents background information about Virtual Profiles to help you understand this application before you start to configure it.

### Restrictions

This release does not support fast switching.

It is recommended that unnumbered addresses be used in virtual template interfaces to ensure that duplicate network addresses are not created on virtual access interfaces.

### Prerequisites

Use of user-specific AAA interface configuration information with Virtual Profiles requires the router to be configured for AAA and requires the AAA server to have user-specific interface configuration AV pairs. The relevant AV pairs (on a RADIUS server) begin as follows:

```
cisco-avpair = "lcp:interface-config=...",
```

The information that follows the equal sign (=) could be any Cisco IOS interface configuration command. For example, the line might be the following:

```
cisco-avpair = "lcp:interface-config=ip address 200.200.200.200 255.255.255.0",
```

Use of a virtual template interface with Virtual Profiles requires a virtual template to be defined specifically for Virtual Profiles.

### Interoperability with Other Cisco Dial Features

Virtual Profiles interoperates with Cisco DDR, Multilink PPP (MLP), and dialers such as ISDN.

#### *DDR Configuration of Physical Interfaces*

Virtual Profiles fully interoperates with physical interfaces in the following DDR configuration states when no other virtual access interface application is configured:

- Dialer Profiles are configured for the interface—The dialer profile is used instead of the Virtual Profiles configuration.
- DDR is not configured on the interface—Virtual Profiles overrides the current configuration.
- Legacy DDR is configured on the interface—Virtual Profiles overrides the current configuration.

**NOTES**

If a dialer interface is used (including any ISDN dialer), its configuration is used on the physical interface instead of the Virtual Profiles configuration.

### *Multilink PPP Effect on Virtual Access Interface Configuration*

As shown in Table 58–1, exactly how a virtual access interface will be configured depends on three factors:

- Whether Virtual Profiles is configured by Virtual Template, by AAA, by both, or by neither. These states are shown as "VP VT only," "VP AAA only," "VP VT and VP AAA," and "No VP at all," respectively, in the table.
- The presence or absence of a dialer interface.
- The presence or absence of MLP. The column label "MLP" is a stand-in for any virtual access feature that supports MLP and clones from a virtual template interface.

In Table 58–1, "(Multilink VT)" means that a virtual template interface is cloned *if* one is defined for MLP or a virtual access feature that uses MLP.

**Table 58–1** *Virtual Profiles Configuration Cloning Sequence*

| Virtual Profiles Configuration | MLP No Dialer | MLP Dialer | No MLP No Dialer | No MLP Dialer |
|---|---|---|---|---|
| VP VT only | VP VT | VP VT | VP VT | VP VT |
| VP AAA only | (Multilink VT)<br>VP AAA | (Multilink VT)<br>VP AAA | VP AAA | VP AAA |
| VP VT and VP AAA | VP VT<br>VP AAA | VP VT<br>VP AAA | VP VT<br>VP AAA | VP VT<br>VP AAA |
| No VP at all | (Multilink VT)* | Dialer† | No virtual access interface is created. | No virtual access interface is created. |

* The Multilink bundle virtual access interface is created and uses the default settings for MLP or the relevant virtual access feature that uses MLP.

† The Multilink bundle virtual access interface is created and cloned from the dialer interface configuration.

The order of items in any cell of the table is important. Where VP VT is shown above VP AAA, it means that first the Virtual Profiles virtual template is cloned on the interface, and then the AAA interface configuration for the user is applied to it. The user-specific AAA interface configuration adds to the configuration and overrides any conflicting physical interface or virtual template configuration commands.

### *Interoperability with Other Features that Use Virtual Templates*

Virtual Profiles also interoperates with virtual access applications that clone a virtual template interface. Each virtual access application can have at most one template to clone from but can clone from multiple AAA configurations.

The interaction between Virtual Profiles and other virtual template applications is as follows:

- If Virtual Profiles is enabled and a virtual template is defined for it, the Virtual Profiles virtual template is used.
- If Virtual Profiles is configured by AAA alone (no virtual template is defined for Virtual Profiles), the virtual template for another virtual access application (VPDN, for example) can be cloned onto the virtual access interface.
- A virtual template, if any, is cloned to a virtual access interface before the Virtual Profiles AAA configuration or AAA Per-User Configuration. AAA Per-User Configuration, if used, is applied last.

## Terminology

The following new or uncommon terms are used in this chapter:

**AV pair**—A configuration parameter on an AAA server; part of the user configuration that the AAA server sends to the router, in response to user-specific authorization requests. The router interprets each AV pair as a Cisco IOS router configuration command and applies the AV pairs in order. In this chapter, the term *AV pair* refers to an interface configuration parameter on a RADIUS server.

An interface configuration AV pair for Virtual Profiles can take a form such as this:

```
cisco-avpair = "lcp:interface-config=ip address 1.1.1.1 255.255.255.255.0",
```

**cloning**—Creating and configuring a virtual access interface by applying configuration commands from a specific virtual template. The virtual template is the source of the generic user information and router-dependent information. The result of cloning is a virtual access interface configured with all the commands in the template.

**virtual access interface**—Instance of a unique virtual interface that is created dynamically and exists temporarily. Virtual access interfaces can be created and configured differently by different applications, such as Virtual Profiles and virtual private dial-up networks.

**virtual template interface**—Generic interface configuration for certain users or for a certain purpose, plus router-dependent information. This takes the form of a list of Cisco IOS interface commands to be applied to the virtual interface as needed.

**virtual profile**—Instance of a unique virtual access interface created dynamically when certain users call in, and torn down dynamically when the call disconnects. A specific user's virtual profile can be configured by a virtual template interface, user-specific interface configuration stored on an AAA server, or both a virtual template interface and user-specific interface configuration from AAA.

Configuration of a virtual access interface begins with a virtual template interface (if any), followed by application of user-specific configuration for the particular user's dial-in session (if any).

## How Virtual Profiles Work—Four Configuration Cases

This section describes Virtual Profiles and the various ways they can work with virtual template interfaces, user-specific AAA interface configuration, and MLP or another feature that requires MLP.

Virtual Profiles separates configuration information into two logical parts:

- Generic—Common configuration for dial-in users plus other router-dependent configuration. This common and router-dependent information can define a virtual template interface stored locally on the router. The generic virtual template interface is independent of and can override the configuration of the physical interface on which a user dialed in.
- User-specific interface information—Interface configuration stored in a users file on an AAA server; for example, the authentication requirements and specific interface settings for a specific user. The settings are sent to the router in the response to the router's request to authenticate the user, and the settings can override the generic configuration. See the section "Virtual Profiles Configured by AAA Configuration Example," later in this chapter.

These logical parts can be used separately or together.

Four separate cases are possible:

- Case 1: Virtual Profiles Configured by Virtual Template—Applies the virtual template.
- Case 2: Virtual Profiles Configured by AAA—Applies the user-specific interface configuration received from the AAA server.
- Case 3: Virtual Profiles Configured by Virtual Template and AAA Configuration—Applies the virtual template and the user-specific interface configuration received from the AAA server.
- Case 4: Virtual Profiles Configured by AAA, and a Virtual Template Is Defined by Another Application—Applies the other application's virtual template interface and then applies the user-specific interface configuration received from the AAA server.

**NOTES**

All cases assume that AAA is configured globally on the router, the user has configuration information in the users file on the AAA server, PPP authentication and authorization proceed as usual, and the AAA server sends user-specific configuration information in the authorization approval response packet to the router.

The cases also assume that AAA works as designed and the AAA server sends configuration information for the dial-in user to the router, even when Virtual Profiles by virtual template is configured.

### *Case 1: Virtual Profiles Configured by Virtual Template*

In the case of Virtual Profiles by virtual template, the software functions as follows:

- If the physical interface is configured for Dialer Profiles (a DDR feature), the router looks for a dialer profile for the specific user.
- If a dialer profile is found, it is used instead of Virtual Profiles.
- If a dialer profile is not found for the user, or legacy DDR is configured, or DDR is not configured at all, Virtual Profiles creates a virtual access interface for the user.

The router applies the configuration commands that are in the virtual template interface to create and configure the virtual profile. The template includes generic interface information and router-specific information, but no user-specific information. No matter whether a user dialed in on a synchronous serial, an asynchronous serial, or an ISDN interface, the dynamically created virtual profile for the user is configured as specified in the virtual template.

Then the router interprets the lines in the AAA server's authorization approval response as Cisco IOS commands to apply to the virtual profile for the user.

Data flows through the virtual profile, and the higher layers treat it as the user's interface.

For example, if a virtual template included only the three commands **ip unnumbered ethernet** 0, **encapsulation ppp,** or **ppp authentication chap,** the virtual profile for any dial-in user would include those three commands.

In Figure 58–1, the dotted box represents the virtual profile configured with the commands that are in the virtual template, no matter which interface the call arrives on.

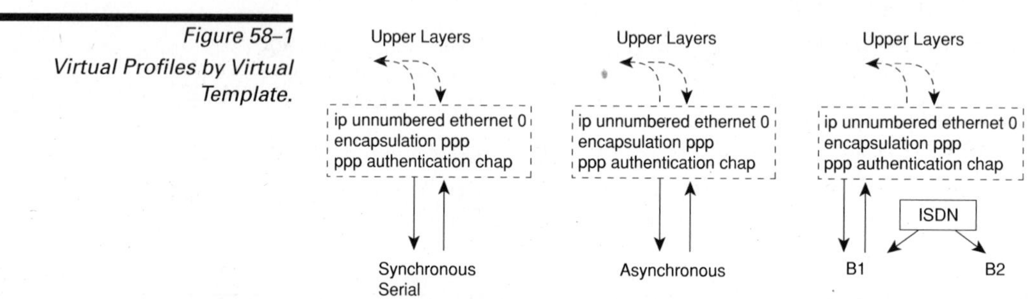


*Figure 58–1 Virtual Profiles by Virtual Template.*

See the section "Configuring Virtual Profiles by Virtual Template," for configuration tasks for this case.

### *Case 2: Virtual Profiles Configured by AAA*

In this case, no dialer profile (DDR feature) is defined for the specific user and no virtual template for Virtual Profiles is defined, but Virtual Profiles by AAA is enabled on the router.

During the PPP authorization phase for the user, the AAA server responds as usual to the router. The authorization approval contains configuration information for the user. The router interprets each of the lines in the AAA server's response as Cisco IOS commands to apply to the virtual profile for the user.

**NOTES**

If MLP is negotiated, the MLP virtual template is cloned first (this is the second row in ), and then interface-specific commands included in the AAA server's response for the user are applied. The MLP virtual template overrides any conflicting interface configuration, and the AAA interface configuration overrides any conflicting configuration from both the physical interface and the MLP virtual template.

The router applies all the user-specific interface commands received from the AAA server.

Suppose, for example, that the router interpreted the AAA server's response as including only the following two commands for this user:

```
ip address 10.10.10.10 255.255.255.255
keepalive 30
```

In Figure 58–2, the dotted box represents the virtual profile configured only with the commands received from the AAA server, no matter which interface the incoming call arrived on. On the AAA RADIUS server, the AV pair might have read as follows, where "\n" means to start a new command line:

```
cisco-avpair = "lcp:interface-config=ip address 10.10.10.10 255.255.255.0\nkeepalive 30",
```

*Figure 58–2*
*Virtual Profiles by AAA Configuration.*

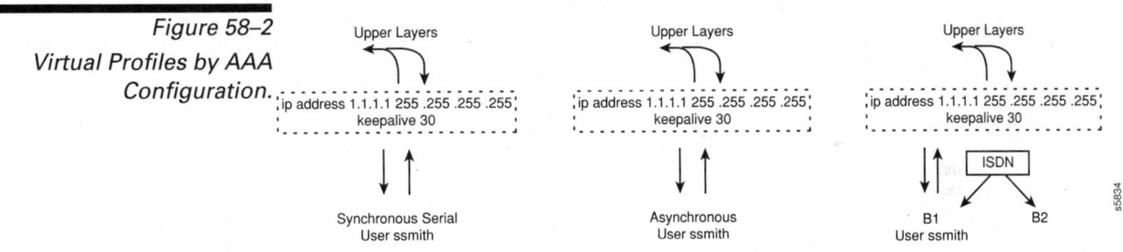


See the section, "Configuring Virtual Profiles by AAA Configuration," for configuration tasks for this case.

### *Case 3: Virtual Profiles Configured by Virtual Template and AAA Configuration*

In this case, no DDR dialer profile is defined for the specific user, a virtual template for Virtual Profiles is defined, Virtual Profiles by AAA is enabled on the router, the router is configured for AAA, and a user-specific interface configuration for the user is stored on the AAA server.

The router performs the following tasks in order:

1. Dynamically creates a virtual access interface cloned from the virtual template defined for Virtual Profiles.
2. Applies the user-specific interface configuration received from the AAA server.

If any command in the user's configuration conflicts with a command on the original interface or a command applied by cloning the virtual template, the user-specific command overrides the other command.

Suppose that the router had the virtual template as defined in Case 1 and the AAA user configuration as defined in Case 2. In Figure 58–3, the dotted box represents the virtual profile configured with configuration information from both sources, no matter which interface the incoming call arrived on. The **ip address** command has overridden the **ip unnumbered** command.

*Figure 58–3 Virtual Profiles by Both Virtual Template and AAA Configuration.*

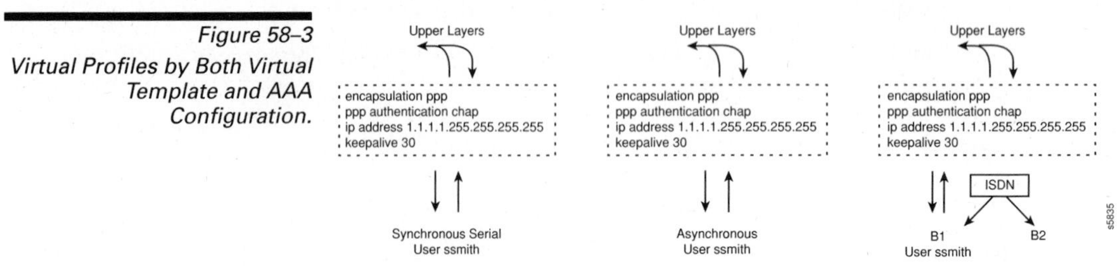


See the section "Configuring Virtual Profiles by Both Virtual Template and AAA Configuration" for configuration tasks for this case.

### Case 4: Virtual Profiles Configured by AAA, and a Virtual Template Is Defined by Another Application

In this case, no DDR dialer profile is defined for the specific user, Virtual Profiles by AAA is configured on the router but no virtual template is defined for Virtual Profiles, and a user-specific interface configuration is stored on the AAA server. In addition, a virtual template is configured for some other virtual access application (VPDN, for example).

The router performs the following tasks in order:

1. Dynamically creates a virtual access interface and clones the virtual template from the other virtual access application onto it.
2. Applies the user-specific interface configuration received from the AAA server.

If any command in the virtual template conflicts with a command on the original interface, the template overrides it.

If any command in the user's AAA interface configuration conflicts with a command in the virtual template, the user's AAA interface configuration overrides the virtual template.

If Per-User Configuration also happens to be configured on the AAA server, that network protocol configuration is applied to the virtual access interface last.

The result is a virtual interface unique to that user.

## Virtual Profiles Configuration Task List

To configure Virtual Profiles for dial-in users, complete the tasks in *one* of the first three sections and then troubleshoot the configuration by performing the tasks in the last section:

- Configuring Virtual Profiles by Virtual Template
- Configuring Virtual Profiles by AAA Configuration
- Configuring Virtual Profiles by Both Virtual Template and AAA Configuration
- Troubleshooting Virtual Profiles Configuration

As indicated earlier in the section "Interoperability with Other Cisco Dial Features," do not define a DDR dialer profile for a user if you intend to define Virtual Profiles for the user.

## Configuring Virtual Profiles by Virtual Template

To configure Virtual Profiles by virtual template, complete these two tasks:

- Create and Configure a Virtual Template Interface
- Specify a Virtual Template Interface for Virtual Profiles

**Notes**

The order in which these tasks is performed is not crucial. However, both tasks must be completed before Virtual Profiles is used.

### Create and Configure a Virtual Template Interface

Because a virtual template interface is a serial interface, all the configuration commands that apply to serial interfaces can also be applied to virtual template interfaces, except **shutdown** and **dialer** commands.

To create and configure a virtual template interface, complete the following tasks beginning in global configuration mode:

| Task | | Command |
|---|---|---|
| **Step 1** | Create a virtual template interface, and enter interface configuration mode. | **interface virtual-template** *number* |
| **Step 2** | Enable IP without assigning a specific IP address on the LAN. | **ip unnumbered ethernet 0** |
| **Step 3** | Enable PPP encapsulation on the virtual template interface. | **encapsulation ppp** |

Other optional PPP configuration commands can be added to the virtual template configuration. For example, you can add the **ppp authentication chap** command.

### Specify a Virtual Template Interface for Virtual Profiles

To specify a virtual template interface as the source of information for Virtual Profiles, complete the following task in global configuration mode.

| Task | Command |
|---|---|
| Specify the virtual template interface as the source of information for Virtual Profiles. | **virtual-profile virtual-template** *number* |

Virtual template numbers range from 1 to 25.

## Configuring Virtual Profiles by AAA Configuration

To configure Virtual Profiles by AAA only, complete these three tasks in any order. All tasks must be completed before Virtual Profiles is used.

- On the AAA server, create user-specific interface configurations for each of the specific users to use this method. See your AAA server documentation for more detailed configuration information about your AAA server.
- Configure AAA on the router.
- Specify AAA as the source of information for Virtual Profiles.

To specify AAA as the source of information for Virtual Profiles, complete the following task in global configuration mode:

| Task | Command |
|---|---|
| Specify AAA as the source of user-specific interface configuration. | **virtual-profile aaa** |

If you also want to use Per-User Configuration for network protocol access lists or route filters for individual users, see Chapter 60, "Per-User Configuration."

In this case, no virtual template interface is defined for Virtual Profiles.

## Configuring Virtual Profiles by Both Virtual Template and AAA Configuration

To configure Virtual Profiles by both virtual template interface and AAA configuration, complete these tasks in any order. All tasks must be completed before Virtual Profiles is used.

- On the AAA server, create user-specific interface configurations for each of the specific users to use this method. See your AAA server documentation for more detailed configuration information about your AAA server.
- Configure AAA on the router.
- Create and Configure a Virtual Template Interface, described in this chapter.
- Specify Virtual Profiles by Both Virtual Templates and AAA, described in this chapter.

## Create and Configure a Virtual Template Interface

To create and configure a virtual template interface, complete the following tasks beginning in global configuration mode:

| Task | | Command |
|---|---|---|
| **Step 1** | Create a virtual template interface, and enter interface configuration mode. | **interface virtual-template** *number* |
| **Step 2** | Enable IP without assigning a specific IP address on the LAN. | **ip unnumbered ethernet** 0 |
| **Step 3** | Enable PPP encapsulation on the virtual template interface. | **encapsulation ppp** |

Because the software treats a virtual template interface as a serial interface, all the configuration commands that apply to serial interfaces can also be applied to virtual template interfaces, except **shutdown** and **dialer** commands. Other optional PPP configuration commands can also be added to the virtual template configuration. For example, you can add the **ppp authentication chap** command.

## Specify Virtual Profiles by Both Virtual Templates and AAA

To specify both the virtual template interface and the AAA Per-User Configuration as sources of information for Virtual Profiles, complete the following tasks in global configuration mode:

| Task | Command |
|---|---|
| Define the virtual template interface as the source of information for Virtual Profiles. | **virtual-profile virtual-template** *number* |
| Specify AAA as the source of user-specific configuration for Virtual Profiles. | **virtual-profile aaa** |

If you also want to use Per-User Configuration for network protocol access lists or route filters for individual users, see Chapter 60.

## TROUBLESHOOTING VIRTUAL PROFILES CONFIGURATION

You can troubleshoot the Virtual Profiles configuration by using the following commands in EXEC mode:

| Task | Command |
|---|---|
| Display information about dial calls and negotiations and virtual profile events. | **debug dialer** |
| Display information about the Per-User Configuration downloaded from the AAA server. | **debug aaa per-user** |
| Display cloning information for a virtual access interface from the time it is cloned from a virtual template to the time it comes down. | **debug vtemplate** |

## VIRTUAL PROFILES CONFIGURATION EXAMPLES

The following sections provide examples for the four cases described in this chapter:

- Virtual Profiles Configured by Virtual Templates Example
- Virtual Profiles Configured by AAA Configuration Example
- Virtual Profiles Configured by Virtual Templates and AAA Configuration Example
- Virtual Profiles Configured by AAA Plus a VPDN Virtual Template on a VPDN Home Gateway Example Example

In these examples, BRI 0 is configured for Legacy DDR, and interface BRI 1 is configured for dialer profiles. Note that interface dialer 0 is configured for Legacy DDR. Interface dialer 1 is a dialer profile.

The intention of the examples is to show how to configure Virtual Profiles. In addition, the examples show the interoperability of DDR and dialer profiles in the respective cases with various forms of Virtual Profiles.

The same user names (John and Rick) occur in all these examples. Note the different configurations allowed to them in each of the four examples.

John is a normal user and can dial in to BRI 0 only. Rick is a privileged user who can dial in to BRI 0 and BRI 1. If Rick dials in to BRI 1, the dialer profile will be used. If Rick dials in to BRI 0, Virtual Profiles will be used. Because John doesn't have a dialer profile, only Virtual Profiles can be applied to him.

### Virtual Profiles Configured by Virtual Templates Example

In this example, the router is configured for Virtual Profiles by a virtual template. (Virtual Profiles does not have any interface-specific AAA configuration.) Comments in the example draw attention to specific features or ignored lines.

In this example, the same virtual template interface applies to both users; they have the same interface configurations.

### *Router Configuration*

```
! Enable AAA on the router.
aaa new-model
aaa authentication ppp default radius
! The following command is required.
aaa authorization network radius
enable secret 5 $1$koOn$/1QAylov6JFAElxRCrL.o/
enable password lab
!
! Specify configuration of Virtual Profiles by virtual template.
! This is the key command for this example.
virtual-profile virtual-template 1
!
! Define the virtual template.
interface Virtual-Template 1
 ip unnumbered ethernet 0
 encapsulation ppp
 ppp authentication chap
!
interface BRI 0
 description Connected to 103
 encapsulation ppp
 no ip route-cache
 dialer rotary-group 0
 ppp authentication chap
!
interface BRI 1
 description Connected to 104
 encapsulation ppp
! Disable fast switching.
 no ip route-cache
 dialer pool-member 1
 ppp authentication chap
!
! Configure dialer interface 0 for DDR for John and Rick.
interface dialer 0
 ip address 1.1.1.1 255.255.255.0
 encapsulation ppp
! Enable legacy DDR.
 dialer in-band
! Disable fast switching.
 no ip route-cache
 dialer map ip 1.1.1.2 name john 1111
 dialer map ip 1.1.1.3 name rick 2222
 dialer-group 1
 ppp authentication chap
!
!
! Configure dialer interface 1 for DDR to dial out to Rick.
interface dialer 1
```

```
 ip address 2.2.2.2 255.255.255.0
 encapsulation ppp
 dialer remote-name rick
 dialer string 3333
 dialer pool 1
 dialer-group 1
! Disable fast switching.
 no ip route-cache
 ppp authentication chap
 dialer-list 1 protocol ip permit
```

## Virtual Profiles Configured by AAA Configuration Example

This example shows the router configuration for Virtual Profiles by AAA and the AAA server configuration for user-specific interface configurations. John and Rick have different IP addresses.

In the AAA configuration Cisco AV pair lines, "\n" is used to indicate the start of a new Cisco IOS command line.

### *AAA Configuration for John and Rick*

```
john Password = "welcome"
     User-Service-Type = Framed-User,
     Framed-Protocol = PPP,
        cisco-avpair = "lcp:interface-config=keepalive 75\nip address 100.100.100.100
255.255.255.0",
rick Password = "emoclew"
     User-Service-Type = Framed-User,
     Framed-Protocol = PPP,
        cisco-avpair = "lcp:interface-config=keepalive 100\nip address 200.200.200.200
255.255.255.0"
```

### *Router Configuration*

```
! Enable AAA on the router.
aaa new-model
aaa authentication ppp default radius
! This is a key command for this example.
aaa authorization network radius
enable secret 5 $1$koOn$/1QAylov6JFAElxRCrL.o/
enable password lab
!
! Specify configuration of Virtual Profiles by aaa.
! This is a key command for this example.
virtual-profiles aaa
!
! Interface BRI 0 is configured for Legacy DDR.
interface BRI 0
 description Connected to 103
 encapsulation ppp
 no ip route-cache
 dialer rotary-group 0
 ppp authentication chap
!
```

```
! Interface BRI 1 is configured for Dialer Profiles.
interface BRI 1
 description Connected to 104
 encapsulation ppp
! Disable fast switching.
 no ip route-cache
 dialer pool-member 1
 ppp authentication chap
!
! Configure dialer interface 0 for DDR for John and Rick.
interface dialer 0
 ip address 1.1.1.1 255.255.255.0
 encapsulation ppp
! Enable legacy DDR.
 dialer in-band
! Disable fast switching.
 no ip route-cache
 dialer map ip 1.1.1.2 name john 1111
 dialer map ip 1.1.1.3 name rick 2222
 dialer-group 1
 ppp authentication chap
!
! Configure dialer interface 1 for DDR to dial out to Rick.
interface dialer 1
 ip address 2.2.2.2 255.255.255.0
 encapsulation ppp
 dialer remote-name rick
 dialer string 3333
 dialer pool 1
 dialer-group 1
! Disable fast switching.
 no ip route-cache
 ppp authentication chap
 dialer-list 1 protocol ip permit
```

### Virtual Profiles Configured by Virtual Templates and AAA Configuration Example

In this example, Virtual Profiles is configured by both virtual templates and AAA configuration. John and Rick can dial in from anywhere and have their same keepalive settings and their own IP addresses.

The remaining AV pair settings are not used by Virtual Profiles. They are the network-protocol access lists and route filters used by AAA-based Per-User Configuration.

In the AAA configuration Cisco AV pair lines, "\n" is used to indicate the start of a new Cisco IOS command line.

#### *AAA Configuration for John and Rick*

```
john Password = "welcome"
     User-Service-Type = Framed-User,
     Framed-Protocol = PPP,
        cisco-avpair = "lcp:interface-config=keepalive 75\nip address 100.100.100.100
255.255.255.0",
```

```
        cisco-avpair = "ip:rte-fltr-out#0=router igrp 60",
        cisco-avpair = "ip:rte-fltr-out#3=deny 171.0.0.0 0.255.255.255",
        cisco-avpair = "ip:rte-fltr-out#4=deny 172.0.0.0 0.255.255.255",
        cisco-avpair = "ip:rte-fltr-out#5=permit any"
rick Password = "emoclew"
     User-Service-Type = Framed-User,
     Framed-Protocol = PPP,
        cisco-avpair = "lcp:interface-config=keepalive 100\nip address 200.200.200.200
255.255.255.0",
        cisco-avpair = "ip:inacl#3=permit ip any any precedence immediate",
        cisco-avpair = "ip:inacl#4=deny igrp 0.0.1.2 255.255.0.0 any",
        cisco-avpair = "ip:outacl#2=permit ip any any precedence immediate",
        cisco-avpair = "ip:outacl#3=deny igrp 0.0.9.10 255.255.0.0 any"
```

### *Router Configuration*

```
! Enable AAA on the router.
aaa new-model
aaa authentication ppp default radius
! This is a key command for this example.
aaa authorization network radius
enable secret 5 $1$koOn$/1QAylov6JFAElxRCrL.o/
enable password lab
!
! Specify use of Virtual Profiles and a virtual template.
! The following two commands are key for this example.
virtual-profile virtual-template 1
virtual-profile aaa
!
! Define the virtual template.
interface Virtual-Template 1
 ip unnumbered ethernet 0
 encapsulation ppp
 ppp authentication chap
!
! Interface BRI 0 is configured for Legacy DDR.
interface BRI 0
 description Connected to 103
 encapsulation ppp
 no ip route-cache
 dialer rotary-group 0
 ppp authentication chap
!
! Interface BRI 1 is configured for Dialer Profiles.
interface BRI 1
 description Connected to 104
 encapsulation ppp
! Disable fast switching.
 no ip route-cache
 dialer pool-member 1
 ppp authentication chap
!
! Configure dialer interface 0 for DDR to dial out to John and Rick.
interface dialer 0
```

```
 ip address 1.1.1.1 255.255.255.0
 encapsulation ppp
 dialer in-band
! Disable fast switching.
 no ip route-cache
 dialer map ip 1.1.1.2 name john 1111
 dialer map ip 1.1.1.3 name rick 2222
 dialer-group 1
 ppp authentication chap
!
! Configure dialer interface 0 for DDR to dial out to Rick.
interface dialer 1
 ip address 2.2.2.2 255.255.255.0
 encapsulation ppp
 dialer remote-name rick
 dialer string 3333
 dialer pool 1
 dialer-group 1
! Disable fast switching.
 no ip route-cache
 ppp authentication chap
!
 dialer-list 1 protocol ip permit
```

## Virtual Profiles Configured by AAA Plus a VPDN Virtual Template on a VPDN Home Gateway Example

Like the Virtual Profiles configured by AAA example earlier in this section, this example shows the router configuration for Virtual Profiles by AAA. The AAA server's users file also includes interface configuration for John and Rick, the two users. Specifically, John and Rick each has his own IP address when in privileged mode.

In this case, however, the router is also configured as the VPDN home gateway. It clones the VPDN virtual template interface first and then clones the Virtual Profiles AAA interface configuration. If Per-User Configuration was configured on this router and the AAA server's users file had network protocol information for the two users, that information would be applied to the virtual access interface last.

In the AAA configuration Cisco AV pair lines, "\n" is used to indicate the start of a new Cisco IOS command line.

### *AAA Configuration for John and Rick*

```
john Password = "welcome"
     User-Service-Type = Framed-User,
     Framed-Protocol = PPP,
        cisco-avpair = "lcp:interface-config=keepalive 75\nip address 100.100.100.100
255.255.255.0",
rick Password = "emoclew"
     User-Service-Type = Framed-User,
     Framed-Protocol = PPP,
        cisco-avpair = "lcp:interface-config=keepalive 100\nip address 200.200.200.200
255.255.255.0"
```

### Router Configuration

```
!Configure the router as the VPDN home gateway.
!
!Enable VPDN and specify the VPDN virtual template to use on incoming calls from the
!network access server.
vpdn enable
vpdn incoming dallas_wan go_blue virtual-template 6
!
!Configure the virtual template interface for VPDN.
interface virtual template 6
ip unnumbered ethernet 0
encapsulation ppp
ppp authentication chap
!
!Enable AAA on the router.
aaa new-model
aaa authentication ppp default radius
aaa authorization network radius
enable secret 5 $1$koOn$/1QAylov6JFAElxRCrL.o/
enable password lab
!
!Specify configuration of Virtual Profiles by aaa.
virtual-profiles aaa
!
!Configure the physical synchronous serial 0 interface.
interface Serial 0
 description Connected to 101
 encapsulation ppp
!Disable fast switching.
 no ip route-cache
 ppp authentication chap
!
!Configure serial interface 1 for DDR. S1 uses dialer rotary group 0, which is
!defined on BRI interface 0.
interface serial 1
 description Connected to 102
 encapsulation ppp
 dialer in-band
! Disable fast switching.
 no ip route-cache
 dialer rotary-group 0
 ppp authentication chap
!
interface BRI 0
 description Connected to 103
 encapsulation ppp
 no ip route-cache
 dialer rotary-group 0
 ppp authentication chap
!
interface BRI 1
 description Connected to 104
 encapsulation ppp
!Disable fast switching.
```

```
 no ip route-cache
 dialer pool-member 1
 ppp authentication chap
!
!Configure dialer interface 0 for DDR to call and receive calls from John and Rick.
interface dialer 0
 ip address 1.1.1.1 255.255.255.0
 encapsulation ppp
!Enable legacy DDR.
 dialer in-band
!Disable fast switching.
 no ip route-cache
 dialer map ip 1.1.1.2 name john 1111
 dialer map ip 1.1.1.3 name rick 2222
 dialer-group 1
 ppp authentication chap
!
!Configure dialer interface 1 for DDR to dial out to Rick.
interface dialer 1
 ip address 2.2.2.2 255.255.255.0
 encapsulation ppp
 dialer remote-name rick
 dialer string 3333
 dialer pool 1
 dialer-group 1
!Disable fast switching.
 no ip route-cache
 ppp authentication chap
 dialer-list 1 protocol ip permit
```

CHAPTER 59

# Virtual Profiles Commands

This chapter describes the commands used to configure Virtual Profiles.

Virtual Profiles is a unique Point-to-Point Protocol (PPP) application that can create and configure a virtual access interface dynamically when a dial-in call is received and tear down the interface dynamically when the call ends. This feature runs on all Cisco IOS platforms that support Multilink PPP.

For configuration tasks and examples, see Chapter 58, "Configuring Virtual Profiles."

## INTERFACE VIRTUAL-TEMPLATE

To associate a virtual template with a virtual template interface, use the **interface virtual-template** global configuration command.

**interface virtual-template** *number*

| *Syntax* | *Description* |
| --- | --- |
| *number* | Number used to identify the virtual template interface. |

### *Default*

Disabled. No virtual template number is defined.

### *Command Mode*

Global configuration

### Usage Guidelines

This command first appeared in Cisco IOS Release 11.2 F.

A virtual template interface is used to provide the configuration for dynamically created virtual access interfaces. It is created by users and can be saved in nonvolatile RAM (NVRAM).

Once the virtual template interface is created, it can be configured in the same way as a serial interface.

### Example

The following example links this virtual template interface with virtual template 1:

```
interface virtual-template 1
 ip unnumbered ethernet 0
 ppp multilink
 ppp authentication chap
```

## VIRTUAL-PROFILE AAA

To enable Virtual Profiles by AAA configuration, use the **virtual-profile aaa** global configuration command.

**virtual-profile aaa**

### Syntax Description

This command has no arguments or keywords.

### Default

Disabled

### Command Mode

Global configuration

### Usage Guidelines

This command first appeared in Cisco IOS Release 11.2 F.

Effect of this command for any specific user depends on the router being configured for AAA and the AAA server being configured for that user's specific configuration information.

### Example

The following example configures Virtual Profiles by AAA configuration only:

```
virtual-profile aaa
```

### Related Commands

Search online to find documentation for related commands.

**aaa authentication**
**virtual-profile virtual-template**

## VIRTUAL-PROFILE VIRTUAL-TEMPLATE

To enable Virtual Profiles by a virtual interface template, use the **virtual-profile virtual-template** global configuration command.

**virtual-profile virtual-template** *number*

| *Syntax* | *Description* |
|---|---|
| *number* | Number of the virtual template to apply, in the range 1 to 30. |

### *Default*

Disabled. No virtual template is defined, and no default virtual template number is used.

### *Command Mode*

Global configuration

### *Usage Guidelines*

This command first appeared in Cisco IOS Release 11.2 F.

When Virtual Profiles are configured by virtual templates only, any interface-specific configuration information that is downloaded from the AAA server is ignored in configuring the virtual access interface for a user.

The **interface virtual-template** command defines a virtual template to be used for Virtual Profiles. Because several virtual templates might be defined for different purposes on the router (such as MLP, PPP over ATM, and Virtual Profiles), it is important to be clear about the virtual template number to use in each case.

### *Example*

The following example configures Virtual Profiles by virtual templates only. The number 2 was chosen because virtual template 1 was previously defined for use by Multilink PPP.

```
virtual-profile virtual-template 2
```

### *Related Commands*

Search online to find documentation for related commands.

**interface virtual-template**

# CHAPTER 60

# Per-User Configuration

This chapter describes a large-scale solution that uses features and commands described in other chapters of this book.

Per-User Configuration provides a flexible, scalable, easily maintained solution for customers with a large number of dial-in users. This solution can tie together the following dial-in features:

- Virtual template interfaces, generic interface configuration, and router-specific configuration information stored in the form of a virtual template interface that can be applied (*cloned*) to a virtual access interface each time any user dials in. This is described in Chapter 54, "Configuring Virtual Template Interfaces."
- AAA per-user security and interface configuration information stored on a separate AAA server and sent by the AAA server to the access server or router in response to authorization requests during the PPP authentication phase. The Per-User Configuration information can add to or override the generic configuration on a virtual interface.
- Virtual Profiles, which can use either or both of the two preceding sources of information for virtual interface configuration. When a user dials in, Virtual Profiles can apply the generic interface configuration and then apply the Per-User Configuration to create a unique virtual access interface for that user. This is described in Chapter 58, "Configuring Virtual Profiles."

This set of features is supported on all platforms that support Multilink PPP.

A virtual access interface created dynamically for any user dial-in session is deleted when the session ends. The resources used during the session are returned for other dial-in uses.

## BACKGROUND INFORMATION

This section provides background information, such as benefits, support, and operational processes.

## Benefits

The Per-User Configuration feature provides these benefits:

- Maintenance ease for service providers with a large number of access servers and a very large number of dial-in users. Service providers do not need to update all their routers and access servers when user-specific information changes; instead, they can update one AAA server.
- Scalability. By separating generic virtual interface configuration on the router from the configuration for each individual, Internet service providers and other enterprises with large numbers of dial-in users can provide a uniquely configured interface for each individual user. In addition, by separating the generic virtual interface configuration from the physical interfaces on the router, the number and types of physical interfaces on the router or access server are not intrinsic barriers to growth.

## Prerequisites

When a specific user dials in to a router, the use of a Per-User Configuration from an AAA server requires that AAA is configured on the router and that a configuration for that user exists on the AAA server.

## Terminology

The following new or uncommon terms are used in this chapter:

**AV pair**—A configuration parameter on an AAA server; part of the user configuration that the AAA server sends to the router, in response to user-specific authorization requests. The router interprets each AV pair as a Cisco IOS router configuration command and applies the AV pairs in order. In this chapter, the term *AV pair* refers to a configuration parameter on either a TACACS+ or a RADIUS server.

On a TACACS server, an AV pair can take forms such as these:

```
rte-fltr-out#0="router igrp 60"
rte-fltr-out#3="permit 0.0.5.6 255.255.0.0"
rte-fltr-out#4="permit any"
```

On a RADIUS server, an AV pair can take forms such as these:

```
cisco-avpair = "lcp:interface-config=ip address 1.1.1.1 255.255.255.255.0",
cisco-avpair = "ip:rte-fltr-out#0=router igrp 60",
cisco-avpair = "ip:rte-fltr-out#1=deny 171.0.0.0 0.255.255.255",
```

**cloning**—Creating and configuring a virtual access interface by applying a specific virtual template interface. The template is the source of the generic user information and router-dependent information. The result of cloning is a virtual access interface configured with all the commands in the template.

**virtual access interface**—Instance of a unique virtual interface that is created dynamically and exists temporarily. Virtual access interfaces can be created and configured differently by different applications, such as Virtual Profiles and virtual private dialup networks.

**virtual profile**—Unique virtual access interface created dynamically when certain users call in, and torn down dynamically when the call disconnects. A specific user's virtual profile can be configured by a virtual template interface, user-specific interface configuration (stored on an AAA server), or both a virtual template interface and user-specific interface configuration from AAA.

Configuration of a virtual access interface begins with a virtual template interface (if any), followed by application of user-specific configuration for the particular user's dial-in session (if any).

**virtual template interface**—Generic configuration of an interface for a certain purpose or configuration common to certain users, plus router-dependent information. This takes the form of a list of Cisco IOS interface commands to be applied to a virtual access interface as needed. Several applications can apply virtual template interfaces, but generally each application uses a single template. Each virtual template interface is identified by number.

## General Operational Processes

In general, the Per-User Configuration process on the Cisco router or network access server proceeds as follows:

1. The user dials in.
2. The authentication and authorization phases occur.
    - If AAA is configured, the router sends an authorization request to the AAA server.
    - If the AAA server has information (AV pairs or other configuration parameters) that defines a configuration for the specific user, the server includes it in the information in the approval response packet.
    - Figure 60–1 illustrates the request and response part of the process that happens when a user dials in, given that AAA is configured and that the AAA server has Per-User Configuration information for the dial-in user.
    - The router looks for AV pairs in the AAA approval response.
    - The router caches the configuration parameters.

**NOTES**

TACACS servers treat authentication and authorization as two phases; RADIUS servers combine authentication and authorization into a single step. For more detailed information, refer to your server documentation.

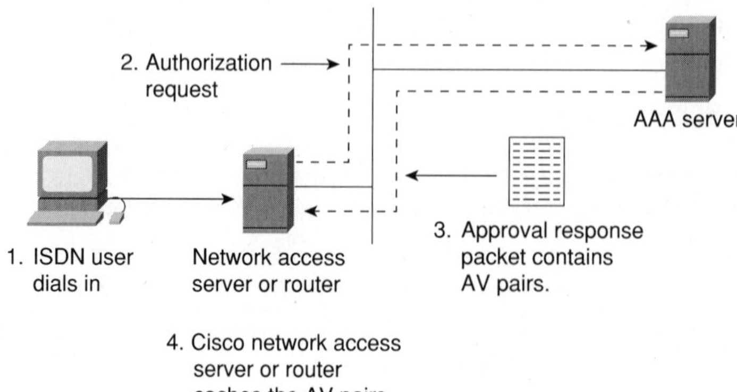


*Figure 60–1*
*Per-User Configuration Authentication and Authorization.*

3. A virtual access interface is created for this user.
   - The router finds the virtual template that is set up for Virtual Profiles, if any, and applies the commands to the virtual access interface.
   - The router looks for the AV pairs to apply to this virtual access interface to configure it for the dial-in user.
   - The AV pairs are sent to the Cisco IOS command-line parser, which interprets them as configuration commands, and applies them to configure this virtual access interface.

The result of this process is a virtual access interface configured uniquely for the dial-in user.

When this user's call ends, the virtual access interface is deleted and its resources are returned for other dial-in uses.

**NOTES**

The use of Virtual Profiles can modify the process that occurs between the user dial-in and the use of AAA configuration information. For more information, see Chapter 58.

## Operational Processes with IP Address Pooling

During IPCP address negotiation, if an IP pool name is specified for a user, the network access server checks whether the named pool is defined locally. If it is, no special action is required and the pool is consulted for an IP address.

If the required pool is not present (either in the local configuration or as a result of a previous download operation), then an authorization call to obtain it is made, using the special username:

```
pools-nas-name
```

where *nas-name* is the configured name of the network access server. In response, the AAA server downloads the configuration of the required pool.

This pool username can be changed using Cisco IOS configuration. For example:

```
aaa configuration config-name nas1-pools-definition.cisco.us
```

This command has the effect of changing the username that is used to download the pool definitions from the default name "pools-*nas-name*" to "nas1-pools-definition.cisco.com."

On a TACACS+ server, the entries for an IP address pool and a user of the pool might be as follows:

```
user = nas1-pools {
     service = ppp protocol = ip {
        pool-def#1 = "aaa 1.0.0.1 1.0.0.3"
        pool-def#2 = "bbb 2.0.0.1 2.0.0.10"
        pool-def#3 = "ccc 3.0.0.1 3.0.0.20"
        pool-timeout=60
    }
}

user = georgia {
    login = cleartext lab
    service = ppp protocol = ip {
                 addr-pool=bbb
    }
}
```

On a RADIUS server, the entries for the same IP address pool and user is as follows:

```
nas1-pools      Password = "cisco" User-Service-Type=Outbound-User
        cisco-avpair = "ip:pool-def#1=aaa 1.0.0.1 1.0.0.3",
        cisco-avpair = "ip:pool-def#2=bbb 2.0.0.1 2.0.0.10",
        cisco-avpair = "ip:pool-def#3=ccc 3.0.0.1 3.0.0.20",
        cisco-avpair = "ip:pool-timeout=60"

georgia Password = "lab"
        User-Service-Type = Framed-User,
        Framed-Protocol = PPP,
                cisco-avpair = "ip:addr-pool=bbb"
```

**NOTES**

This entry specifies a User-Service-Type of Outbound-User. This attribute is supplied by the network access server to prevent ordinary logins from using the well-known username and password combination of nas1-pools/cisco.

Pools downloaded to a Cisco network access server are not retained in nonvolatile memory and automatically disappear whenever the access server or router restarts. Downloaded pools can also be made to time out automatically by adding a suitable AV pair. See the following bullets and the pool-timeout attribute in Table 60–1. Downloaded pools are marked as *dynamic* in the output of the **show ip local pools** command.

To delete downloaded pools, you can do either of the following:

- Manually delete the definition from the network access server. For example, if "bbb" is the name of a downloaded pool, you can enter the Cisco IOS command **no ip local pool bbb**.

  Deleting a pool definition does not interrupt service for current users. If a pool is deleted and then redefined to include a pool address that is currently allocated, the new pool understands and tracks the address as expected.

- Set an AV pair pool-timeout value; this is a more desirable solution.

  The pool-timeout AV pair starts a timer when the pool is downloaded. Once the timer expires, the pools are deleted. The next reference to the pools again causes an authorization call to be made, and the pool definition is downloaded again.

  This method allows definitions to be made and changed on the AAA server and propagated to network access servers.

## Supported Attributes for AV Pairs

Table 60–1 provides a partial list of the Cisco-specific supported attributes for AV pairs that can be used for per-user virtual interface configuration.

**Table 60–1** *Partial List of Cisco-Specific Supported AV Pair Attributes*

| Attribute | Meaning |
|---|---|
| inacl# | An input access list definition. For IP, standard or extended access list syntax can be used, although you cannot mix them within a single list. For IPX, only extended syntax is recognized. The value of this attribute is the text that comprises the body of a named access list definition. |
| outacl#* | An output access list definition. For IP, standard or extended access list syntax can be used. For IPX, only extended syntax is recognized. The value of this attribute is the text that comprises the body of a named access list definition. |
| rte-fltr-in# | An input route filter. For IP, standard or extended access list syntax can be used, although you cannot mix them within a single list. For IPX, only extended syntax is recognized. The first line of this filter must specify a routing process. Subsequent lines comprise the body of a named access list. |
| rte-fltr-out# | An output route filter. For IP, standard or extended access list syntax can be used, although you cannot mix them within a single list. For IPX, only extended syntax is recognized. The first line of this filter must specify a routing process. Subsequent lines comprise the body of a named access list. |
| route#† | Static routes, for IP and IPX.<br>The value is text of the form *destination-address mask* [*gateway*] |

**Table 60–1** *Partial List of Cisco-Specific Supported AV Pair Attributes, Continued*

| Attribute | Meaning |
|---|---|
| sap# | IPX static SAPs. The value is text from the body of an **ipx sap** configuration command. |
| sap-fltr-in# | IPX input SAP filter. Only extended access list syntax is recognized. The value is text from the body of an extended IPX access list configuration command. (The Novell socket number for SAP filtering is 452.) |
| sap-fltr-out# | IPX output SAP filter. Only extended access list syntax is recognized. The value is text from the body of an extended IPX access list configuration command. |
| pool-def# | An IP pool definition. The value is text from the body of an **ip local pool** configuration command. |
| pool-timeout | An IP pool definition. The body is an integer representing a timeout, in minutes. |

* The "outacl" attribute still exists and retains its old meaning.
† The "route" attribute, without a trailing #, is still recognized for backward compatibility with the TACACS+ protocol specification, but if multiple static routes are required in TACACS+, full "route#" names will have to be employed.

Table 60–2 provides examples for each attribute on an AAA TACACS+ server.

**Table 60–2** *ACACS+ Server AV Pair Examples for Each Attribute*

| Attribute | TACACS+ Server Examples |
|---|---|
| inacl# | **IP:**<br>`inacl#3="permit ip any any precedence immediate"`<br>`inacl#4="deny igrp 0.0.1.2 255.255.0.0 any"`<br><br>**IPX:**<br>`inacl#1="deny 3C01.0000.0000.0001"`<br>`inacl#2="deny 4C01.0000.0000.0002"` |
| outacl# | `outacl#2="permit ip any any precedence immediate"`<br>`outacl#3="deny igrp 0.0.9.10 255.255.0.0 any"` |
| rte-fltr-in# | **IP:**<br>`rte-fltr-in#0="router igrp 60"`<br>`rte-fltr-in#3="permit 0.0.3.4 255.255.0.0"`<br>`rte-fltr-in#4="deny any"`<br><br>**IPX:**<br>`rte-fltr-in#1="deny 3C01.0000.0000.0001"`<br>`rte-fltr-in#2="deny 4C01.0000.0000.0002"` |
| rte-fltr-out# | `rte-fltr-out#0="router igrp 60"`<br>`rte-fltr-out#3="permit 0.0.5.6 255.255.0.0"`<br>`rte-fltr-out#4="permit any"` |

**Table 60–2** *ACACS+ Server AV Pair Examples for Each Attribute, Continued*

| Attribute | TACACS+ Server Examples |
|---|---|
| route# | **IP:**<br>`route#1="3.0.0.0 255.0.0.0 1.2.3.4"`<br>`route#2="4.0.0.0 255.0.0.0"`<br><br>**IPX:**<br>`route#1="4C000000 ff000000 30.12.3.4"`<br>`route#2="5C000000 ff000000 30.12.3.5"` |
| sap# | `sap#1="4 CE1-LAB 1234.0000.0000.0001 451 4"`<br>`sap#2="5 CE3-LAB 2345.0000.0000.0001 452 5"` |
| sap-fltr-in# | `sap-fltr-in#1="deny 6C01.0000.0000.0001"`<br>`sap-fltr-in#2="permit -1"` |
| sap-fltr-out# | `sap-fltr-out#1="deny 6C01.0000.0000.0001"`<br>`sap-fltr-out#2="permit -1"` |
| pool-def# | `pool-def#1 = "aaa 1.0.0.1 1.0.0.3"`<br>`pool-def#2 = "bbb 2.0.0.1 2.0.0.10"`<br>`pool-def#3 = "ccc 3.0.0.1 3.0.0.20"` |
| pool-timeout | `pool-timeout=60` |

Table 60–3 provides examples for each attribute on an AAA RADIUS server.

**Table 60–3** *RADIUS Server AV Pair Examples for Each Attribute*

| Attribute | RADIUS Server Examples |
|---|---|
| lcp:interface-config* | `cisco-avpair = "lcp:interface-config=ip address 1.0.0.0 255.255.255.0",` |
| inacl# | `cisco-avpair = "ip:inacl#3=permit ip any any precedence immediate",`<br>`cisco-avpair = "ip:inacl#4=deny igrp 0.0.1.2 255.255.0.0 any",` |
| outacl# | `cisco-avpair = "ip:outacl#2=permit ip any any precedence immediate",`<br>`cisco-avpair = "ip:outacl#3=deny igrp 0.0.9.10 255.255.0.0 any",` |
| rte-fltr-in# | **IP:**<br>`cisco-avpair = "ip:rte-fltr-in#0=router igrp 60",`<br>`cisco-avpair = "ip:rte-fltr-in#3=permit 0.0.3.4 255.255.0.0",`<br>`cisco-avpair = "ip:rte-fltr-in#4=deny any",`<br><br>**IPX:**<br>`cisco-avpair = "ipx:rte-fltr-in=deny 3C01.0000.0000.0001",` |
| rte-fltr-out# | `cisco-avpair = "ip:rte-fltr-out#0=router igrp 60",`<br>`cisco-avpair = "ip:rte-fltr-out#3=permit 0.0.5.6 255.255.0.0",`<br>`cisco-avpair = "ip:rte-fltr-out#4=permit any",` |

**Table 60–3** *RADIUS Server AV Pair Examples for Each Attribute, Continued*

| Attribute | RADIUS Server Examples |
|---|---|
| route# | **IP:**<br>`cisco-avpair = "ip:route=3.0.0.0 255.0.0.0 1.2.3.4",`<br>`cisco-avpair = "ip:route=4.0.0.0 255.0.0.0",`<br><br>**IPX:**<br>`cisco-avpair = "ipx:route=4C000000 ff000000 30.12.3.4",`<br>`cisco-avpair = "ipx:route=5C000000 ff000000 30.12.3.5"` |
| sap# | `cisco-avpair = "ipx:sap=4 CE1-LAB 1234.0000.0000.0001 451 4",`<br>`cisco-avpair = "ipx:sap=5 CE3-LAB 2345.0000.0000.0001 452 5",` |
| sap-fltr-in# | `cisco-avpair = "ipx:sap-fltr-in=deny 6C01.0000.0000.0001",`<br>`cisco-avpair = "ipx:sap-fltr-in=permit -1"` |
| sap-fltr-out# | `cisco-avpair = "ipx:sap-fltr-out=deny 6C01.0000.0000.0001",`<br>`cisco-avpair = "ipx:sap-fltr-out=permit -1"` |
| pool-def# | `cisco-avpair = "ip:pool-def#1=aaa 1.0.0.1 1.0.0.3",`<br>`cisco-avpair = "ip:pool-def#2=bbb 2.0.0.1 2.0.0.10",`<br>`cisco-avpair = "ip:pool-def#3=ccc 3.0.0.1 3.0.0.20",` |
| pool-timeout | `cisco-avpair = "ip:pool-timeout=60"` |

* This attribute is specific to RADIUS servers. It can be used to add Cisco IOS interface configuration commands to a specific user's configuration information.

## AAA Server Configuration for a Per-User Configuration Solution

The configuration requirements and the structure of Per-User Configuration information is set by the specifications of each type of AAA server. Refer to your server documentation for more detailed information. The following sections about TACACS and RADIUS servers are specific to Per-User Configuration.

### Configuring a Freeware TACACS Server for Per-User Configuration

On a TACACS server, the entry in the users file takes a standard form. In the freeware version of TACACS+, the following lines appear in order:

- "User =" followed by the username, a space, and an open brace
- Authentication parameters
- Authorization parameters
- One or more AV pairs
- End brace on a line by itself

The general form of a freeware TACACS user entry is shown by the following general example:

```
user = username {
     authentication parameters go here
     authorization parameters go here
}
```

The freeware TACACS user entry form is also shown by the following examples for specific users:

```
user= tx
  Password= cleartext welcome
  Service= PPP protocol= ip {
        ip:route=10.0.0.0 255.0.0.0
        ip:route=11.0.0.0 255.0.0.0
        ip:route=12.0.0.0 255.0.0.0
        ip:inacl#5=deny 20.0.0.1
}

user= frox
  Password= cleartext lab
  Service= PPP protocol= ip {
        ip:addr-pool=bbb
}
```

For more requirements and detailed information, see your AAA server documentation.

### Configuring a CiscoSecure TACACS Server for Per-User Configuration

The format of an entry in the users file in the AAA database is generally name = value. Some values allow additional subparameters to be specified and, in these cases, the subparameters are enclosed in braces ({}). Following is a simple example of an AAA database showing the default user, one group, two users who belong to the group, and one user who does not:

```
# Sample AA Database 1
unknown_user = {
  password = system #Use the system's password file (/etc/passwd)
}
group = staff {
  # password for staff who do not have their own
  password = des "sefjkAlM7zybE"
  service = shell {
    # allow any commands with any attributes
    default cmd = permit
    default attribute = permit
  }
}
user = joe {  # joe uses the group password

  member = "staff"
}
user = pete {  # pete has his own password
  member = "staff"
  password = des "alkd9Ujiqp2y"
}
user = anita {
  # Use the "default" user password mechanism defined above.
  service = shell {
    cmd = telnet {  # allow telnet to any destination
    }
  }
}
```

### Configuring a RADIUS Server for Per-User Configuration

On a RADIUS server, the format of an entry in the users file includes the following lines in order:

- Username and password
- User service type
- Framed Protocol
- One or more AV pairs

**NOTES**

All these AV pairs are vendor-specific. To use them, RADIUS servers must support the use of vendor-specific AV pairs. Patches for some servers are available from the Cisco Consulting Engineering (CE) customer-support organization.

The structure of an AV pair for Cisco platforms starts with *cisco-avpair* followed by a space, an equal sign, and another space. The rest of the line is within double quotation marks and, for all lines but the last, ends with a comma. Inside the double quotation marks is a phrase indicating the supported attribute, another equal sign, and a Cisco IOS command. The following examples show two quite different partial user configurations on a RADIUS server.

```
tx      Password = "welcome"
        User-Service-Type = Framed-User,
        Framed-Protocol = PPP,
        cisco-avpair = "ip:route=10.0.0.0 255.0.0.0",
        cisco-avpair = "ip:route=11.0.0.0 255.0.0.0",
        cisco-avpair = "ip:route=12.0.0.0 255.0.0.0",
        cisco-avpair = "ip:inacl#5=deny 20.0.0.1"

frox    Password = "lab"
        User-Service-Type = Framed-User,
        Framed-Protocol = PPP,
        cisco-avpair = "ip:addr-pool=bbb"
```

## CONFIGURATION TASKS

Per-User Configuration information exists on AAA servers only and is configured there, as described in section, "AAA Server Configuration for a Per-User Configuration Solution."

For more information about configuring an application that can tie AAA Per-User Configuration information to generic interface and router configuration, see Chapter 58. Virtual profiles are required for combining Per-User Configuration information and generic interface and router configuration information to create virtual access interfaces for individual ISDN B channels.

However, you can monitor and debug the Per-User Configuration settings on the router or access server that are set from an AAA server. Table 60–4 indicates some of the commands to use for each AV pair attribute.

**Table 60–4** *Monitoring and Debugging Per-User Configuration Settings*

| Attribute | Show Commands | Debug Commands |
|---|---|---|
| inacl#<br>outacl# | show ip access-list<br>show ip interface *interface*<br>show ipx access-lists<br>show ipx interface | debug aaa author<br>debug aaa per-user |
| rte-fltr-in#<br>rte-fltr-out# | show ip access-lists<br>show ip protocols | debug aaa author<br>debug aaa per-user |
| route# | show ip route<br>show ipx route | debug aaa author<br>debug aaa per-user |
| sap# | show ipx servers | debug aaa author<br>debug aaa per-user |
| sap-fltr-in#<br>sap-fltr-out# | show ipx access-lists<br>show ipx interface | debug aaa author<br>debug aaa per-user |
| pool-def#<br>pool-timeout | show ip local pool [*name*] | — |

## Per-User Configuration Examples

This section provides TACACS+ and RADIUS variations of two comprehensive examples, which show router or access server configuration and AV pair configuration on an AAA server.

### TACACS+ Freeware Examples

This section provides the TACACS+ freeware versions of the following examples:

- IP Access Lists and Static Routes Using Virtual Profiles over ISDN BRI Example
- IPX Per-User SAP Filters, Using IPXWAN and Virtual Profiles by a Synchronous Interface Example

#### *IP Access Lists and Static Routes Using Virtual Profiles over ISDN BRI Example*

This example provides configurations for the TACACS+ freeware daemon, the network access server, and the peer router named tx. On the TACACS+ AAA server, peer router tx has a configuration that includes static routes and IP access lists.

##### *TACACS+ Freeware Daemon Configuration File*

```
key = tac123
user = tx {
global = cleartext welcome
service = ppp protocol = ip {
```

```
route#1="10.0.0.0 255.0.0.0"
route#2="11.0.0.0 255.0.0.0"
route#3="12.0.0.0 255.0.0.0"
inacl#1="deny 20.0.0.1"
}
}
```

### *Current Network Access Server Configuration*

```
version 11.3
service timestamps debug datetime localtime
service udp-small-servers
service tcp-small-servers
!
hostname sf
!
aaa new-model
aaa authentication ppp default tacacs+
aaa authorization network tacacs+
enable secret 5 $1$koOn$/1QAylov6JFAElxRCrL.o/
enable password lab
!
username tx password 7 15050E0007252621
ip host sf 172.21.114.132
ip domain-name cisco.com
ip name-server 171.69.2.132
ip name-server 198.92.30.32
isdn switch-type basic-5ess
interface Ethernet0
 ip address 172.21.114.132 255.255.255.224
 no ip mroute-cache
 media-type 10BaseT
!

interface Virtual-Template1
 ip unnumbered Ethernet0
 no cdp enable
!
!
interface BRI0
 ip unnumbered Ethernet0
 no ip mroute-cache
 encapsulation ppp
 no ip route-cache
 dialer idle-timeout 300
 dialer map ip 20.0.0.1 name tx broadcast 61482
 dialer-group 1
 no fair-queue
 ppp authentication chap
!
!
ip default-gateway 172.21.114.129
no ip classless
ip route 0.0.0.0 0.0.0.0 172.21.114.129
```

```
!
virtual-profile virtual-template 1
dialer-list 1 protocol ip permit
tacacs-server host 172.21.114.130
tacacs-server key tac123
```

### *Current Peer Configuration for tx*

```
version 11.3
no service pad
!
hostname tx
!
enable secret 5 $1$m1WK$RsjborN1Z.XZuFqsrtSnp/
enable password lab
!
username sf password 7 051C03032243430C
ip host tx 172.21.114.134
ip domain-name cisco.com
ip name-server 171.69.2.132
ip name-server 198.92.30.32
isdn switch-type basic-5ess
!
interface Ethernet0
 ip address 172.21.114.134 255.255.255.224
 no ip route-cache
 shutdown
!
interface BRI0
 ip address 20.0.0.1 255.0.0.0
 encapsulation ppp
 dialer map ip 172.21.114.132 name sf broadcast 61483
 dialer-group 1
 no fair-queue
!
ip default-gateway 172.21.114.129
no ip classless
ip route 172.21.0.0 255.255.0.0 BRI0
dialer-list 1 protocol ip permit
!
line con 0
 exec-timeout 0 0
line vty 0 4
 password lab
 login
end
```

## *IPX Per-User SAP Filters, Using IPXWAN and Virtual Profiles by a Synchronous Interface Example*

This example provides configurations for the TACACS+ daemon and the peer router named ny. On the TACACS+ AAA server, user ny has a configuration that includes inbound and outbound SAP filters.

### *TACACS+ Freeware Daemon User's Configuration File*

key = tac123

```
user = ny {
 global = cleartext welcome
 service = ppp protocol = ipx {
        sap="101 CYBER-01 40.0000.0000.0001 400 10"
        sap="202 CYBER-02 40.0000.0000.0001 401 10"
        sap="303 CYBER-03 40.0000.0000.0001 402 10"
        sap-fltr-out#0="deny 40 101"
        sap-fltr-out#1="deny 40 202"
        sap-fltr-out#2="permit -1"
        sap-fltr-in#0="permit 30 444"
        sap-fltr-in#1="deny -1"
}
```

### *Current Remote Peer (ny) Configuration*

```
version 11.3
!
hostname ny
!
enable password lab
!
username la password 7 140017070F0B272E
ip host NY 172.21.114.131
ip name-server 171.69.2.132
ip name-server 198.92.30.32
ipx routing 0000.0c47.090d
ipx internal-network 30
!
interface Ethernet0
 ip address 172.21.114.131 255.255.255.224
!
!
interface Serial1
 no ip address
 encapsulation ppp
 ipx ipxwan 0 unnumbered peer-ny
 clockrate 4000000
!
ipx sap 444 ZEON-4 30.0000.0000.0001 444 10
ipx sap 555 ZEON-5 30.0000.0000.0001 555 10
ipx sap 666 ZEON-6 30.0000.0000.0001 666 10
!
Current Network Access Server (la) Configuration
version 11.3
service timestamps debug uptime
!
hostname la
!
aaa new-model
aaa authentication ppp default tacacs+
aaa authorization network tacacs+
enable password lab
```

```
!
username ny password 7 044C0E0A0C2E414B
ip host LA 172.21.114.133
ip name-server 198.92.30.32
ip name-server 171.69.2.132
ipx routing 0000.0c47.12d3
ipx internal-network 40
!
interface Ethernet0
 ip address 172.21.114.133 255.255.255.224
!
interface Virtual-Template1
 no ip address
 ipx ipxwan 0 unnumbered nas-la
 no cdp enable
!
interface Serial1
 ip unnumbered Ethernet0
 encapsulation ppp
 ipx ipxwan 0 unnumbered nas-la
 ppp authentication chap
!
ipx sap 333 DEEP9 40.0000.0000.0001 999 10
!
virtual-profile virtual-template 1
tacacs-server host 172.21.114.130
tacacs-server key tac123
```

## RADIUS Examples

This section provides the RADIUS versions of the following examples:

- IP Access Lists and Static Routes Using Virtual Profiles over ISDN BRI Example
- IPX Per-User SAP Filters, Using IPXWAN and Virtual Profiles by a Synchronous Interface Example

### *IP Access Lists and Static Routes Using Virtual Profiles over ISDN BRI Example*

In this example, a remote peer (tx) dials in to a BRI on a Cisco network access server (sf), which requests user configuration information from an AAA server (radiusd).

#### *RADIUS Users File*

```
tx       Password = "welcome"
         User-Service-Type = Framed-User,
         Framed-Protocol = PPP,
         cisco-avpair = "ip:route=10.0.0.0 255.0.0.0",
         cisco-avpair = "ip:route=11.0.0.0 255.0.0.0",
         cisco-avpair = "ip:route=12.0.0.0 255.0.0.0",
         cisco-avpair = "ip:inacl#5=deny 20.0.0.1"
```

### Current Network Access Server Configuration

```
version 11.3
service timestamps debug datetime localtime
service udp-small-servers
service tcp-small-servers
!
hostname sf
!
aaa new-model
aaa authentication ppp default radius
aaa authorization network radius
enable secret 5 $1$koOn$/1QAylov6JFAElxRCrL.o/
enable password lab
!
username tx password 7 15050E0007252621
ip host sf 172.21.114.132
ip domain-name cisco.com
ip name-server 171.69.2.132
ip name-server 198.92.30.32
isdn switch-type basic-5ess
interface Ethernet0
 ip address 172.21.114.132 255.255.255.224
 no ip mroute-cache
 media-type 10BaseT
!
!
interface Virtual-Template1
 ip unnumbered Ethernet0
 no cdp enable
!
!
interface BRI0
 ip unnumbered Ethernet0
 no ip mroute-cache
 encapsulation ppp
 no ip route-cache
 dialer idle-timeout 300
 dialer map ip 20.0.0.1 name tx broadcast 61482
 dialer-group 1
 no fair-queue
 ppp authentication chap
!
ip default-gateway 172.21.114.129
no ip classless
ip route 0.0.0.0 0.0.0.0 172.21.114.129
!
virtual-profile vtemplate 1
dialer-list 1 protocol ip permit
radius-server host 172.21.114.130
radius-server key rad123
```

### Current Peer Configuration for tx

```
version 11.3
no service pad
```

```
!
hostname tx
!
enable secret 5 $1$m1WK$RsjborN1Z.XZuFqsrtSnp/
enable password lab
!
username sf password 7 051C03032243430C
ip host tx 172.21.114.134
ip domain-name cisco.com
ip name-server 171.69.2.132
ip name-server 198.92.30.32
isdn switch-type basic-5ess
!
interface Ethernet0
 ip address 172.21.114.134 255.255.255.224
 no ip route-cache
 shutdown
!
interface BRI0
 ip address 20.0.0.1 255.0.0.0
 encapsulation ppp
 dialer map ip 172.21.114.132 name sf broadcast 61483
 dialer-group 1
 no fair-queue
!
ip default-gateway 172.21.114.129
no ip classless
ip route 172.21.0.0 255.255.0.0 BRI0
dialer-list 1 protocol ip permit
!
line con 0
 exec-timeout 0 0
line vty 0 4
 password lab
 login
!
end
```

### *Outputs of Ping Command from tx*

```
tx# ping 172.21.114.132

Type escape sequence to abort.
Sending 5, 100-byte ICMP Echos to 172.21.114.132, timeout is 2 seconds:
U.U.U
Success rate is 0 percent (0/5)

(fails due to access list deny)
```

### *Radius Debug Output*

```
radrecv: Request from host ac157284 code=1, id=46, length=67
    Client-Id = 172.21.114.132
    Client-Port-Id = 1112670208
    User-Name = "tx"
    CHAP-Password = "\037\317\213\326*\236)#+\266\243\255x\331\370v\334"
```

```
        User-Service-Type = Framed-User
        Framed-Protocol = PPP
    Sending Ack of id 46 to ac157284 (172.21.114.132)
        User-Service-Type = Framed-User
        Framed-Protocol = PPP
        [Vendor 9] cisco-avpair = "ip:route=10.0.0.0 255.0.0.0"
        [Vendor 9] cisco-avpair = "ip:route=11.0.0.0 255.0.0.0"
        [Vendor 9] cisco-avpair = "ip:route=12.0.0.0 255.0.0.0"
        [Vendor 9] cisco-avpair = "ip:inacl#5=deny 20.0.0.1"
```

### *Network Access Server (sf) Show and Debug Commands Output*

```
sf# show debug

General OS:
  AAA Authorization debugging is on
PPP:
  PPP authentication debugging is on
  Multilink activity debugging is on
ISDN:
  ISDN events debugging is on
Dial on demand:
  Dial on demand events debugging is on
VTEMPLATE:
  Virtual Template debugging is on

pr  4 08:30:09: ISDN BR0: received HOST_INCOMING_CALL
        Bearer Capability i = 0x080010
*Apr  4 08:30:09:          ------------------
        Channel ID i = 0x0101
*Apr  4 08:30:09:          IE out of order or end of 'private' IEs --
        Bearer Capability i = 0x8890
*Apr  4 08:30:09:          Channel ID i = 0x89
*Apr  4 08:30:09:          Called Party Number i = 0xC1, '61483'
*Apr  4 08:30:09: ISDN BR0: Event: Received a call from <unknown> on B1 at 64 Kb/s
*Apr  4 08:30:09: ISDN BR0: Event: Accepting the call
%LINK-3-UPDOWN: Interface BRI0:1, changed state to up
*Apr  4 08:30:09: ISDN BR0: received HOST_CONNECT
        Channel ID i = 0x0101
*Apr  4 08:30:09:          ------------------
        Channel ID i = 0x89
*Apr  4 08:30:09: ISDN BR0: Event: Connected to <unknown> on B1 at 64 Kb/s
*Apr  4 08:30:09: PPP BRI0:1: Send CHAP challenge id=30 to remote
*Apr  4 08:30:10: PPP BRI0:1: CHAP response received from tx
*Apr  4 08:30:10: PPP BRI0:1: CHAP response id=30 received from tx
*Apr  4 08:30:10: AAA/AUTHOR/LCP: authorize LCP
*Apr  4 08:30:10: AAA/AUTHOR/LCP: BRI0:1: (0): user='tx'
*Apr  4 08:30:10: AAA/AUTHOR/LCP: BRI0:1: (0): send AV service=ppp
*Apr  4 08:30:10: AAA/AUTHOR/LCP: BRI0:1: (0): send AV protocol=lcp
*Apr  4 08:30:10: AAA/AUTHOR/LCP: BRI0:1: (2084553184): Method=RADIUS
*Apr  4 08:30:10: AAA/AUTHOR (2084553184): Post authorization status = PASS_ADD
*Apr  4 08:30:10: PPP BRI0:1: Send CHAP success id=30 to remote
*Apr  4 08:30:10: PPP BRI0:1: remote passed CHAP authentication.
*Apr  4 08:30:10: VTEMPLATE Reuse vaccess1, New Recycle queue size:0
```

```
*Apr  4 08:30:10: VTEMPLATE set default vaccess1 with no ip address

*Apr  4 08:30:10: Virtual-Access1 VTEMPLATE hardware address 0000.0c46.154a
*Apr  4 08:30:10: VTEMPLATE vaccess1 has a new cloneblk vtemplate, now it has vtemplate
*Apr  4 08:30:10: VTEMPLATE undo default settings vaccess1

*Apr  4 08:30:10: VTEMPLATE ************* CLONE VACCESS1 *****************Apr  4
08:30:10: VTEMPLATE Clone from vtemplate1 to vaccess1
interface Virtual-Access1
no ip address
encap ppp
ip unnumbered ethernet 0
end

%LINK-3-UPDOWN: Interface Virtual-Access1, changed state to up
*Apr  4 08:30:10: AAA/AUTHOR/LCP: authorize LCP
*Apr  4 08:30:10: AAA/AUTHOR/LCP: Virtual-Access1: (0): user='tx'
*Apr  4 08:30:10: AAA/AUTHOR/LCP: Virtual-Access1: (0): send AV service=ppp
*Apr  4 08:30:10: AAA/AUTHOR/LCP: Virtual-Access1: (0): send AV protocol=lcp
*Apr  4 08:30:10: AAA/AUTHOR/LCP: Virtual-Access1: (1338953760): Method=RADIUS
*Apr  4 08:30:10: AAA/AUTHOR (1338953760): Post authorization status = PASS_ADD
*Apr  4 08:30:10: AAA/AUTHOR/FSM: Virtual-Access1: (0): can we start IPCP?
*Apr  4 08:30:10: AAA/AUTHOR/FSM: Virtual-Access1: (0): user='tx'
*Apr  4 08:30:10: AAA/AUTHOR/FSM: Virtual-Access1: (0): send AV service=ppp
*Apr  4 08:30:10: AAA/AUTHOR/FSM: Virtual-Access1: (0): send AV protocol=ip
*Apr  4 08:30:10: AAA/AUTHOR/FSM: Virtual-Access1: (1716082074): Method=RADIUS
*Apr  4 08:30:10: AAA/AUTHOR (1716082074): Post authorization status = PASS_ADD
*Apr  4 08:30:10: AAA/AUTHOR/FSM: Virtual-Access1: we can start IPCP (0x8021)
*Apr  4 08:30:10: MLP Bad link Virtual-Access1
*Apr  4 08:30:10: AAA/AUTHOR/FSM: Virtual-Access1: (0): can we start UNKNOWN?
*Apr  4 08:30:10: AAA/AUTHOR/FSM: Virtual-Access1: (0): user='tx'
*Apr  4 08:30:10: AAA/AUTHOR/FSM: Virtual-Access1: (0): send AV service=ppp
*Apr  4 08:30:10: AAA/AUTHOR/FSM: Virtual-Access1: (0): send AV protocol=unknown
*Apr  4 08:30:10: AAA/AUTHOR/FSM: Virtual-Access1: (2526612868): Method=RADIUS
*Apr  4 08:30:10: AAA/AUTHOR (2526612868): Post authorization status = PASS_ADD
*Apr  4 08:30:10: AAA/AUTHOR/FSM: Virtual-Access1: we can start UNKNOWN (0x8207)
*Apr  4 08:30:10: MLP Bad link Virtual-Access1
*Apr  4 08:30:10: BRI0:1: Vaccess started from dialer_remote_name
*Apr  4 08:30:10: AAA/AUTHOR/FSM: BRI0:1: (0): can we start IPCP?
*Apr  4 08:30:10: AAA/AUTHOR/FSM: BRI0:1: (0): user='tx'
*Apr  4 08:30:10: AAA/AUTHOR/FSM: BRI0:1: (0): send AV service=ppp
*Apr  4 08:30:10: AAA/AUTHOR/FSM: BRI0:1: (0): send AV protocol=ip
*Apr  4 08:30:10: AAA/AUTHOR/FSM: BRI0:1: (3920403585): Method=RADIUS
*Apr  4 08:30:10: AAA/AUTHOR (3920403585): Post authorization status = PASS_ADD
*Apr  4 08:30:10: AAA/AUTHOR/FSM: BRI0:1: we can start IPCP (0x8021)
*Apr  4 08:30:10: AAA/AUTHOR/FSM: BRI0:1: (0): can we start UNKNOWN?
*Apr  4 08:30:10: AAA/AUTHOR/FSM: BRI0:1: (0): user='tx'
*Apr  4 08:30:10: AAA/AUTHOR/FSM: BRI0:1: (0): send AV service=ppp
*Apr  4 08:30:10: AAA/AUTHOR/FSM: BRI0:1: (0): send AV protocol=unknown
*Apr  4 08:30:10: AAA/AUTHOR/FSM: BRI0:1: (3439943223): Method=RADIUS
*Apr  4 08:30:10: AAA/AUTHOR (3439943223): Post authorization status = PASS_ADD
*Apr  4 08:30:10: AAA/AUTHOR/FSM: BRI0:1: we can start UNKNOWN (0x8207)
%LINEPROTO-5-UPDOWN: Line protocol on Interface BRI0:1, changed state to up
```

```
%LINEPROTO-5-UPDOWN: Line protocol on Interface Virtual-Access1, changed state to up
*Apr  4 08:30:13: AAA/AUTHOR/IPCP: Virtual-Access1: start: her address 20.0.0.1, we want
0.0.0.0
*Apr  4 08:30:13: AAA/AUTHOR/IPCP: Virtual-Access1: (0): user='tx'
*Apr  4 08:30:13: AAA/AUTHOR/IPCP: Virtual-Access1: (0): send AV servi*Apr  4 08:30:13:
AAA/AUTHOR/IPCP: Virtual-Access1: (0): send AV service=ppp
*Apr  4 08:30:13: AAA/AUTHOR/IPCP: Virtual-Access1: (0): send AV protocol=ip
*Apr  4 08:30:13: AAA/AUTHOR/IPCP: Virtual-Access1: (0): send AV addr*20.0.0.1
*Apr  4 08:30:13: AAA/AUTHOR/IPCP: Virtual-Access1: (3215797579): Method=RADIUS
*Apr  4 08:30:13: AAA/AUTHOR (3215797579): Post authorization status = PASS_ADD
*Apr  4 08:30:13: AAA/AUTHOR/IPCP: Virtual-Access1: Processing AV service=ppp
*Apr  4 08:30:13: AAA/AUTHOR/IPCP: Virtual-Access1: Processing AV protocol=ip
*Apr  4 08:30:13: AAA/AUTHOR/IPCP: Virtual-Access1: Processing AV addr*20.0.0.1
*Apr  4 08:30:13: AAA/AUTHOR/IPCP: Virtual-Access1: Processing AV route=10.0.0.0 255.0.0.0
*Apr  4 08:30:13: AAA/AUTHOR/IPCP: Virtual-Access1: Processing AV route=11.0.0.0 255.0.0.0
*Apr  4 08:30:13: AAA/AUTHOR/IPCP: Virtual-Access1: Processing AV route=12.0.0.0 255.0.0.0
*Apr  4 08:30:13: AAA/AUTHOR/IPCP: Virtual-Access1: Processing AV inacl#5=deny 20.0.0.1
*Apr  4 08:30:13: AAA/AUTHOR/IPCP: Virtual-Access1: authorization succeeded
*Apr  4 08:30:13: AAA/AUTHOR/IPCP: Virtual-Access1: done: her address 20.0.0.1, we want
20.0.0.1
*Apr  4 08:30:13: AAA/AUTHOR/IPCP: Virtual-Access1: authorization succeeded
*Apr  4 08:30:13: AAA/AUTHOR: Virtual-Access1: parse_cmd 'ip route 10.0.0.0 255.0.0.0
20.0.0.1' ok (0)
*Apr  4 08:30:13: AAA/AUTHOR: Virtual-Access1: enqueue peruser IP txt=no ip route 10.0.0.0
255.0.0.0 20.0.0.1
*Apr  4 08:30:13: AAA/AUTHOR: Virtual-Access1: parse_cmd 'ip route 11.0.0.0 255.0.0.0
20.0.0.1' ok (0)
*Apr  4 08:30:13: AAA/AUTHOR: Virtual-Access1: enqueue peruser IP txt=no ip route 11.0.0.0
255.0.0.0 20.0.0.1
*Apr  4 08:30:13: AAA/AUTHOR: Virtual-Access1: parse_cmd 'ip route 12.0.0.0 255.0.0.0
20.0.0.1' ok (0)
*Apr  4 08:30:13: AAA/AUTHOR: Virtual-Access1: enqueue peruser IP txt=no ip route 12.0.0.0
255.0.0.0 20.0.0.1
*Apr  4 08:30:13: AAA/AUTHOR: parse 'ip access-list standard Virtual-Access1#0' ok (0)
*Apr  4 08:30:13: AAA/AUTHOR: parse 'deny 20.0.0.1' ok (0)
*Apr  4 08:30:13: AAA/AUTHOR: Virtual-Access1: enqueue peruser IP txt=no ip access-list
standard Virtual-Access1#0
*Apr  4 08:30:13: VTEMPLATE vaccess1 has a new cloneblk AAA, now it has vtemplate/AAA
*Apr  4 08:30:13: VTEMPLATE ************* CLONE VACCESS1 *****************

*Apr  4 08:30:13: VTEMPLATE Clone from AAA to vaccess1
interface Virtual-Access1
ip access-group Virtual-Access1#0 in
end

*Apr  4 08:30:13: AAA/AUTHOR: Virtual-Access1: vaccess parse 'interface Virtual-Access1
ip access-group Virtual-Access1#0 in
' ok (0)
*Apr  4 08:30:13: AAA/AUTHOR/FSM: Check for unauthorized mandatory AV's
*Apr  4 08:30:13: AAA/AUTHOR/FSM: Processing AV service=ppp
*Apr  4 08:30:13: AAA/AUTHOR/FSM: Processing AV protocol=unknown
*Apr  4 08:30:13: AAA/AUTHOR/FSM: succeeded
%ISDN-6-CONNECT: Interface BRI0:1 is now connected to  tx
sf#
```

```
sf# show ip access-lists

Standard IP access list Virtual-Access1#0 (per-user)
    deny   20.0.0.1

sf# show ip route

Codes: C - connected, S - static, I - IGRP, R - RIP, M - mobile, B - BGP
       D - EIGRP, EX - EIGRP external, O - OSPF, IA - OSPF inter area
       N1 - OSPF NSSA external type 1, N2 - OSPF NSSA external type 2
       E1 - OSPF external type 1, E2 - OSPF external type 2, E - EGP
       i - IS-IS, L1 - IS-IS level-1, L2 - IS-IS level-2, * - candidate default
       U - per-user static route, o - ODR

Gateway of last resort is 172.21.114.129 to network 0.0.0.0

U    10.0.0.0/8 [1/0] via 20.0.0.1
U    11.0.0.0/8 [1/0] via 20.0.0.1
U    12.0.0.0/8 [1/0] via 20.0.0.1
     20.0.0.0/8 is subnetted, 1 subnets
C       20.0.0.1 is directly connected, Virtual-Access1
     172.21.0.0/16 is subnetted, 1 subnets
C       172.21.114.128 is directly connected, Ethernet0
S*   0.0.0.0/0 [1/0] via 172.21.114.129


sf# show interfaces virtual-access 1

Virtual-Access1 is up, line protocol is up
  Hardware is Virtual Access interface
  Interface is unnumbered.  Using address of Ethernet0 (172.21.114.132)
  MTU 1500 bytes, BW 64 Kbit, DLY 100000 usec, rely 255/255, load 1/255
  Encapsulation PPP, loopback not set, keepalive set (10 sec)
  DTR is pulsed for 5 seconds on reset
  LCP Open, multilink Closed
  Open: IPCP, CDP
  Last input 5d04h, output never, output hang never
  Last clearing of "show interface" counters 00:06:42
  Queueing strategy: fifo
  Output queue 0/40, 0 drops; input queue 0/75, 0 drops
  5 minute input rate 0 bits/sec, 0 packets/sec
  5 minute output rate 0 bits/sec, 0 packets/sec
     76 packets input, 3658 bytes, 0 no buffer
     Received 0 broadcasts, 0 runts, 0 giants
     0 input errors, 0 CRC, 0 frame, 0 overrun, 0 ignored, 0 abort
     141 packets output, 2909 bytes, 0 underruns
     0 output errors, 0 collisions, 0 interface resets
     0 output buffer failures, 0 output buffers swapped out
     0 carrier transitions

sf# show ip interface virtual-access 1

Virtual-Access1 is up, line protocol is up
```

```
  Interface is unnumbered.  Using address of Ethernet0 (172.21.114.132)
  Broadcast address is 255.255.255.255
  Peer address is 20.0.0.1
  MTU is 1500 bytes
  Helper address is not set
  Directed broadcast forwarding is enabled
  Outgoing access list is not set
  Inbound  access list is Virtual-Access1#0
  Proxy ARP is enabled
  Security level is default
  Split horizon is enabled
  ICMP redirects are always sent
  ICMP unreachables are always sent
  ICMP mask replies are never sent
  IP fast switching is disabled
```

```
sf# debug ip packet

IP packet debugging is on
sf#
*Apr  4 08:30:42: IP: s=172.21.114.129 (Ethernet0), d=255.255.255.255, len 186, rcvd 2
*Apr  4 08:30:42: IP: s=20.0.0.1 (Virtual-Access1), d=172.21.114.132, len 104, a*Apr  4
08:30:42: IP: s=20.0.0.1 (Virtual-Access1), d=172.21.114.132, len 104, access denied
*Apr  4 08:30:42: IP: s=172.21.114.132 (local), d=20.0.0.1 (Virtual-Access1), len 4,
sending
*Apr  4 08:30:42: IP: s=20.0.0.1 (Virtual-Access1), d=172.21.114.132, len 104, access
denied
*Apr  4 08:30:44: IP: s=20.0.0.1 (Virtual-Access1), d=172.21.114.132, len 104, access
denied
*Apr  4 08:30:44: IP: s=172.21.114.132 (local), d=20.0.0.1 (Virtual-Access1), len 16,
sending
*Apr  4 08:30:44: IP: s=20.0.0.1 (Virtual-Access1), d=172.21.114.132, len 104, access
denied
```

## *IPX Per-User SAP Filters, Using IPXWAN and Virtual Profiles by a Synchronous Interface Example*

In this example, a remote peer (ny) dials in to a synchronous interface on a Cisco network access server (la), which requests user configuration information from an AAA server (radiusd).

### *RADIUS Users File*

```
ny      Password = "welcome"
        User-Service-Type = Framed-User,
        Framed-Protocol = PPP,
        cisco-avpair = "ipx:sap=101 CYBER-01 40.0000.0000.0001 400 10",
        cisco-avpair = "ipx:sap=202 CYBER-02 40.0000.0000.0001 401 10",
        cisco-avpair = "ipx:sap=303 CYBER-03 40.0000.0000.0001 402 10",
        cisco-avpair = "ipx:sap-fltr-out#20=deny 40 101",
        cisco-avpair = "ipx:sap-fltr-out#21=deny 40 202",
        cisco-avpair = "ipx:sap-fltr-out#22=permit -1",
        cisco-avpair = "ipx:sap-fltr-in#23=permit 30 444",
        cisco-avpair = "ipx:sap-fltr-in#23=deny -1"
```

### *Current Remote Peer (ny) Configuration*

```
version 11.3
!
hostname ny
!
enable password lab
!
username la password 7 140017070F0B272E
ip host NY 172.21.114.131
ip name-server 171.69.2.132
ip name-server 198.92.30.32
ipx routing 0000.0c47.090d
ipx internal-network 30
!
interface Ethernet0
 ip address 172.21.114.131 255.255.255.224
!
!
interface Serial1
 no ip address
 encapsulation ppp
 ipx ipxwan 0 unnumbered peer-ny
 clockrate 4000000
!
ipx sap 444 ZEON-4 30.0000.0000.0001 444 10
ipx sap 555 ZEON-5 30.0000.0000.0001 555 10
ipx sap 666 ZEON-6 30.0000.0000.0001 666 10
!
Current Network Access Server (la) Configuration
version 11.3
service timestamps debug uptime
!
hostname la
!
aaa new-model
aaa authentication ppp default radius
aaa authorization network radius
enable password lab
!
username ny password 7 044C0E0A0C2E414B
ip host LA 172.21.114.133
ip name-server 198.92.30.32
ip name-server 171.69.2.132
ipx routing 0000.0c47.12d3
ipx internal-network 40
!
interface Ethernet0
 ip address 172.21.114.133 255.255.255.224
!
interface Virtual-Template1
 no ip address
 ipx ipxwan 0 unnumbered nas-la
 no cdp enable
!
```

```
interface Serial1
 ip unnumbered Ethernet0
 encapsulation ppp
 ipx ipxwan 0 unnumbered nas-la
 ppp authentication chap
!
ipx sap 333 DEEP9 40.0000.0000.0001 999 10
!
virtual-profile vtemplate 1
radius-server host 172.21.114.130
radius-server key rad123
```

### *RADIUS Debug Output*

```
radrecv: Request from host ac157285 code=1, id=23, length=67
    Client-Id = 172.21.114.133
    Client-Port-Id = 1399128065
    User-Name = "ny"
    CHAP-Password = "%"(\012I$\262\352\031\276\024\302\277\225\347z\274"
    User-Service-Type = Framed-User
    Framed-Protocol = PPP
Sending Ack of id 23 to ac157285 (172.21.114.133)
    User-Service-Type = Framed-User
    Framed-Protocol = PPP
    [Vendor 9] cisco-avpair = "ipx:sap=101 CYBER-01 40.0000.0000.0001 400 10"
    [Vendor 9] cisco-avpair = "ipx:sap=202 CYBER-02 40.0000.0000.0001 401 10"
    [Vendor 9] cisco-avpair = "ipx:sap=303 CYBER-03 40.0000.0000.0001 402 10"
    [Vendor 9] cisco-avpair = "ipx:sap-fltr-out#20=deny 40 101"
    [Vendor 9] cisco-avpair = "ipx:sap-fltr-out#21=deny 40 202"
    [Vendor 9] cisco-avpair = "ipx:sap-fltr-out#22=permit -1"
    [Vendor 9] cisco-avpair = "ipx:sap-fltr-in#23=permit 30 444"
    [Vendor 9] cisco-avpair = "ipx:sap-fltr-in#23=deny -1"
```

### *Network Access Server Show Command Output*

```
la# show ipx servers

Codes: S - Static, P - Periodic, E - EIGRP, N - NLSP, H - Holddown, + = detail
5 Total IPX Servers

Table ordering is based on routing and server info

   Type Name                       Net      Address    Port     Route Hops Itf
s   101 CYBER-01                    40.0000.0000.0001:0400      conn  10  Int
s   202 CYBER-02                    40.0000.0000.0001:0401      conn  10  Int
s   303 CYBER-03                    40.0000.0000.0001:0402      conn  10  Int
S   333 DEEP9                       40.0000.0000.0001:0999      conn  10  Int
P   444 ZEON-4                      30.0000.0000.0001:0444      7/01  11  Vi1


ny# show ipx servers

Codes: S - Static, P - Periodic, E - EIGRP, N - NLSP, H - Holddown, + = detail
5 Total IPX Servers
```

```
Table ordering is based on routing and server info

   Type Name                       Net     Address    Port     Route Hops Itf
P   303 CYBER-03                    40.0000.0000.0001:0402      7/01   11  Se1
P   333 DEEP9                       40.0000.0000.0001:0999      7/01   11  Se1
S   444 ZEON-4                      30.0000.0000.0001:0444      conn   10  Int
S   555 ZEON-5                      30.0000.0000.0001:0555      conn   10  Int
S   666 ZEON-6                      30.0000.0000.0001:0666      conn   10  Int

la# show ipx access-lists

IPX sap access list Virtual-Access1#2
    permit 30 444
    deny FFFFFFFF
IPX sap access list Virtual-Access1#3
    deny 40 101
    deny 40 202
    permit FFFFFFFF
```

**PART 9**

# Cost-Control Solutions

# CHAPTER 61

# Configuring the Bandwidth Allocation Control Protocol

The *Bandwidth Allocation Control Protocol* (*BACP*), described in RFC 2125, provides Multilink PPP peers with the capability to govern link utilization. Once peers have successfully negotiated BACP, they can use the Bandwidth Allocation Protocol (BAP), which is a subset of BACP, to negotiate bandwidth allocation. BAP provides a set of rules governing dynamic bandwidth allocation through call control; a defined method for adding and removing links from a multilink bundle for Multilink PPP is used.

The addition of any link to an existing multilink bundle is controlled by a BAP call or callback request message, and the removal of a link can be controlled by a link-drop message.

BACP is designed to operate in both the virtual interface environment and the dialer interface environment. It can operate over any physical interface that is PPP multilink capable and has a dial capability; at initial release, BACP supports ISDN and asynchronous serial interfaces.

BACP provides the following benefits:

- Allows multilink implementations to interoperate by providing call control through the use of link types, speeds, and telephone numbers.
- Controls thrashing caused by links being brought up and removed in a short period of time.
- Ensures that both ends of the link are informed when links are added or removed from a multilink bundle.

For simplicity, the remaining text of this chapter makes no distinction between BACP and BAP. Only BACP is mentioned.

For a complete description of the PPP BACP commands in this chapter, see Chapter 62, "PPP Bandwidth Allocation Control Protocol Commands."

### Configuration Options

PPP BACP can be configured to operate in the following ways:

- Passive mode—(Default) The system accepts incoming calls; the calls might request callback, addition of a link, or removal of a link from a multilink bundle. The system also monitors the multilink load by default.

  Passive mode is for virtual template interfaces or for dialer interfaces.

- Active Mode—The system initiates outbound calls, sets the parameters for outbound calls, and determines whether links should be added to or removed from a multilink bundle. The system also monitors the multilink load by default.

  Active mode is for dialer interfaces, but not for virtual template interfaces. (If you attempt to configure active mode on a virtual template interface, no calls will be made.)

### Restrictions

A virtual or dialer interface must be configured either to make call requests or to make callback requests, but it cannot be configured to do both.

Support of BACP on virtual interfaces in an MMP environment is restricted to incoming calls on the multilink group. Support of BACP for outgoing calls is provided by dialer interface configuration only.

BACP supports only ISDN and asynchronous serial interfaces.

Dialer support is provided only for legacy DDR dialer configurations; BACP cannot be used in conjunction with the Dialer Profiles DDR feature.

BACP is configured on virtual template interfaces and physical interfaces that are multilink capable. For both the virtual template interfaces and the dialer interfaces, BACP requires Multilink PPP and bidirectional dialing to work between the routers that will negotiate control and allocation of bandwidth for the multilink bundle.

### Prerequisites

BACP requires a system only to have the knowledge of its own phone numbers and link types. A system must be able to provide the phone numbers and link type to its peer to satisfy the call control mechanism. (Certain situations might not be able to satisfy this requirement; numbers might not be present because of security considerations.)

Before you configure BACP on an interface, determine the following important information. The router might be unable to connect to a peer if this information is incorrect:

- Type of link (ISDN or analog) to be used. Link types must match on the local and remote ends of the link.
- Line speed needed to reach the remote peer. The speed configured for the local physical interface must be at least that of the link. The **bandwidth** command or the **dialer map** command with the **speed** keyword can be used.

- Local telephone number to be used for incoming PPP BACP calls, if it is different from a rotary group base number or if incoming PPP BACP calls should be directed to a specific number.

  During negotiations with a peer, PPP BACP might respond with a telephone number *delta*, indicating that the peer should modify certain digits of the dialed phone number and dial again to reach the PPP BACP interface or to set up another link.

## Configuring BACP

BACP can be configured on a virtual template interface or on a dialer interface (including dialer rotary groups and ISDN interfaces).

To configure BACP on a selected interface or interface template, complete the following tasks:

**Step 1** Enable BACP.

Passive mode is in effect, and the values of several parameters are set by default when PPP BACP is enabled.

If you can accept *all* the passive mode parameters, do not go to Step 2.

**Step 2** Modify BACP Passive Mode Default Settings.

or

Configure Active Mode BACP.

**Notes**

You can configure one interface in passive mode and another in active mode so that one interface accepts incoming call requests and makes callback requests (passive mode), and the other interface makes call requests and accepts callback requests (active mode).

A dialer or virtual template interface should be configured to reflect the required dial capability of the interface. A dial-in pool (in passive mode) might have no requirement to dial out but might want remote users to add multiple links, with the remote user incurring the cost of the call. Similarly, a dial-out configuration (active mode) suggests that the router is a client, rather than a server, on that link. The active-mode user incurs the cost of additional links.

---

You might need to configure a base telephone number, if it is applicable to your dial-in environment. This is a number that remote users can dial to establish a connection. Otherwise, individual PPP BACP links might need numbers. Information is provided in the task lists for configuring passive mode or active mode PPP BACP. See the **ppp bap number** command options in the task lists.

You can also troubleshoot BACP configuration and operations and monitor interfaces configured for PPP BACP. See the section "Troubleshooting BACP," and the section "Monitoring Interfaces Configured for BACP," later in this chapter for details. For examples of PPP BACP configuration, see the section "BACP Configuration Examples."

## Enable BACP

To enable PPP bandwidth allocation control and dynamic allocation of bandwidth, complete one of the following tasks in interface configuration mode:

| Task | Command |
|---|---|
| Enable PPP BACP bandwidth allocation negotiation. | **ppp multilink bap** |
| or | |
| Enable PPP BACP bandwidth allocation negotiation and enforce mandatory negotiation of BACP for the multilink bundle. | **ppp multilink bap required** |

When PPP BACP is enabled, it is in passive mode by default and the following settings are in effect:

- Allows a peer to initiate link addition.
- Allows a peer to initiate link removal.
- Requests that a peer initiate link addition.
- Waits 20 seconds before timing out on pending actions.
- Waits three seconds before timing out on not receiving a response from a peer.
- Makes only one attempt to call a number.
- Makes up to three retries for sending a request.
- Searches for and logs up to five free dialers.
- Makes three attempts to send a call status indication.
- Adds only ISDN links to a multilink bundle.
- Monitors load.

The default settings will be in effect in the environment for which the **ppp multilink bap** command is entered:

- Virtual template interface, if that is where the command is entered.

  When the command is entered in a virtual template interface, configuration applies to any virtual access interface that is created dynamically under Multilink PPP, the application that defines the template.
- Dialer interface, if that is where the command is entered.

## Modify BACP Passive Mode Default Settings

To modify the default parameter values or to configure additional parameters in passive mode, complete the following tasks, as needed, in interface configuration mode for the interface or virtual template interface that is configured for PPP BACP:

| Task | Command |
|---|---|
| Modify the timeout on pending actions. | **ppp bap timeout pending** *seconds* |
| Modify the timeout on not receiving a response from a peer. | **ppp bap timeout response** *seconds* |
| Modify the number of attempts to call a number. | **ppp bap max dial-attempts** *number* |
| Modify the number of times to send a call status indication. | **ppp bap max ind-retries** *number* |
| Modify the number of retries of a particular request. | **ppp bap max req-retries** *number* |
| Modify the maximum number of free dialers logged. | **ppp bap max dialers** *number* |
| Specify that only analog links can be added to a multilink bundle<br>or<br>Allow both ISDN and analog links to be added. | **ppp bap link types analog**<br><br>**ppp bap link types isdn analog** |
| For all DDR-capable interfaces in the group, specify a primary telephone number for the peer to call for PPP BACP negotiation, if different from any base number defined on the dialer interface or virtual template interface. | **ppp bap number default** *phone-number* |
| For BRI interfaces on which a different number is provided for each B channel, specify the secondary telephone number. | **ppp bap number secondary** *phone-number* |
| Specify a time to wait between outgoing link-drop requests. | **ppp bap drop timer** *seconds* |
| Disable the default monitoring of load and the validation of peer requests against load thresholds. | **no ppp bap monitor load** |

## Configure Active Mode BACP

To configure active mode BACP, complete the following tasks in interface configuration mode for the dialer interface on which BACP was enabled. For your convenience, the tasks that make BACP function in active mode are presented before the tasks that change default parameters or add parameters.

| Task | Command |
|---|---|
| **Enable Active Mode** | |
| Enable the interface to initiate the addition of links to the multilink bundle. | **ppp bap call request** |
| Enable the interface to initiate the addition of links upon peer request. | **ppp bap callback accept** |
| Enable the interface to drop a link without negotiation after receiving no response to retries to send a drop request. | ppp bap drop after-retries |
| Set the time to wait between outgoing call requests. | ppp bap call timer *seconds* |
| **Modify Default Settings** | |
| Modify the timeout on pending actions. | **ppp bap timeout pending** *seconds* |
| Modify the timeout on not receiving a response from a peer. | **ppp bap timeout response** *seconds* |
| Modify the number of attempts to call a number. | **ppp bap max dial-attempts** *number* |
| Modify the number of times to send a call status indication. | **ppp bap max ind-retries** *number* |
| Modify the number of retries of a particular request. | **ppp bap max req-retries** *number* |
| Modify the maximum number of free dialers logged. | **ppp bap max dialers** *number* |
| Specify that only analog links can be added to a multilink bundle<br>or<br>Allow both ISDN and analog links to be added. | **ppp bap link types analog**<br><br>**ppp bap link types isdn analog** |
| For all DDR-capable interfaces in the group, specify a primary telephone number for the peer to call for PPP BACP negotiation, if different from any base number defined on the dialer interface or virtual template interface. | **ppp bap number default** *phone-number* |
| For BRI interfaces on which a different number is provided for each B channel, specify the secondary telephone number. | **ppp bap number secondary** *phone-number* |

When BACP is enabled, multiple dialer maps to one destination are not needed when they differ only by number. That is, once the initial call has been made to create the bundle, further dialing attempts are realized through the BACP phone number negotiation.

Outgoing calls are supported through the use of dialer maps. However, when an initial incoming call creates a dynamic dialer map, the router can dial out if the peer supplies a phone number. This is achieved by the dynamic creation of static dialer maps for BACP. These temporary dialer maps can be displayed by the **show dialer map** command. These temporary dialer maps last only as long as the BACP group lasts and are removed when the BACP group or the associated map is removed.

## Monitoring Interfaces Configured for BACP

To monitor interfaces configured for PPP BACP, complete the following tasks in EXEC mode:

| Task | Command |
|---|---|
| Display information about all PPP BACP multilink bundle groups or a specific, named multilink bundle group. | **show ppp bap group** [*name*] |
| Display information about the BACP queues. | **show ppp bap queues** |
| Display information about the dialer interface, the multilink bundle, and the group members. | **show ppp multilink** |
| Display BACP numbers dialed and the reasons for the calls. | **show dialer** |
| Display configured dynamic and static dialer maps and dynamically created BACP temporary static dialer maps. | **show dialer map** |

## Troubleshooting BACP

To troubleshoot the BACP configuration and operation, complete the following debug tasks:

| Task | Command |
|---|---|
| Display BACP errors, protocol actions, negotiation events, and transitions. | **debug ppp bap** [**error** \| **event** \| **negotiation**] |
| Display information about events affecting multilink bundles established for BACP. | **debug ppp multilink events** |

## BACP Configuration Examples

This section provides the following BACP configuration examples:

- Basic Examples
- Dialer Rotary Group with Different Dial-In Numbers Example
- Passive Mode Dialer Rotary Group Members with One Dial-In Number Example
- PRI Interface with No Defined PPP BACP Number Example
- BRI Interface with No Defined BACP Number Example

### Basic Examples

The following example configures an ISDN BRI interface for BACP to make outgoing calls and prevent the peer from negotiating link drops:

```
interface bri 0
 ip unnumbered ethernet 0
 dialer load-threshold 10 either
 dialer map ip 172.21.13.101 name bap-peer 12345668899
 encapsulation ppp
 ppp multilink bap
 ppp bap call request
 ppp bap callback accept
 no ppp bap call accept
 no ppp bap drop accept
 ppp bap pending timeout 30
 ppp bap number default 5664567
 ppp bap number secondary 5664568
```

In the following example, a dialer rotary group is configured to accept incoming calls:

```
interface async 1
 no ip address
 encapsulation ppp
 dialer rotary-group 1
 ppp bap number default 5663456
!
! Set the bandwidth to suit the modem/line speed on the remote side.
interface bri 0
 no ip address
 bandwidth 38400
 encapsulation ppp
 dialer rotary-group 1
 ppp bap number default 5663457
!
interface bri 1
 no ip address
 encapsulation ppp
 dialer rotary-group 1
 ppp bap number default 5663458
!
interface dialer1
```

```
 ip unnumbered ethernet 0
 encapsulation ppp
 ppp multilink bap
 ppp bap call accept
 ppp bap link types isdn analog
 dialer load threshold 30
 ppp bap timeout pending 60
```

The following example configures a virtual template interface to use BACP in passive mode:

```
multilink virtual-template 1
!
interface virtual-template 1
 ip unnumbered ethernet 0
 encapsulation ppp
 ppp multilink bap
 ppp authentication chap callin
```

The bundle is created from any multilink-capable interface. In the following example, the bundle is created on a BRI interface:

```
interface bri 0
 no ip address
 encapsulation ppp
 ppp multilink
 ppp bap number default 4000
 ppp bap number secondary 4001
```

## Dialer Rotary Group with Different Dial-In Numbers Example

In this example, a dialer rotary group that has four members, each with a different number, accepts incoming dial attempts. The dialer interface does not have a base phone number; the interface that is used to establish the first link in the multilink bundle will provide the appropriate number from its configuration.

```
interface bri 0
 no ip address
 encapsulation ppp
 isdn spid1 01234567890
 dialer rotary-group 1
 no fair-queue
 no cdp enable
 ppp bap number default 6666666
!
interface bri 1
 no ip address
 encapsulation ppp
 isdn spid1 01234567891
 dialer rotary-group 1
 no fair-queue
 no cdp enable
 ppp bap number default 6666667
!
interface bri 2
```

```
 no ip address
 encapsulation ppp
 isdn spid1 01234567892
 dialer rotary-group 1
 no fair-queue
 no cdp enable
 ppp bap number default 6666668
!
interface bri 3
 no ip address
 encapsulation ppp
 isdn spid1 01234567893
 dialer rotary-group 1
 no fair-queue
 no cdp enable
 ppp bap number default 6666669
!
interface dialer 1
 ip unnumbered Ethernet0
 encapsulation ppp
 dialer in-band
 dialer idle-timeout 300
 dialer-group 1
 no fair-queue
 no cdp enable
 ppp authentication chap
 ppp multilink bap
 ppp bap call accept
 ppp bap callback request
 ppp bap timeout pending 20
 ppp bap timeout response 2
 ppp bap max dial-attempts 2
 ppp bap monitor load
```

### Passive Mode Dialer Rotary Group Members with One Dial-In Number Example

In this example, a dialer rotary group with two members, each with the same number, accepts incoming dial attempts. The dialer interface has a base phone number because each of its member interfaces is in a hunt group and the same number can be used to access each individual interface.

```
interface bri 0
 no ip address
 encapsulation ppp
 isdn spid1 01234567890
 dialer rotary-group 1
 no fair-queue
 no cdp enable
!
interface bri 1
 no ip address
 encapsulation ppp
 isdn spid1 01234567890
 dialer rotary-group 1
 no fair-queue
 no cdp enable
```

```
!
interface dialer 1
 ip unnumbered Ethernet0
 encapsulation ppp
 dialer in-band
 dialer idle-timeout 300
 dialer-group 1
 no fair-queue
 no cdp enable
 ppp authentication chap
 ppp multilink bap
 ppp bap call accept
 ppp bap callback request
 ppp bap timeout pending 20
 ppp bap timeout response 2
 ppp bap max dial-attempts 2
 ppp bap monitor load
 ppp bap number default 6666666
```

### PRI Interface with No Defined PPP BACP Number Example

In the following example, a PRI interface has no BACP number defined and accepts incoming dial attempts (passive mode). The PRI interface has no base phone number defined, so each attempt to add a link would result in a delta of zero being provided to the calling peer. To establish the bundle, the peer should then dial the same number as it originally used.

```
interface serial 0:23
 ip unnumbered Ethernet0
 encapsulation ppp
 dialer in-band
 dialer idle-timeout 300
 dialer-group 1
 no fair-queue
 no cdp enable
 ppp authentication chap
 ppp multilink bap
 ppp bap call accept
 ppp bap callback request
 ppp bap timeout pending 20
 ppp bap timeout response 2
 ppp bap max dial-attempts 2
 ppp bap monitor load
```

### BRI Interface with No Defined BACP Number Example

In the following example, the BRI interface has no base phone number defined. The number that it uses to establish the bundle is that from the dialer map, and all phone delta operations are applied to that number.

```
interface bri 0
 ip unnumbered Ethernet0
 encapsulation ppp
 dialer in-band
 dialer idle-timeout 300
```

```
dialer map ip 10.1.1.1 name bap_peer speed 56 19998884444
dialer-group 1
no fair-queue
no cdp enable
ppp authentication chap
ppp multilink bap
ppp bap call request
ppp bap timeout pending 20
ppp bap timeout response 2
ppp bap max dial-attempts 2
ppp bap monitor load
```

CHAPTER 62

# PPP Bandwidth Allocation Control Protocol Commands

This chapter describes the commands used to configure the Point-to-Point Protocol (PPP) Bandwidth Allocation Control Protocol (BACP) for dial-up solutions on your router.

For information about configuring BACP for dial-up solutions, see Chapter 61, "Configuring the Bandwidth Allocation Control Protocol." For PPP configuration on a router or an access server, see Chapter 25, "Configuring Media-Independent PPP and Multilink PPP," and Chapter 27, "Configuring Asynchronous PPP and SLIP." For PPP commands, see Chapter 26, "Media-Independent PPP and Multilink PPP Commands," and Chapter 28, "Asynchronous PPP and SLIP Commands." For more information about BACP, see RFC 2125.

## PPP BAP CALL

To set PPP BACP call parameters, use the **ppp bap call** interface configuration command. To disable processing of a specific type of incoming connection, use the **no** form of this command.

**ppp bap call** {**accept** | **request** | **timer** *seconds*}
**no ppp bap call** {**accept** | **request** | **timer**}

| *Syntax* | *Description* |
|---|---|
| **accept** | Peer initiates link addition. This is the default. |
| **request** | Local side initiates link addition. |
| **timer** *seconds* | Number of seconds to wait between call requests the router sends, in the range 2 to 120 seconds. No default value is set. |

### Default

**accept**—Peers can initiate the addition of links to a multilink bundle.

The timer is disabled.

### Command Mode

Interface configuration

### Usage Guidelines

This command first appeared in Cisco IOS Release 11.3.

This command can be included in a virtual interface template for configuring virtual interfaces or can be used to configure a dialer interface.

### Example

In the following example, a dialer interface is configured to accept calls. Accepting calls is the default, but the command is included for the sake of the example.

```
interface dialer 1
 ip unnumbered ethernet 0
 encapsulation ppp
 ppp multilink bap
 ppp bap call accept
 ppp bap link types isdn analog
 dialer load threshold 30
 ppp bap timeout pending 60
```

### Related Commands

Search online to find documentation for related commands.

**ppp bap callback**
**ppp bap drop**
**ppp bap link types**

## PPP BAP CALLBACK

To enable PPP BACP callback and set callback parameters, use the **ppp bap callback** interface configuration command. To remove the PPP BACP callback configuration, use the **no** form of this command.

**ppp bap callback** {**accept** | **request** | **timer** *seconds*}
**no ppp bap callback** {**accept** | **request** | **timer**}

| *Syntax* | *Description* |
|---|---|
| **accept** | Local router initiates link addition upon peer notification. |

| | |
|---|---|
| **request** | Local router requests that a peer initiate link addition. |
| **timer** *seconds* | Number of seconds to wait between callback requests the router sends, in the range 2 to 120 seconds. Disabled by default. |

### Default

Callback is disabled, and no callback parameters are set.

The timer is disabled.

### Command Mode

Interface configuration

### Usage Guidelines

This command first appeared in Cisco IOS Release 11.3.

### Example

In the following example, a BRI interface is configured for active mode BACP:

```
interface bri 0
 ip unnumbered ethernet 0
 dialer load-threshold 10 either
 dialer map ip 172.21.13.101 name bap-peer 14085778899
 encapsulation ppp
 ppp multilink bap
 ppp bap call request
 ppp bap callback accept
 no ppp bap call accept
 no ppp bap drop accept
 ppp bap pending timeout 30
 ppp bap number default 5664567
 ppp bap number secondary 5664568
```

### Related Commands

Search online to find documentation for related commands.

**ppp bap call**
**ppp bap drop**
**ppp bap link types**

## PPP BAP DROP

To set parameters for removing links from a multilink bundle, use the **ppp bap drop** interface configuration command. To disable a specific type of default processing, use the **no** form of this command.

> **ppp bap drop** {**accept** | **after-retries** | **request** | **timer** *seconds*}
> **no ppp bap drop** {**accept** | **after-retries** | **request** | **timer**}

| *Syntax* | *Description* |
|---|---|
| **accept** | Peer can initiate link removal. Enabled by default. |
| **after-retries** | Local router can remove the link without BACP negotiation when no response to the drop requests arrives. |
| **request** | Local router can initiate removal of a link. Enabled by default. |
| **timer** *seconds* | Number of seconds to wait between drop requests sent. |

### Default

**accept, request:** Peers can initiate link removal and this router also can initiate link removal.

**no ppp bap drop after-retries:** The link is not dropped when there is no response to drop requests.

**timer:** disabled; no default value is defined.

### Command Mode

Interface configuration

### Usage Guidelines

This command first appeared in Cisco IOS Release 11.3.

The **no ppp bap drop accept** command disables the router's ability to respond favorably to link drop requests from a peer. However, the router can still remove the link when it receives such requests.

The **no ppp bap drop after-retries** command is the default behavior; the **ppp bap drop after-retries** command must be entered explicitly to be effective.

The **no ppp bap drop request** command disables the router's ability to send link drop requests to a peer. However, the peer can still remove the link on its own behalf; for example, when there is too little traffic to justify keeping the link up.

The **ppp bap max** command specifies the maximum number of requests and retries.

### Example

The following partial example sets a 60-second wait between drop requests:

```
ppp bap drop timer 60
```

### Related Commands

Search online to find documentation for related commands.

**ppp bap max**

## PPP BAP LINK TYPES

To specify the types of links that can be included in a specific multilink bundle, use the **ppp bap link types** interface configuration command. To remove a type of interface that was previously allowed to be added, use the **no** form of this command.

**ppp bap link types** [**isdn**] [**analog**]
**no ppp bap link types** [**isdn**] [**analog**]

| *Syntax* | *Description* |
|---|---|
| **isdn** | (Optional) ISDN interfaces can be added to a multilink bundle. This is the default. |
| **analog** | (Optional) Asynchronous serial interfaces can be added to a multilink bundle. |

### *Default*

**isdn**

### *Command Mode*

Interface configuration

### *Usage Guidelines*

This command first appeared in Cisco IOS Release 11.3.

The choice of keywords must suit the interfaces configured for Multilink PPP. For example, if you have configured a dialer rotary with only ISDN interfaces, only the **isdn** keyword would be appropriate. If the configuration allows both ISDN and asynchronous interfaces, both **isdn** and **analog** keywords could be used; the multilink bundle could then consist of both ISDN and asynchronous links. BACP dynamically determines which interfaces are applicable.

### *Example*

In the following example, a dialer interface is configured for passive mode BACP and for both ISDN and asynchronous serial links:

```
interface dialer 1
 ip unnumbered ethernet 0
 encapsulation ppp
 ppp multilink bap
 ppp bap call accept
 ppp bap link types isdn analog
 dialer load threshold 30
 ppp bap timeout pending 60
```

### *Related Commands*

Search online to find documentation for related commands.

ppp bap call
ppp bap callback

### PPP BAP MAX

To set upper limits on the number of retransmissions for PPP BACP, use the **ppp bap max** interface configuration command. To remove any retry limit, use the **no** form of this command.

**ppp bap max** {**dial-attempts** *number* | **ind-retries** *number* | **req-retries** *number* | **dialers** *number*}

**no ppp bap max** {**dial-attempts** | **ind-retries** | **req-retries** | **dialers** *number*}

| *Syntax* | *Description* |
|---|---|
| **dial-attempts** *number* | Maximum number of dial attempts to any destination number, in the range 1 to 3. The default is 1 dial attempt. |
| **ind-retries** *number* | Maximum number of retries of a call status indication message, in the range 1 to 10. The default is 3 indication retries. |
| **req-retries** *number* | Maximum number of retries for a particular request, in the range 1 to 5. The default is 3 request retries. |
| **dialers** *number* | Maximum number of free dialers logged, in the range 1 to 10. The default is 5 dialers. |

#### *Default*

1 dial attempt
3 indication retries
3 request retries
5 searches for free dialers

#### *Command Mode*

Interface configuration

#### *Usage Guidelines*

This command first appeared in Cisco IOS Release 11.3.

In compliance with RFC 2125, the **no** form of this command explicitly removes any status indication retry limit and is displayed in the router configuration.

The **ppp bap max dialers** command works in conjunction with the interface commands **dialer rotor** and **dialer priority**, which can be used to determine free dialers based on the priority or the best available. Dialers include all interfaces that are configured under the dialer group leader (the dialer interface itself). The dialer group leader is displayed as the Master Interface in the **show ppp bap group** output.

BAP bases its link type and phone number decisions on the ordering of the interfaces. This is suited to a mixed media environment of both ISDN and analog interfaces, where it may be desirable to choose the ISDN link over the asynchronous or vice versa.

Note that this also will limit the number of potential phone numbers which can be included in a CallResponse or CallbackRequest; the maximum number is limited to 20. For example, ten BRI interfaces with two numbers per interface.

### *Example*

The following partial example accepts the default number of attempts to dial a number and the default number of indication retries, but configures a limit of four times to send requests:

```
ppp bap max req-retries 4
```

### *Related Commands*

Search online to find documentation for related commands.

**dialer priority**
**dialer rotor**
**ppp bap drop**
**ppp bap monitor load**
**ppp bap timeout**
**show ppp bap group**

## PPP BAP MONITOR LOAD

To validate peer requests to add or remove links against the current bundle load and the defined dialer load threshold, use the **ppp bap monitor load** interface configuration command. To specify that incoming link addition requests are not to be subject to the bundle load threshold, use the **no** form of this command.

**ppp bap monitor load**
**no ppp bap monitor load**

### *Syntax Description*

This command has no arguments or keywords.

### *Default*

Enabled

### *Command Mode*

Interface configuration

### *Usage Guidelines*

This command first appeared in Cisco IOS Release 11.3.

If the load is being monitored and the incoming peer requests that a link be dropped when the current traffic load is above the dialer load (that is, there is enough traffic to justify the current number of links), the router will not drop the link. In addition, when the traffic falls below the threshold, BACP tries to drop a link.

The **no** form of the command indicates that incoming peer requests to add a link are not subject to the bundle load threshold. However, other criteria must be met before a favorable response is sent.

#### *Example*

The following partial example configures BACP not to validate peer requests against the current bundle load and the configured dialer load threshold:

```
no ppp bap monitor load
```

#### *Related Commands*

Search online to find documentation for related commands.

**dialer-load threshold**

### PPP BAP NUMBER

To specify a local telephone number that peers can dial to establish a multilink bundle, use the **ppp bap number** interface configuration command. To remove a previously configured number, use the **no** form of this command.

**ppp bap number** {**default** *phone-number* | **secondary** *phone-number*}
**no ppp bap number** [**default** | **secondary**]

| *Syntax* | *Description* |
|---|---|
| **default** *phone-number* | Primary (base) phone number for this interface, the number that can be used for incoming dial calls. |
| **secondary** *phone-number* | Telephone number for the second B channel. Applies only to BRI interfaces that have a different number for each B channel or to dialer interfaces that are BRIs. |

#### *Default*

No base number is provided.

#### *Command Mode*

Interface configuration

#### *Usage Guidelines*

This command first appeared in Cisco IOS Release 11.3.

If a peer requests that a number be supplied and no PPP BACP default number is defined, it might not be possible for the peer to access the interface. However, the peer can access the interface if it has the number already or the number it dialed originally is the same as the number for establishing a Multilink PPP bundle.

This command is applicable on both the dialer interface and the individual physical interfaces.

**NOTES**

During BACP negotiations between peers, the called party indicates the number to call for BACP if it is different from the number the peer originally dialed. The called party responds with information about the phone number *delta* (the changes to be made in the rightmost digits dialed). This information indicates the number of digits that are different from the number originally dialed and what those digits should be.

For example, if the remote peer dialed 2157659876, and the **ppp bap number** command had the default number 2157659912, the local router would respond "3 | 912." In the response, a vertical bar ( | ) is used to divide the number of digits to change from the number sequence to use instead. In the "3 | 912" response, the local router instructs the calling interface to replace the rightmost three digits with "912" for BACP.

### *Examples*

The following example configures a physical interface with both a default number and a secondary number:

```
interface bri 0
 ip unnumbered ethernet 0
 dialer load-threshold 10 either
 dialer map ip 172.21.13.101 name bap-peer 14085778899
 encapsulation ppp
 ppp multilink bap
 ppp bap call request
 ppp bap callback accept
 no ppp bap call accept
 no ppp bap drop accept
 ppp bap pending timeout 30
 ppp bap number default 5664567
 ppp bap number secondary 5664568
```

In the following example, a PRI with no BAP number defined accepts incoming dial attempts. The PRI interface has no base phone number defined, so each attempt to add a link would result in a delta of zero being provided to the calling peer. The calling peer should then dial the same number as it originally used to establish the bundle.

```
interface serial 0:23
 ip unnumbered Ethernet0
 encapsulation ppp
 dialer in-band
 dialer idle-timeout 300
 dialer-group 1
 no fair-queue
```

```
no cdp enable
ppp authentication chap
ppp multilink bap
ppp bap call accept
ppp bap callback request
ppp bap timeout pending 20
ppp bap timeout response 2
ppp bap max dial-attempts 2
ppp bap monitor load
```

In the following example, a BRI interface with no BAP number defined initiates outgoing dial attempts. The BRI interface has no base phone number defined, so the number that it uses to establish the bundle is that from the dialer map, and all phone delta operations are applied to that number.

```
interface bri 0
 ip unnumbered Ethernet0
 encapsulation ppp
 dialer in-band
 dialer idle-timeout 300
 dialer map ip 10.1.1.1 name bap_peer speed 56 19998884444
 dialer-group 1
 no fair-queue
 no cdp enable
 ppp authentication chap
 ppp multilink bap
 ppp bap call request
 ppp bap timeout pending 20
 ppp bap timeout response 2
 ppp bap max dial-attempts 2
 ppp bap monitor load
!
```

### *Related Commands*

Search online to find documentation for related commands.

**ppp bap call**
**ppp bap callback**

## PPP BAP TIMEOUT

To specify nondefault timeout values for PPP BACP pending actions and responses, use the **ppp bap timeout** interface configuration command. To reset the response timeout to the default value, or to remove a pending timeout entirely, use the **no** form of this command.

**ppp bap timeout** {**pending** *seconds* | **response** *seconds*}
**no ppp bap timeout** {**pending** | **response**}

| *Syntax* | *Description* |
|---|---|
| **pending** *seconds* | Number of seconds to wait before timing out pending actions, in the range 2 to 180 seconds. The default is 20 seconds. |
| **response** *seconds* | Number of seconds to wait for a response before timing out, in the range 2 to 120 seconds. The default is 3 seconds. |

### *Default*

Enabled

**pending**—20 seconds
**response**—3 seconds

### *Command Mode*

Interface configuration

### *Usage Guidelines*

This command first appeared in Cisco IOS Release 11.3.

The **no ppp bap timeout response** command resets the timer to the default value.The **no ppp bap timeout pending** command removes the pending-action timeout entirely (in compliance with the BACP specification).

### *Example*

The following example configures BACP to wait 45 seconds before timing out pending actions:

```
interface dialer 1
 ip unnumbered ethernet 0
 encapsulation ppp
 ppp multilink bap
 ppp bap call accept
 ppp bap link types isdn analog
 dialer load threshold 30
 ppp bap timeout pending 45
```

### *Related Commands*

Search online to find documentation for related commands.

**ppp bap call**
**ppp bap callback**
**ppp bap drop**
**ppp bap max**

### PPP MULTILINK

To enable Multilink PPP (MLP) on an interface and, optionally, to enable dynamic bandwidth allocation, use the **ppp multilink** interface configuration command. To disable Multilink PPP or, optionally, to disable only dynamic bandwidth allocation, use the **no** form of this command.

**ppp multilink** [**bap**]
**no ppp multilink** [**bap** [**required**]]

| *Syntax* | *Description* |
|---|---|
| **bap** | (Optional) Specifies bandwidth allocation control negotiation and dynamic allocation of bandwidth on a link. |
| **required** | Enforces mandatory negotiation of BACP for the multilink bundle. The multilink bundle is disconnected if BACP is not negotiated. |

#### *Defaults*

Disabled. When BACP is enabled, the defaults are to accept calls and to set the timeout pending at 30 seconds.

#### *Command Mode*

Interface configuration

#### *Usage Guidelines*

This command first appeared in Cisco IOS Release 11.3.

The **no** form of the command without the **bap** keyword disables both MLP and BACP on the interface.

This command applies only to interfaces that use PPP encapsulation.

PPP compression is allowed with MLP.

This command with the **bap** keyword must be used prior to configuring any **ppp bap** commands and options. If the **bap required** option is configured and a reject of the options is received, the multilink bundle is torn down.

When BACP negotiation is enabled by this command, the following values are used during negotiations to identify the protocols:

| Protocol | Hexadecimal Value |
|---|---|
| BACP | 0xC02B |
| BAP | 0xC02D |

The **dialer load-threshold** command is used to enable a rotary group to bring up additional links and to add them to a multilink bundle.

When MLP is configured, the **dialer-load threshold 1** command no longer keeps a multilink bundle of any number of links connected indefinitely and the **dialer-load threshold 2** command no longer keeps a multilink bundle of 2 links connected indefinitely. If you want a multilink bundle to be connected indefinitely, you must set a very high idle timer.

### *Related Commands*

Search online to find documentation for related commands.

**dialer-group**
**dialer idle-timeout**
**dialer load-threshold**
**encapsulation ppp**
**ppp authentication**
**ppp bap call**
**ppp bap timeout**
**ppp compress**

## SHOW DIALER MAP

To display configured dynamic and static dialer maps and dynamically created PPP BACP temporary static dialer maps, use the **show dialer map** EXEC command.

**show dialer map**

### *Syntax Description*

This command has no arguments or keywords.

### *Command Mode*

EXEC

### *Usage Guidelines*

This command first appeared in Cisco IOS Release 11.3.

### *Sample Display*

The following is sample output from the **show dialer map** command. The dialer maps are grouped by network address. When multiple dialer maps exist for the same network address, the dialer maps differ only by phone number. In this output, the dialer maps marked "BAP" are temporary dialer maps the PPP BACP creates when a peer calls from a different phone number than is configured or when a peer calls from a number that does not appear in an existing map. The temporary dialer maps allow PPP BACP to make outgoing calls to the peers.

```
bap_peer# show dialer map
```

```
Static dialer map ip 6.1.1.1 name peer_1 on Dialer1
Static dialer map ip 6.1.1.2 name peer_2 on Dialer1
BAP dialer map ip 6.1.1.2 name peer_2 on Dialer1
Dynamic dialer map ip 6.1.1.3 name peer_3 on Dialer1
BAP dialer map ip 6.1.1.3 name peer_3 on Dialer1
```

Table 62–1 describes the significant fields in this output.

**Table 62–1** *Show Dialer Map Field Descriptions*

| Field | Description |
|---|---|
| Static dialer map ip 6.1.1.1 | This is a configured static dialer map to call the specified protocol address. |
| name peer_1 | Name of the remote peer. |
| on Dialer1 | The physical or logical dialer interface on which the static map is configured. |
| BAP dialer map ip 6.1.1.2 | This is a temporary dialer map that was created by PPP BACP for the particular destination with a different phone number from that of any existing maps.<br>It will be removed when the BACP group is removed or the last remaining map to that destination is removed. |
| Dynamic dialer map ip 6.1.1.3 | Dialer map dynamically created when a peer called. |
| BAP dialer map ip 6.1.1.3 name peer_3 | Temporary static dialer map created by PPP BACP when required. It will be removed when the BACP group is removed or when the dynamic dialer map disappears. |

### *Related Commands*

Search online to find documentation for related commands.

**dialer map**

## SHOW PPP BAP

To display the configuration settings and runtime status for a multilink bundle, use the **show ppp bap** EXEC command.

**show ppp bap** {**group** [*name*] | **queues**}

| *Syntax* | *Description* |
|---|---|
| **group** [*name*] | Displays information about all or, optionally, a specific BACP bundle group. |
| **queues** | Displays information about the BACP queues. |

### *Command Mode*

Privileged EXEC

### *Usage Guidelines*

This command first appeared in Cisco IOS Release 11.3.

### *Sample Display*

The following is sample output from the **show ppp bap group** command for the bundle group named *bap-peer*:

```
Group bap-peer (multilink), id 35, peer has precedence, state Idle
Master interface: Dialer1
Outgoing requests: Call, Link Drop
Incoming requests: Call, Callback, Link Drop
Original number dialed 5773926
Transmit queue size threshold is not set
Peer link addition dependent upon load
Timers (secs): Call not set, Callback not set, Link Drop not set,
               Response 30, Pending 20
Retries: Request 3, Dial 1, Indication no limit
Link removal after 3 link drop retries not set
```

Table 62–2 describes the significant fields in this display.

**Table 62–2** *Show PPP BAP Field Descriptions*

| **Field** | **Description** |
|---|---|
| Group bap-peer (multilink), id 35 | Group name and internally assigned ID. "(multilink)" indicates the governing protocol. |
| peer has precedence | In BACP negotiations called "race condition scenarios" in the BACP specification, this peer is deemed to have precedence over the remote peer. |
| state Idle | Internal state. |
| Outgoing requests | Current requests configured for outbound negotiation. |
| Incoming requests | Current requests allowed inbound negotiation. |
| Peer link addition dependent upon load | Router is monitoring the load and subjecting requests to the load settings. |

**Table 62–2** *Show PPP BAP Field Descriptions, Continued*

| Field | Description |
|---|---|
| Timers (secs): Call not set, Callback not set, Link Drop not set, Response 30, Pending 20 | Settings for specified timers. |
| Retries: Request 3, Dial 1, Indication no limit | Limits set on specified types of retransmissions. |
| Link removal after 3 link drop retries not set | The link will not be removed after no response to the link removal request because default behavior was not changed and the relevant link drop parameter was not set. |

### *Related Commands*

Search online to find documentation for related commands.

**show ppp multilink**

## SHOW PPP MULTILINK

To display bundle information for the Multilink PPP bundles, use the **show ppp multilink** EXEC command.

**show ppp multilink**

### *Syntax Description*

This command has no arguments or keywords.

### *Command Mode*

EXEC

### *Usage Guidelines*

This command first appeared in Cisco IOS Release 11.2.

### *Sample Displays*

The following is the output when no bundles are on a system:

```
Router# show ppp multilink

No active bundles
```

The following is sample output when a single Multilink PPP bundle (named *rudder*) is on a system:

```
Router# show ppp multilink
```

```
Bundle rudder, 3 members, first link is BRI0: B-channel 1
0 lost fragments, 8 reordered, 0 unassigned, sequence 0x1E/0x1E rcvd/sent
```

The following is sample output when two active bundles are on a system. Subsequent bundles would be displayed below the previous bundle.

```
Router# show ppp multilink

Bundle rudder, 3 members, first link is BRI0: B-Channel 1
  0 lost fragments, 8 reordered, 0 unassigned, sequence 0x1E/0x1E rcvd/sent
Bundle dallas, 4 members, first link is BRI2: B-Channel 1
  0 lost fragments, 28 reordered, 0 unassigned, sequence 0x12E/0x12E rcvd/sent
```

The following example shows output when a stack group has been created. On stack group member *systema*, Multilink PPP bundle *hansolo* has bundle interface *Virtual-Access4*. Two child interfaces are joined to this bundle interface. The first is a local PRI channel (serial 0:4), and the second is an interface from stack group member *systemb*.

```
systema# show ppp multilink

Bundle hansolo 2 members, Master link is Virtual-Access4
0 lost fragments, 0 reordered, 0 unassigned, 100/255 load
0 discarded,  0 lost received, sequence 40/66 rcvd/sent
members 2
 Serial0:4
 systemb:Virtual-Access6    (1.1.1.1)
```

The following is sample output when the PPP BACP is enabled for the multilink bundle:

```
systema# show ppp multilink

Bundle bap-peer, 1 member, Master link is Virtual-Access1
Bundle under BAP control
Dialer Interface is Dialer1
  0 lost fragments, 0 reordered, 0 unassigned, sequence 0x0/0x0 rcvd/sent
  0 discarded, 0 lost received, 1/255 load

Member links: 1
BRI0:1

Discriminators Local Remote
BRI0:1            24      1
```

Table 62–3 describes significant fields when PPP BACP is enabled.

**Table 62–3** *Show PPP Multilink Field Descriptions*

| **Field** | **Description** |
|---|---|
| Bundle | Configured name of the multilink bundle. |
| 1 member | Number of interfaces in the group. |
| Master link is Virtual-Access1 | Multilink bundle virtual interface. |

**Table 62–3** *Show PPP Multilink Field Descriptions, Continued*

| Field | Description |
|---|---|
| Bundle under BAP control | Multilink bundle is controlled and bandwidth is allocated by BACP. |
| Dialer Interface is Dialer1 | Name of the interface that dials the calls. |
| 1/255 load | Load on the link in the range 1/255 to 255/255. (255/255 is a 100% load.) |
| Member links: 1 | Number of child interfaces. |
| BRI0:1 | Identity of the child interface. Link 1 is using physical interface BRI 0:1. |
| Discriminators Local Remote<br>BRI0:1 24 1 | LCP link discriminators, which are identifiers negotiated for each link in the bundle. This information is specific to BACP. BACP uses these discriminators to determine which link to drop during negotiations. |

CHAPTER 63

# Configuring PPP Callback for DDR

PPP callback provides a client/server relationship between the endpoints of a point-to-point connection. PPP callback allows a router to request that a dial-up peer router call back. The callback feature can be used to control access and toll costs between the routers.

When PPP callback is configured on the participating routers, the calling router (the callback client) passes authentication information to the remote router (the callback server), which uses the host name and dial string authentication information to determine whether to place a return call. If the authentication is successful, the callback server disconnects and then places a return call. The remote username of the return call is used to associate it with the initial call so that packets can be transmitted.

Both routers on a point-to-point link must be configured for PPP callback; one must function as a callback client, and one must be configured as a callback server. The callback client must be configured to initiate PPP callback requests, and the callback server must be configured to accept PPP callback requests and place return calls.

This feature implements the following callback specifications of RFC 1570:

- For the client—Option 0, location is determined by user authentication.
- For the server—Option 0, location is determined by user authentication; Option 1, dialing string; and Option 3, E.164 number.

Return calls are made through the same dialer rotary group but not necessarily the same line as the initial call.

**NOTES**

If the return call fails (because the line is not answered or the line is busy), no retry occurs. If the callback server has no interface available when attempting the return call, it does not retry.

For an example of configuring PPP callback, see section, "PPP Callback Example," later in this chapter. For a complete description of the PPP callback commands in this chapter, see Chapter 64, "PPP Callback Commands for DDR."

## Configuring a Router as a Callback Client

To configure a router interface as a callback client, complete the following tasks beginning in global configuration mode:

| Task | | Command |
|---|---|---|
| **Step 1** | Specify the interface. | **interface** *type number* |
| **Step 2** | Enable DDR. Set parity on synchronous serial interfaces and asynchronous interfaces. | **dialer in-band [no-parity \| odd-parity]** |
| **Step 3** | Enable PPP encapsulation. | **encapsulation ppp** |
| **Step 4** | Enable CHAP or Password Authentication Protocol (PAP) authentication. | **ppp authentication chap**<br>or<br>**ppp authentication pap** |
| **Step 5** | Map the next-hop address to the host name and phone number. | **dialer map** *protocol next-hop-address* **name** *hostname dial-string* |
| **Step 6** | Enable the interface to request PPP callback for this callback map class. | **ppp callback request** |
| **Step 7** | (Optional) Configure a dialer hold queue to store packets for this callback map class. | **dialer hold-queue** *packets* **timeout** *seconds* |

## Configuring a Router as a Callback Server

To configure a router as a callback server, complete the following tasks beginning in global configuration mode:

| Task | | Command |
|---|---|---|
| **Step 1** | Specify the interface and enter interface configuration mode. | **interface** *type number* |

| Task | | Command |
|---|---|---|
| **Step 2** | Enable DDR. Specify parity, if needed, on synchronous or asynchronous serial interfaces. | **dialer in-band** [**no-parity** \| **odd-parity**] |
| **Step 3** | Enable PPP encapsulation. | **encapsulation ppp** |
| **Step 4** | Enable CHAP or PAP authentication. | **ppp authentication** {**chap** \| **pap**} |
| **Step 5** | Map the next-hop address to the host name and phone number, using the name of the map class established for PPP callback on this interface. | **dialer map** *protocol address* **name** *hostname* **class** *classname dial-string* |
| **Step 6** | (Optional) Configure a dialer hold queue to store packets to be transferred when the callback connection is established. | **dialer hold-queue** *number* **timeout** *seconds* |
| **Step 7** | (Optional) Configure a timeout period between calls. | **dialer enable-timeout** *seconds* |
| **Step 8** | Configure the interface to accept PPP callback. | **ppp callback accept** |
| **Step 9** | (ISDN only) Configure the time to wait before another call is placed on a B channel, to allow prior call to be torn down completely. | **isdn fast-rollover-delay** *seconds* |
| **Step 10** | (Optional) Enable callback security, if desired. | **dialer callback-secure** |
| **Step 11** | Return to global configuration mode. | **exit** |
| **Step 12** | Configure a dialer map class for PPP callback. | **map-class dialer** *classname* |
| **Step 13** | Configure a dialer map class as a callback server. | **dialer callback-server** [**username**] |

**NOTES**

On the PPP callback server, the **dialer enable-timeout** functions as the timer for returning calls to the callback client.

## PPP CALLBACK EXAMPLE

The following example configures a PPP callback server and client to call each other.

The PPP callback server is configured on an ISDN BRI interface in a router in Atlanta. The callback server requires an enable timeout and a map class to be defined.

The PPP callback client is configured on an ISDN BRI interface in a router in Dallas. The callback client does not require an enable timeout and a map class to be defined.

### *PPP Callback Server*

```
interface bri 0
 ip address 7.1.1.7 255.255.255.0
 encapsulation ppp
 dialer callback-secure
 dialer enable-timeout 2
 dialer map ip 7.1.1.8 name atlanta class dial1 81012345678901
 dialer-group 1
 ppp callback accept
 ppp authentication chap
!
map-class dialer dial1
 dialer callback-server username
```

### *PPP Callback Client*

```
interface bri 0
 ip address 7.1.1.8 255.255.255.0
 encapsulation ppp
 dialer map ip 7.1.1.7 name dallas 81012345678902
 dialer-group 1
 ppp callback request
 ppp authentication chap
```

# CHAPTER 64

# PPP Callback Commands for DDR

This chapter describes the commands used for configuring PPP callback for DDR and ISDN.

For information about the configuration steps used to configure PPP callback, see Chapter 63, "Configuring PPP Callback for DDR." Many of the **dialer** commands used in this chapter are described in the chapters found in Part V, "Dial-on-Demand Routing." See RFC 1570 for more information about PPP callback.

## DIALER CALLBACK-SECURE

To enable callback security, use the **dialer callback-secure** interface configuration command.

**dialer callback-secure**

### *Syntax Description*

This command has no arguments or keywords.

### *Default*

Disabled

### *Command Mode*

Interface configuration

### *Usage Guidelines*

This command ensures that the initial call is always disconnected at the receiving end and that the return call is made only if the username is configured for callback. If the username (*hostname* in the **dialer map** command) is not configured for callback, the initial call stays up and no return call is made.

### Example

The following partial example configures BRI 0 with the commands required to make it function as the callback server on the shared network. Callback security is enabled on BRI 0.

```
interface BRI0
 ip address 171.1.1.9 255.255.255.0
 encapsulation ppp
 dialer callback-secure
 dialer enable-timeout 2
 dialer map ip 171.1.1.8 name atlanta class dial1 81012345678901
 dialer-group 1
 ppp callback accept
 ppp authentication chap
!
map-class dialer dial1
 dialer callback-server username
```

### Related Commands

Search online to find documentation for related commands.

**dialer callback-server**
**dialer map**
**map-class**
**ppp callback accept**

## DIALER CALLBACK-SERVER

To enable an interface to make return calls when callback is successfully negotiated, use the **dialer callback-server** interface configuration command.

**dialer callback-server** [**username dialstring**]

| *Syntax* | *Description* |
|---|---|
| **username** | (Optional) Identifies the return call by looking up the authenticated host name in a **dialer map** command. This is the default. |
| **dialstring** | (Optional) Identifies the return call during callback negotiation. |

### Default

Disabled. The default keyword is **username**.

### Command Mode

Interface configuration

### Example

The following partial example configures BRI 0 to function as the callback server on the shared network.

```
interface BRI0
 ip address 171.1.1.9 255.255.255.0
 encapsulation ppp
 dialer callback-secure
 dialer enable-timeout 2
 dialer map ip 171.1.1.8 name atlanta class dial1 81012345678901
 dialer-group 1
 ppp callback accept
 ppp authentication chap
!
map-class dialer dial1
 dialer callback-server username
```

### Related Commands

Search online to find documentation for related commands.

**dialer callback-secure**
**dialer enable-timeout**
**dialer hold-queue**
**dialer map**
**map-class**
**ppp callback**

## MAP-CLASS DIALER

To define a class of shared configuration parameters for PPP callback, use the **map-class dialer** global configuration command.

**map-class dialer** *classname*

| *Syntax* | *Description* |
|---|---|
| *classname* | Unique class identifier. |

### Default

Disabled. No class name is provided.

### Command Mode

Global configuration

### Usage Guidelines

The *classname* in the **map-class dialer** command used to specify the class for PPP callback must be the same as the *classname* used in the **dialer map** command.

This command is used on the PPP callback server, not on the callback client.

### *Example*

The following partial example configures BRI 0 to function as the callback server on the shared network. The callback server requires an enable timeout and a map class to be defined.

```
interface BRI0
 ip address 7.1.1.7 255.255.255.0
 encapsulation ppp
 dialer callback-secure
 dialer enable-timeout 2
 dialer map ip 7.1.1.8 name atlanta class dial1 81012345678901
 dialer-group 1
 ppp callback accept
 ppp authentication chap
!
map-class dialer dial1
 dialer callback-server username
```

### *Related Commands*

Search online to find documentation for related commands.

**dialer map**

## PPP CALLBACK

To enable a dialer interface that is not a data terminal ready (DTR) interface to function either as a callback client that requests callback or as a callback server that accepts callback requests, use the **ppp callback** interface configuration command.

**ppp callback** {**accept** | **request**}

| *Syntax* | *Description* |
|---|---|
| **accept** | Enables this dialer interface to accept PPP callback requests (and function as the PPP callback server). |
| **request** | Enables this dialer interface to request PPP callback (and function as the PPP callback client). |

### *Default*

Callback requests are neither accepted nor requested.

### *Command Mode*

Interface configuration

### *Usage Guidelines*

This command first appeared in Cisco IOS Release 11.1.

An interface can request PPP callback only if the interface is configured for PPP authentication with Challenge Handshake Authentication Protocol (CHAP) or Password Authentication Protocol (PAP).

### *Example*

The following example configures a previously defined dialer interface to accept PPP callback requests:

```
ppp callback accept
```

### *Related Commands*

Search online to find documentation for related commands.

**dialer callback-secure**
**map-class dialer**

# Chapter 65

# Configuring Asynchronous Callback

You can configure the Cisco IOS software to call back an asynchronous device that dials in and requests a callback from the router, then disconnects.

Refer to the following sections to configure asynchronous callback:

- Cisco's Implementation of Configuring Asynchronous Callback
- Calling Back PPP Clients
- Calling Back Clients Dialing In and Connecting to the EXEC Prompt
- Calling Back ARA Clients
- Callback Configuration Examples

For a complete description of the commands in this chapter, see Chapter 66, "Asynchronous Callback Commands."

## Cisco's Implementation of Configuring Asynchronous Callback

Asynchronous callback is supported for the following protocols:

- Point-to-Point Protocol (PPP)
- Any device calling in and connecting to the router at the EXEC level
- AppleTalk Remote Access (ARA)

Callback is also supported on other interface types for PPP, including Integrated Services Digital Network (ISDN).

All callback sessions are returned on physical terminal (TTY) lines. ARA is supported on VTY lines, but also is supported on TTY lines if the **vty-arap** command is used. PPP, however, is supported on interfaces. Therefore, to enable PPP callback, you must issue the **autoselect ppp** command on the callback lines.

All current security mechanisms supported in the Cisco IOS software are supported by the callback facility, including the following:

- Terminal Access Controller Access Control System Plus (TACACS+)
- Challenge Handshake Authentication Protocol (CHAP) and Password Authentication Protocol (PAP) for PPP
- Per-user authentication for EXEC callback and ARA callback

The call originator must have the appropriate permissions set on the router before it can initiate a callback session.

Callback is useful for two purposes:

- Cost savings on toll calls

  For example, suppose it costs more to call from clients in Zone A to devices in Zone D than to call from Zone D to Zone A—costs are lower when devices in Zone D call back clients in Zone A.
- Consolidation and centralization of phone billing

  For example, if a corporation has 64 dial-in clients, enabling the corporation's routers to call back these clients consolidates billing. Instead of 64 phone bills, the corporation receives one bill.

## Calling Back PPP Clients

You can call back PPP clients that dial in to asynchronous interfaces. You can enable callback to the following two types of PPP clients:

- Clients that implement PPP callback per RFC 1570 (as an LCP negotiated extension).
- Clients that do not negotiate callback but can put themselves in answer mode, whereby a callback from the router is accepted.

This section describes how to enable callback to each of these types of PPP clients.

### Accept Callback Requests from RFC-Compliant PPP Clients

To accept a callback request from a RFC 1370-PPP-compliant client, perform the following task, in interface (asynchronous) configuration mode:

To configure the Cisco IOS software to call back the originating PPP client, see the section "Enable PPP Callback on Outgoing Lines," later in this chapter.

| Task | Command |
|---|---|
| Enable callback requests from RFC1570-compliant PPP clients on an asynchronous interface. | **ppp callback accept** |

### Accept Callback Requests from Non-RFC-Compliant PPP Clients Placing Themselves in Answer Mode

A PPP client can put itself in answer mode and can still be called back by the router, even though it cannot specifically request callback. To enable callback on the router to this type of client, perform the following task in interface (asynchronous) configuration mode:

| Task | Command |
|---|---|
| Initiate callback requests from non-RFC 1570-compliant PPP clients on an asynchronous interface. | **ppp callback initiate** |

To configure the Cisco IOS software to call back the originating PPP client, see the following section, "Enable PPP Callback on Outgoing Lines."

### Enable PPP Callback on Outgoing Lines

After enabling PPP clients to connect to an asynchronous interface and wait for a callback, you must place one or more TTY lines in PPP mode. Although calls from PPP clients enter through an asynchronous interface, the calls exit the client on a line placed in PPP mode.

To enable PPP client callback on outgoing TTY lines, perform the following steps beginning in global configuration mode:

| Task | | Command |
|---|---|---|
| **Step 1** | Define a chat script to be applied when a PPP client requests callback. | **chat-script** *script-name expect-send* |
| **Step 2** | Specify a per-username callback dial string. | **username** *name* [**callback-dialstring** *telephone-number*] |
| **Step 3** | Specify a per-username rotary group for callback. | **username** *name* [**callback-rotary** *rotary-group-number*] |
| **Step 4** | Specify a per-username line or set of lines for callback. | **username** *name* [**callback-line** [**tty**] *line-number* [*ending-line-number*]] |
| **Step 5** | Enter line configuration mode. | **line** [**tty**] *line-number* [*ending-line-number*] |
| **Step 6** | Configure automatic PPP startup on a line or set of lines. | **autoselect ppp** |

| Task | | Command |
|---|---|---|
| **Step 7** | Enable authentication on the line. | **login** {**authentication** \| **local**} |
| **Step 8** | Apply a chat script to a line or set of lines. | **script callback** *regexp* |
| **Step 9** | Delay the callback for client modems that require a rest period before receiving a callback. | **callback forced-wait** *number-of-seconds* |

A client can issue a callback dial string; that dial string is used *only* if the dial string on the router is specified as NULL, or is not defined.

The recommended PPP chat script follows:

```
chat-script name ABORT ERROR ABORT BUSY "" "ATZ" OK "ATDT \T" TIMEOUT 30 CONNECT \c
```

### Calling Back Clients Dialing In and Connecting to the EXEC Prompt

You can call back clients that dial in to a TTY line and connect to the EXEC prompt. To enable callback, perform the following tasks, beginning in global configuration mode:

| Task | | Command |
|---|---|---|
| **Step 1** | Enable EXEC callback. | **service exec-callback** |
| **Step 2** | Define a chat script to be applied when clients dial in to the EXEC prompt. | **chat-script** *script-name expect-send* |
| **Step 3** | Specify a per-username callback dial string. | **username** *name* [**callback-dialstring** *telephone-number*] |
| **Step 4** | Specify a per-username rotary group for callback. | **username** *name* [**callback-rotary** *rotary-group-number*] |
| **Step 5** | Specify a per-username line or set of lines for callback. | **username** *name* [**callback-line** [**aux** \| **tty**] *line-number* [*ending-line-number*]] |
| **Step 6** | Do not require authentication on EXEC callback. | **username** *name* [**nocallback-verify**] |
| **Step 7** | Enter line configuration mode. | **line** [**tty**] *line-number* [*ending-line-number*] |
| **Step 8** | Apply a chat script to the line or a set of lines. | **script callback** *regexp* |
| **Step 9** | Delay the callback for client modems that require a rest period before receiving a callback. | **callback forced-wait** *number-of-seconds* |

The recommended EXEC chat script is as follows:

```
chat-script name ABORT ERROR ABORT BUSY "" "ATZ" OK "ATDT \T" TIMEOUT 30 CONNECT \c
```

For an example of calling back clients connecting to the EXEC facility, see the section, "Call Back Clients Connecting to the EXEC Prompt Example," later in this chapter.

## Calling Back ARA Clients

You can call back ARA clients. Perform the following steps, starting in global configuration mode. These steps assume you have already enabled AppleTalk routing and enabled ARA.

| Task | | Command |
|---|---|---|
| Step 1 | Enable callback to an ARA client. | **arap callback** |
| Step 2 | Define a chat script to be applied when an ARA client connects to a TTY line and requests callback. | **chat-script** *script-name expect-send* |
| Step 3 | Enter line configuration mode. | **line** [**tty**] *line-number* [*ending-line-number*] |
| Step 4 | Enable ARA on the line. | **arap enable** |
| Step 5 | Configure automatic protocol startup on the line. | **autoselect arap** |
| Step 6 | Enable authentication on the line. | **login** {**authentication** \| **local**} |
| Step 7 | Apply an ARA-specific chat script to a line or set of lines. | **script arap-callback** *regexp* |
| Step 8 | Delay the callback for client modems that require a rest period before receiving a callback. | **callback forced-wait** *number-of-seconds* |
| Step 9 | Exit to global configuration mode. | **exit** |
| Step 10 | Specify a per-username callback dial string. | **username** *name* [**callback-dialstring** *telephone-number*] |
| Step 11 | Specify a per-username rotary group for callback. | **username** *name* [**callback-rotary** *rotary-group-number*] |
| Step 12 | Specify a per-username line or set of lines for callback. | **username** *name* [**callback-line** [**tty**] *line-number* [*ending-line-number*]] |

The recommended ARA chat script follows. The parts of the string that are **bolded** are vendor-specific extensions on the Telebit 3000 modem to disable error control. Refer to the manual for your modem for the specific commands to disable error correction for ARA.

```
chat-script name ABORT ERROR ABORT BUSY "" "ATZ" OK "ATS180=0" OK "ATS181=1" OK "ATDT \T"
TIMEOUT 60 CONNECT \c
```

For an example of calling back a PPP client, see the section "Call Back a PPP Client Example," at the end of this chapter.

## CALLBACK CONFIGURATION EXAMPLES

The following sections provide examples for callback:

- Call Back Clients Connecting to the EXEC Prompt Example
- Call Back an ARA Client Example
- Call Back a PPP Client Example

### Call Back Clients Connecting to the EXEC Prompt Example

The following example shows the process to configure an outgoing callback on the same line as the incoming request. The **login local** command enables local username authentication on lines 4 and 7. Re-authentication is required upon reconnection.

```
service exec-callback
username milarepa callback-dialstring "" password letmein
line 4
 login local
line 7
 login local
```

### Call Back an ARA Client Example

The following example shows the process of configuring callback to an ARA client on line 7. The **login local** command enables local username authentication on lines 4 and 7. Line 7 will always be used for ARA callback, whether the incoming call enters line 4, 7, or 8.

```
appletalk routing
arap callback
arap network 422 router test
username excalibur callback-dialstring "123456" callback-line 7 password guenivere
line 4
 login local
 modem InOut
 autoselect arap
 arap enable
line 7
 login local
 modem InOut
 autoselect arap
 arap enable
line 8
 login local
 modem InOut
 autoselect arap
 arap enable
```

### Call Back a PPP Client Example

The following example shows the process of configuring callback to a PPP client on rotary 77. PAP authentication is enabled for PPP on the asynchronous interfaces. The **login local** command enables local username authentication on lines 7, 8, and 9. The remote PPP client's host name is Ted, and the callback number is fixed at 1234567.

```
username Ted callback-dialstring "1234567" callback-rotary 77
            password Rhoda
interface async7
 ip unnumbered ethernet0
 encapsulation ppp
 no keepalive
 async default ip address 1.1.1.1
 async mode interactive
 ppp callback accept
 ppp authentication pap

interface async8
 ip unnumbered ethernet0
 encapsulation ppp
 no keepalive
 async default ip address 1.1.1.2
 async mode interactive
 ppp callback accept
 ppp authentication pap

interface async9
 ip unnumbered ethernet0
 encapsulation ppp
 no keepalive
 async default ip address 1.1.1.3
 async mode interactive
 ppp callback accept
 ppp authentication pap

line 7
 login local
 modem InOut
 rotary 77
 autoselect ppp

line 8
 login local
 modem InOut
 rotary 77
 autoselect ppp

line 9
 login local
 modem InOut
 rotary 77
 autoselect ppp
```

# CHAPTER 66

# Asynchronous Callback Commands

This chapter describes the commands used to configure the Cisco IOS software to call back an asynchronous device that dials in and requests a callback from the router, then disconnects.

For configuration tasks and examples, see Chapter 65, "Configuring Asynchronous Callback."

## ARAP CALLBACK

To enable an ARA client to request a callback, use the **arap callback** global configuration command.

**arap callback**

### *Syntax Description*

This command has no arguments or keywords.

### *Default*

Callback requests are not accepted on lines configured for ARA.

### *Command Mode*

Global configuration

### *Usage Guidelines*

This command first appeared in Cisco IOS Release 11.1.

This command enables the router to accept callback requests from ARA clients. You first have to enable AppleTalk routing on the router and then enable automatic ARA startup on the line. You can use this command with either local username authentication or TACACS+ authentication.

### *Example*

The following example accepts a callback request from an ARA client:

```
arap callback
```

### *Related Commands*

Search online to find documentation for related commands.

**arap authentication**
**autoselect ara**
**callback forced-wait**
**ppp authentication**
**ppp callback**
**service exec-callback**
**username**

## CALLBACK FORCED-WAIT

To force the Cisco IOS software to wait before initiating a callback to a requesting client, use the **callback forced-wait** global configuration command.

**callback forced-wait**

### *Syntax Description*

This command has no arguments or keywords.

### *Default*

The forced waiting period is not set.

### *Command Mode*

Global configuration

### *Usage Guidelines*

This command first appeared in Cisco IOS Release 11.1.

Use this command when the router is calling back a modem that initiated a call, then dropped the connection, but requires a rest period before subsequent input is accepted.

### *Example*

The following example sets a waiting period during which a callback chat script is delayed from being sent on an outgoing target line:

```
callback-forced-wait
```

### *Related Commands*

Search online to find documentation for related commands.

**arap callback**
**chat-script**
**debug callback**
**ppp callback**
**service exec-callback**
**username**

## PPP CALLBACK

To enable a PPP client to dial in to an asynchronous interface and request a callback, use the **ppp callback** interface configuration command.

**ppp callback {accept | initiate}**

| *Syntax* | *Description* |
|---|---|
| **accept** | Accept callback requests from RFC1570-compliant PPP clients on the interface. |
| **initiate** | Initiate a callback to non-RFC1570-compliant PPP clients dialing in to an asynchronous interface. |

### *Default*

Callback requests are not accepted on asynchronous interfaces.

### *Command Mode*

Interface configuration

### *Usage Guidelines*

This command first appeared in Cisco IOS Release 11.0.

This command enables the Cisco IOS software to accept callback requests entering asynchronous interfaces configured for PPP callback. PPP callback can only be initiated if the interface is configured for authentication using CHAP or PAP.

### *Examples*

The following example accepts a callback request from an RFC-compliant PPP client:

```
ppp callback accept
```

The following example accepts a callback request from a non-RFC-compliant PPP client:

```
ppp callback initiate
```

### *Related Commands*

Search online to find documentation for related commands.

**arap callback**
**autoselect ppp**
**callback-forced-wait**
**ppp authentication**
**username**

## SCRIPT ARAP-CALLBACK

To specify that a chat script start on a line any time an AppleTalk Remote Access (ARA) client requests a callback, use the **script arap-callback** line configuration command. Use the **no** form of this command to disable this feature.

**script arap-callback** *regexp*
**no script arap-callback**

| *Syntax* | *Description* |
|---|---|
| *regexp* | Regular expression that specifies the set of modem scripts that might be executed. The first script name that matches the argument *regexp* is used. |

### *Default*

Not assigned to terminal lines

### *Command Mode*

Line configuration

### *Usage Guidelines*

This command first appeared in Cisco IOS Release 11.1.

This command specifies that if an originating ARA client requests callback, the device will be disconnected and the chat script defined by the argument *regexp* will be executed to call back the client. The first available line specified for callback, and for which a chat script has been applied, will be used for the callback.

Create a chat script using the **chat script** command.

The **script arap-callback** command functions only on physical terminal (TTY) lines. It does not function on virtual terminal (VTY) lines.

### *Example*

The following example specifies that a chat script with a name that includes *usr4* will be activated whenever a client requests a callback on line 4:

```
line 4
 script arap-callback usr4
```

### *Related Commands*

Search online to find documentation for related commands.

**chat-script**
**script activation**
**script callback**
**script connection**
**script dialer**
**script reset**
**script startup**
**start-chat**

## SCRIPT CALLBACK

To specify that a chat script start on a line any time a client requests a callback, use the **script callback** line configuration command. Use the **no** form of this command to disable this feature.

**script callback** *regexp*
**no script callback**

| *Syntax* | *Description* |
|---|---|
| *regexp* | Regular expression that specifies the set of modem scripts that might be executed. The first script name that matches the argument *regexp* is used. |

### *Default*

Not assigned to terminal lines

### *Command Mode*

Line configuration

### *Usage Guidelines*

This command first appeared in Cisco IOS Release 11.1.

This command specifies that if an originating client requests callback, the device will be disconnected and the chat script defined by the argument *regexp* will be executed to call back the client. The first available line specified for callback, and for which a chat script has been applied, will be used for the callback.

Create a chat script using the **chat script** command.

The **script callback** command functions only on physical terminal (tty) lines. It does not function on virtual terminal (vty) lines.

### *Example*

The following example specifies that the chat script with a name that includes *supra4* will be activated whenever a client requests a callback on line 4:

```
line 4
 script callback supra4
```

### *Related Commands*

Search online to find documentation for related commands.

**chat-script**
**script activation**
**script connection**
**script dialer**
**script reset**
**script startup**
**start-chat**

## SERVICE EXEC-CALLBACK

To enable the Cisco IOS software to call back clients who request a callback from the EXEC level, use the **service exec-callback** global configuration command.

**service exec-callback**

### *Syntax Description*

This command has no arguments or keywords.

### *Default*

Callback is not enabled.

### *Command Mode*

Global configuration

### *Usage Guidelines*

This command first appeared in Cisco IOS Release 11.1.

This command enables the Cisco IOS software to return a call to a device that dials in, connects to the EXEC, and requests callback.

### *Example*

The following example enables EXEC level callback:

```
service exec-callback
```

### *Related Commands*

Search online to find documentation for related commands.

**arap callback**
**callback forced-wait**
**debug callback**
**debug confmodem**
**ppp callback**
**username**

CHAPTER 67

# Configuring ISDN Caller ID Callback

ISDN caller ID callback allows the initial incoming call from the client to the server to be rejected based on the caller ID message contained in the ISDN setup message, and it allows a callback to be initiated to the calling destination.

Before Cisco IOS Release 11.2 F, ISDN callback functionality required PPP or Combinet Packet Protocol (CPP) client authentication and client/server callback negotiation to proceed. If authentication and callback negotiation were successful, the callback server had to disconnect the call and then place a return call. Both the initial call and the return call were subject to tolls, and when service providers charge by the minute, even brief calls could be expensive.

This feature is independent of the encapsulation in effect and can be used with various encapsulations, such as PPP, HDLC, Frame Relay, and X.25.

The ISDN caller ID callback feature allows users to control costs because charges do not apply to the initial, rejected call. For a complete description of the ISDN caller ID callback commands in this chapter, see Chapter 68, "ISDN Caller ID Callback Commands."

## RESTRICTIONS

The ISDN caller ID callback feature conflicts with the dialer callback security feature for the Dialer Profiles feature for DDR. If dialer callback security is configured, it takes precedence; ISDN caller ID callback is ignored.

### PREREQUISITES

Caller ID screening requires a local switch that is capable of delivering the caller ID to the router or access server. If you enable caller ID screening but do not have such a switch, no calls will be allowed in.

ISDN caller ID callback requires DDR to be configured and bidirectional dialing to be working between the calling and callback routers. Detailed DDR prerequisites depend on whether you have configured legacy DDR or Dialer Profiles.

For a legacy DDR configuration, ISDN caller ID callback has the following prerequisite:

- A **dialer map** command is configured for the dial string that is used in the incoming call setup message. The dial string is used in the callback.

For a Dialer Profiles configuration, ISDN caller ID callback has the following prerequisites:

- A **dialer caller** command is configured to screen for the dial-in number.
- A **dialer string** command is configured with the number to use in the callback.

### HOW IT WORKS

ISDN caller ID callback allows great flexibility for you to define which calls to accept, which to deny, and which calls to reject initially but for which the router should initiate callback. The feature works by using existing ISDN caller ID screening, which matches the number in the incoming call against numbers configured on the router, determining the best match for number in the incoming call, and then, if configured, initiating callback to the number configured on the router.

When a call is received, the entire list of configured numbers is checked and the configuration of the best match number determines the action:

- If the incoming number is best matched by a number that is configured for callback, then the incoming call is rejected and callback is initiated.
- If the incoming number is best matched by another entry in the list of configured numbers, the call is accepted.
- If the incoming number does not match any entry in the configured list, the call is rejected and no callback is started.

"Don't care" characters are allowed in the caller ID screening configuration on the router and are used to determine the best match.

For more information and examples, see section, "Best Match System Examples," later in this chapter.

#### Callback after the Best Match Is Determined

The details of router activities after it finds a best match with callback depend on the DDR feature that is configured. The ISDN caller ID callback feature works with the following DDR features:

- Legacy DDR
- Dialer Profiles

### *Legacy DDR*

If legacy DDR is configured for the host or user that is identified in the incoming call message, the router performs the following actions:

1. Checks the table of configured numbers for caller ID callback
2. Searches the **dialer map** entries for a number that "best matches" the incoming call string
3. Waits for a configured length of time to expire
4. Initiates callback to the number provided in the **dialer map** command

### *Dialer Profiles*

If the Dialer Profiles feature is configured for the host or user identified in the incoming call message, the router performs the following actions:

1. Searches through all the dialer pool members to match the incoming call number to a **dialer caller** number
2. Initiates a callback to the dialer profile
3. Waits for a configured length of time to expire
4. Calls the number identified in the **dialer string** command associated with the dialer profile.

### Timing and Coordinating Callback on Both Sides

When an incoming call arrives and the router finds a best match configured for callback, the router uses the value configured by the **dialer enable-timeout** command to determine the length of time to wait before making the callback.

The minimum value of the timer is 1 second; the default value of the timer is 15 seconds. The interval set for this feature on this router must be much less than that set for DDR fast call rerouting for ISDN (that interval is set by the **dialer wait-for-carrier** command) on the calling (remote) side. It is recommended that you set the dialer wait-for-carrier timer on the calling side to twice the length of the dialer enable-timeout timer on the callback side.

**NOTES**

The remote site cannot be configured for multiple dial-in numbers because a busy callback number or a rejected call causes the second number to be tried. That number might be located at a different site, defeating the purpose of the callback.

## CONFIGURING ISDN CALLER ID CALLBACK

The required configuration tasks depend whether you have configured legacy DDR or Dialer Profiles. Complete the configuration tasks in the relevant section:

- Configure ISDN Caller ID Callback for Legacy DDR
- Configure ISDN Caller ID Callback for Dialer Profiles

For configuration examples, see section, "ISDN Caller ID Callback Configuration Examples," at the end of this chapter.

### Configure ISDN Caller ID Callback for Legacy DDR

This section provides configuration tasks for the local (server, callback) side and the remote (client, calling) side.

On the callback (local) side, to configure ISDN caller ID callback when legacy DDR is configured, complete the following tasks in interface configuration mode on the callback side:

| Task | Command |
|---|---|
| Configure caller ID screening and callback when a dialer rotary is not configured. | **isdn caller** *remote-number* **callback** |
| or | |
| Configure caller ID screening and callback when a dialer rotary (dialer interface) is configured. | **dialer caller** *remote-number* **callback** |
| Configure the time to wait before initiating callback. | **dialer enable-timeout** *seconds* |

On the calling (remote) side, to set the timer for fast call rerouting, complete the following task in interface configuration mode:

| Task | Command |
|---|---|
| Change the ISDN fast call rerouting timer to double the length of the enable timeout timer. | **dialer wait-for-carrier** *seconds* |

### Configure ISDN Caller ID Callback for Dialer Profiles

This section provides configuration tasks for the local side and the remote side. On the callback (local) side, to configure ISDN caller ID callback when the Dialer Profiles feature is configured, complete the following tasks in interface configuration mode:

| Task | Command |
|---|---|
| Configure caller ID screening and callback. | **dialer caller** *remote-number* **callback** |
| Configure the time to wait before initiating callback. | **dialer enable-timeout** *seconds* |

On the calling (remote) side, to set the timer for fast call rerouting, complete the following task in interface configuration mode:

| Task | Command |
|---|---|
| Change the ISDN fast call rerouting timer to double the length of the enable timeout timer. | **dialer wait-for-carrier** *seconds* |

## Monitoring and Troubleshooting ISDN Caller ID Callback

To monitor and troubleshoot ISDN caller ID callback, perform the following tasks in EXEC mode:

| Task | Command |
|---|---|
| Display information about the status and configuration of the ISDN interface on the router. | **show dialer** |
| Display ISDN events occurring on the user side (on the router) of the ISDN interface. The ISDN events that can be displayed are Q.931 events (call setup and teardown of ISDN network connections). | **debug isdn event** |
| Display Layer 3 signaling messages, protocol transitions and processes, the line protocol state, and the channel IDs for each ISDN interface. | **debug isdn q931** |

## ISDN Caller ID Callback Configuration Examples

This section provides the following examples:

- Best Match System Examples
- Simple Callback Examples
- ISDN Caller ID Callback with Dialer Profiles Example
- ISDN Caller ID Callback with Legacy DDR Examples

### Best Match System Examples

The best match is determined by matching the incoming number against the numbers in the configured callback commands, starting with the right-most character in the numbers and using the letter X for any "don't care" digits in the configured commands. If multiple configured numbers match an incoming number, the best match is the one with the fewest "don't care" digits.

The reason for using a system based on right-most matching is that a given number can be represented in many different ways. For example, all the following items might be used to represent the same number, depending on the circumstances (international call, long-distance domestic call, call through a PBX, and so forth):

```
011 1 408 556 7654
    1 408 556 7654
      408 556 7654
          556 7654
            6 7654
```

### *Best Match Based on the Number of Don't Care Digits*

In the following example, suppose that you have an incoming call from one of those numbers (4085567654), and suppose that you configured the following numbers for callback on the router (disregarding for the moment the commands that can be used to configure callback):

```
556xxxx callback
555xxxx callback
559765x
5577654 callback
xxxxx
```

The first number listed is the best match for the incoming number (in the configured number, the three digits and four Xs all match the incoming number); the line indicates that callback is to be initiated. The last line has five Xs; it is not the best match for the calling number.

**NOTES**

The last number in the preceding list allows calls from any other number to be accepted without callback. When you use such a line, you must make sure that the number of Xs in the line exceeds the number of Xs in any other line. In the last line above, five Xs are used; the other lines use at most four Xs.

The order of configured numbers is not important; the router searches the entire list and then determines the best match.

### *Best Match with No Callback Configured*

In the following example, suppose that a call comes from the same number (4085567654) and only the following numbers are configured:

```
555xxxx callback
559765x
5577654 callback
xxxxx
```

In this case, the best match is in the final line listed, so the incoming call is accepted but callback is not initiated.

### *No Match Configured*

In the following example, suppose that a call comes from the same number (4085567654) and only the following numbers are configured:

```
555xxxx callback
559765x
5577654 callback
```

In this case, there is no match at all, and the call is just rejected.

## Simple Callback Examples

In the following example, callback calls will be made only to numbers in the 555 and 556 exchanges, but any other number can call in:

```
isdn caller 408555xxxx callback
isdn caller 408556xxxx callback
isdn caller xxxxx
```

The following example configures the router to accept a call with a delivered caller ID equal to 4155551234:

```
isdn caller 4155551234
```

The following example configures the router to accept a call with a delivered caller ID equal to 41555512 with any digits in the last two positions:

```
isdn caller 41555512xx
```

The following example configures the router to make a callback to a delivered caller ID equal to 41555512 with any digits in the last two positions. (The router rejects the call initially and then makes the callback.) The router accepts calls from any other numbers.

```
isdn caller 41555512xx callback
isdn caller xxx
```

## ISDN Caller ID Callback with Dialer Profiles Example

The following example shows the configuration of a central site that can place or receive calls from three remote sites over four ISDN BRI lines. Each remote site is on a different IP subnet and has different bandwidth requirements. Therefore, three dialer interfaces and three dialer pools are defined.

```
! This is a Dialer Profile for reaching remote subnetwork 1.1.1.1.
interface Dialer1
 ip address 1.1.1.1 255.255.255.0
 encapsulation ppp
 dialer remote-name Smalluser
 dialer string 4540
 dialer pool 3
 dialer-group 1
 dialer caller 14802616900 callback
 dialer caller 1480262xxxx callback
```

```
!
! This is a Dialer Profile for reaching remote subnetwork 2.2.2.2.
interface Dialer2
 ip address 2.2.2.2 255.255.255.0
 encapsulation ppp
 dialer remote-name Mediumuser
 dialer string 5264540 class Eng
 dialer load-threshold 50 either
 dialer pool 1
 dialer-group 2
 dialer caller 14805364540 callback
 dialer caller 1480267xxxx callback
 dialer enable-timeout 2
!
! This is a Dialer Profile for reaching remote subnetwork 3.3.3.3.
interface Dialer3
 ip address 3.3.3.3 255.255.255.0
 encapsulation ppp
 dialer remote-name Poweruser
 dialer string 4156884540 class Eng
 dialer hold-queue 10
 dialer load-threshold 80
 dialer pool 2
 dialer-group 2
!
! This map class ensures that these calls use an ISDN speed of 56 kbps.
map-class dialer Eng
 isdn speed 56
!
interface bri 0
 encapsulation PPP
!BRI 0 has a higher priority than BRI 1 in dialer pool 1.
 dialer pool-member 1 priority 100
 ppp authentication chap
!
interface bri 1
 encapsulation ppp
 dialer pool-member 1 priority 50
 dialer pool-member 2 priority 50
!BRI 1 has a reserved channel in dialer pool 3; the channel remains inactive
!until BRI 1 uses it to place calls.
 dialer pool-member 3 min-link 1
 ppp authentication chap
!
interface bri 2
 encapsulation ppp
! BRI 2 has a higher priority than BRI 1 in dialer pool 2.
dialer pool-member 2 priority 100
ppp authentication chap
!
interface bri 3
encapsulation ppp
! BRI 3 has the highest priority in dialer pool 2.
```

```
dialer pool-member 2 priority 150
ppp authentication chap
```

### ISDN Caller ID Callback with Legacy DDR Examples

This section provides two examples of caller ID callback with legacy DDR:

- Individual Interface Example
- Dialer Rotary Group Example

#### *Individual Interface Example*

The following example configures a BRI interface for legacy DDR and ISDN caller ID callback:

```
interface bri 0
 description Connected to NTT 81012345678901
 ip address 7.1.1.7 255.255.255.0
 no ip mroute-cache
 encapsulation ppp
 isdn caller 81012345678902 callback
 dialer enable-timeout 2
 dialer map ip 7.1.1.8 name spanky 81012345678902
 dialer-group 1
 ppp authentication chap
```

#### *Dialer Rotary Group Example*

The following example configures BRI interfaces to connect into a rotary group (dialer group) and then configures a dialer interface for that dialer group. This configuration permits IP packets to trigger calls. The dialer interface is configured to initiate callback to any number in the 1-480-261 exchange and to accept calls from two other specific numbers.

```
interface bri 0
 description connected into a rotary group
 encapsulation ppp
 dialer rotary-group 1
!
interface bri 1
 no ip address
 encapsulation ppp
 dialer rotary-group 1
!
interface bri 2
 encapsulation ppp
 dialer rotary-group 1
!
interface bri 3
 no ip address
 encapsulation ppp
 dialer rotary-group 1
!
interface bri 4
 encapsulation ppp
 dialer rotary-group 1
```

```
!
interface Dialer 0
 description Dialer group controlling the BRIs
 ip address 8.1.1.1 255.255.255.0
 encapsulation ppp
 dialer map ip 8.1.1.2 name angus 14802616900
 dialer map ip 8.1.1.3 name moe 14802616901
 dialer map ip 8.1.1.4 name larry 14807362060
 dialer map ip 8.1.1.5 name curly 19165561424
 dialer map ip 8.1.1.6 name shemp 12129767448
 dialer-group 1
 ppp authentication chap
!
 dialer caller 1480261xxxx callback
 dialer caller 19165561424
 dialer caller 12129767448
!
dialer-list 1 protocol ip permit
```

CHAPTER 68

# ISDN Caller ID Callback Commands

This chapter describes the commands needed to configure ISDN caller ID callback.

ISDN caller ID callback allows the initial incoming call from the client to the server to be rejected based on the caller ID message contained in the ISDN setup message, and it allows the server to initiate a callback to the calling client.

For callback configuration tasks and examples, see Chapter 67, "Configuring ISDN Caller ID Callback."

## DIALER CALLER

To configure caller ID screening and optionally to enable ISDN caller ID callback for legacy DDR or the dialer profiles DDR feature, use the **dialer caller** interface configuration command. To disable this feature, use the **no** form of this command.

**dialer caller** *number* [**callback**]
**no dialer caller** *number* [**callback**]

| *Syntax* | *Description* |
|---|---|
| *number* | Remote telephone number for which to screen. Use a letter X to represent a single "don't care" digit. The maximum length of each number is 25 characters. |
| **callback** | (Optional) Enables callback. |

### *Default*

Disabled

### *Command Mode*

Interface configuration

### *Usage Guidelines*

This command first appeared in Cisco IOS Release 11.2.

This command configures the Cisco IOS software to accept calls from the specified number or, used with the **callback** keyword, to reject incoming calls from the specified number but to initiate callback to the number. This command also helps bind a dialer profile to—and thus configure—the interface used for a call.

When the optional **callback** keyword is used, the initial call is rejected (hence, not subject to tolls) and callback is initiated to the calling number.

When Xs are used in the callback number, dialer caller screening is based on a best match system that uses the number of Xs as a criterion. To make callback calls only to specified numbers or ranges of numbers but to accept any other incoming calls, make sure that the number of Xs in any configuration line that uses the **callback** keyword is less than the number of Xs in any configuration line that does not use the keyword.

For example, if you use at most four Xs in the configuration lines with the **callback** keyword, then to accept calls from other numbers use at least five Xs in a configuration line that does not use the **callback** keyword.

**NOTES**

Caller ID screening requires a local switch that is capable of delivering the caller ID to the router or access server. If you enable caller ID screening but do not have such a switch, no calls will be allowed in.

### *Example*

In the following example, callback calls will be made only to numbers in the 555 and 556 exchanges, but any other number can call in:

```
dialer caller 408555xxxx callback
dialer caller 408556xxxx callback
dialer caller xxxxx
```

### *Related Commands*

Search online to find documentation for related commands.

**show dialer**

### ISDN CALLER

To configure ISDN caller ID screening and optionally to enable ISDN caller ID callback for legacy DDR, use the **isdn caller** interface configuration command. To disable this feature, use the **no** form of this command.

**isdn caller** *phone-number* [**callback**]
**no isdn caller** *phone-number* [**callback**]

| *Syntax* | *Description* |
|---|---|
| *phone-number* | Remote telephone number for which to screen. Use a letter X to represent a single "don't care" digit. The maximum length of each number is 25 characters. |
| **callback** | (Optional) Enables callback. |

#### *Default*

Disabled

#### *Command Mode*

Interface configuration

#### *Usage Guidelines*

This command first appeared in Cisco IOS Release 10.0.

This command configures the router to accept calls from the specified number.

**NOTES**

Caller ID screening requires a local switch that is capable of delivering the caller ID to the router. If you enable caller ID screening but do not have such a switch, no calls are allowed in.

When the optional **callback** keyword is used and a call is received from one of the callback numbers, the initial call is rejected (hence, not subject to tolls) and a callback is initiated to that calling number.

When Xs are used in the callback number, dialer caller screening is based on a best match system that uses the *number* of Xs as a criterion. To make callback calls only to specified numbers or ranges of numbers but to accept any other incoming calls, make sure that the number of Xs in any configuration line that uses the **callback** keyword is less than the number of Xs in any configuration line that does not use the keyword.

For example, if you use at most four Xs in the configuration lines with the **callback** keyword, then to accept calls from other numbers use at least five Xs in a configuration line that does not use the keyword.

### Example

In the following example, callback calls will be made only to numbers in the 555 and 556 exchanges, but any other number can call in:

```
isdn caller 408555xxxx callback
isdn caller 408556xxxx callback
isdn caller xxxxx
```

### Related Commands

Search online to find documentation for related commands.

**show dialer**

# CHAPTER 69

# Configuring Snapshot Routing

Snapshot routing enables a single router interface to call other routers during periods when the line protocol for the interface is up (these are called "active periods"). The router dials to all configured locations during such active periods to get routes from all the remote locations.

The router can be configured to exchange routing updates each time the line protocol goes from "down" to "up" or from "dialer spoofing" to "fully up." The router can also be configured to dial the server router in the absence of regular traffic if the active period time expires.

Snapshot routing is useful in two command situations:

- Configuring static routes for DDR interfaces
- Reducing the overhead of periodic updates sent by routing protocols to remote branch offices over a dedicated serial line

For a complete description of the snapshot routing commands in this chapter, see Chapter 70, "Snapshot Routing Commands."

## How Snapshot Routing Works

When configuring snapshot routing, you choose one router on the interface to be the client router and one or more other routers to be server routers. The client router determines the frequency at which routing information is exchanged between routers.

Routing information is exchanged during an active period. During the active period, a client router dials all the remote server routers for which it has a snapshot dialer map defined in order to get routes from all the remote locations. The server router provides information about routes to each client router that calls.

At the end of the active period, the router takes a snapshot of the entries in the routing table. These entries remain frozen during a quiet period. At the end of the quiet period, another active period starts during which routing information is again exchanged. See Figure 69–1.

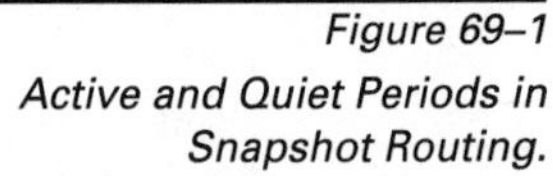

*Figure 69–1*
*Active and Quiet Periods in Snapshot Routing.*

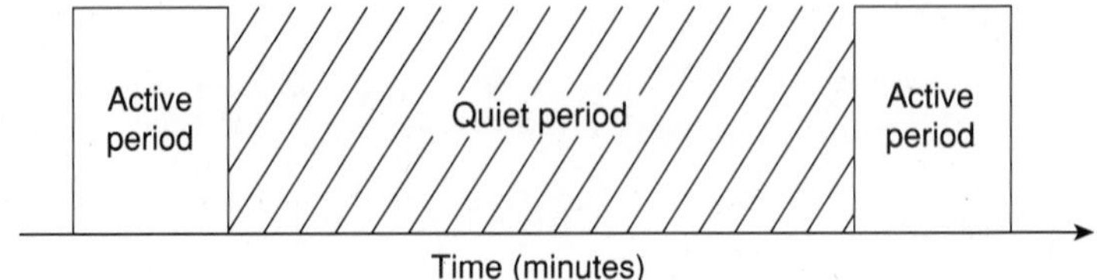


When the router transitions from the quiet period to the active period, the line might not be available for a variety of reasons. For example, the line might be down or busy, or the PVC might be down. If this happens, the router has to wait through another entire quiet period before it can update its routing table entries. This wait might be a problem if the quiet period is very long—for example, 12 hours. To avoid having to wait through the quiet period, you can configure a retry period. If the line is not available when the quiet period ends, the router waits for the amount of time specified by the retry period and then transitions to an active period. See Figure 69–2.

*Figure 69–2*
*Retry Period in Snapshot Routing.*

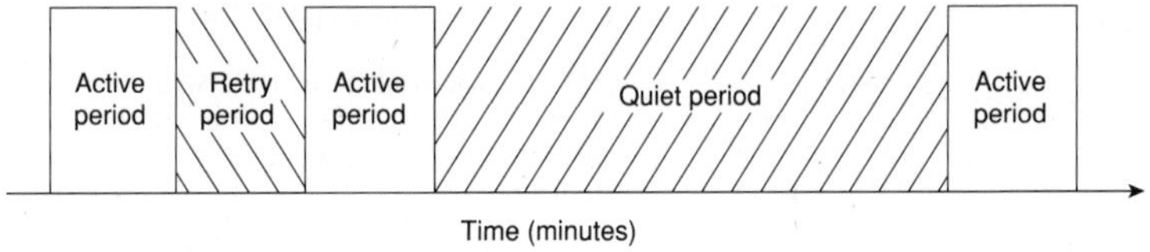


The retry period is also useful in a dial-up environment in which there are more remote sites than router interface lines that dial in to a Primary Rate Interface (PRI) and want routing information from that interface. For example, a PRI has 23 DS-0s available, but you might have 46 remote sites. In this situation, you would have more **dialer map** commands than available lines. The router will try the **dialer map** commands in order and will use the retry time for the lines that it cannot immediately access.

The following routed protocols support snapshot routing. Note that these are all distance-vector protocols.

- AppleTalk—Routing Table Maintenance Protocol (RTMP)
- Banyan VINES—Routing Table Protocol (RTP)
- IP—Routing Information Protocol (RIP), Interior Gateway Routing Protocol (IGRP)
- Novell IPX—RIP, Service Advertisement Protocol (SAP)

## Configuring Snapshot Routing

To configure snapshot routing, perform the tasks described in the following sections:

- Configure the Client Router
- Configure the Server Router

You can also monitor and maintain interfaces configured for snapshot routing. See section, "Monitoring DDR Connections and Snapshot Routing."

For an example of configuring snapshot routing, see section, "Snapshot Routing Configuration Example," later in this chapter.

### Configure the Client Router

To configure snapshot routing on the client router that is connected to a dedicated serial line, perform the following tasks starting in global configuration mode:

| Task | Command |
|---|---|
| **Step 1** Specify a serial interface. | **interface serial** *number* |
| **Step 2** Configure the client router. | **snapshot client** *active-time quiet-time* [**suppress-statechange-updates**] [**dialer**] |

To configure snapshot routing on the client router connected to an interface configured for DDR, perform the following tasks starting in global configuration mode:

| Task | Command |
|---|---|
| **Step 1** Specify a serial interface. | **interface serial** *number* |
| **Step 2** Configure a dialer rotary group. | **dialer rotary-group** *number* |
| **Step 3** Specify a dialer interface. | **interface dialer** *number* |
| **Step 4** Configure the client router. | **snapshot client** *active-time quiet-time* [**suppress-statechange-updates**] [**dialer**] |
| **Step 5** Define a dialer map. | **dialer map snapshot** *sequence-number dial-string* |

Repeat Step 5 for each map you want to define. Maps must be provided for all the remote server routers this client router is to call during each active period.

Because ISDN BRI and PRI automatically have rotary groups, you do not need to define a rotary group when configuring snapshot routing. To configure snapshot routing on the client router over an interface configured for BRI or PRI, perform the following steps:

| Task | | Command |
|---|---|---|
| **Step 1** | Specify a BRI interface. | **interface bri** *number* |
| **Step 2** | Configure the client router. | **snapshot client** *active-time quiet-time* [**suppress-statechange-updates**] [**dialer**] |
| **Step 3** | Define a dialer map. | **dialer map snapshot** *sequence-number dial-string* |

Repeat Step 3 for each map you want to define.

### Configure the Server Router

To configure snapshot routing on the server router that is connected to a dedicated serial line, perform the following tasks starting in global configuration mode:

| Task | | Command |
|---|---|---|
| **Step 1** | Specify a serial interface. | **interface serial** *number* |
| **Step 2** | Configure the server router. | **snapshot server** *active-time* [**dialer**] |

To configure snapshot routing on the associated server router connected to an interface configured for DDR, perform the following tasks beginning in global configuration mode:

| Task | | Command |
|---|---|---|
| **Step 1** | Specify a serial interface. | **interface serial** *number* |
| **Step 2** | Specify a dialer interface. | **interface dialer** *number* |
| **Step 3** | Configure the server router. | **snapshot server** *active-time* [**dialer**] |

The active period for the client router and its associated server routers should be the same.

## MONITORING DDR CONNECTIONS AND SNAPSHOT ROUTING

To monitor DDR connections and snapshot routing, perform the following tasks in privileged EXEC mode:

| Task | Command |
|---|---|
| Display general diagnostics about the DDR interface. | **show dialer** [**interface** *type number*] |
| Display information about the ISDN interface. | **show interfaces bri 0** |

| Task | Command |
|---|---|
| Terminate the snapshot routing quiet period on the client router within two minutes. | **clear snapshot quiet-time** *interface* |
| Display information about snapshot routing parameters. | **show snapshot** *interface* |
| Clear the values of the general diagnostic statistics. | **clear dialer** |

## SNAPSHOT ROUTING CONFIGURATION EXAMPLE

The following example configures snapshot routing on an interface configured for DDR on the client router. In this configuration, a single client router can call multiple server routers. It dials to all different locations during each active period to get routes from all those remote locations.

The absence of the **suppress-statechange-updates** keyword means that routing updates will be exchanged each time the line protocol goes from "down" to "up" or from "dialer spoofing" to "fully up." The **dialer** keyword on the **snapshot client** command allows the client router to dial the server router in the absence of regular traffic if the active period time expires.

```
interface serial 0
 dialer rotary-group 3
!
interface dialer 3
 dialer in-band
 snapshot client 5 360 dialer

dialer map snapshot 2 4155556734
dialer map snapshot 3 7075558990
```

The following commands configure the server router:

```
interface serial 2
 snapshot server 5 dialer
```

# CHAPTER 70

# Snapshot Routing Commands

This chapter describes the commands needed for configuring snapshot routing on the router.

Snapshot routing enables a single router interface to call other routers during periods when the line protocol for the interface is up (these are called "active periods"). The router dials to all configured locations during such active periods to get routes from all the remote locations.

The router can be configured to exchange routing updates each time the line protocol goes from "down" to "up" or from "dialer spoofing" to "fully up." The router can also be configured to dial the server router in the absence of regular traffic if the active period time expires.

Snapshot routing is useful in two command situations:

- Configuring static routes for DDR interfaces
- Reducing the overhead of periodic updates sent by routing protocols to remote branch offices over a dedicated serial line

For configuration tasks and examples, see Chapter 69, "Configuring Snapshot Routing."

## CLEAR SNAPSHOT QUIET-TIME

To end the quiet period on a client router within two minutes, use the **clear snapshot quiet-time** EXEC command.

**clear snapshot quiet-time** *interface*

| *Syntax* | *Description* |
|---|---|
| *interface* | Interface type and number. |

### Command Mode

EXEC

### Usage Guidelines

This command first appeared in Cisco IOS Release 10.3.

The **clear snapshot quiet-time** command places the client router in a state to reenter the active period within two minutes. The two-minute hold period ensures a quiet period of at least two minutes between active periods.

### Example

The following example ends the quiet period on dialer interface 1:

```
clear snapshot quiet-time dialer 1
```

### Related Commands

Search online to find documentation for related commands.

**show snapshot**
**snapshot client**

## DIALER MAP SNAPSHOT

To define a dialer map for Cisco's snapshot routing protocol on a client router connected to a DDR interface, use the **dialer map snapshot** interface configuration command. To delete one or more previously defined snapshot routing dialer maps, use the **no** form of this command.

**dialer map snapshot** *sequence-number dial-string*
**no dialer map snapshot** [*sequence-number*]

| Syntax | Description |
|---|---|
| *sequence-number* | A number in the range from 1 to 254, inclusive, that uniquely identifies a dialer map. |
| *dial-string* | Telephone number of a remote snapshot server to be called during an active period. |

### Default

No snapshot routing dialer map is defined.

### Command Mode

Interface configuration

### Usage Guidelines

This command first appeared in Cisco IOS Release 10.3.

Enter a command for each remote snapshot server router the client router should call during an active period.

Use the **no dialer map snapshot** form of this command to remove all previously defined snapshot dialer maps on the client router; use the **no dialer map snapshot** *sequence-number* form of this command to delete a specified dialer map.

### Examples

The following examples define snapshot dialer maps on a client router:

```
dialer map snapshot 12 4151231234
dialer map snapshot 13 4151231245
```

The following example removes one of the previously defined snapshot routing dialer maps on the client router:

```
no dialer map snapshot 13
```

### Related Commands

Search online to find documentation for related commands.

**dialer rotary-group**
**interface dialer**
**snapshot client**

## SHOW SNAPSHOT

To display snapshot routing parameters associated with an interface, use the **show snapshot** EXEC command.

**show snapshot** [*type number*]

| *Syntax* | *Description* |
|---|---|
| *type number* | (Optional) Interface type and number. |

### Command Mode

EXEC

### Usage Guidelines

This command first appeared in Cisco IOS Release 10.3.

### Sample Display

The following is sample output from the **show snapshot** command:

```
Router# show snapshot serial 1

Serial1 is up, line protocol is up, snapshot up
Options: dialer support
Length of each activation period: 3 minutes
Period between activations:       10 minutes
Retry period on connect failure:  10
For dialer address 240
 Current queue: active, remaining active time: 3 minutes
 Updates received this cycle: ip, ipx, appletalk
For dialer address 1
 Current queue: client quiet, time until next activation: 7 minutes
```

Table 70–1 describes the fields shown in the display.

**Table 70–1** *Show Snapshot Field Descriptions*

| Field | Description |
|---|---|
| Serial1 is up, line protocol is up | Indicates whether the interface hardware is currently active (whether carrier detect is present) and if it has been taken down by an administrator. |
| snapshot up | Indicates whether the snapshot protocol is enabled on the interface. |
| Options: | Option configured on the **snapshot client** or **snapshot server** interface configuration command. It can be one of the following:<br>• dialer support—Snapshot routing is configured with the **dialer** keyword.<br>• stay asleep on carrier up—Snapshot routing is configured with the **suppress-statechange-updates** keyword. |
| Length of each activation period | Length of the active period. |
| Period between activations | Length of the quiet period. |
| Retry period on connect failure | Length of the retry period. |
| For dialer address | Displays information about each dialer rotary group configured with the **dialer map** command. |
| Current queue: | Indicates which period snapshot routing is currently in. It can be one of the following:<br>• active—Routing updates are being exchanged.<br>• client quiet—The client router is in a quiet period, and routing updates are not being exchanged. |

**Table 70–1** *Show Snapshot Field Descriptions, Continued*

| Field | Description |
|---|---|
| | • server quiet—The server router is in a quiet period, awaiting an update from the client router before awakening; routing updates are not being exchanged.<br>• post active—Routing updates are not being exchanged. If the server router receives an update from the client router, it processes it but does not begin an active period. This allows time for resynchronization of active periods between the client and server routers.<br>• no queue—This is a temporary holding queue for new snapshot routing interfaces and for interfaces being deleted. |
| remaining active time<br>time until next activation | Time remaining in the current period. |
| Updates received this cycle | Protocols from which routing updates have been received in the current active period. This line is displayed only if the router or access server is in an active period. |

### SNAPSHOT CLIENT

To configure a client router for snapshot routing, use the **snapshot client** interface configuration command. To disable a client router, use the **no** form of this command.

**snapshot client** *active-time quiet-time* [**suppress-statechange-updates**] [**dialer**]
**no snapshot client** *active-time quiet-time* [**suppress-statechange-updates**] [**dialer**]

| *Syntax* | *Description* |
|---|---|
| *active-time* | Amount of time, in minutes, that routing updates are regularly exchanged between the client and server routers. This can be an integer in the range 5 to 100. There is no default value. A typical value is 5 minutes. |
| *quiet-time* | Amount of time, in minutes, that routing entries are frozen and remain unchanged between active periods. Routes are not aged during the quiet period, so they remain in the routing table as if they were static entries. This argument can be an integer from 8 to 100000. There is no default value. The minimum quiet time is generally the active time plus 3. |
| **suppress-statechange-updates** | (Optional) Disables the exchange of routing updates each time the line protocol goes from "down" to "up" or from "dialer spoofing" to "fully up." |
| **dialer** | (Optional) Used if the client router has to dial up the remote router in the absence of regular traffic. |

### Defaults

Snapshot routing is disabled.

The *active-time* and *quiet-time* arguments have no default values.

### Command Mode

Interface configuration

### Usage Guidelines

This command first appeared in Cisco IOS Release 10.3.

The value of the *active-time* argument must be the same for the client and server routers.

To specify the remote server routers to be called by this client router during each active period, use the **dialer map snapshot** command.

### Example

The following example configures a client router for snapshot routing:

```
interface dialer 1
 snapshot client 5 600 suppress-statechange-updates dialer
```

### Related Commands

Search online to find documentation for related commands.

**clear snapshot quiet-time**
**dialer map snapshot**
**show snapshot**
**snapshot server**

## SNAPSHOT SERVER

To configure a server router for snapshot routing, use the **snapshot server** interface configuration command. To disable a server router, use the **no** form of this command.

**snapshot server** *active-time* [dialer]
**no snapshot server** *active-time* [dialer]

| *Syntax* | *Description* |
|---|---|
| *active-time* | Amount of time, in minutes, that routing updates are regularly exchanged between the client and server routers. This can be an integer in the range 5 to 100. There is no default value. A typical value is 5 minutes. |
| **dialer** | (Optional) Allows the client router to dial up the remote router in the absence of regular traffic. |

### Defaults

Snapshot routing is disabled.

The *active-time* argument has no default value.

### Command Mode

Interface configuration

### Usage Guidelines

This command first appeared in Cisco IOS Release 10.3.

The value of the *active-time* argument must be the same for the client and server routers.

### Example

The following example configures a server router for snapshot routing:

```
interface dialer 1
 snapshot server 5
```

### Related Commands

Search online to find documentation for related commands.

**show snapshot**
**snapshot client**

# CHAPTER 71

# Configuring Accounting

The AAA accounting feature enables you to track the services users are accessing as well as the amount of network resources they are consuming. When **aaa accounting** is activated, the network access server reports user activity to the TACACS+ or RADIUS security server (depending on which security method you have implemented) in the form of accounting records. Each accounting record is comprised of accounting attribute/value (AV) pairs and is stored in a log file on the access control server. This log file can then be analyzed for network management, client billing, and auditing.

## AAA ACCOUNTING TYPES

Cisco IOS Release 11.3 supports five different kinds of accounting:

- Command Accounting
- Connection Accounting
- EXEC Accounting
- Network Accounting
- System Accounting

### Command Accounting

Command accounting provides information about the EXEC shell commands for a specified privilege level that are being executed on a network access server. Each command accounting record includes a list of the commands executed for that privilege level, as well as the date and time each command was executed, and the user who executed it.

The following example shows the information contained in a TACACS+ command accounting record for privilege level 1:

```
Wed Jun 25 03:46:47 1997       172.16.25.15   dpeng  tty3   4082329430/4327528  stop
task_id=3       service=shell   priv-lvl=1      cmd=show version <cr>
```

```
Wed Jun 25 03:46:58 1997      172.16.25.15   dpeng   tty3    4082329430/4327528  stop
task_id=4       service=shell   priv-lvl=1     cmd=show interfaces Ethernet 0 <cr>
Wed Jun 25 03:47:03 1997      172.16.25.15   dpeng   tty3    4082329430/4327528  stop
task_id=5       service=shell   priv-lvl=1     cmd=show ip route <cr>
```

The following example shows the information contained in a TACACS+ command accounting record for privilege level 15:

```
Wed Jun 25 03:47:17 1997      172.16.25.15   dpeng   tty3    4082329430/4327528  stop
task_id=6       service=shell   priv-lvl=15    cmd=configure terminal <cr>
Wed Jun 25 03:47:21 1997      172.16.25.15   dpeng   tty3    4082329430/4327528  stop
task_id=7       service=shell   priv-lvl=15    cmd=interface Serial 0 <cr>
Wed Jun 25 03:47:29 1997      172.16.25.15   dpeng   tty3    4082329430/4327528  stop
task_id=8       service=shell   priv-lvl=15   cmd=ip address 1.1.1.1 255.255.255.0 <cr>
```

**NOTES**

Cisco's implementation of RADIUS does not support command accounting.

### Connection Accounting

Connection accounting provides information about all outbound connections made from the network access server, such as Telnet, local-area transport (LAT), tn3270, packet assembler-disassembler (PAD), and rlogin.

The following example shows the information contained in a RADIUS connection accounting record for an outbound Telnet connection:

```
Wed Jun 25 04:28:00 1997
        NAS-IP-Address = "172.16.25.15"
        NAS-Port = 2
        User-Name = "dpeng"
        Client-Port-DNIS = "4327528"
        Caller-ID = "4082329477"
        Acct-Status-Type = Start
        Acct-Authentic = RADIUS
        Service-Type = Login
        Acct-Session-Id = "00000008"
        Login-Service = Telnet
        Login-IP-Host = "171.68.202.158"
        Acct-Delay-Time = 0
        User-Id = "dpeng"
        NAS-Identifier = "172.16.25.15"

Wed Jun 25 04:28:39 1997
        NAS-IP-Address = "172.16.25.15"
        NAS-Port = 2
        User-Name = "dpeng"
        Client-Port-DNIS = "4327528"
        Caller-ID = "4082329477"
        Acct-Status-Type = Stop
        Acct-Authentic = RADIUS
        Service-Type = Login
```

```
        Acct-Session-Id = "00000008"
        Login-Service = Telnet
        Login-IP-Host = "171.68.202.158"
        Acct-Input-Octets = 10774
        Acct-Output-Octets = 112
        Acct-Input-Packets = 91
        Acct-Output-Packets = 99
        Acct-Session-Time = 39
        Acct-Delay-Time = 0
        User-Id = "dpeng"
        NAS-Identifier = "172.16.25.15"
```

The following example shows the information contained in a TACACS+ connection accounting record for an outbound Telnet connection:

```
Wed Jun 25 03:47:43 1997       172.16.25.15    dpeng   tty3    4082329430/4327528  start
task_id=10      service=connection      protocol=telnet addr=171.68.202.158 cmd=telnet
dpeng-sun
Wed Jun 25 03:48:38 1997       172.16.25.15    dpeng   tty3    4082329430/4327528  stop
task_id=10      service=connection      protocol=telnet addr=171.68.202.158 cmd=telnet
dpeng-sun     bytes_in=4467    bytes_out=96    paks_in=61      paks_out=72 e
lapsed_time=55
```

The following example shows the information contained in a RADIUS connection accounting record for an outbound rlogin connection:

```
Wed Jun 25 04:29:48 1997
        NAS-IP-Address = "172.16.25.15"
        NAS-Port = 2
        User-Name = "dpeng"
        Client-Port-DNIS = "4327528"
        Caller-ID = "4082329477"
        Acct-Status-Type = Start
        Acct-Authentic = RADIUS
        Service-Type = Login
        Acct-Session-Id = "0000000A"
        Login-Service = Rlogin
        Login-IP-Host = "171.68.202.158"
        Acct-Delay-Time = 0
        User-Id = "dpeng"
        NAS-Identifier = "172.16.25.15"

Wed Jun 25 04:30:09 1997
        NAS-IP-Address = "172.16.25.15"
        NAS-Port = 2
        User-Name = "dpeng"
        Client-Port-DNIS = "4327528"
        Caller-ID = "4082329477"
        Acct-Status-Type = Stop
        Acct-Authentic = RADIUS
        Service-Type = Login
        Acct-Session-Id = "0000000A"
        Login-Service = Rlogin
        Login-IP-Host = "171.68.202.158"
        Acct-Input-Octets = 18686
```

```
Acct-Output-Octets = 86
Acct-Input-Packets = 90
Acct-Output-Packets = 68
Acct-Session-Time = 22
Acct-Delay-Time = 0
User-Id = "dpeng"
NAS-Identifier = "172.16.25.15"
```

The following example shows the information contained in a TACACS+ connection accounting record for an outbound rlogin connection:

```
Wed Jun 25 03:48:46 1997       172.16.25.15    dpeng   tty3    4082329430/4327528  start
task_id=12       service=connection       protocol=rlogin addr=171.68.202.158 cmd=rlogin
dpeng-sun /user dpeng
Wed Jun 25 03:51:37 1997       172.16.25.15    dpeng   tty3    4082329430/4327528  stop
task_id=12       service=connection       protocol=rlogin addr=171.68.202.158 cmd=rlogin
dpeng-sun /user dpeng bytes_in=659926 bytes_out=138   paks_in=2378    paks_
out=1251         elapsed_time=171
```

The following example shows the information contained in a TACACS+ connection accounting record for an outbound LAT connection:

```
Wed Jun 25 03:53:06 1997       172.16.25.15    dpeng   tty3    4082329430/4327528  start
task_id=18       service=connection       protocol=lat    addr=VAX        cmd=lat VAX
Wed Jun 25 03:54:15 1997       172.16.25.15    dpeng   tty3    4082329430/4327528  stop
task_id=18       service=connection       protocol=lat    addr=VAX        cmd=lat VAX
bytes_in=0       bytes_out=0      paks_in=0       paks_out=0      elapsed_time=6
```

## EXEC Accounting

EXEC accounting provides information about user EXEC terminal sessions (user shells) on the network access server, including username, date, start and stop times, the access server IP address, and (for dial-in users) the telephone number the call originated from.

The following example shows the information contained in a RADIUS EXEC accounting record for a dial-in user:

```
Wed Jun 25 04:26:23 1997
        NAS-IP-Address = "172.16.25.15"
        NAS-Port = 1
        User-Name = "dpeng"
        Client-Port-DNIS = "4327528"
        Caller-ID = "4082329483"
        Acct-Status-Type = Start
        Acct-Authentic = RADIUS
        Service-Type = Exec-User
        Acct-Session-Id = "00000006"
        Acct-Delay-Time = 0
        User-Id = "dpeng"
        NAS-Identifier = "172.16.25.15"

Wed Jun 25 04:27:25 1997
        NAS-IP-Address = "172.16.25.15"
        NAS-Port = 1
```

```
        User-Name = "dpeng"
        Client-Port-DNIS = "4327528"
        Caller-ID = "4082329483"
        Acct-Status-Type = Stop
        Acct-Authentic = RADIUS
        Service-Type = Exec-User
        Acct-Session-Id = "00000006"
        Acct-Session-Time = 62
        Acct-Delay-Time = 0
        User-Id = "dpeng"
        NAS-Identifier = "172.16.25.15"
```

The following example shows the information contained in a TACACS+ EXEC accounting record for a dial-in user:

```
Wed Jun 25 03:46:21 1997       172.16.25.15    dpeng   tty3    4082329430/4327528  start
task_id=2       service=shell
Wed Jun 25 04:08:55 1997       172.16.25.15    dpeng   tty3    4082329430/4327528  stop
task_id=2       service=shell   elapsed_time=1354
```

The following example shows the information contained in a RADIUS EXEC accounting record for a Telnet user:

```
Wed Jun 25 04:48:32 1997
        NAS-IP-Address = "172.16.25.15"
        NAS-Port = 26
        User-Name = "dpeng"
        Caller-ID = "171.68.202.158"
        Acct-Status-Type = Start
        Acct-Authentic = RADIUS
        Service-Type = Exec-User
        Acct-Session-Id = "00000010"
        Acct-Delay-Time = 0
        User-Id = "dpeng"
        NAS-Identifier = "172.16.25.15"

Wed Jun 25 04:48:46 1997
        NAS-IP-Address = "172.16.25.15"
        NAS-Port = 26
        User-Name = "dpeng"
        Caller-ID = "171.68.202.158"
        Acct-Status-Type = Stop
        Acct-Authentic = RADIUS
        Service-Type = Exec-User
        Acct-Session-Id = "00000010"
        Acct-Session-Time = 14
        Acct-Delay-Time = 0
        User-Id = "dpeng"
        NAS-Identifier = "172.16.25.15"
```

The following example shows the information contained in a TACACS+ EXEC accounting record for a Telnet user:

```
Wed Jun 25 04:06:53 1997        172.16.25.15    dpeng   tty26   171.68.202.158
starttask_id=41      service=shell
```

```
Wed Jun 25 04:07:02 1997     172.16.25.15   dpeng  tty26  171.68.202.158 stoptask_id=41
service=shell   elapsed_time=9
```

## Network Accounting

Network accounting provides information for all PPP, SLIP or ARAP sessions, including packet and byte counts.

The following example shows the information contained in a RADIUS network accounting record for a PPP user who comes in through an EXEC session:

```
Wed Jun 25 04:44:45 1997
        NAS-IP-Address = "172.16.25.15"
        NAS-Port = 5
        User-Name = "dpeng"
        Client-Port-DNIS = "4327528"
        Caller-ID = "408"
        Acct-Status-Type = Start
        Acct-Authentic = RADIUS
        Service-Type = Exec-User
        Acct-Session-Id = "0000000D"
        Acct-Delay-Time = 0
        User-Id = "dpeng"
        NAS-Identifier = "172.16.25.15"

Wed Jun 25 04:45:00 1997
        NAS-IP-Address = "172.16.25.15"
        NAS-Port = 5
        User-Name = "dpeng"
        Client-Port-DNIS = "4327528"
        Caller-ID = "408"
        Acct-Status-Type = Start
        Acct-Authentic = RADIUS
        Service-Type = Framed
        Acct-Session-Id = "0000000E"
        Framed-IP-Address = "10.1.1.2"
        Framed-Protocol = PPP
        Acct-Delay-Time = 0
        User-Id = "dpeng"
        NAS-Identifier = "172.16.25.15"

Wed Jun 25 04:47:46 1997
        NAS-IP-Address = "172.16.25.15"
        NAS-Port = 5
        User-Name = "dpeng"
        Client-Port-DNIS = "4327528"
        Caller-ID = "408"
        Acct-Status-Type = Stop
        Acct-Authentic = RADIUS
        Service-Type = Framed
        Acct-Session-Id = "0000000E"
        Framed-IP-Address = "10.1.1.2"
        Framed-Protocol = PPP
        Acct-Input-Octets = 3075
```

```
        Acct-Output-Octets = 167
        Acct-Input-Packets = 39
        Acct-Output-Packets = 9
        Acct-Session-Time = 171
        Acct-Delay-Time = 0
        User-Id = "dpeng"
        NAS-Identifier = "172.16.25.15"
```

The following example shows the information contained in a TACACS+ network accounting record for a PPP user who first started an EXEC session:

```
Wed Jun 25 04:00:35 1997    172.16.25.15   dpeng  tty4   408/4327528   starttask_id=28
service=shell
Wed Jun 25 04:00:46 1997    172.16.25.15   dpeng  tty4   408/4327528   starttask_id=30
addr=10.1.1.1   service=ppp
Wed Jun 25 04:00:49 1997     172.16.25.15   dpeng   tty4   408/4327528    update
task_id=30      addr=10.1.1.1   service=ppp     protocol=ip     addr=10.1.1.1
Wed Jun 25 04:01:31 1997    172.16.25.15   dpeng  tty4   408/4327528   stoptask_id=30
addr=10.1.1.1   service=ppp     protocol=ip     addr=10.1.1.1   bytes_in=2844
bytes_out=1682  paks_in=36      paks_out=24     elapsed_time=51
Wed Jun 25 04:01:32 1997    172.16.25.15   dpeng  tty4   408/4327528   stoptask_id=28
service=shell   elapsed_time=57
```

The following example shows the information contained in a RADIUS network accounting record for a PPP user who comes in through autoselect:

```
Wed Jun 25 04:30:52 1997
        NAS-IP-Address = "172.16.25.15"
        NAS-Port = 3
        User-Name = "dpeng"
        Client-Port-DNIS = "4327528"
        Caller-ID = "408"
        Acct-Status-Type = Start
        Acct-Authentic = RADIUS
        Service-Type = Framed
        Acct-Session-Id = "0000000B"
        Framed-Protocol = PPP
        Acct-Delay-Time = 0
        User-Id = "dpeng"
        NAS-Identifier = "172.16.25.15"

Wed Jun 25 04:36:49 1997
        NAS-IP-Address = "172.16.25.15"
        NAS-Port = 3
        User-Name = "dpeng"
        Client-Port-DNIS = "4327528"
        Caller-ID = "408"
        Acct-Status-Type = Stop
        Acct-Authentic = RADIUS
        Service-Type = Framed
        Acct-Session-Id = "0000000B"
        Framed-Protocol = PPP
        Framed-IP-Address = "10.1.1.1"
        Acct-Input-Octets = 8630
```

```
Acct-Output-Octets = 5722
Acct-Input-Packets = 94
Acct-Output-Packets = 64
Acct-Session-Time = 357
Acct-Delay-Time = 0
User-Id = "dpeng"
NAS-Identifier = "172.16.25.15"
```

The following example shows the information contained in a TACACS+ network accounting record for a PPP user who comes in through autoselect:

```
Wed Jun 25 04:02:19 1997       172.16.25.15    dpeng   Async5  408/4327528
starttask_id=35      service=ppp
Wed Jun 25 04:02:25 1997      172.16.25.15    dpeng   Async5  408/4327528     update
task_id=35      service=ppp      protocol=ip      addr=10.1.1.2
Wed Jun 25 04:05:03 1997     172.16.25.15   dpeng  Async5 408/4327528    stoptask_id=35
service=ppp      protocol=ip      addr=10.1.1.2    bytes_in=3366    bytes_out=2149
paks_in=42       paks_out=28      elapsed_time=164
```

## System Accounting

System accounting provides information about all system-level events, (for example, when the system reboots, or when accounting is turned on or off).

The following accounting record is an example of a typical TACACS+ system accounting record server indicating that AAA accounting has been turned off:

```
Wed Jun 25 03:55:32 1997       172.16.25.15    unknown unknown unknown start   task_id=25
service=system  event=sys_acct  reason=reconfigure
```

The following accounting record is an example of a TACACS+ system accounting record indicating that AAA accounting has been turned on:

```
Wed Jun 25 03:55:22 1997       172.16.25.15    unknown unknown unknown stop    task_id=23
service=system  event=sys_acct  reason=reconfigure
```

**NOTES**

Cisco's implementation of RADIUS does not support system accounting.

# CONFIGURING AAA ACCOUNTING

This chapter describes the following tasks:

- Enabling Accounting
- Monitoring Accounting

## Prerequisites

Before configuring AAA accounting, you must first:

- Enable AAA on your network access server.
- Define the characteristics of your RADIUS or TACACS+ security server.

## Enabling Accounting

The **aaa accounting** command allows you to create a record for any or all of the accounting functions monitored. To enable AAA accounting, perform the following task in global configuration mode:

| Task | Command |
|---|---|
| Enable accounting. | **aaa accounting** {**system** \| **network** \| **connection** \| **exec** \| **command** *level*} {**start-stop** \| **wait-start** \| **stop-only**} {**tacacs+** \| **radius**} |

For minimal accounting, use the **stop-only** keyword, which instructs the specified authentication system (RADIUS or TACACS+) to send a stop record accounting notice at the end of the requested user process. For more accounting information, use the **start-stop** keyword to send a start accounting notice at the beginning of the requested process and a stop accounting notice at the end of the process. You can further control access and accounting by using the **wait-start** keyword, which ensures that the RADIUS or TACACS+ security server receives the start notice before granting the user's process request.

When **aaa accounting** is activated, the Cisco IOS software issues accounting records for all users on the system, including users whose username string, because of protocol translation, is NULL. To prevent accounting records from being generated for users who do not have usernames associated with them, perform the following task in global configuration mode:

| Task | Command |
|---|---|
| Prevent accounting records from being generated for users whose username string is NULL. | **aaa accounting suppress null-username** |

## Accounting Attribute/Value Pairs

The network access server monitors the accounting functions defined in either TACACS+ attribute/value (AV) pairs or RADIUS attributes, depending on which security method you have implemented.

## MONITORING ACCOUNTING

No specific **show** command exists for either RADIUS or TACACS+. To obtain accounting records displaying information about users currently logged in, perform the following task in EXEC mode:

| Task | Command |
|---|---|
| Step through all active sessions to print all the accounting records for the actively accounted functions. | **show accounting** |

## ACCOUNTING EXAMPLE

In the following sample configuration, RADIUS-style authorization is used to track all usage of the following:

- EXEC commands
- Network services, such as SLIP, PPP, and ARAP
- System-level events not associated with users

```
aaa accounting exec start-stop radius
aaa accounting network start-stop radius
aaa accounting system start-stop radius
```

The **show accounting** command yields the following output for the above configuration:

```
Active Accounted actions on tty0, User billw Priv 1
 Task ID 2, EXEC Accounting record, 00:02:13 Elapsed
 task_id=2 service=shell
 Task ID 3, Connection Accounting record, 00:02:07 Elapsed
 task_id=3 service=connection protocol=telnet address=172.21.14.90 cmd=synth

Active Accounted actions on tty1, User rubble Priv 1
 Task ID 5, Network Accounting record, 00:00:52 Elapsed
 task_id=5 service=ppp protocol=ip address=10.0.0.98

Active Accounted actions on tty10, User bill Priv 1
 Task ID 4, EXEC Accounting record, 00:00:53 Elapsed
 task_id=4 service=shell
```

PART 10

# Virtual Private Dialup Networks

CHAPTER 72

# Configuring Virtual Private Dial-Up Networks

Virtual private dial-up networks allow separate and autonomous protocol domains to share common access infrastructure including modems, access servers, and ISDN routers. VPDN uses the Layer 2 Forwarding protocol (L2F), which permits the tunneling of link level frames.

Using L2F tunneling, an Internet Service Provider (ISP) or other access service can create a virtual tunnel to link a customer's remote sites or remote users with corporate home networks. In particular, a network access server at the ISP's point of presence (POP) exchanges PPP messages with the remote users, and communicates by L2F requests and responses with the customer's home gateway to set up tunnels.

L2F passes protocol-level packets through the virtual tunnel between endpoints of a point-to-point connection.

Frames from the remote users are accepted by the ISP's POP, stripped of any linked framing or transparency bytes, encapsulated in L2F, and forwarded over the appropriate tunnel. The customer's home gateway accepts these L2F frames, strips the L2F encapsulation, and processes the incoming frames for the appropriate interface.

**NOTES**

This implementation of VPDN supports PPP dial-up only.

Cisco routers fast switch Layer 2 Forwarding traffic. In stack group environments in which some L2F traffic is offloaded to a powerful router, fast switching provides improved scalability.

For a complete description of the commands mentioned in this chapter, see Chapter 73, "Virtual Private Dial-Up Network Commands."

## How VPDN Works

Virtual private dial-up networking enables users to configure secure networks that take advantage of Internet Service Providers that tunnel the company's remote access traffic through the ISP cloud.

Remote offices or mobile users can connect to their home network using local dial-up services of third parties. The dial-up service provider agrees to forward the company's traffic from the ISP POP to a company-run home gateway. Network configuration and security remains in the control of the client. The dial-up service provider provides a virtual pipe between the company's sites.

**Notes**

The MMP feature uses L2F to connect multiple PPP sessions for which individual dial-in calls have arrived on different stack group members. L2F provides speed and reliability for the setup and shutdown of Multilink PPP.

A VPDN connection between a remote user and the home LAN is accomplished in the following steps:

1. The remote user initiates a PPP connection to the ISP using the analog telephone system or ISDN.
2. The ISP network access server accepts the connection.
3. The ISP network access server authenticates the end user with CHAP or PAP. The username is used to determine whether the user is a VPDN client. If the user is not a VPDN client, the client accesses the Internet or other contacted service.
4. The tunnel endpoints—the network access server and the home gateway—authenticate *each other* before any sessions are attempted within a tunnel.
5. If no L2F tunnel exists between the network access server and the remote users' home gateway, a tunnel is created. Once the tunnel exists, an unused slot within the tunnel is allocated.
6. The home gateway accepts or rejects the connection. Initial setup can include authentication information required to allow the home gateway to authenticate the user.
7. The home gateway sets up a virtual interface. Link-level frames can now pass through this virtual interface through the L2F tunnel.

Figure 72–1 illustrates a VPDN connection from a remote user, who makes a local call, to the corporate network, through an end-to-end L2F tunnel (shown by the dotted line). The user can even be sent directly to a restricted part or a restricted set of servers on the corporate network based on the user's authentication. In Figure 72–1, the restriction placed on this user is suggested by the arc isolating a part of the corporate network cloud.

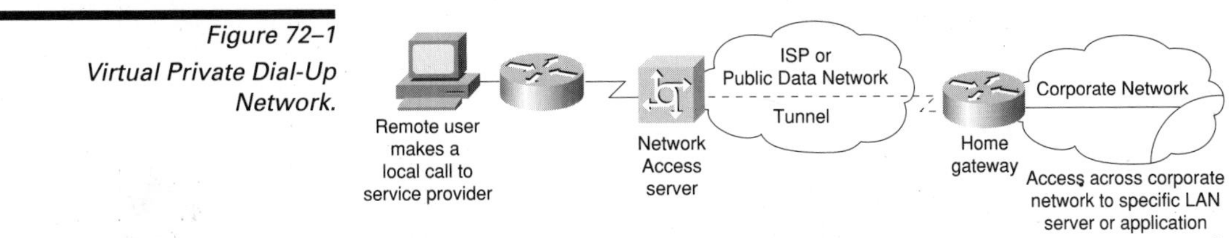


*Figure 72–1 Virtual Private Dial-Up Network.*

## Configuring VPDN on the Home Gateway Router

To configure virtual private dial-up networks on the home gateway router, complete the tasks in the following sections:

- Configure a Virtual Template and Create a Virtual Template Interface
- Configure Incoming VPDN Connections

For more information, see the draft RFC *Level Two Forwarding (Protocol) "L2F,"* which describes the proposed implementation of L2F.

### Configure a Virtual Template and Create a Virtual Template Interface

To configure a virtual template for interfaces on a home gateway access server, perform the following tasks beginning in global configuration mode:

| Task | | Command |
|---|---|---|
| **Step 1** | Create a virtual template interface, and enter interface configuration mode. | **interface virtual-template** *number* |
| **Step 2** | Identify the virtual template interface type and number on the LAN. | **ip unnumbered ethernet 0** |
| **Step 3** | Enable PPP encapsulation on the virtual template interface. | **encapsulation ppp** |
| **Step 4** | Enable PPP authentication on the virtual template interface. | **ppp authentication chap** |

### Configure Incoming VPDN Connections

To configure virtual private dial-up networking on a home gateway router or access server, perform the following tasks in global configuration mode:

| Task | Command |
|---|---|
| Enable virtual private networking. | **vpdn enable** |
| Specify the remote host (the network access server), the local name (the home gateway) to use for authenticating, and the virtual template to use. | **vpdn incoming** *nas-name hgw-name* **virtual-template** *number* |

## Configuring VPDN on the Network Access Server

You can configure the router to authenticate users and also to select the outgoing tunnel based on the home gateway's host name or based on the DNIS information in the incoming calls. In addition, you can configure the tunnel search order:

- Configure the Network Access Server To Authenticate Users
- Configure VPDN Tunnel Lookup Based on Domain Name

  or

- Configure VPDN Tunnel Lookup Based on Dialed Number Information
- Configure VPDN Tunnel Authorization Search Order

### Configure the Network Access Server To Authenticate Users

You can configure the network access to authenticate users before forwarding each connection to the home gateway. This allows you to detect unauthorized users and possibly to lessen the amount of traffic sent over the tunnels. To enable the network access server to authenticate users, complete the following task in global configuration mode:

| Task | Command |
|---|---|
| Enable the network access server to authenticate users. | **vpdn local-authentication** |

### Configure VPDN Tunnel Lookup Based on Domain Name

To configure a network access server to make outgoing L2F connections to a home gateway based on domain name, complete the following tasks in global configuration mode:

| Task | Command |
|---|---|
| Enable virtual private networking. | **vpdn enable** |
| Specify the remote host that is to accept L2F connections. | **vpdn outgoing** *domain-name local-name* **ip** *ip-address* |

### Configure VPDN Tunnel Lookup Based on Dialed Number Information

The network service provider can select a specific VPDN tunnel for outgoing calls from a dial-in user by using the Dialed Number Information Service (DNIS) information provided on ISDN lines.

The ability to select a tunnel based on DNIS provides additional flexibility to network service providers who offer VPDN services and to the corporations that use the services. Instead of having to use only the domain name for tunnel selection, tunnel selection can be based on the dialed number.

With this feature, a corporation—which might have only one domain name—can provide multiple specific phone numbers for users to dial in to the network access server at the service provider's point of presence. The service provider can select the tunnel to the appropriate services or portion of the corporate network based on the dialed number.

To configure a network access server to select outgoing L2F tunnel connections based on DNIS information for virtual private dial-up networking, perform the following tasks in global configuration mode:

| Task | Command |
|---|---|
| Enable virtual private networking. | **vpdn enable** |
| Enable tunnel selection based on DNIS and specify the number to be dialed. | **vpdn outgoing dnis** *number local-name* **ip** *ip-address* |

### Configure VPDN Tunnel Authorization Search Order

When a service provider has multiple AAA servers configured, VPDN tunnel authorization searches based on domain name can be time consuming and might cause the client session to time out.

To provide more flexibility, service providers can now configure the network access server to perform tunnel authorization searches by domain name only, by DNIS only, or by both in a specified order.

To configure the network access server's tunnel authorization searches, perform one of the following tasks in global configuration mode:

| Task | Command |
|---|---|
| Search first on the Dialed Number Information Service (DNIS) information provided on ISDN lines and then search on the domain name. | **vpdn search-order dnis domain** |
| Search first on the domain name and then search on the DNIS information. | **vpdn search-order domain dnis** |
| Search on the domain name only. | **vpdn search-order domain** |
| Search on the DNIS information only. | **vpdn search-order dnis** |

## Monitoring VPDN Virtual Interfaces

To monitor and maintain VPDN virtual interfaces, perform the following task in EXEC mode:

| Task | Command |
|---|---|
| Display information about the active L2F tunnels and the L2F message identifiers. | **show vpdn** |

## VPDN Configuration Examples

In the following example, the network access server is configured to select tunnels based on the dialed number of incoming calls:

```
vpdn enable
vpdn outgoing dnis 4592367 spartan ip 172.34.16.244
```

In the following example, the network access server is configured to select tunnels based on the dialed number of incoming calls and to perform tunnel authorization searches on DNIS only:

```
vpdn enable
vpdn outgoing dnis 4592367 spartan ip 172.34.16.244
vpdn search-order dnis
```

CHAPTER 73

# Virtual Private Dial-Up Network Commands

This chapter describes the commands required to configure virtual private dial-up networks. For information about configuring this feature, see Chapter 72, "Configuring Virtual Private Dial-Up Networks."

## CLEAR VPDN TUNNEL

To shut down a specified tunnel and all the MIDs within it, use the **clear vpdn tunnel** EXEC command.

**clear vpdn tunnel** *network-access-server gateway-name*

| *Syntax* | *Description* |
|---|---|
| *network-access-server* | Name of the network access server at the far end of the tunnel, probably the point of presence of the public data network or the Internet Service Provider's. |
| *gateway-name* | Host name of home gateway at the local end of the tunnel. |

### *Command Mode*

EXEC

### *Usage Guidelines*

This command first appeared in Cisco IOS Release 11.2.

This command is used primarily for troubleshooting. You can use the command to force the tunnel to come down without unconfiguring it (the tunnel could be restarted immediately by a user logging in).

### Example

The following example clears a tunnel between a network access server called orion and a home gateway called sampson:

```
clear vpdn tunnel orion sampson
```

## SHOW VPDN

To display information about active Level 2 Forwarding (L2F) protocol tunnel and Level 2 Forwarding (L2F) message identifiers in a virtual private dial-up network, use the **show vpdn** EXEC command.

**show vpdn**

### Syntax Description

This command has no keywords or arguments.

### Command Mode

EXEC

### Usage Guidelines

This command first appeared in Cisco IOS Release 11.2.

### Sample Display

The following is sample output of the **show vpdn** command:

```
Router# show vpdn

Active L2F tunnels
NAS Name    Gateway Name    NAS CLID    Gateway CLID    State
nas         gateway           4              2          open

L2F MIDs
Name                   NAS Name    Interface    MID      State
phil@cisco.com          nas          As7          1       open
sam@cisco.com           nas          As8          2       open
```

Table 73–1 describes the fields in this sample display.

**Table 73–1** *Show VPDN Field Description*

| Field | Description |
|---|---|
| **Active L2F tunnels** | |
| NAS Name | Host name of the network access server, which is the remote termination point of the tunnel. |

**Table 73–1** *Show VPDN Field Description, Continued*

| Field | Description |
|---|---|
| Gateway Name | Host name of the home gateway, which is local termination point of the tunnel. |
| NAS CLID | A number uniquely identifying the VPDN tunnel on the network access server. |
| Gateway CLID | A number uniquely identifying the VPDN tunnel on the gateway |
| State | Indicates whether the tunnel is open, opening, closing, or closed. |
| **L2F MIDs** | |
| Name | Username of the person from whom a protocol message was forwarded over the tunnel. |
| NAS Name | Host name of the network access server. |
| Interface | Interface from which the protocol message was sent. |
| MID | A number uniquely identifying this user in this tunnel. |
| State | Indicates status for the individual user in the tunnel. The states are: opening, open, closed, closing, and waiting_for_tunnel.<br>The waiting_for_tunnel state means that the user connection is waiting until the main tunnel can be brought up before it moves to the opening state. |

### *Related Commands*

Search online to find documentation for related commands.

**vpdn enable**
**vpdn incoming**
**vpdn outgoing**

## VPDN DOMAIN-DELIMITER

To specify the characters to be used to delimit the domain prefix or domain suffix, use the **vpdn domain-delimiter** global configuration command.

**vpdn domain-delimiter** *characters* [**suffix** | **prefix**]

| *Syntax* | *Description* |
|---|---|
| *characters* | One or more specific characters to be used as suffix or prefix delimiters. Available characters are %, –, @, \ , #, and /. If a backslash (\) is the last delimiter in the command line, enter it as a double backslash (\\). |
| **suffix** \| **prefix** | Usage of the specified characters. |

### *Default*

This command is disabled.

### *Command Mode*

Global configuration

### *Usage Guidelines*

This command first appeared in Cisco IOS Release 11.3.

You can enter one **vpdn domain-delimiter** command to list the suffix delimiters and another **vpdn domain-delimiter** command to list the prefix delimiters. However, no character can be both a suffix delimiter and a prefix delimiter.

This command allows the network access server to parse a list of home gateway DNS domain names and addresses sent by an AAA server. The AAA server can store domain names or IP addresses in the following AV pair:

```
cisco-avpair = "lcp:interface-config=ip address 1.1.1.1 255.255.255.255.0",
cisco-avpair = "lcp:interface-config=ip address bigrouter@excellentinc.com,
```

### *Examples*

The following example lists three suffix delimiters and three prefix delimiters:

```
vpdn domain-delimiter %-@ suffix
vpdn domain-delimiter #/\\ prefix
```

This example allows the following host and domain names:

```
cisco.com#houstonddr
houstonddr@cisco.com
```

### *Related Commands*

Search online to find documentation for related commands.

**vpdn enable**
**vpdn incoming**
**vpdn outgoing**
**vpdn search-order**

## VPDN ENABLE

To enable virtual private dial-up networking on the router and inform the router to look for tunnel definitions in a local database and on a remote authorization server (home gateway), if one is present, use the **vpdn enable** global configuration command.

**vpdn enable**

### *Syntax Description*

This command has no keywords or arguments.

### *Default*

Disabled

### *Command Mode*

Global configuration

### *Usage Guidelines*

This command first appeared in Cisco IOS Release 11.2.

### *Example*

The following example enables virtual private dial-up networking on the router:

```
vpdn enable
```

### *Related Commands*

Search online to find documentation for related commands.

**vpdn incoming**
**vpdn outgoing**

## VPDN FORCE-LOCAL-CHAP

To cause the home gateway to issue its own CHAP challenge even if one has already been issued from the network access server, use the **vpdn force-local-chap** global configuration command. To disable the home gateway's issuing its own CHAP challenge, use the **no** form of this command.

**vpdn force-local-chap**
**no vpdn force-local-chap**

### *Syntax Description*

This command has no arguments or keywords.

### *Default*

The home gateway does not issue its own CHAP challenge.

### Command Mode

Global configuration

### Usage Guidelines

This command first appeared in Cisco IOS Release 11.2.

### Example

The following example configures a virtual template interface on the home gateway and then enables VPDN and forces the home gateway to issue its own CHAP challenge.

```
interface virtual-template 1
ip unnumbered ethernet 0
encapsulation ppp
ppp authentication chap
!
vpdn enable
vpdn incoming world12 troll virtual-template 1
vpdn force-local-chap
```

## VPDN INCOMING

To specify the local name to use for authenticating and the virtual template to use for building interfaces for incoming connections when a Level 2 Forwarding (tunnel) connection is requested from a certain remote host, use the **vpdn incoming** global configuration command.

**vpdn incoming** *remote-name local-name* **virtual-template** *number*

| *Syntax* | *Description* |
| --- | --- |
| *remote-name* | Case-sensitive name of the remote host requesting the connection. |
| *local-name* | Case-sensitive local name to use when authenticating back to the remote host. |
| **virtual-template** *number* | Virtual template to use for building interfaces for incoming calls. |

### Default

Disabled. No host name, IP address, or local name for authentication is provided.

### Command Mode

Global configuration

### Usage Guidelines

This command first appeared in Cisco IOS Release 11.2.

The *remote-name* and *local-name* arguments are case-sensitive.

This command is usually used on a home gateway, not on the network access server in the ISP or public data network.

### *Example*

The following partial example specifies use of local host go_blue and virtual template interface 6 for connections with remote host dallas_wan:

```
vpdn incoming dallas_wan go_blue virtual-template 6
```

## VPDN LOCAL-AUTHENTICATION

To enable local authentication of users on the network access server before the connection is forwarded to the home gateway, use the **vpdn local-authentication** global configuration command. To reset the network access server to the default in which local authentication is disabled, use the **no** form of this command.

**vpdn local-authentication**
**no vpdn local-authentication**

### *Syntax Description*

This command has no arguments and keywords.

### *Default*

This command is disabled.

### *Command Mode*

Global configuration

### *Usage Guidelines*

This command first appeared in Cisco IOS Release 11.3.

### *Example*

In the following example, the network access server is configured to select tunnels based on the dialed number of incoming calls and to authenticate users locally:

```
vpdn enable
vpdn outgoing dnis 4592367 spartan ip 172.34.16.244
vpdn local-authentication
```

### *Related Commands*

Search online for documentation for related commands.

**vpdn enable**
**vpdn outgoing**

### VPDN OUTGOING

To specify use of Dialed Number Information Service (DNIS) or use of a domain name when selecting a tunnel for forwarding traffic to the remote host (the home gateway) on a virtual private dial-up network, use the **vpdn outgoing** global configuration command.

**vpdn outgoing** {**dnis** *dialed-number* | *domain-name*} *local-name* **ip** *ip-address*

| *Syntax* | *Description* |
|---|---|
| **dnis** *dialed-number* | Dialed number to be used for selecting a specific tunnel to be used for forwarding traffic to a home gateway. |
| *domain-name* | Case-sensitive name of the domain to forward traffic to. |
| *local-name* | Case-sensitive local name to use when authenticating the tunnel to the remote host. |
| **ip** *ip-address* | IP address of the remote host (home gateway). |

#### *Default*

Disabled. No remote names and local names are defined.

#### *Command Mode*

Global configuration

#### *Usage Guidelines*

This command first appeared in Cisco IOS Release 11.2

The *domain-name* and *local-name* arguments are case-sensitive.

This command is usually used on a network access server, not on a home gateway.

When use of the Dialed Number Information Service is enabled and a dialed number is provided, the network service provider can use the dialed number to select a specific tunnel destination.

The domain name can be used to choose a tunnel destination. For example, if a user dials in as "joe@company-a.com," then matching on "company-a.com," a tunnel destination can be chosen.

If both DNIS information and a CHAP or PAP name map to a valid tunnel, the DNIS information is used.

If TACACS+ is used to get tunnel information, the string "dnis:" is prepended to the phone number before attempting to look up the information in AAA.

#### *Examples*

The following example selects a tunnel destination based on the domain name:

```
vpdn outgoing chicago-main go-blue ip 172.17.33.125
```

The following example selects a tunnel destination based on the use of DNIS and a specific dialed number:

```
vpdn outgoing dnis 2387765 gocardinal ip 170.16.44.56
```

### *Related Commands*

Search online to find documentation for related commands.

**vpdn enable**
**vpdn incoming**

## VPDN SEARCH-ORDER

To specify how the service provider's network access server is to perform VPDN tunnel authorization searches, use the **vpdn search-order** global configuration command. To remove a prior specification, use the **no** form of the command.

**vpdn search-order {dnis domain | domain dnis | domain | dnis}**
**no vpdn search-order**

| *Syntax* | *Description* |
|---|---|
| **dnis domain** | Search first on the Dialed Number Information Service (DNIS) information provided on ISDN lines and then search on the domain name. |
| **domain dnis** | Search first on the domain name and then search on the DNIS information. |
| **domain** | Search on the domain name only. |
| **dnis** | Search on the DNIS information only. |

### *Default*

When this command is not used, the default is to search first on the Dialed Number Information Service (DNIS) information provided on ISDN lines and then search on the domain name. This is equivalent to using the **vpdn search-order dnis domain** command.

### *Command Mode*

Global configuration

### *Usage Guidelines*

This command first appeared in Cisco IOS Release 11.3.

VPDN authorization searches are performed only as specified.

The configuration shows the **vpdn search-order** command setting only if the command is explicitly configured.

### *Example*

The following example configures a network access server to select a tunnel destination based on the use of DNIS and a specific dialed number, and to perform tunnel authorization searches based on the DNIS information only.

```
vpdn enable
vpdn outgoing dnis 2387765 gocardinal ip 170.16.44.56
vpdn search-order dnis
```

### *Related Commands*

Search online to find documentation for related commands.

**vpdn outgoing**

## VPDN SOURCE-IP

To set the source IP address of the network access server, use the **vpdn source-ip** global configuration command.

**vpdn source-ip** *address*

| *Syntax* | *Description* |
|---|---|
| *address* | IP address of the network access server. |

### *Default*

This command is disabled. No default IP address is provided.

### *Command Mode*

Global configuration

### *Usage Guidelines*

This command first appeared in Cisco IOS Release 11.3.

One source IP address is configured on the network access server. The source IP address is configured per network access server, not per domain.

### *Example*

This example enables VPDN on the network access server and sets an IP source address of 171.4.48.3.

```
vpdn enable
vpdn source-ip 171.4.48.3
```

### *Related Commands*

Search online for documentation for related commands.

**vpdn enable**

PART 11

# Other Network Traffic on ISDN Channels

CHAPTER 74

# Configuring X.25 on ISDN

You can configure X.25 on ISDN in two ways:

- If the ISDN traffic will cross an X.25 network, you configure the ISDN interface as described in Chapter 11, "Setting Up ISDN Basic Rate Service," or in section, "Configuring ISDN PRI," found in Chapter 15, "Configuring Channelized E1 and Channelized T1," making sure to configure that ISDN interface for X.25 addressing and encapsulation.
- If the D channel of an ISDN BRI interface is to carry X.25 traffic, you configure the feature described in this chapter.

Basic Rate Interface (BRI) is an Integrated Systems Digital Network (ISDN) interface, and it consists of two B channels (B1 and B2) and one D channel. The B channels are used to transfer data, voice, and video. The D channel controls the B channels.

ISDN uses the D channel to carry signal information. ISDN can also use the D channel in a BRI to carry X.25 packets. The D channel has a capacity of 16 Kbps, and the X.25 over D channel can utilize up to 9.6 Kbps.

When this feature is configured, a separate X.25-over-D-channel logical interface is created. You can set its parameters without disrupting the original ISDN interface configuration. The original BRI interface will continue to represent the D, B1, and B2 channels.

Because some end-user equipment uses static terminal endpoint identifiers (TEIs) to access this feature, static TEIs are supported. The dialer understands the X.25-over-D-channel calls and initiates them on a new interface.

X.25 traffic over the D channel can be used as a primary interface where low-volume, sporadic interactive traffic is the normal mode of operation. Supported traffic includes IPX, AppleTalk, transparent bridging, XNS, DECnet, and IP.

This feature is not available on the ISDN Primary Rate Interface (PRI).

For a complete description of the commands mentioned in this chapter, see Chapter 75, "X.25 on ISDN Commands."

## X.25 on ISDN D Channel Configuration Tasks

To configure an ISDN BRI interface (and create a special ISDN interface) to carry X.25 traffic on the D channel, complete the following tasks beginning in global configuration mode:

| Task | | Command |
|---|---|---|
| **Step 1** | Specify an ISDN BRI interface. | **interface bri** *number* |
| **Step 2** | Specify a static TEI, if required by the switch. | **isdn x25 static-tei** *number* |
| **Step 3** | Create a configurable interface for X.25 traffic over the ISDN D channel. | **isdn x25 dchannel** |
| **Step 4** | Configure X.25-over-ISDN interface for X.25 traffic. | |

The new X.25-over-ISDN interface is called **interface bri** *number*:0 in configuration displays. It must be configured as an individual X.25 interface.

**Notes**

The **encapsulation x25** command is neither required nor used on this new interface, but other X.25 commands can be used to configure this interface.

If you want to remove the X.25-over-ISDN interface later, use the **no isdn x25 dchannel** command.

## X.25 on ISDN D Channel Configuration Example

The following example creates a BRI 0:0 interface for X.25 traffic over the D channel and then configures the new interface to carry X.25 traffic.

```
interface bri0
 isdn x25 dchannel
 isdn x25 static-tei 8
!
interface bri0:0
 ip address 10.1.1.2 255.255.255.0
 x25 address 31107000000100
 x25 htc 1
 x25 suppress-calling-address
 x25 facility windowsize 2 2
 x25 facility packetsize 256 256
 x25 facility throughput 9600 9600
 x25 map ip 10.1.1.3 31107000000200
```

# CHAPTER 75

# X.25 on ISDN Commands

This chapter describes the commands specific to configuring X.25 on an ISDN BRI D channel.

For ISDN BRI commands, see Chapter 12, "ISDN Basic Rate Service Setup Commands." For information about X.25 configuration tasks, see Chapter 74, "Configuring X.25 on ISDN."

## INTERFACE BRI

To configure a Basic Rate Interface (BRI) interface and enter interface configuration mode, use the **interface bri** global configuration command.

**interface bri** *number*
**interface bri** *slot/port* (Cisco 7500 series)

To configure a BRI subinterface only, use the following form of the **interface bri** global configuration command:

**interface bri** *number.subinterface-number* [**multipoint** | **point-to-point**]
**interface bri** *slot/port.subinterface-number* [**multipoint** | **point-to-point**] (Cisco 7500 series)

To specify the BRI interface that is created by enabling X.25 on a specified ISDN BRI interface, use the **interface bri** command with a subinterface 0 specification:

**interface bri** *number*:0
**interface bri** *slot/port*:0 (Cisco 7200 series)

| *Syntax* | *Description* |
|---|---|
| *number* | Port, connector, or interface card number. The numbers are assigned at the factory at the time of installation or when added to a system, and can be displayed with the **show interfaces** command. |

| | |
|---|---|
| *slot/port* | On the Cisco 7200 series, slot location and port number of the interface. |
| *.subinterface-number* | Subinterface number in the range 1 to 4294967293. The *number* that precedes the period (.) must match the *number* this subinterface belongs to. |
| **multipoint** \| **point-to-point** | (Optional) Specifies a multipoint or point-to-point subinterface. The default is **multipoint**. |
| :0 | The subinterface created by applying the **isdn x25 static-tei** and the **isdn x25 dchannel** commands to the specified BRI interface. This interface must be configured for X.25. |

### Default

The default mode for subinterfaces is multipoint.

### Command Mode

Global configuration

### Usage Guidelines

This command first appeared in Cisco IOS Release 10.3. The capability to carry X.25 traffic on the D channel was added in Cisco IOS Release 11.2 F. This command was modified in Cisco IOS Release 11.2 P to include slot/port syntax for the PA-8B-ST and PA-4B-U port adapters on Cisco 7200 series routers.

Subinterfaces can be configured to support partially meshed Frame Relay networks.

### Example

The following example creates a BRI 0:0 interface for X.25 traffic over the D channel and then configures the new interface to carry X.25 traffic:

```
interface bri0
 isdn x25 dchannel
 isdn x25 static-tei 8
!
interface bri0:0
 ip address 10.1.1.2 255.255.255.0
 x25 address 31107000000100
 x25 htc 1
 x25 suppress-calling-address
 x25 facility windowsize 2 2
 x25 facility packetsize 256 256
 x25 facility throughput 9600 9600
 x25 map ip 10.1.1.3 31107000000200
```

### Related Commands

Search online to find documentation for related commands.

**dialer map**
**dialer-group**
**encapsulation ppp**
**isdn spid1**
**isdn spid2**
**ppp authentication chap**
**ppp authentication pap**
**show interfaces bri**

## ISDN X25 DCHANNEL

To create a configurable interface for X.25 traffic over the ISDN D channel, use the **isdn x25 dchannel** interface configuration command. To remove the interface, use the **no** form of this command.

**isdn x25 dchannel**
**no isdn x25 dchannel**

### *Syntax Description*

This command has no arguments or keywords.

### *Default*

Disabled

### *Command Mode*

Interface configuration

### *Usage Guidelines*

This command first appeared in Cisco IOS Release 11.2 F.

This command creates a new, configurable interface, which can be specified as **interface bri*x*:0** in commands, where *x* is the original BRI interface number.

For example, on a Cisco 4500 router with an MBRI, if the **isdn x25 dchannel** command is configured on bri5, the new interface is bri5:0 and can be used for configuring the other parameters for X.25 over the D channel. These parameters include the addresses, the map statements, and others.

To display the new interface, use the **show running config** command.

### *Example*

The following example creates interface bri 1:0 and configures it for X.25 over the ISDN D channel. This example uses dynamic TEIs, not a static TEI.

```
interface bri1
 isdn x25 dchannel
!
interface bri1:0
```

```
ip address 10.1.1.2 255.255.255.0
x25 address 31107000000100
x25 htc 1
x25 suppress-calling-address
x25 facility windowsize 2 2
x25 facility packetsize 256 256
x25 facility throughput 9600 9600
x25 map ip 10.1.1.3 31107000000200
x25 map ip 10.1.1.4 31107000000800
```

### *Related Commands*

Search online to find documentation for related commands.

**interface bri**

## ISDN X25 STATIC-TEI

To configure a static ISDN Layer 2 terminal endpoint identifier (TEI) for X.25 over the ISDN D channel, use the **isdn x25 static-tei** interface configuration command. Use the **no** form of this command if dynamic TEIs will be used on the interface that is to carry X.25 traffic over the D channel.

**isdn x25 static-tei** *tei-number*

| *Syntax* | *Description* |
|---|---|
| *tei-number* | Terminal endpoint identifier, in the range 0 to 63. |

### *Default*

Disabled

### *Command Mode*

Interface configuration

### *Usage Guidelines*

This command first appeared in Cisco IOS Release 11.2 F.

This command applies to ISDN BRI interfaces only. Only one static TEI is allowed per BRI interface. If a second static TEI is configured, the first static TEI is overwritten.

Some switches require a static TEI be used for X.25 over the ISDN D channel.

When the **isdn x25 dchannel** command is invoked without the **isdn x25 static-tei** command, a dynamic TEI is chosen.

### *Examples*

The following example creates static TEI 8 on the X.25-over-ISDN-D channel:

```
interface bri0
isdn x25 dchannel
isdn x25 static-tei 8
```

Because the **isdn x25 static-tei** command is missing, the following example configuration sets dynamic TEIs for the ISDN channel:

```
interface bri0
isdn x25 dchannel
```

### *Related Commands*

Search online to find documentation for related commands.

**interface bri**
**isdn x25 dchannel**

**PART 12**

# Dial-Related Addressing Services

# CHAPTER 76

# Configuring Network Address Translation

Two of the key problems facing the Internet are depletion of IP address space and scaling in routing. Network Address Translation (NAT) is a feature that allows an organization's IP network to appear from the outside to use a different IP address space than what it is actually using. Thus, NAT allows an organization with nonglobally routable addresses to connect to the Internet by translating those addresses into a globally routable address space. NAT also allows a more graceful renumbering strategy for organizations that are changing service providers or voluntarily renumbering into classless interdomain routing (CIDR) blocks. NAT is also described in RFC 1631. For a complete description of the NAT commands in this chapter, see Chapter 77, "Network Address Translation Commands."

## NAT Business Applications

NAT has several applications. Use it for the following situations:

- You want to connect to the Internet, but not all your hosts have globally unique IP addresses. NAT enables private IP internetworks that use nonregistered IP addresses to connect to the Internet. NAT is configured on the router at the border of a stub domain (referred to as the *inside network*) and a public network such as the Internet (referred to as the *outside network*). NAT translates the internal local addresses to globally unique IP addresses before sending packets to the outside network.
- You must change your internal addresses. Instead of changing them, which can be a considerable amount of work, you can translate them by using NAT.
- You want to do basic load sharing of TCP traffic. You can map a single global IP address to many local IP addresses by using the TCP load distribution feature.

As a solution to the connectivity problem, NAT is practical only when relatively few hosts in a stub domain communicate outside of the domain at the same time. When this is the case, only a small subset of the IP addresses in the domain must be translated into globally unique IP addresses when outside communication is necessary, and these addresses can be reused when no longer in use.

## Benefits of NAT

A significant advantage of NAT is that it can be configured without requiring changes to hosts or routers other than those few routers on which NAT will be configured. As discussed previously, NAT may not be practical if large numbers of hosts in the stub domain communicate outside of the domain. Furthermore, some applications use embedded IP addresses in such a way that it is impractical for a NAT device to translate. These applications may not work transparently or at all through a NAT device. NAT also hides the identity of hosts, which may be an advantage or a disadvantage.

A router configured with NAT will have at least one interface to the inside and one to the outside. In a typical environment, NAT is configured at the exit router between a stub domain and backbone. When a packet is leaving the domain, NAT translates the locally significant source address into a globally unique address. When a packet is entering the domain, NAT translates the globally unique destination address into a local address. If more than one exit point exists, each NAT must have the same translation table. If the software cannot allocate an address because it has run out of addresses, it drops the packet and sends an ICMP Host Unreachable packet.

A router configured with NAT must not advertise the local networks to the outside. However, routing information that NAT receives from the outside can be advertised in the stub domain as usual.

## NAT Terminology

As mentioned previously, the term *inside* refers to those networks that are owned by an organization and that must be translated. Inside this domain, hosts will have address in the one address space, while on the outside, they will appear to have addresses in a another address space when NAT is configured. The first address space is referred to as the *local* address space while the second is referred to as the *global* address space.

Similarly, *outside* refers to those networks to which the stub network connects, and which are generally not under the organization's control. As will be described later, hosts in outside networks can be subject to translation also, and can, thus, have local and global addresses.

To summarize, NAT uses the following definitions:

- **inside local address**—The IP address that is assigned to a host on the inside network. The address is probably not a legitimate IP address assigned by the Network Information Center (NIC) or service provider.
- **inside global address**—A legitimate IP address (assigned by the NIC or service provider) that represents one or more inside local IP addresses to the outside world.

- **outside local address**—The IP address of an outside host as it appears to the inside network. Not necessarily a legitimate address, it was allocated from an address space routable on the inside.
- **outside global address**—The IP address assigned to a host on the outside network by the host's owner. The address was allocated from globally routable address or network space.

## NAT Configuration Task List

Before configuring any NAT translation, you must know your inside local addresses and inside global addresses. The following sections discuss how you can use NAT to perform optional tasks:

- Translating Inside Source Addresses
- Overloading an Inside Global Address
- Translating Overlapping Addresses
- Providing TCP Load Distribution
- Changing Translation Timeouts
- Monitoring and Maintaining NAT

## Translating Inside Source Addresses

Use this feature to translate your own IP addresses into globally unique IP addresses when communicating outside of your network. You can configure static or dynamic inside source translation as follows:

- *Static translation* establishes a one-to-one mapping between your inside local address and an inside global address. Static translation is useful when a host on the inside must be accessible by a fixed address from the outside.
- *Dynamic translation* establishes a mapping between an inside local address and a pool of global addresses.

Figure 76–1 illustrates a router that is translating a source address inside a network to a source address outside the network.

The following process describes inside source address translation, as shown in Figure 130:

1. The user at Host 1.1.1.1 opens a connection to Host B.
2. The first packet that the router receives from Host 1.1.1.1 causes the router to check its NAT table.
    - If a static translation entry was configured, the router goes to Step 3.
    - If no translation entry exists, the router determines that source address (SA) 1.1.1.1 must be translated dynamically, selects a legal, global address from the dynamic address pool, and creates a translation entry. This type of entry is called a *simple entry*.

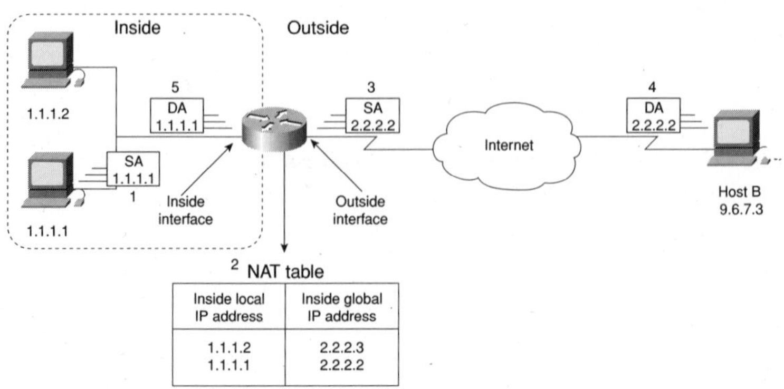


*Figure 76–1*
*NAT Inside Source Translation.*

3. The router replaces the inside local source address of Host 1.1.1.1 with the translation entry's global address, and forwards the packet.
4. Host B receives the packet and responds to Host 1.1.1.1 by using the inside global IP destination address (DA) 2.2.2.2.
5. When the router receives the packet with the inside global IP address, it performs a NAT table lookup by using the inside global address as a key. It then translates the address to the inside local address of Host 1.1.1.1 and forwards the packet to Host 1.1.1.1.
6. Host 1.1.1.1 receives the packet and continues the conversation. The router performs Steps 2 through 5 for each packet.

## Configure Static Translation

To configure static inside source address translation, perform the following tasks beginning in global configuration mode:

| Task | Command |
|---|---|
| Establish static translation between an inside local address and an inside global address. | **ip nat inside source static** *local-ip global-ip* |
| Specify the inside interface. | **interface** *type number* |
| Mark the interface as connected to the inside. | **ip nat inside** |
| Specify the outside interface. | **interface** *type number* |
| Mark the interface as connected to the outside. | **ip nat outside** |

The previous steps are the minimum you must configure. You could configure multiple inside and outside interfaces.

## Configure Dynamic Translation

To configure dynamic inside source address translation, perform the following tasks beginning in global configuration mode:

| Task | Command |
|---|---|
| Define a pool of global addresses to be allocated as needed. | **ip nat pool** *name start-ip end-ip* {**netmask** *netmask* \| **prefix-length** *prefix-length*} |
| Define a standard access list permitting those addresses that are to be translated. | **access-list** *access-list-number* **permit** *source* [*source-wildcard*] |
| Establish dynamic source translation, specifying the access list defined in the prior step. | **ip nat inside source list** *access-list-number* **pool** *name* |
| Specify the inside interface. | **interface** *type number* |
| Mark the interface as connected to the inside. | **ip nat inside** |
| Specify the outside interface. | **interface** *type number* |
| Mark the interface as connected to the outside. | **ip nat outside** |

**NOTES**

The access list must permit only those addresses that are to be translated. (Remember that there is an implicit "deny all" at the end of each access-list.) An access list that is too permissive can lead to unpredictable results.

The following example translates all source addresses passing access list 1 (having a source address from 192.168.1.0/24) to an address from the pool named net-208. The pool contains addresses from 171.69.233.208 to 171.69.233.233.

```
ip nat pool net-208 171.69.233.208 171.69.233.233 netmask 255.255.255.240
ip nat inside source list 1 pool net-208
!
interface serial 0
 ip address 171.69.232.182 255.255.255.240
 ip nat outside
!
interface ethernet 0
 ip address 192.168.1.94 255.255.255.0
```

```
 ip nat inside
!
access-list 1 permit 192.168.1.0 0.0.0.255
```

## Overloading an Inside Global Address

You can conserve addresses in the inside global address pool by allowing the router to use one global address for many local addresses. When this overloading is configured, the router maintains enough information from higher-level protocols (for example, TCP or UDP port numbers) to translate the global address back to the correct local address. When multiple local addresses map to one global address, the TCP or UDP port numbers of each inside host distinguish between the local addresses.

Figure 76–2 illustrates NAT operation when one inside global address represents multiple inside local addresses. The TCP port numbers act as differentiators.

*Figure 76–2 NAT Overloading Inside Global Addresses.*

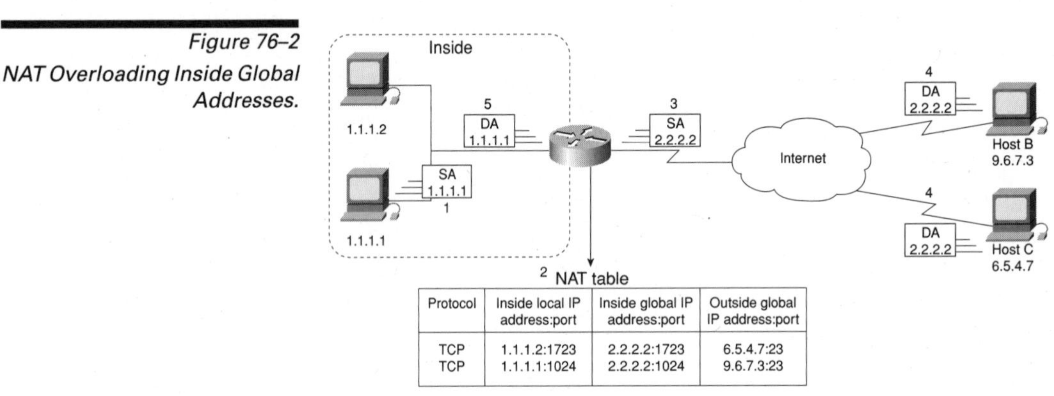


| Protocol | Inside local IP address:port | Inside global IP address:port | Outside global IP address:port |
|---|---|---|---|
| TCP | 1.1.1.2:1723 | 2.2.2.2:1723 | 6.5.4.7:23 |
| TCP | 1.1.1.1:1024 | 2.2.2.2:1024 | 9.6.7.3:23 |

The router performs the following process in overloading inside global addresses, as shown in Figure 131. Both Host B and Host C think they are talking to a single host at address 2.2.2.2. They are actually talking to different hosts; the port number is the differentiator. In fact, many inside hosts could share the inside global IP address by using many port numbers.

1. The user at Host 1.1.1.1 opens a connection to Host B.
2. The first packet that the router receives from Host 1.1.1.1 causes the router to check its NAT table.

   If no translation entry exists, the router determines that address 1.1.1.1 must be translated, and sets up a translation of inside local address 1.1.1.1 to a legal global address. If overloading is enabled, and another translation is active, the router reuses the global address from that translation and saves enough information to be able to translate back. This type of entry is called an *extended entry*.

3. The router replaces the inside local source address 1.1.1.1 with the selected global address and forwards the packet.
4. Host B receives the packet and responds to Host 1.1.1.1 by using the inside global IP address 2.2.2.2.
5. When the router receives the packet with the inside global IP address, it performs a NAT table lookup, using the protocol, inside global address and port, and outside address and port as a key, translates the address to inside local address 1.1.1.1, and forwards the packet to Host 1.1.1.1.
6. Host 1.1.1.1 receives the packet and continues the conversation. The router performs Steps 2 through 5 for each packet.

To configure overloading of inside global addresses, perform the following tasks beginning in global configuration mode:

| Task | Command |
|---|---|
| Define a pool of global addresses to be allocated as needed. | **ip nat pool** *name start-ip end-ip* {**netmask** *netmask* \| **prefix-length** *prefix-length*} |
| Define a standard access list. | **access-list** *access-list-number* **permit** *source* [*source-wildcard*] |
| Establish dynamic source translation, identifying the access list defined in the prior step. | **ip nat inside source list** *access-list-number* **pool** *name* **overload** |
| Specify the inside interface. | **interface** *type number* |
| Mark the interface as connected to the inside. | **ip nat inside** |
| Specify the outside interface. | **interface** *type number* |
| Mark the interface as connected to the outside. | **ip nat outside** |

**NOTES**

The access list must permit only those addresses that are to be translated. (Remember that there is an implicit "deny all" at the end of each access list.) An access list that is too permissive can lead to unpredictable results.

The following example creates a pool of addresses named net-208. The pool contains addresses from 171.69.233.208 to 171.69.233.233. Access list 1 allows packets having the source address from 192.168.1.0 to 192.168.1.255. If no translation exists, packets matching access list 1 are translated to an address from the pool. The router allows multiple local addresses (192.168.1.0 to 192.168.1.255) to use the same global address. The router retains port numbers to differentiate the connections.

```
ip nat pool net-208 171.69.233.208 171.69.233.233 netmask 255.255.255.240
ip nat inside source list 1 pool net-208 overload
!
interface serial0
 ip address 171.69.232.182 255.255.255.240
 ip nat outside
!
interface ethernet0
 ip address 192.168.1.94 255.255.255.0
 ip nat inside
!
access-list 1 permit 192.168.1.0 0.0.0.255
```

## Translating Overlapping Addresses

The NAT overview discusses translating IP addresses, perhaps because your IP addresses are not legal, officially assigned IP addresses. Perhaps you chose IP addresses that officially belong to another network. The case of an address used both illegally and legally is called *overlapping*. You can use NAT to translate inside addresses that overlap with outside addresses. Use this feature if your IP addresses in the stub network are legitimate IP addresses belonging to another network, and you want to communicate with those hosts or routers.

Figure 76–3 shows how NAT translates overlapping networks.

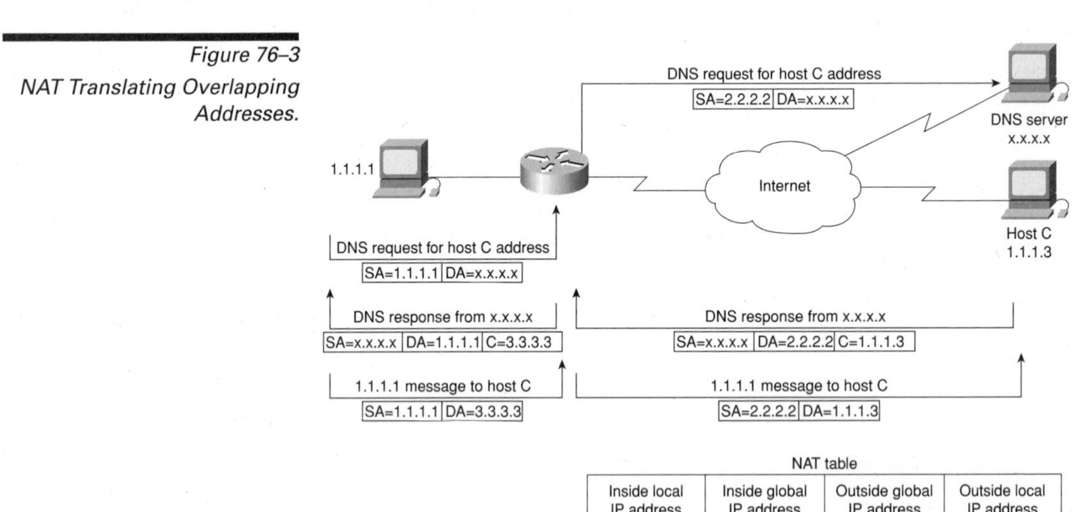


| Inside local IP address | Inside global IP address | Outside global IP address | Outside local IP address |
|---|---|---|---|
| 1.1.1.1 | 2.2.2.2 | 1.1.1.3 | 3.3.3.3 |

*Figure 76–3 NAT Translating Overlapping Addresses.*

The router performs the following process when translating overlapping addresses:

1. The user at Host 1.1.1.1 opens a connection to Host C by name, requesting a name-to-address lookup from a DNS server.
2. The router intercepts the DNS reply and translates the returned address if there is an overlap (that is, the resulting legal address resides illegally in the inside network). To translate the return address, the router creates a simple translation entry mapping the overlapping address 1.1.1.3 to an address from a separately configured, outside local address pool.

   The router examines every DNS reply from everywhere, ensuring that the IP address is not in the stub network. If it is, the router translates the address.
3. Host 1.1.1.1 opens a connection to 3.3.3.3.
4. The router sets up translations mapping inside local and global addresses to each other, and outside global and local addresses to each other.
5. The router replaces the source address with the inside global address and replaces the destination address with the outside global address.
6. Host C receives the packet and continues the conversation.
7. The router does a lookup, replaces the destination address with the inside local address, and replaces the source address with the outside local address.
8. Host 1.1.1.1 receives the packet, and the conversation continues, using this translation process.

## Configure Static Translation

To configure static outside source address translation, perform the following tasks beginning in global configuration mode:

| Task | Command |
|---|---|
| Establish static translation between an outside local address and an outside global address. | **ip nat outside source static** *global-ip local-ip* |
| Specify the inside interface. | **interface** *type number* |
| Mark the interface as connected to the inside. | **ip nat inside** |
| Specify the outside interface. | **interface** *type number* |
| Mark the interface as connected to the outside. | **ip nat outside** |

### Configure Dynamic Translation

To configure dynamic outside source address translation, perform the following tasks beginning in global configuration mode.

| Task | Command |
|---|---|
| Define a pool of local addresses to be allocated as needed. | **ip nat pool** *name start-ip end-ip* {**netmask** *netmask* \| **prefix-length** *prefix-length*} |
| Define a standard access list. | **access-list** *access-list-number* **permit** *source* [*source-wildcard*] |
| Establish dynamic outside source translation, specifying the access list defined in the prior step. | **ip nat outside source list** *access-list-number* **pool** *name* |
| Specify the inside interface. | **interface** *type number* |
| Mark the interface as connected to the inside. | **ip nat inside** |
| Specify the outside interface. | **interface** *type number* |
| Mark the interface as connected to the outside. | **ip nat outside** |

**NOTES**

The access list must permit only those addresses that are to be translated. (Remember that there is an implicit "deny all" at the end of each access list.) An access list that is too permissive can lead to unpredictable results.

In the following example, the addresses in the local network are being used legitimately by someone else on the Internet. An extra translation is required to access that external network. Pool net-10 is a pool of outside local IP addresses. The statement `ip nat outside source list 1 pool net-10` translates the addresses of hosts from the outside overlapping network to addresses in that pool.

```
ip nat pool net-208 171.69.233.208 171.69.233.223 prefix-length 28
ip nat pool net-10 10.0.1.0 10.0.1.255 prefix-length 24
ip nat inside source list 1 pool net-208
ip nat outside source list 1 pool net-10
!
interface serial 0
 ip address 171.69.232.192 255.255.255.240
 ip nat outside
!
interface ethernet0
 ip address 192.168.1.94 255.255.255.0
 ip nat inside
access-list 1 permit 192.168.1.0 0.0.0.255
```

## PROVIDING TCP LOAD DISTRIBUTION

Another use of NAT is unrelated to Internet addresses. Your organization may have multiple hosts that must communicate with a heavily used host. Using NAT, you can establish a virtual host on the inside network that coordinates load sharing among real hosts. Destination addresses that match an access list are replaced with addresses from a rotary pool. Allocation is done in a round-robin basis, and only when a new connection is opened from the outside to the inside. Non-TCP traffic is passed untranslated (unless other translations are in effect). Figure 76–4 illustrates this feature.

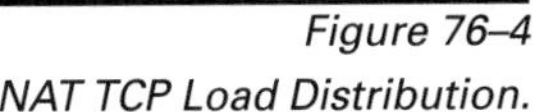

*Figure 76–4*
*NAT TCP Load Distribution.*

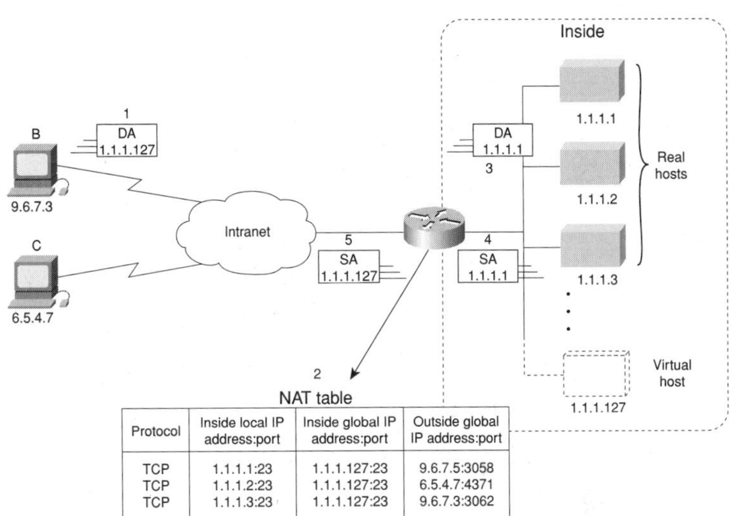


| Protocol | Inside local IP address:port | Inside global IP address:port | Outside global IP address:port |
|---|---|---|---|
| TCP | 1.1.1.1:23 | 1.1.1.127:23 | 9.6.7.5:3058 |
| TCP | 1.1.1.2:23 | 1.1.1.127:23 | 6.5.4.7:4371 |
| TCP | 1.1.1.3:23 | 1.1.1.127:23 | 9.6.7.3:3062 |

The router performs the following process when translating rotary addresses:

1. The user on Host B (9.6.7.3) opens a connection to virtual host at 1.1.1.127.
2. The router receives the connection request and creates a new translation, allocating the next real host (1.1.1.1) for the inside local IP address.
3. The router replaces the destination address with the selected real host address and forwards the packet.
4. Host 1.1.1.1 receives the packet and responds.
5. The router receives the packet, performs a NAT table lookup using the inside local address and port number, and the outside address and port number as the key. The router then translates the source address to the address of the virtual host and forwards the packet.

The next connection request will cause the router to allocate 1.1.1.2 for the inside local address.

To configure destination address rotary translation, perform the following tasks beginning in global configuration mode. This allows you to map one virtual host to many real hosts. Each new TCP session opened with the virtual host will be translated into a session with a different real host.

| Task | Command |
|---|---|
| Define a pool of addresses containing the addresses of the real hosts. | **ip nat pool** *name start-ip end-ip* {**netmask** *netmask* \| **prefix-length** *prefix-length*} **type rotary** |
| Define an access list permitting the address of the virtual host. | **access-list** *access-list-number* **permit** *source* [*source-wildcard*] |
| Establish dynamic inside destination translation, identifying the access list defined in the prior step. | **ip nat inside destination list** *access-list-number* **pool** *name* |
| Specify the inside interface. | **interface** *type number* |
| Mark the interface as connected to the inside. | **ip nat inside** |
| Specify the outside interface. | **interface** *type number* |
| Mark the interface as connected to the outside. | **ip nat outside** |

**NOTES**

The access list must permit only those addresses that are to be translated. (Remember that there is an implicit "deny all" at the end of each access list.) An access list that is too permissive can lead to unpredictable results.

In the following example, the goal is to define a virtual address, connections to which are distributed among a set of real hosts. The pool defines the addresses of the real hosts. The access list defines the virtual address. If a translation does not already exist, TCP packets from serial 0 (the outside interface) whose destination matches the access list are translated to an address from the pool.

```
ip nat pool real-hosts 192.168.15.2 192.168.15.15 prefix-length 28 type rotary
ip nat inside destination list 2 pool real-hosts
!
interface serial 0
 ip address 192.168.15.129 255.255.255.240
 ip nat outside
!
interface ethernet 0
 ip address 192.168.15.17 255.255.255.240
 ip nat inside
!
access-list 2 permit 192.168.15.1
```

## CHANGING TRANSLATION TIMEOUTS

By default, dynamic address translations time out after some period of non-use. You can change the default values on timeouts, if necessary. When overloading is not configured, simple translation entries time out after 24 hours. To change this value, perform the following task in global configuration mode:

| Task | Command |
|---|---|
| Change the timeout value for dynamic address translations that do not use overloading. | **ip nat translation timeout** *seconds* |

If you have configured overloading, you have finer control over translation entry timeout because each entry contains more context about the traffic that is using it. To change timeouts on extended entries, perform one or more of the following tasks in global configuration mode:

| Task | Command |
|---|---|
| Change the UDP timeout value from 5 minutes. | **ip nat translation udp-timeout** *seconds* |
| Change the DNS timeout value from 1 minute. | **ip nat translation dns-timeout** *seconds* |
| Change the TCP timeout value from 24 hours. | **ip nat translation tcp-timeout** *seconds* |
| Change the Finish and Reset timeout value from 1 minute. | **ip nat translation finrst-timeout** *seconds* |

## MONITORING AND MAINTAINING NAT

By default, dynamic address translations will time out from the NAT translation table at some point. You can clear the entries before the timeout by performing one of the following tasks in EXEC mode:

| Task | Command |
|---|---|
| Clear all dynamic address translation entries from the NAT translation table. | **clear ip nat translation** |
| Clear a simple dynamic translation entry containing an inside translation, or both inside and outside translation. | **clear ip nat translation inside** *global-ip local-ip* [**outside** *local-ip global-ip*] |
| Clear a simple dynamic translation entry containing an outside translation. | **clear ip nat translation outside** *local-ip global-ip* |

| Task | Command |
|---|---|
| Clear an extended dynamic translation entry. | **clear ip nat translation** *protocol* **inside** *global-ip global-port local-ip local-port* [**outside** *local-ip local-port global-ip global-port*] |

You can display translation information by performing one of the following tasks in EXEC mode:

| Task | Command |
|---|---|
| Display active translations. | **show ip nat translations [verbose]** |
| Display translation statistics. | **show ip nat statistics** |

## NAT Configuration Examples

The following are NAT configuration examples.

### Dynamic Inside Source Translation Example

The following example translates all source addresses passing access list 1 (having a source address from 192.168.1.0/24) to an address from the pool named net-208. The pool contains addresses from 171.69.233.208 to 171.69.233.233.

```
ip nat pool net-208 171.69.233.208 171.69.233.233 netmask 255.255.255.240
ip nat inside source list 1 pool net-208
!
interface serial 0
 ip address 171.69.232.182 255.255.255.240
 ip nat outside
!
interface ethernet 0
 ip address 192.168.1.94 255.255.255.0
 ip nat inside
!
access-list 1 permit 192.168.1.0 0.0.0.255
```

### Overloading Inside Global Addresses Example

The following example creates a pool of addresses named net-208. The pool contains addresses from 171.69.233.208 to 171.69.233.233. Access list 1 allows packets having the source address from 192.168.1.0 to 192.168.1.255. If no translation exists, packets matching access list 1 are translated to an address from the pool. The router allows multiple local addresses (192.168.1.0 to 192.168.1.255) to use the same global address. The router retains port numbers to differentiate the connections.

```
ip nat pool net-208 171.69.233.208 171.69.233.233 netmask 255.255.255.240
ip nat inside source list 1 pool net-208 overload
```

```
!
interface serial0
 ip address 171.69.232.182 255.255.255.240
 ip nat outside
!
interface ethernet0
 ip address 192.168.1.94 255.255.255.0
 ip nat inside
!
access-list 1 permit 192.168.1.0 0.0.0.255
```

## Translating Overlapping Address Example

In the following example, the addresses in the local network are being used legitimately by someone else on the Internet. An extra translation is required to access that external network. Pool net-10 is a pool of outside local IP addresses. The statement `ip nat outside source list 1 pool net-10` translates the addresses of hosts from the outside overlapping network to addresses in that pool.

```
ip nat pool net-208 171.69.233.208 171.69.233.223 prefix-length 28
ip nat pool net-10 10.0.1.0 10.0.1.255 prefix-length 24
ip nat inside source list 1 pool net-208
ip nat outside source list 1 pool net-10
!
interface serial 0
 ip address 171.69.232.192 255.255.255.240
 ip nat outside
!
interface ethernet0
 ip address 192.168.1.94 255.255.255.0
 ip nat inside
!
access-list 1 permit 192.168.1.0 0.0.0.255
```

## TCP Load Distribution Example

In the following example, the goal is to define a virtual address, connections to which are distributed among a set of real hosts. The pool defines the addresses of the real hosts. The access list defines the virtual address. If a translation does not already exist, TCP packets from serial 0 (the outside interface) whose destination matches the access list are translated to an address from the pool.

```
ip nat pool real-hosts 192.168.15.2 192.168.15.15 prefix-length 28 type rotary
ip nat inside destination list 2 pool real-hosts
!
interface serial 0
 ip address 192.168.15.129 255.255.255.240
 ip nat outside
!
interface ethernet 0
 ip address 192.168.15.17 255.255.255.240
 ip nat inside
!
access-list 2 permit 192.168.15.1
```

CHAPTER 77

# Network Address Translation Commands

This chapter describes the commands that enable the Network Address Translation (NAT) feature, which allows an organization's IP network to appear from the outside to use different IP address space than what it is actually using.

For configuration tasks and examples, see Chapter 76, "Configuring Network Address Translation."

## CLEAR IP NAT TRANSLATION

To clear dynamic Network Address Translation (NAT) translations from the translation table, use the **clear ip nat translation** EXEC command.

**clear ip nat translation** {* | [**inside** *global-ip local-ip*] [**outside** *local-ip global-ip*]}
**clear ip nat translation** *protocol* **inside** *global-ip global-port local-ip local-port* [**outside** *local-ip global-ip*]

| *Syntax* | *Description* |
|---|---|
| * | Clears all dynamic translations. |
| **inside** *global-ip* | (Optional) When used without the arguments *protocol*, *global-port*, and *local-port*, clears a simple translation that also contains the specified *local-ip* address. When used with the arguments *protocol*, *global-port*, and *local-port*, clears an extended translation. |
| **outside** *local-ip* | (Optional) Clears an entry that contains this local IP address and the specified *global-ip* address. |
| *protocol* | (Optional) Clears an entry that contains this protocol and the specified *global-ip* address, *local-ip* address, *global-port*, and *local-port*. |

| | |
|---|---|
| *global-port* | (Optional) Clears an entry that contains this *global-port* and the specified *protocol*, *global-ip* address, *local-ip* address, and *local-port*. |
| *local-port* | (Optional) Clears an entry that contains this *local-port* and the specified *protocol*, *global-ip* address, *local-ip* address, and *global-port*. |

### *Command Mode*

EXEC

### *Usage Guidelines*

This command first appeared in Cisco IOS Release 11.2.

Use this command to clear entries from the translation table before they time out.

### *Example*

The following example shows the NAT entries before and after the UDP entry being cleared:

```
router# show ip nat translation
Pro Inside global       Inside local        Outside local       Outside global
udp 171.69.233.209:1220 192.168.1.95:1220 171.69.2.132:53     171.69.2.132:53
tcp 171.69.233.209:11012 192.168.1.89:11012 171.69.1.220:23   171.69.1.220:23
tcp 171.69.233.209:1067 192.168.1.95:1067 171.69.1.161:23     171.69.1.161:23

router# clear ip nat translation udp inside 171.69.233.209 1220 192.168.1.95 1220
171.69.2.132 53 171.69.2.132 53

router# show ip nat translation
Pro Inside global       Inside local        Outside local       Outside global
tcp 171.69.233.209:11012 192.168.1.89:11012 171.69.1.220:23   171.69.1.220:23
tcp 171.69.233.209:1067 192.168.1.95:1067 171.69.1.161:23     171.69.1.161:23
```

### *Related Commands*

Search online to find documentation for related commands.

**ip nat**
**ip nat inside destination**
**ip nat inside source**
**ip nat outside source**
**ip nat pool**
**ip nat translation**
**show ip nat statistics**
**show ip nat translations**

## IP NAT

To designate that traffic originating from or destined for the interface is subject to Network Address Translation (NAT), use the **ip nat** interface configuration command. To prevent the interface from being able to translate, use the **no** form of this command.

**ip nat {inside | outside}**
**no ip nat {inside | outside}**

| *Syntax* | *Description* |
|---|---|
| **inside** | Indicates the interface is connected to the inside network (the network subject to NAT translation). |
| **outside** | Indicates the interface is connected to the outside network. |

### *Default*

Traffic leaving or arriving at this interface is not subject to network address translation.

### *Command Mode*

Interface configuration

### *Usage Guidelines*

This command first appeared in Cisco IOS Release 11.2.

Only packets moving between "inside" and "outside" interfaces can be translated. You must specify at least one inside interface and outside interface for each border router where you intend to use NAT.

### *Example*

The following example translates between inside hosts addressed from either the 192.168.1.0 or 192.168.2.0 networks to the globally unique 171.69.233.208/28 network:

```
ip nat pool net-208 171.69.233.208 171.69.233.223 prefix-length 28
ip nat inside source list 1 pool net-208
!
interface ethernet 0
 ip address 171.69.232.182 255.255.255.240
 ip nat outside
!
interface ethernet 1
 ip address 192.168.1.94 255.255.255.0
 ip nat inside
!
access-list 1 permit 192.168.1.0 0.0.0.255
access-list 1 permit 192.168.2.0 0.0.0.255
```

### *Related Commands*

Search online to find documentation for related commands.

**clear ip nat translation**
**ip nat inside destination**
**ip nat inside source**
**ip nat outside source**
**ip nat pool**

**ip nat translation**
**show ip nat statistics**
**show ip nat translations**

## IP NAT INSIDE DESTINATION

To enable Network Address Translation (NAT) of the inside destination address, use the **ip nat inside destination** global configuration command. To remove the dynamic association to a pool, use the **no** form of this command.

**ip nat inside destination list** {*access-list-number* | *name*} **pool** *name*
**no ip nat inside destination list** {*access-list-number* | *name*}

| *Syntax* | *Description* |
|---|---|
| **list** *access-list-number* | Standard IP access list number. Packets with destination addresses that pass the access list are translated using global addresses from the named pool. |
| **list** *name* | Name of a standard IP access list. Packets with destination addresses that pass the access list are translated using global addresses from the named pool. |
| **pool** *name* | Name of the pool from which global IP addresses are allocated during dynamic translation. |

### *Default*

No inside destination addresses are translated.

### *Command Mode*

Global configuration

### *Usage Guidelines*

This command first appeared in Cisco IOS Release 11.2.

This command has two forms: dynamic and static address translation. The form with an access list establishes dynamic translation. Packets from addresses that match the standard access list are translated using global addresses allocated from the pool named with the **ip nat pool** command.

Alternatively, the syntax form with the keyword **static** establishes a single static translation.

### *Examples*

The following example translates between inside hosts addressed to either the 192.168.1.0 or 192.168.2.0 networks to the globally unique 171.69.233.208/28 network:

```
ip nat pool net-208 171.69.233.208 171.69.233.223 prefix-length 28
ip nat inside destination list 1 pool net-208
!
```

```
interface ethernet 0
 ip address 171.69.232.182 255.255.255.240
 ip nat outside
!
interface ethernet 1
 ip address 192.168.1.94 255.255.255.0
 ip nat inside
!
access-list 1 permit 192.168.1.0 0.0.0.255
access-list 1 permit 192.168.2.0 0.0.0.255
```

*Related Commands*

Search online to find documentation for related commands.

**clear ip nat translation**
**ip nat**
**ip nat inside source**
**ip nat outside source**
**ip nat pool**
**ip nat translation**
**show ip nat statistics**
**show ip nat translations**

### IP NAT INSIDE SOURCE



To enable Network Address Translation (NAT) of the inside source address, use the **ip nat inside source** global configuration command. To remove the static translation or remove the dynamic association to a pool, use the **no** form of this command.

**ip nat inside source** {**list** {*access-list-number* | *name*} **pool** *name* [**overload**] | **static** *local-ip global-ip*}

**no ip nat inside source** {**list** {*access-list-number* | *name*} **pool** *name* [**overload**] | **static** *local-ip global-ip*}

| *Syntax* | *Description* |
|---|---|
| **list** *access-list-number* | Standard IP access list number. Packets with source addresses that pass the access list are dynamically translated using global addresses from the named pool. |
| **list** *name* | Name of a standard IP access list. Packets with source addresses that pass the access list are dynamically translated using global addresses from the named pool. |
| **pool** *name* | Name of the pool from which global IP addresses are allocated dynamically. |

| | |
|---|---|
| **overload** | (Optional) Enables the router to use one global address for many local addresses. When overloading is configured, each inside host's TCP or UDP port number distinguishes between the multiple conversations using the same local IP address. |
| **static** *local-ip* | Sets up a single static translation; this argument establishes the local IP address assigned to a host on the inside network. The address could be randomly chosen, allocated from RFC 1918, or obsolete. |
| *global-ip* | Sets up a single static translation; this argument establishes the globally unique IP address of an inside host as it appears to the outside world. |

### *Default*

No NAT translation of inside source addresses occurs.

### *Command Mode*

Global configuration

### *Usage Guidelines*

This command first appeared in Cisco IOS Release 11.2.

This command has two forms: dynamic and static address translation. The form with an access list establishes dynamic translation. Packets from addresses that match the standard access list are translated using global addresses allocated from the pool named with the **ip nat pool** command.

Alternatively, the syntax form with the keyword **static** establishes a single static translation.

### *Example*

The following example translates between inside hosts addressed from either the 192.168.1.0 or 192.168.2.0 networks to the globally unique 171.69.233.208/28 network:

```
ip nat pool net-208 171.69.233.208 171.69.233.223 prefix-length 28
ip nat inside source list 1 pool net-208
!
interface ethernet 0
 ip address 171.69.232.182 255.255.255.240
 ip nat outside
!
interface ethernet 1
 ip address 192.168.1.94 255.255.255.0
 ip nat inside
!
access-list 1 permit 192.168.1.0 0.0.0.255
access-list 1 permit 192.168.2.0 0.0.0.255
```

### *Related Commands*

Search online to find documentation for related commands.

**clear ip nat translation**
**ip nat**
**ip nat inside destination**
**ip nat outside source**
**ip nat pool**
**ip nat translation**
**show ip nat statistics**
**show ip nat translations**

## IP NAT OUTSIDE SOURCE

To enable Network Address Translation (NAT) of the outside source address, use the **ip nat outside source** global configuration command. To remove the static entry or the dynamic association, use the **no** form of this command.

**ip nat outside source** {**list** {*access-list-number* | *name*} **pool** *name* | **static** *global-ip local-ip*}
**no ip nat outside source** {**list** {*access-list-number* | *name*} **pool** *name* | **static** *global-ip local-ip*}

### *Syntax Description*

| | |
|---|---|
| **list** *access-list-number* | Standard IP access list number. Packets with source addresses that pass the access list are translated using global addresses from the named pool. |
| **list** *name* | Name of a standard IP access list. Packets with source addresses that pass the access list are translated using global addresses from the named pool. |
| **pool** *name* | Name of the pool from which global IP addresses are allocated. |
| **static** *global-ip* | Sets up a single static translation. This argument establishes the globally unique IP address assigned to a host on the outside network by its owner. It was allocated from globally routable network space. |
| *local-ip* | Sets up a single static translation. This argument establishes the local IP address of an outside host as it appears to the inside world. The address was allocated from address space routable on the inside (RFC 1918). |

### *Default*

No translation of source addresses coming from the outside to the inside network occurs.

### *Command Mode*

Global configuration

### Usage Guidelines

This command first appeared in Cisco IOS Release 11.2.

You might have IP addresses that are not legal, officially assigned IP addresses. Perhaps you chose IP addresses that officially belong to another network. The case of an address used illegally and legally is called *overlapping*. You can use NAT to translate inside addresses that overlap with outside addresses. Use this feature if your IP addresses in the stub network happen to be legitimate IP addresses belonging to another network, and you need to communicate with those hosts or routers.

This command has two forms: dynamic and static address translation. The form with an access list establishes dynamic translation. Packets from addresses that match the standard access list are translated using global addresses allocated from the pool named with the **ip nat pool** command.

Alternatively, the syntax form with the keyword **static** establishes a single static translation.

### Example

The following example would translate between inside hosts addressed from the 9.114.11.0 network to the globally unique 171.69.233.208/28 network. Further packets from outside hosts addressed from the 9.114.11.0 network (the true 9.114.11.0 network) are translated to appear to be from the network 10.0.1.0/24.

```
ip nat pool net-208 171.69.233.208 171.69.233.223 prefix-length 28
ip nat pool net-10 10.0.1.0 10.0.1.255 prefix-length 24
ip nat inside source list 1 pool net-208
ip nat outside source list 1 pool net-10
!
interface ethernet 0
 ip address 171.69.232.182 255.255.255.240
 ip nat outside
!
interface ethernet 1
 ip address 9.114.11.39 255.255.255.0
 ip nat inside
!
access-list 1 permit 9.114.11.0 0.0.0.255
```

### Related Commands

Search online to find documentation for related commands.

**clear ip nat translation**
**ip nat**
**ip nat inside destination**
**ip nat inside source**
**ip nat pool**
**ip nat translation**
**show ip nat statistics**
**show ip nat translations**

### IP NAT POOL

To define a pool of IP addresses for Network Address Translation (NAT), use the **ip nat pool** global configuration command. To remove one or more addresses from the pool, use the **no** form of this command.

**ip nat pool** *name start-ip end-ip* {**netmask** *netmask* | **prefix-length** *prefix-length*} [**type rotary**]

**no ip nat pool** *name start-ip end-ip* {**netmask** *netmask* | **prefix-length** *prefix-length*} [**type rotary**]

| *Syntax* | *Description* |
|---|---|
| *name* | Name of the pool. |
| *start-ip* | Starting IP address that defines the range of addresses in the address pool. |
| *end-ip* | Ending IP address that defines the range of addresses in the address pool. |
| **netmask** *netmask* | Network mask that indicates which address bits belong to the network and subnetwork fields and which bits belong to the host field. Specify the netmask of the network to which the pool addresses belong. |
| **prefix-length** *prefix-length* | Number that indicates how many bits of the netmask are ones (how many bits of the address indicate network). Specify the netmask of the network to which the pool addresses belong. |
| **type rotary** | (Optional) Indicates that the range of address in the address pool identify real, inside hosts among which TCP load distribution will occur. |



#### *Default*

No pool of addresses is defined.

#### *Command Mode*

Global configuration

#### *Usage Guidelines*

This command first appeared in Cisco IOS Release 11.2.

This command defines a pool of addresses using start address, end address, and either netmask or prefix length. The pool could define either an inside global pool, an outside local pool, or a rotary pool.

#### *Example*

The following example translates between inside hosts addressed from either the 192.168.1.0 or 192.168.2.0 networks to the globally unique 171.69.233.208/28 network:

```
ip nat pool net-208 171.69.233.208 171.69.233.223 prefix-length 28
ip nat inside source list 1 pool net-208
```

```
!
interface ethernet 0
 ip address 171.69.232.182 255.255.255.240
 ip nat outside
!
interface ethernet 1
 ip address 192.168.1.94 255.255.255.0
 ip nat inside
!
access-list 1 permit 192.168.1.0 0.0.0.255
access-list 1 permit 192.168.2.0 0.0.0.255
```

*Related Commands*

Search online to find documentation for related commands.

**clear ip nat translation**
**ip nat**
**ip nat inside destination**
**ip nat inside source**
**ip nat outside source**
**ip nat translation**
**show ip nat statistics**
**show ip nat translations**

## IP NAT TRANSLATION

To change the amount of time after which Network Address Translation (NAT) translations time out, use the **ip nat translation** global configuration command. To disable the timeout, use the **no** form of this command.

**ip nat translation {timeout | udp-timeout | dns-timeout | tcp-timeout | finrst-timeout}** *seconds*

**no ip nat translation {timeout | udp-timeout | dns-timeout | tcp-timeout | finrst-timeout}**

| *Syntax* | *Description* |
|---|---|
| **timeout** | Specifies that the timeout value applies to dynamic translations except for overload translations. Default is 86400 seconds (24 hours). |
| **udp-timeout** | Specifies that the timeout value applies to the UDP port. Default is 300 seconds (5 minutes). |
| **dns-timeout** | Specifies that the timeout value applies to connections to the Domain Name System (DNS). Default is 60 seconds. |
| **tcp-timeout** | Specifies that the timeout value applies to the TCP port. The default is 86400 seconds (24 hours). |

**finrst-timeout** Specifies that the timeout value applies to Finish and Reset TCP packets, which terminate a connection. Default is 60 seconds.

*seconds* Number of seconds after which the specified port translation times out. Default values are listed in the Defaults section.

### Defaults

**timeout** is 86400 seconds (24 hours)
**udp-timeout** is 300 seconds (5 minutes)
**dns-timeout** is 60 seconds (1 minute)
**tcp-timeout** is 86400 seconds (24 hours)
**finrst-timeout** is 60 seconds (1 minute)

### Command Mode

Global configuration

### Usage Guidelines

This command first appeared in Cisco IOS Release 11.2.

When port translation is configured, there is finer control over translation entry timeouts because each entry contains more context about the traffic that is using it. Non-Domain Name System UDP translations time out after 5 minutes; DNS times out in 1 minute. TCP translations time out in 24 hours unless an RST or FIN is seen on the stream, in which case they time out in 1 minute.



### Example

The following example causes UDP port translation entries to time out after 10 minutes:

```
ip nat translation udp-timeout 600
```

### Related Commands

Search online to find documentation for related commands.

**clear ip nat translation**
**ip nat**
**ip nat inside destination**
**ip nat inside source**
**ip nat outside source**
**ip nat pool**
**show ip nat statistics**
**show ip nat translations**

## SHOW IP NAT STATISTICS

To display Network Address Translation (NAT) statistics, use the **show ip nat statistics** EXEC command.

**show ip nat statistics**

### Syntax Description

This command has no arguments or keywords.

### Command Mode

EXEC

### Usage Guidelines

This command first appeared in Cisco IOS Release 11.2.

### Sample Display

The following is sample output from the **show ip nat statistics** command:

```
router# show ip nat statistics
Total translations: 2 (0 static, 2 dynamic; 0 extended)
Outside interfaces: Serial0
Inside interfaces: Ethernet1
Hits: 135  Misses: 5
Expired translations: 2
Dynamic mappings:
-- Inside Source
access-list 1 pool net-208 refcount 2
 pool net-208: netmask 255.255.255.240
        start 171.69.233.208 end 171.69.233.221
        type generic, total addresses 14, allocated 2 (14%), misses 0
```

Table 77–1 describes the significant fields in the display.

**Table 77–1** *Show IP NAT Statistics Field Descriptions*

| Field | Description |
|---|---|
| Total translations | Number of translations active in the system. This number is incremented each time a translation is created and is decremented each time a translation is cleared or times out. |
| Outside interfaces | List of interfaces marked as outside with the **ip nat outside** command. |
| Inside interfaces | List of interfaces marked as inside with the **ip nat inside** command. |
| Hits | Number of times the software does a translations table lookup and finds an entry. |
| Misses | Number of times the software does a translations table lookup, fails to find an entry, and must try to create one. |
| Expired translations | Cumulative count of translations that have expired since the router was booted. |

### Related Commands

Search online to find documentation for related commands.

**clear ip nat translation**
**ip nat**
**ip nat inside destination**
**ip nat inside source**
**ip nat outside source**
**ip nat pool**
**ip nat translation**
**show ip nat statistics**
**show ip nat translations**

## SHOW IP NAT TRANSLATIONS

To display active Network Address Translation (NAT) translations, use the **show ip nat translations** EXEC command.

**show ip nat translations [verbose]**

| *Syntax* | *Description* |
|---|---|
| verbose | (Optional) Displays additional information for each translation table entry, including how long ago the entry was created and used. |

### *Command Mode*

EXEC

### *Usage Guidelines*

This command first appeared in Cisco IOS Release 11.2.

### *Sample Displays*

The following is sample output from the **show ip nat translations** command. Without overloading, two inside hosts are exchanging packets with some number of outside hosts.

```
router# show ip nat translations
Pro Inside global      Inside local       Outside local      Outside global
--- 171.69.233.209     192.168.1.95       ---                ---
--- 171.69.233.210     192.168.1.89       ---                --
```

With overloading, a translation for a DNS transaction is still active, and translations for two Telnet sessions (from two different hosts) are also active. Note that two different inside hosts appear on the outside with a single IP address.

```
router# show ip nat translations
Pro Inside global      Inside local       Outside local      Outside global
udp 171.69.233.209:1220 192.168.1.95:1220 171.69.2.132:53    171.69.2.132:53
tcp 171.69.233.209:11012 192.168.1.89:11012 171.69.1.220:23  171.69.1.220:23
tcp 171.69.233.209:1067 192.168.1.95:1067 171.69.1.161:23    171.69.1.161:23
```

The following is sample output that includes the **verbose** keyword:

```
router# show ip nat translations verbose
```

Part XII Command Reference

```
Pro Inside global      Inside local       Outside local      Outside global
udp 171.69.233.209:1220 192.168.1.95:1220 171.69.2.132:53    171.69.2.132:53
        create 00:00:02, use 00:00:00, flags: extended
tcp 171.69.233.209:11012 192.168.1.89:11012 171.69.1.220:23  171.69.1.220:23
        create 00:01:13, use 00:00:50, flags: extended
tcp 171.69.233.209:1067 192.168.1.95:1067 171.69.1.161:23    171.69.1.161:23
        create 00:00:02, use 00:00:00, flags: extended
```

Table 77–2 describes the significant fields in the display.

**Table 77–2** *Show IP NAT Translations Field Descriptions*

| Field | Description |
|---|---|
| Pro | Protocol of the port identifying the address. |
| Inside global | Legitimate IP address (assigned by the NIC or service provider) that represents one or more inside local IP addresses to the outside world. |
| Inside local | IP address assigned to a host on the inside network; probably not a legitimate address assigned by the NIC or service provider. |
| Outside local | IP address of an outside host as it appears to the inside network; probably not a legitimate address assigned by the NIC or service provider. |
| Outside global | IP address assigned to a host on the outside network by its owner. |
| create | How long ago the entry was created (in hours:minutes:seconds). |
| use | How long ago the entry was last used (in hours:minutes:seconds). |

### *Related Commands*

Search online to find documentation for related commands.

**clear ip nat translation**
**ip nat**
**ip nat inside destination**
**ip nat inside source**
**ip nat outside source**
**ip nat pool**
**ip nat translation**
**show ip nat statistics**

CHAPTER 78

# Configuring Easy IP

The Easy IP (Phase 1) feature combines Network Address Translation (NAT) and PPP/Internet Protocol Control Protocol (IPCP). This feature enables a Cisco router to automatically negotiate its own registered WAN interface IP address from a central server and to enable all remote hosts to access the global Internet using this single registered IP address. Because Easy IP (Phase 1) uses existing port-level multiplexed NAT functionality within the Cisco IOS software, IP addresses on the remote LAN are invisible to the Internet.

For a complete description of the Easy IP commands in this chapter, see Chapter 79, "Easy IP Commands."

**NOTES**

Simple translations, either static or dynamic, are not supported in non-Plus Cisco IOS software images. In order to enable dynamic or static simple translation along with Easy IP (Phase 1), you need to obtain the full NAT Plus Cisco IOS software image.

## BENEFITS

Easy IP (Phase 1) provides the following benefits:

- Reduced Internet access costs through the use of dynamically allocated IP addresses
- Simplified router configuration and IP address management
- Conserved registered IP addresses
- Dynamic IP address allocation for remote workstations
- Remote LAN IP address privacy

## List of Terms

**PPP/Internet Protocol Control Protocol (IPCP)**—Defined in RFC 1332, this protocol provides the ability to dynamically configure IP addresses over Point-to-Point Protocol (PPP). A Cisco IOS Easy IP (Phase 1) router uses PPP/IPCP to dynamically negotiate its own registered WAN interface IP address from a central access server or Dynamic Host Configuration Protocol (DHCP) server.

**Network Address Translation (NAT)**—Operates on a router that connects two or more networks together. In Easy IP (Phase 1), at least one of these networks (designated as "inside" or "LAN") is addressed with private addresses that must be converted into a registered address before packets can be forwarded to the other registered network (designated as "outside" or "WAN"). Within the context of Easy IP (Phase 1), port-level multiplexed NAT is used to translate all internal private addresses to a single outside registered IP address.

## How Easy IP Works

Easy IP (Phase 1) assumes that all clients have statically configured IP addresses. The PPP/IPCP address negotiation functionality in Easy IP is used to assign an IP address from a central device (PPP/IPCP option 3—"IP Address") to the Easy IP router.

Figure 78–1 shows a typical scenario for using the Easy IP feature.

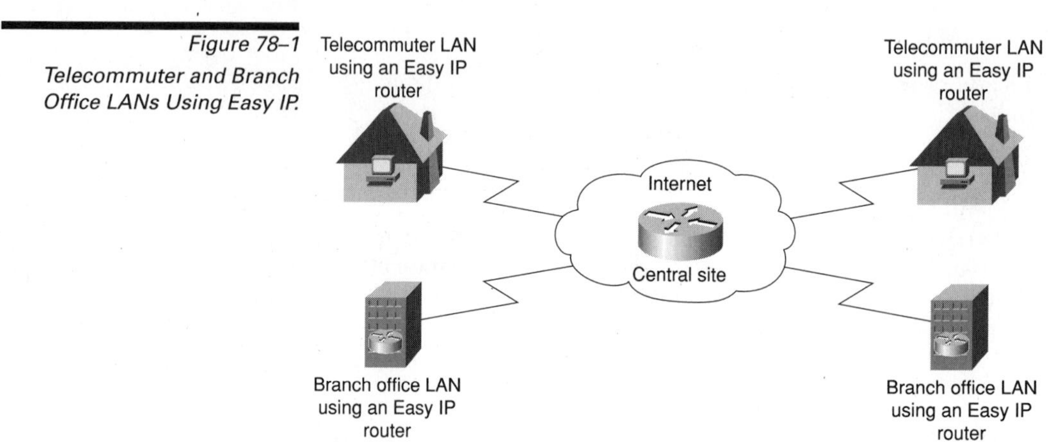


*Figure 78–1 Telecommuter and Branch Office LANs Using Easy IP.*

Steps 1 through 4 illustrate how Easy IP (Phase 1) works.

**Step 1** When a SOHO host generates "interesting" traffic (as defined by access control lists) for dial-up (first-time only), the Easy IP router requests a single registered IP address from the central site's access server via PPP/IPCP. See Figure 78–2.

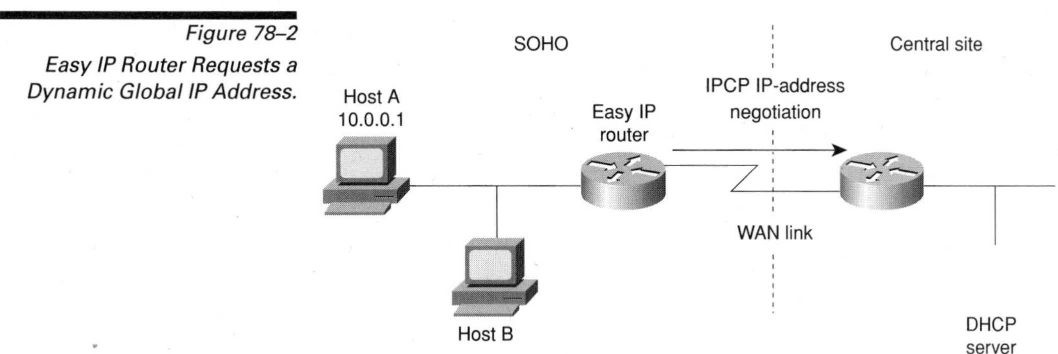


*Figure 78–2*
*Easy IP Router Requests a Dynamic Global IP Address.*

**Step 2** The central site router replies with a dynamic global address from a local DHCP IP address pool. See Figure 78–3.

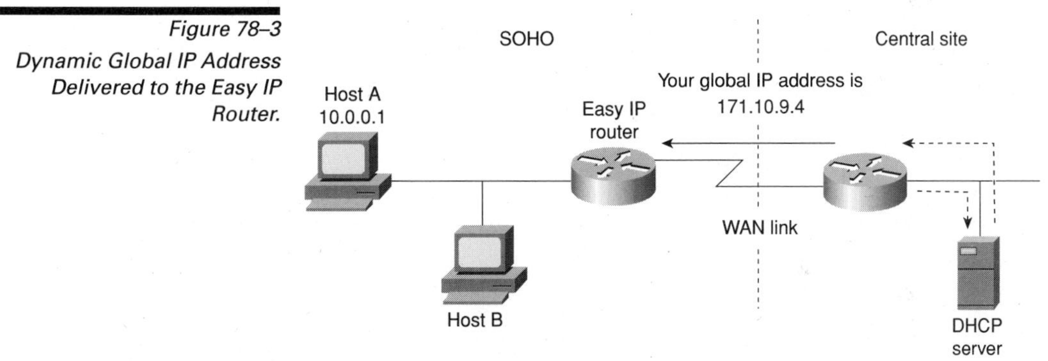


*Figure 78–3*
*Dynamic Global IP Address Delivered to the Easy IP Router.*

**Step 3** The Easy IP router uses port-level NAT functionality to automatically create a translation that associates the WAN interface's registered IP address with the client's private IP address. See Figure 78–4.

**Step 4** The remote hosts contain multiple static IP addresses while the Easy IP router obtains a single registered IP address using PPP/IPCP. The Easy IP router then creates port-level multiplexed NAT translations between these addresses so that each remote host address (inside private address) is translated to a single external address assigned to the Easy IP router. This many-to-one address translation is also called port-level multiplexing or port address translation (PAT). Note that the NAT port-level multiplexing function can be used to conserve global addresses by allowing the remote routers to use one global address for many local addresses. See Figure 78–5.

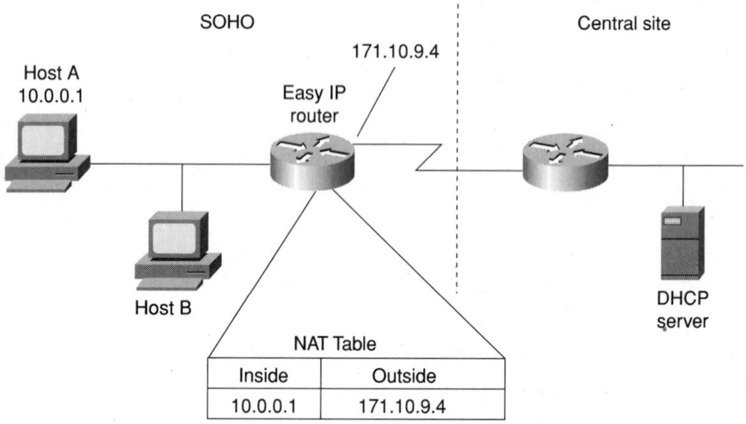
SOHO
Central site
171.10.9.4
Host A
10.0.0.1
Easy IP
router
Host B
DHCP
server
NAT Table
Inside
Outside
10.0.0.1
171.10.9.4

*Figure 78–4*
*Port-Level NAT Functionality Used for IP Address Translation.*

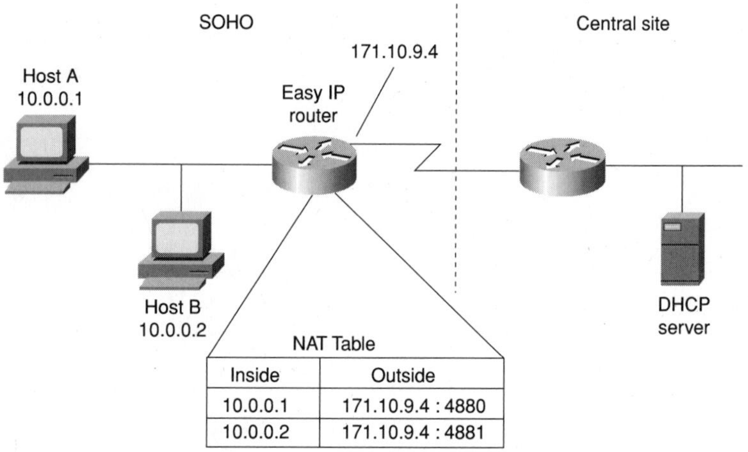
SOHO
Central site
171.10.9.4
Host A
10.0.0.1
Easy IP
router
Host B
10.0.0.2
DHCP
server
NAT Table
Inside
Outside
10.0.0.1
171.10.9.4 : 4880
10.0.0.2
171.10.9.4 : 4881

*Figure 78–5*
*Multiple Private Internal IP Addresses Are Bound to a Single Global IP Address.*

## PREREQUISITES

Complete the following tasks before using Easy IP (Phase 1):

- Configure the Integrated Services Digital Network (ISDN) switch type and service provider identifier (SPID) (if using ISDN).
- Configure the static route from LAN to WAN interface.

For information about configuring ISDN switch types, see Chapter 11, "Setting Up ISDN Basic Rate Service." For information about NAT, see Chapter 76, "Configuring Network Address Translation."

## EASY IP CONFIGURATION TASK LIST

In its most simple configuration, an Easy IP (Phase 1) router or access server will have a single LAN interface and a single WAN interface. Based on this model, you must complete the following tasks to use Easy IP (Phase 1):

- Define the NAT Pool
- Configure the LAN Interface
- Define NAT for the LAN Interface
- Configure the WAN Interface
- Enable PPP/IPCP Negotiation
- Define NAT for the Dialer Interface
- Configure the Dialer Interface

For configuration examples, see section, "Easy IP Configuration Examples," later in this chapter.

### Define the NAT Pool

The first step in enabling Easy IP (Phase 1) is to create a pool of internal IP addresses to be translated. To define the NAT pool, perform the following tasks in global configuration mode:

| Task | | Command |
|---|---|---|
| **Step 1** | Define a standard access list permitting those addresses that are to be translated. | **access-list** *access-list-number* **permit** *source* [*source-wildcard*] |
| **Step 2** | Establish dynamic source translation, identifying the access list defined in the prior step. | **ip nat inside source list** *access-list-number* **interface** *dialer-name* **overload** |

For information about configuring NAT, see Chapter 76.

### Configure the LAN Interface

To configure the LAN interface, perform the following tasks in interface configuration mode:

| Task | | Command |
|---|---|---|
| **Step 1** | Select a specific LAN interface. | **interface** *type number* |
| **Step 2** | Define the IP address and subnet mask for this interface. | **ip address** *address mask* |

### Define NAT for the LAN Interface

To ensure that the LAN interface is connected to the inside network (and therefore subject to NAT), perform the following task in interface configuration mode:

| Task | Command |
|---|---|
| Define the interface as internal for network address translation. | **ip nat inside** |

For information about configuring NAT, see Chapter 76.

### Configure the WAN Interface

To configure the WAN interface, perform the following tasks in interface configuration mode:

| Task | | Command |
|---|---|---|
| **Step 1** | Select the WAN interface. | **interface** *type number* |
| **Step 2** | Remove any associated IP address from this interface. | **no ip address** |
| **Step 3** | Select PPP as the encapsulation method for this interface. | **encapsulation ppp** |
| **Step 4** | Bind the WAN interface to the dialer interface. | **dialer pool-member** *number* |

### Enable PPP/IPCP Negotiation

To enable PPP/IPCP negotiation on the dialer interface, perform the following tasks in interface configuration mode:

| Task | | Command |
|---|---|---|
| **Step 1** | Select the dialer interface. | **interface** *dialer-name* |
| **Step 2** | Enable PPP/IPCP negotiation for this interface. | **ip address negotiated** |

### Define NAT for the Dialer Interface

To define that the dialer interface is connected to the outside network, perform the following tasks in interface configuration mode:

| Task | | Command |
|---|---|---|
| **Step 1** | Select the dialer interface. | **interface** *dialer-name* |
| **Step 2** | Define the interface as external for network address translation. | **ip nat outside** |

For information about configuring NAT, see Chapter 76.

### Configure the Dialer Interface

To configure the dialer interface information, perform the following tasks in interface configuration mode:

| Task | | Command |
|---|---|---|
| **Step 1** | Select the dialer interface. | **interface** *dialer-name* |
| **Step 2** | Specify for a dialer interface the length of time the interface waits for a carrier before timing out. | **dialer wait-for-carrier-time** *seconds* |
| **Step 3** | Create a dialer hold queue and specify the number of packets to be held in it. | **dialer hold-queue** *packets* |
| **Step 4** | Specify the remote router CHAP authentication name. | **dialer remote-name** *name* |
| **Step 5** | Specify the amount of idle time that can pass before calls to the central access server are disconnected. | **dialer idle-timeout** *seconds* |
| **Step 6** | Specify the telephone number required to reach the central access server. | **dialer string** *string* |
| **Step 7** | Specify the dialing pool to use. | **dialer pool** *number* |
| **Step 8** | Assign the dialer interface to a dialer group. | **dialer-group** *number* |

## Easy IP Configuration Examples

The following example shows how to configure BRI interface 0 (shown as interface bri0) to obtain its IP address via PPP/IPCP address negotiation:

```
! The following command defines the NAT pool.
ip nat inside source list 101 interface dialer1 overload
!
! The following commands define the ISDN switch type.
isdn switch type vn3
isdn tei-negotiation first-call
```

```
!
!The following commands define the LAN address and subnet mask.
interface ethernet0
 ip address 10.0.0.4 255.0.0.0

!The following command defines ethernet0 as internal for NAT.
 ip nat inside
!
!The following commands binds the physical interface to the dialer1 interface.
interface bri0
 no ip address
 encapsulation ppp
 dialer pool-member 1
!
interface dialer1
!
!The following command enables PPP/IPCP negotiation for this interface.
 ip address negotiated
 encapsulation ppp
!
!The following command defines dialer1 interface as external for NAT.
 ip nat outside
 dialer remote-name dallas
 dialer idle-timeout 180
!
!The following command defines the dialer string for central access server.
 dialer string 4159991234
 dialer pool 1
 dialer-group 1
!
!The following commands define the static route to the WAN interface.
ip route 0.0.0.0 0.0.0.0 dialer1
access-list 101 permit ip 10.0.0.0 0.255.255.255 any
dialer-list 1 protocol ip list 101
```

The following example shows how to configure an asynchronous interface (interface async1) to obtain its IP address via PPP/IPCP address negotiation:

```
! This command defines the NAT pool.
ip nat inside source list 101 interface dialer 1 overload
!
!The following commands define the LAN IP address and subnet mask.
interface ethernet0
 ip address 10.0.0.4 255.0.0.0
!
!The following command defines ethernet0 as internal for NAT.
 ip nat inside
!
!The following commands bind the physical dialer1 interface.
interface async1
 no ip address
 encapsulation ppp
 async mode dedicated
 dialer pool-member 1
```

```
!
interface dialer1
!
!The following command enables PPP/IPCP negotiation for this interface.
 ip address negotiated
 encapsulation ppp
!
!The following command defines dialer1 interface as external for NAT.
 ip nat outside
 dialer wait-for-carrier-time 30
 dialer hold-queue 10
 dialer remote-name dallas
 dialer idle-timeout 180
!
!The following command defines the dialer string for central access server.
 dialer string 4159991234
 dialer pool 1
 dialer-group 1
!
!The following commands define the static route to the WAN interface.
ip route 0.0.0.0 0.0.0.0 dialer1
access-list 101 permit ip 10.0.0.0 0.255.255.255 any
dialer-list 1 protocol ip list 101
```

# CHAPTER 79

# Easy IP Commands

This chapter describes the commands used for configuring Easy IP (Phase 1). For configuration tasks and examples, see Chapter 78, "Configuring Easy IP."

## IP ADDRESS NEGOTIATED

To specify that the IP address for a particular interface is obtained via PPP/IPCP address negotiation, use the **ip address negotiated** interface configuration command. Use the **no** form of this command to disable this feature.

**ip address negotiated**
**no ip address negotiated**

### *Syntax Description*

This command has no arguments or keywords.

### *Command Mode*

Interface configuration

### *Usage Guidelines*

This command first appeared in Cisco IOS Release 11.3.

Use the **ip address negotiated** interface command to enable a Cisco router to automatically negotiate its own registered WAN interface Internet Protocol (IP) address from a central server (via PPP/IPCP) and to enable all remote hosts to access the global Internet using this single registered IP address.

### Example

The following example configures an asynchronous interface (interface async1) to obtain its IP address via PPP/IPCP address negotiation:

```
interface async1
 ip address negotiated
 encapsulation ppp
```

### Related Commands

Search online to find documentation for related commands.

**encapsulation ppp**
**ip address**
**ip unnumbered**

## IP NAT INSIDE SOURCE

To enable Network Address Translation (NAT) of the inside source address, use the **ip nat inside source** global configuration command. To remove the static translation or remove the dynamic association to a pool, use the **no** form of this command.

**ip nat inside source** {**list** {*access-list-number* | *name*} {**pool** *name* | **interface** *dialer-name*} [**overload**] | **static** *local-ip global-ip*}
**no ip nat inside source** {**list** {*access-list-number* | *name*} {**pool** *name* | **interface** *dialer-name*} [**overload**] | **static** *local-ip global-ip*}

| *Syntax* | *Description* |
|---|---|
| **list** *access-list-number* | Standard IP access list number. Packets with source addresses that pass the access list are dynamically translated using global addresses from the named pool. |
| **list** *name* | Name of a standard IP access list. Packets with source addresses that pass the access list are dynamically translated using global addresses from the named pool. |
| **pool** *name* | Name of the pool from which global IP addresses are allocated dynamically. |
| **interface** *dialer-name* | Name of the dialer interface on which the PPP/IPCP address negotiation takes place. |
| **overload** | (Optional) Enables the router to use one global address for many local addresses. When overloading is configured, each inside host's TCP or UDP port number distinguishes between the multiple conversations using the same local IP address. |

| *Syntax* | *Description* |
|---|---|
| **static** *local-ip* | Sets up a single static translation. This argument establishes the local IP address assigned to a host on the inside network. The address could be randomly chosen, allocated from RFC 1918, or obsolete. |
| *global-ip* | Sets up a single static translation. This argument establishes the globally unique IP address of an inside host as it appears to the outside world. |

**NOTES**

Simple translations, either static or dynamic, are not supported in non-Plus Cisco IOS software images. In order to enable dynamic or static simple translation along with Easy IP (Phase 1), you need to obtain the full NAT Plus Cisco IOS software image.

### Default

No NAT translation of inside source addresses occurs.

### Command Mode

Global configuration

### Usage Guidelines

This command first appeared in Cisco IOS Release 11.2 F.

This command has two forms: dynamic and static address translation. The form with an access list establishes dynamic translation. Packets from addresses that match the standard access list are translated using global addresses allocated from the pool named with the **ip nat pool** command.

Alternatively, the syntax form with the keyword **static** establishes a single static translation.

### Example

The following example translates between inside hosts addressed from either the 192.168.1.0 or 192.168.2.0 networks to the globally unique 171.69.233.208/28 network:

```
ip nat pool net-208 171.69.233.208 171.69.233.223 prefix-length 28
ip nat inside source list 1 pool net-208
!
interface ethernet 0
 ip address 171.69.232.182 255.255.255.240
 ip nat outside
!
interface ethernet 1
 ip address 192.168.1.94 255.255.255.0
 ip nat inside
!
access-list 1 permit 192.168.1.0 0.0.0.255
access-list 1 permit 192.168.2.0 0.0.0.255
```

*Related Commands*

Search online to find documentation for related commands.

**clear ip nat translation**
**ip nat**
**ip nat inside destination**
**ip nat outside source**
**ip nat pool**
**ip nat translation**
**show ip nat statistics**
**show ip nat translations**

**PART 13**

# Appendixes

# APPENDIX A

# Configuring Modem Support and Chat Scripts

This appendix contains information to help you set modem strings and troubleshoot your modem connections to Cisco routers. For information about configuring a line to support modems, see Chapter 5, "Configuring Modem Support and Asynchronous Devices."

## MODEM SETTINGS FOR USE IN STRINGS

Table A–1 contains required settings and EC/compression settings for specific modem types. Use this information to create your modem scripts. Table A–2 contains information for setting AUX ports and general comments. See Table A–3 for a legend of symbols used in these two tables.

**Table A–1** *Required Settings and EC/Compression Settings*

| Settings Required for All Modems | | | | | Settings for EC/Compression | | | | | |
|---|---|---|---|---|---|---|---|---|---|---|
| **Modem** | **FD** | **AA** | **CD** | **DTR** | **RTS/CTS Flow** | **LOCK DTE Speed** | **Best Error** | **Best Comp** | **No Error** | **No Comp** |
| Codex 3260 | &F | S0=1 | &C1 | &D3 | *FL3 | *SC1 | *SM3 | *DC1 | *SM1 | *DC0 |
| USR Courier USR Sportster | &F | S0=1 | &C1 | &D3 | &H1&R2 | &B1 | &M4 | &K1 | &M0 | &K0 |
| Global Village Teleport Gold | &F | S0=1 | &C1 | &D3 | \Q3 | \J0 | \N7 | %C1 | \N0 | %C0 |

**Table A–1** *Required Settings and EC/Compression Settings, Continued*

| Settings Required for All Modems | | | | | Settings for EC/Compression | | | | | |
|---|---|---|---|---|---|---|---|---|---|---|
| **Modem** | **FD** | **AA** | **CD** | **DTR** | **RTS/CTS Flow** | **LOCK DTE Speed** | **Best Error** | **Best Comp** | **No Error** | **No Comp** |
| Telebit T1600/T3000/WB | &F1 | S0=1 | &C1 | &D3 | S58=2 S68=2 | S51=6 | S180=2 S181=1 | S190=1 | S180=0 S181=1 | S190=0 |
| Telebit T2500 (ECM) | &F | S0=1 | &C1 | &D3 | S58=2 S68=2 | S51=6 | S95=2 | S98=1 S96=1 | S95=0 | S98=0 S96=0 |
| Telebit Trailblazer | &F | S0=1 | &C1 | | | | | | | |
| AT&T Paradyne Dataport | &F | S0=1 | &C1 | &D3 | \Q3 | ---> | \N7 | %C1 | \N0 | %C0 |
| Hayes modems Accura/ Optima | &F | S0=1 | &C1 | &D3 | &K3 | &Q6 | &Q5 | &Q9 | &Q6 | <--- |
| Microcom QX4232 series | &F | S0=1 | &C1 | &D3 | \Q3 | \J0 | \N6 | %C1 | \N0 | %C0 |
| Motorola UDS FastTalk II | &F | S0=1 | &C1 | &D3 | \Q3 | \J0 | \N6 | %C1 | \N0 | %C0 |
| Multitech MT1432 MT932 | &F | S0=1 | &C1 | &D3 | &E4 | $BA0 | &E1 | &E15 | &E0 | &E14 |
| Digicom Scout Plus | &F | S0=1 | &C1 | &D3 | *F3 | *S1 | *E9 | <--- | *E0 | <--- |
| Digicom SoftModem | &F | S0=1 | &C1 | &D3 | &K3 | ---> | \N5 | %C1 | \N0 | %C0 |

**Table A–1** *Required Settings and EC/Compression Settings, Continued*

| Settings Required for All Modems | | | | | Settings for EC/Compression | | | | | |
|---|---|---|---|---|---|---|---|---|---|---|
| Modem | FD | AA | CD | DTR | RTS/CTS Flow | LOCK DTE Speed | Best Error | Best Comp | No Error | No Comp |
| Viva 14.4/9642c | &F | S0=1 | &C1 | &D3 | &K3 | ---> | \N3 | %M3 | \N0 | %M0 |
| ZyXel U-1496E | &F | S0=1 | &C1 | &D3 | &H3 | &B1 | &K4 | <--- | &K0 | <--- |
| Supra V.32bis/28.8 | &F | S0=1 | &C1 | &D3 | &K3 | ---> | \N3 | %C1 | \N0 | %C0 |
| ZOOM 14.4 | &F | S0=1 | &C1 | &D3 | &K3 | ---> | \N3 | %C2 | \N0 | %C0 |
| Intel External | &F | S0=1 | &C1 | &D3 | \Q3 | \J0 | \N3 | %C1 "H3 | \N0 | %C0 |
| Practical Peripherals | &F | S0=1 | &C1 | &D3 | &K3 | ---> | &Q5 | &Q9 | &Q6 | <--- |

**Table A–2** *AUX and Platform Specific Settings*

| | Settings for Use with AUX Port | | Other Settings | | |
|---|---|---|---|---|---|
| Modem | No Echo | No Res | CAB-MDCE | Write Memory | Comments |
| Codex 3260 | E0 | Q1 | &S1 | &W | |
| USR Courieræ USR Sportster | E0 | Q1 | *NA* | &W | |
| Global Village Teleport Gold | E0 | Q1 | *NA* | &W | |

**Table A–2** *AUX and Platform Specific Settings, Continued*

| Modem | Settings for Use with AUX Port | | Other Settings | | Comments |
|---|---|---|---|---|---|
| | No Echo | No Res | CAB-MDCE | Write Memory | |
| Telebit T1600/T3000/WB | E0 | Q1 | &S4 | &W | All Telebit modems need to have the speed set explicitly. These examples use 38400 bps. Using what Telebit calls "UNATTENDED ANSWER MODE" is the best place to start a dial in only modem. |
| Telebit T2500 (ECM) | E0 | Q1 | &S1 | &W | |
| Telebit Trailblazer | E0 | Q1 | *NA* | &W | Use "ENHANCED COMMAND MODE" on the T2500. |
| AT&T Paradyne Dataport | E0 | Q1 | *NA* | &W | Almost all Microcom modems have similar configuration parameters. |
| Hayes modems Accura/ Optima | E0 | Q1 | *NA* | &W | |
| Microcom QX4232 series | E0 | Q1 | *NA* | &W | |
| Motorola UDS FastTalk II | E0 | Q1 | *NA* | &W | |
| Multitech MT1432 MT932 | E0 | Q1 | &S1 | &W | |
| Digicom Scout Plus | E0 | Q2 | &B2 | &W | |
| Digicom SoftModem | E0 | Q1 | &S1 | &W | |
| Viva 14.4/9642c | E0 | Q1 | &S1 | &W | |

**Table A–2** *AUX and Platform Specific Settings, Continued*

| | Settings for Use with AUX Port | | Other Settings | | |
|---|---|---|---|---|---|
| **Modem** | **No Echo** | **No Res** | **CAB-MDCE** | **Write Memory** | **Comments** |
| ZyXel U-1496E | E0 | Q1 | &S1 | &W | Additional information on ftp.zyxel.com |
| Supra V.32bis/28.8 | E0 | Q1 | &S1 | &W | |
| ZOOM 14.4 | E0 | Q1 | &S1 | &W | |
| Intel External | E0 | Q1 | *NA* | &W | |
| Practical Peripherals | E0 | Q1 | *NA* | &W | Based on PC288LCD. May vary. |

Table A–3 contains a legend of symbols used in Table A–1 and Table A–2.

**Table A–3** *Legend to Symbols Used in Modem Chart*

| Symbol | Meaning |
|---|---|
| *NA* | This option is not available on the noted modem. |
| --> | The command noted on the right will handle that function. |
| <-- | The command on the left will handle that function. |
| AUX port | These parameters are only required for pre-9.21 AUX ports or any other port without modem control set. |

## MODEM TROUBLESHOOTING TIPS

Table A–4 contains troubleshooting tips on modem access and control.

**Table A–4** *Modem Troubleshooting Tips*

| Problem | Likely Cause |
|---|---|
| Connection refused. | Someone already has a connection to that port<br>-or-<br>an XEC is running on that port |

**Table A–4** *Modem Troubleshooting Tips, Continued*

| | |
|---|---|
| | -or-<br>the modem failed to lower CD after a call disconnected, resulting in an EXEC that remained active after disconnect.<br>To force the line back into an idle state, clear the line from the console and try again. If it still fails, ensure that you have set **modem inout** command for that line. If you don't have modem control, either turn off EXEC on the line (by using the **exec-timeout** line configuration command) before making a reverse connection or configure the modem using an external terminal. As a last resort, disconnect the modem, clear the line, make the Telnet connection, and then attach the modem. This prevents a misconfigured modem from denying you line access. |
| Connection appears to hang. | Try entering "^U" (clear line), "^Q" (XON), and press Return a few times to try to establish terminal control. |
| EXEC does not come up, autoselect is on. | Press Return to enter EXEC. |
| Modem does not hang up after entering **quit**. | The modem is either not receiving DTR information, or you have not set up modem control on the router. |
| Interrupt another user's session when you dial in. | The modem is either not dropping CD on disconnect, or you have not set up modem control on the Cisco router. |
| Connection hangs after entering "+++" on the dialing modem, followed by an ATO. | The answering modem saw and interpreted the "+++" when it was echoed to you. This is a bug in the answering modem, common to many modems. There may be a switch to work around this problem; check the modem's documentation. |
| Losing data. | You may have Hardware Flow Control only on for either the router's line (DTE) or the modem (DCE). Hardware Flow Control should be on for both or off for both, but not for only one. |
| Using MDCE. | Turn MDCE into an MMOD by moving pin 6 to pin 8 because most modems use CD and not DSR to indicate the presence of carrier. You can also program some modems to provide carrier info via DSR. |

## Sample Modem Scripts

Listed below are several modem command strings that are appropriate for use with your access server or router. For use with the access server, **Speed=xxxxxx** is a suggested value only. Set the DTE speed of the modem to its maximum capability. This can be done by making a reverse Telnet connection in the EXEC mode to the port on the access server where the modem is connected, then sending an **at** command followed by a carriage return.

In the following example, the modem is attached to asynchronous interface 2 on the access server. The IP address indicated as the server-ip-address is the IP address of the Ethernet 0 interface. The administrator connects from the EXEC to asynchronous interface 2, which has its IP address assigned from Ethernet 0.

```
2511> telnet server-ip-address port-number
                192.156.154.42    2002
```

AST Premium Exec Internal Data/Fax (MNP 5)

```
Init=AT&F&C1&D3\G0\J0\N3\Q2S7=60S0=1&W
Speed=9600
```

ATi 9600etc/e (V.42bis)

```
Init=AT&FW2&B1&C1&D3&K3&Q6&U1S7=60S0=1&W
Speed=38400
```

AT&T Paradyne KeepInTouch Card Modem (V.42bis)

```
Init=AT&FX6&C1&D3\N7\Q2%C1S7=60S0=1&w
Speed=57600
```

AT&T ComSphere 3800 Series (V.42bis)

```
Init=AT&FX6&C1&D2\N5\Q2%C1"H3S7=60S0=1&W
Speed=57600
```

AT&T DataPort Fax Modem (V.42bis)

```
Init=AT&FX6&C1&D2\N7\Q2%C1S7=60S0=1&W
Speed=38400
```

Boca Modem 14.4K/V.32bis (V.42bis)

```
Init=AT&FW2&C1&D3&K3&Q5%C1\N3S7=60S36=7S46=138S95=47S0=1&W
Speed=57600
```

CALPAK MXE-9600

```
Init=AT&F&C1&D3S7=60S0=1&W
Speed=9600
```

Cardinal 2450MNP (MNP 5)

```
Init=AT&F&C1&D3\J0\N3\Q2\V1%C1S7=60S0=1&w
Speed=9600
```

Cardinal 9650V32 (MNP)

```
Init=AT&F&B1&C1&D3&H1&I1&M6S7=60S0=1&W
```

Cardinal 9600V42 (V.42bis)

```
Init=AT&FW2&C1&D3&K3&Q5\N3%C1%M3S7=60S46=138S48=7S95=3S0=1&W
Speed=38400
```

Cardinal 14400 (V.42bis)

```
Init=AT&F&C1&D3&K3&Q5\N3%C1%M3S7=60S46=138S48=7S95=47S0=1&W
Speed=57600
```

COMPAQ SpeedPAQ 144 (V.42bis)

```
Init=AT&F&C1&D3&K3&Q5\J0\N3%C1S7=60S36=7S46=2S48=7S95=47S0=1&W
Speed=57600
```

Data Race RediMODEM V.32/V.32bis

```
Init=AT&F&C1&D3&K3&Q6\J0\N7\Q3\V2%C1S7=60 Speed=38400S0=1&W
```

Dell NX20 Modem/Fax (MNP)

```
Init=AT&F&C1&D3%C1\J0\N3\Q3\V1W2S7=60S0=1&W
Speed=9600
```

Digicom Systems (DSI) 9624LE/9624PC (MNP 5)

```
Init=AT&F&C1&D3*E1*F3*S1S7=60S0=1&W
```

Digicom Systems (DSI) 9624LE+ (V.42bis)

```
Init=AT&F&C1&D3*E9*F3*N6*S1S7=60S0=1&W
Speed=38400
```

Everex Evercom 24+ and 24E+ (MNP 5)

```
Init=AT&F&C1&D3\J0\N3\Q2\V1%C1S7=60S0=1&W
```

Everex EverFax 24/96 and 24/96E (MNP 5)

```
Init=AT&F&C1&D3\J0\N3\Q2\V1%C1S7=60S0=1&W
Speed=9600
```

Everex Evercom 96+ and 96E+ (V.42bis)

```
Init=AT&FW2&C1&D3\J0\N3\Q2\V2%C1S7=60S0=1&W
Speed=38400
```

Freedom Series V.32bis Data/FAX Modem

```
Init=AT&F&C1&D3&K3&Q6\J0\N7\Q3\V2%C1S7=60S0=1&W
Speed=38400
```

Gateway 2000 TelePath

```
Init=AT&FW2&C1&D3&K3&Q5\N3%C1S7=60S36=7S46=138S48=7S95=47S0=1&W
Speed=38400
```

Gateway 2000 Nomad 9600 BPS Internal Modem

```
Init=AT&F&C1&D3%C1\J0\N3\Q2S7=60S0=1&W
Speed=38400
```

GVC SM-96V (V.42bis)

```
Init=AT&F&C1&D3%C1\J0\N6\Q2\V1S7=60S0=1&W
Speed=38400
```

GVC SM-144V (V.42bis)

```
Init=AT&F&C1&D3%C1\J0\N6\Q2\V1S7=60S0=1&W
Speed=57600
```

Hayes Smartmodem Optima 9600 (V.42bis)

```
Init=AT&FW2&C1&D3&K3&Q5S7=60S46=138S48=7S95=47S0=1&W
Speed=38400
```

Hayes Smartmodem Optima 14400 (V.42bis)

```
Init=AT&FW2&C1&D3&K3&Q5S7=60S46=138S48=7S95=47S0=1&W
Speed=57600
```

Hayes Optima 28800 (V.34)

```
Init=AT&FS0=1&C1&D3&K3&Q6&Q5&Q9&W
Speed=115200
```

Hayes V-series Smartmodem 9600/9600B (V.42)

```
Init=AT&F&C1&D3&K3&Q5S7=60S0=1&W
Speed=9600
```

Hayes V-series ULTRA Smartmodem 9600 (V.42bis)

```
Init=AT&F&C1&D3&K3&Q5S7=60S46=2S48=7S95=63S0=1&W
Speed=38400
```

Hayes V-series ULTRA Smartmodem 14400 (V.42bis)

```
Init=AT&FW2&C1&D3&K3&Q5S7=60S38=10S46=2S48=7S95=63S0=1&W
Speed=38400
```

Hayes ACCURA 24 EC (V.42bis)

```
Init=AT&FW2&C1&D3&K3&Q5S7=60S36=7S46=138S48=7S95=47S0=1&W
```

Hayes ACCURA 96 EC (V.42bis)

```
Init=AT&FW2&C1&D3&K3&Q5S7=60S36=7S46=138S48=7S95=47S0=1&W
Speed=38400
```

Hayes ACCURA 144 EC (V.42bis)

```
Init=AT&FW2&C1&D3&K3&Q5S7=60S36=7S46=138S48=7S95=47S0=1&W
Speed=57600
```

Hayes ISDN System Adapter

```
Init=AT&FW1&C1&D3&K3&Q0S7=60S0=1&W
Speed=57600
```

IBM 7855 Modem Model 10 (MNP)

```
Init=AT&F&C1&D3\N3\Q2\V1%C1S7=60S0=1&W
```

IBM Data/Fax Modem PCMCIA (V.42bis)

```
Init=AT&F&C1&D3&K3&Q5%C3\N3S7=60S38=7S46=138S48=7S95=47S0=1&W
Speed=57600
```

Identity ID9632E

```
Init=AT&F&C1&D3S7=60S0=1&W
Speed=9600
```

Infotel V.42X (V.42bis)

```
Init=AT&F&C1&D3S7=30S36=7S0=1&W
Speed=9600
```

Infotel V.32 turbo (V.42bis)

```
Init=AT&FW1&C1&D3&K3&Q5S7=60S0=1&w
Speed=38400
```

Infotel 144I (V.42bis)

```
Init=AT&F&C1&D3&K3&Q5\N3%C1S7=60S36=7S46=138S48=7S95=47S0=1&W
Speed=38400
```

Intel 9600 EX (V.42bis)

```
Init=AT&F&C1&D3\J0\N3\Q2\V2%C1"H3S7=60S0=1&W
Speed=38400
```

Intel 14400 EX (V.42bis)

```
Init=AT&F&C1&D3\J0\N3\Q2\V2%C1"H3S7=60S0=1&W
Speed=38400
```

Macronix MaxFax 9624LT-S
```
Init=AT&F&C1&D3&K3&Q9\J0\N3\Q3%C1S7=60S36=7S46=138S48=7S95=47S0=1&W
Speed=9600
```
Megahertz T3144 internal (V.42bis)
```
Init=AT&F&C1&D3%C1\J0\N3\Q2\V2S7=60S0=1&W
Speed=57600
```
Megahertz T324FM internal (V.42bis)
```
Init=AT&F&C1&D3%C1\J0\N3\Q2\V1S7=60S46=138S48=7S0=1&W
Speed=9600
```
Megahertz P2144 FAX/Modem (V.42bis)
```
Init=AT&F&C1&D3%C1\J0\N7\Q2\V2S7=60S0=1&W
Speed=38400
```
Megahertz T396FM internal (V.42bis)
```
Init=AT&FW2&C1&D3%C1\J0\N7\Q2\V2S7=60S0=1&W
Speed=38400
```
Megahertz CC3144 PCMCIA card modem (V.42bis)
```
Init=AT&F&C1&D3&K3&Q5%C3\N3S7=60S38=7S46=138S48=7S95=47S0=1&W
Speed=57600
```
Microcom AX/9624c (MNP 5)
```
Init=AT&F&C1&D3\G0\J0\N3\Q2%C1S7=60S0=1&W
Speed=9600
```
Microcom AX/9600 Plus (MNP 5)
```
Init=AT&F&C1&D3\J0\N3\Q2S7=60S0=1&W
```
Microcom QX/V.32c (MNP 5)
```
Init=AT&F&C1&D3\J0%C3\N3\Q2S7=60S0=1&W
Speed=38400
```
Microcom QX/4232hs (V.42bis)
```
Init=AT&F&C1&D3\J0%C3\N3\Q2-K0\V2S7=60S0=1&W
Speed=38400
```
Microcom QX/4232bis (V.42bis)
```
Init=AT&F&C1&D3\J0%C3\N3\Q2-K0\V2W2S7=60S0=1&W
Speed=38400
```
Microcom Deskporte 28800 (V.34)
```
Init=AT&F&c1&q1E0S0=1&W
Speed=115200
```
Microcom MicroPorte 542 (V.42bis)
```
Init=AT&F&C1&D3&Q5S7=60S46=138S48=7S95=47S0=1&W
Speed=9600
```
Microcom MicroPorte 1042 (V.42bis)
```
Init=AT&F&C1&D3%C3\J0-M0\N6\Q2\V2S7=60S0=1&W
Speed=9600
```
Microcom MicroPorte 4232bis (V.42bis)
```
Init=AT&F&C1&D3%C3%G0\J0-M0\N6\Q2\V2S7=60S0=1&W
Speed=38400
```

Microcom DeskPorte FAST

```
Init=ATX4S7=60-M1\V4\N2L1S0=1&W
Speed=57600
```

Motorola/Codex 3220 (MNP)

```
Init=AT&F&C1&D3*DC1*FL3*MF0*SM3*XC2S7=60S0=1&W
```

Motorola/Codex 3220 Plus (V.42bis)

```
Init=AT&F&C1&D3*DC1*EC0*MF0*SM3*XC2S7=60S0=1&W
Speed=38400
```

Motorola/Codex 326X Series (V.42bis)

```
Init=AT&F&C1&D3*FL3*MF0*SM3*TT2*XC2S7=60S0=1&W
Speed=38400
```

MultiTech MultiModem V32EC (V.42bis)

```
Init=AT&FX4&C1&D3$BA0&E1&E4&E15#L0S7=60S0=1&W
Speed=38400
```

MultiTech MultiModem V32 (no MNP or V.42)

```
Init=AT&F&C1&D3S7=60S0=1&W
Speed=9600
```

MultiTech MultiModem 696E (MNP)

```
Init=AT&F&C1&D3$BA0&E1&E4&E15S7=60S0=1&W
```

MultiTech MultiModem II MT932 (V.42bis)

```
Init=AT&FX4&C1&D3$BA0&E1&E4&E15#L0S7=60S0=1&W
Speed=38400
```

MultiTech MultiModem II MT1432 (V.42bis)

```
Init=AT&FX4&C1&D3#A0$BA0&E1&E4&E15#L0S7=60S0=1&W
Speed=57600
```

NEC UltraLite 14.4 Data/Fax Modem (V.42bis)

```
Init=AT&F&C1&D3&K3&Q4\J0\N7\Q2W2%C1S7=60S0=1&W
Speed=38400
```

Practical Peripherals PC28800SA (V.42bis)

```
Init=AT&F&C1&D3&K3&Q5S7=60S36=7S46=2S48=7S95=47S0=1&W
Speed=115200
```

Practical Peripherals PM9600SA (V.42bis)

```
Init=AT&F&C1&D3&K3&Q5S46=138S48=7S7=60S0=1&W
Speed=38400
```

Practical Peripherals PM14400FX (V.42bis)

```
Init=AT&F&C1&D3&K3&Q5S7=60S36=7S46=2S48=7S95=47S0=1&W
Speed=57600
```

Practical Peripherals PM14400SA (V.42bis)

```
Init=AT&F&C1&D3&K3&Q5S7=60S36=7S46=2S48=7S95=47S0=1&W
Speed=57600
```

Prometheus ProModem 9600 Plus (V.42)

```
Init=AT&F&C1&D3*E7*F3S7=60S0=1&W
```

Prometheus ProModem Ultima (V.42bis)

```
Init=AT&F&C1&D3*E9*F3*N6*S1S7=60S0=1&W
Speed=38400
```

Racal Datacomm ALM 3223 (V.42bis)

```
Init=AT&F&C1&D3\M0\N3\P2\Q1\V1S7=60S0=1&W
Speed=38400
```

Supra FAXModem V.32bis (V.42bis)

```
Init=AT&FN1W2&C1&D1&K3&Q5\N3%C1S7=60S36=7S48=7S95=45S0=1&W
Speed=57600
```

Telebit T1600 (V.42bis)

```
Init=AT&FX2&C1&D3&R3S7=60S51=6S58=0S59=15S68=2S180=2S190=1S0=1&W
Speed=38400
```

Telebit T2500 (V.42bis)

```
Init=AT~&FX2S7=60S51=5S52=2S66=1S68=2S97=1S98=3S106=1S131=1S0=1&W

Telebit T3000 (V.42bis)
Init=AT&FX2&C1&D3S51=6S59=7S68=2S7=60S0=1&W
Speed=38400
```

Telebit QBlazer (V.42bis)

```
Init=AT&FX2&C1&D3S59=7S68=2S7=60S0=1&W
Speed=38400
```

Texas Instruments V.32bis Internal Modem

```
Init=AT&F&C1&D3%C1\J0\N7\Q2\V2S7=60S0=1&W
Speed=38400
```

Toshiba T24/DF Internal

```
Init=AT&F&C1&D3\J0\N3\Q2%C1S7=60S36=7S46=138S48=7S0=1&W
Speed=9600
```

Universal Data Systems FasTalk V.32/42b (V.42bis)

```
Init=AT&F&C1&D3\J0\M0\N7\V1\Q2%C1S7=60S0=1&W
Speed=38400
```

Universal Data Systems V.32 (no MNP or V.42)

```
Init=AT&F&C1&D2S7=60S0=1&W
Speed=9600
```

Universal Data Systems V.3224 (MNP 4)

```
Init=AT&F&C1&D2\J0\N3\Q2S7=60S0=1&W
```

Universal Data Systems V.3225 (MNP 5)

```
Init=AT&F&C1&D2\J0\N3\Q2%C1S7=60S0=1&W
```

Universal Data Systems V.3227 (V.42bis)

```
Init=AT&F&C1&D2\J0\M0\N7\Q2%C1S7=60S0=1&W
Speed=38400
```

Universal Data Systems V.3229 (V.42bis)

```
Init=AT&F&C1&D3\J0\M0\N7\Q2%C1S7=60S0=1&W
Speed=38400
```

U.S. Robotics Sportster 9600 (V.42bis)

```
Init=AT&FX4&A3&B1&D3&H1&I0&K1&M4S7=60S0=1&W
Speed=38400
```

U.S. Robotics Sportster 14400 (V.42bis)

```
Init=AT&FX4&A3&B1&D3&H1&I0&K1&M4S7=60S0=1&W
Speed=57600
```

U.S. Robotics Sportster 14400 (V.42bis) x

```
Init=AT&FX4&B1&C1&D2&H1&K1&M4E0X7Q0V1S0=1&W
Speed=57600
```

U.S. Robotics Sportster 28800 (V.34)

```
Init=AT&FS0=1&C1&D2&H1&R2&N14&B1&W
Speed=115200
```

U.S. Robotics Courier 28800 (V.34)

```
Init=AT&FS0=1&C1&D2&H1&R2&N14&B1&W
Speed=115200
```

U.S. Robotics Courier V.32bis (V.42bis)

```
Init=AT&FX4&A3&C1&D2&M4&H1&K1&B1S0=1&W
Speed=38400
```

U.S. Robotics Courier HST Dual Standard (V.42bis)

```
Init=AT&FB0X4&A3&C1&D2&M4&H1&K1&B1&R2&S1S0=1&W
Speed=115200
```

U.S. Robotics Courier HST (V.42bis)

```
Init=AT&FB0X4&A3&C1&D2&M1&H1&K1&B1S0=1&W
Speed=115200
```

U.S. Robotics WorldPort 2496 FAX/Data (V.42bis)

```
Init=AT&FX4&C1&D3%C1"H3\J0-J1\N3\Q2\V2S7=60S0=1&W
Speed=57600
```

U.S. Robotics WorldPort 9696 FAX/Data (MNP 5)

```
Init=AT&FX4&C1&D3%C1\J0\N3\Q2\V2S7=60S0=1&W
```

U.S. Robotics WorldPort 9600 (MNP 5)

```
Init=AT&FX4&C1&D3%C1\J0\N3\Q2\V2S7=60S0=1&W
```

U.S. Robotics WorldPort 14400 (V.42bis)

```
Init=AT&FX4&A3&B1&C1&D3&H1&K1&M4S7=60S0=1&W
Speed=57600
```

Ven-Tel PCM 9600 Plus (MNP)

```
Init=AT&FB0&C1&D3\N3\Q3%B0%C1%F1S7=60S0=1&W
```

ViVa 9642e (V.42bis)

```
Init=AT&F&C1&D3&K3&Q5\N3%C3S7=60S36=7S46=138S48=7S95=47S0=1&W
Speed=38400
```

ViVa 14.4/FAX (V.42bis)

```
Init=AT&F&C1&D3&K3&Q5\N3%C3S7=60S36=7S46=138S48=7S95=47S0=1&W
Speed=38400
```

ZOOM V.32 turbo (V.42bis)

```
Init=AT&FW1&C1&D3&K3&Q5%C1\N3S7=60S36=7S46=138S48=7S95=47S0=1&W
Speed=38400
```

ZOOM V.32bis (V.42bis)

```
Init=AT&FW1&C1&D3&K3&Q9%C1\N3S7=60S36=7S95=47S0=1&W
Speed=38400
```

Zyxel U-1496 (V.42bis)

```
Init=AT&FX6&B1&C1&D2&N0&K4&H3S7=60S0=1&W
Speed=57600
```

**APPENDIX B**

# X.3 PAD Parameters

A PAD is a packet assembler/disassembler, which is a device that collects data from a group of terminals and periodically outputs the data in packets (data organized in a special format). A PAD also does the reverse. That is, it can take data packets from a host and return them into a character stream that can be transmitted to the terminals. A PAD is defined by ITU-T Recommendations X.3, X.28, and X.29.

**NOTES**

The ITU-T carries out the functions of the former Consultative Committee for International Telegraph and Telephone (CCITT).

ITU-T Recommendation X.3 specifies the parameters for terminal-handling functions such as baud rate, flow control, character echoing, and other functions, for a connection to an X.25 host. The X.3 parameters are similar in function to the Telnet options.

ITU-T Recommendation X.29 specifies a protocol for setting the X.3 parameters via a network connection. When a connection is established, the destination host can request that the PAD or terminal change its parameters using the X.29 protocol. A PAD can refuse to do this, in which case a terminal user can change the parameter later. A PAD cannot tell the destination host to change its X.3 parameters, but it can communicate that its own parameters were changed.

Along with Recommendations X.3 and X.29, the ITU-T also provides Recommendation X.28 to specify the user interface for locally controlling a PAD; however, the communication server is not a PAD, and this recommendation is not supported.

This appendix discusses the X.3 PAD parameters. Chapter 23, "Configuring the Cisco PAD Facility for X.25 Connections," explains how to make PAD connections and how to switch between connections.

## X.3 PAD Parameters

Following are descriptions of the X.3 parameters. Default values are noted in the descriptions. The default value for any parameter not so noted is zero for outgoing connections or not set for incoming PAD connections. For incoming PAD connections, the communication server sends an X.29 SET PARAMETER packet to set the noted defaults.

Since the X.3 parameters describe the user's terminal, which exists on only one side of the connection, the PAD protocols are not always symmetric.

Some of the commands described in this section require ASCII decimal values.

### Parameter 1: Escape from Data Transfer

Parameter 1 determines whether or not the communication server will be allowed to escape from data transfer mode in order to send PAD command signals. Because the EXEC mode uses a two-character escape sequence, and there is no way to set the escape character on a Telnet connection, this parameter is refused on translation sessions.

Cisco's legacy PAD mode does not support this parameter. However, Cisco's X.28 standard user interface does support this parameter.

### Parameter 2: Local Echo Mode

Parameter 2 determines whether or not PAD is required to perform local echo of characters. This parameter can be negotiated end-to-end on translation sessions. On incoming PAD connections, software turns local echo off on the remote PAD to support the Cisco-user interface. See Table B–1 for local echo mode values and their descriptions.

**Table B–1** *PAD Local Echo Mode Values*

| Value | Description |
|---|---|
| 0 | No local echo (incoming PAD connection default). |
| 1 | Local echo on (outgoing connection default). |

### Parameter 3: Data Forward Character

Parameter 3 sets up a packet forwarding mask; that is, it selects which character causes PAD to forward a packet either before expiration of the Idle Timer (see parameter 4) or when in local editing mode. See Table B–2 for data forward character values and their descriptions.

**Table B–2** *PAD Data Forward Character Values*

| Value | Description |
|---|---|
| 0 | None—full packet. |
| 1 | Forward packet upon receipt of an alphanumeric character. |

**Table B–2** *PAD Data Forward Character Values, Continued*

| Value | Description |
|---|---|
| 2 | Forward packet upon receipt of a RETURN (outgoing connection default). |
| 4 | Forward packet upon receipt of ESCAPE, BEL, ENQ, or ACK. |
| 8 | Forward packet upon receipt of DEL, CAN, OR DC2. |
| 16 | Forward packet upon receipt of ETX or EOT. |
| 32 | Forward packet upon receipt of HT, LT, VT, or FF. |
| 64 | All other characters in the ASCII chart. |

As X.3 supports a wider variety of dispatch characters than Telnet does, parameter changes to or from the default causes a translation session to negotiate in or out of line mode on the Telnet connection.

A forwarding mask can be statically set using the **terminal dispatch-character** terminal **parameter-setting** EXEC command. This command can set any character or characters as the forwarding mask, and overrides (when logical) any values set by parameter 3.

## Parameter 4: Idle Timer

Parameter 4 controls the amount of time the software waits for new data before sending a packet in the absence of a data forwarding character. See Table B–3 for PAD Idle Timer values and their descriptions.

**Table B–3** *PAD Idle Timer Values*

| Value | Description |
|---|---|
| 0 | No timer. |
| 1-255 | Delay value in twentieths of a second (default for both connection types is 1). |

## Parameter 5: Device Control

Parameter 5 selects whether PAD can transmit flow control (ASCII XON/XOFF) characters during data transfer to the terminal to control the terminal and data flow. Flow control is not directly supported on communication servers because data must make network hops to travel to the final destination. However, depending on the type of incoming connection, setting this parameter can cause similar negotiations to be sent over the connection, thereby attempting to change the state of the flow control option at the device closest to the user.

### Parameter 6: PAD Service Signals

Parameter 6 selects whether or not PAD is required to transmit service signals. Because the communication server does not use Recommendation X.28 for its user interface, this parameter is ignored.

Cisco's legacy PAD mode does not support this parameter. However, Cisco's X.28 standard user interface does support this parameter.

### Parameter 7: Action upon Receipt of a BREAK Signal

Parameter 7 defines the action of the PAD after receiving a BREAK signal from the terminal. See Table B–4 for PAD BREAK signal values and their descriptions.

**Table B–4** *PAD BREAK Signal Values*

| Value | Description |
|---|---|
| 0 | Ignore the BREAK signal. |
| 1 | Transmit an interrupt packet to notify the remote host or another PAD that the BREAK signal has been generated. |
| 2 | Transmit a Reset packet to reset the virtual circuit. |
| 4 | Transmit an X.29 Break indication to the remote host, or to a PAD (outgoing connection default). |
| 8 | Escape from data transfer mode. |
| 16 | Discard output to the terminal by setting parameter 8 to a value of 1. |
| 21 | Combination of values 1, 4, and 16 (incoming connection default). |

The PAD protocols allow you to send a special X.29 Indication of Break packet, send an Interrupt packet, perform a reset operation, act as if the recall character had been typed, or begin discarding output to the user. Combinations of these options are also allowed, as long as they make sense. Common options are to begin discarding output and send both an X.25 Interrupt packet and an X.29 Indication of Break packet; these options are supported. All other options are not supported and are silently ignored.

### Parameter 8: Discard Output

Parameter 8 indicates to the PAD whether to discard received packets rather than disassemble and transmit them. This parameter works in conjunction with parameter 7. If value 16 is chosen for parameter 7, all output is discarded after reception of the BREAK signal. Setting parameter 8 to zero restores normal data delivery to the terminal. See Table B–5 for PAD discard output values and their descriptions.

This parameter can also be set and unset manually using the PAD **resume** EXEC command.

**Table B–5** *PAD Discard Output Values*

| Value | Description |
|---|---|
| 0 | Normal data delivery to the terminal (outgoing connection default). |
| 1 | Discard all output to the terminal. Set by parameter 7; see previous description. |

## Parameter 9: Return Padding

Parameter 9 determines whether or not PAD can provide padding (insert filler characters) upon receipt of a Return character from the terminal.

## Parameter 10: Line Folding (Not Supported)

Line folding means inserting a LINE FEED at a certain point that then places subsequent characters on the next line. Parameter 10 determines selection of this function and specification of the line length.

Neither Cisco's legacy PAD mode or Cisco's X.28 standard user interface supports this parameter.

## Parameter 11: Baud Rate

Parameter 11 is a read-only value that determines the baud rate transmitted across the interface between PAD and the terminal. See Table B–6 for PAD baud rate values and their descriptions.

**Table B–6** *PAD Baud Values*

| Value | Description (in bits per second) |
|---|---|
| 10 | 50 |
| 5 | 75 |
| 9 | 100 |
| 0 | 110 |
| 1 | 134.5 |
| 6 | 150 |
| 8 | 200 |
| 2 | 300 |
| 4 | 600 |
| 3 | 1200 |
| 7 | 1800 |
| 11 | 75/1200 |

**Table B–6** *PAD Baud Values, Continued*

| Value | Description (in bits per second) |
|---|---|
| 12 | 2400 |
| 13 | 4800 |
| 14 | 9600 |
| 15 | 19200 |
| 16 | 48000 |
| 17 | 56000 |
| 18 | 64000 |

## Parameter 12: Input Flow Control

Parameter 12 determines whether or not the terminal can transmit ASCII XON/XOFF (transmission on and off) characters to PAD during the data transfer mode. Flow control is not directly supported on communication servers because data must make network hops to travel to the final destination. However, depending on the type of incoming connection, setting this parameter can cause similar negotiations to be sent over the connection, thereby attempting to change the state of the flow control option at the device closest to the user.

## Parameter 13: LINE FEED Insertion

Parameter 13 determines the procedure for inserting the LINE FEED character upon receipt of a Return character. The PAD also responds to a value that results from the addition of any of the values in Table B–7.

**Table B–7** *PAD Line FEED Signal Values*

| Value | Description |
|---|---|
| 0 | Do not insert the LINE FEED character (outgoing connection default). |
| 1 | Insert a LINE FEED after transmitting RETURN to the terminal. |
| 2 | Insert a LINE FEED after echoing RETURN to the terminal. |
| 4 | Insert a LINE FEED after echoing RETURN to the remote host. |

## Parameter 14: LINE FEED Padding

Parameter 14 determines whether or not PAD can provide padding (insert filler characters) upon receipt of a LINE FEED character from the terminal. This function is generally provided by the end user's operating system.

### Parameter 15: Local Editing

Parameter 15 enables or disables a PAD editing function for the terminal in data transfer mode. Enabling the editing function disables the Idle Timer (see parameter 4). The user at the terminal can make corrections and display the line buffer containing the characters to be transmitted when the forwarding character (see parameter 3) is received. See Table B–8 for PAD local editing function values and their descriptions.

**Table B–8** *PAD Local Editing Function*

| Value | Description |
|---|---|
| 0 | Disables editing capabilities in data transfer mode. Any characters entered become part of the data stream and are transmitted (default for both connection types). |
| 1 | Enables editing capabilities in the data transfer mode, which suspends the following PAD operations:<br>1) Full packet data forwarding until the edit buffer is full<br>2) Forwarding of DATA packets upon expiration of the Idle Timer |

Parameters 16, 17, and 18 provide the editing functions.

### Parameter 16: Character Delete

Parameter 16 allows you to select a character that will delete characters while in PAD editing mode. This character is valid only if parameter 15 is set to one. See Table B–9 for PAD line display editing function values and their descriptions.

**Table B–9** *PAD Line Display Editing Function*

| Value | Description |
|---|---|
| 0-127 | Select one character from the ASCII character set to represent the delete character. Default is character 18 (CTRL-R). |

### Parameter 17: Line Delete

Parameter 17 allows you to select a character that will delete a line while in PAD editing mode. This character is valid only if parameter 15 is set to one. See Table B–10 for PAD line delete editing function values and their descriptions.

**Table B–10** *PAD Line Delete Editing Function*

| Value | Description |
|---|---|
| 0-127 | Select one character from the ASCII character set to represent the delete character. Default is character 21 (CTRL-U). |

### Parameter 18: Line Display

Parameter 18 allows you to select a character that will display a line while in PAD editing mode. This character is valid only if parameter 15 is set to one. See Table B–11 for PAD line display editing function values and their descriptions.

**Table B–11** *PAD Line Display Editing Function*

| Value | Description |
|---|---|
| 0-127 | Select one character from the ASCII character set to represent the delete character. Default is character 18 (CTRL-R). |

### Parameter 19: Edit PAD Service Signals

Cisco's legacy PAD mode does not support this parameter. However, Cisco's X.28 standard user interface does support this parameter.

### Parameter 20: Echo Mask

Cisco's legacy PAD mode does not support this parameter. However, Cisco's X.28 standard user interface does support this parameter.

### Parameter 21: Parity treatment (Not Supported)

Neither Cisco's legacy PAD mode nor Cisco's X.28 user interface supports this parameter.

### Parameter 22: Page Wait (Not Supported)

Neither Cisco's legacy PAD mode nor Cisco's X.28 user interface supports this parameter.

# APPENDIX C

# Regular Expressions

This appendix explains regular expressions and how to use them in Cisco IOS software configurations. It also provides details for composing regular expressions. This appendix has the following sections:

- General Concepts
- Using Regular Expressions
- Creating Regular Expressions
- Practical Examples

## GENERAL CONCEPTS

A regular expression is a pattern to match against an input string. You specify the pattern that a string must match when you compose a regular expression. Matching a string to the specified pattern is called "pattern matching." Pattern matching either succeeds or fails.

For example, you can specify in an X.25 routing table that incoming packets with destination addresses beginning with 3107 are routed to serial interface 0. In this example, the pattern to match is the *3107* specified in the X.25 routing table. The string is the initial portion of the destination address of any incoming X.25 packet. When the destination address string matches *3107* pattern, then pattern matching succeeds and the Cisco IOS software routes the packet to serial interface 0. When the initial portion of the destination address does not match *3107*, then pattern matching fails and the software does not route the packet to serial interface 0.

If a regular expression can match two different parts of an input string, it will match the earliest part first.

## Using Regular Expressions

Cisco configurations use several implementations of regular expressions. Generally, you use regular expressions in the following ways:

- To specify chat scripts for asynchronous lines in the dial-on-demand routing (DDR) feature
- To specify routes in a routing table for the X.25 switching feature
- To filter packets and routing information in the DECnet and BGP protocols

### Specifying Chat Scripts

On asynchronous lines, chat scripts send commands for modem dialing and logging in to remote systems. You use a regular expression in the **modem chat-script** command to specify the name of the chat script that the Cisco IOS software is to execute on a particular asynchronous line. You can also use regular expressions in the **dialer map** command to specify a "modem" script or "system" script to be used for a connection to one or multiple sites on an asynchronous interface.

### Specifying Routes in a Routing Table

As described in the "General Concepts" section, you can use regular expressions to help specify routes in an X.25 routing table. When you create entries in an X.25 routing table, you can use regular expressions in the **x25 route** command to help specify routes for incoming calls. When a router or access server receives an incoming call that should be forwarded to its destination, the Cisco IOS software consults the X.25 routing table to determine the route. The software compares the X.121 network interface address (or destination address) field and the Call User Data (CUD) field of the incoming packet with the routing table to determine the route. When the destination address and the CUD of the incoming packet match the X.121 and CUD regular expressions you specified in the routing table, the access server or router forwards the call.

### Filtering Packets and Routing Information

You can use regular expressions in access lists for both DECnet and Border Gateway Protocol (BGP). In DECnet, you can use regular expressions in the **access-list** command to filter *connect initiate* packets. With these packets, you can filter packets by DECnet object type, such as MAIL. In BGP, you use regular expressions in the **ip as-path access-list** command for path filtering by neighbor. Using regular expressions, you specify an access list filter on both incoming and outbound updates based on the BGP autonomous system paths.

## Creating Regular Expressions

A regular expression can be a single-character pattern or a multiple-character pattern. That is, a regular expression can be a single character that matches the same single character in the input string or multiple characters that match the same multiple characters in the input string. This section describes creating both single-character patterns and multiple-character patterns. It also discusses creating more complex regular expressions using multipliers, alternation, anchoring, and parentheses.

## Single-Character Patterns

The simplest regular expression is a single character that matches itself in the input string. For example, the single-character regular expression **3** matches a corresponding *3* in the input string. You can use any letter (A–Z, a–z) or number (0–9) as a single-character pattern. The following examples are single-character, regular-expression patterns:

```
A
k
5
```

You can use a keyboard character other than a letter or a number—such as an exclamation point (!) or a tilde (~)—as a single-character pattern, but certain keyboard characters have special meaning when used in regular expressions. Table C–1 lists the keyboard characters with special meaning.

**Table C–1** *Characters with Special Meaning*

| Character | | Special Meaning |
|---|---|---|
| period | . | Matches any single character, including white space |
| asterisk | * | Matches 0 or more sequences of the pattern |
| plus sign | + | Matches 1 or more sequences of the pattern |
| question mark | ? | Matches 0 or 1 occurrences of the pattern |
| caret | ^ | Matches the beginning of the input string |
| dollar sign | $ | Matches the end of the input string |
| underscore | _ | Matches a comma (,), left brace ({), right brace (}), left parenthesis, right parenthesis, the beginning of the input string, the end of the input string, or a space |
| brackets | [] | Designates a range of single-character patterns |
| hyphen | - | Separates the endpoints of a range |
| parentheses | () | (Border Gateway Protocol (BGP) specific) Designates a group of characters as the name of a confederation |



To use these special characters as single-character patterns, remove the special meaning by preceding each character with a backslash (\). The following examples are single-character patterns matching a dollar sign, an underscore, and a plus sign, respectively:

```
\$
\_
\+
```

You can specify a range of single-character patterns to match against a string. For example, you can create a regular expression that matches a string containing one of the following letters: *a*, *e*, *i*, *o*, and *u*. One and only one of these characters must exist in the string for pattern matching to succeed. To specify a range of single-character patterns, enclose the single-character patterns in square brackets ([ ]). The order of characters within the brackets is not important. For example, **[aeiou]** matches any one of the five vowels of the lowercase alphabet, while **[abcdABCD]** matches any one of the first four letters of the lowercase or uppercase alphabet.

You can simplify ranges by typing only the endpoints of the range separated by a dash (—). Simplify the previous range as follows:

```
[a-dA-D]
```

To add a hyphen as a single-character pattern in your range, include another hyphen and precede it with a backslash:

```
[a-dA-D\-]
```

You can also include a right square bracket (]) as a single-character pattern in your range. To do so, enter the following:

```
[a-dA-D\-\]]
```

The previous example matches any one of the first four letters of the lower- or uppercase alphabet, a hyphen, or a right square bracket.

You can reverse the matching of the range by including a caret (^) at the start of the range. The following example matches any letter *except* the ones listed:

```
[^a-dqsv]
```

The following example matches anything except a right square bracket (]) or the letter *d*:

```
[^\]d]
```

## Multiple-Character Patterns

When creating regular expressions, you can also specify a pattern containing multiple characters. You create multiple-character regular expressions by joining letters, numbers, or keyboard characters that do not have special meaning. For example, **a4%** is a multiple-character regular expression. Precede keyboard characters that have special meaning with a backslash (\)when you want to remove their special meaning.

With multiple-character patterns, order is important. The regular expression **a4%** matches the character *a* followed by the number *4* followed by a % sign. If the input string does not have *a4%*, in that order, pattern matching fails. The multiple-character regular expression **a.** uses the special meaning of the period character (.) to match the letter *a* followed by any single character. With this example, the strings *ab*, *a!*, or *a2* are all valid matches for the regular expression.

You can remove the special meaning of the period character by preceding it with a backslash. In the expression **a\.** only the string *a.* matches the regular expression.

You can create multiple-character regular expressions containing all letters, all digits, all special keyboard characters, or a combination of letters, digits, and other keyboard characters. The following examples are all valid regular expressions:

```
telebit
3107
v32bis
```

## Multipliers

You can create more complex regular expressions that instruct the Cisco IOS software to match multiple occurrences of a specified regular expression. To do so, you use some special characters with your single- and multiple-character patterns. Table C–2 lists the special characters that specify "multiples" of a regular expression.

**Table C–2** *Special Chacters Used as Multipliers*

| **Character** | | **Description** |
|---|---|---|
| asterisk | * | Matches 0 or more single- or multiple-character patterns. |
| plus sign | | Matches 1 or more single- or multiple-character patterns. |
| question mark | ? | Matches 0 or 1 occurrences of the single- or multiple-character pattern. |

The following example matches any number of occurrences of the letter *a*, including none:

```
a*
```

The following pattern requires that at least one letter *a* be present in the string to be matched:

```
a+
```

The following pattern matches the string *bb* or *bab*:

```
ba?b
```

The following string matches any number of asterisks (*):

```
\**
```

To use multipliers with multiple-character patterns, enclose the pattern in parentheses. In the following example, the pattern matches any number of the multiple-character string *ab*:

```
(ab)*
```

As a more complex example, the following pattern matches one or more instances of alphanumeric pairs (but not none; that is, an *empty string* is not a match):

```
([A-Za-z][0-9])+
```

The order for matches using multipliers (*, +, or ?) is longest construct first. Nested constructs are matched from outside to inside. Concatenated constructs are matched beginning at the left side of the construct. Thus, the regular expression matches *A9b3*, but not *9Ab3*, because the letter appears first in the construct.

## Alternation

Alternation allows you to specify alternative patterns to match against a string. You separate the alternative patterns with a vertical bar (|). Exactly one of the alternatives can match the input string. For example, the regular expression **codex|telebit** matches the string *codex* or the string *telebit*, but not both *codex* and *telebit*.

### Anchoring

You can instruct the Cisco IOS software to match a regular-expression pattern against the beginning or the end of the input string. That is, you can specify that the beginning or end of an input string contain a specific pattern. You "anchor" these regular expressions to a portion of the input string using the special characters shown in Table C–3.

**Table C–3** *Special Characters Used for Anchoring*

| Character | Description |
|---|---|
| ^ | Matches the beginning of the input string |
| $ | Matches the end of the input string |

Note another use for the ^ symbol. As an example, the following regular expression matches an input string only if the string starts with *abcd*:

```
^abcd
```

whereas the following expression is a range that matches any single letter, as long as it is not the letters *a*, *b*, *c*, or *d*:

```
[^abcd]
```

With the following example, the regular expression matches an input string that ends with *.12*:

```
$\.12
```

Contrast these anchoring characters with the special character underscore (_). Underscore matches the beginning of a string (^), the end of a string ($), parentheses ( ( ) ), space ( ), braces ({ }), comma (,), or underscore (_). With the underscore character, you can specify that a pattern exist anywhere in the input string. For example, _1300_ matches any string that has *1300* somewhere in the string. The string's *1300* can be preceded by or end with a space, brace, comma, or underscore. So, while *{1300_* matches the regular expression, *21300* and *13000* do not.

Using the underscore character, you can replace long regular-expression lists. For example, you can replace the following list of regular expressions with simply _1300_:

```
^1300$
^1300(space)
(space)1300
{1300,
,1300,
{1300}
,1300,
(1300
```

### Parentheses for Recall

As shown in the "Multipliers" section, you use parentheses with multiple-character regular expressions to multiply the occurrence of a pattern. You can also use parentheses around a single- or multiple-character pattern to instruct the IOS software to remember a pattern for use elsewhere in the regular expression.

To create a regular expression that recalls a previous pattern, you use parentheses to instruct memory of a specific pattern and a backslash (\) followed by an integer to reuse the remembered pattern. The integer specifies the occurrence of a parentheses in the regular expression pattern. If you have more than one remembered pattern in your regular expression, then \1 uses the first remembered pattern and \2 uses the second remembered pattern, and so on.

The following regular expression uses parentheses for recall:

```
a(.)bc(.)\1\2
```

This regular expression matches the letter *a* followed by any character (call it character #1) followed by *bc*, followed by any character (character #2), followed by character #1 again, followed by character #2 again. In this way, the regular expression can match *aZbcTZT*. The software identifies character #1 as *Z* and character #2 as*T*, and then uses *Z* and *T* again later in the regular expression.

The parentheses do not change the pattern; they only instruct the software to recall that part of the matched string. The regular expression **(a)b** still matches the input string *ab*, and (^3107) still matches a string beginning with *3107*, but now the Cisco IOS software can recall the *a* of the *ab* string and the starting *3107* of another string for use later.

## PRACTICAL EXAMPLES

This section shows you practical examples of regular expressions. The examples correspond with the various ways you can use regular expressions in your configurations.

### Specifying Chat Scripts Example

The following example uses regular expressions in the **chat-script** command to specify chat scripts for lines connected to Telebit and U.S. Robotics modems. The regular expressions are **telebit.*** and **usr.***. When the chat script name (the string) matches the regular expression (the pattern specified in the command), then the Cisco IOS software uses that chat script for the specified lines. For lines 1 and 6, the Cisco IOS software uses the chat script named *telebit* followed by any number of occurrences (*) of any character (.). For lines 7 and 12, the software uses the chat script named *usr* followed by any number of occurrences (*) of any character (.).

```
! Some lines have Telebit modems
line 1 6
chat-script telebit.*
! Some lines have US Robotics modems
line 7 12
chat-script usr.*
```

### X.25 Switching Feature Example

In the following X.25 switching feature example, the **x25 route** command causes all X.25 calls to addresses whose first four Data Network Identification Code (DNIC) digits are 1111 to be routed to serial interface 3. Note that the first four digits (^1111) are followed by a regular expression pattern that the Cisco IOS software is to remember for use later. The \1 in the rewrite pattern recalls the portion of the original address matched by the digits following the 1111, but changes the first four digits (1111) to 2222.

```
x25 route ^1111(.*) substitute-dest 2222\1 interface serial 3
```

### DECnet Access List Example

In the following DECnet example, the regular expression is **^SYSTEM$**. The access list permits access to all connect initiate packets that match the access identification of SYSTEM.

```
access-list 300 permit 0.0 63.1023 eq id ^SYSTEM$
```

### BGP IP Access Example

The following BGP example contains the regular expression **^123.***. The example specifies that BGP neighbor with IP address 128.125.1.1 is not sent advertisements about any path through or from the adjacent autonomous system 123.

```
ip as-path access-list 1 deny ^123 .*

router bgp 109
network 131.108.0.0
neighbor 129.140.6.6 remote-as 123
neighbor 128.125.1.1 remote-as 47
neighbor 18.125.1.1 filter-list 1 out
```

# Index

## Symbols



## Numerics



## A

## B

## E

## G

## H

**N**

## T

## W-Z